Psychology

The Science of Behavior

fifth edition

Neil R. Carlson
The University of Massachusetts

William Buskist
Auburn University

ALLYN AND BACON

Boston ■ London ■ Toronto ■ Sydney ■ Tokyo ■ Singapore

Vice President and Editor-in-Chief, Social Sciences: *Sean Wakely*
Series Editor: *Carolyn Merrill*
Senior Development Editor: *Marilyn Freedman*
Series Editorial Assistant: *Alyssa Dorrie*
Vice President Field Marketing: *Joyce Nilsen*
Composition and Prepress Buyer: *Linda Cox*
Manufacturing Buyer: *Megan Cochran*
Cover Administrator: *Linda Knowles*
Production Administrator: *Mary Beth Finch*
Editorial-Production Service: *Woodstock Publishers' Services*
Copyeditor: *Leslie Brunetta*
Photo Researcher: *Helane Manditch-Prottas*
Text Designer: *Carol Somberg for Omegatype Typography, Inc.*
Cover Designer: *Susan Paradise*

Library of Congress Cataloging-in-Publication Data
Carlson, Neil R., 1942-
      Psychology : the science of behavior / Neil R. Carlson, William
Buskist. — 5th ed.
          p.   cm.
      Includes bibliographical references (p. 639) and indexes.
      ISBN 0-205-19345-5 (hardcover)
      1. Psychology.   I. Buskist, William.   II. Title.
BF121.C35   1997
150—dc20   96–34118
                                                   CIP

Printed in the United States of America
10 9 8 7 6 5 4 3 2 1   01 00 99 98 97 96

The photo credits appear on pages 682–683. They should be considered
an extension of the copyright page.

DEDICATION ■

From Neil Carlson

Dedicated to the memory of my father
Fritz Helmer Carlson
1910–1996

and in celebration of the birth of Alexander Pierre Nils Le Floch

From William Buskist

Dedicated to the memory of my grandmother, Marion E. Short
and my uncle, Dr. Kenneth Trout

Brief Contents

Contents

Preface xv
To the Reader xviii

v

Chapter 7
Perception   198

Chapter 8
Memory   230

Chapter 9
Consciousness   268

Chapter 10
Language   300

Chapter 11   Intelligence and Thinking   332

Chapter 13 Motivation and Emotion   412

Chapter 14 Personality   446

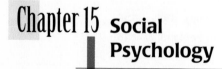

Chapter 15 Social Psychology   482

Preface

This fifth edition of *Psychology: The Science of Behavior* has two authors: Neil Carlson and William Buskist. Our collaboration has been fun, and, we think, fruitful. Although we share the same basic philosophy about the goals of psychology as an experimental and natural science, we have challenged each other to sharpen and refine our thinking—and our writing.

In this book we have tried to convey our own fascination with the pursuit of knowledge. We have tried to explain how psychologists go about discovering the causes of behavior, and, of course, we have summarized the important things we have learned. We have tried to integrate findings across different subdisciplines and show the student that all of what we do is related, even though different psychologists concern themselves with different phenomena, or with different levels of analysis of these phenomena. One of the book's major themes is that behavior can best be understood in the context of its adaptive significance. It continues to combine a scholarly survey of research with applications of research results to problems that confront us today. Using the discovery method to take students inside the research process, we foster a critical understanding of the logic and significance of empirical findings. This approach is featured prominently in special sections, "Evaluating Scientific Issues," described below.

Major Content Changes

When we began preparing the fifth edition of this book, we were pleased to have the opportunity to improve it. Aided by the helpful suggestions of students and instructors who had used the earlier editions, we had a clear plan for what should be done. The fifth edition offers a new organization that emphasizes the biological underpinning of behavior and maintains the standards of clarity and scholarship to which students and instructors have become accustomed. The book now contains eighteen chapters. We have added two new chapters: Chapter 3—*Evolution, Heredity, and Behavior*—re-

flects psychology's increasing interest in understanding how evolutionary and genetic variables affect behavior. Chapter 16—*Life-Style, Stress, and Health*—addresses psychology's expanding role in understanding the impact of life-style on both mental and physical health. The topics of intelligence and thinking are combined in one chapter, as are motivation and emotion. A full chapter on language provides expanded coverage, including neurological mechanisms of language comprehension and production, and discussion of cognitive and social factors have been expanded throughout. In all chapters, we reorganized outlines that we thought could be clarified and generally tried to be sure that the text is as easy to read and understand as we could make it. The result is, we think, a significant improvement on previous editions.

Pedagogical Aids

The new edition offers the best pedagogical features of past editions, along with new improvements. Each chapter now begins with a *preview* that gives students a survey of what the chapter discusses. These previews are designed both to engage students' interest and to present the scope of the chapter. The chapter preview is followed by an *opening vignette,* a lively narrative that illustrates examples of phenomena covered in the chapter. As in previous editions, we have provided summaries where they will do the most good: just after a sizable chunk of material. Each chapter contains several of these *interim summaries,* found after each major heading. They provide students with a place to relax a bit and review what they have just read. Taken together, they provide a much longer summary than students would tolerate at the end of a chapter and will, we believe, serve them better. New *thought questions,* designed to entice students to apply what they have learned to everyday issues, now follow each interim summary. In this edition, *new terms and their definitions* are printed in the margin, so that a student can see at a glance what new vocabulary is being introduced and can quickly scan the terms and definitions to review for an exam. In addition, all figures are explicitly referred to in what we think are the best locations. *Figure references* are in boldface italic type so that the student can easily find his or her place in the text after examining the figure.

Each chapter of this edition contains two special features: a critical-thinking section called "Evaluating Scientific Issues" and a new section called "Biology and Culture." Examples of the issues covered in *Evaluating Scientific Issues* include subliminal self-help tapes, hypnosis and criminal investigation, "physiological" versus "psychological" drug addiction, the cancer-prone personality, clinical versus actuarial diagnosis, and the existence of a language-acquisition device in the brain. The *Biology and Culture* sections highlight the interaction of biology (evolution, genetics, and physiology) and culture (learning, experience, and socialization) with examples from cross-cultural research. Examples include thinking critically about ethnocentrism, the deaf community, cultural contexts for remembering, and cultural differences in the definition of intelligence.

Ancillary Materials

Experience with the first four editions guided the revision of the supplements. The instructor's section and annotations in the special *Annotated Instructor's Edition* were written by Bill Buskist, who also prepared the newly expanded *Instructor's Resource Manual.* We think that these supplements will serve as a handy guide to the topical coverage in the text and a useful resource for teaching creatively and effectively. Allyn and Bacon also makes available to adopters a wide array of additional supplementary materials, including a package of *overhead transparencies,* many in full color. Allyn and Bacon's exclusive CNN videocassettes and videodisks, which include brief, up-to-the-minute segments on topics related to psychology, such as brain research; an extensive video library, including *The Brain* and *The Mind,* also available as teaching modules. Adopters can also obtain **PsychScience**, a program for Macintosh or PC that provides students with the opportunity to participate in on-line experiments. They can also obtain *presentation software for the IBM,* as well as a special CD-ROM multimedia study aid. The *Strategic Learning Package,* by Mary and Neil Carlson, provides students with thorough studying and self-testing exercises. This package includes a printed study guide and a set of *computerized exercises* (available for both PC and Macintosh computers) that

review vocabulary, present self-tests, and provide interactive review of figures and diagrams. The learning objectives and practice test questions featured in the study guide are reflected in the *Test Bank,* written by Bill Buskist. Questions of varying difficulty are provided for each learning objective. The test bank is also available in computerized form, in both PC and Macintosh formats. See your Allyn and Bacon representative for more information on these and other ancillary materials that are available with this book.

Acknowledgments

As the writers we get to think of the book as "ours," but it belongs to many other people. We acknowledge their contributions and thank them. Three editors at Allyn and Bacon, Laura Pearson, Sean Wakely, and Carolyn Merrill, sponsored this edition. They found reviewers to read successive approximations of the final version of the text, gathered a group of people to create the ancillary material, and convinced the management to put their best people to work on the production of the book. Sue Gleason, senior developmental editor, and Marilyn Freedman, freelance developmental editor, carefully read our first drafts and suggested changes that made the book much more interesting—and much more clear. They also provided us with those necessary social reinforcers to keep our enthusiasm high during such a long project. Mary Beth Finch, production editor, assembled the team that designed and produced the book. Barbara Gracia, of Woodstock Publishers' Services, managed the book's production and somehow managed to remain calm and collected (at least when we spoke with her) despite an extremely tight production schedule. Helane Manditch-Prottas read the manuscript and found photos to accompany the text. Jay Alexander of I-Hua Graphics drew the superb illustrations. Leslie Brunetta, our copy editor, attacked the manuscript with her red pencil and helped us tighten and clarify our prose.

Many colleagues assisted us by reading drafts of chapters of the book, evaluating them, and suggesting changes. These people played an important part in shaping this edition. Their names are listed below. We also wish to acknowledge again our colleagues who read and evaluated the previous edition.

Finally, we thank our families for tolerating our spending so much time on the book and for putting up with our grouchiness when work seemed to be going slowly. Without their love and understanding we could never have finished this project.

Reviewers of the Fifth Edition

Elaine Baker
Marshall University

John Broida
University of Southern Maine

James Calhoun
University of Georgia

Robert Ennis
Golden West College

Valerie Farmer
Illinois State University

Mark Fineman
Southern Connecticut State University

Robert Fischer
Ball State University

Nelson Freedman
Queen's University

Mary Hogan
University of Texas, El Paso

William Overman
University of North Carolina, Wilmington

Norman Remley
Texas Christian University

Jefferson Singer
Connecticut College

Dale Swartzentruber
Ohio Wesleyan University

James Todd
Eastern Michigan University

Andrea Wesley
University of Southern Mississippi

Susan Whitbourne
University of Massachusetts, Amherst

Lois Willoughby
Miami-Dade Community College

Reviewers of the Fourth Edition

Daniel Ash
Jefferson Community College, Lousiville

David Berger
State University of New York, Cortland

John Broida
University of Southern Maine

J. Timothy Cannon
University of Scranton

Dennis Cogan
Texas Tech University

Kim Dolgin
Ohio Wesleyan University

Robert Ennis
Golden West College

Edwin Fisher
Center for Health Behavior Research, St. Louis

Gabriel Frommer
Indiana University, Bloomington

James Holland
University of Pittsburgh

Janice Kennedy
Georgia Southern University

Joseph Lowman
University of North Carolina

Jack Marr
Georgia Institute of Technology

Edmund Martin
Georgia Institute of Technology

Dale McAdam
University of Rochester

Linda Musun-Miller
University of Arkansas, Little Rock

Irvin Perline
Mesa Community College

Terry Steele
University of Wisconsin, Oshkosh

Robert Wallace
University of Hartford

Eric Zillmer
Drexel University

To the Reader

You purchased this book because it was assigned to you, and now you will be spending a considerable amount of time reading it. We hope that you will enjoy it; learning about psychology can be fun. If it were not, we would never have finished writing this book, and we would long ago have tired of lecturing about it to our students.

When we took our first psychology course as undergraduates, we were surprised to learn that psychological investigation was actually a scientific enterprise. Like most of our fellow students, we had thought that psychologists knew all there was to know about the real, often hidden, reasons for our behavior, and that we would now learn all their secrets. We had never really considered where this knowledge came from. We quickly learned that psychologists knew much less about the important questions than we thought they did, but their pursuit of knowledge was more interesting than we had suspected it could be.

It is the fascination and excitement of the pursuit of knowledge that we try to convey in our lectures, and which we have tried to convey in this book. The scientific method is an outstandingly successful intellectual achievement. It permits the practitioner to enjoy a mixture of speculation, logical deduction, and empirical data collection. Those of us who enjoy gadgets can spend time with computers and other hardware. Those of us who enjoy watching social interactions can design experiments that present interesting situations and observe our subjects' behavior. And afterward, we can teach our students about what we discovered, and how we discovered it.

There are some things you should know about the book before you start reading. Each chapter is preceded by a table of contents and a brief overview of the material to be discussed. These overviews tell you what to expect when you read the chapter and help you keep track of your progress.

Because every discipline has its own vocabulary—and psychology is no exception—important terms are specially marked in the text. Each one appears in **boldface** where the definition or description is given. Succinct definitions of these terms are provided at the bottom of each page.

The book contains tables, graphs, diagrams, drawings, and photographs. They are there to illustrate important points, and in some cases, to say something that cannot be said with words alone. We are always annoyed when illustrations accompany text without a clear indication of when we should stop reading and consult them. If we look at the illustration too soon, we will not understand it. If we look at it too late, we will have struggled with text that we could have understood more clearly had we only looked at the illustration first. Therefore, we have added explicit references so that you will be spared this kind of annoyance. These are in boldface italics, like this: (See *Figure 5.10.*). If you wait until you see a figure or table reference before looking away from the text, you will be consulting the illustration at the most appropriate time. Sometimes it is best to look at a figure more than once; in such cases we provide more than one reference to it. Some photographs that illustrate general rather than specific points are not numbered; you can look at these whenever you find a convenient stopping place.

Rather than provide a long summary at the end of each chapter we have provided interim summaries—reviews of the information that has just been presented. These summaries divide chapters into more easily managed chunks. When you reach an interim summary in your reading, take the opportunity to relax and think about what you have read. You might even want to take a five-minute break after reading the interim summary, then read it once again to remind yourself of what you just read, and go on to the next section. If you read the material this way, you will learn it with much less effort than you would otherwise have to expend.

The study guide that accompanies this text (consult your instructor regarding availability) is an excellent aid to actively learning the material in the book. By thinking about and answering the study questions, you will be sure not to have missed some important points. In addition, each chapter in the study guide includes two short self-tests so you can assess your comprehension of the material. An interactive computer program that is included with the study guide will also help you review the material in the book.

Although this book has two authors, and although we read each others' words and suggested ways to clarify what the other person had written, each of us is ultimately responsible for what he wrote. You will see that the book is written in the first person; we wrote "I" and "me" rather than "we" and "us." Each of us has illustrated points with examples from our own lives or those of people we know, and these narratives demand personal pronouns. If you want to know which of us wrote a particular narrative, write (or E-mail) to us and we will be happy to tell you.

We have not met you, but we feel as if we have been talking to you while working on this book. Writing is an unsocial activity in the sense that it is done alone. It is even an antisocial activity when the writer must say, "No, I'm too busy writing to talk with you now." So as we wrote this book, we consoled ourselves by imagining that you were listening to us. You will get to meet us, or at least do so vicariously, through our words, as you read this book. If you then want to make the conversation two-way, please write to Neil Carlson at the Department of Psychology, Tobin Hall, University of Massachusetts, Amherst, MA 01003 (e-mail: nrc@psych.umass.edu) or to William Buskist at the Department of Psychology, Auburn University, Auburn, Alabama, 36849 (e-mail: buskiwf@mail.auburn.edu). We hope to hear from you.

Chapter 1

The Science
of Psychology

Chapter Outline

What Is Psychology?

Explaining Behavior • The Goals of Psychological Research • Fields of Psychology

Psychology is the science of behavior, and psychologists try to explain behavior by discovering its causes. In addition, some psychologists try to apply the discoveries of psychological research to practical problems. Scientific psychology consists of many subfields, each investigating different types of behaviors or searching for different types of causes.

The Rise of Psychology as a Science

Philosophical Roots of Psychology • Biological Roots of Psychology

The science of psychology is rooted in philosophy and biology. Philosophers developed the principles of materialism and empiricism, which made it possible to conceive of studying the human mind—and eventually, behavior. Biologists developed experimental methods that enabled us to study the brain and discover its role in the control of behavior.

Major Trends in the Development of Psychology

Structuralism • Ebbinghaus: Pioneer in Research on Human Memory • Functionalism • Freud's Psychodynamic Theory • Behaviorism • Gestalt Psychology • Humanistic Psychology • Reaction Against Behaviorism: The Cognitive Revolution • The Biological Revolution

The first laboratory of experimental psychology was established by Wilhelm Wundt in Germany in 1879. Wundt's structuralism was soon abandoned, but other laboratories developed new methods to study the causes of behavior. Hermann Ebbinghaus developed methods to measure learning and memory objectively. Charles Darwin's principle of natural selection led to the development of functionalism, which in turn inspired the development of behaviorism, a movement in psychology that insisted that only observable behavior could be studied scientifically. Sigmund Freud's psychodynamic theory and humanistic psychologists have had wide appeal with the general public. More recently, cognitive psychologists have restored an emphasis on the study of mental processes. New developments in the research methods of neurobiology have strengthened the biological emphasis in psychological research.

René, a lonely, intelligent young man of eighteen years, had secluded himself in Saint-Germain, a village to the west of Paris. He had recently suffered a nervous breakdown and chose the retreat to recover. Even before coming to Saint-Germain, he had heard of the fabulous Royal Gardens built for Henri IV and Marie de Médicis, and one sunny day he decided to visit them. The guard stopped him at the gate; but when he identified himself as a student at the King's School at La Flèche, he was permitted to enter. The gardens consisted of a series of six large terraces overlooking the Seine River, planted in the symmetrical, orderly fashion so loved by the French. Grottoes were cut into the limestone hillside at the end of each terrace; René entered one of them. He heard eerie music accompanied by the gurgling of water but, at first, could see nothing in the darkness. As his eyes became accustomed to the gloom, he could make out a figure illuminated by a flickering torch. He approached the figure, which he soon recognized as that of a young woman. As he drew closer, he saw that she was actually a bronze statue of Diana, bathing in a pool of water. Suddenly, the Greek goddess fled and hid behind a bronze rose bush. As René pursued her, an imposing statue of Neptune rose in front of him, barring the way with his trident.

René was delighted. He had heard about the hydraulically operated mechanical organs and the moving statues, but he had not expected such realism. As he walked back toward the entrance to the grotto, he saw the plates buried in the ground that controlled the valves operating the machinery. He spent the rest of the afternoon wandering through the grottoes, listening to the music and being entertained by the statues.

During his stay in Saint-Germain, René visited the Royal Gardens again and again. He had been thinking about the relation between the movements of animate and inanimate objects, which had concerned philosophers for some time. He thought he saw in the apparently purposeful, but obviously inanimate, movements of the statues an answer to some important questions. Even after he left Saint-Germain, he revisited the grottoes in his memory; and he went so far as to name his daughter Francine after their designers, the Francini brothers of Florence.

What is psychology? If you asked this question of several people, you would receive several different answers. In fact, if you asked this question of several *psychologists,* you would still receive more than one answer. Psychologists are probably the most diverse group of people in our society to share the same title. They engage in research, teaching, counseling, and psychotherapy; they advise industry and governmental agencies about personnel matters, the design of products, advertising and marketing, and legislation; they devise and administer tests of personality, achievement, and ability. Psychologists study a wide variety of phenomena, including physiological processes within the nervous system, genetics, environmental events, personality characteristics, mental abilities, and social interactions. And yet psychology is a new discipline; the first person to call himself a psychologist was still alive in 1920. According to the latest census, there are 119,000 people in the United States alone who are employed as psychologists. That is quite a large number for a field that is a little more than one hundred years old.

This chapter describes the nature of psychology, its goals, and its history.

What Is Psychology?

In this book, we will study the science of psychology. The primary emphasis is on discovering the causes of behavior. Of course, I shall describe the applications of these discoveries to the treatment of mental disorders and the improvement of society, but my focus will be on the way psychologists discover the facts that make these applications possible.

As the title of this book says, **psychology** is the science of behavior. The word *psychology* comes from two Greek words, *psukhe,* meaning "breath" or "soul," and *logos,* meaning "word" or "reason." The modern meaning of *psycho-* is "mind" and the modern meaning of *-logy* is "science"; thus, the word *psychology* literally means "the science of the mind." But I just said that psychology is the science of *behavior.* Early

psychology The scientific study of the causes of behavior; also, the application of the findings of psychological research to the solution of problems.

The research interests of psychologists vary widely. For example, one psychologist might be interested in applying the principles of visual perception to the design of displays and controls, and another may be interested in romantic attraction.

in the development of psychology, people conceived of the mind as an independent, free-floating spirit. Later, they described it as a characteristic of a functioning brain whose ultimate function was to control behavior. Thus, the focus turned from the mind, which cannot be directly observed, to behavior, which can. And because the brain is the organ that both contains the mind and controls behavior, psychology very soon incorporated the study of the brain.

Explaining Behavior

The ultimate goal of research in psychology is to understand human behavior: to explain why people do what they do. Different kinds of psychologists are interested in different kinds of behaviors and different levels of explanation. Not all of them study humans; some conduct research using laboratory animals or study the behavior of wild animals in their natural habitats. Research using animals has provided many insights into the factors that affect human behavior.

How do psychologists "explain" behavior? First, we must describe it. We must become familiar with the things that people (or other animals) do. We must learn how to categorize and measure behavior so that we can be sure that different psychologists in different places are observing the same phenomena. Next, we must discover the *causes* of the behavior we observe—those events responsible for its occurrence. If we can discover the events that caused the behavior to occur, we have "explained" it. Events that cause other events (including behavior) to occur are called **causal events.** (Be careful; the word is *cau-sal,* not *ca-su-al.*)

Different psychologists are interested in different behaviors. For example, one psychologist might be interested in visual perception and another might be interested in romantic attraction. Even when they are interested in the same behavior, different psychologists might study different categories of causal events. Some look inside the organism in a literal sense, seeking physiological causes, such as the activity of nerve cells or the secretions of glands. Others look inside the organism in a metaphorical sense, explaining behavior in terms of hypothetical mental states, such as anger, fear, curiosity, or love. Still others look only for events in the environment (including things that other people do) that cause behaviors to occur.

The Goals of Psychological Research

Why do psychologists want to explain behavior? One good reason is intellectual curiosity. An essential part of human nature seems to be a need to understand what makes things work—and what could be more interesting than trying to understand our fellow human beings? But psychological research is more than an idle endeavor of curious scientists; it holds the promise of showing us how to solve our most important and pressing problems.

Human behavior is at the root of most of the world's problems: poverty, crime, overpopulation, drug addiction, bigotry, pollution, war. If global warming does adversely affect our planet, or if forests and lakes die because of acid rain, it will be because of our *behavior*—it is we who produce the polluting chemicals and spew them into the atmosphere. Health-related problems—such as cardiovascular disease, some forms of cancer, and a large number of stress-related illnesses—are caused (or at least aggravated) by an individual's behavior. Smoking, obesity, lack of exercise, poor diet, unsanitary personal habits, and stressful life-styles are responsible for much of the illness found around the world. Inappropriate agricultural practices, inefficient distribution of food, and wars and tribal conflicts—which you will note are the products of human *behaviors*—are responsible for much of the hunger and starvation that exists in the world today. If

causal event An event that causes another event to occur.

people's behavior could be changed, people's living conditions could be drastically improved.

These problems are still with us; psychological research has not yet given us all the answers. In some cases, we know what must be done to solve a problem, but we do not yet know how to get people to do it. I hope that while reading this book and learning what psychologists have discovered about human behavior, you will think about what can be done. Perhaps you will be one of those who discover important principles of behavior or apply them to solving the problems that we face.

Fields of Psychology

Psychologists come in many varieties. Some of us are scientists, trying to discover the causes of behavior. Some of us are practitioners of *applied psychology,* applying what our scientific colleagues have learned to the solution of problems in the world outside the laboratory. (Of course, some psychologists perform both roles.) This section describes the various fields of psychological research and the areas of applied psychology.

Areas of Psychological Research

Most research psychologists are employed by colleges or universities or by private or governmental research laboratories. Research psychologists differ from one another in two principal ways: in the types of *behavior* they investigate and in the *causal events* they analyze. That is, they explain different types of behaviors, and they explain them in terms of different types of causes. For example, two psychologists might both be interested in memory, but they might attempt to explain memory in terms of different causal events—one may focus on physiological events while the other may focus on environmental events.

To explore the areas of psychology, let's look at an important behavioral problem: drug abuse. As you know, drug abuse is one of the most serious problems that we presently face. Alcohol abuse can lead to divorce, loss of jobs, automobile accidents, birth defects, and cirrhosis of the liver. Smoking can lead to lung cancer, heart attacks, and strokes. Heroin addiction can lead to fatal overdoses. Addicts who

---

physiological psychology The branch of psychology that studies the physiological basis of behavior.

psychophysiology The measurement of physiological responses, such as blood pressure and heart rate, to infer changes in internal states, such as emotions.

comparative psychology The branch of psychology that studies the behaviors of a variety of organisms in an attempt to understand the adaptive and functional significance of the behaviors and their relation to evolution.

behavior analysis The branch of psychology that studies the effect of the environment on behavior—primarily, the effects of the consequences of behaviors on the behaviors themselves.

---

take their drugs intravenously run a serious risk of contracting and spreading AIDS. Why do people use these drugs and subject themselves to these dangers? What can psychological research tell us about the causes of—and possible solutions to—the problem of drug abuse?

Physiological psychology examines the physiology of behavior. It looks for causal events in an organism's physiology, especially in the nervous system and its interaction with glands that secrete hormones. Physiological psychologists study almost all behavioral phenomena that can be observed in nonhuman animals, including learning, memory, sensory processes, emotional behavior, motivation, sexual behavior, and sleep. Physiological psychologists usually study animals because most physiological experiments cannot ethically be performed using humans.

Physiological psychologists have much to tell us about drug abuse. Most importantly, they have discovered that all drugs having the potential for addiction act on a particular system in the brain that is involved in our reactions to pleasurable events such as encountering food, warmth, and sexual contact. Some drugs artificially activate this system, providing effects on behavior similar to those that pleasurable events naturally produce. Understanding how these drugs affect the brain may help us develop medications to help addicts break their habit.

Psychophysiology is the measurement of people's physiological reactions, such as heart rate, blood pressure, electrical resistance of the skin, muscle tension, and electrical activity of the brain. These measurements provide an indication of a person's degree of arousal or relaxation. Most psychophysiologists investigate phenomena such as stress and emotions. A practical application of their techniques is the lie detector test.

An important contribution of psychophysiologists to the study of drug abuse is the development of methods used to assess people's level of excitability and their reactivity to various drugs and various kinds of environmental events. These methods are used to understand why some people are more likely than others to become drug addicts.

Comparative psychology is the study of the behavior of members of a variety of species in an attempt to explain behavior in terms of evolutionary adaptation to the environment. Comparative psychologists study behavioral phenomena similar to those studied by physiological psychologists. They are more likely than most other psychologists to study inherited behavioral patterns, such as courting and mating, predation and aggression, defensive behaviors, and parental behaviors.

Comparative studies of the effects of drugs have shown that all species of mammals tested so far react like humans to addictive drugs. If laboratory animals are given the chance to inject these drugs into a vein, they will become addicted to them.

Behavior analysis is the branch of psychology that studies the effect of the environment on behavior. Behavior analysts are primarily interested in learning and motivation.

They believe that behaviors are controlled by their consequences and by nothing else. Behaviors that produce pleasant outcomes tend to be repeated, whereas those that produce unpleasant consequences (or no consequences at all) are less likely to be repeated. Behavior analysts do their research in the laboratory or in applied settings, such as schools, homes, and businesses. Their findings have been applied to teaching, business management, and psychotherapy.

Behavior analysts have contributed much to the study of drug addiction. They have developed methods for studying the way that pleasurable events (including the effects of drugs) lead people to repeat certain behaviors. They have discovered that some of the negative effects of addictive drugs, including withdrawal symptoms, are learned. They have developed methods that can indicate the abuse potential of newly developed drugs before they are tried on people. Psychotherapists have applied the discoveries of behavior analysts to the treatment of people with drug addictions.

Behavior genetics is the branch of psychology that studies the role of genetics in behavior. The genes we inherit from our parents include a blueprint for the construction of a human brain. Each blueprint is a little different, which means that no two brains are exactly alike. Therefore, no two people will act exactly alike, even in identical situations. Behavior geneticists study the role of genetics in behavior by examining similarities in physical and behavioral characteristics of blood relatives, whose genes are more similar than those of unrelated individuals. They also perform breeding experiments with laboratory animals to see what aspects of behavior can be transmitted to an animal's offspring. (Of course, genetic differences are only one of the causes of individual differences. People have different experiences, too, and these experiences will affect their behavior.)

One of the major contributions of behavior genetics to the study of drug abuse has been the development of strains of laboratory animals that are especially susceptible to the effects of drugs. Comparisons of these animals with others who tend not to become addicted may help us understand the physiological mechanisms involved in drug dependence.

Cognitive psychology is the study of mental processes and complex behaviors such as perception, attention, learning and memory, verbal behavior, concept formation, and problem solving. To cognitive psychologists, the events that cause behavior consist of functions of the human brain that occur in response to environmental events. Their explanations involve characteristics of inferred mental processes, such as imagery, attention, and mechanisms of language. Most of them do not study physiological mechanisms, but recently, some have begun collaborating with neurologists and other professionals involved in brain scanning. The study of the biology of cognition has been greatly aided by the development of harmless brain-scanning methods that permit us to measure the activity of various parts of the human brain. (These methods are described in Chapter 4.) Cognitive psychologists almost exclusively study humans, although some of them have begun to study animal cognition as well.

The primary contribution of cognitive psychology to the study of drug addiction has been the development of therapeutic methods that have proved themselves useful in the treatment of addictive behaviors. Cognitive behavior therapists have discovered the importance of teaching people coping strategies that enable them to better resist the temptations of addictive drugs.

Experimental neuropsychology is closely allied with both cognitive psychology and physiological psychology. This branch of psychology is generally interested in the same phenomena studied by cognitive psychologists, but it attempts to discover the particular brain mechanisms responsible for cognitive processes. One of the principal research techniques is to study the behavior of people whose brains have been damaged by natural causes, such as diseases, strokes, or tumors. Experimental neuropsychologists have developed many tests that are useful in assessing behavioral and cognitive deficits caused by abnormal brain functions. For example, they have developed tests that show the effects that the intake of alcohol, nicotine, and other drugs by pregnant women have on the development of their babies.

Developmental psychology is the study of physical, cognitive, emotional, and social development, especially of children. Some developmental psychologists study phenomena of adolescence or adulthood—in particular, the effects of aging. The causal events they study are as comprehensive as all of psychology: physiological processes, cognitive processes, and social influences.

Developmental psychologists have contributed to our understanding of the development of drug-taking behavior. In addition, their research on infant development has made it possible for neuropsychologists to develop tests to assess behavioral and cognitive deficits caused by brain damage caused by addictive drugs.

Social psychology is the study of the effects of people on people. Social psychologists explore phenomena such as perception (of oneself as well as of others), cause-and-effect relations in human interactions, attitudes and opinions, inter-

behavior genetics The branch of psychology that studies the role of genetics in behavior.

cognitive psychology The branch of psychology that studies complex behaviors and mental processes such as perception, attention, learning and memory, verbal behavior, concept formation, and problem solving.

experimental neuropsychology The branch of psychology that attempts to understand human brain functions by studying patients whose brains have been damaged by accident or disease.

developmental psychology The branch of psychology that studies the changes in behavioral, perceptual, and cognitive capacities of organisms as a function of age and experience.

social psychology The branch of psychology devoted to the study of the effects people have on each other's behavior.

personal relationships, group dynamics, and emotional behaviors, including aggression and sexual behavior.

Drug addiction is more than a physiological problem: It is also a social problem. For example, children who begin smoking do not do so because their first cigarette gives them pleasure—this experience is usually *unpleasant.* Instead, they smoke because their peers do, and because smoking is portrayed so attractively in advertisements. Social influences are also involved in addictions to alcohol and the illegal drugs. If we want to try to do something about these influences, we must first understand them.

Personality psychology is the study of individual differences in temperament and patterns of behavior. Personality psychologists look for causal events in a person's past history, both genetic and environmental. Some personality psychologists are closely allied with social psychologists; others work on problems related to adjustment to society and hence study problems of interest to clinical psychologists.

Personality differences certainly play a role in a person's susceptibility to drug addiction. One of the major contributions of personality psychologists to our understanding of drug addiction has been the development of tests of personality that can be used to study the factors involved in susceptibility to drug abuse.

Cross-cultural psychology is the study of the impact of culture on behavior. Because the ancestors of people of different racial and ethnic groups lived in different environments that presented different problems and opportunities, different cultures have developed different strategies for adapting to their environments. These strategies show themselves in laws, customs, myths, religious beliefs, and ethical principles. The importance of cross-cultural research, and the interaction between biological and cultural factors on people's behavior, are explored in a special section entitled "Biology and Culture" found in each of the rest of the chapters of this book.

Undoubtedly, cross-cultural research can teach us much about drug addiction. Some cultures have traditions of drug use that generally do not lead to drug abuse; others have more problems when their members encounter these drugs. While some differences may be genetic (for example, differences in the ability to metabolize alcohol or in the sensitivity of nerve cells to particular drugs), many of the differences can best be understood by studying the customs and habits surrounding drug use.

Clinical psychology is the study of mental disorders and problems of adjustment. Most clinical psychologists are practitioners who attempt to help people solve their problems, whatever the causes. The rest are scientists who look for a wide variety of causal events, including genetic factors, physiological factors, and environmental factors such as parental upbringing, interactions with siblings, and other social stimuli. They also do research on evaluating and improving methods of psychotherapy.

Clinical psychologists (and other mental health professionals, such as psychiatrists) are the people we call on to apply to individuals what we have learned about the causes of a disorder. Their contribution to addressing the problem of drug addiction has been an important one: the development of therapeutic methods used to prevent and treat drug abuse.

Fields of Applied Psychology

Not all psychologists do research. In fact, *most* psychologists work outside the laboratory, applying the findings of research psychologists to problems related to people's behavior. This section describes some of the most important fields of applied psychology.

As we saw in the previous subsection, some *clinical psychologists* perform research devoted to discovering the causes of mental disorders and problems of adjustment. But most clinical psychologists are applied psychologists, dedicated to improving human functioning, especially that of individuals in distress. They are primarily engaged in psychological assessment and psychotherapy. Clinical psychologists work in private practice (on their own or as part of a joint practice), in hospitals and mental health clinics, as part of government services, in work organizations, and sometimes as professors.

Clinical neuropsychologists specialize in the identification and treatment of the behavioral consequences of nervous system disorders and injuries. They typically work in a hospital, closely associated with neurologists (physicians who specialize in diseases of the nervous system), although some teach or have private practices.

Health psychologists use their skills to promote behaviors and lifestyles that maintain health and prevent illness. They are employed in hospitals, health maintenance organizations, government agencies, universities, and private practice.

School psychologists were among the first of applied psychologists. The field of school psychology is related to clinical psychology. As the name implies, school psychologists deal with the behavioral problems of students at school. The school psychologist deals with all aspects of school life—

personality psychology The branch of psychology that attempts to categorize and understand the causes of individual differences in patterns of behavior.

cross-cultural psychology The branch of psychology that studies the effects of culture on behavior.

clinical psychology The branch of psychology devoted to the investigation and treatment of abnormal behavior and mental disorders.

clinical neuropsychologist A psychologist who specializes in the identification and treatment of the behavioral consequences of nervous system disorders and injuries.

health psychologist A psychologist who works to promote behaviors and lifestyles that improve and maintain health and prevent illness.

school psychologist A psychologist who deals with the behavioral problems of students at school.

learning, social relations, testing, violence, substance abuse, neglect.

Consumer psychologists help organizations who manufacture products or who buy products or services. Consumer psychologists study the motivation, perception, learning, cognition, and purchasing behavior of individuals in the marketplace and their use of products once they reach the home. Some consumer psychologists take a marketer's perspective, some take a consumer's perspective, and some adopt a more or less neutral perspective, especially if they work at a university.

Community psychologists are concerned with the welfare of individuals in the social system—usually, disadvantaged persons. In general, the community psychologist favors the modification and improvement of "the system" rather than treating the individual person as a problem.

Organizational psychologists, members of one of the largest and oldest fields of applied psychology, deal with the workplace. Their predecessors formerly concentrated on industrial work processes (such as the most efficient way to shovel coal), but organizational psychologists now spend more effort analyzing modern plants and offices. Most are employed by large companies and organizations, but almost a third are employed in universities.

Engineering psychologists (sometimes also called ergonomists or human factors psychologists) mainly focus on the ways that people and machines work together. They study machines ranging from cockpits to computers, from robots to CD players, from transportation vehicles for the disabled to telephones. If the machine is well designed, the task can be much easier, more enjoyable, and safer. Engineering psychologists help designers and engineers design better machines.

Interim Summary

What Is Psychology?

Psychology is the science of behavior, and psychologists study a large variety of behaviors in humans and other animals. They attempt to explain these behaviors by studying the events that cause them. Different psychologists are interested in different behaviors and in different categories of causes.

Psychology has twelve major branches. Physiological psychologists study the role of the brain in behavior. Psychophysiologists study people's physiological reactions, such as changes in heart rate and muscle tension. Comparative psychologists study the evolution of behavior by comparing the behavioral capacities of various species of animals. Behavior analysts study the relation of the environment to behavior—in particular, the effects of the consequences of behavior. Behavior geneticists study the genetics of behavior. Cognitive psychologists study complex human behaviors such as cognition, memory, and attention. Experimental neuropsychologists study the behavior of people who have brain damage. Developmental psychologists study the development of behavior throughout the life span. Social psychologists study the effects of people on the behavior of other people. Personality psychologists study individual differences in temperament and patterns of behavior. Cross-cultural psychologists study the impact of culture on behavior. Clinical psychologists study the causes of and methods of treatment of mental disorders and problems of adjustment.

Psychology is a profession as well as a scientific discipline. Applied psychologists apply the findings of psychological research to solving problems. Clinical psychologists help people with their mental and behavior problems. Clinical neuropsychologists help people with the behavioral effects of disorders of the nervous system. Health psychologists help promote healthy behaviors and lifestyles. School psychologists work with students in the school. Consumer psychologists advise people who buy or sell goods and services. Community psychologists work to change the social system in ways that improve people's welfare. Organizational psychologists help organizations become more efficient and effective. Engineering psychologists help design machines that are safer and easier to operate.

Thought Questions

- Before you read the previous section, how would you have answered the question, "What is psychology?" Would your answer be different now?
- What problems would you like psychologists to work on? If you wanted to be a psychologist, which field do you think you would be most interested in? What questions might you want to answer?

The Rise of Psychology as a Science

Although philosophers and other thinkers have been concerned with psychological issues for a long time, the science of psychology is comparatively young; it started in Germany in the late nineteenth century. In order to understand

consumer psychologist A psychologist who helps organizations that manufacture products or that buy products or services.

community psychologist A psychologist who works for the welfare of individuals in the social system, attempting to improve the system rather than treating people as problems.

organizational psychologist A psychologist who works for increasing the efficiency and effectiveness of organizations.

engineering psychologist A psychologist who studies the ways that people and machines work together and helps design machines that are safer and easier to operate.

how this science came into being, we must first trace its roots back through philosophy and the natural sciences, because these disciplines provided the methods we use to study human behavior. These roots took many centuries to develop. Let us examine them now and see how they set the stage for the emergence of the science of psychology in the late nineteenth century.

Philosophical Roots of Psychology

Each of us is conscious of our own existence. Furthermore, we are aware of this consciousness. Although we often find ourselves doing things that we had not planned to do (or had planned *not* to do), by and large we feel that we are in control of our behavior. That is, we have the impression that our conscious mind controls our behavior. We consider alternatives, make plans, and then act. We get our bodies moving; we engage in behavior.

Consciousness is a private experience, and yet its study has a long history. Even though we can experience only our own consciousness directly, we assume that our fellow human beings are also conscious, and, to at least some extent, we attribute consciousness to other animals as well. To the degree that our behaviors are similar, we tend to assume that our mental states, too, resemble one another. Much earlier in the history of our species, people were very generous in attributing a life-giving *animus,* or spirit, to anything that seemed to move or grow independently. Because they believed that the movements of their own bodies were controlled by their minds or spirits, they inferred that the sun, moon, wind, tides, and other moving objects were similarly animated. This primitive philosophy is called **animism** (from the Latin *animare,* "to quicken, enliven, endow with breath or soul"). Even gravity was explained in animistic terms: Rocks fell to the ground because the spirits within them wanted to be reunited with Mother Earth.

Obviously, our interest in animism is historical. No educated person in our society believes that rocks fall because they "want to." Rather, we believe that they fall because of the existence of natural forces inherent in physical matter, even if we do not understand what these forces are. But note that different interpretations can be placed on the same events. Surely, we are just as prone to subjective interpretations of natural phenomena, albeit more sophisticated ones, as our ancestors were. In fact, when we try to explain why people do what they do, we tend to attribute at least some of their behavior to the action of a motivating spirit—namely, a will. In our daily lives, this explanation of behavior may often suit our needs. However, on a scientific level, we need to base our explanations on phenomena that can be observed and measured objectively. We cannot objectively and directly observe "will."

The best means we have to ensure objectivity is the scientific method (described in Chapter 2). Psychology as a

Animism attempts to explain natural phenomena by supernatural means. This engraving depicts the ancient Greek explanation for the movement of the sun across the sky.

science must be based on the assumption that behavior is strictly subject to physical laws, just as any other natural phenomenon is. The rules of scientific research impose discipline on humans whose natural inclinations might lead them to incorrect conclusions. It seemed natural for our ancestors to believe that rocks had spirits, just as it seems natural for people nowadays to believe that behavior can be affected by a person's will. In contrast, the idea that feelings, emotions, imagination, and other private experiences are the products of physical laws of nature did not come easily; it evolved through many centuries.

Although the history of Western philosophy properly begins with the ancient Greeks, we will begin here with René Descartes (1596–1650), a seventeenth-century French philosopher and mathematician. (Yes, this is the same René I talked about in the opening vignette.) Descartes has been

René Descartes (1596–1650)

animism The belief that all animals and all moving objects possess spirits providing their motive force.

called the father of modern philosophy and of a biological tradition that led to modern physiological psychology. Descartes advocated a sober, impersonal investigation of natural phenomena using sensory experience and human reasoning. He assumed that the world was a purely mechanical entity that, having once been set in motion by God, ran its course without divine interference. Thus, to understand the world, one had only to understand how it was constructed. This stance challenged the established authority of the Church, which believed that the purpose of philosophy was to reconcile human experiences with the truth of God's revelations.

To Descartes, animals were mechanical devices; their behavior was controlled by environmental stimuli. His view of the human body was much the same: It was a machine. Thus, Descartes was able to describe some movements as automatic and involuntary. For example, the application of a hot object to a finger would cause an almost immediate withdrawal of the arm away from the source of stimulation. Reactions like this did not require participation of the mind; they occurred automatically. Descartes called these actions **reflexes** (from the Latin *reflectere*, "to bend back upon itself"). Energy coming from the outside source would be reflected back through the nervous system to the muscles, which would contract. The term is still in use today, but, of course, we explain the operation of a reflex differently. (See *Figure 1.1*.)

What set humans apart from the rest of the world, according to Descartes, was their possession of a mind. The mind was a uniquely human attribute and was not subject to the laws of the universe. Thus, Descartes was a proponent of **dualism,** the belief that all reality can be divided into two distinct entities: mind and matter. He distinguished between "extended things," or physical bodies, and "thinking things," or minds. Physical bodies, he believed, do not think, and minds are not made of ordinary matter. Although Descartes

was not the first to propose dualism, his thinking differed from that of his predecessors in one important way: He was the first to suggest that a link exists between the human mind and its purely physical housing. Although later philosophers pointed out that this theoretical link actually contradicted his belief in dualism, the proposal of an interaction between mind and matter was absolutely vital to the development of a psychological science.

Descartes reasoned that mind and body could interact. The mind controlled the movements of the body, while the body, through its sense organs, supplied the mind with information about what was happening in the environment. Descartes hypothesized that this interaction between mind and body took place in the pineal body, a small organ situated on top of the brain stem, buried beneath the large cerebral hemispheres of the brain. When the mind decided to perform an action, it tilted the pineal body in a particular direction, causing fluid to flow from the brain into the proper set of nerves. This flow of fluid caused the appropriate muscles to inflate and move. How did Descartes come up with this mechanical concept of the body's movements?

Western Europe in the seventeenth century was the scene of great advances in the sciences. It was not just the practical application of science that impressed Europeans; it was the beauty, imagination, and fun of it as well. Craftsmen constructed many elaborate mechanical toys and devices during this period. As we saw in the opening vignette, the young René Descartes was greatly impressed by the moving statues in the Royal Gardens (Jaynes, 1970). These devices served as models for Descartes as he theorized about how the body worked. He conceived of the muscles as balloons. They became inflated when a fluid passed through the nerves that connected them to the brain and spinal cord, just as water flowed through pipes to activate the statues. This inflation was the basis of the muscular contraction that causes us to move.

This story illustrates one of the first times that a technological device was used as a model for explaining how the nervous system works. In science, a **model** is a relatively simple system that works on known principles and is able to do at least some of the things that a more complex system can do. For example, when scientists discovered that elements of the nervous system communicate by means of electrical impulses, researchers developed models of the brain based on telephone switchboards and, more recently, computers. Abstract models, which are completely mathematical in their properties, have also been developed.

Figure 1.1

Descartes's diagram of a withdrawal reflex.

reflex An automatic response to a stimulus, such as the blink reflex to the sudden approach of an object toward the eyes.

dualism The philosophical belief that reality consists of mind and matter.

model A relatively simple system that works on known principles and is able to do at least some of the things that a more complex system can do.

Although Descartes's model of the human body was mechanical, it was controlled by the nonmechanical (in fact, nonphysical) mind. Thus, humans were born with a special capability that made them greater than simply the sum of their physical parts. Their knowledge was more than merely a physical phenomenon.

With the work of the English philosopher John Locke (1632–1704), the mechanization of the whole world became complete. Locke did not exempt the mind from the mechanical laws of the material universe. Descartes's *rationalism* (pursuit of truth through reason) was replaced by **empiricism**—pursuit of truth through observation and experience. A prevalent belief in the seventeenth century was that ideas were innately present in an infant's mind. Locke rejected this belief. Instead, he proposed that all knowledge must come through experience; it is empirically derived. (In Greek, *empeiria* means "experience.") His model of the mind was a tablet of soft clay, smooth at birth and ready to accept the writings of experience upon it.

Locke believed that our knowledge of complex experiences was nothing more than linkages of simple, primary sensations: simple ideas combined to form complex ones. In contrast, the Irish bishop, philosopher, and mathematician George Berkeley (1685–1753) believed that our knowledge of events in the world did not come simply from direct experience but instead was the result of inferences based on the accumulation of past experiences. In other words, we must learn how to perceive. For example, our visual perception of depth involves several elementary sensations, such as observing the relative movements of objects as we move our head and the convergence of our eyes (turning inward toward each other or away) as we focus on near or distant objects. Although our knowledge of visual depth seems to be immediate and direct, it is actually a secondary, complex response constructed from a number of simple elements. Our perceptions of the world can also involve integrating the activity of different sense organs, such as when we see, hear, feel, and smell the same object.

As you can see, the philosophers Locke and Berkeley were grappling with the workings of the human mind and the way in which people acquire knowledge. They were dealing with the concept of learning. (In fact, modern psychologists are still concerned with the issues that Berkeley raised.) As philosophers, they were trying to fit a nonquantifiable variable—reason—into the equation.

empiricism   The philosophical view that all knowledge is obtained through the senses.

materialism   A philosophical belief that reality can be known only through an understanding of the physical world, of which the mind is a part.

doctrine of specific nerve energies   Johannes Müller's observation that different nerve fibers convey specific information from one part of the body to the brain or from the brain to one part of the body.

With the work of the Scottish philosopher James Mill (1773–1836), the pendulum took its full swing from *animism* (physical matter animated by spirits) to *materialism*—mind composed entirely of matter. **Materialism** is the belief that reality can be known only through an understanding of the physical world, of which the mind is a part. Mill worked on the assumption that humans and animals were fundamentally the same. Both humans and animals were thoroughly physical in their makeups and were completely subject to the physical laws of the universe. Essentially, he agreed with Descartes's approach to understanding the human body but rejected the concept of an immaterial mind. Mind, to Mill, was as passive as the body. It responded to the environment in precisely the same way. The mind, no less than the body, was a machine.

Biological Roots of Psychology

René Descartes and his model of muscular physiology provides a good beginning for a discussion of the biological roots of psychology. Descartes's concept was based on an actual working model (the moving statue) whose movements seemed similar to those of human beings. Recognition of that similarity served as "proof" of his theory; he did not have the means available to offer a scientific proof. But technological development soon made experimentation and manipulation possible. Truth need not only be reasoned; it could be demonstrated and verified. Descartes's hydraulic model of muscular movement was shown to be incorrect by Luigi Galvani (1737–1798), an Italian physiologist who discovered that muscles could be made to contract by applying an electrical current directly to them or to the nerves that were attached to them. The muscles themselves contained the energy needed for them to contract. They did not have to be inflated by pressurized fluid.

It is in the work of the German physiologist Johannes Müller (1801–1858) that we note a definite transition from the somewhat sporadic, isolated instances of research into human physiology to the progressively more direct and precise exploration of the human body. Müller was a forceful advocate of applying experimental procedures to the study of physiology. He recommended that biologists should do more than observe and classify; they should remove or isolate animals' organs, test their responses to chemicals, and manipulate other conditions in order to see how the organism worked. His most important contribution to what would become the science of psychology was his **doctrine of specific nerve energies.** He noted that the basic message sent along all nerves was the same—an electrical impulse. And the impulse itself was the same, regardless of whether the message concerned, for example, a visual perception or an auditory one. What, then, accounts for the brain's ability to distinguish different kinds of sensory information? That is, why do we see what our eyes detect, hear what our ears detect, and so on? After all, the optic nerves and the auditory nerves both send the same kind of message to the brain.

Johannes Müller (1801–1858)

The answer is that the messages are sent over different channels. Because the optic nerves are attached to the eyes, the brain interprets impulses received from these nerves as visual sensations. You have probably already noticed that rubbing your eyes causes sensations of flashes of light. When you rub your eyes, the pressure against them stimulates visual receptors located inside. As a result of this stimulation, messages are sent through the optic nerves to the brain. The brain interprets these messages as sensations of light.

Müller's doctrine had important implications. If the brain recognizes the nature of a particular sensory input by means of the particular nerve that brings the message, then perhaps the brain is similarly specialized, with different parts having different functions. In other words, if different nerves convey messages about different kinds of information, then those regions of the brain that receive these messages must have different functions. Müller's ideas have endured, forming the basis for investigations into the functions of the nervous system. For centuries, philosophers had identified thinking or consciousness as the distinguishing feature of the human mind and had concluded that the mind was located in the brain. Now the components of the nervous system were being identified and their means of operation were being explored.

Pierre Flourens (1774–1867), a French physiologist, provided experimental evidence for the implications of Müller's doctrine of specific nerve energies. He operated on animals, removing various parts of the nervous system. He found that the resulting effects depended on which parts were removed. He observed what the animal could no longer do and concluded that the missing capacity must have been the function of the part that he had removed. For example, if an animal could not move its leg after part of its brain was removed, then that region must normally control leg movements. This

---

experimental ablation   The removal or destruction of a portion of the brain of an experimental animal for the purpose of studying the functions of that region.

---

method of removal of part of the brain, called **experimental ablation** (from the Latin *ablatus*, "carried away"), was soon adopted by neurologists, and it is still used by scientists today. Through experimental ablation, Flourens claimed to have discovered the regions of the brain that control heart rate and breathing, purposeful movements, and visual and auditory reflexes.

The first person to apply the logic of Flourens's method to humans was Paul Broca (1824–1880). In 1861, Broca, a French surgeon, performed an autopsy on the brain of a man who had had a stroke several years previously. The stroke (damage to the brain caused in this case by a blood clot) had caused the man to lose the ability to speak. Broca discovered that the stroke had damaged part of the cerebral cortex on the left side of the man's brain. He suggested that this region of the brain is a center for speech.

Although subsequent research has found that speech is not controlled by a single "center" in the brain, the area that Broca identified is indeed necessary for speech production. The comparison of postmortem anatomical findings with a patient's behavioral and intellectual deficits has become an important means of studying the functions of the brain. Psychologists can operate on the brains of laboratory animals, but they obviously cannot operate on the brains of humans. Instead, they must study the effects of brain damage that occurs from natural causes.

In 1870, the German physiologists Gustav Fritsch and Eduard Hitzig introduced the use of electrical stimulation as a tool for mapping the functions of the brain. The results of this method complemented those produced by the experimental destruction of nervous tissue and provided some answers that the method of experimental ablation could not. For example, Fritsch and Hitzig discovered that applying a small electrical shock to different parts of the cerebral cortex caused movements of different parts of the body. In fact, the body appeared to be "mapped" on the surface of the brain. (See *Figure 1.2.*)

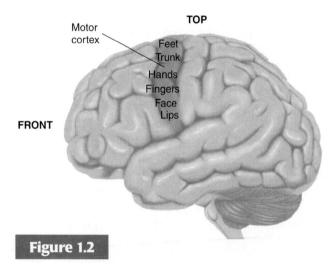

Figure 1.2

Cortical motor map. Stimulation of various parts of the motor cortex causes contraction of muscles in various parts of the body.

Hermann von Helmholtz (1821–1894)

The work of the German physicist and physiologist Hermann von Helmholtz (1821–1894) did much to demonstrate that mental phenomena could be explained by physiological means. This extremely productive scientist made contributions to both physics and physiology. He actively disassociated himself from natural philosophy, from which many assumptions about the nature of the mind had been derived. Müller, under whom Helmholtz had conducted his first research, believed that human organs were endowed with a vital immaterial force that coordinated physiological behavior, a force that was not subject to experimental investigation. Helmholtz would allow no such assumptions about unproved (and unprovable) phenomena. He advocated a purely scientific approach, with conclusions based on objective investigation and precise measurement.

Until Helmholtz's time, scientists believed that the transmission of impulses through nerves was as fast as the speed of electricity in wires; under this assumption, transmission would be virtually instantaneous, considering the small distances that impulses have to travel within the human body. Helmholtz successfully measured the speed of the nerve impulse and found that it was only about ninety feet per second, which is considerably slower than the speed of electricity in wires. This finding suggested to later researchers that the nerve impulse is more complex than a simple electrical current passing through a wire, which is indeed true.

Helmholtz also attempted to measure the speed of a person's reaction to a physical stimulus, but he abandoned this attempt because there was too much variability from person to person. However, this variability interested scientists who followed him; they tried to explain the reason for individual differences in behavior. Because both the velocity of nerve impulses and a person's reactions to stimuli could be mea-

sured, researchers theorized that mental events themselves could be the subject of scientific investigation. Possibly, if the proper techniques could be developed, one could investigate what went on within the human brain. Thus, Helmholtz's research was very important in setting the stage for the science of psychology.

In Germany, a contemporary of von Helmholtz's, Ernst Weber (1795–1878), began work that led to the development of a method for measuring the magnitude of human sensations. Weber, an anatomist and physiologist, found that people's ability to tell the difference between two similar stimuli—such as the brightness of two lights, the heaviness of two objects, or the loudness of two tones—followed orderly laws. This regularity suggested to Weber and his followers that the study of perceptual phenomena could be as scientific as that of physics or biology. In Chapter 6, we will consider the study of the relation between the physical characteristics of a stimulus and the perceptions they produce, a field called **psychophysics,** or the physics of the mind.

Interim Summary

The Rise of Psychology as a Science

We can see that by the mid-nineteenth century, philosophy had embraced two concepts that would lead to the objective investigation of the human mind: the principles of materialism and empiricism. Materialism maintained that the mind was made of matter; thus, all natural phenomena, including human behavior, could be explained in terms of physical entities: the interaction of matter and energy. Empiricism emphasized that all knowledge was acquired by means of sensory experience; no knowledge was innate. By directing attention to the tangible, sensory components of human activity, these concepts laid the foundation for a scientific approach in psychology. At this time, the divisions between science and philosophy were still blurred. But subsequent developments in the natural sciences, especially in biology and physiology, provided the necessary ingredients that, united with the critical, analytical components of philosophy, formed the scientific discipline of psychology. These ingredients were experimentation and verification.

To summarize our history thus far, we turn to the nineteenth-century French philosopher and mathematician Auguste Comte. His *law of three stages,* which traced human intellectual development, offers us an interesting analogy. Humans had moved from a theological stage (the world and human destiny explained in terms of gods and spirits), through a transitional stage (explanations given in terms of essences, final causes, and other abstractions), to the modern positive stage (explanations given in terms of natural laws and empirical evidence). We can relate the development of the study of the human mind to Comte's three stages. Beginning with animism, we moved through theology and philosophy, and from there into the arenas of biology and physiology. This progression led us to the laboratory of Ernst Weber and the development of psychophysics.

psychophysics The branch of psychology that measures the quantitative relation between physical stimuli and perceptual experience.

Thought Questions

- Explaining things, whether scientifically or through myths and legends, seems to be a human need. It seems that people would rather invent a myth to explain a phenomenon than simply say, "I don't know." Can you think of a possible explanation for this need?
- Which of the philosophers and biologists described in this section appeal to you the most? Would you like to know more about any of them and of their times? What questions would you like to ask them if it were possible to meet them?

Major Trends in the Development of Psychology

Psychology began in Germany in the late nineteenth century with Wilhelm Wundt (1832–1920). Wundt was the first person to call himself a psychologist. He shared the conviction of other German scientists that all aspects of nature, including the human mind, could be studied scientifically. His book *Principles of Physiological Psychology* was the first textbook of psychology.

The fact that Germany was the birthplace of psychology had as much to do with social, political, and economic influences as with the abilities of its scientists and scholars. The German university system was well established, and professors were highly respected members of society. The academic tradition in Germany emphasized a scientific approach to a large number of subject areas, such as history, phonetics, archaeology, aesthetics, and literature. Thus, in contrast to French and British scholars, who adopted the more tradi-

tional, philosophical approach to the study of the human mind, German scholars were open to the possibility that the human mind could be studied scientifically. Experimental physiology, one of the most important roots of experimental psychology, was well established there. A more mundane and practical factor that favored Germany as the birthplace of psychology was that its universities were well financed; there was money to support researchers who wanted to expand scientific investigation into new fields. It was in this climate that Müller, Helmholtz, and Wundt conducted their research.

Structuralism

Wundt defined psychology as the "science of immediate experience," and his approach was called **structuralism.** Its subject matter was the *structure* of the mind, built from the elements of consciousness, such as ideas and sensations. Its raw material was supplied by trained observers who described their own experiences. The observers were taught to engage in **introspection** (literally, "looking within"); they observed stimuli and described their experiences. Wundt and his associates made inferences about the nature of mental processes by seeing how changes in the stimuli caused changes in the verbal reports of their trained observers.

Wundt was particularly interested in the problem that had intrigued George Berkeley: How did basic sensory information give rise to complex perceptions? His trained observers attempted to ignore complex perceptions and report only the elementary ones. For example, the sensation of seeing a patch of red is immediate and elementary, whereas the perception of an apple is complex.

Wundt was an ambitious and prolific scientist who wrote many books and trained many other scientists in his laboratory. However, his method did not survive the test of time; structuralism died out in the early twentieth century. The major problem with his approach was the difficulty encountered by observers in reporting the raw data of sensation, data unmodified by experience. In addition, the emphasis of psychological investigation shifted from the study of the human mind to the study of human behavior. More recently, psychologists have resumed the study of the human mind, but we now have better methods for studying it than were available to Wundt. Although structuralism has been supplanted, Wundt's contribution must be acknowledged. He established psychology as an experimental science, independent of philosophy. He trained a great number of psychologists, many of whom established their own laboratories and continued the evolution of the new discipline.

Wilhelm Wundt (1832–1920)

structuralism Wundt's system of experimental psychology; it emphasized introspective analysis of sensation and perception.

introspection Literally, "looking within," in an attempt to describe one's own memories, perceptions, cognitive processes, or motivations.

Ebbinghaus: Pioneer in Research on Human Memory

Most of the pioneers of psychology founded *schools,* groups of people having a common belief in a particular theory and methodology. (In this context, the word *school* refers to a branch of a particular academic discipline, not a building or institution. For example, structuralism was a school of psychology.) The exception to this trend was Hermann Ebbinghaus (1850–1909). In 1876, after receiving his Ph.D. in philosophy but still unattached to an academic institution, Ebbinghaus came across a secondhand copy of a book by Gustav Fechner in which he described his mathematical approach to the measurement of human sensation. Intrigued by Fechner's research, Ebbinghaus decided to attempt to measure human memory: the processes of learning and forgetting.

Working alone, Ebbinghaus devised methods to measure memory and the speed with which forgetting occurred. He realized that he could not compare the learning and forgetting of two prose passages or two poems, because some passages would undoubtedly be easier to learn than others. Therefore, he devised a relatively uniform set of materials—nonsense syllables, such as *juz, bul,* and *gof.* He printed the syllables on cards and read through a set of them, with the rate of presentation controlled by the ticking of a watch. After reading the set, he paused a fixed amount of time, then read the cards again. He recorded the number of times he had to read the cards to be able to recite them without error. He measured forgetting by trying to recite the nonsense syllables on a later occasion—minutes, hours, or days later. The number of syllables he remembered was an index of the percentage of memory that had been retained.

Ebbinghaus's approach to memory was entirely empirical; he devised no theory of why learning occurs and was interested only in gathering facts through careful, systematic observation. However, despite the lack of theory, his work made important contributions to the development of the science of psychology. He introduced the principle of eliminating variable errors by making observations repeatedly on different occasions (using different lists each time) and calculating the average of these observations. **Variable errors** include errors caused by random differences in the subject's mood or alertness or by uncontrollable changes in the environment. He constructed graphs of the rate at which the memorized lists of nonsense syllables were forgotten, which provided a way to measure mental contents across time. As we will see in Chapter 8, Ebbinghaus's research provided a

variable error An error caused by random differences in experimental conditions, such as the subject's mood or changes in the environment.

functionalism The strategy of understanding a species' structural or behavioral features by attempting to establish their usefulness with respect to survival and reproductive success.

model of systematic, rigorous experimental procedures that modern psychologists still emulate.

Functionalism

After structuralism, the next major trend in psychology was functionalism. This approach, which began in the United States, was in large part a protest against the structuralism of Wundt. Structuralists were interested in what they called the components of consciousness (ideas and sensations); functionalists focused on the process of conscious activity (perceiving and learning). Functionalism grew from the new perspective on nature supplied by Charles Darwin and his followers. Proponents of **functionalism** stressed the biological significance (the purpose, or *function*) of natural processes, including behaviors. The emphasis was on overt, observable behaviors, not on private mental events.

Charles Darwin (1809–1882) proposed the theory of evolution in his book *On the Origin of Species by Means of Natural Selection,* published in 1859. As you know, his work, more than that of any other person, revolutionized biology. The concept of *natural selection* showed how the consequences of an animal's characteristics affect its ability to survive. Instead of simply identifying, describing, and naming species, biologists now began to look at the adaptive significance of the ways in which species differed.

Darwin's theory suggested that behaviors, like other biological characteristics, could best be explained by understanding their role in the adaptation of an organism (a human or other animal) to its environment. Thus, behavior has a biological context. Darwin assembled evidence that behaviors, like body parts, could be inherited. In *The Expression of the Emotions in Man and Animals,* published in 1872, he proposed that the facial gestures that animals make in expressing emotions were descended from movements that previously had other functions. New areas of exploration were opened for psychologists by the ideas that an evolutionary continuity existed among the various species of animals and that behaviors, like parts of the body, had evolutionary histories.

The most important psychologist to embrace functionalism was William James (1842–1910). As James said, "My thinking is first, last, and always for the sake of my doing." That is, thinking was not an end in itself; its function was to produce useful behaviors. Although James was a champion of experimental psychology, he did not appear to enjoy doing research, instead spending most of his time reading, thinking, teaching, and writing during his tenure as professor of philosophy (later, professor of psychology) at Harvard University. His course entitled "The Relations Between Physiology and Psychology" was the first course in experimental psychology to be offered in the United States.

James was a brilliant writer and thinker. Although he did not produce any important experimental research, his teaching and writing influenced those who followed him. His the-

William James (1842–1910)

ory of emotion is one of the most famous and durable psychological theories. It is still quoted in modern textbooks of psychology. (Yes, you will read about it later in this book.) Psychologists still find it worthwhile to read James's writings; he supplied ideas for experiments that still sound fresh and new today.

Unlike structuralism, functionalism was not supplanted; instead, its major tenets were absorbed by its successor, behaviorism. One of the last of the functionalists, James Angell (1869–1949), described its basic principles:

1. Functional psychology is the study of mental *operations* and not mental *structures*. (For example, the mind remembers; it does not contain a memory.) It is not enough to compile a catalog of what the mind does; one must try to understand what the mind accomplishes by this doing.

2. Mental processes are not studied as isolated and independent events but as part of the biological activity of the organism. These processes are aspects of the organism's adaptation to the environment and are a product of its evolutionary history. For example, the fact that we are conscious implies that consciousness has adaptive value for our species.

3. Functional psychology studies the relation between the environment and the response of the organism to the environment. There is no meaningful distinction between mind and body; they are part of the same entity.

Freud's Psychodynamic Theory

While psychology was developing as a fledgling science, an important figure, Sigmund Freud (1856–1939), was formulating a theory of human behavior that would greatly affect psychology and psychiatry and radically influence intellectuals of all kinds. Freud began his career as a neurologist, so his

work was firmly rooted in biology. He soon became interested in behavioral and emotional problems and began formulating his psychodynamic theory of personality, which would evolve over his long career. Although his approach was based on observation of patients and not on scientific experiments, he remained convinced that the biological basis of his theory would eventually be established.

Freud and his theory are discussed in detail in Chapter 14; I mention him here only to mark his place in the history of psychology. His theory of the mind included structures, but his structuralism was quite different from Wundt's. He devised his concepts of ego, superego, id, and other mental structures through talking with his patients, not through laboratory experiments. His hypothetical mental operations included many that were unconscious and hence not available to introspection. And unlike Wundt, Freud emphasized function; his mental structures served biological drives and instincts and reflected our animal nature.

Behaviorism

The next major trend in psychology, behaviorism, directly followed from functionalism. It went farther in its rejection of the special nature of mental events, denying that unobservable and unverifiable mental events were properly the subject matter of psychology. Behaviorists believe that because psychology is the study of observable behaviors, mental events, which cannot be observed, are outside the realm of psychology. **Behaviorism** is thus the study of the relation between people's environments and their behavior, without appeal to hypothetical events occurring within their heads.

One of the first behaviorists was Edward Thorndike (1874–1949), an American psychologist who studied the behavior of animals. He noticed that some events, usually those that one would expect to be pleasant, seemed to "stamp in" a response that had just occurred. Noxious events seemed to "stamp out" the response, or make it less likely to occur. (Nowadays, we call these processes *reinforcement* and *punishment;* they are described in more detail in Chapter 5.) Thorndike defined the **law of effect** as follows:

> Any act which in a given situation produces satisfaction becomes associated with that situation, so that when the situation recurs the act is more likely than before to recur also. Conversely, any act which in a given situation produces discomfort becomes disassociated from that situation, so that when the situation recurs the act is less likely than before to recur. (Thorndike, 1905, p. 203)

behaviorism A movement in psychology that asserts that the only proper subject matter for scientific study in psychology is observable behavior.

law of effect Thorndike's observation that stimuli that occur as a consequence of a response can increase or decrease the likelihood of making that response again.

The law of effect is certainly in the functionalist tradition. It observes that the consequences of a behavior act back upon the organism, affecting the likelihood that the behavior that just occurred will occur again. An organism does something, and the consequences of this action make that action more likely. This process is very similar to the principle of natural selection. Just as organisms that successfully adapt to their environments are more likely to survive and breed, behaviors that cause useful outcomes become more likely to recur.

Although Thorndike insisted that the subject matter of psychology was behavior, his explanations contained mentalistic terms. For example, in his law of effect he spoke of "satisfaction," which is certainly not a phenomenon that can be directly observed. Later behaviorists threw out terms like *satisfaction* and *discomfort* and replaced them with more objective terms that reflected the behavior of the organism rather than any feelings it might have.

Another major figure in the development of the behavioristic trend was not a psychologist at all but a physiologist: Ivan Pavlov (1849–1936), a Russian who studied the physiology of digestion (for which he later received a Nobel Prize). In the course of studying the stimuli that produce salivation, he discovered that hungry dogs would salivate at the sight of the attendant who brought in their dishes of food. Pavlov found that a dog could be trained to salivate at completely arbitrary stimuli, such as the sound of a bell, if the stimulus was quickly followed by the delivery of a bit of food into the animal's mouth.

Pavlov's discovery had profound significance for psychology. He showed that through experience an animal could learn to make a response to a stimulus that had never caused this response before. This ability, in turn, might explain how organisms learn cause-and-effect relations in the environment. In contrast, Thorndike's law of effect suggested an explanation for the adaptability of an individual's behavior to its particular environment. So from Thorndike's and Pavlov's studies two important behavioral principles had been discovered.

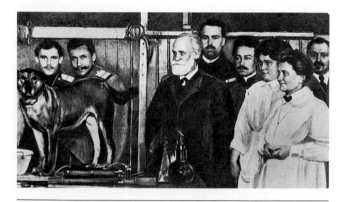

Ivan Pavlov (1849–1936) in his laboratory with some of his collaborators. His research revealed valuable, though unsought, information about the principles of learning.

John B. Watson (1878–1958)

Behaviorism as a formal school of psychology began with the publication of a book by John B. Watson (1878–1958), *Psychology from the Standpoint of a Behaviorist.* Watson was a professor of psychology at the Johns Hopkins University. He was a popular teacher and writer and was a very convincing advocate of behaviorism. Even after leaving Johns Hopkins and embarking on a highly successful career in advertising, he continued to lecture and write magazine articles about psychology.

According to Watson, psychology was a natural science whose domain was restricted to observable events: the behavior of organisms. He believed that the elements of consciousness studied by the structuralists were too subjective to lend themselves to scientific investigation. He defined psychology as the objective study of stimuli and the behaviors they produced. Even thinking was reduced to a form of behavior—talking to oneself:

> Now what can we observe? We can observe *behavior—what the organism does or says.* And let us point out at once: that saying is doing—that is, *behaving.* Speaking overtly or to ourselves (thinking) is just as objective a type of behavior as baseball. (Watson, 1930, p. 6)

Behaviorism is still very much in evidence today in psychology. Its advocates included the late B. F. Skinner (1904–1990), one of the most influential psychologists of the twentieth century. Behaviorism has given birth to the technology of teaching machines (which have since been replaced by computers), the use of behavior modification in instruction of the mentally retarded, and the use of behavior therapy to treat mental disorders. Research on the nature of the basic principles that Thorndike and Pavlov discovered still continues.

Psychologists, including modern behaviorists, have moved away from the strict behaviorism of Watson; mental processes such as imagery and attention are again considered to be proper subject matter for scientific investigation. But Watson's emphasis on objectivity in psychological research remains. Even those modern psychologists who most vehe-

B. F. Skinner (1904–1990)

The founders of Gestalt psychology realized that some phenomena— such as the apparent movement created by lights that flashed on and off in sequence—could only be understood by analyzing the relation between events across time.

mently protest against what they see as the narrowness of behaviorism use the same principles of objectivity to guide their research. As research scientists, they must uphold the principles of objectivity that evolved from empiricism to functionalism to behaviorism. A psychologist who studies private mental events realizes that these events can only be studied indirectly, by means of behavior—verbal reports of inner experiences. Psychologists realize that these reports are not pure reflections of these mental events; like other behaviors, these responses can be affected by many factors. But as much as possible, they strive to maintain an objective stance to ensure that their research findings will be valid and capable of being verified.

Gestalt Psychology

The structuralism of Wilhelm Wundt was not the only German influence on the development of psychology. In 1911, a German psychologist, Max Wertheimer (1880–1943), bought a toy that presented a series of pictures in rapid succession. Each picture was slightly different from the one that preceded it, and the resulting impression was that of continuous motion—like a movie. Wundt and his followers insisted that if we want to understand the nature of human consciousness we must *analyze* it—divide it into its individual elements. But Wertheimer and his colleagues realized that the perception of a motion picture was not that of a series of individual still pictures. Instead, viewers saw continuity in time and space. They saw objects that retained their identity as they moved from place to place. Asking people to study these pictures one at a time and to describe what they saw (the structuralist approach) would never explain the phenomenon of the motion picture.

Wertheimer and his colleagues attempted to discover the *organization* of cognitive processes, not their elements. They called their approach **Gestalt psychology.** *Gestalt* is a German word that roughly translates into "unified form" or "overall shape." (In German, all nouns begin with a capital letter; thus, we write *Gestalt* rather than *gestalt*.) Gestalt psychologists insisted that perceptions resulted from patterns of interactions among many elements—patterns that could exist across both space and time. For example, a simple melody consists of a pattern of different notes, played one at a time. If the melody is played in different keys, so that the individual notes are different, people can still recognize it. Clearly, they recognize the relations the notes have to each other, not just the notes themselves.

Although the Gestalt school of psychology no longer exists, its insistence that elements of an experience interact— that the whole is not simply the sum of its parts—has had a profound influence on the development of modern psychology. Gestalt psychology did not disappear because of some inherent fatal flaw in its philosophy or methodology. Instead, many of its approaches and ideas were incorporated into other areas of psychology.

Humanistic Psychology

For many years, philosophers and other intellectuals have been concerned with what they see as the special nature of humanity—with free will and spontaneity, with creativity and consciousness. As the science of psychology developed, these concerns received less attention because researchers could not agree on objective ways to study them. Humanistic

Gestalt psychology A movement in psychology that emphasized that cognitive processes could be understood by studying their organization, not their elements.

psychology developed during the 1950s and 1960s as a reaction against both behaviorism and psychoanalysis. Although psychoanalysis certainly dealt with mental phenomena that could not be objectively measured, it saw people as products of their environment and of innate, unconscious forces. Humanistic psychologists insist that human nature goes beyond environmental influences, and that conscious processes, not unconscious ones, are what psychologists should study. In addition, they note that psychoanalysis seems preoccupied with disturbed people, ignoring positive phenomena such as happiness, satisfaction, love, and kindness.

Humanistic psychology is an approach to the study of human behavior that emphasizes human experience, choice and creativity, self-realization, and positive growth. The father of humanistic psychology, Abraham Maslow (1908–1970), wrote, "What a man *can* be, he *must* be. He must be true to his own nature . . . [to a] desire to become more and more what one idiosyncratically is, to become everything that one is capable of becoming" (1970, p. 46).

Humanistic psychologists emphasize the positive sides of human nature and the potential we all share for personal growth. In general, humanistic psychologists do not believe that we will understand human consciousness and behavior through scientific research. Thus, the humanistic approach has not had a significant influence on psychology as a science. Its greatest impact has been on the development of methods of psychotherapy based on a positive and optimistic view of human potential.

Reaction Against Behaviorism: The Cognitive Revolution

The emphasis on behaviorism restricted the subject matter of psychology to observable behaviors. For many years, concepts such as consciousness were considered to be outside the domain of psychology. As one psychologist put it, "psychology, having first bargained away its soul and then gone out of its mind, seems now . . . to have lost all consciousness" (Burt, 1962, p. 229). During the past three decades many psychologists have protested against the restrictions of behaviorism and have turned to the study of consciousness, feelings, imagery, and other private events. Much of *cognitive psychology* uses an approach called **information processing**—information received through the senses is "processed" by various sys-

tems of neurons in the brain. Some systems store the information in the form of memory, and other systems control behavior. Some systems operate automatically and unconsciously, while others are conscious and require effort on the part of the individual. Because the information-processing approach was first devised to describe the operations of complex physical systems such as computers, the modern model of the human brain is, for most cognitive psychologists, the computer. As you will learn in Chapter 7, another model (neural networks) is beginning to replace the computer.

Although cognitive psychologists now study mental structures and operations, they have not gone back to the introspective methods that structuralists such as Wundt employed. They use objective research methods, just as behaviorists do. For example, several modern psychologists have studied the phenomenon of imagery. If you close your eyes and imagine what the open pages of this book look like, you are viewing a *mental image* of what you have previously seen. This image exists only within your brain, and it can be experienced by you and no one else. I have no way of knowing whether your images are like mine any more than I know whether the color red looks the same to you as it does to me. The *experience* of imagery cannot be shared.

But behaviors that are based upon images can indeed be measured. For example, Kosslyn (1973, 1975) asked a group of people to memorize several drawings. Then, he asked them to imagine one of them, focusing their attention on a particular feature of the image. Next, he asked them a question about a detail of the image that was either "near" the point they were focusing on or "far" from it. For example, if they were picturing a boat, he might ask them to imagine that they were looking at its stern (back). Then he might ask them whether the boat had a rudder at the stern, or whether a rope was fastened to its bow (front). Because the bow is at the opposite end of the boat, it should be located at the "opposite end" of the image.

Kosslyn found that people could very quickly answer a question about a feature of the boat that was near the place they were focusing on, but they took longer to answer a question about a part that was farther away. It was as if they had to scan their mental image to get from one place to the other. (See *Figure 1.3*.)

Figure 1.3

A drawing used in the imagery study by Kosslyn.
(From Kosslyn, S. M. Perception and Psychophysics, 1973, 14, 90–94. Reprinted with permission.)

humanistic psychology An approach to the study of human behavior that emphasizes human experience, choice and creativity, self-realization, and positive growth.

information processing An approach used by cognitive psychologists to explain the workings of the brain; information received through the senses is processed by systems of neurons in the brain.

Because we cannot observe what is happening within a person's head, the concept of imagery remains hypothetical. However, this hypothetical concept very nicely explains and organizes some concrete results—namely, the amount of time it takes for a person to give an answer. Although the explanation for the results of this experiment is phrased in terms of private events (mental images), the behavioral data (how long it takes to answer the questions) are empirical and objective.

The Biological Revolution

Although psychology is firmly rooted in biology, the biological approach to behavior has become so strong in the past few years that it can properly be called a revolution. During the early and mid-twentieth century, the dominance of behaviorism led to a de-emphasis of biological factors in the study of behavior. At the time, scientists had no way of studying what went on in the brain, but that did not prevent people from spinning elaborate theories of how the brain controlled behavior. Behaviorists rejected such speculation. They acknowledged that the brain controlled behavior, but because we could not see what was happening inside the brain, we should refrain from inventing physiological explanations that could not be verified.

Cognitive psychologists inherited from early behaviorists a suspicion of the value of biology in explaining behavior. Thus, the cognitive revolution did not lead to a renewed interest in biology. But the extraordinary advances in neurobiology in the late twentieth century have revolutionized psychology. Neurobiologists (biologists who study the nervous system) and scientists and engineers in allied fields have developed ways to study the brain that were unthinkable just a few decades ago. We can study fine details of nerve cells, discover their interconnections, analyze the chemicals they use to communicate with each other, produce drugs that block the action of these chemicals or mimic their effects, see the internal structure of a living human brain, and measure the activity of different parts of the brain—regions as small as a few cubic millimeters—while people are watching visual displays, listening to words, or performing various kinds of cognitive tasks. In addition, it seems as though every day a new gene is discovered that plays a role in a particular behavior, and drugs are being designed to duplicate or block the effects of these genes.

Interim Summary

Major Trends in the Development of Psychology

We can see that psychology has come a long way in a relatively short time. The first laboratory of experimental psychology was established in 1879, a little over a century ago. Wilhelm Wundt established psychology as a discipline that was independent of philosophy. At about the same time, Ebbinghaus contributed important methods for objectively measuring learning and forgetting. Even though Wundt's structuralism did not last, interest in psychology continued to grow. It took on added breadth and scope with the emergence of functionalism, which grew out of Darwin's theory of evolution, and its stress on the adaptive value of biological phenomena. Functionalism gave rise to the objectivity of behaviorism, which still dominates the way we do research.

The cognitive revolution began because some psychologists believed that a strict emphasis on observable behavior missed some of the complexity of human cognition and behavior—an opinion that modern behaviorists contest. The biological revolution in psychology manifests itself in the increased interest of psychologists in all fields—not just physiological psychology—in the role of biological factors in behavior.

Thought Questions

- Although psychology began in Germany, it soon migrated to North America, where it flourished. Can you think of any characteristics of North American society that might explain why psychology developed faster there than elsewhere in the world?
- As you have learned, psychologists study a wide variety of behaviors. Do you think that there are any behaviors that psychologists cannot explain (or should not try to explain)?

Suggestions for Further Reading

Butterfield, H. *The Origins of Modern Science: 1300–1800.* New York: Macmillan, 1959.

Whitehead, A. N. *Science and the Modern World.* New York: Macmillan, 1925.

These books by Butterfield and Whitehead describe the history of science in general. Whitehead's is old, but it is a classic.

Benjamin, L. T. *A History of Psychology: Original Sources and Contemporary Research.* New York: McGraw-Hill, 1988.

Schultz, D., and Schultz, S. E. *A History of Modern Psychology,* 4th ed. New York: Academic Press, 1987.

Several books describe the history of psychology, including its philosophical and biological roots, and you may wish to read one of them and then expand your reading from there to learn more. The books by Benjamin and Schultz are excellent introductions.

Chapter 2

The Ways and Means of Psychology

Chapter Outline

The Scientific Method in Psychology

Identifying the Problem: Getting an Idea for Research • Designing an Experiment • Performing an Experiment • Correlational Studies • Single-Subject Research • Generality • *Evaluating Scientific Issues: Format for Critical Thinking*

The scientific method is the most effective procedure for understanding natural phenomena and cause-and-effect relations. Starting with hypotheses—guesses about the way variables are related—researchers use experiments and observational studies to investigate phenomena. Experimenters must use valid and reliable operational definitions of independent and dependent variables. They must avoid confounding variables if their results are to be clear and understandable. Finally, they hope to generalize the results of their research beyond the particular subjects they have studied.

Ethics

Research with Human Subjects • Research with Animal Subjects • *Biology and Culture: Cross-Cultural Research*

Psychologists must abide by the ethical principles set forth by governmental agencies and professional societies. Human subjects must give informed consent prior to participating in a study. They must be treated with dignity and care for their well-being. Animals used in research must be housed properly and treated humanely.

Understanding Research Results

Descriptive Statistics: What Are the Results? • Inferential Statistics: Are the Results Significant?

Once researchers have collected data from a study, they analyze the results. They first describe the data using descriptive statistics, such as measures of central tendency, variability, and correlation. Next, they use inferential statistics to determine whether the results are statistically significant. They estimate the likelihood that the results could have occurred by chance.

During her summer vacations, Carlotta works for her parents, who own a small business employing about a dozen people. The employees place electronic components on circuit boards; the company works on orders too small to be done by large, automated factories.

Last summer, after her first year of college, Carlotta decided to try to help increase the company's productivity. Naturally, if a worker could complete more boards in a day, the company would earn more money—and the worker would receive a larger bonus. One evening, she spent a few hours working on a circuit board, adjusting the angle at which the board rested in a holder fastened to the workbench. Then, after discussing the project with her parents, she designed an experiment, using the principles she had learned in her introductory psychology course.

That evening, she adjusted all the holders to a new angle, which she thought would be better than the original one. The next morning, she met with the employees before they began work. "As you can see, I have adjusted the circuit board holders. I think you'll find the new angle more comfortable, and I hope that you'll be able to finish more boards. I'll see how many you complete over the next few days, and if you're able to do more, then we'll know that the new angle is better." At the end of the day, the workers, eager to know how they had done, gathered around Carlotta as she totaled the production figures. Suddenly, she grinned and said triumphantly, "It worked! We finished almost 20 percent more circuit boards." The workers, sharing her enthusiasm, congratulated her as they left for home.

Carlotta continued to collect data for the rest of the week and then met with her friend Paul, who had taken a statistics course. They used a statistical test to compare the production figures for the four days prior to the change with figures for the four days after the change, and they found that without a doubt the production had increased significantly. Unfortunately, a week later, she discovered that production had fallen back to its earlier level. A week after that, it was actually 5 percent lower! She consulted with her parents and then readjusted the angle of the holders back to the previous position. After a week, production was back to normal. "I can't understand what happened," she said. "I did everything right."

As soon as she returned to school in September, Carlotta sought out her psychology professor, Dr. P., and told her what had happened. She insisted that she had diligently applied the rules of the scientific method, so her experiment should have worked. Dr. P. smiled and said, "You've come across the Hawthorne effect."

"I've never heard of that. Who is Hawthorne?"

"Hawthorne is a place, not a person. Over forty years ago, the managers of the Hawthorne Plant of the Western Electric Company tried to see whether raising the level of lighting would increase productivity. They found that it did but that the changes were only temporary. They went on to do some more investigating and found that productivity went up even if they *lowered* the level of lighting. What was actually happening was this: The people knew that their performance was being monitored and that an experiment was being done. This knowledge probably made them work just a little harder. They may even have been pleased that management was trying to improve their working conditions and tried to return the favor. Of course, the effect didn't last indefinitely, and, eventually, production returned to normal. When industrial psychologists design experiments, they must be careful not to obtain results contaminated by the Hawthorne effect."

"I get it. I thought I was manipulating only one independent variable—the angle of the circuit board holder—but I was introducing a new one: the fact of being observed."

"Exactly. People are not passive participants in an experiment. They have their own expectations and reactions to being observed."

Psychologists attempt to explain behavior. As scientists, we believe that behavior, like other natural phenomena, can be studied objectively. The scientific method permits psychologists to discover the nature and causes of behavior. This approach has become the predominant method of investigation for a very practical reason: It works better than any other method we have discovered. The results obtained by following the scientific method are the ones that are most likely to turn out to be correct.

In this chapter you will learn how the scientific method is used in psychological research. What you learn here will help you understand the research described in the rest of the book. But even more than that, what you learn here can be applied to everyday life. Knowing how a psychologist can be misled by the results of improperly conducted research can help us all avoid being misled by more casual observations.

Does following the steps of the scientific method guarantee that the results of a study will be important? No, it does not. The results of some properly performed studies are trivial or have no relevance to what goes on in more natural environments. The scientific method guarantees only that the particular question being asked will be answered. When a scientist asks a trivial question, nature returns a trivial answer.

The scientific method applies to *all* psychological research. "Scientific" does not mean "technical"; thus, no area of psychological investigation is inherently more "scientific" than any other. For example, the physiological analysis of hunger is not inherently more scientific than an investigation of the social factors affecting a person's willingness to help someone else. Scientists do not necessarily need a laboratory or any special apparatus to conduct their research. Depending on the question being asked, a scientist might need no more than a pad of paper, a pencil, and some natural phenomenon—such as another person's behavior—to observe.

The Scientific Method in Psychology

The goal of psychological research is to discover the causes of behavior. To do so we need to describe behaviors and the events that are responsible for their occurrence in a language that is both precise enough to be understood by others and general enough to apply to a wide variety of situations. As we saw in Chapter 1, this language takes the form of explanations, which are general statements about the events that cause phenomena to occur. The nature of these general statements will become clear as we see how psychologists use the scientific method.

There are three major types of scientific research. **Naturalistic observations**—observations of people or animals in their natural environment—are the least formal and are constrained by the fewest rules. Naturalistic observations pro-

vide the foundations of the biological and social sciences. For example, Charles Darwin's observation and classification of animals, plants, and fossils during his voyage around the world provided him with the raw material for his theory of evolution. **Correlational studies** are observational in nature, but they involve more formal measurement—of environmental events, of individuals' physical and social characteristics, and of their behavior. Researchers examine the *relations* of these measurements in an attempt to discover the causes of the observed behaviors. **Experiments** go beyond mere measurement. A psychologist performing an experiment *makes things happen* and observes the results. As we will see, only an experiment can positively identify cause-and-effect relations.

The **scientific method** consists of a set of rules that dictate the general procedure a scientist must follow in his or her research. These rules are not arbitrary; as we will see, they are based on logic and common sense. The following five steps summarize the rules of the scientific method that apply to experiments, the most rigorous form of scientific research. As we will see later, many of these rules also apply to observational studies. Some new terms introduced here without definition will be described in detail later in this chapter.

1. *Identify the problem and formulate hypothetical cause-and-effect relations among variables.* This step involves identifying *variables* (particular behaviors and particular environmental and physiological events) and describing the relations among them in general terms. Consider the following *hypothesis*: "Loss of self-esteem increases a person's susceptibility to propaganda." This statement describes a relation between two variables—self-esteem and susceptibility to propaganda—and states that a decrease in one causes an increase in the other.

2. *Design the experiment.* Experiments involve the manipulation of *independent variables* and the observation of *dependent variables.* For example, if we wanted to test the hypothesis about the relation between self-esteem and susceptibility to propaganda, we would have to do something to lower people's self-esteem (the independent vari-

naturalistic observation The observation of the behavior of people or other animals in their natural environments.

correlational study The observation of two or more variables in the behavior or other characteristics of people or other animals.

experiment A study in which the experimenter changes the value of an independent variable and observes whether this manipulation affects the value of a dependent variable. Only experiments can confirm the existence of cause-and-effect relations among variables.

scientific method A set of rules that govern the collection and analysis of data gained through observational studies or experiments.

able) and see whether that experience altered their susceptibility to propaganda (the dependent variable). Each variable must be *operationally defined,* and the independent variable must be *controlled* so that only it, and no other variable, is responsible for any changes in the dependent variable.

3. *Perform the experiment.* The researcher must organize the material needed to perform the experiment, train the people who will perform the research, recruit volunteers whose behavior will be observed, and assign each of these volunteers to a *treatment group* or a *control group.* The experiment is performed and the observations are recorded.

4. *Evaluate the hypothesis by examining the data from the study.* Do the results support the hypothesis, or do they suggest that it is wrong? This step often involves special mathematical procedures used to determine whether an observed relation is *statistically significant.*

5. *Communicate the results.* Once psychologists have learned something about the causes of a behavior from an experiment or observational study, they must tell others about their findings. In most cases, the scientists write an article that includes a description of the procedure and results and a discussion of their significance. They send the article to one of the many journals that publish results of psychological research. In addition, researchers often present their findings at conferences or professional conventions. As a result, other psychologists will be able to incorporate these findings into their own thinking and hypothesizing.

Following these simple steps decreases the chances that we will be misled by our observations and come to incorrect conclusions from our research. As we shall see in Chapter 11, people have a tendency to accept some types of evidence even though the rules of logic indicate that we should not. This tendency usually serves us well in our daily lives, but it can lead us to make the wrong conclusions when we try to understand the true causes of natural phenomena, including our own behavior.

The scientific method insists that scientists report the details of their research so that other investigators can repeat, or *replicate,* the study. **Replication** is one of the great strengths of science; it ensures that erroneous results and incorrect conclusions are weeded out. When scientists publish a study, they know that if the findings are important enough, their col-

leagues will try to replicate it (perhaps with some minor variations) to be sure that the results were not just a statistical fluke—or the result of some unsuspected errors in the design or execution of the study. This knowledge encourages scientists to be careful and honest in their research because those who are not careful and honest will eventually be discovered.

Now that you have a general idea of what the scientific method is, let us describe its components and the rules that govern it.

Identifying the Problem: Getting an Idea for Research

Science is a very competitive enterprise. Most scientists want to make names for themselves. They want to discover and explain interesting phenomena and have other scientists acknowledge their importance. They may hope that the public at large will be affected by the fruits of their research. But only a few scientists become well known, even among their colleagues. What makes a scientist great? Obviously, greatness is not achieved simply by following the rules. The scientific method is not difficult to understand or to master, and the laboratory methods required for even the most technical research can be learned after only a few years of study. A great scientist certainly needs to be hard working and dedicated—perhaps even obstinate and relentless. But above all, a successful scientist needs to have *good ideas.* Where do they come from?

Hypotheses

A hypothesis is the starting point of any study. It is an idea, phrased as a general statement, that a scientist wishes to test through scientific research. In the original Greek, *hypothesis* means "suggestion," and the word still conveys the same meaning. When scientists form a hypothesis, they are simply suggesting that a relation exists among various phenomena (like the one that might exist between loss of self-esteem and a person's susceptibility to propaganda). Thus, a **hypothesis** is a tentative statement about a cause-and-effect relation between two or more events.

Hypotheses do not spring out of thin air; they occur to a scientist as a result of research or scholarship. Research breeds more research. That is, worthwhile research does not merely answer questions; it suggests new questions to be asked—new hypotheses to be tested. Productive and creative scientists formulate new hypotheses by thinking about the implications of studies that they have performed or that have been performed by others. The best of them see ideas that others have missed and translate these ideas into research projects.

Theories

A **theory,** a set of statements designed to explain a set of phenomena, is an elaborate form of hypothesis. In fact, a theory can be a way of organizing a system of related hypotheses to

replication Repetition of an experiment or observational study to see whether previous results will be obtained.

hypothesis A statement, usually designed to be tested by an experiment, that tentatively expresses a cause-and-effect relationship between variables.

theory A set of statements designed to explain a set of phenomena; more encompassing than a hypothesis.

Some of the earliest scientific theories involved the movements of celestial bodies.

problems in new ways and by showing how findings that did not appear to be related to each other can be explained by a single concept. There is even a scientific journal, *Psychological Review,* that is devoted to articles of theoretical significance.

Naturalistic Observations

Naturalists are people who carefully observe animals in their natural environment, disturbing them as little as possible. Naturalistic observations, then, are what naturalists see and record. All sciences—physical, biological, and social—begin with simple observation. For example, people described mountains, volcanoes, canyons, plains, and the multitude of rocks and minerals found in these locations long before they attempted to understand their formation. Thus, observation and classification of the landscape and its contents began long before the development of the science of geology.

The subject of psychology is behavior. In order to understand our behavior, or the behavior of other animals, we first have to know something about that behavior. Much of what we know about behavior comes from ordinary experience: observing other people, listening to their stories, watching films, reading novels. In effect, we perform naturalistic observations all our lives. But careful, systematic observations permit trained observers, already well informed about a particular topic, to discover subtly different categories of behavior and to develop hypotheses about their causes.

For example, suppose we were interested in studying the social behavior of preschoolers. We want to know what types of personality variables might exist at that age, under what conditions children share their toys or fight over them, how they react to newcomers to the group, and so on. The best way to begin to get some ideas is to watch groups of children. We would start taking notes, classifying behaviors into categories and seeing what events provoked them—and what the effects

explain some larger aspect of nature. A good theory fuels the creation of new hypotheses. (More accurately, a good scientist, contemplating a good theory, thinks of more good hypotheses to test.) For example, Albert Einstein's theory of relativity states that time, matter, and energy are interdependent. Changes in any one will produce changes in the others. The hypotheses suggested by this theory revolutionized science; the field of nuclear physics largely rests on experiments arising from Einstein's theory.

A good theory is one that generates *testable hypotheses*— hypotheses that can potentially be supported or proved wrong by scientific research. Some theories are so general or so abstract that they do not produce testable hypotheses and hence cannot be subjected to scientific rigor. For example, Sigmund Freud theorized that behavior was motivated by conflicts between mental structures such as the id and the superego. Because there is no way to observe these structures, there is no way to test these ideas scientifically.

The framework for most psychological research is larger in scope than a hypothesis but smaller in scope than a full-fledged theory. For example, the frustration-aggression hypothesis suggests that people (or other animals) tend to become aggressive when they do not achieve a goal that they have been accustomed to achieving. This hypothesis makes a prediction that might fit many different situations. Indeed, many experiments have been performed to test this hypothesis under different conditions.

Even though the frameworks that most psychologists construct fall short of constituting theories, they serve a similar function by stimulating researchers to think about old

Much can be learned through careful observation of animals in their natural environment. The results of such observations often suggest hypotheses to be tested by subsequent studies.

of these behaviors might be. These observations would teach us how to categorize and measure the children's behavior and would help us develop hypotheses that we (or other psychologists) could test in experiments or more formal observational studies.

The important feature of naturalistic observations is that the observer remains in the background, trying not to interfere with the people (or animals) being observed. In some cases, psychologists *do* interfere with a situation in a natural setting. For example, Chapter 15 describes some experiments designed to discover what factors determine whether bystanders come to the aid of people who have been hurt or who are in some other sort of distress. An "accident" is staged, and the behavior of passers-by is surreptitiously observed. Although studies such as these take place outside the laboratory—at job sites or on the street—they are experiments, not naturalistic observations.

Designing an Experiment

Although naturalistic observations enable a psychologist to classify behaviors into categories and provide hypothetical explanations for these behaviors, only an experiment can determine whether these explanations are correct. Let us see how to design an experiment. We will learn about the operational definition and control of experimental variables.

variable A measure capable of assuming any of several values.

manipulation Setting the value of an independent variable in an experiment to see whether the value of the dependent variable is affected.

experimental group A group of subjects in an experiment, the members of which are exposed to a particular value of the independent variable, which has been manipulated by the experimenter.

control group A comparison group used in an experiment, the members of which are exposed to the naturally occurring or zero value of the independent variable.

independent variable The variable that is manipulated in an experiment as a means of determining cause-and-effect relations. Manipulation of an independent variable demonstrates whether it affects the value of the dependent variable.

dependent variable The event whose value is measured in an experiment. Manipulation of independent variables demonstrates whether they affect the value of dependent variables.

nominal fallacy The false belief that one has explained the causes of a phenomenon by identifying and naming it; for example, believing that one has explained lazy behavior by attributing it to "laziness."

Variables

The hypothesis proposed earlier—"Loss of self-esteem increases a person's susceptibility to propaganda"—describes a relation between lowered self-esteem and susceptibility to propaganda. Scientists refer to these two components as **variables:** things that have a particular *value,* which can vary. Scientists either *measure* or *manipulate* the values of variables. **Manipulate** literally means "to handle" (from *manus,* "hand"). Psychologists use the word *manipulate* to refer to setting the value of a variable for experimental purposes. The results of this manipulation determine whether the hypothesis is true or false.

To test the self-esteem hypothesis with an experiment, we would assemble two groups of volunteers to serve as subjects. We would present subjects in the **experimental group** with a situation designed to lower their self-esteem. We would treat subjects in the **control group** in a way that would not alter their self-esteem. We would then measure the susceptibility to propaganda of all the subjects and see whether the behavior of the subjects in the experimental group differed from the behavior of the subjects in the control group. (See *Figure 2.1.*)

This experiment examines the effect of one variable on another. The variable that we manipulate (self-esteem) is called the **independent variable.** The variable that we measure (susceptibility to propaganda) is the **dependent variable.** An easy way to keep the names of these variables straight is to remember that a hypothesis describes how the value of a *dependent* variable *depends* on the value of an independent variable. Our hypothesis proposes that susceptibility to propaganda depends on the level of a person's self-esteem. (See *Figure 2.2.*)

We want to understand the causes of behavior in more than one specific situation. Thus, the variables that hypotheses deal with are expressed in general terms. Independent and dependent variables are *categories* into which various behaviors are classified. For example, we would probably label all of the following behaviors as "interpersonal aggression": hitting, kicking, and throwing something at someone. Presumably, these behaviors would have very similar causes. A psychologist must know enough about a particular type of behavior to be able to classify it correctly.

Although one of the first steps in psychological investigation involves naming and classifying behaviors, we must be careful to avoid committing the nominal fallacy. The **nominal fallacy** refers to the erroneous belief that one has explained an event simply by naming it. (*Nomen* means "name.") Classifying a behavior does not explain it; classifying only prepares us to examine and discover events that cause a behavior. For example, suppose that we see a man frown and shout at other people without provocation, criticize their work when it is really acceptable, and generally act unpleasantly toward everyone around him. Someone says, "Boy, he's really angry today!" Does this statement explain his behavior?

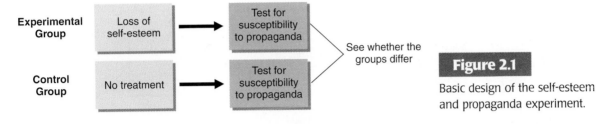

Figure 2.1

Basic design of the self-esteem and propaganda experiment.

It does not; it only *describes* the behavior. Instead of saying he is angry, we might better say that he is "engaging in angry or hostile behavior." This statement does not pretend to explain why he is acting the way he is. To say that he is angry suggests that an internal state is responsible for his behavior—that anger is causing his behavior. But all we have observed is his behavior, not his internal state. Even if he is experiencing feelings of anger, these feelings still do not explain his behavior. What we really need to know is *what events made him act the way he did*. Perhaps he has a painful toothache. Perhaps he just learned that he was passed over for a promotion. Perhaps he had a terrible fight with his wife. Perhaps he just read a book that advised him to be more assertive. Events like these are causes of both the behavior and the feelings. Unless they are discovered, we cannot say that we have explained his behavior.

Of course, many events may precede any behavior. Some of these events are completely unrelated to the observed behavior. I get off the train because the conductor announces my stop, not because one person coughs, another turns the page of her newspaper, another crosses his legs, or another looks at her watch. The task of a psychologist is to determine which of the many events that occurred before a particular behavior caused that behavior to happen.

Operational Definitions

Hypotheses are phrased in general terms, but when we design an experiment (step 2 of the scientific method) we need to decide what *particular* variables we will manipulate and measure. For example, in order to lower the self-esteem of subjects in our proposed experiment, we must arrange a particular

situation that has this effect. Similarly, we must measure the subjects' susceptibility to propaganda in a particular way. In other words, generalities such as "self-esteem" and "susceptibility to propaganda" must be translated into specific operations.

This translation of generalities into specific operations is called an **operational definition:** Independent variables and dependent variables are defined in terms of the operations an experimenter performs to set their values or to measure them. In our proposed experiment, the operational definition of the independent and dependent variables might be the following:

Independent variable: Subjects' self-esteem was lowered by arranging for the subjects to accidentally knock over a precariously placed pile of color slides. The experimenter responded politely but showed some distress, letting it be known that she had just spent a lot of time arranging them for a talk and now will now have to arrange them all over again.

Dependent variable: Subjects' susceptibility to propaganda was measured by measuring their opinions on a particular topic, then by showing them a propaganda film on the topic, and finally by measuring their opinions again. The measure of any change in opinion toward that expressed by the film indicates the degree of susceptibility.

Providing an operational definition of variables is a hallmark of well-conducted research. If research is to be understood, evaluated, and possibly replicated by other people (step 5 of the scientific method), the investigator must provide others with a thorough and adequate description of the procedures used to manipulate the independent variable and to measure the dependent variable. For example, a complete definition of the dependent variable (susceptibility to propaganda) would have to include a detailed description of the opinion test used and of the propaganda film the subjects watched. (See *Figure 2.3.*)

There are many ways to translate a general concept into a set of operations. Using a particular operational definition, the experimenter may or may not succeed in manipulating the independent variable or in measuring the dependent

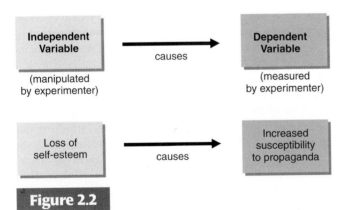

Figure 2.2

Independent and dependent variables.

operational definition The definition of a variable in terms of the operations the experimenter performs to measure or manipulate it.

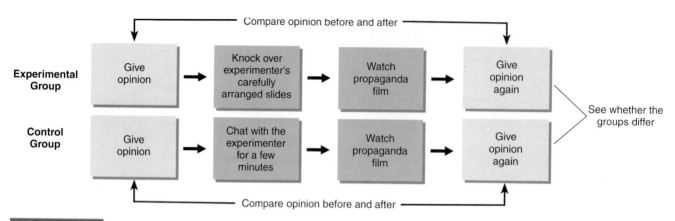

Figure 2.3

Details of the self-esteem and propaganda experiment.

variable. For example, there is certainly no single definition of self-esteem. Another investigator, using a different set of operations to lower a person's self-esteem, might obtain results that are different from ours. Which operational definition is correct? Which set of results should we believe? These questions bring up the issue of *validity.*

The **validity** of an operational definition refers to how appropriate it is—how accurately it represents the variable whose value has been manipulated or measured. Obviously, only experiments that use valid operational definitions of their variables can provide meaningful results. Let us consider my operational definition of lowered self-esteem: the result of accidentally causing a lot of extra trouble for a kind, hardworking experimenter. How can we know whether we actually succeeded in lowering our subjects' self-esteem in our experiment? Perhaps, after the experiment is finished, we could ask our subjects some questions about their self-esteem. If subjects in the experimental group said that they felt clumsy, blamed themselves for doing something that caused extra work for someone, and felt bad because they had not been more careful, then our confidence in the validity of the operational definition is increased. But because the term *self-esteem* does not have a precise definition, we can never be absolutely certain.

Given enough time, the validity of an operational definition will emerge (or so we hope). If different investigators define the variable in slightly different ways but their experiments yield similar results, we become more confident that the research is leading to an understanding of the phenomena we are studying.

> **validity**   The degree to which the operational definition of a variable accurately reflects the variable it is designed to measure or manipulate.
>
> **confounding of variables**   An inadvertent alteration of more than one variable during an experiment. The results of an experiment involving confounded variables permit no valid conclusions about cause and effect.

Control of Independent Variables

A scientist performs an experiment by manipulating the value of the independent variable (such as the level of a person's self-esteem) and then observing whether this change affects the dependent variable (such as susceptibility to propaganda). If an effect is seen, the scientist can conclude that there is a cause-and-effect relation between the variables. That is, changes in the value of the independent variable cause changes in the value of the dependent variable.

In designing an experiment, the experimenter must manipulate the value of the independent variable—and *only* the independent variable. For example, if we want to determine whether noise has an effect on people's reading speed, we must choose our source of noise carefully. If we use the sound from a television set to supply the noise and find that it slows people's reading speed, we cannot conclude that the effect was caused purely by "noise." We might have selected an interesting program, thus distracting the subjects' attention from the material they were reading. If we want to do this experiment properly, we should use noise that is neutral and not a source of interest by itself—for instance, noise like the *sssh* sound that is heard when an FM radio is tuned between stations.

In this example, we intended to test the effects of an independent variable (noise) on a dependent variable (reading speed). By using a television to provide the noise, we were inadvertently testing the effects of other variables besides noise on reading speed. We introduced extra, unwanted variables in addition to the independent variable.

One of the meanings of the word *confound* is "to fail to distinguish." If an experimenter inadvertently introduces one or more extra, unwanted independent variables, he or she cannot distinguish the effects of any one of them on the dependent variable. That is, the effects of the variables will be confounded. There are many ways in which **confounding of variables** can occur. The best way to understand the problems that can arise is to examine some of the mistakes that an experimenter can make.

When I was a graduate student, I accompanied several fellow students to hear a talk that was presented by a visitor to the zoology department. He described research he had conducted in a remote area of South America. He was interested in determining whether a particular species of bird could recognize a large bird that normally preys upon it. He had constructed a set of cardboard models that bore varying degrees of resemblance to the predator: from a perfect representation, to two models of noncarnivorous birds, to a neutral stimulus (a triangle, I think). The experimenter somehow restrained each bird he was testing and suddenly presented it with each of the test stimuli, in decreasing order of similarity to the predator—that is, from predator to harmless birds to triangle. He observed a relation between the amount of alarm that the birds showed and the similarity that the model bore to the predator. The most predatorlike model produced the greatest response. (See *Figure 2.4.*)

As one of us pointed out—to the embarrassment of the speaker and his hosts—the study contained a fatal flaw that made it impossible to conclude whether a relation existed between the independent variable (similarity of the model to the predator) and the dependent variable (amount of alarm). Can you figure it out? Reread the previous paragraph, consult Figure 2.4, and think about the problem for a while before you read on.

Here is the answer. To test the birds' responses to the models, the investigator presented each model at a different time *but always in the same order.* Very likely, even if the birds had been shown the *same* model again and again, they would have exhibited less and less of a response. We very commonly observe this phenomenon, called *habituation,* when a stimulus is presented repeatedly. The last presentation produces a much smaller response than the first. Consequently, we do not know whether the decrease in signs of alarm occurred be-

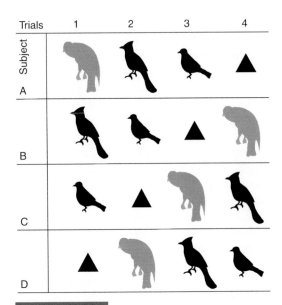

Figure 2.5

Counterbalancing in the predator experiment. The predator experiment could be improved by changing the order of presentation of the models.

cause the stimuli looked less and less like the predator or because the birds' responses simply habituated. The investigator's trip to South America was a waste of time, at least insofar as this experiment was concerned.

Could the zoologist have carried out his experiment in a way that would have permitted a relation to be inferred? Yes, he could have; perhaps the solution has occurred to you already. Here is the answer: The experimenter should have presented the stimuli in different orders to different birds. Some birds would see the predator first, others would see the triangle first, and so on. Then he could have calculated the average amount of alarm that the birds showed to each of the stimuli, having the assurance that the results would not be contaminated by habituation. This procedure is called **counterbalancing.** To *counterbalance* means to "weigh evenly," and counterbalancing would have been accomplished if the investigator had made sure that each of the models was presented equally often (to different birds, of course) as the first, second, third, or fourth stimulus. The effects of habituation would thus be spread equally among all the stimuli. (See *Figure 2.5.*)

Let us look at another example of confounding of independent variables. Suppose we believe that a particular oil extracted from a tropical bean might reduce aggressiveness. We

Stimuli arranged in order of similarity to predator

Figure 2.4

A schematic representation of the flawed predator experiment.

counterbalancing A systematic variation of conditions in an experiment, such as the order of presentation of stimuli, so that different subjects encounter them in different orders; prevents confounding of independent variables with time-dependent processes such as habituation or fatigue.

decide to test our hypothesis by feeding this oil to a group of rats. We mix the oil with some rat food and feed this mixture to members of the experimental group. Members of the control group receive the same food without the additive. A month later, we test the aggressiveness of each rat in a competitive situation. To do so, we take its food away for several hours so that it will be hungry, and then place it in a small cage with another hungry rat. The cage contains a dish of food so small that only one rat at a time can eat from it. Our measure of aggressiveness is the amount of time a rat manages to gain access to the food dish.

Suppose we find that rats in the experimental group spend less time at the food dish in the competitive situation than do rats in the control group. Can we conclude that the oil reduces aggressiveness? Not necessarily. If the results are to be valid, the only difference between the two groups of rats should be that the experimental rats ate some of the oil while the control rats did not. But suppose that the oil tastes bad. In this case, the rats in the experimental group might eat less food. At the end of the month they might be weakened by partial starvation so that they cannot compete effectively with healthy rats that have been eating a normal diet. Or perhaps the oil tasted good—so good that the animals in the experimental group ate more than those in the control group. In this case, they might be less hungry than their competitors during the test and hence less motivated to fight for the food.

To perform this experiment properly, we would have to prepare two diets that tasted the same and contained the same number of calories. We might have to add an ordinary oil (such as corn oil) to the food we feed to the control rats to match the total fat content of the experimental group's diet, and we might have to add a flavoring agent to both diets to mask any unpleasant (or particularly tasty) flavor of the special oil. And we would have to weigh the animals daily and measure the amount of food they ate; if the groups differed in either measure we would have to adjust the diets and start again.

As you will begin to appreciate, it is often difficult to be sure that independent variables are not confounded. We must be certain that when we manipulate the independent variable that variable only, *and no other variable,* is affected.

Performing an Experiment

Having carefully designed a study, we must then decide how best to conduct it. This brings us to step 3 of the scientific method: Perform the experiment. We must decide what subjects will be used, what instructions will be given, and what equipment and materials will be used. We must ensure that the data collected will be accurate; otherwise, all effort will be in vain.

reliability   The repeatability of a measurement; the likelihood that if the measurement was made again it would yield the same value.

Reliability of Measurements

If the procedure described by an operational definition gives consistent results under consistent conditions, the procedure is said to have high **reliability.** For example, measurements of people's height and weight are extremely reliable. Measurements of their academic aptitude (by means of standard, commercial tests) are also reliable, but somewhat less so.

Note, however, that a reliable operational definition may or may not be *valid.* For example, suppose that we operationally define "susceptibility to propaganda" as the length of a person's thumb; the longer someone's thumb is, the more susceptible that person is to propaganda. Although this measurement can be made accurately and reliably, it is nonsensical. (Of course, most examples of reliable but invalid operational definitions are more plausible than this one.) Achieving reliability is usually much easier than achieving validity. Reliability is mostly a result of care and diligence on the part of researchers in the planning and execution of their studies.

Let's look at an example of a variable that can decrease the reliability of an operational definition. Suppose that in our study of the effects of lowered self-esteem on susceptibility to propaganda we hire several experimenters to collect the data. Suppose further that some of these people are pleasant and kind, whereas others are rude and arrogant. Presumably, subjects who knock over the slides belonging to the nice experimenters will feel bad and lose self-esteem. But what about the subjects who knock over the slides belonging to the nasty ones? These subjects will probably be less upset with themselves and might even be pleased that they were responsible for making extra work for someone so unpleasant. The pleasantness of the experimenter is an extraneous factor that could affect the reliability of our definition of self-esteem.

Alert, careful experimenters can control most of the extraneous factors that might affect the reliability of their measurements. Conditions throughout the experiment should always be as consistent as possible. For example, the same instructions should be given to each person who participates in the experiment, all mechanical devices should be in good repair, and all assistants hired by the experimenter should be well trained in performing their tasks. Noise and other sources of distraction should be kept to a minimum.

Another issue that affects reliability is the degree of subjectivity involved in making a measurement. Our definition of lowered self-esteem is *objective;* that is, even a nonexpert could follow our procedure and obtain the same results. But researchers often attempt to study variables whose measurement is *subjective;* that is, it requires practical judgment and expertise. For example, suppose that a psychologist wants to count the number of friendly interactions that a child makes with other children in a group. This measurement requires someone to watch the child and count the number of times a friendly interaction occurs. But it is difficult to be absolutely specific about what constitutes a friendly interaction and what does not. What if the child looks at another child and their gazes meet? One observer may say that the look conveyed

Measurement of subjective phenomena, such as the occurrence of friendly interactions, requires that the criteria be specified as precisely as possible.

interest in what the other child was doing and so should be scored as a friendly interaction. Another observer may disagree.

The solution in this case is, first, to try to specify as precisely as possible the criteria to be used for defining an interaction as friendly in order to make the measurement as objective as possible. Then, two or more people should watch the child's behavior and score it independently; that is, neither person should be aware of the other person's ratings. If their ratings agree, we can say that the scoring system has high **interrater reliability.** If they disagree, interrater reliability is low, and there is no point in continuing the study. Instead, the rating system should be refined, and the raters should be trained to apply it consistently. Any investigator who performs a study that requires some degree of skill and judgment in measuring the dependent variables must do what is necessary to produce high interrater reliability.

Selecting the Subjects

So far, we have dealt with what we, as researchers, would do—what hypothesis we would test, how we would design the experiment, and how we would obtain valid and reliable measurements. Now let's turn to the people who will participate in our experiment: our subjects. How do we choose them? How do we assign them to the experimental or control group? These decisions must be carefully considered because

just as independent variables can be confounded, so can variables that are inherent in subjects whose behavior is being observed.

Consider the following example: Suppose a professor wants to determine which of two teaching methods works best. She teaches two courses in introductory psychology, one that meets at 8 A.M. and another that meets at 4 P.M. She uses one teaching method for the morning class and another for the afternoon class. At the end of the semester she finds that the final examination scores were higher for her morning class. She concludes that from now on she will use that particular teaching method for all of her classes.

What is the problem? The two groups of subjects for the experiment are not equivalent. People who sign up for a class that meets at 8 A.M. are likely to differ in some ways from those who sign up for a 4 P.M. class. Some people prefer to get up early while others prefer to sleep late. Perhaps the school schedules some kinds of activities (such as athletic practice) late in the afternoon, which means that students interested in participating in these activities will not be able to enroll in the 4 P.M. class. For many reasons, the students in the two classes will probably not be equivalent. Therefore, we cannot conclude that the differences in their final examination scores were caused solely by the differences in the teaching methods.

Subjects must be carefully assigned to the various groups used in an experiment. The usual way to assign them is by **random assignment.** One way to accomplish random assignment is to list the names of the available subjects and then to toss a coin for each one to determine the subject's assignment to one of two groups. (More typically, the assignment is made by computer or by consulting a list of random numbers.) We can expect people to have different abilities, personality traits, and other characteristics that may affect the outcome of the experiment. But if people are randomly assigned to the experimental conditions, these differences should be equally distributed across the groups.

Researchers must remain alert to the problem of confounding subject variables even after they have designed an experiment and randomly assigned subjects to the groups. Some problems will not emerge until the investigation is actually performed. Suppose that an experimenter was interested in learning whether anger decreases a person's ability to concentrate. The experimenter acts very rudely toward the subjects in the experimental group, which presumably makes them angry, but treats the subjects in the control group politely. After the rude or polite treatment, the subjects watch a video screen that shows a constantly changing display of pat-

interrater reliability The degree to which two or more independent observers agree in their ratings of another organism's behavior.

random assignment An assignment of subjects to the various groups of an experiment by random means, thereby ensuring comparable groups.

terns of letters. Subjects are instructed to press a button whenever a particular letter appears. This vigilance test is designed to reveal how carefully subjects are paying attention to the letters.

The design of this experiment is sound. Assuming that the subjects in the experimental group are really angry and that our test is a valid measure of concentration, we should be able to make conclusions about the effects of anger on concentration. However, the experiment, as performed under real conditions, may not work out the way it was designed. Suppose that some of our "angry" subjects simply walk away. All experimenters are required to tell subjects that they are free to leave at any time; some angry subjects might well do so. If they do, we will now be comparing the behavior of two groups of subjects of somewhat different character—a group of people who are willing to submit to the experimenter's rude behavior and a group of randomly selected people, some of whom would have left had they been subjected to the rude treatment. Now the experimental group and control group are no longer equivalent. (See *Figure 2.6.*)

The moral of this example is that an experimenter must continue to attend to the possibility of confounded variables even after the experiment is under way. The solution in this case? There probably is none. Because we cannot force subjects to continue to participate, there is a strong possibility that some of them will leave. Some psychological variables are, by their very nature, difficult to investigate.

Subjects' Expectations

Subjects in a psychology experiment are not simply passive participants whose behavior is controlled solely by the independent variables manipulated by the experimenter. In the opening vignette, we saw that Carlotta learned this fact when she tried to improve production at her parents' company. Subjects who are participating in experiments know that they are being observed, and this knowledge is certain to affect their behavior. In fact, some subjects may try to outwit the experimenter by acting in a way that is opposite to what they think is expected. However, most subjects will try to cooperate because they do not want to ruin the experiment for the investigator. They may even try to figure out what question is being asked so that they can act accordingly. Because the study is being run by a psychologist, some subjects are unlikely to take what he or she says at face value and will look for motives hidden behind an apparently simple task. Actually, most experiments are not deceptive at all; they are what they appear to be.

"Deceptive" studies do not always succeed in fooling the subjects. For example, suppose you are a participant in an experiment that was represented as being a learning study. On the table in front of you is an assortment of knives and pistols. The experimenter says, "Oh, ignore them. Someone else left them here. They have nothing to do with this study." Do you believe her? Probably not, and you will undoubtedly try to figure out how the presence of these weapons is supposed to affect your behavior. You may suspect that the psychologist is trying to determine whether the presence of weapons will increase your hostility. With this suspicion in mind, you may (1) act naturally, so that you will not spoil the experiment; (2) act aggressively, to help the experimenter get the results you think she wants; or (3) act nonaggressively, to prove that you are immune to the effects of objects associated with violence. The results of this study may not show the effects of the presence of weapons on aggression but, rather, show the relative numbers of people who select strategy 1, 2, or 3 in response to the knowledge that they are being observed.

Experimenters must always remember that their subjects do not merely react to the independent variable in a simple-minded way. As you will see in Chapter 15, these considerations are especially important in social psychology experiments. In some of these studies, the experimenter or the experimenter's assistants act out roles designed to provide a particular kind of social situation to which the subjects are exposed. Obviously, the subjects' interpretation of these situations affects their behavior.

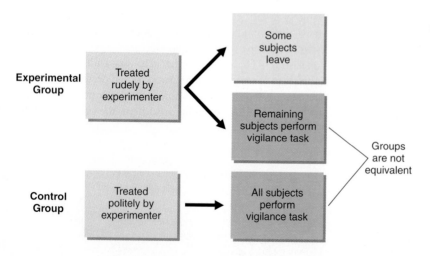

Figure 2.6

A possible problem with the anger and concentration experiment: loss of subjects from the experimental group.

Single-Blind Experiments. A special problem is posed by experiments in which subjects' behavior might be affected by their knowledge of the independent variable. For example, suppose that we want to study the effects of a stimulant drug, such as amphetamine, on a person's ability to perform a task that requires fine manual dexterity. We will administer the drug to one group of subjects and leave another group untreated. (Of course, the experiment will have to be supervised by a physician, who will prescribe the drug.) We will count how many times each subject can thread a needle in a ten-minute period (our operational definition of fine manual dexterity). We will then see whether taking the drug had any effect on the number of needle threadings.

But there is a problem in our design. For us to conclude that a cause-and-effect relation exists, the treatment of the two groups must be identical except for the single variable that is being manipulated. In this case the mere administration of a drug may have effects on behavior, independent of its pharmacological effects. The behavior of subjects who know that they have just taken amphetamine is very likely to be affected by this knowledge as well as by the drug circulating in their bloodstreams.

To solve this problem, we should give pills to the members of both groups. People in one group will receive amphetamine, and those in the other group will receive an inert pill—a **placebo.** (The word comes from the Latin *placere,* "to please." A physician sometimes gives a placebo to anxious patients to placate them.) Subjects will not be told which pill they receive. By using this improved experimental procedure, called a **single-blind study,** we can infer that any observed differences in needle-threading ability of the two groups were produced solely by the pharmacological effects of amphetamine.

Double-Blind Experiments. In a single-blind experiment, only the subjects are kept ignorant of their assignment to a particular experimental group; the experimenter knows which treatment each subject receives. Now let us look at an example in which it is important to keep both the experimenter and the subjects in the dark. Suppose we believe that if patients with mental disorders take a particular drug, they will be more willing to engage in conversation. We give the drug to some patients and administer a placebo to others. We talk with all the patients afterward and rate the quality of the conversation. But "quality of conversation" is a difficult dependent variable to measure, and the rating is therefore likely to be subjective. The fact that we, the experimenters, know which patients received the drug means that we may tend to give higher ratings to the quality of conversation with those patients. Of course, we would not intentionally cheat, but even honest people tend to perceive results in a way that favors their own preconceptions.

The solution to this problem is simple. Just as the patients should not know whether they are receiving a drug or a placebo, neither should the experimenter. That is, we should use the **double-blind procedure.** Someone else should administer the pill, or the experimenter should be given a set of identical-looking pills in coded containers so that both experimenter and patient are unaware of the nature of the contents. Now the ratings cannot be affected by any preconceived ideas the experimenter may have.

The double-blind procedure does not apply only to experiments that use drugs as the independent variable. Suppose that the experiment just described attempted to evaluate the effects of a particular kind of psychotherapy, not a drug, on the willingness of a patient to talk. If the same person does both the psychotherapy and the rating, that person might tend to see the results in a light that is most favorable to his or her own expectations. In this case, then, one person should perform the psychotherapy and another person should evaluate the quality of conversation with the patients. The evaluator will not know whether a particular patient has just received psychotherapy or is a member of the control (untreated) group.

Even scientists who perform studies with laboratory animals may have to use a single-blind or double-blind procedure. Let's consider a case that calls for a single-blind procedure. Suppose that we want to know whether a particular drug will affect an animal's ability to learn a particular task. Just before we train the animals in the experimental group, we give them the drug. But how do we administer the drug? Suppose we have to put a pill into the animal's mouth and make the animal swallow it. Or suppose we administer the drug by injecting it with a hypodermic syringe. Either of these procedures might affect the animal's behavior in the learning task. To avoid this problem, we have to administer placebo pills or injections to animals in the control group.

The expectations of experimenters can influence results in studies with laboratory animals as much as in studies with human subjects. Rosenthal and Fode (1963) demonstrated the influence of expectations by having students train rats to learn the way through a maze. They told half the students that they had "stupid" rats and the other half that they had "smart" rats. In fact, there were no differences in the animals' abilities. However, an analysis of the results indicated that the "smart" animals learned faster than the "stupid" ones. The students' expectations clearly affected their rats' performances. Presumably, the students who had "smart"

placebo An inert substance that cannot be distinguished from a real medication by the patient or subject; used as the control substance in a single-blind or double-blind experiment.

single-blind study An experiment in which the experimenter but not the subject knows the value of the independent variable.

double-blind study An experiment in which neither the subject nor the experimenter knows the value of the independent variable.

rats took better care of them, which affected the animals' performances.

Correlational Studies

If we want to be sure that a cause-and-effect relation exists, we must perform an experiment in which we manipulate the independent variable and measure its effects on the dependent variable. But there are some variables—especially subject variables—that a psychologist cannot manipulate. For example, a person's sex, genetic history, income, social class, family environment, and personality are obviously not under the psychologist's control. Nevertheless, these variables are important and interesting because they often affect people's behavior. Because they cannot be manipulated, they cannot be investigated in an experiment. A different method must therefore be used to study them: a correlational study.

The basic principle of a correlational study is simple: In each member of a group of people we measure two or more variables as they are found to exist, and we determine whether the variables are related by using a statistical procedure called *correlation*. Correlational studies are often done to investigate the effects of personality variables on behavior. For example, we may ask whether shyness is related to daydreaming. Our hypothesis is that shy people tend to daydream more than do less shy people. We decide how to assess a person's shyness and the amount of daydreaming that he or she engages in each day, and we then take the measure of these two variables for a group of people. If shy people tend to daydream more (or less) than do people who are not shy, we can conclude that the variables are related.

Suppose that we do, in fact, find that shy people spend more time daydreaming. Such a finding tells us that the variables are related—we say they are *correlated*—but it does not permit us to make any conclusions about cause and effect. Shyness may have caused the daydreaming, or daydreaming may have caused the shyness, or perhaps some other variable that we did not measure caused both shyness and an increase in daydreaming. In other words, *correlations do not necessarily indicate cause-and-effect relations.* (See *Figure 2.7.*)

A good illustration of this principle is provided by a correlational study that attempted to determine whether membership in the Boy Scouts would affect a person's subsequent participation in community affairs (Chapin, 1947). The investigator compared a group of men who had once been Boy Scouts with a group of men who had not. He found that the men who had been Boy Scouts tended to join more community affairs groups later in life.

The investigator concluded that the experience of being a Boy Scout increased a person's tendency to join commu-

Daydreaming keeps a person from making many contacts with other people; experiences in fantasies are more successful and gratifying than those in real life.

He does not know how to respond in the company of other people.

Person has poor social skills; finds contacts with other people uncomfortable.

He turns to daydreaming because he receives no gratification from social contacts.

Figure 2.7

An example of a correlation. Correlations do not necessarily indicate cause-and-effect relations: Daydreaming could cause shyness, or shyness could cause daydreaming.

Correlation is not causation. Does being a Boy Scout increase people's tendency to join community organizations later, or do young people who like to join groups continue to do so when they are adults? Without performing an experiment, we cannot tell.

than companies that do not. Can we conclude that the heavy use of computers is the cause of the increased productivity? No, we cannot; correlation does not prove causation. Is it likely that the two types of small companies (those that make heavy use of computers and those that do not) are identical in all other ways? Probably not. For example, companies that make heavy use of computers can afford to do so, and they can probably afford to make other investments that might increase productivity. In addition, these companies may also have managers who are up-to-date in other respects, and having modern ideas about other aspects of running a company may also improve productivity. The use of computers may indeed increase productivity, but the information presented does not permit us to come to this conclusion.

Can anything be done to reduce some of the uncertainty inherent in correlational studies? The answer is yes. When attempting to study the effects of a variable that cannot be altered (such as sex, age, socioeconomic status, or personality characteristics), we can use a procedure called **matching.** Rather than selecting subjects randomly, we *match* the subjects in each of the groups on all of the relevant variables except the one being studied. For instance, if we want to study the effects of shyness on daydreaming, we may gather two groups of subjects, shy and nonshy. We select the subjects in each group in such a way that the effects of other variables are minimized. We make sure that the average age, intelligence, income, and personality characteristics (other than shyness) of the two groups are the same. If we find that, say, the shy group is, on average, younger than the nonshy group, we will replace some of the people in the shy group with older shy people until the average age is the same.

If, after following this matching procedure, we find that shyness is still related to daydreaming, we can be more confident that the relation is one of cause and effect and that the differences between the two variables are not caused by a third variable. The limitation of the matching procedure is that we may not know all the variables that should be held constant. If, unbeknownst to us, the two groups are not matched on an important variable, then the results will be misleading. In any case, even the matching procedure does not permit us to decide which variable is the cause and which is the effect; we still do not know whether shyness causes daydreaming or daydreaming causes shyness.

The strengths and limitations of correlational studies will become evident in subsequent chapters in this book. For example, almost all studies that attempt to discover the environmental factors that influence personality characteristics or the relation between these characteristics and people's behavior are correlational.

nity organizations. However, this conclusion is not warranted. All we can say is that people who join the Boy Scouts in their youth tend to join community organizations later in life. It could be that people who, for one reason or another, are "joiners" tend to join the Boy Scouts when they are young and community organizations when they are older. To determine cause and effect, we would have to perform an experiment. For example, we would make some boys join the Boy Scouts and prevent others from doing so, and then see how many organizations they voluntarily joined later in life. Because we cannot interfere in people's lives in such a way, we can never be certain that being a Boy Scout increases a person's tendency to join community organizations later.

The news media often report the results of correlational studies. We are led to believe that because two variables are correlated, one event causes another. But this conclusion may not be true. For example, a news magazine reported a study that found that small companies that make heavy use of computers have productivity-per-employee levels 2.5 times greater

matching A systematic selection of subjects in groups in an experiment or (more often) a correlational study to ensure that the mean values of important subject variables of the groups are similar.

Single-Subject Research

Not all investigations use groups of subjects. **Single-subject research** investigates the behavior of individuals, and for some phenomena this method is very effective. Single-subject research can involve either experiments or correlational studies. Consider an example of a single-subject experiment. Suppose that we are investigating a potential food additive. We feed a small amount to a rat, who immediately has a convulsion and dies. We now strongly suspect that the compound is poisonous. Perhaps we will try it on one more rat to be sure that the first one was not about to die anyway. If the second rat dies, we probably will not bother to do further testing. The response is so closely tied to the administration of the compound that we conclude that one event caused the other. There is no point in carrying out a full-fledged testing procedure involving an experimental group given the drug and a control group given a placebo.

In single-subject research, individual subjects can serve as their own controls. Suppose that we wanted to see whether a particular hormone affected a rat's level of activity. We would house a rat in a cage that contained a running wheel in which the animal could exercise. An electric counter connected to the wheel would keep track of how many revolutions the wheel made each day. We would record the animal's activity for several days and wait until this measure had stabilized. Once it had, we would start giving the rat an injection of a placebo each day. At first, the injections might affect the animal's activity level, but eventually the animal would become habituated to the injections. Next, we would start giving the rat injections of the hormone. We might try several different doses to see whether different concentrations of the hormone had different effects. Following each change in dose, we would wait until the animal's activity level had stabilized before moving on to the next dose. Finally, we would begin administering the placebo again.

Figure 2.8 shows some hypothetical results. We see the rat's habituation to the effects of a daily injection on days 1 through 6 and the effects of various doses of the hormone. We also see that the animal's activity level returns to normal soon after the injections contain no hormone. This return to the baseline level of activity assures us that the hormone has not had long-term effects on the animal's behavior. (See *Figure 2.8.*)

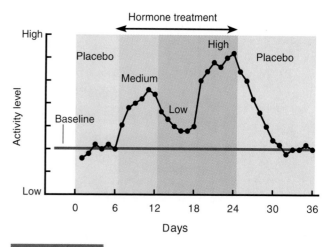

Figure 2.8

Results of a hypothetical single-subject experiment.

In another type of single-subject study, a **case study**, psychologists take advantage of events that have occurred outside their control. For example, some colleagues and I studied a woman who had sustained a serious skull fracture in an automobile accident (Margolin, Marcel, and Carlson, 1985). The damage to her brain made it impossible for her to read, although her vision was almost normal. We gave her lists of words, such as *rose, violet, carrot, petunia,* and *daffodil,* and asked her to choose the one that did not belong with the others. She would point to the word *carrot* even though she could not read it. Her performance indicates that people can have some idea of the meaning of words even though they cannot say the words to themselves.

Obviously, we cannot fracture the skulls of a group of people to study phenomena like this. Instead, we study patients whose brains have been damaged by accident or disease. We compare their performance before and after the brain damage occurred. Usually, we do not meet the patients until after the brain damage occurs, so we must compare their performance with our estimate of what it was previously. In some cases, our estimate is certain to be reasonably accurate. For example, if we meet a patient who cannot read but who received a college education, we can be sure that the inability to read was caused by the brain damage.

Case studies are also performed by clinical psychologists and other mental health professionals, who observe the behavior of clients and listen to what they have to say about their lives. Clinicians often try to correlate events in the client's past with the client's present behavior and personality. Studies like these are called **retrospective studies** ("backward looking"), and their validity depends heavily on the client's memory of past events. Because recollections are often faulty, one must be cautious about accepting the conclusions of retrospective studies whose results cannot be independently verified. And because these studies are correlational and not experimental, we cannot be sure that the events that occurred in the past were the causes of the client's present behavior.

single-subject research   An experiment or correlational study concerning the behavior of individual subjects rather than comparisons of the average performance of groups of subjects.

case study   Observation of the behavior of individuals having special characteristics, such as psychological or neurological disorders.

retrospective study   A research technique that requires subjects to report what happened in the past.

Case studies can have yet another drawback: The people who are studied may not be representative of the population as a whole. For example, many mental health professionals used to believe that homosexuality was a psychological disorder, caused by unhealthy family relationships. They made this conclusion because they found that most of their homosexual clients reported that they had experienced such relationships during childhood. However, this conclusion is not justified. People do not consult mental health professionals unless they have some sort of problem; thus, the professionals are unlikely to see happy, untroubled people in their practices. Instead, they see a nonrepresentative sample of the population. In fact, research has shown that mentally healthy homosexuals are no more likely than anyone else to have had unhappy childhoods. (Chapter 13 reviews the evidence.)

Generality

When we carry out an experiment or a correlational study, we probably assume that our subjects are representative of the larger population. In fact, a representative group of subjects is usually referred to as a **sample** of the larger population. If we study the behavior of a group of five-year-old children, we want to make conclusions about five-year-olds in general. We want to be able to **generalize** our specific results to the population as a whole—to conclude that the results tell us something about human nature in general, not simply about our particular subjects.

Many researchers recruit their subjects from introductory courses in psychology. The results of studies that use these students as subjects can be generalized only to other groups of students who are similarly recruited. In the strictest sense, the results cannot be generalized to students in other courses, to adults in general, or even to all students enrolled in introductory psychology—after all, students who volunteer to serve as subjects may be different from those who do not. Even if we used truly random samples of all age groups of adults in our area, we could not generalize the results to people who live in other geographical regions. If our ability to generalize is really so limited, is it worthwhile to do psychological research?

But we are not so strictly limited, of course. Most psychologists assume that a relation among variables that is observed in one group of humans will also be seen in other groups as long as the sample of subjects is not especially unusual. For example, we may expect data obtained from prisoners to have less generality than data obtained from college students.

The problems associated with generalizing occur in correlational studies just as often as they do in experiments. In one famous case, the limitations of generalizing were demonstrated with a vengeance. During the United States presidential campaign of 1948 poll takers predicted, from a sampling of the populace, that Thomas E. Dewey would easily defeat Harry S Truman. Of course, they were embarrassingly wrong. The sample of subjects had been drawn from telephone directories. In 1948, fewer Americans had telephones, and those

Figure 2.9

Truman, the winner of the 1948 U.S. presidential election, appears to enjoy the premature headline proclaiming Dewey's victory. The *Chicago Daily Tribune* based its news story on the opinion polls instead of waiting for the verdict from the voting polls. Modern polling techniques are much more accurate, but they are still not infallible.

who did tended to be wealthier than those who did not. A much higher proportion of people who did not have telephones voted for Truman. Hence, the samples drawn by poll takers were not representative of the population to which they wanted to generalize—United States voters. (See *Figure 2.9*.)

Evaluating Scientific Issues

Format for Critical Thinking

In each of the subsequent chapters in this book, you will find a section called "Evaluating Scientific Issues." These sections present a controversial issue or an unanswered question and then examine the quality of the evidence concerning the issue. Each section begins with a description of the controversy. In most cases, this description includes an assertion that a certain state of affairs is true. For example, the section in Chapter 6 evaluates the assertion that subliminal messages can be used in teaching or advertising, and the section in Chapter 12 evaluates the assertion that television viewing impairs children's cognitive development.

sample A selection of items from a larger population—for example, a group of subjects selected to participate in an experiment.

generalization The conclusion that the results obtained from a sample apply also to the population from which the sample was taken.

After presenting the assertion, I will describe the evidence in favor of it. Next, I will present contrary evidence along with a critique of the evidence in favor of the assertion. The critiques refer back to the rules of the scientific method, described in this chapter. I will then accept or reject the assertion—or we will see that more evidence is needed before a decision can be made.

The point of these sections is to help you develop your ability to think critically—to learn to evaluate controversies by examining the nature and quality of the evidence and by drawing from the evidence only those conclusions that logically follow from it. Unfortunately, many people misuse or misinterpret research findings or misrepresent falsehoods as rigorous scientific truths in attempts to alter our attitudes and opinions or to sell us something. For example, advertisers will cite the opinions of scientific "experts." But there is no certified board of experts who are always right; we need to know the basis for the experts' opinions. That is, we need to know what the evidence is and understand how to evaluate it.

People who try to convince us of something often use nonscientific arguments. They may say something like "Everyone knows that . . ." or "Contrary to what so-called 'experts' say, common sense tells us that . . ." (The rule seems to be: If you cannot find an expert to quote, then condemn experts as "living in an ivory tower" or being "out of touch with reality.") People trying to convince us of something will also cite their personal experiences or offer testimonials of other people. If the cases they cite are rich with personal details, it is difficult not to be swayed by them.

Although some of you will eventually become psychologists, most of you will not. Nevertheless, I hope that by reading this book you will come to appreciate that being able to apply the scientific method to issues in psychological research will help you to evaluate critically other issues that you will encounter in everyday life.

Interim Summary

The Scientific Method in Psychology

The scientific method allows us to determine the causes of natural phenomena. There are three basic forms of scientific research: naturalistic observations, experiments, and correlational studies. Only experiments permit us to be certain that a cause-and-effect relation exists. An experiment tests the truth of a hypothesis, which is a tentative statement about a relation between an independent variable and a dependent variable. Hypotheses come from information gathered through naturalistic observations, from previous experiments, or from formal theories.

To perform an experiment, a scientist alters the value of the independent variable and measures changes in the dependent variable. Because a hypothesis is stated in general terms, the scientist must specify the particular operations that he or she will perform to manipulate the independent variable and to measure the dependent variable. That is, the experimenter must provide operational definitions, which may require some ingenuity and hard work. Operational definitions are a necessary part of the procedure by which a hypothesis is tested; they also can eliminate confusion by giving concrete form to the hypothesis, making its meaning absolutely clear to other scientists.

Validity is the degree to which an operational definition produces a particular value of an independent variable or measures the value of a dependent variable. Reliability refers to the consistency and precision of an operational definition. Researchers achieve high reliability by carefully controlling the conditions of their studies and by ensuring that procedures are followed correctly. Measurement involving subjectivity requires researchers to seek high interrater reliability.

When designing an experiment, experimenters must be sure to control extraneous variables that may confound their results. If an extra variable is inadvertently manipulated and if this extra variable has an effect on the dependent variable, then the results of the experiment will be invalid. Confounding of subject variables can be caused by improperly assigning subjects to groups or by treatments that cause some subjects to leave the experiment. Another problem involves subjects' expectations. Most subjects in psychological research try to figure out what the experimenter is trying to accomplish, and their conclusions can affect their behavior. If knowledge of the experimental condition could alter the subjects' behavior, the experiment should be conducted with a single-blind procedure. And if that knowledge might also alter the experimenter's assessment of the subjects' behavior, a double-blind procedure should be used.

Correlational studies involve assessing relations among variables that the researcher cannot readily manipulate, such as personality characteristics, age, and sex. The investigator attempts to hold these variables constant by matching members in each of the groups on all relevant variables except for the one being studied. The problem is that investigators may miss a variable that affects the outcome. And, of course, even a well-designed correlational study cannot determine which variable is the cause and which is the effect.

Not all studies involve comparisons of the behavior of groups of subjects. Single-subject research consists of the detailed observation of individual subjects under different conditions. Case studies involve careful observations of the behavior of specific people, such as those with psychological or neurological disorders. Retrospective case studies ask subjects to recall events from earlier in their lives.

Researchers are almost never interested only in the particular subjects they study; they want to be able to generalize their results to a larger population. The confidence that researchers can have in their generalizations depends on the nature of the variables being studied and on the composition of the sample group of subjects.

Thought Questions

- How might you apply the four steps of the scientific method to a question of your own—for example, whether time spent studying affects a student's grades?
- What is the relation between theories and hypotheses?
- Suppose that you were interested in studying the effects of sleep deprivation on learning ability. Which of these two variables would be the independent variable and which would be the dependent variable? How might you operationally define these variables?
- What is the difference between description and explanation in psychology?
- In what ways might an operational definition be reliable yet not valid? Valid yet not reliable?

Ethics

Because psychologists must study living subjects, they must obey ethical rules as well as scientific rules. Great care is needed in the treatment of human subjects because we can hurt people in very subtle ways. For example, reconsider the hypothetical experiment on anger and concentration. For the experiment to be scientifically valid, we must make the subjects angry. How would this be done? How would the subjects be likely to react? Is it possible that the experimenter's rude behavior would have negative, long-lasting effects on the subjects?

Research with Human Subjects

In the United States, federal regulations state that all departments of psychology that engage in federally funded research must have a committee that reviews the ethics of all studies using humans. The committee must review the studies before they are performed to ensure that subjects will be treated properly. In addition, the American Psychological Association (APA) has developed ethical guidelines for human research.

The APA guidelines direct all psychologists conducting human research to treat their subjects with respect. Two guidelines direct researchers not to coerce potential subjects into participating in research. Thus, a course instructor cannot require students to participate as subjects in psychological research as a condition of completing the class. In addition, researchers must give all potential participants every opportunity to decline or withdraw from a study without fear of being punished for doing so.

The guidelines also require that researchers obtain the **informed consent** of potential subjects *before* they participate in research. Informed consent can be given only after the potential subject reads a written statement prepared by the researcher that discloses those aspects of the research that might affect a person's willingness to participate in the study. The statement also states the requirements of the subject's participation during the course of the study and the kind of compensation (usually extra class credit) provided by the researcher for that participation. The informed consent statement constitutes a contract between subject and researcher and is signed by both of them.

Sometimes the design of a study requires that subjects remain unaware of the true nature of the research. As we saw earlier, knowing the purpose of the experiment may bias subjects' responses. Such behavior would invalidate the results of the study. Thus, in some situations, deception is necessary to protect the integrity of the research. According to the APA guidelines, deception is justified as long as the researcher satisfies the following conditions:

- The participant is provided with a sufficient explanation of this action as soon as the research is completed.
- The deception does not otherwise psychologically or physically harm potential subjects.
- The dignity of the subjects is maintained.

Informed consent requires that potential subjects understand exactly what is expected of them during the course of the research and that the investigator protects participants from physical and psychological discomfort, harm, and danger. If stress or danger is possible, the participant must be so informed and every step must be taken to minimize any potentially negative effects.

Another APA guideline concerns **confidentiality,** or the privacy of subjects concerning their participation in research. This guideline specifies that all steps must be taken to assure that subjects' participation is confidential. If any possibility exists that someone other than the researchers may have access to the data, the subjects must be informed of this possibility before they provide their informed consent to participate.

Finally, after participating in research, subjects must receive a **debriefing,** in which they are fully informed of the true nature and purpose of the research and its potential scientific value. If the experimenters are concerned that other potential subjects may learn of the nature of the research before the project is completed, they may delay the debriefing session until the study is finished. However, if they do so, they must take special care that no damage is caused by the delay.

Research with Animal Subjects

Although most psychologists study the behavior of their fellow humans, some study the behavior of other animals. Any-

informed consent Agreement to participate as a subject in an experiment after being informed about the nature of the research and any possible adverse effects.

confidentiality Privacy of subjects and nondisclosure of their participation in a research project.

debriefing Full disclosure to research participants of the true nature and purpose of a research project after its completion.

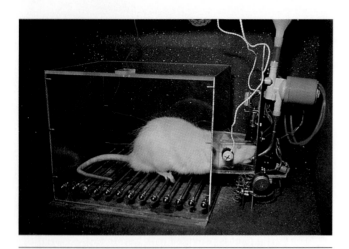

Should animals be used in psychological research? Most psychologists and other researchers strongly believe that animal research, conducted humanely, is necessary and ethically justified. This rat is receiving a drink of a sweet liquid during its participation in a learning task.

time we use another species of animal for our own purposes, we should be sure that what we are doing is both humane and worthwhile. A good case can be made that such psychological research qualifies on both counts. Humane treatment is a matter of procedure. We know how to maintain laboratory animals in good health in comfortable, sanitary conditions. For experiments that involve surgery, we know how to administer anesthetics and analgesics so that animals do not suffer. Most industrially developed societies have very strict regulations about the care of animals and require approval of the procedures that will be used in the experiments in which they participate. There is no excuse for mistreating animals in our care. In fact, the vast majority of laboratory animals *are* treated humanely.

Whether an experiment is worthwhile is more difficult to say. We use animals for many purposes. We eat their meat and their eggs and drink their milk; we turn their hides into leather; we extract insulin and other hormones from their organs to treat people with diseases; we train them to do useful work on farms or to entertain us. These are all forms of exploitation. Even having a pet is a form of exploitation: It is we—not they—who decide that they will live in our homes. The fact is, we have been using other animals throughout the history of our species.

Pet owning causes much more suffering among animals than scientific research does. As Miller (1983) notes, pet owners are not required to receive permission to house their pets from boards of experts that include veterinarians, nor are they subject to periodic inspections to be sure that their

homes are clean and sanitary, that their pets have enough space to exercise properly, and that their diets are appropriate. Scientific researchers are. Miller also notes that fifty times more dogs and cats are killed by humane societies each year because they have been abandoned by their former owners than are used in scientific research.

The use of animals in research and teaching is a special target of animal rights activists. Nicholl and Russell (1990) examined twenty-one books written by such activists and calculated the number of pages devoted to concern for different uses of animals. Next, they compared the relative concern the authors showed for these uses to the numbers of animals actually involved in each of these categories. The authors showed relatively little concern for animals used for food, hunting, or furs or for those killed in pounds. However, although only 0.3 percent of the animals were used for research and education, 63.3 percent of the pages are devoted to this use. In terms of pages per million animals used, the authors showed 665 times more concern for research and education than for food and 231 times more than for hunting. Even the use of animals for furs (which consumes two-thirds as many animals as research and education) attracted 41.9 times less attention per animal.

Our species is beset by medical, mental, and behavioral problems, many of which can be solved only through research involving animals. In fact, research with laboratory animals has produced important discoveries about the possible causes or potential treatments of neurological and mental disorders, including Parkinson's disease, schizophrenia, manic-depressive illness, anxiety disorders, obsessive compulsive disorders, anorexia nervosa, obesity, and drug addictions. Although much progress has been made, these problems are still with us and cause much human suffering. Unless we continue our research with laboratory animals, these problems will not be solved. Some people have suggested that instead of using laboratory animals in our research, we could use tissue cultures or computer simulations. Unfortunately, tissue cultures or computer simulations are not substitutes for living organisms. We have no way to study behavioral problems such as addictions in tissue cultures, nor can we program a computer to simulate the workings of an animal's nervous system. If we could, we would already have all the answers.

Biology and Culture

Cross-Cultural Research

Although most psychologists study members of their own cultures, **cross-cultural psychologists** are interested in the effects of cultures on behavior. The term *culture* traditionally refers to a group of people who live together in a common environment, who share customs, religious beliefs and practices, and who often resemble each other ge-

cross-cultural psychology A branch of psychology that studies the effects of culture on behavior.

netically. However, definitions of culture can vary widely. For example, the "North American culture" includes people of diverse ethnic and religious backgrounds, political beliefs, and economic statuses, while the "Fore people" includes a small, fairly homogeneous group of people living in the highlands of New Guinea. Within a broadly defined culture, we can identify subcultures based on ethnicity, age, political beliefs, and other characteristics by which people define themselves.

Cross-cultural research provides an opportunity for psychologists to test the generality of the results of a study performed with members of a particular culture. If similar studies performed with members of different cultures produce similar results, we can be more confident that we have discovered a general principle that applies broadly to members of our species. On the other hand, if the studies yield different results in different cultures, we need to carry out further research. Obviously, differences among cultures affect the variables we are interested in. We need to perform further cross-cultural research to identify these differences.

Cultures differ with respect to two major classes of variables: biological and ecological. Biological variables include such factors as diet, genetics, and endemic diseases. Ecological variables include such factors as geography, climate, political systems, population density, religion, cultural myths, and education. Behavioral differences among people of different cultures result from differences in biological and ecological variables.

Identifying the cultural variables responsible for behavioral differences is a difficult process. In cross-cultural research, culture is considered to be a treatment variable—something like an independent variable (Berry et al., 1992). But cultures, like people, differ in many ways, and people are born into their cultures, not assigned to them by psychologists performing experiments. Thus, cross-cul-

Population density, revealed by satellite photos of North America at night, is an important ecological cultural variable.

tural comparisons are subject to the same limitations that affect other correlational studies.

Psychologists who do cross-cultural research have investigated social behaviors, personality differences, problem solving, intellectual abilities, perceptual abilities, and esthetics. This book examines research that demonstrates the interplay between biology and culture, such as the role of the environment in brain development, the effects of cultural differences in child-rearing practices, cultural definitions of intelligence, cultural differences in emotional expressions, and expressions of mental disorders in different cultural contexts. The sections entitled "Biology and Culture" should help you appreciate the effects of variables that people within a culture are rarely aware of because they are an implicit part of their own lives.

Some cultures are small and relatively homogeneous, such as these Fore people living in the highlands of New Guinea, dressed for a festival.

Interim Summary

Ethics

Because psychologists study living organisms, they must follow ethical principles in the treatment of their subjects. The American Psychological Association has developed ethical guidelines that require informed consent, confidentiality, and a postexperiment debriefing. Subjects may withdraw their consent to participate at any time before or during an experiment without any penalty. If deception is necessary, the experimenter must be certain that the subjects will not be harmed psychologically or physically and that their dignity will be maintained. Committees review all psychological research before giving their consent for it to be carried out to assure that these guidelines are met.

Research that involves the use of laboratory animals is also guided by ethical principles. It is incumbent on all scientists using these animals to see that they are housed comfortably and treated humanely, and laws have been enacted to ensure that they are. Such research has already produced many benefits to humankind and promises to continue to do so.

Thought Questions

■ In your opinion, should ethical rules be absolute or should they be flexible? Suppose that a researcher proposed to perform an experiment whose results could have important and beneficial consequences for society. However, the proposed study would violate ethical guidelines because it would involve a moderate degree of psychological discomfort for the participants. Should the researcher be given permission to perform the experiment? Should an exception be made because of the potential benefits to society?

■ Why do you think some people apparently are more upset about using animals for research and teaching than for other purposes?

Understanding Research Results

The study is finished. Now what do we do? We have a collection of data—numbers representing the measurements of behavior we have made. What did we find? Was our hypothesis supported? To answer these questions, we must analyze the data we have collected. We will use some statistical methods to do so.

Descriptive Statistics: What Are the Results?

In most of the examples I have cited so far, the behavior of groups of subjects was observed and measured. Once a study is finished, we need some way to compare these measurements. To do so, we will use **descriptive statistics,** mathematical procedures that permit us to summarize sets of numbers. Using these procedures, we will calculate measures that summarize the performance of the subjects in each group. Then

---

descriptive statistics Mathematical procedures for organizing collections of data, such as determining the mean, the median, the range, the variance, and the correlation coefficient.

measure of central tendency A statistical measure used to characterize the value of items in a sample of numbers.

mean A measure of central tendency; the sum of a group of values divided by their number; the arithmetic average.

median A measure of central tendency; the midpoint of a group of values arranged numerically.

---

we can compare these measures to see whether the groups of subjects behaved differently (step 4 of the scientific method). We can also use these measures to describe the results of the experiment to others (step 5 of the scientific method). You are already familiar with some descriptive statistics. For example, you know how to calculate the average of a set of numbers; an average is a common measure of *central tendency.* You might be less familiar with measures of *variability,* which tell us how groups of numbers differ from one another, and with measures of *relations,* which tell us how closely related two sets of numbers are.

Measures of Central Tendency

When we say that the average weight of an adult male in North America is 173 pounds or that the average density of population in the United States is 63.9 people per square mile, we are using a **measure of central tendency,** a statistic that represents many observations. There are several different measures of central tendency, but the most common is the average, also called the **mean.** The mean of a set of observations is calculated by adding the individual values and dividing by the number of observations. The mean is the most frequently used measure of central tendency in reports of psychological experiments.

Although the mean is usually selected to measure central tendency, it is not the most precise measure, especially if a set of numbers contains a few especially high or low values. The most representative measure of central tendency is the *median.* For this reason, we usually read "median family income" rather than "mean family income" in newspaper or magazine articles. To calculate the **median** of a set of numbers, we arrange them in numerical order and find the midpoint. For example, the median of the numbers 1, 2, and 6 is 2.

To understand why the median is the best representative of a set of numbers that contains some extreme values, consider a small town of one hundred families. Ninety-nine of the families, all of whom work in the local textile mill, make between $15,000 and $20,000 per year. However, the income of one family is $2 million per year (an extreme value, to be sure). This family consists of a popular novelist and her husband, who moved to the area because of its mild climate. The *mean* income for the town as a whole, considering the novelist as well as the mill workers, is $37,325 per year. In contrast, the *median* income for the town is $17,500 per year. Clearly, the median represents the typical family income of the town better than the mean does.

Why, then, would we ever bother to use the mean rather than the median? As we will see later in this chapter, the mean is used to calculate other important statistics and has special mathematical properties that often make it more useful than the median.

Measures of Variability

Many experiments produce two sets of numbers, one consisting of the experimental group's scores and one of the control group's scores. If the mean scores of these two groups differ, the experimenter can conclude that the independent variable had an effect. However, the experimenter must decide whether the difference between the two groups is larger than what would probably occur by chance. To make this decision, the experimenter calculates a **measure of variability**—a statistic that describes the degree to which scores in a set of numbers differ from each other. The psychologist then uses this measure as a basis for comparing the means of the two groups.

Two sets of numbers can have the same mean or median and still be very different. For example, the mean and median of both sets of numbers listed in Table 2.1 are the same, but the numbers are clearly different. The variability of the scores in set B is greater. (See *Table 2.1*.)

One way of stating the difference between the two sets of numbers is to say that the numbers in set A range from 8 to 12 and the numbers in set B range from 0 to 20. The **range** of a set of numbers is simply the largest number minus the smallest. Thus, the range of set A is 4 and the range of set B is 20.

The range is not used very often to describe the results of psychological experiments because another measure of variability—the standard deviation—has more useful mathematical properties. To calculate the standard deviation of a set of numbers, you first calculate the mean and then find the difference between each number and the mean. These difference scores are squared (that is, multiplied by themselves) and then summed. The mean of this total is called the *variance;* the **standard deviation** is the square root of the variance. The more different the numbers are from each other, the larger the standard deviation will be. (See *Table 2.2*.)

Measurement of Relations

In correlational studies, the investigator measures the degree to which two variables are related. For example, suppose that a psychologist has developed a new aptitude test and wants to sell the test to college admissions committees for screening applicants. Before the committees will consider buying the test, the psychologist must show that a person's score on the

test is related to his or her subsequent success in college. To do so, the psychologist will give the test to a group of freshmen entering college and later obtain their average grades. The psychologist will then measure the relation between test scores and grades.

Table 2.2

Calculation of the Variance and Standard Deviation of Two Sets of Numbers Having the Same Mean

Sample A

Score	Difference Between Score and Mean	Difference Squared
8	10 − 8 = 2	4
9	10 − 9 = 1	1
10	10 − 10 = 0	0
11	11 − 10 = 1	1
12	12 − 10 = 2	4
Total: 50	Total:	10
Mean: 50/5 = 10	Mean (variance):	10/5 = 2
	Square root (standard deviation):	1.41

Sample B

Score	Difference Between Score and Mean	Difference Squared
0	10 − 0 = 10	100
5	10 − 5 = 5	25
10	10 − 10 = 0	0
15	15 − 10 = 5	25
20	20 − 10 = 10	100
Total: 50	Total:	250
Mean: 50/5 = 10	Mean (variance):	250/5 = 25
	Square root (standard deviation):	5

Table 2.1

Two Sets of Numbers Having the Same Mean and Median but Different Ranges

Sample A	Sample B
8	0
9	5
10 ← Median	10 ← Median
11	15
12	20
Total: 50	Total: 50
Mean: 50/5 = 10	Mean: 50/5 = 10
Range: 12 − 8 = 4	Range: 20 − 0 = 20

---

measure of variability A statistical measure used to characterize the dispersion in values of items in a sample of numbers.

range The difference between the highest score and the lowest score of a sample.

standard deviation A statistic that expresses the variability of a measurement; square root of the sum of the squared deviations from the mean.

Table 2.3

Test Scores and Average Grades of Ten Students

Student	Test Score	Average Grade[a]
A. C.	15	2.8
B. F.	12	3.2
G. G.	19	3.5
L. H.	8	2.2
R. J.	14	3.0
S. K.	11	2.6
P. R.	13	2.8
A. S.	7	1.5
J. S.	9	1.9
P. V.	18	3.8

[a]0 = F; 4 = A

Let's suppose that we give the test to ten students entering college and later obtain their average grades. We will have two scores for each person, as shown in *Table 2.3*. We can examine the relation between these variables by plotting the scores on a graph. For example, student R. J. received a test score of 14 and earned an average grade of 3.0. We can represent this student's score as a point on the graph shown in Figure 2.10. The horizontal axis represents the test score, and the vertical axis represents the average grade. We put a point on the graph that corresponds to R. J.'s score on both of these measures. (See *Figure 2.10.*)

We do this for each of the remaining students and then look at the graph, called a **scatterplot,** to determine whether the two variables are related. When we examine the scatterplot, we see that the points tend to be located along a diagonal line that runs from the lower left to the upper right, indicating that a rather strong relation exists between a student's test score and average grade. (See *Figure 2.10.*) High scores are associated with good grades, low scores with poor grades.

Although scatterplots are useful, we need a more convenient way to communicate the results to others, so we calculate the **correlation coefficient,** a number that expresses the strength of a relation. Calculating this statistic for the two sets of scores gives a correlation of +.9 between the two variables.

The size of a correlation coefficient can vary from 0 (no relation) to 1.0 (perfect relation). A perfect relation means that if we know the value of a person's score on one measure, then we can predict exactly what his or her score will be on the other. Thus, a correlation of +.9 is very close to perfect; our hypothetical aptitude test is an excellent predictor of how well a student will do in college.

Correlations can be negative as well as positive. A *negative* correlation indicates that high values on one measure are associated with low values on the other and vice versa. An example of a negative correlation is the relation between people's mathematical ability and the amount of time it would take them to solve a series of math problems. People with the highest level of ability will take the least amount of time to solve the problems. For purposes of prediction a negative correlation is just as good as a positive one. A correlation of −.9 is an almost perfect relation, but in this case high scores on one measure predict low scores on the other. Examples of scatterplots illustrating high and low correlations, both positive and negative, are shown in *Figure 2.11.*

If the points in a scatterplot fall along a line, the relation is said to be *linear.* But many relations are nonlinear. For example, consider the relation between level of illumination and reading speed. Obviously, it is impossible to read in the dark. As the light level increases, people's reading speed will increase, but once an adequate amount of light falls on a page, further increases in light will have no effect. Finally, the light becomes so bright and dazzling that people's reading speed will decline. (See *Figure 2.12.*) A correlation coefficient cannot accurately represent a nonlinear relation such as this because the mathematics involved in calculating this measure assume that the relation is linear. Scientists who discover nonlinear relations in their research usually present them in graphs or express them as nonlinear mathematical formulas.

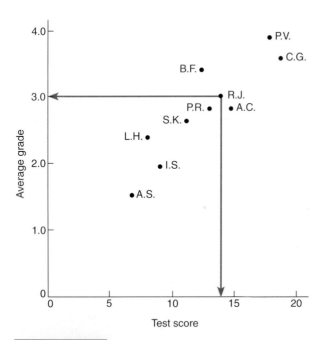

Figure 2.10

A scatterplot of the test scores and average grades of ten students. An example of graphing one data point (student R. J.) is shown by the red lines.

scatterplot A graph of items that have two values; one value is plotted against the horizontal axis and the other against the vertical axis.

correlation coefficient A measurement of the degree to which two variables are related.

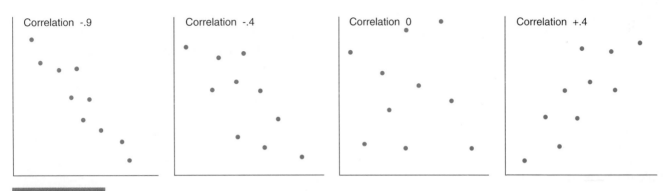

Figure 2.11

Scatterplots of variables having several different levels of correlation.

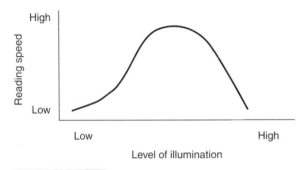

Figure 2.12

A nonlinear relation. Results of a hypothetical experiment investigating the relation between level of illumination and reading speed. A correlation coefficient cannot adequately represent this kind of relation.

Inferential Statistics: Are the Results Significant?

When we perform an experiment, we select a sample of subjects from a larger population. In doing so, we hope that the results will be similar to those we might have obtained had we used all members of the population in the experiment. We randomly assign the subjects to groups in an unbiased manner, alter only the relevant independent variables, and measure the dependent variable using a valid and reliable method. After the experiment is completed, we must examine the results and decide whether a relation really exists between independent and dependent variables. That is, we must decide whether the results are **statistically significant**—not simply due to chance. To do so, we will use *inferential statistics*. As we saw, descriptive statistics enable us to summarize our data. **Inferential statistics** enable us to determine whether the results are statistically significant.

The concept of statistical significance is not an easy one to grasp, so I want to make sure you understand the purpose of this discussion. Recall our hypothesis that loss of self-esteem increases people's susceptibility to propaganda. We mea-

sure people's opinions about a particular subject and then arrange for members of the experimental group (but not of the control group) to "accidentally" knock over the pile of color slides. Next, we show a propaganda film to the subjects in both groups and then measure their opinions again. To see whether viewing the film changed their opinions, we calculate the mean opinion change for both groups. If the means are different, we can conclude that the loss of self-esteem *does* affect people's susceptibility to propaganda.

But how different is different? Suppose that we tested two groups of people, both treated exactly the same way. Would the mean scores of the two groups be precisely the same? Of course not. *By chance*, they would be at least slightly different. Suppose that we find that the mean score for the group that was subjected to a loss of self-esteem is lower than the mean score for the control group. How much lower would it have to be before we could rightfully conclude that the difference between the groups was significant?

Assessment of Differences Between Samples

The obvious way to determine whether two group means differ significantly is to look at the size of the difference. If it is large, then we can be fairly confident that the independent variable had a significant effect. If it is small, then the difference is probably due to chance. What we need are guidelines to help us determine when a difference is large enough to be statistically significant.

The following example will explain how these guidelines are constructed. A few years ago, I performed a simple correlational study. I distributed cards to students in one of my classes to collect some data that I could analyze to explain

statistical significance The likelihood that an observed relation or difference between two variables is not due to chance factors.

inferential statistics Mathematical procedures for determining whether relations or differences between samples are statistically significant.

some statistical concepts. I will use the data I collected for that purpose here, too.

The seventy-six students in the class had an average height of 67.2 inches. I performed a correlational study to test the following hypothesis: People whose first names end in vowels will, on the average, be shorter than people whose first names end in consonants. (I will tell you later why I expected this hypothesis to be confirmed.)

I divided the subjects into two groups: those whose first names ended in vowels and those whose first names ended in consonants. Table 2.4 contains a listing of these two groups. Indeed, the means for the two groups differed by 4.1 inches. (See *Table 2.4*.)

A difference of 4.1 inches seems large, but how can we be sure that it is not due to chance? What we really need to know

Table 2.4

Height (in Inches) of Selected Samples of Students

Name Ends in Consonant		Name Ends in Vowel
65	61	67
67	68	68
71	70	62
72	65	63
73	73	62
65	60	64
74	70	60
74	72	63
67	63	61
69	67	69
68	73	63
75	66	65
72	71	69
71	72	71
65	64	69
66	69	65
70	73	70
72	75	63
72	72	63
71	66	64
62	71	65
62	68	63
80	70	66
	75	62
		72
		65
		66
		65
		65

Total: 3257
Mean: 3257/47 = 69.3

Total: 1890
Mean: 1890/29 = 65.2
Difference between means: 69.3 − 65.2 = 4.1

Table 2.5

Height (in Inches) of a Random Division of a Class into Two Groups

Group A		Group B	
65	71	63	62
72	63	62	63
72	74	70	65
69	72	70	75
61	71	65	71
69	65	64	80
66	71	75	71
70	67	63	68
66	72	70	71
65	66	75	73
66	72	67	62
65	73	65	72
64	63	68	65
72	69	63	72
63	62	69	66
65	60	67	73
62	70	68	65
67	68	60	73
69		61	
64		74	

Total: 2561
Mean: 67.4

Total: 2586
Mean: 68.1

Difference: −0.7

is how large a difference there would be if the means had been calculated from two groups that were randomly selected. For comparison, I divided the class into two random groups by shuffling the cards with the students' names on them and dealing them out into two piles. Then I calculated the mean height of the people whose names were in each of the piles. This time, the difference between the means was 0.7 inch. (See *Table 2.5*.)

I divided the cards into two random piles five more times, calculating the means and the difference between the means each time. The differences ranged from 0.2 to 0.7 inch. (See *Table 2.6*.) It began to look as though a mean difference of 4.1 inches was bigger than what would be expected by chance.

Next, I divided the cards into two random piles 1000 times. (I used my computer to do the chore.) *Not once* in 1000 times was the difference between the means greater than 3.0 inches. Therefore, I can conclude that if the class is divided randomly into two groups, the chance that the means of their heights will differ by 4.1 inches is much less than one time in a thousand, or 0.1%. Thus, I can safely say that when I divided the students into two groups according to the last letters of their first names, I was dividing them in a way that was somehow related to their height. The division was *not* equivalent to random selection; a person's height *really is* related to the last letter of his or her first name.

Table 2.6

Mean Heights (in Inches) of Five Random Divisions of the Class into Two Groups

Group A	Group B	Difference
67.6	67.9	-0.3
68.1	67.4	0.7
67.8	67.6	0.2
67.9	67.5	0.4
68.0	67.4	0.6

Figure 2.13 presents a frequency distribution of the differences between the means of the two groups for 1000 random divisions of the class. The height of a point on the graph represents the number of times (the frequency) that the difference between the means fell into that particular range. For example, the difference between the means fell between –0.2 and +0.2 inch 170 times. (See *Figure 2.13.*)

Suppose that the difference between the means in our observational study had been smaller than 4.1 inches—say, 2.3 inches. Would we conclude that the difference represented a real relation, or would we decide that the difference was due to chance? A look at Figure 2.13 will help us decide.

We can see that only 15 out of 1000 times (1.5 percent) is the difference between the means of the two groups as large as or larger than 2.3 inches: 11 + 4 = 15. (See *Figure 2.13.*) Therefore, if we obtain a difference of 2.3 inches between the means of the groups and conclude that people whose first names end in vowels tend to be shorter than people whose first names end in consonants, *the likelihood of our being wrong is only 1.5 percent.* The calculations show that we will obtain a difference of at least 2.3 inches between the means

purely by chance only 1.5 percent of the time. Because 1.5 percent is a small number, we are fairly safe in concluding that the relation is statistically significant.

The method used to determine the statistical significance of my original findings from the group of seventy-six students employs the same principles that researchers use to determine whether the results observed in a given experiment represent a real difference or are just due to chance. In this example we considered two possibilities: (1) that the difference between the means was due to chance, and (2) that the difference between the means occurred because the last letter of a person's first name is related to his or her height. We found that a difference of 4.1 inches would be expected less than one time in a thousand. Therefore, we rejected alternative 1 and concluded that alternative 2 was correct. The results supported my original hypothesis.

Ordinarily, psychologists who conduct experiments or correlational studies like this one do not use their computers to divide their subject's scores randomly 1000 times. Instead, they calculate the mean and standard deviation for each group and consult a table that statisticians have already prepared for them. The table (which is based upon special mathematical properties of the mean and standard deviation) will tell them how likely it is that their results could have been obtained by chance. In other words, the table tells them how likely it is that the last letter of a person's first name is *not* related to his or her height. If the likelihood is low enough, they will conclude that the results they obtained are statistically significant. Most psychologists consider a 5 percent probability to be statistically significant but are much more comfortable with 1 percent or less.

It is important to realize that statistical tests help us decide whether results are representative of the larger population but not whether they are *important*. In general usage, the word *significant* does mean "important," but *statistical* significance simply means that the results appear not to be caused

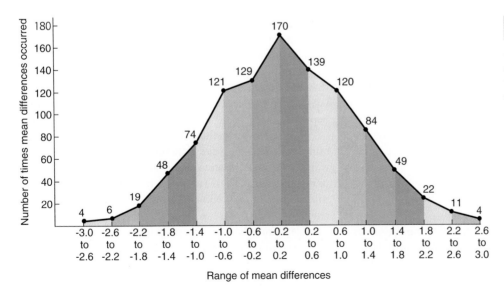

Figure 2.13

A frequency distribution. This distribution illustrates the number of occurrences of various ranges of mean differences in height. The group of 76 people was divided randomly into 2 sets of numbers 1000 times.

Although individuals vary widely in height, men are taller, on the average, than women—and this explains the finding in my classroom observational study.

by chance. For example, suppose that a school board decides to perform an experiment to try a new teaching method. The researchers find that the test scores of students who were taught by the new method are higher than those of students who were taught by the old one. The difference is statistically significant, but it is very small. (A small difference can be statistically significant if the variability within the groups is low enough or if the groups of subjects are very large.) Because changing all classes over to the new method is very expensive, the school system would probably decide to continue with the present method.

Oh yes, I should now tell you why I originally hypothesized that the last letter of a person's first name is related to his or her height. Females are more likely than males to have first names that end in a vowel (Paula, Anna, Marie, etc.). Because females tend to be shorter than males, I expected that a group of students whose first names ended in vowels would be shorter, on average, than those whose first names end in consonants. Indeed, that was what I found.

Interim Summary

Understanding Research Results

Psychologists need ways to communicate their results to others accurately and concisely. They typically employ three kinds of descriptive statistics: measures of central tendency, variability, and relations. The most common examples of these measures are the mean, the median, the standard deviation, and the correlation coefficient.

If psychologists test a hypothesis by comparing the scores of two groups of subjects, they must have some way of deter-

mining whether the observed difference in the mean scores is larger than what would be expected by chance. My example was a correlational study; I certainly did not *manipulate* my students' names—they already had them when they came to my class. However, the procedure I followed is based upon the same logic that a psychologist would use in assessing the significance of the results of an experiment.

Psychologists perform experiments by observing the performance of two or more groups of subjects who have been exposed to different conditions, each representing different values of the independent variable. Next, they calculate the group means and standard deviations of the values of the dependent variable that were measured. Finally, they determine the statistical significance of the results. To do so, they plug means and standard deviations into a formula and consult a special table that statisticians have devised. The table indicates the likelihood of getting such results when the independent variable actually has *no effect* on the dependent variable. If the probability of obtaining these results by chance is sufficiently low, the psychologists will reject the possibility that the independent variable had no effect and decide in favor of the alternative—that it really did have an effect on the dependent variable.

The scientific method consists of a logical system of inquiry with sensible rules that must be followed if a person wants to draw accurate conclusions about the causes of natural phenomena. These rules were originally devised by philosophers who attempted to determine how we can understand reality. By our natures, we are all intuitive psychologists, trying to understand why other people do what they do, so it is especially important to realize how easily we can be fooled about the actual causes of behavior. Thus, everyone, not just professional psychologists, should know the basic steps of the scientific method.

Thought Questions

- Can you think of some variables that you would expect to be positively and negatively correlated?

- What does it mean to say that a study produced statistically significant results?
- Why might the results of a study be statistically significant but nevertheless unimportant?

Suggestions for Further Reading

Christensen, L. B. *Experimental Methodology,* 6th ed. Boston: Allyn and Bacon, 1994.

Kiess, H. O., and Bloomquist, D. W. *Psychological Research Methods: A Conceptual Approach.* Boston: Allyn and Bacon, 1985.

Several standard textbooks discuss the scientific method in psychological research. The Christensen book covers ethical and practical issues as well as theoretical ones, and the Kiess and Bloomquist book describes statistical tests.

Barber, T. X. *Pitfalls in Human Research.* New York: Pergamon Press, 1976.

McCain, G., and Segal, E. M. *The Game of Science,* 4th ed. Belmont, CA: Brooks/Cole, 1981.

Both of these books are rather entertaining accounts of the whys and wherefores of the scientific method. Most of us enjoy reading about the mistakes of others, perhaps thinking that we could have done things better. Barber's book allows us to indulge in this activity; it discusses specific instances of studies that were flawed.

Bell, J. *Evaluating Psychological Information: Sharpening Your Critical Thinking Skills.* Boston: Allyn and Bacon, 1991.

Bell's book provides what the title claims: an excellent way to sharpen your critical thinking skills. It is full of exercises to help you accomplish that goal.

Chapter 3

Evolution, Heredity, and Behavior

Chapter Outline

The Development of Evolutionary Theory

The Voyage of the Beagle • The Origin of Species

Heredity and environment interact to influence our behavior. To understand these influences, many psychologists study evolution, genetics, and events in the immediate environment that affect behavior. Our understanding of biological evolution stems from Darwin's work on natural selection.

Natural Selection and Evolution

Natural Selection • Natural Selection in Human Evolution

Natural selection occurs because individual organisms vary physically, behaviorally, and genetically. Some physical and behavioral characteristics provide a competitive advantage for survival and reproduction. If these characteristics have a genetic basis, they are likely to increase in frequency in successive generations. In human evolution, natural selection has favored an upright posture and increases in brain size. These two factors contributed to the exploration and settling of new environments, and eventually, to culture.

Heredity and Genetics

Basic Principles of Genetics • The Importance of Genetic Diversity • Influences of Gender on Heredity • Mutations and Chromosomal Aberrations • Genetic Disorders • Genetic Counseling • Heredity and Behavior Genetics • *Evaluating Scientific Issues: The Genetics of Alcoholism*

Genes contain instructions for the synthesis of protein molecules. These molecules control bodily development and regulate physiological processes. Sexual reproduction provides for genetic diversity through the recombination of genes. Genetic diversity increases the chance that some members of a species may survive environmental changes. The expression of a gene depends on its interaction with other genes, the sex of the individual possessing that gene, and the environmental conditions under which that individual lives. Changes in genetic material caused by mutations or chromosomal aberrations produce changes in gene expression and play a primary role in the cause of genetic disorders. Twin research, adoption studies, and artificial selection studies using animals are the primary ways that psychologists and other scientists study the relation between genes and behavior. Research suggests that genetic factors may be involved in alcoholism.

Sociobiology

Reproductive Strategies and the Biological Basis of Parenting • The Biological Basis of Altruism • Reciprocal Altruism • Evaluation of Sociobiology • *Biology and Culture: Thinking Critically about Ethnocentrism*

Sociobiology, the study of the biological basis of social behavior, represents an extension of Darwin's work to the explanation of complex human behavior. Sex differences in the resources that parents invest in procreation and caring for their offspring have led to the evolution of four different patterns of selecting mates and rearing offspring. Altruism increases the reproductive success of other individuals with whom one may have many genes in common. We are likely to engage in altruistic acts toward others who may later be in a position to return the favor to us or to our relatives. Sociobiologists have been criticized for neglecting the role of the environment in determining human behavior. When thinking critically about whether human social behaviors, such as those related to ethnocentrism, are genetically or environmentally based, we must be careful to avoid several logical pitfalls. Behavior is due to the complex interaction of evolutionary, genetic, and environmental variables.

*E*ven in summer, the waters of the North Atlantic off Maine's Acadia National Park are chilly. But the cold water is not unpleasant enough to dissuade thousands of tourists from wading, swimming, and body surfing at the park's Sand Beach, a small stretch of sand and pebbles surrounded on each side by massive rocks.

The people who venture into the waters off this beach do so at no small personal risk. Staying in the cold water for too long can lead to *hypothermia,* a condition in which the body's core temperature is lowered. If the body's core temperature drops too far, even simple physical movements become extremely difficult to execute. This poses a life-threatening problem for swimmers who find themselves far from shore.

Sand Beach is also well-known for a powerful riptide, a strong current moving away from the shore. People caught in this riptide often find themselves pulled far from shore in only a few minutes.

Some time ago, two college students, Scott and Mike, spent the summer traveling from coast to coast and from Canada to Mexico. Their trip eventually led them to Acadia National Park. Like many young people who visit the park, they felt compelled to swim in the North Atlantic.

The waves were breaking pretty well that day, and Scott and Mike, along with about twenty others, spent much of the early afternoon body surfing. Both Mike and Scott were getting tired; they decided that they would catch one more wave before calling it a day. Because it was to be their last ride of the day, they wanted to make it a good one. They waited patiently for just the right wave. After several minutes, Mike noticed that they had drifted far from shore.

"Hey, Scott," he said. "We're pretty far out—we'd better head back in before this riptide makes us sharkbait."

Scott agreed. "Yeah, you're right; it's a little scary out here."

Just as they started swimming toward shore, they heard a voice behind them, pleading, "Wait, don't leave me out here! Help me, I'm starting to drown!"

Both Mike and Scott were surprised; they thought they were the only people who had drifted out. They both whirled around in just enough time to see a man's head sink below the surface.

Mike and Scott immediately swam toward the drowning swimmer. Mike reached him first and tried to get behind him. But he swam too close—the drowning swimmer latched on to him, attempting to climb on top of him in his desperate effort to reach the air. Scott grabbed the man from behind and pulled him off Mike.

Mike warned the man, "Stop fighting us or we'll leave you here." The man, gulping for air, reluctantly relaxed, floating on his back while Scott towed him toward shore.

Mike and Scott spent the next fifteen minutes taking turns towing him. They both screamed for help, but they were too far away; the pounding surf muffled their pleas.

Mike and Scott were getting very tired and scared. They could feel their bodies weakening. They had been in the chilly water for a long time. They knew that they were beginning to feel the effects of hypothermia—they began to wonder whether they were going to make it to the shore.

But they kept taking turns towing the man and yelling for help.

Finally, their pleas were heard. A lifeguard swimming atop a surfboard appeared. "Help me get him up on the board," he said.

After the man was on the board, he turned to Mike and Scott. "You guys all right?" he asked.

They both nodded. "We're almost there; we'll make it," Scott replied.

Mike and Scott started swimming slowly. They managed to catch a good-sized wave that brought them crashing onto the shore. They crawled several yards out of the surf. Simultaneously, they collapsed. They lay on the sand and pebbles, tired and dazed by what they had just experienced.

The Development of Evolutionary Theory

From my early youth I have had the strongest desire to understand and explain whatever I observed—that is, to group all facts under some general laws. . . . Therefore, my success as a man of science, whatever this may have amounted to, has been determined, as far as I can judge, by complex and diversified mental qualities and conditions. Of these, the most important have been—the love of science—unbounded patience in long reflecting over any subject—industry in observing and collecting facts—and a fair share of invention and common sense. With such moderate abilities as I possess, it is truly surprising that I should have influenced to a considerable extent the belief of scientific men on some important points.(Darwin, 1887, pp. 67–71)

These are humble words from a man who has influenced the course of scientific thought more than has any other individual since Copernicus (who, in 1543, proposed that the sun, not the earth, was at the center of the universe). Charles Darwin argued that, over time, organisms originate and become adapted to their environments by biological means. Today, his concept of **biological evolution**—changes that take place in the genetic and physical characteristics of a population or group of organisms over time—stands as the primary explanation of the origin of life (Mayr, 1978).

The scope of Darwin's work transcends biology and has influenced other natural sciences, especially psychology. In the past two decades, psychologists have become increasingly aware of the many ways that biology influences behavior. As you will see in this chapter, many behavioral differences among organisms, both within and across species, correspond to genetic and other biological differences. Understanding these differences and their evolution allows psychologists to understand behavior in terms of its possible origins and **adaptive significance**—its effectiveness in aiding the organism to adapt to changing environmental conditions.

Consider *gregariousness*, the tendency to form groups or to be sociable. People tend to form social units. We live in families, have circles of friends, and join groups, such as churches, fraternities and sororities, and political organizations. To understand the adaptive significance of this tendency, we must ask ourselves two questions. First, what events and conditions in a person's lifetime might contribute to an individual's gregariousness—what function does gre-

gariousness serve in helping people adapt to the changing circumstances of life? And second, what events and conditions in the evolution of our species favored gregariousness—what functions has gregariousness served in the history of humankind? These are important questions because a complete understanding of gregariousness, like any behavior, requires that we understand both the past and present conditions that influence it.

In other words, psychologists might research how *past environmental conditions* favored gregariousness over a more solitary existence as a means of organizing human culture and how the *immediate environment* influences day-to-day sociability. They are interested in understanding both **ultimate causes** (from the Latin *ultimatus,* "to come to an end") of behavior—events and conditions that, over successive generations, have slowly shaped the behavior of our species—and **proximate causes** (from the Latin *proximus,* "near"), namely immediate environmental variables that affect behavior.

By understanding how adaptive behavior developed through the long-term process of evolution, psychologists are able to gain a more thorough understanding of our ability to adjust to changes in our immediate environment (Skinner, 1987). To understand the present, we must understand the past—the history of the individual and the history of our species. We behave as we do because we are members of the human species—an ultimate cause—and because we have learned to act in special ways—a proximate cause. Both biology and environment contribute to our personal development.

Considering the role of evolutionary factors in behavior is becoming so widespread that a new subfield within psychology, **evolutionary psychology,** is beginning to emerge

biological evolution Changes that take place in the genetic and physical characteristics of a population or group of organisms over time.

adaptive significance The effectiveness of behavior in aiding organisms to adjust to changing environmental conditions.

ultimate causes Evolutionary conditions that have slowly shaped the behavior of a species over generations.

proximate causes Immediate environmental events and conditions that affect behavior.

evolutionary psychology The branch of psychology that studies the ways in which an organism's evolutionary history contributes to the development of behavioral patterns and cognitive strategies related to reproduction and survival during its lifetime.

(Tooby and Cosmides, 1989). This area of psychology investigates how an organism's evolutionary history contributes to the development of behavior patterns and cognitive strategies related to reproduction and survival during its lifetime (Leger, 1991). As we will see throughout this book, evolutionary psychology has made significant contributions to our understanding of behavior.

If evolutionary psychology succeeds in its quest to understand the relation between evolution and development, we might also arrive at a clearer understanding of the psychological adaptations of our species that have given rise to, and continue to augment, the on-going evolution of culture. **Culture** is the sum of socially transmitted knowledge, customs, and behavior patterns common to a particular group of people. Psychology's contribution to this understanding will be an explanation of how thinking and behaving shape cultural adaptations to changing environmental conditions. Arriving at such knowledge requires that the contribution of the evolutionary process be understood. No theory of behavior can be complete without considering the role of evolution.

In this chapter, I will discuss the development of Darwin's theory of evolution and explain how evolution operates. I will also discuss the general principles of heredity and genetics, the basic means by which biological and many behavioral characteristics are passed from one generation to the next. Finally, I will examine sociobiology, a branch of biology that seeks to identify and understand evolutionary influences on social behavior.

The story of how Charles Darwin developed his theory illustrates the mix of hard work, intellect, and good fortune that often makes scientific discovery possible. In fact, Darwin's work is an excellent example of how observation and experimentation can lead to scientific breakthroughs.

The Voyage of the Beagle

After receiving a degree in theology from Christ's College, Cambridge (England) in 1831, Darwin met Captain Robert Fitz Roy. The captain was looking for someone to serve as an unpaid naturalist and traveling companion during a five-year voyage on board the HMS *Beagle,* a ten-gun brig converted to an ocean-going research vessel. The *Beagle's* mission was to explore and survey the coast of South America and to make longitudinal measurements worldwide. Darwin was eager to volunteer, but his father was strongly opposed. Fortunately for Darwin, his father appended his refusal with a challenge, "If you can find any man of common sense who advises you to go, I will give my consent." Darwin later recounted that his uncle, whom Darwin's father thought was "one of the most sensible men in the world," defended Darwin, and his father immediately consented (Darwin, 1887, p. 36).

culture The sum of socially transmitted knowledge, customs, and behavior patterns common to a particular group of people.

Charles Darwin (1809–1882)

Darwin went to London and made arrangements for the voyage. He was to learn later that Fitz Roy nearly rejected him because of the shape of his nose! Fitz Roy believed that the nose indicated a person's character. Fitz Roy suspected that anyone having a nose like Darwin's could not "possess sufficient energy and determination for the voyage." In the end, though, Darwin's aristocratic standing and his references convinced Fitz Roy to allow him aboard (Engel, 1962; Gould, 1977). Darwin later noted, "I think he was afterwards well satisfied that my nose had spoken falsely" (Darwin, 1887, p. 36).

During the voyage, Darwin observed the flora and fauna of South America, Australia, South Africa, and the islands of the Pacific, South Atlantic, and Indian Oceans. He spent most of his time doing what he enjoyed most—collecting. He collected creatures and objects of every sort: marine animals, reptiles, amphibians, land mammals, birds, insects, plants, rocks, minerals, fossils, and seashells. These specimens, which were sent back to England at various stages of the trip, were later examined by naturalists from all over Europe.

Darwin did not form his theory of evolution while at sea. Although he was impressed by the tremendous amount of diversity among seemingly related animals, he believed in *creationism,* the view that all living things were designed by God and are nonevolving (Gould, 1985).

The Origin of Species

Upon his return home to England in 1836, Darwin continued to marvel at the many ways animals and plants adapt to their environments. He sifted through his collections, often discussing his findings and ideas with other scientists. He carefully reviewed the work of earlier naturalists who had developed their own theories on evolution. (Darwin was not the first person to propose a theory of evolution, but he was

(a)

(b)

(c)

(d)

Figure 3.1

Varieties of pigeons believed to have been produced through artificial selection. (a) The wild rock pigeon, believed to be the ancestor of each of the other breeds of pigeons shown here. (b) Blue grizzle frillback. (c) English pouter. (d) Indian Fantail.

the first to amass weighty evidence in its favor.) He became interested in **artificial selection,** a procedure in which particular animals are mated to produce offspring who possess especially desirable characteristics. For example, if a rancher wished to develop cattle that yielded the largest steaks, then he or she would examine the available breeding stock and permit only the "beefiest" ones to reproduce. If this process is repeated over many generations of animals, the cattle should become beefier. In other words, in artificial selection people select which animals will breed and which will not based on specific, desirable characteristics of the animals. Darwin was intrigued with artificial selection and, in fact, bred pigeons for a while. (See *Figure 3.1.*)

As he pondered whether there might be a natural process corresponding to the role humans play in artificial selection, Darwin's views on evolution began slowly to change. In his own words,

> without any theory [I] collected facts on a wholesale scale, more especially with domesticated productions, by printed enquiries, by conversation with skillful breeders and gardeners, and by extensive reading ... (and) soon perceived that selection was the keystone of man's success in making useful races of animals and plants. But how selection could be applied to organisms living in a state of nature remained for some time a mystery to me. (Darwin, 1887, p. 53)

It would be another year and a half before Darwin's intensive study of artificial selection would bear fruit. Darwin recalls the event in his autobiography:

> I happened to read for amusement Malthus on *Population,* and being well prepared to appreciate the struggle for existence which everywhere goes on from long continued observation of plants and animals, it at once struck me that under these circumstances favourable

variations would tend to be preserved, and unfavourable ones to be destroyed. The result would be the formation of a new species. (Darwin, 1887, p. 54)

What struck Darwin was the idea of **natural selection,** or the consequence of the fact that organisms reproduce differentially: Within any given population, some members of a given species will produce more offspring than will others. Any animal that possesses a characteristic that helps it to survive or adapt to changes in its environment is likely to live longer and to produce more offspring than are animals that do not have this characteristic.

Darwin was well aware of the significance of his discovery but did not publish his theory until twenty years later. Why did he wait so long? Among other things, he devoted considerable time gathering supportive evidence. He took great pains to develop a clear, coherent, and accurate case for his theory. He examined and reexamined his specimens, carefully studied current research and theory in the natural sciences, conducted his own research on artificial selection, and perhaps most importantly, tested his ideas on his closest colleagues, whom he often met at a pub in London.

Darwin might have been even slower in publishing his theory had it not been for an intriguing coincidence. In 1858, he received a manuscript from Alfred Russell Wallace, another naturalist, outlining a theory of natural selection iden-

artificial selection A procedure in which animals are deliberately mated to produce offspring that possess particularly desirable characteristics.

natural selection The consequence of the fact that organisms reproduce differentially, which is caused by behavioral differences among them. Within any given population, some animals—the survivors—will produce more offspring than will other animals.

tical to his own. What was he to do? If he published his theory now, it would look like he had stolen the idea from Wallace; if he did not publish it, his twenty years of painstaking toil would be wasted. He presented the dilemma to his colleagues, who suggested that he and Wallace make a joint presentation of their separate works before a learned society—the Linnean Society—so that each might lay equal claim to the theory of natural selection. This was done, and a year later Darwin published his "abstract," which we know today as *The Origin of Species.* The book sold out on its first day of publication and has been selling steadily ever since.

Natural Selection and Evolution

Darwin's theory of evolution has four basic premises (Mayr, 1978).

1. The world's animal and plant communities are dynamic, not static: They change over time with new forms originating and others becoming extinct.

2. The evolutionary process is gradual and continuous. New species arise through slow and steady environmental changes that gradually "perfect" each species to its surroundings. When sudden and dramatic changes occur in the environment, a species' ability to adapt is usually challenged. Some species adapt and live, others become extinct.

3. All organisms descended from an original and common ancestor. Over time, the process of natural selection has created different species, each specifically adapted to its ecological niche.

4. Natural selection not only causes changes within populations during changing environmental conditions; it also acts to maintain the status quo under relatively constant environmental conditions.

According to Jacob (1977), natural selection results from two characteristics of life. First, *reproduction* produces offspring that are slightly different from their parents. Second, *interaction with a changing environment* requires that living

---

reproductive success The number of viable offspring an individual produces relative to the number of viable offspring produced by other members of the same species.

variation The differences found across individuals of any given species in terms of their genetic, biological (size, strength, physiology), and psychological (intelligence, sociability, behavior) characteristics.

genotype An organism's genetic makeup.

phenotype The outward expression of an organism's genotype; an organism's physical appearance and behavior.

---

things adapt behaviorally to its vagaries or risk injury, illness, or death. The interaction of these factors causes differential reproduction, and ultimately evolution. Evolution, then, is a process strongly influenced by behavioral adaptations to changing environments.

Natural Selection

The essence of Malthus's essay, which Darwin was reading when the idea of natural selection first occurred to him, was that the earth's food supply grows slower than populations of living things. The resulting scarcity of food produces competition among animals, with the less-fit individuals losing the struggle for life. For example, wolves who are fleet of foot are better able to capture prey than are slower packmates. Fast wolves will therefore tend to outlive and outreproduce slower wolves. (See *Figure 3.2.*) If a wolf's tendency to run fast is a genetically controlled trait, it will be passed on to its offspring. These offspring will be more likely to catch prey and will therefore live longer and have more opportunities to reproduce.

The ability of an individual to produce offspring defines that individual's **reproductive success**—the number of viable offspring it produces relative to the number of viable offspring produced by other members of the same species. Contrary to popular interpretation, "survival of the fittest" does not always mean survival of the most physically fit or of the strongest. The evolutionary "bottom line" is not physical strength but reproductive success. Physical strength is only one factor that might contribute to such success. In humans, for example, good looks, charm, and intelligence play an important role in an individual's ability to attract a mate and reproduce.

Two aspects of natural selection, *variation* and *competition,* are the critical factors that determine whether any particular animal and its offspring will enjoy reproductive success. Let's take a look at each of these aspects, beginning with variation.

Variation

The characteristic of **variation** includes differences among members of a species, including physical characteristics such as size, strength, or physiology, and behavioral characteristics, such as intelligence or sociability. What factors are responsible for these sorts of variations? First, an individual organism's genetic makeup, or its **genotype,** differs from that of all other individuals (except in the case of identical twins). As a result of these genetic differences, an individual organism's physical characteristics and behavior, or its **phenotype,** also varies from every other individual.

Every individual's phenotype is produced by the interaction of its genotype with the environment. In essence, the genotype determines how much the environment can influence an organism's development and behavior. For instance, identical twins have exactly the same genotype. If they are

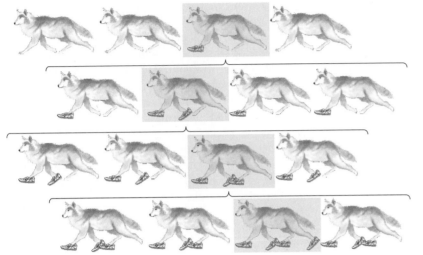

Figure 3.2

Natural selection at work. Wolves that are fast will be better at escaping predators, capturing game, and reproducing than their slower packmates. Because of the adaptive advantage that running fast confers upon a wolf's survival and reproductive success, the genotype for running speed will be passed on and increase in frequency across future generations.

separated at birth and one twin has a better diet than the other, their phenotypes will be different: The better-fed twin is likely to be taller and stronger. However, no matter how much better one twin's diet is than the other's, neither will ever become extremely tall or very muscular if the twins do not possess the genes for tallness and muscularity. Likewise, neither twin will realize his or her full potential for tallness and muscularity if he or she does not eat a nutritional diet. In this example, both the genotype (the genes related to tallness and muscularity) and a favorable environment (a well-balanced, nutritional diet) must be present for either twin to reach his or her full growth potential.

The interaction of genetic and environmental factors in determining a phenotype is made especially clear in the case of dermatographia, an inherited trait in which genetic factors permit the skin to react to surface pressure. Although this trait is genetic, without the environmental factor of pressure, the phenotype—welting of the skin—will not be expressed.

Phenotypes and the genotypes responsible for them may or may not be selected, depending on the particular advantage they confer. Consider, for example, Darwin's finches, thirteen species of finch that Darwin discovered in the Galapagos Islands, located off the west coast of South America. A striking physical difference among these birds is beak size. Some finches have a small, thin beak phenotype and others have a large, thick beak phenotype. Birds having small, thin beaks feed on small seeds covered by weak shells, and birds having large, thick beaks feed on large seeds covered by tough shells.

In a study that investigated the relationship between rainfall, food supply, and finch population on one island, Peter Grant (1986) discovered that the amount of rainfall and the size of the food supply directly affected the mortality of finches having certain kinds of beaks. During droughts, small seeds became scarce. As a result, the finches having small, thin beaks died at a higher rate than finches having bigger, thicker beaks. During the next few years, the number of finches having bigger, thicker beaks increased—just as the principle of natural selection would predict. During times of plentiful

rain, small seeds became abundant, and the number of finches having small, thin beaks became more plentiful in subsequent years.

Grant's study makes two important points. First, although evolution occurs over the long run, natural selection can produce important changes in the short run—in the space of only a few years. Second, phenotypic variation, in this case, differences in beak size, can produce important selective advantages that affect survival. Imagine if all the finches had had small, thin beaks. During the drought, most, if not all, these finches might have died. None would be left to reproduce; these finches would have become extinct on this island. Fortunately, there was phenotypic variation in beak size among the finches. And because phenotypic variation is caused by genetic variation (different genotypes give rise to different phenotypes), some finches—those having large, thick beaks—had an advantage. Their food supply (the larger seeds) was relatively unaffected by the drought, enabling them to outsurvive and outreproduce the finches having small, thin beaks.

You might think that *all* finches should have developed large, thick beaks. However, when rain is plentiful and small seeds are abundant, birds having small, thin beaks find it easier to feed. Under these environmental conditions, these birds have a phenotypic (and genotypic) advantage.

Competition

The second aspect of natural selection is **competition**. Because individuals of a given species share the same environment, competition within a species for food, mates, and territory is inevitable. Every fish captured and eaten by one bald eagle is a fish that cannot be captured and eaten by another bald eagle. If one bald eagle finds a suitable mate, then there is one fewer potential mate for other bald eagles.

competition   A striving or vying with others who share the same ecological niche for food, mates, and territory.

Competition also occurs between species when members of different species vie for similar ecological resources, such as food and territory. For example, yellow-headed blackbirds and red-winged blackbirds eat the same foods and occupy the same type of breeding territories; thus, they compete for these resources. Such competition does not involve competition for mates (yellow-headed blackbirds do not court red-winged blackbirds and vice versa). However, although these species do not compete for mates, their competition for other resources indirectly influences reproductive success because the ability to find and court a suitable mate depends on the ability to stake out and defend a territory having an adequate food supply. The probability of a yellow-headed blackbird finding a mate and successfully rearing a family depends not only on its success in competing against other yellow-headed blackbirds, but also on its success in competing against red-winged blackbirds.

Natural selection works because the members of any species have different phenotypes. Because these phenotypes are caused by different genotypes, successful individuals will pass on their genes to the next generation. Over time, competition for food and other resources will allow only the best-adapted phenotypes (and their corresponding genotypes) to survive, thereby producing evolutionary change.

Natural Selection in Human Evolution

Reconstruction of human evolution is a difficult job, something akin to assembling a giant jigsaw puzzle whose pieces have been scattered throughout the world. Some of the pieces may have been lost forever; others have become damaged beyond recognition; and those few that are found force continual reinterpretation of how the other pieces might fit the puzzle. Some of our past will likely remain a mystery forever. At best, all we can do is make an educated guess about the evolution and lifestyles of our ancestors.

Many biologists and natural historians of Darwin's time believed that natural selection applied to all animals, including humans. Others insisted that although natural selection applied to other animals, it did *not* apply to humans. However, through study of the fossil record and recent developments in genetic research, we now know that our species is related genetically to other mammals. The gorilla and the chimpanzee are our closest living relatives, and together we appear to have descended from a common ancestor.

Our evolution from this ancestor appears to have begun in Africa about 2 million years ago (Clark, 1993). The earliest humans have been labeled *Homo habilis* (literally "handy man"). *Homo habilis* was small (only about 1.3 meters tall and about 40 kilograms in weight), but was bipedal (able to

walk upright on two feet). Compared to its predecessor, a species called *Australopithecus, Homo habilis* had a larger brain and more powerful hands. The strong hands were well suited to making simple stone tools; hence the name handy man. It is easy to see why natural selection favored such adaptively significant traits. They helped these early humans adapt to the environment in terms of creating shelter against the elements, catching and preparing food, and making weapons for self-defense.

About 1.6 million years ago, *Homo habilis* was succeeded by *Homo erectus* ("upright man"). *Homo erectus* had a much larger brain and stood more erect than *Homo habilis* and had a more complex life-style. *Homo erectus* was the first of our ancestors to establish regular base camps, which probably served as centers for social activities, including the preparation and eating of food. *Homo erectus* created more efficient and stronger tools than did *Homo habilis,* successfully hunted big game, and discovered and used fire. Fire enabled these early humans to cook food, remain warm in cold weather, and protect themselves from predators. *Homo erectus's* use of fire, coupled with their social nature, and their ability to hunt big game permitted them to explore and settle new environments, including Europe, Asia, and other parts of Africa.

The earliest known *Homo sapiens* ("intelligent man") appears to have arisen about 500,000 years ago. The best known of the early *Homo sapiens, Homo sapiens neanderthalensis,* lived throughout Europe and Central Asia between approximately 300,000 and 35,000 years ago. Neanderthals constructed small huts from bones and animal skins and sometimes burned bones as fuel. They were skilled big game hunters, toolmakers, and clothiers, and they had cultural rituals for burying their dead. In one Neanderthal burial site unearthed in France, a small boy was found positioned on his left side with a small pillow of flints under his head and an ax positioned by his right hand. Similar Neanderthal burial sites have been discovered, suggesting that these humans possessed cultural traditions not previously found in the prehistoric record.

Scientists believe that Neanderthals and modern humans (*Homo sapiens sapiens*) overlapped each other, although the origin of *Homo sapiens sapiens* is unclear. It seems to have arisen between 200,000 and 100,000 years ago. What is clear, though, is that the *Homo sapiens sapiens* line has survived to flourish in all parts of the world, despite the presence of hostile climate, terrain, and predators. (See *Figure 3.3.*)

The remarkable success of the human species in adapting to a variety of ecological niches stems from the fact that natural selection has favored two important human characteristics: **bipedalism,** the ability to move about the environment on two feet, and **encephalization,** increased brain size. The ability to walk upright, which appears to have evolved in our early hominid ancestors over 4 million years ago (Boaz, 1993), not only allowed greater mobility, it also freed the hands for grabbing, holding, and throwing objects. The ability to grasp objects, in combination with an expanding capacity for learning and remembering new skills provided by a larger brain, led

bipedalism The ability to move about the environment on two feet.

encephalization Increases in brain size.

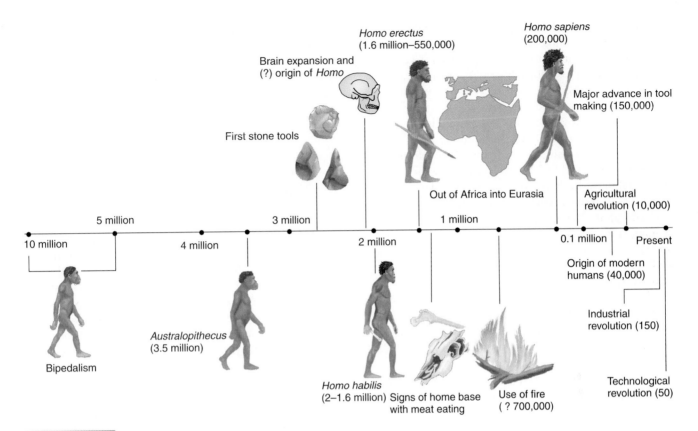

Figure 3.3

Major milestones in human evolution. The ability to walk upright freed the hands for tool use and other manipulative skills. Increased brain size accompanied increased intelligence. These two adaptations combined probably contributed significantly to all other major adaptations in human evolution.

(Adapted from Lewin, R. Human Evolution: An Illustrated Introduction. *Cambridge, MA: Blackwell Scientific Publications, Inc. 1984.)*

to advances in toolmaking, food gathering, hunting, and escaping predators. Humans who were able to fashion and use tools for hunting and self-defense lived longer and enjoyed greater reproductive success than did their less talented counterparts.

As the brain became larger, more of its volume became devoted to thinking, reasoning, decision making, and other complex cognitive functions. Another important ability that emerged from encephalization was planning—the capacity to anticipate future events and to take into account the effects

Cultural evolution includes the development of specific kinds of tools to accomplish specific tasks such as cutting, producing steel, and processing and storing complex information.

that those events might have on an individual or group of individuals. Such planning might have involved the organization of hunts, the institution of social customs and events (such as weddings and funerals), and the planting and harvesting of crops. Over time, the interaction of bipedalism and encephalization permitted humans to exploit new environments and establish well-organized communities.

Advances in tool making and hunting, combined with the use of fire for cooking, protection, and warmth, were adaptive; they helped humans live longer. The increased life span of humans may have aided the gradual accumulation of wisdom as the older members of early human communities began to share their knowledge with younger members through language. Although the fossil record cannot tell us when language first developed, we can be sure that those who were able to communicate with others through language had a distinct advantage over those who could not.

Language originated and subsequently evolved because of its immensely adaptive significance. As Skinner (1986) noted, language not only provided a simple means of warning others of danger, but also provided a means of communicating important information to others, such as the location of a good hunting spot or instructions on how to craft a tool. But perhaps the most important advantage conferred by language was its ability to reinforce the already strong social tendencies of early humans. It is not difficult to imagine a group of early humans sitting around a campfire eating the catch of the day and enjoying simple conversation. These conversations ultimately led to the development and transmission of cultural traditions. There is little doubt that language helps form strong bonds between individuals and families. Indeed, language is the foundation upon which all human cultures are built.

As cultures continued evolving, humans gained an increasing ability to control and modify their environment. The same intellectual resourcefulness that permitted early humans to discover and use fire and to invent useful tools prompted the agricultural revolution of 10,000 years ago, the industrial revolution of 150 years ago, and the technological revolution that began only 50 years ago with the invention of the transistor, the integrated circuit, and the computer. **Cultural evolution,** or the adaptive changes of cultures in response to changes in the environment over time, is possible only because humans have been genetically endowed with a capacity for learning and language. As cultural anthropologist Marvin Harris (1991) has noted, our capacity for learning has evolved because (1) it leads to "a more flexible and rapid method of achieving reproductive success" and (2) it allows entire groups of people to "adjust or take advantage of novel opportunities in a single generation without having to wait for the appearance and spread of genetic mutations" (p. 27). For example, advances in medicine have allowed us to control

cultural evolution   The adaptive changes of cultures in response to environmental changes over time.

life-threatening diseases such as polio, smallpox, malaria, tetanus, typhoid fever, and diphtheria. It would take hundreds of thousands of years, maybe even millions, to evolve immunities to these diseases. Let's not forget, though, that cultural evolution is a mixed blessing. With it has come pollution, many social ills and injustices (for example, racism), and overpopulation.

Interim Summary

Natural Selection and Evolution

Understanding behavior completely requires that psychologists learn more about both proximate causes of behavior—how animals adapt to environmental changes through learning—and ultimate causes of behavior—historical events and conditions in the evolution of a species that have shaped its behavior. Evolutionary psychology is a relatively new subfield of psychology that is devoted to the study of how evolution and genetic variables influence adaptive behavior.

Darwin's voyage on the *Beagle* and his subsequent thinking and research in artificial selection led him to develop the idea of biological evolution, which explains how genetic and physical changes occur in groups of animals over time. The primary element of biological evolution is natural selection: the tendency of some members of a species to produce more offspring than other members do. Members of a species vary genetically, such that some possess specific traits to a greater or lesser extent than other individuals do. If any of these traits gives an animal a competitive advantage over other members of the species—for example, a better ability to escape predators, find food, or attract mates—then that animal is also more likely to have greater reproductive success. Its offspring will then carry its genes into future generations. Two important adaptations during the course of human evolution are *bipedalism,* the ability to walk upright, and *encephalization,* an increase in brain size. The combination of these two factors allowed early humans to explore and settle new environments and led to advances in tool making, hunting, food gathering, and self-defense. Encephalization appears to have been associated with language development and cultural evolution. The study of the evolution of our species suggests the nature of the circumstances under which adaptive behavior first emerged and those circumstances that have been important for its continued expression to the present time.

Thought Questions

- In what ways are psychology and biology related disciplines? How does understanding biological aspects of behavior contribute to our understanding of psychological aspects of behavior?
- How do ultimate and proximate causes of behavior influence human behavior—for example, eating?
- What might be the effects of reducing genetic variability in a population of organisms?

- What argument might be made to support the suggestion that the human species is no longer evolving via natural selection? Is this a valid argument? Explain.
- How might the course of human evolution have been different had natural selection not favored encephalization?

Heredity and Genetics

Darwin's work unveiled the process of natural selection and pointed out new frontiers for exploration and experimentation. One of the most important of these frontiers is **genetics,** the study of "the structure and function of genes and the way in which genes are passed from one generation to the next" (Russell, 1992, p. 2). Genetics, then, also involves the study of how the genetic makeup of an organism influences its physical and behavioral characteristics. Closely related to genetics are the principles of **heredity,** the sum of the traits and tendencies inherited from a person's parents and other biological ancestors. Although Darwin had built a strong case for natural selection, he could not explain a key tenet of his theory—inheritance. He knew that individual differences occurred within a given species and that those differences were subject to natural selection. But he did not know how adaptations were passed from parent to offspring. Six years after *The Origin of Species* was published, Gregor Mendel, an Austrian monk who conducted experimental cross-breeding studies with pea plants, uncovered the basic principles of heredity. Mendel demonstrated conclusively how height, flower color, seed shape, and other traits of pea plants could be transmitted from one generation to the next. His work has since been applied to studying heredity in thousands of plants and animals.

Basic Principles of Genetics

Genes are segments of genetic material called **DNA (deoxyribonucleic acid)**—strands of sugar and phosphate that are connected by nucleotide molecules of adenine, thymine, guanine, and cytosine. DNA is configured like a twisted ladder:

genetics The study of the genetic makeup of organisms and how it influences their physical and behavioral characteristics.

heredity The sum of the traits and tendencies inherited from a person's parents and other biological ancestors.

genes Small units of chromosomes that direct the synthesis of proteins and enzymes.

DNA Deoxyribonucleic acid. The DNA structure resembles that of a twisted ladder. Strands of sugar and phosphates are connected by rungs made from adenine and thymine and guanine and cytosine.

the sugar and phosphate form the sides and the four nucleotides form the rungs. (See *Figure 3.4.*) The particular sequence of these nucleotide molecules actually directs the synthesis of protein molecules that regulate the biological and physical development of the body and all of its organs.

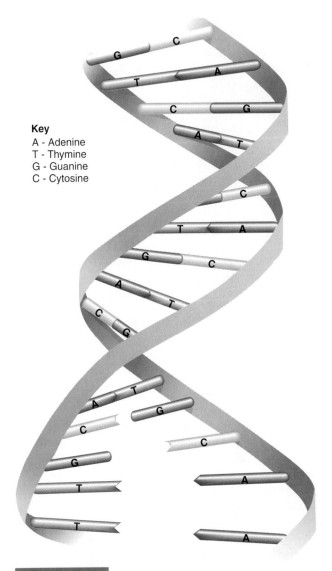

Key
A - Adenine
T - Thymine
G - Guanine
C - Cytosine

Figure 3.4

The structure and composition of DNA. DNA resembles a twisted ladder whose sides are composed of molecules of sugar and phosphate and whose rungs are made of combinations of four nucleotide bases: adenine, thymine, guanine, and cytosine. Genes are segments of DNA that direct the synthesis of proteins and enzymes according to the particular sequences of nucleotide bases that they contain. In essence, genes serve as "recipes" for the synthesis of these proteins and enzymes, which regulate the cellular and other physiological processes of the body, including those responsible for behavior.

(Based on Watson, J. D. Molecular Biology of the Gene. Menlo Park: Benjamin, 1976.)

Some protein molecules regulate cell development and others regulate the chemical interactions that occur within cells.

Genes as "Recipes" for Protein Synthesis

Genes can only influence our development and behavior through protein synthesis. Proteins are strings of amino acids, arranged in a chain. Each sequence of nucleotides (adenine, thymine, guanine, and cytosine) specifies a particular amino acid. Thus, in a sense, genes are "recipes" consisting of different nucleotide sequences. In this case, the recipe is for combining the proteins necessary to create and develop physiological structures and for behavior—how those structures might function in response to environmental stimulation.

Strictly speaking, though, there are no genes for behavior, only for the physical structures and physiological processes that are related to behavior. For example, when we refer to a gene for schizophrenia (a mental disorder characterized by irrational thinking, delusions, hallucinations, and perceptual distortions), we are really referring to a gene that contains instructions for synthesizing particular proteins, which, in turn, are responsible for the development of specific physiological processes that are sensitive to certain stressful environmental conditions.

Genes also direct the synthesis of **enzymes,** which govern the processes that occur within every cell in the body, and thus control each cell's structure and function. As we will see later, a faulty gene may contain instructions for synthesis of faulty enzymes, which produces serious physiological and behavioral problems.

Chromosomes and Meiosis

Genes are located on **chromosomes,** the rodlike structures made of DNA found in the nucleus of every cell. In essence, genes are particular regions of chromosomes that contain the recipes for particular proteins. Each set of chromosomes contains a different sequence of genes. We inherit twenty-three individual chromosomes from each of our parents, giving us twenty-three pairs—forty-six individual chromosomes—in most cells of the body. One pair of chromosomes, the **sex chromosomes,** contains the instructions for the development of male or female sex characteristics—those characteristics that distinguish males from females.

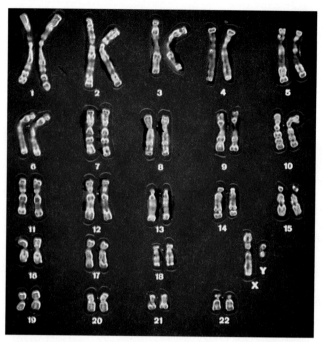

(a)

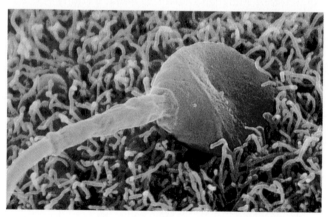

(b)

(a) Human chromosomes. The presence of a Y chromosome indicates that this sample came from a male. A sample from a female would include two X chromosomes. (b) Fertilization—a human sperm penetrating an egg.

enzymes Proteins that regulate the structure of bodily cells and the processes occurring within those cells.

chromosomes Rodlike structures in the nuclei of living cells; contain genes.

sex chromosomes The chromosomes that contain the instructional code for the development of male or female sex characteristics.

meiosis The form of cell division by which new sperm and ova are formed. The chromosomes within the cell are randomly rearranged so that new sperm and ova contain twenty-three individual chromosomes, or half of that found in other bodily cells.

Sexual reproduction involves the union of a sperm, which carries genetic instructions from the male, with an ovum (egg), which carries genetic instructions from the female. Sperms and ova differ from the other bodily cells in at least two very important ways. First, new bodily cells are created by simple division of existing cells. Second, all twenty-three pairs of chromosomes divide in two, making copies of themselves. The copies pull apart, and the cell splits into two cells, each having a complete set of twenty-three pairs of chromosomes. Sperms and ova are formed by a special form of cell division called **meiosis.** The twenty-three pairs of chromosomes break apart into two groups, with one member of each pair joining one of the groups. The cell splits into two cells, each of which contains twenty-three *individual* chromosomes. The assignment of the members of each pair of chromosomes to a particular group is a random process; thus, a single individual can produce 2^{23} (8,388,608) different ova or sperms.

Although brothers and sisters may resemble each other, they are not exact copies. Because the union of a particular sperm with an ovum is apparently random, a couple can produce 8,388,608 × 8,388,608, or 70,368,774,177,664 different children. Only identical twins are genetically identical. Identical twins occur when a fertilized ovum divides, giving rise to two identical individuals. Fraternal twins are no more similar than any two siblings. They occur when a woman produces two ova, both of which are fertilized (by different sperms, of course).

Sex is determined by the twenty-third pair of chromosomes: the *sex chromosomes*. There are two different kinds of sex chromosomes, X chromosomes and Y chromosomes. Females have a pair of X chromosomes (XX); males have one of each type (XY). Because women's cells contain only X chromosomes, each of their ova contains a single X chromosome (along with twenty-two other single chromosomes). Because men's cells contain both an X chromosome and a Y chromosome, half of the sperm they produce contain an X chromosome and half contain a Y chromosome. Thus, the sex of a couple's offspring depends on which type of sperm fertilizes the ovum. A Y-bearing sperm produces a boy, and an X-bearing sperm produces a girl. (See *Figure 3.5.*)

Dominant and Recessive Alleles

Each pair of chromosomes contains pairs of genes: One gene in each pair is contributed by each parent. Sometimes individual genes in each pair are identical, and sometimes they are different. Alternative forms of genes are called **alleles.** (*Allele,* like *alias,* comes from the Greek *allos,* "other.") Consider eye color. The pigment found in the iris of the eye is produced by a particular gene. If parents each contribute the same allele for eye color to their child, the gene combination is called *homozygous* (from the Greek *homo,* "same" and *zygon,* "yolk"). However, if the parents contribute different alleles, the gene combination is said to be *heterozygous* (from the Greek *hetero,* "different"). Heterozygous gene combinations produce phenotypes controlled by the **dominant allele** —the allele that has a more powerful influence on the expression of the trait. The allele for brown eyes is dominant. When a child inherits the allele for brown eye color from one parent and the allele for blue eye color from the other parent, the child will have brown eyes. Brown eyes is said to be a *dominant* trait. The blue eye color controlled by the **recessive allele**—the allele that has a weaker effect on the expression of a trait—is not expressed. Only if both of a child's alleles for eye color are of the blue type will the child have blue eyes. Thus, blue eyes is said to be a *recessive* trait. Inheritance of two alleles for brown eyes will, of course, result in brown eyes. (See

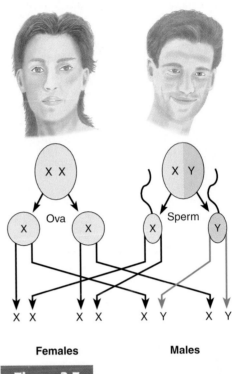

Figure 3.5

Determination of sex. The sex of human offspring depends on whether the sperm that fertilizes the ovum carries an X or a Y chromosome.

Figure 3.6.) Other eye colors, such as hazel or black, are produced by the effects of other genes, which influence the dominant brown allele to code for more (black) or less (hazel) pigment in the iris.

It is important to remember that the genetic contributions to our personal development and behavior are extremely complex. One reason for this complexity is that protein synthesis is often under *polygenic* control, that is, influenced by many pairs of genes, not just a single pair. The inheritance of behavior is even more complicated, because different environments influence the expression of polygenic traits. Consider, for example, the ability to run. Running speed for any individual is the joint product of genetic factors that produce proteins for muscle, bone, blood, oxygen metabolism, and motor

alleles Alternative forms of the same gene.

dominant allele The form of the gene that controls the expression of a trait. When a gene pair contains two dominant alleles or when it contains both a dominant and a recessive allele, the trait regulated by the dominant gene will be expressed.

recessive allele The form of the gene that does not influence the expression of a trait unless it is paired with another recessive allele.

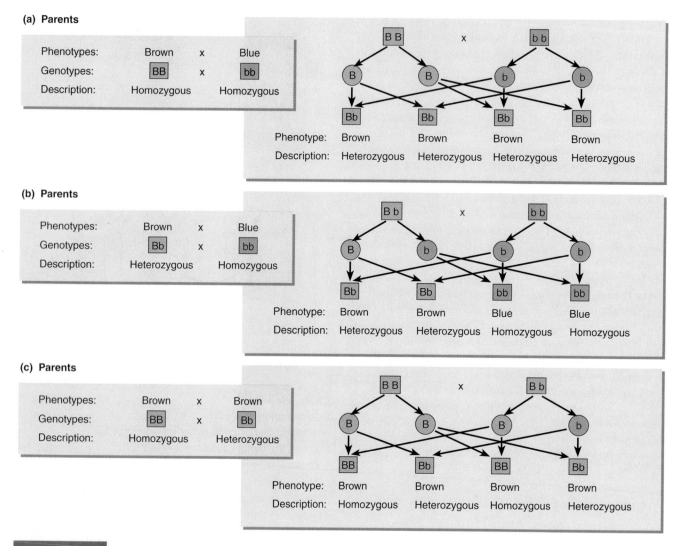

(a) Parents

Phenotypes:	Brown	x	Blue
Genotypes:	BB	x	bb
Description:	Homozygous		Homozygous

(b) Parents

Phenotypes:	Brown	x	Blue
Genotypes:	Bb	x	bb
Description:	Heterozygous		Homozygous

(c) Parents

Phenotypes:	Brown	x	Brown
Genotypes:	BB	x	Bb
Description:	Homozygous		Heterozygous

Figure 3.6

Patterns of inheritance for eye color. (a) If one parent is homozygous for the dominant eye color (BB), and the other parent is homozygous for the recessive eye color (bb), then all their children will be heterozygous for eye color (Bb) and will have brown eyes. (b) If one parent is heterozygous (Bb), and the other parent is homozygous recessive (bb), then their children will have a 50 percent chance of being heterozygous (brown eyes) and a 50 percent chance of being homozygous recessive (blue eyes). (c) If one parent is homozygous dominant (BB), and the other parent is heterozygous (Bb), then their children will have a 50 percent chance of being homozygous for the dominant eye color (BB) and will have brown eyes, and a 50 percent chance of being heterozygous (Bb) for the trait and will have brown eyes.
(Adapted from Klug, W. S., and Cummings, M. R. Concepts of Genetics. 2nd ed. Glenview, IL: Scott, Foresman, 1986.)

---

coordination (to name but a few) and environmental factors such as exercise patterns, age, nutrition, accidents, and so on.

The Importance of Genetic Diversity

As we saw, no two individuals, except identical twins, are genetically identical. Such genetic diversity is a characteristic of all species that reproduce sexually.

Can you think of many organisms that reproduce asexually? Yeast and fungi may come to mind, and if you are familiar with horticultural practices, you may know that nurseries often reproduce plants and trees through grafting, which is an asexual process. But when we examine the world around us, we find that the overwhelming majority of species reproduce sexually. Why?

The answer is that sexual reproduction increases a species' ability to adapt to environmental changes. Sexual reproduction leads to genetic diversity, and genetically diverse species have a better chance of adapting to a changing environment. When the environment changes, some members of a genetically diverse species may have genes that enable them to survive in the new environment. These genes manufacture proteins that give rise to physical structures, physiological processes, and, ultimately, adaptively significant behavior that can withstand particular changes in the environment.

This reasoning explains why so many insects, such as cockroaches, have survived our species' best efforts to exterminate them. The lifespan of insects is very short, so that even in a short period of time, many different generations are born and die. When we attempt to alter their environment, as we do when we apply an insecticide to their habitat, we may kill many of them. However, some survive because they had the right combination of genes (and hence, the necessary physiological processes and behavior patterns) to resist the toxic effects of the poison. The survivors then reproduce. Our reaction is to attempt to develop a new poison to which this generation of insects is not resistant. The result is sort of an evolutionary "arms race" in which both insects and humans produce newer and more powerful adaptations in response to each other (Dawkins, 1986). Natural selection, then, has favored species that reproduce sexually because of the adaptive value of genetic diversity.

Influences of Gender on Heredity

An individual's sex plays a crucial role in influencing the expression of certain traits. A good example is hemophilia, an increased tendency to bleed from even minor injuries. The blood of people who do not have hemophilia will begin to clot in the first few minutes after they sustain a cut. In contrast, the blood of people who have hemophilia may not do so for thirty minutes or even several hours. Hemophilia is caused by a recessive gene on the X chromosome that fails to produce a protein necessary for normal blood clotting. Because females have two X chromosomes, they can carry an allele for hemophilia but still have normal blood clotting if the other allele is normal. Males, however, have only a single X chromosome, which they receive from their mothers. If the gene for blood clotting carried on this chromosome is faulty, they develop hemophilia.

The gene for hemophilia is an example of a *sex-linked gene,* so named because this gene resides only on the sex chromosomes. There also are sex-related genes that express themselves in both sexes, although the phenotype appears more frequently in one sex than in the other. These genes are called *sex-influenced genes.* For example, pattern baldness (thin hair across the top of the head) develops in men if they inherit either or both alleles for baldness, but this trait is not

seen in women, even when they inherit both alleles. The expression of pattern baldness is influenced by an individual's sex hormones, which are different for men and women. The effects of these hormones on expression of pattern baldness explains why it is much more common among men than women. (Yes, it is true that pattern baldness can be expressed in women—fortunately, very rarely.)

Mutations and Chromosomal Aberrations

Changes in genetic material are caused by mutations or chromosomal aberrations. **Mutations** are accidental alterations in the DNA code within a single gene. Mutations are the original source of genetic diversity. Although most mutations have harmful effects, some may produce characteristics that are beneficial in certain environments. Mutations can be either spontaneous, occurring naturally, or the result of human-made factors such as high-energy radiation.

Hemophilia provides one of the most famous examples of mutation. Although hemophilia has appeared many times in human history, no other case of hemophilia has had as far-reaching effects as the spontaneous mutation that was passed among the royal families of nineteenth-century Europe. Through genealogical analysis, researchers have discovered that this particular mutant gene arose with Queen Victoria (1819–1901). She was the first in her family line to bear affected children—two female carriers and an afflicted son. The tradition that dictates that nobility marry only other nobility caused the mutant gene to spread rapidly throughout the royal families. (See *Figure 3.7.*)

The second type of genetic change, **chromosomal aberration,** involves either changes in parts of chromosomes or a change in the total number of chromosomes. An example of a disorder caused by a chromosomal aberration—in this case, a partial deletion of the genetic material in chromosome 5—is the *cri-du-chat syndrome.* Infants who have this syndrome have gastrointestinal and cardiac problems, are severely mentally retarded, and make crying sounds resembling a cat's mewing (hence its name, "cry of the cat"). In general, the syndrome's severity appears to be related directly to the amount of genetic material that is missing. Psychologists and developmental disability specialists have discovered that early special education training permits many individuals having this syndrome to learn self-care and communication skills. This fact highlights an important point about genetics and behavior: Even behavior that has a genetic basis can often be modified to some extent through training or experience.

Genetic Disorders

Many genes decrease an organism's viability—its ability to survive. These "killer genes" are actually quite common. On the average, each of us has two to four of them. Fortunately, these lethal genes are usually recessive, and there are so many

---

mutations Accidental alterations in the DNA code within a single gene. Mutations can either be spontaneous and occur naturally or be the result of environmental factors, such as exposure to high-energy radiation.

chromosomal aberration The rearrangement of genes within chromosomes or a change in the total number of chromosomes.

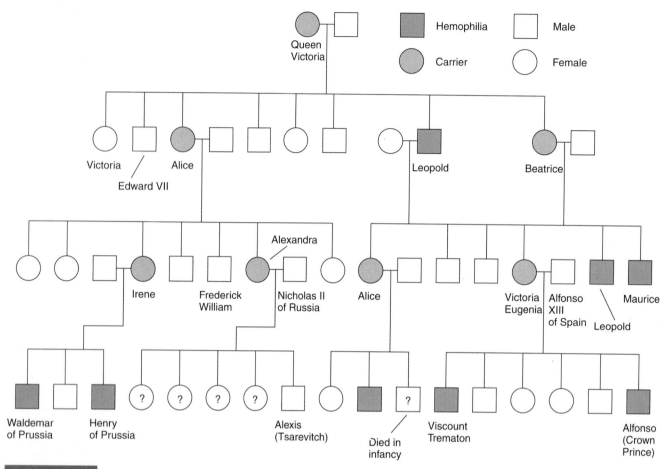

Figure 3.7

Genealogical analysis of the inheritance of hemophilia among European royal families. The gene for this disorder likely originated with Queen Victoria of England. She was the first woman in the English royal family to bear an afflicted son or a carrier daughter. Circles represent females; squares represent males.
(Adapted from Winchester, A. M. Genetics: A Survey of the Principles of Heredity. *Boston: Houghton-Mifflin, 1972.)*

different types that most couples do not carry the same ones. (If these genes were dominant and we had two to four of them, we would be dead!) When a child inherits the dominant healthy gene from one parent and the recessive lethal gene from the other, the destructive effects of the lethal gene are not expressed.

A few lethal genetic disorders are caused by a dominant gene, however. Different dominant lethal genes express themselves at different times in the life span. A fetus may die and be spontaneously aborted before a woman even realizes that she is pregnant, a baby may be stillborn, or the lethal genes may not be expressed until adulthood.

> **Down syndrome** A genetic disorder caused by a chromosomal aberration resulting in an extra twenty-first chromosome. People having Down syndrome are generally short, have broad skulls and round faces, and suffer impairments in physical, psychomotor, and cognitive development.

There are many human genetic disorders. Here are several of the more common ones that impair mental functioning and behavior and so are of special interest to psychologists.

Down syndrome is caused by a chromosomal aberration consisting of an extra twenty-first chromosome. People having Down syndrome are generally short, have broad skulls and round faces, and show impaired physical, psychomotor, and cognitive development. About 15 percent of children born with this condition die before their first birthdays, usually from heart and respiratory complications. The frequency of Down syndrome increases with the age of the mother (Rischer and Easton, 1992). About 40 percent of all Down syndrome children are born to women over forty. To a lesser extent, the age of the father also increases the chances of Down syndrome. Although people having Down syndrome are mentally retarded, special educational training permits many of them to hold jobs involving simple tasks, such as sorting. Although Down syndrome is caused by a chromosomal aberration, it is *not* a hereditary disorder.

Huntington's chorea does not emerge until the afflicted person is between thirty and forty years old. It is caused by a dominant lethal gene that results in degeneration in certain parts of the brain. Before the onset of this disease, an individual may be healthy in every respect. After onset, however, the individual experiences slow but progressive mental and physical deterioration, including loss of coordination and motor ability. Death generally occurs five to fifteen years after onset. Because age of onset for Huntington's chorea is long after sexual maturity, this lethal gene can be passed from parent to child before the parent even knows that he or she has the gene.

Individuals having **phenylketonuria (PKU)** are homozygous for a recessive gene responsible for synthesis of a faulty enzyme, which renders them unable to break down phenylalanine, an amino acid found in many foods. As a result, blood levels of phenylalanine increase, causing severe brain damage and mental retardation. PKU is one of the many diseases for which infants are routinely tested before they leave the hospital. Infants diagnosed as having PKU are placed on a low-phenylalanine diet shortly after birth. If this diet is carefully followed, brain development will be normal.

Genetic Counseling

Couples having a family history of genetic disorders often seek **genetic counseling,** the process of determining the likelihood that a couple may produce a child having a genetic disorder. Individuals who suspect that they may have a genetic disorder may also seek such counseling.

The first step in genetic counseling is generally a pedigree analysis of the family or families involved. This analysis identifies any family history of genetic disorders and provides an estimate of the likelihood that a genetic disorder is present. If a family history of genetic disorders is discovered, the genetic counselor discusses the probability of the couple having a child who has a disorder. In the case of an individual, the counselor may recommend screening for the disorder.

In the case of prospective parents who have a family history of a genetic disorder, the counselor will generally recommend further analysis, this time to detect if either or both persons is a carrier for the gene causing the disorder. *Carrier detection* is a biochemical procedure in which people can be tested for the presence of particular proteins or enzymes produced by the genes in question. If high levels of one of these substances is found, the person may be a carrier. Carrier detection is also accomplished through DNA probes that detect whether the gene in question is normal or defective. The use of DNA probes is a relatively recent development in genetic counseling, and probes have not yet been developed for all genetic disorders.

Once the genetic counselor informs the couple of the likelihood of producing a child who has a genetic disorder, the couple must then make the difficult decision of whether to have children. For example, a couple having a strong family history of PKU is likely to have a child who has PKU. However, the couple may decide to have a child anyway, knowing that PKU is treatable and that many people who have PKU lead happy, healthy, and productive lives so long as they control their diets.

In instances in which the woman is already pregnant, the fetus can be tested for genetic disorders. In fact, such testing is often recommended for pregnant women over thirty-five or for those whose family pedigrees reveal a genetic problem. The most common prenatal detection method is *amniocentesis,* which involves removal and examination of fetal cells found in the amniotic fluid surrounding the fetus, usually during the sixteenth week of pregnancy. The chromosomes in the fetal cells are examined for incomplete, missing, or extra chromosomes. In addition, amniocentesis allows parents to know the sex of their unborn child, which may be relevant in the case of sex-linked disorders. Because amniocentesis is a complicated and expensive test, it is usually only used in cases in which the likelihood of genetic disorder is known to be high.

Genetic counseling provides parents with objective information with which they can make rational decisions about having a child or continuing a pregnancy. This situation is particularly difficult as it involves sensitive personal and moral issues.

Heredity and Behavior Genetics

Because each of us is born into a different environment and each of us possesses a unique combination of genetic instructions, we differ considerably from one another. Consider, for instance, your classmates. They come in different sizes and shapes, vary in personality and intelligence, and possess unequal artistic and athletic abilities. To what extent are these sorts of differences attributable to heredity or to the environment? If all your classmates had been reared in identical environments, any differences between them would necessarily be due to genetics. Conversely, if all your classmates had come from the same fertilized egg but were subsequently raised in different environments, any differences in their personal characteristics would necessarily be due only to the environment.

Huntington's chorea A genetic disorder caused by a dominant lethal gene in which a person experiences slow but progressive mental and physical deterioration.

phenylketonuria (PKU) A genetic disorder caused by a particular pair of homozygous recessive genes and characterized by the inability to break down phenylalanine, an amino acid found in many high protein foods. The resulting high blood levels of phenylalanine cause mental retardation.

genetic counseling A form of counseling in which people receive information regarding their family history of genetic disorders.

Heritability is a statistical term that refers to the amount of variability in a trait in a given population that is due to genetic differences among the individuals in that population. Heritability is sometimes confused with *inheritance,* the tendency of a given trait to be passed from parent to individual offspring. But heritability does not apply to individuals; it pertains only to the variation of a trait in a specific population. The more that a trait in a given population is influenced by genetic factors, the greater its heritability. The scientific study of heritability—of the effects of genetic influences on behavior—is called **behavior genetics.** As noted by one of this field's most prolific researchers, Robert Plomin (1990), behavior genetics is intimately involved with providing an explanation of why people differ. As we will see below, behavior geneticists attempt to account for the roles that both heredity and the environment play in individual differences in a wide variety of physical and mental abilities.

Studying Genetic Influences

Although farmers and animal breeders had experimented with artificial selection for thousands of years, only within the last 150 years has the relation between heredity and behavior been formally studied in the laboratory. Of course, Mendel's careful analysis of genetic influences on specific characteristics gave us the first good clue that traits were actually heritable. A cousin of Darwin's, Francis Galton (1869), stimulated further interest in this field with his studies showing that intelligence tends to run in families: If parents are intelligent, then, in general, so are their children. The search for genetic bases of behavior has been active ever since. In fact, the search to understand the relative contributions of heredity and environment to human behavior is among the most heavily researched areas in psychology today. Two primary tools of behavioral geneticists are artificial selection and twin research.

Artificial Selection in Animals. Any heritable trait can be selected in a breeding program. The heritability of many traits in animals, such as aggression, docility, preference for alcohol, running speed, and mating behaviors, can be studied by means of artificial selection.

Consider, for example, the classic study that Robert Tryon (1940) conducted concerning maze learning. Tryon wished to determine whether genetic variables influenced learning. He began his study with a large sample of genetically diverse rats. He trained them to learn a maze and recorded the number of errors each rat made in the process. He then selected

two groups of rats—those that learned the fastest (bright) and those that learned the slowest (dull). He mated "bright" rats with other "bright" rats and "dull" rats with other "dull" rats. To ensure that the rats were not somehow learning the maze from their mothers, he "adopted out" some of the pups: Some of the bright pups were reared by dull mothers and some of the dull pups were reared by bright mothers. He found that parenting made little difference in his results, so this factor can be discounted.

Tryon continued this sequence of having rats learn the maze and selectively breeding the best with the best (bright) and the worst with the worst (dull) over many generations. Soon, the maze performance of each group was virtually nonoverlapping. (See *Figure 3.8.*) He concluded that maze learning in rats could be manipulated through artificial selection.

Later studies showed that Tryon's results were limited by the standard laboratory cage environment in which rats lived when they were not running the maze. For example, Cooper and Zubek (1958) demonstrated that differences in maze ability were virtually eliminated when bright and dull strains of rats were reared in either enriched environments designed to stimulate learning (cages containing geometric objects, such as tunnels, ramps, and blocks) or impoverished environments designed to inhibit learning (cages containing only food and water dishes). However, Cooper and Zubek's rats who were reared in the standard laboratory cage performed similarly to Tryon's rats: The bright rats outperformed the dull rats. Thus, changing the environmental conditions in which the rats lived had an important result—reducing the effects of genetic differences between the bright and dull rats. This finding makes good sense when you consider the fact that genes are not expressed in the absence of an environment.

Tryon's research demonstrated that over successive generations a trait can be made to become more or less likely in a given population, but we do not know precisely why. We do

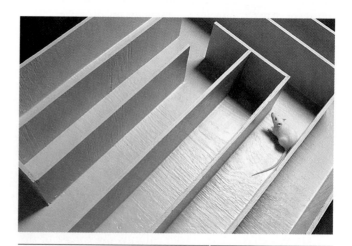

Tryon's selective breeding study showed that a rat's ability to navigate successfully through a maze was affected by genetic factors.

heritability The amount of variability in a given trait in a given population at a given time due to genetic factors.

behavior genetics The study of genetic influences on behavior, largely through research involving artificial selection procedures and investigations into the similarities and differences between twins.

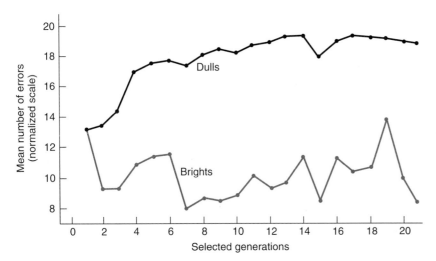

Figure 3.8

Results from Tryon's 1940 artificial breeding research of rats' ability to learn a maze. Within a few generations, differences in the rats' ability to negotiate the maze became distinct.

(Adapted from Tryon, R. C. Genetic differences in maze-learning ability in rats. Yearbook of the National Society for the Study of Education, 1940, 39, 111–119.)

not know whether genes related to learning or genes related to other traits were selected. Tryon's rats may have been neither especially bright nor especially dull. Perhaps each of these strains differed in its capacity to be motivated by the food reward that awaited them at the end of the maze.

The day may not be too far off when actually manipulating specific genes to assess their influence on behavior becomes a reality. The rapidly emerging field of *molecular genetics* is mapping the sequence of nucleotide bases on human chromosomes. The results of this mapping will help scientists understand how specific DNA sequences can influence physiological processes that affect behavior, emotion, remembering, and thinking and play a crucial role in identifying specific genes involved in psychological disorders (Plomin and Rende, 1991). Until that day comes, however, artificial breeding studies will continue to be an important source of information about hereditary influences on behavior. As we will see in the "Evaluating Scientific Issues" section, artificial selection has played a prominent role in our understanding of the role genetics plays in alcoholism.

Twin Studies. There are two barriers to studying the effects of heredity on behavioral traits in humans. First, ethical considerations prevent psychologists and geneticists from manipulating people's genetic history or restricting the type of environment in which they are reared. For example, we cannot artificially breed people to learn the extent to which shyness or other personality characteristics are inherited or deprive the offspring of intelligent people of a good education to see if their intelligence will be affected. Second, in most cases, the enormous variability in human environments effectively masks any correlation that might exist between genetics and trait expression.

Psychologists have been able to circumvent these barriers by taking advantage of an important quirk of nature—multiple births. In fact, in the arsenal of the behavior geneticist, twin research is the most powerful weapon in the study of human genetics (Fulker and Cardon, 1993).

Recall that identical twins, also called *monozygotic (MZ) twins,* arise from a single fertilized ovum, called a zygote, that splits into two genetically identical cells. Fraternal, or *dizygotic (DZ) twins,* develop from the separate fertilization of two ova. DZ twins are no more alike genetically than any two siblings. Because MZ twins are genetically identical, they should be more similar to one another in terms of their psychological characteristics (such as personality or intelligence) than either DZ twins or nontwin siblings.

Concordance research, which examines the degree of similarity in traits expressed between twins, supports this ra-

Research with identical twins has provided psychologists with information about the role of heredity in behavioral traits.

concordance research Research that studies the degree of similarity between twins in traits expressed. Twins are said to be concordant for a trait if either both or neither twin expresses it and discordant if only one twin expresses it.

tionale. Twins are *concordant* for a trait if both of them express it or if neither does, and they are *discordant* if only one expresses it. If concordance rates (which can range from 0 percent to 100 percent) of any given trait are substantially higher for MZ twins than for DZ twins, heredity is likely involved in the expression of that trait. Table 3.1 compares concordance values between MZ and DZ twins for several traits. (See *Table 3.1.*) When we observe a trait exhibiting a high concordance for MZ twins but a low one for DZ twins, we can conclude that the trait is strongly affected by genetics. This is especially true for a trait such as blood type, which has a heritability of 100 percent. If the concordance rates are similar, the effect of heredity is low. For example, consider the characteristic of religious beliefs. In this case, a high concordance value (that is, both twins having similar beliefs) probably reflects the fact that they acquired their beliefs from their parents. In fact, the concordance rate for religious beliefs of DZ twins is generally just as high as that of MZ twins (Loehlin and Nichols, 1976). Thus, religious beliefs are not inherited.

Twin studies have been used to study a wide range of psychological phenomena. This research has shown that genetic factors affect cognitive abilities such as language ability, mathematical ability, and vocabulary skills; personality traits such as extroversion (the tendency to be outgoing) and emotional stability; personality development; and the occurrence of psychological disorders such as schizophrenia and mental retardation (Bouchard and Propping, 1993). Further evidence for genetic influences on trait expression comes from extensive analyses of twin studies concerning heredity and intelligence (Bouchard and McGue, 1981).

Table 3.1

Comparison of Concordance Rates Between Monozygotic (MZ) and Dizygotic (DZ) Twins for Various Traits

Trait	Concordance	
	MZ	DZ
Blood types	100%	66%
Eye color	99	28
Mental retardation	97	37
Measles	95	87
Idiopathic epilepsy	72	15
Schizophrenia	69	10
Diabetes	65	18
Identical allergy	59	5
Tuberculosis	57	23

Source: Klug, W. S., and Cummings, M. R. *Concepts of Genetics.* 2nd ed. Glenview, IL: Scott, Foresman, 1986.

Evaluating Scientific Issues

The Genetics of Alcoholism

Chances are that you know an alcoholic—someone who is addicted to alcohol. If you do, then you know from first-hand experience the kinds of physical, personal, and social costs often associated with this disorder. For example, consider just a few of the many possibilities: increased risk of being injured in an accident; liver damage; loss of employment; marital discord; and estrangement from family members, friends, and coworkers. Cross-cultural research has shown that alcoholism is no respecter of geographic boundaries—it is prevalent worldwide (Helzer and Canino, 1992).

Because alcohol is available to just about everyone and because alcoholism is such a serious problem, psychologists and other scientists have long searched for causes of this disorder. Although the search is still underway, many researchers believe that genetic factors play an important role in alcoholism. This conclusion is based on data gathered from three lines of research: twin studies, adoption studies, and artificial breeding studies of animals (for a recent review, see Begleiter and Kissin, 1995).

■ Twin Studies

Twin studies have consistently shown that concordance rates for alcohol use and for alcoholism are higher for MZ twins than for DZ twins. For example, in a study of nearly 4,000 Australian twins, Heath, Meyer, and Martin (1990) found that compared to DZ twins, MZ twins were more similar in their frequency of drinking and in the amount of alcohol consumed while drinking. Pickens et al. (1991), in a study of American twins and their genetic risk for alcoholism, found statistically significant differences in concordance rates for males: They found 76 percent for MZ twins and 61 percent for DZ twins. Concordance rates for females were much lower and not statistically significant: The researchers found 36 percent for MZ twins and 25 percent for DZ twins. The results of a related study (McGue, Pickens, and Svikis, 1992) support these findings: Concordance rates for males (77 percent for MZ twins and 54 percent for DZ twins) were higher than those for females (39 percent for MZ twins and 42 percent for DZ twins). The results of these two studies suggest that males are more likely than females to have a genetic predisposition for alcoholism.

■ Adoption Studies

Adoption studies concerning alcoholism involve children separated from their biological parents at birth or shortly thereafter. The children studied bear no genetic relation to their adoptive parents or siblings. For example, in an adoption study conducted in Sweden involving nearly 1000 males, Cloninger and his colleagues (1981) reported that sons of alcoholic biological parents were more likely to become alcoholics than were sons of nonalcoholic biological parents, even when they were reared by nonalcoholic adoptive parents. A study of Swedish females found similar results (Bohman et al., 1981). Cloninger (1987) has also shown that drinking patterns of male and female alcoholics tend to differ. Whereas male alcoholics may become either steady (drinking daily or almost every day) or binge (sprees of heavy drinking followed by periods of nondrinking) drinkers, female alcoholics tend to become binge drinkers.

■ Artificial Selection Studies

Artificial selection studies using rats as subjects also suggest a genetic basis for alcoholism. In these studies, specific strains of rats are bred for their preference for alcohol. One strain, called the P (preference for alcohol) line, voluntarily drinks alcohol, prefers drinking alcohol to other liquids, shows increased blood-alcohol levels while drinking, will make specific responses to obtain alcohol in an experimental setting, develops a tolerance for alcohol, and develops a physical dependency on alcohol (that is, they show signs of withdrawal when alcohol is no longer available). In contrast, the NP (no preference for alcohol) strain shows none of these characteristics (Lumeng et al., 1995). Examination of the brains of these two strains of rats shows distinct differences in the chemical composition of specific brain regions, suggesting that specific brain mechanisms are related to susceptibility to alcoholism. This finding supports the possible role of genes in alcoholism.

■ Conclusions

Have you noticed anything interesting about the evidence just presented regarding the relationship between genetics and alcoholism? Perhaps you noticed that the three lines of research reviewed are convergent—twin studies, adoption studies, and artificial breeding studies each independently suggest that there is a genetic basis for alcoholism. Convergent evidence is important in science, for it shows that when a relationship between two variables is examined from different approaches, the conclusions are still the same. We are thus more likely to believe that a relationship between heredity and alcoholism really exists.

However, I did not present any evidence suggesting the existence of a particular gene or set of genes for alcoholism because research in that area is still in its preliminary stages. Several years ago, researchers claimed to discover such a gene (e. g., Blum et al., 1990). More recent research evidence suggests that this discovery may have been marred by methodological problems (Gelernter, Goldman, and Risch, 1993). This is clearly a problem that will be addressed by future research. There is no doubt, though, that alcoholism has a tendency to run in families. In fact, about 25 percent of the male relatives of alcoholics are also alcoholics. This number is five times as large as that for males in the general population (Cotton, 1979; Plomin, 1990). But these numbers raise an important question: If genetics are involved in alcoholism, why aren't more of the male relatives of alcoholics themselves alcoholics—shouldn't all of them abuse alcohol? The answer is no.

Remember that genes are expressed in an environment. Different environments affect genes in different ways. A person who has the gene (or set of genes) for alcoholism will not become an alcoholic if he or she does not first consume alcohol—the environmental factor of alcohol must be present. Thus, a person may have this gene and have parents who are alcoholics, but if he or she never consumes alcohol, there is no chance that he or she will become an alcoholic. In Plomin's (1990) words, "it is unlikely that genes drive us to drink."

Clearly, environmental factors must also play a crucial role in the development of alcoholism. Twin and adoption studies do not unequivocally rule out the influence of the drinking habits of family and friends or the tendency of culture or religion to affect if and how a particular person consumes alcohol. Artificial selection studies do not rule out individual characteristics, such as emotionality, which may be selected coincidentally with a preference for alcohol and, in turn, influence the tendency to drink. Nevertheless, the three lines of research we have discussed—twin studies, adoption studies, and artificial selection—strongly suggest that genetic factors play an important role in alcoholism.

Interim Summary

Heredity and Genetics

The instructions for the synthesis of protein molecules, which oversee the development of the body and all of its processes, are contained in genes. Genes are found on chromosomes, which consist of DNA and are found in every cell. We inherit twenty-three individual chromosomes, each of which contains thousands of genes, from each parent. This means that our genetic blueprint represents a recombination of the genetic instructions that our parents inherited from their parents. Such recombination makes for tremendous genetic diversity. Genetically diverse species have a better chance of adapting to a changing environment than do genetically nondiverse species because some members of the species may have genes that enable them to survive in a new environment.

The expression of a gene depends on several factors, including its interaction with other genes (polygenic traits), the sex of the individual carrying the particular gene, and the environmental conditions under which that individual lives. Changes in genetic material caused by mutations or chromosomal aberrations lead to changes in the expression of a particular gene. For example, hemophilia, an increased tendency to bleed from even minor injuries, is the result of a mutation, and Down syndrome, which involves impaired mental, physical, and psychomotor development, is the result of a chromosomal aberration.

Behavior genetics is the study of how genes influence behavior. Psychologists and other scientists use artificial selection studies of animals, twin studies, and adoption studies to investigate the possible relationship between genes and behavior in humans. Alcoholism is one area in which behavior genetics has begun to shed light on the dynamics of this relationship. When taken together, the results from twin studies, adoption studies, and artificial selection using animals suggest that alcoholism has a genetic basis.

Thought Questions

- How would you explain the fact that I have blue eyes but my sister has brown eyes?
- In scientific terms, what does it mean to say that there is a gene for shyness?
- How might the gene related to the development of athletic ability interact with environmental variables to produce a specific phenotype (for example, a specific level of athletic ability in a specific individual)?
- How would you design a study to assess the genetic basis of human aggression? Could you use more than one approach to gathering this information, and, if so, what would these other approaches entail?

Sociobiology

Sociobiology is the study of the genetic bases of social behavior. Sociobiology represents the synthesis of research findings regarding social behavior from many other fields of science, including those from evolutionary psychology and behavior genetics. (Evolutionary psychology and behavior genetics are broader fields than sociobiology in the sense that both are concerned with other phenomena, such as intelligence and cognition, in addition to social behavior.) Sociobiologists are especially interested in understanding the evolutionary roots of our modern-day social actions. More often than not, sociobiologists study the evolutionary bases of social behavior in nonhuman animals and then extrapolate from those species to humans. Sociobiology represents an interface between the biological sciences and psychology. However, not all psychologists are ardent supporters of sociobiology. As we will see, some think that sociobiology is too

simplistic and that its emphasis on genetics inadequately explains the complexities of human behavior.

Reproductive Strategies and the Biological Basis of Parenting

Among the most important social behaviors related to the survival of a species are those related to reproduction and parenting. Indeed, a focal point of sociobiological research and theory has been understanding more about the different kinds of social organization that result from particular **reproductive strategies**—systems of mating and rearing offspring.

You are likely quite accustomed to thinking about sex and family in terms of **monogamy**: the mating of one female and one male. If mating is successful, the individuals share in the raising of the child or children. But monogamy is just one of several reproductive strategies sexual creatures employ in mating and rearing of offspring (Barash, 1982). Three other major classes of reproductive strategy are also possible. (See *Figure 3.9.*) **Polygyny** involves one male mating with more than one female; **polyandry** entails one female mating with more than one male; and **polygynandry** involves several females mating with several males.

According to Trivers (1972), these four reproductive strategies evolved because of important sex differences in the resources that parents invest in conceiving and rearing their offspring. **Parental investment** is the time, physical effort, and risks to life involved in procreation and in the feeding, nurturing, and protecting of offspring. Parental investment is a critical factor in mate selection. An individual who is willing and able to make a greater investment is generally more sought after as a mate and is often more selective or discriminating when selecting a mate (Trivers, 1972).

In some species, competition for mates leads to **sexual selection**—selection for traits specific to sex, such as body

---

sociobiology The study of the genetic bases of social behavior.

reproductive strategies Different systems of mating and rearing offspring. These include monogamy, polygyny, polyandry, and polygynandry.

monogamy The mating of one female and one male.

polygyny The mating of one male with more than one female.

polyandry The mating of one female with more than one male.

polygynandry The mating of several females with several males.

parental investment The resources, including time, physical effort, and risks to life that a parent spends in procreation and in the feeding, nurturing, and protecting of offspring.

sexual selection Selection for traits specific to sex, such as body size or particular patterns of behavior.

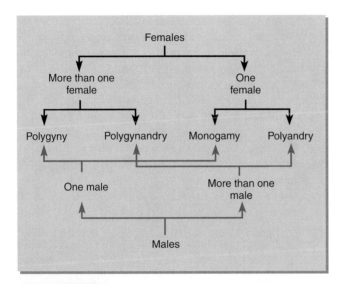

Figure 3.9

Reproductive strategies. Different numbers of males mating with different numbers of females yields the four reproductive strategies of monogamy, polygyny, polyandry, and polygynandry.

size or particular patterns of behavior. For example, in some animals, such as buffalo, females select mates based on the male's ability to survive the skirmishes of the rutting (mating) season. In general, the larger and more aggressive males win these battles and gain access to more females and enjoy greater reproductive success.

You may be surprised to learn that polygyny is by far the most common reproductive strategy among humans. In fact, 84 percent of human societies practice polygyny or allow men who are either wealthy or powerful to practice it (Badcock, 1991). Monogamy is the next most popular reproductive strategy, with about 15 percent of all human cultures practicing it. Polyandry and polygynandry are both rare. Combined, these two reproductive strategies dominate in fewer than 1 percent of all human cultures.

Let's now consider each reproductive strategy individually, beginning with polygyny.

Polygyny: High Female and Low Male Parental Investment

In many species, the female makes the greater parental investment. According to sociobiological theory, whether one is an ova producer or a sperm producer defines the nature of one's parental investment. The fundamental asymmetry between the sexes has been aptly captured by sociobiologists Martin Daly and Margo Wilson (1978, p. 48): "Although each parent contributes almost equally to the genetic resources of the new creature they create, not all contributions are equitable. The female provides the raw materials for the early differentiation and growth of their progeny. Here at the very fundament of

sexuality, is love's labor divided, and it is the female who contributes the most."

Among most mammals (including humans), there can be little doubt that the costs associated with reproduction are higher for females than for males. First, females have fewer opportunities than males to reproduce. Generally, females produce only one ovum or a few ova periodically, whereas males produce vast quantities of sperm over substantially shorter time intervals. Second, females carry the fertilized ovum in their bodies during a long gestation period, continuously diverting a major portion of their own metabolic resources to nourish the rapidly growing fetus. Females also assume all the risks that accompany pregnancy and childbirth, including physical discomfort and possible death. The male's contributions to reproduction are, at a minimum, the sperm and the time needed for intercourse. Third, after the offspring is born, females may continue to devote some of their metabolic resources to the infant by nursing it. Just as important, they usually devote more time and physical energy than males to caring for the newborn.

In addition, a female can only bear a certain number of offspring in a lifetime, regardless of the number of males with whom she mates. In contrast, a male is limited in his reproductive success only by the number of females he can impregnate. For example, consider the differences between females and males in our species. If a woman became pregnant once a year for 10 years, she would have 10 children—only a fraction of the number of children that a man is capable of fathering over the same interval. Suppose that a man impregnated a different woman every month for 10 years—he would have fathered 120 children. This example is hardly an exaggeration. According to the *Guinness Book of World Records,* the largest number of live births to one woman is 69 (she had several multiple births). In contrast, King Ismail of Morocco is reported to have fathered 1056 children.

In many polygynous species, intense competition for the opportunity to mate occurs among males. The competition

Although extremely rare, if not nonexistent in Western cultures, polyandry is practiced in some Eastern cultures. Shown here is a Nepalese wedding ceremony in which two men are being married to the same woman.

Large male elephant seals are more successful in competing for females than are smaller males. But is there a point at which larger size could become maladaptive?

almost always involves some sort of physical confrontation. That is, males fight among themselves for the opportunity to mate. Usually, the larger, stronger, and more aggressive male wins, which means that only he will mate with the available females in the local vicinity. If one of the smaller, weaker males attempts to mate with a female, he is generally chased away by the victorious male.

Because females in polygynous species invest so heavily in their offspring, they are usually highly selective of their mates, choosing to mate with only those males who possess specific attributes, such as physical size, strength, and aggressiveness. Such selectivity makes adaptive sense for both her and her progeny. After all, bearing the offspring of the victor means that her male offspring will tend to possess the same adaptively significant attributes as their father and thus be more likely to win their own quests for mating privileges. And, as a result, genes for large size, increased strength, and aggressiveness will continue to have greater representation in future generations than will genes for less adaptive attributes.

However, sexual selection may reach a point of diminishing returns. Consider the elephant seal. Male elephant seals have evolved to be several times larger than female elephant seals. The largest males almost always win mating privileges—with up to several dozen females. But growing to the point at which the male's mobility while foraging for food and fighting is impaired is maladaptive. An overly large male will be unable to find ample food to sustain his size and will be unlikely to win contests with leaner and more agile competitors. Thus, the male's adaptive attributes are kept in check by the costs of getting too large.

Monogamy: Shared, But Not Always Equal, Parental Investment

Monogamy has evolved in those species whose environments have favored the contributions of both parents to the survival and reproductive success of their offspring. In other words,

under some conditions, two individuals sharing parental duties enjoy more reproductive success than does one individual who must do it all alone. For example, foxes are monogamous. They must provide food, milk, and protection for their offspring. A single fox attempting to fulfill these responsibilities puts the pups at risk. Providing food is better accomplished by two parents than one. A single fox parent would find it difficult to hunt for food with the pups tagging along. Leaving the pups in the den would put them at risk of predation and wandering off and getting lost. However, if both parents are able to share in hunting and protection, the chances of the pups surviving and reaching sexual maturity are enhanced.

Although both parents in monogamous species share offspring-rearing duties, each parent may not make an equal contribution toward that end. Like females in polygynous species, females in monogamous species generally have greater parental investment in the offspring, for many of the same reasons: the limited opportunity for mating relative to that for males, pregnancy and its accompanying risks, providing milk to the newborns, and the time and energy spent in caring for them. As a result, very few monogamous species, including our own, are *exclusively* monogamous. In fact, there is a strong tendency in most monogamous species toward patterns of reproductive behavior and parental investment that resemble those of polygynous species.

For example, in monogamous species, females tend to be more careful than males in selecting a mate, and males tend to be more sexually promiscuous than females (Badcock, 1991). In our own species, men tend to engage in premarital sexual intercourse more often than do females (Kinsey, Pomeroy, and Martin, 1948; Kinsey, Pomeroy, Martin, and Gebhard, 1953; Hunt, 1974), although this gap appears to be decreasing (Wolfe, 1980). Men also tend to have more premarital and extramarital sexual partners (Symons, 1979). Unmarried women tend to seek long-term sexual relationships, while unmarried men tend to prefer more diversity and casualness in their sexual relationships (Tavris and Sadd, 1977).

In our evolutionary past, those females who carefully selected their mates produced more offspring than did those who were less choosy. Males who successfully mated with a number of females produced more offspring than did males who mated with fewer females. From a sociobiological perspective, females tend to be more interested in the quality of their offspring, which, of course, leads females to be selective about the quality of the father and the kinds of resources he brings to the relationship. In contrast, males tend to be more interested in the sheer number of matings.

However, keep in mind that human sexual behavior, although a product of natural selection, is subject to strong cultural influences, which explains why monogamy is the dominant reproductive strategy in western cultures. Specific legal, moral, and cultural sanctions punish sexual arrangements that deviate from monogamous marriages.

Remember, too, that we tend to think of reproductive success today not in terms of the mere number of children we have (although among some religious subcultures, this is still

We do not usually measure our reproductive success by the number of children we produce. For personal reasons, a couple may choose to limit their family size but do their best to ensure that their child matures into a happy, healthy, and responsible adult.

an important measure of success), but in terms of raising healthy, happy, and well-adjusted children. Although most people have the biological capacity to produce a large number of children, many do not have the psychological or financial wherewithal to do so. Some people fear that a large family will reduce the amount of money they can make and will therefore lower their quality of life. Others see a large family as an impediment to obtaining other career goals and life aspirations. And still others simply have no desire to have any children at all.

Polyandry: High Male and Low Female Parental Investment

Polyandry is a rare reproductive strategy among humans and nonexistent in other mammals. It is more prevalent among species that lay eggs. Once the eggs are laid, then either the male or the female may take care of them, although in many instances, the male makes the greater investment of time and effort.

An example of polyandry in humans is found among some of the people who live in remote Himalayan villages. These people are extremely poor and live in a harsh environment, which makes their primary livelihood, farming, difficult. In order to prevent the dissolution of family farms through marriage, families that have more than one son limit the number of marriages to only one per generation—several brothers may share the same wife. A female tends to marry

more than one man (most often brothers) to guarantee that she will be adequately supported. In other words, the male's primary investment—the farm, which is the source of food and some income for the family—is guarded jealously through polyandry.

Polygynandry: Group Parental Investment

Many primates, such as chimpanzees, live in colonies in which few or no barriers are placed on which female mates with which male. In other words, the colonies are promiscuous—during periods of mating, intercourse is frequent and indiscriminate. What is the advantage of such a reproductive strategy?

The primary advantage seems to be the cooperation of males and females in the colony with respect to rearing offspring. Because the males in the colony are not sure which offspring belong to them, it is in their best interest to help rear and protect all the offspring and defend their mothers. The unity in the colony and the lack of aggression among the males contributes directly to the general welfare of all colony members. Females and males have access to many mates, and the offspring are well cared for.

However, a form of monogamy called a *consortship* is sometimes observed in polygynandrous species. For instance, a particular male chimpanzee may ward off other male suitors from a particular female, resulting in an exclusive sexual union. If successful, he is guaranteed the certainty of which offspring are his, albeit at some cost. There is a chance that he could be seriously injured in protecting his mate from other males, and therefore he becomes less useful as a parental investor in his offspring or those of the colony.

Incestuous Relationships: A Universal Taboo

Different reproductive strategies have evolved because the environmental conditions under which various species have evolved are different. But the environments are not so different among species that each species requires its own unique reproductive strategy. Courtship rituals may vary across species, but these rituals still conform to one of the four reproductive strategies discussed above. When more than one species have in common the same reproductive strategy, we may assume that their evolutionary histories with respect to behavior leading to successful mating and childrearing are similar.

Actually, all reproductive strategies have one element in common: avoidance of **incest**—the mating of kin who share many of the same genes. Avoidance of incest appears to have evolved for a very good reason: Closely related relatives are likely to share the same recessive genes that cause genetic disorders. Thus, animals that avoid incestuous matings have an

incest The mating of close relatives who share many of the same genes.

evolutionary advantage over those that do not; they produce healthier offspring who themselves are more likely to live to sexual maturity and produce offspring of their own.

How do individual species members refrain from incestuous matings? Sociobiologists have observed two mechanisms. The first involves migration of individuals away from their birthplaces before sexual maturity, effectively insuring that they will not court close relatives and copulate with them during the mating season. This mechanism is common in many nonhuman mammals—for example, bear and deer. To a small extent, it is also found in some human cultures.

The second mechanism involves the ability to recognize close genetic relatives and to avoid them as potential mates. This mechanism is common in human culture. However, some researchers have shown that this mechanism appears to extend beyond close genetic relatives and apply more generally to those individuals with whom a person has had an extended and close association during childhood and adolescence. Several studies have investigated mating patterns of members of different Israeli *kibbutzim,* villages in which children are raised collectively (Spiro, 1958; Talmon, 1972, Shepher, 1983; and Durham, 1991). Researchers did not find a single instance of a marriage that had occurred between members of the same kibbutz. Durham (1991) suggests that children may develop a natural aversion to becoming sexually attracted to those individuals with whom they are raised. Presumably, the tendency to develop this aversion is inherited.

In addition, all human cultures have *taboos* against incest. A taboo is a societal rule prohibiting the members of a given culture from engaging in specific behaviors—in this case, mating with one's close relatives. Taboos are products of cultural evolution and are socially transmitted through language from one generation to the next.

Incest taboos are probably of secondary importance, serving to reinforce the natural aversion we have toward incest or mating with nonrelatives with whom we were raised. For example, in one study (Shepher, 1983), the elders actually encouraged the children of the kibbutz to marry so that the children would not end up living far from home. But despite the absence of a taboo—and despite encouragement by the elders—none of the children married each other.

The Biological Basis of Altruism

Reproductive and parenting behaviors are not the only social behaviors studied by sociobiologists. A particularly interest-

---

altruism The unselfish concern of one individual for the welfare of another.

inclusive fitness The reproductive success of those who share common genes.

kin selection A type of selection that favors altruistic acts aimed at individuals who share some of the altruist's genes, such as parents, siblings, grandparents, grandchildren, and, under certain conditions, distant relatives.

---

ing and important social behavior that is central to sociobiological theory is **altruism,** the unselfish concern of one individual for the welfare of another. Examples of altruistic behavior abound in our culture, and in their most extreme form are represented when one person risks his or her life to save the life of another. Remember Scott and Mike from the opening vignette? They saved a man from drowning in the Atlantic Ocean—they risked their lives to save someone else's life. Examples of altruism are not limited to our species. In fact, they are common throughout the animal kingdom. Consider, for example, the honey bee that sacrifices its life on behalf of its hivemates by stinging an intruder, or the prairie dog that gives an alarm call that warns other prairie dogs of the predator but increases its own chances of being captured. In each case, the altruist's chances of survival and reproductive success are lowered while that of the other individuals are raised.

Kin Selection

Sociobiologists seek ultimate causes—in particular, the consequences of natural selection—to explain altruism. They assert that natural selection has favored the evolution of organisms that show altruistic tendencies. However, there is an important problem here. On the surface, altruism poses an enigma to evolutionary theory. Recall that natural selection favors only those phenotypes that enhance one's reproductive success. How could altruistic behavior have evolved given that, by definition, it is less adaptive than selfish or competitive behavior?

Geneticist William D. Hamilton (1964, 1970) suggested an answer to this question in a series of mathematical papers. Hamilton's insights stemmed from examining natural selection from the perspective of the gene instead of from the perspective of the whole, living organism. He argued that natural selection does not favor mere reproductive success but rather **inclusive fitness,** or the reproductive success of those individuals who share many of the same genes. Altruistic acts are generally aimed at close relatives such as parents, siblings, grandparents, and grandchildren. The closer the family relation is, the more likely the genetic similarity among the individuals involved. Such biologic favoritism toward relatives is called **kin selection** (Maynard Smith, 1964).

The message here is clear: Under the proper circumstances, individuals behave altruistically toward others with whom they share a genetic history, with the willingness to do so decreasing as the relative becomes more distant. In this view, altruism is not necessarily a conscious act but rather an act driven by a biological prompt that has been favored by natural selection. Natural selection would favor this kind of altruism simply because organisms who share genes also help each other survive.

Parenting is a special case of kin selection and an important contributor to one's survival and reproductive success. In the short run, parents' altruistic actions promote the continued survival of their offspring. In the long run, these actions increase the likelihood that the offspring, too, will become parents and that their genes will survive in successive generations. Such cycles continue according to biological schedule, generation after generation. In the words of sociobiologist David Barash (1982),

> It is obvious why genes for parenting have been selected: All living things are the offspring of parents who themselves were parents! It is a guaranteed, unbroken line stretching back into time. [Genes] that inclined their bearers to be less successful parents left fewer copies of themselves than did those [genes] that were more successful. (pp. 69–70)

What is at stake, of course, is not the survival of individual organisms but the survival of the genes carried by those organisms. Hamilton's insightful contribution to sociobiological theory was to show that altruistic behavior has a *genetically selfish basis*. In other words, genes allow organisms to maximize their inclusive fitness through altruistic behavior directed at other organisms sharing the same genes (Dawkins, 1986). You carry copies of genes that have been in your family line for thousands of years. When the opportunity presents itself, you will most likely carry on the tradition—reproducing and thus projecting your biological endowment into yet another generation. But you did not reach sexual maturity on your own; the concern for your welfare by your parents, brothers, sisters, grandparents, and perhaps an aunt or uncle has contributed to your chances of being reproductively successful. Genes not projected into the next generation simply disappear.

Reciprocal Altruism

Kin selection explains altruism toward relatives, but what about altruism directed toward nonrelatives? What about the kind of altruism that Scott and Mike showed toward the drowning swimmer? Do sociobiologists have an explanation for a person's altruistic actions toward a nonrelative? According to Trivers (1971), the answer is yes. This kind of altruism, called **reciprocal altruism,** is the expression of a crude biological version of the golden rule.

Reciprocal altruism has evolved apparently because it increases the chances that altruistic behavior will be reciprocated. In other words, if you do something altruistic toward someone else, that person is likely to return the favor should he or she be in such a position in the future to do so.

Generally speaking, certain conditions must be satisfied before such reciprocity is likely. First, giving aid must carry with it a low risk to the altruist but a high benefit for the recipient. In other words, altruists behave *as if* they have calculated a cost–benefit ratio for their action: The lower the cost to them and the greater the benefit for others, the more likely the altruistic act. Second, there must be a good chance that the situation *could* be reversed. If the altruist is not likely ever to benefit from similar action on the part of the original recipient, the chances of altruism are lowered. And third, the recipient must be able to recognize the altruist. We are more likely to render assistance to people with whom we are most familiar.

The kind of altruism shown by Scott and Mike does not meet these criteria. In their situation, they both faced high risk, the chance that the circumstances could be reversed was low (the man they aided was unlikely to help them some day), and the person they aided was a stranger to them. Why then did Scott and Mike rescue the drowning man?

Here we see the strong influence of culture on behavior. Both Scott's and Mike's parents had taught them to help others who need help. Indeed, both Scott and Mike had a long history of helping others, albeit in less dramatic situations. Thus, their reactions to the drowning man appear to be automatic. In addition to having the capacity to behave altruistically under certain circumstances, we also have the inherited capacity *to learn* to behave altruistically under still other circumstances. It is not surprising to learn that all cultures have a version of the golden rule. Altruism and other forms of reciprocation appear to be highly valued and adaptive traits for individuals in any culture to possess.

Evaluation of Sociobiology

We have seen that sociobiology is the extension of evolutionary theory and genetics to the study of social behavior. Research supports much sociobiological theory, particularly that concerning nonhuman animals (Barash, 1982). Nonetheless, sociobiology has been at the center of a fierce scientific controversy ever since E. O. Wilson published *Sociobiology: The New Synthesis* in 1975, the official birth date of this discipline. Although Wilson's work, which is based chiefly on studies of nonhuman animal behavior, has generated an enormous outpouring of scientific research, it has also roused a number of serious charges (Montagu, 1980). Wilson's *On Human Nature* (1978), which extended sociobiological theory to human affairs, ignited even more criticism. Most of the criticism focuses on the extension of the theory to human behavior.

Some critics argue that technological innovations developed through cultural evolution have rendered the sociobiological account of human behavior irrelevant. They point out that because the environment we now live in is so different from the one in which we evolved, cultural evolution, not biological evolution, shapes human behavior. In response, sociobiologists agree that cultural practices play an important role in shaping human behavior today, but they also argue that natural selection favored the particular genotypes that made culture possible. Sociobiologists argue that understanding natural selection and its role in human evolution is critical to understanding how human culture evolved.

reciprocal altruism Altruism in which people behave altruistically toward one another because they are confident that such acts will be reciprocated toward either them or their kin.

Another criticism of sociobiology is that it draws simplistic analogies between research done with nonhuman animals and human behavior. This criticism maintains that we cannot learn anything important about human social behavior from research focusing on nonhuman animals. Sociobiologists reply that our understanding of human genetics and physiology is a direct result of research involving nonhuman animals and that advances in understanding human social behavior are likely to follow a similar avenue.

Sociobiologists are also criticized for explaining human social behavior only in terms of genetic determinants and for ignoring environmental factors such as experience and cultural influences. Sociobiologists point out that genes and environmental factors interact to produce any given phenotype. They stress that genes only endow organisms with a behavioral capacity; it is the environment that actually shapes specific behaviors.

The most intense criticism of sociobiology is political, not scientific. Opponents argue that sociobiology sanctions the superiority of one group over another, be it a race, a gender, or a political organization. After all, they argue, if one group of individuals is genetically superior to another, then there are "natural" grounds for justifying the "survival of the fittest" and one group's unethical and immoral domination of another. An example is Hitler's quest for world domination in the name of Aryan superiority. Sociobiologists flatly deny such allegations and argue that it is the critics and not they who have confused the term "natural" with the terms "good" and "superior." Sociobiologists contend that they study the biological bases of social behavior only to understand it further, not to find justification for particular cultural practices and customs. Wilson has eloquently stated the sociobiological defense:

> The purpose of sociobiology is not to make crude comparisons between animal species or between animals and men. . . . Its purpose is to develop general laws of the evolution and biology of social behavior, which might then be extended in a disinterested manner to the study of human beings. . . . It is vital not to misconstrue the political implications of such generalizations. To devise a naturalistic description of human social behavior is to note a set of facts for further investigation, not to pass a value judgment or to deny that a great deal of the behavior can be deliberately changed if individual societies wish. . . . Human behavior is dominated by culture in the sense that the greater part, perhaps all, of the variation between societies is based on differences in cultural experiences. . . . To understand the evolutionary history . . . is to understand in a deeper manner the construction of human nature, to learn what we really are and not just what we hope

we are, as viewed through the various prisms of our mythologies (Wilson, in Barash, 1982, pp. xiv–xv).

Biology and Culture

Thinking Critically about Ethnocentrism

As I write this chapter, there are over fifty wars occurring throughout the world. Although the newspaper headlines and the lead stories on television news shows have focused mainly on the civil war and "ethnic cleansing" in the former Yugoslavia, tension and conflict are present in many places in today's world, just as they seem always to have been. A reading of any world history text quickly leaves the impression that human history is a history of war and destruction based on **ethnocentrism,** the idea that one's own cultural, national, racial, or religious group is superior to or more deserving than others. But ethnocentrism does not only result in war; it is also present in disagreements between politico-religious groups (such as those between Israelis and Palestinians), gang fighting over turf (such as that between the Bloods and the Crypts), rivalry between college athletic teams (for bragging rights), and even the friendly jostling that sometimes occurs between high school seniors and younger students (as is hinted at by the expression "Seniors rule").

■ **How Prevalent is Ethnocentrism?**
In a study aimed at distinguishing ethnocentrists from nonethnocentrists, Silverman (1987) presented people with a hypothetical choice. They were to imagine themselves in a position of imminent danger and having only one means of escape—by boat. There was a catch, though. Two boats were departing and they had to make a choice of which to take. If they took the westbound boat, they would be depriving another person, of different ethnic origin, the chance to escape the danger. If they chose the eastbound boat, they would be depriving someone of similar ethnic origin the chance. About 70 percent of Silverman's subjects made the ethnocentric choice and deprived someone ethnically dissimilar to themselves of a place on the boat.

The results of this study are in general agreement with the assertion of sociobiologists that ethnocentrism is widespread. Sociobiologists argue that ethnocentrism plays a central role in aggression such as feuds and war (Wilson, 1978). Ethnocentrism's suspected role in aggression coupled with its apparent prevalence has led sociobiologists to search for its origins.

■ **What Are the Origins of Ethnocentrism?**
What are the origins of ethnocentrism, and why can't we live more peacefully with each other? Is our ethnocen-

ethnocentrism The idea that one's own cultural, national, racial, or religious group is superior to or more deserving than others.

Wars, violent conflicts, and protests are often marked by ethnocentrism.

terms—as "beasts" and "wild savages"—by eighteenth- and nineteenth-century Americans. And in the former Yugoslavia, Serbs and Bosnian Muslims view each other as being "unfit." Trying to justify our ethnocentrism through such thinking will not lead us to the truth regarding its origins. It will only contribute to its persistence.

The third step might be to avoid committing what might be called the *universality fallacy,* or the belief that because a behavior, such as aggression, is common or universal, that there *must* be a specific genetic component to the behavior. Many behaviors are common among the world's people—for example, automobile driving, swimming, and kite-flying—but we certainly do not talk of having a gene for these behaviors. And that is probably because these behaviors are more innocuous than those involved in aggression; there is no perceived need to justify them politically or morally. Closely related to the universality fallacy is the *naturalistic fallacy,* which is the belief that because a behavior is natural it is also right. We must remember, though, that the concepts of "rightness" and "wrongness" are inventions of human culture. Belching, for example, is a natural behavior, but most people in Western civilization consider such behavior rude or inappropriate under many circumstances, such as at the dinner table, at the theater, or in the classroom. The ability to think in terms of right and wrong seems to be a characteristic that has evolved only in our species. And we tend to develop and apply moral concepts as narrowly or as broadly as we deem a particular situation warrants.

In a study designed to shed some light on the evolutionary and environmental origins of ethnocentrism, Irwin (1987) investigated the social patterns of the Netsilingmiut Inuit tribe, their neighboring groups of Inuit, and Native Americans. The study involved two important components: a computer simulation of the genetic relatedness of tribal members and tribal migration patterns and an analysis of historical records. Irwin found that acts of sharing, cooperation, and altruism, such as food sharing, gift exchange, and wife sharing took place among tribal members but less so between the Netsilingmiut and members of other tribes. Thus, as the probability of genetic relatedness with others decreased, the Netsilingmiut showed a slight tendency toward ethnocentrism. This was true even though they spoke the same language and shared other cultural customs with the other tribes.

However, when the historical records of social patterns between Inuit as a general population and Native Americans were examined, a stronger tendency toward ethnocentrism was found. In this case, the groups spoke different languages and were presumably very different in other ways, such as each group's physical features, style of dress, and body markings. No evidence of altruism between these groups was found. And, whereas war among different Inuit tribes did not involve the killing of women

trism genetically determined—is there a gene or set of genes for ethnocentrism? Or is our ethnocentrism learned, perhaps through socialization processes? These are important questions whose answers have far-reaching implications for how we think about getting along with others.

How should we *personally* proceed to answer these types of questions? Our first step might be to examine the way we have framed the question. We have posed the question in a mutually exclusive frame—as if ethnocentrism must be due to genetics *or* to environmental factors, and to nothing else. But, as we have seen in this chapter, physical and psychological traits are the result of the *interaction* of genetic and environmental factors; neither alone is sufficient for trait expression. Perhaps by reframing the question to read simply, "In what ways do genetics *and* learning influence ethnocentrism?" we may cast a broader intellectual net in our search for an answer.

The second step might be to sort out other issues that could be involved in the question. For example, are we looking for the causes of ethnocentrism or a way to justify it? Hitler's quest for world domination, the U.S. government's callous treatment of Native Americans during the eighteenth- and nineteenth-centuries, and the ethnic cleansing in the former Yugoslavia are examples of ethnocentric thinking that have been justified, presumably by one group's "natural" or biological superiority over the other. In Hitler's view, Jewish people (and all other non-Aryans) were biologically inferior to the Aryan race. Native Americans were often described in less than human and children, war between Inuit and Native Americans "were often genocidal." Irwin noted that, in general, the tendency toward aggression increases as the differences between groups of people increase.

This latter point is telling. The ability to recognize another person or group as being closely biologically related is correlated with particular patterns of social interaction. For example, we tend to behave altruistically toward people who we *know* are our relatives (kin selection). We also tend to behave altruistically toward people with whom we are *familiar* (reciprocal altruism). However, we tend to be less altruistic toward persons we consider strangers or with whom we are otherwise unacquainted. You can probably still remember your parents admonitions to be wary of strangers ("Don't get in a car with a stranger," "Don't let strangers in the house," and "Don't pick up hitchhikers" are all bits of advice that parents frequently give their children.) And the more different others are from us, the less likely our tendency to behave altruistically—or, in other words, the greater the tendency to behave in ethnocentric ways.

Thus, it is likely that biological evolution has been an important factor influencing our social behavior. But it certainly has not been the only factor (Durham, 1991). Our genetic endowment allows for a capacity to learn— for our behavior to be changed by our experiences. Our social interactions with others—with parents, friends, teachers, and so on—can leave an indelible impression on us regarding not only how we behave with them, but also how we behave with others, including strangers. Is ethnocentrism an inherited tendency? Probably so. Does the environment play a role in ethnocentrism? Absolutely. Ethnocentrism is *not* a destiny; it may become more or less characteristic of our behavior depending on our experience with others.

Interim Summary

Sociobiology

The discovery of the genetic basis for social behavior is the primary goal of sociobiology. Sociobiologists have been especially interested in studying social behavior related to reproduction and the rearing of offspring. Different reproductive strategies are believed to have evolved because of sex differences in the resources that parents invest in procreative and childrearing activities. These resources include the time, physical effort, and risks to life involved in procreation and in the feeding, nurturing, and protecting of offspring. Polygynous and monogamous strategies tend to require greater female investment, polyandrous strategies tend to require greater male investment, and polygynandrous strategies tend to require investment on the part of members of a large group, such as a colony of chimpanzees. Despite these differences, all reproductive strategies entail avoidance of incest, either through migration or the recognition of closely related genetic kin or those individuals with whom one was raised. All human cultures have taboos against incest.

Altruism has also been an important topic of study among sociobiologists because it represents an intriguing scientific puzzle, which, on the surface, would seem difficult to explain by appealing to natural selection. After all, why would natural selection favor a trait that lowers one's own reproductive success while increasing the reproductive success of others? The answer to this question may be found in inclusive fitness, or the reproductive success of those who share many of the same genes. Altruistic behavior generally involves one organism risking its life either for others with whom it shares some genes (kin selection) or who are likely to be in the position of later returning the favor (reciprocal altruism).

Sociobiology has been criticized on the grounds that natural selection is no longer a factor in human evolution, that research on animal social behavior is not relevant to understanding human social behavior, that environmental factors play a greater role in shaping human behavior than genetic factors, and that sociobiology is simply a way to justify the superiority of one group over another. Sociobiologists reply that natural selection has shaped and continues to shape the evolution of culture, that findings from animal research can be generalized to humans, that genes and environment interact to determine behavior, and, finally, that sociobiology is an attempt to understand human social behavior, not to justify it.

Ethnocentrism, or the belief that one's own cultural, national, racial, or religious group is superior to others, is a common view throughout the world. Some scientists have debated whether ethnocentrism is genetic or learned. However, this debate disregards other possibilities, such as the role of gene-environment interaction. You should also know the implications of taking a position on the issue—perhaps one's position is based not so much on sound reasoning as on trying to justify one's own ethnocentric view of the world. You should also be aware that just because a behavior is common to many cultures or seems "natural" does not necessarily mean that it is due to genetics or that it is moral.

Thought Questions

- Do you believe that human social behavior has a genetic component? What is the rationale for your answer?
- How might ethnocentrism have influenced human evolution? What factors contribute to its continued presence throughout the world?

Suggestions for Further Reading

Darwin, C. *The Origin of Species by Means of Natural Selection.* London: Murray, 1859.

This book contains the full argument that Darwin marshalled in defense of evolution by natural selection. It is a must for serious students of evolutionary psychology.

Dawkins, R. *The Blind Watchmaker.* New York: Norton, 1986.

This book addresses many common misconceptions and erroneous beliefs regarding Darwin's theory.

Gould, S. J. *Ever since Darwin: Reflections in Natural History.* New York: Norton, 1977.

Gould, S. J. *The Panda's Thumb: More Reflections in Natural History.* New York: Norton, 1980.

Gould, S. J. *Eight Little Piggies.* New York: Norton, 1993.

These three books are collections of Gould's essays written originally for the magazine *Natural History.* Evolution, the history of evolutionary biology, and genetic determinism are the common threads running through these books. Gould is a gifted and witty author; reading his work is a pleasure.

Russell, P. J. *Genetics.* New York: HarperCollins, 1992.

A very good introductory presentation of the basic principles of genetics.

Plomin, R. *Nature and Nurture: An Introduction to Behavioral Genetics.* Pacific Grove, CA: Brooks/Cole, 1990.

This very brief book (144 pages), authored by one of the field's preeminent scholars, is an excellent, simple-to-read introduction to the field of behavior genetics. The relevance of behavior genetics to understanding the origins of common behaviors and problems comes across especially clearly.

Wilson, E. O. *Sociobiology: The New Synthesis.* Cambridge: Harvard University Press, 1975.

This well-written and engaging graduate-level text represents the evolutionary argument for the biological basis of social behavior. The last chapter contains applications of the theory to humans.

Chapter 4

Biology of Behavior

Chapter Outline

The Brain and Its Components

Structure of the Nervous System • Cells of the Nervous System • The Action Potential • Synapses • A Simple Neural Circuit • Neuromodulators: Action at a Distance

The central nervous system consists of the brain and the spinal cord. The peripheral nervous system consists of nerves that connect the central nervous system to sense organs, muscles, and glands. The primary functions of the brain are to control behavior and to regulate the physiological processes of the body. Circuits of neurons (nerve cells) accomplish these functions, supported by glial cells. Neurons communicate with each other by releasing chemicals called transmitter substances. The message transmitted from place to place— the action potential—is a change in the electrochemical properties of the neuron. Synapses, the junctions between neurons, are either excitatory or inhibitory: Excitatory synapses increase a neuron's activity, and inhibitory synapses decrease it. Neuromodulators, such as the opioids, affect behavior by altering the activity of large groups of neurons.

Study of the Brain

Research Methods of Physiological Psychology • Assessment of Damage to the Human Brain • *Biology and Culture: Environmental Effects on Brain Development*

Physiological psychologists study the physiological control of behavior by conducting research with laboratory animals. Neuropsychologists study humans with brain injuries. The development of scanning devices has revolutionized study of the living human brain. The development of the nervous system is influenced by both genetic and environmental variables.

Control of Behavior

Organization of the Cerebral Cortex • Lateralization of Function • Vision: The Occipital and Temporal Lobes • Audition: The Temporal Lobe • Somatosensation and Spatial Perception: The Parietal Lobe • Planning and Moving: The Frontal Lobe • Surgical Treatment of Seizure Disorders

The cerebral cortex, the outer layer of the cerebral hemispheres, receives sensory information, controls perceptual and learning processes, and formulates plans and actions. Some brain functions are lateralized— controlled primarily by one side of the brain. Each of the four lobes of the brain is involved with specific

activities: The occipital lobe and the temporal lobe control seeing; the temporal lobe controls hearing; the parietal lobe controls perception of the body and the space around it; and the frontal lobe controls motor activities, planning, attending to emotionally related stimuli, spontaneous behavior, and speech. Seizure disorders (also known as epilepsy*) are sometimes treated by surgical removal of scarred or damaged regions of the brain that periodically excite neighboring neurons and cause a storm of neural activity. The surgery is performed under local anesthetic so that the behavior of the conscious patient can be observed to be sure that only the damaged brain tissue is removed.*

Control of Internal Functions and Automatic Behavior

The Brain Stem • The Cerebellum • Structures within the Cerebral Hemispheres

The more primitive parts of the brain control homeostasis and species-typical behaviors, such as those involved in fighting, foraging, and reproduction. The cerebellum plays a crucial role in the execution of movement. The thalamus functions as a relay station for sensory information on its way to the cerebral cortex. The hypothalamus controls the autonomic nervous system and the endocrine system. Endocrine glands secrete hormones, which affect physiological functions and behavior. The limbic system regulates the expression of emotion, defense, and aggression and is involved in learning and memory.

Drugs and Behavior

Effects of Drugs on Synaptic Transmission • Drugs That Cause Sedation • Drugs That Cause Excitation • Drugs That Modify Perceptions or Produce Hallucinations • Psychotherapeutic Drugs • *Evaluating Scientific Issues: "Physiological" Versus "Psychological" Drug Addiction*

Drugs that affect behavior do so by facilitating or interfering with synaptic transmission. Drugs that cause sedation, such as tranquilizers and alcohol, depress the activity of the nervous system. Drugs that cause excitation, such as cocaine and amphetamine, increase the activity of the nervous system. Some hallucinogenic drugs alter synapses that release particular transmitter substances and others mimic the effects of certain neuromodulators. Psychotherapeutic drugs reduce the symptoms of mental disorders by acting on specific transmitter substances. Although the side effects of addictive drugs (tolerance and withdrawal symptoms) are important, they are not responsible for addiction. Addiction is caused by the effects of drugs on neurons in the brain that are involved in reinforcement (reward).

iss S. was a sixty-year-old woman who had history of high blood pressure, which was not responding well to the medication she was taking. One evening, she was sitting in her reclining chair reading the newspaper when the phone rang. She got out of her chair and walked to the phone. As she did, she began to feel giddy and stopped to hold on to the kitchen table. She had no memory of what happened after that.

The next morning, a neighbor, who usually stopped by to have coffee with her, found her lying on the floor, mumbling incoherently. She called an ambulance, which took Miss S. to a hospital.

Two days after her admission, the neurological resident in charge of her case told a group of us that she had had a stroke in the back part of the right side of the brain. He attached a CT scan to an illuminated viewer mounted on the wall and showed us a white spot caused by the accumulation of blood in a particular region of her brain. (You can look at the scan yourself; it is shown in Figure 4.20.)

We then went to see Miss S. in her hospital room. Miss S. was awake but seemed a little confused. The resident greeted her and asked how she was feeling. "Fine, I guess," she said. "I still don't know why I'm here."

"Can you see the other people in the room?"

"Why, sure."

"How many are there?"

She turned her head to the right and began counting. She stopped when she had counted the people at the foot of her bed. "Seven," she reported. "What about us?" asked a voice from the left of her bed. "What?" she said, looking at the people she had already counted. "Here, to your left. No, toward your left!" the voice repeated. Slowly, rather reluctantly, she began turning her head to the left. The voice kept insisting, and finally, she saw who was talking. "Oh," she said, "I guess there are more of you."

The resident approached the left side of her bed and touched her left arm. "What is this?" he asked. "Where?" she said. "Here," he answered, holding up her arm and moving it gently in front of her face. "

"Oh, that's an arm."

"An arm? Whose arm?"

"I don't know." She paused. "I guess it must be yours."

"No, it's yours. Look, it's a part of you." He traced with his fingers from her arm to her shoulder.

"Well, if you say so," she said, sounding unconvinced.

When we returned to the residents' lounge, the chief of neurology said that we had seen a classic example of unilateral (one-sided) neglect, caused by damage to a particular part of the brain. "I've seen many cases like this," he explained. "People can still perceive sensations from the left side of their bodies, but they just don't pay attention to them. A woman will put makeup on only the right side of her face, and a man will shave only half of his beard. When they put on a shirt or a coat, they will use their left hand to slip it over their right arm and shoulder, but then they'll just forget about their left arm and let the garment hang from one shoulder. They also don't look at things located toward the left—or even at the left halves of things. Once I saw a man who had just finished eating breakfast. He was sitting in his bed, with a tray in front of him. There was half a pancake on his plate. 'Are you all done?' I asked. 'Sure,' he said. I turned the plate around so that the uneaten part was on his right. He gave a startled look and said, 'Where the hell did that come from?' "

The human brain is the most complex object we know of. As far as our species is concerned, it is the most important 3½ pounds of living tissue in the world. It is also the only object capable of studying itself. (If it could not do so, this chapter could not exist.) Our perceptions, our thoughts, our memories, our emotions, and our desires all reside in our brains. If a surgeon transplants a heart, a liver, or a kidney—or even all three organs—we do not ask ourselves whether the identity of the recipient has been changed. But if a brain transplant were feasible (it isn't), we would undoubtedly say that the owner of the brain was getting a new body rather than the reverse. If Sally's hopelessly damaged brain were removed to make room for Jane's brain, Sally's body would now contain Jane's memories, thoughts, and personality. Jane would live on and Sally's passing would be mourned, even though her body still lived.

The Brain and Its Components

The brain contains anywhere between 10 billion and 100 billion nerve cells—no one knows for sure—and about as many helper cells, which take care of important support and housekeeping functions. For many decades, neuroscientists have known that the brain contains many different types of nerve cells. These cells differ in shape, size, and the kinds of chemicals they produce.

In recent years, neuroscientists have learned that the nerve cells of the brain are organized in *modules*—clusters of nerve cells that communicate with each other. Of course, individual modules do not stand alone; they are connected to other neural circuits, receiving information from some of them, processing this information, and sending the results on to other modules. Particular modules have particular functions, just as the transistors, resistors, and capacitors in a computer chip do. In order to understand how the brain works, we have to understand how individual nerve cells work, how they connect with each other to form modules, and just what these modules do. Next, we have to understand the more complex neural circuits formed by connections among large numbers of modules. We will be working on this task for many years to come.

Let's take a quick look at the overall structure of the nervous system and then examine its elements—neurons and helper cells—in more detail.

Structure of the Nervous System

The brain has two primary functions: control of behavior and regulation of the body's physiological processes. How does it accomplish these tasks?

Let's begin with a brief overview of the structure of the nervous system. The brain cannot act alone. It needs to receive information from the body's sense receptors, and it must be connected with the muscles and glands of the body if it is to affect behavior and physiological processes. The nervous system consists of two divisions. The brain and the spinal cord make up the **central nervous system.** The **spinal cord** is a long, thin collection of nerve cells attached to the base of the brain and running the length of the spinal column. The spinal cord contains circuits of nerve cells that control some simple reflexes, such as automatically pulling away from a painfully hot object. The central nervous system communicates with the rest of the body through the **nerves**—bundles of fibers that transmit information in and out of the central nervous system. The nerves, which are attached to the spinal cord and to the base of the brain, make up the **peripheral nervous system.** (See *Figure 4.1.*)

The human brain has three major parts: the *brain stem,* the *cerebellum,* and the *cerebral hemispheres.* Figure 4.2 shows a view of the left side of the brain. The lower part of the cerebellum and brain stem projects beneath the left cerebral hemisphere; the upper part is normally hidden. (See *Figure 4.2.*)

If the human brain is removed from the skull, it looks as if it has a handle or stem. The **brain stem** is one of the most primitive regions of the brain, and its functions are correspondingly basic ones—primarily control of physiological functions and automatic behaviors. In fact, the brains of some animals, such as amphibians, consist primarily of a brain stem and a simple cerebellum.

The pair of **cerebral hemispheres** constitutes the largest part of the human brain. The cerebral hemispheres contain the parts of the brain that evolved most recently—and thus are involved in behaviors of particular interest to psychologists. The **cerebellum,** attached to the back of the brain stem, looks like a miniature version of the cerebral hemispheres. Its primary function is to control and coordinate movements. (See *Figure 4.2.*)

central nervous system The brain and the spinal cord.

spinal cord A long, thin collection of nerve cells attached to the base of the brain and running the length of the spinal column.

nerve A bundle of nerve fibers that transmit information between the central nervous system and the body's sense organs, muscles, and glands.

peripheral nervous system The cranial and spinal nerves; that part of the nervous system peripheral to the brain and spinal cord.

brain stem The "stem" of the brain, including the medulla, pons, and midbrain.

cerebral hemisphere The largest part of the brain; covered by the cerebral cortex and containing parts of the brain that evolved most recently.

cerebellum A pair of hemispheres resembling the cerebral hemispheres but much smaller and lying beneath and in back of them; controls posture and movements, especially rapid ones.

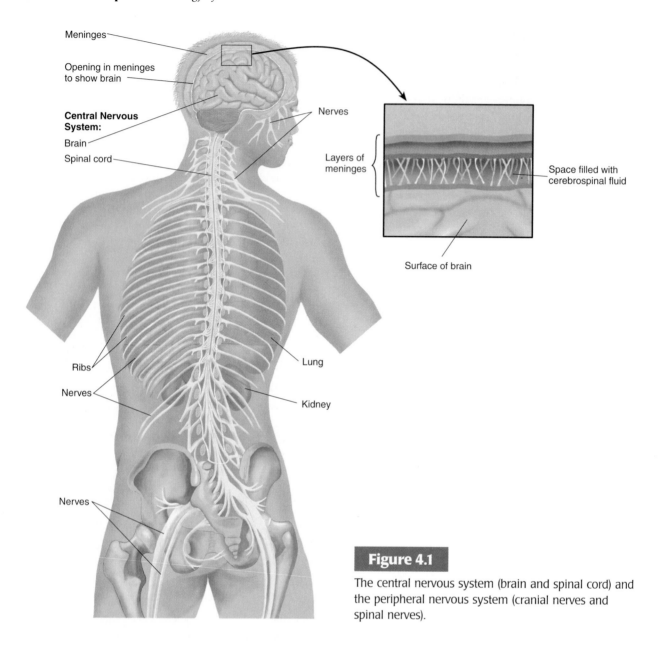

Meninges

Opening in meninges to show brain

Central Nervous System:

Brain

Spinal cord

Nerves

Layers of meninges

Space filled with cerebrospinal fluid

Surface of brain

Ribs

Nerves

Lung

Kidney

Nerves

Figure 4.1

The central nervous system (brain and spinal cord) and the peripheral nervous system (cranial nerves and spinal nerves).

Because the central nervous system is vital to an organism's survival, it is exceptionally well protected. The brain is encased in the skull, and the spinal cord runs through the middle of a column of hollow bones known as **vertebrae.**

vertebra One of the bones that encase the spinal cord and constitute the vertebral column.

meninges The three-layered set of membranes that enclose the brain and spinal cord.

cerebrospinal fluid (CSF) The liquid in which the brain and spinal cord float; provides a shock-absorbing cushion.

cerebral cortex The outer layer of the cerebral hemispheres of the brain, approximately 3 mm thick.

(Refer to *Figure 4.1.*) Both the brain and the spinal cord are enclosed by a three-layered set of membranes called the **meninges.** (*Meninges* is the plural of *meninx,* the Greek word for "membrane." You have probably heard of meningitis, which is an inflammation of the meninges.) The brain and spinal cord do not come into direct contact with the bones of the skull and vertebrae. Instead, they float in a clear liquid called **cerebrospinal fluid (CSF).** This liquid fills the space between two of the meninges, thus providing a liquid cushion surrounding the brain and spinal cord and protecting them from being bruised by the bones that encase them.

The surface of the cerebral hemispheres is covered by the **cerebral cortex.** (The word *cortex* means "bark" or "rind.") The cerebral cortex consists of a thin layer of tissue approxi-

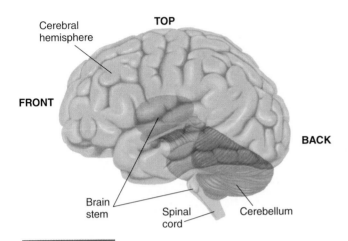

Cerebral hemisphere

TOP

FRONT

BACK

Brain stem

Spinal cord

Cerebellum

Figure 4.2

The three major parts of the brain: brain stem, cerebellum, and cerebral hemisphere. Only the left side of the brain is shown.

mately 3 millimeters thick. It is often referred to as **gray matter** because of its appearance. It contains billions of nerve cells. (The structure and functions of nerve cells are described in the next section.) It is in the cerebral cortex that perceptions take place, memories are stored, and plans are formulated and executed. The nerve cells in the cerebral cortex are connected to other parts of the brain by a layer of nerve fibers called the **white matter** because of the shiny white appearance of the substance that coats and insulates them. Figure 4.3 shows a slice of the brain. As you can see, the gray matter and white matter are distinctly different. (See *Figure 4.3.*)

The human cerebral cortex is very wrinkled; it is full of bulges separated by grooves. The bulges are called *gyri* (singular, *gyrus*), and the large grooves are called *fissures*. Fissures and gyri expand the amount of surface area of the cortex and greatly increase the number of nerve cells it can contain. Animals with the largest and most complex brains, including humans and the higher primates, have the most wrinkled brains and, thus, the largest cerebral cortexes. (See *Figure 4.3.*)

The peripheral nervous system consists of the nerves that connect the central nervous system with sense organs, muscles, and glands. Nerves carry both incoming and outgoing information. The sense organs detect changes in the environment and send signals through the nerves to the central nervous system. The brain sends signals through the nerves to the muscles (causing behavior) and the glands (producing adjustments in internal physiological processes).

Nerves are bundles of many thousands of individual fibers, all wrapped in a tough, protective membrane. Under a microscope, nerves look something like telephone cables, with their bundles of wires. (See *Figure 4.4.*) Like the individual wires in a telephone cable, nerve fibers transmit messages through the nerve, from a sense organ to the brain or from the brain to a muscle or gland.

As we saw earlier, some nerves are attached to the spinal cord and others are attached directly to the brain. The **spinal nerves,** attached to the spinal cord, serve all of the body below the neck, conveying sensory information from the body and carrying messages to muscles and glands. The twelve pairs of **cranial nerves,** attached to the brain, primarily serve muscles and sense receptors in the neck and head. For example, when you taste food, the sensory information gets from your tongue to your brain through one set of cranial nerves. Other sets of cranial nerves bring sensory information to the brain from the eyes, ears, and nose. When you chew food, the command to chew reaches your jaw muscles through another set of cranial nerves. Still other cranial nerves control the eye muscles, the tongue, the neck muscles, and the muscles we use for speech. (Refer to *Figure 4.1.*)

Cells of the Nervous System

Neurons, or nerve cells, are the elements of the nervous system that bring sensory information to the brain, store memories, reach decisions, and control the activity of the muscles. They are assisted in their task by another kind of cell: the **glia.** Glia (or *glial cells*) get their name from the Greek word for glue. At one time, scientists thought that glia simply held neurons—the important elements of the nervous system—in place. They do that, but they also do much more. During development of the brain, some types of glial cells form long fibers that guide developing neurons from their place of birth to their final resting place. Other types of glia manufacture chemicals that neurons need to perform their tasks and absorb chemicals that might impair neurons' functioning. Others form protective insulating sheaths around nerve fibers. Still others serve as the brain's immune system, protecting it from invading microorganisms that might infect it.

gray matter The portions of the central nervous system that are abundant in cell bodies of neurons rather than axons.

white matter The portions of the central nervous system that are abundant in axons rather than cell bodies of neurons. The color derives from the presence of the axons' myelin sheaths.

spinal nerve A bundle of nerve fibers attached to the spinal cord; conveys sensory information from the body and carries messages to muscles and glands.

cranial nerve A bundle of nerve fibers attached to the base of the brain; conveys sensory information from the face and head and carries messages to muscles and glands.

neuron A nerve cell; consists of a cell body with dendrites and an axon whose branches end in terminal buttons that synapse with muscle fibers, gland cells, or other neurons.

glial cell A cell of the central nervous system that provides support for neurons and supplies them with some essential chemicals.

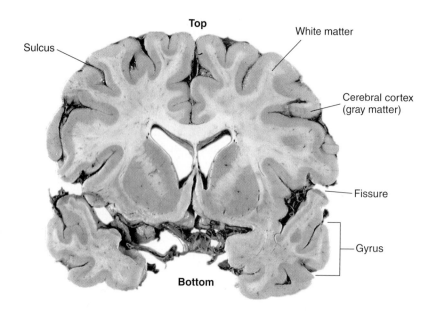

Top

Sulcus

White matter

Cerebral cortex
(gray matter)

Fissure

Gyrus

Bottom

Figure 4.3

A photograph of a slice of a human brain showing fissures and gyri and the layer of cerebral cortex that follows these convolutions.
(Harvard Medical School/Betty G. Martindale.)

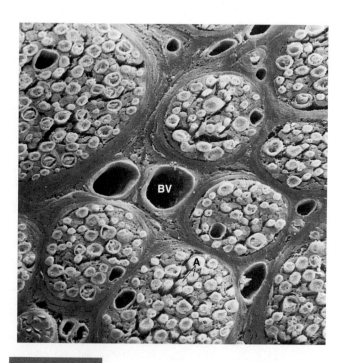

BV

A

Figure 4.4

Nerves. A nerve consists of a sheath of tissue that encases a bundle of individual nerve fibers (also known as *axons*). BV = blood vessel; A = individual axons.

(From Tissues and Organs: A Text-Atlas of Scanning Electron Microscopy, *by Richard G. Kessel and Randy H. Kardon. Copyright © 1979 by W. H. Freeman and Co. Reprinted by permission.)*

lism and maintenance of the cell. The soma also receives messages from other neurons. (See *Figure 4.5.*)

2. The **dendrites,** the treelike growths attached to the soma, function principally to receive messages from other neurons. (*Dendron* means "tree.") They transmit the information they receive down their "trunks" to the soma. (See *Figure 4.5.*)

3. The nerve fiber, or **axon,** carries messages away from the soma toward the cells with which the neuron communicates. (See *Figure 4.5.*) These messages, called *action potentials,* consist of brief changes in the electrical charge of the axon. For convenience, an action potential is usually referred to as the *firing* of an axon.

4. The **terminal buttons** are located at the ends of the "twigs" that branch off the ends of axons. (See *Figure 4.5.*) Terminal buttons secrete a chemical called a **transmitter substance** whenever an action potential travels down the axon (whenever the axon fires). (These chemicals are often referred to as *neurotransmitters.*) The transmitter substance affects the activity of the other cells with

But let's get back to neurons. The four principal parts of a neuron are shown in Figure 4.5.

1. The **soma,** or cell body, is the largest part of the neuron and contains the mechanisms that control the metabo-

soma   A cell body; the largest part of a neuron.

dendrite   A treelike part of a neuron on which the terminal buttons of other neurons form synapses.

axon   A long, thin part of a neuron attached to the soma; divides into a few or many branches, ending in terminal buttons.

terminal button   The rounded swelling at the end of the axon of a neuron; releases transmitter substance.

transmitter substance   A chemical released by the terminal buttons that causes the postsynaptic neuron to be excited or inhibited.

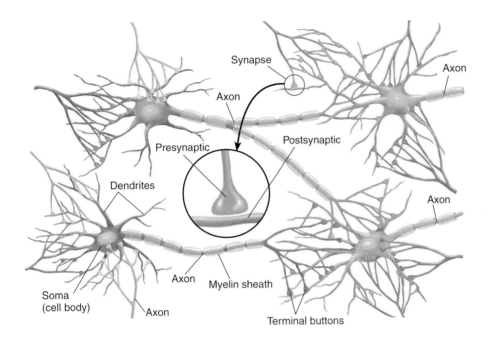

Figure 4.5

The principal parts of a neuron and its connections with other neurons (synapses).

which the neuron communicates. Thus, the message is conveyed *chemically* from one neuron to another. Most drugs that affect the nervous system and hence alter a person's behavior do so by affecting the chemical transmission of messages between cells.

Many axons, especially long ones, are insulated with a substance called *myelin.* The white matter located beneath the cerebral cortex gets its color from the **myelin sheaths** around the axons that travel through these areas. Myelin, part protein and part fat, is produced by special cells that individually wrap themselves around segments of the axon, leaving small bare patches of the axon between them. (See *Figure 4.5.*) The principal function of myelin is to insulate axons from each other and thus to prevent the scrambling of messages. It also increases the speed of the action potential.

The symptoms of a particular neurological disease prove just how important the myelin sheath is. In some cases, people's immune systems go awry and begin to attack parts of their own bodies. One of these disorders is called *multiple sclerosis,* because an autopsy of the brain and spinal cord will show numerous patches of hardened, damaged tissue. (*Skleros* is Greek for "hard.") The immune systems of people who have multiple sclerosis attack a protein in the myelin sheath of axons in the central nervous system, stripping it away. Although most of the axons survive this assault, they can no longer function normally, and so—depending on where the damage occurs—people who have multiple sclerosis suffer from various sensory and motor impairments.

The Action Potential

The message carried by the axon—the action potential—involves an electrical current, but it does not travel down the

axon the way electricity travels through a wire. Electricity travels through a wire at hundreds of millions of meters per second. But as we saw in Chapter 1, Helmholtz discovered that the axon transmits information at a much slower rate—less than 100 meters per second.

The membrane of an axon is electrically charged. When the axon is resting (that is, when no action potential is occurring), the outside is charged at +70 millivolts (thousandths of a volt) with respect to the inside. An **action potential** is an abrupt, short-lived reversal in the electrical charge of an axon. This temporary reversal begins at the end of the axon that attaches to the soma and is transmitted to the end that divides into small branches capped with terminal buttons.

The electrical charge of the axon occurs because of an unequal distribution of positively and negatively charged particles inside the axon and in the fluid that surrounds it. These particles, called **ions,** are produced when various substances—including ordinary table salt—are dissolved in water. Normally, ions cannot penetrate the membrane that surrounds axons. However, the axonal membrane contains special submicroscopic proteins that serve as ion channels or ion transporters. **Ion channels** can open or close; when they

myelin sheath The insulating material that encases most large axons.

action potential A brief electrochemical event that is carried by an axon from the soma of the neuron to its terminal buttons; causes the release of a transmitter substance.

ion A positively or negatively charged particle; produced when many substances dissolve in water.

ion channel A special protein molecule located in the membrane of a cell; controls the entry or exit of particular ions.

are open, a particular ion can enter or leave the axon. **Ion transporters** work like pumps. They use the energy resources of the cell to transport particular ions into or out of the axon. (See *Figure 4.6.*)

The outside of the membrane is positively charged (and the inside is negatively charged) because the axon contains more negatively charged ions and fewer positively charged ions. When an axon is resting, its ion channels are closed, so ions cannot move in or out of the axon. An action potential is caused by the opening of some ion channels in the membrane at the end of the axon nearest the soma. The opening of these ion channels permits positively charged sodium ions to enter, which reverses the membrane potential at that location. This reversal causes nearby ion channels to open, which produces another reversal at *that* point. The process continues all the way to the terminal buttons located at the other end of the axon.

Note that an action potential is a *brief* reversal of the membrane's electrical charge. As soon as the charge reverses, the ion channels close and another set of ion channels open for a short time, letting positively charged potassium ions *out* of the axon. This outflow of positive ions restores the normal electrical charge. Thus, an action potential resembles the "wave" that sports fans often make in a stadium during a

game. People in one part of the stadium stand up, raise their arms over their heads, and sit down again. People seated next to them see that a wave is starting, so they do the same—and the wave travels around the stadium. Everyone remains at the same place, but the effect is that of something circling in the stands around the playing field. Similarly, electricity does not really travel down the length of an axon. Instead, the entry of positive ions in one location reverses the charge at that point and causes ion channels in the adjacent region to open, and so on. (See *Figure 4.7.*)

You may be wondering what happens to the sodium ions that enter the axon and the potassium ions that leave it. This is where the ion transporters come in. The ion transporters pump sodium ions out of the axon and pump potassium ions back in, restoring the normal balance. (See *Figure 4.7.*)

Synapses

Neurons communicate with other cells by means of synapses. A **synapse** is the conjunction of a terminal button of one neuron and the membrane of another cell—neuron, muscle cell, or gland cell. Let us first consider synapses between one neuron and another. The terminal button belongs to the **presynaptic neuron**—the neuron that sends the message. As we saw, when terminal buttons become active, they release a chemical called a transmitter substance. The neuron that receives the message (that is, detects the transmitter substance) is called the **postsynaptic neuron.** (Refer to inset, *Figure 4.5.*) A neuron receives messages from many terminal buttons, and in turn its terminal buttons form synapses with many other neurons. The drawing in Figure 4.5 is much simplified; thousands of terminal buttons can form synapses with a single neuron.

Figure 4.8 illustrates the relation between a motor neuron and a muscle. A **motor neuron** is one that forms synapses with a muscle and controls its contractions. When the axon of a motor neuron fires, all the muscle fibers with which it forms synapses will contract with a brief twitch. (See *Figure 4.8.*) A muscle consists of thousands of individual muscle

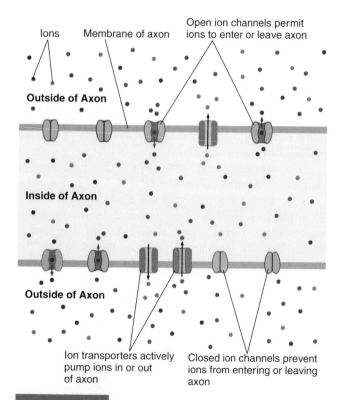

Figure 4.6

Ion channels and ion transporters. These structures regulate the numbers of ions found inside and outside the axon. An unequal distribution of positively and negatively charged ions is responsible for the axon's electrical charge.

ion transporter A special protein molecule located in the membrane of a cell; actively transports ions into or out of the cell.

synapse The junction between the terminal button of one neuron and the membrane of a muscle fiber, a gland, or another neuron.

presynaptic neuron A neuron whose terminal buttons form synapses with and excite or inhibit another neuron.

postsynaptic neuron A neuron with which the terminal buttons of another neuron form synapses and that is excited or inhibited by that neuron.

motor neuron A neuron whose terminal buttons form synapses with muscle fibers. When an action potential travels down its axon, the associated muscle fibers will twitch.

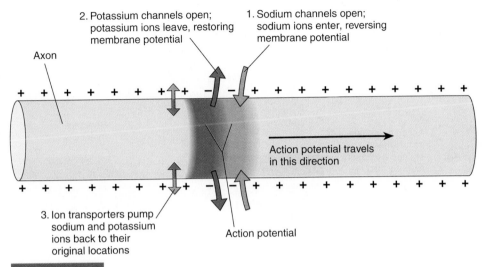

2. Potassium channels open; potassium ions leave, restoring membrane potential

1. Sodium channels open; sodium ions enter, reversing membrane potential

Axon

Action potential travels in this direction

3. Ion transporters pump sodium and potassium ions back to their original locations

Action potential

Figure 4.7

Movement of sodium and potassium ions during the action potential. Sodium ions are represented by red arrows, potassium ions by green arrows.

fibers. It is controlled by a large number of motor neurons, each of which forms synapses with different groups of muscle fibers. The strength of a muscular contraction, then, depends on the rate of firing of the axons that control it. If they fire at a high rate, the muscle contracts forcefully; if they fire at a low rate, the muscle contracts weakly.

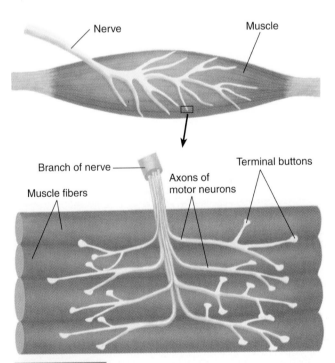

Nerve

Muscle

Branch of nerve

Terminal buttons

Axons of motor neurons

Muscle fibers

Figure 4.8

Synapses between terminal buttons of the axon of a motor neuron and a muscle.

There are basically two types of synapses: *excitatory synapses* and *inhibitory synapses*. Excitatory synapses do just what their name implies. When the axon fires, the terminal buttons release a transmitter substance that excites the postsynaptic neurons with which they form synapses. The effect of this excitation is to make it more likely that the axons of the postsynaptic neurons will fire. Inhibitory synapses do just the opposite. When they are activated, they *lower* the likelihood that the axons of the postsynaptic neurons will fire.

The rate at which a particular axon fires is determined by the activity of the synapses on the dendrites and soma of the cell. If the excitatory synapses are more active, the axon will fire at a high rate. If the inhibitory synapses are more active, it will fire at a low rate or, perhaps, not at all. (See *Figure 4.9.*)

How do molecules of transmitter substance exert their excitatory or inhibitory effect on the postsynaptic neuron? When an action potential reaches a terminal button, it causes the terminal button to release a small amount of transmitter substance into the **synaptic cleft,** a fluid-filled space between the terminal button and the membrane of the postsynaptic neuron. The transmitter substance causes reactions in the postsynaptic neuron that either excite or inhibit it. These reactions are triggered by special submicroscopic protein molecules embedded in the postsynaptic membrane called **receptor molecules.** (See *Figure 4.10.*)

synaptic cleft A fluid-filled gap between the presynaptic and postsynaptic membranes; the terminal button releases transmitter substance into this space.

receptor molecule A special protein molecule located in the membrane of the postsynaptic neuron that responds to molecules of the transmitter substance. Receptors such as those that respond to opiates are sometimes found elsewhere on the surface of neurons.

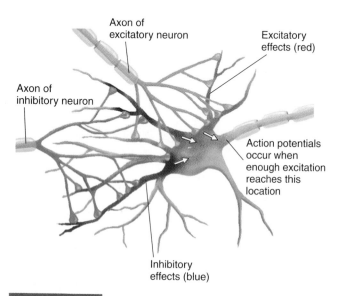

Axon of
excitatory neuron

Excitatory
effects (red)

Axon of
inhibitory neuron

Action potentials
occur when
enough excitation
reaches this
location

Inhibitory
effects (blue)

Figure 4.9

Interaction between the effects of excitatory and inhibitory
synapses. The rate of firing of the axon of neuron C is
controlled by these two factors.

A molecule of a transmitter substance attaches to a receptor molecule the way a key fits in a lock. After their release
from a terminal button, molecules of transmitter substance
find their way to the receptor molecules, attach to them, and
activate them. Once they are activated, the receptor molecules
produce excitatory or inhibitory effects on the postsynaptic
neuron. They do so by opening ion channels. The ion channels found at excitatory synapses permit sodium ions to enter
the neuron; those found at inhibitory synapses permit potassium ions to leave it. (See *Figure 4.11.*)

The excitation or inhibition produced by a synapse is
short-lived; the effects soon pass away, usually in a fraction of
a second. At most synapses, the effects are terminated by a
process called **reuptake**. The transmitter substance is released
by the terminal button and is quickly taken up again, so it
therefore has only a short time to stimulate the postsynaptic
receptor molecules. (See *Figure 4.12.*) The rate at which the
terminal button takes back the transmitter substance determines how prolonged the effects of the chemical on the postsynaptic neuron will be. The faster the transmitter substance
is taken back, the shorter its effects will be on the postsynaptic neuron. As we will see, some drugs affect the nervous system by slowing down the rate of reuptake, thus prolonging
the effects of the transmitter substance.

reuptake The process by which a terminal button retrieves
the molecules of transmitter substance that it has just released; terminates the effect of the transmitter substance on
the receptors of the postsynaptic neuron.

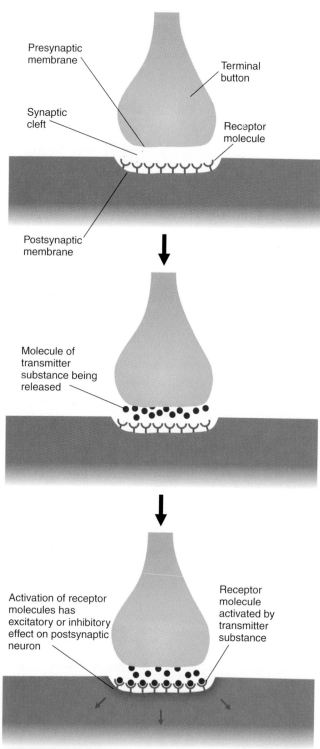

Presynaptic
membrane

Terminal
button

Synaptic
cleft

Receptor
molecule

Postsynaptic
membrane

Molecule of
transmitter
substance being
released

Activation of receptor
molecules has
excitatory or inhibitory
effect on postsynaptic
neuron

Receptor
molecule
activated by
transmitter
substance

Figure 4.10

The release of a transmitter substance from a terminal
button. *Top:* Before the arrival of an action potential. *Middle:*
Just after the arrival of an action potential. Molecules of
transmitter substance have been released. *Bottom:*
Activation of receptor molecules. The molecules of
transmitter substance diffuse across the synaptic cleft and
some of them activate receptor molecules in the

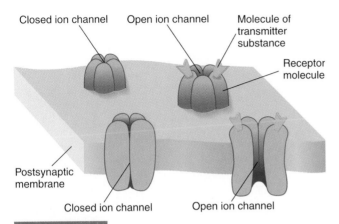

Closed ion channel   Open ion channel   Molecule of transmitter substance

Receptor molecule

Postsynaptic membrane

Closed ion channel   Open ion channel

Figure 4.11

Detailed view of receptor molecules in the postsynaptic neuron. When activated by molecules of a transmitter substance, the receptor molecules allow sodium ions to enter the postsynaptic neuron, causing excitation, or allow potassium ions to leave, causing inhibition.

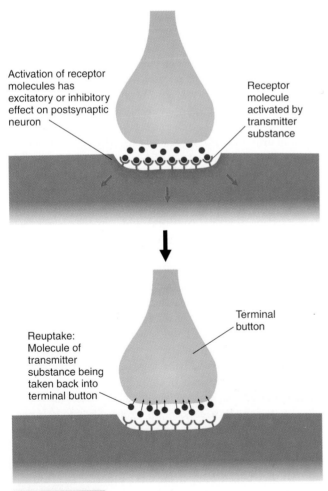

Activation of receptor molecules has excitatory or inhibitory effect on postsynaptic neuron

Receptor molecule activated by transmitter substance

Terminal button

Reuptake: Molecule of transmitter substance being taken back into terminal button

Figure 4.12

Reuptake of molecules of transmitter substance.

A Simple Neural Circuit

Let's try to put together what we know about neurons, action potentials, and synapses by seeing how a simple neural circuit works. The interconnections of the billions of neurons in our central nervous system provide us with the capacities for perception, decision making, memory, and action. Although we do not yet know enough to draw a "neural wiring diagram" for such complex functions, we can do so for some of the simpler reflexes that are triggered by certain kinds of sensory stimuli. For example, when your finger touches a painfully hot object, your hand withdraws. When your eye is touched, your eyes close and your head draws back. When a baby's cheek is touched, it turns its mouth toward the object, and if the object is of the appropriate size and texture, the baby begins to suck. All these activities occur quickly, without thought.

A simple withdrawal reflex, which is triggered by a noxious stimulus (such as contact with a hot object), requires three types of neurons. **Sensory neurons** detect the noxious stimulus and convey this information to the spinal cord. **Interneurons**, located entirely within the brain or spinal cord, receive the sensory information and in turn stimulate the motor neurons that cause the appropriate muscle to contract. (See *Figure 4.13.*) The sequence is simple and straightforward. A noxious stimulus applied to the skin produces a burst of action potentials in the sensory neurons. Their axons fire, and their terminal buttons, located within the spinal cord, release an excitatory transmitter substance. The chemical stimulates the interneurons and causes them to fire. The interneurons excite the motor neurons, and these neurons cause the muscle to contract. (See *Figure 4.13.*)

The next example adds a bit of complexity to the circuit. Suppose you have removed a hot casserole from the oven. As you start over to the table to put it down, the heat begins to penetrate the rather thin potholders you are using. The pain caused by the hot casserole triggers a withdrawal reflex that tends to make you drop it. And yet you manage to keep hold of it long enough to get to the table and put it down. What prevented your withdrawal reflex from making you drop the casserole on the floor?

As we saw earlier, the activity of a neuron depends on the relative activity of the excitatory and inhibitory synapses on it. The pain from the hot casserole increases the activity of excitatory synapses on the motor neurons, which tends to cause the hand to open. However, this excitation is counteracted by inhibition from another source—the brain. The brain contains neural circuits that recognize what a disaster it would be if you dropped the casserole on the floor. These neural circuits

sensory neuron A neuron that detects changes in the external or internal environment and sends information about these changes to the central nervous system.

interneuron A neuron located entirely within the central nervous system.

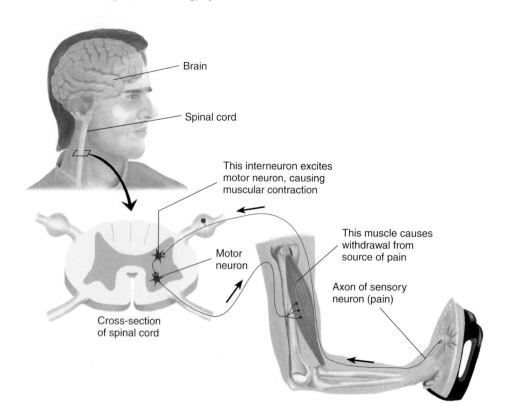

Brain

Spinal cord

This interneuron excites motor neuron, causing muscular contraction

This muscle causes withdrawal from source of pain

Motor neuron

Axon of sensory neuron (pain)

Cross-section of spinal cord

Figure 4.13

A schematic representation of the elements of a withdrawal reflex. Although this figure shows just one sensory neuron, one interneuron, and one motor neuron, in reality, many thousands of each type of neuron would be involved.

send information to the spinal cord that prevents the withdrawal reflex from making you drop the dish.

Figure 4.14 shows how this information reaches the spinal cord. As you can see, an axon from a neuron in the brain reaches the spinal cord, where it forms a synapse with an inhibitory interneuron. When the neuron in the brain becomes active, it excites this inhibitory interneuron. The interneuron releases an inhibitory transmitter substance, which decreases the rate of firing of the motor neuron, preventing your hand from opening. This circuit provides an example of a contest between two competing tendencies: to drop the casserole and to hold on to it. (See *Figure 4.14.*) Complex decisions about behavior are made within the brain by much more complicated circuits of neurons, but the basic principles remain the same.

Neuromodulators: Action at a Distance

As you just learned, terminal buttons excite or inhibit postsynaptic neurons by releasing transmitter substances. These chemicals travel a very short distance and affect receptor

neuromodulator A substance secreted in the brain that modulates the activity of neurons that contain the appropriate receptor molecules.

opioid A neuromodulator whose action is mimicked by a natural or synthetic opiate, such as opium, morphine, or heroin.

molecules located on a small patch of the postsynaptic membrane. But some neurons release chemicals that get into the general circulation of the brain and stimulate receptor molecules on many thousands of neurons, some located a considerable distance away. The chemicals these neurons release are called **neuromodulators,** because they modulate the activity of the neurons they affect.

We can think of neuromodulators as the brain's own "drugs." Because these chemicals diffuse widely in the brain, they can activate or inhibit many different circuits of neurons, thus exerting several behavioral and physiological effects. These effects act together to help achieve a particular goal.

The best-known neuromodulator is a category of chemicals called *endorphins,* or **opioids** ("opiumlike substances"). Opioids are neuromodulators that stimulate special receptor molecules (opioid receptors) located on neurons in several parts of the brain. Their behavioral effects include decreased sensitivity to pain and a tendency to persist in ongoing behavior. Opioids are released while an animal is engaging in important species-typical behaviors, such as mating or fighting. The behavioral effects of opioids ensure that a mating animal or an animal fighting to defend itself is less likely to be deterred by pain; thus, conception is more likely to occur and a defense is more likely to be successful.

Many years ago, people discovered that eating or smoking the sap of the opium poppy decreased their sensitivity to pain, so they began using it for this purpose. They also discovered that the sap produced pleasurable effects: People who took it enjoyed the experience and wanted to take more. In recent times, chemists have discovered that the sap of the

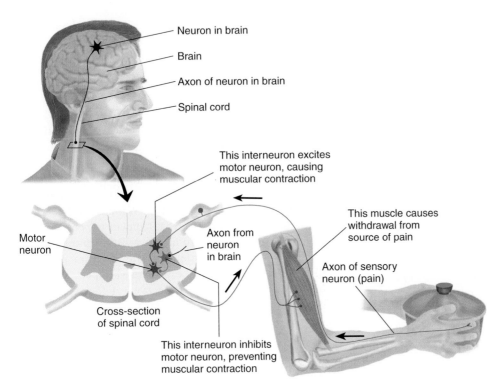

Neuron in brain

Brain

Axon of neuron in brain

Spinal cord

This interneuron excites motor neuron, causing muscular contraction

This muscle causes withdrawal from source of pain

Motor neuron

Axon from neuron in brain

Axon of sensory neuron (pain)

Cross-section of spinal cord

This interneuron inhibits motor neuron, preventing muscular contraction

Figure 4.14

A schematic representation of a withdrawal reflex being inhibited by the brain.

opium poppy contains a class of chemicals called *opiates*. They also learned how to extract and concentrate them and to produce synthetic versions with even greater potency. In the mid-1970s, neurobiologists learned that opiates produce their effect by stimulating special *opioid receptor molecules* located on neurons in the brain (Pert, Snowman, and Snyder, 1974). Soon after that, they discovered the brain's opioids (Terenius and Wahlström, 1975). Thus, opiates mimic the effects of a special category of neuromodulators that the brain uses to regulate some types of species-typical behaviors. I will say more about opiates later in this chapter.

The brain produces other neuromodulators. Some help organize the body's response to stress, while others reduce anxiety and promote sleep. Some promote eating, while others help end a meal. Undoubtedly, many other neuromodulators are waiting to be discovered.

Interim Summary

The Brain and Its Components

The brain has two major functions: control of behavior and regulation of the body's physiological processes.

The central nervous system consists of the spinal cord and the three major divisions of the brain: the brain stem, the cerebellum, and the cerebral hemispheres. The cerebral cortex, which covers the cerebral hemispheres, is wrinkled by fissures and gyri. The brain communicates with the rest of the body through the peripheral nervous system, which includes the spinal nerves and cranial nerves.

The basic element of the nervous system is the neuron, with its soma, dendrites, axon, and terminal buttons. Neurons are assisted in their tasks by glia, which provide physical support, aid in the development of the nervous system, provide neurons with chemicals they need, remove unwanted chemicals, provide myelin sheaths for axons, and protect neurons from infections.

One neuron communicates with another (or with muscle or gland cells) by means of synapses. A synapse is the junction of the terminal button of the presynaptic neuron with the membrane of the postsynaptic neuron. Synaptic communication is chemical; when an action potential travels down an axon (when the axon "fires"), it causes a transmitter substance to be released by the terminal buttons. An action potential consists of a brief change in the electrical charge of the axon, produced by a brief entry of positively charged sodium ions into the axon followed by a brief exit of positively charged potassium ions. Ions enter the axon through ion channels, and ion transporters eventually restore the proper concentrations of ions inside and outside the cell.

Molecules of the transmitter substance released by terminal buttons either excite or inhibit the firing of the postsynaptic neuron. The combined effects of excitatory and inhibitory synapses on a particular neuron determine the rate of firing of that neuron. As we have seen, the reflex is the simplest element of behavior, and it illustrates the contest between excitation and inhibition.

Neuromodulators resemble transmitter substances but travel farther and are dispersed more widely. They are released by terminal buttons and modulate the activity of many neurons. The best-known neuromodulators are the opioids, which are released when an animal is engaged in important behavior. The opiates, extracted from the sap of the opium poppy or produced in a laboratory, stimulate the brain's opioid receptors.

Thought Questions

- The brain is the seat of our perceptions, thoughts, memories, and feelings. Why, then, do we so often refer to our hearts as the location of our feelings and emotions? For example, why do you think we say, "He acted with his heart, not with his head"?
- As we saw, opioids are useful neuromodulators because they encourage an animal to continue fighting or mating. Can you think of other behaviors that might be influenced by neuromodulators? Can you think of mental or behavioral problems that might be caused if too much or too little of these neuromodulators were secreted?

Study of the Brain

Most of our knowledge of the functions of the nervous system was obtained through research using laboratory animals. For example, all that we know about neurons and their functions was learned through animal research. In addition, research using laboratory animals has produced important discoveries about the causes and treatments of neurological and mental disorders, many of which I discuss in this book. Thanks to such research, we now have drugs that help people with neurological disorders such as Parkinson's disease and mental disorders such as schizophrenia, depression, and obsessive compulsive disorders. As we saw in Chapter 2, all research using live animals must follow strict regulations designed to protect the animals' health and well-being.

The easiest way to justify research with animals is to point to actual and potential benefits to human health. However, we can also justify this research by employing a less practical, but perhaps equally important, argument. One of the things that characterizes our species is a quest for an understanding of our world. For example, astronomers study the universe and try to uncover its mysteries. Even if their discoveries never lead to practical benefits such as better drugs or faster methods of transportation, the fact that they enrich our understanding of the beginning and the fate of our universe justifies their efforts. The pursuit of knowledge is itself a worthwhile endeavor. Surely the attempt to understand the

brain lesion Damage to a particular region of the brain.

stereotaxic apparatus A device used to insert an electrode into a particular part of the brain for the purpose of recording electrical activity, stimulating the brain electrically, or producing localized damage.

universe within us—our nervous system, which is responsible for all that we are or can be—is also valuable.

Research Methods of Physiological Psychology

Physiological psychologists now have at their disposition a range of research methods that would have been impossible to imagine just a few decades ago. We have ways to identify neurons that contain particular chemicals. We have ways to take photographs of particular ions entering neurons when the appropriate ion channels open. We have ways to inactivate individual genes to see what happens to behavior when they no longer function. In fact, just listing and briefly describing these methods would take up an entire chapter. In this section, I will describe only the most important research methods, which will give you a taste of the research performed by physiological psychologists.

The earliest research method of physiological psychology—and the one that is still most commonly used—involves correlating a behavioral deficit with damage to a specific part of the nervous system. The investigator produces a **brain lesion,** an injury to a particular part of the brain, and then studies the effects of the lesion on the animal's behavior. If particular behaviors are disrupted, the damaged part of the brain must be involved in those behaviors.

To produce a brain lesion, the researcher anesthetizes an animal and prepares it for surgery, drills a hole in its skull, and destroys part of its brain. In most cases, the region under investigation is located deep within the brain. To reach this region, the investigator must use a special device called a **stereotaxic apparatus** to insert a fine wire (called an electrode) into a particular location in the brain. (The term *stereotaxic* refers to the ability to manipulate an object in three-dimensional space.) The researcher passes an electrical current through the electrode, which produces heat that destroys a small portion of the brain around the tip of the electrode. After a few days, the animal recovers from the operation, and the researcher can assess its behavior. (See *Figure 4.15.*)

A stereotaxic apparatus can also be used to insert wires for recording the electrical activity of neurons in particular regions of the brain. As we saw earlier, neurons transmit information by means of electrical charges; the electrode detects these charges. The electrode is then attached to an electrical connector cemented to the animal's skull, and the incision in the scalp is sewn up. The connector is later attached to a wire leading to electronic devices that record the brain's electrical activity while the animal is performing various behaviors. (See *Figure 4.16.*)

An electrode placed in an animal's brain can be used to lead electrical current into the brain as well as out of it. If an electrical connector on the animal's skull is attached to an electrical stimulator, current can be sent to a portion of the animal's brain. This current activates neurons located near the

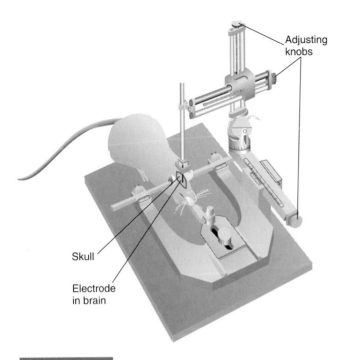

Figure 4.15

A stereotaxic apparatus, used to insert a wire into a specific portion of an animal's brain.

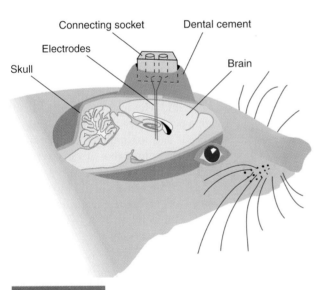

Figure 4.16

A permanently attached set of electrodes in an animal's brain and a connecting socket cemented to the skull.

tip of the electrode. The experimenter can then see how this artificial stimulation affects the animal's behavior. One example of an experiment that uses this technique is shown in Figure 4.17. A rat presses a lever attached to an electrical switch that turns on a stimulator. The stimulator sends a brief pulse of electricity through an electrode placed in the rat's brain. If the tip of the electrode is located in certain parts of the brain,

the animal will press the lever again and again. (See *Figure 4.17.*) This finding suggests that these parts of the brain play a role in reward mechanisms.

Neurosurgeons sometimes use stereotaxic apparatuses to operate on humans. For example, destruction of a particular region near the center of the cerebral hemispheres can alleviate the tremors (trembling) that occur in some cases of Parkinson's disease. Neurosurgeons can also insert electrodes into the human brain and record the electrical activity of particular regions to try to find locations that might be responsible for triggering epileptic seizures.

Brain functions—and hence, behavior—can be affected by a variety of chemicals. For example, particular drugs or particular hormones can affect behavior by altering the activity of particular types of neurons in the brain. Physiological psychologists can learn how these chemicals produce their behavioral effects by administering them to laboratory animals and studying the responses of neurons in their brains. These chemicals can even be injected directly into specific areas of the brain, using a stereotaxic apparatus.

After a brain lesion has been made, or after an electrode has been placed in an animal's brain and its behavior has been observed, the researcher must verify the location of the lesion or electrode. To do so, he or she humanely kills the animal with an overdose of an anesthetic, removes the brain, and uses special *histological* procedures to slice the brain, dye the cells and fiber tracts, and examine the slices under a microscope. (The prefix *histo-* refers to body tissue.) *Figure 4.18* is a photograph of a slice of a mouse's brain showing the location of a lesion made with a stereotaxic apparatus.

Although physiological psychologists regularly use many other techniques, they most frequently produce lesions, record the electrical activity of the nervous system, stimulate the brain, and administer drugs and hormones while carrying out their experiments. These methods illustrate the basic types of approaches to research in physiological psychology.

Assessment of Damage to the Human Brain

Physiological psychologists know the approximate location of the brain lesions of their laboratory animals because they placed them there. In addition, they can confirm the precise location of the lesions by examining slices of the animals' brains under a microscope after behavioral testing is completed.

Study of the human brain is a different matter. Neuropsychologists attempt to understand human brain functions by studying the behavior of people whose brains have been damaged. Most human brain lesions are the result of natural causes, such as a stroke. A **stroke** (also known as a

stroke A cerebrovascular accident; damage to the brain caused by a blood clot in a cerebral artery or rupture of a cerebral blood vessel.

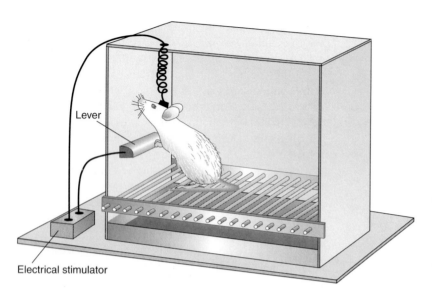

Lever

Electrical stimulator

Figure 4.17

An example of an electrical stimulation experiment. When the rat presses the switch, it receives a brief pulse of electricity to its brain through electrodes like those shown in Figure 4.16.

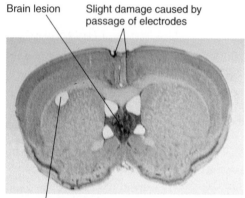

Brain lesion   Slight damage caused by passage of electrodes

Hole made in tissue to identify left and right sides of brain

Figure 4.18

A thin slice of a mouse brain, stained with a dye that shows the location of cell bodies. The arrow indicates the location of a lesion made with a stereotaxic apparatus.

cerebrovascular accident, or *CVA*) occurs when a blood clot obstructs an artery in the brain or when a blood vessel in the brain bursts open. In the first case, the clot blocks the supply of oxygen and nutrients to a particular region and causes that region to die. In the second case, the blood that accumulates in the brain directly damages neural tissue, partly by exerting pressure on the tissue and partly through its toxic effects on cells. The most common causes of strokes are high blood pressure and high levels of cholesterol in the blood.

CT scanner   A device that uses a special X-ray machine and a computer to produce images of the brain that appear as slices taken parallel to the top of the skull.

In order to relate brain damage to behavioral changes, neuropsychologists must know just where the damage is. But until recently, the only way they could determine the location of the damage was to examine the brain after the patient died. To do so, they needed the family's permission. Often, the patient lived for many years, and some families would not grant permission to perform an autopsy.

The development of several different diagnostic machines has provided solutions to these problems and has revolutionized neuropsychological research. The machine most commonly used is the **CT scanner.** (See *Figure 4.19.*) (*CT* stands for *computerized tomography. Tomos,* meaning "cut," describes the CT scanner's ability to produce a picture that looks like a slice of the brain.) The scanner sends a narrow beam of X rays through a person's head. The beam is moved around the patient's head, and a computer calculates the amount of radiation that passes through it at various points along each angle. The result is a two-dimensional image of a "slice" of the person's head, parallel to the top of the skull.

Using the CT scanner, an investigator can determine the approximate location of a brain lesion in a living patient. Knowing the results of behavioral testing and the location of the brain damage, the neuropsychologist can compare them and make inferences about the normal function of the damaged brain tissue. Figure 4.20 shows several CT scans of the brain of a patient with a lesion caused by a stroke—Miss S., whose case I described in the opening vignette. The scans are arranged from the bottom of the brain (scan 1) to the top (scan 6). You can easily see the lesion, a white spot, in the lower left corner of scan 5. (See *Figure 4.20.*)

Two other machines, the *MRI scanner* and the *PET scanner* (for "magnetic resonance imagery" and "positron emission tomography," respectively), are also used to examine the living human brain. At present, the MRI scanner is more expensive than the CT scanner, but it provides pictures of the brain that show much more detail. It does so with the use of

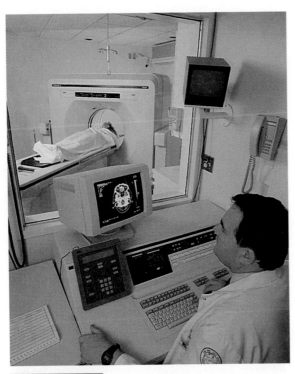

Figure 4.19

A patient being placed in a computerized tomography (CT) scanner.

magnetic fields and radio waves rather than with X rays. Figure 4.21 shows an MRI scan of the head. As you can see, this image is extremely realistic and detailed. (See *Figure 4.21.*)

The PET scanner is used to investigate chemical processes within the brain. A person is given a harmless dose of a radioactive substance, which enters the brain. The chemical accumulates in particular regions of the brain; the location depends on the specific chemical. Figure 4.22 shows PET scans after the use of a chemical that becomes concentrated in regions of the brain that contain the most activity. As you can see, different regions become active when the person sees images, hears sounds, or talks. (See *Figure 4.22.*)

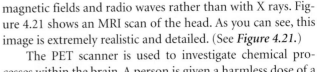

Biology and Culture

Environmental Effects on Brain Development

The nature–nurture controversy is one of the oldest in psychology. Normally, this controversy revolves around the origins of a particular behavior, talent, or personality trait. People ask, "Is it caused by biological or social factors?" "Is it innate or learned?" "Is it a result of hereditary or cultural influences?" "Should we look for an explanation in the brain or in the environment?" Almost always,

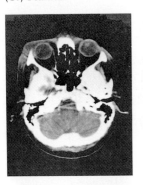
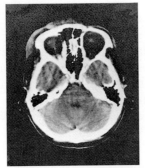
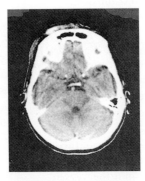
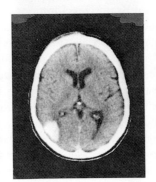
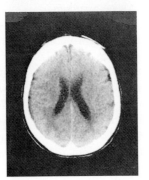

Figure 4.20

A set of CT scans from a patient with a brain lesion caused by a stroke (the white spot in the lower left corner of scan 5). Because left and right are traditionally reversed on CT scans, the brain lesion is actually in the *right* hemisphere.
(Courtesy of Dr. J. McA. Jones, Good Samaritan Hospital, Portland, Oregon.)

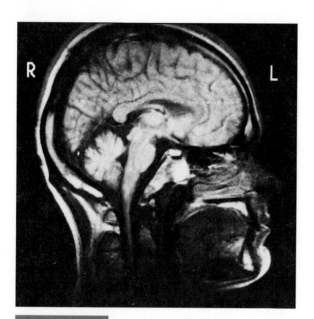

Figure 4.21

An MRI scan of a human brain.
(Philips Medical Systems.)

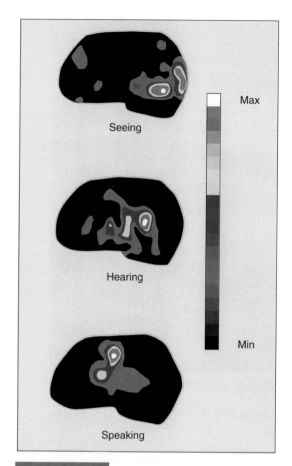

Figure 4.22

PET scans of the left side of the brain showing the regions having the highest amount of activity. The scans show that different regions of the brain are activated by different tasks.
(Discover, 1989, 10(3), p. 61. Reprinted by permission of the publisher.)

biology, innateness, heredity, and the brain are placed on the "nature" side of the equation. Society, learning, culture, and the environment are placed on the "nurture" side. Rarely does anyone question whether these groups of items really form a true dichotomy.

As you will see throughout the rest of this book, most modern psychologists consider the nature–nurture issue to be a relic of the past. That is, they believe that *all* behaviors, talents, and personality traits are the products of *both* types of factors: biological and social, hereditary and cultural, physiological and environmental. The task of the modern psychologist is not to find out which one of these factors is more important but to discover the particular roles played by each of them and to determine the ways in which they interact. But too often, physiology is assumed to be determined entirely by heredity.

As you know, the body develops according to a program established by the genes. The only way that genes can influence our personalities and behavior is through their effect on physical development. Brain development obviously plays a critical role in this regard, but the endocrine system and the structure of other parts of our bodies have important effects, too. For example, having a male or female body certainly influences our behavior and affects the way we are treated by other people.

Most people believe that heredity is the sole influence on normal development of the brain. Many people are familiar with the fact that brain development can be disrupted by drugs taken by a pregnant woman or by diseases that she contracts. But few people consider the possibility that environmental factors have important influences on the normal development of the brain.

■ Evidence for the Effects of Experience on Brain Development

Studies using humans and laboratory animals show that interactions between hereditary and environmental factors—between nature and nurture—begin very early in life. For example, more than twenty-five years ago, Rosenzweig and his colleagues began a research program designed to see what effects environmental stimulation would have on the development of the brain (see Rosenzweig, 1984, for a review). The experimenters divided litters of rats and placed the animals into two kinds of environments: enriched and impoverished. The enriched environment contained such things as running wheels, ladders, slides, and "toys" that the animals could explore and manipulate. The experimenters changed these objects every day to maximize the animals' experiences and to ensure that they would learn as much as possible. The impoverished environments were plain cages in a dimly illuminated, quiet room.

Rosenzweig and his colleagues found many differences in the brains of the animals raised in the two environments. The brains of rats raised in the enriched environment had a thicker cerebral cortex, a better blood supply, more protein content, and more acetylcholine (a transmitter substance that appears to play an important role in learning). Subsequent studies have found changes on a microscopic level as well. Greenough and Volkmar (1973) found that the neurons of rats raised in the enriched environment had larger and more complex dendritic trees. Turner and Greenough (1985) found that synapses in their cerebral cortexes were larger and that more synapses were found on each of their neurons. Changes occur even in the adult brain. Sirevaag et al. (1988) found that when rats were placed in an enriched environment between the ages of thirty and sixty days (young adulthood), the capillaries in their visual cortexes grew more branches and their surface areas increased, presumably to accommodate the growth that was stimulated by the experience.

Environmental stimulation does not begin at the time of birth. While in the uterus, fetuses feel the movements of their mothers' bodies and hear the sounds of their mothers' voices and sounds from the external environment that pass through the abdominal wall. After they are born, infants receive much environmental stimulation when they are nursed, when they are bathed, when their diapers are changed, and when they are simply held and cuddled. This stimulation clearly contributes to normal development. When infants are born prematurely and must be placed in isolators, they are deprived of the stimulation that occurs in the uterus and receive less handling than do normal, full-term infants. Several studies have found that gentle stroking of premature infants can reduce the effects of this environmental deprivation; it increases their growth rates and rates of motor development (Solkoff et al., 1969; Solkoff and Matuszak, 1975). According to evidence from experiments using infant rats reviewed by Schanberg and Field (1987), stroking and handling an infant may stimulate the release of hormones necessary for normal growth and development (including development of the brain).

Specific types of experiences can affect the development of specific parts of the brain. For example, Nobel laureates David Hubel and Torsten Wiesel found that if one eye of a young animal is closed during a critical period of brain development that occurs shortly after birth, normal synaptic connections are not established between that eye and the visual cortex—a fact that can easily be seen by microscopic examination of the brain. The eye effectively becomes blind (Wiesel, 1982). Even simple learning tasks can affect brain development. Spinelli and his colleagues (Spinelli and Jensen, 1979; Spinelli, Jensen, and DiPrisco, 1980) trained young animals to move one of their forelegs whenever they saw a particular visual stimulus. The training caused significant changes in the development of the visual cortex and in the part of the somatosensory cortex

that analyzed information coming from the animals' wrists, where a tactile stimulus was presented.

As we will see in Chapter 12, development of the male and female sex organs is controlled by the secretion of particular sex hormones during fetal development. These hormones also affect brain development and influence sex-related behavior in adults. Research by Moore and her colleagues (reviewed by Moore, 1992) indicates that at least some of the effects of heredity on sexual behavior are indirect. Female rats spend a considerable amount of time licking the genital region of their offspring. This behavior is very useful because it stimulates urination and permits the mother to ingest the water and minerals that are released so they can be recycled in her milk. Moore and her colleagues discovered that mothers spent much more time licking their male offspring and wondered whether this licking could have any effects on the males' sexual behavior later in life. Indeed, it did. First, the experimenters found that a male sex hormone was responsible for the presence of an odor in the male pups' urine, which was attractive to the mothers. Next, they found that if the mothers could not smell the odor, they failed to give the males special attention—and that, as a result, the males showed decreases in their sexual behavior in adulthood. But if the experimenters stroked the genitals of the male pups with a small brush each day, the animals showed normal sexual behavior when they grew up.

In this example there are several steps between heredity and behavior. The genes are responsible for the presence of the male sex hormone in the rat, which has the effect of making the urine of male pups especially attractive to the mother. She spends more time licking their genitals, which somehow affects their sexual development. Evidence indicates that the licking affects the development of the genitals and a group of neurons in the spinal cord; whether the licking also affects brain development has not yet been determined.

■ Conclusions

I have reviewed only a few of the many effects of environment on physiological development that researchers have discovered so far. It is clear that the brain does not develop in a vacuum. For example, the genes contain a program for the development of the visual system of the brain, but this program depends on the eyes' receiving visual stimulation. The genes also contain a program for the development of sex organs and the neural circuits necessary for sexual behavior. But normal development in rats depends on the responsiveness of the mother to an odor produced only by male pups. Not only has the nature–nurture issue become a relic of the past, but also so has the assumption that physiology is solely a product of heredity. Interactions between genes and environment begin to occur early in development and undoubtedly continue throughout the life span.

Interim Summary

Study of the Brain

Most of the methods we now have for treating neurological disorders and severe mental disorders were developed as results of research using laboratory animals, and future developments will require further research. Physiological psychologists usually study laboratory animals. They use a stereotaxic apparatus to destroy parts of the brain in animals or to place electrodes within an animal's brain to record electrical activity there or to stimulate it. They also investigate the effects of drugs or hormones on brain functions and behavior. Neuropsychologists study people who have sustained brain damage, correlating their behavioral deficits with the location of their lesions, usually determined by a CT scan or an MRI scan. PET scans permit researchers to study the activity level of specific regions of the living human brain.

The nature–nurture controversy was important in the past, when psychologists asked whether particular behaviors, talents, or personality traits were caused by hereditary factors ("nature") or by experience ("nurture"). The controversy is now over because psychologists realize that almost all characteristics are affected by *both* factors. What is less generally recognized is that the normal development of the brain—which was generally assumed to be programmed solely by hereditary factors—is also affected by the environment.

Thought Questions

- Would you like to have an electrode placed in your brain so that you could see what reinforcing ("rewarding") brain stimulation feels like?
- Suppose it were necessary to make an MRI scan of your brain. Would you want to see the scans afterward?
- Suppose you had a PET scanner and lots of volunteers. You could present various types of stimuli while PET scans were being taken, and you could have the volunteers perform various types of mental tasks and behaviors that did not involve their moving around. What kinds of experiments would you perform?
- Although the basic program that controls brain development is contained in our chromosomes, environmental factors can also influence this process. Why do you think the process of development is not completely automatic and programmed? What is the point of letting the environment influence it? Would we be better off if development *were* simply automatic, or does such flexibility have some potential benefits?

Control of Behavior

As I have already said, the brain has two roles: controlling the movements of the muscles and regulating the physiological functions of the body. The first role looks outward toward the environment and the second looks inward. The outward-looking role includes several functions: perceiving events in the environment, learning about them, making plans, and acting. The inward-looking role requires the brain to measure and regulate internal characteristics such as body temperature, blood pressure, and nutrient levels. The outward-looking role is, of course, of particular interest to psychology. So in this section, we will examine the portions of the brain that control behavior. The following section describes the brain's regulatory functions.

Organization of the Cerebral Cortex

If we want to understand the brain functions most important to the study of behavior—perceiving, learning, planning, and moving—we should start with the cerebral cortex.

Regions of Primary Sensory and Motor Cortex

We become aware of events in our environment by means of the five major senses: vision, audition, olfaction, gustation (taste), and the somatosenses ("body" senses: touch, pain, and temperature). Three areas of the cerebral cortex receive information from the sensory organs. The **primary visual cortex,** which receives visual information, is located at the back of the brain, on the inner surfaces of the cerebral hemispheres. The **primary auditory cortex,** which receives auditory information, is located on the inner surface of a deep fissure in the side of the brain. The **primary somatosensory cortex,** a vertical strip near the middle of the cerebral hemispheres, receives information from the body senses. As Figure 4.23 shows, different regions of the primary somatosensory cortex receive information from different regions of the body. In addition, the base of the somatosensory cortex receives information concerning taste. (See *Figure 4.23.*)

The three regions of primary sensory cortex in each hemisphere receive information from the opposite side of the body. Thus, the primary somatosensory cortex of the left hemisphere learns what the right hand is holding, the left primary visual cortex learns what is happening toward the person's right, and so on. The connections between the sensory organs and the cerebral cortex are said to be **contralateral** (*contra,* "opposite"; *lateral,* "side.")

primary visual cortex The region of the cerebral cortex that receives information directly from the visual system; located in the occipital lobes.

primary auditory cortex The region of the cerebral cortex that receives information directly from the auditory system; located in the temporal lobes.

primary somatosensory cortex The region of the cerebral cortex that receives information directly from the somatosensory system (touch, pressure, vibration, pain, and temperature); located in the front part of the parietal lobes.

contralateral Residing in the side of the body opposite the reference point.

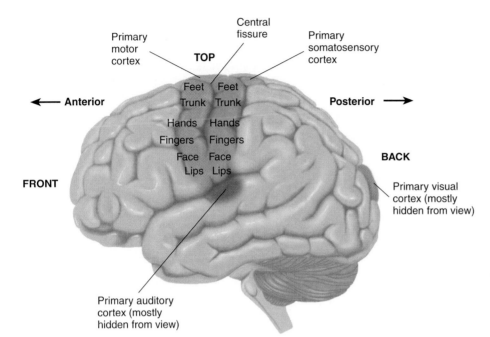

Primary motor cortex

Central fissure

TOP

Primary somatosensory cortex

← **Anterior**

Posterior →

Feet Feet
Trunk Trunk
Hands Hands
Fingers Fingers
Face Face
Lips Lips

BACK

FRONT

Primary visual cortex (mostly hidden from view)

Primary auditory cortex (mostly hidden from view)

Figure 4.23

A side view of the human brain showing the primary sensory and motor areas of the cerebral cortex.

The region of the cerebral cortex most directly involved in the control of movement is the **primary motor cortex,** located just in front of the primary somatosensory cortex. (Note that in this context *motor* is used in its original sense and refers to *movement,* not to mechanical engines.) Neurons in different parts of the primary motor cortex are connected to muscles in different parts of the body. The connections, like those of the sensory regions of the cerebral cortex, are contralateral; the left primary motor cortex controls the right side of the body and vice versa. Thus, for example, if a surgeon electrically stimulates the "hand" region of the left primary motor cortex, the patient's right hand will move. (See *Figure 4.23.*) I like to think of the strip of primary motor cortex as the keyboard of a piano, with each key controlling a different movement. (We will see shortly who the "player" of this piano is.)

Association Cortex

The regions of primary sensory and motor cortex occupy only a small part of the cerebral cortex. The rest of the cerebral cortex accomplishes what is done between sensation and action: perceiving, learning and remembering, planning, and acting. These processes take place in the *association areas* of the cerebral cortex. The *central fissure* provides an important dividing line between the **anterior** (front) part of the cerebral cortex and the **posterior** (back) regions. (See *Figure 4.23.*) The anterior region is involved in movement-related activities, such as planning and executing behaviors. The posterior part is involved in perceiving and learning.

Discussing the various regions of the cerebral cortex is easier if we have names for them. In fact, the cerebral cortex is divided into four areas, or *lobes,* named for the bones of the skull that cover them: the frontal lobe, parietal lobe, temporal lobe, and occipital lobe. (See *Figure 4.24.*) Of course, the

brain contains two of each lobe, one in each hemisphere. The **frontal lobe** (the "front") includes everything in front of the central fissure. The **parietal lobe** (the "wall") is located on the side of the cerebral hemisphere, just behind the central fissure, in back of the frontal lobe. The **temporal lobe** (the "temple") juts forward from the base of the brain, beneath the frontal and parietal lobes. The **occipital lobe** (*ob,* "in back of"; *caput,* "head") lies at the very back of the brain, behind the parietal and temporal lobes.

Each primary sensory area of the cerebral cortex sends information to adjacent regions, called the **sensory association**

primary motor cortex The region of the cerebral cortex that directly controls the movements of the body; located in the back part of the frontal lobes.

anterior Toward the front.

posterior Toward the back.

frontal lobe The front portion of the cerebral cortex, including Broca's speech area and the motor cortex; damage impairs movement, planning, and flexibility in behavioral strategies.

parietal lobe The region of the cerebral cortex behind the frontal lobe and above the temporal lobe; contains the somatosensory cortex; is involved in spatial perception and memory.

temporal lobe The portion of the cerebral cortex below the frontal and parietal lobes and containing the auditory cortex.

occipital lobe The rearmost portion of the cerebral cortex; contains the primary visual cortex.

sensory association cortex Those regions of cerebral cortex that receive information from the primary sensory areas.

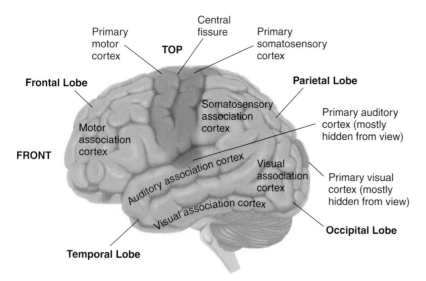

Primary
motor
cortex

Central
fissure

TOP

Primary
somatosensory
cortex

Frontal Lobe

Parietal Lobe

Somatosensory
association
cortex

Primary auditory
cortex (mostly
hidden from view)

Motor
association
cortex

FRONT

Auditory association cortex

Visual
association
cortex

Primary visual
cortex (mostly
hidden from view)

Visual association cortex

Occipital Lobe

Temporal Lobe

Figure 4.24

The four lobes of the cerebral cortex and the locations of the association cortex.

cortex. Circuits of neurons in the sensory association cortex analyze the information received from the primary sensory cortex; perception takes place there, and memories are stored there. The regions of the sensory association cortex located closest to the primary sensory areas receive information from only one sensory system. For example, the region closest to the primary visual cortex analyzes visual information and stores visual memories. Regions of the sensory association cortex located far from the primary sensory areas receive information from more than one sensory system; thus, they are involved in several kinds of perceptions and memories. These regions make it possible to integrate information from more than one sensory system. For example, we can learn the connection between the sight of a particular face and the sound of a particular voice. (See *Figure 4.24.*)

Just as regions of the sensory association cortex of the posterior part of the brain are involved in perceiving and remembering, the frontal association cortex is involved in the planning and execution of movements. The anterior part of the frontal lobe—known as the **prefrontal cortex**—contains the **motor association cortex**. The motor association cortex controls the primary motor cortex; thus, it directly controls behavior. If the primary motor cortex is the keyboard of the piano, then the motor association cortex is the piano player. Obviously, we behave in response to events happening in the world around us. Therefore, the sensory association cortex of the posterior part of the brain sends information about the

environment to the motor association cortex (prefrontal cortex), which translates the information into plans and actions. (See *Figures 4.24* and *4.25.*)

Lateralization of Function

Although the two cerebral hemispheres cooperate with each other, they do not perform identical functions. Some functions are *lateralized*—located primarily on one side of the brain. In general, the left hemisphere participates in the *analysis* of information—the extraction of the elements that make up the whole of an experience. This ability makes the left hemisphere particularly good at recognizing *serial events*—events whose elements occur one after the other. The left hemisphere is also involved in controlling serial behaviors. (In a few people the functions of the left and right hemispheres are reversed.) The serial functions performed by the left hemisphere include verbal activities, such as talking, understanding the speech of other people, reading, and writing. These abilities are disrupted by damage to the various regions of the left hemisphere. (I will say more about language and the brain in Chapters 9 and 10.)

In contrast, the right hemisphere is specialized for *synthesis*; it is particularly good at putting isolated elements together to perceive things as a whole. For example, our ability to draw sketches (especially of three-dimensional objects), read maps, and construct complex objects out of smaller elements depends heavily on circuits of neurons located in the right hemisphere. Damage to the right hemisphere disrupts these abilities.

We are not aware of the fact that each hemisphere perceives the world differently. Although the two cerebral hemispheres perform somewhat different functions, our perceptions and our memories are unified. This unity is accomplished by the **corpus callosum**, a large band of axons that connects the two cerebral hemispheres. The corpus callosum connects corresponding parts of the left and right hemi-

prefrontal cortex The anterior part of the frontal lobe; contains the motor association cortex.

motor association cortex Those regions of the cerebral cortex that control the primary motor cortex; involved in planning and executing behaviors.

corpus callosum A large bundle of axons ("white matter") that connects the cortex of the two cerebral hemispheres.

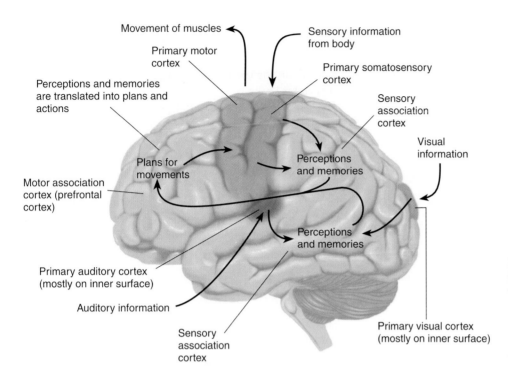

Movement of muscles
Primary motor cortex
Sensory information from body
Primary somatosensory cortex
Sensory association cortex
Perceptions and memories are translated into plans and actions
Visual information
Plans for movements
Perceptions and memories
Motor association cortex (prefrontal cortex)
Perceptions and memories
Primary auditory cortex (mostly on inner surface)
Auditory information
Sensory association cortex
Primary visual cortex (mostly on inner surface)

Figure 4.25

The relation between the association cortex and the regions of primary sensory and motor cortex. Arrows refer to the flow of information.

spheres: The left and right temporal lobes are connected, the left and right parietal lobes are connected, and so on. Because of the corpus callosum, each region of the association cortex knows what is happening in the corresponding region of the opposite side of the brain.

Figure 4.26 shows a brain that has been sliced through the middle, from top to bottom. We see the inner surface of

the right hemisphere. The corpus callosum has been cut; if we looked at it closely we would see the ends of millions of severed axons. We also see the names of several structures that have not yet been discussed. Do not worry about them; I will describe them soon. (See *Figure 4.26.*)

If the corpus callosum unites the two hemispheres and permits them to interchange information, what would hap-

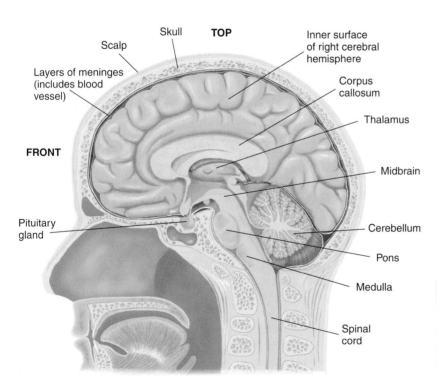

Scalp
Skull
TOP
Inner surface of right cerebral hemisphere
Layers of meninges (includes blood vessel)
Corpus callosum
Thalamus
FRONT
Midbrain
Pituitary gland
Cerebellum
Pons
Medulla
Spinal cord

Figure 4.26

A view of a brain that has been sliced through the midline. The corpus callosum unites the cerebral cortex of the two hemispheres.

pen if the corpus callosum were cut? In fact, neurosurgeons sometimes deliberately cut the corpus callosum to treat a certain type of epilepsy. I will describe the interesting effects of this operation on perceptions and consciousness in Chapter 9.

Vision: The Occipital and Temporal Lobes

The primary business of the occipital lobe—and the lower part of the temporal lobe—is seeing. (Refer to *Figure 4.24.*) Total damage to the primary visual cortex, located in the inner surface of the posterior occipital lobe, produces blindness. Because the visual field is "mapped" onto the surface of the primary visual cortex, a small lesion in the primary visual cortex produces a "hole" in a specific part of the field of vision.

The visual association cortex is located in the rest of the occipital lobe and in the lower portion of the temporal lobe. (Refer to *Figure 4.24.*) Damage to the visual association cortex will not cause blindness. In fact, visual acuity may be very good; the person may be able to see small objects and may even be able to read. However, the person will not be able to *recognize* objects by sight. For example, when looking at a drawing of a clock, the person may say that he or she sees a circle, two short lines forming an angle in the center of a circle, and some dots spaced along the inside of the circle, but will not be able to recognize what the picture shows. On the other hand, if the person is handed a real clock, he or she will immediately recognize it by touch. This fact tells us that the person has not simply forgotten what clocks are. Similarly, the person may fail to recognize his or her spouse by sight but will be able to do so from the sound of the spouse's voice. This deficit in visual perception is called **visual agnosia** (*a-*, "without"; *gnosis*, "knowledge"). I will have more to say about it in Chapter 7.

Audition: The Temporal Lobe

The temporal lobe contains both the primary auditory cortex and the auditory association cortex. The primary auditory cortex is hidden from view on the inner surface of the upper temporal lobe. The auditory association cortex is located on the lateral surface of the upper temporal lobe. (Refer to *Figure 4.24.*) Damage to the primary auditory cortex leads to hearing losses, while damage to the auditory association cortex produces more complex deficits. Damage to the left auditory association cortex causes severe language deficits. People with such damage are no longer able to comprehend speech, presumably because they have lost the circuits of neurons

that decode speech sounds. However, the deficit is more severe than that. They also lose the ability to produce meaningful speech; their speech becomes a jumble of words. I will say more about the language deficits produced by brain damage in Chapter 10.

Damage to the right auditory association cortex does not seriously affect speech perception or production, but it does affect the ability to recognize nonspeech sounds, including patterns of tones and rhythms. The damage can also impair the ability to perceive the location of sounds in the environment. As we will see later, the right hemisphere is very important in the perception of space. The contribution of the right temporal lobe to this function is to participate in perceiving the placement of sounds.

Somatosensation and Spatial Perception: The Parietal Lobe

The primary sensory function of the parietal lobe is perception of the body. (Refer to *Figure 4.24.*) However, the association cortex of the parietal lobe is involved in much more than somatosensation. Damage to a particular region of the association cortex of the left parietal lobe can disrupt the ability to read or write without causing serious impairment in the ability to talk and understand the speech of other people. Damage to another part of the parietal lobe impairs a person's ability to draw. When the left parietal lobe is damaged, the primary deficit seems to be in the person's ability to make precise hand movements; their drawing looks shaky and sloppy. In contrast, the primary deficit produced by damage to the right parietal lobe is perceptual. The person can analyze a picture into its parts but has trouble integrating these parts into a consistent whole. Thus, he or she has difficulty drawing a coherent picture. (See *Figure 4.27.*)

The right parietal lobe also plays a role in people's ability to pay attention to stimuli located toward the opposite (left) side of the body. As we saw in the opening vignette, Miss S. displayed a symptom called unilateral neglect. A CT scan of her brain (shown in Figure 4.20) reveals that her stroke damaged part of the association cortex of the right parietal lobe.

Most neuropsychologists believe that the left parietal lobe plays an important role in our ability to keep track of the location of the moving parts of our own body, whereas the right parietal lobe helps us keep track of the space around us. People with right parietal lobe damage usually have difficulty with spatial tasks, such as reading a map. People with left parietal lobe damage usually have difficulty identifying parts of their own bodies by name. For example, when asked to point to their elbows, they may actually point to their shoulders.

People with damage to the left parietal lobe often have difficulty performing arithmetic calculations. This deficit is probably related to other spatial functions of the parietal lobe. For example, try to multiply 55 by 12 without using

visual agnosia The inability of a person who is not blind to recognize the identity or use of an object by means of vision; usually caused by damage to the brain.

Drawing by patients with left-hemisphere damage

Model for patients to copy

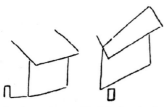

Drawing by patients with right-hemisphere damage

Figure 4.27

Attempts to copy a drawing of a house by patients with damage to the left and right parietal lobes.

(From Gainotti, G., and Tiacci, C. Neuropsychologia, 1970, 8, 289–303.)

pencil and paper. Close your eyes and work on the problem for a while. Try to analyze how you did it.

Most people report that they try to imagine the numbers arranged one above the other as they would be if paper and pencil were being used. In other words, they "write" the problem out mentally. Apparently, damage to the parietal lobes makes it impossible for people to keep the imaginary numbers in place and remember what they are.

Planning and Moving: The Frontal Lobe

Although the principal function of the frontal lobe is motor activity, it is also involved in planning, changing strategies, being aware of oneself, evaluating emotionally related stimuli, and performing a variety of spontaneous behaviors. It also contains a region involved in the control of speech. (Refer to *Figure 4.24.*)

Damage to the primary motor cortex produces a very specific effect: paralysis of the side of the body opposite to the brain damage. If a portion of the region is damaged, then only the corresponding parts of the body will be paralyzed. However, damage to the prefrontal cortex produces more complex behavioral deficits.

1. *Slowing of thoughts and behavior and loss of spontaneity.* The person will *react* to events in the environment but

shows deficits in *initiating* behavior. When a person with damage to the prefrontal cortex is asked to say or write as many words as possible, he or she will have great difficulty coming up with more than a few, even though he or she has no problem understanding words or identifying objects by name.

2. *Perseveration.* People with damage to the frontal lobes tend to have difficulty changing strategies. If given a task to solve, they may solve it readily; but they will fail to abandon the strategy and learn a new one if the problem is changed.

3. *Loss of self-awareness and changes in emotional reactions.* People with damaged frontal lobes often have rather bland personalities. They seem indifferent to events that would normally be expected to affect them emotionally. For example, they may show no signs of distress at the death of a close relative. They have little insight into their own problems and are uncritical of their performance on various tasks. They do not even seem to be bothered by pain, although they may say that they still feel it.

4. *Deficiencies in foresight and planning.* In terms of daily living, the most important consequences of damage to the frontal lobes are probably lack of foresight and difficulty planning. A person with frontal lobe damage might perform fairly well on a test of intelligence but be unable to hold a job. Presumably, planning is related to the general motor functions of the frontal lobes. Just as we can use the posterior regions of the brain to imagine something we have perceived, we can use the frontal region to imagine something we might do. Perhaps we test various possible actions by imagining ourselves doing them and guessing what the consequences of these actions might be. When people's frontal lobes are damaged, they often do or say things that have unfavorable consequences because they have lost their ability to plan their actions.

As we saw in Chapter 1, Paul Broca discovered that damage to a region of the left frontal lobe disrupts speech. This region, which we now call Broca's area, lies just in front of the "face" region of the primary motor cortex. (See *Figure 4.28.*) Thus, Broca's area controls the muscles used for talking. Circuits of neurons located in Broca's area appear to contain the memories of the sequences of muscular movements that are needed to pronounce words. I will have more to say about the effects of lesions in Broca's area in Chapter 10.

Surgical Treatment of Seizure Disorders

The neural circuits in the brain must maintain a close balance between excitation and inhibition. If there is too much inhibition, the brain cannot do its work. If there is too much excitation, neural activity gets out of control and causes a *seizure disorder* (otherwise known as "epilepsy"). During a seizure, the neurons in the brain fire wildly and uncontrollably, dis-

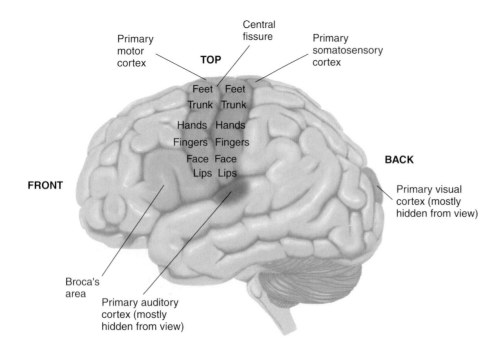

Primary
motor
cortex

Central
fissure

Primary
somatosensory
cortex

TOP

Feet   Feet
Trunk Trunk
Hands Hands
Fingers Fingers
Face Face
Lips Lips

BACK

FRONT

Primary visual
cortex (mostly
hidden from view)

Broca's
area

Primary auditory
cortex (mostly
hidden from view)

Figure 4.28

Broca's area, located just in front
of the face region of the primary
motor cortex. This region is
involved in the control of speech.

rupting normal brain functions. Most seizure disorders can be controlled by drugs, but occasionally neurosurgeons must perform an operation known as *seizure surgery.*

Most seizure disorders are caused by the presence of one or more *seizure foci* in the brain—regions of scar tissue that irritate the brain tissue surrounding them. From time to time, excitation spreads throughout the brain, causing a seizure. Seizure surgery involves removing the abnormal brain tissue that contains a seizure focus. One of the pioneers of seizure surgery, the late Wilder Penfield, developed the operation, which has provided us with some interesting information about the functions of the human brain (Penfield and Jasper, 1954). The patient's head is first shaved. Then, with the patient under local anesthesia, the surgeon cuts the scalp and saws through the skull so that a piece of bone can be removed and the brain itself exposed. The patient is conscious throughout the entire procedure.

When removing the damaged part of the brain, the surgeon wants to cut away all the abnormal tissue—including the seizure focus—while sparing healthy neural tissue that performs important functions, such as the comprehension and production of speech. For this reason, Penfield first stimulated parts of the brain to determine what functions they performed so he could decide which regions he could safely remove. Penfield touched the tip of a metal electrode to various parts of the brain and observed the effects of stimulation on the patient's behavior. For example, stimulation of one part of the brain produced movement, and stimulation of another part produced sensations of sounds. Stimulation of parts of the brain involved in verbal communication stopped the patient's ongoing speech and disrupted the ability to understand what the surgeon and his associates were saying. Penfield placed a sterile, numbered piece of paper on each

point he stimulated. He then photographed the exposed brain with its numbered locations before removing the slips of paper and proceeding with the surgery. After the operation, he could compare his notes about the patient's behavior with the photograph of the patient's brain showing the locations of the points of stimulation. (See *Figure 4.29.*)

Because seizure surgery often involves the removal of a substantial amount of brain tissue (usually from one of the temporal lobes), we might expect it to cause behavioral deficits. But in most cases, the reverse is true; people's performance on tests of neuropsychological functioning usually increases. How can the removal of brain tissue improve a person's performance?

The answer is provided by looking at what happens in the brain not *during* seizures but *between* them. Between seizures, the excitatory activity caused by a seizure focus is held in check by a compensatory increase in inhibitory activity. That is, inhibitory synapses in the region surrounding the seizure focus become more active. (This phenomenon is known as *interictal inhibition; ictus* means "stroke" in Latin.) A seizure occurs when the excitation overcomes the inhibition.

The problem is that the compensatory inhibition does more than hold the excitation in check; it also suppresses the normal functions of a rather large region of brain tissue surrounding the seizure focus. Thus, even though the focus may be small, its effects are felt over a much larger area—even between seizures. Removing the seizure focus and some surrounding brain tissue eliminates the source of the irritation and makes the compensatory inhibition unnecessary. Freed from interictal inhibition, the brain tissue located near the site of the former seizure focus can now function normally, and the patient's neuropsychological abilities will show an improvement.

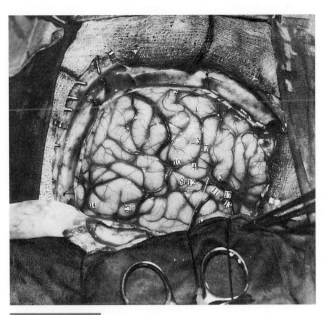

Figure 4.29

The appearance of the cortical surface of a conscious patient whose brain has been stimulated. The points of stimulation are indicated by the numbered tags placed there by the surgeon.

(From "Case M. M.," in Wilder Penfield, The Mystery of the Mind: A Critical Study of Consciousness and the Human Brain, *with Discussions by William Feindel, Charles Hendel, and Charles Symonds. Copyright © 1975 by Princeton University Press. Figure 4, p. 24 reprinted by permission of Princeton University Press.)*

Interim Summary

Control of Behavior

Anatomically, the cerebral cortex is divided into four lobes: frontal, parietal, occipital, and temporal. Functionally, the cerebral cortex is organized into five major regions: the three regions of the primary sensory cortex (visual, auditory, and somatosensory), the primary motor cortex, and the association cortex. The association cortex consists of sensory regions that are responsible for perceiving and learning and the motor regions that are responsible for planning and acting.

Suppose that you see a rose and then pick it and smell it. The visual stimulation is transmitted from the eyes to the brain through the optic nerves, one of the pairs of cranial nerves. The information is sent to the primary visual cortex in the occipital lobe. Your perception of the rose causes you to remember how beautiful one looks in a vase on your desk. This memory, located in the visual association cortex, causes messages to be sent forward to the motor association cortex (the "piano player") in your frontal lobes. There, plans are made to pick the rose so you can display it on your desk. Impulses are sent to your primary motor cortex and from there

to the muscles that control your legs. As you move toward the rose, new sensory information received by the posterior lobes informs the frontal lobes about the appropriate movements. You reach for the rose and pick it.

When you pick the rose, you feel the stem with your fingers. The somatosensory information is transmitted from your fingers to the spinal cord by means of a spinal nerve. It is then sent up through the spinal cord and is relayed to the primary somatosensory cortex. Next, your frontal lobes direct your hand to bring the rose under your nose and then command your muscles to make you sniff in some air to smell the rose. Information about the aromatic molecules is transmitted to your brain through the olfactory nerves, another pair of cranial nerves.

The right and left hemispheres are involved with somewhat different functions; that is, some brain functions are lateralized. The left hemisphere is mostly concerned with analysis—with the extraction of information about details of perception, such as the series of sounds that constitute speech or the symbols that constitute writing. The right hemisphere is mostly concerned with synthesis—with putting together a perception of the general form and shape of things from smaller elements that are present at the same time. The two hemispheres share information through the corpus callosum, a large bundle of axons.

The frontal lobes are concerned with motor functions, including the planning of strategies for action. A region of the left frontal cortex (Broca's area) is specialized for control of speech. The three lobes behind the central fissure are generally concerned with perceiving, learning, and remembering: somatosensory information in the parietal lobe, visual information in the occipital and lower temporal lobes, and auditory information in the upper temporal lobe. The other functions of these lobes are related to these perceptual processes; for example, the parietal lobes are concerned with perception of space as well as knowledge about the body.

Seizure disorders (also known as *epilepsy*) are sometimes treated by surgical removal of scarred or damaged regions of the brain that periodically excite neighboring neurons and cause a storm of neural activity. The surgery is performed under local anesthetic so that the behavior of the conscious patient can be observed to be sure that only the damaged brain tissue is removed.

Thought Questions

- If you were to have a stroke (and let's hope you don't), in which region of the cerebral cortex and in which hemisphere would you prefer the brain damage to be located? Why?
- Damage to the anterior or posterior corpus callosum produces different behavioral deficits. Why do you think this is so?
- Suppose you suspected that someone had a lesion in the left parietal lobe. What behavioral tests would you

devise to try to determine whether the person did indeed have a lesion there?

■ Explain why a brain lesion that impairs a person's speech often also affects movements of the right side of the body.

Control of Internal Functions and Automatic Behavior

So far, I have discussed brain regions involved in perceiving, remembering, planning, and acting. I have talked primarily about the role of the cerebral cortex in these activities. However, there is much more to the brain than the cerebral cortex. After all, the cortex consists of only the outer 3 millimeters of the surface of the cerebral hemispheres. What roles do the brain stem, the cerebellum, and the interior of the cerebral hemispheres play?

As we shall see, the primary function of the cerebellum is to help the cerebral hemispheres control movements and to initiate some automatic movements—such as postural adjustment—on its own. The brain stem and much of the interior of the cerebral hemispheres are involved in homeostasis and control of species-typical behaviors. **Homeostasis** (from the root words *homoios,* "similar," and *stasis,* "standstill") refers to maintaining a proper balance of physiological variables such as temperature, concentration of fluids, and the amount of nutrients stored within the body. **Species-typical behaviors** are the more-or-less automatic behaviors exhibited by most members of a species that are important to survival, such as eating, drinking, fighting, courting, mating, and caring for offspring.

The Brain Stem

The brain stem contains three structures: the *medulla,* the *pons,* and the *midbrain.* Figure 4.30 shows a view of the left

homeostasis The process by which important physiological characteristics (such as body temperature and blood pressure) are regulated so that they remain at their optimum level.

species-typical behavior A behavior seen in all or most members of a species, such as nest building, special food-getting behaviors, or reproductive behaviors.

medulla The part of the brain stem closest to the spinal cord; controls vital functions such as heart rate and blood pressure.

pons The part of the brain stem just anterior to the medulla; involved in control of sleep.

midbrain The part of the brain stem just anterior to the pons; involved in control of fighting and sexual behavior and in decreased sensitivity to pain during these behaviors.

side of the brain. The brain has been rotated slightly so that we can see some of the front of the brain stem and the cerebral hemispheres are shown lightly so that the details of the brain stem can be seen. We also see the *thalamus,* the *hypothalamus,* and the *pituitary gland,* which I will describe later. (See *Figure 4.30.*)

The brain stem contains circuits of neurons that control functions vital to the survival of the organism in particular and of the species in general. For example, circuits of neurons in the **medulla,** the part of the brain stem closest to the spinal cord, control heart rate, blood pressure, rate of respiration, and—especially in simpler animals—crawling or swimming motions. And circuits of neurons in the **pons,** the part of the brain just above the medulla, control some of the stages of sleep. Circuits of neurons in the **midbrain** control movements used in fighting and sexual behavior and decrease sensitivity to pain while engaged in these activities. (See *Figure 4.30.*)

The Cerebellum

The cerebellum plays an important role in the control of movement. It receives sensory information, especially about the position of body parts, so it knows what the parts of the body are doing. It also receives information from the cortex of the frontal lobes, so it knows what movements the frontal lobes intend to accomplish. The cerebellum is basically a computer that compares the location of the body parts with the intended movements and assists the frontal lobes in executing these movements. Without the cerebellum, the frontal lobes would produce jerky, uncoordinated, inaccurate movements—which is exactly what happens when a person's cerebellum is damaged. Besides helping the frontal lobes accomplish their tasks, the cerebellum monitors information regarding posture and balance, to keep us from falling down when we stand or walk, and produces eye movements that compensate for changes in the position of the head.

Recently, researchers have discovered that the cerebellum may also play a role in people's cognitive abilities. For a long time, neurologists have known that cerebellar damage can interfere with people's ability to speak, but the deficit seems to involve control of the speech muscles rather than the cognitive abilities involved in language. However, a few years ago, researchers making PET scans of the brains of people working on various types of cognitive tasks discovered that parts of their cerebellums became active—even when the people were not moving. Many neuroscientists now suspect that as we learn more about the cerebellum we will discover that its functions are not limited to motor tasks.

Structures within the Cerebral Hemispheres

So far, we have been directing most of our attention to the surface of the brain. Now let's see what's inside.

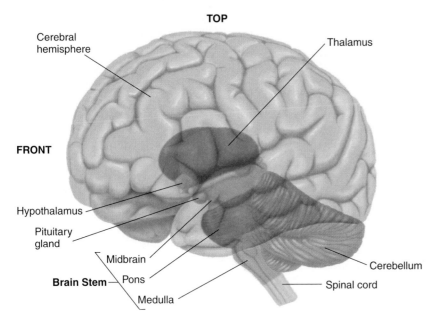

TOP

Cerebral hemisphere

Thalamus

FRONT

Hypothalamus

Pituitary gland

Midbrain

Brain Stem — Pons

Medulla

Cerebellum

Spinal cord

The divisions of the brain stem: the medulla, the pons, and the midbrain. The thalamus, hypothalamus, and pituitary gland are attached to the end of the brain stem.

The Thalamus

If you stripped away the cerebral cortex and the white matter that lies under it, you would find the **thalamus,** located in the heart of the cerebral hemispheres. (*Thalamos* is Greek for "inner chamber.") The thalamus is divided into two parts, one in each cerebral hemisphere. Each part looks rather like a football, with the long axis oriented from front to back. (See *Figure 4.30.*)

The thalamus performs two basic functions. The first—and most primitive—is similar to that of the cerebral cortex. Parts of the thalamus receive sensory information, other parts integrate the information, and still other parts assist in the control of movements through their influence on circuits of neurons in the brain stem. However, the second role of the thalamus—that of a relay station for the cortex—is even more important. As the cerebral hemispheres evolved, the cerebral cortex grew in size and its significance for behavioral functions increased. The thalamus took on the function of receiving sensory information from the sensory organs, performing some simple analyses, and passing the results on to the primary sensory cortex. Thus, all sensory information (except for olfaction, which is the most primitive of all sensory systems) is sent to the thalamus before it reaches the cerebral cortex.

The Hypothalamus

Hypo- means "less than" or "beneath," and as its name suggests, the **hypothalamus** is located below the thalamus, at the base of the brain. The hypothalamus is a small region, consisting of less than 1 cubic centimeter of tissue (smaller than a grape). Its relative importance far exceeds its relative size. (See *Figure 4.30.*)

The hypothalamus, like the brain stem, participates in homeostasis and species-typical behaviors. It receives sensory information, including information from receptors inside the organs of the body; thus, it is informed about changes in the organism's physiological status. It also contains specialized sensors that monitor various characteristics of the blood that flows through the brain, such as temperature, nutrient content, and amount of dissolved salts. In turn, the hypothalamus controls the **pituitary gland,** an *endocrine gland* attached by a stalk to the base of the hypothalamus.

Hormones are chemicals produced by *endocrine glands* (from the Greek *endo-*, "within," and *krinein*, "to secrete"). **Endocrine glands** secrete hormones into the blood supply, which carries them to all parts of the body. **Hormones** are similar to transmitter substances or neuromodulators, except that they act over much longer distances. Like transmitter substances and neuromodulators, they produce their effects by stimulating receptor molecules. These receptor molecules are located on (or in) particular cells. The presence of a hormone causes physiological reactions in these cells, which are

thalamus A region of the brain near the center of the cerebral hemispheres. All sensory information except smell is sent to the thalamus and then relayed to the cerebral cortex.

hypothalamus A region of the brain located just above the pituitary gland; controls the autonomic nervous system and many behaviors related to regulation and survival, such as eating, drinking, fighting, shivering, and sweating.

pituitary gland An endocrine gland attached to the hypothalamus at the base of the brain.

endocrine gland A gland that secretes a hormone.

hormone A chemical substance secreted by an endocrine gland that has physiological effects on target cells in other organs.

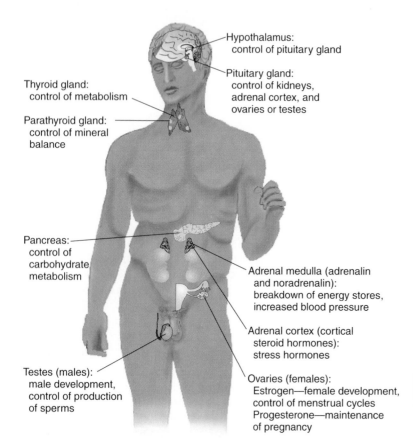

Hypothalamus: control of pituitary gland

Pituitary gland: control of kidneys, adrenal cortex, and ovaries or testes

Thyroid gland: control of metabolism

Parathyroid gland: control of mineral balance

Pancreas: control of carbohydrate metabolism

Adrenal medulla (adrenalin and noradrenalin): breakdown of energy stores, increased blood pressure

Adrenal cortex (cortical steroid hormones): stress hormones

Testes (males): male development, control of production of sperms

Ovaries (females): Estrogen—female development, control of menstrual cycles Progesterone—maintenance of pregnancy

Figure 4.31

The location and primary functions of the principal endocrine glands.

known as **target cells.** Almost every cell of the body contains hormone receptors of one kind or other. This includes neurons; hormones that affect behavior do so by altering the activity of particular groups of neurons in the brain. For example, the sex hormones have important effects on behavior and will be discussed in later chapters.

The pituitary gland has been called the "master gland" because the hormones it secretes act on target cells in other endocrine glands; thus, the pituitary gland controls the activity of other endocrine glands. By controlling the pituitary gland, the hypothalamus controls the entire endocrine system. *Figure 4.31* shows some of the endocrine glands and the functions they regulate.

target cell A cell whose physiological processes are affected by a particular hormone; contains special receptor molecules that respond to the presence of the hormone.

autonomic nervous system (ANS) The portion of the peripheral nervous system that controls the functions of the glands and internal organs.

sympathetic branch The portion of the autonomic nervous system that activates functions that accompany arousal and expenditure of energy.

parasympathetic branch The portion of the autonomic nervous system that activates functions that occur during a relaxed state.

The hypothalamus also controls much of the activity of the **autonomic nervous system,** which consists of nerves that control the functions of the glands and internal organs. The nerves of the autonomic nervous system control activities such as sweating, shedding tears, salivating, secreting digestive juices, changing the size of blood vessels (which alters blood pressure), and secreting some hormones. The autonomic nervous system has two branches. The **sympathetic branch** directs activities that involve the expenditure of energy. For example, activity of the sympathetic branch can increase the flow of blood to the muscles when we are about to fight someone or run away from a dangerous situation. The **parasympathetic branch** controls quiet activities, such as digestion of food. Activity of the parasympathetic branch stimulates the secretion of digestive enzymes and increases the flow of blood to the digestive system. (See *Figure 4.32.*)

Psychophysiologists can monitor the activity of the autonomic nervous system and its relation to psychological phenomena such as emotion. For example, when a person is angry, his or her heart rate and blood pressure rise. The lie detector (described in Chapter 13) works by recording emotional responses controlled by the autonomic nervous system.

The homeostatic functions of the hypothalamus can involve either internal physiological changes or behavior. For example, the hypothalamus is involved in the control of body temperature. It can directly lower body temperature by causing sweating to occur, or it can raise it by causing shivering to

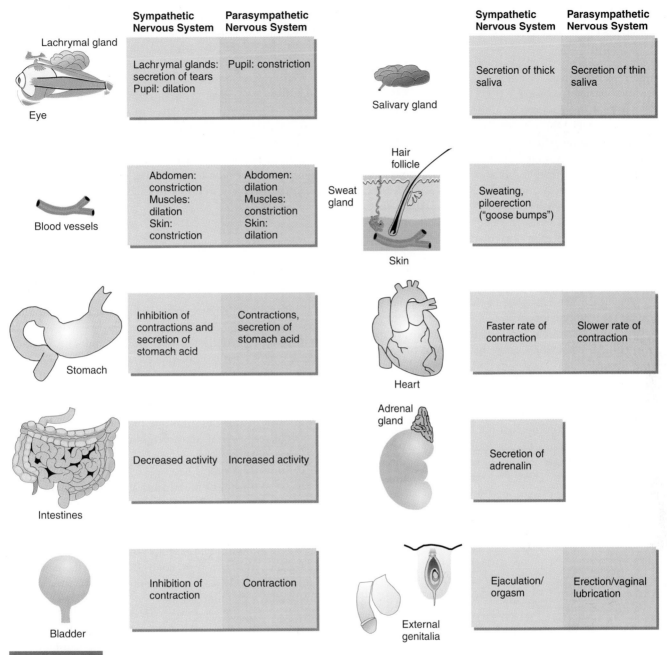

	Sympathetic Nervous System	Parasympathetic Nervous System
Eye (Lachrymal gland)	Lachrymal glands: secretion of tears Pupil: dilation	Pupil: constriction
Blood vessels	Abdomen: constriction Muscles: dilation Skin: constriction	Abdomen: dilation Muscles: constriction Skin: dilation
Stomach	Inhibition of contractions and secretion of stomach acid	Contractions, secretion of stomach acid
Intestines	Decreased activity	Increased activity
Bladder	Inhibition of contraction	Contraction

	Sympathetic Nervous System	Parasympathetic Nervous System
Salivary gland	Secretion of thick saliva	Secretion of thin saliva
Skin (Hair follicle, Sweat gland)	Sweating, piloerection ("goose bumps")	
Heart	Faster rate of contraction	Slower rate of contraction
Adrenal gland	Secretion of adrenalin	
External genitalia	Ejaculation/orgasm	Erection/vaginal lubrication

Figure 4.32

The autonomic nervous system and the organs it controls. Sympathetic nerves are shown in red and pink; parasympathetic nerves are shown in dark and light blue.

occur. If these measures are inadequate, it can send messages to the cerebral cortex that will cause the person to engage in a learned behavior, such as turning on an air conditioner or putting another log on the fire. Damage to the hypothalamus can cause impaired regulation of body temperature, changes in food intake, sterility, and stunting of growth.

The Limbic System

The **limbic system,** a set of structures located in the cerebral hemispheres, plays an important role in learning and in the expression of emotion. The limbic system consists of several regions of the **limbic cortex**—the cerebral cortex located around the edge of the cerebral hemispheres where they join

limbic system A set of interconnected structures of the brain important in emotional and species-typical behavior; includes the amygdala, hippocampus, and limbic cortex.

limbic cortex The cerebral cortex located around the edge of the cerebral hemispheres where they join with the brain stem; part of the limbic system.

with the brain stem. (*Limbus* means "border"; hence the term *limbic* system.) Besides the limbic cortex, the most important components of the limbic system are the *amygdala* and the *hippocampus.* The amygdala and the hippocampus get their names from their shapes; *amygdala* means "almond" and *hippocampus* means "sea horse."

Figure 4.33 shows a view of the right hemisphere of the brain, rotated slightly and seen from the left. We can see the limbic cortex, located on the inner surface of the right cerebral hemisphere. The left hippocampus and amygdala, located in the middle of the temporal lobe, are shown projecting out into the place where the missing left hemisphere would be. We can also see the right hippocampus and amygdala, "ghosted in." We also see a structure that does not belong to the limbic system—the corpus callosum. As we saw earlier, the corpus callosum consists of a band of nerve fibers that enables the left and right cerebral hemispheres to communicate with each other. (See *Figure 4.33.*)

Damage to the **amygdala,** a cluster of neurons located deep in the temporal lobe, affects emotional behavior—especially negative emotions, such as those caused by painful, threatening, or stressful events. In addition, the amygdala controls physiological reactions that help provide energy for short-term activities such as fighting or fleeing. However, if these reactions are prolonged, they can lead to stress-related illnesses. If an animal's amygdala is destroyed, it no longer reacts emotionally to events that normally produce stress and anxiety. We might think that an animal would be better off if it did not become "stressed out" by unpleasant or threatening situations. However, research has shown that animals with damaged amygdalas cannot survive in the wild. The animals

fail to compete successfully for food and other resources, and often act in ways that provoke attacks by other animals. I will discuss the role of the amygdala in emotion and stress in Chapters 13 and 16.

The **hippocampus,** a collection of structures located just behind the amygdala, plays an important role in memory. People with lesions of the hippocampus lose the ability to learn anything new. For them, "yesterday" is always the time before their brain damage occurred; everything after that slips away, just as the memory of dreams often slips away from a person soon after awakening. I will have more to say about this form of amnesia in Chapter 8, which discusses human memory.

Interim Summary

Control of Internal Functions and Automatic Behavior

The more primitive parts of the brain control homeostasis and species-typical behaviors. The brain stem, which consists of the medulla, the pons, and the midbrain, contains neural circuits that control vital physiological functions and produce automatic movements such as those used in locomotion, fighting, and sexual behavior. The cerebellum assists the cerebral cortex in carrying out movements; it coordinates the control of muscles, resulting in smooth movements. It also regulates postural adjustments and appears to play some role in cognitive abilities.

Within the cerebral hemispheres, the thalamus participates in the control of movements and relays sensory information to the cerebral cortex. The hypothalamus receives sensory information from sense receptors elsewhere in the body and also contains its own specialized receptors, such as those used to monitor body temperature. It controls the pituitary gland, which, in turn, controls most of the endocrine glands of the body, and it also controls the internal organs through the autonomic nervous system. Hormones, secreted by endocrine glands, are chemicals that act on hormone receptors in target cells and produce physiological reactions in these cells. The hypothalamus can control homeostatic processes directly and automatically through its control of the pituitary gland and the autonomic nervous system, or it can cause neural circuits in the cerebral cortex to execute more complex, learned behavior.

The amygdala and the hippocampus, both located within the temporal lobe, are important parts of the limbic system. The amygdala is involved in emotions and emotional

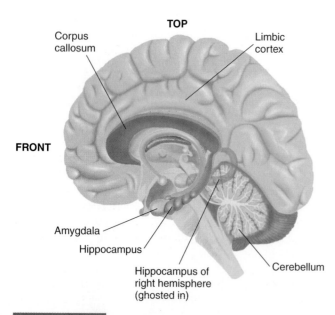

TOP

Corpus callosum

Limbic cortex

FRONT

Amygdala

Hippocampus

Hippocampus of right hemisphere (ghosted in)

Cerebellum

Figure 4.33

The principal structures of the limbic system.

amygdala A part of the limbic system of the brain located deep in the temporal lobe; damage causes changes in emotional and aggressive behavior.

hippocampus A part of the limbic system of the brain, located in the temporal lobe; plays important roles in learning.

behaviors, such as defense and aggression, and it plays an important role in physiological reactions that have beneficial effect in the short run but can lead to stress-related illnesses if they become chronic. The hippocampus is involved in learning and memory; people with damage to this structure can recall old memories but are unable to learn anything new.

Thought Questions

- The cerebellum is one of the largest parts of the brain and contains billions of neurons. What does this fact suggest about the complexity of the task of coordinating movements of the body?
- Suppose that you wanted to build a lie detector. You would monitor reactions that might indicate emotional responses produced by the act of lying. What behavioral and physiological functions would you want to record?
- Tranquilizers reduce negative emotional reactions. In what part (or parts) of the brain do you think these drugs might act? Why?

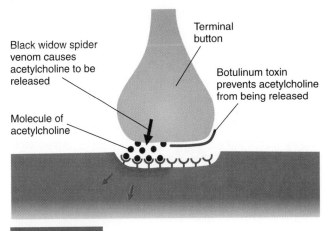

Figure 4.34

Drugs that affect the release of a neurotransmitter, acetylcholine. Black widow spider venom causes acetylcholine to be released. Botulinum toxin prevents the release of acetylcholine from the terminal buttons.

Drugs and Behavior

Long ago, people discovered that the sap, fruit, leaves, bark, or roots of various plants could alter their perceptions and behavior, could be used to treat diseases, or could be used as poisons to kill animals for food. Many of the chemicals found in plants are still used for their behavioral effects, and many other chemicals have been artificially produced in modern laboratories.

Effects of Drugs on Synaptic Transmission

How do drugs affect the nervous system? As we saw, communication between neurons involves the release of transmitter substances. Neurons release many different kinds of transmitter substances, and various drugs can affect the production or release of one or more of these chemicals. Drugs can also mimic the effects of transmitter substances on receptor molecules, block these effects, or interfere with the reuptake of a transmitter substance once it is released. Through these mechanisms, a drug can alter the perceptions, thoughts, and behaviors controlled by particular transmitter substances. Let's examine some of these effects.

Stimulating or Inhibiting the Release of Transmitter Substances

Some drugs stimulate certain terminal buttons to release their transmitter substance continuously, even when the axon is not firing. Other drugs prevent certain terminal buttons from re-

leasing their transmitter substance when the axon fires. The effects of most of these drugs are more or less specific to one transmitter substance. Because different classes of neurons release different transmitter substances, these drugs affect only a selected set of neurons. An example of a stimulating drug is the venom of the black widow spider, which causes the release of a transmitter substance called *acetylcholine*. In contrast, botulinum toxin, a poison that is sometimes present in improperly canned food, prevents the release of acetylcholine. An adult will almost certainly survive the bite of a black widow spider; the symptoms are severe abdominal cramps. However, an extremely small amount of botulinum toxin— less than a millionth of a gram—is fatal. The victim becomes paralyzed and suffocates to death. (See *Figure 4.34.*)

Stimulating or Blocking Postsynaptic Receptor Molecules

Transmitter substances produce their effects by stimulating postsynaptic receptor molecules, which excite or inhibit postsynaptic neurons by opening ion channels and permitting ions to enter or leave the neurons. Some drugs duplicate the effects of particular transmitter substances by directly stimulating particular kinds of receptor molecules. If we use the lock-and-key analogy to describe the effects of a transmitter substance on a receptor molecule, then a drug that stimulates receptor molecules works like a master key, turning the receptor molecules on even when the transmitter substance is not present. For example, nicotine stimulates acetylcholine receptors located on neurons in certain regions of the brain. In low doses, this stimulation has a pleasurable (and addictive) excitatory effect; in high doses, it can cause convulsions and death. (See *Figure 4.35.*)

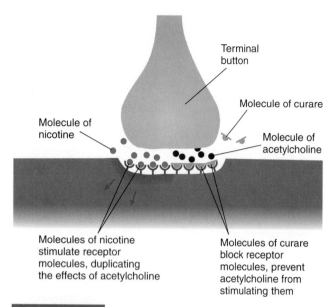

Figure 4.35

Drugs that interact with receptor molecules in the postsynaptic membrane. Nicotine directly stimulates the receptor molecules. Curare blocks receptor molecules and thus prevents acetylcholine from activating them.

Some drugs block receptor molecules, making them inaccessible to the transmitter substance and thus inhibiting synaptic transmission. A drug that blocks receptor molecules "plugs up" the lock so that the key will no longer fit into it. For example, a poison called curare was discovered by South American Indians, who use it on the darts of their blowguns. This drug blocks the acetylcholine receptors that are located on muscle fibers. The curare prevents synaptic transmission in muscles. The paralyzed victim is unable to breathe and consequently suffocates. (See *Figure 4.35.*)

Some medically useful chemicals work by blocking receptor molecules. For example, antipsychotic drugs alleviate the symptoms of schizophrenia, a serious mental disorder, by blocking receptor molecules in the brain that are normally stimulated by a transmitter substance called *dopamine*. This fact has led some investigators to suggest that the symptoms of schizophrenia may be caused by malfunctions of neurons that release dopamine. I will discuss antipsychotic drugs later in this chapter and then in more detail in Chapters 17 and 18.

Inhibiting Reuptake

The effects of most transmitter substances are kept brief by the process of reuptake. Molecules of the transmitter substance are released by a terminal button, they stimulate the

barbiturate A drug that causes sedation; one of several derivatives of barbituric acid.

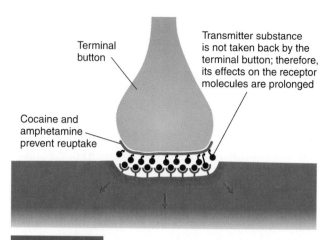

Figure 4.36

Drugs that block reuptake. Cocaine and amphetamine block the reuptake of certain transmitter substances, thus prolonging their effects on the receptor molecules in the postsynaptic membrane.

receptor molecules in the postsynaptic membrane for a fraction of a second, and then they are pumped back into the terminal button. Some drugs inhibit the process of reuptake so that molecules of the transmitter substance continue to stimulate the postsynaptic receptor molecules for a long time. Therefore, inhibition of reuptake increases the effect of the transmitter substance. The excitatory effects of cocaine and amphetamine are produced by their ability to inhibit the reuptake of certain transmitter substances, including dopamine. (See *Figure 4.36.*)

Drugs That Cause Sedation

Some drugs depress behavior, causing relaxation, sedation, or even loss of consciousness. In most cases, the depression is caused by stimulation of a class of receptor molecules that is normally activated by neuromodulators produced by the brain. **Barbiturates** depress the brain's activity by stimulating a particular category of neuromodulator receptors. In low doses, barbiturates have a calming effect. In progressively higher doses, they produce difficulty in walking and talking, unconsciousness, coma, and death. Barbiturates are abused by people who want to achieve the relaxing, calming effect of the drugs, especially to counteract the anxiety and irritability that can be produced by stimulants. They are occasionally prescribed as sleep medications, but they are a very poor choice for this purpose because they suppress dreaming and produce a particularly unrefreshing sleep. In addition, a dose of a barbiturate sufficient to induce sleep is not that much lower than a fatal dose; thus, these drugs do not have much of a safety factor. Ideally, the therapeutic dose of a drug is much lower than a fatal dose.

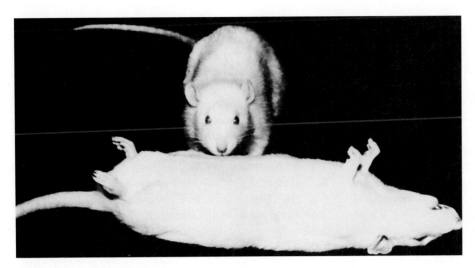

Figure 4.37

The effects of an antialcohol drug. Both rats received an injection of alcohol, but the one in the back also received an injection of the alcohol antagonist and appears to be perfectly sober.
(Photo courtesy of Steven M. Paul, National Institute of Mental Health, Bethesda, Md.)

Many **antianxiety drugs** are members of a family known as the **benzodiazepines**, which include the well-known tranquilizer Valium *(diazepam)*. These drugs, too, stimulate some sort of neuromodulator receptors located on neurons in various parts of the brain—including the amygdala. The benzodiazepines are very effective in reducing anxiety and are sometimes used to treat people who are afflicted by periodic attacks of severe anxiety. In addition, some benzodiazepines serve as sleep medications. These behavioral effects suggest that they mimic the effects of neuromodulators involved in the regulation of mood and the control of sleep.

By far the most commonly used depressant drug is ethyl alcohol, the active ingredient in alcoholic beverages. This drug has effects similar to those of the barbiturates: Larger and larger doses of alcohol reduce anxiety, disrupt motor coordination, and then cause unconsciousness, coma, and finally death. The effects of alcohol and barbiturates are additive: A moderate dose of alcohol plus a moderate dose of barbiturates can be fatal.

The primary effect of alcohol appears to be similar to that of the benzodiazepines: It stimulates some type of neuromodulator receptor. Suzdak et al. (1986) discovered a drug that reverses alcohol intoxication, presumably by blocking some type of neuromodulator receptor. Figure 4.37 shows two rats who received injections of enough alcohol to make them pass out. The one facing us also received an injection of the antialcohol drug and appears completely sober. (See *Figure 4.37.*)

This wonder drug is not likely to reach the market soon. Although the behavioral effects of alcohol may be mediated by neuromodulator receptors, alcohol has other, potentially fatal effects on all cells of the body. Alcohol destabilizes the membrane of cells, interfering with their functions. Thus, a person who takes some of the antialcohol drug could go on to drink himself or herself to death without becoming drunk in the process.

Alcohol is a dangerous drug because of its high potential for addiction. I will discuss the problem of addiction (to alcohol and other drugs) in further detail in Chapter 17.

Drugs That Cause Excitation

Several categories of drugs stimulate the central nervous system and thus activate behavior. Because of the effects some of these drugs have on the neural circuits involved in reinforcement (reward), they tend to be abused. Two very popular stimulant drugs, amphetamine and cocaine, have almost identical effects: They inhibit the reuptake of dopamine and thus strengthen the effectiveness of synapses that use this transmitter substance. As we shall see in Chapter 13, reinforcing stimuli—such as food for a hungry animal, water for a thirsty one, or sexual contact for a sexually aroused one—exert their behavioral effects largely by increasing the activity of a circuit of dopamine-secreting neurons. Thus, amphetamine and cocaine mimic the effects of reinforcing stimuli. Free-base cocaine (crack) is particularly addictive. The drug has an immediate effect on the reuptake of dopamine and produces such a profound feeling of euphoria and pleasure that the person wants to repeat the experience again and again.

Cocaine and amphetamine, if taken in large enough doses for a few days, can produce the symptoms of paranoid schizophrenia—a serious mental disorder. Heavy users of these drugs suffer from hallucinations and their thoughts become confused and difficult to control. They may come to

antianxiety drug　A "tranquilizer," which reduces anxiety. The most common include chlordiazepoxide (Librium) and diazepam (Valium).

benzodiazepine　A class of drug having anxiolytic ("tranquilizing") effects; examples are Librium and Valium.

believe that they are being attacked or plotted against. In fact, an experienced clinician cannot distinguish the drug-induced symptoms from those that occur in people who really have the psychosis. This fact has suggested to some investigators that schizophrenia may be caused by overactivity of dopamine-secreting synapses; this hypothesis will be discussed in more detail in Chapter 17.

Opiate drugs have both excitatory and inhibitory effects on behavior. All of these effects occur because these drugs mimic the effects of the body's own opioid neuromodulators: They stimulate opioid receptors located on neurons in various parts of the brain. The inhibitory effects include analgesia (reduced sensitivity to pain), hypothermia (lowering of body temperature), and sedation. The pain reduction is accomplished by neurons in the midbrain, the hypothermia by neurons in the hypothalamus, and the sedation by neurons in the medulla. A fatal overdose of an opiate kills its victim by inhibiting the activity of circuits of neurons in the medulla that control breathing, heart rate, and blood pressure. But it is the excitatory effects of opiates that induce people to abuse them. Some opioid receptors are located on dopamine-secreting neurons involved in reinforcement (reward). When a person takes an opiate such as heroin, the activity of these neurons produces feelings of euphoria and pleasure, similar to those produced by cocaine or amphetamine. These excitatory effects, and not the inhibitory ones, are responsible for addiction.

Drugs That Modify Perceptions or Produce Hallucinations

Throughout history, people have enjoyed changing their consciousness now and then by taking drugs, fasting, meditating, or chanting. Even children enjoy spinning around and making themselves dizzy—presumably for the same reasons. Chemicals found in several different plants produce profound changes in consciousness. Behaviorally, these changes are difficult to specify. Large doses of drugs such as marijuana or LSD tend to make laboratory animals become sedated, but the animals give no sign of having their consciousnesses altered. But then, how could they? Only humans can describe the consciousness-altering effects of the drugs.

Drugs can affect consciousness in several different ways. We have the clearest understanding of one category of drugs: those that affect synapses that use a transmitter substance called *serotonin*. Serotonin plays an important role in the control of dreaming. Normally, we dream only when we are asleep, in a particular stage called *REM sleep* (for the rapid eye movements that occur then). During the rest of the day, circuits of serotonin-secreting neurons inhibit the mechanisms responsible for dreaming, thus preventing them from becoming active. Drugs such as LSD, psilocybin, and DMT suppress the activity of serotonin-secreting neurons, permitting dream mechanisms to become active. As a result, hallucinations occur. These hallucinations are often interesting and even awe-inspiring, but sometimes produce intense fear and anxiety.

Not all hallucinogenic drugs interfere with serotonin-secreting synapses. Cocaine and amphetamine, which affect dopamine-secreting synapses, also produce hallucinations. However, the hallucinations produced by cocaine and amphetamine take some time to develop, and they are primarily auditory. LSD-induced hallucinations take place immediately and are primarily visual, as dreams are. The two types of hallucinations undoubtedly occur for different reasons.

THC (tetrahydrocannabinol), the active ingredient in marijuana, exerts its behavioral effects by stimulating THC receptors—specific neuromodulator receptors present in particular regions of the brain. THC produces analgesia and sedation, stimulates appetite, reduces nausea caused by drugs used to treat cancer, relieves asthma attacks, decreases pressure within the eyes in patients with glaucoma, and reduces the symptoms of certain motor disorders. On the other hand, THC interferes with concentration and memory, alters visual and auditory perception, and distorts perceptions of the passage of time (Howlett, 1990).

Devane et al. (1992) discovered that the brain produces a neuromodulator that activates the THC receptor: a fatlike substance that they named *anandamide,* from the Sanskrit word *ananda,* or "bliss." We do not yet know how it is released or what physiological functions it performs. But now that the THC receptor has been identified and the natural neuromodulator has been found, researchers also hope to find drugs that have the therapeutic effects of THC but not its adverse effects on cognition.

Psychotherapeutic Drugs

The symptoms of some serious mental disorders can be reduced or even eliminated by various psychotherapeutic drugs. Cocaine and amphetamine—drugs that stimulate synapses that use dopamine—can induce the symptoms of schizophrenia: hallucinations, delusions, and a disordered thought process. In contrast, drugs that block dopamine receptors can be used to reduce or even eliminate these symptoms. These antipsychotic drugs, such as chlorpromazine (Thorazine) and clozapine (Clozaril), have made it possible to discharge people who would otherwise have been unable to care for themselves from mental hospitals.

Another important category of psychotherapeutic drugs includes the antidepressant medications. Depression—extreme, intense feelings of sadness and hopelessness—can result from tragedies in a person's life, but it can sometimes arise without any obvious external cause, presumably as a result of biochemical abnormalities within the brain. The antidepressant medications, such as fluoxetine (Prozac), tend to stimulate synapses that use serotonin. They have saved many lives that otherwise would have been lost through suicide.

Yet another drug is used to treat a special category of depression in which a person's mood fluctuates between periods of severe depression and periods of *mania*, a state of excited, unrealistic elation. This drug is a simple inorganic compound called lithium carbonate. The biochemical cause of its therapeutic effects is unknown.

Evaluating Scientific Issues

"Physiological" Versus "Psychological" Drug Addiction

As we all know, some drugs have very potent reinforcing effects, which lead some people to abuse them or even to become addicted to them. Many people (psychologists, health professionals, and lay people) believe that "true" addiction is caused by the unpleasant physiological effects that occur when an addict tries to stop taking the drug. For example, Eddy et al. (1965) defined physical dependence as "an adaptive state that manifests itself by intense physical disturbances when the administration of a drug is suspended" (p. 723). In contrast, they defined psychic dependence as a condition in which a drug produces "a feeling of satisfaction and a psychic drive that requires periodic or continuous administration of the drug to produce pleasure or to avoid discomfort" (p. 723). Most people regard the latter as less important than the former. But, as we shall see, the reverse is true.

■ Evidence for Physiological Addiction

For many years, heroin addiction has been considered as the prototype for all drug addictions. People who habitually take heroin (or other opiates) become physically dependent on the drug; that is, they show *tolerance* and *withdrawal symptoms*. **Tolerance** is the decreased sensitivity to a drug that comes from its continued use; the drug user must take larger and larger amounts of the drug in order for it to be effective. Once a person has taken an opiate regularly enough to develop tolerance, that person will suffer withdrawal symptoms if he or she stops taking the drug. **Withdrawal symptoms** are primarily the opposite of the effects of the drug itself. That is, heroin produces euphoria; withdrawal from it produces *dysphoria*—a feeling of anxious misery. (*Euphoria* and *dysphoria* mean "easy to bear" and "hard to bear," respectively.) Heroin produces constipation; withdrawal from it produces nausea, cramping, and diarrhea. Heroin produces relaxation; withdrawal from it produces agitation.

Most investigators believe that the withdrawal symptoms are produced by the body's attempt to compensate for the unusual condition of heroin intoxication. That is, most systems of the body, including those controlled by the brain, are regulated so that they stay at an optimal

value. When a drug artificially changes these systems for a prolonged time, homeostatic mechanisms begin to produce the opposite reaction, which partially compensates for the disturbance from the optimal value. These compensatory mechanisms account for the fact that more and more heroin must be taken in order to achieve the effects that were produced when the person first started taking the drug. They also account for the symptoms of withdrawal: When the person stops taking the drug, the compensatory mechanisms make themselves felt, unopposed by the action of the drug.

■ How Important Is Physiological Addiction?

Heroin addiction has provided such a striking example of drug dependence that some authorities have concluded that "real" addiction does not occur unless a drug causes tolerance and withdrawal. Without doubt, withdrawal symptoms make it difficult for a person to stop taking heroin—they help keep the person hooked. But withdrawal symptoms do not explain why a person becomes a heroin addict in the first place; that fact is explained by the drug's reinforcing effect. Certainly, people do not start taking heroin so that they will become physically dependent on it and feel miserable when they go without it. Instead, they begin taking it because it makes them feel good.

Even though the withdrawal effects of heroin make it difficult to stop taking the drug, these effects alone are not sufficient to keep most people hooked. In fact, when the cost of the habit gets too high, some addicts stop taking heroin "cold turkey." Doing so is not as painful as most people believe; withdrawal symptoms have been described as similar to a bad case of the flu—unpleasant, but survivable. After a week or two, when their nervous systems adapt to the absence of the drug, these addicts recommence their habit, which now costs less to sustain. If their only reason for taking the drug was to avoid unpleasant withdrawal symptoms, they would be incapable of following this strategy. The reason that people take—and continue to take—drugs such as heroin is that the drugs give them a pleasurable "rush"; in other words, the drugs have a reinforcing effect on their behavior.

There are two other kinds of evidence that contradict the assertion that drug addiction is caused by physical dependence. First, some very potent drugs, including cocaine, do not produce physical dependency. That is, people who take the drug do not show tolerance; and if they stop, they do not show any withdrawal symptoms. As a

tolerance   The decreased sensitivity to a drug resulting from its continued use.

withdrawal symptom   An effect produced by discontinuance of use of a drug after a period of continued use; generally opposite to the drug's primary effects.

result, experts believed for many years that cocaine was a relatively innocuous drug, not in the same league as heroin. Obviously, they were wrong; cocaine is even more addictive than heroin. As a matter of fact, laboratory animals who can press a lever and give themselves injections of cocaine are more likely to die than are those who can give themselves injections of heroin. Second, some drugs produce physical dependence (tolerance and withdrawal symptoms) but are not abused (Jaffe, 1985). The reason they are not abused is that they do not have reinforcing effects on behavior—they are just not any fun to take.

■ What Should We Conclude?

The most important lesson we can learn from the misguided distinction between "physiological" and "psychological" addiction is that we should never underestimate the importance of "psychological" factors. After all, given that behavior is controlled by circuits of neurons in the brain, even "psychological" factors involve physiological mechanisms. People often pay more attention to physiological symptoms than psychological ones—they consider them more *real*. But behavioral research indicates that an exclusive preoccupation with physiology can hinder our understanding of the causes of addiction.

Interim Summary

Drugs and Behavior

Many chemicals found in nature have behavioral effects, and many more have been synthesized in the laboratory. Drugs can facilitate or interfere with synaptic activity. Facilitators include drugs that cause the release of a transmitter substance (such as the venom of the black widow spider); drugs that directly stimulate postsynaptic receptor molecules, thus duplicating the effects of the transmitter substance itself (such as nicotine); and drugs that inhibit the reuptake of a transmitter substance (such as amphetamine and cocaine). Drugs that interfere with synaptic activity include those that inhibit the release of a transmitter substance (such as botulinum toxin) and those that block receptor molecules (such as curare).

There are several major categories of drugs that affect behavior. Alcohol, barbiturates, and tranquilizers depress the activity of the brain by stimulating various types of receptor molecules. Amphetamine and cocaine stimulate the brain primarily by retarding the reuptake of dopamine. The opiates duplicate the effects of the brain's opioids, decreasing sensitivity to pain and producing intensely enjoyable feelings of euphoria and pleasure. LSD, psilocybin, and related drugs inhibit the activity of synapses that use serotonin. The hallu-

cinogenic effects of these drugs may be related to dreaming, which is controlled by circuits of serotonin-secreting neurons. The physiological effects of marijuana are produced by a compound called THC, which stimulates receptors that are normally activated by a natural neuromodulator called anandamide.

Some drugs having behavioral effects are useful in treating mental disorders. Psychotherapeutic drugs include those that reduce the symptoms of schizophrenia and those that relieve depression. Antischizophrenic drugs block dopamine receptors, and antidepressant drugs generally facilitate the action of serotonin.

Opiates produce tolerance and withdrawal symptoms, which make their habitual use increasingly expensive and make quitting more difficult. But the primary reason for addiction is the reinforcing effect, not the unpleasant symptoms produced when an addict tries to quit. Tolerance appears to be produced by homeostatic mechanisms that counteract the effects of the drug. The distinction between "physiological" addiction (complete with tolerance and withdrawal effects) and "psychological" addiction (lacking these effects) has obscured the true cause of addiction: the reinforcing effect of the drug. Cocaine was once thought to be relatively harmless because it does not produce "real" (that is, physiological) addiction; obviously, we now know better.

Thought Questions

■ Suppose that someone takes a drug for anxiety. Suppose further that he is planning on going out for drinks with friends. His wife advises him to enjoy an evening with his friends but not to have any drinks. Why is this suggestion a good one?

■ Many useful drugs have been found in nature, and more are yet to be discovered. What are some of the consequences of deforestation, especially of tropical forests that have an especially rich diversity of species? Who owns the resources and the drugs that are discovered? The indigenous people who live there? The governments of the countries where the resources are located? The pharmaceutical companies that extract them and develop purified forms of them?

■ If you were in charge of the research department of a pharmaceutical company, what new behaviorally active drugs would you seek? Analgesics? Antianxiety drugs? Antiaggressive drugs? Memory-improving drugs? Should behaviorally active drugs be taken only by people who clearly have afflictions such as schizophrenia, depression, or obsessive compulsive disorder, or should we try to find drugs that help people who want to improve their intellectual performance or social adjustment or simply to feel happier?

Suggestions for Further Reading

Grilly, D. M. *Drugs and Human Behavior,* 2nd ed. Boston: Allyn and Bacon, 1994.

Julien, R. M. *A Primer of Drug Action: A Concise, Nontechnical Guide to the Actions, Uses, and Side Effects of Psychoactive Drugs,* 7th ed. San Francisco: W. H. Freeman, 1995.

If you are interested in learning more about the effects of drugs that are often abused, you may want to read these books, both of which contain much helpful information about the effects of popular drugs and their use and abuse in society.

Carlson, N. R. *Foundations of Physiological Psychology,* 3rd ed. Boston: Allyn and Bacon, 1995.

My introductory textbook of physiological psychology discusses the topics presented in this chapter in more detail.

Chapter 5

Learning
and Behavior

Chapter Outline

Learning is an adaptive process in which the tendency to perform a particular behavior is changed by experience. As environmental conditions change, we learn new behaviors and eliminate old ones. However, changes in behavior do not always reflect learning, and learning may occur without obvious changes in behavior.

Habituation

Habituation—the simplest form of learning—involves learning not to respond to insignificant events that occur repeatedly. Habituation helps an organism's behavior become sensitive to more important stimuli, such as those involving survival and procreation.

Classical Conditioning

Pavlov's Serendipitous Discovery • The Biological Significance of Classical Conditioning • Basic Principles of Classical Conditioning • Conditional Emotional Responses • What Is Learned in Classical Conditioning?

In classical conditioning, an organism's behavior is elicited by one stimulus—the conditional stimulus—that predicts the occurrence of another stimulus—the unconditional stimulus. Different relations between the conditional and unconditional stimuli may lead to extinction, spontaneous recovery, generalization, and discrimination of the conditional response. Classical conditioning plays an important role in emotion.

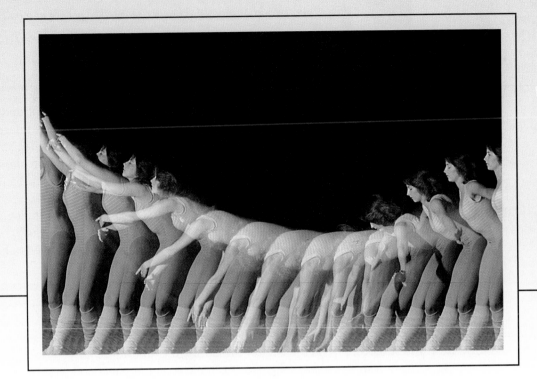

Operant Conditioning

The Law of Effect • Skinner and Operant Behavior • The Three-Term Contingency • Reinforcement, Punishment, and Extinction • Other Operant Procedures and Phenomena • *Biology and Culture: Learning, Superstition, and Ritualistic Behavior*

Operant conditioning enables an organism's behavior to be modified by its consequences. Positive and negative reinforcement increase the frequency of a behavior and punishment and extinction decrease it. New, complex behaviors can be acquired through the process of shaping. Superstition and ritualistic behavior occur in many species when such behaviors are accidentally reinforced.

Conditioning of Complex Behaviors

Aversive Control of Behavior • Observation and Imitation • The Analysis of Human Behavior • *Evaluating Scientific Issues: What Is Insight?* • Some Thoughts on Behavior Analysis and Cognitive Psychology

Punishment and negative reinforcement are effective means of controlling operant behavior, but they may produce undesirable side effects. An aversion to a flavor can be conditioned by a single pairing of the flavor with illness—a finding that has had useful applications with cancer patients, people addicted to drugs, and even wildlife that prey on domestic animals. Insight was once thought to involve a sudden—almost magical—solution to a problem. Research using animals has shown that insight may not be so sudden after all: Insight seems to require previous experience with the elements of the problem.

*A*hmad Wahl, a successful lawyer, wanted to get rid of a bad habit. He was an excellent speaker and writer, and when he heard someone make a grammatical error, he was quick to point it out. Afterward, he regretted doing so because he either embarrassed the other person or made him or her angry. He liked to think of himself as friendly, kind, and tolerant; his habit of correcting people's grammar conflicted with this aspect of his self-image.

One day, he was discussing a real estate transaction with a client, a psychologist. The client happened to commit a grammatical error, and before Ahmad could stop himself, he corrected her. He apologized immediately and said that he had tried to stop the bad habit but never seemed to think of remaining silent until afterward, when it was too late.

"If you really want to break that habit, I know how to do it," said the psychologist, May Lin Lee. "In fact, I'd be willing to bet that you can get rid of it within two weeks."

"Really? I thought psychoanalysis took a long time. That's why I never tried to find a psychologist to help me."

"I'm not a psychoanalyst; in fact, hardly any psychologists are. I'm a behavior analyst. I use some basic principles of learning that psychologists have discovered to help people change their behavior. Your little habit will be easy to get rid of."

"If you can really help me, I'll exchange my professional services for yours. How about a swap? If you succeed, I won't bill you for the closing on your house."

May Lin smiled. "It's a deal," she said. She took a piece of paper and wrote a few lines. "Here," she said. "Read this contract, and then sign it."

Ahmad read what she had written and then looked at her suspiciously. "That's all there is to it? I have to burn a ten-dollar bill every time I correct someone's grammar?" She nodded. "Don't you want to talk to me to find out if I've got some kind of complex that's making me criticize others?"

"No, that's all you have to do. And I want you to make a note on your appointment calendar every time you have to burn a ten-dollar bill. Oh, make sure you carry a good supply of them with you and a lighter or a pack of matches. You have to burn the money right away."

Ahmad looked unconvinced, but he signed the paper.

A week later he called May Lin, as he had agreed to do. "I can't understand it," he said. "I really think it's working. I had to burn one bill the first day, two the second, none the third, one the fourth, and one the fifth. That was the last. This morning, I talked with a client who made more grammatical errors than I could count, and I didn't correct any of them. But I can't understand this—if I can make myself burn ten-dollar bills, why couldn't I exercise enough willpower before to stop correcting people?"

"Breaking a habit is not really a matter of willpower; that's a misconception most people have. What you need to do is arrange the contingencies in your environment so that they reinforce desirable behaviors or, as in your case, punish undesirable ones. Psychologists have learned that behaviors are changed most effectively when they are reinforced or punished immediately. Somehow—and for our purposes it really doesn't matter how—you had acquired the habit of correcting people. Later in life, you began feeling bad about the effect this behavior had on other people and on your own self-image. But the immediate effect of correcting someone was probably a reinforcing one—a feeling that you had demonstrated your superiority, perhaps. The bad feeling you had afterward came too late to have a direct effect on your behavior. So I had you do something that was certain to have an unpleasant effect on you. The immediate punishing effect of the loss of the money outweighed the reinforcing effect of your demonstrating your superiority. And once you started realizing you were beating your habit, the satisfaction you derived from that accomplishment started reinforcing your remaining silent."

"You know, you're right. The past few days, I've almost been hoping that people will make grammatical errors so that I can pride myself on keeping quiet."

Ahmad called May Lin a week later to tell her that he had not burned any more ten-dollar bills.

We are what we are because of history—both our ancestors' history and the history of our own lives. The process of natural selection shaped the evolution of our species: Mutations introduced variability, and those changes that produced favorable consequences were maintained. Behavior is similarly selected: Behaviors that produce favorable consequences are repeated, but those that produce unfavorable consequences tend not to recur. In other words, we learn from experience.

Learning is an adaptive process in which the tendency to perform a particular behavior is changed by experience. As conditions change, we learn new behaviors and eliminate old ones.

Learning cannot be observed directly; it can only be inferred from changes in behavior. But not all changes in behavior are caused by learning. For example, your performance on an examination or the skill with which you operate an automobile can be affected by your physical or mental condition—such as fatigue, fearfulness, or preoccupation. Moreover, learning may occur without noticeable changes in observable behavior taking place. In some cases, learning is not apparent—at least, not right away—from our observable behavior. In other cases, we may never have the opportunity to demonstrate what we have learned. For example, although you may have received training in how to change a flat tire in a driver's education class, your behavior will not be noticeably different unless you need to change a flat tire. In still other cases, you may not be sufficiently motivated to demonstrate something you have learned. For example, a teacher might pose a question to the class. Although you know the answer, you do not say anything because you get nervous when speaking in front of others.

Learning takes place within the nervous system. Experience alters the structure and chemistry of the brain, and these changes affect the individual's subsequent behavior. Performance is the behavioral change (or new behavior) produced by the internal change.

This chapter considers three kinds of learning: habituation, classical conditioning, and operant conditioning. All three involve cause-and-effect relations between behavior and the environment. We learn which stimuli are trivial and which are important, and we learn to make adaptive responses and to avoid maladaptive ones. We learn to recognize those conditions under which a particular response is useful and those under which a different response is more appropriate. The types of learning described in this chapter serve as the building blocks for more complex behaviors, such as problem solving and thinking, which I will describe in later chapters.

The extent to which we learn a behavior is reflected in the skill with which we perform that behavior.

Habituation

Many events may cause us to react automatically. For example, a sudden, unexpected noise causes an **orienting response:** We become alert and turn our heads toward the source of the sound. However, if the noise occurs repeatedly, we gradually cease to respond to it; we eventually ignore it.

learning An adaptive process in which the tendency to perform a particular behavior is changed by experience.

orienting response Any response by which an organism directs appropriate sensory organs (eyes, ears, nose) toward the source of a novel stimulus.

Habituation, learning *not* to respond to an unimportant event that occurs repeatedly, is the simplest form of learning. Even animals that have very primitive nervous systems are capable of habituation. For example, if we tap the shell of a land snail with a pencil, a withdrawal response occurs—the body is withdrawn into the shell. After half a minute or so, the body extends out of the shell and the snail will continue with whatever it was doing. If we tap the shell again, the withdrawal response occurs again, but this time the snail will stay inside its shell for a shorter period. Another tap will cause another withdrawal response, but for even less time. Eventually, the withdrawal response will stop completely. The withdrawal response will have habituated.

From an evolutionary perspective, habituation makes adaptive sense. If a once-novel stimulus occurs again and again without any important result, the stimulus has no significance to the organism. Obviously, responding to a stimulus of no importance wastes time and energy. Consider what would happen to a land snail in a rainstorm if the withdrawal response never habituated—the snail would remain in its shell until the rain stopped falling. And consider how distracting it would be to have your attention diverted every time a common household noise occurred.

The simplest form of habituation is temporary, and is known as *short-term habituation*. Suppose that we tap a snail's shell again and again until the withdrawal response habituates. If we tap it again the next day, we will find that the withdrawal response reoccurs and continues for several more taps. It takes just as long for habituation to occur as it did the day before. And if we repeat our experiment every day afterward, the same thing will happen; the snail does not remember what happened previously.

Animals that have more complex nervous systems are capable of *long-term habituation*. For example, a hunting dog may be frightened the first few times it hears the sound of a shotgun, but it soon learns not to respond to the blast. This habituation carries across from day to day and even from one hunting season to the next. Likewise, your behavior has habituated to stimuli that you have probably not thought about for a long time. When people move to new houses or apartments, they often complain about being kept awake by unfamiliar noises. But after a while, they no longer notice them.

Habituation is a simple but useful form of learning: It permits us to remain relatively free from distraction by petty events, and we are able to get more important things done.

Classical Conditioning

Unlike habituation, classical conditioning involves learning about the conditions that predict that a significant event will occur. We acquire much of our behavior through classical conditioning. For example, if you are hungry and smell a favorite food cooking, your mouth is likely to water. If you see someone with whom you have recently had a serious argument, you are likely to experience again some of the emotional reactions that occurred during the encounter. If you hear a song that you used to listen to with a loved one, you are likely to experience a feeling of nostalgia.

Let's consider how classical conditioning takes place. Suppose that you have an uninflated balloon directly before you. Someone starts inflating the balloon with a pump; the balloon gets larger and larger. What are you likely to do? You will probably grimace and squint your eyes partly shut—you realize that the balloon is about to burst in your face.

Now consider how a person learns to flinch defensively at the sight of a tightly stretched balloon. Suppose that we inflate a balloon in front of a young boy who has never seen one before. The boy will turn his eyes toward the enlarging balloon, but he will not flinch. When the balloon explodes, the noise and the blast of air will cause a defensive startle reaction: He will squint, grimace, raise his shoulders, and suddenly move his arms toward his body. A bursting balloon is an important stimulus, one that causes an automatic, *unlearned* defensive reaction. (See *Figure 5.1.*)

We will probably not have to repeat the experience many times for the boy to learn to react the way we all do—flinching defensively before the balloon actually bursts. A previously neutral stimulus (the overinflated balloon), followed by an important stimulus (the explosion that occurs when the balloon bursts), can now trigger the defensive flinching response by itself. The defensive flinching response has been *classically conditioned* to the sight of an overinflated balloon. (See *Figure 5.2.*)

Pavlov's Serendipitous Discovery

In December 1904, the Russian physiologist Ivan Pavlov was awarded the Nobel Prize in physiology and medicine for his work on the digestive system. Invited to Stockholm to accept the award and to deliver an acceptance speech, the 55-year-old Pavlov did not speak of his pioneering work on digestion (Babkin, 1949). Instead, his address, entitled "The First Sure Steps along the Path of a New Investigation," focused on his more recent work involving conditional reflexes or "involuntary" responses. Pavlov's new line of research was to take him far from the research for which he was awarded the Nobel Prize, and today he is remembered more for his work in psychology than in physiology. But it was while studying the digestive system that Pavlov stumbled on the phenomenon that was to make him one of the most famous psychologists of all time. Let's pick up Pavlov's story as it unfolded nearly one hundred years ago.

habituation The simplest form of learning; learning not to respond to an unimportant event that occurs repeatedly.

Figure 5.1

The process of classical conditioning. The child watches the balloon expand until it bursts, which causes a defensive startle reaction.

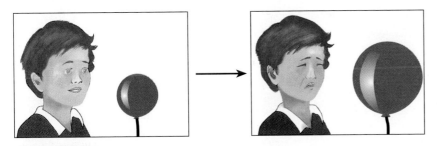

Figure 5.2

The conditional response. After the child's first experience with a bursting balloon, the mere sight of an inflated balloon elicits a defensive reaction.

Pavlov's chief ambition as a physiologist was to discover the neural mechanisms controlling glandular secretions during digestion. He measured the secretions during the course of a meal. For example, he inserted a small tube in a duct in an animal's mouth and collected drops of saliva as they were secreted by the salivary gland. It was while conducting routine studies of salivation in dogs that his interest in digestion became forever sidetracked by a serendipitous discovery.

Pavlov's strategy was to study salivary processes in individual dogs over many test sessions. During each session, he placed dry food powder inside the dog's mouth and then collected the saliva. All went well until the dogs became experienced subjects. After several testing sessions, the dogs began salivating *before* being fed, usually as soon as they saw the laboratory assistant enter the room with the food powder. What Pavlov discovered was a form of learning in which one stimulus predicts the occurrence of another. In this case, the appearance of the laboratory assistant predicted the appearance of food.

Rather than ignoring this phenomenon or treating it as a confounding variable that needed to be controlled, Pavlov designed experiments to discover exactly why the dogs were salivating before being given the opportunity to eat. He suspected that salivation might be triggered by stimuli that were initially unrelated to eating. Somehow, these neutral stimuli came to control what is normally a natural reflexive behavior. After all, dogs do not naturally salivate when they see labora-

tory assistants. Pavlov's new chief ambition was to understand the variables that controlled this unexpected behavior.

To do so, he placed an inexperienced dog in a harness and occasionally gave it small amounts of food powder. (See *Figure 5.3*.) Just prior to placing the food powder in the dog's mouth, Pavlov sounded a bell, a buzzer, or some other auditory stimulus. At first, the dog showed only a startle response to the sound, perking its ears and turning its head toward the sound. The dog salivated only when the food powder was placed in its mouth. But after only a dozen or so pairings of the bell and food powder, the dog began to salivate when the bell rang. Placing the food powder in the dog's mouth was no longer necessary to elicit salivation; the sound by itself was sufficient. Pavlov showed that a neutral stimulus can elicit a response similar to the original reflex when the stimulus predicts the occurrence of a significant stimulus (in this case, food powder). This type of learning is called **classical conditioning**. (Pavlov performed such an impressive and authoritative series of experiments that this form of learning is called "classical" out of respect for his work. It is also sometimes referred to as *Pavlovian conditioning*.)

Pavlov demonstrated that conditioning occurred only when the food powder followed the bell within a short time.

classical conditioning The process by which a response normally elicited by one stimulus (the UCS) comes to be controlled by another stimulus (the CS) as well.

Figure 5.3

Pavlov's original procedure for classical conditioning. The experimenter rings a bell and then presents the food. Saliva is collected in a tube.

If there was a long delay between the sound and the food powder or if the sound followed the food powder, the animal never learned to salivate when it heard the sound. Thus, the sequence and timing of events are important factors in classical conditioning. Classical conditioning provides us with a way to learn cause-and-effect relations between environmental events. We are able to learn about the stimuli that warn us that an important event is about to occur. Obviously, warning stimuli must occur prior to the event about which we are being warned.

Figure 5.4 shows the basic classical conditioning procedure—the special conditions that must exist for an organism to respond to a previously neutral stimulus. (See *Figure 5.4.*) A stimulus, such as food, that naturally elicits reflexive behavior, such as salivation, is called an **unconditional stimulus (UCS)**. The reflexive behavior itself is called the **uncondi-**tional response (UCR). If, for a certain dog, a bell signals food, then the bell may also come to elicit salivation through classical conditioning. Another dog may hear the sound of an electric can opener just before it is fed, in which case that sound will come to elicit salivation. A neutral stimulus paired with the unconditional stimulus that eventually elicits a response is called a **conditional stimulus (CS)**. The behavior elicited by a conditional stimulus is called a **conditional response (CR).** In the case of Pavlov's dogs, food powder was the UCS. It elicited the UCR, salivation. At first, when Pavlov presented the sound of the bell or buzzer, the dogs did not salivate; the sound was merely a neutral stimulus, not a CS. However, with repeated pairings of the sound and the food powder, the sound became a CS, reliably eliciting the CR—salivation.

The Biological Significance of Classical Conditioning

Salivation is an innate behavior and is adaptive because it facilitates digestion. Through natural selection, the neural circuitry that underlies salivation has become part of the genetic endowment of many species. Pavlov's experiments demonstrated that an innate reflexive behavior, such as salivation, can be elicited by novel stimuli. Thus, a response that is naturally under the control of appropriate environmental stimuli, such as salivation caused by the presence of food in the mouth, can also come to be controlled by other kinds of stimuli.

unconditional stimulus (UCS) In classical conditioning, a stimulus, such as food, that naturally elicits a reflexive response, such as salivation.

unconditional response (UCR) In classical conditioning, a response, such as salivation, that is naturally elicited by the UCS.

conditional stimulus (CS) In classical conditioning, a stimulus which, because of its repeated association with the UCS, eventually elicits a conditional response (CR).

conditional response (CR) In classical conditioning, the response elicited by the CS.

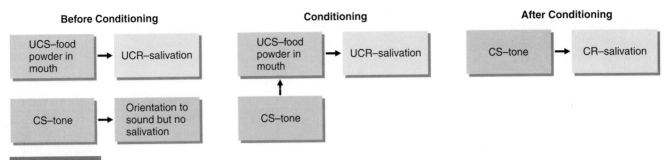

Before Conditioning

UCS–food powder in mouth → UCR–salivation

CS–tone → Orientation to sound but no salivation

Conditioning

UCS–food powder in mouth → UCR–salivation

CS–tone

After Conditioning

CS–tone → CR–salivation

Figure 5.4

Basic components of the classical conditioning procedure. Prior to conditioning, the UCS but not the CS, elicits a response (the UCR). During conditioning, the CS is presented in conjunction with the CS. Once the conditioning is completed, the CS alone elicits a response (the CR).

Classical conditioning accomplishes two functions. First, the ability to learn to recognize stimuli that predict the occurrence of an important event allows the learner to make the appropriate response faster and perhaps more effectively. For example, hearing the buzz of a wasp near your head may make you duck and allow you to avoid being stung. Seeing a rival increases an animal's heart rate and the flow of blood to its muscles, makes it assume a threatening posture, and causes the release of hormones that prepare it for vigorous exercise. Indeed, Hollis (1982) found that male Siamese fighting fish were more likely to win fights if they were given a stimulus (CS) warning that an intruding male (UCS) would soon enter their territory. She and her colleagues (Hollis, Cadieus, and Colbert, 1989) also found that male blue gouramis (another species of fish) were more likely to mate and less likely to attack when they received a stimulus (CS) warning them of the approach of a female (UCS).

The second function of classical conditioning is even more significant. Through classical conditioning, stimuli that were previously unimportant acquire some of the properties of the important stimuli with which they have been associated and thus become able to modify behavior. A neutral stimulus becomes desirable when it is associated with a desirable stimulus or it becomes undesirable when it is associated with an undesirable one. In a sense, the stimulus takes on symbolic value. For example, we respond differently to the sight of a stack of money than to a stack of paper napkins. The reason for the special reaction to money is that money has, in the past, been associated with desirable commodities, such as food, clothing, automobiles, electronic devices, and so on.

Basic Principles of Classical Conditioning

Pavlov's research soon led to the discovery of several interesting phenomena that still bear the names he gave them seventy years ago (Pavlov, 1927). These include *acquisition, extinction, spontaneous recovery, stimulus generalization,* and *discrimination.*

Acquisition

In laboratory experiments, a single pairing of the CS with the UCS is not usually sufficient for learning to take place. Only with repeated CS–UCS pairings does conditional responding gradually appear (although there are important exceptions, as we'll soon see). The learning phase of classical conditioning, during which the CS gradually increases in frequency or strength, is called **acquisition**. (During this phase, the CS is *acquired.*) The left side of Figure 5.5 shows a learning curve that illustrates the course of acquisition of a conditional eyeblink response in two human subjects. (See *Figure 5.5.*) In this study, a tone (CS) was paired with a puff of air into the eye (UCS). The puff of air caused the subjects' eyes to blink automatically (UCR). Conditioning was measured as the per-

Advertisers often use classical conditioning to associate their products with happy and attractive young people. What is the message that this advertiser is attempting to send to passing motorists?

acquisition In classical conditioning, the time during which a CR first appears and increases in frequency.

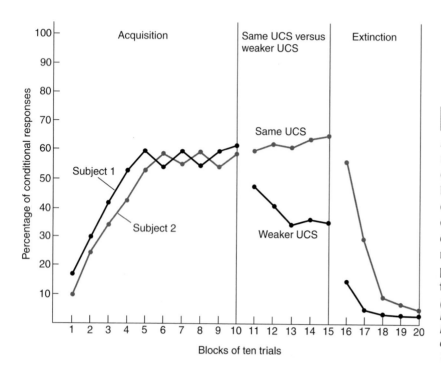

Figure 5.5

Acquisition and extinction of a conditional response. The left panel shows the learning curve for acquisition of an eyeblink response by two people. The middle panel shows a decrease in the percentage of CRs (eyeblinks) elicited by the CS (tone) when the intensity of the UCS (puff of air) was reduced. The right panel shows the extinction curves produced when the CS (tone) was no longer followed by the UCS (puff of air).

(Adapted from Trapold, M. A. and Spence, K. W. Performance changes in eyelid conditioning as related to the motivational and reinforcing properties of the UCS. Journal of Experimental Psychology, 1960, 59, p. 212.)

centage of trials in which conditional eyeblinks (CR) occurred. Note that at the beginning of the experiment, the tone elicited very few CRs. During the first fifty trials, the percentage of CRs increased rapidly but finally stabilized.

Two factors that influence the strength of the CR are the *intensity of the UCS* and the *timing of the CS and UCS*. The intensity of the UCS can determine how quickly the CR will be acquired: more intense UCSs usually produce more rapid learning. For example, rats will learn a conditioned fear response faster if they receive higher levels of a painful stimulus (Annau and Kamin, 1961). Classical conditioning of a salivary response in dogs occurs faster when the animals are given larger amounts of food (Wagner et al., 1964).

Generally speaking, the more intense the UCS, the stronger the CR. Look at the middle panel of Figure 5.5. (See *Figure 5.5*.) After 100 conditioning trials, Subject 1 was given a less intense puff of air, while Subject 2 received the same UCS intensity as before. The percentage of CRs elicited from Subject 1 decreased soon after the intensity of the air puff was diminished and leveled off at about 35 percent. This value represents the highest level of conditional responding that can be maintained by the weaker UCS.

The second factor affecting the acquisition of the CR is the timing of the CS and UCS. Classical conditioning occurs fastest when the CS occurs shortly before the UCS and both stimuli end at the same time. In his experiments on salivary

conditioning, Pavlov found that one-half second was the optimal delay between the onset of the CS and the onset of the UCS. With shorter or longer delays between the CS and UCS, conditioning generally was slower and weaker. (See *Figure 5.6*.)

Extinction and Spontaneous Recovery

Once a classically conditioned response has been acquired, what happens to that response if the CS continues to be presented but is no longer followed by the UCS? This procedure, called **extinction**, eventually eliminates the CR. Returning to

extinction   In classical conditioning, the elimination of a response that occurs when the CS is repeatedly presented without being followed by the UCS.

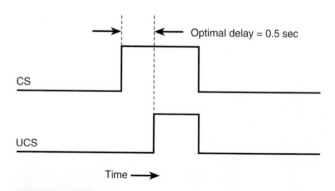

Figure 5.6

The timing of the CS and UCS in classical conditioning. The CS precedes the UCS by a brief interval of time, and both stimuli end simultaneously.

our classically conditioned eyeblink response, suppose that after we reduce the intensity of the UCS, we stop presenting the UCS (the puff of air). However, we do continue to present the CS (the tone). The third panel of Figure 5.5 shows the results of our extinction procedure. (See *Figure 5.5.*) CRs become less frequent, and eventually they cease altogether. Note that extinction occurs more rapidly for Subject 1, which indicates that extinction is affected by the UCS intensity. Thus, once CRs are formed, they do not necessarily remain a part of an organism's behavior.

It is important to realize that extinction occurs only when the CS occurs but the UCS does not. For example, the eyeblink response will extinguish only if the tone is presented without the puff of air. If *neither* stimulus is presented, extinction will not occur. In other words, the subject must learn that the CS no longer predicts the occurrence of the UCS—and that cannot happen if neither stimulus is presented.

Once a CR has been extinguished, it may not disappear from the organism's behavior permanently. Pavlov demonstrated that after responding had been extinguished, the CR would often suddenly reappear the next time the dog was placed in the experimental apparatus. Pavlov referred to the CR's reappearance after a "time out" period as **spontaneous recovery**. He also found that if he began presenting the CS and the UCS together again, the animals would acquire the conditional response very rapidly—much faster than they did in the first place.

Stimulus Generalization and Discrimination

No two stimuli are exactly alike. Once a response has been conditioned to a CS, similar stimuli will also elicit that response. The more closely the other stimuli resemble the CS, the more likely they will elicit the CR. For example, Pavlov discovered that once a dog learned to salivate when it heard a bell, it would salivate when it heard a bell having a different tone or when it heard a buzzer. This phenomenon is called **generalization**: A response produced by a particular CS will also occur when a similar CS is presented. Of course, there are limits to generalization. A dog that learns to salivate when it hears a bell will probably not salivate when it hears a door close in the hallway.

In addition, an organism can be taught to distinguish between similar but different stimuli—a phenomenon called **discrimination**. (The term *discrimination* means "to distin-

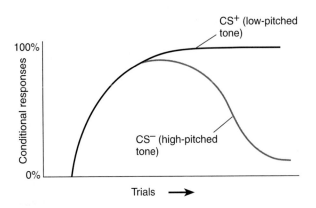

Figure 5.7

Behavior produced through discrimination training. The CS⁺ is always followed by the UCS (a puff of air directed toward the eye); the CS⁻ is always presented without the UCS.

guish.") Discrimination training is accomplished by using two different CSs during training. One CS is *always* followed by the UCS; the other CS is *never* followed by the UCS. For example, suppose that we regularly direct a puff of air at an animal's eye during each trial in which a low-pitched tone (CS⁺) is sounded, but on trials in which a high-pitched tone (CS⁻) is sounded, we present no air puff. At first, increased amounts of blinking will occur in response to both stimuli (generalization). Gradually, however, fewer and fewer blinks will occur after the CS⁻, but they will continue to be elicited by the CS⁺. (See *Figure 5.7.*) Discrimination, then, involves learning the difference between two or more stimuli. An animal learns that differences among stimuli are important—it learns when to respond to one stimulus and when not to respond to a different stimulus.

Conditional Emotional Responses

Many stimuli are able to arouse emotional responses, such as feelings of disgust, contempt, fear, anger, sadness, tenderness, longing, or sexual desire. Many of these stimuli, such as a place, a phrase, a song, or someone's voice and face, originally had no special significance. But because these stimuli were paired with other stimuli that elicited strong emotional reactions, they came, through classical conditioning, to take on emotional significance.

If you read or hear words such as *enemy, ugly, bitter,* or *failure,* you are likely to experience at least a weak negative emotional response. In contrast, the words *gift, win, happy,* and *beauty* may elicit positive responses. These words had no effect on you before you learned what they meant. They took on their power through being paired with pleasant or unpleasant events or perhaps with descriptions of such events.

spontaneous recovery After an interval of time, the reappearance of a response that had previously been extinguished.

generalization In classical conditioning, CRs elicited by stimuli that resemble the CS used in training.

discrimination In classical conditioning, the appearance of a CR when one stimulus is presented (the CS+) but not another (the CS−)

Staats and Staats (1957) found that if people read neutral nonsense words such as *yof* or *laj* while hearing positive or negative words, they later said that they liked those that had been associated with the positive words and disliked those that had been associated with the negative ones. The researchers found that this procedure could even affect people's ratings of the pleasantness of names such as Tom or Bill or nationalities such as Italian or Swedish (Staats and Staats, 1958). Berkowitz (1964) found that when people had received unpleasant electrical shocks while in the company of another person, they later acted in a hostile manner toward that person. Thus, classical conditioning may play a role in the development of ethnic prejudices and personal dislikes (and, of course, of positive reactions as well). We are often not aware of the reason for our emotional reactions. We simply feel them and conclude that there is something "nice" or something "nasty" about the stimulus (or the person).

Many people are troubled by behaviors that they wish they could stop or by thoughts and fears that bother them. **Phobias** are unreasonable fears of specific objects or situations, such as spiders, automobiles, or enclosed spaces. Presumably, at some time early in life, the person having the phobia was exposed to the now-fearsome object in conjunction with a stimulus that elicited pain or fear. For example, being stuck in a hot, overcrowded elevator with a group of frightened and sweating fellow passengers might be expected to lead to a fear of elevators or perhaps even to produce a full-fledged phobia.

Classical conditioning can occur even without direct experience with the conditional and unconditional stimuli. For example, a child of a parent who has a snake phobia can develop the same fear simply by observing signs of fear in his or her parent. The child need not be attacked or menaced by a snake. In addition, people can develop phobias vicariously—by hearing about or reading stories that vividly describe unpleasant episodes. The imaginary episode that we picture as we hear or read a story (UCS) can provide imaginary stimuli (CSs) that lead to *real* conditional emotional responses (CRs).

Fetishes, unusual sexual attachments to objects such as articles of clothing, also develop through classical conditioning. These attachments probably occur because of a prior association of a stimulus that most people find neutral with sexual stimuli. One possible scenario is that of a teenage boy looking at sexually arousing pictures of women wearing high-heeled shoes. His arousal may become conditioned to the shoes worn by the women, and the boy may subsequently become a shoe fetishist. Of course, fetishism cannot be that simple; there must be other factors operating, too. Some people are undoubtedly more susceptible than others to develop-

Through classical conditioning, we come to respond emotionally to particular stimuli. Conditional emotional responses such as crying are often elicited by significant events such as defeat in an important game.

ing fetishes. For example, women very rarely develop them. Nevertheless, the process by which the attachment occurs most likely involves classical conditioning.

In a rather unusual study of fetishes, Rachman and Hodgson (1968) conditioned a sexual response to an object popular among fetishists, women's knee-length boots. Their subjects, young single males, were first shown a color slide of the boots, then a slide of an attractive, naked woman. Sexual arousal was measured by a device called a *plethysmograph*, which measures changes in an object's size. In this case, the plethysmograph was attached to the men's penises to make an accurate record of the size of their erections.

The pairing of the boots as a conditional stimulus and the pictures of naked women as unconditional stimuli resulted in classical conditioning: The subjects' penises enlarged in response to the slide of the boots alone. The subjects' responses also generalized to color slides of shoes. Repeated presentation of the boots alone (without the naked women) eventually led to decreases in the males' sexual arousal. That is, the conditioned response was extinguished.

If classical conditioning is responsible for the development of phobias and fetishes, then perhaps a knowledge of the principles of learning can be used to eliminate them. In fact, therapists have done exactly that; I will discuss the therapeutic procedures they have devised in Chapter 18.

What Is Learned in Classical Conditioning?

Recent research has shown that for classical conditioning to occur, the CS must be a reliable predictor of the UCS (Rescorla, 1988). Imagine yourself as the subject in a classical conditioning demonstration involving a tone as the CS, a puff of

phobia Unreasonable fear of specific objects or situations, such as insects, animals, or enclosed spaces, learned through classical conditioning.

fetish Unusual sexual attachment to objects such as articles of clothing, learned through classical conditioning.

air into your left eye as the UCS, and an eyeblink as the CR. Your psychology professor asks you to come to the front of the class and seats you in a comfortable chair. Occasionally, a tone sounds for a second or two, and then a brief but strong puff of air hits your eye. The puff of air makes you blink. Soon you begin to blink during the tone, before the puff occurs. Now consider all the other stimuli in the classroom— your teacher explaining the demonstration to the class, your classmates' questions, squeaks from students moving in their chairs, and so on. Why don't any of these sounds become CSs? Why do you blink only during the tone? After all, some of these stimuli occur at the same time as the puff of air. The answer is that among the stimuli present during the demonstration, only the tone reliably predicts the puff of air. All the other stimuli are poor forecasters of the UCS. The neutral stimulus becomes a CS only when the following conditions are satisfied:

- The CS must regularly occur prior to the presentation of the UCS.
- The CS does *not* regularly occur when the UCS is absent.

This is just another way of saying what I've said before: The key factor in classical conditioning is the reliability of the CS in predicting the presentation of the UCS (Rescorla, 1966).

Consider another example. The smell of food is more likely to elicit feelings of anticipation and excitement about supper than is the smell of your mother's cologne or the sound of the furnace because the smell of the food is the best predictor of a meal about to be served. Likewise, the sound of footsteps behind you as you are walking is more apt to make you afraid than the sound of a car passing by or the wind blowing in the trees because the footsteps are better predictors of being mugged or threatened with danger.

Interim Summary

Habituation and Classical Conditioning

So far, we have considered two forms of learning: habituation and classical conditioning. Habituation screens out stimuli that experience has shown to be unimportant. This form of learning allows organisms to respond to more important stimuli, such as those related to survival and reproduction.

Classical conditioning occurs when a neutral stimulus occurs just before an unconditional stimulus (UCS)—one that automatically elicits a behavior. The response that an organism makes in response to the unconditional stimulus (the UCR) is already a natural part of its behavior; what the organism learns to do is to make it in response to a new stimulus (the conditional stimulus, or CS). When the response is made to the CS, it is called the conditional response, or CR.

The relationship between the conditional stimulus and unconditional stimulus determines the nature of the conditional response. Acquisition of the conditional response is in-

fluenced by the intensity of the unconditional stimulus and the delay between the conditional stimulus and unconditional stimulus. Extinction occurs when the conditional stimulus is still presented but is no longer followed by the unconditional stimulus. However, the conditional response may show spontaneous recovery later, even after a delay. Generalization occurs when stimuli similar to the conditional stimulus used in training elicit the conditional response. Discrimination involves training the organism to make a conditional response only after a particular conditional stimulus occurs.

Through classical conditioning, stimuli that were previously neutral with respect to an organism's behavior can be made to become important. This importance can have profound effects on a limitless variety of behaviors. For example, the importance of money, established through classical conditioning, affects a broad range of our behavior. Many of the emotions we feel when we encounter a person, place, or object that has been previously associated with a pleasant or unpleasant situation are acquired through classical conditioning. This phenomenon explains why we sometimes feel a touch of nostalgia when we hear a song that reminds us of a friend we have not seen for a long time. Classical conditioning can also establish various classes of stimuli as objects of fear (phobia) or of sexual attraction (fetishes). For classical conditioning to occur, the conditional stimulus must not only occur immediately before the unconditional stimulus, but it must also reliably predict the occurrence of the unconditional stimulus.

Thought Questions

- Can you think of a personal situation in which an orienting response might *not* habituate? Describe this situation.
- Do you think it would take longer for a response to habituate to a stimulus associated with danger (for example, the lights and sounds signaling that a train is approaching) or to a stimulus associated with a nondangerous situation, such as the hourly chiming of a grandfather clock? Explain.
- Reflect for a few moments on a recent situation in which you felt a strong emotion. What aspects of the situation contributed to this emotion? Can you describe the situation in terms of the elements of the classical conditioning paradigm?
- Under what set of conditions might the emotion you just described be generalized to other situations? Under what set of conditions would this emotion not be generalized to other situations?

Operant Conditioning

Habituation and classical conditioning teach us about stimuli in the environment: We learn to ignore unimportant stimuli, and we learn about those that predict the occurrence

Students' raising of their hands in response to their teacher's questions is reinforced by the opportunity to speak and receive attention from their teacher.

of important ones. These forms of learning deal with relations between one stimulus and another. In contrast, **operant conditioning** teaches us the relations between environmental stimuli and our own behavior. (The term *operant* refers to the fact that an organism learns through responding— through *operating* on the environment.) The principle behind operant conditioning is already familiar to you: When a particular action has good consequences, the action will tend to be repeated; when a particular action has bad consequences, the action will tend not to be repeated.

The Law of Effect

As we saw in Chapter 1, operant conditioning was first discovered in the basement of a house in Cambridge, Massachusetts, by a twenty-four-year-old man who would later become one of this century's most influential educational psychologists, Edward L. Thorndike. Thorndike placed a hungry cat inside a "puzzle box." The animal could escape and eat some food only after it operated a latch that opened the door. At first, the cat engaged in random behavior: meowing, scratching, hissing, pacing, and so on. Eventually, the cat would accidentally activate the latch and open the door. On successive trials, the animal's behavior would become more and more efficient until it was operating the latch without hesitation. Thorndike called this process "learning by trial and accidental success."

Thorndike explained that the cat learned to make the correct response because only the correct response was followed by a favorable outcome: escape from the box and the opportunity to eat some food. The occurrence of the favorable outcome strengthens the response that produced it. Thorndike called this relation between a response and its consequences the **law of effect**.

As you can see, the law of effect is analogous to the concept of natural selection, a point made by Thorndike himself. Natural selection determines which members of a species will survive and reproduce. The law of effect determines which responses will survive and become part of the organism's behavioral repertoire. As Skinner (1981, 1990) noted, it is a sort of selection by consequences. The ability to adjust behavior to fit particular changes in the environment is highly adaptive.

The impact of Thorndike's discovery of the law of effect on the early development of scientific psychology would be difficult to overstate. It affected research in the study of learning in one very important way: It stimulated an enormous number of experimental studies aimed at understanding behavior-environment interactions, a line of research that is known today as *behavior analysis*. Nowhere was this effect more evident than in the work of B. F. Skinner, to which we now turn.

Skinner and Operant Behavior

Although Thorndike discovered the law of effect, Harvard psychologist Burrhus Frederic Skinner championed the laboratory study of the law of effect and advocated the application of behavior analysis and its methods to solving human problems (Skinner, 1953, 1971; Mazur, 1994). He devised objective methods for studying behavior, invented apparatus and methods for observing it, and created his own philosophy for interpreting it (Bolles, 1979). Moreover, he wrote several books for the general public, including a novel, *Walden Two*, that showed how his discoveries might be used for bettering society (Skinner, 1948).

One of Skinner's most important inventions was the **operant chamber**, an apparatus in which an animal's behavior can be easily observed, manipulated, and automatically recorded. (See *Figure 5.8.*) For example, an operant chamber used for rats is constructed so that a particular behavior, such as pressing on a lever, will occasionally cause a pellet of food to be delivered. An operant chamber used for pigeons is built

operant conditioning A form of learning in which behavior is affected by its consequences. Favorable consequences strengthen the behavior and unfavorable consequences weaken the behavior.

law of effect Thorndike's idea that the consequences of a behavior determine whether that behavior is likely to be repeated.

operant chamber An apparatus in which an animal's behavior can be easily observed, manipulated, and automatically recorded.

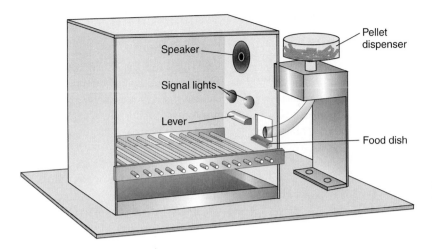

Speaker

Signal lights

Lever

Pellet dispenser

Food dish

Figure 5.8

An operant chamber. (This operant chamber is used for lever pressing in rats.)

so that a peck at a plastic disk on the front wall will occasionally open a drawer that contains some grain. Behavior analysts who study human behavior use special devices suitable to the unique characteristics of their human subjects (Baron, Perone, and Galizio, 1991). In this case, instead of giving their subjects some food, they give them points (as in a video game) or points exchangeable for money.

Behavior analysts manipulate environmental events to determine their effects on *response rate*, the number of responses emitted during a given amount of time. Events that increase response rate are said to *strengthen* responding; events that decrease response rate *weaken* responding. To measure response rate, Skinner devised the **cumulative recorder**, a device that records each response as it occurs in time.

The invention of the operant chamber and the cumulative recorder represent clear advances over Thorndike's research methods because subjects can (1) emit responses more freely over a greater time period and (2) be studied for longer periods of time without interference produced by the experimenter handling or otherwise interacting with them between trials. Under highly controlled conditions such as these, behavior analysts have been able to discover a wide range of important behavioral principles.

The Three-Term Contingency

Behavior does not occur in a vacuum. Sometimes a response will have certain consequences; sometimes it will not. Suppose that you want to teach your dog to bark whenever you say the word speak. You get a few pieces of food that the dog likes. Then you attract its attention and say, "Speak!" while waving a piece of food in front of it. The dog begins to show signs of excitement at the sight of the food and finally lets out a bark. Immediately, you give it the food. Then you bring out another piece of food and again say, "Speak!" This time the dog probably barks a little sooner. After several trials, the dog will bark whenever you say, "Speak!" even if no food is visible. You do not give your dog a piece of food whenever it barks. You only do so if you have just said, "Speak!" If the dog barks

at other times, you ignore it or even tell it to be quiet. Your dog learns to discriminate between times when barking will get him a piece of food and times when it will not. The word *speak* serves as a **discriminative stimulus**—a stimulus that indicates that behavior will have certain consequences and thus sets the occasion for responding.

Our daily behavior is guided by many different kinds of discriminative stimuli. For example, consider answering the telephone. The phone rings, you pick it up and say, "Hello," into the receiver. Most of the time, someone on the other end of the line begins to speak. Have you ever picked up a telephone when it was *not* ringing and said, "Hello"? Doing so would be absurd, because there would be no one on the other end of the line with whom to speak. We answer the phone (make a response) only when the phone rings (the preceding event) because, in the past, someone with whom we enjoy talking has been at the other end of the line (the following event).

Skinner referred formally to the relationship among these three items—the preceding event, the response, and the following event—as the **three-term contingency**. He also made the following observations about these components. (See *Figure 5.9.*)

- The preceding event—the *discriminative stimulus*—sets the occasion for responding because, in the past, when that stimulus occurred, the response was followed by

cumulative recorder A mechanical device connected to an operant chamber for the purpose of recording operant responses as they occur in time.

discriminative stimulus In operant conditioning, the stimulus that sets the occasion for responding because, in the past, a behavior has produced certain consequences in the presence of that stimulus.

three-term contingency The relation among discriminative stimuli, behavior, and the consequences of that behavior. A motivated organism emits a specific response in the presence of a discriminative stimulus because, in the past, that response has been reinforced only when the discriminative stimulus is present.

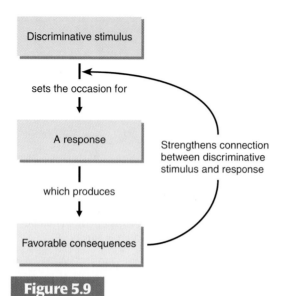

Figure 5.9

The three-term contingency.

certain consequences. If the phone rings, we are likely to answer it because we have learned that doing so has particular (and generally favorable) consequences.

- The *response* we make—in this case, picking up the phone and saying, "Hello," when the phone rings—is called an *operant behavior.*

- The *following event*—the voice on the other end of the line—is the consequence of the operant behavior.

In other words, an operant behavior occurs in the presence of discriminative stimuli and is followed by certain consequences. These consequences are *contingent* upon behavior; that is, they are produced by that behavior. In the presence of discriminative stimuli, a consequence will occur *if and only if* an operant behavior occurs. In the absence of a discriminative stimulus, the operant behavior will have no effect. Once an operant behavior is established, it tends to persist whenever the discriminative stimulus occurs, even if other aspects of the environment change (Nevin, 1988; Mace et al. 1990). Of course, motivational factors can affect a response. For example, if your dog is not hungry, it might not bother to bark when you say, "Speak!" and you might not bother to answer the telephone if you are doing something you do not want to interrupt. I will discuss the role of motivation in behavior in Chapter 13.

---

positive reinforcement An increase in the frequency of a response that is regularly and reliably followed by an appetitive stimulus.

negative reinforcement An increase in the frequency of a response that is regularly and reliably followed by the termination of an aversive stimulus.

Reinforcement, Punishment, and Extinction

Behavior analysts study behavior-environment interactions by manipulating the relations among components of the three-term contingency. Of the three elements, the consequence is the most frequently manipulated variable. In general, operant behaviors can be followed by five different kinds of consequences: positive reinforcement, negative reinforcement, punishment, response cost, and extinction. These consequences are always defined in terms of their effect on responding.

Positive Reinforcement

Positive reinforcement is an increase in the frequency of a response that is regularly and reliably followed by an appetitive stimulus. An *appetitive stimulus* is any stimulus that an organism seeks out. If an appetitive stimulus follows a response and increases the frequency of that response, we call it a *positive reinforcer.* For example, the opportunity to eat some food can reinforce a hungry pigeon's pecking of a plastic disk. Money or other rewards (including social rewards) can reinforce a person's behavior. Suppose that you visit a new restaurant and really enjoy your meal. You are likely to visit the restaurant several more times because you like the food. This example illustrates positive reinforcement. Your enjoyment of the food (the appetitive stimulus) reinforces your going to the restaurant and ordering dinner (the response).

Negative Reinforcement

Negative reinforcement is an increase in the frequency of a response that is regularly and reliably followed by the termination of an *aversive stimulus.* An aversive stimulus is unpleasant or painful. If an aversive stimulus is terminated (ends or is turned off) as soon as a response occurs and thus

Our use of umbrellas when it is raining out is a negatively reinforced behavior. Opening an umbrella blocks the rain that would otherwise fall on us.

increases the frequency of that response, we call it a *negative reinforcer*. For example, after you have walked barefoot across a stretch of hot pavement, the termination of the painful burning sensation negatively reinforces your response of sticking your feet into a puddle of cool water. Or suppose that a woman staying in a rented house cannot get to sleep because of the unpleasant screeching noise that the furnace makes. She goes to the basement to discover the source of the noise and finally kicks the side of the oil burner. The noise ceases. The next time the furnace screeches, she immediately goes to the basement and kicks the side of the oil burner. This example, too, illustrates negative reinforcement. The unpleasant noise (the aversive stimulus) is terminated when the woman kicks the side of the oil burner (the response).

It is important to remember that both positive and negative reinforcement *increase* the likelihood that a given response will occur again. However, positive reinforcement involves the *occurrence* of an *appetitive* stimulus, whereas negative reinforcement involves the *termination* of an *aversive* stimulus. Negative reinforcement is thus *not* the same as punishment (which I describe next).

Punishment

Punishment is a decrease in the frequency of a response that is regularly and reliably followed by an aversive stimulus. If an aversive stimulus follows a response and decreases the frequency of that response, we call it a *punisher*. For example, receiving a painful bite would punish the response of sticking your finger into a parrot's cage. Parents often attempt to punish the behavior of their children or pets by scolding them. Consider a woman who returns home from work and discovers that her dog has soiled the carpet. The dog runs to greet her, and she says, "Bad dog," and slaps him. When she comes home the next day, she calls her dog; but he stays where he is, hiding under the bed. Why do you think the dog hides?

This example illustrates punishment, but not of the response that the woman intends. The response she punishes is the one that the dog has just made: running up to her when she enters the door. Because the dog soiled the rug some time ago, that response is not punished.

Although punishment is effective in reducing or suppressing undesirable behavior, it can also produce several negative side effects:

- Unrestrained use of physical force (for example, child abuse) may cause serious bodily injury.
- Punishment often induces fear, hostility, and other undesirable emotions in people receiving punishment. It may result in retaliation against the punisher.
- Through punishment, organisms learn only which response *not* to make. Punishment does not teach the organism desirable responses.

Reinforcement and punishment are most effective in maintaining or changing behavior when a stimulus *immediately* follows the behavior. The example of the woman and

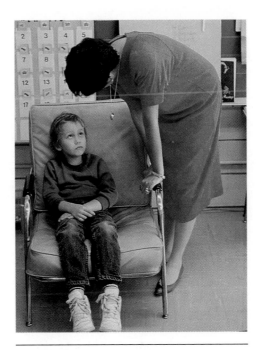

Punishment occurs when a punishing stimulus immediately follows a response. This teacher is scolding a child for misbehaving.

the dog illustrates this principle. It may occur to you that many organisms—particularly humans—can tolerate a long delay between their work and the reward that they receive for it. This ability appears to contradict the principle that reinforcement must occur immediately. However, the apparent contradiction can be explained by a phenomenon called conditioned reinforcement, which I will discuss later in this chapter.

Why is immediacy of reinforcement or punishment essential for learning? The answer is found by examining the function of operant conditioning: learning about the consequences of our own behavior. Normally, causes and effects are closely related in time; you do something, and something immediately happens, good or bad. The consequences of our action teach us whether to repeat that action. Events that follow a response by a long delay were probably not caused by that response.

Response Cost

Response cost is a decrease in the frequency of a response that is regularly and reliably followed by the termination of an appetitive stimulus. Response cost is a form of punish-

punishment A decrease in the frequency of a response that is regularly and reliably followed by an aversive stimulus.

response cost A decrease in the frequency of a response that is regularly and reliably followed by the termination of an appetitive stimulus.

ment. For example, suppose that you are enjoying a conversation with an attractive person that you have just met. You make a disparaging remark about a well-known politician. Your new friend's smile suddenly disappears. You quickly change the topic and never bring it up again. The behavior (disparaging remark) is followed by the removal of an appetitive stimulus (your new friend's smile). The removal of the smile punishes the disparaging remark.

Response cost is often referred to as *time-out from positive reinforcement* (or simply *time-out*) when it is used to remove a person physically from an activity that is reinforcing to that person. For example, suppose that a young boy is tormenting his little sister while they are watching television. Their mother might say to him, "That's enough! No more television for you today! Go to your room!" The boy can no longer engage in the activity he enjoys (watching television) after he is sent out of the room.

It is important not to confuse punishment with negative reinforcement. Punishment causes a behavior to *decrease,* whereas negative reinforcement causes a behavior to *increase.* (That is probably a good rule to memorize.)

As we have just seen, there are four types of operant conditioning—two kinds of reinforcement and two kinds of punishment—caused by the occurrence or termination of appetitive or aversive stimuli. (See *Figure 5.10.*) Another way

to change behavior through operant conditioning is extinction, which involves no consequence at all.

Extinction

Extinction is a decrease in the frequency of a previously reinforced response because it is no longer followed by a reinforcer. Behavior that is no longer reinforced decreases in frequency—it is said to *extinguish.* For example, a rat whose lever pressing was reinforced previously with food will eventually stop pressing the lever when food is no longer delivered. People soon learn to stop dropping money into vending machines that don't work. A young boy will stop telling his favorite "knock-knock" joke if no one laughs at it any more.

Extinction is not the same as forgetting. Forgetting takes place when a behavior is not rehearsed (or a person does not think about a particular memory) for a long time. Extinction takes place when an organism makes a response that is no longer reinforced. If the organism does not have an opportunity to make that response, it will not extinguish. For example, if you go out of town for a few weeks, you will not forget how to operate the vending machine where you often buy a candy bar. But if you put money in the machine and do not receive anything in return, your response will extinguish.

Extinction makes good sense. If a response no longer "works," there is no point in persisting in making it. In fact, doing so expends energy unnecessarily and keeps an organism from discovering a different response that will work.

Other Operant Procedures and Phenomena

The basic principles of reinforcement, punishment, and extinction described above are used in other operant procedures to teach an organism a new response, to teach it when or when not to respond, or to teach it how to respond in a particular way. Let's examine some of these other operant procedures.

Shaping

Most behavior is acquired through an organism's interaction with reinforcing and punishing events in its environment. In fact, Skinner developed a technique, called **shaping,** to teach new behaviors to his subjects. Shaping involves reinforcing any behavior that *successively approximates* the desired response. Suppose that we want to train a rat to press a lever when a red light is lit (the discriminative stimulus) in an operant chamber. Although the rat has used its paws to manip-

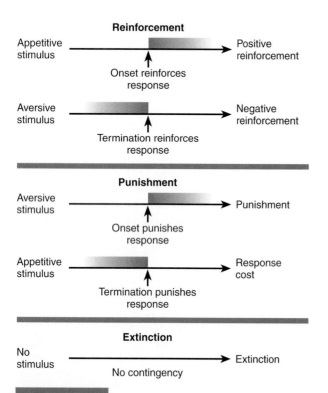

Figure 5.10

Reinforcement, punishment, and extinction produced by the onset, termination, or omission of appetitive or aversive stimuli. The upward pointing arrows indicate the occurrence of a response.

extinction A decrease in the frequency of a previously reinforced response because it is no longer followed by a reinforcer.

shaping The reinforcement of behavior that successively approximates the desired response until that response is fully acquired.

ulate many things during its lifetime, it has never before pressed a lever in an operant chamber. And when it is first placed in the chamber, it is not likely to press the lever even once on its own.

The lever on the wall of the chamber is attached to an electrical switch that is wired to electronic control equipment or a computer. A mechanical dispenser can automatically drop molded pellets of food, about the size of a very small pea, into a dish in the chamber. Thus, the delivery of a food pellet can be made dependent on the rat's pressing the lever.

Before we can shape lever pressing, we must make the rat hungry. We do so by letting the animal eat only once a day. When that time comes around, we know that it is hungry. We place the animal in the operant chamber and then train it to eat the food pellets as they are dispensed from the pellet dispenser. As each pellet is delivered, the dispenser makes a clicking sound. This sound is important. No matter where the rat is in the operant chamber, it can hear the sound, which indicates that the food pellet has been dispensed. Once the rat is hungry and has learned where to obtain food, we are ready to shape the desired response. We make the operation of the pellet dispenser contingent on the rat's behavior. We start by giving the rat a food pellet for just facing in the direction of the lever. Next, we wait until the rat makes a move toward the lever. Finally, we give the rat a piece of food only if it actually touches the lever. Soon, our rat performs like Thorndike's cats: It makes the same response again and again.

Shaping is a formal training procedure, but something like it also occurs in the world outside the laboratory. A teacher praises poorly formed letters produced by a child who is just beginning to print. As time goes on, only more accurately drawn letters bring approval. The method of successive approximations can also be self-administered. Consider the acquisition of skills through trial and error. To begin with, you must be able to recognize the *target behavior*—the behavior displayed by a person having the appropriate skill. Your first attempts produce behaviors that vaguely resemble those of a skilled performer, and you are satisfied by the results of these attempts. In other words, the stimuli that are produced by your behavior serve as reinforcers for that behavior. As your skill develops, you become less satisfied with crude approximations to the final behavior; you are satisfied only when your behavior improves so that it more closely resembles the target behavior. Your own criteria change as you become more skilled. Skills such as learning to draw a picture, catching a baseball, or making a bed are all behaviors that are acquired through shaping. After all, when a child learns these skills, he or she first learns behaviors that only approximate the final level of skill that he or she will eventually obtain. This process is perfectly analogous to the use of changing criteria in training an animal to perform a complex behavior.

intermittent reinforcement The occasional reinforcement of a particular behavior; produces responding that is more resistant to extinction.

Complex behaviors, such as riding a bicycle, are not learned all at once. Instead, they are shaped; that is, we first learn behaviors that only approximate the level of skill ultimately needed to perform the behavior properly.

Intermittent Reinforcement

So far, we have considered situations in which a reinforcing stimulus is presented after each response (or, in the case of extinction, not at all). But usually, not every response is reinforced. Sometimes a kind word is ignored; sometimes it is appreciated. Not every fishing trip is rewarded with a catch, but some are, and that is enough to keep a person trying. As we'll see, the effects of intermittent reinforcement on behavior are very different from those of continuous reinforcement.

The term **intermittent reinforcement** refers to situations in which not every occurrence of a response is reinforced. The relation between responding and reinforcement usually follows one of two patterns: Each response has a certain probability of being reinforced, or responses are reinforced after particular intervals of time have elapsed.

Probability-based patterns require a variable number of responses for each reinforcer. Consider the performance of an archer shooting arrows at a target. Suppose that the archer hits the bull's-eye one-fifth of the time. On average, he will have to make five responses for every reinforcement (hitting the bull's-eye); the ratio of responding to reinforcement is five to one. The number of reinforcers the archer receives is directly proportional to the number of responses he makes. If he shoots more arrows (that is, if his rate of responding increases), he will receive more reinforcers—assuming that he does not get tired or careless.

Behavior analysts refer to this pattern of intermittent reinforcement as a *ratio schedule of reinforcement*. In the laboratory, the apparatus controlling the operant chamber may be programmed to deliver a reinforcer after every fifth response (a ratio of five to one), after every tenth, after every two hundredth, or after any desired number. If the ratio is constant—for example, if a reinforcer is programmed to be delivered following every tenth response—the animal will respond rapidly, receive the reinforcer, pause a little while, and then begin responding again. This type of ratio schedule is called a **fixed-ratio schedule** (specifically, a *fixed-ratio 10 schedule*).

If the ratio is variable, averaging a particular number of responses but varying from trial to trial, the animal will respond at a steady, rapid pace. For example, we might program a reinforcer to be delivered, on the average, after every fifty responses. This type of ratio schedule is called a **variable-ratio schedule** (specifically, *a variable-ratio 50 schedule*). A slot machine is programmed to deliver money on a variable-ratio schedule of reinforcement. Variable in this instance means that the person cannot predict how many responses will be needed for the next payoff.

The second type of pattern of reinforcement involves time. A response is reinforced, but only after a particular time interval has elapsed. A good example of behavior that is reinforced on such a schedule is fishing. One form of fishing consists of casting a lure into the water and retrieving it in such a way that it resembles a minnow (the bait). If no fish are present, none will be caught; during these times responses will not be reinforced. But every now and then, a hungry, eager-to-bite fish will swim by. If a lure is moving through the water at the same time a hungry fish is present, the angler may get a fish. After a fish is caught, another may come by soon or not for a long time. The only way to find out is to cast the lure. Clearly, the number of reinforcers anglers receive is *not* proportional to the number of casts made. Casting the lure more often will not necessarily mean catching more fish because the opportunities for catching one come only now and then.

Of course, if the angler waits too long between casts, he or she may miss catching a fish when it swims by.

This second pattern of intermittent reinforcement is called an *interval schedule of reinforcement*. After various intervals of time, a response will be reinforced. If the time intervals are fixed, the animal will stop responding after each reinforcement. It learns that responses made immediately after reinforcement are never reinforced. Then it will begin responding a little while before the next reinforcer is available. This type of interval schedule is called a **fixed-interval schedule**.

If the time intervals are variable, the animal (like the angler) will respond at a slow, steady rate. That way, it will not waste energy on useless responses, but it will not miss any opportunities for reinforcement either. This type of interval schedule is called a **variable-interval schedule.** In a variable-interval sixty-second schedule of reinforcement, a reinforcer would be delivered immediately following the first response after different time intervals had elapsed. The interval might be thirty seconds at one time, and ninety seconds at another, but, on the average, it will be sixty seconds. An animal whose behavior is reinforced by this schedule would learn not to pause immediately after a reinforcer was delivered. Instead, it would steadily respond throughout the interval, regardless of the length of the interval.

Schedules of reinforcement are important because they show us that different reinforcement contingencies affect the pattern and rate of responding. (See *Figure 5.11*.) Think about your own behavior. How would you perform in classes in which your grades were determined by a midterm and a final, or by weekly quizzes, or by unannounced quizzes that occur at variable intervals? What kind of schedule of reinforcement is a salesperson on while waiting on potential cus-

fixed-ratio schedule   A schedule of reinforcement in which reinforcement occurs only after a fixed number of responses have been made since the previous reinforcement (or the start of the session).

variable-ratio schedule   A schedule of reinforcement similar to a fixed-ratio schedule but characterized by a variable response requirement having a particular mean.

fixed-interval schedule   A schedule of reinforcement in which the first response that is made after a fixed interval of time since the previous reinforcement (or the start of the session) is reinforced.

variable-interval schedule   A schedule of reinforcement similar to a fixed-interval schedule but characterized by a variable time requirement having a particular mean.

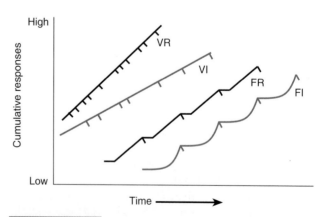

Figure 5.11

Rate of responding as controlled by each of the following schedules: Variable-ratio, variable-interval, fixed-ratio, and fixed-interval. The steepness of each curve represents speed of responding: The steeper the curve, the faster the responding. A pause in responding is represented by a horizontal line. The tick marks under each line represent delivery of a reinforcer.

tomers? Some people work at a slow, steady rate, but others work furiously after long periods of inactivity. Can it be that in the past their work habits were shaped by different schedules of reinforcement?

Resistance to Extinction and Intermittent Reinforcement

Suppose that we train two pigeons to peck at a plastic disk mounted on the wall of an operant chamber by reinforcing these responses with the opportunity to eat a small amount of food. We train the animals for twenty daily sessions of thirty minutes each, but we train the two animals differently. We give the first bird some food every time it pecks the disk. We train the second bird the same way at first, but then we begin reinforcing every third response on the average—that is, we institute a variable-ratio 3 schedule. Each day, we increase the number of responses required for reinforcement until the bird is making an average of fifty responses for each reinforcer.

Now, suppose that we stop reinforcing responding altogether; we put both birds on an extinction schedule. We find that the behavior of the first bird, accustomed to receiving food each time it responds, soon extinguishes. However, the second bird persists and makes thousands of responses before it finally quits. Why?

The behavior of the birds illustrates the following rule: A response that has been reinforced intermittently is more re-

---

Highly skilled professional athletes, such as Michael Jordan, make complicated plays seem easy. We often fail to appreciate the many thousands of hours of practice and study that make the learning of such graceful behaviors possible.

sistant to extinction. The more responses an organism has had to make for each reinforcement, the longer it will respond during extinction. Continuous reinforcement (that is, reinforcement after every response) is very different from extinction. The very first nonreinforced response signals that conditions have changed. In contrast, intermittent reinforcement and extinction are more similar. An organism whose behavior has been reinforced intermittently has had a lot of experience making nonreinforced responses. The animal cannot readily detect the fact that responses are no longer being reinforced—that the contingencies have changed. Therefore, the behavior extinguishes more slowly.

As you know, some people keep trying, even if they have difficulty succeeding. Other people seem to give up when they encounter the smallest difficulty. Perhaps one of the reasons for differences in people's perseverance is their past experience with different types of schedules of reinforcement. I will explore this possibility further in Chapter 13, which considers the variables that affect motivation.

Generalization and Discrimination

In classical conditioning, generalization means that stimuli resembling the CS also elicit the CR. In operant conditioning, **generalization** means that stimuli resembling a discriminative stimulus also serve as discriminative stimuli for a particular response.

In operant conditioning, as in classical conditioning, generalization can be reduced through discrimination training. In classical conditioning, discrimination means that CRs occur only in response to certain CSs and not to other similar stimuli. In operant conditioning, **discrimination** means that responding occurs only when a particular discriminative stimulus is present—one that was present while responding was reinforced in the past. Responding does *not* occur when discriminative stimuli associated with extinction or punishment are present.

Through discrimination training, organisms can be trained to recognize very complex similarities; that is, they can learn to recognize particular concepts. For example, Herrnstein and Loveland (1964) trained pigeons to respond to the concept of a human being. First, they trained the birds to peck at a translucent plastic disk. Then they assembled a set of more than a thousand color slides. Some of the slides contained photographs of humans, depicted in a wide variety of scenes and poses. Other slides did not contain human figures. Herrnstein and Loveland selected a group of slides, with and without human figures, from the larger set and projected them on the translucent disk, where the birds could see them.

generalization In operant conditioning, the occurrence of responding when a stimulus similar (but not identical) to the discriminative stimulus is present.

discrimination In operant conditioning, responding only when a specific discriminative stimulus is present but not when similar stimuli are present.

Figure 5.12

A pigeon trained by Herrnstein and Loveland (1964), would be able to respond correctly to the presence of a human being in one of these two slides.

Then they started discrimination training. When a human figure was projected, pecking was reinforced; that is, food was presented only if the pigeon pecked the disk when a slide containing a human being was shown. When the projected image was that of a scene that did not contain a human, pecking was not reinforced (no food was presented). Thus, a disk containing no human figure was the discriminative stimulus that signaled extinction. (See *Figure 5.12.*)

The birds quickly learned to respond to the concept of a human being. Their performance on the original set of slides generalized to slides that they had not seen before. The birds became as good as the experimenters at detecting whether a human figure was present in an image. In fact, in one instance, the birds outperformed the humans. They pecked when they saw a slide that supposedly did not contain a human. When the experimenters looked at the slide more carefully, they dis-

primary reinforcer A biologically significant appetitive stimulus, such as food or water.

primary punisher A biologically significant aversive stimuli, such as pain.

conditioned (or secondary) reinforcer (or punisher)
A stimulus that acquires its reinforcing (or punishing) properties through association with a primary reinforcer (or punisher). Sometimes referred to as a secondary reinforcer (or punisher).

covered a tiny image of a person hidden away in a corner that they had missed when they had first sorted the slides.

Obviously, recognizing certain kinds of similarities between different categories of stimuli is a very important task in our everyday lives. When we encounter a problem to solve—for example, diagnosing a puzzling disease or improving a manufactured product—we attempt to discover elements of the situation that are similar to those we have seen in other situations and try to apply the strategies that have been successful in the past. That is, we try to generalize old solutions to new problems.

Discriminative stimuli can exert powerful control over responding because of their association with the consequences of such responding. In or out of the laboratory, we learn to behave appropriately to environmental conditions. For example, we usually talk about different things with different people. We learn that some friends do not care for sports, so we do not talk about this topic with them because we will receive few reinforcers (such as nods or smiles). Instead, we discuss topics that have interested them in the past.

Conditioned Reinforcement and Punishment

We have studied reinforcement mainly in terms of *primary reinforcers* and *primary punishers*. **Primary reinforcers** are biologically significant appetitive stimuli, such as food when one is hungry. **Primary punishers** are biologically significant aversive stimuli, such as those that produce pain. Behavior can also be reinforced with a wide variety of other stimuli: money, a smile, a hug, kind words, a pat on the back, or prizes and awards. These stimuli, called **conditioned reinforcers** (or *secondary reinforcers*), acquire their reinforcing properties through association with primary reinforcers. Because it can be exchanged for so many different kinds of primary reinforcers in our society, money is the most common conditioned reinforcer among humans. That money is a conditioned reinforcer can be demonstrated by asking yourself whether you would continue to work if you could no longer exchange money for food, drink, shelter, medical services, and other items. Likewise, **conditioned punishers** acquire their punishing effects through association with aversive events. For example, the sight of a flashing light on top of a police car serves as a conditioned punisher to a person who is driving too fast because such a sight precedes an unpleasant set of stimuli: a lecture by a police officer and a speeding ticket.

A stimulus becomes a conditioned reinforcer or punisher by means of classical conditioning. That is, if a neutral stimulus occurs regularly just before an appetitive or aversive stimulus, then the neutral stimulus itself becomes an appetitive or aversive stimulus. The primary reinforcer or punisher serves as the UCS because it produces the UCR—good or bad feelings. After classical conditioning takes place, these good or bad feelings are produced by the CS—the conditioned reinforcer or punisher. Once that happens, the stimulus can reinforce or punish behaviors by itself. Thus, operant conditioning often involves aspects of classical conditioning.

For most people, handshakes, smiles, awards, and other forms of social approval serve as important forms of conditioned reinforcement.

Conditioned reinforcement and punishment are very important. They permit an organism's behavior to be affected by stimuli that are not biologically important in themselves but that are regularly associated with the onset or termination of biologically important stimuli. Indeed, stimuli can even become conditioned reinforcers or punishers by being associated with other conditioned reinforcers or punishers. The speeding ticket is just such an example. If an organism's behavior could only be controlled by primary reinforcers and punishers, its behavior would not be very flexible. The organism would never learn to perform behaviors that had only long-range benefits. Instead, its behavior would be controlled on a moment-to-moment basis by a very limited set of stimuli. Conditioned reinforcers and punishers, such as money, grades, smiles, and frowns, allow for behavior to be altered by a wide variety of contingencies.

Biology and Culture

Learning, Superstition, and Ritualistic Behavior

Are you a superstitious person? Do you have a lucky charm or an object of clothing that you feel brings you good luck? Do you have a special routine or ritual that you or your family follows before an important event? Many people—in every culture—do. Some rituals have even become codified into culturewide practices, such as celebrations and ceremonies, for instance, weddings and baptisms. How do superstitions and rituals come to be? Why do they exist and what functions do they serve?

■ Learning and Genes

We learned in Chapters 3 and 4 that behavior is shaped by the continual interaction between an organism's ge-

netic endowment and its environment. Genetic differences and environmental differences give rise to particular patterns of behavior. In turn, these behavior patterns help adapt an animal to its environment. Ernst Mayr (1974), an American biologist, has provided a useful descriptive framework for understanding how these two factors—genes and environment—interact to determine how and what organisms may learn. He has argued that the type of *genetic program*, the specific set of genetic instructions an organism inherits at birth, determines the extent to which an organism's behavior may be changed by environmental factors, or how much it may be capable of learning.

Across species, the capacity to learn varies along a continuum. At one end are species having *closed genetic programs* and at the other end are those having *open genetic programs*. Species having closed programs, such as insects and some amphibians and reptiles, generally have short life spans, mature quickly, and receive little or no care from their parents. At birth, these animals are genetically predisposed to respond in certain ways in particular situations. Consider the courtship ritual of a fish called the three-spined stickleback. The ritual is characterized by a "zig-zag dance" in which the movements of the dance are stimulated by specific behaviors performed by each fish. These fish do not learn to dance; they dance flawlessly at the first opportunity for mating. (See *Figure 5.13.*) Keep in mind, though, that saying that a species possesses a closed genetic program does not mean that members of that species are not capable of learning. It simply means that the capacity for learning of that species is severely restricted compared to that of other species. For instance, even honey bees can learn to discriminate objects on the basis of color, but obviously they cannot learn most of the sorts of things that you and I can—or even that the family cat or dog can.

Species having open genetic programs, which include many mammals and birds, generally have longer life spans and extended periods of immaturity and parental care. For these organisms, experience can leave an indelible impression on behavior. Learning is the means by which organisms having open genetic programs adapt to their environments. Humans, of course, possess an open genetic program. Courtship rituals vary from one culture to the next; they are not stereotyped, as is the zig-zag dance of the stickleback. Consider the Sandalu bachelor ritual, practiced among unmarried males of the Laiapu Enga of New Guinea (Schwab, 1995). The purpose of the ritual is two-fold. First, it is to purify the eyes from the pollution caused by looking at the private parts of a female. (Sometimes the men see a woman's genitals underneath her grass skirt as she dances in the garden.) The function of the ritual restores the male's worthiness to marry. Second, the ritual is performed to increase the man's fertility.

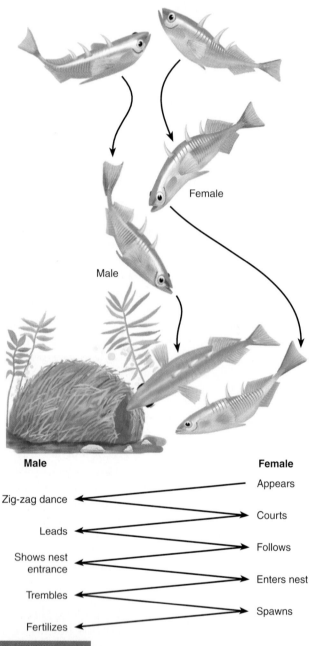

Male **Female**

Zig-zag dance ← Appears

Leads ← Courts

Shows nest entrance ← Follows

Trembles ← Enters nest

Fertilizes ← Spawns

Figure 5.13

The zig-zag courtship dance of the three-spine stickleback. Each part of the dance is triggered by a response made by the other fish.

(From The Study of Instinct *by Niko Tinbergen, Oxford University Press, 1951, p.49 [Figure 47].)*

The ritual itself involves a series of stages that unfold over several days. The young men seclude themselves near a creek where they bathe, chant and sing a ritual incantation in praise of the Sandalu ceremony, adopt new names, spit to rid themselves of the effects of bad language, and wash both eyes and eyelids with water while saying a spell (for example, "I have seen the private parts of a woman.

. . . Take this off my eyes; let it go down the river."). They then participate in a ceremony designed to induce dreaming. Finally, during the "firenight," when the women come dancing into the camp, a man gives his girlfriend a "firestick," which is a public announcement of engagement. He later sings her love songs at her home.

Although in general the courtship rituals of the three-spined stickleback and the Laiapu Enga seem to have the same purpose—procreation—the basis of each ritual is very different. The zig-zag dance is the result of a genetic program that produces a nervous system that responds in a stereotyped manner to a particular situation: the presence of a receptive mate during the mating season. The Sandalu bachelor ritual (and most other human behavior) is the result of a genetic program that produces a nervous system that can be altered in many ways by interaction with the environment. Thus, humans have an inherited capacity for their behavior to be modified through interaction with their environments.

In North America, people learn the courtship rituals that are valued by their cultures just as the Laiapu Enga learn the courtship ritual that is valued by their culture. In fact, all cultural customs and rituals exist because their practice is reinforced by members of the culture (Guerin, 1992, 1995). Thus, rituals often accompany courtship and reproductive behaviors because of our inherited capacity for our behavior to be affected by its consequences—we live in a culture in which rituals of this nature are reinforced.

■ The Origins of Superstitious and Ritualistic Behavior

How might particular cultural practices such as the Sandalu bachelor ritual (and practices of our own that the Laiapu Enga people would think peculiar) arise? What are their origins, and what possible adaptive value might they have?

In this chapter, you have learned that whenever an organism encounters an appetitive stimulus, the behavior it has just performed becomes more likely. Normally, the behavior is instrumental in obtaining a reinforcer; there is a cause-and-effect relation between response and reinforcement. We learn to press the button on a drinking fountain because that response makes the water flow. A duck learns to swim up to people on shore because doing so often results in the people throwing food. But the response does not have to *cause* the appetitive stimulus for the behavior to be affected.

Consider the following example, based on an experiment by Skinner (1948). We place a hungry pigeon inside an operant chamber and program the apparatus to dispense a bit of food every fifteen seconds. After a few minutes, we look in on the bird and find it spinning around frantically, counterclockwise. We remove the bird and replace it with another one. We find that after receiving several pieces of food, the second pigeon is standing in the middle of the floor, bobbing its head up and down like a mechanical toy. A third bird persists in flapping its wings.

Skinner explained these behaviors in the following way: When a reinforcer is intermittently given to an animal regardless of what the animal does, it will seldom just wait quietly for more. Instead, the animal will tend to persist in what it was doing when the reinforcement occurred. Perhaps the first pigeon was turning around when the food dispenser was first operated. The pigeon heard the noise, turned toward its source, and saw the food. It ate, waited in the vicinity of the food dispenser, and finally turned to go. Just then, another bit of food was delivered, so the bird went back to eat it. The next time, the pigeon turned away a little sooner and made a couple of revolutions before some food was dispensed again. From then on, the pigeon went into a spin after each reinforcement. From the bird's point of view, the response was what brought the food. Under these conditions, the birds have acquired **superstitious behaviors**—behaviors that appear to cause certain events but in reality do not.

We humans probably acquire superstitious behaviors in the same way. We perform a behavior that is followed by a reinforcer. From our point of view, it was the behavior that produced the reinforcer. For example, we do well on a test after studying for it while listening to the radio. The next time we study for a test, we turn on the radio. Most baseball pitchers perform a little ritual before throwing the ball to the batter, such as scuffing the ground with their shoes, rubbing the ball, tugging on their hats, and turning the ball in the glove. Baseball pitchers do these things because, in the past, they may have done so just before throwing strikes. Whether the behaviors are relevant or irrelevant, those that precede success will tend to be repeated.

Of course, we can only speculate about the kinds of environmental conditions that have given rise to supersti-

tious behaviors and rituals that are part of all human cultures. Probably, these behaviors were inadvertently reinforced sometime long ago and then taught to subsequent generations.

The precise origins of the Sandalu ritual are unknown (Schwab, 1995). But for our purposes (and for the Laiapu Enga), these origins are not important. What is important for us to know is that this ritual, like any other ritual, helps bind a community of people together—indeed, the bachelors' participation in the ritual is reinforced by the community through social approval. While we may think the Sandalu ritual strange—perhaps even silly—it has for many centuries served as a centerpiece of Laiapu Enga culture, binding these people together in close-knit communities. In fact, only recently, and partly through the influence of western civilization, has the Sandalu bachelor ritual been abandoned and replaced with more "modern" courtship rituals. As the Laiapu Enga's social environment has changed, so has their behavior. In essence, the behavior of the Laiapu Enga has adapted to western influences, a behavioral change that could occur only because of the open genetic system of our species.

Interim Summary

Operant Conditioning

The law of effect specifies a relation between behavior and its consequences. If a stimulus that follows a response makes that response become more likely, we say that the response was reinforced. If the stimulus makes the response become less likely, we say that it was punished. The reinforcing or punishing stimulus must follow the behavior almost immediately if it is to be effective.

The process of operant conditioning helps adapt an organism's behavior to its environment. Skinner described the relation between behavior and environmental events as a three-term contingency: In the presence of discriminative stimuli, a consequence will occur if and only if an operant response occurs.

A reinforcer is an appetitive stimulus that follows an operant response and causes that response to occur more frequently in the future. A punisher is an aversive stimulus that follows an operant response and causes it to occur less frequently in the future. But if an aversive stimulus is *terminated* after a response occurs, the response is reinforced through a process called negative reinforcement. And the termination of an appetitive stimulus can punish a response through a process called response cost. Extinction occurs when operant

A superstitious behavior: Will crossing her fingers help this student do well on her test?

superstitious behavior A behavior that occurs in response to the noncontingent occurrence of an appetitive stimulus; appears to cause a certain event but in reality does not.

responses are emitted but not reinforced, which makes sense because organisms must be able to adapt their behavior to changing environments.

Complex responses, which are unlikely to occur spontaneously, can be shaped by the method of successive approximations. Teachers use this process to train students to perform complex behaviors; something similar occurs when, in the course of learning a new skill, we become satisfied only when we detect signs of improvement.

Schedules of reinforcement, which were originally designed to study the principles of learning in the laboratory, have their counterparts in the world outside the laboratory. Researchers have developed various types of schedules of reinforcement, which have different effects on the rate and pattern of responding. When a response is reinforced intermittently, it is more resistant to extinction, probably because an intermittent reinforcement schedule resembles extinction more than a continuous reinforcement schedule does.

Discrimination involves the detection of essential differences between stimuli or situations so that responding occurs only when appropriate. Generalization is another necessary component of all forms of learning because no two stimuli, and no two responses, are precisely the same. Thus, generalization embodies the ability to apply what is learned from one experience to similar experiences.

The major difference between classical conditioning and operant conditioning is in the nature of the contingencies: Classical conditioning involves a contingency between stimuli (CS and UCS), whereas operant conditioning involves a contingency between the organism's behavior and an appetitive or aversive stimulus. The two types of conditioning complement each other. The pairings of neutral stimuli with appetitive and aversive stimuli (classical conditioning) determine which stimuli become conditioned reinforcers and punishers.

A species' capacity for learning varies along a continuum according to its genetic program. Species having closed genetic programs learn little, if anything, through interaction with the environment; the behavior of its members may be said to be genetically predisposed. The mating ritual of the three-spine stickleback is an example of such behavior. In contrast, species having open genetic systems learn a great deal through interaction with the environment. That is why behavior varies from individual to individual and from culture to culture. Human superstition and rituals, such as the Sandalu bachelor ritual, are reinforced by the cultures in which they are performed.

Thought Questions

- The law of effect is often extolled as a universal principle of behavior. Can you think of an example in which the law of effect is *not* applicable to an instance of behavior?
- Suppose that you run into a friend while walking along the street. You stop and talk to each other for a few minutes. How would you explain your interactions

with your friend in terms of the three-term contingency?
- Reflect for a moment on the activities in which you have engaged so far today. Where appropriate, explain how the principles of positive reinforcement, negative reinforcement, punishment, response cost, and extinction have operated to influence your behavior today. Give specific, concrete examples and explain them using references to specific environmental events.
- How might you (and the rest of your class) shape your psychology instructor's behavior so that he or she stands only at the far left side of the room while lecturing?
- Many people have had the embarrassing experience of mistaking a stranger for a friend. For example, you may catch a glimpse of your "friend" walking down the other side of the street, call out her name, and wave rather excitedly only to discover as your look more closely that the person is not who you thought she was. How would you explain this event using the principles of behavior discussed in this section?

Conditioning of Complex Behaviors

So far, we have considered rather simple examples of reinforced behaviors. But people and many other animals are able to learn very complex behaviors. Consider the behavior of a young girl learning to print letters. She sits at her school desk, producing long rows of letters. What kinds of reinforcing stimuli maintain her behavior? Why is she devoting her time to a task that involves so much effort? The answer is that her behavior produces stimuli—printed letters—which serve as conditioned reinforcers. In previous class sessions, the teacher demonstrated how to print the letters and praised the girl for printing them herself. The act of printing was reinforced, and the printed letters that this act produces come to serve as conditioned reinforcers. The child prints a letter, sees that it looks close to the way it should, and her efforts are reinforced by the sight of the letter. Doing something correctly or making progress toward that goal can provide an effective reinforcer.

This fact is often overlooked by people who take a limited view of the process of reinforcement, thinking that it has to resemble the delivery of a small piece of food to an animal being taught a trick. Some people even say that because reinforcers are rarely delivered to humans immediately after they perform a behavior, operant conditioning must not play a major role in human learning. This assertion misses the point that, especially for humans, reinforcers can be very subtle events.

An everyday term for the conditioned reinforcement that shapes and maintains our behavior when we perform a behavior correctly is *satisfaction*. Usually, we work hard at some task because it "gives us satisfaction." An artist who produces a fine painting gains satisfaction from the image that emerges as she works on it and receives even stronger satisfaction from looking at the finished product. This satisfaction derives from experience. The artist has learned to recognize good pieces of art; when she produces one herself, she provides her own conditioned reinforcer.

Aversive Control of Behavior

Your own experience has probably taught you that punishment can be as effective as positive reinforcement in changing behavior. Aversive control of behavior seems to permeate our society. From fines given to speeding motorists to the prison sentences given to felons, our society uses punishment to try to control the behavior of its citizens. Aversive control of behavior is common for two main reasons. First, it can be highly effective in inducing behavior change, producing nearly immediate results. A person given a fine for running a stop sign is likely, at least for a short while, to heed the sign's instruction. The very effectiveness of punishment as a means of behavior change can serve as an immediate reinforcer for the person doing the punishing.

Second, society cannot always control the positive reinforcers that shape and maintain the behavior of its members. However, it can and does control aversive stimuli that may be used to punish misconduct. For example, suppose that a young person's peers encourage antisocial behaviors such as theft. Society has no control over reinforcers provided by the peer group, but it can control stimuli to punish the antisocial behaviors, such as fines and imprisonment.

How Punishers Work

How does a punishing stimulus suppress behavior? Punishment, like reinforcement, usually involves a discriminative stimulus. A child's shouting is usually punished in the classroom but not outdoors during recess. A dog chases a porcupine, gets stuck with quills, and never chases one again. However, it continues to chase the neighbor's cat.

Most aversive stimuli elicit some sort of protective or defensive response, such as cringing, freezing, hiding, or running away. The response depends on the species of animal and, of course, on the situation. If you slap your dog for a misdeed, the dog will cower down and slink away, looking clearly "apologetic," because you are in a position of dominance. However, if the dog is struck by a stranger, it may very well react by attacking the person. Both types of behaviors are known as *species-specific defense reactions* (Bolles, 1970).

Suppose that a dog sees a porcupine for the first time. The sight of the animal elicits an approach response. The dog chases the porcupine, which stops and emits its own species-specific defense reactions: It bristles its quills and starts swinging its tail back and forth. The dog approaches and gets a face full of quills. The pain elicits a withdrawal response: The dog runs away. The next time the dog sees a porcupine, it

Punishment takes many forms. This motorist is receiving a citation for having violated a traffic law.

runs toward it, seeing only a medium-sized animal that attracts its interest. But as soon as the dog gets close enough to see the porcupine clearly, it stops and turns away.

Here is what might have happened. A stimulus (the sight of the porcupine) was present at the time the dog received a painful stimulus that elicited a species-specific defense reaction. Through the process of classical conditioning, the stimulus became linked to the response. The next time the dog spots the porcupine, the sight of the porcupine elicits the defensive withdrawal response. (See *Figure 5.14.*)

Escape and Avoidance

Negative reinforcement teaches organisms to make responses that terminate aversive stimuli. These responses can make a stimulus cease (for example, the woman who kicked the oil burner and made the unpleasant noise stop), or the organism can simply run away. In either case, psychologists call the be-

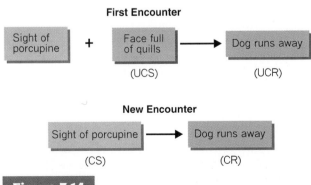

Figure 5.14

A schematic diagram of the way an aversive stimulus may punish a behavior by classical conditioning of a defensive withdrawal response.

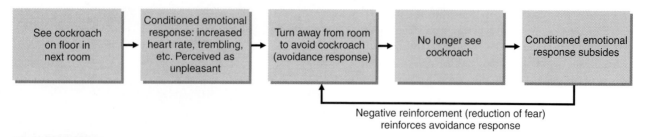

Figure 5.15

Maintenance of a phobia through negative reinforcement—reduction of fear by an avoidance response.

havior an **escape response**: The organism endures the effects of the aversive stimulus until its behavior terminates the stimulus. In some cases, the animal can do more than escape the aversive stimulus; it can learn to do something to *prevent* it from occurring. This type of behavior is known as an **avoidance response**.

Avoidance responses usually require some warning that the aversive stimulus is about to occur in order for the organism to be able to make the appropriate response soon enough. Suppose that you meet a man at a party who backs you against the wall and engages you in the most boring conversation you have ever had. In addition, his breath is so bad that you are afraid you will pass out. You finally manage to break away from him (an escape response). A few days later, you attend another party. You begin walking toward the buffet table and see the same man (discriminative stimulus) standing nearby. You decide that you will get some food later and turn away to talk with some friends at the other end of the room (an avoidance response).

As we saw earlier, phobias can be considered to be conditioned emotional responses—fears that are acquired through classical conditioning. But unlike most classically conditioned responses, phobias are especially resistant to extinction. If we classically condition an eyeblink response in a rabbit and then repeatedly present the CS alone, without the UCS (puff of air), the response will extinguish. However, if a person has a phobia for cockroaches, the phobia will not extinguish easily even if he or she encounters cockroaches and nothing bad happens. Why does the response persist?

Most psychologists believe that the answer lies in a subtle interaction between operant and classical conditioning. The sight of a cockroach makes a person having a cockroach phobia feel frightened; that is, he or she experiences an unpleasant conditional emotional response. The person runs out of

the room, leaving the cockroach behind and reducing the unpleasant feelings of fear. This reduction in an aversive stimulus reinforces the avoidance response and perpetuates the phobia. (See *Figure 5.15.*)

Conditioning of Flavor Aversions

You have probably eaten foods that made you sick and now avoid them on the basis of their flavor alone. (Does any particular flavor come to mind?) The association of a substance's flavor with illness, which is often caused by eating that substance, leads to **conditioned flavor-aversion learning**.

The study of flavor aversion learning is important not only because it is a real-life experience, but also because it has taught psychologists about unique relations that may exist between certain CSs and certain UCSs. As we just saw, punishment is a result of classical conditioning—a species-typical defensive response becomes classically conditioned to a discriminative stimulus. This is exactly how conditioned flavor aversions are acquired. The flavor is followed by an unconditional stimulus (sickness) that elicits the unpleasant responses of the autonomic nervous system, such as cramping and retching. Then, when the animal encounters the flavor again, the experience triggers unpleasant internal reactions that cause the animal to stop eating the food.

Many learning researchers once believed that nearly any CS could be paired with nearly any UCS to produce nearly any CR. However, in a now classic experiment, John Garcia and his colleague, Robert A. Koelling, showed that animals are more prepared to learn some types of relations among stimuli than others.

In the first phase of their experiment, Garcia and Koelling (1966) permitted rats to drink saccharine-flavored water from a tube. Each lick from the tube produced three CSs: taste, noise, and bright lights. This phase ensured that rats were equally familiar with each of the CSs. In the next phase, the rats were divided into four groups, each experiencing either "bright-noisy" water or "tasty" water. Each CS was paired with illness or electric shock. (See *Figure 5.16.*)

After several trials, the experimenters measured the amount of saccharine-flavored water the rats consumed. (See *Figure 5.17.*) They found that the rats learned the association between flavor and illness but not between flavor and pain produced by electric shock. Likewise, the rats learned the

escape response An operant response acquired through negative reinforcement that terminates an aversive stimulus.

avoidance response An operant response acquired through negative reinforcement that prevents an aversive stimulus from occurring.

conditioned flavor-aversion learning A type of learning in which a substance is avoided because its flavor has been associated with illness.

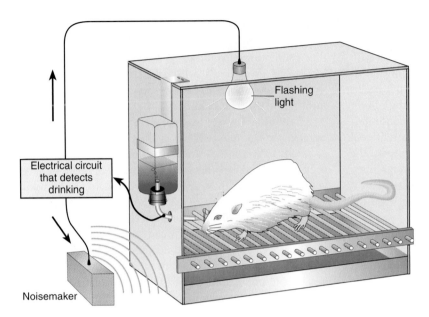

Figure 5.16

Conditioned flavor aversion. A rat drinks "bright-noisy" water in the experiment conducted by Garcia and Koelling (1966). The light flashes and the noisemaker clatters each time the rat's tongue touches the waterspout.

association between the "bright-noisy water" and shock-induced pain but not between the "bright-noisy water" and illness. The results make sense; after all, the animal has to taste the flavor that makes it sick, not hear it, and in the world outside the laboratory, a particular flavor does not usually indicate that you are about to receive an electric shock.

This experiment provides two important conclusions: (1) Rats can learn about associations between internal sensations (being sick) and novel tastes and (2) the interval between the two stimuli can be very long. These facts suggest that the brain mechanisms responsible for a conditioned flavor aversion are different from the ones that mediate an aversion caused by stimuli applied to the outside of the body (such as a painful foot shock). It appears that conditioned flavor aversions serve to protect animals from poisonous foods by enabling them to learn to avoid eating them. Because few naturally occurring poisons cause sickness immediately, neural mechanisms that mediate conditioned flavor aversions must be capable of learning the association between events that are separated in time. Most other cause-and-effect relations involve events that

occur close in time; hence the neural mechanisms that mediate an organism's ability to learn about them operate under different time constraints.

Some animals have eating habits quite different from those of rats; they eat foods that they cannot taste or smell. For example, some birds eat seeds that are encased in a tasteless husk. They do not have teeth, so they cannot break open the husk and taste the seed. Thus, they cannot use odor or taste as a cue to avoid a poison. However, Wilcoxon, Dragoin, and Kral (1971) found that quail (a species of seed-eating birds) can form a conditioned aversion to the sight of food that earlier made them sick.

People can also acquire conditioned flavor aversions. A friend of mine often took trips on airplanes with her parents when she was a child. Unfortunately, she usually got airsick. Just before takeoff, her mother would give her some spearmint-flavored chewing gum to help relieve the pressure on her eardrums that would occur when the plane ascended. Yes, she developed a conditioned flavor aversion to spearmint gum. In fact, the odor of the gum still makes her feel nauseated.

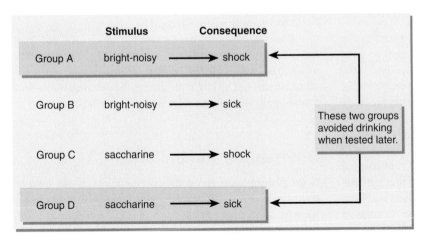

Figure 5.17

The results of the experiment conducted by Garcia and Koelling (1966).

(Adapted from Garcia, J. and Koelling, R. Relation of cue to consequence in avoidance learning. Psychonomic Science, 1966, 4, 123–124.)

Conditioned flavor aversions, like most learning situations, involve both classical and operant conditioning. From one point of view, we can say that the aversive stimuli produced by the poison punish the behavior of eating a particular food. That is, the flavor serves as a discriminative stimulus for a punishment contingency (operant conditioning). But it also serves as a conditioned stimulus for a classical conditioning situation: The flavor is followed by an unconditional stimulus (the poison) that elicits unpleasant responses of the autonomic nervous system, such as cramping and retching. Then, when the animal encounters the flavor at a later date, it experiences unpleasant reactions that cause it to leave the source of the stimulus and avoid the food.

As we just saw, conditioned flavor aversions occur when particular flavors are followed by feelings of nausea—even several hours later. This phenomenon has several implications for situations outside the laboratory.

An unfortunate side effect of chemotherapy or radiation therapy for cancer is nausea. Besides killing the rapidly dividing cells of malignant tumors, both chemotherapy and radiation kill the rapidly dividing cells that line the digestive system—and thus cause nausea and vomiting. Knowing what we know about conditioned flavor aversions, we might predict that chemotherapy or radiation therapy would cause a conditioned aversion to the foods a patient ate during the previous meal. Bernstein (1978) showed that this prediction is correct. She gave ice cream to some cancer patients who were about to receive a session of chemotherapy and found that several months later, 75 percent of these patients refused to eat ice cream of the same flavor. In contrast, control subjects who did not taste it before their chemotherapy said that they liked it very much. Only one trial was necessary to develop the conditioned flavor aversion. Even when patients have a clear understanding that the drugs are responsible for their aversion and that the food is really wholesome, they still cannot bring themselves to eat it (Bernstein, 1991). Thus, a conditioned food aversion is not a result of cognitive processes such as reasoning or expectation.

Experiments such as the one I just described indicate that cancer patients run a real risk of developing aversions to the foods they normally eat. And because cancer patients tend to have appetite problems and to lose weight, these aversions can have serious consequences. In fact, questionnaires and interviews reveal that cancer patients do develop aversions to the foods that they normally eat—even if their treatment sessions occur several hours after the previous meal (Bernstein, Webster, and Bernstein, 1982; Mattes, Arnold, and Boraas, 1987). When patients receive many treatment sessions, they are likely to develop aversions to a wide variety of foods.

Because a treatment that produces nausea may cause the development of a conditioned flavor aversion to the last thing a person has eaten, Broberg and Bernstein (1987) attempted to attach the aversion to a flavor other than one that patients encounter in their normal diets. The experimenters had cancer patients eat a coconut or root beer Lifesaver (a sugared candy) after the last meal before a chemotherapy session, hoping that the unique flavor would serve as a scapegoat, thus preventing a conditioned aversion to patients' normal foods. The procedure worked; the patients were much less likely to show an aversion to the food eaten during the last meal before the treatment.

Conditioned flavor aversions can also have useful applications. For example, psychologists have applied conditioned aversions to wildlife control. In regions where coyotes have been attacking sheep, they have left chunks of dog food laced with an emetic drug wrapped in pieces of fresh sheepskin. The coyotes eat the bait, get sick, and develop a conditioned aversion to the smell and taste of sheep (Gustavson and Gustavson, 1985). These methods can help protect endangered species as well as livestock. Mongooses have been introduced into some islands in the Caribbean, where they menace the indigenous population of sea turtles. Nicolaus and Nellis (1987) found that a conditioned aversion to turtle eggs could be established in mongooses by feeding them eggs into which an emetic drug had been injected.

Evidence suggests that for some species, conditioned flavor aversions can become cultural traditions. Gustavson and Gustavson (1985) reported that after adult coyotes had developed a conditioned aversion to a particular food, their offspring, too, avoided that food. Apparently, the young coyotes learned from their mothers what food was fit to eat. However, Nicolaus, Hoffman, and Gustavson (1982) found that adult raccoons having a conditioned aversion to chickens did not teach their offspring to avoid chickens. In fact, after seeing the young raccoons kill and eat chickens, the adults overcame their aversion and began preying on chickens again.

And sometimes wild animals find a way to outwit psychologists. Gustavson and Gustavson (1985) tell the story of the bears in Mount Rainier National Park who had developed a taste for the contents of garbage cans. The psychologists sprayed the garbage several times each day with a mint-flavored emetic drug, hoping that the bears would leave the area after they developed an aversion to the garbage. The bears soon stopped eating the garbage, but then they began menacing campers who were preparing or eating their meals, which consisted of mint-free food. The psychologists admitted defeat. The park rangers captured the bears and transported them to a remote part of the park.

Understanding the basic principles of classical and operant conditioning is relevant to everyday life. The importance of the basic principles of learning is shown by the fact that all of them—including conditioned flavor aversions—have found applications to problems outside the laboratory.

Observation and Imitation

Normally, we learn about the consequences of our own behavior or about stimuli that directly affect us. But we can also learn by a less direct method: observing the behavior of others. Video game machines usually have instructions printed on them and often flash instructions on the screen. But it is much easier to learn how to play the game by watching someone who has had experience with it. Likewise, one of the best ways to improve your tennis game (besides taking lessons) is to watch the pros play.

Nature provides clear examples that imitation does seem to be an innate tendency. Many species of birds must learn to sing the song of their species; if they are raised apart from other birds of their species, they will never sing or they will sing a peculiar song that bears little resemblance to that of normally raised birds (Marler, 1961). However, if they hear the normal song played over a loudspeaker, they will sing it properly when they become adults. They have learned the song, but clearly there were no external reinforcement contingencies; nothing in the environment reinforced their singing of the song. (This phenomenon also provides an excellent example of the distinction between learning and performance. A baby bird hears the proper song but does not sing it until adulthood. The changes that take place in its brain do not manifest themselves in behavior for many months.)

Classically conditioned behaviors, as well as operantly conditioned behaviors, can be acquired through observation. For example, suppose that a young girl sees her mother show signs of fear whenever she encounters a dog. The girl herself will likely develop a fear of dogs, even if she never sees another one. In fact, Bandura and Menlove (1968) reported that children who were afraid of animals—in this case, dogs—were likely to have a parent who feared dogs, but they usually could not remember having had unpleasant direct experiences with them. As we will see in Chapter 13, we tend to imitate—and feel—the emotional responses of people we observe. Perhaps when we see someone we know well show signs of fear, we imitate these responses ourselves, and the responses become classically conditioned to the important stimulus present at the time.

Under normal circumstances, learning by observation may not require external reinforcement. In fact, there is strong evidence that imitating the behavior of other organisms may be reinforcing in itself. However, in some cases in which the ability to imitate is absent, it can be learned through reinforcement. For example, Baer, Peterson, and Sherman (1967) studied three severely retarded children who had never been seen to imitate the behavior of other people. When the experimenters first tried to induce the children to do what they themselves did, such as clap their hands, the children were unresponsive. Next, the experimenters tried to induce and reinforce imitative behavior in the children. An experimenter would look at a child, say, "Do this," and perform a behavior. If the child made a similar response, the child was immediately praised and given a piece of food. At first, the children were physically guided to make the response. If the behavior to be imitated was clapping, the experimenter would clap his or her hands, hold the child's hands and clap them together, and then praise the child and give him or her some food.

The procedure worked. The children learned to imitate the experimenters' behaviors. But more important, the children had not simply learned to mimic a specific set of responses. They had acquired the general tendency to imitate. When the researchers performed new behaviors and said, "Do this," the children would imitate them.

Obviously, teaching retarded children is much more effective when the children pay attention to their teachers and imitate their behaviors when requested to do so. The procedure I have just described has proved to be useful for teaching retarded children behaviors that will help them lead more productive lives. But the theoretical significance of this demonstration is also important. The experiment indicates that imitation, as a general tendency, is subject to reinforcement (and presumably to punishment, as well). An organism can learn more than simply making a certain response to a certain stimulus; it can learn a strategy that can be applied to many different situations. Social learning theory emphasizes the importance of learning through observation and will be discussed in Chapter 14. We'll also discuss the role of imitation in language acquisition by children in Chapter 10.

The Analysis of Human Behavior

As I noted earlier, behavior analysts study both humans and nonhuman animals (Navarick, Bernstein, and Fantino, 1990; Hyten and Reilly, 1992). Although there is still much research being done with nonhumans, behavior analysts have become increasingly interested in studying behavior that is unique to humans, such as certain social and verbal behaviors (Hake, 1982; Baron et al., 1991). To provide you with an overview of the considerable breadth of research in this area, I will now briefly describe three current areas of operant research that focus on human behavior: instructional control of behavior, stimulus equivalence, and drug use and abuse.

Instructional Control

Human behavior is influenced not only by reinforcement, but also by the interactions of reinforcement with *rules*, that is, verbal descriptions of the relation between behavior and reinforcement. In fact, much of our everyday behavior involves following rules of one sort or another. Cooking from a recipe, following directions to a friend's house, and obeying the speed limit are common examples. Because rules have the potential to influence our behavior in almost any situation, behavior analysts are interested in learning more about how rules and reinforcement interact.

One way to investigate this interaction is to give subjects rules that are false—that is, rules that are inaccurate descriptions of the behavior required for reinforcement (Galizio, 1979; Baron and Galizio, 1983). In such experiments, people may behave in accordance with either the rule or the reinforcement requirement. For example, in one study (Buskist

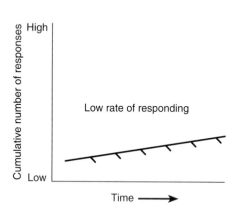

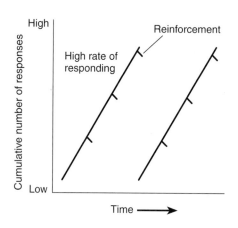

Figure 5.18

Typical cumulative records of operant responses of people who have been trained on a fixed-interval schedule of reinforcement. Some people respond at a very slow rate (left), and others respond at a fast rate (right). The tick marks under each line represent delivery of a reinforcer.

and Miller, 1986), one group of college students was told that the schedule in effect was a fixed-interval 15-second (FI 15) schedule, when in fact, it was a fixed-interval 30-second (FI 30-sec) schedule. Recall that in a fixed interval schedule, a response will be reinforced only after a certain amount of time has passed since the last reinforcement. Another group was told the truth about the schedule.

At first, the misinformed students responded according to the instructions, making one response about every 15 seconds. However, because the rule directly contradicted the actual reinforcement schedule, they soon learned to respond about once every 30 seconds. The students abandoned the rule they had been given by the experimenter in favor of the actual reinforcement contingency. The group of students who were told the truth responded accordingly.

A third group of students, also exposed to the FI 30-second schedule, was told that the schedule in effect was a FI 60-second schedule. The rule given to these students was ambiguous, but it was not exactly false. If the students made a response every 60 seconds, they would receive a reinforcer every time. These students could have received a reinforcer every 30 seconds, but they never learned to do so. The point is that rules can be influential in controlling behavior not only when they are true, but also when they are ambiguous. The problem, of course, is that ambiguous instructions often lead to inefficient behavior, as they did in this case.

Other researchers have shown that people sometimes generate their own rules about the consequences of their behavior (Lowe, 1979). Some researchers, such as Fergus Lowe, argue that our ability to verbally describe the consequences of our behavior explains why humans often respond differently from other animals when placed under similar reinforcement contingencies (Lowe, Beasty, and Bentall, 1983). When ex-

posed to FI schedules, animals do not respond immediately after each reinforcement. As time passes, though, responding gradually increases until the next reinforcer is delivered. Humans, on the other hand, tend to follow one of two strategies: responding very slowly or responding very rapidly. (See *Figure 5.18.*) Those people who respond slowly often describe the schedule as interval-based—which it is—and they respond accordingly. Those who respond rapidly usually describe the schedule as ratio-based—which it is not—and they respond accordingly. Thus, the language one uses may indeed exert some control over one's own behavior. The extent to which language and other behaviors interact is the subject of ongoing experimental and theoretical work (Hayes, 1989; Cerruti, 1990).

Stimulus Equivalence

Probably the hottest area of operant research using humans is **stimulus equivalence**, the emergence of novel behavior without direct reinforcement of that behavior (Fields, 1993; Fields et al., 1995). The experiments designed to study stimulus equivalence are extremely complex, so I will not describe them in detail here. Instead, I will give you a brief overview.

Suppose that you were asked to learn the relationship among a group of symbols: A, B, and C. Suppose further that after training *without reinforcement*, you discovered that A = B and A = C. How then would you respond to the following question: Does B = C? You would probably reason that if A = B and A = C, then B, too, is equal to C. But notice that you were never trained or received any direct reinforcement for learning that B = C. Rather, the equivalent relationship between B and C *emerged* from your previous learning; hence, the term *stimulus equivalence.*

Stimulus equivalence is an important area of research because it represents one way we learn to use and understand symbols, such as language. For example, let A represent a picture of a dog, B represent the spoken word *dog*, and C represent the printed word *dog*. Suppose that we teach a child to point to the picture of the dog (A) and say the word *dog* (B). In this case, the child learns that A = B and B = A. Next, suppose that we teach the child to point to the picture of the dog (A) when he sees the printed word *dog* (C). The child learns

stimulus equivalence A type of learning in which stimuli become equivalent even though the organism has never observed a relation between them; may be involved in learning how to read and manipulate symbols.

behavior pharmacology The study of how drugs influence behavior; combines the principles of operant conditioning with the principles of drug action.

Training: A = B

The child learns that the animal
is called "dog"

Training: A = C

The child learns that the written
word *dog* refers to the animal

Testing: B = C?

The child says "dog" when he
sees the word *dog*

Figure 5.19

Stimulus equivalence.

that A = C and that C = A. What we are really interested in, though, is whether the child will have learned that the spoken word *dog* (B) is equivalent to, or means the same thing as, the printed word *dog* (C). (See *Figure 5.19.*)

This is precisely what children learn under these circumstances, even though the equivalent relationship, B = C, has not been *directly* trained (Sidman and Tailby, 1982). Rather, it emerged as a consequence of the child's learning history. Understanding how stimulus equivalence develops is likely to lead to a better understanding of language development.

Drug Use and Abuse

Soon after Skinner outlined the principles of operant behavior, others were quick to apply them to the study of drug action and drug taking (Thompson and Schuster, 1968). In fact, Skinner's three-term contingency is now partly the basis of an entirely separate discipline of pharmacology known as **behavioral pharmacology**, the study of how drugs influence behavior. In this field, the terms *discriminative stimuli, responding,* and *consequences* translate into *drugs as discriminative stimuli, the direct effects of drugs on behavior,* and *the reinforcing effects of drugs,* respectively.

Perhaps the most interesting discovery in behavioral pharmacology is the finding that most psychoactive drugs function as reinforcers in both humans and animals. When administered as a consequence of responding, these drugs will induce and maintain high rates of responding (Griffiths, Bigelow, and Henningfield, 1980). There is a very high correlation between drugs that will maintain animal responding in experimental settings and those that are abused by humans (Griffiths et al., 1980). Cocaine, for example, maintains very high rates of responding and drug consumption, to the point that food and water consumption decreases to life-threatening levels. (Unlimited access to cocaine in rhesus monkeys can lead, in some cases, to death.) These findings have allowed psychologists to study the *abuse potential* of newly

available drugs in order to predict their likelihood of becoming drugs of abuse. The realization that drugs are reinforcers has, in turn, led behavior pharmacologists to treat cocaine dependence in people successfully by scheduling reinforcement for non-drug taking behavior (Higgins, Budney, and Bickel, 1994).

Just as the phone ringing can serve as a discriminative stimulus for you answering it, the stimulus effects of drugs can also exert control over human behaviors that are reinforced by nondrug stimuli. People become more sociable under the influence of alcohol not only because the drug reduces their inhibitions, but also because people have some successful social interactions while under the drug's effects. These interactions reinforce their sociability. In fact, many laboratory studies have shown that certain drugs actually increase social responding and social reinforcement (Higgins, Hughes, and Bickel, 1989).

Human behavior under schedules of reinforcement has become a significant weapon in the arsenal of drug researchers for developing models of drug use and abuse (Bickel and DeGrandpre, 1994). Continued research in behavioral pharmacology is likely to lead to more breakthroughs in understanding behavioral changes produced by drugs. I will have more to say about drugs and drug use in Chapters 16 and 17.

Evaluating Scientific Issues

What Is Insight?

Many problems we have to solve in our daily lives require us to make responses that we have never made before and that we have never seen anyone else make, either. We often think about a problem, looking at the elements and trying to imagine various solutions. We try various responses in our heads, but none seem to work. Suddenly, we think of a new approach; maybe this one will work! We try it, and it does. We say that we have solved the problem through insight.

But what is insight? Some people see it as almost a magical process: a sudden flash of inspiration, a bolt from the blue, an answer coming from nowhere. Most people regard insight as a particularly human ability— or, at least, as an ability that belongs to our species and, perhaps, some of the higher primates.

■ Insight in Other Primates

During the early part of this century, the German psychologist Wolfgang Köhler studied the problem-solving behaviors of chimpanzees. In one famous example (Köhler, 1927/1973), he hung some bananas from the ceiling of an animal's cage, just high enough to be out of reach. The cage also contained a large box. Sultan, one of the chimps, first tried to jump up to reach the bananas, then paced around the cage, stopped in front of the box, pushed it toward the bananas, climbed onto the box, and retrieved and ate the fruit. (See *Figure 5.20.*) Later, when the bananas were suspended even higher, he stacked up several boxes, and on one occasion when no boxes were present, he grabbed Köhler by the hand, led him over to the bananas, and climbed on top of him. (Sorry, but I do not have a picture of that.)

Köhler believed that the insightful problem-solving behavior shown by the chimpanzees was different from the behavior of Thorndike's cats as they learned to escape the puzzle boxes. The cats clearly showed trial-and-error behavior, coming upon the solution by accident. The escape from the box served as a reinforcing stimulus, and eventually the animals learned to operate the latch efficiently. But the behavior of the chimpanzees seemed very different. They suddenly came upon a solution, often after looking at the situation (and, presumably, thinking about it). Köhler saw no accidental trial-and-error behavior. Perhaps some processes other than operant conditioning are responsible for the kind of insight that primates can display. Perhaps insight is a behavior that is not subject to the principles of learning outlined in this chapter.

■ A Behavioral Analysis of Insight

More recent work suggests that insight may be less mysterious than it appears. Insight may actually be based on combinations of behaviors initially learned through trial and error. In one study (Epstein, Kirshnit, Lanza, and Rubin, 1984), the experimenters used operant procedures (with food as the reinforcer) to teach a pigeon two behaviors: (1) to push a box toward a target (a green spot placed at various locations on the floor) and (2) to climb onto a box and peck at a miniature model of a banana, which was suspended overhead. Once these behaviors had been learned, the experimenters confronted the pigeon

Figure 5.20

Insightful behavior by a chimpanzee in an experiment similar to the one performed by Köhler. The chimpanzee piles boxes on top of each other to reach the banana hanging overhead.

Insightful behavior by a pigeon. The pigeon moves the box toward the banana overhead, pushes the box into position under the banana, mounts the box, and pecks the banana.

(From Norman Baxley/© 1984 Discover Publications.)

with a situation in which the box was in one part of the chamber and the banana was in another.

> At first, the bird appeared to be confused: It stretched toward the banana, turned back and forth from the banana to the box, and so on. Then, rather suddenly, it began to push the box toward the banana, sighting the banana and readjusting the path of the box as it pushed. Finally, it stopped pushing when the box was near the banana, climbed onto the box, and pecked the banana. (Epstein, 1985, p. 132)

The pigeon acted much the way that Sultan did. In a subsequent experiment, Epstein (1987) taught a pigeon to (1) peck at a model of a banana, (2) climb onto a box, (3) open a door, and (4) push a box toward a target. When the pigeon was confronted with a banana hanging above its head and a box behind a door, it combined all four behaviors: It opened the door, pushed the box out and moved it under the banana, climbed the box, and pecked the banana. (See *Figure 5.21.*)

Insightful behavior generally involves combining and adapting behaviors in a new context. We know from the experiments by Epstein and his colleagues that pigeons will show insightful behavior only after they have learned the individual behaviors that must go together to solve a problem. For example, only if pigeons have learned to push a box toward a goal will they move it under a model banana hanging from the top of the cage. It is not enough to have learned to push a box; they must have learned to push it toward a goal. Presumably, the chimpanzees' experience with moving boxes around and climbing on them was necessary for them to solve the hanging banana problem.

■ What Should We Conclude?

In Chapter 2, you learned about the pitfall called the *nominal fallacy*, in which we tend to think that we have explained a phenomenon simply by naming it. So, too, we must realize that simply labeling behavior as insightful does not help us to understand it. If we do not know what behaviors an animal has already learned, a novel and complex sequence of behaviors that solves a problem seems to come from nowhere. To understand the necessary conditions for insight to occur, we need to know more than what is happening during the current situation; we also need to know what kinds of learning experiences the animal has had in the past.

The scientist's challenge is to dissect even the most complex behaviors and try to understand their causes. Perhaps chimpanzees, like humans, are capable of solving problems by using some sort of mental imagery, testing possible solutions in their heads before actually trying them. But neither humans nor chimpanzees will be able to think about objects they have never seen or imagine themselves performing behaviors they have never performed or seen others perform. Naturally, humans, chimpanzees, and pigeons will be able to perform different kinds of behaviors and perceive different kinds of relations in their environments, because of their different habitats and because of differences in the complexities of their brains. But the raw material for problem solving—including the thinking that may accompany some forms of insightful behavior—must come from previous experience. And that, of course, is what this chapter has been all about.

Some Thoughts on Behavior Analysis and Cognitive Psychology

The success of behavior analysis in discovering laws of behavior that accurately describe and predict behavior across species and across experimental settings is one of psychology's foremost achievements. These laws are valued not only for their theoretical elegance, but also for their application in understanding behavior in everyday life.

But as your experiences in previous chapters have demonstrated, few, if any, approaches or perspectives in psychology go unchallenged. Such is the case with behavior analysis. From early in this century to about the mid-1960s, the behavioral perspective dominated studies of learning and behavior. Gradually, though, many researchers became dissatisfied with this approach and its strict emphasis on environmental determinants of learning. Some psychologists believed that thoughts, perceptions, emotions, and so on are important causes of behavior. As a result, their research has focused on understanding *cognition*, or the mental processes by which organisms acquire and store information about their environment and how that information is subsequently used to make plans and solve problems. Although we will examine cognitive psychology in detail in later chapters, I include here a glimpse of how it has challenged the behavior-analytic perspective.

In the cognitive view, behavior is not due solely to environmental causes, but also to internal events: processing information about the environment, storing it in memory, and then manipulating that information when it becomes useful in solving a problem or making a decision (Neisser, 1967). Cognitive psychologists argue that for any organism, learning depends on three things: its capacity to form mental representations of its environment, its ability to manipulate those representations, and its ability to implement the results of such manipulations as it interacts with the environment. Even operant behavior, then, has a cognitive component (Rescorla, 1991).

Behavior analysts respond that there is no solid evidence that such internal representations actually exist. They accuse cognitive psychologists of talking about "internal surrogates" of the real world as if they actually exist when, in fact, they are simply hypothetical constructs (Skinner, 1978, 1990). After all, no one has ever directly observed an internal representation; the very best that we can do is to observe behavior directly and then make *inferences* about what cognitive pro-

cesses seem to be responsible for the behavior, a conviction also held by cognitive psychologists. But it is these very inferences about cognition to which behavior analysts take exception. Because we cannot gather direct evidence that such things exist, how can we be sure that we are not on a wild goose chase, looking for and talking about things that do not exist? Behavior analysts do believe that such events as thoughts exist, but they do not view them as *causes* of behavior; instead thoughts are viewed as behaviors that are influenced by environmental variables. (Of course, these thoughts can go on to influence *other* behaviors. Behavior analysts do not deny the importance of thinking.)

The debate between cognitive psychologists and behavior analysts has been and will continue to be lively. It has been a useful one, as differences in perspective can often be. If nothing else, cognitive psychology has exposed some of the boundaries of the behavior-analytic position (its emphasis on only observable behavior) and defined new frontiers in need of exploration (cognitive processes). The debate has also been a productive one, with both behavior analysts and cognitive psychologists designing research and conducting experiments to bolster their respective positions. This chapter has given you an overview of the behavioral position and the research that supports it. The next several chapters will fill you in on the work of today's cognitive psychologists.

Interim Summary

Conditioning of Complex Behaviors

Much behavior is under the control of aversive contingencies, which specify particular behaviors that are instrumental in either escaping or avoiding aversive stimuli. For instance, you may escape the clutches of a would-be mugger by running away, or you may avoid getting mugged altogether by staying in well-illuminated areas at night.

The phenomenon of conditioned flavor aversions illustrates how natural selection can affect the brain mechanisms involved in learning. Because there is a delay between tasting a poison and getting sick, the rule that a reinforcing or punishing stimulus must immediately follow the response cannot apply. Indeed, organisms are able to learn the association between flavor and illness over a long interval. Psychologists have used conditioned flavor aversions to help cancer patients undergoing chemotherapy to form aversions to distinct flavors that are not part of the patients' normal diets. Psychologists have also applied conditioned flavor aversions to controlling wildlife predation on domestic animals.

Behavior analysts study the behavior of many species, but of late, behaviors especially important to our species have come under close scrutiny. How instructions control behavior, how people learn what symbols such as words stand for, and how different classes of drugs, especially those most likely to be abused, affect behavior are three areas of research receiving the most empirical attention.

The effects of reinforcing and punishing stimuli on behavior can be complex and subtle. We are able to acquire both operantly and classically conditioned responses through observation and imitation. In addition, we can learn to modify and combine responses learned in other contexts to solve new problems. The fact that pigeons, too, can exhibit insight suggests that not all instances of insight learning require "thinking" in the sense of imagining the behavior before it is performed. Of course, pigeons are unlikely to learn the individual behaviors necessary for solving, say, the hanging banana problem unless someone deliberately teaches them. Chimpanzees' ability to manipulate objects and observe the behavior of others allows them to engage in much more flexible behaviors than most other species can.

Cognitive psychologists disagree with behavior analysts about the determinants of behavior. While behavior analysts argue that behavior is governed by external causes, such as discriminative stimuli and environmentally based reinforcers and punishers, cognitive psychologists maintain that behavior is controlled by internal causes, such as thoughts, images, feelings, and perceptions. Both groups of psychologists continue to design and conduct research to support their positions, creating new fuel to drive one of the most important debates in modern psychology.

Thought Questions

- Skinner might argue that many of the laws that govern behavior in our culture are based more on aversive control of behavior (punishment, response cost, negative reinforcement) than on positive reinforcement. Would you agree or disagree with this position? Why or why not?

- Negative reinforcement is often a difficult concept for many students to grasp. Sometimes it helps to further understanding of this principle by generating examples that show negative reinforcement in action. Can you think of any personal examples in which your behavior has been negatively reinforced? Can you identify the stimuli in these examples that serve as the negative reinforcers and can you state which aspects of your behavior were influenced by these stimuli?

- What important behaviors have you learned, wholly or partially, from first observing them being performed by others? Would you have been able to learn these behaviors as well or as quickly had you not first had the opportunity to see them being performed by someone else? Why or why not?

Suggestions for Further Reading

Mazur, J.E. *Learning and Behavior.* Englewood Cliffs, NJ: Prentice-Hall, 1994.

An excellent book written for upper-division courses in behavior analysis. This text presents an overview of classical and operant conditioning and is up-to-date on research and theoretical positions in behavior analysis.

Skinner, B.F. *Science and Human Behavior.* New York: The Free Press, 1953.

This book, although originally published over forty years ago, is still a valuable interpretation of the behavior-analytic position. The basic principles of operant conditioning and their application to understanding a wide range of behaviors are explained interestingly and clearly. This book is an excellent choice if you wish to know more about Skinner's views.

Skinner, B.F. *Upon Further Reflection.* Englewood Cliffs, NJ: Prentice-Hall, 1987.

This little book is an anthology of Skinner's more recent ideas. In the preface, Skinner notes that the book is committed to the "experimental analysis of behavior and its use in the interpretation of human affairs." The topics he discusses range from why we are not acting to save the world to cognitive science to behaviorism to education. This book, too, is thought-provoking and clearly written.

Chapter 6

Sensation

Chapter Outline

Sensory Processing

Transduction • Sensory Coding • Psychophysics • *Evaluating Scientific Issues: Subliminal Self-Help*

The primary function of the sense organs is to provide information that can guide behavior. The translation of information about environmental events into neural activity is called transduction. In the nervous system, sensory information must be translated into one of two types of neural code: anatomical or temporal. Psychophysics is the study of the relation between the physical characteristics of stimuli and the perceptions they produce. The term subliminal perception refers to the behavioral effects of a stimulus that cannot be consciously detected. There is no evidence that information presented subliminally can produce useful, practical learning.

Vision

Light • The Eye and Its Functions • Transduction of Light by Photoreceptors • Adaptation to Light and Dark • Eye Movements • Color Vision

Light is a form of electromagnetic radiation. Images of the visual scene are focused on the retina, the inner layer at the back of the eye. Photoreceptors, specialized neurons located in the retina, contain chemicals called photopigments that transduce light into neural activity. Chemical changes in the photopigments are responsible for our ability to see in dim or bright light. The eyes make small involuntary movements that prevent the image from fading and two types of voluntary movements. Light can vary in wavelength, intensity, and purity. Three types of cones in the retina, each most sensitive to a particular wavelength of light, detect colors. Most genetic defects affecting color vision cause the inability to produce one of the three photopigments found in cones.

Audition

Sound • The Ear and Its Functions • Detecting and Localizing Sounds in the Environment • *Biology and Culture: The Deaf Community*

Sound waves can vary in frequency, intensity, and complexity, giving rise to differences in perceptions of pitch, loudness, and timbre. The bones of the middle ear transmit sound vibrations from the eardrum to the

cochlea, which contains the auditory receptors—the hair cells. The auditory system detects individual frequencies by means of place coding and rate coding. Left–right localization is accomplished by two means: arrival time and differences in intensity. The Deaf community consists of deaf people who can comfortably and effectively communicate with each other through sign language.

Gustation

Receptors and the Sensory Pathway • The Four Qualities of Taste

Taste receptors on the tongue respond to bitterness, sourness, sweetness, and saltiness and, together with the olfactory system, provide us with information about complex flavors.

Olfaction

Anatomy of the Olfactory System • The Dimensions of Odor

The olfactory system detects the presence of aromatic molecules. The discovery of a family of receptor molecules suggests that several hundred different types of receptors may be involved in olfactory discrimination and thus that odor may have several hundred dimensions.

The Somatosenses

The Skin Senses • The Internal Senses • The Vestibular Senses

Sensory receptors in the skin provide information about touch, pressure, vibration, changes in temperature, and stimuli that cause tissue damage. Pain perception helps protect us from harmful stimuli. Sensory endings located in the internal organs, joints, and muscles convey information about our own movements and about events occurring in our organs. The vestibular system helps us maintain our balance and makes compensatory eye movements to help us maintain fixation when our heads move.

Nine-year-old Sara tried to think of something else, but the throbbing pain in her thumb was relentless. Earlier in the day, her brother had slammed the car door on it.

"Why does it have to hurt so much, Daddy?" she asked piteously.

"I wish I could help you, sweetheart," he answered. "Pain may be useful, but it sure isn't fun."

"What do you mean, useful?" she asked in astonishment. "You mean it's good for me?" She looked at her father reproachfully.

"Well, this probably isn't the time to tell you about the advantages of pain, because it's hard to appreciate them when you're suffering." A glimmer of interest began to grow in her eyes. For as long as she could remember, Sara loved to have her father explain things to her, even when his explanations got a little confusing.

"You know," he said, "there are some people who never feel any pain. They are born that way."

"Really?" Her eyes widened. "They're lucky!"

"No, they really aren't. Without the sense of pain, they keep injuring themselves. When they touch something hot, they don't know enough to let go, even when their hand is getting burned. If the water in the shower gets too hot, they don't realize they're getting scalded. If their shoes don't fit right, they get huge blisters without knowing what's happening. If they fall and sprain an ankle—or even break a bone—they don't feel that something bad has happened to them, and their injury will just get worse. Some people who have no ability to feel pain have died when their appendix burst because they didn't know that something bad was happening inside them."

Sara looked thoughtful. Her father's explanation seemed to be distracting her from her pain.

"Parents of children who can't feel pain say that it's difficult to teach them to avoid danger. When a child does something that causes pain, she quickly learns to avoid repeating her mistake. Remember when you were three years old and walked on the grill of the heater in the cabin floor? You had just gotten out of the shower, and you burned the bottoms of your feet."

"I *think* so," she said. "Yes, you bought me a bag of candy corn to make me forget how much it hurt."

"That's right. Your mom and I had told you that the grill was dangerous when the heater was on, but it took an actual experience to teach you to stay away. We feel pain when parts of our bodies are damaged. The injured cells make a chemical that's picked up by nerve endings, and the nerves send messages to the brain to warn it that something bad is happening. Our brains automatically try to get us away from whatever it is that hurts us—and we also learn to become afraid of it. After you burned your feet on the grill, you stayed away from it even when you were wearing shoes.

"Kids who can't feel pain can learn to stay away from dangerous things, but it's not an automatic, gut-level kind of learning. They have to pay attention all the time, and if they let down their guard, it's easy for them to injure themselves. Pain isn't fun, but it's hard to survive without it."

"I guess so," said Sara reluctantly. She looked at her bandaged thumb, and the sudden realization of how much it hurt brought tears to her eyes again. "But the pain could go away now, because it's already taught me everything I need to know."

Behavior does not exist in a vacuum, nor do our thoughts and emotions. Our actions are provoked, informed, and guided by events that occur in our environment, and we think about—and have feelings about—what is happening there. Our senses are the means by which we experience the world; everything we learn is detected by sense organs and transmitted to our brains by sensory nerves. Without sensory input, a human brain would be utterly useless; it would learn nothing, think no thoughts, have no experiences, and control no behaviors.

Vision, to most people, is the most important sense modality. Through it, we recognize family and friends, see their facial expressions and gestures, learn to read, perceive objects that are beyond our reach, and find our way around our environment. It provides us with information about the size, shape, color, and movement of objects nearby and at a distance. Through vision, we receive some of our most powerful aesthetic experiences, in the form of art and other beautiful images—experiences rivaled only by the hearing of music that we appreciate.

The other senses also contribute to the richness of experience. Because of the role that speech plays in human culture, audition is extremely important for social behavior. With vision, it provides information about distant events, as does the sense of smell, which can tell us about sources of aromatic molecules far upwind. The other senses deal with events occurring immediately nearby, for instance the taste of our favorite foods or the touch of a loved one. The body senses are closely tied to our own movements. When we feel an object, the experience is active, not passive; we move our hands over it to determine its shape, texture, and temperature. And information from specialized organs in the inner ear and from receptors in the muscles and joints is actually produced by our own movements. This information helps us to maintain our balance as we engage in our everyday activities.

Our senses are the means by which we experience the world.

Sensory Processing

Experience is traditionally divided into two classes: sensation and perception. Most psychologists define **sensation** as the detection of simple properties of stimuli, such as brightness, color, warmth, and sweetness. **Perception** is the detection of objects (both animate and inanimate), their locations, their movements, and their backgrounds. According to these definitions, seeing the color red is a *sensation*, but seeing a red

sensation The detection of the elementary properties of a stimulus.

perception The detection of the more complex properties of a stimulus, including its location and nature; involves learning.

apple is a *perception*. Similarly, seeing a movement is a sensation, but seeing a baseball coming toward us and realizing that we will have to move to the left to catch it is a perception. Psychologists used to believe that perceptions depended heavily on learning whereas pure sensations involved innate, "prewired" physiological mechanisms. However, neither behavioral nor physiological research has been able to establish a clear boundary between "simple" sensations and "complex" perceptions. Indeed, research has shown that experience is essential to the development of some of the most elementary features of sensory systems.

This chapter describes our sensory mechanisms: the visual, auditory, gustatory, olfactory, and somatosensory systems. According to tradition, we have five senses, but in fact, we have several more. For example, the somatosensory system includes separate components that are able to detect touch, warmth, coolness, vibration, physical damage (pain), head tilt, head movement, limb movement, muscular contraction, and various events occurring within our bodies. Whether we choose to call each of these components "senses" is a matter of terminology.

Transduction

The brain, floating in cerebrospinal fluid and swaddled in its protective sheath of meninges and sheltered in the thick skull, is isolated from the world around us. The only sense receptors that the brain possesses detect such things as temperature and salt concentration of the blood, and these receptors

Table 6.1		
The Types of Transduction Accomplished by the Sense Organs		
Location of Sense Organ	**Environmental Stimuli**	**Energy Transduced**
Eye	Light	Radiant energy
Ear	Sound	Mechanical energy
Vestibular system	Tilt and rotation of head	Mechanical energy
Tongue	Taste	Recognition of molecular shape
Nose	Odor	Recognition of molecular shape
Skin, internal organs	Touch	Mechanical energy
	Temperature	Thermal energy
	Vibration	Mechanical energy
	Pain	Chemical reaction
Muscle	Stretch	Mechanical energy

cannot inform it about what is going on outside. Useful actions require information about the external world, and such information is gathered by the sense organs located outside the brain.

Sense organs detect the presence of environmental stimuli provided by light, sound, odor, taste, or mechanical contact. This information is transmitted to the brain through neural impulses—action potentials carried by the axons in sensory nerves. The task of the sense organs is to transmit signals to the brain that are coded in such a way as to faithfully represent the events that have occurred in the environment. The task of the brain is to analyze this information and reconstruct what has occurred.

Transduction (literally, "leading across") is the process by which the sense organs convert energy from environmental events into neural activity. Each sense organ responds to a particular form of energy given off by an environmental stimulus and translates that energy into neural firing to which the brain can respond. The means of transduction are as diverse as the kinds of stimuli we can perceive. In most senses, specialized neurons called **receptor cells** release chemical transmitter substances that stimulate other neurons, thus altering the rate of firing of their axons. In the somatosenses ("body senses"), dendrites of neurons respond directly to physical stimuli without the intervention of specialized receptor cells. However, some of these neurons do have specialized endings that enable them to respond to particular kinds of sensory information. *Table 6.1* summarizes the types of transduction accomplished by our sense organs.

transduction The conversion of physical stimuli into changes in the activity of receptor cells of sensory organs.

receptor cell A neuron that directly responds to a physical stimulus, such as light, vibrations, or aromatic molecules.

Sensory Coding

As we saw in Chapter 4, nerves are bundles of axons, each of which can do no more than transmit action potentials. These action potentials are fixed in size and duration; they cannot be altered. Thus, different stimuli cannot be translated into different types of action potentials. Yet we can detect an enormous number of different stimuli with each of our sense organs. For example, we are capable of discriminating among approximately 7.5 million different colors. We can also recognize touches to different parts of the body, and we can further

We are capable of distinguishing among approximately 7.5 million different colors.

discriminate the degree of pressure involved and the sharpness or bluntness, softness or hardness, and the temperature of the object touching us. But how, then, if action potentials cannot be altered, do the sense organs tell the brain that, for instance, a red apple or a yellow lemon has been seen—or that the right hand is holding a small, cold object or a large, warm one? The information from the sense organs must somehow be coded in the activity of axons carrying information from the sense organs to the brain.

A *code* is a system of symbols or signals representing information. Spoken English, written French, semaphore signals, magnetic fields on a recording tape, and the electrical zeros and ones in the memory of a computer are all examples of codes. As long as we know the rules of a code, we can convert a message from one medium to another without losing any information. Although we do not know the precise rules by which the sensory systems transmit information to the brain, we do know that they take two general forms: *anatomical coding* and *temporal coding*.

Anatomical Coding

Since the early 1800s, when Johannes Müller formulated his doctrine of specific nerve energies (discussed in Chapter 1), we have known that the brain learns what is happening through the activity of specific sets of neurons. Sensory organs located in different places in the body send their information to the brain through different nerves. Because the brain has no direct information about the physical energy impinging on a given sense organ, it uses **anatomical coding** to interpret the location and type of sensory stimulus according to which incoming nerve fibers are active. For example, if you rub your eyes, you will mechanically stimulate the light-sensitive receptors located there. This stimulation produces action potentials in the axons of the nerves that connect the eyes with the brain (the *optic nerves*). The visual system of the brain has no way of knowing that the light-sensitive receptors of the eyes have been activated by an unnatural stimulus. As a result, the brain acts as if the neural activity in the optic nerves was produced by light—so you see stars and flashes. Experiments performed during surgery have shown that artificial stimulation of the nerves that convey taste produces a sensation of taste, electrical stimulation of the auditory nerve produces a sensation of a buzzing noise, and so forth.

We use forms of anatomical coding to distinguish not only among the sense modalities themselves, but also among stimuli of the same sense modality. Obviously, sensory coding for the body surface is anatomical: Different nerve fibers serve different parts of the skin. Thus, we can easily discriminate a touch on the arm from a touch on the knee. As we saw in Chapter 4, the primary somatosensory cortex contains a neural "map" of the skin. Receptors in the skin in different parts of the body send information to different parts of the primary somatosensory cortex. Similarly, the primary visual cortex maintains a map of the visual field.

Temporal Coding

Temporal coding is the coding of information in terms of time. The simplest form of temporal code is *rate*. By firing at a faster or slower rate according to the intensity of a stimulus, an axon can communicate quantitative information to the brain. For example, a light touch to the skin can be encoded by a low rate of firing and a more forceful touch by a high rate. Thus, the firing of a particular set of neurons (an anatomical code) tells *where* the body is being touched; the rate at which these neurons fire (a temporal code) tells *how intense* that touch is. As far as we know, all sensory systems use rate of firing to encode the intensity of stimulation. The nervous system may use more complex forms of temporal codes, but this possibility has yet to be scientifically established.

Psychophysics

As you learned in Chapter 1, nineteenth-century Europe was the birthplace of **psychophysics,** the systematic study of the relation between the physical characteristics of stimuli and the sensations they produce (the "physics of the mind"). To study perceptual phenomena, scientists had to find reliable ways to measure people's sensations. We will examine two of these methods—the just-noticeable difference and the procedures of signal detection theory—in the following subsections.

The Principle of the Just-Noticeable Difference

In Germany, Ernst Weber (1795–1878), an anatomist and physiologist, investigated the ability of humans to discriminate between various stimuli. He measured the **just-noticeable difference (jnd)**—the smallest change in the magnitude of a stimulus that a person can detect. He discovered a principle that held true for all sensory systems: The jnd is directly related to the magnitude of that stimulus. For example, when he presented subjects with two metal objects and asked them to say whether they differed in weight, the subjects reported that the two weights felt the same unless they differed by a factor of 1 in 40. That is, a person could just barely distin-

---

anatomical coding A means by which the nervous system represents information; different features are coded by the activity of different neurons.

temporal coding A means by which the nervous system represents information; different features are coded by the pattern of activity of neurons.

psychophysics A branch of psychology that measures the quantitative relation between physical stimuli and perceptual experience.

just-noticeable difference (jnd) The smallest difference between two similar stimuli that can be distinguished. Also called difference threshold.

guish a 40-gram weight from a 41-gram weight, an 80-gram weight from an 82-gram weight, or a 400-gram weight from a 410-gram weight. Psychologically, the difference between a 40-gram weight and a 41-gram weight is equivalent to the difference between an 80-gram weight and an 82-gram weight: one jnd. Different senses had different ratios. For example, the ratio for detecting differences in the brightness of white light is approximately 1 in 60. These ratios are called **Weber fractions.**

Gustav Fechner (1801–1887), another German physiologist, used Weber's concept of the just-noticeable difference to measure people's sensations. Assuming that the jnd was the basic unit of a sensory experience, he measured the absolute magnitude of a sensation in jnds.

Suppose we want to measure the strength of a person's sensation of light of a particular intensity. We seat the subject in a darkened room facing two disks of frosted glass, each having a light bulb behind it; the brightness of the light bulb is adjustable. One of the disks serves as the sample stimulus, the other as the comparison stimulus. (See *Figure 6.1.*) We start with the sample stimulus and the comparison stimulus turned off completely and increase the brightness of the comparison stimulus until our subject can just detect a difference. That value is one jnd. Then we set the sample stimulus to that intensity (one jnd) and again increase the brightness of the comparison stimulus just until our subject

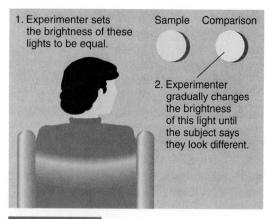

Figure 6.1

The method for determining a just-noticeable difference (jnd).

Weber fraction The ratio between a just-noticeable difference and the magnitude of a stimulus; reasonably constant over the middle range of most stimulus intensities.

threshold The point at which a stimulus, or a change in the value of a stimulus, can just be detected.

difference threshold An alternate name for just-noticeable difference (jnd).

absolute threshold The minimum value of a stimulus that can be detected.

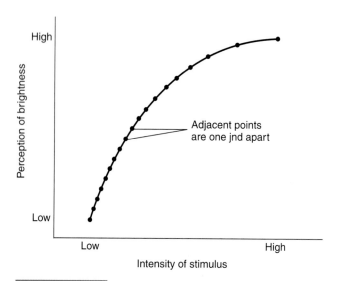

Figure 6.2

A hypothetical range of perceived brightness (in jnds) as a function of intensity.

can again tell them apart. The new value of the comparison stimulus is two jnds. We continue making these measurements until our stimuli are as bright as we can make them or until they become uncomfortably bright for our subject. Finally, we construct a graph indicating the strength of a sensation of brightness (in jnds) in relation to the intensity of a stimulus. The graph, which relates strength of a sensory experience to physical intensity, might look something like *Figure 6.2.*

Signal Detection Theory

Psychophysical methods rely heavily on the concept of a **threshold,** the line between not perceiving and perceiving. The just-noticeable difference can also be called a **difference threshold,** the minimum detectable difference between two stimuli. An **absolute threshold** is the minimum value of a stimulus that can be detected—that is, discriminated from no stimulus at all. Thus, the first comparison in the experiment I just described—using a dark disk as the sample stimulus—measured an absolute threshold. The subsequent comparisons measured difference thresholds.

Even early psychophysicists realized that a threshold was not an absolutely fixed value. When an experimenter flashes a very dim light, a subject may report seeing it on some trials but not on others. By convention, the threshold is the point at which a subject detects the stimulus 50 percent of the time. This definition is necessary because of the inherent variability of the activity in the nervous system. Even when they are not being stimulated, neurons are never absolutely still; they fire every now and then. If a very weak stimulus occurs when neurons in the visual system happen to be quiet, the brain is likely to detect it. But if the neurons happen to be firing, the effects of the stimulus are likely to be lost in the "noise."

According to signal detection theory, we must discriminate between the signal, conveying information, and noise, contributed by background stimuli and random activity of our own nervous systems.

An alternative method of measuring a person's sensitivity to changes in physical stimuli takes account of random changes in the nervous system (Green and Swets, 1974). According to **signal detection theory,** every stimulus event requires discrimination between *signal* (stimulus) and *noise* (consisting of both background stimuli and random activity of the nervous system).

Suppose you are seated in a quiet room, facing a small warning light. The experimenter tells you that when the light flashes, you *may* hear a faint tone one second later. Your task is to say "yes" or "no" after each flash of the warning light, according to whether or not you hear the tone. At first the task is easy: Some flashes are followed by an easily heard tone; others are followed by silence. You are confident about your yes and no decisions. But as the experiment progresses, the tone gets fainter and fainter, until it is so soft that you have doubts about how you should respond. The light flashes. What should you say? Did you really hear a tone or were you just imagining it?

At this point your *response bias*—your tendency to say "yes" or "no" when you are not sure whether you detected the stimulus—can have an effect. According to the terminology of signal detection theory, *hits* are saying "yes" when the stimulus is presented; *misses* are saying "no" when it is presented; *correct negatives* are saying "no" when the stimulus is not presented; and *false alarms* are saying "yes" when the stimulus is not presented. Hits and correct negatives are correct responses; misses and false alarms are incorrect responses. (See *Figure 6.3.*) Suppose you want to be very sure that you are correct when you say "yes" because you would feel foolish saying you have heard something that is not there. Your response bias is

to err in favor of making hits and avoiding false alarms, even at the risk of making misses. Alternatively, your response bias might be to err in favor of detecting all stimuli, even at the risk of making false alarms.

A person's response bias can seriously affect an investigator's estimate of the threshold of detection. A conservative person will appear to have a higher threshold than will someone who does not want to let a tone go by without saying "yes." Therefore, signal detection theorists have developed a method of assessing people's sensitivity, regardless of their initial response bias. They deliberately manipulate the response biases and observe the results of these manipulations on the people's judgments.

Suppose you are a subject in the experiment just described, and the experimenter promises you a dollar every time you make a hit, with no penalty for false alarms. You would undoubtedly tend to say "yes" on every trial, even if you were not sure you had heard the tone; after all, you have nothing to lose and everything to gain. In contrast, suppose the experimenter announced that she would fine you a dollar every time you made a false alarm and give you nothing for making hits. You would undoubtedly say "no" every time, because you would have *everything* to lose and *nothing* to gain: You would be extremely conservative in your judgments.

Now consider your response bias under a number of intermediate conditions. If you receive a dollar for every hit but are also fined fifty cents for every miss, you will say "yes" whenever you are reasonably sure you heard the tone. If you receive fifty cents for every hit but are fined a dollar for each

Judgment

	"Yes"	"No"
Light *did* flash	Hit	Miss
Light *did not* flash	False alarm	Correct negative

Event

Figure 6.3

Four possibilities in judging the presence or absence of a stimulus.

signal detection theory A mathematical theory of the detection of stimuli, which involves discriminating a signal from the noise in which it is embedded and which takes into account subjects' willingness to report detecting the signal.

false alarm, you will be more conservative. But if you are sure you heard the tone, you will say "yes" to earn fifty cents. (I should note that there are other, less expensive ways to change people's response biases besides offering them payment, which is fortunate for researchers on limited budgets.) *Figure 6.4* graphs your performance over this range of payoff conditions.

The graph in Figure 6.4 is a **receiver operating characteristic curve (ROC curve)**, named for its original use in research at the Bell Laboratories to measure the intelligibility of speech transmitted through a telephone system. The curve shows performance when the sound is difficult to detect. If the sound were louder, so that you rarely doubted whether you heard it, you would make almost every possible hit and very few false alarms. The few misses you made would be under the low-payoff condition, when you wanted to be absolutely certain you heard the tone. The few false alarms would occur when guessing did not matter because the fine for being wrong was low or nonexistent. The ROC curve (magenta) reflecting this new condition is shown with the original one (blue) in Figure 6.5. The difference between the two curves demonstrates that the louder tone is easier to detect. Detectability is measured by the relative distances of the curves from a 45-degree line. (See *Figure 6.5*.)

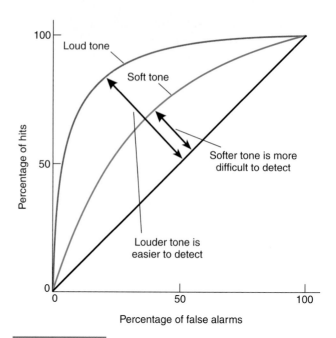

Figure 6.5

Two ROC curves, obtained by presenting a more discriminable stimulus (black curve) and a less discriminable stimulus (blue curve).

The signal detection method is the best way to determine a person's sensitivity to the occurrence of a particular stimulus. Note that the concept of threshold is not used. Instead, a stimulus is more or less detectable. The person *decides* whether a stimulus occurred, and the consequences of making hits or false alarms can bias this decision. Signal detection theory emphasizes that sensory experience involves factors other than the activity of the sensory systems, such as motivation and prior experience.

Evaluating Scientific Issues

Subliminal Self-Help

As you undoubtedly know, the market is full of self-help aids: books, audiocassettes, videocassettes, courses, and seminars on how to increase your productivity, improve your self-image, enhance your memory, reduce stress, quit smoking, become fit, and lose weight. If you are afraid that achieving these goals might take some effort on your part, don't worry—no work is necessary. Or so say the makers of subliminal *self-help cassettes (that is, audio- or videocassettes containing messages so faint that they cannot be consciously heard or seen).*

The United States Armed Forces spends billions of dollars each year training their personnel, and they support research directed at developing more effective educa-

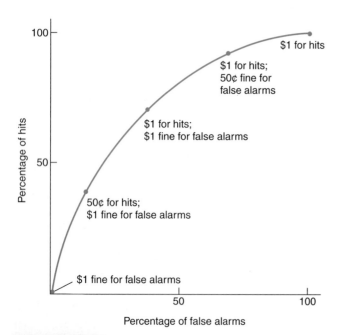

Figure 6.4

A receiver operating characteristic (ROC) curve. The percentage of hits and false alarms in judging the presence of a stimulus under several payoff conditions.

receiver operating characteristic curve (ROC curve)
A graph of hits and false alarms of subjects under different motivational conditions; indicates people's ability to detect a particular stimulus.

tional methods. In 1984, the Army Research Institute asked the National Academy of Sciences/National Research Council to investigate several methods purported to improve people's performance—including the use of subliminal self-help procedures. These investigations provide an objective, scientific evaluation of subliminal self-help procedures (Druckman and Bjork, 1991).

■ Claims about Subliminal Self-Help Tapes

According to the vendor of a subliminal self-help audio cassette, *Building Self-Confidence,* the message provided by the tape reaches

> the subconscious mind, which is the seat of all memories, knowledge and emotions. The unconscious mind has a powerful influence on conscious actions, thoughts, feelings, habits, and behaviors, and actually controls and guides your life. If you want to make real, lasting changes and improvements in any area of your life, you must reach the subconscious mind where the changes begin. (Druckman and Bjork, 1991, p. 107)

The tape is rather pleasant to listen to; all one hears is the sound of surf washing on a beach, with the cries of sea gulls in the distance. But according to the manufacturer, the tape contains a voice making positive statements such as: "I am a secure person. I believe in myself more and more every day, and my confidence naturally rises to the surface in every situation." The voice is inaudible, masked by the sound of the surf. To profit from these messages, says a notice on the carton, "Simply play the tapes while you work, play, drive, read, exercise, relax, watch TV, or even as you sleep. No concentration is required for the tapes to be effective" (Druckman and Bjork, 1991, pp. 107–108).

By the late 1980s, there were at least 2000 vendors of subliminal self-help tapes in North America, having sales of more than $50 million a year (Oldenburg, 1990). One catalog of such tapes even promises to help restore hearing. Imagine, a deaf person restoring his or her hearing by listening to a subliminal message on an audiotape! What a remarkable achievement—to say the least.

Several vendors offer subliminal videotapes in which they present visual information so briefly that it cannot be consciously detected. One manufacturer even supplies an electronic device that plugs into a television set and superimposes subliminal messages on ordinary programs, so that the viewer can effortlessly engage in self-improvement while watching reruns of, say, *The Brady Bunch* or *The Love Boat.*

■ Evidence in Support of Subliminal Self-Help Tapes

How would one determine whether subliminal self-help tapes work? Having read Chapter 2, you know that one would perform a double-blind study. One group of subjects would listen to tapes that contained the message, while another group would listen to tapes that contained only the background noise. Neither the experimenters nor the subjects would know which tapes contained a hidden message. The experimenters would make measurements of the personal characteristics relevant to the tapes before and after the course of treatment. For example, if the tape helped people lose weight, we would weigh them. If it helped cure acne or helped make people become better bowlers (no, I'm not making this up), we would count their pimples or record their bowling scores. You will probably not be surprised to learn that the vendors of subliminal self-help tapes have *not* performed studies such as these.

What kind of evidence *do* the manufacturers provide? They provide *testimonials.* "Bless you! I'm listening to my tape on pain reduction. It is marvelous. I had almost instant relief from pain on first using it a few days ago. It's much cheaper than a doctor and much better than medication. Phenomenal is what it has done for my spirits" (Druckman and Bjork, 1991, p. 113).

We need not doubt the sincerity of the satisfied customers; vendors do not usually need to write their own testimonials. But can testimonials be taken as evidence that subliminal self-help really works? Let's evaluate the evidence.

■ Does the Evidence Support Subliminal Self-Help Claims?

If a person is convinced that he or she received help from a subliminal tape, can we conclude that the system really works? Research—and simple logic—indicate that the answer is no. At least three phenomena can account for the fact that some customers will say that they are satisfied. First, simply making a purchase indicates a commitment to self-improvement. In fact, some people with emotional or behavioral problems show improvements in their feelings and behavior as soon as they register for psychotherapy—even before the therapy actually begins (Rachman and Wilson, 1980). Second, social psychologists learned long ago that once people have expended some effort toward reaching a goal, they tend to justify their effort by perceiving positive results. (We will encounter experiments that provide several examples of this phenomenon in Chapter 15.) Finally, if a person expects an effect to occur, he or she is easily convinced that it really did.

The effect of expectation is demonstrated by a study carried out to follow up a famous hoax. In 1957, an advertising expert claimed that he had inserted subliminal visual messages in a showing of *Picnic,* a popular film. The messages, which said "Eat Popcorn" and "Drink Coke," supposedly caused people to rush to the refreshment stand and purchase these items. As you can imagine, this event received much attention and publicity. Several years later, the advertising expert revealed that he had invented the episode in an attempt to get some favorable publicity for his firm (Weir, 1984).

In 1958, long before the advertising expert admitted his hoax, the Canadian Broadcasting Corporation commissioned a study to determine whether a subliminal message could really work (Pratkanis, Eskenazi, and Greenwald, 1990). At the beginning of a television show, an announcer described the alleged "Popcorn" study and told the viewers that a test of subliminal persuasion would follow, with an unspecified message appearing on the screen. In fact, the message was "Phone now." According to the telephone company, no increase in rate of phone calls occurred. But many viewers wrote to the television network to say that they had felt compelled to do *something,* such as eat or drink. Obviously, the specific message to "Phone now" did not get across to the viewers, but the expectation that they should feel some sort of compulsion made many of them report that they did.

Is there any objective, scientific evidence that subliminal perception can occur? The answer is yes, there is. But the information transmitted by this means is very scanty. *Subliminal* literally means "below threshold," after the Latin *limen,* "threshold." The term **subliminal perception** refers to the behavioral effect of a stimulus that falls below the threshold of conscious detection. That is, although the person denies having detected a stimulus, the stimulus has a measurable effect on his or her behavior. But the effects are subtle, and special procedures are required to demonstrate them. For example, if the word *nurse* is first flashed on a screen, it becomes easier for the viewer to recognize a related word, such as *doctor,* but not an unrelated word, such as *chair.* This phenomenon, called *semantic priming,* occurs even when the priming stimulus *(nurse)* is presented so rapidly that the subjects deny having seen it, meaning that it can occur subliminally (Marcel, 1983).

Results such as these simply indicate that perception is a complex process—that when a stimulus is too weak to give rise to a conscious perception, it may still be strong enough to leave some traces in the brain that affect people's perception of other stimuli. And this effect has a threshold of its own; if a word is presented too briefly, it has no effect at all on the perception of other words. The phenomenon is a real one that involves the sense receptors and normal physiological processes. (I describe the relation between consciousness, perception, and memories in more detail in Chapters 8 and 9.)

Psychologists have examined very few of the many thousands of different subliminal self-help tapes that are available, but those they have examined seem to be ineffective. Some, according to Merikle (1988), contain stimuli that are simply too weak for the human ear to detect under any conditions. Others, when subjected to spectrographic analysis (which detects the presence of "voice-prints" in the sound track) were found to contain no message at all.

Perhaps this fact explains the results of the experiment by Pratkanis, Eskenazi, and Greenwald (1990). The experimenters recruited volunteers to listen to either a subliminal tape designed to improve memory or one designed to improve self-esteem. After the subjects listened to the tapes for five weeks, the experimenters asked them whether their memories or self-esteem had improved. About half of the subjects said that they had—but none of the objective tests of memory or self-esteem administered by the experimenters showed any effect. Besides, the experimenters had switched tapes for half of the subjects: Some of those who thought they had received a memory tape actually received a self-esteem tape and vice versa. The switch made no difference at all in the satisfaction ratings. Thus, a person's satisfaction is no indication that subliminal perception has really taken place.

■ What Should We Conclude?

Only one conclusion seems possible: If you have been thinking about purchasing subliminal self-help tapes, save your money—unless you think you will be content with a placebo effect caused by commitment to change, a need to justify your efforts, and expectation of good results.

Interim Summary

Sensory Processing

We experience the world through our senses. Our knowledge of the world stems from the accumulation of sensory experience and subsequent learning. All sensory experiences are the result of energy from events that is transduced into activity of receptors, which are specialized neurons. Transduction causes changes in the activity of axons of sensory nerves, and these changes in activity inform the sensory mechanisms of the brain about the environmental event. The information received from the receptors is transmitted to the brain by means of two coding schemes: anatomical coding and temporal coding.

To study the nature of experience scientifically, we must be able to measure it. In nineteenth-century Germany, Weber devised the concept of the just-noticeable difference, and Fechner used the jnd to measure the magnitude of sensations. In the twentieth century, signal detection theory gave rise to methods that enabled psychologists to assess people's sensitivity to stimuli despite individual differences in response bias. The methods of psychophysics apply to all sensory modalities, including sight, smell, taste, hearing, and touch.

The makers of subliminal self-help tapes suggest that material that is presented below the detection threshold can improve a variety of skills and attitudes. Evidence suggests, however, that the testimonials of satisfied customers are a result of commitment to change, a need to justify one's efforts,

subliminal perception The perception of a stimulus, as indicated by a change in behavior, at an intensity insufficient to produce a conscious sensation.

and expectation of good results. Subliminal perception does occur as long as the stimulus is not *too* weak, but the effects are subtle and are unlikely to produce useful changes in people's behavior.

Thought Questions

- What sense modalities would you least want to lose? Why?
- If you could design a new sense modality, what kind of information would it detect? What advantages would this new ability provide? Or do you think that our sensory organs already detect all the useful information that is available? Why or why not?

Vision

The visual system performs a remarkable job. We take for granted the fact that in a quick glance we can recognize what there is to see: people, objects, and landscapes in depth and full color. Researchers who have tried to program computers to recognize scenes visually realize just how complex this task is. This section begins our tour of the visual system. We will consider the eye and its functions in this chapter and explore the nature of visual perception in Chapter 7. But first, let's start with the stimulus: light.

Light

As we all know, the eye is sensitive to light. But what is light? Light consists of radiant energy similar to radio waves. As the radiant energy is transmitted from its source, it oscillates. For example, the antenna that broadcasts the programs of my favorite FM station transmits radio waves that oscillate at 88.5 MHz (megahertz, or million times per second). Because radiant energy travels at 186,000 miles per second, the waves transmitted by this antenna are approximately 11 feet apart. (One 88.5 millionth of 186,000 miles equals 11.09 feet.) Thus, the **wavelength** of the signal from the station—the distance between the waves of radiant energy—is 11 feet. (See *Figure 6.6.*)

The wavelength of visible light is much shorter, ranging from 380 through 760 nanometers (a nanometer, nm, is a billionth of a meter). When viewed by a human eye, different wavelengths of visible light have different colors: for instance, 380-nm light looks red and 760-nm light looks violet.

All other radiant energy is invisible to our eyes. Ultraviolet radiation, X rays, and gamma rays have shorter wavelengths than visible light has, whereas infrared radiation, radar, and (as we saw) radio waves have longer wavelengths. The entire range of wavelengths is known as the *electromagnetic spectrum*; the part our eyes can detect—the part we see as light—is referred to as the *visible spectrum*. (See *Figure 6.7.*)

The definition of the visible spectrum is based on the human visual system. Some other species of animals would

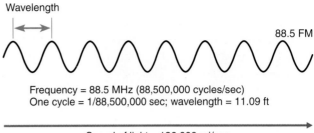

Frequency = 88.5 MHz (88,500,000 cycles/sec)
One cycle = 1/88,500,000 sec; wavelength = 11.09 ft

Speed of light = 186,000 mi/sec

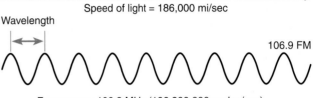

Frequency = 106.9 MHz (106,900,000 cycles/sec)
One cycle = 1/106,900,000 sec; wavelength = 9.82 ft

Figure 6.6

Wavelength versus vibration. Because the speed of light is constant, faster vibrations produce shorter wavelengths.

undoubtedly define the visible spectrum differently. For example, bees can see ultraviolet radiation that is invisible to us. Some plants have taken advantage of this fact and produce flowers that contain dyes that reflect ultraviolet radiation, presenting patterns that attract bees to them. Some snakes (notably, pit vipers such as the rattlesnake) have special organs that detect infrared radiation. This ability enables them to find their prey in the dark by detecting the heat emitted by small mammals in the form of infrared radiation.

The Eye and Its Functions

The eyes are important and delicate sense organs—and they are well protected. Each eye is housed in a bony socket and can be covered by the eyelid to keep dust and dirt out. The eyelids are edged by eyelashes, which help keep foreign matter from falling into the open eye. The eyebrows prevent sweat on the forehead from dripping into the eyes. Reflex mechanisms provide additional protection: The sudden approach of an object toward the face or a touch on the surface of the eye causes automatic eyelid closure and withdrawal of the head.

Figure 6.8 shows a cross section of a human eye. The transparent **cornea** forms a bulge at the front of the eye and admits light. The rest of the eye is coated by a tough white membrane called the **sclera** (from the Greek *skleros,* "hard").

wavelength The distance between adjacent waves of radiant energy; in vision, most closely associated with the perceptual dimension of hue.

cornea The transparent tissue covering the front of the eye.

sclera The tough outer layer of the eye; the "white" of the eye.

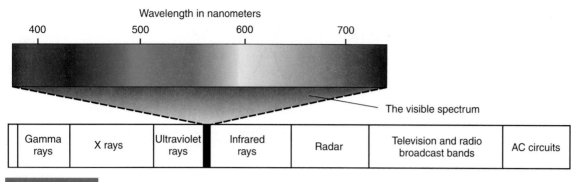

Figure 6.7

The electromagnetic spectrum.

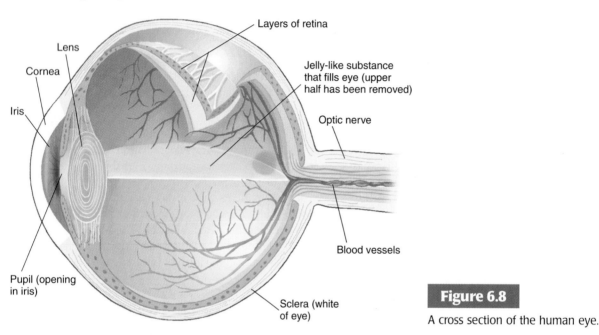

Figure 6.8

A cross section of the human eye.

The **iris** consists of two bands of muscles that control the amount of light admitted into the eye. The brain controls these muscles and thus regulates the size of the pupil, constricting it in bright light and dilating it in dim light. The space immediately behind the cornea is filled with *aqueous humor*, which simply means "watery fluid." This fluid is constantly produced by tissue behind the cornea that filters the fluid from the blood. In place of blood vessels, the aqueous humor nourishes the cornea and other portions of the front of the eye; this fluid must circulate and be renewed. (If aqueous humor is produced too quickly or if the passage that re-

turns it to the blood becomes blocked, the pressure within the eye can increase and cause damage to vision—a disorder known as *glaucoma*.) Because of its transparency, the cornea must be nourished in this unusual manner. Our vision would be less clear if we had a set of blood vessels across the front of our eyes. (See *Figure 6.8.*)

The curvature of the cornea and of the **lens,** which lies immediately behind the iris, causes images to be focused on the inner surface of the back of the eye. Although this image is upside-down and reversed from left to right, the brain compensates for this alteration and interprets the information appropriately. The shape of the cornea is fixed, but the lens is flexible; a special set of muscles can alter its shape so that the eye can obtain images of either nearby or distant objects. This change in the shape of the lens to adjust for distance is called **accommodation.**

Normally, the length of the eye matches the refractive power of the cornea and the lens so that the image of the visual scene is sharply focused on the retina. However, for some people these two factors are not matched, and the image on

iris The pigmented muscle of the eye that controls the size of the pupil.

lens The transparent organ situated behind the iris of the eye; helps focus an image on the retina.

accommodation Changes in the thickness of the lens of the eye that focus images of near or distant objects on the retina.

To a nearsighted person, distant objects are blurry and out of focus.

the retina is therefore out of focus. These people need an extra lens in front of their eyes (in the form of eyeglasses or contact lenses) to correct the discrepancy and bring the image into focus. People whose eyes are too long (front to back) are said to be *nearsighted;* they need a concave lens to correct the focus. People whose eyes are too short are said to be *farsighted;* they need a convex lens. As people get older, the lenses of their eyes become less flexible and it becomes difficult for them to focus on objects close to them. These people need reading glasses with convex lenses (or bifocals, if they already wear glasses). (See *Figure 6.9.*)

The **retina,** which lines the inner surface of the back of the eye, performs the sensory functions of the eye. Embedded in the retina are over 130 million **photoreceptors**—specialized neurons that transduce light into neural activity. The information from the photoreceptors is transmitted to neurons that send axons toward one point at the back of the eye—the **optic disk.** All axons leave the eye at this point and join the optic nerve, which travels to the brain. (See *Figures 6.8* and *6.10.*) Because there are no photoreceptors directly in front of the optic disk, this portion of the retina is blind. If you have not located your own *blind spot,* you might want to try the demonstration shown in *Figure 6.11.*

Before the seventeenth century, scientists thought that the lens sensed the presence of light. Johannes Kepler (1571–1630), the astronomer who discovered the true shape of the planets' orbits around the sun, is credited with the suggestion that the retina, not the lens, contained the receptive tissue of the eye. It remained for Christoph Scheiner (another German astronomer) to demonstrate in 1625 that the lens is simply a focusing device. (I suppose that astronomers had a special interest in vision and gave some thought to it during the long nights spent watching the sky.) Scheiner obtained an ox's eye from a slaughterhouse. After carefully peeling the sclera away from the back the eye, he was able to see an upside-down image of the world through the thin, translucent membrane that remained. As an astronomer, he was familiar with the

fact that convex glass lenses could cast images, so he recognized the function of the lens of the eye.

Figure 6.12 shows a cross section of the retina. The retina has three principal layers. Light passes successively through the *ganglion cell layer* (front), the *bipolar cell layer* (middle), and the *photoreceptor layer* (back). Early anatomists were surprised to find the photoreceptors in the deepest layer of the retina. As you might expect, the cells that are located above the photoreceptors are transparent. (See *Figure 6.12.*)

Photoreceptors respond to light and pass the information on by means of a transmitter substance to the **bipolar cells,** the neurons with which they form synapses. Bipolar cells transmit this information to the **ganglion cells,** neurons whose axons travel across the retina and through the optic nerves. Thus, visual information passes through a three-cell chain to the brain: photoreceptor → bipolar cell → ganglion cell → brain.

A single photoreceptor responds only to light that reaches its immediate vicinity, but a ganglion cell can receive information from many different photoreceptors. The retina also contains neurons that interconnect both adjacent photore-

retina   The tissue at the back inside surface of the eye that contains the photoreceptors and associated neurons.

photoreceptor   A receptive cell for vision in the retina; a rod or a cone.

optic disk   A circular structure located at the exit point from the retina of the axons of the ganglion cells that form the optic nerve.

bipolar cell   A neuron in the retina that receives information from photoreceptors and passes it on to the ganglion cells, from which axons proceed through the optic nerves to the brain.

ganglion cell   A neuron in the retina that receives information from photoreceptors by means of bipolar cells and from which axons proceed through the optic nerves to the brain.

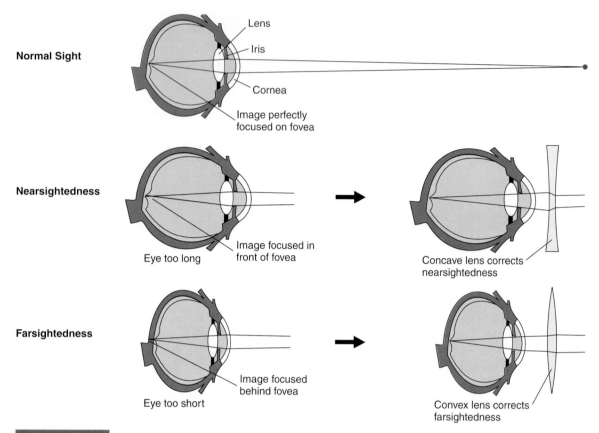

Figure 6.9

Lenses used to correct nearsightedness and farsightedness.

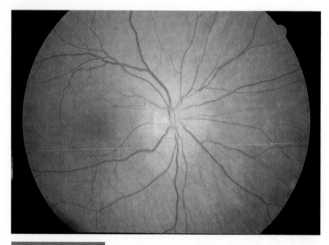

Figure 6.10

A view of the back of the eye. The photograph shows the retina, the optic disk, and blood vessels.

(Courtesy of Douglas G. Mollerstuen, New England Medical Center.)

ceptors and adjacent ganglion cells. (See *Figure 6.12.*) The existence of this neural circuitry indicates that some kinds of information processing are performed in the retina.

The human retina contains two general types of photoreceptors: 125 million rods and 6 million cones, so called because of their shapes. **Rods** function mainly in dim light; they are very sensitive to light but are insensitive to differences between colors. **Cones** function when the level of illumination is bright enough to see things clearly. They are also responsible for color vision. The **fovea,** a small pit in the back of the retina approximately 1 millimeter in diameter, contains only cones. (Refer to *Figure 6.8.*) Most cones are connected to only one ganglion cell apiece. As a consequence, the fovea is responsible for our finest, most detailed vision. When we look at a point in our visual field, we move our eyes so that the image of that point falls directly on the cone-packed fovea.

Farther away from the fovea, the number of cones decreases and the number of rods increases. Up to one hundred rods may converge on a single ganglion cell. A ganglion cell that receives information from so many rods is sensitive to very low levels of light. Rods are therefore responsible for our sensitivity to very dim light, but they provide poor acuity.

rod A photoreceptor that is very sensitive to light but cannot detect changes in hue.

cone A photoreceptor that is responsible for acute daytime vision and for color perception.

fovea A small pit near the center of the retina containing densely packed cones; responsible for the most acute and detailed vision.

Figure 6.11

A test for the blind spot. With the left eye closed, look at the + with your right eye and move the page back and forth, toward and away from yourself. At about 20 centimeters, the colored circle disappears from your vision because its image falls on your blind spot.

Transduction of Light by Photoreceptors

Although light-sensitive sensory organs have evolved independently in a wide variety of animals—from insects to fish to mammals—the chemistry is essentially the same in all species: A molecule derived from vitamin A is the central ingredient in the transduction of the energy of light into neural activity. (Carrots are said to be good for vision because they contain a substance that the body easily converts to vitamin A.) In the absence of light, this molecule is attached to another molecule, a protein. The two molecules together form a **photopigment.** The photoreceptors of the human eye contain four kinds of photopigments (one for rods and three for cones), but their basic mechanism is the same. When a photon (a particle of light) strikes a photopigment, the photopigment splits apart into its two constituent molecules. This event starts the process of transduction. The splitting of the photopigment causes a series of chemical reactions that stimulate the photoreceptor and cause it to send a message to the bipolar cell with which it forms a synapse. The bipolar cell sends a message to the ganglion cell, which then sends one on to the brain. (See *Figure 6.13.*)

Intact photopigments have a characteristic color. **Rhodopsin,** the photopigment of rods, is pink (*rhodon* means "rose" in Greek). However, once the photopigments are split apart by the action of light, they lose their color—they become bleached. Franz Boll discovered this phenomenon in 1876 when he removed an eye from an animal and pointed it toward a window that opened out onto a brightly lit scene. He then examined the retina under dim light and found that the image of the scene was still there. The retina was pink where little light had fallen and pale where the image had been bright. It was Boll's discovery that led investigators to suspect that a chemical reaction was responsible for the transduction of light into neural activity.

After light has caused a molecule of photopigment to split and become bleached, energy from the photoreceptor's metabolism causes the two molecules to recombine. The photopigment is then ready to be bleached by light again. Each photoreceptor contains many thousands of molecules of photopigment. The number of intact, unbleached molecules of photopigment in a given cell depends on the relative rates at which they are being split by light and being put back

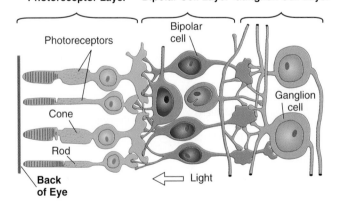

Figure 6.12

The cells of the retina.

(Redrawn by permission of the Royal Society and the authors from Dowling, J. E., and Boycott, B. B. Proceedings of the Royal Society (London), 1966, Series B, 166, 80–111.)

photopigment A complex molecule found in photoreceptors; when struck by light, it splits apart and stimulates the membrane of the photoreceptor in which it resides.

rhodopsin The photopigment contained by rods.

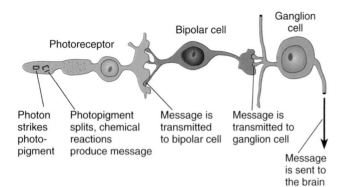

Figure 6.13

Transduction of light into neural activity. A photon strikes a photoreceptor and causes the photopigment to split apart. This event initiates the transmission of information to the brain.

together by the cell's energy. The brighter the light, the more bleached photopigment there is.

Adaptation to Light and Dark

Think, for a moment, about how difficult it can be to find a seat in a darkened movie theater. If you have just come in from the bright sun, your eyes do not respond well to the low level of illumination. However, after a few minutes, you can see rather well—your eyes have adapted to the dark. This phenomenon is called **dark adaptation.**

In order for light to be detected, photons must split molecules of rhodopsin or one of the other photopigments. When high levels of illumination strike the retina, the rate of regeneration of rhodopsin falls behind the rate of the bleaching process. With only a small percentage of the rhodopsin molecules intact, the rods are not very sensitive to light. If you enter a dark room after being in a brightly lit room or in sunlight, there are too few intact rhodopsin molecules for your eyes to respond immediately to dim light. The probability that a photon will strike an intact molecule of rhodopsin is very low. However, after a while, the regeneration of rhodopsin overcomes the bleaching effects of the light energy. The rods become full of unbleached rhodopsin, and a photon passing through a rod is likely to find a target. The eye has become dark adapted.

Eye Movements

Our eyes are never completely at rest, even when our gaze is fixed on a particular place called the *fixation point*. Our eyes

dark adaptation The process by which the eye becomes capable of distinguishing dimly illuminated objects after going from a bright area to a dark one.

make fast, aimless, jittering movements, similar to the fine tremors our hands and fingers make when we try to keep them still. They also make occasional slow movements away from the target they are fixed on, which are terminated by quick movements that bring the image of the fixation point back to the fovea.

Although the small, jerky movements that the eyes make when at rest are random, they appear to serve a useful function. Riggs, Ratliff, Cornsweet, and Cornsweet (1953) devised a way to project *stabilized images* on the retina—images that remain in the same location on the retina. They mounted a small mirror in a contact lens worn by the subject and bounced a beam of light off it. They then projected the image onto a white screen in front of the subject, bounced it off several more mirrors, and finally directed it toward the subject's eye. (See *Figure 6.14.*) The path of the light was arranged so that the image on the screen moved in perfect synchrony with the eye movements. If the eye moved, so did the image; thus, the image that the experimenters projected always fell on precisely the same part of the retina despite the subject's eye movements. Under these conditions, details of visual stimuli began to disappear. At first, the image was clear, but then a

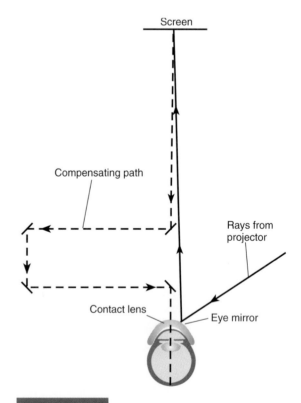

Figure 6.14

A procedure for stabilizing an image on the retina.
(From Riggs, L. A., Ratliff, F., Cornsweet, J. C., and Cornsweet, T. N. Journal of the Optical Society of America, 1953, 43, 495–501. Reprinted with permission.)

"fog" drifted over the subject's field of view, obscuring the image. After a while, some images could not be seen at all.

These results suggest that elements of the visual system are not responsive to an unchanging stimulus. The photoreceptors or the ganglion cells, or perhaps both, apparently cease to respond to a constant stimulus. The small, involuntary movements of our eyes keep the image moving and thus keep the visual system responsive to the details of the scene before us. Without these involuntary movements, our vision would become blurry soon after we fixed our gaze on a single point and our eyes became still.

The eyes also make three types of "purposive" movements: conjugate movements, saccadic movements, and pursuit movements. **Conjugate movements** are cooperative movements that keep both eyes fixed on the same target—or, more precisely, that keep the image of the target object on corresponding parts of the two retinas. If you hold up a finger in front of your face, look at it, and then bring your finger closer to your face, your eyes will make conjugate movements toward your nose. If you then look at an object on the other side of the room, your eyes will rotate outward, and you will see two separate blurry images of your finger. As you will learn in Chapter 7, conjugate eye movements assist in depth perception—in the perception of distance.

When you scan the scene in front of you, your gaze travels from point to point as you examine important or interesting features. As you do so, your eyes make jerky **saccadic movements**—you shift your gaze abruptly from one point to another. For example, when you read a line in this book, your eyes stop several times, moving very quickly between each stop. You cannot consciously control the speed of movement between stops; during each *saccade* the eyes move as fast as they can.

Much of the time, the scene in front of us contains moving objects: objects blown by the wind, automobiles, airplanes, animals, other people. When we concentrate on one of these objects, we fix our gaze on it and track its movements with our eyes. These tracking movements, which follow the object we are watching, are called **pursuit movements.**

Color Vision

Among mammals, only primates have full color vision. A bull does not charge a red cape; he charges what he sees as an annoying gray object being waved at him. Among nonmammals, many birds and fishes also have excellent color vision; the brightly colored lure may really appeal to the fish as much as to the angler who buys it.

As we saw, light (as we humans define it) consists of radiant energy having wavelengths between 380 and 760 nm. Light of different wavelengths gives rise to sensations of different colors. How can we tell the difference between different wavelengths of light? Experiments have shown that there are three types of cones in the human eye, each containing a dif-

The spectral colors, contained in a rainbow, do not include all the colors we can see. Thus, differences in wavelength do not account for all the differences in the colors we can perceive.

ferent type of photopigment. Each type of photopigment is most sensitive to light of a particular wavelength. That is, light of a particular wavelength most readily causes a particular photopigment to split. Thus, different types of cones are stimulated by different wavelengths of light. Information from the cones enables us to perceive colors.

Wavelength is related to color, but the terms are not synonymous. For example, the *spectral colors* (the colors we see in a rainbow, which contains the entire spectrum of visible radiant energy) do not include all the colors that we can see, such as brown, pink, and the metallic colors silver and gold. The fact that not all colors are found in the spectrum means that differences in wavelength alone do not account for the differences in the colors we can perceive.

The Dimensions of Color

Most colors can be described in terms of three physical dimensions: wavelength, intensity, and purity. Three perceptual dimensions—hue, brightness, and saturation—corresponding to these physical dimensions describe what we see. The **hue** of most colors is determined by wavelength; for example,

conjugate movement The cooperative movement of the eyes, which ensures that the image of an object falls on identical portions of both retinas.

saccadic movement The rapid movement of the eyes that is used in scanning a visual scene, as opposed to the smooth pursuit movements used to follow a moving object.

pursuit movement The movement that the eyes make to maintain an image of a moving image upon the fovea.

hue A perceptual dimension of color, most closely related to the wavelength of a pure light.

Table 6.2		
Physical and Perceptual Dimensions of Color		
Perceptual Dimension	Physical Dimension	Physical Characteristics
Hue	Wavelength	Frequency of oscillation of light radiation
Brightness	Intensity	Amount of energy of light radiation
Saturation	Purity	Intensity of dominant wavelength relative to total radiant energy

light having a wavelength of 540 nm is perceived as green. A color's **brightness** is determined by the intensity, or amount of energy, of the light that is being perceived, all other factors being equal. A color of maximum brightness dazzles us with a lot of light. A color of minimum brightness is simply black. The third perceptual dimension of color, **saturation,** is roughly equivalent to purity. A fully saturated color consists of light of only one wavelength—for example, pure red or pure blue. Desaturated colors look pastel or washed out. (See *Table 6.2.*)

Saturation is probably the most difficult dimension of color to understand. White light consists of a mixture of all wavelengths of light. Although its components consist of light of all possible hues, we perceive it as being colorless. White light is completely desaturated; no single wavelength is dominant. If we begin with light of a single wavelength (a pure, completely saturated color) and then mix in some white light, the result will be a less saturated color. For example, when white light is added to red light (700 nm), the result is pink light. The dominant wavelength of 700 nm gives the color a reddish hue, but the addition of white light to the mixture decreases the color's saturation. In other words, pink is a less saturated version of red. *Figure 6.15* illustrates how a color having a particular dominant wavelength (hue) can vary in its brightness and saturation.

Color Mixing

Vision is a *synthetic* sensory modality. It synthesizes (puts together) rather than analyzes (takes apart). When two wavelengths of light are present, we see an intermediate color rather than the two components. (In contrast, the auditory system is *analytical.* If a high note and a low note are played together on a piano, we hear both notes instead of a single, intermediate tone.) The addition of two or more lights of different wavelengths is called **color mixing.** Color mixing is an additive process and is very different from paint mixing. So are its results. If we pass a beam of white light through a prism, we break it into the spectrum of the different wavelengths it contains. If we recombine these colors by passing them through another prism, we obtain white light again. (See *Figure 6.16.*)

Color mixing must not be confused with pigment mixing—what we do when we mix paints. An object has a particular color because it contains pigments that absorb some wavelengths of light (converting them into heat) and reflect other wavelengths. For example, the chlorophyll found in the leaves of plants absorbs less green light than light of other wavelengths. When a leaf is illuminated by white light, it reflects a high proportion of green light and appears green to us.

When we mix paints, we are subtracting colors, not adding them. Mixing two paints yields a darker result. For example, adding blue paint to yellow paint yields green paint, which certainly looks darker than yellow. But mixing two beams of light of different wavelengths always yields a brighter color. For example, when red and green light are shone together on a piece of white paper, we see yellow. In fact, we cannot tell a pure yellow light from a synthesized one made of the proper intensities of red and green light. To our eyes, both yellows appear identical.

To reconstitute white light, we do not even have to recombine all the wavelengths in the spectrum. If we shine a blue light, a green light, and a red light together on a sheet of white paper and properly adjust their intensities, the place where all three beams overlap will look perfectly white. A color television or a computer display screen uses this system. When white appears on the screen, it actually consists of tiny dots of red, blue, and green light. (See *Figure 6.17.*)

brightness A perceptual dimension of color, most closely related to the intensity or degree of radiant energy emitted by a visual stimulus.

saturation A perceptual dimension of color, most closely associated with purity of a color.

color mixing The perception of two or more lights of different wavelengths seen together as light of an intermediate wavelength.

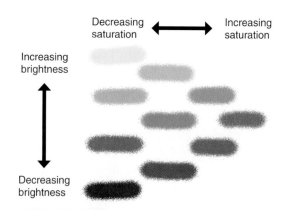

Figure 6.15

Hue, brightness, and saturation. The colors shown have the same dominant wavelength (hue) but different saturation and brightness.

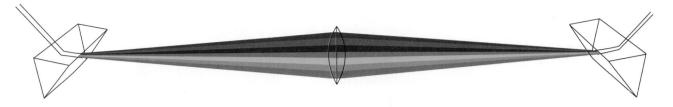

Figure 6.16

Color mixing. White light can be split into a spectrum of colors with a prism and recombined through another prism.

Figure 6.17

Additive color mixing and paint mixing. When blue, red, and green light of the proper intensity are all shone together, the result is white light. When red, blue, and yellow paints are mixed together, the result is a dark gray.

Color Coding in the Retina

In 1802, Thomas Young, a British physicist and physician, noted that the human visual system can synthesize any color from various amounts of almost any set of three colors of different wavelengths. Young proposed a **trichromatic theory** ("three color" theory) of color vision. He hypothesized that the eye contains three types of color receptors, each sensitive to a different hue, and that the brain synthesizes colors by combining the information received by each type of receptor. He suggested that these receptors were sensitive to three of the colors that people perceive as "pure": blue, green, and red. (His theory ignored the fact that people also perceive yellow as a pure color; more about this fact later.) Young's suggestion was incorporated into a more elaborate theory of color vision by Hermann von Helmholtz.

Experiments in recent years have shown that the cones in the human eye do contain three types of photopigments, each of which preferentially absorbs light of a particular wavelength: 420, 530, and 560 nm. Although these wavelengths actually correspond to blue-violet, green, and yellow-green, most investigators refer to these receptors as *blue, green,* and *red* cones. To simplify the discussion here, I too will pretend that the three cones respond to these three pure

hues. Red and green cones are present in about equal proportions. There are far fewer blue cones.

The eye uses the principle of the color television screen but in reverse: Instead of displaying colors, it analyzes them. If a spot of white light shines on the retina, it stimulates all three types of cones equally, and we perceive white light. If a spot of pure blue, green, or red light shines on the retina, it stimulates only one of the three classes of cones, and a pure color is perceived. If a spot of yellow light shines on the retina, it stimulates red and green cones equally well but has little effect on blue cones. (You can see from Figure 6.18 that yellow is located between red and green.) Stimulation of red and green cones, then, is the signal that yellow light has been received.

Several scientists after Young and Helmholtz devised theories that took account of the fact that people also perceive yellow as a psychologically pure hue. Late in the nineteenth century, Ewald Hering, a German physiologist, noted that the four primary hues appeared to belong to pairs of opposing colors: red/green and yellow/blue. We can imagine a

trichromatic theory The theory that color vision is accomplished by three types of photoreceptors, each of which is maximally sensitive to a different wavelength of light.

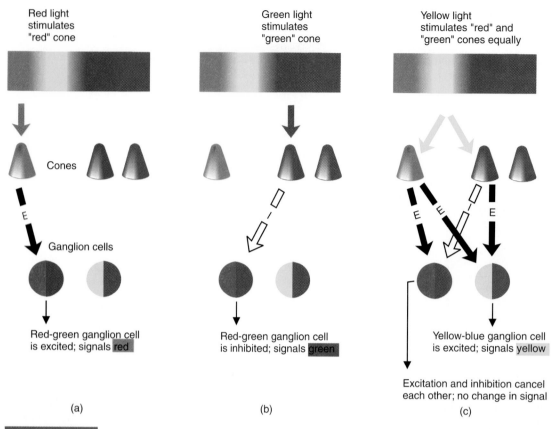

Red light stimulates "red" cone

Green light stimulates "green" cone

Yellow light stimulates "red" and "green" cones equally

Cones

Ganglion cells

Red-green ganglion cell is excited; signals red

Red-green ganglion cell is inhibited; signals green

Yellow-blue ganglion cell is excited; signals yellow

Excitation and inhibition cancel each other; no change in signal

(a) (b) (c)

Figure 6.18

Color coding in the retina. (a) Red light stimulating a "red" cone, which causes excitation of a red/green ganglion cell. (b) Green light stimulating a "green" cone, which causes inhibition of a red/green ganglion cell. (c) Yellow light stimulating "red" and "green" cones equally. The stimulation of "red" and "green" cones causes excitation of a yellow/blue ganglion cell. The arrows labeled E and I represent neural circuitry within the retina that translates excitation of a cone into excitation or inhibition of a ganglion cell. For clarity, only some of the circuits are shown.

bluish green or a yellowish green, or a bluish red or a yellowish red. However, we cannot imagine a greenish red or a yellowish blue. Hering originally suggested that we cannot imagine these blends because there are two types of photoreceptors, one kind responding to green and red and the other kind responding to yellow and blue. (I will explain the reasoning behind this statement shortly.)

Hering's hypothesis about the nature of photoreceptors was wrong, but his principle describes the characteristics of the information the retinal ganglion cells send to the brain. Two types of ganglion cells encode color vision: *red/green cells* and *yellow/blue cells*. Both types of ganglion cells fire at a steady rate when they are not stimulated. If a spot of red light shines on the retina, excitation of the red cones causes the red/green ganglion cells to begin to fire at a high rate. Con-

versely, if a spot of green light shines on the retina, excitation of the green cones causes the red/green ganglion cells to begin to fire at a slow rate. Thus, the brain learns about the presence of red or green light by the increased or decreased rate of firing of axons attached to red/green ganglion cells. Similarly, yellow/blue ganglion cells are excited by yellow light and inhibited by blue light. Because red and green light, and yellow and blue light, have opposite effects on the rate of axon firing, this coding scheme is called an **opponent process**.

Figure 6.18 provides a schematic explanation of the opponent-process coding that takes place in the retina. Stimulation of a red cone by red light excites the red/green ganglion cell, whereas stimulation of a green cone by green light inhibits the red/green ganglion cell. (See *Figure 6.18a* and *6.18b*.) If the photoreceptors are stimulated by yellow light, both the red and green cones are stimulated equally. Because of the neural circuitry between the photoreceptors and the ganglion cells, the result is that the yellow/blue ganglion cell is excited, signaling yellow. (See *Figure 6.18c*.)

opponent process The representation of colors by the rate of firing of two types of neurons: red/green and yellow/blue.

Figure 6.19

A negative afterimage. Stare for approximately 30 seconds at the cross in the center of the left figure; then quickly transfer your gaze to the cross in the center of the right figure. You will see colors that are complementary to the originals.

The retina contains red/green and yellow/blue ganglion cells because of the nature of the connections between the cones, bipolar cells, and ganglion cells. The brain detects various colors by comparing the rates of firing of the axons in the optic nerve that signal red or green and yellow or blue. Now you can see why we cannot perceive a reddish green or a bluish yellow: An axon that signals red or green (or yellow or blue) can either increase or decrease its rate of firing. It cannot do both at the same time. A reddish green would have to be signaled by a ganglion cell firing slowly and rapidly at the same time, which is obviously impossible.

Negative Afterimages

Figure 6.19 demonstrates an interesting property of the visual system: the formation of a **negative afterimage.** Stare at the cross in the center of the image on the left for approximately thirty seconds. Then quickly look at the cross in the center of the white rectangle to the right. You will have a fleeting experience of seeing the red and green colors of a radish—colors that are complementary, or opposite, to the ones on the left. (See *Figure 6.19.*) Complementary items go together to make up a whole. In this context, *complementary colors* are those that make white (or shades of gray) when added together.

The most important cause of negative afterimages is adaptation in the rate of firing of retinal ganglion cells. When ganglion cells are excited or inhibited for a prolonged period of time, they later show a *rebound effect,* firing faster or slower than normal. For example, the green of the radish in Figure 6.19 inhibits some red/green ganglion cells. When this region of the retina is then stimulated with the neutral-colored light reflected off the white rectangle, the red/green ganglion cells—no longer inhibited by the green light—fire faster than normal. Thus, we see a red afterimage of the radish.

Defects in Color Vision

Approximately one in twenty males has some form of defective color vision. These defects are sometimes called *color blindness,* but this term should probably be reserved for the very few people who cannot see any color at all. Males are affected more than females because many of the genes for pro-

ducing photopigments are located on the X chromosome. Because males have only one X chromosome (females have two), a defective gene there will always be expressed.

There are many different types of defective color vision. Two of the three described here involve the red/green system. People with these defects confuse red and green. Their primary color sensations are yellow and blue; red and green both look yellowish. Figure 6.20 shows one of the figures from a commonly used test for defective color vision. A person who confuses red and green will not be able to see the 5. (See *Figure 6.20.*)

The most common defect, called **protanopia** (literally, "first-color defect"), appears to result from a lack of the photopigment for red cones. The fact that people with protanopia have relatively normal acuity suggests that they have red cones but that these cones are filled with green photopigment (Boynton, 1979). If red cones were missing, almost half of the cones would be gone from the retina, and vision would be less acute. To a protanope, red looks much darker than green. The second form of red/green defect, called **deuteranopia** ("second-color defect"), appears to result from the opposite kind of substitution: Green cones are filled with red photopigment.

The third form of color defect, called **tritanopia** ("third-color defect"), involves the yellow/blue system and is much rarer: It affects fewer than 1 in 10,000 people. Tritanopes see the world in greens and reds; to them, a clear blue sky is a bright green, and yellow looks pink. The faulty gene that causes tritanopia is not carried on a sex chromosome; therefore, it is equally common in males and females. This defect appears to involve loss of blue cones. But because there are far

negative afterimage The image seen after a portion of the retina is exposed to an intense visual stimulus; a negative afterimage consists of colors complementary to those of the physical stimulus.

protanopia A form of hereditary anomalous color vision; caused by defective "red" cones in the retina.

deuteranopia A form of hereditary anomalous color vision; caused by defective "green" cones in the retina.

tritanopia A form of hereditary anomalous color vision; caused by a lack of "blue" cones in the retina.

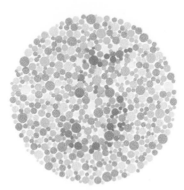

Figure 6.20

A figure commonly used to test for defective color vision. People with red/green color blindness will fail to see the 5.

(Courtesy of American Optical Corporation.)

fewer of these than of red and green cones to begin with, investigators have not yet determined whether the cones are missing or are filled with one of the other photopigments.

Interim Summary

Vision

Imagine yourself watching an ice-skating competition on television with a friend. Right now your eyes are directed toward the television screen. The cornea and lens of your eyes cast an image of the screen on your retinas, which contain photoreceptors: rods and cones. Because the room and the television screen are brightly illuminated, only your cones are gathering visual information; your rods work only when the light is very dim. The energy from the light that reaches the cones in your retinas is transduced into neural activity when photons strike molecules of photopigment, splitting them into their two constituents. This event causes the cones to send information through the bipolar cells to the ganglion cells. The axons of the ganglion cells travel through the optic nerves and form synapses with neurons in the brain.

Vision requires the behavior of looking, which consists of moving our eyes and head. The eyes have a repertoire of movements that function for visual perception. Experiments using stabilized images show that small, involuntary movements keep an image moving across the photoreceptors, thus preventing them from adapting to a constant stimulus. (As you will see later in this chapter, other sensory systems also respond better to changing stimuli than to constant ones.) As the skaters glide across the ice your eyes follow them with pursuit movements. Now your friend says something, so you turn your head toward him. Your eyes make rapid saccadic movements so that you can look directly at your friend's face. These movements are conjugate in nature, so that each eye is fixed on the same point. Because your friend is closer to you than the television screen, you must also accommodate for the change in distance, adjusting the focus of the lenses of your eyes.

When an image of the visual scene—your friend's face or the television screen—is cast upon the retina, each part of the image has a different color, which can be specified in terms of its hue (dominant wavelength), brightness (intensity), and saturation (purity). Information about color is encoded tri-chromatically by your cones; the red, green, and blue cones respond in proportion to the amount of the appropriate wavelength contained in the light striking them. This information is transformed into an opponent-process coding, signaled by the firing rates of red/green and yellow/blue ganglion cells, and is transmitted to the brain. If you stare for a while at the television screen and then look at a blank wall, you will see a negative afterimage of the screen. If you are a male, the chances are about one in twenty that you will have some defect in red/green color vision. If this is the case, your red or green cones contain the wrong photopigment. Male or female, chances are very slim that you will have a blue/yellow confusion, caused by the absence of functioning blue cones.

Thought Question

- Why is color vision useful? Birds, some fish, and some primates have full, three-cone color vision. Considering our own species, what benefits derive from the evolution of color vision?

Audition

Vision involves the perception of objects in three dimensions, at a variety of distances, and with a multitude of colors and textures. These complex stimuli may occur at a single point in time or over an extended period. They may also involve an unchanging scene or a rapidly changing one. The other senses analyze much simpler stimuli (such as an odor or a taste) or depend on time and stimulus change for the development of a complex perception. For example, to perceive a solid object in three dimensions by means of touch, we must manipulate it—turn it over in our hands or move our hands over its surface. The stimulus must change over time for a full-fledged perception of form to emerge. The same is true for audition: We hear nothing meaningful in an instant.

Most people consider the sense of hearing second in importance only to vision. In some ways it is *more* important. A blind person can converse and communicate with other people almost as well as a sighted person. Deafness is much more likely to produce social isolation. A deaf person cannot easily join in the conversation of a group of people who do not know sign language. Although our eyes can transmit much more information to the brain, our ears are used for some of our most important forms of social communication.

Sound

Sound consists of rhythmical pressure changes in air. As an object vibrates, it causes the air around it to move. When the object is in the phase of vibration in which it moves toward you, it compresses molecules of air; as it moves away, it pulls the molecules of air farther apart. As a pressure wave arrives

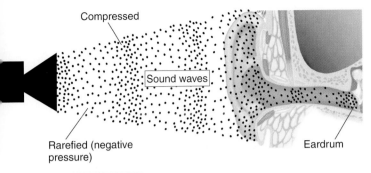

Compressed

Sound waves

Rarefied (negative pressure)

Eardrum

Figure 6.21

Sound waves. Changes in air pressure from sound waves move the eardrum in and out. Air molecules are closer together in regions of higher pressure and farther apart in regions of lower pressure.

at your ear, it bends your eardrum in. The following wave of negative pressure (when the molecules are pulled farther apart) causes your eardrum to bulge out. (See *Figure 6.21*.)

Sound waves are measured in frequency units of cycles per second called **hertz (Hz)**. The human ear perceives vibrations between approximately 30 and 20,000 Hz. Sound waves can vary in intensity and frequency. These variations produce corresponding changes in sensations of loudness and pitch. Consider a loudspeaker, a device that contains a paper cone moved back and forth by a coil of wire located in a magnetic field. Alternations in the electrical current transmitted from an amplifier to this coil cause the coil (and the paper cone) to move back and forth. If the cone begins vibrating more rapidly, the pitch of the sound increases. If the vibrations become more intense (that is, if the cone moves in and out over a greater distance), the loudness of the sound increases. (See *Figure 6.22*.) A third perceptual dimension, *timbre*, corresponds to the complexity of the sound vibration. I will discuss timbre in a later section of this chapter.

Sound consists of rhythmical pressure changes in air, which can convey an incredible diversity of auditory sensations.

The Ear and Its Functions

When people refer to the ear, they usually mean what anatomists call the *pinna*—the flesh-covered cartilage attached to the side of the head. (*Pinna* means "wing" in Latin.) But the pinna performs only a small role in audition. It helps funnel sound through the *ear canal* toward the middle and inner ear, where the business of hearing gets done. (See *Figure 6.23*.)

The *eardrum* is a thin, flexible membrane that vibrates back in forth in response to sound waves and passes these vibrations on to the receptor cells in the inner ear. The eardrum is attached to the first of a set of three middle ear bones called the **ossicles** (literally, "little bones"). The three ossicles are known as the *hammer*, the *anvil*, and the *stirrup*, because of their shapes. These bones act together, in lever fashion, to transmit the vibrations of the eardrum to the fluid-filled structure of the inner ear that contains the receptive organ.

The bony structure that contains the receptive organ is called the **cochlea** (*kokhlos* means "snail," which accurately describes its shape; see *Figure 6.23*). The cochlea is filled with a liquid. A bony chamber attached to the cochlea (the *vestibule*) contains two openings, the oval window and the round window. The last of the three ossicles (the stirrup) presses against a membrane behind an opening in the bone surrounding the cochlea called the **oval window**, thus transmitting sound waves into the liquid inside the cochlea, where it can reach the receptive organ for hearing. The cochlea is divided into two parts by the **basilar membrane**—a sheet of tissue that contains the auditory receptor cells. As the footplate of the stirrup presses back and forth against the membrane behind the oval window, pressure changes in the fluid above the basilar membrane cause the basilar membrane to vibrate back and forth. Because the basilar membrane varies in its width and flexibility, different frequencies of sound cause different parts of the basilar membrane to vibrate. High-frequency sounds cause the end near the oval window to vibrate, medium-frequency sounds cause the middle to vibrate, and low-frequency sounds cause the tip to vibrate. (See *Figure 6.24*.)

hertz (Hz) · The primary measure of the frequency of vibration of sound waves; cycles per second.

ossicle One of the three bones of the middle ear (the hammer, anvil, and stirrup) that transmit acoustical vibrations from the eardrum to the membrane behind the oval window of the cochlea.

cochlea A snail-shaped chamber set in bone in the inner ear, where audition takes place.

oval window An opening in the bone surrounding the cochlea. The stirrup presses against a membrane behind the oval window and transmits sound vibrations into the fluid within the cochlea.

basilar membrane A membrane that divides the cochlea of the inner ear into two compartments. The receptive organ for audition resides here.

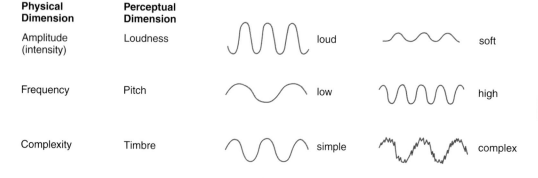

Physical Dimension	Perceptual Dimension				
Amplitude (intensity)	Loudness		loud		soft
Frequency	Pitch		low		high
Complexity	Timbre		simple		complex

Figure 6.22

The physical and perceptual dimensions of sound waves.

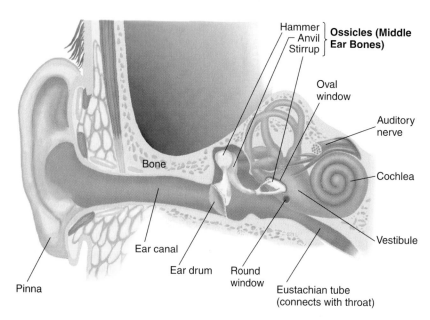

Figure 6.23

Anatomy of the auditory system.

In order for the basilar membrane to vibrate freely, the fluid in the lower chamber of the cochlea must have somewhere to go—unlike gases, liquids cannot be compressed. Free space is provided by the **round window**. When the basilar membrane flexes down, the displacement of the fluid causes the membrane behind the round window to bulge out. In turn, when the basilar membrane flexes up, the membrane behind the round window bulges in. (See *Figure 6.24.*)

Some people suffer from a middle ear disease that causes bone to grow over the round window. Because their basilar membrane cannot easily flex back and forth, these people have a severe hearing loss. However, their hearing can be restored by a surgical procedure called *fenestration* ("window making") in which a tiny hole is drilled in the bone where the round window should be.

Sounds are detected by special neurons known as auditory hair cells, located on the basilar membrane. **Auditory hair cells** transduce mechanical energy caused by the flexing of the basilar membrane into neural activity. These cells possess hairlike protrusions called **cilia** ("eyelashes"). The ends of the cilia are embedded in a fairly rigid shelf (the **tectorial membrane**) that hangs over the basilar membrane like a balcony. When sound vibrations cause the basilar membrane to flex back and forth, the cilia are stretched. This pull on the cilia is translated into neural activity. (See *Figure 6.25.*)

When a mechanical force is exerted on the cilia of the auditory hair cells, the electrical charge across their membrane is altered. The change in the electrical charge causes a transmitter substance to be released at a synapse between the auditory hair cell and the dendrite of a neuron of the auditory nerve. The release of the transmitter substance excites the neuron, which transmits messages through the auditory nerve to the brain. (See *Figure 6.25.*)

round window   An opening in the bone surrounding the cochlea. Movements of the membrane behind this opening permit vibrations to be transmitted through the oval window into the cochlea.

auditory hair cell   The sensory neuron of the auditory system; located on the basilar membrane.

cilium   A hairlike appendage of a cell; involved in movement or in transducing sensory information. Cilia are found on the receptors in the auditory and vestibular systems.

tectorial membrane   A membrane located above the basilar membrane; serves as a shelf against which the cilia of the auditory hair cells move.

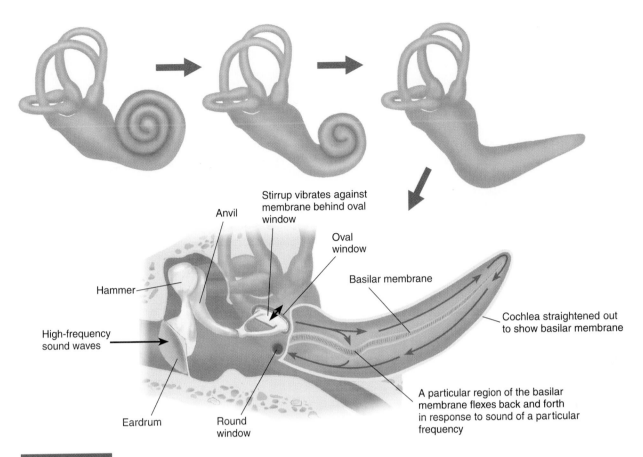

Stirrup vibrates against membrane behind oval window

Anvil

Oval window

Basilar membrane

Hammer

Cochlea straightened out to show basilar membrane

High-frequency sound waves

A particular region of the basilar membrane flexes back and forth in response to sound of a particular frequency

Eardrum

Round window

Figure 6.24

Responses to sound waves. When the stirrup pushes against the membrane behind the oval window, the membrane behind the round window bulges outward. Different high-frequency and medium-frequency sound vibrations cause flexing of different portions of the basilar membrane. In contrast, low-frequency sound vibrations cause the tip of the basilar membrane to flex in synchrony with the vibrations.

Detecting and Localizing Sounds in the Environment

As we saw, sounds can differ in loudness, pitch, and timbre. They also have sources; they come from particular locations. How does the ear distinguish these characteristics? As we will see, the ear's ability to distinguish sounds by their timbre depends on its ability to distinguish loudness and pitch. So let's examine these two characteristics first.

Loudness and Pitch

Scientists originally thought that the neurons of the auditory system represented pitch by firing in synchrony with the vibrations of the basilar membrane. However, they subsequently learned that axons cannot fire rapidly enough to represent the high frequencies that we can hear. A good, young ear can hear frequencies of more than 20,000 Hz, but axons cannot fire more than 1000 times per second. Therefore, high-frequency sounds, at least, must be encoded in some other way.

As we saw, high-frequency and medium-frequency sounds cause different parts of the basilar membrane to vi-

brate. Thus, sounds of different frequencies stimulate different groups of auditory hair cells located along the basilar membrane. At least for high-frequency and medium-frequency sounds, therefore, the brain is informed of the pitch of a sound by the activity of different sets of axons from the auditory nerve. When medium-frequency sound waves reach the ear, the middle of the basilar membrane vibrates, and auditory hair cells located in this region are activated. In contrast, high-frequency sounds activate auditory hair cells located at the base of the basilar membrane, near the oval window. (Refer to *Figure 6.24.*)

Two kinds of evidence indicate that pitch is detected in this way. First, direct observation of the basilar membrane has shown that the region of maximum vibration depends on the frequency of the stimulating tone (von Békésy, 1960). Second, experiments have found that damage to specific regions of the basilar membrane causes loss of the ability to perceive specific frequencies. The discovery that some antibiotics damage hearing (for example, deafness is one of the possible side effects of an antibiotic used to treat tuberculosis) has helped auditory researchers investigate the anatomi-

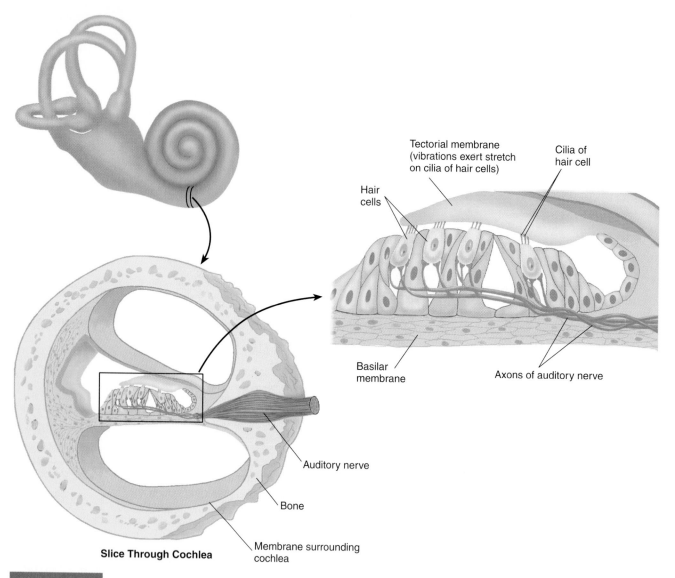

Tectorial membrane
(vibrations exert stretch
on cilia of hair cells)

Cilia of
hair cell

Hair
cells

Basilar
membrane

Axons of auditory nerve

Auditory nerve

Bone

Slice Through Cochlea

Membrane surrounding
cochlea

Figure 6.25

The transduction of sound vibrations in the auditory system.

cal coding of pitch. Stebbins et al. (1969) administered an antibiotic to different groups of animals for varying times. Next, they tested the animals' ability to perceive tones of different frequencies. Afterward, they removed the animals' cochleas and examined them. They found that the longer the animals were exposed to the antibiotic, the more of their hair cells were killed. Damage started at the end of the basilar membrane nearest the oval window and progressed toward the other end. The experimenters compared the various groups of animals and found that the hearing loss was proportional to the amount of damage to the hair cells. The loss began with the highest frequencies and progressed toward the lower frequencies. Thus, the hair cells nearest the oval window are responsible for detecting high-pitched sounds.

Although high-frequency and medium-frequency sounds are detected because they cause different regions of the basilar

membrane to vibrate, low-frequency sounds are detected by a different method. Kiang (1965) recorded the electrical activity of single axons in the auditory nerve and found many that responded to particular frequencies. Presumably, these axons were stimulated by hair cells located on different regions of the basilar membrane. However, he did not find any axons that responded uniquely to particular frequencies lower than 200 Hz—and yet tones lower than 200 Hz are easily perceived. How, then, are the lower frequencies encoded?

The answer is this: Frequencies lower than 200 Hz cause the very tip of the basilar membrane to vibrate in synchrony with the sound waves. Neurons that are stimulated by hair cells located there are able to fire in synchrony with these vibrations, thus firing at the same frequency as the sound. The brain "counts" these vibrations (so to speak) and thus detects low-frequency sounds. As you may have recognized, this process is an example of temporal coding. (Refer to *Figure 6.24.*)

The best evidence that low frequencies are detected in this way comes from an experiment performed many years ago by Miller and Taylor (1948). These investigators used white noise as a stimulus. White noise consists of a random mixture of all the perceptible frequencies of sound—it sounds like the *sssh* heard when a television or FM radio is tuned between stations. White noise stimulates *all* regions of the basilar membrane because it contains all frequencies of sound.

Miller and Taylor presented people with white noise that passed through a hole in a rotating disk. By spinning the disk at various speeds, the investigators could divide the noise into extremely brief pulsations, which could be presented at various time intervals. Thus, a "pitch" was artificially created by setting the pulsation of the white noise at a certain speed. When the frequency of the pulsation was less than 250 Hz, the subjects could accurately identify its pitch. However, above 250 Hz, the perception of pitch disappeared. Because the white noise stimulated all parts of the basilar membrane, the low-frequency sounds must have been detected by neurons that fired in synchrony with the pulsations. The medium-frequency and high-frequency sounds could not be differentiated by frequency of pulsation alone.

What about loudness? The axons of the cochlear nerve appear to inform the brain of the loudness of a stimulus by altering their rate of firing. More intense vibrations stimulate the auditory hair cells more intensely. This stimulation causes them to release more transmitter substance, which results in a higher rate of firing by the axons in the auditory nerve.

This explanation works for the axons involved in place coding of pitch; in this case, pitch is signaled by which neurons fire, and loudness is signaled by their rate of firing. However, the neurons that signal lower frequencies do so with their rate of firing. If they fire more frequently, they signal a higher pitch. Obviously, they cannot signal both loudness and pitch by the same means. Therefore, most investigators believe that the loudness of low-frequency sounds is signaled by the number of auditory hair cells that are active at a given time. A louder sound excites a larger number of hair cells.

Timbre

You can easily distinguish between the sounds of a violin and a clarinet, even if they are playing tones of the same pitch and loudness. So, clearly, pitch and loudness are not the only characteristics of a sound. Sounds can vary greatly in complexity. They can start suddenly or gradually increase in loudness, be short or long, and seem thin and reedy or full and vibrant. The enormous variety of sounds that we can distinguish is in large part due to an important characteristic of sound called timbre.

The combining, or synthesis, of two or more simple tones, each consisting of a single frequency, can produce a complex tone. For example, an electronic synthesizer produces a mixture of sounds of different frequencies, each of which can be varied in amplitude (intensity). Thus, it can synthesize the

complex sounds of a clarinet or violin or can assemble completely new sounds not produced by any other source. Conversely, complex sounds that have a regular sequence of waves can be reduced by means of analysis into several simple tones. Figure 6.26 shows a waveform produced by the sound of a clarinet (upper curve). The curves beneath it show the amplitude and frequency of the simple waves that can be shown, mathematically, to produce the waveform of the sound made by a clarinet. (See *Figure 6.26.*)

An analysis like the one shown in Figure 6.26 specifies the timbre of a sound. We can tell a clarinet from another instru-

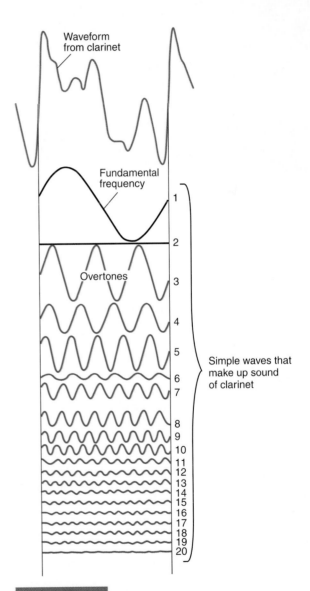

Figure 6.26

Analysis of timbre. The shape of a sound wave from a clarinet is shown at the top. The waveforms under it show the frequencies into which it can be analyzed. *(Copyright © 1977 by CBS Magazines. Reprinted from* Stereo Review, *June 1977, by permission.)*

The sound of a musical instrument such as a clarinet can be analyzed mathematically into a series of simple tones. The ear performs this analysis automatically.

Relative loudness is the most effective means of perceiving the location of high-frequency sounds. Acoustic energy, in the form of vibrations, does not actually pass through solid objects. Low-frequency sounds can easily make a large solid object such as a wall vibrate, setting the air on the other side in motion and producing a *new* sound across the barrier. But large solid objects cannot vibrate rapidly, so they effectively damp out high-frequency sounds. Thus, they cast a "sound shadow," just as opaque objects cast a shadow in the sunlight. The head is one such large solid object, and it damps out high-frequency sounds so that they appear much louder to the ear nearer the source of the sound. Thus, if a source on your right produces a high-frequency sound, your right ear will receive more intense stimulation than your left ear will. The brain uses this difference to calculate the location of the source of the sound. (See *Figure 6.27.*)

The second method involves detecting differences in the arrival time of sound pressure waves at each eardrum. This method works best for frequencies below approximately 3000 Hz. A 1000-Hz tone produces pressure waves approximately 1 foot apart. Because the distance between a person's eardrums is somewhat less than half that, a source of 1000-Hz sound lo-

ment because each instrument produces sounds consisting of a unique set of simple tones called **overtones.** Their frequencies are multiples of the **fundamental frequency,** or the basic pitch of the sound. **Timbre** is the distinctive combination of overtones with the fundamental frequency. The fundamental frequency causes one part of the basilar membrane to flex, while each of the overtones causes another portion to flex. During a complex sound many different portions of the basilar membrane are flexing simultaneously. Thus, the ear analyzes a complex sound, just as the person who devised Figure 6.26 did. Information about the fundamental frequency and each of the overtones is sent to the brain through the auditory nerve, and the person hears a complex tone having a particular timbre. When you consider that we can listen to an orchestra and identify several instruments playing simultaneously, you can appreciate the complexity of the analysis performed by the auditory system.

Locating the Source of a Sound

When we hear an unexpected sound, we usually turn our heads quickly to face its source. Even newborn infants can make this response with reasonably good accuracy. And once our faces are oriented toward the source of the sound, we can detect changes in its location by as little as 1 degree. To do so, we make use of two qualities of sound: relative loudness and difference in arrival time.

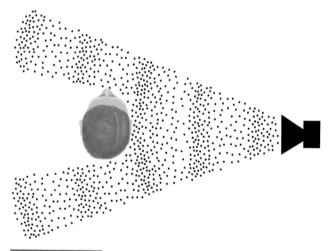

Figure 6.27

Localizing the source of high-frequency sounds. The head casts a "sound shadow" for high-frequency sound vibrations. The brain uses the difference in loudness to detect the location of the source of the sound.

overtone A component of a complex tone; one of a series of tones whose frequency is a multiple of the fundamental frequency.

fundamental frequency The lowest, and usually most intense, frequency of a complex sound; most often perceived as the sound's basic pitch.

timbre A perceptual dimension of sound, determined by the complexity of the sound—for example, as shown by a mathematical analysis of the sound wave.

Left eardrum pulled out   Right eardrum pushed in

Both eardrums pushed in

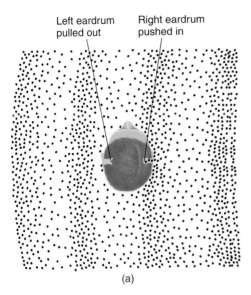

(a)

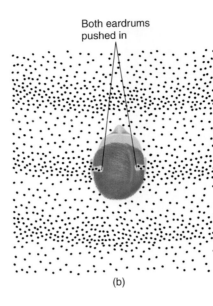

(b)

Figure 6.28

Localizing the source of medium-frequency and high-frequency sounds through differences in arrival time. (a) Source of a 1000-Hz tone to the right. The pressure waves on each eardrum are out of phase; one eardrum is pushed in, while the other is pushed out. (b) Source of a sound directly in front. The vibrations of the eardrums are synchronized.

cated to one side of the head will cause one eardrum to be pushed in while the other eardrum is being pulled out. In contrast, if the source of the sound is directly in front of the listener, both eardrums will move in synchrony. (See *Figure 6.28.*)

Researchers have found that when the source of a sound is located to the side of the head, as in Figure 6.28(a), axons in the right and left auditory nerves will fire at different times. The brain is able to detect this disparity, which causes the sound to be perceived as being off to one side. In fact, the brain can detect differences in firing times of a fraction of a millisecond (a thousandth of a second). The easiest stimuli to locate are those that produce brief clicks, which cause brief bursts of neural activity. Apparently, it is easiest for the brain to compare the arrival times of single bursts of incoming information.

Biology and Culture

The Deaf Community

Deafness profoundly affects a person's ability to communicate with others. Just imagine trying to join a group of people whose voices you cannot hear. But these difficulties disappear in the company of other deaf people; it is only in the company of people who have normal hearing that deafness hinders a person's ability to communicate (Erting et al., 1989; Sachs, 1989; Schein, 1989).

Deafness is unlike other sensory disabilities. Deaf people aren't just people who have a particular sensory loss—they share a common language. As we saw in Chapter 2, the term *culture* usually refers to a group of people who live close together in a common environment—who share customs, religious beliefs, and practices—and who

often resemble each other genetically. Certainly, deaf people are extremely diverse. They live in different environments, have different religious beliefs, and are genetically unrelated. Nevertheless, deaf people have their own culture. What unites the Deaf community is the ability of its members to communicate with each other visually, through sign language. The Deaf community can provide a remedy for the most important disadvantage of deafness: the inability to communicate easily with other people. (Of course, other deficits remain, such as the inability to listen to music.)

Not all deaf people are members of the Deaf community. People who are *postlingually deaf*—people who become deaf late in life, after they have learned oral and written language—are unlikely to learn sign language and join the Deaf community. (In this context, *lingual,* from the word for "tongue," refers to the acquisition of spoken language.) In addition, some *prelingually deaf* people—people who are born deaf or who become deaf during infancy—never learn sign language, primarily because they are "mainstreamed" in community schools or attend a school for the deaf that teaches oral communication.

What is a sign language? It is *not* English; nor is it French or Spanish or Chinese. The most common sign language in North America is ASL—American Sign Language. ASL is a full-fledged language, having signs for nouns, verbs, adjectives, adverbs, and all the other parts of speech contained in oral languages. People can converse rapidly and efficiently by means of sign language, can tell jokes, and can even make puns based on the similarity between signs. They can also use their language ability to think in words.

The grammar of ASL is based on its visual, spatial nature. For example, if a person makes the sign for *John* in one place and later makes the sign for *Mary* in another place, she can place her hand in the *John* location and move it toward the *Mary* location while making the sign

Communication by means of American Sign Language is as rapid, efficient, and rich in nuance and detail as that of any spoken language.

for *love*. As you undoubtedly figured out for yourself, she is saying, "John loves Mary." Signers can also modify the meaning of signs through facial expressions or the speed and vigor with which they make a sign. Thus, many of the prepositions, adjectives, and adverbs found in spoken languages do not require specific words in ASL. The fact that sign languages are based on three-dimensional hand and arm movements accompanied by facial expressions means that their grammars are very different from those of spoken languages. Thus, a word-for-word translation from a spoken language to a sign language (or vice versa) is impossible.

There is no single, universal sign language. Deaf people from North America cannot communicate with deaf people from Great Britain. (They can write to each other, of course, but written English bears no relation to ASL or to the sign language used in Great Britain.) However, deaf people in France and North America can understand each other reasonably well, because ASL is partly based on the sign language that was used in France in the early nineteenth century.

Several attempts have been made (invariably, by people who are *not* deaf) to "improve" sign languages. Deaf people resent such attempts, just as you or I would if a foreigner tried to improve the English language by cleaning up its inconsistencies. Most people cherish their native languages, and deaf people are particularly proud of theirs.

Education of the Deaf poses special problems. Deafness follows the so-called "90-percent rule." That is, 90 percent of deaf children have parents who can hear, 90 percent of deaf people marry other deaf people, and 90 percent of deaf parents have children who can hear. Most parents of deaf children, not being themselves deaf, know nothing about the Deaf community. Thus, they are unable to transmit to their children the most important characteristic of this community: a sign language. The current preference for "mainstreaming" children who have disabilities—that is, placing them in ordinary neighborhood schools with the rest of the population—means that most of their teachers have no experience educating the deaf. In fact, most of their teachers have never even *met* a deaf child before. Some deaf people do not learn a sign language until late childhood or adolescence, when they finally meet other deaf people. Others never learn it.

Some schools for the deaf use the *oralist approach* to education. Children are taught to communicate orally with the rest of the population by reading lips and speaking. Both tasks are extremely difficult. Try watching a news broadcast with the sound turned off to see how much you can understand. Ask a friend to say, "bear, bar, pear," and see if you can see the difference. Of course, you could get better with years of practice, but even a very skilled lip-reader must do a lot of guessing and anticipating. And you would be starting out knowing English as a native language, so you would know what words to look out for and anticipate. A deaf child taught with the oralist approach starts out with no knowledge of language at all, which makes the process doubly difficult. Also, learning to lip-read and to speak (without the opportunity to hear yourself) takes so much time that not much of the day is left over for other academic subjects.

Most people in the Deaf community, who communicate with each other by means of signing, have negative feelings toward oral communication. The difficult task of deciphering lip movements makes them feel tense. They realize that their pronunciation is imperfect and that their voices sound strange to others. They feel at a disadvantage with respect to hearing people in a spoken conversation. In contrast, they feel relaxed and at ease when communicating with other deaf people. A young man wrote about his experience when he entered Gallaudet University, an institution for the deaf that uses sign language.

> As I made my way through many educational and enjoyable semesters, learning a "new" way of communicating, I was enthralled. I was able to understand a person 100 percent of the time without having to lipread or depend on notes. It is a special feeling to relax and listen when in the past you have had to pay so much attention to the person you were speaking with that you could never really relax. (Mentkowski, 1983, p. 1)

Like other people who closely identify with their cultures, members of the Deaf community feel pride in their common heritage and react to perceived threats. Some deaf people say that if they were given the opportunity to hear, they would refuse it. Some deaf parents have expressed happiness when they learned that their children were born deaf, too. They no longer needed to fear that their children would not be a part of their own Deaf culture.

A recent technological development, the cochlear implant, is perceived by most members of the Deaf community as a serious threat to their culture. A cochlear implant is an electronic device surgically implanted in the inner ear that can enable deaf people to hear. It is most useful for two groups: people who became deaf in adulthood and very young children. Cochlear implants in postlingually deaf adults pose no threat to the Deaf community because these people never were members of the culture. But putting a cochlear implant in a young child means that the child's early education will be committed to the oralist approach. In addition, many deaf people resent the implication that deafness is something that needs to be repaired. They see themselves as different but not at all defective.

Interim Summary

Audition

Were you to sit at a synthesizer, you would have at your fingertips the means to produce a vast array of sounds. You would also have at your disposal (in your head) an auditory system sophisticated enough to differentiate among those sounds. The physical dimensions of the synthesizer's sound—amplitude, frequency, and complexity—would be translated into the perceptual dimensions of loudness, pitch, and timbre for sounds ranging from 30 to 20,000 Hz. Sound pressure waves put the process in motion by setting up vibrations in the eardrum, which are passed on to the ossicles. Vibrations of the stirrup against the membrane behind the oval window create pressure changes in the fluid within the cochlea that cause the basilar membrane to flex back and forth. This vibration causes the auditory hair cells on the basilar membrane to move relative to the tectorial membrane. The resulting pull on the cilia of the hair cells stimulates them to secrete a transmitter substance that excites neurons of the auditory nerve. This process informs the brain of the presence of a sound.

Two different methods of detection enable the brain to recognize the pitch of a sound. Different high-frequency and medium-frequency sounds are perceived when different parts of the basilar membrane vibrate in response to these frequencies. Low-frequency vibrations are detected when the tip of the basilar membrane vibrates in synchrony with the sound, which causes some axons in the auditory nerve to fire at the same frequency.

To locate the source of a sound (for example, if your synthesizer is hooked up to different speakers), you have available two means: Low-frequency sounds are located by differences in the arrival time of the sound waves in each ear. High-frequency sounds are located by differences in intensity caused by the "sound shadow" cast by your head.

As you produce sounds of more and more complex timbre, the auditory system will analyze them into their constituent frequencies, each of which causes a particular part of the basilar membrane to vibrate. All these functions proceed automatically, so that when you press some keys on your synthesizer, your brain will then hear what you have played, whether it resembles the sound of a clarinet or some new combination of fundamental frequency and overtones.

The Deaf community consists of deaf people who communicate visually by means of a sign language. The social isolation that a deaf person feels in the society of oral communicators disappears in the company of other people who can sign. Communication by sign languages is as accurate and efficient as it is by spoken languages.

Thought Questions

- A naturalist once noted that when a male bird stakes out his territory, he sings with a very sharp, staccato song that says, in effect, "Here I am, and stay away!" In contrast, if a predator appears in the vicinity, many birds will emit alarm calls that consist of steady whistles that start and end slowly. Knowing what you do about the two means of localizing sounds, why do these two types of calls have different characteristics?
- If you had a child who was born deaf, would you send your child to a school that taught sign language or to one that emphasized speaking and lip-reading? Why? Now imagine that you are deaf (or, if you are deaf, that you are hearing). Would your answer change?

Gustation

We have two senses specialized for detecting chemicals in our environment: taste and smell. Together, they are referred to as the **chemosenses**. Taste, or **gustation**, is the simplest of the sense modalities. We can perceive only four qualities of taste: *sourness, sweetness, saltiness,* and *bitterness*. Taste is not the same as flavor; the flavor of a food includes its odor as well as its taste. You have probably noticed that the flavors of foods are diminished when you have a head cold. This loss of flavor occurs not because your taste buds are inoperative but because congestion with mucus makes it difficult for odor-laden air to reach your receptors for the sense of smell. Without their characteristic odors to serve as cues, onions taste much like apples (although apples do not make your eyes water).

chemosense One of the two sense modalities (gustation and olfaction) that detect the presence of particular molecules present in the environment.

gustation The sense of taste.

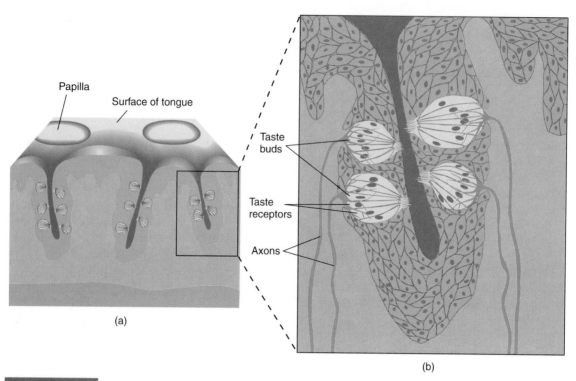

Papilla

Surface of tongue

Taste buds

Taste receptors

Axons

(a)

(b)

Figure 6.29

The tongue. (a) Papillae on the surface of the tongue. (b) Taste buds.

Receptors and the Sensory Pathway

The tongue has a somewhat corrugated appearance, being marked by creases and bumps. The bumps are called **papillae** (from the Latin, meaning "nipple"). Each papilla contains a number of taste buds (in some cases as many as 200). A **taste bud** is a small organ that contains a number of receptor cells,

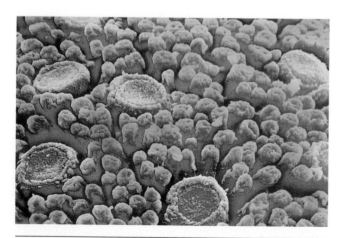

A photograph of taste buds taken with a scanning electron microscope.

each of which is shaped rather like a segment of an orange. The cells have hairlike projections called *microvilli* that protrude through the pore of the taste bud into the saliva that coats the tongue and fills the trenches of the papillae. (See *Figure 6.29.*) Molecules of chemicals dissolved in the saliva stimulate the receptor cells, probably by interacting with special receptors on the microvilli that are similar to the postsynaptic receptors found on other neurons. The receptor cells form synapses with dendrites of neurons that send axons to the brain through three different cranial nerves.

The Four Qualities of Taste

The surface of the tongue is differentially sensitive to taste. The tip is most sensitive to sweet and salty substances; the sides to sour substances; and the back of the tongue, the back of the throat, and the soft palate overhanging the back of the tongue to bitter substances. (See *Figure 6.30.*)

The physical properties of the molecules that we taste determine the nature of the taste sensations. Different molecules stimulate different types of receptors. For example, all

papilla A small bump on the tongue that contains a group of taste buds.

taste bud A small organ on the tongue that contains a group of gustatory receptor cells.

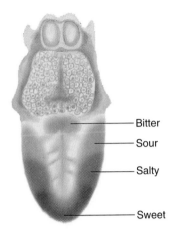

Bitter

Sour

Salty

Sweet

Figure 6.30

Sensitivity of different regions of the tongue to different tastes.

substances that taste salty ionize (break into charged particles) when they dissolve. The most important salty substance is, of course, table salt—sodium chloride (NaCl). Other chlorides, such as lithium or potassium chloride, and some other salts, such as bromides or sulfates, are also salty in taste; but none tastes quite as salty as sodium chloride. This finding suggests that the specific function of salt-tasting receptors is to identify sodium chloride. Sodium plays a unique role in the regulation of our body fluid. If the body's store of sodium falls, we cannot retain water, and our blood volume will fall. The result can be heart failure. Loss of sodium stimulates a strong craving for the salty taste of sodium chloride.

Both bitter and sweet substances seem to consist of large, nonionizing molecules. Scientists cannot predict, merely on the basis of shape, whether a molecule will taste bitter or sweet (or neither). Some molecules (such as saccharin) stimulate both sweet and bitter receptors; they taste sweet at the front of the tongue and bitter at the back of the palate and throat. Most likely, the function of the bitterness receptor is to avoid ingesting poisons. Many plants produce alkaloids that serve to protect them against being eaten by insects or browsing animals. Some of these alkaloids are poisonous to humans, and most of them taste bitter. In contrast, the sweetness receptor enables us to recognize the sugar content of fruits and other nutritive plant foods. When sweet-loving animals gather and eat fruit, they tend to disperse the seeds and help propagate the plant; thus, the presence of sugar in the fruit is to the plant's advantage as well.

Most sour tastes are produced by acids—in particular, by the hydrogen ion (H+) contained in acid solutions. The sourness receptor probably serves as a warning device against substances that have undergone bacterial decomposition, most of which become acidic. In earlier times, most wholesome,

natural foods tasted either sweet or salty, not bitter or sour. (Nowadays, we can mix sweet-tasting and sour-tasting substances to make tasty beverages, such as lemonade.)

Olfaction

The sense of smell—**olfaction**—is one of the most interesting and puzzling of the sense modalities. It is unlike other sense modalities in two important ways. First, people have difficulty describing odors in words. Second, odors have a powerful ability to evoke old memories and feelings, even many years after an event. At some time in their lives, most people encounter an odor that they recognize as having some childhood association, even though they cannot identify it. The phenomenon may occur because the olfactory system sends information to the limbic system, a part of the brain that plays a role in both emotions and memories.

Olfaction, like audition, seems to be an analytical sense modality. That is, when we sniff air that contains a mixture of familiar odors, we can usually identify the individual components. The molecules do not blend together and produce a single odor the way lights of different wavelengths produce a single color.

Although other animals, such as dogs, have more sensitive olfactory systems than humans do, we should not underrate our own. We can smell some substances at lower concentrations than our most sensitive instruments can detect. One reason for the difference in sensitivity between our olfactory system and those of other mammals is that other mammals put their noses where odors are the strongest—just above ground level. For example, watch a dog following an odor trail. The dog sniffs along the ground, where the odors of the passing animal will have clung. Even a bloodhound's nose would not be very useful if it were located five feet above the ground, as ours is.

Odors play a very important role in the lives of most mammals. Although we do not make use of olfaction in identifying one another, we do use it to avoid some dangers, such as food that has spoiled. In fact, the odor of rotten meat will trigger vomiting—a useful response if some of the rotten meat has been swallowed. Other animals recognize friend and foe by means of smell and use odors to attract mates and repel rivals. And the reproductive behavior of laboratory mammals—and even the menstrual cycles of women—can be influenced by the odors emitted by other animals of the same species.

Anatomy of the Olfactory System

Figure 6.31 shows the anatomy of the olfactory system. The receptor cells lie in the **olfactory mucosa**, one-inch-square patches of mucous membrane located on the roof of the nasal sinuses, just under the base of the brain. (See *Figure 6.31.*) The

olfaction The sense of smell.

olfactory mucosa The mucous membrane lining the top of the nasal sinuses; contains the cilia of the olfactory receptors.

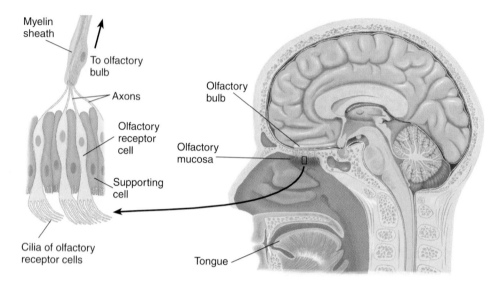

Figure 6.31

The olfactory system.

receptor cells have cilia that are embedded in the olfactory mucosa. They also have axons that pass through small holes in the bone above the olfactory mucosa and form synapses with neurons in the olfactory bulbs. The **olfactory bulbs** are stalk-like structures located at the base of the brain that contain neural circuits that perform the first analysis of olfactory information.

The interaction between odor molecule and receptor appears to be similar to that of transmitter substance and post-synaptic receptor on a neuron. That is, when a molecule of an odorous substance fits a receptor molecule located on the cilia of a receptor cell, the cell becomes excited. This excitation is passed on to the brain by the axon of the receptor cell. Thus, similar mechanisms may detect the stimuli for taste and olfaction.

Unlike information from all other sensory modalities, olfactory information is not sent to the thalamus and then relayed to a specialized region of the cerebral cortex. Instead, olfactory information is sent directly to several regions of the limbic system—in particular, to the amygdala and to the limbic cortex of the frontal lobe.

The Dimensions of Odor

We know that there are four qualities of taste and that a color can be specified by hue, brightness, and saturation. Recent research in molecular biology suggests that the olfactory system uses up to a thousand different receptor molecules, located in the membrane of the receptor cells, to detect different categories of odors (Jones and Reed, 1989; Buck and Axel, 1991; Axel, 1995). Presumably, the presence of molecules of a substance with a particular odor produces a particular pattern of activity in the olfactory system. That is, the molecules will

strongly stimulate some receptors, weakly stimulate others, and stimulate still others not at all. This pattern of stimulation is transmitted to the brain, where it is recognized as belonging to a particular odor. Researchers do not yet know exactly which molecules stimulate which receptors; nor do they know how the information from individual olfactory receptor cells is put together.

Interim Summary

Gustation and Olfaction

Both gustation and olfaction are served by cells having receptors that respond selectively to various kinds of molecules. Taste buds have four kinds of receptors, responding to molecules that we perceive as sweet, salty, sour, or bitter. To most organisms, sweet and moderately salty substances taste pleasant, whereas sour or bitter substances taste unpleasant. Sweetness and saltiness receptors permit us to detect nutritious foods and sodium chloride. Sourness and bitterness receptors help us avoid substances that might be poisonous.

Olfaction is a remarkable sense modality. Olfactory information combines with information about taste to provide us with the flavor of a food present in our mouths. We can distinguish countless different odors and can recognize smells from childhood, even when we cannot remember when or where we first encountered them. Although we recognize similarities between different odors, most seem unique. Unlike visual stimuli, odors do not easily blend. For example, when visiting a carnival, we can distinguish the odors of popcorn, cotton candy, crushed grass, and diesel oil in a single sniff. The detection of different odors appears to be accomplished by up to a thousand different receptor molecules located in the membrane of the olfactory receptor cells.

Thought Questions

- Bees and birds can taste sweet substances, but cats and alligators cannot. Obviously, the ability to taste partic-

olfactory bulbs   Stalk-like structures located at the base of the brain that contain neural circuits that perform the first analysis of olfactory information.

ular substances is related to the range of foods a species eats. If, through the process of evolution, a species develops a greater range of foods, what do you think comes first, the food or the receptor? Would a species start eating something having a new taste (say, something sweet) and later develop the appropriate taste receptors, or do the taste receptors evolve first and then lead the animal to a new taste?

■ Odors have a peculiar ability to evoke memories—a phenomenon vividly described by Marcel Proust in his novel *Remembrance of Things Past.* Have you ever encountered an odor that you knew was somehow familiar, but you couldn't say exactly why? Can you think of any explanations? Might this phenomenon have something to do with the fact that the sense of olfaction developed very early during the evolutionary development of our brain?

The Somatosenses

The body senses, or **somatosenses,** include our ability to respond to touch, vibration, pain, warmth, coolness, limb position, muscle length and stretch, tilt of the head, and changes in the speed of head rotation. The number of sense modalities represented in this list depends on one's definition of a sense modality. However, it does not really matter whether we say that we respond to warmth and coolness by means of one sense modality or two different ones; the important thing is to understand how our bodies are able to detect changes in temperature.

Many experiences require simultaneous stimulation of several different sense modalities. For example, taste and odor alone do not determine the flavor of spicy food; mild (or sometimes not-so-mild) stimulation of pain detectors in the mouth and throat gives Mexican food its special characteristic. Sensations such as tickle and itch are apparently mixtures of varying amounts of touch and pain. Similarly, our perception of the texture and three-dimensional shape of an object that we touch involves cooperation among our senses of pressure, muscle and joint sensitivity, and motor control (to manipulate the object). If we handle an object and find that it moves smoothly in our hand, we conclude that it is slippery. If, after handling this object, our fingers subsequently slide across each other without much resistance, we perceive a feeling of oiliness. If we sense vibrations when we move our fingers over an object, it is rough. And so on. If you close your eyes as you manipulate some soft and hard, warm and cold, and smooth and rough objects, you can make yourself aware of the separate sensations that interact and give rise to a complex perception.

The following discussion of the somatosenses groups them into three major categories: the skin senses, the internal senses, and the vestibular senses.

The Skin Senses

The entire surface of the human body is *innervated* (supplied with nerve fibers) by the dendrites of neurons that transmit somatosensory information to the brain. Cranial nerves convey information from the face and front portion of the head (including the teeth and the inside of the mouth and throat); spinal nerves convey information from the rest of the body's surface. All somatosensory information is detected by the dendrites of neurons; the system uses no separate receptor cells. However, some of these dendrites have specialized endings that modify the way they transduce energy into neural activity.

Figure 6.32 shows the sensory receptors found in hairy skin and in smooth, hairless skin (such as skin on the palms of the hands or the soles of the feet). The most common type of skin sensory receptor is the **free nerve ending,** which resembles the fine roots of a plant. Free nerve endings infiltrate the middle layers of both smooth and hairy skin and surround the hair follicles in hairy skin. If you bend a single hair on your forearm, you will see how sensitive the free nerve endings are. (Try it; then see *Figure 6.32.*)

The largest of the special receptive endings, called the **Pacinian corpuscle,** is actually visible to the naked eye. (See *Figure 6.32.*) Pacinian corpuscles are very sensitive to touch. When they are moved, their axons fire a brief burst of impulses. Pacinian corpuscles are thought to be the receptors that inform us about vibration.

Other specialized receptors detect other sensory qualities, including warmth, coolness, and pain.

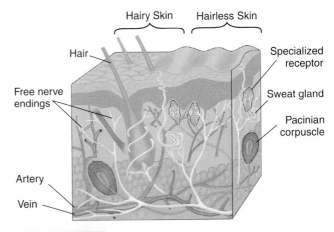

Figure 6.32

Sensory receptors in hairy skin (left) and in hairless skin (right).

somatosense Bodily sensations; sensitivity to such stimuli as touch, pain, and temperature.

free nerve ending An unencapsulated (naked) dendrite of somatosensory neurons.

Pacinian corpuscle A specialized, encapsulated somatosensory nerve ending, which detects mechanical stimuli, especially vibrations.

Temperature

There is general agreement that different sensory endings produce the sensations of warmth and coolness. Detectors for coolness appear to be located closer to the surface of the skin. If you suddenly place your foot under a stream of rather hot water, you may feel a brief sensation of cold just before you perceive that the water is really hot. This sensation probably results from short-lived stimulation of the coolness detectors located in the upper layers of the skin.

Our temperature detectors respond best to *changes* in temperature. Within reasonable limits, the air temperature of our environment comes to feel "normal." Temporary changes in temperature are perceived as warmth or coolness. Thus, our temperature detectors adapt to the temperature of our environment. This adaptation can be easily demonstrated. If you place one hand in a pail of hot water and the other in a pail of cold water, the intensity of the sensations of heat and cold will decrease after a few minutes. If you then plunge both hands into a pailful of water that is at room temperature, it will feel hot to the cold-adapted hand and cold to the hot-adapted hand. It is mainly the change in temperature that is signaled to the brain. Of course, there are limits to the process of adaptation. Extreme heat or cold will continue to feel hot or cold, however long we experience it.

Pressure

Sensory psychologists speak of touch and pressure as two separate senses. They define *touch* as the sensation of very light contact of an object with the skin and *pressure* as the sensation produced by more forceful contact. Sensations of pressure occur only when the skin is actually moving, which means that the pressure detectors respond only while they are being bent. Just how the motion stimulates the neurons is not known. If you rest your forearm on a table and place a small weight on your skin, you will feel the pressure at first, but eventually you will feel nothing at all, if you keep your arm still. You fail to feel the pressure not because your brain "ignores" incoming stimulation but because your sensory endings actually cease sending impulses to your brain. Studies that have measured the very slow, very minute movements of a weight sinking down into the skin have shown that sensations of pressure cease when the movements stop. With the addition of another weight on top of the first one, movement and sensations of pressure begin again (Nafe and Wagoner, 1941). A person will feel a very heavy weight indefinitely, but the sensation is probably one of pain rather than pressure.

Sensitivity to subtle differences in touch and pressure varies widely across the surface of the body. The most sensitive regions are the lips and the fingertips. The most common measure of the tactile discrimination of a region of skin is the **two-point discrimination threshold.** To determine this measure, an experimenter touches a person with one or both legs of a pair of dividers and asks the person to say whether the sensation is coming from one or two points. (See *Figure 6.33.*)

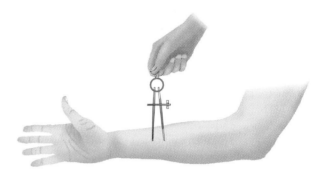

Figure 6.33

The method for determining the two-point discrimination threshold.

The farther apart the legs of the dividers must be before the person reports feeling two separate sensations, the lower the sensitivity of that region of skin.

Pain

Pain is a complex sensation involving not only intense sensory stimulation but also an emotional component. That is, a given sensory input to the brain might be interpreted as pain in one situation and as pleasure in another. For example, when people are sexually aroused, they become less sensitive to many forms of pain and may even find such intense stimulation pleasurable.

Physiological evidence suggests that the sensation of pain is quite different from the emotional reaction to pain. Opiates such as morphine diminish the sensation of pain by stimulating opioid receptors on neurons in the brain; these neurons block the transmission of pain information to the brain. In contrast, some tranquilizers (such as Valium) depress neural systems that are responsible for the emotional reaction to pain but do not diminish the intensity of the sensation. Thus, people who have received a drug like Valium will report that they feel the pain just as much as they did before but that it does not bother them much.

Evidence from surgical procedures also supports the distinction between sensation and emotion. Prefrontal lobotomy (a form of brain surgery), like the use of tranquilizers such as Valium, blocks the emotional component of pain but does not affect the primary sensation. Therefore, operations similar to prefrontal lobotomy (but much less drastic) are sometimes performed to treat people who suffer from chronic pain that cannot be alleviated by other means.

Many noxious stimuli elicit two kinds of pain—an immediate sharp, or "bright," pain followed by a deep, dull,

two-point discrimination threshold The minimum distance between two small points that can be detected as separate stimuli when pressed against a particular region of the skin.

sometimes throbbing pain. Some stimuli elicit only one of these two kinds of pain. For example, a pinprick will produce only the superficial "bright" pain, whereas a hard blow from a blunt object to a large muscle will produce only the deep, dull pain. Different sets of axons mediate these two types of pain.

Pain—or the fear of pain—is one of the most effective motivators of human behavior. However, it also serves us well in the normal course of living. As unpleasant as pain is, we would have difficulty surviving without it. (Remember Sara, the nine-year-old girl whose encounter with pain was described in the opening vignette?) For example, pain tells us if we have sprained an ankle, broken a bone, or have an inflamed appendix.

A particularly interesting form of pain sensation occurs after a limb has been amputated. After their limbs are gone, up to 70 percent of amputees report that they feel as though their missing limbs still existed, and that they often hurt. This phenomenon is referred to as the **phantom limb** (Melzak, 1992). People who have phantom limbs report that the limbs feel very real, and they often say that if they try to reach out with their missing limbs, it feels as though they were responding. Sometimes, they perceive the limbs as sticking out, and they may feel compelled to avoid knocking them against the side of a doorframe or sleeping in a position that would make the limbs come between them and the mattress. People have reported all sorts of sensations in phantom limbs, including pain, pressure, warmth, cold, wetness, itching, sweatiness, and prickliness.

The classic explanation for phantom limbs has been activity of the sensory axons belonging to the amputated limbs. Presumably, this activity is interpreted by the nervous system as coming from the missing limbs. When nerves are cut and connections cannot be reestablished between the proximal and distal portions, the cut ends of the proximal portions form nodules known as *neuromas*. The treatment for phantom pain has been to cut the nerves above these neuromas, to cut the bundles of nerve fibers that bring the information from these nerves into the spinal cord, or to make lesions in somatosensory pathways in the spinal cord, thalamus, or cerebral cortex. Sometimes these procedures work for a while, but, unfortunately, the pain often returns.

Melzak suggests that the phantom limb sensation is inherent in the organization of the parietal cortex. As we saw in Chapter 4, the parietal cortex is involved in our awareness of our own bodies. Indeed, people who have sensory neglect, caused by lesions of the right parietal lobe, have been known to push their own legs out of bed, believing that they actually belong to someone else. Melzak reports that some people who were born missing limbs nevertheless experience phantom limb sensations, which would suggest that our brains are genetically programmed to provide sensations for all four limbs—even if we do not have them.

The Internal Senses

Sensory endings located in our internal organs, bones and joints, and muscles convey painful, neutral, and in some cases pleasurable sensory information. For example, the internal senses convey the pain of arthritis, the perception of the location of our limbs, and the pleasure of a warm drink descending to our stomachs.

Muscles contain special sensory endings. One class of receptors, located at the junction between muscles and the tendons that connect them to the bones, provides information about the amount of force the muscle is exerting. These receptors protect the body by inhibiting muscular contractions when they become too forceful. During competition, some weight lifters have received injections of a local anesthetic near the tendons of some muscles to eliminate this protective mechanism. As a result, they are able to lift even heavier weights. Unfortunately, if they use this tactic, some tendons may snap or some bones may break.

Another set of stretch detectors consists of spindle-shaped receptors distributed throughout the muscle. These receptors, appropriately called **muscle spindles,** inform the

Information from the internal senses, along with visual information, tells these skaters about the location and movements of their bodies and helps them gauge the force they need to exert to perform their intricate maneuvers.

phantom limb Sensations that appear to originate in a limb that has been amputated.

muscle spindle A muscle fiber that functions as a stretch receptor; arranged parallel to the muscle fibers responsible for contraction of the muscle, it detects muscle length.

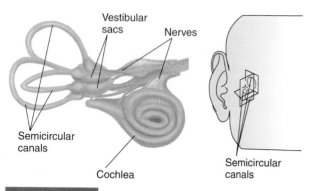

Vestibular sacs

Nerves

Semicircular canals

Cochlea

Semicircular canals

Figure 6.34

The three semicircular canals and two vestibular sacs located in the inner ear.

brain about changes in muscle length. People are not conscious of the specific information provided by the muscle spindles, but the brain uses the information from these receptors and from joint receptors to keep track of the location of parts of the body and to control muscular contractions.

The Vestibular Senses

What we call our "sense of balance" in fact involves several senses, not just one. If we stand on one foot and then close our eyes, we immediately realize how important a role vision plays in balance. The **vestibular apparatus** of the inner ear provides only part of the sensory input that helps us remain upright.

The three **semicircular canals**—located in the inner ear—oriented at right angles to one another, detect changes in rotation of the head in any direction. (See *Figure 6.34.*) These canals contain a liquid. Rotation of the head makes the liquid flow, stimulating the receptor cells located in the canals.

Another set of inner ear organs, the **vestibular sacs**, contain crystals of calcium carbonate that are embedded in a gelatinlike substance attached to receptive hair cells. In one sac the receptive tissue is on the wall; in the other, it is on the floor. When the head tilts, the weight of the calcium carbonate crystals shifts, producing different forces on the cilia of the hair cells. These forces change the activity of the hair cells, and the information is transmitted to the brain. (See *Figure 6.34.*)

vestibular apparatus The receptive organs of the inner ear that contribute to balance and perception of head movement.

semicircular canal One of a set of three organs in the inner ear that respond to rotational movements of the head.

vestibular sac One of a set of two receptor organs in each inner ear that detect changes in the tilt of the head.

The vestibular sacs are very useful in maintaining an upright head position. They also participate in a reflex that enables us to see clearly even when the head is being jarred. When we walk, our eyes are jostled back and forth. The jarring of the head stimulates the vestibular sacs to cause reflex movements of the eyes that partially compensate for the head movements. People who lack this reflex because of localized brain damage must stop walking in order to see things clearly—for example, to read a street sign.

Interim Summary

The Somatosenses

The somatosenses gather several different kinds of information from different parts of the body. The skin senses of temperature, touch and pressure, vibration, and pain inform us about the nature of objects that come in contact with our skin. Imagine a man attempting to climb a rock cliff. As he reaches for a firm handhold overhead, the Pacinian corpuscles in his fingers detect vibration caused by movement of his fingers over the rock, which helps him determine its texture and find cracks into which he can insert anchors for his rope. Perhaps temperature receptors in his fingers tell him whether the rock is exposed to the sun and has warmed up or whether it is in the cool shade. If he cuts his skin against some sharp rock, free nerve endings give rise to sensations of pain. Presumably he is too intent on his task to notice sensations from his internal organs, although he would certainly feel a painful stimulus like a kidney stone. And if he thinks that he is slipping, he will most assuredly feel a queasy sensation caused by his internal reaction to a sudden release of adrenaline. As he climbs, he relies heavily on sensory receptors in his muscles and joints, which inform his brain of the movement and location of his arms and legs. The vestibular senses help him keep his balance. When he reaches the top and enjoys a hot cup of tea, he can savor a comfortable, warm feeling going from his mouth and throat to his stomach.

Thought Questions

- Our fingertips and our lips are the most sensitive parts of our bodies; relatively large amounts of the primary somatosensory cortex are devoted to analyzing information from these parts of the body. It is easy to understand why our fingertips are so sensitive: We use them to explore objects by touch. But why are our lips so sensitive? Does it have something to do with eating?
- Why can slow, repetitive vestibular stimulation (like that provided by a boat ride in stormy weather) cause nausea and vomiting? Can you think of any useful functions that this response might serve?

Suggestions for Further Reading

Bruce, V., and Green, P. *Visual Perception: Physiology, Psychology and Ecology.* London: Lawrence Erlbaum Associates, 1990.

Gregory, R. L. *Eye and Brain: The Psychology of Seeing,* 4th ed. Princeton, NJ: Princeton University Press, 1990.

Many books have been written about vision and visual perception. An excellent starting point is the inexpensive paperback by Gregory. Gregory knows his subject thoroughly and writes with wit and style. The book contains excellent illustrations, many in color. The book by Bruce and Green is also fine and discusses some topics not covered in the Gregory book.

Gulick, W. L., Gescheider, G. A., and Frisina, R. D. *Hearing: Physiological Acoustics, Neural Coding, and Psychoacoustics.* New York: Oxford University Press, 1989.

Yost, W. A. *Fundamentals of Hearing: An Introduction,* 3rd ed. San Diego: Academic Press, 1994.

There are many excellent books on hearing. I can especially recommend these two for their thoroughness and accuracy.

Matlin, M., and Foley, H. J. *Perception,* 3rd ed. Boston: Allyn and Bacon, 1992.

Sekuler, R., and Blake, R. *Perception,* 2nd ed. New York: McGraw-Hill, 1990.

Both of these books provide good introductions to the functions of the sensory systems. The book by Matlin and Foley has an excellent chapter on taste, with many applications for food and beverage tasting.

Chapter 7

Perception

Chapter Outline

Visual perception is a rapid, automatic, unconscious process. We experience the results of this process, not its steps. The function of visual perception is to guide our action. This guidance can occur immediately, or it can provide us with memories that we can use much later.

Brain Mechanisms of Visual Perception

The Primary Visual Cortex • The Visual Association Cortex • Effects of Brain Damage on Visual Perception

The visual system of the brain is arranged hierarchically. Information is analyzed at each level, and the results are passed on to the next level for further analysis. The primary visual cortex contains a "map" of the retina and hence, of the visual field. Visual images are broken down into small pieces, each analyzed by clusters of neurons that provide information about such features as lines, edges, and colors. Particular regions of the first level of the visual association cortex are responsible for the analysis of details of shape, color, location, and movement. The second level of the visual association cortex contains regions that recognize three-dimensional objects and the objects' location and direction of movement. Brain damage to a person's visual association cortex disrupts specific perceptual abilities, such as the perception of common objects, faces, colors, movements, and spatial locations.

Perception of Form

Figure and Ground • Organization of Elements: Gestalt Laws of Grouping • Models of Pattern Perception • *Evaluating Scientific Issues: Does the Brain Work Like a Computer?* • Top-Down Processing: The Role of Context

The Gestalt organizational laws of proximity, similarity, good continuation, closure, and common fate describe how the grouping of elements of the visual scene help us distinguish between figure and ground—objects and their backgrounds. Psychologists have proposed several models—templates, prototypes, and distinctive features—to explain how we can recognize particular patterns of visual stimuli and thus identify

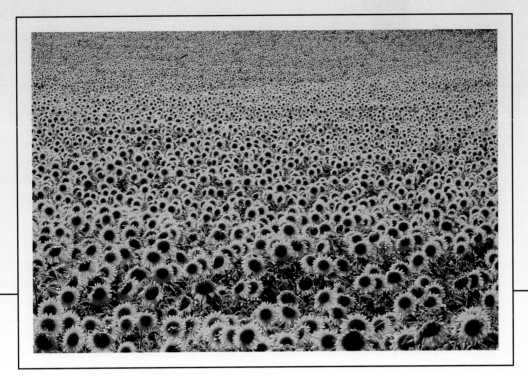

particular objects. *The fact that we can recognize complex objects such as faces as quickly as we can recognize simple geometric shapes suggests that the visual system performs many tasks at the same time. Cognitive research and research using computers provides evidence that the brain is a parallel processor. New models called* neural networks *have elements with properties similar to those of neurons. Bottom-up processing assembles a complex perception from simple elements provided by clusters of neurons in the primary visual cortex. Top-down processing refers to the powerful effect that context can have on the interpretation of the information about these simple elements.*

Perception of Space and Motion

Depth Perception • *Biology and Culture: Effects of Experience on Visual Perception* • Constancies of Visual Perception • Perception of Motion

Although perceiving the shapes of objects is an important task, we must also perceive their locations in space and their movements for our own behavior to be effective. Depth perception is accomplished by both binocular and monocular cues. A person's culture may affect his or her visual perceptions, but probably not in a fundamental way. When there are changes in the brightness of the light that illuminates an object or when an object rotates or its distance from us changes, our perception of the object remains relatively constant. The perception of motion enables us to predict the future locations of objects. We can perceive shapes of objects even when we have only scanty information about the movements of their parts. We can also perceive nonexistent movement when two objects are alternately illuminated.

r. L., a young neuropsychologist, was presenting the case of Mrs. R. to a group of medical students doing a rotation in the neurology department at the medical center. The chief of the department had shown them Mrs. R.'s CT scans, and now Dr. L. was addressing the students. He told them that Mrs. R.'s stroke had not impaired her ability to talk or to move about, but it had affected her vision.

A nurse ushered Mrs. R. into the room and helped her find a seat at the end of the table.

"How are you, Mrs. R.?" asked Dr. L.

"I'm fine. I've been home for a month now, and I can do just about everything that I did before I had my stroke."

"Good. How is your vision?"

"Well, I'm afraid that's still a problem."

"What seems to give you the most trouble?"

"I just don't seem to be able to recognize things. When I'm working in my kitchen, I know what everything is as long as no one moves anything. A few times my husband tried to help me by putting things away, and I couldn't see them any more." She laughed. "Well, I could see them, but I just couldn't say what they were."

Dr. L. took some objects out of a paper bag and placed them on the table in front of her.

"Can you tell me what these are?" he asked. "No," he said, "please don't touch them."

Mrs. R. stared intently at the objects. "No, I can't rightly say what they are."

Dr. L. pointed to one of them, a wristwatch. "Tell me what you see here," he said.

Mrs. R. looked thoughtful, turning her head one way and then the other. "Well, I see something round, and it has two things attached to it, one on the top and one on the bottom." She continued to stare at it. "There are some things inside the circle, I think, but I can't make out what they are."

"Pick it up."

She did so, made a wry face, and said, "Oh. It's a wristwatch." At Dr. L.'s request, she picked up the rest of the objects, one by one, and identified each of them correctly.

"Do you have trouble recognizing people, too?" asked Dr. L.

"Oh, yes!" she sighed. "While I was still in the hospital, my husband and my son both came in to see me, and I couldn't tell who was who until my husband said something—then I could tell which direction his voice was coming from. Now I've trained myself to recognize my husband. I can usually see his glasses and his bald head, but I have to work at it. And I've been fooled a few times." She laughed. "One of our neighbors is bald and wears glasses, too, and one day when he and his wife were visiting us, I thought he was my husband, so I called him 'honey.' It was a little embarrassing at first, but everyone understood."

"What does a face look like to you?" asked Dr. L.

"Well, I know that it's a face, because I can usually see the eyes, and it's on top of a body. I can see a body pretty well, by how it moves." She paused a moment. "Oh, yes, I forgot, sometimes I can recognize a person by how he moves. You know, you can often recognize friends by the way they walk, even when they're far away. I can still do that. That's funny, isn't it? I can't see people's faces very well, but I can recognize the way they walk."

Dr. L. made some movements with his hands. "Can you tell what I'm doing?" he asked.

"Yes, you're mixing something—like some cake batter."

He mimed the gestures of turning a key, writing, and dealing out playing cards, and Mrs. R. recognized them without any difficulty.

"Do you have any trouble reading?" he asked.

"Well, a little, but I don't do too badly."

Dr. L. handed her a magazine, and she began to read the article aloud—somewhat hesitantly, but accurately. "Why is it," she asked, "that I can see the *words* all right but have so much trouble with *things* and with people's faces?"

Take a look around you—look around the room or out the window. Think of what you are seeing—shapes, figures, background, shadows, areas of light and dark—as you move and as your eyes move. Your knowledge of the objects and their relative location is extensive, and you have a good idea of what they will feel like, even if you have not touched them. If the lighting suddenly changes (if lamps are turned on or off or if a cloud passes in front of the sun), the amount of light reflected by the objects in the scene changes too, but your perception of the objects remains the same—you see them as having the same shape, color, and texture as before. Similarly, you do not perceive an object as increasing in size as you approach it, even though the image it casts upon your retina does get larger. These perceptions of form, movement, and space are the topics of this chapter.

As we saw in Chapter 6, the primary function of the sense organs is to provide information to guide behavior. In doing so, the visual system performs many remarkable tasks. The brain receives fragments of information from approximately 1 million axons in each of the optic nerves. It combines and organizes these fragments into the perception of a scene—objects having different forms, colors, and textures, residing at different locations in three-dimensional space. Even when our bodies or our eyes move, exposing the photoreceptors to entirely new patterns of visual information, our perception of the scene before us does not change. We see a stable world, not a moving one, because the brain keeps track of our own movements and those of our eyes and compensates for the constantly changing patterns of neural firing that these movements cause.

Perception is the process by which we recognize what is represented by the information provided by our sense organs. This process gives unity and coherence to this input. Perception is a rapid, automatic, unconscious process; it is not a deliberate one in which we puzzle out the meaning of what we see. We do not first *see* an object and then *perceive* it; we simply perceive the object. Yes, occasionally we see something ambiguous and must reflect about what it might be or gather further evidence to determine what it is, but this situation is more problem solving than perception. If we look at a scene carefully, we can describe the elementary sensations that are present, but we do not become aware of the elements before we perceive the objects and the background of which they are a part. Our awareness of the process of visual perception comes only after it is complete; we are presented with a finished product, not the details of the process.

The distinction between sensation and perception is not easy to make; in some respects the distinction is arbitrary. Probably because of the importance we give to vision and because of the richness of the information provided by our visual system, psychologists make a more explicit distinction between visual sensation and perception than they do for any other sensory system. Hence, this chapter will focus primarily on visual perception. I will discuss the most important task of auditory perception—recognizing spoken words—in Chapter 10.

Brain Mechanisms of Visual Perception

Although the eyes contain the photoreceptors that detect areas of different brightnesses and colors, perception takes place in the brain. As we saw in Chapter 6, the optic nerves send visual information to the thalamus, which relays the information to the primary visual cortex, located in the occipital lobe at the back of the brain. In turn, neurons in the primary visual cortex send visual information to two successive levels of the visual association cortex. The first level, located in the occipital lobe, surrounds the primary visual cortex. The second level is divided into two parts, one in the middle of the parietal lobe and one in the lower part of the temporal lobe. (See *Figure 7.1.*)

Visual perception by the brain is often described as a hierarchy of information processing. According to this scheme,

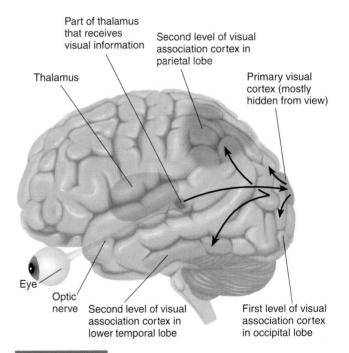

Part of thalamus that receives visual information

Second level of visual association cortex in parietal lobe

Primary visual cortex (mostly hidden from view)

Thalamus

Eye

Optic nerve

Second level of visual association cortex in lower temporal lobe

First level of visual association cortex in occipital lobe

Figure 7.1

The visual system of the brain. Arrows represent the flow of visual information. Sensory information from the eye is transmitted through the optic nerve to the thalamus, and from there it is relayed to the primary visual cortex. The results of the analysis performed there are sent to the visual association cortex of the occipital lobe (first level) and then on to that of the temporal lobe and parietal lobe (second level). At each stage, additional analysis takes place.

perception A rapid, automatic, unconscious process by which we recognize what is represented by the information provided by our sense organs.

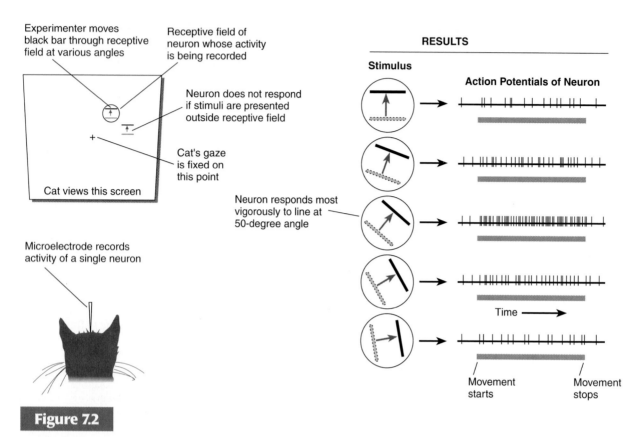

Experimenter moves black bar through receptive field at various angles

Receptive field of neuron whose activity is being recorded

Neuron does not respond if stimuli are presented outside receptive field

Cat's gaze is fixed on this point

Cat views this screen

Microelectrode records activity of a single neuron

RESULTS

Stimulus

Action Potentials of Neuron

Neuron responds most vigorously to line at 50-degree angle

Time

Movement starts

Movement stops

Figure 7.2

Responses of a single neuron to lines of particular orientations that are passed through its receptive field.

circuits of neurons analyze particular aspects of visual information and send the results of their analysis on to another circuit, which performs further analysis. At each step in the process, successively more complex features are analyzed. Eventually, the process leads to the perception of the scene and of all the objects in it. The higher levels of the perceptual process interact with memories: The viewer recognizes familiar objects and learns the appearance of new, unfamiliar ones.

The Primary Visual Cortex

Our knowledge about the characteristics of the earliest stages of visual analysis has come from investigations of the activity of individual neurons in the thalamus and primary visual cortex. For example, David Hubel and Torsten Wiesel have inserted *microelectrodes*—extremely small wires having microscopically sharp points—into various regions of the visual system of cats and monkeys to detect the action potentials produced by individual neurons (Hubel and Wiesel, 1977, 1979). The signals detected by the microelectrodes are electronically amplified and sent to a recording device so that they can be studied later.

After positioning a microelectrode close to a neuron, Hubel and Wiesel presented various stimuli on a large screen in front of the anesthetized animal. The anesthesia makes the animal unconscious but does not prevent neurons in the visual system from responding. The researchers moved a stimulus around on the screen until they located the point where it had the largest effect on the electrical activity of the neuron. Next, they presented stimuli of various shapes to learn which ones produced the greatest response from the neuron.

From their experiments, Hubel and Wiesel (1977, 1979) concluded that the geography of the visual field is retained in the primary visual cortex. That is, the surface of the retina is "mapped" on the surface of the primary visual cortex. However, this map on the brain is distorted, with the largest amount of area given to the center of the visual field. The map is actually like a mosaic—a picture made of individual tiles or pieces of glass. Each "tile" (it is usually called a *module*) consists of a block of tissue, approximately 0.5 x 0.7 mm in size and containing approximately 150,000 neurons. All of the neurons within a module receive information from the same small region of the retina. The primary visual cortex contains approximately 2500 of these modules.

Because each module in the visual cortex receives information from a small region of the retina, that means that it receives information from a small region of the visual field—the scene that the eye is viewing. If you looked at the scene before you through a soda straw, you would see the amount of information received by an individual module. Hubel and

receptive field   That portion of the visual field in which the presentation of visual stimuli will produce an alteration in the firing rate of a particular neuron.

Wiesel found that neural circuits within each module analyzed various characteristics of their own particular part of the visual field—that is, of their **receptive field.** Some circuits detected the presence of lines passing through the region and signaled the *orientation* of these lines (that is, the angle they made with respect to the horizon). Other circuits detected the thickness of these lines. Others detected movement and its direction. Still others detected colors.

Figure 7.2 shows a recording of the responses of an orientation-sensitive neuron in the primary visual cortex. This neuron is located in a cluster of neurons that receive information from a small portion of the visual field. (That is, the neuron has a small receptive field.) The neuron responds when a line oriented at 50 degrees to the vertical is placed in this location—especially when the line is moving through the receptive field. This response is specific to that orientation; the neuron responds very little when a line having a 70-degree or 30-degree orientation is passed through the receptive field. Other neurons in this cluster share the same receptive field but respond to lines of different orientations. Thus, the orientation of lines that pass through this receptive field is signaled by an increased rate of firing of particular neurons in the cluster. (See *Figure 7.2.*)

Because each module in the primary visual cortex receives information about only a restricted area of the visual field, the information must be combined somehow for perception to take place. This combination takes place in the visual association cortex.

The Visual Association Cortex

The first level of the visual association cortex, which surrounds the primary visual cortex, contains several subdivisions, each of which contains a map of the visual scene. Each subdivision receives information from different types of neural circuits within the modules of the primary visual cortex.

One subdivision receives information about the orientation and widths of lines and edges and is involved in perception of shapes. Another subdivision receives information about movement and keeps track of the relative movements of objects (and may help compensate for movements of the eyes as we scan the scene in front of us). Yet another subdivision receives information concerning color (Livingstone and Hubel, 1988; Zeki, 1993). (See *Figures 7.1* and *7.3.*)

The two regions of the second level of the visual association cortex put together the information gathered and processed by the various subregions of the first level. Information about shape, movement, and color are combined in the visual association cortex in the lower part of the temporal lobe. Three-dimensional form perception takes place here. The visual association cortex in the parietal lobe is responsible for perception of the *location* of objects. It integrates information from the first level of the visual association cortex with information from the motor system and the body senses about movements of the eyes, head, and body (Ungerleider and Mishkin, 1982). (See *Figures 7.1* and *7.3.*)

Researchers have studied the anatomy and functions of the visual association cortex in laboratory animals. They have also used PET scans to discover the locations of comparable subregions in the human brain. For example, when a person looks at a display containing irregular patches of different colors, one region of the visual association cortex becomes active. When a person looks at a display containing moving black-and-white squares, another region becomes active. Presumably, these regions are involved in the analysis of color and movement, respectively. (See *Figure 7.4.*)

As you will see in the next section, neuropsychologists have discovered that specific visual deficits can be caused by damage to various parts of the visual system. This finding, along with the results of PET scans, suggests that the organization of the visual association cortex of the human brain is similar to that of other primates studied in the laboratory.

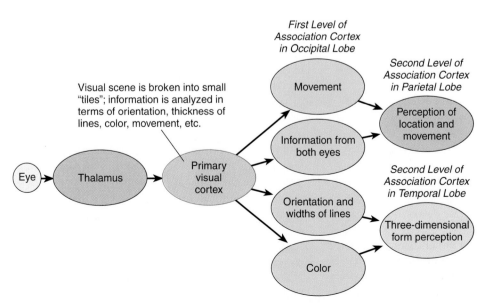

Figure 7.3

A schematic diagram of the types of analyses performed on visual information in the primary visual cortex and the various regions of the visual association cortex.

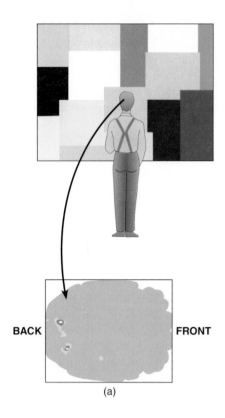

(a)

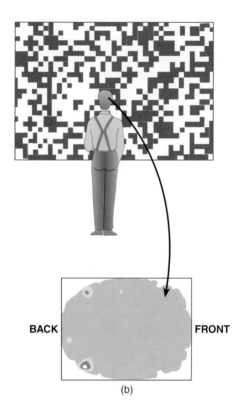

(b)

Figure 7.4

PET scans of the human brain showing regions of increased metabolic activity (indicating increased neural activity) when the subjects looked at multicolored patterns (a) and moving black and white rectangles (b).
(Adapted from Zeki, S. La Recherche, 1990, 21, 712–721.)

Effects of Brain Damage on Visual Perception

The effects of damage to the primary visual cortex and to the visual association cortex support the general outline just described. When the primary visual cortex is damaged, a person becomes blind in some portion of the visual field. The exact location depends on where the brain damage is. However, even if the person loses a considerable amount of his or her sight, the person will be able to perceive objects and their backgrounds. This finding supports the conclusion that perception takes place in the visual association cortex and not in the primary visual cortex.

Try a simple demonstration that illustrates this principle. Roll up a piece of paper so that it forms a small tube and look through it as you would through a telescope. Move the tube around so that you can scan the scene in front of you. Although you see only a part of the scene at any one time, you have no difficulty perceiving what is present. Your experience is like that of a person who has extensive damage to the primary visual cortex but whose visual association cortex has been spared: The result is a limited visual field but good perceptual ability.

In contrast, damage to the visual association cortex does not disrupt the person's ability to see fine details, but it does produce varying amounts of difficulty in perceiving shapes and objects or in perceiving particular visual characteristics. For example, damage to part of the visual association cortex can disrupt color vision—a condition known as **achromatop**-

sia (literally, "vision without color"). A person who has achromatopsia can still see normally, but everything looks as if it had been filmed in black and white. Damage to only one side of the brain produces achromatopsia in the contralateral (opposite) visual field. Total achromatopsia occurs only after bilateral damage. (See *Figure 7.5.*)

Damage to another subregion of the visual association cortex can make it difficult for a person to perceive movements and to keep track of moving objects. For example, Zihl et al. (1991) studied a woman who had sustained bilateral damage to a region of the first level of the visual association cortex. The woman could see; she could recognize the shape, color, and location of objects in her environment. However, she had great difficulty perceiving movements. She was unable to cross a street without traffic lights because she could not judge the speed at which cars were moving. When the investigators asked her to try to detect movements of a visual target in the laboratory, she said, "First the target is completely at rest. Then it suddenly jumps upwards and downwards" (p. 2244). She was able to see that the target was constantly changing its position, but she had no sensation of the movement.

Damage to the visual association cortex in the parietal lobe can make it difficult for a person to keep track of the location of objects in the visual scene. This deficit is called

achromatopsia The inability to discriminate among different hues; caused by damage to the visual association cortex.

Figure 7.5

A photograph illustrating the way the world would look to a person who had achromatopsia in the right visual field, caused by damage on the left side of the brain to the region of the visual association cortex shown in Figure 7.4a.

Balint's syndrome, after its discoverer. People who have Balint's syndrome can recognize individual objects when they look directly at them but are unable to see where they are located. The scene in front of them is a jumble of individual objects, arranged in no particular order.

Damage to the visual association cortex of the temporal lobe can disrupt the ability to recognize objects without affecting the ability to see colors, movements, or fine details. This deficit is called **visual agnosia.** People who have visual agnosia may have normal visual acuity, but they cannot successfully recognize objects visually by their shape. For example, a brain-damaged patient studied by Benson and Greenberg (1969) was initially believed to be blind but was subsequently observed to navigate his wheelchair around the halls of a hospital. Testing revealed that he could pick up threads placed on a sheet of white paper. He could discriminate among stimuli that differed in size, brightness, or hue but could not distinguish stimuli that differed only in shape. Surprisingly, many people who have visual agnosia can read—just like Mrs. R., who was described in the opening vignette. (And as we shall see in Chapter 10, many people who are unable to read because of brain damage have no difficulty recognizing objects by sight. These results indicate that different brain mechanisms are involved in the recognition of words and objects.)

One form of visual agnosia makes it difficult or impossible for a person to recognize particular faces—a disorder called **prosopagnosia** (from the Greek *prosōpon,* meaning "face"). For example, Mrs. R. was unable to recognize her husband by sight but could identify him by his voice as soon as he spoke. She could even recognize friends at a distance by observing the way they walked. Most people who have prosopagnosia have difficulty recognizing other complex visual stimuli

as well (Damasio, Tranel, and Damasio, 1990). They can easily recognize *categories* of objects (such as automobiles, animals, or houses) but have difficulty distinguishing between particular *individual* stimuli (their car, their dog, or their house). One woman who had prosopagnosia could no longer distinguish between different makes of cars and so had to find her own in a parking lot by looking for the correct license plate. (Obviously, she could still distinguish numbers and letters.) Another person, a farmer, could no longer tell his cows apart.

Interim Summary

Brain Mechanisms of Vision

Visual information proceeds from the retina to the thalamus, and then to the primary visual cortex. The primary visual cortex is organized into modules ("tiles"), each of which receives information from a small region of the retina. Neural circuits within each module analyze specific information from their part of the visual field, including the orientation and width of lines, color, and movement.

The different types of information analyzed by the neural circuits in the modules of the primary visual cortex are sent to separate maps of the visual field in the first level of the visual association cortex. The information from these maps is combined in the second level of the visual association cortex: form perception in the base of the temporal lobe and spatial perception in the parietal lobe.

Damage to specific regions of the primary visual cortex causes blindness in corresponding parts of the visual field. Damage to parts of the first level of the visual association cortex causes achromatopsia (lack of color vision) or difficulty in perceiving movements. Damage to the visual association cortex of the parietal lobe causes Balint's syndrome, a deficit in spatial perception. Damage to the visual association cortex of the temporal lobe can disrupt form perception without affecting the ability to see colors, movements, or fine details—a condition called visual agnosia.

Thought Questions

- Would you rather that your primary visual cortex or your visual association cortex be partially (not totally) damaged? What would the symptoms be, and which would you find less disabling?

Balint's syndrome A syndrome caused by bilateral damage to the parieto-occipital region of the brain; includes difficulty in perceiving the location of objects and reaching for them under visual guidance.

visual agnosia The inability of a person who is not blind to recognize the identity of an object visually; caused by damage to the visual association cortex.

prosopagnosia A form of visual agnosia characterized by difficulty in the recognition of people's faces; caused by damage to the visual association cortex.

■ If you had one of the perceptual deficits described in this section, what coping strategies might you adopt? Suppose that you could not identify people by sight, or recognize your automobile. Suppose that you could not recognize common objects but could read. How could you arrange things so that you would function at a high level of independence? Suppose you had complete achromatopsia. What would you miss seeing? What difficulties would you face and how would you cope with them?

Perception of Form

When we look at the world, we do not see patches of colors and shades of brightness. We see *things*—cars, streets, people, desks, books, trees, dogs, chairs, walls, flowers, clouds, televisions. We see where each object is located, how large it is, and whether it is moving. We recognize familiar objects and also recognize when we see something we have never seen before. The visual system is able to perceive shapes, determine distances, and detect movements; it tells us what something is, where it is located, and what it is doing. This section considers the first task: perceiving an object's form.

Figure and Ground

Most of what we see can be classified as either object or background. *Objects* are things having particular shapes and particular locations in space. (In this context, people can be considered as objects.) *Backgrounds* are essentially formless and serve mostly to help us judge the location of objects we see in front of them. Psychologists use the terms **figure** and **ground** to label an object and its background, respectively. The classification of an item as a figure or as a part of the background is not an intrinsic property of the item. Rather, it depends on the behavior of the observer. If you are watching some birds fly overhead, they are figures and the blue sky and the clouds behind them are part of the background. If, instead, you are watching the clouds move, then the birds become background. If you are looking at a picture hanging on a wall, it is an object. If you are looking at a person standing between you and the wall, the picture is part of the background. Sometimes, we receive ambiguous clues about what

figure   A visual stimulus that is perceived as a self-contained object.

ground   A visual stimulus that is perceived as a formless background against which objects are seen.

Gestalt psychology   A branch of psychology that asserts that the perception of objects is produced by particular configurations of the elements of stimuli.

Figure 7.6

A drawing in which figure and ground can be reversed. You can see either two faces against a white background or a goblet against a dark background.

is object and what is background. For example, does *Figure 7.6* illustrate two faces or a wine goblet?

What are the characteristics of the complex patterns of light—varying in brightness, saturation, and hue—that give rise to perceptions of figures, of *things?* One of the most important aspects of form perception is the existence of a *boundary.* If the visual field contains a sharp and distinct change in brightness, color, or texture, we perceive an edge. If this edge forms a continuous boundary, we will probably perceive the space enclosed by the boundary as a figure. (See *Figure 7.7.*)

Organization of Elements: Gestalt Laws of Grouping

As we just saw, most figures are defined by a boundary. But the presence of a boundary is not necessary for the perception of form. *Figure 7.8* shows that when small elements are arranged in groups, we tend to perceive them as larger figures. And *Figure 7.9* demonstrates *illusory contours*—lines that do not exist. In this figure, the orientation of the pie-shaped objects and the three 45-degree segments make us perceive two triangles, one on top of the other. The one that looks like it is superimposed on the three black circles even appears to be brighter than the background.

The tendency to perceive elements as belonging together has been recognized for many years. Earlier in this century, a group of psychologists organized a theory of perception called **Gestalt psychology.** *Gestalt* is the German word for "form." They maintained that the task of perception was to recognize

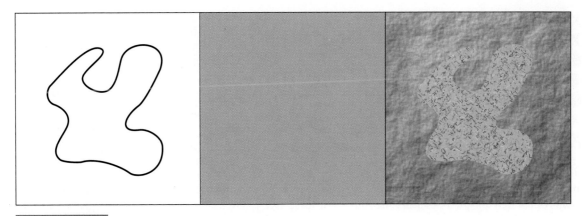

Figure 7.7

Form perception and boundaries. We immediately perceive even an unfamiliar figure when its outline is closed.

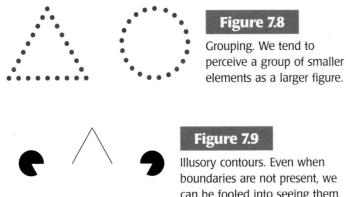

Figure 7.8

Grouping. We tend to perceive a group of smaller elements as a larger figure.

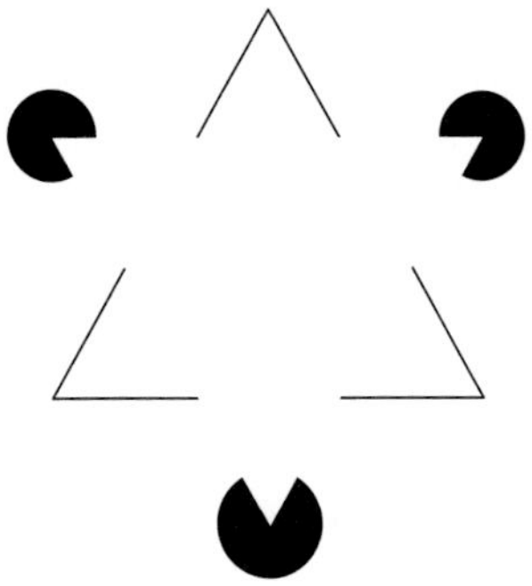

Figure 7.9

Illusory contours. Even when boundaries are not present, we can be fooled into seeing them. The triangle with its point down looks brighter than the surrounding area.

objects in the environment according to the organization of their elements. They argued that in perception the whole is more than the sum of its parts. Because of the characteristics of the visual system of the brain, visual perception cannot be understood simply by analyzing the scene into its elements. Instead, what we see depends on the *relations* of these elements to one another.

Elements of a visual scene can combine in various ways to produce different forms. Gestalt psychologists have observed that several principles of grouping can predict the combination of these elements. The fact that our visual system groups and combines elements is useful because we can then perceive forms even if they are fuzzy and incomplete. The real world presents us with objects partly obscured by other objects and with backgrounds that are the same color as parts of the objects in front of them. The outlines of objects are very often not distinct. As I look out the window of my office, I see a large bush against a background of trees. It is

summer, and I see countless shades of green in the scene before me. I cannot distinguish the bush from the trees behind it simply by differences in color. However, I can clearly see the outline of the bush because of subtle differences in its texture (the leaves are smaller than those of the tree) and because the wind causes its branches to move in a pattern different from that of the tree branches. The laws of grouping discovered by Gestalt psychologists describe my ability to distinguish this figure from its background.

The **law of proximity** states that elements that are closest together will be perceived as belonging together. *Figure 7.10* demonstrates this principle. The pattern on the left looks like four vertical columns because the dots are closer to their neighbors above and below them than to those located to the right and to the left. The pattern on the right looks like four horizontal rows.

The **law of similarity** states that elements that look similar will be perceived as part of the same form. We can easily see the diamond inside the square in *Figure 7.11*.

Figure 7.10

The Gestalt principle of proximity. Different spacing of the dots produces five vertical or five horizontal lines.

law of proximity   A Gestalt law of organization; elements located closest to each other are perceived as belonging to the same figure.

law of similarity   A Gestalt law of organization; similar elements are perceived as belonging to the same figure.

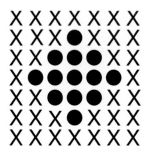

Figure 7.11

The Gestalt principle of similarity. Similar elements are perceived as belonging to the same form.

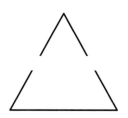

Figure 7.13

The Gestalt principle of closure. We tend to supply missing information to close a figure and separate it from its background. Lay a pencil across the gaps and see how strong the perception of a complete triangle becomes.

Good continuation refers to predictability or simplicity. Which of the two sets of colored dots best describes the continuation of the line of black dots in *Figure 7.12?* If you see the figure the way I do, you will choose the colored dots that continue the curve down and to the right. It is simpler to perceive the line as following a smooth course than as suddenly making a sharp bend.

Often, one object partially hides another, but we nevertheless perceive the incomplete image. The **law of closure** states that our visual system often supplies missing information and "closes" the outline of an incomplete figure. For example, *Figure 7.13* looks a bit like a triangle, but if you place a pencil on the page so that it covers the gaps, the figure undeniably looks like a triangle. (Try it.)

The final Gestalt law of organization relies on movement. The **law of common fate** states that elements that move in the same direction will be perceived as belonging together

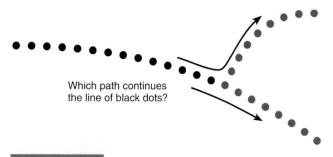

Which path continues the line of black dots?

Figure 7.12

The Gestalt principle of good continuation. It is easier to perceive a smooth continuation than an abrupt shift.

good continuation A Gestalt law of organization; given two or more interpretations of elements that form the outline of the figure, the simplest interpretation will be preferred.

law of closure A Gestalt law of organization; elements missing from the outline of a figure are "filled in" by the visual system.

law of common fate A Gestalt law of organization; elements that move together give rise to the perception of a particular figure.

template A hypothetical pattern that resides in the nervous system and is used to perceive objects or shapes by a process of comparison.

and forming a figure. In the forest, an animal is camouflaged if its surface is covered with the same elements found in the background—spots of brown, tan, and green—because its boundary is obscured. There is no basis for grouping the elements on the animal. As long as the animal is stationary, it remains well hidden. However, once it moves, the elements on its surface will move together, and the animal's form will quickly be perceived.

And how did I distinguish the bush from the trees? You will recall that the primary cues were differences in leaf size and in the movement induced by the wind, examples of similarity and common fate, respectively.

Models of Pattern Perception

Most of the psychologists who are currently studying perception call themselves cognitive psychologists. They are interested in the mental processes responsible for perception—the steps that take place between the time the eye is exposed to a stimulus and the time a perception of the image is formed, ready for the person to act on. They collect behavioral data and try to make inferences about the nature of these mental processes. Let us examine some of the models they have devised to explain the process of pattern perception.

Templates and Prototypes

One possible explanation for our ability to recognize shapes of objects is that as we gain experience looking at things, we acquire **templates,** which are special kinds of memories used by the visual system. A template (pronounced *TEM-plit*) is a type of pattern used to manufacture a series of objects. For example, a cookie cutter is a template used to cut out identical shapes from a flat piece of dough. Perhaps the visual system reverses the process; when a particular pattern of visual stimulation is encountered, it searches through its set of templates and compares each of them with the pattern provided by the stimulus. If it finds a match, it knows that the pattern is a familiar one. Connections between the appropriate template and memories in other parts of the brain could provide the name of the object and other information about it, such as its function, when it was seen before, and so forth.

The template model of pattern recognition has the virtue of simplicity. However, most psychologists do not believe that it could actually work—the visual system would have to store

The template model for pattern recognition seems inadequate for explaining how we can recognize a human hand, in its many sizes, colors, and positions.

an unreasonably large number of templates. Consider a familiar object, such as a human hand. Hold your own hand out in front of you and look at it. Turn it around, wiggle your fingers, clench your fist, and see how many different patterns you can project on the retinas of your eyes. No matter what you do, you continue to recognize the pattern as belonging to your hand. How many different templates would your visual memory have to contain just to recognize a hand? And suppose the hand were more or less hairy, were darker or lighter, had longer or shorter fingers—I think you get the point.

A more flexible model of pattern perception suggests that patterns of visual stimulation are compared with prototypes rather than templates. **Prototypes** (Greek for "original model") are idealized patterns of a particular shape; they resemble templates but are used in a much more flexible way. The visual system does not look for exact matches between the pattern being perceived and the memories of shapes of objects but accepts a degree of disparity; for instance, it accepts the various patterns produced when we look at a particular object from different viewpoints.

Most psychologists believe that pattern recognition by the visual system does involve prototypes, at least in some form. For example, you can undoubtedly identify maple trees, fir trees, and palm trees when you see them. In nature, each

tree looks different from all the others, but maples resemble other maples more than they resemble firs, and so on. A reasonable assumption is that your visual system has memories of the prototypical visual patterns that represent these objects. Recognizing particular types of trees, then, is a matter of finding the best fit between stimulus and prototype.

The visual system of the brain may indeed contain generic prototypes that help us recognize objects we have never seen before: coffee cups, maple trees, human faces. But we do more than recognize categories of objects; we can recognize *particular* coffee cups, maple trees, or human faces. In fact, we can learn to recognize enormous numbers of objects. Think of how many different people you can recognize by sight, how many buildings in your town you can recognize, how many pieces of furniture in your house and in your friends' houses you are familiar with—the list will be very long. Standing (1973) showed people 10,000 color slides and found that they could recognize most of them weeks later, *even though they had seen them just once.*

I strongly suspect that many objects have to be represented by more than one prototype, such as profile and frontal views of a face. Perhaps there are even various levels of prototypes: generic ones such as maples or human faces and more specific ones such as the tree in your backyard or the face of a friend. In fact, evidence from studies of nonhuman primates suggests that familiarity with categories of objects may lead to the development of specific types of prototypes.

Humphrey (1974) showed monkeys pictures of other animals and used habituation to see how the monkeys categorized what they saw. The method he used was first developed to study the perceptual abilities of human infants, and it is described in more detail in Chapter 10. Briefly, if a monkey (or a baby) sees the same picture twice in succession, it spends less time looking at the picture the second time. Humphrey found that when monkeys were shown a series of pictures of different monkeys, they spent a considerable amount of time examining each one, as if each picture was novel and interesting. (After all, they were acquainted with monkeys and could certainly recognize different faces.) However, if the monkeys were shown a series of four-legged animals such as pigs and cows, they quickly lost interest; it was as if they were looking at the same picture again and again. Over the next few months, Humphrey showed the monkeys pictures of various species of animals. The experience seemed to sharpen the monkeys' ability to recognize the animals. In fact, not only could they tell the difference between pigs and cows, but also they could distinguish between one pig and another or one cow and another. It was as if the experience with many individuals led to the development of more and more specific prototypes of categories of four-legged animals.

prototype A hypothetical idealized pattern that resides in the nervous system and is used to perceive objects or shapes by a process of comparison; recognition can occur even when an exact match is not found.

We can recognize particular objects as well as general categories of objects.

Distinctive Features

How complete does the information in a prototype have to be? Does a prototype have to contain a detailed representation of an image of the object it represents, or can the information be represented in some shorthand way? Some psychologists suggest that the visual system encodes images of familiar patterns in terms of **distinctive features**—collections of important physical features that specify particular items. For example, Figure 7.14 contains several examples of the letter *N*. Although the examples vary in size and style, you have no trouble recognizing them. (See *Figure 7.14.*) How do you do so? Perhaps your visual system contains a specification of the distinctive features that fit the criterion for an *N*: two parallel vertical lines connected by a diagonal line sloping downward from the top of the left one to the bottom of the right one.

An experiment by Neisser (1964) supports the hypothesis that perception involves analysis of distinctive features. Figure 7.15 shows one of the tasks he asked people to do. The figure shows two columns of letters. Scan through them until you find the letter *Z*, which occurs once in each column. (See *Figure 7.15.*)

> **distinctive feature** A physical characteristic of an object that helps distinguish it from other objects.

N N N N *N*
N N N *N* *N*

Figure 7.14

Distinctive features. We easily recognize all of these items as the letter N.

GDOROC	IVEMXW
COQUCD	XVIWME
DUCOQG	VEMIXW
GRUDQO	WEXMVI
OCDURQ	XIMVWE
DUCGRO	IVMWEX
ODUCQG	VWEMXI
CQOGRD	IMEWXV
DUZORQ	EXMZWI
UCGROD	IEMWVX
QCUDOG	EIVXWM
RQGUDO	WXEMIV
DRGOQC	MIWVXE
OQGDRU	IMEVXW
UGCODQ	IEMWVX
ODRUCQ	IMWVEX
UDQRGC	XWMVEI
ORGCUD	IWEVXM

Figure 7.15

A letter-search task. Look for the letter Z hidden in each column.

(Adapted from Neisser, U. Scientific American, 1964, 210, 94–102.)

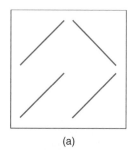
(a)

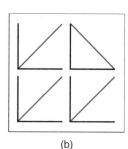
(b)

Figure 7.16

Contextual cues. Perceiving a simple stimulus is facilitated by contextual cues. The line that does not match the other three is more easily recognized in (b).

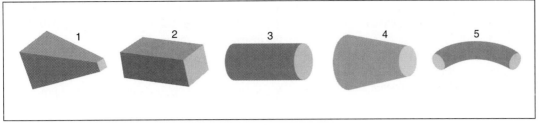

(a) Geons

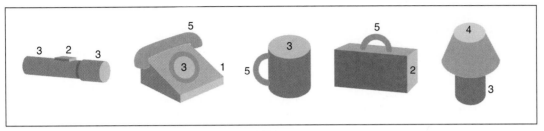

(b) Objects

Figure 7.17

Geons for perception. (a) Several different geons. (b) The combination of two or three geons (indicated by the numbers) into common three-dimensional objects.
(Adapted from Biederman, I. In An Invitation to Cognitive Science. Vol. 2: Visual Cognition and Action, *edited by D. N. Osherson, S. M. Kosslyn, and J. Hollerbach. Cambridge, MA: MIT Press, 1990.)*

Chances are good that you found the letter in the left column much faster than you did the one in the right column, just as Neisser's subjects did. Perhaps you guessed why: The letters in the left column have few features in common with those found in the letter *Z*, so the *Z* stands out from the others. In contrast, the letters in the right column have many features in common with the target letter, and thus the *Z* is camouflaged, so to speak. (See *Figure 7.15.*)

There are some phenomena that cannot easily be explained by the distinctive-features model. The model suggests that the perception of an object consists of analysis and synthesis; the visual system first identifies the component features of an object and then adds up the features to determine what the object is. We might expect, then, that more complex objects, having more distinctive features, would take longer to perceive. But often, the addition of more features, in the form of contextual cues, *speeds up* the process of perception. Figure 7.16 contains two sets of four items. One item in each is different from the other three. Look at the two sets, and see which types of items are easier to distinguish. (See *Figure 7.16.*) As you can see, the patterns in both sets differ with respect to only one feature: the tilt of the diagonal line. But the addition of the horizontal and vertical lines in Figure 17.16b makes the perceptual task much easier. We see a triangle and three right angles bisected by a diagonal line; the triangle just pops out as being different. If we perceived individual features (such as the diagonal lines) before perceiving more complex figures (such as triangles and bisected right angles) that are composed of these features, then we should perceive simpler figures faster than we perceive more complex ones. The fact that we do not

means that a perception is not simply an assembly of individual features.

The distinctive-features model appears to be a reasonable explanation for the perception of letters, but what about more natural stimuli, which we encounter in places other than the written page? Biederman (1987, 1990) suggests a model of pattern recognition that combines some aspects of prototypes and distinctive features. He suggests that the shapes of objects that we encounter can be constructed from a set of thirty-six different shapes that he refers to as **geons.** *Figure 7.17* illustrates a few geons and some objects that can be constructed from them. Perhaps, Biederman suggests, the visual system recognizes objects by identifying the particular sets and arrangements of geons that they contain.

Even if Biederman is correct that our ability to perceive categories of common objects involves recognition of geons, it seems unlikely that the geons are involved in perception of *particular* objects. For example, it is difficult to imagine how we could perceive faces of different people as assemblies of different sets of geons. The geon hypothesis appears to work best for the recognition of prototypes of generic categories: telephones or flashlights in general rather than the telephone on your desk or the flashlight a friend lent you.

Biederman points out that particular features of figures—cusps and joints formed by the ends of line segments—are of

geon According to Biederman, an elementary shape that can serve as a prototype in recognizing objects; a given object can consist of one or more individual geons.

critical importance in recognizing drawings of objects. Presumably, the presence of these joints enables the viewer to recognize the constituent geons. Figure 7.18 shows two sets of degraded images of drawings of five common objects. One set, (a), shows the locations of cusps and joints; the other, (b), does not. Biederman (1990) found that people found the items with cusps and joints much easier to recognize. (See *Figure 7.18.*)

Evaluating Scientific Issues

Does the Brain Work Like a Serial Computer?

As we saw in Chapter 1, when we try to understand something very complicated (such as the functions of the human brain), we tend to think in terms of things that are familiar to us. For example, René Descartes used the moving statues in the Royal Gardens as a basis for his hydraulic model of the nervous system. He saw an analogy between the nerves, muscles, and brain of the body and the pipes, cylinders, and valves of the statues, and he suggested that their principles of operation might be similar. Although cognitive psychology has a history that dates back to the early part of this century, most of its philosophy and methodology have developed during the past thirty years. During this time, the best-known physical device that performs functions similar to those of the human brain has been the general-purpose serial computer. Thus, it is the computer that provided (and still provides) much of the inspiration for the models of human brain function constructed by cognitive psychologists.

■ Using Computers to Model Cognitive Processes

To understand the thought processes that guide the development of models inspired by computers, we must understand something about how modern general-purpose computers work. They consist of four major parts (and countless other parts that I will not talk about).

- *Input devices* and *output devices* (or, collectively, *I/O devices*) permit us to communicate with the computer—to give it instructions or data and to learn the results of its computations.

- *Memory* permits information to be stored in the computer. This information can contain instructions or data we have given the computer or the intermediate steps and final results of its calculations.

- A *central processor* contains the electronic circuits necessary for the computer to perform its functions: to

read the information received by the input devices and to store it in memory, to *execute the steps* specified by the instructions contained in its programs, and to *display the results* by means of the output devices. (See *Figure 7.19.*)

Modern general-purpose computers can be programmed to store any kind of information that can be coded in numbers or words, can solve any logical problem that can be explicitly described, and can compute any mathematical equations that can be written. Therefore—in principle, at least—they can be programmed to do the things we do: perceive, remember, make deductions, solve problems. The power and flexibility of computers seem to make them an excellent basis for constructing models of mental processes. For example, psychologists, linguists, and computer scientists have constructed computer-inspired models of visual pattern perception, speech comprehension, reading, control of movement, and memory.

The construction of computer programs that simulate human mental functions is called **artificial intelligence.** Such an enterprise can help clarify the nature of mental functions. For instance, to construct a program and simulate perception and classification of certain types of patterns, the investigator must specify precisely what the task of pattern perception requires. If the program fails to rec-

Figure 7.18

Incomplete figures. (a) Without cusps and joints. (b) With cusps and joints. Which set of objects is easier to recognize?

(From Biederman, I. Higher-level vision. In An Invitation to Cognitive Science. Vol. 2: Visual Cognition and Action, edited by D. N. Osherson, S. M. Kosslyn, and J. Hollerbach. Cambridge, MA: MIT Press,

(a)   (b)

artificial intelligence A field of study in which computer programs are designed to simulate human cognitive abilities with the expectation that the endeavor will help the investigator understand the mechanisms that underlie these abilities.

ognize the patterns, then the investigator knows that something is wrong with the model or with the way it has been implemented in the program. The investigator revises the model, tries again, and keeps working until it finally works (or until he or she gives up the task as being too ambitious). So far, no program is advanced enough to deal with more than a small fraction of the patterns a human can recognize.

Ideally, the task of discovering what steps are necessary in a computer program to simulate some human cognitive abilities tells the investigator the kinds of processes the brain must perform. However, there is usually more than one way to accomplish a particular goal. Critics of artificial intelligence have pointed out that it is entirely possible to write a program that performs a task that the human brain performs—and comes up with exactly the same results—but does the task in an entirely different way. In fact, some say, given the way that computers work and what we know about the structure of the human brain, the computer program is *guaranteed* to work differently.

■ How Does a Serial Computer Work?

Serial computers work one step at a time. Each step takes time. A complicated program will contain more steps and will take more time to execute. But we do some things extremely quickly that computers take a very long time to do. One of the best examples (appropriately enough,

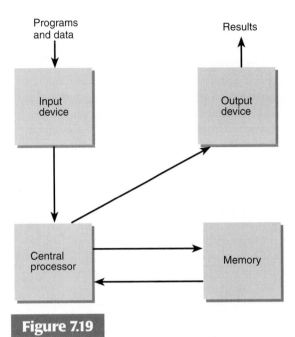

Figure 7.19

The major components of a general-purpose serial computer.

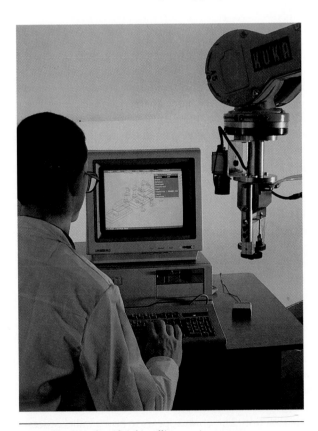

An application of artificial intelligence: A computer controls a robot arm equipped with visual and tactile sensors.

given the subject of this chapter) is visual perception. We can recognize a complex figure about as quickly as we can a simple one. For example, it takes about the same amount of time to recognize a friend's face as it does to identify a simple triangle. The same is not true at all for a serial computer. A computer must "examine" the scene through an input device something like a television camera. Information about the brightness of each point of the picture must be converted into a number and stored in a memory location. Then the program examines each memory location, one at a time, and does calculations that determine the locations of lines, edges, textures, and shapes; finally, it tries to determine what these shapes represent. Recognizing a face takes *much* longer than recognizing a triangle.

■ An Alternative: The Parallel Processor

If the brain were a serial device, its maximum speed would probably be around ten steps per second, considering the rate at which neurons can fire (Rumelhart et al., 1986). This rate is extremely slow, compared with modern serial computers. Obviously, when we perceive visual images, our brain does not act like a serial device.

Instead, the brain appears to be a **parallel processor,** in which many different modules (collections of circuits of neurons) work simultaneously at different tasks. A complex task is broken down into many smaller ones, and separate modules work on each of them. Because the brain consists of many billions of neurons, it can afford to devote different clusters of neurons to different tasks.

parallel processor A computing device that can perform several operations simultaneously.

With so many things happening at the same time, the task gets done quickly.

■ The Emerging Model: Neural Networks

It is one thing to say that the brain consists of many different modules, all working in parallel on separate pieces of a complicated task (such as recognizing someone's face), and another thing to explain how these modules work. Recently, psychologists have begun to devise models of mental functions that are based, more or less, on the way the brain seems to be constructed. These models are called **neural networks.**

Investigators have discovered that when they construct a network of simple elements interconnected in certain ways, the network does some surprising things. The elements have properties like those of neurons. They are connected to each other through junctions similar to synapses. Like synapses, these junctions can have either excitatory or inhibitory effects. When an element receives a critical amount of excitation, it sends a message to the elements with which it communicates, and so on. Some of the elements of a network have input lines that can receive signals from the "outside," which could represent a sensory organ or the information received from another network. Other elements have output lines, which communicate with other networks or control muscles, producing behavior. Thus, particular patterns of input can represent particular stimuli, and particular patterns of output can represent responses. (See *Figure 7.20.*)

Investigators do not construct physical networks. Instead, they write computer programs that simulate them. The programs keep track of each element and the state of each of its inputs and outputs and calculate what would happen if a particular pattern of input is presented. Neural networks can be taught to "recognize" particular stimuli. They are shown a particular stimulus, and their output is monitored. If the response on the output lines is incorrect, the network is given a signal indicating the correct response. This signal causes the strength of some of the junctions to be changed, just as learning is thought to alter the strength of synapses in the brain. After several trials, the network learns to make correct responses.

If the network uses a sufficiently large number of elements, it can be trained to recognize several different patterns, producing the correct response each time one of the patterns is shown to it. In addition, it will even recognize the patterns if they are altered slightly, or if only parts of the patterns are shown. Thus, neural networks can recognize not only particular patterns but also variations on that pattern. Thus, they act as if they had learned general *prototypes*, not specific *templates*.

neural network A model of the nervous system based on interconnected networks of elements that have some of the properties of neurons.

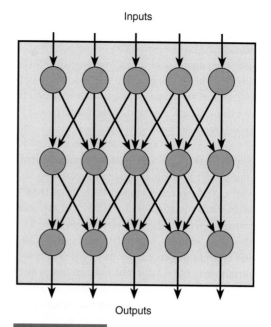

Inputs

Outputs

Figure 7.20

A very simple neural network used as a model of brain function. The circles are elements having properties similar to those of neurons. The connections (arrows) can be excitatory or inhibitory, depending on the particular model.

Visual perception, then, consists of a series of analyses, beginning with simple features and progressing to more complex ones. Each level of analysis involves a different neural network. In the primary visual cortex the networks are small and local. Each one analyzes simple features—such as orientation of lines and edges, color, and movement—within a restricted part of the visual field. In the subregions of the visual association cortex of the occipital lobes, larger networks process the information they receive from the primary visual cortex. For example, the region that receives information about orientation of lines and edges recognizes shapes and patterns: squares, circles, ice cream cones, dogs, cats, faces. Other networks of neurons in the visual association cortex of the temporal lobes put all the information together and perceive the entire, three-dimensional scene, with objects having particular shapes, colors, and textures. The locations of the objects in the visual scene are determined by a network of neurons in the parietal lobes.

So what is the answer to the question posed at the beginning of this section? *Does* the brain work like a computer? The answer seems to be that it does, but not like the most familiar kind of computer, which cognitive psychologists first used as a basis for constructing models of brain function. The brain appears to be a parallel processor made up of collections of neural networks.

Top-Down Processing: The Role of Context

We must often perceive objects under conditions that are less than optimum; the object is in a shadow, camouflaged against a similar background, or obscured by fog. Nevertheless, we usually manage to recognize the item correctly. We are often helped in our endeavor by the context in which we see the object. For example, look at the four items in *Figure 7.21*. Can you tell what they represent? Now, look at *Figure 7.23*. With the aid of a context, the items are easily recognized.

Palmer (1975) showed that even more general forms of context can aid in the perception of objects. He first showed his subjects familiar scenes, such as a kitchen. (See *Figure 7.22*.) Next, he used a device called a tachistoscope to show them drawings of individual items and asked the subjects to identify them. (The word comes from *takhistos*, "most swift," and *skopein*, "to see.") A **tachistoscope** can present visual stimuli very briefly so that they are very difficult to perceive. Sometimes, the subjects saw an object that was appropriate to the scene, such as a loaf of bread. Other times, they saw an inappropriate but similarly shaped object, such as a mailbox. (See *Figure 7.22*.)

Palmer found that when the objects fit the context that had been set by the scene, the subjects correctly identified about 84 percent of them. But when they did not, performance fell to about 50 percent. Performance was intermediate in the no-context control condition, under which subjects did not first see a scene. Thus, compared with the no-context control condition, an appropriate context facilitated recognition and an inappropriate one interfered with it.

The context effects demonstrated by experiments such as Palmer's are not simply examples of guessing games. That is, people do not think to themselves, "Let's see, that shape could be either a mailbox or a loaf of bread. I just saw a picture of a kitchen, so I guess it's a loaf of bread." The process is rapid, unconscious, and automatic; thus, it belongs to the category of perception rather than to problem solving, which is much slower and more deliberate. Somehow, seeing a kitchen scene sensitizes the neural circuits responsible for the perception of loaves of bread and other items we have previously seen in that context.

Psychologists distinguish between two categories of information-processing models of pattern recognition: *bottom-up processing* and *top-down processing*. In **bottom-up processing,** also called *data-driven processing*, the perception is constructed out of the elements—the bits and pieces—of the stimulus, beginning with the image that falls on the retina. The information is processed by successive levels of the visual sys-

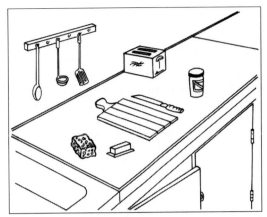

Contextual scene

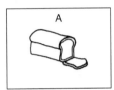 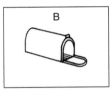

Target object (presented very briefly)

Figure 7.22

Stimuli from the experiment by Palmer (1975). After looking at the contextual scene, the subjects were shown one of the stimuli below it very briefly, by means of a tachistoscope.

(From Palmer, S. E. Memory and Cognition, 1975, 3, 519–526. Reprinted by permission of the Psychonomic Society, Inc.)

tem until the highest levels (the "top" of the system) are reached, and the object is perceived. **Top-down processing** refers to the use of contextual information—to the use of the "big picture." Presumably, once the kitchen scene is perceived, information is sent from the "top" of the system down through lower levels. This information excites neural circuits responsible for perceiving those objects normally found in kitchens and inhibits others. Then, when the subject sees a drawing of a loaf of bread, information starts coming up through the successive levels of the system and finds the appropriate circuits already warmed up, so to speak.

Haenny and Schiller (1988) obtained direct evidence that watching for a particular stimulus can, indeed, warm up neural circuits in the visual system. They trained monkeys to look at a pattern of lines oriented at a particular angle, to remember that pattern, and then to pick it out from a series of

Figure 7.21

Simple elements that are difficult to recognize without a context.

tachistoscope A device that can present visual stimuli for controlled (usually very brief) durations of time.

bottom-up processing A perception based on successive analyses of the details of the stimuli that are present.

top-down processing A perception based on information provided by the context in which a particular stimulus is encountered.

Figure 7.23

An example of top-down processing. The context facilitates our recognition of the items shown in Figure 7.21.
(Adapted from Palmer, S. E. In Explorations in Cognition, *edited by D. A. Norman, D. E. Rumelhart, and the LNR Research Group. San Francisco: W. H. Freeman, 1975.)*

different patterns presented immediately afterward. A correct response would be rewarded by a sip of fruit juice.

While the animals were performing the task, the experimenters recorded the activity of individual neurons in the visual association cortex. They found that watching for a pattern of lines having a particular orientation affected the responsiveness of the neurons. For example, if the monkeys were watching for a pattern containing lines oriented at 45 degrees, neurons that detected lines of that orientation responded more vigorously than normal when that pattern was presented again. Haenny, Maunsell, and Schiller (1988) found that this enhancement could even be produced by letting the monkeys feel the orientation of a pattern of grooves in a metal plate they could not see; when a subsequent visual pattern contained lines whose orientation matched that of the grooves, a larger neural response was seen.

In most cases, perception consists of a combination of top-down and bottom-up processing. Figure 7.24 shows several examples of objects that can only be recognized by a combination of both forms of processing. Our knowledge of the configurations of letters in words provides us with the contexts that permit us to organize the flow of information from the bottom up. (See *Figure 7.24.*)

Interim Summary

Perception of Form

Perception of form requires, first, recognition of figure and ground. The Gestalt organizational laws of proximity, similarity, good continuation, and common fate describe some of the ways in which we distinguish figure from ground even when the outlines of the figures are not explicitly bounded by lines.

Psychologists have advanced two major hypotheses about the mechanism of pattern perception, or visual recognition of particular shapes. The first hypothesis suggests that our brain contains templates of all the shapes we can perceive. We compare a particular pattern of visual input with these templates until we find a fit. But how many different patterns can the brain hold? The second hypothesis suggests that our brain contains prototypes, which are more flexible than simple templates. Some psychologists believe that prototypes are collections of distinctive features (such as the two

parallel lines and the connecting diagonal of the letter *N*). Others prefer the neural network model, asserting that the ability of neural networks to learn to recognize patterns of input is the best explanation for form perception.

Until very recently, cognitive psychologists based their information-processing models of the human brain on the modern serial computer. However, just because a function can be simulated by a computer program does not mean that the brain and the computer perform the function in the same way. In fact, they do not. The brain consists of billions of interconnected elements that operate rather slowly. However, by doing many things simultaneously, the brain can perform complex operations in a brief amount of time. Thus, recent attempts to devise models of mental functions—especially those involving pattern recognition, which is an essential feature of perception—have employed neural networks. This approach uses assemblies of elements having properties similar to those of neurons.

Perception involves both bottom-up and top-down processing. Our perceptions are influenced not only by the details of the particular stimuli we see, but also by their relations

TAE CAT
RED
SPOT
EISH

Figure 7.24

Examples of combined top-down/bottom-up processing. The effect of context enables us to perceive the letters despite the missing or ambiguous features. Note that a given letter may be perceived in more than one way, depending on the letters surrounding it.

(Adapted from McClelland, J. J., Rumelhart, D. E., and Hinton, G. E. In Parallel Distributed Processing. Vol. I: Foundations, *edited by D. E. Rumelhart, J. L. McClelland, and the PDP Research Group. © 1986 the Massachusetts Institute of Technology; published by The MIT Press, Cambridge, Mass.)*

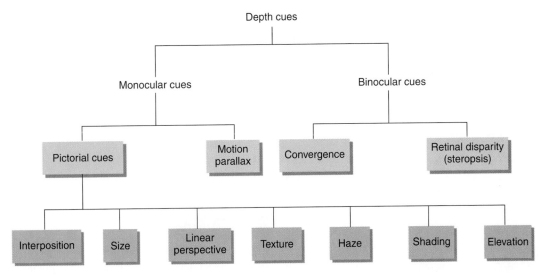

Figure 7.25

The principal monocular and binocular depth cues. *(Adapted from Matlin, M. W., and Foley, H. J. Sensation and Perception, 3rd ed. Boston: Allyn and Bacon, 1992.)*

to each other and our expectations. Thus, we may perceive a shape either as a loaf of bread in the kitchen or as a mailbox alongside a country road.

Thought Questions

- Explore your environment a little and look for examples of figure and ground. Can you change your focus of attention and make items previously seen as figures become part of the background and vice versa? Can you find some examples of when the Gestalt principles of grouping help you perceive particular objects?
- How many unique objects do you think you can recognize? How many more do you think you will learn to recognize during the years ahead of you? Think of the efficiency of the coding of this information in the computer contained in your head.
- What principles do you use when you try to assemble the pieces of a complex picture-puzzle? Can you relate these principles to the concepts of templates, prototypes, and distinctive features?
- People who want to appear thinner are often advised to wear clothes having vertical stripes, while those who want to appear heavier are advised to wear clothes having horizontal stripes. Can you think of an explanation for such advice?

Perception of Space and Motion

Besides being able to perceive the forms of objects in our environment, we are able to judge quite accurately their relative location in space and their movements. Perceiving where things are and perceiving what they are doing are obviously important functions of the visual system.

Depth Perception

Depth perception requires that we perceive the distance of objects in the environment from us and from each other. We do so by means of two kinds of cues: binocular ("two-eye") and monocular ("one-eye"). Binocular cues arise from the fact that the visual fields of both eyes overlap. Only animals that have eyes on the front of the head (such as primates, cats, and some birds) can obtain binocular cues. Animals that have eyes on the sides of their heads (such as rabbits and fish) can obtain only monocular cues.

One monocular cue involves movement and thus must be experienced in the natural environment or in a motion picture. The other monocular cues can be represented in a drawing or a photograph. In fact, most of these cues were originally discovered by artists and only later studied by psychologists. Artists wanted to represent the world realistically, and they studied their visual environments to identify the features that indicated distance of objects from the viewer. Art historians can show us the evidence of their discoveries.

Figure 7.25 shows the ten most important sources of distance cues (terms highlighted in color).

Binocular Cues

An important cue about distance is supplied by **convergence**. Recall from Chapter 6 that the eyes make conjugate movements so that both look at (*converge* on) the same point of the visual scene. If an object is very close to your face, your eyes are turned inward. If it is farther away, they look more nearly straight ahead. Thus, the eyes can be used like range finders. The brain controls the extraocular muscles, so it knows the angle between them, which is related to the distance between

convergence The result of conjugate eye movements whereby the fixation point for each eye is identical; feedback from these movements provides information about the distance of objects from the viewer.

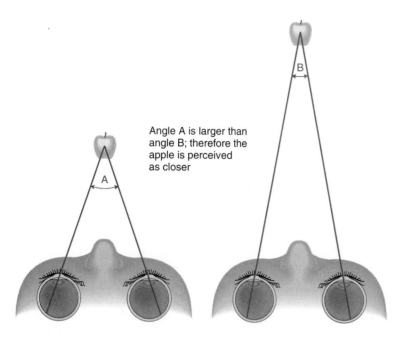

Angle A is larger than angle B; therefore the apple is perceived as closer

Figure 7.26

Convergence. When the eyes converge on a nearby object, the angle between them is greater than when they converge on a distant object. The brain uses this information in perceiving the distance of an object.

the object and the eyes. Convergence is most important for perceiving the distance of objects located close to us—especially those we can reach with our hands. (See *Figure 7.26.*)

Another important factor in the perception of distance is the information provided by **retinal disparity.** (*Disparity* means "unlikeness" or "dissimilarity.") Hold up a finger of one hand at arm's length and then hold up a finger of the other hand midway between your nose and the distant finger. If you look at one of the fingers, you will see a double image of the other one. (Try it.) Whenever your eyes are pointed toward a particular point, the images of objects at different distances will fall on different portions of the retina in each eye. The amount of disparity produced by the images of an object on the two retinas provides an important clue about its distance from us.

The perception of depth resulting from retinal disparity is called **stereopsis.** A *stereoscope* is a device that shows two slightly different pictures, one to each eye. The pictures are taken by a camera equipped with two lenses, located a few inches apart, just as our eyes are. When you look through a stereoscope, you see a three-dimensional image. An experiment by Julesz (1965) demonstrated that retinal disparity is what produces the effect of depth. Using a computer, he produced two displays of randomly positioned dots in which the location of some dots differed slightly. If some of the dots in one of the displays were displaced slightly to the right or the

left, the two displays gave the impression of depth when viewed through a stereoscope.

Figure 7.27 shows a pair of these random-dot stereograms. If you look at them very carefully, you will see that some of the dots near the center have been moved slightly to the left. (See *Figure 7.27.*) Some people can look at these figures without using a stereoscope and see depth. If you want to try this, hold the book at arm's length and look at the space between the figures. Now pretend you are looking "through" the book, into the distance. Each image will become double, since your eyes are no longer converged properly. If you keep looking, you might make two of these images fuse into one, located right in the middle. Eventually, you might see a small square in the center of the image, raised above the background.

Electrical recordings of individual neurons in the visual system of the brain have found a class of cells that receive information from both eyes and respond only when there is a

Figure 7.27

A pair of random-dot stereograms.

(From Julesz, B. Texture and visual perception. Scientific American, *1965, 12, 38–48. Copyright © 1965 by Scientific American, Inc. All rights reserved.)*

retinal disparity   The fact that points on objects located at different distances from the observer will fall on slightly different locations on the two retinas; provides the basis for stereopsis, one of the forms of depth perception.

stereopsis   A form of depth perception based on retinal disparity.

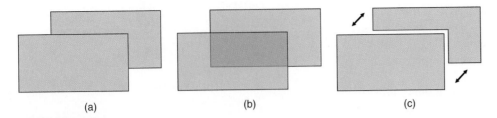

(a)   (b)   (c)

Figure 7.28

Use of the principle of good form in the perception of depth. The two objects shown in (a) could be two identical rectangles, one in front of the other, as shown in (b) or a rectangle and an L-shaped object, as shown in (c). The principle of good form states that we will see the ambiguous object in its simplest (best) form—in this case, a rectangle. As a result, the shape to the right is perceived as being partly hidden and thus farther away from us.

slight disparity between the image of an object on both retinas. (This effect would occur if an object was slightly nearer or farther from you than the point at which you are gazing.) Thus, some neurons at this level apparently compare the activity of neurons with corresponding receptive fields for both eyes and respond when there is a disparity. These neurons participate in stereopsis.

Monocular Cues

One of the most important sources of information about the relative distance of objects is **interposition** (*interposed* means "placed between"). If one object is placed between us and another object so that the closer object partially obscures our view of the more distant one, we can immediately perceive which object is closer to us.

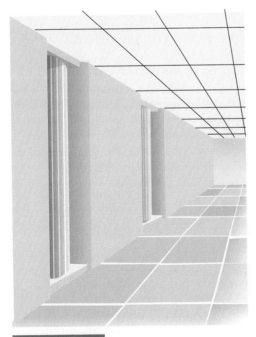

Figure 7.29

Principle of perspective. Perspective gives the appearance of distance and makes the two columns look similar in size.

Obviously, interposition works best when we are familiar with the objects and know what their shapes should look like. But it even works with unfamiliar objects. Just as the Gestalt law of good continuation plays a role in form perception, the *principle of good form* affects our perception of the relative location of objects: We perceive the object having the simpler border as being closer. Figure 7.28 (a) can be seen either as two rectangles, located one in front of the other (Figure 7.28 (b)), or a rectangle nestled against an L-shaped object (Figure 7.28 (c)). Because we tend to perceive an ambiguous drawing according to the principle of good form, we are more likely to perceive Figure 7.28 (a) as two simple shapes—rectangles—one partly hiding the other. (See *Figure 7.28.*)

Another important monocular distance cue is provided by our familiarity with the *sizes* of objects. For example, if an automobile casts a very small image on our retinas, we will perceive it as being far away. Knowing how large cars are, our visual system can automatically compute the approximate distance from the size of the retinal image.

Figure 7.29 shows two columns located at different distances. The drawing shows **linear perspective:** the tendency for parallel lines that recede from us to converge at a single point. Because of perspective, we perceive the columns as being the same size even though they produce retinal images of different sizes. We also perceive the segments of the wall between the columns as rectangular, even though the image they cast on the retina does not contain any right angles. (See *Figure 7.29.*)

In a natural environment that has not been altered by humans, we seldom see actual converging lines that denote perspective. For example, earlier in our evolutionary history people did not see streets, large buildings, and railroad tracks. Did we acquire the ability to use perspective cues only after

interposition A monocular cue of depth perception; an object that partially occludes another object is perceived as closer.

linear perspective A monocular cue of depth perception; the arrangement or drawing of objects on a flat surface such that parallel lines receding from the viewer are seen to converge at a point on the horizon.

producing these features of the landscape, or is there a counterpart of perspective to be found in nature? As we will see later, this is one of the questions being studied by cross-cultural psychologists interested in the role of experience in visual perception.

Texture, especially the texture of the ground, provides another cue we use to perceive the distance of objects sitting on the ground. A coarser texture looks closer, and a finer texture looks more distant. (See *Figure 7.30.*) The earth's atmosphere, which always contains a certain amount of haze, can also supply cues about the relative distance of objects or parts of the landscape. Parts of the landscape that are farther away become less distinct because of haze in the air. Thus, **haze** provides a monocular distance cue. (See *Figure 7.31.*)

The patterns of light and shadow in a scene—its **shading**—can provide us with cues about the three-dimensional shapes of objects. Although the cues shading provides do not usually tell us much about the absolute distances of objects from us, they can tell us which *parts* of objects are closer and which are farther. Figure 7.32 illustrates the power of this phenomenon. Some of the circles look as if they bulge out toward us; others look as if they were hollowed out (dimpled). The only difference is the direction of the shading. Our visual system appears to interpret such stimuli as if they were illuminated from above. Thus, the top of a convex (bulging) object will be light and the bottom will be in shadow. If you turn the book upside down, the bulges and dimples will reverse. (See *Figure 7.32.*)

When we are able to see the horizon, we perceive objects near it as being distant and those above or below it as being nearer to us. Thus, **elevation** provides an important monocular depth cue. For example, cloud B and triangle B in *Figure*

Cues from atmospheric haze. Variation in detail, owing to haze, produces an appearance of distance.

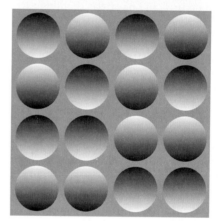

Figure 7.32

Depth cues supplied by shading. If the tops of the circles are dark, they look like depressions. If the bottoms are dark, they appear as bumps.

7.33 appear farther away from us than do cloud A and triangle A.

So far, all the monocular distance cues discussed have been those that can be rendered in a drawing or captured by a camera. However, another important source of distance information depends on our own movement. Try the following demonstrations: If you focus your eyes on an object close to you and move your head from side to side, your image of the scene moves back and forth behind the nearer object. If you focus your eyes on the background while moving your head

Figure 7.30

Texture cues. Variations in texture can produce an appearance of distance. The stones diminish in size toward the top of the photo; we therefore perceive the top of the photo as being farther away from us.

texture A monocular cue of depth perception; the fineness of detail present in the surfaces of objects or in the ground or floor of a scene.

haze A monocular cue of depth perception; objects that are less distinct in their outline and texture are seen as farther from the viewer.

shading A monocular cue of depth perception; determines whether portions of the surface of an object are perceived as concave or convex.

elevation A monocular cue of depth perception; objects nearer the horizon are seen as farther from the viewer.

from side to side, the image of the nearer object passes back and forth across the background. Head and body movements cause the images from the scene before us to change; the closer the object, the more it changes relative to the background. The information contained in this relative movement helps us perceive distance.

Figure 7.34 illustrates the kinds of cues supplied when we move with respect to features in the environment. The top part of the figure shows three objects at different distances from the observer: a man, a house, and a tree. The lower part shows the views that the observer will see from five different places (P_1–P_5). The changes in the relative locations of the objects provide cues concerning their distance from the observer. (See *Figure 7.34.*) The phenomenon is known as

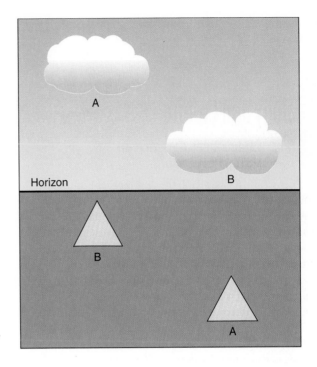

Figure 7.33

Depth cues supplied by elevation. The objects nearest the horizontal line appear farthest away from us.

(Adapted from Matlin, M. W., and Foley, H. J. Sensation and Perception, 3rd ed. Boston: Allyn and Bacon, 1992.)

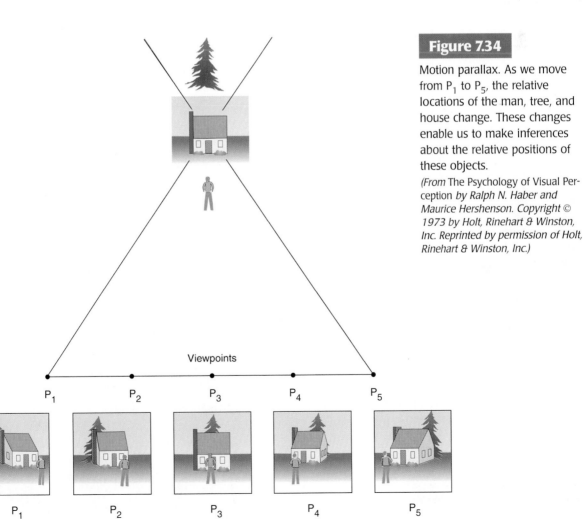

Figure 7.34

Motion parallax. As we move from P_1 to P_5, the relative locations of the man, tree, and house change. These changes enable us to make inferences about the relative positions of these objects.

(From The Psychology of Visual Perception by Ralph N. Haber and Maurice Hershenson. Copyright © 1973 by Holt, Rinehart & Winston, Inc. Reprinted by permission of Holt, Rinehart & Winston, Inc.)

motion parallax. (*Parallax* comes from a Greek word meaning "change.")

Biology and Culture

Effects of Experience on Visual Perception

As we saw in Chapter 4, the development of the nervous system is shaped by an interplay between heredity and environment. In fact, normal development of the sensory systems of the brain *requires* experience. For example, we saw that if one of an animal's eyes is covered during the first few months after it is born, particular sets of neural connections fail to develop in the brain. As a result, the animal is unable to perceive normally with that eye after it is uncovered. If development of the brain can be so drastically affected by temporarily blocking visual input, perhaps smaller changes in sensory input can produce less dramatic changes in perceptual ability.

The development of visual perception certainly involves learning. From birth onwards, we explore our environment with our eyes. The patterns of light and dark, color and movement, produce changes in the visual system of the brain. Many psychologists and anthropologists have wondered what role culture plays in the development of perceptual abilities. As we saw in Chapter 2, cultures differ with respect to two major classes of variables: biological and ecological. Biological variables, which include factors such as diet, genetics, and diseases common in a particular region, may affect perceptual development, but these variables have not received much interest from cross-cultural researchers. Ecological variables—particularly those associated with geography, cultural codes, and education—have received more attention.

Consider geographical variables. The visual stimulation we receive, particularly during infancy, affects the development of our visual system. If our environment lacks certain features—certain visual patterns—we may fail to recognize the significance of these features if we encounter them later in life. We might expect that people living in a treeless environment having no tall vertical features but instead vast, sweeping vistas would perceive the world differently from inhabitants of dense forests who are surrounded by vertical features but very seldom encounter open fields.

A second set of ecological variables that may affect perceptual development comes from cultural codes found in pictorial representations. For example, as we saw earlier in this chapter, artists have learned to represent all the monocular depth cues (except for those produced by movement) in their paintings. But not all cues are repre-

Perhaps people from cultures whose art does not use linear perspective will not recognize this device when they see it in paintings from another culture.

motion parallax A cue of depth perception. As we pass by a scene, objects closer to us pass in front of objects farther away.

sented in the traditional art of all cultures. For example, many cultures do not use linear perspective. Does the absence of particular cues in the art of a particular culture mean that people from this culture will not recognize them when they see them in paintings from another culture?

The answer to this question is not yet known. According to Berry et al. (1992), some reports suggest that Asians who are unfamiliar with art that incorporates linear perspective are more likely to misperceive the true shape of rectangles drawn in perspective. (Refer to *Figure 7.29.*) But to be sure, more cross-cultural research will have to be done.

The effects on perception of another cultural code—language—has received much attention. In the mid-nineteenth century, the British statesman William Gladstone noted that the writings of the ancient Greeks did not contain words for brown or blue. Perhaps the ancient Greeks did not perceive these colors. Magnus (1880) investigated this hypothesis by gathering both linguistic and perceptual data. He sent questionnaires and color chips to Western residents of European colonies and asked them to test the abilities of the native people to distinguish among the various colors. He assumed that language would reflect perceptual ability. If a language did not contain words to distinguish between certain colors, then the people who belonged to that culture would not be able to distinguish these colors perceptually.

Magnus was surprised to discover very few cultural differences in people's ability to perceive various colors. Linguistic differences did not appear to reflect perceptual differences. The issue emerged again in the mid-twentieth century with the principle of **linguistic relativity.** Briefly stated, this principle asserts that language used by the members of a particular culture is related to these people's thoughts and perceptions. The best-known proponent of this principle, Benjamin Whorf, stated that "the background linguistic system . . . of each language is not merely a reproducing instrument for voicing ideas but rather is itself a shaper of ideas, the program and guide for the individual's mental activity, for his analysis of impressions, for his synthesis of his mental stock-of-trade" (Whorf, 1956, p. 212).

Proponents of linguistic relativity suggested that color names were cultural conventions—that members of a given culture could divide the countless combinations of hue, saturation, and brightness that we call colors into any number of different categories. Each category was assigned a name, and when members of that culture looked out at the world, they perceived each of the colors they saw as belonging to one of these categories.

Two anthropologists tested this hypothesis (Berlin and Kay, 1969; Kay, 1975). Berlin and Kay studied a wide range of languages and found the following eleven primary color terms: black, white, red, yellow, green, blue, brown, purple, pink, orange, and gray. (Of course, the words for these terms are different in different languages. For example, Japanese speakers say *aka*, Navahos say *lichi*, Eskimos say *anpaluktak*, and English speakers say *red*.) The authors referred to these as *focal colors*. Not all languages used all eleven (as English does). In fact, some languages used only two: black and white. If a language contained words for three primary colors, they were black, white, and red. If it contained words for six primary colors, they were black, white, red, yellow, green, and blue. The fact that all cultures agree about what categories of colors deserve names suggests that the physiology of the visual system—and not arbitrary cultural conventions—is responsible for the selection of color names.

Other evidence strongly suggests that this conclusion is correct. Heider (1971) found that both children and adults found it easier to remember a color chip of a focal color (such as red or blue) than one of a nonfocal color (such as turquoise or peach). Rosch (formerly Heider) studied members of the Dani culture of New Guinea. The language of the Dani people has only two basic color terms: *mili* ("black") and *mola* ("white"). Rosch assembled two sets of color chips, one containing focal colors and the other containing nonfocal colors. She taught her subjects arbitrary names that she made up for the colors. Even though the subjects had no words in their language for any of the colors, the group learning names for focal colors learned the names faster and remembered them better (Heider, 1972; Rosch, 1973).

So far, there is little evidence that perception is shaped by cultural codes. What about the other major ecological variable: geography? Does growing up in an environment having particular types of visual features affect the development of the visual system? So far, cross-cultural studies of this issue have revealed a few modest differences. For example, people who live in "carpentered worlds"—that is, worlds in which buildings are built from long, straight pieces of material that normally join each other in right angles—are more likely to be subject to the Müller-Lyer illusion. This illusion is shown in Figure 7.35. Look at the two vertical lines and decide which is longer. (See *Figure 7.35.*) Actually, the lines are of equal length.

Segall, Campbell, and Herskovits (1966) presented the Müller-Lyer illusion (and several others) to groups of subjects from Western and non-Western cultures. Most investigators believe that the Müller-Lyer illusion is a result of our experience with the angles formed by the intersection of walls, ceilings, and floors. The angled lines can be seen as examples of linear perspective. (See *Figure 7.36.*) In fact, Segall and his colleagues *did* find that people from "carpentered" cultures were more susceptible to

linguistic relativity The hypothesis that the language a person speaks is related to his or her thoughts and perceptions.

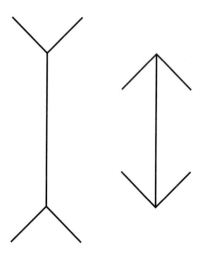

Figure 7.35

The Müller-Lyer illusion. The two vertical lines are actually equal in length, but the one on the left appears to be longer.

Figure 7.36

The impact of culture on the Müller-Lyer illusion. People from "non-carpentered" cultures that lack rectangular corners are less likely to be susceptible to this illusion. Although the two vertical lines are actually the same height, the one on the right looks shorter.

this illusion. So experience with straight lines forming right angles does seem to affect people's perception.

In summary, the human visual system seems to provide us with an accurate representation of the world—a representation that is shared by members of other cultures. When we consider the importance of accurate perception, we should not be surprised that the process of

evolution has been so successful. As we will see in subsequent chapters, culture has powerful effects on such phenomena as social roles and definitions of intelligence. It also strongly influences the interpretation and emotional impact of what we see. But, by and large, we all see the same world.

Constancies of Visual Perception

An important characteristic of the visual environment is that it is almost always changing as we move, as objects move, and as lighting conditions change. However, despite the changing nature of the image the visual environment casts on our retinas, our perceptions remain remarkably constant.

Brightness Constancy

Experiments have shown that people can judge the whiteness or grayness of an object very well, even if the level of illumination changes. If you look at a sheet of white paper either in bright sunlight or in shade, you will perceive it as being white, although the intensity of its image on your retina will vary. If you look at a sheet of gray paper in sunlight, it may in fact reflect more light to your eye than will a white paper located in the shade, but you will still see the white paper as white and the gray paper as gray. This phenomenon is known as **brightness constancy**.

Katz (1935) demonstrated brightness constancy by constructing a vertical barrier and positioning a light source so that a shadow was cast to the right of the barrier. In the shadow, he placed a gray square card on a white background. In the lighted area on the left of the barrier, he placed a number of shades of gray and asked subjects to choose one that matched the gray square in the shadow. (See *Figure 7.37.*) His subjects matched the grays not in terms of the light that the cards actually reflected but in terms of the light they *would have* reflected had both been viewed under the same level of illumination. In other words, the subjects compensated for the dimness of the shadow. The match was not perfect, but it was much closer than it would have been if perception of brightness had been made solely on the basis of the amount of light that fell on the retina.

The perception of white and gray, then, is not a matter of absolutes; rather, they are perceived relative to the surrounding environment. For example, we perceive a ceiling painted a rather dark off-white color as pure white unless a piece of white paper is placed next to it for comparison. When I lecture to my classes, I use an overhead projector that permits me to project notes and diagrams onto a screen at the front of the room. If I put a small piece of paper on the projector,

brightness constancy The tendency to perceive objects as having constant brightness even when they are observed under varying levels of illumination.

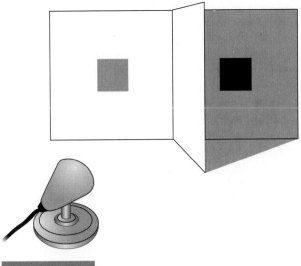

Brightness constancy as demonstrated by the experiment by Katz (1935).

point to the image it casts on the screen, and ask the students the color of the image, they invariably say black. Then I turn off the projector, so that the entire screen has the color they just perceived as black. Now, they tell me, the screen is white.

Form Constancy

When we approach an object or when it approaches us, we do not perceive it as getting larger. Even though the image of the object on the retina gets larger, we perceive this change as being due to a decrease in the distance between ourselves and the object. Our perception of the object's size remains relatively constant.

The unchanging perception of an object's size and shape when it moves relative to us is called **form constancy**. (People

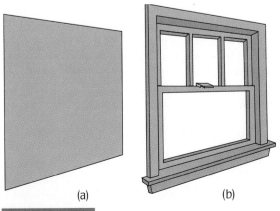

(a)   (b)

Form constancy. (a) This figure can be perceived as a trapezoid. (b) Because we recognize this figure as a window, we perceive its shape as rectangular.

also refer to *size constancy,* but size is simply one aspect of form.) In the nineteenth century, Hermann von Helmholtz suggested that form constancy was achieved by **unconscious inference**—a mental computation of which we are unaware. We know the size and shape of a familiar object. Therefore, if the image it casts upon our retina is small, we perceive it as being far away; if the image is large, we perceive it as being close. (As we saw in the subsection on perception of distance, size is an important monocular cue.) In either case, we perceive the object itself as being the same size.

Form constancy also works for rotation. The drawing of Figure 7.38 (a) could be either a trapezoid or a rectangle rotated away from us. However, the extra cues clearly identify the drawing in Figure 7.38 (b) as a window, and experience tells us that windows are rectangular rather than trapezoidal; thus, we perceive it as rectangular. Obviously, this effect will not be seen in members of cultures that do not have buildings fitted with rectangular windows. (See *Figure 7.38.*)

The process just described works for familiar objects. However, we often see unfamiliar objects whose size we do not already know. If we are to perceive the size and shape of unfamiliar objects accurately, we must know something about their distance from us. An object that produces a large retinal image is perceived as big if it is far away and small if it is close. Apparently, the visual system performs this computation—another instance of unconscious inference. Figure 7.39 illustrates this phenomenon. Although the two mailboxes are exactly the same size, the one that appears to be farther away looks larger. (See *Figure 7.39.*) If you turn the book upside down and look at the figure again, the appearance of depth is greatly diminished, and the two mailboxes appear to be approximately the same size.

Perception of Motion

Detection of movement is one of the most primitive aspects of visual perception. This ability is seen even in animals whose visual systems do not obtain detailed images of the environment. Of course, our visual system can detect more than the mere presence of movement. We can see what is moving in our environment and can detect the direction in which it is moving.

Adaptation and Long-Term Modification

One of the most important characteristics of all sensory systems is that they show adaptation and rebound effects. For example, when you stare at a spot of color, the adaptation of

form constancy The tendency to perceive objects as having a constant form, even when they are rotated or their distance from the observer changes.

unconscious inference A mental computation of which we are unaware that plays a role in perception.

Figure 7.39

Effect of perceived distance. Although both mailboxes are exactly the same size, the upper one looks larger because of the depth cues (perspective and texture) that surround it. If you turn the book upside-down and look at the picture, thus disrupting the depth cues, the mailboxes look the same size.

neurons in your visual system will produce a negative after-image if you shift your gaze to a neutral background; and if you put your hand in some hot water, warm water will feel cool to that hand immediately afterward.

Motion, like other kinds of stimuli, can give rise to adaptation and aftereffects. The first time I recorded an EEG, I remember watching the paper pass by the pens as they traced their record of the electrical activity of a person's brain. I turned the machine off, and, suddenly, the paper seemed to go backward. At first I thought that the paper was really going in reverse, but I realized that it never seemed to get anywhere. That is, I perceived the paper as moving, but at the same time

The combat soldier's survival depends on the ability to detect movement in the environment.

I could see that it was clearly remaining in the same spot. The phenomenon is difficult to describe; you really need to see it for yourself. You may not have an EEG machine available to you, but if you spend a minute or two watching an old-fashioned phonograph record turning around, it will appear to turn backward if you suddenly stop its movement.

This phenomenon was first reported in writing in 1834 by a Mr. Adams who noticed it after watching the descent of a waterfall. (Because Mr. Adams's report preceded mine, the phenomenon has been called the *waterfall phenomenon*, not the *EEG-machine phenomenon*.) Recently, Tootell et al. (1995) presented subjects with a display showing a series of concentric rings moving outwards, like the ripples in a pond. When the rings suddenly stopped moving, the subjects had the impression of the opposite movement—that the rings were moving inward. During this time, the experimenters scanned the subjects' brains to measure their metabolic activity. The scans showed increased activity in the motion-sensitive region of the visual association cortex, which lasted as long as the illusion did. Thus, the neural circuits that give rise to this illusion appear to be located in the same region that responds to actual moving stimuli.

A study by Ball and Sekuler (1982) suggests that even the long-term characteristics of the system that detects movement can be modified by experience. The experimenters trained people to detect extremely small movements. Each subject sat in front of a display screen. A series of dots appeared, scattered across the face of the screen, and either all moved an extremely small distance or all remained stationary. The dots always moved in the same direction, but the direction was different for each person in the experiment. After several sessions, the experimenters assessed the subjects' sensitivity to detecting movements of the dots. They found that each person was especially good at detecting movement *only in the direction in which he or she had been trained;* the training did not increase their detection of movements in other directions. The effect was still present when the subjects were tested again ten weeks later.

The fact that the subjects learned to detect a small movement in a particular direction, and not small movements in general, shows that particular aspects of their visual systems were modified by experience. Did they acquire new sets of feature detectors, or were parallel networks of neurons modified in some way? As yet, we have no way of knowing the nature of the changes to the visual system.

Interpretation of a Moving Retinal Image

As you read this book, your eyes are continuously moving. Naturally, the eye movements cause the image on your retina to move. You can also cause the retinal image to move by holding the book close to your face, looking straight ahead, and moving it back and forth. (Try it.) In the first case, when you were reading normally, you perceived the book as being still. In the second case, you perceived it as moving. Why does your brain interpret the movement differently in these two cases? Try another demonstration. Pick a letter on this page, stare at it, and then move the book around, following the letter with your eyes. This time you will perceive the book as moving, even though the image on your retina remains stable. Thus, perception of movement requires coordination between movements of the image on the retina and those of the eyes.

Obviously, the visual system must know about eye movements in order to compensate for them in interpreting the significance of moving images on the retina. Another simple demonstration suggests the source of this information. Close your left eye and look slightly down and to the left. Gently press your finger against the outer corner of the upper eyelid of your right eye and make your right eye move a bit. The scene before you appears to be moving, even though you know better. This sensation of movement occurs because your finger—not your eye muscles—moved your eye. When your eye moves normally, perceptual mechanisms in your brain compensate for this movement. Even though the image on the retina moves, you perceive the environment as being stationary. However, if the image moves because the object itself moves or because you push your eye with your finger, you perceive movement. (See *Figure 7.40.*)

Besides perceiving absolute movements, we perceive the movements of objects relative to one another. Sometimes, we can be fooled. You may have sat in an automobile at a stoplight when the vehicle next to you started to roll backward. For a moment, you were uncertain whether you were moving forward or the other vehicle was moving backward. Only by looking at nonmoving objects such as buildings or trees could you be sure.

In general, if two objects of different size are seen moving relative to each other, the smaller one is perceived as moving and the larger one as standing still. We perceive people at a distance moving against a stable background and flies moving against an unmoving wall. Thus, when an experimenter moves a frame that encloses a stationary dot, we tend to see the dot move, not the frame. This phenomenon is also encountered when we perceive the moon racing behind the clouds, even though we know that the clouds, not the moon, are moving.

Perception of movement can even help us perceive three-dimensional forms. Johansson (1973) demonstrated just how much information we can derive from movement. He dressed actors in black and attached small lights to several points on their bodies, such as their wrists, elbows, shoulders, hips, knees, and feet. He made movies of the actors in a darkened room while they were performing various behaviors, such as walking, running, jumping, limping, doing push-ups, and dancing with a partner who was also equipped with lights. Even though observers who watched the films could only see a pattern of moving lights against a dark background, they could readily perceive the pattern as belonging to a moving human and could identify the behavior the actor was performing. Subsequent studies (Kozlowski and Cutting, 1977; Barclay, Cutting, and Kozlowski, 1978) showed that people could even tell, with reasonable accuracy, the sex of the actor wearing the lights. The cues appeared to be supplied by the relative amounts of movement of the shoulders and hips as the person walked.

As we saw earlier, perception of the shape of objects, their color, their location, and their movement appears to involve different brain mechanisms. In addition, the recognition of shape from movement appears to be at least somewhat independent of the perception of static form. People with prosopagnosia, who cannot recognize even their spouses' faces, can often recognize people at a distance by observing the way they walk.

Combining Information from Successive Fixations

As you saw in Chapter 6, when examining a scene, our eyes do not roam slowly around; rather, they make rapid steplike movements called *saccades*. After each saccade, the eyes rest for a while, gathering information before moving again. These stops are called *fixations*. The visual system combines the information from each fixation and perceives objects too large or too detailed to see in a single glance. Obviously, in doing so, it must keep track of the locations of each of the fixations.

Figure 7.41 illustrates an *impossible figure*. That is, an artist can draw lines that, at first glance, represent a three-dimensional object. However, careful inspection shows that the object cannot possibly exist. (See *Figure 7.41.*) But the drawing in Figure 7.42 creates a very different impression; it does not look at all like a unified three-dimensional object. (See *Figure 7.42.*) The difference in the two impressions is that the details of the larger figure cannot be gathered in a single glance. Apparently, when we look from one end of the figure to the other, the information we gather from the first fixation is slightly modified to conform to the image of the second one. Of course, the two images do not exactly match, as a careful inspection shows.

Clearly, what we see during one fixation affects what we see in another. Long ago, psychologists discovered that if they presented two visual stimuli, one after the other, the second stimulus could sometimes erase the image of the first. That is,

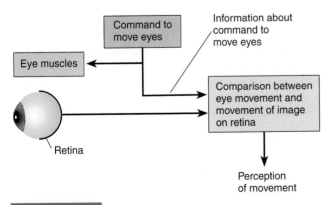

Figure 7.40

A schematic representation of the brain mechanisms responsible for the interpretation of a moving retinal image. This system must compensate for eye movements.

Figure 7.41

An impossible figure. Only after carefully studying the figure do we see that it cannot be a drawing of a real three-dimensional object.

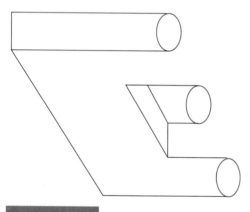

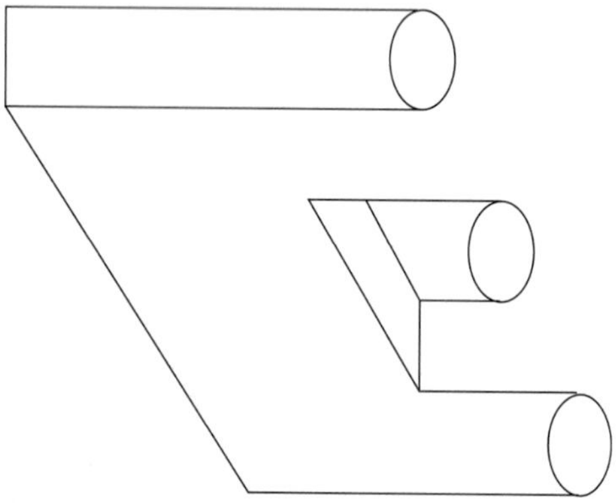

Figure 7.42

An unconvincing impossible figure. When the legs are short enough so that the entire figure can be perceived during a single fixation, the figure does not look paradoxical.

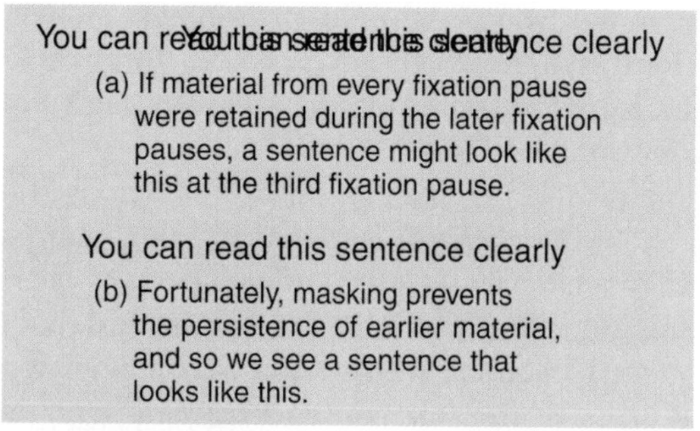

You can re**You can see this clearly**nce clearly

(a) If material from every fixation pause were retained during the later fixation pauses, a sentence might look like this at the third fixation pause.

You can read this sentence clearly

(b) Fortunately, masking prevents the persistence of earlier material, and so we see a sentence that looks like this.

Figure 7.43

The role of backward masking. If each saccade did not erase the remaining image from the previous fixation, we probably would not be able to read. *(From Margaret W. Matlin,* Sensation and Perception, *2nd ed. Copyright © 1988 by Allyn and Bacon. Reproduced with permission.)*

under the appropriate conditions, the subject would fail to perceive the image that came first. This phenomenon is known as **backward masking** (Werner, 1935).

Normally, backward masking can be demonstrated only in the laboratory, where the shape and intensity of the stimuli and the time interval between them can be carefully controlled. However, Breitmeyer (1980) suggests that the explanation for this phenomenon lies in the nature of the saccadic movements made by the eyes when gathering information about the visual environment. For example, consider the saccadic movements your eyes make as you read a line of text in this book. You do not stop and look at each letter or even at each word; instead, you make several fixations on each line. During each one, your visual system gathers information and begins decoding the letters and words. Your eyes move on, and you perceive more words. Breitmeyer suggests that each saccade erases the image remaining from the previous fixation, leaving only the information that has been analyzed by the visual system. *Figure 7.43* illustrates what might happen if this erasure did not occur.

Perception of Movement in the Absence of Motion

If you sit in a darkened room and watch two small lights that are alternately turned on and off, your perception will be that of a single light moving back and forth between two different locations. You will not see the light turn off at one position and then turn on at the second position. If the distance and timing are just right, the light will appear to stay on at all times, quickly moving between the positions. This response is known as the **phi phenomenon**. Theater marquees, "moving" neon signs, and some computer animations make use of it.

This characteristic of the visual system accounts for the fact that we perceive the images in motion pictures and on tele-

backward masking   The ability of a stimulus to interfere with the perception of a stimulus presented just before it.

phi phenomenon   The perception of movement caused by the turning on of two or more lights, one at a time, in sequence; often used on theater marquees; responsible for the apparent movement of images in movies and television.

This lithograph Convex and Concave, *by M. C. Escher shows how contradictory depth clues can be combined to provide an "impossible" scene.*

vision as continuous rather than separate. The images actually jump from place to place, but we see smooth movement.

Interim Summary

Perception of Space and Motion

Our visual system accomplishes a remarkable feat: It manages to perceive objects accurately even in the face of movement and changes in levels of illumination. Because the size and shape of a retinal image vary with the location of an object relative to the eye, accurate form perception requires depth perception—perception of the locations of objects in space. Depth perception comes from binocular cues (from convergence and retinal disparity) and monocular cues (from interposition, size, linear perspective, texture, haze shading, elevation, and the effects of head and body movements).

A person's culture may affect his or her perceptions, but probably not in a fundamental way. The Whorf hypothesis, which suggested that language could strongly affect the way we perceive the world, has not been supported by empirical research. It is possible that experience with some environmental features, such as particular geographical features or buildings composed of straight lines and right angles, may have some influence on the way people perceive the world.

We perceive the brightness of an object relative to that of objects around it; thus, objects retain a constant brightness under a variety of conditions of illumination. In addition, our perception of the relative distance of objects helps us maintain form constancy.

Because our bodies may well be moving while we are visually following some activity in the outside world, the visual system has to make further compensations. It keeps track of the commands to the eye muscles and compensates for the direction in which the eyes are pointing. Movement is perceived when objects move relative to one another. In particular, a smaller object is likely to be perceived as moving across a larger one. Movement is also perceived when our eyes follow a moving object, even though its image remains on the same part of the retina.

Movement supplies important cues about an object's three-dimensional shape. In fact, we are much more sensitive to complex movements than we commonly realize, as illustrated by the demonstration using the movies of actors wearing lights. Sometimes, we can even recognize a friend at a distance by the way that person walks.

Because a complex scene, covering a large area, cannot be seen in a single glance, the visual system must combine information from successive fixations. The phenomenon of backward masking suggests that the image received from the previous fixation is erased immediately after a saccade so that blurring does not occur.

The phi phenomenon describes our tendency to see an instantaneous disappearance of an object and its reappearance somewhere else as movement of that object. Because of the phi phenomenon, we perceive television shows and movies as representations of reality, not as a series of disconnected images.

Thought Questions

- Why do you suppose that artists often hold their thumbs in front of them while looking at the scene they are painting?
- You have undoubtedly tried to see the hidden three-dimensional images in the "magic paintings" that became popular several years ago. What phenomenon described in this section accounts for the existence of these images?
- When we ride in an automobile and can see the sun or moon through a side window, why does it look like these objects are following us?

Suggestions for Further Reading

Matlin, M. W., and Foley, H. J. *Perception,* 3rd ed. Boston: Allyn and Bacon, 1992.

Sekuler, R., and Blake, R. *Perception,* 2nd ed. New York: McGraw-Hill, 1990.

Two of the books that I recommended at the end of Chapter 6 discuss visual perception as well as sensory processes.

Chapter 8

Memory

Chapter Outline

Overview and Sensory Memory

Iconic Memory • Echoic Memory

Memory involves the cognitive process of encoding, storage, and retrieval of information. Encoding involves putting stimulus information in a form that can be used by our memory system. Storage involves maintaining it in memory and retrieval involves locating and using it. Sensory memory stores newly perceived information for very brief periods. Although sensory memory appears to exist for all senses, visual (iconic) and auditory (echoic) memories have received the most empirical attention.

Short-Term or Working Memory

Encoding of Information: Interaction with Long-Term Memory • Primacy and Recency Effects • The Limits of Working Memory • Varieties of Working Memory • Loss of Information from Short-Term Memory

Information may enter working memory (also called short-term memory) from both sensory memory and long-term memory. Working memory works very well for items at the beginning and end of lists. Working memory holds about seven items and lasts for about twenty seconds, unless the information is rehearsed. Verbal and visual information in working memory appears to be represented both phonologically and acoustically and is subject to manipulation by thought processes. An important cause of loss of information in working memory is displacement of older information to make room for newer information.

Learning and Encoding in Long-Term Memory

The Consolidation Hypothesis • The Levels of Processing Hypothesis • Improving Long-Term Memory Through Mnemonics

Long-term memory likely involves permanent structural changes in the brain. Our ability to retrieve information from long-term memory is often determined by how that information is learned or encoded. Rehearsal helps us store information permanently, although some types of rehearsal seem to be more effective than others. Special techniques, called mnemonics, improve storage and retrieval of information in long-term memory.

Organization of Long-Term Memory

Episodic and Semantic Memory • Explicit and Implicit Memory • The Biological Basis of Long-Term Memory

Research has distinguished among permanent memories for autobiographical information, conceptual information, information of which we are aware, and information of which we may be unaware. Studies involving amnesic persons strongly suggest that the biological basis of long-term memory involves the hippocampus.

Remembering

Remembering and Recollecting • How Long Does Memory Last? • *Biology and Culture: Cultural Contexts for Remembering* • Reconstruction: Remembering as a Creative Process • Remembering and Emotion Remembering and Interference • *Evaluating Scientific Issues: Hypnosis, Remembering, and Criminal Investigation*

In many instances, remembering is automatic—we do not have to put forth much conscious effort to retrieve a memory. In other cases, though, we must actively search for and use cues that aid our retrieval of a memory. Forgetting of information is greatest during the first few years after it is learned and decreases slowly afterwards. Remembering is influenced by aspects of culture, such as teaching practices and societal mores. Remembering complex information is often inaccurate because it involves reconstruction of information from existing memories. Remembering is strongly influenced by mood and emotion-provoking experiences. Information contained in other memories may interfere with recall of a particular memory. Hypnosis may help people recall information, but it also may bias the accuracy of the information that is actually remembered.

I accompanied Fred, my graduate student, to the Veteran's Administration Hospital in a nearby town, where he had been studying several patients.

We met Mr. P. in the lounge. Fred introduced us, and we walked to the room where he had set up his equipment. We sat down and chatted.

"How long have you been here?" Fred asked Mr. P.

"Oh, about a week."

"Uh-huh. What brought you here?"

"I'm having some work done on my teeth. I'll be going back home in a couple of days. I have to help my father on the farm."

I knew that Mr. P. had actually been in the hospital for eleven years.

He had been an alcoholic for a long time before that, and he was brought to the hospital in a severely malnourished condition. He was diagnosed with Korsakoff's syndrome, a state of physical and mental deterioration caused by excessive consumption of alcohol. Fred pointed to a slide projector and screen and asked Mr. P. whether he had seen them before.

He looked at them and said, "No, I don't think so."

Fred looked at me and said, "Say, have you met Dr. Carlson?"

Mr. P. turned around, stood up, and extended his hand. "No, I don't believe I have. How do you do, sir?" he said. We shook hands, and I greeted him in return.

"Mr. P., a few days ago you saw some pictures here," said Fred. Mr. P. looked doubtful but said politely, "Well, if you say so." Fred dimmed the lights and showed him the first slide.

Two pictures of two different automobiles were projected on the screen, side by side.

"Which one did you see before?" Fred asked.

"Neither of them."

"Well," Fred persisted, "point to the one you might have seen." Mr. P. looked nonplussed but pointed to the one on the right. Fred made a notation in his notebook and then showed the next slide, which showed views of two different trees.

"Which one?" he asked.

Silently, Mr. P. pointed to the one on the left. After showing eighteen pairs of slides, Fred said, "That's it, Mr. P. Thanks for helping me. By the way, have you met Dr. Carlson?" Mr. P. looked at Fred and then followed his gaze, turned around, and saw me. He stood up, and we shook hands and introduced ourselves.

As we left the hospital, I asked Fred how Mr. P. had done. "He got seventeen correct!" he exulted.

Overview

In this chapter, we will attempt to understand the *structure* of **memory**—the cognitive processes of encoding, storing, and retrieving information. **Encoding** refers to the active process of putting stimulus information into a form that can be used by our memory system. **Storage** refers to the process of maintaining information in memory. **Retrieval** refers to the active processes of locating and using information stored in memory.

When psychologists refer to the structure of memory, they are referring to two approaches to understanding memory—a literal one and a metaphorical one (Howard, 1995). Literally, physiological psychologists and other neuroscientists are trying to discover the physiological changes that occur in the brain when an organism learns something. To them, the structure of memory refers to these physiological changes. Cognitive psychologists study the structure of memory in a metaphorical sense. They have developed conceptual, infor-

memory The cognitive processes of encoding, storing, and retrieving information.

encoding The process by which sensory information is converted into a form that can be used by the brain's memory system.

storage The process of maintaining information in memory.

retrieval The active processes of locating and using stored information.

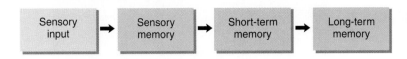

Figure 8.1

The information-processing model of human memory.

mation-processing models of memory. Most of the research described in this chapter involves these kinds of models. However, we will also examine research on the physiological nature of memory.

Recall from Chapter 5 that learning is the tendency for behavior to change as a result of experience; learning and experience produce changes in the structure of the brain. The ability to learn allows us to engage in an enormous variety of behaviors in response to an enormous variety of situations. A lapse of time may occur between the act of learning and a change in behavior caused by learning. For example, I may observe that a new restaurant has opened and then, some days later, visit that restaurant when I want to eat out. The usefulness of memory, then, manifests itself in behavior. Presumably, the sight of the restaurant has induced some changes in my brain, which we refer to as a memory. Later, when I think about what restaurant I would like to visit, I think about the new restaurant (that is, I retrieve the memory) and I act. This chapter describes the encoding, storage, and retrieval of memories.

Memory is selective. We perceive an enormous amount of information each day but can later remember only a portion of it. Research suggests that we possess at least three forms of memory: sensory memory, short-term memory, and long-term memory (Atkinson and Shiffrin, 1968). **Sensory memory** is memory in which representations of the physical features of a stimulus are stored for a very brief time—perhaps for a second or less. This form of memory is difficult to distinguish from the act of perception. The information contained in sensory memory represents the original stimulus fairly accurately and contains all or most of the information that has just been perceived. For example, sensory memory contains a brief image of a sight we have just seen or a fleeting echo of a sound we have just heard. Normally, we are not aware of sensory memory; no analysis seems to be performed on the information while it remains in this form. The function of sensory memory appears to be to hold information long enough for it to be transferred to the next form of memory, short-term memory.

Short-term memory is an immediate memory for stimuli that have just been perceived. As we will soon see, its ca-

pacity is limited in terms of the number of items that it can store and of its duration. We can remember a new item of information, such as a telephone number, by rehearsing it. However, once we stop rehearsing the information, we may not be able to remember it later. Information soon leaves short-term memory, and unless it is stored in long-term memory, it will be lost forever.

To demonstrate the fact that short-term memory can hold only a limited amount of information for a limited time, read the following numbers to yourself just once, and then close your eyes and recite them back.

1 4 9 2 3 0 7

You probably had no trouble remembering them. Now, try the following set of numbers, and go through them only once before you close your eyes.

7 2 5 2 3 9 1 6 5 8 4

Very few people can repeat eleven numbers; in fact, you may not have even bothered to try once you saw how many numbers there were. Even if you practice, you will probably not be able to recite more than seven to nine independent pieces of information that you have seen only once. Thus, short-term memory has definite limits. However, as we will see, there are ways to organize new information so that you can remember more than seven to nine items, but in such cases the items can no longer be considered independent.

If you wanted to, you could recite the eleven numbers again and again until you had memorized them. You could rehearse the information in short-term memory until it was eventually stored in **long-term memory**—memory in which information is represented on a permanent or near-permanent basis. Unlike short-term memory, long-term memory has no known limits; and, as its name suggests, it is relatively durable. Presumably, it occurs because of physical changes that take place in the connections among neurons in the brain. If we stop thinking about something we have just perceived (that is, something contained in short-term memory), we may not remember the information later. However, information in long-term memory need not be continuously rehearsed. We can stop thinking about it until we need the information at a future time.

Some cognitive psychologists argue that no real distinction exists between short-term and long-term memory; instead, they see them as different phases of a continuous process. These psychologists object to the conception of memory as a series of separate units with information flowing from one to the next. Figure 8.1 illustrates this simple *information-processing model* of memory. (See ***Figure 8.1***.) As we will see, psychologists have discovered that memory may be more complex than this model would have us believe.

sensory memory Memory in which representations of the physical features of a stimulus are stored for very brief durations.

short-term memory An immediate memory for stimuli that have just been perceived. It is limited in terms of both capacity (7 ± 2 chunks of information) and duration (less than 20 seconds).

long-term memory Memory in which information is represented on a permanent or near-permanent basis.

Sensory Memory

Under most circumstances, we are not aware of sensory memory. Information we have just perceived remains in sensory memory just long enough to be transferred to short-term memory. In order for us to become aware of sensory memory, information must be presented very briefly so that we can perceive its aftereffects. For example, a thunderstorm at night provides us with an opportunity to become aware of visual sensory memory. When a bright flash of lightning reveals a scene, we *see* things before we *recognize* them. That is, we see something first, then study the image it leaves behind. Although we probably have a sensory memory for each sense modality, research efforts so far have focused on the two most important forms: iconic (visual) and echoic (auditory) memory.

Iconic Memory

Visual sensory memory, called **iconic memory** (*icon* means "image"), is a form of sensory memory that briefly holds a visual representation of a scene that has just been perceived. To study this form of memory, Sperling (1960) presented visual stimuli to people by means of a tachistoscope. As you may recall from Chapter 7, a tachistoscope is an apparatus for presenting visual stimuli for extremely brief durations. Sperling flashed a set of nine letters on the screen for fifty milliseconds. (See *Figure 8.2*.) He then asked people to recall as many letters as they could, a method known as the whole-report procedure. On average, they could remember only four or five letters, but they insisted that they could see more. However, the image of the letters faded too fast for people to identify them all.

To determine whether the capacity of iconic memory accounted for this limitation, Sperling used a partial-report procedure. He asked people to name the letters in only one of the three horizontal rows. Depending on whether a high, middle, or low tone was sounded, they were to report the letters in the top, middle, or bottom line. (See *Figure 8.2*.) When the subjects were warned beforehand to which line they should attend, they had no difficulty naming all three letters correctly. But then Sperling sounded the tone *after* he flashed the letters on the screen. The subjects had to select the line from the mental image they still had: *They had to retrieve the information from iconic memory.* With brief delays, they recalled the requested line of letters with perfect accuracy. For example, after seeing all nine letters flashed on the screen, they would hear the high tone, direct their attention to the top line of letters in their iconic memory, and "read them off." These results indicated that their iconic memory contained an image of all nine letters.

iconic memory A form of sensory memory that holds a brief visual image of a scene that has just been perceived.

Images to which we are briefly exposed, such as a bolt of lightning, linger momentarily in iconic memory.

Sperling also varied the delay between flashing the nine letters on the screen and sounding the high, medium, or low tone. If the delay was longer than one second, people could report only around 50 percent of the letters. This result indicated that the image of the visual stimulus fades quickly from iconic memory. It also explains why subjects who were asked to report all nine letters failed to report more than four or five. They had to scan their iconic memory, identify each letter, and store each letter in short-term memory. This process took time, and during this time, the image of the letters was fading. Although their iconic memory originally contained all nine letters, there was time to recognize and report only four or five before the mental image disappeared.

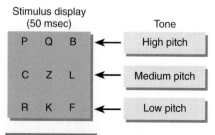

Figure 8.2

The critical features of Sperling's iconic memory study.

(Adapted from Sperling, G. The information available in brief visual presentations. Psychological Monographs, 1960, 74, 1–29.)

Echoic Memory

Auditory sensory memory, called **echoic memory,** is a form of sensory memory for sounds that have just been perceived. It is necessary for comprehending many sounds, particularly those that constitute speech. When we hear a word pronounced, we hear individual sounds, one at a time. We cannot identify the word until we have heard all the sounds, so acoustical information must be stored temporarily until all the sounds have been received. For example, if someone says "mallet," we may think of a kind of hammer; but if someone says "malice," we will think of something entirely different. The first syllable we hear—mal—has no meaning by itself in English, so we do not identify it as a word. However, once the last syllable is uttered, we can put the two syllables together and recognize the word. At this point, the word enters short-term memory. Echoic memory holds a representation of the initial sounds until the entire word has been heard.

Darwin, Turvey, and Crowder (1972) investigated echoic memory with a partial-report procedure similar to the one Sperling employed. On each trial, they presented three different sets of numbers simultaneously, from three different locations (to the left and right of the person and straight ahead). The numbers were spoken at a rate of three per second. After presenting the numbers, the experimenters presented a visual stimulus that indicated the location of the sounds the people should repeat. If the cue came soon after the numbers, subjects could accurately repeat what they had just heard from that direction. However, if the delay exceeded four seconds, they did just as poorly as they did using the whole-report procedure. Thus, the experimenters concluded that echoic memory lasts less than four seconds.

Interim Summary

Sensory Memory

Memory exists in three forms: sensory, short-term, and long-term. The characteristics of each differ, which suggests that they differ physiologically as well. Sensory memory is very limited—it provides temporary storage until the newly perceived information can be stored in short-term memory. Short-term memory contains a representation of information that has just been perceived, such as an item's name. Although the capacity of short-term memory is limited, we can rehearse the information as long as we choose, thus increasing the likelihood that we will remember it indefinitely (that is, that it will enter long-term memory).

Information in sensory memory lasts for only a short time. The partial-report procedure shows that when a visual stimulus is presented in a brief flash, all of the information is available for a short time. If the viewer's attention is directed to one line of information within a few hundred milliseconds of the flash, the information can be transferred into short-term memory. Echoic memory appears to operate similarly.

Thought Questions

- It is easy to understand how we can rehearse verbal information in short-term memory—we simply say the information to ourselves again and again. But much of the information we learn is not verbal. Can we rehearse nonverbal information in short-term memory? How do we do so?
- Suppose your iconic memory malfunctioned. Instead of holding information only briefly, your iconic memory retained information for longer periods of time. What complications or problems might follow from such a malfunction? Would there be any advantages to this sort of malfunction?

Short-Term or Working Memory

Short-term memory has a limited capacity, and most of the information that enters it is subsequently forgotten. What, then, is its function? Before I attempt to answer this question, let us examine its nature a little more closely.

Encoding of Information: Interaction with Long-Term Memory

So far, the story I have been telling about memory has been simple: Information in sensory memory enters short-term memory, where it may be rehearsed for a while. The rehearsal process keeps the information in short-term memory long enough for it to be transferred into long-term memory. After that, a person can stop thinking about the information; it can be recalled later, when it is needed.

This simple story is actually inaccurate. First of all, information does not simply "enter short-term memory." For example, read the letters below. Put them into your short-term memory, and keep them there for a few seconds while you look away from the book.

P X L M R

How did you keep the information in short-term memory? You would probably say that you repeated the letters to yourself. You may even have whispered or moved your lips. You are able to say the names of these letters because many years ago you learned them. But that knowledge is stored in long-term memory. Thus, when you see some letters, you retrieve information about their names from long-term memory, and then you hear yourself rehearse those names (out loud or silently, "within your head"). The five letters you looked at contain only visual information; their names came

echoic memory A form of sensory memory for sounds that have just been perceived.

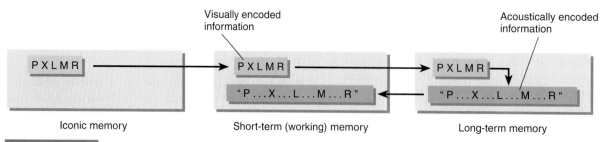

Figure 8.3

Relations between iconic memory, short-term memory, and long-term memory. Letters are read, transformed into their acoustic equivalents, and rehearsed as "sounds" in the head. Information can enter short-term memory from both iconic memory and long-term memory. Visual information enters short-term memory from iconic memory, but what is already known about that information (such as names of letters) is moved from long-term memory to short-term memory.

from your long-term memory, which means that the information put into short-term memory actually came from long-term memory.

To convince yourself that you used information stored in long-term memory to remember the five letters, study the symbols below, look away from the book, and try to keep them in short-term memory for a while.

$$\zeta \cap \partial \ni \wp$$

Could you do so? I certainly can't. I never learned the names of these symbols, so I have no way of rehearsing them in short-term memory. Perhaps, then, Figure 8.3 more accurately represents the successive stages of the memory process than does the diagram you saw in Figure 8.1.(See *Figure 8.3.*)

You can see now that short-term memory is more than a simple way station between perception and long-term memory. Information can enter short-term memory from two directions: from sensory memory or from long-term memory. In Figure 8.3 this feature is represented by arrows pointing to short-term memory from both iconic memory and long-term memory. (See *Figure 8.3.*) Perhaps another example will clarify the process further. When we are asked to multiply 7 by 19, information about the request enters our short-term memory from our sensory memory. Actually performing the task, though, requires that we retrieve some information from long-term memory. What does *multiply* mean? What is a *7* and a *19*? At the moment of the request, such information is not being furnished through our senses; it is available only from long-term memory. Note, however, that information is not recalled directly from long-term memory. It is first moved into short-term memory and is then recalled.

The fact that short-term memory contains both new information and information retrieved from long-term memory has led some psychologists to prefer the term **working memory** (Baddeley, 1986, 1993). In fact, from now on, I will use the terms *short-term memory* and *working memory* interchangeably. Working memory does indeed seem to work on what we have just perceived. In fact, working memory repre-

sents a sort of behavior that takes place within our head. It represents our ability to remember what we have just perceived and to think about it in terms of what we already know (Haberlandt, 1994). We use it to remember what a person says at the beginning of a sentence until we finally hear the end. We use it to remember whether any cars are coming up the street after looking left and then right. We use it to think about what we already know and to come to conclusions on the basis of this knowledge.

Primacy and Recency Effects

Imagine yourself as a participant in a memory study. You are asked to listen to the experimenter as she slowly reads words, one at a time, off a long list of words. As soon as she finishes reading the list, you are asked to write down each word that you can remember. (This task is called a *free-recall task.*) Which words in the list do you think that you are most likely to remember? If you are like most subjects in free-recall tasks like this one, you will remember the words at the beginning and the end of the list and forget the words in between. The tendency to remember the words at the beginning of the list is called the **primacy effect;** the tendency to remember words at the end of the list is called the **recency effect.**

What causes these effects? Research that has addressed this question points to two factors (Atkinson and Shiffrin, 1968). The primacy effect appears to be due to the fact that words earlier in a list have the opportunity to be rehearsed

working memory   Another name for short-term memory.

primacy effect   The tendency to remember initial information. In the memorization of a list of words, the primacy effect is evidenced by better recall of the words early in the list.

recency effect   The tendency to recall later information. In the memorization of a list of words, the recency effect is evidenced by better recall of the last words in the list.

more than do words in the other parts of a list. This makes good sense—the first words get rehearsed more because, at the experiment's outset, these are the only words available to rehearse. The rehearsal permits them to be stored in long-term memory. As more and more words on the list are presented, short-term memory becomes more and more full, so words that come later have more competition for rehearsal time. Because the first words on the list are rehearsed the most, they are remembered better.

What about the recency effect? As Atkinson and Shiffrin (1968) point out, because the words at the end of the list were the last to be heard, they are still available in short-term memory. Thus, when you are asked to write the words on the list, the last several words are still available in short-term memory, even though they did not undergo as much rehearsal as words at the beginning of the list.

The primacy and recency effects are important because they demonstrate that memory is not a random process. Information is not just plucked from the environment and stored away randomly in the brain. Instead, the processing of information is much more orderly; it follows predictable patterns and is dependent on the contributions of rehearsal and short-term memory.

The Limits of Working Memory

How long does information remain in working memory? The answer to this question was provided in a classic study conducted by Lloyd and Margaret Peterson (1959). The experimenters presented people with a stimulus composed of three consonants, such as *JRG*. Not surprisingly, with rehearsal, people easily recalled it thirty seconds later. The Petersons

Unless we actively rehearse the material we are studying, we are unlikely to remember it for very long: It is relegated to short-term memory, in which information is stored for relatively short periods of time.

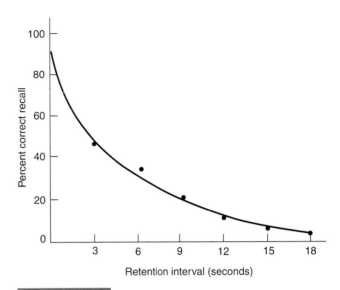

Figure 8.4

Limits of recall from working memory. Percent correct in the recall of the stimulus as a function of the duration of the distractor task used in the study by Peterson and Peterson.
(Adapted from Peterson, L. M., and Peterson, M. J. Short-term retention of individual verbal items. Journal of Experimental Psychology, *1959, 58, 193–198.)*

then made the task a bit more challenging: They prevented their subjects from rehearsing. After they presented the subjects with *JRG*, they asked them to count backward by three from a three-digit number they gave them immediately after they had presented the set of consonants. For example, they might present subjects with *JRG*, then say, "397." The subjects would count out loud, "397 . . . 394 . . . 391 . . . 388 . . . 385," and so on until the experimenters signaled them to recall the consonants. The accuracy of a subject's recall was determined by the length of the interval between presentation of the consonants and when recall was requested. (See *Figure 8.4.*) When rehearsal was disrupted by backward counting—which prevented subjects from rehearsing information in short-term memory—the consonants remained accessible in memory for only a few seconds. After a fifteen- to eighteen-second delay between the presentation of the consonants and the recall signal, recall dropped to near zero. So, for now we can conclude that, once attended to, stimuli remain in working memory for less than twenty seconds *unless they are rehearsed*.

And what is the capacity of working memory? A while ago, I asked you to try to repeat eleven numbers, which you were almost certainly unable to do. In fact, Miller (1956), in a paper entitled "The Magical Number Seven, Plus or Minus Two," demonstrated that people could retain, on the average, about seven pieces of information in their short-term memories: seven numbers, seven letters, seven words, or seven tones of a particular pitch. If we can remember and think about only seven pieces of information at a time, how can we manage to write novels, design buildings, or even carry on simple conversations? The answer comes in a particular form of encoding of information that Miller called **chunking,** a process by which information is simplified by rules, which make it easily remembered once the rules are learned.

A simple demonstration illustrates this phenomenon. Read the ten numbers printed below and see whether you have any trouble remembering them.

1 3 5 7 9 2 4 6 8 0

These numbers are easy to retain in short-term memory because we can remember a rule instead of ten independent numbers. In this case, the rule concerns odd and even numbers. The actual limit of short-term memory is seven *chunks,* not necessarily seven individual items. Thus, the total amount of information we can store in short-term memory depends on the particular rules we use to organize it.

In life outside the laboratory (and away from the textbook), we are seldom required to remember a series of numbers. The rules that organize our short-term memories are much more complex than those that describe odd and even numbers. But the principles of chunking apply to more realistic learning situations. For example, say the group of words below, look away from the page, and try to recite the words from memory.

along got the was door crept locked slowly he until passage the he to which

No doubt you found the task hopeless; there was just too much information to store in short-term memory. Now try the following group of words:

He slowly crept along the passage until he got to the door, which was locked.

This time you were probably much more successful. Once the same fifteen words are arranged in a sequence that makes sense, they are not difficult to store in short-term memory.

The capacity of short-term memory for verbal material is not measured in letters, syllables, or words. Instead, the limit depends on how much *meaning* the information has. The first set of words above merely contains fifteen different words. Because few people can immediately recite back more than five to nine independent items, we are not surprised to find that we cannot store fifteen jumbled words in short-term memory. However, when the items are related, we can store many more of them. We do not have to string fifteen words together in a meaningless fashion. Instead, we can let the

image of a man creeping down a passage toward a locked door organize the new information. Thus, we can read or hear a sentence such as the one above, understand what the sentence means, and remember that meaning.

Varieties of Working Memory

So far, I have been referring to short-term or working memory in the singular. But evidence suggests that working memory can contain a variety of sensory information: visual, auditory, somatosensory, gustatory, and olfactory. It can also contain information about movements that we have just made (motor memories), and it possibly provides the means by which we rehearse movements that we are thinking about making. Is all this information contained in a single system, or do we have several independent working memories?

Most research on the nature of working memory has concentrated on visual or verbal material; few studies have investigated working memory for nonspeech sounds, touch, odors, or other types of information. Although each sensory modality may have a separate form of working memory associated with it, so far we have solid evidence for only two types of information in working memory: verbal and visual.

Phonological Working Memory

Much of the information we receive can be encoded verbally. For example, we can see or smell a rose and think the word *rose;* we can feel the prick of a thorn and think the word *sharp;* and so on. Thus, seeing a rose, smelling a rose, and feeling a thorn can all result in words running through our working memory. How is verbal information stored in working memory? Evidence suggests that the short-term storage of words, whether originally presented visually or acoustically, occurs in **phonological short-term memory**—short-term or working memory for verbal information. The Greek word *phōnē* means both "sound" and "voice"; as the name implies, phonological coding could involve either the auditory system of the brain or the system that controls speech. As we shall see, it involves both.

An experiment by Conrad (1964) showed how quickly visually presented information becomes encoded acoustically. He briefly showed people lists of six letters and then asked them to write the letters. The errors the subjects made were almost always acoustical rather than visual. For instance, they sometimes wrote *B* when they had seen *V* (these letters sound similar), but they rarely wrote *F* when they had seen *T* (these letters look similar). The results suggest that the subjects read the letters, encoded them acoustically ("heard them in their minds"), and remembered them by rehearsing the letters as sounds. During this process, they might easily mistake a *V* for a *B*.

The fact that the errors seem to be acoustical may reflect a form of acoustical coding in working memory. That is, phonological memory may be produced by activity in the au-

chunking A process by which information is simplified by rules, which make it easily remembered once the rules are learned. For example, the string of letters TWAABCFBI are easier to remember if a person learns the rule that organizes them into smaller "chunks": TWA, ABC, and FBI.

phonological short-term memory Short-term memory for verbal information.

ditory system—say, circuits of neurons in the auditory association cortex. However, we *say* words as well as hear them. Thus, as Hintzman (1967) suggested, the coding may be articulatory. (In this context, *articulation* refers to coordinated movements of the muscles involved in speech.) Rather than hearing words echo in our heads, we may be feeling ourselves say them.

People often talk to themselves. Sometimes, they talk aloud; sometimes, they whisper or simply move their lips. At other times, no movements can be detected, but people still report that they are *thinking* about saying something. They are engaging in **subvocal articulation,** an unvoiced speech utterance. For example, read the sentence below and rehearse it a few times as if you were trying to memorize it. (It is the beginning of the poem "Jabberwocky" from *Through the Looking-Glass,* by Lewis Carroll.)

'Twas brillig, and the slithy toves

Did gyre and gimble in the wabe.

If you pay close attention to what you are doing, you will probably find that you not only "hear" the words, but also say them to yourself. In fact, you may even make small movements of your tongue and lips. Studies have shown that actual movements are not necessary for verbal rehearsal; people can learn to keep their tongues and lips absolutely still while retaining verbal information in short-term memory (Garrity, 1977). But even though no actual movement may occur, it is still likely that activity occurs in the neural circuits in the brain that normally control speech. When we close our eyes and imagine seeing something, the mental image is undoubtedly caused by the activity of neurons in the visual association cortex. Similarly, when we imagine saying something, the "voice in our head" is probably controlled by the activity of neurons in the motor association cortex.

Conrad (1970) attempted to determine whether subvocal articulation played a role in phonological working memory by repeating his 1964 experiment using deaf children as subjects. The children had been deaf from birth and thus could not confuse the letters because of their sounds. Nevertheless, some of the children made "acoustical" errors. The children who made these errors were those who were rated by their teachers as being the best speakers. Therefore, the results suggested that the deaf children who could speak the best encoded the letters in terms of the movements they would make to pronounce them.

This study provides clear evidence for an articulatory code in working memory. Of course, people who can both hear and speak may use both acoustic and articulatory codes: They may simultaneously hear a word and feel themselves saying it in their heads.

Baddeley (1986) suggests that the auditory system and the articulatory system of the brain cooperate in a looplike fashion. For example, when we see a printed word, we say it, out loud or silently. Suppose that we say it to ourselves silently. Doing so obviously involves activity of circuits of neurons that control articulation. Information concerning this activity is communicated within the brain to circuits of neurons in the auditory system, and the word is "heard." Information is then transmitted back to the articulatory system, where the word is silently repeated again. The loop continues until the person's attention turns to something else or until it is replaced with new information. (See *Figure 8.5.*)

The best neurological evidence for the existence of phonological short-term memory comes from a disorder called conduction aphasia, which is usually caused by damage to a region of the left parietal lobe. **Conduction aphasia** appears as a profound deficit in phonological working memory. People who have conduction aphasia can talk and can comprehend what others are saying, but they are very poor at repeating precisely what they hear. When they attempt to repeat words that other people say, they often get the meaning correct but use different words. For example, if asked to repeat the sentence, "The cement truck ran over the bicycle," a person who has conduction aphasia may reply, "The concrete mixer got into an accident with a bike."

Most investigators believe that conduction aphasia is caused by brain damage that disrupts the connections between two regions of the cerebral cortex that play important

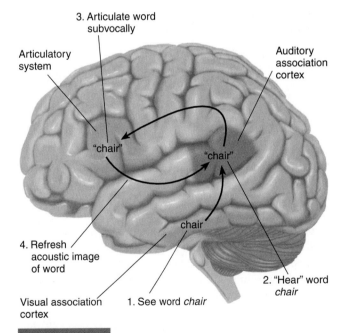

3. Articulate word subvocally

Articulatory system

Auditory association cortex

"chair"

"chair"

chair

4. Refresh acoustic image of word

Visual association cortex

1. See word *chair*

2. "Hear" word *chair*

Figure 8.5

The articulatory loop. A hypothetical explanation of phonological working memory.

subvocal articulation An unvoiced speech utterance.

conduction aphasia An inability to remember words that are heard, although they usually can be understood and responded to appropriately. This disability is caused by damage to Wernicke's and Broca's areas.

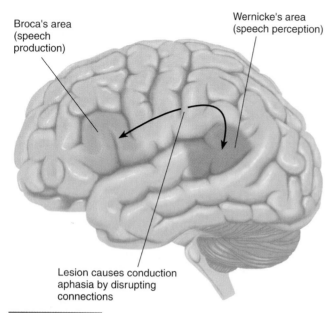

Broca's area
(speech
production)

Wernicke's area
(speech perception)

Lesion causes conduction
aphasia by disrupting
connections

Figure 8.6

A diagram showing how conduction aphasia is caused.

roles in people's language ability. These two regions are *Wernicke's area,* which is concerned with the perception of speech, and *Broca's area,* which is concerned with the production of speech. (I describe these areas in more detail in Chapter 10.) As we saw, phonological working memory appears to involve both articulatory and acoustical coding. Because the brain damage that produces conduction aphasia disconnects regions of the brain involved in speech perception and production, perhaps the damage disrupts acoustical short-term memory by making such subvocal verbal rehearsal difficult or impossible. (See *Figure 8.6.*)

Visual Working Memory

Verbal information can be received by means of the visual system or the auditory system—that is, we can hear words or read them. As we saw in the previous section, both forms of input produce acoustic and articulatory codes in phonological working memory. But much of the information we receive from the visual system is nonverbal. We recognize objects, perceive their locations, and find our way around the environment. We can look at objects, close our eyes, and then sketch or describe them. We can do the same with things we saw in the past. Thus, we apparently possess a working memory that contains visual information, either obtained from the immediate environment by means of the sense organs or retrieved from long-term memory.

The chunking of information in working memory does not have to consist of words. Much of what we see is familiar; we have seen the particular items—or similar items—before. Thus, our visual working memory does not have to encode all the details, the way a photograph copies all the details in the

scene gathered by the lens of a camera. For example, our short-term memory of the sight of a dog does not have to store every visual feature we saw, such as four legs, whiskers, ears, a tail. Instead, we already have mental images of dogs in our long-term memory. When we see a dog, we can select a prototype that fits the bill, filling in a few features to represent the particular dog we just saw.

DeGroot (1965) performed an experiment that provides a nice example of the power of encoding visual information in working memory. He showed chessboards to expert players and to novices. If the positions of the pieces represented an actual game in progress, the experts could glance at the board for a few seconds and then look away and report the position of each piece; the novices could not. However, if the same number of pieces had been placed haphazardly on the board, the experts recognized immediately that their positions made no sense, and they could not remember their positions any better than a nonexpert could. Thus, their short-term memories for the positions of a large number of chess pieces depended on organizational rules stored in long-term memory as a result of years of playing chess. Novices could not remember the location of the pieces in either situation because they lacked long-term memories for patterns of chess pieces on a board.

Humans have a remarkable ability to manipulate visual information in working memory. For example, Shepard and

One advantage that experienced chess players have over novice chess players is their superior long-term memory for different patterns of chess pieces on the playing board. This information helps them to anticipate the possible moves their opponent might make as well as to plan complicated advances of their own pieces.

Metzler (1971) presented people with pairs of drawings that could be perceived as three-dimensional constructions made of cubes. A person's task was to see whether the shape on the right was identical to the one on the left; some were, and some were not. Even when the shapes were identical, the one on the right was sometimes drawn as if it had been rotated. For example, in Figure 8.7(a) the shape on the right has been rotated clockwise 80 degrees, but in Figure 8.7(b) the two shapes are different. (See *Figure 8.7.*)

Shepard and Metzler found that people were very accurate in judging whether the pairs of shapes were the same or different. However, they took longer to decide when the right-hand shape was rotated. They reported that they formed an image of one of the drawings in their heads and rotated it until it was aligned the same way as the other one. If their rotated image coincided with the drawing, they recognized them as having the same shape. If they did not, they recognized them as being different. Look at Figure 8.7 to see whether you would use the same strategy. The data supported what the subjects said—the more the shape was rotated, the longer it took for people to rotate the image of one of the shapes in working memory and compare it with the other one. (See *Figure 8.8.*)

This study and many others like it indicate that we can manipulate images just as we can manipulate physical ob-

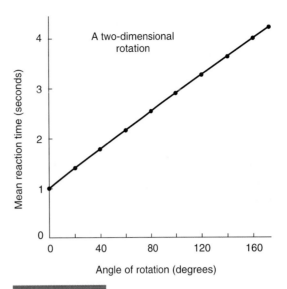

Figure 8.8

The results from the mental rotation task study. Mean reaction time is shown as a function of angle of rotation.

(Adapted from Shepard, R. N., and Metzler, J. Mental rotation of three-dimensional objects. Science, *1971, 171, 701–703. Copyright 1971 by the American Association for the Advancement of Science.)*

jects. A very important human trait is the ability to build things: houses, tools, machines, bridges, and so on. The planners of these objects must be able to picture the shapes of the parts and how they will go together. An architect, a designer, or an engineer can make drawings to supplement visual working memory, but most drawings serve to refine and elaborate images that are already at least somewhat developed. When a mason builds a wall from fieldstones, he looks at the rocks and imagines how they should be put together so that they will fit tightly; surely, this task involves rotating images of three-dimensional objects.

Loss of Information from Short-Term Memory

The essence of short-term memory is its transience; hence, its name. Information enters from sensory memory and from long-term memory, is rehearsed, thought about, modified, and then leaves. Some of the information controls ongoing behavior and some of it causes changes in long-term memory, but ultimately, it is lost from short-term memory. What causes it to leave? The simplest possibility is that it *decays*—it fades away. Of course, rehearsal allows one to refresh information indefinitely, thus preventing the decay from eliminating the information.

The most important cause appears to be *displacement*. As you already know, short-term memory has a capacity of

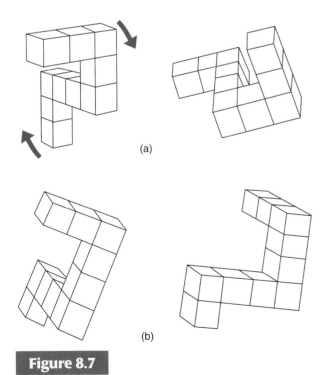

Figure 8.7

The mental rotation task. (a) The shape on the right is identical to the one on the left but rotated 80 degrees clockwise. (b) The two shapes are different.

(Adapted from Shepard, R. N., and Metzler, J. Mental rotation of three-dimensional objects. Science, *1971, 171, 701–703. Copyright 1971 by the American Association for the Advancement of*

around seven independent items. Once this capacity is reach-ed, either additional information will have to be ignored or some information already in short-term memory will have to be displaced to make room available for the new information.

One of the best examples of displacement of information in short-term memory comes from an experiment conducted by Waugh and Norman (1965). The people in this study heard lists of sixteen digits. The last digit, accompanied by a tone, was called the *probe digit.* When people heard it, they had to think back to the previous occurrence of the same digit and tell the experimenter the digit that followed that one.

For example, look at the sequence of numbers listed below. The last one, a 9, was accompanied by a tone, which told the person that it was the probe. If you examine the list, you will see that the earlier occurrence of a 9 was followed by a 4. Thus, the target, or correct, response was "four."

2 6 7 5 1 3 7 2 6 3 9 4 5 8 1 9

Notice that the 4 is separated from the second 9 by three numbers (5, 8, and 1). Waugh and Norman presented many different lists in which the location of the correct response varied. The distance between the target and the probe ranged from one to twelve items.

The experimenters ran two conditions in their study. In one condition the lists were presented rapidly, at four digits per second. In the other they were presented slowly, at only one digit per second. The reason for this manipulation was to determine whether any effects they observed were caused by the mere passage of time rather than by displacement. Figure 8.9 shows the results. Clearly, the more items that came be-

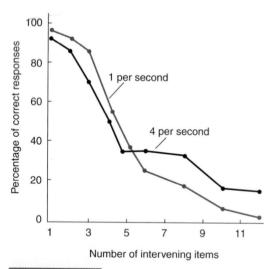

Figure 8.9

Displacement of information in short-term memory. The graph shows the percentage of correct responses as a function of intervening items presented at two different rates of time.

(Adapted from Waugh, N. C., and Norman, D. A. Primary memory. Psychological Review, 1965, 72, 89–104.)

tween the target and the probe, the less likely it was that the target would be remembered. Furthermore, the curves looked approximately the same for either the fast or the slow rate of presentation. Thus, the critical variable seems to be the *number* of items between the target and the probe, not the *time* that had elapsed. (See *Figure 8.9.*)

The results clearly indicate that new information displaces old information in short-term memory. But if you look carefully at the graph again, you will also see some evidence for decay. At the longest delays (six or more intervening items), subjects performed more poorly when the items were presented slowly. Perhaps information in short-term memory does decay, but the effect is much less important than displacement. (See *Figure 8.9.*)

Interim Summary

Short-Term or Working Memory

Information in short-term memory is encoded accord-ing to previously learned rules. Information in long-term memory determines the nature of the encoding. Because short-term memory contains information retrieved from long-term memory as well as newly perceived information, many researchers conceive of it as working memory. Working memory is not simply a way station between sensory mem-ory and long-term memory; it is where thinking occurs. When presented with a list of items, we tend to remember the items at the beginning of the list (the primacy effect) and at the end of the list (the recency effect) better than items in the middle of the list. The primacy effect presumably occurs be-cause we have a greater opportunity to rehearse items early in the list and thus store them in long-term memory, and the re-cency effect occurs because we can retrieve items at the end of the list from short-term memory.

Working memory lasts for about twenty seconds and has a capacity of about seven items—give or take two. We often simplify large amounts of information by organizing it into "chunks" of information, which can then be more easily re-hearsed and remembered.

Although each sensory system probably has a working memory associated with it, psychologists have devoted most of their attention to two kinds: phonological and visual work-ing memory. The existence of acoustical errors (rather than visual ones) in the task of remembering visually presented let-ters suggests that information is represented phonologically in short-term memory. Because deaf people (but only those who can talk) also show this effect, the code appears to be articula-tory. Phonological working memory is encoded acoustically as well. People who have conduction aphasia show a specific deficit in phonological short-term memory, apparently be-cause their brain damage interrupts direct communication between Wernicke's area and Broca's area.

Visual working memory is also important and has been demonstrated in the laboratory by the ability of chess masters to remember a board and by the ability to perform mental rotation of shapes. Mental manipulation of shapes is an important component of our ability to design and construct tools, buildings, bridges, and other useful objects.

As the Waugh and Norman study showed, the loss of information from short-term memory appears to be primarily a result of displacement; new information pushes out old information. However, a small amount of simple decay may also occur.

Thought Questions

- Suppose that someone has sustained a brain injury that prohibits her from putting information into, and getting information out of, long-term memory. Would this injury affect only her long-term memory, or would her short-term memory be affected, too? Can you think of an experiment that you could perform that would answer this question?
- Take a few moments to imagine the shortest route you can take to get from your home to your favorite restaurant. In terms of how your short-term memory operates, explain how you are able to accomplish this bit of mental imagery.

Learning and Encoding in Long-Term Memory

Information that is present in short-term memory may or may not be available later. But once information has successfully made its way into long-term memory, it remains relatively stable. Of course, we do forget things, but our brains have the remarkable ability to store vast amounts of information for a very long time.

What kinds of information can be stored in long-term memory? To answer this question, let us consider the kinds of things we can learn. First, we can learn to recognize things: objects, sounds, odors, textures, and tastes. Thus, we can remember perceptions received by all of our sensory systems, which means that we have visual memories, auditory memories, olfactory memories, somatosensory memories, and gustatory memories. These memories can be combined and interconnected, so that hearing a soft "meow" in the dark elicits an image of a cat. Perceptual memories can also contain information about the order in which events occurred, so that we can remember the plot of a movie we saw or hear the melody of a song in our heads.

Second, we can learn from experience. We can learn to make new responses—as when we learn to operate a new machine, ride a bicycle, or say a new word—or we can learn to make old responses in new situations. Perceptual memories presumably involve alterations in circuits of neurons in the sensory association cortex of the brain—visual memories in the visual cortex, auditory memories in the auditory cortex, and so on. Memories that involve combinations of perceptual information presumably involve the establishment of connections between different regions of the association cortex. For example, the sound of a "meow" elicits the memory of the cat's image by means of connections between the auditory association cortex and the visual association cortex that were previously established by our experiences with cats. Motor memories (memories for particular behaviors) presumably involve alterations in circuits of neurons in the motor association cortex of the frontal lobes. Thus, learning to perform particular behaviors in particular situations likely involves the establishment of connections between the appropriate regions of the sensory and motor cortexes.

Memory involves both active and passive processes. Sometimes, we use deliberate strategies to remember something (encode the information into long-term memory), as when we rehearse the lines of a poem or memorize famous dates for a history course. At other times, we simply observe and remember without any apparent effort, as when we tell a friend about an interesting experience we had. And memories can be formed even without our being aware of having learned something. What factors determine whether we can eventually remember an experience?

The Consolidation Hypothesis

The traditional view of memory is that it consists of a two-stage process (not counting sensory memory). Information enters short-term memory from the environment, where it is stored temporarily. Then if the material is rehearsed long enough, it is transferred into long-term memory. Once the information is in long-term memory, we can safely stop thinking about it. The transfer of information from short-term memory into long-term memory has been called **consolidation** (Hebb, 1949). Presumably, short-term memory consists of the activity of neurons that encodes the information received from the sense organs. Once this activity subsides, the information is forgotten. Through rehearsal (for example, by means of the articulatory loop), the neural activity can be sustained; and if enough time passes, the activity causes structural changes in the brain. These structural changes are more or less permanent and solid (hence, the term consolidation). They are responsible for long-term memory.

Some of the best evidence in favor of the consolidation hypothesis comes from events that disrupt brain functioning. From the earliest times people have observed that a blow to the head can affect memory. Let us consider an imaginary case.

José, a baseball player, is standing on first base. The pitcher delivers the ball from the stretch, and José runs

---

consolidation The process by which information in short-term memory is transferred to long-term memory, presumably because of physical changes that occur in neurons in the brain.

toward second base. The catcher sees him running, jumps to his feet, and throws the ball to second base just as José is sliding into the base. The ball is thrown wide to the right, and hits José just above the ear. He regains consciousness in the dugout, sees his teammates gathered around him, and sits up slowly.

"What happened to me?" he asks. He sits for a while, dazed, then shakes his head tentatively and decides that he will be all right.

"I'm OK. I'll go back on base." He leaves the dugout and heads for first base.

"Hey!" one of his teammates yells. "You were on second—you stole second base."

José looks at him incredulously but notes that the other teammates are nodding. It must be true. He hustles out to second base, puzzled.

In many similar incidents, people have been hit on the head and have forgotten what happened immediately before the injury. A blow to the head makes the brain bump against the inside of the skull, and this movement apparently disrupts its normal functioning. The blow disrupts short-term memory but not long-term memory. A lack of memory for events, particularly episodic or autobiographical ones that occurred just before an injury, is called **retrograde amnesia.** (*Retro-* means "backward": in this case, backward in time.) José had stood on first base long enough to form a memory for having been there. As soon as the pitcher began his delivery toward home plate, José dashed toward second base. His memory of his attempt to steal second base was in short-term memory and was destroyed when the normal functioning of his brain was temporarily disrupted.

This example is an uncomplicated one, chosen to illustrate some important principles. Actually, head injury often disrupts people's memories for a period of time afterward; if the injury is severe enough, retrograde amnesia can extend back for a period of days or even weeks. Obviously, the loss of memories in that case involves more than short-term memories. Why recent long-term memories are more vulnerable to injury than older long-term memories is a mystery.

Events like those in my simple story support two of the assumptions of the consolidation hypothesis. Because only recently perceived information is disrupted by a minor head injury, (1) short-term memory and long-term memory appear to be physiologically different and (2) the transfer of information from short-term memory to long-term memory seems to take time. Information stored in fragile short-term memory is eventually consolidated into more stable long-term memory.

The Levels of Processing Hypothesis

The consolidation hypothesis makes several assertions about the learning process. It asserts that short-term memory and long-term memory are physiologically different. The evidence I presented in the previous section supports this assertion, and few investigators doubt that information that has just been perceived is stored in the brain in a different way than information that was perceived some time ago. However, some other features of the original consolidation hypothesis have been challenged. First, the hypothesis asserts that all information gets into long-term memory only after passing through short-term memory. Second, it asserts that the most important factor determining whether a particular piece of information reaches long-term memory is the amount of time it spends in short-term memory.

Craik and Lockhart (1972) have pointed out that the act of rehearsal may effectively keep information in short-term memory but does not necessarily result in the establishment of long-term memories. They suggested that people engage in two different types of rehearsal: maintenance rehearsal and elaborative rehearsal. **Maintenance rehearsal** is the rote repetition of verbal information—just repeating an item over and over. This behavior serves to maintain the information in short-term memory but does not necessarily result in lasting changes. In contrast, when people engage in **elaborative rehearsal,** they think about the information and relate it to what they already know. Elaborative rehearsal involves more than new information. It involves deeper processing: forming associations, attending to the meaning of the information, thinking about that information, and so on. Thus, we *elaborate* on new information by recollecting related information already in long-term memory. Here's a practical example: You are more likely to remember information for a test by processing it deeply or meaningfully; simply rehearsing over the material to be tested will not do.

The effectiveness of elaboration in remembering was nicely demonstrated in an experiment conducted by Craik and Tulving (1975). The investigators gave subjects a set of cards, each containing a printed sentence including a missing word, denoted by a blank line, such as "The _____ is torn." After reading the sentence, the subjects looked at a word flashed on a screen, then pressed a button as quickly as possible to signify whether the word fit the sentence. In this example, *dress* will fit, but *table* will not. The sentences varied in complexity. Some were very simple:

> She cooked the _____ .
>
> The ——— is torn.

retrograde amnesia The loss of the ability to retrieve memories of one's past, particularly memories of episodic or autobiographical events.

maintenance rehearsal The rote repetition of information; repeating a given item over and over again.

elaborative rehearsal The processing of information on a meaningful level, such as forming associations, attending to the meaning of the material, thinking about it, and so on.

Others were complex:

The great bird swooped down and carried off the struggling ———— .

The old man hobbled across the room and picked up the valuable ———— .

The sentences were written so that the same word could be used for either a simple or a complex sentence: "She cooked the chicken" or "The great bird swooped down and carried off the struggling chicken." All subjects saw a particular word once, in either a simple or a complex sentence.

The experimenters made no mention of a memory test, so there was no reason for the subjects to try to remember the words. However, after responding to the sentences, they were presented with them again and were asked to recall the words they had used. The experimenters found that the subjects were twice as likely to remember a word if it had previously fit into a sentence of medium or high complexity than if it had fit into a simple one.

These results suggest that a memory is more effectively established if the item is presented in a rich context—one that is likely to make us think about the item and imagine an action taking place. Consider the different images conjured up by these two sentences (also from Craik and Tulving, 1975):

He dropped the watch.

The old man hobbled across the room and picked up the valuable watch.

The second sentence provides much more information. The word *watch* is remembered in the vivid context of a hobbling old man, and the word *valuable* suggests that the watch is interesting. Perhaps, because the man is old, the watch is too; it might be a large gold pocket watch attached to a gold chain. The image that is evoked by the more complex sentence provides the material for a more complex memory. This complexity makes the memory more distinctive and thus helps us pick it out from all the other memories we have. When the incomplete sentence is presented again, it easily evokes a memory of the image of the old man and of the watch.

Craik and Lockhart (1972) proposed a framework for understanding the process by which information enters long-term memory. They suggested that memory is a by-product of perceptual analysis. A central processor, analogous to the central processing unit of a computer, can analyze sensory information on several different levels. They conceived of the levels as being hierarchically arranged, from shallow (superfi-

cial) to deep (complex). A person can control the level of analysis by *paying attention* to different features of the stimulus. If a person focuses on the superficial sensory characteristics of a stimulus, then these features will be stored in memory. If the person focuses on the meaning of a stimulus and the ways in which it relates to other things the person already knows, then these features will be stored in memory. For example, consider the word written below.

tree

You can see that the word is written in black type, that the letters are lowercase, that the bottom of the stem of the letter t curves upward to the right, and so on. Craik and Lockhart referred to these characteristics as *surface features* and to the analysis of these features as **shallow processing.** Maintenance rehearsal is an example of shallow processing. In contrast, consider the *meaning* of the word *tree*. You can think about how trees differ from other plants, what varieties of trees you have seen, what kinds of foods and what kinds of wood they provide, and so on. These features refer to a word's meaning and are called *semantic features*. Their analysis is called **deep processing.** Elaborative rehearsal is an example of deep processing. According to Craik and Lockhart, deep processing generally leads to better retention than surface processing does.

Among the evidence cited by Craik and Lockhart to support their model were the results from a study conducted by Hyde and Jenkins (1969). These researchers asked people to analyze lists of words. Some people were asked to analyze surface features—to count the letters in each word or to see whether the word contained the letter *e*. Others were asked to analyze deeper features—to think about the word and decide how pleasant or unpleasant they found it to be. As you can see in Figure 8.10, the people who engaged in a deeper level of processing remembered more words. (See *Figure 8.10.*)

Knowledge, Encoding, and Learning

You might think that memory is related to knowledge: As we gain more knowledge over time, our recall of that knowledge improves. That would explain why memories of adults are generally superior to those of children. However, merely possessing knowledge does not always facilitate recall; even the brightest people have problems with remembering things. What seems to be more important is what happens during the encoding of information. Remember, encoding involves getting material into memory. More than that, how we encode information is likely to affect our ability to remember it later. We have already seen that, to some degree, encoding information involves paying attention to it. We have also seen that if we can make material more meaningful during encoding, we may decrease the likelihood of forgetting that information later.

Automatic Versus Effortful Processing. Psychologists and educators have long known that retrieval is enhanced by the ex-

shallow processing The analysis of the superficial characteristics of a stimulus, such as its size or shape.

deep processing The analysis of the complex characteristics of a stimulus, such as its meaning or its relationship to other stimuli.

(a)   (b)

Taking notes while studying from a text (a) is a more active method of processing information than is merely highlighting important passages in the text (b). Note-taking is a form of deep processing, and highlighting is a form of shallow processing.

tent to which one practices or rehearses information. Practicing or rehearsing information, through either shallow or deep processing, is called **effortful processing**. As a student, you know that the more you concentrate on your studies, the more likely it becomes that you will do well on an exam. But

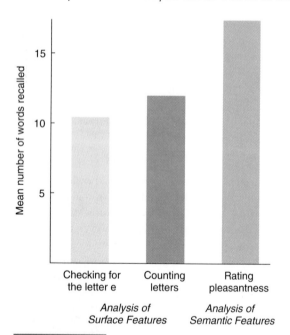

Figure 8.10

Shallow versus deep processing. Mean number of words recalled after performing tasks that required analysis of surface features or analysis of semantic features.

(Based on Craik, F. I. M., and Lockhart, R. S. Levels of processing: A framework for memory research. Journal of Verbal Learning and Verbal Behavior, *1972,* 11, *671–684.)*

your experience also tells you that you have stored information in memory that you never rehearsed in the first place. Somehow, without any effort, information gets encoded into your memory. This formation of memories of events and experiences with little or no attention or effort is called **automatic processing**.

Information that is automatically processed includes frequency (How many times have you read the word *encode* today?), time (When did you meet your best friend for the first time?), and place (Where in the textbook is the graph of Sperling's data located?). Automatic processing helps us to learn things with relative ease, which makes life a lot less taxing than having continually to process information effortfully. Unfortunately, perhaps because of its complexity, most textbook learning is effortful, not automatic.

Encoding Specificity.   When encoding is not automatic, it is effortful, and the most useful effort we can expend would be an attempt to make the new material meaningful. We can think of making new or difficult material meaningful as elaborative encoding; you encountered this idea earlier as elaborative rehearsal. There are two conclusions that I'll offer concerning elaborative encoding. First, it seems clear that more rehearsal is better than less.

The second conclusion concerns **encoding specificity**, the principle that *how* we encode information determines our

effortful processing Practicing or rehearsing information through either shallow or deep processing.

automatic processing The formation of memories of events and experiences with little or no attention or effort.

encoding specificity The principle that how we encode information determines our ability to retrieve it later.

ability to retrieve it later. For example, suppose that someone reads you a list of words that you are to recall later. The list contains the word *beet,* along with a number of terms related to music, such as *melody, tune,* and *jazz.* When asked if the list contained the names of any vegetables, you may report that it did not. Because of the musical context, you encoded *beet* as *beat* and never thought of the tuberous vegetable while you were rehearsing the list (Flexser and Tulving, 1978).

Many experiments have made the point that meaningful elaboration during encoding is helpful and probably necessary for the formation of useful memories. Imagine, for example, trying to remember the following passage:

> With hocked gems financing him, our hero bravely defied all scornful laughter that tried to prevent his scheme. "Your eyes deceive," he had said, "An egg, not a table correctly typifies this unexplored planet." Now three sturdy sisters sought proof. Forging along, sometimes through calm vastness, yet more often over turbulent peaks and valleys, days became weeks as many doubters spread fearful rumors about the edge. At last, from nowhere welcomed winged creatures appeared, signifying momentous success.

How do you think you would have done on this task? Could you have remembered this passage very well? Probably not, for it is phrased rather oddly. However, what if, *before* you read the paragraph, you were told that it had a title: "Columbus Discovers America"? Do you think you might have encoded the story differently and so improved your recall? (Read the passage over again and you will see that the "hocked gems" refer to the means by which Queen Isabella financed the expedition, the "sturdy sisters" refer to the three ships, and the "winged creatures" refer to the birds that signaled the proximity of land.) Dooling and Lachman (1971) found that people who were told the title of a story such as this one remembered the information much better. But if they were given the title *after* they had read and processed the story, their recall was not improved (Bransford and Johnson, 1972). Apparently, the time to make information meaningful is during encoding.

Criticisms of the Levels of Processing Hypothesis

The concept of processing depth has been useful in guiding research efforts to understand how we learn and remember. However, many psychologists have noted that the distinction between shallow and deep processing has never been rigorously defined. The difference between looking at the shape of the letters of a word and thinking about its meaning is clear, but most instances of encoding cannot be so neatly categorized. The term *depth* seems to be a metaphor. It roughly describes the fact that information is more readily remembered when we think about it in relation to what we already know, but it is not exact and specific enough to satisfy most memory theorists.

Another problem with trying to understand exactly what is meant by terms such as *depth of processing* is that no matter

what we may ask a person to do when we present a stimulus (for example, "Count the letters"), we have no way of knowing what else he or she may be doing that may aid recall of that item. In other words, researchers may not be able to control the depth to which a person processes information because they have no way of peering into his or her head and knowing exactly how the information is being manipulated. For each of us, our memory, its processes, and its contents are private. Memory, like all cognitive processes, is not an observable phenomenon.

Some psychologists have criticized the assertion that tasks that encourage people to focus on superficial features of stimuli inevitably lead to poorer memory than do tasks that encourage them to focus on deeper features. For example, after reading something new, people can often remember exactly where the information appeared on a page (Rothkopf, 1971). I have had students tell me, after failing to answer a question on a test, that they could picture the page on which the answer could be found, but they just could not remember what the words said. This example indicates good retention of information that had undergone shallow processing but poor retention of information that had undergone deep processing.

Improving Long-Term Memory Through Mnemonics

When we can imagine information vividly and concretely, and when it fits into the context of what we already know, it is easy to remember later. People have known this fact for millennia and have devised *mnemonic systems* (from the Greek *mnemon,* meaning "mindful") for remembering things in order to take advantage of it. All **mnemonic systems**—special techniques or strategies consciously used to improve memory—make use of information already stored in long-term memory to make memorization an easier task.

Mnemonic systems do not simplify information; in fact, they make it more elaborate. More information is stored, not less. However, the additional information makes the material easier to recall. Furthermore, mnemonic systems organize new information into a cohesive whole so that retrieval of part of the information ensures retrieval of the rest of it. These facts suggest that the ease or difficulty with which we learn new information depends not on *how much* we must learn but on *how well it fits with what we already know.* The better it fits, the easier it is to retrieve.

Method of Loci

In Greece before the sixth century B. C., few people knew how to write, and those who did had to use cumbersome clay tablets. Consequently, oratory skills and memory for long epic poems (running for several hours) were highly prized, and

mnemonic system A special technique or strategy consciously employed in an attempt to improve memory.

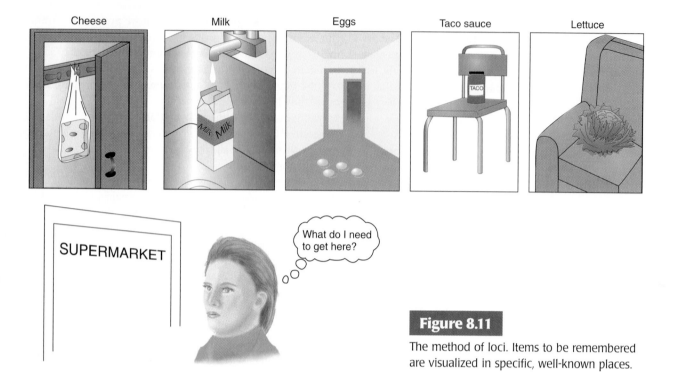

some people earned their livings by using them. Because people could not carry around several hundred pounds of clay tablets, they had to keep important information in their heads. To do so, the Greeks devised the **method of loci,** a mnemonic system in which items to be remembered are mentally associated with specific physical locations. (The word *locus* means "place"; the plural is *loci,* pronounced "low sigh.")

To use the method of loci, would-be memory artists had to memorize the inside of a building. In Greece, they would wander through public buildings, stopping to study and memorize various locations and arranging them in order, usually starting with the door of the building. After memorizing the locations, they could make the tour mentally, just as you could make a mental tour of your house to count the rooms. To learn a list of words, they would visualize each word in a particular location in the memorized building and picture the association as vividly as possible. For example, for the word *love,* they might imagine an embracing couple leaning against a particular column in a hall of the building. To recall the list, they would imagine each of the locations in sequence, "see" each word, and say it. To store a speech, they would group the words into concepts and place a "note" for each concept at a particular location in the sequence.

Suppose that you wish to remember a short shopping list without writing it down. Your list consists of five items:

method of loci A mnemonic system in which items to be remembered are mentally associated with specific physical locations or landmarks.

peg-word method A mnemonic system in which items to be remembered are associated with a set of mental pegs that one already has in memory, such as key words of a rhyme.

cheese, milk, eggs, taco sauce, and lettuce. First, you would think of a familiar place, perhaps your house. Next, you would mentally walk through your house, visually placing different items from your list at locations—*loci*—in the house: a package of cheese hanging from a coat rack, milk dripping from the kitchen faucet, eggs lying in the hallway, a bottle of taco sauce on the kitchen chair, and a head of lettuce on the sofa. (See *Figure 8.11.*) Then, in the grocery store, you mentally retrace your path through the house and note what you have stored at the different loci. Any familiar location will do the trick as long as you can visually and vividly imagine the items to be remembered in the various landmarks.

Peg-Word Method

A similar technique, the **peg-word method,** involves the association of items to be remembered with a set of mental pegs that are already stored in memory (Miller, Galanter, and Pribram, 1960). As with the method of loci, the goal involves visually associating the new with the familiar. In the peg-word method, the familiar material is a set of "mental pegs" that you already have in memory. One example is to take the numbers from one to ten and rhyme each number with a peg word; for example, one is a bun, two is a shoe, three is a tree, four is a door, five is a hive, and so on. Returning to your grocery list, you might imagine the package of cheese in a hamburger *bun,* a *shoe* full of milk, eggs dangling from a *tree,* taco sauce on a *door,* and the lettuce on top of a bee *hive.* (See *Figure 8.12.*) In the grocery store, you review each peg word in order and recall the item associated with it. At first, this technique may seem silly, but there is ample research suggesting that it actually works (Marshark et al., 1987).

Cheese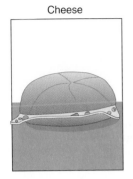

Milk

Eggs

Taco sauce

Lettuce

SUPERMARKET

What do I need to get here?

Figure 8.12

The peg-word method. Items to be remembered are associated with nouns that rhyme with numbers.

Narrative Stories

Another useful aid to memory is to place information into a **narrative,** in which items to be remembered are linked together by a story. Bower and Clark (1969) showed that even inexperienced people can use this method. The investigators asked people to try to learn twelve lists of ten concrete nouns each. They gave some of the people the following advice:

> A good way to learn the list of items is to make up a story relating the items to one another. Specifically, start with the first item and put it in a setting which will allow other items to be added to it. Then, add the other items to the story in the same order as the items appear. Make each story meaningful to yourself. Then, when you are asked to recall the items, you can simply go through your story and pull out the proper items in their correct order. (Bower and Clark, 1969, p. 181)

Here is a typical narrative, described by one of the subjects (list words are italicized): "A *lumberjack darted* out of the forest, *skated* around a *hedge* past a *colony* of *ducks.* He tripped on some *furniture,* tearing his *stocking* while hastening to the *pillow* where his *mistress* lay."

People in the control group were merely asked to learn the lists and were given the same amount of time as the people in the "narrative" group to study them. Both groups could remember a particular list equally well immediately afterward. However, when all the lists had been learned, recall of

all 120 words was far superior in the group that had constructed narrative stories.

Obviously, mnemonic systems have their limitations. They are useful for memorizing information that can be reduced to a list of words, but not all information can easily be converted to such a form. For example, if you were preparing to take an examination on the information in this chapter, figuring out how to encode it into lists would probably take you more time than studying and learning it by more traditional methods, such as those suggested in the study guide.

Long-term memory has no known limits. Shakespearean actors, like these actors performing a scene from The Taming of the Shrew, *may remember their parts long after their performances are over.*

narrative A mnemonic system in which items to be remembered are linked together by a story.

Interim Summary

Learning and Encoding in Long-Term Memory

Long-term memory appears to consist of physical changes in the brain—probably within the sensory and motor association cortex. Consolidation of memories is likely caused by rehearsal of information, which sustains particular neural activities and leads to permanent structural changes in the brain. Data from head injuries provide evidence that long-term and short-term memory are physiologically different: Short-term memories probably involve neural activity (which can be prolonged by rehearsal), whereas long-term memories probably involve permanent structural changes.

Craik and Lockhart's model of memory points out the importance of elaboration in learning. Maintenance rehearsal, or simple rote repetition, is usually less effective than elaborative rehearsal, which involves deeper, more meaningful processing. These theorists assert that long-term memory is a by-product of perceptual analysis. The level of processing can be shallow or deep and is controlled by changes in the amount of attention we pay to information. Having read a description of Craik and Tulving's experiment, you can probably remember the end of the sentence "The great bird swooped down and carried off the struggling _____."

Encoding of information to be stored in long-term memory may take place automatically or effortfully. Automatic processing of information is usually related to the frequency, timing, and place (location), of events. Textbook learning entails effortful processing, most likely because of its complexity. The principle of encoding specificity—how we encode information into memory—determines the ease with which we are able to retrieve that information at a later time. To produce the most durable and useful memories, information should be encoded in ways that are meaningful. However, critics of the levels of processing model point out that shallow processing sometimes produces very durable memories, and the distinction between shallow and deep has proved to be impossible to define explicitly.

Mnemonic systems are strategies used to enhance memory and usually employ information that is already contained in long-term memory and visual imagery. For example, to use the method of loci to remember a grocery list, you would simply imagine each item on the list appearing at a specific location, say, at various places in your home. Other mnemonic systems include the peg-word method, which involves visually associating items to be remembered with a specific set of "mental pegs," such as parts of a rhyme, and narrative stories, which involve weaving a story around the to-be-remembered items. Mnemonics are useful for remembering lists of items but are less useful for more complex material, such as textbook information.

Thought Questions

■ Suppose that a friend comes to you for advice about studying for an upcoming English test. He explains to you that half of the test involves multiple-choice questions over key terms and the other half involves essay questions about the narrative of several short stories. Based on what you now know about encoding and memory, what suggestions might you offer him regarding how to prepare for the test? (Hints: Is there a difference between how rote information is best encoded and how more elaborate, complex information is best encoded? What role might the idea of levels of processing play in studying for a test?)

The Organization of Long-Term Memory

As we just saw, consolidation is not a simple, passive process. Many investigators believe that long-term memory consists of more than a simple pool of information. Instead, it is organized—different kinds of information are encoded differently and stored in different ways.

Episodic and Semantic Memory

Long-term memory contains more than exact records of sensory information that has been perceived. It also contains information that has been transformed—organized in terms of meaning. A study by Sachs (1967) showed that as a memory of verbal material gets older, specific sensory information becomes less important than the specific words. She had subjects read a passage of prose. At varying intervals after reading a particular sentence in the passage (the *test sentence*), Sachs interrupted the subjects, presented them with another sentence (the *comparison sentence*), and asked them whether it had appeared in the passage. The comparison sentence was sometimes the same as the test sentence and sometimes different. Differences might involve meaning or only word order. For example:

Test sentence: He sent a letter about it to Galileo, the great Italian scientist.

Comparison sentence, different meaning: Galileo, the great Italian scientist, sent him a letter about it.

Comparison sentence, same meaning but different word order: He sent Galileo, the great Italian scientist, a letter about it.

The results shown in Figure 8.13 reveal that the subjects accurately recognized changes when there was no delay between the test sentence and the comparison sentence. When a delay was introduced, they had difficulty remembering the specific word order of the original sentence but made very few errors in meaning, even with a 160-syllable delay. (See *Figure 8.13*.) Thus, as the sentence enters long-term memory,

(a)   (b)

Remembering the correct spelling of a word involves semantic memory—memory for academic-type information (a). Remembering important life events, such as an important social event, involves episodic memory—memory for specific events that occurred at a specific time (b).

information about its *form* disappears faster than information about its *meaning*.

This distinction between information about specific items (such as word order) and more general information about meaning has led to the suggestion that there are two

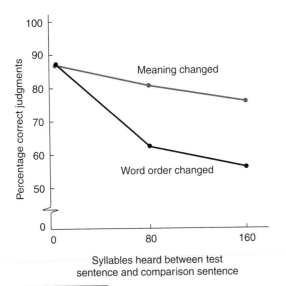

Figure 8.13

Memory for sensory information versus meaning. Percentage of correct judgments as a function of the delay between the test sentence and the comparison sentence. As memory for verbal material gets older, specific sensory information becomes less important than specific words.

(Based on data of Sachs, J. S. Recognition memory of syntactic and semantic aspects of connected discourse. Perception and Psychophysics, *1967,* 2, *437–442.)*

kinds of long-term memory: episodic memory and semantic memory (Tulving, 1972). **Episodic memory** provides us with a record of our life experiences. Events stored there are autobiographical; episodic memory consists of memory about specific things we have done, seen, heard, felt, tasted, and so on. They are tied to particular contexts: this morning's breakfast, my fifteenth birthday party, the first time I went skiing, and so forth. **Semantic memory** consists of conceptual information; it is a long-term store of data, facts, and information, including vocabulary. Your knowledge of what psychology is, how human sensory systems operate, and how behavior is affected by its consequences are now part of your semantic memory. (If not, you need to review some of the material presented earlier in this book!) In other words, semantic memory contains information of the "academic" type. Semantic memories appear to interact with episodic ones. For example, when I come to work at the university, I park my car in the lot adjacent to the building. When I leave the building each evening, I have to remember where I parked my car that day. My semantic memory tells me that I always park in Lot 40. However, because I park in a different space each day, I must use information in episodic memory to find my car again. In particular, I must remember the most recent episode in which I parked the car.

The distinction between episodic and semantic memory reflects the fact that we make different uses of things we have learned: We describe things that happened to us or talk about facts we have learned. However, we cannot necessarily conclude that episodic memory and semantic memory are differ-

episodic memory A type of long-term memory that serves as a record of our life's experiences.

semantic memory A type of long-term memory that contains data, facts, and other information, including vocabulary.

ent memory systems. They may simply be different kinds of information stored in the same system. For example, I am a native English speaker, but I have also learned to speak French. Do I have an English memory system and a French memory system? Most likely not. Instead, my memory contains the information needed to recognize and speak both English and French words and to understand their meanings. The same system can handle both kinds of words. Calling a particular memory "semantic" may simply mean that we have forgotten some details about when we learned the information, not that it is part of a different system. In fact, Tulving (1983, 1984) suggests that episodic memory is a part of semantic memory, not a separate, independent system.

Explicit and Implicit Memory

For many years, most cognitive psychologists have studied memory as a conscious operation. People were presented with lists of words, facts, episodes, or other kinds of stimuli and were asked to recognize or recollect them later. In many cases, the response was a verbal one. More recently, psychologists have come to appreciate the fact that an unconscious memory system, which is capable of controlling complex behaviors, also exists. Most psychologists use the terms explicit memory and implicit memory to refer to this distinction. **Explicit memory** is memory of which we are aware; we know that we have learned something, and we can talk about what we have learned to others. (For this reason, some psychologists prefer to use the term *declarative memory*.) **Implicit memory** is unconscious; we cannot talk directly about its contents. However, the contents of implicit memory can affect our behavior—even our verbal behavior. (Some psychologists use the term *procedural memory* because this system is responsible for remembering "how to" skills, such as bicycle riding.) The distinction between implicit and explicit memory is important because retrieval cues seem to influence implicit memory more than explicit memory and the level of processing seems to influence explicit memory more than implicit memory (Blaxton, 1989; Roediger, 1990).

Implicit memory appears to operate automatically. It does not require deliberate attempts on the part of the learner to memorize something. It does not seem to contain facts; instead, it controls behaviors. If someone asks us a question about a fact or about something we have experienced, the question evokes images in the explicit memory system that we can then describe in words. For example, suppose that someone asks us which is larger, a boat or a bee. We have probably never answered that question before. But we can easily do so, perhaps by picturing both of these objects and comparing their size.

In contrast, implicit memory is not something about which we can answer questions. Suppose we learn to ride a bicycle. We do so quite consciously and develop episodic memories about our attempts: who helped us learn, where we rode, how we felt, how many times we fell, and so on. But we also

Experienced ice skaters, such as this speed racer, use implicit, or procedural, memories. The skill is performed automatically without the need for deliberate, conscious recall of the movements required to perform the skill.

learn to ride. We learn to make automatic adjustments with our hands and bodies that keep our center of gravity above the wheels. Most of us cannot describe the rules that govern our behavior. For example, what do you think you must do if you start falling to the right while riding a bicycle? Many cyclists would say that they compensate by leaning to the left. But they are wrong; what they really do is turn the handlebars to the right. Leaning to the left would actually make them fall faster, because it would force the bicycle even farther to the right. The point is that although they have learned to *make* the appropriate movements, they cannot necessarily describe in words what these movements are.

The acquisition of specific behaviors and skills is probably the most important form of implicit memory. Driving a car, turning the pages of a book, playing a musical instrument, dancing, throwing and catching a ball, sliding a chair backward as we get up from the dinner table—all these skills involve coordination of movements with sensory information received from the environment and from our own moving body parts. We do not need to be able to describe these activi-

explicit memory Memory that can be described verbally and of which a person is therefore aware.

implicit memory Memory that cannot be described verbally and of which a person is therefore not aware.

ties in order to perform them. We may not be aware of all the movements involved while we are performing them. Implicit memory may have evolved earlier than explicit memory. Our ancient ancestors were able to adapt their behavior to their environment long before they were able to talk.

A good example of learning without awareness is provided by an experiment conducted by Graf and Mandler (1984). These investigators showed people a list of six-letter words and had some of them engage in a task that involved elaborative processing: They were to think about each word and to decide how much they liked it. Other people were given a task that involved processing superficial features: They were asked to look at the words and decide whether they contained particular letters. Later, their explicit and implicit memories for the words were assessed. In both cases the basic task was the same, but the instructions to the subjects were different. People were shown the first three letters of each word. For example, if one of the words had been *define*, they would have been shown a card on which was printed *def*. Several different six-letter words besides *define* begin with the letters *def*, such as *deface, defame, defeat, defect, defend, defied,* and *deform*, so there are several possible responses. The experimenters assessed explicit memory by asking people to try to remember the words they had seen previously, using the first three letters as hints. They assessed implicit memory by asking the people

to say the first word that came to mind that started with the three letters on the card.

Figure 8.14 shows that deliberate processing (shallow or deep processing) had a striking effect on the explicit memory task but not on the implicit memory task. When people used the three letters as cues for deliberate retrieval, they were much more successful if they had thought about whether they liked the word than if they simply paid attention to the occurrence of particular letters. However, when people simply said the first word that came to mind, the way they had studied the words had little effect on the number of correct words that "popped into their heads." (See *Figure 8.14.*)

The Biological Basis of Long-Term Memory

Psychologists agree that long-term memory involves more or less permanent changes in the structure of the brain (Fuster, 1995). Much of what we know about the biology of human memory has been derived from studies of people who suffer from memory loss—amnesia—or from studies of animals in which amnesia is surgically induced to learn more about the specific brain mechanisms involved in memory (Spear and Riccio, 1994).

Human Anterograde Amnesia

Damage to particular parts of the brain can permanently impair people's ability to form new long-term memories, a phenomenon known as **anterograde amnesia.** The brain damage can be caused by the effects of long-term alcoholism, severe malnutrition, stroke, head trauma, or surgery (Parkin, 1991). In general, people with anterograde amnesia can still remember events that occurred prior to the damage. They can talk about things that happened before the onset of their amnesia, but they cannot remember what has happened since. They never learn the names of people they subsequently meet, even if they see them daily for years. As we saw in the opening vignette, Mr. P. had been in the hospital for eleven years, but he thought he had actually been there for about a week. And he could not remember meeting me fifteen minutes after we were introduced.

One of the most famous cases of anterograde amnesia is that of patient H. M. (Scoville and Milner, 1957; Milner, 1970; Corkin, Sullivan, Twitchell, and Grove, 1981). H. M.'s case is interesting because his amnesia is both severe and relatively pure, being uncontaminated by other neuropsychological deficits. In 1953, when H. M. was twenty-seven, a neurosur-

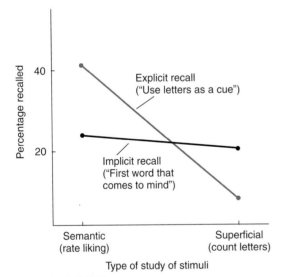

Figure 8.14

Explicit versus implicit memory. The graph shows the percentage of words recalled as a function of the type of study procedure. Deliberate processing improved performance of the explicit memory task but had little effect on the implicit memory task.

(Based on data from Graf, P., and Mandler, G. Activation makes words more accessible, but not necessarily more retrievable. Journal of Verbal Learning and Verbal Behavior, *1984, 23, 553–568.)*

anterograde amnesia A disorder caused by brain damage that disrupts a person's ability to form new long-term memories of events that occur after the time of the brain damage.

geon removed part of the temporal lobe on both sides of his brain. The surgery was performed to alleviate very severe epilepsy, which was not responding to drug treatment. The surgery cured the epilepsy, but it caused anterograde amnesia. (This type of operation is no longer performed.)

H. M. can carry on conversations and talk about general topics not related to recent events. He can also talk about his life prior to the surgery. However, he cannot talk about anything that has happened since 1953. He lives in an institution where he can be cared for and spends most of his time solving crossword puzzles and watching television. H. M. is aware that he has a memory problem. For example, here is his response to an investigator's question.

> Every day is alone in itself, whatever enjoyment I've had, and whatever sorrow I've had. . . . Right now, I'm wondering. Have I done or said anything amiss? You see, at this moment everything looks clear to me, but what happened just before? That's what worries me. It's like waking from a dream; I just don't remember. (Milner, 1970, p. 37)

Clearly, H. M.'s problem lies in his ability to store new information in long-term memory, not in his short-term memory. His verbal short-term memory is normal; he can repeat seven numbers forward and five numbers backward, which is about average for the general population. At first, investigators concluded that the problem was in memory consolidation and that the part of the brain that was destroyed during surgery was essential for carrying out this process. But subsequent evidence suggests that the brain damage disrupts explicit memory without seriously damaging implicit memory.

Many studies performed with H. M. and with other people with anterograde amnesia have shown that implicit learning can still take place. For example, Figure 8.15 shows two sets of drawings. Almost no one can recognize these drawings when they see set I or II. However, once they have seen the complete drawings, they can recognize the elephant and the umbrella if they later see only the incomplete versions. So can H. M.; seeing the complete versions leads to a long-term memory that aids his recognition (Milner, 1970). (See *Figure 8.15*.)

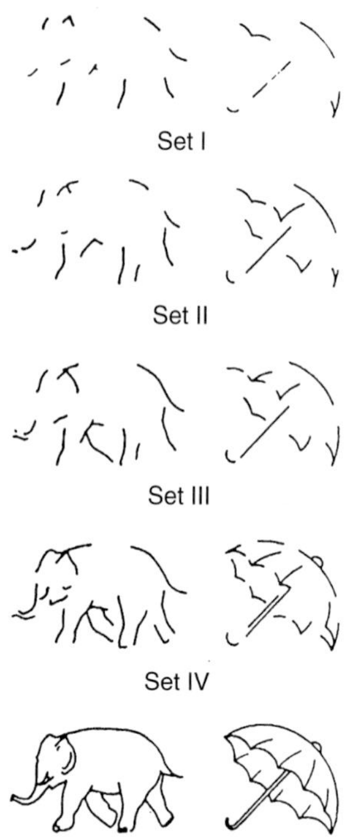

Other investigators have found that people with anterograde amnesia can learn to solve puzzles, perform visual discriminations, and make skilled movements that require hand-eye coordination (Squire, 1987). Clearly, their brains are still capable of undergoing the kinds of changes that constitute long-term memory. But the people fail to remember having performed the tasks previously. For example, they may learn the task on one occasion. The next day, the experimenter brings them to the experimental apparatus and asks if they have ever seen it before. Like Mr. P. in the opening vignette, the subjects say no, they have not. They have no explicit, episodic memory for having spent some time learning

hippocampus A structure in the limbic system, located deep in the temporal lobe, which plays an important role in memory.

Figure 8.15

Broken drawings used to study implicit memory. Two sets of the different versions of broken drawings presented to patient H. M.

(Reprinted with permission of author and publisher from Gollin, E. S. Developmental studies of visual recognition of incomplete objects. Perceptual and Motor Skills, 1960, 11, 289–298.)

the task. But then they go on to perform the task well, clearly demonstrating the existence of implicit long-term memory.

Graf, Squire, and Mandler (1984) showed lists of six-letter words to amnesic and nonamnesic people and asked them to rate how much they liked them. (As you will recall, this task maximizes the formation of explicit memory but has no effect on implicit memory.) They then administered two types of memory tests. In the explicit memory condition, they asked people to recall the words they had seen. In the implicit memory condition, they presented cards containing the first three letters of the words and asked people to say the first word that started with those letters that came into their minds. As Figure 8.16 shows, the amnesic people explicitly remembered fewer words than the nonamnesic people in the control group, but both groups performed well on the implicit memory task. (See *Figure 8.16*.)

The evidence I have presented so far suggests that the brain damage causing anterograde amnesia disrupts the formation of new *explicit* memories but spares the ability to form new *implicit* memories. The fact that amnesic patients can remember facts and describe experiences that occurred before the brain injury indicates that their ability to recall explicit memories acquired earlier is not severely disrupted. What parts of the brain are involved in the functions necessary for establishing new explicit memories? The most important part seems to be the **hippocampus**, a structure located deep within the temporal lobe that forms part of the limbic system. (Refer to *Figure 4.33*.)

The hippocampus, like many structures of the brain, is not fully mature at birth. In fact, it is not until a child is two to three years old that most of these structures are fully developed. As a result, many cognitive activities, such as the for-

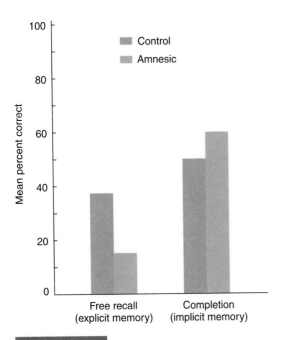

Figure 8.16

Explicit and implicit memory of amnesic patients and nonamnesic people. The performance of amnesic patients was impaired when they were instructed to try to recall the words they had previously seen but not when they were asked to say the first word that came into their minds.
(Adapted from Graf, P., Squire, L. R., and Mandler, G. The information that amnesic patients do not forget. Journal of Experimental Psychology: Learning, Memory, and Cognition, 1984, 10, 164–178.)

mation of semantic memories, are not well developed until this age. One reason that few people remember events that occurred during infancy may be the immaturity of the hippocampus.

The hippocampus receives information from all association areas of the brain and sends information back to them. In addition, the hippocampus has two-way connections with many regions in the interior of the cerebral hemispheres. Thus, the hippocampal formation is in a position to know—and to influence—what is going on in the rest of the brain (Gluck and Myers, 1995). Presumably, it uses this information to influence the establishment of explicit long-term memories.

Anterograde Amnesia in Animals

Given that a key difference between implicit and explicit long-term memory seems to be whether we are able to talk about the memories, can we conclude that only humans have an explicit memory system? The answer seems to be no. Damage to the hippocampus produces memory impairments in animals that resemble those that occur in humans.

As we just saw, people with anterograde amnesia can learn to perform a variety of tasks as long as the tasks do not involve explicit memories. Therefore, it should come as no surprise that similar brain damage in laboratory animals does not interfere with most tests of memory. But suppose that we tried to devise a task that involved learning similar to that of which the human explicit memory system is capable. As we saw earlier, the explicit memory system contains both semantic and episodic information. Remember, the term *semantic* refers exclusively to verbal information; because nonhuman animals cannot talk, we could hardly design a task to assess their semantic memory. But perhaps animals are able to remember episodes. What distinguishes episodic information from semantic information? The primary distinction seems to be that episodic information is organized in a context. In fact, I think I will repeat that word to show how important it is: *context.*

In an earlier section, I gave some examples of episodic memories—this morning's breakfast, my fifteenth birthday party, and the first time I went skiing. Episodic memories consist of collections of perceptions of events organized in time and identified by a particular *context.* For example, consider my memory of this morning's breakfast. I put on my robe, walked downstairs, filled the coffee maker with ten cups of water, put the coffee grinder on the counter and plugged it in, went to the cupboard and took out the container of coffee beans, . . . well, you probably are not interested in all the details. The point is that the memory contains many events, organized in time. But how do I know that I am talking about today's breakfast, not yesterday's? My memory contains many details about many breakfasts, and, if I want to, I can describe many of them. The distinguishing feature among them is the context: today's breakfast, yesterday's breakfast, the first breakfast we had in a hotel room in Paris, and so on.

Can animals perform tasks that require them to learn the order in which events occur and to distinguish between different contexts? The answer seems to be yes. Olton and Samuelson (1976) devised a task that required animals to remember a recent episode. They constructed a maze consisting of a central platform and eight arms radiating away from it. They placed a small piece of food at the end of each arm and then put a hungry rat on the central platform. The animal began exploring the arms of the maze, finding and eating the food. As soon as the rat ate all eight pieces of food, the experimenters removed the rat and ended the trial. (See *Figure 8.17.*) After twenty sessions, most animals foraged for the food efficiently, entering each arm only once. Even when a series of doors was used to prevent the animals from visiting the arms in a particular order (say, simply working their way clockwise around the maze), the animals avoided retracing their steps (Olton, Collison, and Werz, 1977). Clearly, this performance required them to retain a particular episode in memory—the arms of the maze that have been visited that day. Yesterday's sequence was different and must not be confused with today's. (You can see that this task is similar to our ability to remember exactly where we parked our car on a given day.)

Olton and Samuelson found that surgical destruction of the hippocampus impaired the rats' performance. These im-

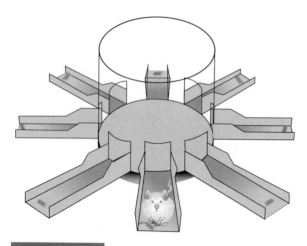

Figure 8.17

The eight-arm radial maze used by Olton and his colleagues.

paired rats learned that food was to be found at the ends of the arms of the maze and would eagerly run out to the ends of the arms. However, they visited the arms in an aimless fashion, often entering arms that they had already visited during the trial. Thus, damage to the hippocampus appears to disrupt an animal's ability to remember episodic information, just as it does in humans.

How does damage to the hippocampus disrupt memory? Most likely, damage to the hippocampus interferes with structural and chemical processes at the synaptic level. As we saw in Chapter 7, recent work with neural networks suggests that networks of simple elements that have properties similar to those of neurons can be taught to recognize stimuli or to connect the recognition of a stimulus with the production of a particular response. Learning in these networks is accomplished when the strength of the inhibitory or excitatory connections between the elements increases or decreases. Thus, learning in real circuits of neurons could be accomplished by changes in the synapses that connect them. For example, synapses could become larger or smaller, entirely new synapses could be established, or more transmitter substance could be produced and released by some synapses. Damage to the hippocampus disrupts these processes.

Interim Summary

The Organization of Long-Term Memory

Episodic and semantic memory refer to different degrees of specificity in long-term memories: We can remember the time and place we learned an episodic memory but not a semantic memory. The study by Sachs (using the "Galileo" sentences) provided behavioral evidence in support of this distinction. Most psychologists believe that the distinction is important but do not believe that episodic and semantic memories are parts of different systems. Another distinc-

tion—between explicit and implicit memory—has received much attention. Graf and Mandler's study showed that conscious processing of information influences explicit memory more than implicit memory. Actively thinking about information enhances memory more than does simply being exposed to it (for example, studying words at some deeper level in contrast to merely looking at them).

Much of what we have learned about the biological basis of memory comes from studies involving humans with brain damage and from laboratory studies in which animals undergo surgical procedures that produce amnesia. Anterograde amnesia appears to be a deficit of explicit memory, but not a major impairment of implicit memory. People with anterograde amnesia cannot talk about events that took place after their brain damage occurred, but they can learn to perform many tasks that do not require verbal rules, such as recognizing fragmentary pictures. The behavior of laboratory animals also demonstrates this distinction between episodic and other kinds of memories. If a rat's hippocampus has been destroyed, the animal cannot remember which arm of a maze it has just entered to eat a piece of food. The important feature of episodic memory appears to be the ability to use the present context to organize information in memory.

Thought Questions

- Does it make sense to you to suppose that there are different kinds of memory for different kinds of information and that different kinds of information require different kinds of encoding to be remembered? Can you propose alternative ways for thinking about how long-term memory might be organized (in contrast to the system we have described in this chapter)? Try it. (You may find it helpful to compose a list of all the categories of information people can remember—people, places, things, words, events, and so on—and all the ways that remembering can take place—fast, slow, with or without much effort, with or without awareness, using or not using retrieval cues, and so on.)
- In the past two decades, many researchers have wondered whether nonhuman animals can think. We learned in this chapter that animals can remember and forget information. Does this mean that they can also think? (Define what you mean by think.) What sort of evidence would you need to gather in order to be able to say that because animals possess memory, they also can think?

Remembering

So far, I have described research and theorizing on the act of learning and the nature of long-term memory. But what do we know about remembering—getting information out of long-term memory?

Remembering and Recollecting

Remembering is an automatic process. The word *automatic* means "acting by itself." But this definition implies that no special effort is involved. Thinking about examinations you may have taken—and the efforts you made to remember what you had studied—you may want to dispute that statement. Of course you are right; sometimes, we work very hard to remember something. What is automatic is the retrieval of information from memory in response to the appropriate stimulus. What is sometimes effortful is the attempt to come up with the thoughts (the internal stimuli) that cause the information to be retrieved.

The retrieval of implicit memories is automatic: When the appropriate stimulus occurs, it automatically evokes the appropriate response. For example, when I open my car door, I do not have to think about how the latch works; my hand moves to the appropriate place, my fingers move into the proper position, and I make the necessary movements. But explicit memories, too, are retrieved automatically. Whisper your name to yourself. How did you manage to remember what your name is? How did you retrieve the information needed to move your lips in the proper sequence? Those questions simply cannot be answered by introspection. The information just pops out at us when the proper question is asked (or, more generally, when the appropriate stimulus is encountered).

Reading provides a particularly compelling example of the automatic nature of memory retrieval. When an experienced reader looks at a familiar word, the name of the word occurs immediately, and so does the meaning. In fact, it is difficult to look at a word and not think of its name. Figure 8.18 contains a list of words that can be used to demonstrate a phenomenon known as the *Stroop effect* (Stroop, 1935; Macleod, 1991, 1992). Look at the words in Figure 8.18 and, as quickly as you can, say the *names of the colors in which the words are printed;* do not read the words themselves. (See *Figure 8.18.*)

Most people cannot completely ignore the words and simply name the colors; the tendency to think of the words and pronounce them is difficult to resist. The Stroop effect indicates that even when we try to suppress a well-practiced memory, it tends to be retrieved automatically when the appropriate stimulus occurs.

But what about the fact that some memories seem to be difficult to recall? For most people, remembering information is effortless and smooth. It is something we do unconsciously and automatically—most of the time. Occasionally, though, our memory of a name or a place or something else fails. The experience is often frustrating because we *know* that the information is "in there someplace," but we just cannot seem to get it out: "Oh, *what* is his name? I can see his face, he has a mustache, and he's skinny. It seems like his name starts with a 'D': Don? No. Dave? Nope. Dennis? No, that's not it either—what *is* his name?!" Now I remember, his name is Doug. Doug Hoisington, a friend of mine in New York. This phenomenon is known as the **tip-of-the-tongue phenome-**

blue blue blue green
green yellow red
yellow yellow blue
red green yellow
yellow green yellow
yellow red yellow
green blue yellow
red blue green green
blue blue green red

Figure 8.18

The Stroop effect. Name the color in which the words are printed as quickly as you can; you will find it difficult to ignore what the words say.

non and has fascinated psychologists since the days of William James (1893). It was first studied carefully during the 1960s (Brown and McNeill, 1966), and since then, we have learned a good deal about it (Brown, 1991). It is a common, if not universal, experience; it occurs about once a week and increases with age; it often involves proper names and knowing the first letter of the word; and is solved during the experience about 50 percent of the time.

The active search for stimuli that will evoke the appropriate memory, as exemplified in the tip-of-the-tongue phenomenon, has been called *recollection* (Baddeley, 1982). Recollection may be aided by contextual variables, including physical objects, suggestions, or other verbal stimuli. These contextual variables are called **retrieval cues.** For example, as I was about to leave my house this morning, I remembered that I needed to stop by the grocery store on my way home from school later in the day to buy something, but I couldn't remember what it was that I was supposed to buy. So I went into the kitchen and began looking for clues (retrieval cues). Right away, I noticed the toaster and remembered that I was out of bread—that is what I needed to get at the store.

tip-of-the-tongue phenomenon An occasional problem with retrieval of information that we are sure we know but cannot immediately remember.

retrieval cues Contextual variables, including physical objects, or verbal stimuli, that improve the ability to recall information from memory.

As you might guess, the usefulness of retrieval cues often depends on encoding specificity. Encoding specificity is quite general in its impact on retrieval. In one rather strange example, skilled scuba divers served as subjects and learned lists of words either underwater or on land (Godden and Baddeley, 1975). Their ability to recall the lists was later tested in either the same or a different environment. The variable of interest was *where* subjects learned the list: in or out of the water. When lists were learned underwater, they were recalled much better underwater than on land, and lists learned on land were recalled better on land than in the water. The context in which information is learned or processed influences our ability to recollect that information. The implication for studying is clear: To improve recall of material to be tested, the best study strategy is to review the material under conditions similar to those that will prevail during the test. If you are going to take all your psychology tests in a specific room, then you should study for those tests in that room.

How Long Does Memory Last?

The question, "How long does memory last?" has fascinated psychologists and other researchers for many years. In fact, in 1895, Hermann Ebbinghaus reported the results of the first experiment to determine memory duration. (I mentioned Ebbinghaus in Chapter 1, in the discussion of the history of psychology.) Using himself as a subject, Ebbinghaus memorized thirteen nonsense syllables such as *dax, wuj, lep,* and *pib.* He then studied how long it took him to relearn the original list after intervals varying from a few minutes up to thirty-one days. Figure 8.19 shows what he found. Much of what he learned was forgotten very quickly—usually within a day or two. But even after thirty-one days, he could still recall some of the original information. (See *Figure 8.19.*)

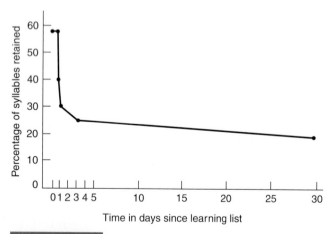

Figure 8.19

Ebbinghaus's (1885) forgetting curve.

(Adapted from Ebbinghaus, H. Memory: A Contribution to Experimental Psychology. *(Translated by H. A. Ruger and C. E. Bussenius), 1885/1913, New York: Teacher's College, Columbia University.)*

Researchers have found that there is little decline for recall of information such as names and faces, even after fifty years.

Ebbinghaus's research dealt with remembering nonsense syllables. What about remembering aspects of real life? For example, how long might you remember the important experiences of your youth? Research by Bahrick addressed this issue by testing the memories of people of different ages, all of whom had accumulated similar information at different times in their past (Bahrick, 1983, 1984a, 1984b). For example, Bahrick was interested in peoples' ability to recall the names and faces of high school classmates, Spanish learned in high school or college, or significant aspects of a small town in which they had all been raised.

The recall tests were given to everyone in the study at about the same time. And, of course, the retention intervals for the older people were much longer than those for younger people. Bahrick found that his subjects remembered considerable amounts of information without further use, elaboration, or rehearsal even almost fifty years after originally learning it. In fact, retention scores showed little decline for the period between three years and nearly fifty years after learning. (See *Figure 8.20.*) About the only factor that significantly affected people's ability to recall the information was the degree to which the original material was learned (which again shows us the importance of initial encoding). In general, the rate of forgetting of this kind of information which also includes people's names, music, and special situations is greatest in the first few years after it is learned and decreases slowly afterwards (Kausler, 1994).

Biology and Culture

Cultural Contexts for Remembering

Memory consists of a network of physical changes in our brains. As we have new experiences, biochemical changes

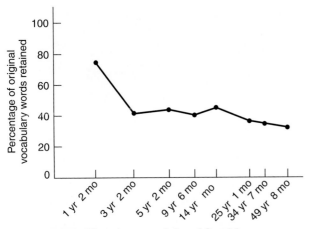

Figure 8.20

The forgetting curve for Spanish vocabulary.
(Adapted from Bahrick, H. P. Semantic memory content in permastore: Fifty years of memory for Spanish learned in school. Journal of Experimental Psychology: General, 1984, 113, 1–29.)

occur in the brain that produce alterations in the neurons that constitute this network. Of course, different people have different experiences, so the physical changes in their brains are different, too. Although it is true that many people "know" the same things—the basic rules of arithmetic, the fact that the sun rises in the east, and so on—it is also true that how we use our memory, how we get information out of our memory, and the personal meaning of that information differs considerably from person to person. We should not be surprised to learn, then, that culture provides an important context for remembering.

In fact, some researchers, such as Jayanthi Mistry and Barbara Rogoff (1994), argue that "remembering is an activity that is defined . . . in terms of its function in the social and cultural system" (p. 141). In their view, the act of remembering cannot be separated from its cultural context. In support of this position, let's consider two studies that compared the remembering abilities of Guatemalan Mayan and American children.

In the first study (Rogoff and Waddell, 1982), the children were given a test of free recall of lists of material they had learned earlier. Not surprisingly, the American children performed better—after all, if there is one thing that American children learn in school, it is how to remember lists of information: names, dates, places, events, and so on. Mayan children receive no such training. In their agriculturally based culture, this sort of information is of little practical value.

To compare how children from these two cultures would perform on a task that was not biased toward the experiences common to children in either culture, Rogoff and Waddell had the Mayan and American children watch a local experimenter place twenty small toy objects (cars, animals, and so on) in a model of a country village. After the children viewed the scene for a few minutes, the objects were removed and mixed in with sixty other objects from which the twenty items had been originally selected. After a short delay, each child was asked to reconstruct the scene the way the experimenter had constructed it. This time, the Mayan children performed as well as the American children. (In fact, they did slightly better.) The cross-cultural differences were eliminated when the American children were not permitted to use well-practiced, culturally based mnemonic strategies. The Mayan children did not have defective memories; their culture simply had not prepared them for learning long lists of unrelated items.

Cultural customs also seem to affect remembering. In a second study, Rogoff and Waddell asked American and Mayan children to recall a story five minutes after hearing it told in their respective native languages by a local teenager. Although the story was taken from Mayan oral history, neither the Mayan nor the American children had heard the story before. Interestingly, though, the American children seemed to remember the story better than did the Mayan children, as evidenced by their retelling of the story to an adult. For example, consider the responses of one child from each culture (as cited in Mistry and Rogoff, 1994).

As retold by the Mayan child:

When the angel came, cha (so I have been told), from Heaven, well, when the angel came, he came to see the flood (The adult listener prompts: What else?) He ate the flesh of the people . . . . (and then?) He didn't return right away, cha . . . . (What else?) That's all. He threw up, cha, he threw up cha, the flesh. "I like the flesh," he said, cha . . . . (What else?) "Now you're going to become a buzzard," they told him, cha . . . . (With further prompts, the retelling continued similarly). (p. 140)

Here is the same story as retold by an American child:

. . . There once was a buzzard and he was an angel in heaven and God sent him down to . . . . to take all the dead animals and um, and so the buzzard went down and he ate the animals and then he was so full he couldn't get back up to heaven and so he waited another day and then he flew back up to heaven and God said, "You're not an angel anymore," and he goes, "Why?" And . . . and he said that "you ate the raw meat and now you're a buzzard and you'll have and . . . and you'll have to eat the garbage," and . . . and he goes, "I didn't eat anything," and God said, "Open your mouth and let's see," and then he opened his mouth and there was all the raw meat and he goes, "It's true I did eat, I did eat the meat," and God goes, "That's . . . that's why you're the buzzard now," and the . . . and the . . . and . . . and so the buzzard flew down and he, um, then he ate all the trash and everything. (p. 139)

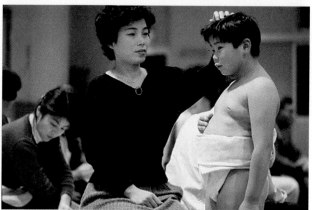

The culture in which we are raised plays an important role in providing us with learning experiences and memories of those experiences.

If you were asked to say which of these children retold the story better, clearly you would say the American child did. In fact, you would probably express some surprise at the Mayan child's *inability to remember* the story any better than he did. What you do not know, though, is that in Mayan culture children do not speak openly to adults. When they cannot avoid speaking to an adult, they must include the word *cha* (so I have been told) in their conversation to show to the adult that they are not behaving disrespectfully by having superior knowledge. Thus, the Mayan child may have remembered the story, but the discomfort produced by having to retell it to an adult interfered with his ability to provide the adult with the story's details. In contrast, the American child, who undoubtedly was used to speaking freely to adults, *appeared* to have a better memory for the story.

Remembering or verbally expressing a memory is not an activity that occurs independently of cultural practices and rules. Culture influences remembering to the extent that it provides the context for what information is learned, the strategies for learning it, and social contingencies for expressing it.

Reconstruction: Remembering as a Creative Process

Much of what we recall from long-term memory is not an accurate representation of what actually happened previously. It is a plausible account of what might have happened or even of what we think *should* have happened. An early experiment by Bartlett (1932) called attention to this fact. He had people read a story or essay or look at a picture. Then he asked them on several later occasions to retell the prose passage or draw the picture. Each time, the people "remembered" the original a little differently. If the original story had contained peculiar and unexpected sequences of events, people tended to retell it in a more coherent and sensible fashion, as if their memories had been revised to make the

Leading questions using words such as "hit," "bumped," or "smashed" can lead eyewitnesses to remember events differently. Eyewitness accounts are often inaccurate descriptions of the events as they actually occurred.

information accord more closely with their own conceptions of reality. Bartlett concluded that people remember only a few striking details of an experience and that during recall they reconstruct the missing portions in accordance with their own expectations. (These expectations would, of course, be contained in semantic memory.)

Many studies have confirmed Bartlett's conclusions and have extended his findings to related phenomena. Experiments by Spiro (1977, 1980) illustrated that people will remember even a rather simple story in different ways, according to their own conceptions of reality. Two groups of people read a story about an engaged couple in which the man was opposed to having children. In one version, the woman was upset when she learned his opinion because she wanted to have children. In the other version, the woman also did not want to have children.

After reading the story, people were asked to fill out some forms. While collecting the forms, the experimenter either said nothing more about the story or "casually mentioned" that the story was actually a true one and added one of two different endings: The couple got married and have been happy ever since, or the couple broke up and never saw each other again.

Two days, three weeks, or six weeks later, the subjects were asked to recall the story they had read. If at least three weeks had elapsed, people who had heard an ending that contradicted the story tended to "remember" information that resolved the conflict. For example, if they had read that the woman was upset to learn that the man did not want children but were later told that the couple was happily married, people were likely to "recall" something that would have resolved the conflict, such as that the couple had decided to adopt a child rather than have one of their own. If people had read that the woman also did not want children but were later told that the couple broke up, then they were likely to "remember" that there was a difficulty with one set of parents. In contrast, people who had heard an ending that was consistent with the story they had read did not remember any extra facts; they did not need them to make sense of the story. For example, if they had heard that the couple disagreed about having a child and later broke up, no new "facts" had to be added.

When asking people to recall details from the story, Spiro also asked them to indicate how confident they were about the accuracy of particular details. He found that people were most confident about details that had actually not occurred but had been added to make more sense of the story. Thus, a person's confidence in the accuracy of a particular memory is not necessarily a good indication of whether the event actually occurred.

Loftus (1979) has investigated the variables that affect the recall of details from episodic memory. Her research indicates that the kinds of questions used to elicit the information can have a major effect on what people remember. In courts of law, attorneys are not permitted to ask witnesses leading questions—questions that suggest what the answer should be. Loftus's research showed that even subtle changes in a question can affect people's recollections. For example, Loftus and Palmer (1974) showed people films of car accidents and asked them to estimate vehicles' speeds when they *contacted, hit, bumped, collided,* or *smashed* each other. As Figure 8.21 shows, the people's estimates of the vehicles' speeds were directly related to the force of the impact suggested by the verb, such as *hit,* that appeared in the question. (See *Figure 8.21.*)

In a similar experiment, when people were asked a week after viewing the film whether they saw any broken glass (there was none), people in the *smashed* group were most likely to say yes. Thus, a leading question that encouraged them to remember the vehicles going faster also encouraged them to remember that they saw nonexistent broken glass. The question appears to have modified the memory itself.

Another experiment indicates that even very subtle leading questions can affect people's recollections. Loftus and Zanni (1975) showed people short films of an accident involving several vehicles. Some people were asked, "Did you see *a* broken headlight?"; others were asked, "Did you see *the* broken headlight?" The particular question biased the people's responses: Although the film did not show a broken headlight, twice as many people who heard the article *the* said that they remembered seeing one.

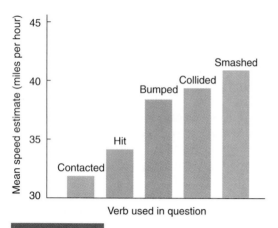

Figure 8.21

Leading questions and recall. Mean estimated speed of vehicles as recalled by people in the study by Loftus and Palmer (1974).

(Based on data from Loftus, E. F., and Palmer, J. C. Reconstruction of automobile destruction: An example of the interaction between language and memory. Journal of Verbal Learning and Verbal Behavior, 1974, 13, 585–589.)

Experiments such as these have important implications for eyewitness testimony in courts of law. A judge can prevent an attorney from asking leading questions during a trial, but he or she cannot undo the effects of leading questions put to the witness during pretrial investigations. Experiments like the ones I have cited in this section indicate that learning new information and recalling it later are active processes—we do not simply place an item of information in a mental filing cabinet and pick it up later. We organize and integrate information in terms of what we already know about life and have come to expect about particular experiences. Thus, when we recall the memory later, it may contain information that was not part of the original experience.

At first, this phenomenon may appear to be maladaptive because it means that eyewitness testimony cannot be regarded as infallible, even when a witness is trying to be truthful. However, it probably reflects the fact that information about an episode can be more efficiently stored by means of a few unique details. The portions of an episode that are common to other experiences, and hence resemble information already stored in long-term memory, need not be retained. If every detail of every experience had to be encoded uniquely in long-term memory, perhaps we would run out of storage space. Unfortunately, this process sometimes leads to instances of faulty remembering.

Remembering and Emotion

Research also suggests that recall of memory is better when people's moods or emotional states match their emotional states when they originally learned the material. This phenom-

enon is called **state-dependent memory.** The experimental procedure used in tests of state-dependent memory usually requires manipulation of a person's mood by hypnosis (Bower, 1981), through drugs (Eich, Weingartner, Stillman, and Gillin, 1975), or by changing environmental contexts, as exemplified earlier in the study involving scuba divers who learned word lists either underwater or on land (Godden and Baddeley, 1975). Next, the person is given a list of items to memorize. Later, when the person may or may not be experiencing the same mental or emotional state, he or she is asked to recall the items on the list.

In addition, what we remember about emotional events seems to differ from what we seem to recall about unusual or neutral events. Consider the results of a study by Christianson and Loftus (1991) in which three groups of people viewed a slide show. The slides were identical except for one slide appearing in the middle of the series. For one group (emotional), this slide showed a woman injured near a bicycle. For another group (unusual), the slide was of a woman carrying a bicycle. The third group (neutral) saw a slide of a woman riding a bicycle. When asked to recall the central and peripheral details of this target slide, people in the emotional condition recalled more of the central details than did people in the neutral condition, but remembered fewer of the peripheral details. That is, in the emotional condition, people recalled seeing the injured woman and the bicycle, but not other details shown in the slide, such as the surrounding scenery. People in the unusual condition recalled both kinds of details poorly. One reason that the central details of emotional events may be recalled better is because they capture our attention—and divert it away from the peripheral details.

A phenomenon first described by Colegrove (1899) suggests that events that produce strong emotional reactions can facilitate the storage of vivid episodic memories. He found that most of the people he questioned were able to describe in great detail what they were doing and what was happening around them when they heard the news of the assassination of Abraham Lincoln. Brown and Kulik (1977) obtained the same results when they questioned people about important events during the twentieth century, such as the assassination of John F. Kennedy. They called the phenomenon **flashbulb memory,** because it was as if the emotional event firmly imprinted the details of the episode in people's memories.

Are flashbulb memories different from other types of episodic memory? Does a powerful emotion really cause the details of an episode to be recorded indelibly and accurately? Neisser (1982) suggests not. He describes a "flashbulb" mem-

state-dependent memory The tendency to recall information better when our mental or emotional state at retrieval matches that during encoding.

flashbulb memory A lucid memory for an event or experience that occurred during a particularly emotional experience.

ory of his own, which occurred when he learned that Pearl Harbor was bombed in December 1941. For many years, he assumed that his memory was a faithful reflection of the events that he witnessed. But when he later thought about the episode in more detail, he discovered inconsistencies that proved that his memory was inaccurate. Once again, we see that the vividness of a memory is not a reliable indication of its accuracy.

Remembering and Interference

Although long-term memory appears to last for a long time, you have probably heard the notion that people forget some things they once knew because too much time has elapsed since the memory was last used and so has *decayed*. Although psychologists argued in favor of this idea many years ago, most psychologists today hold that memory failure occurs for other reasons. One popular alternative explanation for memory failure is *interference*.

The finding that some memories may interfere with the retrieval of others is well established. An early study by Jenkins and Dallenbach (1924) showed that people are less likely to remember information after an interval of wakefulness than after an interval of sleep, presumably because of new memories that are formed when one is awake. (See *Figure 8.22*.)

Subsequent research soon showed that there are two types of interference in retrieval. Sometimes we experience **retroactive interference**—when we try to retrieve information, other information, which we have learned more recently,

interferes. Figure 8.23 diagrams how researchers test for the effects of retroactive interference. (See *Figure 8.23*.) The experimental group first learns a list of words (we'll call the list "A"). Next, during the retention interval, the experimental group learns a second list of words, "B." Finally, the experimental group is asked to recall the first list of words ("A"). Meanwhile, the control group learns only the words in list "A"—the group is not asked to learn the words in list "B" during the retention interval. However, the control group is asked to recall the words in list A immediately following the retention interval. If the experimental group recalls fewer words during the test than does the control group, retroactive interference is said to have occurred in the people in that group.

You may have a hard time recalling the presents you received on your seventh birthday because you have had many birthdays since. If your seventh birthday had been just yesterday, you would likely show perfect recall. When memories that interfere with retrieval are formed *after* the learning that is being tested, we have retroactive interference.

At other times, retrieval is impaired by **proactive interference,** in which our ability to recall new information is reduced because of information we learned previously. Figure 8.23 illustrates the experimental procedure used to test for proactive interference. (See *Figure 8.23*.) In this procedure, the experimental group learns the words in both list "A" and list "B." The control group learns only the words in list "B." Both groups then experience a retention interval before they are asked to recall the words in list "B." If the experimental group recalls fewer words in list "B" during the test than does the control group, proactive interference is said to have occurred.

Let us assume that you took Spanish for two years in high school, and that you are now taking a French class in college. You find that some of the knowledge and study skills from high school are beneficial. But occasionally, you discover that when you try to recall some French, Spanish pops up instead. Indeed, one reason that you may not be able to recall with certainty what birthday presents you received last year is that you have had so many birthdays before.

As reasonable and intuitive as the principle of interference may be, it has not gone unchallenged. Researchers agree that interference can affect retrieval, but some argue that the kinds of recall tasks people are asked to perform in the laboratory are most likely to be affected by interference. In real life, such effects may not be so powerful. For example, meaningful prose, such as the kind found in novels, is resistant to interference. Laboratory studies most often use lists of nonsense syllables and unrelated words.

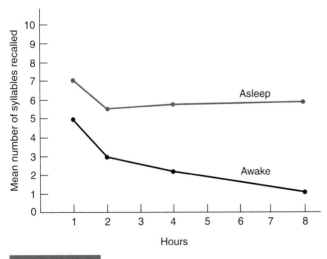

Figure 8.22

Interference in memory retrieval. The mean number of nonsense syllables recalled after sleeping or staying awake for varying intervals of time.

(Adapted from Jenkins, J. G., and Dallenbach, K. M. Oblivescence during sleep and waking. American Journal of Psychology, 1924, 35, 605–612.)

retroactive interference Interference in recall that occurs when recently learned information disrupts our ability to remember older information.

proactive interference Interference in recall that occurs when previously learned information disrupts our ability to remember newer information.

Retroactive Interference

Group	Initial learning	Retention interval	Retention test
Experimental	Learn A	Learn B	Recall A
Control	Learn A		Recall A

Proactive Interference

Group	Initial learning	Retention interval	Retention test
Experimental	Learn A Learn B		Recall B
Control	Learn B		Recall B

Figure 8.23

Retroactive and proactive interference.

Evaluating Scientific Issues

Hypnosis, Remembering, and Criminal Investigation

In many criminal investigations—particularly those in which little or no physical evidence is available—the memory of witnesses becomes particularly important. Their ability to remember events and faces can determine the success or failure of the investigation—and of the subsequent prosecution, should a suspect be brought to trial. But memories of eyewitnesses are fallible, especially when the events in question are fast-paced, confusing, and frightening. It is not surprising that many criminal investigators have turned to hypnosis in an attempt to improve the recollection of crime witnesses.

■ Hypnotic Memory Enhancement

Some police departments employ officers trained in hypnosis or hire professionals as consultants. If victims of crime or witnesses to crimes cannot supply the investigators with sufficient details to identify the criminal, they may be hypnotized to help them recollect facts that they are unable to recall. Several methods are used in this effort. The most common is to ask the witness to relax, imagine himself or herself at the scene of the crime, try to see things as they were, and describe all that happens. Almost always, the witness is told that hypnosis is a significant aid to memory and that he or she will become aware of information that was previously available only to the subconscious mind.

Sometimes, the hypnotist uses a method called the *television technique,* so named because of its resemblance to the methods used in broadcasts of sporting or news events. Witnesses are told to "zoom in" on details they have forgotten (such as the criminal's face or the license plates of the car involved in an accident) or to "freeze the frame" to examine fleeting details at their leisure (Reiser and Nielsen, 1980).

Police hypnotists have reported some successes with their techniques. One of the most famous was the capture and conviction of the kidnappers in the Chowchilla case (Kroger and Doucé, 1979). In July 1976, three masked men kidnapped a busload of children in Chowchilla, California, and transferred them to a subterranean chamber they had prepared in an abandoned quarry. Eventually, the bus driver and two of the older boys managed to dig their way out, and the other children were rescued. The driver had seen the license plates on the two vans the criminals had used to transport him and the children, but the most he could remember during the subsequent investigation was three numbers (out of seven) from one of them.

Under hypnosis, the bus driver suddenly remembered the two license plate numbers, which the police investigated. It turned out that one of the numbers was completely wrong, but the other one was correct except for one digit. The police found the kidnappers, who were then arrested, convicted, and sentenced to life imprisonment.

■ How Can Hypnosis Assist Memory?

Some advocates of hypnotic memory enhancement have made outrageous claims about its efficacy. But what can hypnosis actually do? First, it cannot possibly help people remember events that they did not witness. It can only help people recollect information that they have already learned and are having trouble recalling. In other words, hypnosis only helps if the information has been perceived and has left a trace in the brain. It cannot enhance memories themselves; it can only enhance their recollection. The bus driver in the Chowchilla case was able to remember three more numbers from one of the license plates only because he had actually seen the plates—and had, in fact, tried to memorize them at the time.

As we shall see in Chapter 9, hypnosis does not enable a person to do anything that he or she could not do, if properly motivated, when not hypnotized. That is, hypnosis does not give a person any special powers or abilities that he or she does not already possess. The same thing is true for recalling memories.

In fact, some investigators have developed methods for improving recall of memories that do not involve hypnosis but are based on the research findings of cognitive psychologists interested in memory. These methods appear to work just as well as hypnosis. The guided memory method of Malpass and Devine (1981) instructs witnesses to visualize the original environmental setting in which the events occurred and to try to imagine their mood, thoughts, and feelings at the time. Such a reconstruction often provides state-dependent retrieval cues that help witnesses recall details they thought they had forgotten. The cognitive interview of Geiselman et al. (1984) also encourages a re-creation of the original environment and, in addition, has the witness try to describe the episode from different perspectives.

■ The Dangers of Hypnotic Memory Enhancement

Many people believe that even if hypnosis does not endow someone with special powers, it should perhaps be used routinely just in case it helps a witness to remember some unreported information. However, as Orne et al. (1988) point out, hypnosis does more than help people recollect memories. It can modify existing memories, increase people's confidence in their recollections, and even implant false memories. For example, in one case, a hypnotist interviewing a victim who had been raped by a masked man asked her to mentally "take off" his mask and report what his face looked like. She did, and the authorities even attempted to convict a man on the basis of her "eyewitness identification" (Orne et al., 1988). Because the victim never saw the man's face, her hypnotic visualization of it was completely imaginary.

Most witnesses to a crime want very much to help the police in their investigation. The eagerness of the witness, who may even be the victim of the crime, along with a belief in the mythical powers of hypnosis and the expertise of the hypnotist, sometimes leads the witness to "see" details that were never present at the scene of the crime. In one case, after being hypnotized, a witness to a murder identified a person as the murderer. However, testimony later showed that the witness was 270 feet away. Under the lighting conditions present at the time, this witness could not possibly have seen the murderer's face beyond 25 feet (People v. Kempinski, 1980).

Laurence and Perry (1983) demonstrated that, through suggestion, hypnosis can induce false memories that people later sincerely come to believe. The researchers hypnotized people and asked them whether they had been awakened by some loud noises on a particular night. (They first ascertained that, in fact, the people had not been awakened then.) Most of the people reported that yes, they had heard some loud noises. When the people were interviewed by another experimenter later, in a nonhypnotized condition, 48 percent said that they had heard some loud noises on the night in question. Even after the experimenter told them that the hypnotist had *suggested* that the noises had occurred, almost half of them still insisted that the noises had occurred. One said, "I'm pretty certain I heard them. As a matter of fact, I'm pretty damned certain. I'm positive I heard these noises" (Laurence and Perry, 1983, p. 524).

The results of this and other studies (Laurence and Perry, 1988) strongly suggest that the testimony of people who have been hypnotized by investigators to "help refresh their memories" is not always trustworthy. Fuzzy details become clear memories of events, and the witnesses become convinced that these events actually occurred. As we saw earlier, research on eyewitness testimony has shown that leading questions can affect the memories of people who are not hypnotized. Hypnosis magnifies this effect; under hypnosis people are especially suggestible, and subtle hints made by the examiner can inadvertently change the way they recollect an event.

The eyewitness testimony of a person who appears to believe sincerely what he or she is saying is extremely compelling. Thus, it has a strong effect on a jury. If, in addition, the person's testimony is full of precise details about the episode, the effects on a jury are even more powerful. Because an interview under hypnosis tends to fill in missing details, often with events that never really happened, and increases the witness's confidence in what he or she remembers, the potential dangers of permitting a previously hypnotized witness to testify before a jury should be obvious.

■ What Should We Conclude?

The Council on Scientific Affairs of the American Medical Association (1985) concludes that although hypnosis may be useful in providing leads to guide further investigation, the dangers of contaminating the recollection of witnesses are very real. In fact, most courts in North America do not permit witnesses to testify once they have been hypnotized. Thus, if the police hypnotize a witness, they run the risk of rendering the person's testimony inadmissible. Even if the only goal of hypnosis is to provide clues, the police must be wary of the results of the interview. If they place too much credence in the statements of a hypnotized witness, they may end up following false leads and neglecting more productive ones. They may even be deliberately misled by a witness who stands to gain by doing so. Contrary to popular belief, there is no way to be sure that a person is hypnotized and not merely pretending to be; and even genuinely hypnotized people can lie. Justice would probably best be served if, instead of interviewing people under hypnosis, the police pursued methods based on scientific research of the memory process.

Interim Summary

Remembering

Remembering is an automatic process, although we may sometimes work hard at generating thoughts that will help this process along. As Bahrick's research shows, forgetting information occurs primarily in the first few years after it is learned and the rate of forgetting decreases slowly thereafter. Once we have learned something and retained it for a few years, chances are that we will remember it for a long time afterwards. Remembering information is influenced by how cultures teach their members to learn about the world. In addition, a culture's customs governing social interaction may also influence what people tell others about what they have learned.

Recalling a memory of a complex event entails a process of reconstruction that uses old information. And, as Loftus's research has established, our ability to recall information from episodic memory is influenced by retrieval cues, such as the questions people are asked in courts of law to establish how an event occurred. Sometimes, the reconstruction introduces new "facts" that we perceive as memories of what we previously perceived. This reconstructive process undoubtedly makes more efficient use of the resources we have available for storage of long-term memories.

Remembering is strongly influenced by contextual variables involving mood and emotion. In fact, remembering is easier when an individual's mood during the attempt to recall information is the same as it was when that information was originally learned. We also tend to remember the circumstances that we were in when we first hear of a particularly emotional event such as an assassination attempt, a natural disaster, or an invasion of one country by another.

Sometimes recollecting one memory is made more difficult by the information contained in another memory, a phenomenon known as interference. In retroactive interference, information that we have recently learned interferes with our recollection of information learned earlier. In proactive interference, information that we learned a while ago interferes with information we have learned more recently. Although interference has been demonstrated in the laboratory, interference may not operate so obviously in real life. Prose and other forms of everyday language appear to be more resistant to interference than are the nonsense syllables that people who participate in memory experiments are often required to learn.

Hypnosis has sometimes been used to improve the recall of persons who witness crimes. But, as research has shown, this can be a risky practice, if only because hypnotic suggestions given to the witness may bias his or her recall of the events. That is, hypnosis may modify a person's memory, increase a person's confidence in his or her recollections, and suggest false, but believable, memories. For these reasons, the testimony of witnesses who have been hypnotized to enhance their memories of a crime is not credible or admissible in court.

Thought Questions

- Recall a particularly important event in your life. Think about the activities that led up to this event and how it has affected your life since. How much of the information that you recall about this event is accurate? How many of the details surrounding this event have you reconstructed? How would you go about finding the answers to these questions?
- The chapter described an anecdote offered by Neisser suggesting that flashbulb memories may not always be accurate. How would you design a study to provide a more formal analysis of the accuracy of flashbulb memories?

Suggestions for Further Reading

Luria, A. R. *The Mind of a Mnemonist.* New York: Basic Books, 1968.

Given the importance of learning and forgetting in almost everyone's life, it is not surprising that many popular books have been written about human memory. This book is the great Russian neurologist's account of a man with an extraordinary memory.

Loftus, E. F. *Memory.* Reading, MA: Addison-Wesley, 1980.

Loftus, E. F., and Ketcham, K. *The Myth of Repressed Memory.* New York: St. Martin's, 1994.

Elizabeth Loftus is an internationally recognized authority on remembering. She has researched and written extensively on the errors people make in recalling events. The first book listed above discusses the tricks our memories can play on us when we try to remember what we have seen. The second book deals with case studies of individuals who purportedly were able to recall significant events that had been "repressed" because of their traumatic nature. As Loftus and Ketcham note, such repressed memories likely never existed in the first place.

Haberlandt, K. *Cognitive Psychology.* Boston: Allyn and Bacon, 1994.

Spear, N. E., and Riccio, D. C. *Memory: Phenomena and Principles.* Boston: Allyn and Bacon, 1994.

The first book is an upper-level undergraduate text that contains a well-written and thoughtful consideration of memory and its processes. The book's discussion of memory is placed in the larger context of cognitive psychology, so you can expect to find coverage of several other topics as well, especially language, decision making, reasoning, and problem solving. The second book focuses entirely on memory. You can expect to find the well-articulated answers to almost any question you might have about memory in this book.

Cermak, L. S. *Improving Your Memory.* New York: W. W. Norton, 1975.

If you are interested in improving your own memory, there are dozens of books to choose from. Cermak's is one of the best.

Chapter 9

Consciousness

Chapter Outline

Consciousness as a Social Phenomenon

Can We Understand Consciousness? • The Adaptive Significance of Consciousness • Consciousness and the Ability to Communicate

Although consciousness is a subjective phenomenon, it is a natural phenomenon that can be studied scientifically. Consciousness may be explained as a product of our ability to communicate symbolically with other people.

Selective Attention

Auditory Information • Visual Information • Brain Mechanisms of Selective Attention • *Biology and Culture: Control of Consciousness*

Our ability to focus on particular categories of stimuli or stimuli in particular locations is called selective attention. PET studies show that attention to a particular characteristic of a visual stimulus increases the activity of particular regions of the visual association cortex involved in the analysis of that characteristic. For many centuries, people of various cultures have discovered drugs and developed behavioral methods of increasing or decreasing their consciousness.

Consciousness and the Brain

Isolation Aphasia: A Case of Global Unawareness • Visual Agnosia: Lack of Awareness of Visual Perceptions • The Split-Brain Syndrome

Studies of people with brain damage show that some mental processes can be lost from awareness. It is sometimes possible for people to perceive objects they are unaware of or to lose the ability to understand words while retaining the ability to recognize and repeat them. People with split brains (those whose corpus callosum has been cut) cannot talk about perceptions or other mental processes that occur in their right hemispheres.

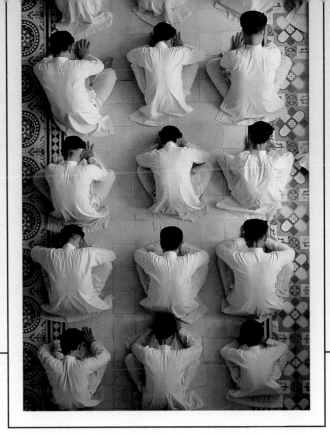

Hypnosis

Hypnotic phenomena include hallucinations and other changes in consciousness, posthypnotic suggestibility, and posthypnotic amnesia. The behavior of a hypnotized subject depends on the suggestions of the hypnotist and the subject's expectations. Hypnosis is related to people's ability to participate actively in a story that interests them and may be related to their ability to empathize with other people. There is no evidence that hypnotized people can be induced to perform acts that they would never perform when they were not hypnotized. Hypnosis has been used to relieve pain, to help people break maladaptive habits, and as an adjunct to psychotherapy.

Sleep

Sleep consists of slow-wave sleep and REM sleep. One of the most important functions of slow-wave sleep may be to permit the cerebral cortex to rest. In adults, REM sleep may be involved somehow in learning, and it may play a role in brain development. Dreaming occurs during REM sleep. REM sleep behavior disorder and cataplexy are neurological disorders that involve the mechanisms of REM sleep. The brain contains two biological clocks that control circadian rhythms and rhythms of slow-wave sleep and REM sleep.

*L*averne J. had brought her grandfather to see Dr. M., a neuropsychologist. Mr. J.'s stroke had left him almost completely blind; all he could see was a tiny spot in the middle of his visual field. Dr. M. had learned about his condition from his neurologist and had asked him to come to his laboratory so that he could do some tests for his research project.

Dr. M. helped Mr. J. find a chair and sit down. Mr. J., who walked with the aid of a cane, gave it to his granddaughter to hold for him. "May I borrow that?" asked Dr. M. Laverne nodded and handed it to him. "The phenomenon I'm studying is called blindsight," he said. "Let me see if I can show you what it is."

"Mr. J., please look straight ahead. Keep looking that way, and don't move your eyes or turn your head. I know that you can see a little bit straight ahead of you, and I don't want you to use that piece of vision for what I'm going to ask you to do. Fine. Now, I'd like you to reach out with your right hand and point to what I'm holding."

"But I don't see anything—I'm blind!" said Mr. J., obviously exasperated.

"I know, but please try, anyway."

Mr. J. shrugged his shoulders and pointed. He looked startled when his finger encountered the end of the cane, which Dr. M. was pointing toward him.

"Gramps, how did you do that?" asked Laverne, amazed. "I thought you were blind."

"I am!" he said, emphatically. "It was just luck."

"Let's try it just a couple more times, Mr. J.," said Dr. M. "Keep looking straight ahead. Fine." He reversed the cane, so that the handle was pointing toward Mr. J. "Now I'd like you to grab hold of the cane."

Mr. J. reached out with an open hand and grabbed hold of the cane.

"Good. Now put your hand down, please." He rotated the cane 90 degrees, so that the handle was oriented vertically. "Now reach for it again."

Mr. J. did so. As his arm came up, he turned his wrist so that his hand matched the orientation of the handle, which he grabbed hold of again.

"Good. Thank you, you can put your hand down." Dr. M. turned to Laverne. "I'd like to test your grandfather now, but I'll be glad to talk with you later."

After the formal test session was over, Dr. M. met with Laverne. "Let me tell you a little bit about blindsight. Your grandfather's stroke damaged the visual cortex of the brain and some of the nerve fibers that bring information to it from the eyes. He has lost almost all of what we could call the mammalian visual system—the visual system of the brain that began evolving when mammals split off from their ancestors. That system is primarily responsible for our visual processes. But the brain that primitive mammals inherited from their ancestors already had a visual system—the one found in amphibians and reptiles. That system still exists in our brains today. Mainly, it helps us detect movements that occur off to the side. It directs our attention to things that we're not looking at but that might be important to us. Your grandfather's stroke did not damage his primitive visual system. That system still works, as you saw. Although it can only detect simple shapes that are clearly isolated from their background, it can direct his hand movements toward objects in his blind field."

Laverne nodded. "Yes, I can understand that, but why did Gramps say that he couldn't see the cane, when he obviously could?"

"Now you're getting to the interesting part. When we say that we can *see* something, we mean that we are conscious of having perceived it." Laverne nodded. "Research from the past few years—with people like your grandfather, whose brains have been damaged in some way—indicates that consciousness is a property of particular parts of the brain, not of the brain as a whole. We're not sure just what parts they are, or exactly how they work, but they seem to be related to our ability to communicate—with others and with ourselves. The primitive visual system evolved long before the brain functions necessary for consciousness evolved. Therefore, the primitive visual system is not connected with the systems responsible for consciousness; only the new mammalian visual system is. When we see something with the newer system, we are aware of what we see. But when your grandfather's remaining visual system—the primitive one—detects something, he is not conscious of seeing anything because that system is not connected with those responsible for awareness."

"I think I understand," said Laverne. She paused, looking reflective. "I've never thought of consciousness as something that you could study scientifically. Do you think your research can find out how it works?"

"Well, that will probably take a long time, but I like to think my research takes us a few steps in that direction."

What is consciousness and why are we conscious? How do we direct our consciousness from one event to another, paying attention to some stimuli and ignoring others? What do we know about the brain functions responsible for consciousness? What is hypnosis—can another person really take control of our own thoughts and behavior? Why do we regularly undergo the profound alteration in consciousness called sleep? We do not yet have all the answers to these questions, but we have made much progress. This chapter explores the nature of human consciousness: knowledge of our own existence, behavior, perceptions, and thoughts.

When do we become aware of our own existence?

Consciousness as a Social Phenomenon

Why are we aware of ourselves: of our thoughts, our perceptions, our actions, our memories, and our feelings? Is some purpose served by our ability to realize that we exist, that events occur, that we are doing things, and that we have memories? Philosophers have puzzled over this question for centuries without finding a convincing answer. Psychologists neglected the problem of consciousness for many years. Early behaviorists denied that there was anything to explain. The only subject matter for psychological investigation was behavior, and consciousness was not behavior. More recently, investigators have begun to apply the methods of inquiry developed by psychology and neuroscience, and, finally, we seem to be making some progress.

Can We Understand Consciousness?

Historically, people have taken three philosophical positions about the nature of consciousness (Flanagan, 1992). The first, and earliest, position is that consciousness is not a natural phenomenon. (*Natural* phenomena are those subject to the laws of nature that all scientists attempt to discover: laws involving matter and purely physical forces.) This position says

that consciousness is something supernatural and miraculous, not to be understood by the human mind.

The second position is that consciousness is a natural phenomenon but also that, for various reasons, we cannot understand it. Consciousness exists because of the nature of the human brain, but just how this occurs is not known. Some people say that we can never understand consciousness because our brains are simply not capable of doing so; it would take a more complex brain than ours to understand the biology of subjective awareness. Others say that we are probably capable of understanding consciousness but that at present we lack the means to study it scientifically. Still others say that, in principle, everything can be explained—including all aspects of the human brain—but that *consciousness* is a vague, poorly defined term. Before we can hope to study it with any success, we must define just what it is we want to study.

The third position is that people are indeed conscious, that this consciousness is produced by the activity of the human brain, and that there is every reason for us to be optimistic about our ability to understand this phenomenon.

The Adaptive Significance of Consciousness

What might the function of consciousness be? One of the most important principles to emerge from the study of evolution is that all characteristics of living organisms have (or had) useful functions. Sometimes these functions are not apparent. If they are not, it is prudent to admit our ignorance and keep trying to discover them. To discover the functions of consciousness, we must not confuse consciousness with complex mental processes such as perceiving, remembering, or thinking. Consciousness is the *awareness* of these processes, not the processes themselves. Thus, consciousness is a characteristic that exists *in addition to* functions such as perception, memory, thinking, and planning.

It is difficult to see why a living organism having elaborate behavioral abilities plus consciousness would have any advantages over one that possessed the same abilities but lacked consciousness. If the behavior of these two types of organisms were identical in all situations, then they should be equally successful. So let us put aside the search for useful functions of consciousness itself. A more fruitful approach might be to conceive of consciousness as a byproduct of another characteristic of the human brain that *does* have useful functions. But what might this characteristic be?

Let us consider what we know about consciousness. First, although the word *consciousness* is a noun, it does not refer to a thing. The word *life* is a noun, too, but modern biologists know better than to look for "life." Instead, they study the characteristics of living organisms. Similarly, "consciousness" does not exist. What exist are humans having the ability to do something in particular: be conscious. So, then, what does it mean to be conscious? Consciousness is a private experience, which cannot be shared directly. We experience our own consciousness but not that of others. We conclude that other people are conscious because they are like us and because they can *tell us* that they, too, are conscious.

In my opinion, it is no coincidence that the only evidence we have of consciousness in other people comes through the use of language. I believe that the most likely explanation for consciousness lies in its relation to deliberate, symbolic communication. Our ability to communicate (through words, signs, or other symbolic means) provides us with self-awareness. Thus, consciousness—like communication—is, I believe, primarily a social phenomenon.

Consciousness and the Ability to Communicate

How does the ability to communicate symbolically give rise to consciousness? To answer this question, let us consider what

can be accomplished through verbal communication. We can ask other people to help us get something we need. We can share our knowledge with others by describing our past experiences. We can make plans with other people to accomplish tasks that are beyond the abilities of a single person. We can warn other people of our intentions and in so doing avoid potential conflicts. In other words, we can express our needs, thoughts, perceptions, memories, intentions, and feelings to other people.

All of these accomplishments require two general capacities. First, we must be able to translate private events—our needs, thoughts, and other processes—into symbolic expressions. This means that the brain mechanisms we employ for communicating with others must receive input from the systems of the brain involved in perceiving, thinking, remembering, and so on. Second, our words (or other symbols) must have an effect on the person listening. Once the words are decoded in the listener's brain, they must affect the listener's own thoughts, perceptions, memories, and—ultimately—behavior. For example, if we describe an event that we witnessed, our listener will be able to imagine that event, too. The episode will become part of our listener's memory.

Of course, the world is not divided into talkers and listeners. We are all capable of expressing our thoughts symbolically and of decoding the symbols other people express. Having both of these capabilities enables us to communicate with ourselves, privately. We can make plans in words, think about the consequences of these plans in words, and use words to produce behaviors—all without actually *saying* the words. We *think* them.

As we saw in Chapter 8, thinking in words appears to involve subvocal articulation. Thus, the brain mechanisms that permit us to understand words and produce speech are the same ones we use to think in words. Similarly, investigators have noted that when deaf people are thinking to themselves, they often make small movements with their hands, just as those of us who can hear and speak sometimes talk to ourselves under our breath. Apparently, we exercise our expressive language mechanisms, whatever they may be, when we think.

So what does all this have to do with consciousness? My thesis is this: The ability to communicate with ourselves symbolically gives rise to consciousness. We are conscious of those private events we can talk about, to ourselves or to other people: our perceptions, needs, intentions, memories, and feelings.

Are humans the only living organisms having self-awareness? Probably not. The evolutionary process is incremental: New traits and abilities—including the ability of humans to communicate symbolically—build upon ones that already exist. Most forms of communication among animals other than humans—for example, mating displays and alarm calls—are automatic and probably do not involve consciousness. However, other forms of communications can be learned, just as we learn our own language. Certainly, your dog can learn to communicate with you. The fact that it can learn to tell you when it wants to eat, go for a walk, or play suggests that it, too, may be conscious. Obviously, our ability to communicate symbolically far surpasses that of any other species; thus, our consciousness is much more highly developed.

Could a computer ever be conscious? In principle, I do not see any reason to reject this possibility. I think most people would admit that alien species from another planetary system could be conscious. Their brains would be different from ours, so the design of our brain is not the only one capable of consciousness. Perhaps, then, the thought of a conscious computer is not farfetched, either. The computer would have to possess devices that enabled it to perceive events in its environment, think about these events, remember them, and so on. It would also have to communicate symbolically with us (or with other computers), describing its perceptions, thoughts, and memories. Furthermore, when we described our own mental events, our words would have to evoke thoughts and perceptions in the computer, just as they do in the brain of a human.

I cannot prove any of these speculations. But everything we know about consciousness—including information we have gained from the study of the human brain—is consistent with what I have written here. In any event, this discussion may have given you some food for thought.

Interim Summary

Consciousness as a Social Phenomenon

Consciousness, as it is defined here, can be viewed as a byproduct of our ability to communicate symbolically by using words or other signs. Its physiological basis is the activity of language mechanisms of the brain. The private use of language (thinking to oneself) is clearly conscious. Private nonverbal processes are conscious if we can describe them—that is, if their activities are available to the neural mechanisms of language. In the same way, we are conscious of *external* events only if we can think (and verbalize) about our perceptions of them.

This view of human self-awareness is only one of several, and it may finally be proved wrong. However, it does help present a unified picture of a variety of phenomena related to consciousness. Its primary value is that it relates a private and mysterious phenomenon to a set of behaviors that can be observed and studied.

Thought Questions

- What do you think about the possibility that members of other species may be conscious? What evidence would you look for to answer this question?
- If my thesis is correct, babies acquire consciousness as they acquire language. Do you think this conclusion is somehow related to the fact that we cannot remember what happened to us when we were very young?
- What would happen if a person were raised in isolation and never came in contact with (or communi-

cated with) another person? That person would not be able to talk. What would that person's mental life be like? Would he or she be conscious?

Selective Attention

We do not become conscious of all the stimuli detected by our sensory organs. For example, if an angler is watching a large trout circling underneath an artificial fly she has gently cast on the water, she probably will not notice the chirping of birds in the woods behind her or the temperature of the water surrounding her legs or the floating twigs drifting by with the current. Her attention is completely devoted to the behavior of the fish, and she is poised to respond with the appropriate movements of her fly rod if the fish takes the bait. The process that controls our awareness of particular categories of events in the environment is called **selective attention.**

As we saw in Chapter 8, sensory memory receives more information than it can transfer into short-term (working) memory. For example, Sperling (1960) found that although people could remember only about four or five of the nine letters he flashed on the screen if they tried to remember them all, they could *direct their attention* to any of the three lines of letters contained in sensory memory and identify them with perfect accuracy. The topic of Chapter 8 was memory; that chapter discussed the nature of sensory memory and the fate of information that entered short-term memory. In this chapter, I will discuss the nature of the process of attention and the fate of information that *does not* enter short-term memory.

The process of selective attention determines which events we become conscious of. Attention may be controlled automatically, as when an intense stimulus (such as a loud sound) captures our attention. It may be controlled by instructions ("Pay attention to that one over there!"). Or it may be controlled by the demands of the particular task we are performing. (For example, when we are driving a car, we pay special attention to other cars, pedestrians, road signs, and so on.) Our attentional mechanisms serve to enhance our responsiveness to certain stimuli and to tune out irrelevant information.

Attention plays an important role in memory. By exerting control over the information that reaches short-term memory, it determines what information ultimately becomes stored in explicit long-term memory. (As you will recall, *explicit memory* is the portion of long-term memory that we can talk about—that we can become conscious of.) But the storage of information in *implicit memory* does not require

selective attention The process that controls our awareness of, and readiness to respond to, particular categories of stimuli or stimuli in a particular location.

. . . ate everything on his plate, and then asked for another . . .

Figure 9.1

Dichotic listening and shadowing. A person listens to two different spoken messages simultaneously and continuously repeats back what one voice is saying.

conscious attention. Not all the information we do not pay attention to is lost.

Why does selective attention exist? Why do we not simply process *all* the information that is being gathered by our sensory receptors—after all, it sometimes happens that we miss something important because our attention is occupied elsewhere. According to Broadbent (1958), the answer is that the brain mechanisms responsible for conscious processing of this information have a limited capacity. There is only so much information that these mechanisms can handle at one particular moment. Thus, we need some system to serve as a gatekeeper, controlling the flow of information to this system. The nature of this gatekeeper—selective attention—is still the subject of ongoing research (Neisser, 1967; Treisman, 1993).

Auditory Information

The first experiments that investigated the nature of attention took advantage of the fact that we have two ears. Cherry (1953) devised a test of selective attention called **dichotic listening,** a task that requires a person to listen to one of two messages presented simultaneously, one to each ear. (*Dichotic* means "divided into two parts.") He placed headphones on his subjects and presented recordings of different spoken messages to each ear. He asked the subjects to **shadow** the message presented to one ear—to continuously repeat back what that voice was saying. Shadowing ensured that they would pay attention to only that message. (See *Figure 9.1.*)

What happened to the information that entered the unattended ear? In general, it appeared to be lost. When questioned about what that ear had heard, subjects responded

that they had heard something, but they could not say what it was. Even if the voice presented to the unshadowed ear began to talk in a foreign language, they did not notice the change.

These results suggest that a channel of sensory input (in this case, one ear) can simply be turned off. Perhaps neurons in the auditory system that detect sound from the unattended ear are inhibited so that they cannot respond to sounds presented to that ear. (See *Figure 9.2(a).*)

The story is not so simple. Other evidence shows that selective attention is not achieved by simply closing a sensory channel. Some information, by its very nature, can break through into consciousness. For example, if a person's name is presented to the unattended ear, he or she will very likely hear it and remember it later (Moray, 1959). Or if the message presented to the unattended ear contains sexually explicit words, people tend to notice them immediately (Nielsen and Sarason, 1981). The fact that some kinds of information presented to the unattended ear can grab our attention indicates that even unattended information undergoes some verbal analysis.

This stock exchange broker must keep track of several different conversations and selectively attend to each of them, one after the other.

dichotic listening A task that requires a person to listen to one of two different messages being presented simultaneously, one to each ear, through headphones.

shadowing The act of continuously repeating verbal material as soon as it is heard.

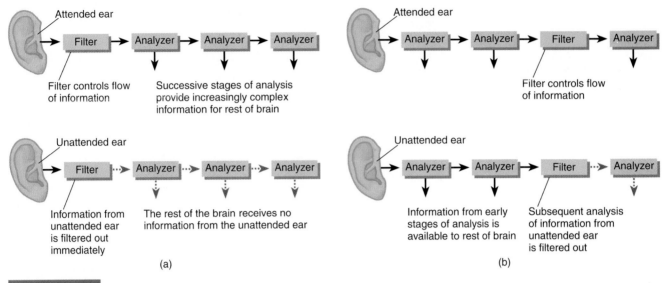

Figure 9.2

Models of selective attention in the dichotic listening task. (a) Filtering of unattended sensory information immediately after it is received by the sensory receptors. This model cannot explain the fact that some information presented to the unattended ear enters consciousness. (b) Filtering of unattended sensory information after some preliminary analysis.

If the unattended information is "filtered out" at some level, this filtration must not occur until *after* the sounds are identified as words. (See *Figure 9.2(b)*.)

Several studies have shown that information presented to the unattended ear can affect our behavior even if we do not become conscious of the information. To put it another way, the information can produce implicit memories—memories of which we are unaware. Von Wright, Anderson, and Stenman (1975) showed that words previously presented along with an unpleasant electrical shock would produce an emotional reaction when the words were presented to the unattended ear. Even when the subject was not consciously attending to the voice, the information produced a nonverbal response—a classically conditioned emotional reaction. Thus, the unattended information could trigger the recall of an implicit memory.

McKay (1973) showed that information presented to the unattended ear can influence verbal processing even when the listener is not conscious of this information. In the attended ear, subjects heard sentences such as the following:

They threw stones toward the bank yesterday.

While this sentence was being presented, the subjects heard the word *river* or *money* in the unattended ear. Later, they were asked which of the following sentences they had heard:

They threw stones toward the side of the river yesterday.

They threw stones toward the savings and loan association yesterday.

Of course, the subjects had heard neither of these sentences. But as Sachs (1967) has shown (Chapter 8), people quickly forget the particular words a sentence contains, although they do remember the sentence's meaning much longer. McKay found that the subjects' choices were determined by whether the word *river* or *money* was presented to the unattended ear. They did not specifically recall hearing the words presented to the unattended ear, but obviously these words had affected their perception of the meaning of the word *bank*.

Besides being able to notice and remember some characteristics of information received by the unattended sensory channel, we are able to store information temporarily as it comes in. No doubt you have had the following sort of experience. You are intently reading or thinking about something, when you become aware that someone has asked you a question. You look up and say, "What?" but then answer the question before the other person has had a chance to repeat it. You first became aware that you had just been asked a question, but you did not know what had been asked. However, when you thought for a moment, you remembered what the question was—you heard it again in your mind's ear, so to speak. The information, held in temporary storage, was made accessible to your verbal system.

Treisman (1960) showed that people can follow a message that is being shadowed even if it switches from one ear to the other. Suppose a person is shadowing a message presented to the left ear, while the message to the right ear is unshadowed. (See *Figure 9.3*.) In the example given in Figure 9.3, the person will probably say "crept out of the swamp" and

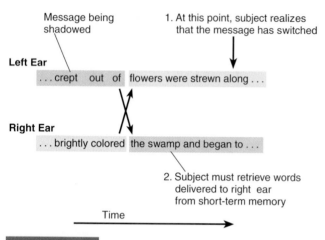

Message being shadowed

1. At this point, subject realizes that the message has switched

Left Ear

... crept   out   of   flowers were strewn along ...

Right Ear

... brightly colored   the swamp and began to ...

2. Subject must retrieve words delivered to right ear from short-term memory

Time

Figure 9.3

Shadowing a message that switches ears. When the message switches, the person must retrieve some words from memory that were heard by the unattended ear.

not "crept out of flowers." Apparently, the switch occurs when the message begins to make no sense. However, by the time the person realizes that "crept out of flowers" makes no sense, the rest of the message, "the swamp," has already been presented to the right ear. Because the person is able to continue the message without missing any words, he or she must be able to retrieve some words from memory. Thus, even though an unshadowed message cannot be remembered later, it produces some trace that can be retrieved if attention is directed to it soon after the words are presented.

Selective attention to auditory messages has practical significance outside the laboratory. For example, sometimes we

Figure 9.4

The cocktail-party phenomenon. We can follow a particular conversation even when other conversations are going on around us.

have to sort out one message from several others without the benefit of such a distinct cue; we seldom hear one voice in one ear and another voice in the other. We might be trying to converse with one person while we are in a room with several other people who are carrying on their own conversations. Even in a situation like the one shown in Figure 9.4, we can usually sort out one voice from another—an example of the *cocktail-party phenomenon*. (See *Figure 9.4.*) In this case, we are trying to listen to the person opposite us and to ignore the cross conversation of the people to our left and right. Our ears receive a jumble of sounds, but we are able to pick out the ones we want, stringing them together into a meaningful message and ignoring the rest. This task takes some effort; following one person's conversation in such circumstances is more difficult when what he or she is saying is not very interesting. If we overhear a few words of another conversation that seems more interesting, it is hard to strain out the cross conversation.

Visual Information

More recent experiments have studied the nature of visual attention. These experiments have shown that we can successfully attend to the *location* of the information or to the *nature* of the information (revealed by its physical features, such as form or color).

Let us consider location first. Sperling's studies on sensory memory were probably the first to demonstrate the role of attention in selectively transferring visual information into verbal short-term memory (or, for our purposes, into consciousness). Other psychologists have studied this phenomenon in more detail. For example, Posner, Snyder, and Davidson (1980) had subjects watch a computer-controlled video display screen. A small mark in the center of the screen served as a fixation point for the subjects' gaze. They were shown a warning stimulus near the fixation point followed by a target stimulus—a letter displayed to the left or the right of the fixation point. The warning stimulus consisted of either an arrow pointing right or left or simply a plus sign. The arrows served as cues to the subjects to expect the letter to occur either to the right or to the left. The plus sign served as a neutral stimulus, containing no spatial information. The subjects' task was to press a button as soon as they detected the letter.

Eighty percent of the time, the arrow accurately pointed toward the location in which the letter would be presented. However, 20 percent of the time, the arrow pointed *away from* the location in which it would occur. The advance warning clearly had an effect on the subjects' response times: When they were correctly informed of the location of the letter, they responded faster; and when they were incorrectly informed, they responded more slowly. (See *Figure 9.5.*)

This study shows that selective attention can affect the detection of visual stimuli: If a stimulus occurs where we expect it, we perceive it more quickly; if it occurs where we do *not* expect it, we perceive it more slowly. Thus, people can fol-

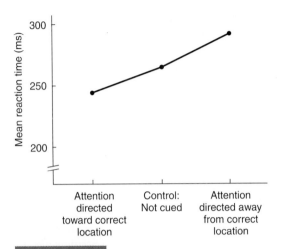

Figure 9.5

Location as a cue for selective attention. Mean reaction time in response to a letter displayed on a screen after subjects received a cue directing attention toward the location in which the letter appears was less than when no cue or an incorrect cue was received.

low instructions to direct their attention to particular locations in the visual field. Because the subjects' gaze remained fixed on the center of the screen in this study, this movement of attention was independent of eye movement. How does this focusing of attention work neurologically? The most likely explanation seems to be that neural circuits that detect a particular kind of stimulus are somehow sensitized, so that they can more easily detect that stimulus. In this case, the mechanism of selective attention sensitized the neural circuits that detect visual stimuli in a particular region.

The second dimension of visual attention is the nature of the object being attended to (Vecera and Farah, 1994; Desimone and Duncan, 1995). Sometimes, two events happen in close proximity, but we can watch one of them while ignoring the other. For example, Neisser and Becklen (1975) showed subjects a videotape that presented a situation similar to the one confronted by a person trying to listen to the voice of one person at a cocktail party. The videotape contained two different actions presented one on top of the other: a basketball game and a hand game, in which people try to slap their opponents' hands, which are resting on top of theirs. The subjects could easily follow one scene and remember what had happened in it; however, they could not attend simultaneously to both scenes. (See *Figure 9.6.*)

It is possible that the selective attention exercised by Neisser and Becklen's subjects was controlled by eye movements as their gaze followed the actions of one of the games. However, Rock and Gutman (1981) found that people can pay attention to one of two *shapes,* even when the shapes overlap. They presented overlapping outlines of shapes of fa-

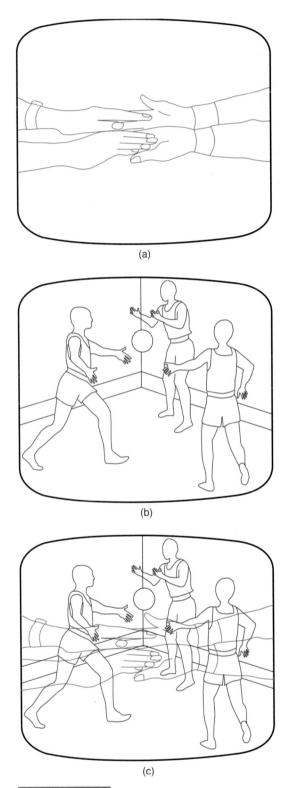

Figure 9.6

Drawings of the scenes from the videotapes in Neisser and Becklen's study. (a) The hand game. (b) The basketball game. (c) The two games superimposed.

(From Neisser, U., and Becklen, R. Cognitive Psychology, 1975, 7, 480–494. Reprinted with permission.)

miliar objects and meaningless forms, drawn in different colors (red and green). They asked the subjects to pay attention to only one of the colors. Afterward, on a recognition test, they showed the subjects all the forms they had seen. The subjects recognized only those shapes that they had been instructed to pay attention to. Even when the nonattended figures consisted of a familiar shape, they failed to recognize them. (See *Figure 9.7.*)

What happens to visual information that people do not pay attention to? Is it simply lost? As we saw in the section on attention to auditory stimuli, some processing of unattended auditory information does occur, and implicit memories can be established of sounds we do not consciously notice. The same can be said of unattended visual information. For example, Neisser (1969) asked subjects to read lines of text printed in black but to ignore the lines of text printed in red, which appeared just below each black line. Afterward, the subjects could remember nothing of the text printed in red, unless their own name appeared there—this they noticed and remembered. Apparently, our own name tends to jump out at us in print just as it shouts at us when presented acoustically to the unattended ear.

Brain Mechanisms of Selective Attention

As we saw, one possible explanation for selective attention is that some components of the brain's sensory system are temporarily sensitized, which enhances their ability to detect particular categories of stimuli. For example, if a person were watching for changes in shapes, colors, or movements (that is, if the person's attention were focused on one of these attributes), we might expect to see increased activity in the portions of the visual cortex devoted to the analysis of shapes, colors, or movements.

This result is exactly what Corbetta et al. (1991) found. These investigators had subjects look at a computerized display containing thirty colored rectangles, which could change in shape, color, or speed of movement. The subjects were

asked to say whether they detected a change. On some trials, the subjects were told to pay attention only to one attribute: shape, color, or speed of movement. The stimuli were counterbalanced so that the same set of displays were presented during each condition. Thus, the only difference between the conditions was the type of stimulus change the subjects were watching for.

The investigators used a PET scanner to measure brain activity while the subjects were watching the display. They found that paying attention to shape, color, or speed of movement caused activation of different regions of the visual association cortex. The locations corresponded almost precisely to the regions other studies have shown to be activated by shapes, colors, or movements. Thus, selective attention toward different attributes of visual stimuli is accompanied by activation of the appropriate regions of the visual association cortex. (See *Figure 9.8.*)

Luck et al. (1993) obtained similar results in a study using monkeys. They recorded the activity of single neurons in the visual association cortex. When a cue indicated that the monkey should be watching for a stimulus to be presented in a particular location, neurons that received input from the appropriate part of the visual field began firing more rapidly, even before the stimulus was presented. These neurons seemed to be "primed" for detecting a stimulus in their part of the visual field.

Biology and Culture

Control of Consciousness

A craving for at least occasional changes in consciousness seems to be a widespread trait among members of our species. Every culture has its means for altering consciousness—even children enjoy spinning around to make themselves dizzy. Some means of altering consciousness have become commonplace, such as the ingestion of coffee, tea, alcohol, or tobacco. Many people use drugs that our society has outlawed, such as marijuana or cocaine. The expectations and customs of a society substantially influence the effects that drugs have on a person's consciousness. For example, when coffee drinking was associated with religious rituals long ago, it undoubtedly caused a much more striking change in consciousness than it does now when it is dispensed into a paper cup from the local vending machine. Similarly, when smoking tobacco was a part of Native American rites, it almost certainly induced a greater change in consciousness than it does in the average cigarette smoker today.

The urge to alter, expand, or even escape from one's consciousness does not require the use of drugs. Since the beginning of history, people have developed ways to change their consciousnesses by means of self-control.

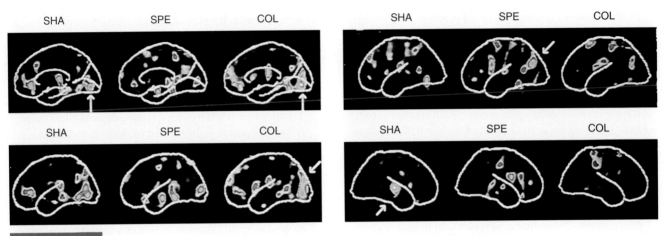

Figure 9.8

PET scans of visual selective attention. The arrows indicate regions of the brain that were activated the most. The three-letter abbreviations above each scan indicate the stimulus dimension to which the person was paying attention. Abbreviations: SHA = shape; SPE = speed of movement; COL = color.
(From Corbetta, M., Miezin, F.M., Dobmeyer, S., Shulman, G.L., and Petersen, S.E. Journal of Neuroscience, 1991, 11, 2383–2402.)

For example, the ancient Hebrews and early Christians often fasted for many days, undoubtedly because of the effects that their altered metabolism had on their consciousnesses. In earlier times, there was also much more emphasis on ritualized chants and movements, such as those of the early Jewish Hasidim and Cabalists. In fact, the Christian Pentecostal sect and the Jewish Hasidic sects today practice dances and chanting that would not seem strange to thirteenth-century mystics, and these rituals encourage the "taking over" of one's consciousness.

The one function that all methods of changing consciousness have in common is an alteration in *attention*. The various exercises can be divided into those that withdraw attention from the stimuli around us and those that increase attention to events that have become so commonplace that we no longer notice them—including our own behaviors that have become automatic and relatively nonconscious. We refer to exercises in both categories as *meditation*. Forms of meditation have developed in almost every culture. Zen Buddhism, Yoga, Sufism, and Taoism are best known and most influential in Eastern societies, where they first developed, but there is also a tradition of meditation and contemplation in the Western world, still carried on by the Christian monasteries. Even the ritualized recitation of the Rosary and the clicking of the beads serve to focus a person's attention on the prayer he or she is chanting.

■ Techniques for Withdrawing Attention

The goal of most meditation exercises is to remove attention from all sensory stimuli—to think of absolutely nothing. The various techniques require that the meditator direct his or her attention to a single object (such as a specially prepared symbol), to a spoken or imagined word or phrase (such as a prayer or mantra), to a monotonous sound (such as the rushing of a waterfall), or to a repetitive movement (such as breathing or touching the tips of each of the four fingers with the thumb). A Tibetan monk might say, "*Om mani padme hum*"; a Christian monk might say, "Lord Jesus Christ, have mercy on me"; and a Sufi might say, "*La illa ill' Allahu.*" Although the theologies are different, the basic effect of all the chants is the same.

By concentrating on an object, a sound, or a repetitive movement, we can learn to ignore other stimuli. We achieve this kind of focus to some degree when we read a

Different cultures have discovered different ways to alter their consciousness through meditating or engaging in repetitive movements. These Islamic Dervish monks, members of the Mevlevi sect (often called Whirling Dervishes*) are participating in a dance in which spinning facilitates a trance-like state that connects them with Allah.*

book intently or attempt to solve a problem. The difference is that the book or problem supplies a changing form of stimulation. Thoughts, words, images, and ideas flow through our minds. In contrast, a person attempting to achieve a meditative trance selects an inherently static object of attention that leads to habituation. By concentrating on this unchanging source of information, continually bringing his or her attention back to it, the person achieves a state of utter concentration on *nothing*.

Withdrawal of attention appears to have two primary goals: to reduce verbal control over nonverbal functions of the brain and to produce afterward a "rebound phenomenon"—a heightening of awareness and an increase in attention. The second goal is identical to that of consciousness-increasing exercises.

■ Techniques for Increasing and Dishabituating Consciousness

Habituation to most stimuli in our environment enables us to concentrate on those stimuli that are important to our survival. For instance, I can remember very little about showering, shaving, and dressing this morning or about driving back and forth between my home and office. When driving along a highway I do not concentrate on the position of my hands on the steering wheel, its texture under my fingers, or the road vibrations transmitted through my body. Neither do I notice the shape of the windshield, the color of the hood, the outline of the guardrails as I go past them, or any of the myriad other

Doing something dangerous heightens self-awareness and awareness of one's surroundings.

stimuli to which I could attend. Sometimes I drive over a very familiar route and suddenly arrive at my destination without being able to remember anything about the journey, or at least large parts of it. Obviously, I did all the right things, because I got there, but for all I can remember about the trip, I may as well have been unconscious. My attention is left free for noticing dangers that I must either respond to or be injured by. The relative infrequency of automobile accidents attests to the efficiency of our attentional mechanisms in monitoring the information that we must process in order to survive.

However, given our awareness that we all must grow older and eventually die, habituation to everything around us would prevent us from making the most of life. The beautiful things and special moments may not contain stimuli that are important to our survival, but they are certainly important to the enjoyment of life. Techniques for increasing awareness help reduce habituation.

The easiest way to reduce habituation and automatic functioning is to encounter novel stimuli. If we go to new places and have new experiences, we are more likely to be aware of what is going on around us. Moreover, there is a worthwhile side effect: When we return home, many of the old stimuli seem fresh and new again, at least for a while. We recover from some of our habituation.

Another way to notice things is to do them differently. Many ancient traditions suggest doing routine tasks in a different order or with the unaccustomed hand and making oneself concentrate on just what happens. By analyzing the details of the habituated stimuli, we force them into consciousness. For example, if this morning I had shaved before showering, tried to hold my toothbrush in my left hand, and had put the left pant leg on before the right, I might have remembered more details of the start of my day.

Doing something dangerous, or at least something that places great demands on skill and coordination, can also heighten awareness by presenting unexpected stimuli to which we must react. Activities such as driving a car too fast, rock climbing, skiing, and hang gliding require us to be aware of what is going on around us and to remain vigilant at all times. Many people report that they never feel so "alive" as when they are in danger.

Finally, as I mentioned earlier, a very effective means of increasing our attention to the world around us is to remove ourselves from it temporarily. Almost all the meditative traditions, new and old, stress that the world appears to be more real after a period of withdrawal of attention from it. This heightened awareness undoubtedly occurs because attentional mechanisms, which have been suppressed by concentration on an unchanging stimulus, now "rebound," and we notice much more than we previously did.

Interim Summary

Attention

As we saw in the first section of this chapter, consciousness can be analyzed as a social phenomenon derived through evolution of the brain mechanisms responsible for our ability to communicate with each other (and, in addition, with ourselves). However, because our verbal mechanisms can contain only a limited amount of information at one time, we cannot be conscious of all the events that take place in our environment. The process of selective attention determines which stimuli will be noticed and which will be ignored. The factors that control our attention include novelty, verbal instructions, and our own assessment of the significance of what we are perceiving.

Dichotic listening experiments show that what is received by the unattended ear is lost within a few seconds unless something causes us to take heed of it; after those few seconds we cannot say what that ear heard. However, the study using the classically conditioned response to the electrical shock indicates that even unattended information can produce implicit (as opposed to explicit) memories.

Studies using visually presented information indicate that attention can focus on location or on shape: We can pay attention to particular objects or to stimuli that occur in a particular place. A PET study found that when people pay attention to particular characteristics of visual stimuli, the activity of particular regions of the brain is enhanced.

Techniques of meditation have been used since the beginning of history and include methods for increasing or decreasing attention to the external world. In meditative techniques, a person pays strict attention to a simple stimulus such as a visual pattern, a word, or a monotonous, repetitive movement. As the response to the repeated stimulus habituates, the person is left with a relatively empty consciousness. The withdrawal of attention causes a rebound that leads the practitioner to look at his or her surroundings with revitalized awareness.

Thought Questions

- Have you ever had an experience similar to the one I described in this section, in which someone asks you a question that you weren't paying attention to, and then, before it could be repeated, you realize what it was? How long do you think the unattended information lasts before it is eventually lost? Can you think of an experiment that would permit you to find out?
- Let's reconsider the cocktail-party phenomenon. Suppose that someone is carrying on a conversation and then happens to overhear a word or two from another conversation that seems much more interesting than the present one. Wanting to be polite, the person tries to ignore the other conversation, but finds it difficult. Should we regard this example as a failure of the person's attentional mechanism, or is it actually useful that we usually don't become so absorbed in one thing that we miss out on potentially interesting information?
- Why do we feel that paying attention to something not very interesting takes some effort—that it requires work? And if we concentrate on something for a long time, we feel tired. Where does this tiredness take place? Do some circuits of neurons become "weary"? Why, then, do we not become tired when we are concentrating just as hard on something that interests us?

Consciousness and the Brain

As we have already seen, brain damage can alter human consciousness. For example, Chapter 8 described the phenomenon of anterograde amnesia, caused by brain damage—particularly, to the hippocampus. Although people with this defect cannot form new verbal memories, they can learn some kinds of tasks. However, they remain unaware that they have learned something, even when their behavior indicates that they have. The brain damage does not prevent all kinds of learning, but it does prevent conscious awareness of what has been learned.

If human consciousness is related to speech, then it is probably related to the brain mechanisms that control comprehension and production of speech. This hypothesis suggests that for us to be aware of a piece of information, the information must be transmitted to neural circuits in the brain responsible for our communicative behavior. Several reports of cases of human brain damage support this suggestion.

Isolation Aphasia: A Case of Global Unawareness

Geschwind, Quadfasel, and Segarra (1968) described the case of a woman who had suffered severe brain damage from inhaling carbon monoxide from a faulty water heater. The damage spared the primary auditory cortex, the speech areas of the brain, and the connections between these areas. However, the damage destroyed large parts of the visual association cortex and isolated the speech mechanisms from other parts of the brain. In fact, the syndrome they reported is referred to as **isolation aphasia,** a language disturbance that includes an inability to comprehend speech or to produce

isolation aphasia A language disturbance that includes an inability to comprehend speech or to produce meaningful speech without affecting the ability to repeat speech and to learn new sequences of words; caused by brain damage that isolates the brain's speech mechanisms from other parts of the brain.

meaningful speech, but also an ability to repeat speech and to learn new sequences of words. Thus, although the woman's brain's speech mechanisms could receive auditory input and could control the muscles used for speech, they received no information from the other senses or from the neural circuits that contain memories concerning past experiences and the meanings of words.

The woman remained in the hospital for nine years, until she died. During this time, she made few movements except with her eyes, which were able to follow moving objects. She gave no evidence of recognizing objects or people in her environment. She did not spontaneously say anything, answer questions, or give any signs that she understood what other people said to her. By all available criteria, she was not conscious of anything that was going on. However, the woman could *repeat* words that were spoken to her. And if someone started a poem she knew, she would finish it. For example, if someone said, "Roses are red, violets are blue," she would respond, "Sugar is sweet, and so are you." She even learned new poems and songs and would sing along with the radio. Her case suggests that consciousness is not simply activity of the brain's speech mechanisms; it is activity prompted by information received from other parts of the brain concerning memories or events presently occurring in the environment.

Visual Agnosia: Lack of Awareness of Visual Perceptions

The case I just described was of a woman who appeared to have completely lost her awareness of herself and her environment. In other instances, people have become unaware of particular kinds of information. For example, as we saw in the opening vignette of this chapter, people with a particular kind of blindness caused by brain damage can point to objects that they cannot see—or rather, that they are not aware of seeing. Two colleagues and I studied a young man with a different kind of disconnection between perception and awareness. His brain had been damaged by an inflammation of the blood vessels and he consequently suffered from **visual agnosia,** the inability to recognize the identity of an object visually (Margolin, Friedrich, and Carlson, 1985). The man had great difficulty identifying common objects by sight. For example, he could not say what a hammer was by looking at it, but he quickly identified it when he was permitted to pick it up and feel it. He was not blind; he could walk around without bumping into things, and he had no trouble making visually guided movements to pick up an object that he wanted to identify. The simplest conclusion was that his disease had damaged the neural circuits responsible for visual perception.

However, the simplest conclusion was not the correct one. Although the patient had great difficulty visually recog-

visual agnosia   The inability of a person who is not blind to recognize the identity of an object visually; caused by damage to the visual association cortex.

nizing objects or pictures of objects, he often made hand movements that appeared to be related to the object he could not identify. For example, when we showed him a picture of a pistol, he stared at it with a puzzled look, then shook his head and said that he couldn't tell what it was. While continuing to study the picture, he clenched his right hand into a fist and began making movements with his index finger. When we asked him what he was doing, he looked at his hand, made a few tentative movements with his finger, then raised his hand in the air and moved it forward each time he moved his finger. He was unmistakably miming the way a person holds and fires a pistol. "Oh!" he said. "It's a gun. No, a pistol." Clearly, he was not aware what the picture was until he paid attention to what his hand was doing. On another occasion, he looked at a picture of a belt and said it was a pair of pants. We asked him to show us where the legs and other parts of the pants were. When he tried to do so, he became puzzled. His hands went to the place where his belt buckle would be (he was wearing hospital pajamas) and moved as if he were feeling one. "No," he said. "It's not a pair of pants—it's a belt!"

The patient's visual system was not normal, yet it functioned better than we could infer from only his verbal behavior. That is, his perceptions were much more accurate than his words indicated. The fact that he could mime the use of a pistol or feel an imaginary belt buckle with his hands indicated that his visual system worked well enough to initiate appropriate nonverbal behaviors, though not the appropriate words. Once he felt what he was doing, he could name the object. The process might involve steps such as those shown in *Figure 9.9.*

Although the patient had lost his ability to read, speech therapists were able to teach him to use finger spelling to read. He could not say what a particular letter was, but he could learn to make a particular hand movement when he saw it. After he had learned the finger-spelling alphabet used by deaf people, he could read slowly and laboriously by making hand movements for each letter and feeling the words that his hand was spelling out.

This case supports the conclusion that consciousness is synonymous with a person's ability to talk about his or her perceptions or memories. In this particular situation, disruption of the normal interchange between the visual perceptual system and the verbal system prevented the patient from being directly aware of his own visual perceptions. Instead, it was as if his hands talked to him, telling him what he had just seen.

The Split-Brain Syndrome

One surgical procedure demonstrates dramatically how various brain functions can be disconnected from each other and from verbal mechanisms. It is used for people who have severe epilepsy that cannot be controlled by drugs. In these people, violent storms of neural activity begin in one hemisphere and are transmitted to the other by the corpus callo-

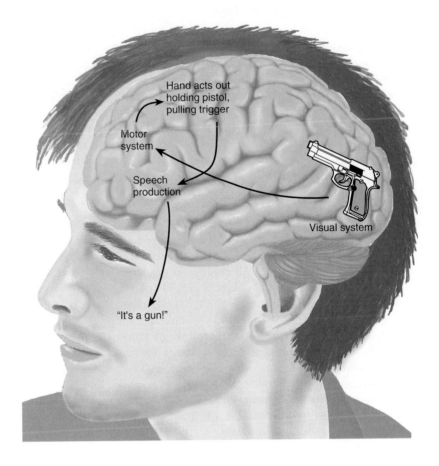

Figure 9.9

Hypothetical exchanges of information within the brain of a patient with visual agnosia.

sum, the large bundle of axons that connect corresponding parts of the cortex on one side of the brain with those on the other. Both sides of the brain then engage in wild neural firing and stimulate each other, causing an epileptic seizure. These seizures can occur many times each day, preventing the patient from leading a normal life. Neurosurgeons discovered that the **split-brain operation**—cutting the corpus callosum to disconnect the two cerebral hemispheres—greatly reduces the frequency of the epileptic seizures. (See *Figure 9.10.*)

Sperry (1966) and Gazzaniga and his associates (Gazzaniga, 1970; Gazzaniga and LeDoux, 1978) have studied split-brain patients extensively. Normally, the cerebral cortex of the left and right hemispheres exchange information through the corpus callosum. With one exception (described later), each hemisphere receives sensory information from the opposite side of the body and controls muscular movements on that side. The corpus callosum permits these activities to be coordinated, so that each hemisphere knows what is going on in the other hemisphere. After the two hemispheres are disconnected, they operate independently; their sensory mechanisms, memories, and motor systems can no longer exchange

split-brain operation A surgical procedure that severs the corpus callosum, thus abolishing the direct connections between the cortex of the two cerebral hemispheres.

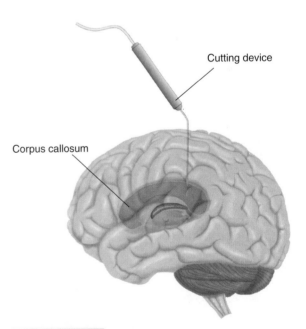

Figure 9.10

The split-brain operation. Holes are drilled in the top of the skull and a cutting device is introduced between the left and right cerebral hemispheres, severing the corpus callosum.

information. The effects of these disconnections are not obvious to a casual observer, for the simple reason that only one hemisphere—in most people, the left—controls speech. The right hemisphere of an epileptic person with a split brain can understand speech reasonably well, but it is poor at reading and spelling. And because Broca's speech area is located in the left hemisphere, the right hemisphere is totally incapable of producing speech.

Because only one side of the brain can talk about what it is experiencing, a casual observer will not detect the independent operations of the right side of a split brain. Even the patient's left brain has to learn about the independent existence of the right brain. One of the first things that these patients say they notice after the operation is that their left hand seems to have a mind of its own. For example, patients may find themselves putting down a book held in the left hand, even if they are reading it with great interest. At other times, they surprise themselves by making obscene gestures with the left hand. Because the right hemisphere controls the movements of the left hand, these unexpected movements puzzle the left hemisphere, the side of the brain that controls speech.

One exception to the crossed representation of sensory information is the olfactory system. When a person sniffs a flower through the left nostril, only the left brain receives a sensation of the odor. Thus, if the right nostril of a patient with a split brain is closed and the left nostril is open, the patient will accurately identify odors verbally. If the odor enters the right nostril, the patient will say that he or she smells nothing. But, in fact, the right brain has perceived the odor and can identify it. This ability is demonstrated by an experiment in which the patient is told to reach for some objects hidden from view by a partition. If asked to use the left hand, with the left nostril closed, he or she will select the object that corresponds to the odor—a plastic flower for a floral odor, a toy fish for a fishy odor, a model tree for the odor of pine, and so forth. But if the left nostril is closed, the right hand fails this test, because it is connected to the left hemisphere, which did not smell the odor. (See *Figure 9.11.*)

Sometimes, the hands conflict and attempt to do different things—or even to fight one another. One study even reported that a man with a split brain attempted to beat his wife with one hand and protect her with the other. Did he *really* want to hurt her? Yes and no, I guess.

As we saw in Chapter 4, the left hemisphere, besides giving us the ability to read, write, and speak, is good at other tasks that require verbal abilities, such as mathematics and logic. The right hemisphere excels at tasks of perception and has a much greater artistic ability. If a patient with a split brain tries to use his or her right hand to arrange blocks to duplicate a geometrical design provided by the experimenter, the hand will hopelessly fumble around with the blocks. Often, the left hand (controlled by the right hemisphere) will brush the right hand aside and easily complete the task. It is as if the right hemisphere gets impatient with the clumsy ineptitude of the hand controlled by the left hemisphere.

The effects of cutting the corpus callosum reinforce the conclusion that consciousness depends on the ability of speech mechanisms in the left hemisphere to receive infor-

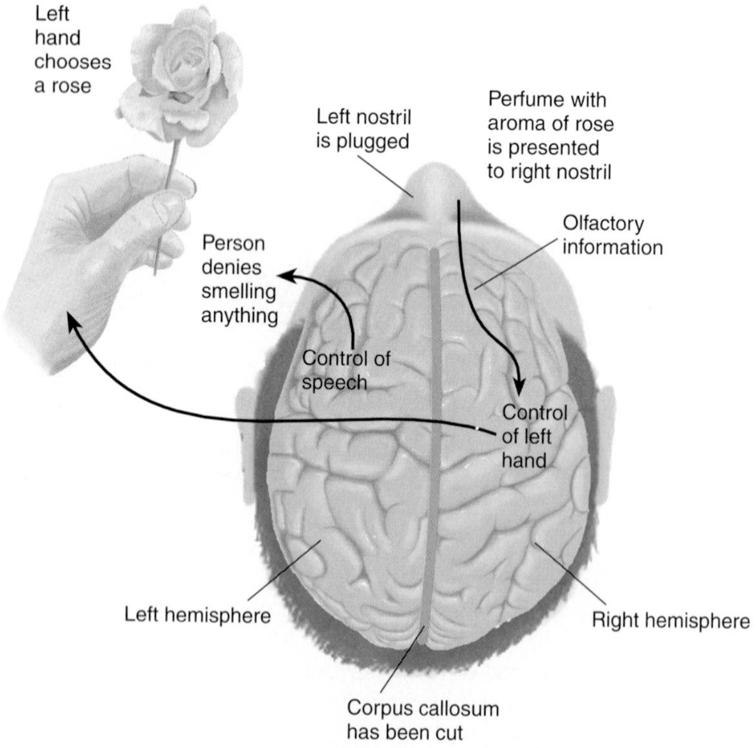

Figure 9.11

Identification of an object by a person with a split brain in response to an olfactory stimulus.

Left hand chooses a rose

Left nostril is plugged

Perfume with aroma of rose is presented to right nostril

Olfactory information

Person denies smelling anything

Control of speech

Control of left hand

Left hemisphere

Right hemisphere

Corpus callosum has been cut

mation from other regions of the brain. If such communication is interrupted, then some kinds of information can never reach consciousness.

Interim Summary

Consciousness and the Brain

The suggestion that consciousness is a function of our ability to communicate with each other receives support from some cases of human brain damage. As we saw, people with blindsight can point to objects they say they cannot see; people with isolation aphasia can perceive speech and talk without apparent awareness; and a patient with a particular form of visual agnosia can make appropriate hand movements when looking at objects that cannot be consciously recognized. Thus, brain damage can disrupt a person's awareness of perceptual mechanisms without disrupting other functions performed by these mechanisms. And although a person whose corpus callosum has been severed can make perceptual judgments with the right hemisphere, he or she cannot talk about them and appears to be unaware of them.

Thought Questions

■ Some people with split brains have reported that they can use only one hand to hold a book while reading. If they use the other hand, they find themselves putting the book down even though they want to continue reading. Which hand puts the book down? Why does it do so?

■ When a stimulus is presented to the right hemisphere of a person with a split brain, the person (speaking with his or her left hemisphere) claims to be unaware of it. Thus, the left hemisphere is unaware of stimuli perceived only by the right hemisphere. Because the right hemisphere cannot talk to us, should we conclude that it lacks conscious self-awareness? If you think it *is* conscious, has the surgery produced two independent consciousnesses where only one previously existed?

Hypnosis

Hypnosis is a specific and unusual form of verbal control that apparently enables one person to control another person's behavior, thoughts, and perceptions. Under hypnosis, a person can be induced to bark like a dog, act like a baby, or tolerate being pierced with needles. Although these examples are interesting and amusing, hypnosis is important to psychology because it provides insights about the nature of consciousness and has applications in the fields of medicine and psychotherapy.

Hypnosis, or *mesmerism,* was discovered by Franz Anton Mesmer (1734–1815), an Austrian physician. He found that when he passed magnets back and forth over people's bodies (in an attempt to restore their "magnetic fluxes" and cure them of disease), they would often have convulsions and enter a trancelike state during which almost miraculous cures could be achieved. As Mesmer discovered later, the patients were not affected directly by the magnetism of the iron rods; they were responding to his undoubtedly persuasive and compelling personality. We now know that convulsions and trancelike states do not necessarily accompany hypnosis, and we also know that hypnosis does not cure physical illnesses. Mesmer's patients apparently had psychologically produced symptoms that were alleviated by suggestions made while they were hypnotized.

The Induction of Hypnosis

A person undergoing hypnosis can be alert, relaxed, tense, lying quietly, or exercising vigorously. There is no need to move an object in front of someone's face or to say "You are getting sleepy"; an enormous variety of techniques can be used to induce hypnosis in a susceptible person. The only essential feature seems to be the subject's understanding that he or she is to be hypnotized. Moss (1965) reported having sometimes simply said to a well-practiced subject, in a normal tone of voice, "Please sit in that chair and go into hypnosis," and the subject complied within a few seconds. Sometimes, this approach even worked on volunteers who had never been hypnotized before. (Of course, these people had some expectations about what the word *hypnosis* means; their behavior conformed to their expectations.)

Characteristics of Hypnosis

Hypnotized people are very suggestible; their behavior will conform with what the hypnotist says, even to the extent that they may appear to misperceive reality. Under hypnosis, people can be instructed to do things that they would not be ex-

Is a hypnotized person really under the control of the hypnotist, or is the person simply acting out a social role?

pected to do under normal conditions, such as acting out imaginary scenes or pretending to be an animal. Hypnotized people can be convinced that an arm cannot move or is insensitive to pain, and they then act as if that is the case; hypnosis can thus be used to induce paralysis or anesthesia. They can also be persuaded to have positive or negative hallucinations—to see things that are not there or *not* to see objects that *are* there.

One of the most dramatic phenomena of hypnosis is **posthypnotic suggestibility,** in which a person is given instructions under hypnosis and follows those instructions after returning to a nonhypnotized state. For example, a hypnotist might tell a man that he will become unbearably thirsty when he sees the hypnotist look at her watch. She might also admonish him not to remember anything upon leaving the hypnotic state, so that **posthypnotic amnesia** is also achieved. After leaving the hypnotic state, the man acts normally and professes ignorance of what he perceived and did during hypnosis, perhaps even apologizing for not having succumbed to hypnosis. The hypnotist later looks at her watch, and the man suddenly leaves the room to get a drink of water.

Studies indicate that when changes in perception are induced in hypnotized people, the changes occur not in the people's actual perceptions but in their verbal reports about their perceptions. For example, Miller, Hennessy, and Leibowitz (1973) used the *Ponzo illusion* to test the effects of hypnotically induced blindness. Although the two parallel horizontal lines in the left portion of Figure 9.12 are the same length, the top one looks longer than the bottom one. This effect is produced by the presence of the slanted lines to the left and right of the horizontal ones; if these lines are not present, the horizontal lines appear to be the same length. (See *Figure 9.12.*) Through hypnotic suggestion, the experimenters made the slanted lines "disappear." But even though the subjects reported that they could not see the slanted lines, they still perceived the upper line as being longer than the lower one. This result indicates that the visual system continues to process sensory information during hypnotically induced blindness; otherwise, the subjects would have perceived the lines as being equal in length. The reported blindness appears to occur not because of altered activity in the visual system but because of altered activity in the verbal system (and in consciousness).

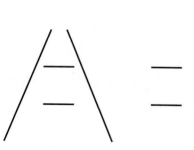

Figure 9.12

The Ponzo illusion and hypnotic blindness. The short horizontal lines are actually the same length. Even when a hypnotic suggestion made the slanted lines disappear, the visual system still perceived the illusion.

Hypnosis as a Social Role

Hypnosis has been called a special case of learning, a transference of the superego, a goal-directed behavior shaped by the hypnotist, a role-playing situation, and a restructuring of perceptual–cognitive functioning. In other words, no one yet knows exactly what it is. Hypnosis has been described as a state of enhanced suggestibility, but that is simply a description, not an explanation. Several investigators have advanced theories of hypnosis. I will discuss one that makes sense from an evolutionary standpoint.

All the behavioral and perceptual phenomena discussed so far in this book have obvious survival value for the organism; that is, functional analysis of a behavioral phenomenon usually points to a plausible reason for the occurrence of the behavior. Therefore, if hypnotic phenomena occurred only when a person was hypnotized, it would be difficult to understand why the brain happened to evolve in such a way that it is susceptible to hypnosis. Does it seem plausible that this susceptibility first manifested itself in the eighteenth century when Mesmer discovered the phenomenon of hypnosis? A theory of hypnosis by Barber (1979) indicates that at least some aspects of hypnosis are related to events that can happen every day.

Barber argues that hypnosis should not be viewed as a special state of consciousness, in the way that sleep is a state of consciousness that differs from waking; rather, the hypnotized person should be seen as acting out a social role. The phenomena of hypnosis are social behaviors, not manifestations of a special state of consciousness. Hypnotized people willingly join with the hypnotist in enacting a role expected of them. Some of the rules governing this role are supplied by the direct instructions of the hypnotist, others are indirectly implied by what the hypnotist says and does, and still others consist of expectations that the people already have about what hypnotized people do.

People's expectations about hypnosis do indeed play an important role in their behavior while under hypnosis. In lectures to two sections of an introductory psychology class, Orne (1959) told one section (falsely) that one of the most prominent features of hypnosis was rigidity of the preferred (that is, dominant) hand. Later, he arranged a demonstration of hypnosis during a meeting of students from both sections. Several of the students who had heard that the dominant hand became rigid showed this phenomenon when hypnotized, but none of the students who had not heard this myth developed a rigid hand. Similarly, if people become willing to follow a hypnotist's suggestions, perhaps they do so because

posthypnotic suggestibility   The tendency of a person to perform a behavior suggested by the hypnotist some time after the person has left the hypnotic state.

posthypnotic amnesia   A failure to remember what occurred during hypnosis; induced by suggestions made during hypnosis.

they believe that this suggested behavior is what is supposed to happen. Perhaps people willingly follow a hypnotist's suggestion to do something silly (such as bark like a dog) because they know that hypnotized people are not responsible for their behavior.

If hypnosis can be described as role playing, then why are so many people willing to play this role? Barber (1975) submits that the suspension of self-control that occurs during hypnosis is very similar to our "participation" in the story of a movie or novel. When we go to a movie or read a book, we generally do so with the intent of becoming swept up in the story. We willingly let the filmmaker or author lead us through a fantasy. When we hear a story or read a book, we even imagine the scenes and the events that occur in them. We feel happy when good things happen to characters that we identify with and like, and we feel sad when bad things happen to them. Certainly, we express a full range of emotions while watching a good movie or reading a good book. In fact, one of the criteria we use to judge a movie or book is whether it causes us to enter this fantasy world; if it does not, we regard the work as a poor one. Perhaps these imagined events are similar to the hallucinations experienced during hypnosis.

The proposal that hypnosis is related to our ability to participate vicariously in a story provides at least a starting point for a functional explanation. One of the ways that we can affect other people's behavior verbally is to get them to imagine themselves in our place; this phenomenon is called *empathy*. It is easier to obtain assistance from others if they can imagine themselves in our place and thus see how important their help is to our well-being. Surely, the ability to think about another person's situation empathetically facilitates cooperation and assistance. Perhaps our moral codes owe their existence at least partly to this phenomenon.

Many hypnotic phenomena are striking and would seem impossible to achieve without hypnosis. However, researchers have successfully demonstrated all of them without hypnosis. If people are given carefully worded instructions that strongly motivate them to cooperate with the experimenter, they can learn to ignore painful stimuli, act as if they were children, imagine themselves seeing nonexistent objects, fail to remember lists of words they have just read, and so on. The essential difference is that they realize that they are pretending, whereas hypnotized people generally believe that their behavior is involuntary.

Susceptibility to Hypnosis

Not everyone can be hypnotized. In fact, the ability to be hypnotized appears to be a stable trait; if a person can be hypnotized on one occasion, he or she probably can be hypnotized on another. However, attempts to relate personality traits to hypnotic susceptibility have yielded few definitive results. Susceptibility does not appear to be related strongly to any particular personality type (Hilgard, 1979). What does appear to be related to susceptibility to hypnosis is the ability to

produce vivid mental images, a high capacity for becoming involved in imaginative activities, and a rich, vivid imagination (Kihlstrom, 1985). You can readily see that such people would be likely to participate vicariously in a story.

As we saw in Chapter 4, the left hemisphere is more involved in sequential tasks, including verbal tasks, and the right hemisphere is more involved in simultaneous tasks, including picture perception and perception of space. In addition, several studies have indicated that the right hemisphere is more involved in social interactions (Kolb and Whishaw, 1990). There are some hints that hypnosis may be related to the functions of the right hemisphere. For example, Sackheim, Paulus, and Weiman (1979) found that students who are easily hypnotized tend to sit on the right side of the classroom. In this position, they see most of the front of the room with their right hemispheres, so perhaps their choice represents a preference for right-hemisphere involvement in perceptual tasks. This preference may represent a generally increased sensitivity to social roles, including those involved in hypnosis. I hasten to add that this hypothesis is speculative and may very well be wrong, but at least it points the way to some hypotheses that can be tested experimentally.

Evaluating Scientific Issues

Can Hypnosis Cause Antisocial Behavior?

Dramatic demonstrations of the apparent power that a hypnotist exerts over a hypnotized person have led some observers to conclude that people can be induced to commit antisocial acts—even crimes—while under hypnosis. Others assert quite the contrary: that people will never perform an act while hypnotized that violates their moral codes. Who is right? How much freedom of action does a hypnotized person have while following the suggestions of the hypnotist?

■ Evidence for Hypnotic Coercion

Toward the end of the nineteenth century, several experiments suggested that a hypnotized person can indeed be coerced into doing something dangerous or immoral. However, as Laurence and Perry (1988) note, the experiments are not very convincing, because the "harm" that the subjects caused was symbolic rather than real. A neurologist, Giles de la Tourette, gave a hypnotized woman a ruler, saying that it was in fact a pistol (Ladame, 1887). He implanted the posthypnotic suggestion that the next time she saw a certain person, she would shoot him. The victim then entered the room, and the woman "shot him." He fell to the floor, shouting, "I am dead." Another person was told that a piece of chalk was really a knife and that a door was a person. The subject willingly stabbed the door—that is, the person—to death (Liégois, 1889).

Although many people believe that hypnosis enables one to do things he or she would not otherwise do, no reliable evidence supports this belief.

More recent experiments have induced subjects to perform much more convincing dangerous acts or acts of violence. For example, Rowland (1939) placed an agitated rattlesnake in a box and asked hypnotized subjects to reach inside and pick it up. Three of the four subjects tried to do so, banging their hands against an invisible sheet of glass that protected the front of the box; the fourth subject came out of hypnosis and refused to reach for the snake. The investigator also ordered two of the subjects to throw some sulfuric acid at him, and they did so. Of course, he was protected by another invisible sheet of glass. Rowland concluded that "persons in deep hypnosis will allow themselves to be exposed to unreasonably dangerous situations" and "will perform acts unreasonably dangerous to others" (p. 117).

Some reports of unethical use of hypnosis outside the laboratory provide further evidence for hypnotic coercion. For example, Kline (1972) reported the case of a physician who successfully used hypnosis to seduce some of his female patients. He hypnotized them repeatedly, establishing a close personal relationship and gradually introducing erotic suggestions. Several of his patients complied with his suggestions and had sexual relations with him. He was eventually caught when a patient who served as his unpaid assistant and mistress began talking about their sexual episodes in her sleep. Her husband made tape recordings of her descriptions and prosecuted the physician.

■ **Evaluating the Evidence for Hypnotic Coercion**
The studies (and the case of seduction) I just cited may seem convincing, but we cannot necessarily conclude from them that a person may be coerced through hypnosis into doing something that he or she would not otherwise do. To begin with, how can we be sure that the people really perceive the act they are being asked to commit as dangerous? After all, they know that they are participating in an experiment being carried out by a

respected scientist. Would that person really expose them to the danger of a rattlesnake bite or let himself receive a faceful of sulfuric acid? As Orne and Evans (1965) said about experiments like the one by Rowland (1939):

> If these actions are to be designated as antisocial or self-destructive it must be shown that they are perceived as such by subjects.... A subject is aware of certain realities imposed by the experimental situation. It is as clear to a subject as it is to any scientist that no reputable investigator can risk injuring a subject during the course of an experiment.... Consequently, any requested behavior which appears to a subject to be dangerous at face value may be reinterpreted in the context of a laboratory situation. (Orne and Evans, 1965, p. 191)

Orne and Evans performed an improved version of the experiment by Rowland. They told hypnotized subjects to put their hand into a beaker of fuming concentrated nitric acid and pick up a coin that had just been placed there. In fact, the beaker *really did* contain concentrated nitric acid. As soon as a subject put his or her hand into the acid, the experimenter grabbed it and submerged it in a basin of soapy lukewarm water, which washed off the acid before any harm could be done. (Before beginning the experiment, Orne practiced this "rescue operation" to be sure that the subjects would not get hurt. Nevertheless, I doubt that most review boards would permit such an experiment today.)

All five subjects complied with the experimenters' request. But did they really *perceive* this act as dangerous? As the experimenters found out, they did not. When they were questioned afterward, they said that "they were quite convinced that they would not be harmed because the context was an experimental one, presumably being conducted by responsible experimenters. All subjects appeared to assume that some form of safety precautions had been taken during the experiment" (Orne and Evans, 1965, p. 199). And they were absolutely right; that is precisely what the experimenters had done.

Orne and Evans's experiment also contained two unhypnotized control groups. The subjects in one group were asked to pretend that they were hypnotized. All five subjects in this group reached into the beaker of acid for the coin. Subjects in another group were given no instructions concerning hypnosis but were simply asked to perform the task. *All five of them complied!* Thus, even though the task would seem to be convincingly dangerous, the subjects told themselves that it could not possibly be dangerous and did what the experimenters told them to. (As we saw in Chapter 2, subjects are not passive participants in experiments; what they do often depends on how they interpret the situation.)

But suppose that an experimenter could arrange a situation that convinced subjects that they were being asked to perform an act that was truly antisocial or dangerous. Would hypnosis compel them to do so? Milgram (1963, 1974) instructed subjects to press a button that supposedly delivered an electric shock to a "trainee" (hidden behind a wall) whenever he made a wrong answer in a learning task. (In fact, the "trainee" never received a shock.) As noises, pleas, and finally screams came through the wall, most of the subjects continued to press the button under the instructions of the experimenter. Even after silence suggested that the "trainee" had died, an overwhelming majority of the subjects continued to push the button while the experimenter turned up the voltage, demanding through the intercom that the apparently dead "trainee" respond.

Most of the button-pushing subjects actually were convinced that they were delivering shocks to the poor "trainee." They were upset and distressed by the "trainee's" cries. Some of them tried to stop the experiment, but they continued when the experimenter said that they had to go on. This experiment would seem to be a good demonstration of the power of hypnosis—except for the fact that none of the subjects were hypnotized. (The experiment is described in more detail in Chapter 15.)

Results such as these show why it is imperative that appropriate control groups be used in any experiment that attempts to determine whether hypnosis can induce people to commit antisocial acts. Even if hypnotized people perform acts that they believe to be antisocial or dangerous, how can we be sure that they would not have performed them *without* being hypnotized? An experiment by Coe, Kobayashi, and Howard (1973) found that several unhypnotized subjects were quite willing to become involved in a scheme to sell heroin. One subject later revealed that he had planned to attack a confederate of the experimenters (someone hired to play a role in the study) and steal the money involved in the transaction. Clearly, if people commit an antisocial act when hypnotized, we cannot conclude that they did so *because* they were hypnotized unless the members of the control group fail to do so. And in the experiment by Coe et al., this was not the case.

What about the use of hypnosis for seduction? Again, without a control group, we cannot conclude that hypnosis was necessary. For example, how can we be sure that the physician described by Kline (1972) would not have managed to seduce some women without hypnotizing them? After all, most seductions do not involve hypnosis.

■ **What Can We Conclude?**

I think it is unlikely that any experiment that follows proper ethical guidelines will be able to tell us whether hypnosis can be used to induce people to perform acts that violate their moral codes. First, the context of the experimental setting is a rather good guarantee that the subject will be protected from harm and prevented from harming another person. Second, it is difficult to determine just what a person's moral code is. Sometimes, people surprise us by their willingness to perform antisocial acts. And even if they believe that an act is harmful to someone else and that performing the act would violate

their own moral code, they may tell themselves that whatever they do, it will be the experimenter's fault—and thus perform the act anyway. What they tell themselves will, of course, be absolutely correct. Suppose that an experimenter instructs a subject to do something that would seem to harm someone else. The subject complies, something goes wrong, and the other person really is hurt. Who is to blame? Obviously, it is the experimenter, not the subject.

The issue of hypnosis and antisocial behavior is an interesting one, but it will probably never be resolved. Even the scientific method cannot provide answers to every question we ask.

Uses of Hypnosis

Hypnosis can play a useful role in medicine, dentistry, and psychotherapy. The analgesia (insensitivity to pain) produced by hypnosis is more effective than that produced by morphine, tranquilizers such as Valium, or acupuncture (Stern et al., 1977). Thus, it can be used to suppress the pain of childbirth or of having one's teeth drilled or to prevent gagging when a dentist is working in a patient's mouth. It is also useful in reducing the nausea caused by the drugs used in chemotherapy for cancer. However, because not all people can be hypnotized, and because the induction of hypnosis takes some time, few physicians or dentists use hypnosis to reduce pain—drugs are easier to administer. Hypnosis can also be used to help people break a bad habit such as smoking. As we have seen, hypnosis is a useful tool for research into human consciousness. Finally, hypnosis is often used in psychotherapy to help patients discuss painful memories whose inaccessibility is impeding progress.

Reputable societies such as the American Medical Association and the American Psychological Association are opposed to the use of hypnosis for memory enhancement in criminal investigations. As we saw in the "Evaluating Scientific Issues" section of Chapter 8, hypnotic suggestions can alter people's memories or establish entirely new ones—which would render a witness's testimony invalid. But this characteristic of hypnosis has been exploited by clinicians to help their clients overcome the long-term effects of painful memories, such as those responsible for phobias (Baker, 1990). The therapist hypnotizes the client and has the client imagine the time and setting in which the traumatic event occurred. Then the therapist describes a different, more pleasant episode and suggests that the client will now remember the event differently. When this method successfully changes client's memories, they often find that their phobias are eliminated.

Interim Summary

Hypnosis

Hypnosis is a form of verbal control over a person's consciousness in which the hypnotist's suggestions affect some of the person's perceptions and behaviors. Although some people have viewed hypnosis as a mysterious, trancelike state, investigations have shown it to be similar to many phenomena of normal consciousness. There is no single way to induce hypnosis, and the responses depend very much on what the hypnotist says.

Barber asserts that being hypnotized is similar to participating vicariously in a narrative, which is something we do whenever we become engrossed in a novel, a movie, a drama, or even the recounting of a friend's experience. When we are engrossed in this way, we experience genuine feelings of emotion, even though the situation is not "real."

Although researchers have devised some ingenious experiments, we still do not know whether hypnosis can induce people to perform behaviors that they would not otherwise perform. For one thing, they will almost always assume that the experimenter has taken steps to protect them and prevent them from harming someone else. For another, many *unhypnotized* people perform what would appear to be antisocial acts; thus, the compliance rate is usually quite similar in experimental and control groups. Finally, even people who would not normally perform antisocial or distasteful acts may do so because they (correctly) assume that the experimenter is responsible for what they do.

Whatever its causes, hypnosis has been shown to be useful in reducing pain, eliminating bad habits, and helping people talk about painful thoughts and memories. However, as we saw in Chapter 8, most investigators distrust the use of hypnosis to refresh the memories of witnesses of crimes.

Thought Questions

- People with autism appear to lack the ability to empathize with others. In fact, they seem not to comprehend that other people have their own mental lives and consciousness. Do you think that autistic people can be hypnotized? If not, why not?
- Some people prefer explanations that demystify puzzling phenomena such as hypnosis. Others resist such explanations; for them, an interesting phenomenon is spoiled by an explanation that places it in the realm of physics and biology. How do you feel about these two viewpoints?

Sleep

Sleep is not a state of unconsciousness. It is a state of *altered* consciousness. During sleep, we have dreams that can be just as vivid as waking experiences, and yet we forget most of them as soon as they are over. Our amnesia leads us to think—incorrectly—that we were unconscious while we were asleep. In fact, there are two distinct kinds of sleep—and thus, two states of altered consciousness.

We spend approximately one-third of our lives sleeping—or trying to. You may therefore think that the reason we sleep is clearly understood by scientists who study this phenomenon. And yet, despite the efforts of many talented researchers, we are still not sure why we sleep. Many people are preoccupied with sleep or with the lack of it. Collectively, they consume tons of drugs each year in an attempt to get to sleep. Advertisements for nonprescription sleep medications imply that a night without a full eight hours of sleep is a physiological and psychological disaster. Is this worry justified? Does missing a few hours—or even a full night—of sleep actually harm us? As we will see, the answer seems to be no.

The Stages of Sleep

Sleep is not uniform. We can sleep lightly or deeply; we can be restless or still; we can have vivid dreams, or our consciousness can be relatively blank. Researchers who have studied sleep have found that its stages usually follow an orderly, predictable sequence.

Most sleep research takes place in sleep laboratories. Because a person's sleep is affected by his or her surroundings, a sleep laboratory contains one or more small bedrooms, furnished and decorated to be as homelike and comfortable as possible. The most important apparatus of the sleep laboratory is the **polygraph,** a machine located in a separate room that records on paper the output of various devices that can be attached to the sleeper. For example, the polygraph can record the electrical activity of the brain through small metal disks pasted to the scalp, producing an **electroencephalogram (EEG).** It can record electrical signals from muscles, producing an **electromyogram (EMG)** or from the heart, producing an **electrocardiogram (EKG).** Or it can record eye movements through small metal disks attached to the skin around the eyes, producing an **electro-oculogram (EOG).** Other special transducers can detect respiration, sweating, skin or body temperature, and a variety of other physiological states.

Let us look at a typical night's sleep of a male college student on his third night in the laboratory. (Of course, we would obtain similar results from a female, with one excep-

polygraph An instrument that records changes in physiological processes such as brain activity, heart rate, and breathing.

electroencephalogram (EEG) The measurement and graphical presentation of the electrical activity of the brain, recorded by means of electrodes attached to the scalp.

electromyogram (EMG) The measurement and graphical presentation of the electrical activity of muscles, recorded by means of electrodes attached to the skin above them.

electrocardiogram (EKG) The measurement and graphical presentation of the electrical activity of the heart, recorded by means of electrodes attached to the skin.

electro-oculogram (EOG) The measurement and graphical presentation of the electrical activity caused by movements of the eye, recorded by means of electrodes attached to the skin adjacent to the eye.

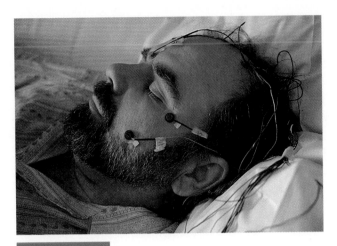

Figure 9.13

A subject prepared for a night's sleep in a sleep laboratory.

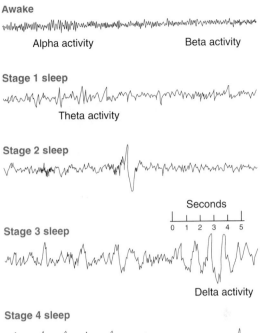

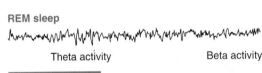

Figure 9.14

An EEG recording of the stages of sleep.
(From Horne, J.A. Why We Sleep: The Functions of Sleep in Humans and Other Mammals. *Oxford, England: Oxford University Press, 1989. Copyright 1988 Oxford University Press. By permission of Oxford University Press.)*

tion, which I will note later.) The EEG electrodes are attached to his scalp, EMG electrodes to his chin, EKG electrodes to his chest, and EOG electrodes to the skin around his eyes. (See *Figure 9.13.*) Wires connected to these electrodes are plugged into the amplifiers of the polygraph. The output of each amplifier causes a pen on the polygraph to move up and down while a long, continuous sheet of paper moves by.

The EEG record distinguishes between alert and relaxed wakefulness. When a person is alert, the tracing looks rather irregular, and the pens do not move very far up or down. The EEG in this case shows high-frequency (15–30 Hz), low-amplitude electrical activity called **beta activity.** When a person is relaxed and perhaps somewhat drowsy, the record shows **alpha activity,** a medium-frequency (8–12 Hz), medium-amplitude rhythm. (See *Figure 9.14.*)

The technician leaves the room, the lights are turned off, and the student closes his eyes. As he relaxes and grows drowsy, his EEG changes from beta activity to alpha activity. The first stage of sleep (stage 1) is marked by the presence of some **theta activity,** EEG activity of 3.5–7.5 Hz. This stage is actually a transition between sleep and wakefulness; the EMG shows that the student's muscles are still active, and his EOG indicates slow, gentle, rolling eye movements. The eyes slowly

beta activity   The irregular, high-frequency activity of the electroencephalogram, usually indicating a state of alertness or arousal.

alpha activity   Rhythmical, medium-frequency activity of the electroencephalogram, usually indicating a state of quiet relaxation.

theta activity   EEG activity of 3.5–7.5 Hz; occurs during the transition between sleep and wakefulness.

delta activity   The rhythmical activity of the electroencephalogram, having a frequency of less than 3.5 Hz, indicating deep (slow-wave) sleep.

slow-wave sleep   Sleep other than REM sleep, characterized by regular, slow waves on the electroencephalograph.

open and close from time to time. Soon, the student is fully asleep. As sleep progresses, it gets deeper and deeper, moving through stages 2, 3, and 4. The EEG gets progressively lower in frequency and higher in amplitude. (See *Figure 9.14.*) Stage 4 consists mainly of **delta activity,** characterized by relatively high-amplitude waves occurring at less than 3.5 Hz. Our sleeper becomes less responsive to the environment, and it becomes more difficult to awaken him. Environmental stimuli that caused him to stir during stage 1 produce little or no reaction during stage 4. The sleep of stages 3 and 4 is called **slow-wave sleep.**

Stage 4 sleep is reached in less than an hour and continues for as much as a half hour. Then, suddenly, the EEG begins to indicate lighter levels of sleep, back through stages 3 and 2 to the activity characteristic of stage 1. The sleeper's heartbeat becomes irregular and his respiration alternates between shallow breaths and sudden gasps. The EOG shows that the subject's eyes are darting rapidly back and forth, up and down. The EEG record looks like that of a person who is

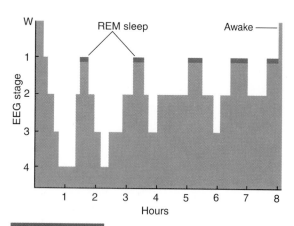

Figure 9.15

Typical progression of stages during a night's sleep. The dark blue shading indicates REM sleep.

(From Hartmann, E. The Biology of Dreaming, 1967. Courtesy of Charles C Thomas, Publisher, Springfield, Illinois.)

Principal Characteristics of REM Sleep and Slow-Wave Sleep

Rem Sleep	Slow-Wave Sleep
Rapid EEG waves	Slow EEG waves
Muscular paralysis	Lack of muscular paralysis
Rapid eye movements	Slow or absent eye movements
Penile erection or vaginal secretion	Lack of genital activity
Dreams	

awake and active. Yet the sleeper is fast asleep. Although his EMG is generally quiet, indicating muscular relaxation, his hands and feet twitch occasionally. (See *Figure 9.14.*)

At this point, the subject is dreaming. He has entered another stage of sleep, called **rapid eye movement (REM) sleep.** The first episode of REM sleep lasts about twenty to thirty minutes and is followed by approximately one hour of slow-wave sleep. As the night goes on, the episodes of REM sleep get longer and the episodes of slow-wave sleep get shorter, but the total cycle remains at approximately ninety minutes. A typical night's sleep consists of four or five of these cycles. *Figure 9.15* shows a record of a person's stages of sleep; the colored shading indicates REM sleep.

As I noted, although a person in REM sleep exhibits rapid eye movements and brief twitches of the hands and feet, the EMG shows that the facial muscles are still. In fact, physiological studies have shown that, aside from occasional twitching, a person actually becomes paralyzed during REM sleep. Males are observed to have partial or full erections. In addition, women's vaginal secretions increase at this time. These genital changes are usually not associated with sexual arousal or dreams of a sexual nature. Table 9.1 lists the principal characteristics of REM sleep and slow-wave sleep. (See *Table 9.1.*)

Functions of Sleep

Sleep is one of the few universal behaviors. All mammals, all birds, and some cold-blooded vertebrates spend part of each day sleeping. Sleep is seen even in species that would seem to be better off without sleep. For example, the Indus dolphin (*Platanista indi*) lives in the muddy waters of the Indus estu-

ary in Pakistan (Pilleri, 1979). Over the ages, it has become blind, presumably because vision is not useful in the animal's environment. (It has an excellent sonar system, which it uses to navigate and find prey.) However, despite the dangers caused by sleeping, sleep has not disappeared. The Indus dolphin never stops swimming; doing so would result in injury, because of the dangerous currents and the vast quantities of debris carried by the river during the monsoon season. Pilleri captured two Indus dolphins and studied their habits. He found that they slept a total of seven hours a day, in very brief naps of four to sixty seconds each. If sleep did not perform an important function, we might expect that it, like vision, would have been eliminated in this species through the process of natural selection.

The universal nature of sleep suggests that it performs some important functions. But just what are they? The simplest explanation for sleep is that it serves to repair the wear and tear on our bodies caused by moving and exercising. Perhaps our bodies just get worn out by performing waking activities for sixteen hours or so.

One approach to discovering the functions of sleep is the deprivation study. Consider, for example, the function of eating. The effects of starvation are easy to detect: The person loses weight, becomes fatigued, and will eventually die if he or she does not eat again. By analogy, it should be easy to discover why we sleep by seeing what happens to a person who goes without sleep.

Unfortunately, deprivation studies have not obtained persuasive evidence that sleep is needed to keep the body functioning normally. Horne (1978) reviewed over fifty experiments in which humans had been deprived of sleep. He reported that most of them found that sleep deprivation did not interfere with people's ability to perform physical exercise. In addition, they found no evidence of a physiological stress response to sleep deprivation. If people encounter stressful situations that cause illness or damage to various organ systems, changes can be seen in such physiological measures as blood levels of cortisol and epinephrine. (The physiology of stress is described in more detail in Chapter 16.) Generally, these changes did not occur.

rapid eye movement (REM) sleep A period of sleep during which dreaming, rapid eye movements, and muscular paralysis occur and the EEG shows beta activity.

Although sleep deprivation does not seem to damage the body, and sleep does not seem to be necessary for athletic exercise, sleep may be required for normal brain functioning. Several studies suggest that sleep-deprived people are able to perform normally on most intellectual tasks, as long as the tasks are short. They perform more poorly on tasks that require a high level of cortical functioning after two days of sleep deprivation (Horne and Pettitt, 1985). In particular, they perform poorly on tasks that require them to be watchful, alert, and vigilant.

During stage 4 sleep, the metabolic activity of the brain decreases to about 75 percent of the waking level (Sakai et al., 1979). Thus, stage 4 sleep appears to give the brain a chance to rest. In fact, people are unreactive to all but intense stimuli during slow-wave sleep and, if awakened, act groggy and confused—as if their cerebral cortex has been shut down and has not yet resumed its functioning. These observations suggest that during stage 4 sleep the brain is, indeed, resting.

Sleep deprivation studies of humans suggest that although the brain may need slow-wave sleep in order to recover from the day's activities, the rest of the body does not. Another way to determine whether sleep is needed for restoration of physiological functioning is to look at the effects of daytime activity on nighttime sleep. If the function of sleep is to repair the effects of activity during waking hours, then we should expect that sleep and exercise are related. That is, we should sleep more after a day of vigorous exercise than after a day spent quietly at an office desk.

In fact, the relation between sleep and exercise is not very compelling. For example, Ryback and Lewis (1971) found no changes in slow-wave or REM sleep of healthy subjects who spent six weeks resting in bed. If sleep repairs wear and tear, we would expect these people to sleep less. Adey, Bors, and Porter (1968) studied the sleep of *completely* immobile quadriplegics and paraplegics and found only a small decrease in slow-wave sleep as compared to uninjured people.

Although bodily exercise has little effect on sleep, *mental* exercise seems to increase the demand for slow-wave sleep. In an ingenious study, Horne and Minard (1985) found a way to increase mental activity without affecting physical activity and without causing stress. The investigators told volunteers to show up for an experiment in which they were supposed to take some tests designed to test reading skills. In fact, when the people turned up, they were told that the plans had been changed. They were invited for a day out, at the expense of the experimenters. (Not surprisingly, they willingly accepted.) They spent the day visiting an art exhibition, a shopping center, a museum, an amusement park, a zoo, and an interesting mansion. After a scenic drive through the countryside they watched a movie in a local theater. They were driven from place to place and certainly did not become overheated by exercise. After the movie, they returned to the sleep laboratory. They said they were tired, and they readily fell asleep. Their sleep duration was normal, and they awoke feeling refreshed. However, their slow-wave sleep—particularly stage 4 sleep—was increased.

Dreaming

One of the most fascinating aspects of sleep is the fact that we enter a fantasy world several times each night during which we perceive imaginary events and perform imaginary behaviors. Why do we do so?

States of Consciousness During Sleep

A person who is awakened during REM sleep and asked whether anything was happening will almost always report a dream. The typical REM sleep dream resembles a play or movie—it has a narrative form. Conversely, reports of narrative, storylike dreams are rare among people awakened from slow-wave sleep. In general, mental activity during slow-wave sleep is more nearly static; it involves situations rather than stories and generally unpleasant ones. For example, a person awakened from slow-wave sleep might report a sensation of being crushed or suffocated.

Unless the sleep is heavily drugged, almost everyone has four or five bouts of REM sleep each night, with accompanying dreams. Yet if the dreamer does not happen to awaken while the dream is in progress, it is lost forever. Some people who claimed not to have had a dream for many years slept in a sleep laboratory and found that, in fact, they did dream. They were able to remember their dreams because the investigator awakened them during REM sleep.

The reports of people awakened from REM and slow-wave sleep clearly show that people are conscious during sleep, even though they may not remember any of their experiences then. Lack of memory for an event does not mean that it never happened; it only means that there is no permanent record accessible to conscious thought during wakefulness. Thus, we can say that slow-wave sleep and REM sleep reflect two different states of consciousness.

Functions of Dreams

There are two major approaches to the study of dreaming: a psychological analysis of the contents of dreams, and psychobiological research on the nature and functions of REM sleep. Let us consider the psychological analysis first.

Symbolism in Dreams. Since ancient times, people have regarded dreams as important, using them to prophesy the future, decide whether to go to war, or determine the guilt or innocence of a person accused of a crime. In this century, Sigmund Freud proposed a very influential theory about dreaming. He said that dreams arise out of inner conflicts between unconscious desires (primarily sexual ones) and prohibitions against acting out these desires, which we learn from society. According to Freud, although all dreams represent unfulfilled wishes, their contents are disguised and expressed symbolically. The *latent content* of the dream (from the Latin word for "hidden") is transformed into the *manifest content* (the actual story line or plot). Taken at face value, the manifest content is innocuous, but a knowledgeable psychoanalyst can supposedly recognize unconscious desires disguised as symbols in the dream. For example, climbing a set of stairs or shooting a gun might represent sexual intercourse. The problem with Freud's theory is that it is not disprovable; even if it is wrong, a psychoanalyst can always provide a plausible interpretation of a dream that reveals hidden conflicts disguised in obscure symbols.

Hall (1966), who agrees that symbols can be found in dreams, does not believe that they are usually hidden. For example, a person may plainly engage in sexual intercourse in one dream and have another dream that involves shooting a gun. Surely the "real" meaning of shooting the gun need not be hidden from a dreamer who has undisguised dreams of sexual intercourse at other times or who has an uninhibited sex life during waking. Why should this person disguise sexual desires while dreaming? As Hall says, people use their own symbols, not those of anyone else. They represent what the dreamer thinks, and therefore, their meaning is usually not hidden from the dreamer.

Hobson (1988) proposed an explanation for dreaming that does not involve unconscious conflicts or desires. As we will see later, research using laboratory animals has shown that REM sleep occurs when a circuit of acetylcholine-secreting neurons in the pons becomes active, stimulating rapid eye movements, activation of the cerebral cortex, and muscular paralysis. (Yes, other animals engage in REM sleep, and they appear to dream, too.) The activation of the visual system produces both eye movements and images. In fact, several experiments have found that the particular eye movements that a person makes during a dream correspond reasonably well with the content of a dream; that is, the eye movements are those that one would expect a person to make if the imaginary events were really occurring (Dement, 1974). The images evoked by the cortical activation often incorporate memories

Marc Chagall's painting depicts images and symbols that could occur in a dream. Freud's assertion that dreams provide an opportunity for unconscious desires to be expressed symbolically is challenged by many psychologists today.

of episodes that have occurred recently or of things that a person has been thinking about lately. Presumably, the circuits responsible for these memories are more excitable because they have recently been active. Hobson suggests that although the activation of these brain mechanisms produces fragmentary images, our brains try to tie these images together and make sense of them by creating a more or less plausible story.

We still do not know whether the particular topics we dream about are somehow related to the functions that dreams serve or whether the purposes of REM sleep are fulfilled by the physiological changes in the brain—regardless of the plots of our dreams. Given that we do not really know for sure why we dream, this uncertainty is not surprising. But the rapid progress being made in most fields of brain research suggests that we will have some answers in the not-too-distant future.

Effects of REM Sleep Deprivation.   As we saw, total sleep deprivation impairs people's ability to perform tasks that require them to be alert and vigilant. What happens when only REM sleep is disrupted? People who are sleeping in a laboratory can be selectively deprived of REM sleep. An investigator awakens them whenever their polygraph records indicate that they have entered REM sleep. The investigator must also awaken control subjects just as often at random intervals to eliminate any effects produced by being awakened several times.

If someone is deprived of REM sleep for several nights and is then allowed to sleep without interruption, the onset of REM sleep becomes more frequent. It is as if a need for REM sleep builds up, forcing the person into this state more often. When the person is no longer awakened during REM sleep, a rebound phenomenon is seen: The person engages in many more bouts of REM sleep than normal during the next night or two, as if catching up on something important that was missed.

Researchers have discovered that the effects of REM sleep deprivation are not very striking. In fact, medical journals contain reports of several patients who showed little or no REM sleep after sustaining damage to the brain stem (Lavie et al., 1984; Gironell, de la Calzada, and Sagales, 1995). The lack of REM sleep did not appear to cause serious side effects. One of the patients, after receiving his injury, completed high school, attended law school, and began practicing law.

Several investigators have suggested that REM sleep may play a role in learning. For example, Greenberg and Pearlman (1974) suggest that REM sleep helps integrate memories of events of the previous day—especially those dealing with emotionally related information—with existing memories. Crick and Mitchson (1983) suggest that REM sleep helps flush useless information from memory to prevent the storage of useless clutter. Many studies using laboratory animals have shown that deprivation of REM sleep does impair the ability to learn a complex task. However, although the animals learn the task more slowly, they still manage to learn it. Thus, REM sleep is not *necessary* for learning. If REM sleep does play a role in learning, it appears to be a subtle one—at least, in the adult. As we shall see in the next subsection, REM sleep may be important for brain development.

Role of REM Sleep in Brain Development. REM sleep begins early in development. Studies of human fetuses and infants born prematurely indicate that REM sleep begins to appear thirty weeks after conception and peaks at around forty weeks (Roffwarg, Muzio, and Dement, 1966; Petre-Quadens and De Lee, 1974; Inoue et al., 1986). REM sleep of fetuses was recorded harmlessly by using ultrasound to watch eye movements. Approximately 70 percent of a newborn infant's sleep is REM sleep. By six months of age, this proportion has declined to approximately 30 percent. By eight years of age, it has fallen to approximately 22 percent. By late adulthood, it is less than 15 percent.

Researchers have long been struck by the fact that the highest proportion of REM sleep is seen during the most active phase of brain development. Perhaps, then, REM sleep plays a role in this process. Of course, no one has experimented on infants by depriving them of REM sleep to see whether their brain development was impaired. But such studies have been carried out on laboratory animals. For example, Mirmiran (1995) described a series of studies he and his colleagues performed with infant rats. They injected the rats with drugs that suppressed REM sleep during the second and third weeks of life and found that the animals showed behavioral abnormalities as adults. In addition, their cerebral cortexes and brain stems were smaller than those of control subjects.

Of course, we cannot be sure that the effects of the drugs on brain development were caused by the REM sleep deprivation. The drugs may have had other effects beside REM sleep suppression that were responsible for these effects. However, Marks et al. (1995) deprived kittens of REM sleep without using drugs and found abnormalities in the development of the animals' visual systems. Thus, the hypothesis that REM sleep aids brain development seems to be reasonable and merits further study. Exactly what role REM sleep might play is still not known.

Brain Mechanisms of Sleep

If sleep is a behavior, then some parts of the brain must be responsible for its occurrence. In fact, researchers have discovered several brain regions that have special roles in sleep and biological rhythms.

Let us first consider biological rhythms. All living organisms show rhythmic changes in their physiological processes and behavior. Some of these rhythms are simply responses to environmental changes. For example, the growth rate of plants is controlled by daily rhythms of light and darkness. In animals, some rhythms are controlled by internal "clocks," located in the brain. Mammals have two biological clocks that play a role in sleep. One of these controls **circadian rhythms**— rhythms that oscillate once a day (*circa*, about; *dies*, day). The second clock, which controls the cycles of slow-wave

Late-term fetuses and newborn infants spend much time in REM sleep, which has led some investigators to hypothesize that this activity plays a role in brain development.

and REM sleep, oscillates several times a day.

The clock that controls circadian rhythms is located in a small pair of structures located at the bottom of the hypothalamus: the *suprachiasmatic nuclei (SCN)*. The activity of neurons in the SCN oscillates once each day; the neurons are active during the day and inactive at night. These changes in activity control daily cycles of sleep and wakefulness. If people are placed in a windowless room with constant lighting, they will continue to show circadian rhythms, controlled by the oscillations of their suprachiasmatic nuclei. However, because this biological clock is not very accurate, people's circadian rhythms will eventually get out of synchrony with the day/night cycles outside the building. But within a few days after leaving the building, their rhythms will become resynchronized with those of the sun. This resynchronization is accomplished by a direct connection between the eyes and the SCN. Each morning, when we see the light of the sun (or turn on the room lights), our biological clock resets and begins ticking off the next day.

The second biological clock in the mammalian brain runs considerably faster, and it runs continuously, unaffected by periods of light and darkness. In humans, this clock cycles with a ninety-minute period. The first suggestion that a ninety-minute cycle occurs throughout the day came from the observation that infants who are fed on demand show regular feeding patterns (Kleitman, 1961). Later studies found ninety-minute cycles of rest and activity, including such activities as eating, drinking, smoking, heart rate, oxygen consumption, stomach motility, urine production, and performance on various tasks that make demands on a person's ability to pay attention. Kleitman termed this phenomenon the **basic rest-activity cycle (BRAC).** (See Kleitman, 1982, for a review.)

circadian rhythm A daily rhythmical change in behavior or physiological process.

basic rest-activity cycle (BRAC) A 90-minute cycle (in humans) of waxing and waning alertness controlled by a biological clock in the pons; during sleep, it controls cycles of REM sleep and slow-wave sleep.

During the night, the clock responsible for the BRAC controls the alternating periods of REM sleep and slow-wave sleep.

Studies using laboratory animals have found that the clock responsible for the BRAC is located somewhere in the pons. The pons also contains neural circuits that are responsible for REM sleep. The neurons that begin a period of REM sleep release acetylcholine. The release of this transmitter substance activates several other circuits of neurons. One of these circuits activates the cerebral cortex and causes dreaming. Another activates neurons in the midbrain and causes rapid eye movements. Yet another activates a set of inhibitory neurons that paralyzes us and prevents us from acting out our dreams. The location of the two biological clocks is shown in *Figure 9.16.*

The first hint that REM sleep was turned on by acetylcholine-secreting neurons came from the observation that overdoses of insecticides that excite such neurons also cause visual hallucinations, like those of dreaming. Subsequent research using laboratory animals confirmed this suspicion. These acetylcholine-secreting neurons (referred to as *REM-ON* neurons) are normally inhibited by neurons that secrete another transmitter substance, serotonin. Thus, drugs that decrease the activity of serotonin-secreting neurons will permit the REM-ON neurons to become active. LSD is one of these drugs, and this fact explains why people who take LSD experience visual hallucinations similar to the ones that occur during dreams. On the other hand, drugs that increase the activity

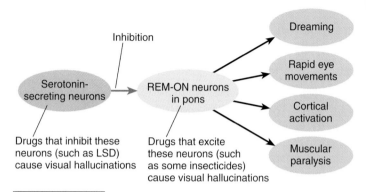

Figure 9.17

Control of REM sleep. REM sleep is produced by activation of the acetylcholine-secreting REM-ON neurons located in the pons. These neurons are normally inhibited by serotonin-secreting neurons.

of serotonin-secreting neurons will suppress REM sleep. All antidepressant drugs have this effect, which suggests that excessive amounts of REM sleep may play a role in mood disorders. This hypothesis will be explored in more detail in Chapter 17. (See *Figure 9.17.*)

What about the brain mechanisms responsible for slow-wave sleep? The most important brain region seems to be the **preoptic area,** located just in front of the hypothalamus, at the base of the brain. (This region is named for the fact that it is located anterior to the point where some axons in the optic nerves cross to the other side of the brain.) If the preoptic area is destroyed, an animal will sleep much less (McGinty and Sterman, 1968; Szymusiak and McGinty, 1986). If it is electrically stimulated, an animal will become drowsy and fall asleep (Sterman and Clemente, 1962a, 1962b).

Sleep Disorders

Sleep does not always go smoothly, and some of the brain mechanisms responsible for sleep can malfunction, causing medical problems that manifest themselves while a person is awake. Fortunately, some of the things that sleep researchers have learned can help people with sleep-associated disorders.

Insomnia

Insomnia is a problem that is said to affect at least 20 percent of the population at some time (Raybin and Detre, 1969). However, I must emphasize that there is no single definition of insomnia that can apply to all people. The amount of sleep that individuals require is quite variable. A short sleeper may feel fine with five hours of sleep; a long sleeper may still feel unrefreshed after ten hours. Insomnia must be defined in relation to a person's particular sleep needs.

Ironically, the most important cause of insomnia seems to be sleeping medication. Insomnia is not a disease that can

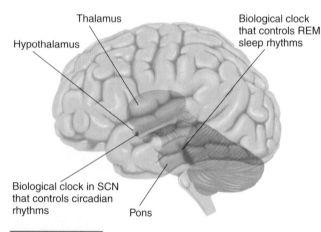

Figure 9.16

Two biological clocks in the human brain. The suprachiasmatic nucleus (SCN) of the hypothalamus is responsible for circadian rhythms. The clock in the pons is responsible for the basic rest-activity cycle (BRAC) and cycles of REM sleep and slow-wave sleep.

preoptic area   A region at the base of the brain just in front of the hypothalamus; contains neurons that appear to control the occurrence of slow-wave sleep.

be corrected with a medicine, in the way that diabetes can be treated with insulin. Insomnia is a symptom. If it is caused by pain or discomfort, the physical ailment that leads to the sleeplessness should be treated. If it is secondary to personal problems or psychological disorders, these problems should be dealt with directly. Patients who receive sleeping medications develop a tolerance to them and suffer rebound symptoms if they are withdrawn (Weitzman, 1981). That is, the drugs lose their effectiveness, so the patient requests larger doses from the physician. If a patient attempts to sleep without his or her accustomed medication or even takes a smaller dose one night, he or she is likely to experience a withdrawal effect: a severe disturbance of sleep. The patient becomes convinced that the insomnia is even worse than before and turns to more medication for relief. This common syndrome is called *drug dependency insomnia.* Kales et al. (1979) found that withdrawal of some sleeping medications produced a rebound insomnia after the drugs were used for as few as three nights.

A common cause of insomnia, especially in older people, is *sleep apnea* (*apnea* means "without breathing"): They cannot sleep and breathe at the same time. When they fall asleep, they stop breathing, the content of carbon dioxide in their blood builds up, and they awaken, gasping for air. After breathing deeply for a while, they go back to sleep and resume the cycle. Some people who suffer from sleep apnea are blessed with a lack of memory for this periodic sleeping and awakening; others are aware of it and dread each night's sleep. Fortunately, some types of sleep apnea in adults can be corrected by throat surgery.

Insomnia can neither kill nor disable you. If a more basic problem, such as depression, seems to be causing your insomnia, get professional help. If there are no obvious causes and the insomnia is not severe, try doing your worrying (or whatever else it is that may interfere with sleep) *before* going to bed. Make bed a place where you sleep, not where you worry. Establish and follow a regular routine when you get ready for bed. If you do not fall asleep in a reasonable amount of time, do not lie there fretting. *Get up and do something else,* and do not go back to bed until you feel drowsy. Even if you are up most of the night, stay up until you feel sleepy enough to doze off as soon as you get into bed. Remember that you will survive even if you miss a night's sleep. Make yourself get up at a regular time each morning; if you do, you will eventually find it easier to fall asleep at night. Avoid taking naps; they make it more difficult to establish a strong daily pattern of sleep and wakefulness. Finally, remember that stimulants such as caffeine or depressants such as alcohol can be important sources of sleep disorders.

Disorders Associated with REM Sleep

Two important characteristics of REM sleep are dreaming and paralysis. The paralysis results from a brain mechanism that prevents us from acting out our dreams. In fact, damage to specific regions of the pons of a cat's brain will produce just that result: The cat, obviously asleep, acts as if it were participating in a dream (Jouvet, 1972). It walks around stalking imaginary prey and responding defensively to imaginary predators.

This phenomenon can occur in humans, too. Several years ago, Schenck et al. (1986) reported the existence of an interesting syndrome: **REM sleep behavior disorder,** the absence of the paralysis that normally occurs during REM sleep. Consider the following case:

> I was a halfback playing football, and after the quarterback received the ball from the center he lateraled it sideways to me and I'm supposed to go around end and cut back over tackle and—this is very vivid—as I cut back over tackle there is this big 280-pound tackle waiting, so I, according to football rules, was to give him my shoulder and bounce him out of the way . . . when I came to I was standing in front of our dresser and I had [gotten up out of bed and run and] knocked lamps, mirrors and everything off the dresser, hit my head against the wall and my knee against the dresser. (Schenck, Bundlie, Ettinger, and Mahowald, 1986, p. 294)

As we saw, studies using laboratory animals have shown that the neural circuitry that controls the paralysis that accompanies REM sleep is located in the pons. In humans, REM sleep behavior disorder seems to be produced by damage to this region (Culebras and Moore, 1989).

Dreams and muscular paralysis are fine when a person is lying in bed. But some people have periodic attacks of a sleep-related disorder called **cataplexy** (*kata-,* "down"; *plessein,* "to strike"). They are struck down by paralysis while actively going about their business. They fall to the ground and lie there, paralyzed but fully conscious. Attacks of cataplexy generally last less than a minute. The attacks are usually triggered by strong emotional states, such as anger, laughter, or even lovemaking. People who have cataplectic attacks tend also to enter REM sleep as soon as they fall asleep, in contrast to the normal ninety-minute interval.

Cataplexy is a biological disorder, probably involving inherited abnormalities in the brain. In fact, researchers have even developed breeds of dogs that are subject to attacks of cataplexy so that they can study this disorder in the laboratory. As we saw, brain mechanisms responsible for REM sleep are normally inhibited by serotonin-secreting neurons. Cataplexy can be treated by drugs that increase the activity of these neurons, thus increasing the inhibition.

REM sleep behavior disorder A neurological disorder characterized by absence of the paralysis that normally occurs during REM sleep; the patient acts out his or her dreams.

cataplexy A neurological disorder in which the person collapses, becoming temporarily paralyzed but not unconscious; usually triggered by anger or excitement; apparently related to the paralysis that normally accompanies REM sleep.

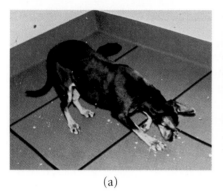 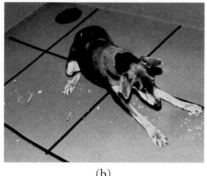 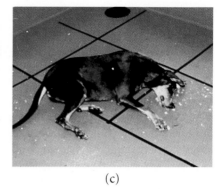

(a)   (b)   (c)

A dog undergoing a cataplectic attack triggered by its excitement at finding some food on the floor. (a) Sniffing the food. (b) Muscles beginning to relax. (c) Dog is temporarily paralyzed, as it would be during REM sleep.

Disorders Associated with Slow-Wave Sleep

Several phenomena occur during the deepest phase (stage 4) of slow-wave sleep. These events include sleepwalking, sleeptalking, night terrors, and enuresis.

Sleepwalking can be as simple as getting out of bed and right back in again or as complicated as walking out of a house and climbing into a car. (Fortunately, sleepwalkers apparently do not try to drive.) We know that sleepwalking is not the acting out of a dream because it occurs during stage 4 of slow-wave sleep, when the EEG shows high-amplitude slow waves and the person's mental state generally involves a static situation, not a narrative. Sleepwalkers are difficult to awaken; once awakened, they are often confused and disoriented. However, contrary to popular belief, it is perfectly safe to wake them up.

Sleepwalking is *not* a manifestation of some deep-seated emotional problem. Most sleepwalkers are children, who almost invariably outgrow this behavior. The worst thing to do, according to sleep researchers, is to try to get them treated for it. Of course, a house inhabited by a sleepwalker should be made as safe as possible, and the doors should be kept locked at night. For some reason, sleepwalking runs in families; Dement (1974) tells of a family whose grown members were reunited for a holiday celebration. In the middle of the night they awoke to find that they had all gathered in the living room—during their sleep.

Sleeptalking sometimes occurs as part of a REM sleep dream, but it more usually occurs during other stages of sleep. Often, one can carry on a conversation with the sleeptalker, indicating that the person is very near the boundary between sleep and waking. During this state, sleeptalkers are sometimes very suggestible. So-called truth serums are used in an attempt to duplicate this condition, so that the person being questioned is not on guard against giving away secrets and is not functioning well enough to tell elaborate lies. Unfortunately for the interrogators (and fortunately for the rest of the population), there are no foolproof, reliable truth serums.

Night terrors, like sleepwalking, occur most often in children. In this disorder, the child awakes, screaming with terror. When questioned, the child does not report a dream and often seems confused. Usually, the child falls asleep quickly without showing any aftereffects and seldom remembers the event the next day. Night terrors are not the same as nightmares, which are simply frightening dreams from which one happens to awaken. Apparently, night terrors are caused by sudden awakenings from the depths of stage 4 sleep. The sudden, dramatic change in consciousness is a frightening experience for the child. The treatment for night terrors, like that for sleepwalking, is no treatment at all.

The final disorder of slow-wave sleep, *enuresis,* or "bed wetting," is fairly common in young children. Most children outgrow it, just as they outgrow sleepwalking or night terrors. Emotional problems can trigger enuresis, but bed wetting does not itself indicate that a child is psychologically unwell. The problem with enuresis is that, unlike the other stage 4 phenomena, there are aftereffects that must be cleaned up. Parents dislike having their sleep disturbed and get tired of frequently changing and laundering sheets. The resulting tension in family relationships can make the child feel anxious and guilty and can thus unnecessarily prolong the disorder.

Fortunately, a simple training method often cures enuresis. A moisture-sensitive device is placed under the bed sheet; when it gets wet, it causes a bell to ring. Because a child releases only a few drops of urine before the bladder begins to empty in earnest, the bell wakes the child in time to run to the bathroom. In about a week, most children learn to prevent their bladders from emptying and manage to wait until morning. Perhaps what they really learn is not to enter such a deep level of stage 4 sleep in which the mechanism that keeps the bladder from emptying seems to break down.

Interim Summary

Sleep

Sleep consists of several stages of slow-wave sleep, characterized by increasing amounts of delta activity in the EEG, and REM sleep. REM sleep is characterized by beta activity in the EEG, rapid eye movements, general paralysis (with twitching movements of the hands and feet), and dreaming. Sleep is a behavior, not simply an altered state of consciousness. Although evidence suggests that sleep is not necessary for repairing the wear and tear caused by physical exercise, it may play an important role in providing an opportunity for the brain to rest.

Although narrative dreams occur only during REM sleep, people often are conscious of static situations during slow-wave sleep. Freud suggested that dreams provided the opportunity for unconscious conflicts to express themselves through symbolism in dreams. Hobson suggested that dreams are the attempts of the brain to make sense of hallucinations produced by the activation of the cerebral cortex. The function of REM sleep in adults is uncertain, but it may be involved somehow in learning. Fetuses and infants engage in much more REM sleep than adults do, which suggests that REM sleep may play a role in brain development. Some experimental research supports this suggestion.

The brain contains two biological clocks. One, located in the suprachiasmatic nucleus of the hypothalamus, controls circadian (daily) rhythms. This clock is reset when light strikes the retina in the morning. The second clock, located in the pons, controls the basic rest-activity cycle, which manifests itself in changes in activity during the day and alternating periods of slow-wave sleep and REM sleep during the night. A circuit of acetylcholine-secreting neurons in the pons, normally inhibited by serotonin-secreting neurons, turns on REM sleep. Slow-wave sleep is controlled by neurons in the preoptic area.

Insomnia appears to be a symptom of a variety of physical and emotional disorders, not a disease. Although it is often treated by sleep medications, these drugs cause more sleep problems than they cure. Two neurological disorders involve mechanisms of REM sleep. REM sleep behavior disorder occurs when brain damage prevents the paralysis that normally keeps us from acting out our dreams. Cataplectic attacks are just the opposite. They are caused by activation at inappropriate times of the mechanism that causes paralysis during REM sleep. Drugs that stimulate serotonin-secreting neurons are useful in treating cataplexy. The disorders of slow-wave sleep include sleepwalking, sleeptalking, and night terrors. Sleepwalking and night terrors are primarily disorders of childhood and are best left untreated. Sleeptalking is generally harmless (unless the talker gives away important secrets in his or her sleep), so it probably should not even be considered a disorder.

Thought Questions

- What is accomplished by dreaming? Some researchers believe that the subject matter of a dream does not matter—it is the REM sleep itself that is important. Others believe that the subject matter *does* count. Some researchers believe that if we remember a dream, the dream failed to accomplish all of its functions; others say that remembering is useful because it can give us some insights into our problems. What do you think of these controversies?

- Some people report that they are "in control" of some of their dreams—that they feel as if they decide what comes next and are not simply swept along passively. Have you ever had this experience? And have you ever had a "lucid dream," in which you were aware of the fact that you were dreaming?

- Until recently (that is, in terms of the evolution of our species), our ancestors tended to go to sleep when the sun set and wake up when it rose. Once our ancestors learned how to control fire, they undoubtedly stayed up somewhat later, sitting in front of a fire. But it was only with the development of cheap, effective lighting that many members of our species adopted the habit of staying up late and waking several hours after sunrise. Considering that the neural mechanisms of sleep evolved long ago, do you think the changes in our daily rhythms affect any of our physical and intellectual abilities?

Suggestions for Further Reading

Wallace, B., and Fisher, L.E. *Consciousness and Behavior*, 3rd ed. Boston: Allyn and Bacon, 1991.

This book provides more information about a variety of topics related to consciousness, including some that I did not discuss in this chapter, such as extrasensory perception (ESP).

Jaynes, J. *The Origin of Consciousness in the Breakdown of the Bicameral Mind*. Boston: Houghton Mifflin, 1976.

Jaynes's book presents the provocative hypothesis that human consciousness is a recent phenomenon that emerged long after the evolution of the human brain, as we know it now. You do not need to agree with Jaynes's thesis to enjoy reading this scholarly book.

Winson, J. *Brain and Psyche: The Biology of the Unconscious*. Garden City, N.Y.: Anchor Press/Doubleday, 1985.

Winson, a neurophysiologist, attempts to explain the physiology of unconscious phenomena.

Baker, R.A. *They Call It Hypnosis*. Buffalo, N.Y.: Prometheus Books, 1990.

Laurence, J.-R., and Perry, C. *Hypnosis, Will, and Memory: A Psycho-Legal History*. New York: Guilford Press, 1988.

Sheehan, P.W., and McConkey, K.M. *Hypnosis and Experience: The Exploration of Phenomena and Process*. Hillsdale, N.J.: Lawrence Erlbaum Associates, 1982.

If you would like to learn more about hypnosis, you will enjoy reading any of these books. The Sheehan and McConkey book provides a more advanced, scholarly approach.

Cohen, D.B. *Sleep and Dreaming: Origins, Nature and Functions*. New York: Pergamon Press, 1979.

Horne, J. *Why We Sleep: The Functions of Sleep in Humans and Other Mammals*. Oxford: Oxford University Press, 1988.

Both of these books about sleep are excellent and interesting.

Chapter 10

Language

Chapter Outline

Speech and Comprehension

Perception of Speech • Understanding the Meaning of Speech • Brain Mechanisms of Verbal Behavior

Language permits us to communicate perceptions, thoughts, and memories. Words have meanings (semantics), and they are arranged into sentences that follow specific rules (syntax). Context plays an important role in the complex task of identifying individual words from continuous speech. Both semantics and syntax provide meaning. Studies of patients with brain damage and PET studies of people engaging in verbal behavior suggest that some parts of the brain play special roles in language-related behaviors.

Reading

Scanning of Text • Phonetic and Whole-Word Recognition: Evidence from Neuropsychology • Understanding the Meanings of Words and Sentences

Reading allows words to be transmitted anywhere in the world and to be preserved for future generations. The eye-tracking device allows researchers to study people's eye movements during reading. Reading is accomplished by whole-word recognition and by decoding the sounds that are represented by letters and groups of letters. Brain damage can produce acquired dyslexias, disrupting one or both of these processes. Developmental dyslexias may involve abnormal development of parts of the left hemisphere that play a special role in language abilities. The phenomenon of semantic priming has permitted researchers to investigate the interactions of neural circuits responsible for recognizing and understanding spoken and written words.

Language Acquisition by Children

Perception of Speech Sounds by Infants • The Prespeech Period and the First Words • The Two-Word Stage • How Adults Talk to Children • Acquisition of Adult Rules of Grammar • Acquisition of Meaning • *Evaluating Scientific Issues: Is There a Language Acquisition Device?* • *Biology and Culture: Communication with Other Primate Species*

By the time babies are born, they have already learned something about language from what they have heard while in their mother's uterus. Language is very much a social behavior; babies learn to carry on "conversations" with caregivers even before they can utter real words, and they use movements, facial expressions, and sounds to communicate. During the two-word stage, children begin to combine words creatively, saying things they have never heard. Infants learn how to communicate verbally from adults and older children, who use a special form of address known as child-directed speech. Some researchers believe that the human brain contains a language acquisition device that already contains universal rules of grammar. The question of whether language abilities are uniquely human is being addressed by researchers who have succeeded in teaching other primates some aspects of language.

*D*r. W. ushered Mr. and Mrs. V. into the office and introduced us. Most people would not guess that Mr. V. had suffered brain damage; he walked normally, had normal control of his hands, and spoke without difficulty. Well, his speech was sometimes hesitant, but it would be easy to attribute that to his personality; he was somewhat shy and seemed content to let his wife do most of the talking.

Several months earlier, Mr. V. had been savagely beaten on the head with a tire iron. While he was visiting a friend, a stranger broke into the apartment, attacked him, and fled. His skull was fractured, and surgery was necessary to remove bone fragments and to stop the bleeding within his brain.

Mr. V. was in a coma for several days, but once he regained consciousness, his recovery was rapid. However, although his vision was only slightly impaired, he had lost the ability to read. His job as production supervisor in a factory obviously required him to read, so he could not go back to work. He continued to hope that his occupational therapist would be able to help him regain his ability, so he had not officially retired from his job. Remarkably—and this is why I was particularly interested in meeting him—he could still write. Mrs. V. told the story.

"It was about six months after F. got out of the hospital. We were standing in the kitchen, which is right next to the utility room. The washing machine had broken, and a repairman was there fixing it. F. wanted to tell me something he didn't want the repairman to overhear, so he picked up a pencil and a pad of paper and wrote me a note. I started reading it and all of a sudden we realized what had happened. F. could write! It nearly bowled us both over. How could he write if he couldn't read?"

We tested Mr. V. and found that his wife was correct. Mr. V. could not read even the simplest words. He would stare at them, take off his glasses and put them on again, and complain that his eyes were bothering him. However, when we showed him pictures of objects and designs, he had no trouble recognizing them and perceiving fine details. *Words* were what he had trouble with. But when we asked him to write, he was able to do so. His spelling was not very good, and his handwriting was even worse than mine, but we could certainly recognize what he had written. We asked him to write several sentences, each on a different piece of paper. We then shuffled the papers and asked him to try to read them. He could not.

A case similar to that of Mr. V. was first reported in the late nineteenth century by a French neurologist, J. Dejerine. Dejerine concluded that damage to his patient's brain prevented information from the visual system from reaching structures in the left hemisphere that were involved with the comprehension of words. The right hemisphere was intact, so the patient could still perceive and recognize objects. Subsequent research proved him to be correct. Dejerine's observations provided the first proof that the left hemisphere was specialized for reading as well as for the production and comprehension of speech.

***

With the exception of sexual behavior (without which our species would not survive), communication is probably the most important of all human social behaviors. Our use of language can be private—we can think to ourselves in words or write diaries that are meant to be seen by no one but ourselves—but language evolved through social contacts among our early ancestors. Speaking and writing are clearly social behaviors: We learn these skills from other people and use them to communicate with them.

Besides using language to communicate with others, we use it as a tool in our own remembering and thinking. As we saw in Chapter 8, we often encode information in memory verbally. In fact, Schiano and Watkins (1981) determined that people could retain a longer series of pictures of objects in short-term memory when the things the pictures showed had short names and when the names sounded very different from one another. Presumably, shorter names took less "room" in short-term memory, and different-sounding names were less

People's earliest attempts at written communication took the form of stylized pictures. These petrogylphs are located in southern Utah, in the southwest United States.

likely to be confused. In addition, we can extend our long-term memory for information by writing notes and consulting them later. Language also enables us to think about very complex and abstract issues by encoding them in words and then manipulating the words according to logical rules.

The acts of speaking, listening, writing, and reading are behaviors and, like other behaviors, we can study them. Linguists have studied the "rules" of language and have described precisely what we do when we speak or write. In contrast, researchers in **psycholinguistics,** a branch of psychology devoted to the study of verbal behavior, are more concerned with human cognition than with the particular rules that describe language. Psycholinguists are interested in how children acquire language—how verbal behavior develops and how children learn to speak from their interactions with adults. They also study how adults use language and how verbal abilities interact with other cognitive abilities. These issues, rather than the concerns of linguists, are the focus of this chapter.

Speech and Comprehension

The ability to engage in verbal behavior confers decided advantages on our species. Through listening and reading, we can profit from the experiences of others, even from those of people who died long ago. Through talking and writing, we can share the results of our own experiences. We can request from other people specific behaviors and information that are helpful to us. We can give information to other people so that their behavior will change in a way that benefits them (or us). Consider the effects of the following sentences:

> Please hold that knot for me while I tie another one.
>
> Which way am I supposed to turn this?
>
> Whenever you do that, I get very angry.
>
> Can I have some milk, Mommy?
>
> The sink is full of dirty dishes.
>
> I love you.

Understanding the speech of others is one of the most complex tasks that we can do. The rest of this section discusses our ability to recognize words, understand the grammatical structure of the phrases and sentences we hear, and comprehend their meaning. As we shall see, several brain regions play special roles in this process.

Perception of Speech

When we speak to someone, we produce a series of sounds in a continuous stream, punctuated by pauses and modulated by stress and changes in pitch. We write sentences as sets of words, with spaces between them. But we *say* sentences as a string of sounds, emphasizing (*stressing*) some, quickly sliding over others, raising the pitch of our voice on some, lowering it on others. We maintain a regular rhythmic pattern of stress. We pause at appropriate times—for example, between phrases—but we do not pause after pronouncing each word. Thus, speech does not come to us as a series of individual words; we must extract the words from a stream of speech (Liberman et al., 1967; Miller and Eimas, 1995).

Recognition of Speech Sounds

The human auditory system performs a formidably complex task in enabling us to recognize speech sounds. These sounds vary according to the sounds that precede and follow them, the speaker's accent, and the stress placed on the syllables in which they occur. **Phonemes** are the elements of speech—the smallest units of sound that contribute to the meaning of a word. For example, the word *pin* consists of three phonemes: /p/ + /i/ + /n/. Thus, the first step in recognizing speech sounds appears to be the identification of phonemes.

Many experiments have investigated how we discriminate among phonemes. Let us consider just one distinction

psycholinguistics A branch of psychology devoted to the study of verbal behavior.

phoneme The minimum unit of sound that conveys meaning in a particular language, such as /p/.

that we can detect: **voice-onset time,** the delay between the initial sound of a voiced consonant and the onset of vibration of the vocal cords. *Voicing* is the vibration of your vocal cords. The distinction between voiced and unvoiced consonants permits us to distinguish between /p/ and /b/, between /k/ and /g/, and between /t/ and /d/. Try to figure out the difference yourself by saying *pa* and *ba.* Pay attention to what the sounds are like, not to how you move your lips to make them.

The difference is very subtle. When you say *pa,* you first build up a little pressure in your mouth. When you open your lips, a puff of air comes out. The *ah* sound does not occur immediately, because the air pressure in your mouth and throat keeps air from leaving your lungs for a brief time. Your vocal cords do not vibrate until air from your lungs passes through them. When you say *ba,* you do not first build up pressure. Your vocal cords start vibrating as soon as your lips open. The delay in voicing that occurs when you say *pa* is very slight: only 0.06 second. Try saying *pa* and *ba* aloud a few more times and note the difference. Your vocal cords will start vibrating just a little later when you say *pa.*

Lisker and Abramson (1970) presented subjects with a series of computer-generated sounds consisting of a puff followed by an *ah.* The sounds varied only in one way: the amount of time between the puff and the *ah.* When we speak, we make a puff for *pa* but not for *ba.* However, even though the computer always produced a puff, subjects reported that they heard *ba* when the delay was short and *pa* when it was long. As Figure 10.1 shows, subjects discriminated between the phonemes /p/ and /b/ strictly according to the delay in voicing. (Negative delays mean that the *ah* sound started *before* the puff.) Note how sharp the discrimination is. Obviously, the auditory system is capable of detecting very subtle differences. (See *Figure 10.1.*)

Although the fundamental unit of speech—logically and descriptively—is the phoneme, research suggests that *psychologically* the fundamental unit is larger. For example, the two syllables *doo* and *dee* each consist of two phonemes. When we hear them spoken, we hear the same phoneme /d/ at the beginning. But Liberman, Cooper, Shankweiler, and Studdert-Kennedy (1967) analyzed the sounds of the syllables and found that the beginning phonemes were *not* the same. In fact, they could not cut out a section of a tape recording of the two syllables that would sound like /d/.

Results like these suggest that the fundamental unit of speech consists of groups of phonemes, such as syllables. An experiment conducted by Ganong (1980) supports this suggestion. He found that the perception of a phoneme is affected by the sounds that follow. He used a computer to synthesize a novel sound that fell between those of the phonemes /g/ and /k/. When the sound was followed by *ift,* the subjects heard the

word *gift,* but when it was followed by *iss,* they heard *kiss.* These results suggest that we recognize speech sounds in pieces larger than individual phonemes.

Recognition of Words in Continuous Speech: The Importance of Context

The perception of continuous speech involves different mechanisms from those used in the perception of isolated syllables. Because speech is full of hesitations, muffled sounds, and sloppy pronunciations, many individual words are hard to recognize out of context. For example, when Pollack and Pickett (1964) isolated individual words from a recording of normal conversations and played them back to other people, those people correctly identified the words only 47 percent of the time. When they presented the same words in the context of the original conversation, the subjects identified and understood almost 100 percent of them. Miller, Heise, and Lichten (1951) found that subjects understood strings of words such as "who brought some wet socks" in a noisy environment but failed to understand strings such as "wet brought who socks some." These findings confirm that the context of speech provides important cues to aid our recognition of words.

The effect of context on the perception of words is an example of top-down processing. (This concept was discussed in Chapter 7.) Other contexts also affect word perception. For example, although we tend to think of a conversation as involving only sounds, we also use other types of cues present in the environment to help us understand what someone is saying. If we are standing at a snack shop at a beach and someone says, "I scream," we are likely to hear it as "ice cream" (Reynolds and Flagg, 1983).

Understanding the Meaning of Speech

The meaning of a sentence (or of a group of connected sentences that are telling a story) is conveyed by the words that are chosen, the order in which they are combined, the affixes that are attached to the beginnings or ends of the words, the pattern of rhythm and emphasis of the speaker, and knowledge about the world shared by the speaker and the listener. Let us examine some of these features.

Syntax

If we want a listener to understand our speech, we must follow the "rules" of language. We must use words with which the listener is familiar and combine them in specific ways. For example, if we say, "The two boys looked at the heavy box," we can expect to be understood; but if we say, "Boys the two looking heavily the box at," we will not be. Only the first sentence follows the rules of English grammar.

---

voice-onset time The delay between the initial sound of a voiced consonant (such as the puffing sound of the phoneme /p/) and the onset of vibration of the vocal cords.

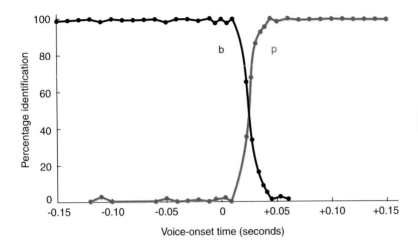

Figure 10.1

Discriminating between two phonemes. Identification of a sound as *ba* or *pa* as a function of voice-onset time.

(From Lisker, L., and Abramson, A. Proceedings of the Sixth International Congress of Phonetic Sciences, Prague, 1967. Prague: Academia, 1970. Reprinted with permission.)

All languages have a *syntax*, or *grammar*. They all follow certain principles, which linguists call **syntactical rules,** for combining words to form phrases, clauses, or sentences. (*Syntax*, like *synthesis*, comes from the Greek *syntassein*, "to put together.") Syntax provides important information. Consider the following sentence: *A little girl picked the pretty flowers*. A linguist (or an English teacher) can analyze the sentence and identify the part of speech for each word. However, linguists and English teachers could *understand* sentences like this one while they were still children—even before they learned the names *articles, noun phrases*, and so on. Our understanding of syntax is automatic. We are no more conscious of this process than a child is conscious of the laws of physics when he or she learns to ride a bicycle.

The automatic nature of syntactical analysis is nicely illustrated by experiments performed with artificial grammars. For example, Reber and Allen (1978) devised a set of rules for combining the letters *M, V, R, T,* and *X*. For example, *MVRXR* and *VXTTV* were "grammatical," but *MXVTR* and *VMRTX* were "ungrammatical." (The rules were rather complex.) They asked subjects to look at twenty "grammatical" strings of letters, printed on index cards. The subjects were told to "pay the utmost attention to the letter strings" but were not instructed to do anything else. Later, the subjects were presented with fifty different strings of letters, half of which were "grammatical" and half of which were not. Some of the "grammatical" strings were ones they had already seen, and some were new to them. The subjects were asked to indicate whether the strings were "grammatical."

The subjects did quite well; they correctly identified 81 percent of the strings of letters. Obviously, they had learned the rules, because they could recognize whether sequences they had never seen were correct. But despite their excellent performance, they could not express the rules verbally. The subjects made statements like the following: "The shapes of the items began to make sense." ". . . almost all my decisions are based on things looking either very right or very wrong. Sometimes for some reason things came out and glared at me

saying, 'bad, bad, bad,' other times the letters just flowed together and I knew it was an ok item."

In Chapter 8, we saw that some memories (*implicit memories*) cannot be described verbally, whereas others (*explicit memories*) can. Apparently, the syntactic rules are learned implicitly. Later, we can be taught to talk about these rules and recognize their application (and, for example, construct diagrams of sentences), but this ability is not needed to speak and understand the speech of others. In fact, Knowlton, Ramus, and Squire (1991) found that patients with anterograde amnesia were able to learn an artificial grammar even though they had lost the ability to form explicit memories. In contrast, as Gabrieli, Cohen, and Corkin (1988) observed, such patients are unable to learn the meanings of new words. Thus, learning syntax and word meaning appears to involve different types of memory—and consequently, different brain mechanisms.

I have no intention of describing the syntactical rules of the English language; they are very complicated and would not tell you much about the psychology of verbal behavior. However, becoming acquainted with the types of cues we attend to in trying to understand things people say (or write) is useful. Syntactical cues are signaled by *word order, word class, function words, affixes, word meanings,* and *prosody*.

Word order is important in English. For example, if we say, "The A Xs the B," we are indicating that the agent is A, the object is B, and the thing being done is X. For example, in the sentences *The boy hit the ball* and *The ball hit the boy,* word order tells us who does what to whom.

Word class refers to the grammatical categories (such as noun, pronoun, verb, adjective) that we learn about in school. But a person need not learn to categorize these words deliberately in order to recognize them and use them appropriately. For example, when we hear a sentence containing the

syntactical rule A grammatical rule of a particular language for combining words to form phrases, clauses, and sentences.

word *pretty,* we recognize that it refers to a person or a thing. Consider these two sentences: *The pretty girl picked the straw-berries* and *The tablecloth was pretty.* Although the word *pretty* is used in two different ways, at the beginning or end of the sentence, we have no trouble identifying what the word refers to.

Words can be classified as function words or content words. **Function words** include determiners, quantifiers, prepositions, and words in similar categories: *a, the, to, some, and, but, when,* and so on. **Content words** include nouns, verbs, and most adjectives and adverbs: *apple, rug, went, caught, heavy, mysterious, thoroughly, sadly.* Content words express meaning; function words express the relations between content words and thus are very important syntactical cues. As we shall see later, people with a particular type of brain damage lose the ability to comprehend syntax. Included with this deficit is the inability to understand function words or to use them correctly in speech.

Affixes are sounds that we add to the beginning (*pre-fixes*) or end (*suffixes*) of words to alter their grammatical function. For example, we add the suffix *-ed* to the end of a regular verb to indicate the past tense (*drop/dropped*); we add *-ing* to a verb to indicate its use as a noun (*sing/singing*); and we add *-ly* to an adjective to indicate its use as an adverb (*bright/brightly*). We are very quick to recognize the syntacti-cal function of words with affixes like these. For example, Ep-stein (1961) presented people with word strings such as the following:

a vap koob desak the citar molent um glox nerf

A vapy koob desaked the citar molently um glox nerfs.

The people could more easily remember the second string than the first, even though letters had been added to some of the words. Apparently, the addition of the affixes *-y, -ed,* and *-ly* made the words seem more like a sentence and they thus became easier to categorize and recall.

---

function word A preposition, article, or other word that conveys little of the meaning of a sentence but is important in specifying its grammatical structure.

content word A noun, verb, adjective, or adverb that conveys meaning.

affix A sound or group of letters that is added to the beginning of a word (prefix) or its end (suffix).

semantics The meanings and the study of the meanings represented by words.

prosody The use of changes in intonation and emphasis to convey meaning in speech besides that specified by the particular words; an important means of communication of emotion.

deep structure The essential meaning of a sentence, without regard to the grammatical features (surface structure) of the sentence that are needed to express it in words.

The *meaning* of a word—its **semantics**—provides important cues to the syntax of a sentence. (*Semantics* comes from the Greek *sema,* "sign.") For example, consider the following set of words: *Frank discovered a louse combing his beard.* The *syntax* of this sentence is ambiguous. It does not tell us whether Frank was combing Frank's beard, the louse was combing the louse's beard, or the louse was combing Frank's beard. But our knowledge of the world and of the usual meanings of words tells us that Frank was doing the combing, because people, not lice, have beards and combs.

Just as function words help us determine the syntax of a sentence, content words help us determine its meaning. For example, even with its function words removed, the following set of words still makes pretty good sense: *man placed wooden ladder tree climbed picked apples.* You can probably fill in the function words yourself and get *The man placed the wooden ladder against the tree, climbed it, and picked some apples.* We can often guess at function words, which is fortunate, because they are normally pronounced quickly and without emphasis and are therefore the most likely to be poorly pronounced.

The final syntactic cue is called prosody. **Prosody** refers to the use of stress, rhythm, and changes in pitch that accompany speech. Prosody can emphasize the syntax of a word or group of words or even serve as the primary source of syntactic information. For example, in several languages (including English), a declarative sentence can be turned into a question by means of prosody. Read the following sentences aloud to see how you would indicate to a listener which is a statement and which is a question.

You said that.

You said that?

In written communication, prosody is emphasized by punctuation marks. For example, a comma indicates a short pause, a period indicates a longer one along with a fall in the pitch of voice, and a question mark indicates an upturn in the pitch of voice near the end of the sentence. These devices serve as only partial substitutes for the real thing. Thus, because writers cannot rely on the cues provided by prosody, they must be especially careful to see that the syntax of their sentences is conveyed by other cues: word order, word class, function words, affixes, and word meaning.

Relation Between Semantics and Syntax

There is more than one way to say something, and, sometimes, a particular sentence can mean more than one thing. In Chapter 8, I described an experiment by Sachs that showed that we soon forget the particular form a sentence takes but remember its meaning much longer. Noam Chomsky (1957, 1965), a noted linguist, suggested that newly formed sentences are represented in the brain in terms of their meaning, which he called their **deep structure.** The deep structure represents the kernel of what the person intended to say. In order to say the sentence, the brain must transform the deep structure into the appropriate **surface structure:** the particular form the sentence takes.

An example of a "slip of the tongue" recorded by Fromkin (1973) gives us some clues about the way a sentence's deep structure can be transformed into a particular surface structure.

Rosa always date shranks.

The speaker actually intended to say, "Rosa always dated shrinks" (meaning psychiatrists or clinical psychologists). We can speculate that the deep structure of the sentence's verb phrase was something like this: *date* [past tense] + *shrink* [plural]. The words in brackets represent the names of the syntactical rules that are to be used in forming the surface structure of the sentence. Obviously, the past tense of *date* is *dated*, and the plural of *shrink* is *shrinks*. However, something went wrong during the transformation of the deep structure (meaning) into the surface structure (words and syntax). Apparently, the past tense rule got applied to the word *shrink*, resulting in *shrank*. The plural rule also got applied, making the nonsense word *shranks*. (See *Figure 10.2.*)

Most psychologists agree that the distinction between surface structure and deep structure is important. As we saw in Chapter 8, people with a language disorder known as conduction aphasia have difficulty repeating words and phrases, but they can *understand* them. In other words, they can retain the deep structure, but not surface structure, of other people's speech. Later in this chapter we will encounter more neuropsychological evidence in favor of the distinction. However, most psychologists disagree with Chomsky about the particular nature of the cognitive mechanisms through which deep structure is translated into surface structure (Tannhaus, 1988; Bohannon, 1993; Hulit and Howard, 1993).

Knowledge of the World

Comprehension of speech also involves knowledge about the world and about particular situations that we may encounter (Carpenter, Miyake, and Just, 1995). Schank and Abelson (1977) suggested that this knowledge is organized into **scripts,** which specify various kinds of events and interactions that people have witnessed or have learned about from others. Once the speaker has established which script is being referred to, the listener can fill in the details. For example, consider the following sentences (Hunt, 1985): *I learned a lot about the bars in town yesterday. Do you have an aspirin?* To understand what the speaker means, you must be able to do more than simply understand the words and analyze the sentence structure. You must know something about bars; for example, that they serve alcoholic beverages and that "learning about them" probably involves some drinking. You must also realize that drinking these beverages can lead to a headache and that aspirin is a remedy for headaches.

Hunt notes that when we describe an event to someone else, we usually do not spell out all the details. For example, consider this story: *Tony was hungry. He went to the restaurant and ordered a pizza. When he was finished, he found he had forgotten to take his wallet with him. He was embarrassed.* To understand it, you must know that after eating in a restaurant, you are expected to pay and also that because Tony had forgotten his wallet, he had no money with him.

Brain Mechanisms of Verbal Behavior

Studies of people with brain damage and PET studies of people engaged in verbal behavior suggest that mechanisms involved in perceiving, comprehending, and producing speech are located in different areas of the cerebral cortex. These studies have furthered our understanding of the processes of normal verbal behavior. Let us examine some of these mechanisms.

Speech Production: Evidence from Broca's Aphasia

In order to produce meaningful speech, we need to convert perceptions, memories, and thoughts into speech. The neural mechanisms that control speech production appear to be located in the frontal lobes. Damage to a region of the motor association cortex in the left frontal lobe (Broca's area) disrupts the ability to speak: It causes **Broca's aphasia,** a language disorder characterized by slow, laborious, nonfluent speech. (See *Figure 10.3.*) When trying to talk with patients who have Broca's aphasia, most people find it hard to resist supplying the words the patients are obviously groping for. But although these patients often mispronounce words, the ones they man-

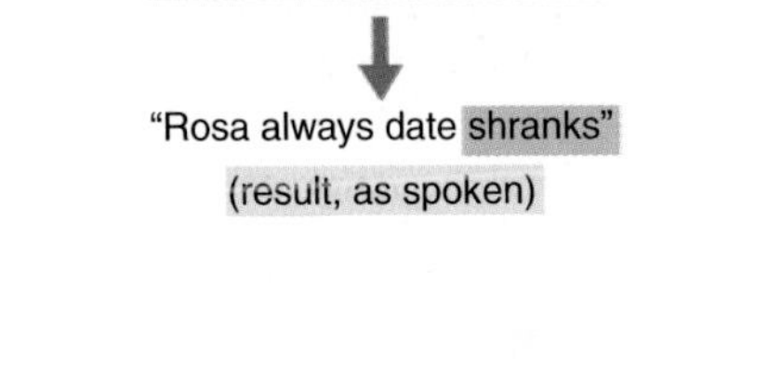

Rosa always date [past tense] shrink [plural]
(what the speaker intended to say)

↓

Rosa always date shrink [past tense] [plural]
(error in transformation process)

↓

(grammatical rules applied)

↓

"Rosa always date shranks"
(result, as spoken)

Figure 10.2

Deep structure and surface structure. A possible explanation for the error in the sentence *Rosa always date shranks.*

surface structure The grammatical features of a sentence.

script The characteristics (events, rules, and so on) that are typical of a particular situation; assists the comprehension of verbal discourse.

Broca's aphasia Severe difficulty in articulating words, especially function words, caused by damage that includes Broca's area, a region of the frontal cortex on the left (speech-dominant) side of the brain.

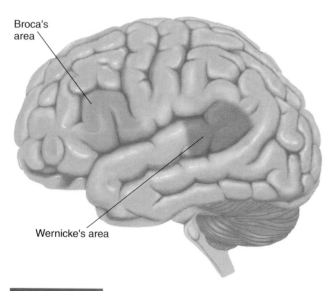

Broca's area

Wernicke's area

Figure 10.3

The locations of Broca's area and Wernicke's area.
(Wernicke's area will be described later.)

age to come out with are meaningful. They have something to say, but the damage to the frontal lobe makes it difficult for them to express these thoughts.

Here is a sample of speech from a man with Broca's aphasia, who is telling the examiner why he has come to the hospital. As you will see, his words are meaningful, but what he says is certainly not grammatical. The dots indicate long pauses.

> Ah . . . Monday . . . ah Dad and Paul [patient's name] . . . and Dad . . . hospital. Two . . . ah doctors . . . , and ah . . . thirty minutes . . . and yes . . . ah . . . hospital. And, er Wednesday . . . nine o'clock. And er Thursday, ten o' clock . . . doctors. Two doctors . . . and ah . . . teeth. Yeah, . . . fine. (Goodglass, 1976, p. 278)

Lesions that produce Broca's aphasia must be centered in the vicinity of Broca's area. However, damage restricted to the cortex of Broca's area does not appear to produce Broca's aphasia; the damage must extend to surrounding regions of the frontal lobe and to the underlying subcortical white matter (H. Damasio, 1989; Naeser et al., 1989).

Wernicke (1874) suggested that Broca's area contains motor memories—in particular, memories of the sequences of muscular movements that are needed to articulate words. Talking involves rapid movements of the tongue, lips, and jaw, and these movements must be coordinated with each other and with those of the vocal cords; thus, talking requires some very sophisticated motor control mechanisms. Obviously, circuits of neurons somewhere in our brain will, when properly

agrammatism   A language disturbance; difficulty in the production and comprehension of grammatical features, such as proper use of function words, word endings, and word order. Often seen in cases of Broca's aphasia.

activated, cause these sequences of movements to be executed. Because damage to the lower left frontal lobe (including Broca's area) disrupts the ability to articulate words, this region is the most likely candidate for the location of these "programs." The fact that this region is located just in front of the part of the primary motor cortex that controls the muscles used for speech certainly supports this conclusion.

In addition to their role in the production of words, neural circuits located in the lower left frontal lobe appear to perform some more complex functions. Damage to Broca's area often produces **agrammatism:** loss of the ability to produce or comprehend speech that employs complex syntactical rules. For example, people with Broca's aphasia rarely use function words. In addition, they rarely use grammatical markers such as *-ed* or auxiliaries such as *have* (as in *I have gone*). A study by Saffran, Schwartz, and Marin (1980) illustrates this difficulty. The following quotations are from agrammatic patients attempting to describe pictures:

> *Picture of a boy being hit in the head by a baseball*
>   The boy is catch . . . the boy is hitch . . . the boy is hit the ball. (p. 229)

> *Picture of a girl giving flowers to her teacher*
>   Girl . . . wants to . . . flowers . . . flowers and wants to . . . . The woman . . . wants to . . . The girl wants to . . . the flowers and the woman. (p. 234)

So far, I have described Broca's aphasia as a disorder in speech *production*. In an ordinary conversation, Broca's aphasics seem to understand everything that is said to them. They appear to be irritated and annoyed by their inability to express their thoughts well, and they often make gestures to supplement their scanty speech. The striking disparity between their speech and their comprehension often leads people to assume that their comprehension is normal. But their comprehension is *not* normal. To test agrammatic people for speech comprehension, Schwartz, Saffran, and Marin (1980) showed them a pair of drawings, read a sentence aloud, and then asked them to point to the appropriate picture. The patients heard forty-eight sentences such as *The clown applauds the dancer* and *The robber is shot by the cop*. For the first sample sentence, one picture showed a clown applauding a dancer, and the other showed a dancer applauding a clown. On average, the brain-damaged people responded correctly to only 62 percent of the pictures (chance would be 50 percent). In contrast, the performance of normal people is around 100 percent on such a simple task.

The correct picture in the study by Schwartz and her colleagues was specified by a particular aspect of grammar: word order. The agrammatism that accompanies Broca's aphasia appears to disrupt patients' ability to use grammatical information, including word order, to decode the meaning of a sentence. Thus, their deficit in comprehension parallels their deficit in production. If they heard a sentence such as *The mosquito was swatted by the man,* they would understand that it concerns a man and a mosquito and the action of swatting. Because of their knowledge of men and mosquitoes, they would have no trouble figuring out who is doing what to whom. But a sentence such as *The cow was kicked by the horse* does not provide any extra cues; if the grammar is not understood, neither is the meaning of the sentence.

Other experiments have shown that people with Broca's aphasia have difficulty carrying out a sequence of commands, such as "Pick up the red circle and touch the green square with it" (Boller and Dennis, 1979). This finding, along with the other symptoms described in this section, suggests that an important function of the left frontal lobe is sequencing—of movements of the muscles of speech (producing words) and of words (comprehending and producing grammatical speech).

Speech Comprehension: Evidence from Wernicke's Aphasia

Comprehension of speech obviously begins in the auditory system, which is needed to analyze sequences of sounds and to recognize them as words. *Recognition* is the first step in comprehension. Recognizing a spoken word is a complex perceptual task that relies on memories of sequences of sounds. This task appears to be accomplished by neural circuits in the upper part of the left temporal lobe—a region that has come to be known as **Wernicke's area.** (Refer to *Figure 10.3.*)

Brain damage in the left hemisphere that invades Wernicke's area as well as the surrounding region of the temporal and parietal lobes produces a disorder known as Wernicke's aphasia. (See *Figure 10.4.*) The symptoms of **Wernicke's aphasia** are poor speech comprehension and production of meaningless speech. Unlike Broca's aphasia, Wernicke's aphasia is fluent and unlabored; the person does not strain to articulate words and does not appear to be searching for them. The patient maintains a melodic line, with the voice rising and falling normally. When you listen to the speech of a person with Wernicke's aphasia, it appears to be grammatical. That is, the person uses function words such as *the* and *but* and employs complex verb tenses and subordinate clauses. However, the person uses few content words, and the words that he or she strings together just do not make sense. In the extreme, speech deteriorates into a meaningless jumble, illustrated by the following example:

> *Examiner:* What kind of work did you do before you came into the hospital?
>
> *Patient:* Never, now mista oyge I wanna tell you this happened when happened when he rent. His—his kell come down here and is—he got ren something. It hap-

Wernicke's area A region of auditory association cortex located in the upper part of the left temporal lobe; involved in the recognition of spoken words.

Wernicke's aphasia A disorder caused by damage to the left temporal and parietal cortex, including Wernicke's area; characterized by deficits in the perception of speech and by the production of fluent but rather meaningless speech.

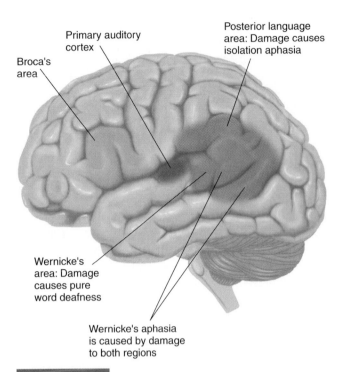

Figure 10.4

The location of brain damage that produces Wernicke's aphasia, pure word deafness, and isolation aphasia.

pened. In thesse ropiers were with him for hi—is friend—like was. And it just happened so I don't know, he did not bring around anything. And he did not pay it. And he roden all o these arranjen from the pedis on from iss pescid. In these floors now and so. He hadn't had em round here. (Kertesz, 1981, p. 73)

Because of the speech deficit of people with Wernicke's aphasia, when we try to assess their ability to comprehend speech, we must ask them to use nonverbal responses. That is, we cannot assume that they do not understand what other people say to them just because they do not give the proper answer. A commonly used test of comprehension assesses their ability to understand questions by pointing to objects on a table in front of them. For example, they are asked to "Point to the one with ink." If they point to an object other than the pen, they have not understood the request. When tested this way, people with severe Wernicke's aphasia do indeed show poor comprehension.

Because Wernicke's area is a region of the auditory association cortex, and because a comprehension deficit is so prominent in Wernicke's aphasia, this disorder has been characterized as a *receptive* aphasia. Wernicke suggested that the region that now bears his name is the location of memories of the sequences of sounds that constitute words. This hypothesis is reasonable; it suggests that the auditory association cortex of Wernicke's area recognizes the sounds of words, just as the visual association cortex in the lower part of the temporal lobe recognizes the sight of objects.

But why should damage to an area responsible for the ability to recognize spoken words disrupt people's ability to speak? Wernicke's aphasia, like Broca's aphasia, actually appears to consist of several deficits. The abilities that are disrupted include *recognition of spoken words, comprehension of the meaning of words,* and the *ability to convert thoughts into words.* Let us consider each of these abilities in turn.

Remember, *recognizing* a word is not the same as *comprehending* it. If you hear a foreign word several times, you will learn to recognize it; but unless someone tells you what it means, you will not comprehend it. Recognition is a perceptual task; comprehension involves retrieval of additional information from long-term memory. Damage to Wernicke's area produces a deficit in *recognition;* damage to the surrounding temporal and parietal cortex produces a deficit in production of meaningful speech and comprehension of the speech of others.

Brain damage that is restricted to Wernicke's area produces an interesting syndrome known as **pure word deafness** —a disorder of auditory word recognition, uncontaminated by other problems. Although people with pure word deafness are not deaf, they cannot understand speech. As one patient put it, "I can hear you talking, I just can't understand what you're saying." Another said, "It's as if there were a bypass somewhere, and my ears were not connected to my voice" (Saffran, Marin, and Yeni-Komshian, 1976, p. 211). These patients can recognize nonspeech sounds such as the barking of a dog, the sound of a doorbell, the chirping of a bird, and so on. Often, they can recognize the emotion expressed by the intonation of speech even though they cannot understand what is being said. More significantly, their own speech is excellent. They can often understand what other people are saying by reading their lips. They can also read and write, and, sometimes, they ask people to communicate with them in writing. Clearly, pure word deafness is not an inability to comprehend the meaning of words; if it were, people with this disorder would not be able to read people's lips or read words written on paper.

What happens if the region around Wernicke's area is damaged, but Wernicke's area itself is spared? The person will exhibit all of the symptoms of Wernicke's aphasia *except* a deficit in auditory word recognition. (We already encountered this disorder in Chapter 9.) Damage to the region surrounding Wernicke's area (which I will henceforth refer to as the *posterior language area*) produces a disorder known as **isolation aphasia,** an inability to comprehend speech or to produce meaningful speech accompanied by the ability to repeat speech and learn new sequences of words. (See *Figure 10.4.*) The difference between isolation aphasia and Wernicke's aphasia is that patients with isolation aphasia can repeat what other people say to them; thus, they obviously can recognize words. However, *they cannot comprehend the meaning of what they hear and repeat; nor can they produce meaningful speech of their own.* Apparently, the sounds of words are recognized by neural circuits in Wernicke's area, and this in-

Recognition is not the same as comprehension. If you encounter a foreign word several times you will learn to recognize it, but you will need additional information to learn to comprehend it.

formation is transmitted to Broca's area so that the words can be repeated. (In fact, a bundle of axons does directly connect these two regions.) But because the posterior language area is destroyed, the meaning of the words cannot be comprehended. (See *Figure 10.5.*)

Word Recognition and Production: PET Studies

The results of studies using the PET-scanning method are generally consistent with the results of studies of language-impaired patients with brain damage. First, several studies have found that patients with Broca's aphasia show abnormally low activity in the lower left frontal lobe, while patients with Wernicke's aphasia show low activity in the temporal/parietal area of the brain (Karbe et al., 1990, 1991; Metter et al., 1989, 1990). These results explain the fact that lesions in the depths of the brain can sometimes produce aphasia; these

pure word deafness The ability to hear, to speak, and (usually) to write, without being able to comprehend the meaning of speech; caused by bilateral temporal lobe damage.

isolation aphasia A language disturbance that includes an inability to comprehend speech or to produce meaningful speech accompanied by the ability to repeat speech and to learn new sequences of words; caused by brain damage to the left temporal/parietal cortex that spares Wernicke's area.

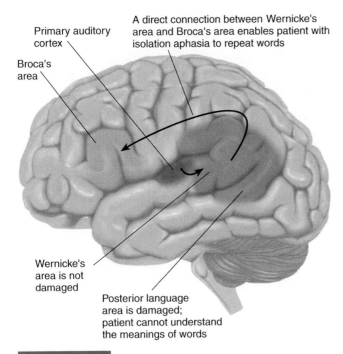

Primary auditory cortex

A direct connection between Wernicke's area and Broca's area enables patient with isolation aphasia to repeat words

Broca's area

Wernicke's area is not damaged

Posterior language area is damaged; patient cannot understand the meanings of words

Figure 10.5

Connections among regions of the brain that play a special role in language. The arrows provide an explanation of the ability of people with isolation aphasia to repeat words without being able to understand them.

lesions disrupt the activity of the frontal or temporal/parietal cortex and produce language disturbances.

Other studies have used PET scanners to investigate the neural activity of normal people while they performed verbal tasks. Several have shown that all kinds of auditory stimuli, including clicks, tones, and words played backwards, activate the region of the primary auditory cortex. In contrast, only the sound of words activates the left posterior temporal lobe—the region of Wernicke's area (Mazzitta et al., 1982; Lauter et al., 1985; Wise et al., 1991; Petersen and Fiez, 1993).

Figure 10.6 shows PET scans from a study by Petersen et al. (1988). Listening passively to a list of nouns activated the primary auditory cortex and Wernicke's area, while repeating the nouns activated the primary motor cortex and Broca's area. When people were asked to think of verbs that were appropriate to use with the nouns, even more intense activity was seen in Broca's area. (See *Figure 10.6.*) (Other parts of the

brain were activated as well; if you are interested in a discussion of these regions and their participation in verbal behavior, see Petersen and Fiez, 1993.)

What Is Meaning?

As we have seen, Wernicke's area is involved in the analysis of speech sounds and, thus, in the recognition of words. Brain damage to the posterior language area that surrounds Wernicke's area does not disrupt people's ability to recognize words, but it does disrupt their ability to understand them or to produce meaningful speech of their own. What, exactly, do we mean by *meaning*? And what types of brain mechanisms are involved?

Words refer to objects, actions, or relations in the world. Thus, the meaning of a word (its *semantics*) is defined by particular memories associated with it. For example, knowing the meaning of the word *tree* means being able to imagine the physical characteristics of trees: what they look like, what the wind sounds like blowing through their leaves, what the bark feels like, and so on. It also means knowing facts about trees: about their roots, buds, flowers, nuts, wood, and the chlorophyll in their leaves. These memories are not stored in the primary speech areas but in other parts of the brain, especially regions of the association cortex. Different categories of memories may be stored in particular regions of the brain, but they are somehow tied together, so that hearing the word *tree* activates all of them.

In thinking about the brain's verbal mechanisms involved in recognizing words and comprehending their meaning, I find that the concept of a dictionary serves as a useful analogy. Dictionaries contain entries (the words) and definitions (the meanings of the words). In the brain, there are at least two types of entries: auditory and visual. That is, we can look up a word according to how it sounds or looks (in writing). Consider just one type of entry: the sound of a word. We hear a familiar word and understand its meaning. How do we do so?

First, we must recognize the sequence of sounds that constitute the word—we find the auditory entry for the word in our "dictionary." As we saw, this entry appears to be located in Wernicke's area. Next, the memories that constitute the meaning of the word must be activated. Presumably, Wernicke's area is connected—through the posterior language area—with the neural circuits that contain these memories. (See *Figure 10.7.*)

The process works in reverse when we describe our thoughts or perceptions in words. Suppose that we want to tell

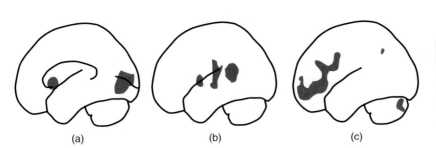

(a)   (b)   (c)

Figure 10.6

PET scans of subjects from the study by Petersen et al. (1988). (a) Listening passively to a list of nouns. (b) Silently reading a list of nouns. (c) Thinking of verbs related to a list of nouns.

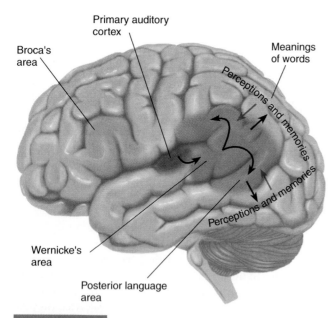

Broca's area

Primary auditory cortex

Meanings of words

Perceptions and memories

Perceptions and memories

Wernicke's area

Posterior language area

Figure 10.7

Words into thoughts and thoughts into words. The "dictionary" in the brain relates the sounds of words to their meanings and permits us to comprehend the meanings of words and translate our own thoughts into words. Black arrows represent comprehension of words; red arrows represent translation of thoughts or perceptions into words.

someone about a tree that we just planted. Thoughts about the tree (for example, a visual image of it) occur in our association cortex—the visual association cortex, in this example. Information about the activity of these circuits is sent first to the posterior language area and then to Broca's area, which causes the words to be set into a grammatical sentence and pronounced. (See *Figure 10.7.*)

What evidence do we have that meanings of words are represented by neural circuits in various regions of association cortex? The best evidence comes from the fact that damage to particular regions of the sensory association cortex can damage particular kinds of information and thus abolish particular kinds of meanings. For example, I met a patient who had recently sustained a stroke that had damaged a part of her right parietal lobe that plays a role in spatial perception. She was alert and intelligent and showed no signs of aphasia. However, she was confused about directions and other spatial relations. Although she could point to the ceiling and to the floor if I asked her to, she could not say which was above the other. Similarly, although her perception of other people appeared to be normal, she could not say whether a person's head was at the top or bottom of the body. I wrote a set of multiple-choice questions that evening, and the next day I gave her a test. When a question contained a word that dealt with space, she failed to understand what it meant. For example, she chose the following statements:

A tree's branches are *under* its roots.

The sky is *down.*

But when a question did not deal with space, she had no trouble choosing the correct alternative. For example, she chose the following statements:

After exchanging pleasantries, they got *down* to business.

He got sick and threw *up.*

Consider the use of the word *up* in the last sentence. It does not refer to a direction (actually, when we vomit, we usually point our mouths *down,* for obvious reasons). Instead, the word is simply part of a phrase. Similarly, getting *down* to business does not imply that the business has just gotten closer to the floor.

Damage to other regions of the brain can disrupt particular categories of meaning in speech. For example, damage to part of the association cortex of the *left* parietal lobe can produce an inability to name the body parts. This disorder is called autotopagnosia, or "poor knowledge of one's own topography." (A better name would have been *autotopanomia,* "poor *naming* of one's own topography.") People who can otherwise converse normally cannot reliably point to their elbows, knees, or cheeks when asked to do so, and they cannot name body parts when the examiner points to them. However, they have no difficulty understanding the meaning of other words.

Interim Summary

Speech and Comprehension

Language, the second most important human social behavior, is an orderly system of communication. The recognition of words in continuous speech is a complex process. Phonemes are recognized even though their pronunciation is affected by neighboring sounds, by accents and speech peculiarities, and by stress. Studies have shown that we distinguish between voiced and unvoiced consonant phonemes by means of voice-onset time. Research has also shown that the primary unit of analysis is not individual phonemes but groups of phonemes—perhaps syllables. Our recognition of words in continuous speech is far superior to our ability to recognize them when they have been isolated. We use contextual information in recognizing what we hear.

Meaning is a joint function of syntax and semantics. All users of a particular language observe syntactical rules that establish the relations of the words in a sentence to one another. These rules are not learned explicitly. In fact, research indicates that people can learn to apply rules of an artificial grammar without being able to say just what these rules are. The most important features that we use to understand syntax are word order, word class, function words, affixes, word meanings, and prosody. Content words refer to objects, actions, and the characteristics of objects and actions and thus can express meaning even in some sentences having ambiguous syntax.

Chomsky has suggested that speech production entails the transformation of deep structure into surface structure. Most psychologists disagree with the details of Chomsky's explanation but consider the distinction between deep and surface structure to be an interesting and important insight.

Speech comprehension requires more than an understanding of syntax and semantics; it also requires knowledge of the world. We must share some common knowledge about the world with a speaker if we are to understand what the speaker is referring to.

The effects of brain damage suggest that memories of the sounds of words are located in Wernicke's area and that memories of the muscular movements needed to produce them are located in Broca's area. Thus, Wernicke's area is necessary for speech perception, and Broca's area is necessary for its production. Wernicke's aphasia (caused by damage that extends beyond the boundaries of Wernicke's area) is characterized by fluent but meaningless speech that is scarce in content words but rich in function words. Presumably, function words and other syntactical features of speech related to motor operations involve mechanisms in the frontal lobes; as we saw, Broca's aphasia (caused by damage that extends beyond the boundaries of Broca's area) is characterized by nonfluent but meaningful speech that is scarce in function words but rich in content words.

Damage restricted to Wernicke's area does not produce aphasia; instead, it produces pure word deafness, a deficit in speech comprehension unaccompanied by other language difficulties. Damage to the temporal/parietal region surrounding Wernicke's area produces isolation aphasia—loss of the ability to produce meaningful speech or to comprehend the speech of others but retention of the ability to *repeat* speech. The results of studies of patients with brain damage have been supported by PET studies. Understanding the meaning of words requires other areas of the cortex, which contain memories of the relations between words and the concepts they denote.

Thought Questions

- Suppose that you were asked to determine the abilities and deficits of people with aphasia. What tasks would you include in your examination to test for the presence of particular deficits?
- What are the thoughts of a person with severe Wernicke's aphasia like? These people produce speech having very little meaning. Can you think of any ways that you could test these people to see if their thoughts were any more coherent than their words?

Reading

Speech first developed as a means of communication between two or more people facing each other—or at least within earshot of each other. The invention of writing, which made it possible for people to communicate across both space and time, was an important turning point in civilization. The first system of writing appears to have been developed around 4000 B.C. in ancient Sumeria (the location of present-day Iran and Iraq), apparently in response to the need to keep records of ownership and of business transactions. The earliest forms of writing were stylized drawings of real objects *(pictographs)*, but most cultures soon developed symbols based on sounds. For example, Egyptian hieroglyphic writing used some symbols as pictographs but used others phonetically, to spell out people's names or words that denoted concepts not easily pictured.

With the notable exception of Chinese (and other Asian writing systems based on Chinese), most modern languages use alphabetic writing systems in which a small number of symbols represent (more or less) the sounds used to pronounce words. For example, most European languages are represented by the Roman alphabet, originally developed to represent the sounds of Latin and subsequently adopted by tribes of people ruled or influenced by the Roman Empire. The Roman alphabet was adapted from the Greek alphabet, which in turn was adapted from the Phoenician alphabet. For example, the letter D has its origin in the Phoenician symbol *daleth*, which meant "door." At first, the symbol literally indicated a door, but it later came to represent the phoneme /d/. The Greeks adopted the symbol and its pronunciation but changed its name to *delta*. Finally, the Romans took it, alter-

When people read Chinese, the amount of time they fixate on each character is proportional to its complexity—the number of brush strokes used to make it.

Phoenician
"daleth"

Greek
"delta"

Hebrew
"daleth"

Cyrillic (Russian)

Roman

Medieval

DDDD*Dd*
Modern

Figure 10.8

The evolution of the letter D.

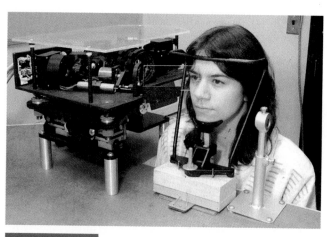

Figure 10.9

A woman seated in front of an eye tracker.

ing its shape into the one we recognize in our own language today. (See *Figure 10.8.*)

Scanning of Text

As we saw in Chapter 6, our eyes make rapid jumps, called *saccades*, as we scan a scene. These same rapid movements occur while we read. In fact, a French ophthalmologist discovered saccadic eye movements while watching people read (Javal, 1879).

The study of eye movements made during reading has been greatly facilitated by the development of a device called an eye tracker. An **eye tracker** consists of an apparatus that holds a person's head in a fixed position and a special video camera that keeps track of the person's gaze by focusing on an eye and monitoring the position of the pupil. The subject reads material presented by a computer on a video. (See *Figure 10.9.*)

We do not perceive things while the eyes are actually moving but during the brief **fixations** that occur between saccades. The average fixation has a duration of about 250 milliseconds (ms, 1/1000 of a second), but their duration can vary considerably. Figure 10.10 shows the pattern of fixations made by good and poor readers. The ovals above the text indicate the location of the fixations (which occur just below the ovals, on the text itself), and the numbers indicate their duration (in milliseconds). All of the good reader's fixations were made in the forward direction, whereas the poor reader looked back and examined previously read words several times (indicated by the arrows). In addition, the good reader took, on average, considerably less time to examine each word. (See *Figure 10.10.*)

What do we look at when we read? College students fixate on most words when they are asked to read text carefully enough to understand its meaning. They fixate on 80 percent

of the content words but on only 40 percent of the function words (Just and Carpenter, 1980). Of course, function words are generally shorter than content words, but the difference is not simply a matter of size. Readers are more likely to skip over short function words such as *and* or *the* than over short content words such as *ant* or *run* (Carpenter and Just, 1983).

Eye movements provide an excellent window into the dynamics of the reading process. Apparently, as we read a sentence, we analyze it word by word (Rayner and Pollatsek, 1989). Of course, some words contribute more to our understanding than do others. And sometimes, we must wait to see how a sentence turns out to understand the beginning. The more unusual a word is, the longer a reader fixates on it; presumably, we take longer to recognize and understand unusual words. For example, the word *sable* receives a longer fixation than the word *table*. The word that follows an unusual word does not receive a longer-than-usual fixation, which indicates that the reader finishes processing the word before initiating the next saccade (Thibadeau, Just, and Carpenter, 1982).

Besides spending a longer time fixating on unusual words, readers spend more time fixating on *longer* words. In fact, if word familiarity is held constant, the amount of time a word receives is proportional to its length (Carpenter and Just, 1983). (See *Figure 10.11.*) In addition, Just, Carpenter, and Wu (1983) found that the amount of time that Chinese readers spent fixating on a Chinese character was proportional to the number of brush strokes used to make it. All Chinese characters are of approximately the same size, so the increased fixation time appears to reflect the complexity of a word rather than the amount of space it occupies.

Phonetic and Whole-Word Recognition: Evidence from Neuropsychology

Most psychologists who study the reading process believe that readers have two basic ways to recognize words: phonetic

eye tracker A device that measures the location of a person's gaze while he or she observes a visual display.

fixation A brief interval between saccadic eye movements during which the eye does not move; visual information is gathered during this time.

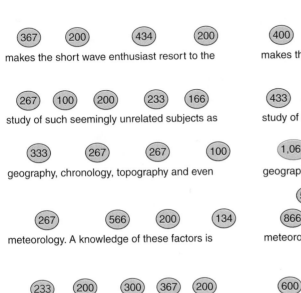
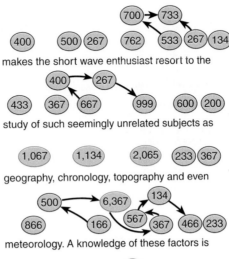

Figure 10.10

The pattern of fixations made by two readers. The ovals are placed above the locations of the fixations; the numbers within them indicate the durations of the fixations (in milliseconds). Arrows indicate backtracking to words already examined. (a) A good reader. (b) A poor reader.

(From Marcel Adam Just and Patricia A. Carpenter, The Psychology of Reading and Language Comprehension. *Copyright © 1987 by Allyn and Bacon. After Buswell (1937). Reproduced with permission.)*

and whole-word recognition. **Phonetic reading** involves the decoding of the sounds that letters or groups of letters make. For example, I suspect that you and I would pronounce *pra-glet* in approximately the same way. Our ability to pronounce this nonsense word depends on our knowledge of the relation between letters and sounds in the English language. We use such knowledge to "sound the word out." But do we have to "sound out" familiar, reasonably short words such as *table* or *grass*? It appears that we do not; we recognize each of these words as a whole. We engage in **whole-word reading**—reading by recognizing a word as a whole.

If a reader is relatively inexperienced, he or she will have to sound out most words and, consequently, will read rather slowly. Experienced readers will have had so much practice looking at words that they will quickly recognize most of them as individual units. In other words, during reading, phonetic and whole-word reading are engaged in a race. If the word is familiar, the whole-word method will win. If the word is unfamiliar, the whole-word method will fail, and the phonetic method will have enough time to come to completion.

Figure 10.12 illustrates some elements of the reading process. The diagram is an oversimplification of a very complex process, but it helps organize some of the facts that investigators have obtained. It considers only reading and pronouncing single words, not understanding the meaning of text. When we see a familiar word, we normally recognize it as a whole and say it aloud. If we see an unfamiliar word or a pronounceable nonword, we must try to read it phonetically. We recognize each letter and then sound it out, based on our knowledge of phonetics. (See *Figure 10.12.*)

Whole-word recognition is not only faster than phonetic decoding, but is also absolutely necessary in a language (such as English) in which spelling is not completely phonetic. Consider the following pairs of words: *cow/blow, bone/one, post/cost, limb/climb.* Obviously, no single set of phonological rules can account for the pronunciation of both members of each pair. (*Phonology*—loosely translated as "laws of sound" —refers to the relation between letters and the sounds they represent in a particular language.) But all these words are fam-

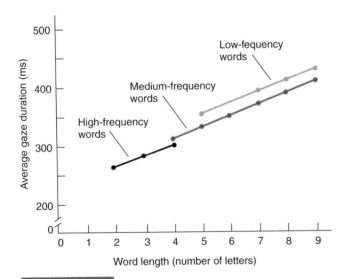

Figure 10.11

Average gaze duration as a function of word length.

(From Marcel Adam Just and Patricia A. Carpenter, The Psychology of Reading and Language Comprehension. *Copyright © 1987 by Allyn and Bacon. After Carpenter and Just, 1983. Reproduced with permission.)*

phonetic reading   Reading by decoding the phonetic significance of letter strings; "sound reading."

whole-word reading   Reading by recognizing a word as a whole; "sight reading."

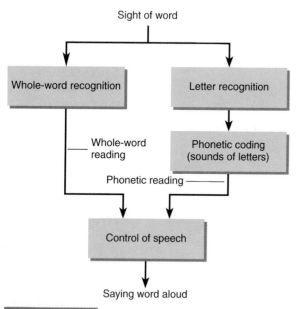

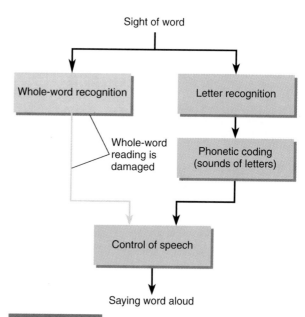

Figure 10.12

A simplified model of the reading process, showing whole-word and phonetic reading. The model considers only reading a single word aloud. Whole-word reading is used for most familiar words; phonetic reading is used for unfamiliar words and for nonwords such as *glab, trisk,* or *chint.*

Figure 10.13

A hypothetical explanation of surface dyslexia. Only phonetic reading remains.

iliar and easy to read. If we did not have the ability to recognize words as wholes, we would not be able to read irregularly spelled words, which are rather common in our language.

The best evidence that proves that people can read words without sounding them out comes from studies of patients with acquired dyslexias. *Dyslexia* means "faulty reading." *Acquired* dyslexias are those caused by damage to the brains of people who already know how to read. In contrast, *developmental* dyslexias are reading difficulties that become apparent

Most school systems teach children to read phonetically so that they can sound out words they do not recognize.

when children are learning to read. Developmental dyslexias may involve anomalies in brain circuitry, and I will discuss them later.

Although investigators have reported several types of acquired dyslexias, I will mention just three of them here. All of these disorders are caused by damage to the left parietal lobe or left temporal lobe, but the anatomy of dyslexias is not well understood. **Surface dyslexia** is a deficit in whole-word reading (Marshall and Newcombe, 1973; McCarthy and Warrington, 1990). The term *surface* reflects the fact that people with this disorder make errors related to the visual appearance of the words and to pronunciation rules, not to the meaning of the words, which is metaphorically "deeper" than the appearance. Because patients with surface dyslexia have difficulty recognizing words as wholes, they are obliged to sound them out. Thus, they can easily read words with regular spelling, such as *hand, table,* or *chin.* However, they have difficulty reading words with irregular spelling, such as *sew, pint,* and *yacht.* In fact, they may read these words as *sue, pinnt,* and *yatchet.* They have no difficulty reading pronounceable nonwords, such as *glab, trisk,* and *chint.* (See *Figure 10.13.*)

Patients with **phonological dyslexia** have the opposite problem; they can read by the whole-word method but cannot

surface dyslexia A reading disorder in which people can read words phonetically but have difficulty reading irregularly spelled words by the whole-word method.

phonological dyslexia A reading disorder in which people can read familiar words but have difficulty reading unfamiliar words or pronounceable nonwords because they cannot sound out words.

sound out words. Thus, they can read words that they are already familiar with, but they have great difficulty figuring out how to read unfamiliar words or pronounceable nonwords (Beauvois and Dérouesné, 1979; Dérouesné and Beauvois, 1979). People with phonological dyslexia may be excellent readers if they have already acquired a good reading vocabulary before their brain damage occurs. (See *Figure 10.14.*)

Phonological dyslexia provides evidence that whole-word reading and phonological reading involve different brain mechanisms. Phonetic reading, which is the only way we can read nonwords or words we have not yet learned, entails some sort of letter-to-sound decoding. It also requires more than decoding of the sounds produced by single letters, because, for example, some sounds are transcribed as two-letter sequences (such as *th* or *sh*) and the addition of the letter *e* to the end of a word lengthens an internal vowel (*can* becomes *cane*).

As we saw earlier in this chapter, recognizing a spoken word is different from understanding it. For example, patients with transcortical sensory aphasia can repeat what is said to them even though they show no signs of understanding what they hear or say. Another language disorder resembles isolation aphasia, except that the words in question are written, not spoken (Schwartz, Marin, and Saffran, 1979; Lytton and Brust, 1989). People with this disorder, called **direct dyslexia,** can read words aloud *even though they cannot understand the words they are saying.* After sustaining a stroke that damaged his left frontal and temporal lobes, Lytton and Brust's patient lost the ability to communicate verbally; his speech was meaningless and he was unable to comprehend what other people said to him. However, he could read words with which he was already familiar. He could *not* read pronounceable nonwords; thus, he had lost the ability to read phonetically. His comprehension deficit seemed complete; when the investigators presented him with a word and several pictures, one of which corresponded to the word, he read the word correctly but had no idea which picture went with it.

The symptoms of developmental dyslexias resemble those of acquired dyslexias. Developmental dyslexias first manifest themselves in childhood. They tend to occur in families, which suggests the presence of a genetic (and hence biological) component. Several studies have found evidence that brain abnormalities in a portion of Wernicke's area may be responsible for such reading difficulty (Galaburda and Kemper, 1979; Galaburda et al., 1985; Galaburda, 1993). In addition, Galaburda, Menard, and Rosen (1994) found evidence that structural differences in the auditory system of the brain may play a role in this disorder.

Geschwind and Behan (1984) have found that there is an association between dyslexia, left-handedness, and various immune disorders, such as thyroid and bowel diseases, diabetes, and rheumatoid arthritis. They suggest that a genetic abnormality, besides predisposing people for immune disorders, may also affect the development of parts of the left hemisphere of the brain. Their hypothesis is interesting and has some support, but much research remains to be done to test it experimentally. And almost certainly, there are several types of developmental dyslexias having several different causes.

As we saw earlier, PET studies have shown that the auditory association cortex is activated by the sound of words but not by other sounds. Petersen et al. (1990) obtained similar results using visual stimuli. These investigators presented people with four types of visual stimuli: unfamiliar letterlike forms, strings of consonants, pronounceable nonwords, and real words. They found that although all visual stimuli activated the primary visual cortex, one region of the visual association cortex was activated only by pronounceable nonwords or by real words. Their finding suggests that this region plays a role in recognition of familiar combinations of letters. Presumably, damage to this region, or faulty development of the neural circuits located there, is responsible for some forms of dyslexia. (See *Figure 10.15.*)

Understanding the Meanings of Words and Sentences

Recognizing a word is a matter of perception. The primary task is a visual one. But as we saw in the previous section, when we encounter an unfamiliar word, we use phonological codes to "sound out the word." Once we recognize a word, the next step in the reading process is understanding its meaning.

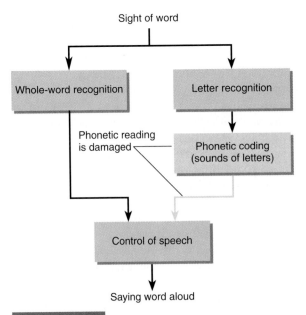

Figure 10.14

A hypothetical explanation of phonological dyslexia. Only whole-word reading remains.

direct dyslexia   A language disorder caused by brain damage in which people can read words aloud without understanding them.

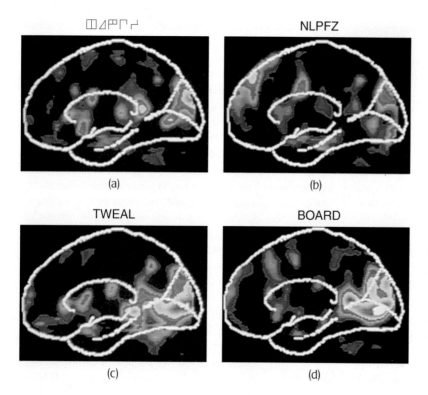

(a) NLPFZ (b)

TWEAL (c) BOARD (d)

Figure 10.15

PET scans of the medial surface of the brains of people reading letterlike forms (a), strings of consonants (b), pronounceable nonwords (c), and real words (d).

(From Petersen, S. E., Fox, P. T., Snyder, A. Z., and Raichle, M. E. Science, 1990, 249, 1041–1044. Reprinted with permission.)

We learn the meanings of words through experience. The meanings of content words involve memories of objects, actions, and their characteristics; thus, the meanings of content words involve visual, auditory, somatosensory, olfactory, and gustatory memories. These memories of the meanings of words are distributed throughout the brain. For example, our understanding of the meaning of the word *apple* involves memories of the sight of an apple, the way it feels in our hands, the crunching sound we hear when we bite into it, and the taste and odor we experience when we chew it. Our understanding of the meanings of adjectives, such as the word *heavy,* involves memories of objects that are difficult or impossible to lift. The image evoked by the phrase *heavy package* undoubtedly involves memories of our own experience with heavy packages, whereas the one evoked by the phrase *heavy rocket* (with which we have had no personal experience) is understood in terms of visual size and bulk.

What about the understanding of abstract content words, such as the nouns *honesty* and *justice?* These words are probably first understood as adjectives: An *honest student* is one who does not cheat on exams or plagiarize while writing papers, an *honest bank clerk* does not steal money, and so on. Our understanding of these words depends on our direct experience with such people or our vicarious experience with them through stories we read or hear about. By itself, the word *honesty* is abstract; it does not refer to anything concrete.

The understanding of most function words is also abstract. For example, the word *and* serves to link two or more things being discussed; the word *or* indicates a choice; the word *but* indicates that a contradiction will be expressed in the next phrase. The meanings of such words are difficult to imagine or verbalize, rather like the rules of grammar. The meanings of prepositions, such as *in, under,* or *through,* are more concrete and are probably represented by images of objects in relation to each other.

As we read (or hear) a sentence, the words and phrases we encounter activate memories that permit us to understand their meanings. Unless we deliberately pause to figure out an obscure allusion (which should not happen very often in the case of good writing and speaking), this activation is an automatic, unconscious process. When we read the sentence *She opened her mouth to let the dentist examine her aching tooth,* we very quickly picture a specific scene. Our understanding depends not only on comprehension of the specific words, but also on our knowledge of dental chairs, dentists, toothaches and their treatment, and so on.

A phenomenon known as semantic priming gives us some hints about the nature of activation of memories triggered by the perception of words and phrases. **Semantic priming** is a facilitating effect on the recognition of words having meanings related to a word encountered earlier. It involves similarities in the *meanings* of words. If a person reads a particular word, he or she can more easily read a second word that is related in meaning to the first. For example, if a person sees the word *bread,* he or she will be more likely to successfully recognize a fuzzy image of the word *butter* or an image that is presented very briefly by means of a tachistoscope

semantic priming A facilitating effect on the recognition of words having meanings related to a word that was presented previously.

(Johnston and Dark, 1986). Presumably, the brain contains circuits of neurons that serve as "word detectors" involved in visual recognition of particular words (Morton, 1979; McClelland and Rumelhart, 1981). Reading the word *bread* activates word detectors and other neural circuits involved in memories of the word's meaning. Apparently, the activation spreads to circuits denoting related concepts, such as butter. Thus, our memories must be linked according to our experience regarding the relations between specific concepts.

Figure 10.16 suggests how neural representations of concepts may be linked together. The concept *piano* has many different features, including the sounds a piano makes, its size, the shapes it can have, its components, the people who interact with it, and so on. Depending on the context in which it is perceived, the word *piano* can activate various subsets of these features. For example, the sentences *The piano was tuned* and *The piano was lifted* activate neural representations of different features. (See *Figure 10.16.*)

Context effects, an example of top-down processing, have been demonstrated through semantic priming. For example, Zola (1984) asked people to read sentences such as the following while he recorded their eye movements with an eye tracker.

1. Movie theaters must have adequate popcorn to serve their patrons.
2. Movie theaters must have buttered popcorn to serve their patrons.

Zola found that people made a significantly shorter fixation on the word *popcorn* in sentence 2. Let us consider why they did so. The word *adequate* is not normally associated with the word *popcorn*, so the people who read sentence 1 were unprepared for this word when they got to it. However, *buttered* certainly goes with *popcorn*, especially in the context of a movie theater. Thus, the context of the sentence must have provided some activation of the word detector for *popcorn*, making it easier for people to recognize the word.

Semantic priming studies have also shed some light on another aspect of the reading process—the development of a *mental model*. Many investigators believe that as a person reads some text, he or she generates a mental model of what the text is describing (Johnson-Laird, 1983). For example, if the text contains a narrative, the reader will imagine the scenes and actions that are being recounted. Glenberg, Meyer, and Lindem (1987) had subjects read the following sentences. Some subjects read the words *put on*; others saw *took off*.

> John was preparing for a marathon in August. After doing a few warm-up exercises, he *put on/took off* his sweatshirt and went jogging. He jogged halfway around the lake without too much difficulty.

After the subjects had read the last sentences, the experimenters flashed the word *sweatshirt* on a screen and measured the subjects' reaction times. Those subjects who had read *put on* recognized the word faster than did those who had read *took off*. Presumably, the mental model of the first

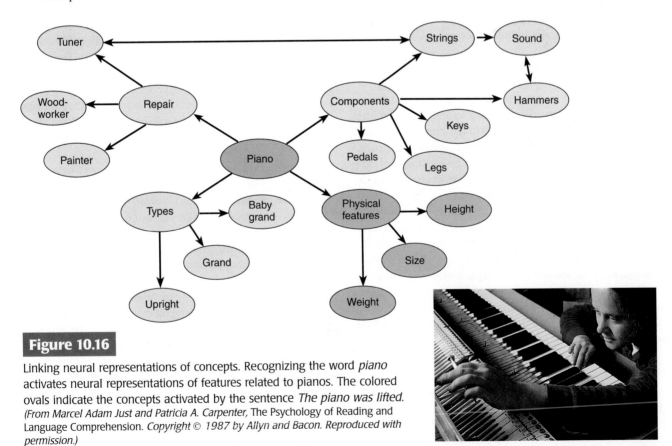

Figure 10.16

Linking neural representations of concepts. Recognizing the word *piano* activates neural representations of features related to pianos. The colored ovals indicate the concepts activated by the sentence *The piano was lifted.* *(From Marcel Adam Just and Patricia A. Carpenter,* The Psychology of Reading and Language Comprehension. *Copyright © 1987 by Allyn and Bacon. Reproduced with permission.)*

group of subjects contained a man wearing a sweatshirt; thus, the word detector for *sweatshirt* was primed.

Interim Summary

Reading

Writing allows people to communicate with other people they have never met—and who may not even be alive at the time the writing takes place. Recognition of written words is a complex perceptual task. The eye-tracking device allows researchers to study people's eye movements and fixations and to learn from these behaviors some important facts about the nature of the reading process. For example, we analyze a sentence word by word as we read it, taking longer to move on from long words or unusual ones.

Once a word has been perceived, recognition of its pronunciation and meaning takes place. Long or unfamiliar words are sounded out—that is, they are read phonologically. In contrast, short, familiar words are recognized as wholes. In fact, only whole-word reading will enable us to know how to pronounce words such as *cow* and *blow,* or *bone* and *one*, which have irregular spellings. In an experienced reader, both whole-word and phonetic reading take place simultaneously. If a word is recognized as a whole, the reader moves on to the next one; if not, he or she continues to decode it phonologically. The distinction between these two forms of recognition is supported by behavioral data and by studies of people with acquired dyslexias. People with surface dyslexia have difficulty with whole-word reading, while people with phonological dyslexia have difficulty sounding out unfamiliar words or pronounceable nonwords. In addition, people with direct dyslexia can read words but cannot understand their meaning. Developmental dyslexias appear to be caused by abnormal development of parts of the left hemisphere, and they may be caused by genetic defects that also affect the immune system and predispose a person toward left-handedness.

The meanings of words are learned through experience. Concrete content words are represented by memories of objects, actions, and their characteristics. Abstract content words are probably first understood as adjectives that refer to properties of concrete concepts. Function words are understood by their grammatical roles or by the relations they represent. The phenomenon of semantic priming suggests that some neural circuits (word detectors) recognize the visual form of words, while other circuits encode various aspects of the meanings of words. Connections between these circuits are responsible for our ability to recognize associations in meaning. Thus, semantic priming has been used to study the processes of word recognition and comprehension of meaning.

Thought Questions

- Suppose someone close to you received a head injury that caused phonological dyslexia. What would you do to try to help her read better? (It would probably be best to build on her remaining abilities.) Suppose she needed to learn to read some words she had never seen before. How would you help her do so?
- Young children often move their lips while they read. Why do you think they do so?

Language Acquisition by Children

How do children learn to communicate verbally with other people? How do they master the many rules needed to transform a thought into a coherent sentence? How do they learn the meanings of thousands of words? And *why* do they do all these things? Do other people shape children's babble into words by appropriately reinforcing their behavior, or do innate mechanisms ensure the acquisition of language without reinforcement? This section addresses these and other questions related to children's verbal development.

Perception of Speech Sounds by Infants

Language development starts even before birth. Although the sounds that reach a fetus are somewhat muffled, speech sounds can still be heard. And some learning appears to take place prenatally. The voice that a fetus hears best and most often is obviously that of its mother. Consequently, a newborn infant prefers its mother's voice to that of others (DeCasper and Fifer, 1980). DeCasper and Spence (1986) even found that newborn infants preferred hearing their mothers reading a passage they had read aloud several times before their babies were born to hearing them read a passage they had never read before. Presumably, the infants had learned something about the rhythm and intonation of the passage they had heard *in utero*.

An infant's auditory system is remarkably well developed. Wertheimer (1961) found that newborn infants still in the delivery room can turn their heads toward the source of a sound. Infants two or three weeks of age can discriminate between the sound of a voice and other sounds. By the age of two months, babies can tell an angry voice from a pleasant one; an angry voice produces crying, whereas a pleasant one causes smiling and cooing.

Psychologists have developed a clever technique to determine what sounds a very young infant can perceive. A special pacifier nipple is placed in the baby's mouth. The nipple is connected by a plastic tube to a pressure-sensitive switch that converts the infant's sucking movements into electrical signals. These signals can be used to turn on auditory stimuli. Each time the baby sucks, a particular sound is presented. (See *Figure 10.17.*)

If the auditory stimulus is novel, the baby usually begins to suck at a high rate. If the stimulus remains the same, its

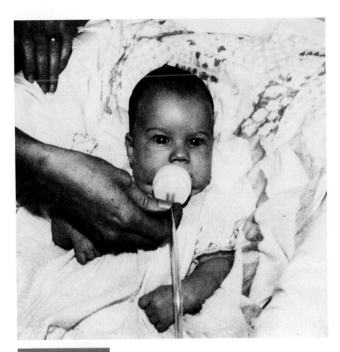

Figure 10.17

A procedure used to investigate auditory perception by infants. The baby's sucking action on the nipple turns on the tape recorder for a while.

Table 10.1	
Examples of Responses Infants Make to Various Speech Sounds	
First Age of Occurrence	Response
Newborn	Is startled by a loud noise
	Turns head to look in the direction of sound
	Is calmed by the sound of a voice
	Prefers mother's voice to a stranger's
	Discriminates among many speech sounds
1-2 mo	Smiles when spoken to
3-7 mo	Responds differently to different intonations (e.g., friendly, angry)
8-12 mo	Responds to name
	Responds to "no"
	Recognizes phrases from games (e.g., "Peekaboo," "How big is baby?")
	Recognizes words from routines (e.g., waves to "bye-bye")
	Recognizes some words

Source: Berko Gleason, J. *The Development of Language.* New York: Macmillan Publishing Company, 1993. Used by permission.

novelty wears off (habituation occurs) and the rate of sucking decreases. With another new stimulus, the rate of sucking again suddenly increases, unless the baby cannot discriminate the difference. If the stimuli sound the same to the infant, the rate of sucking remains low after the change.

Using this technique, Eimas et al. (1971) found that one-month-old infants could tell the difference between the sounds of the consonants *b* and *p*. Like Lisker and Abramson (1970) in the study discussed earlier, they presented the sounds *ba* and *pa*, synthesized by a computer. The infants, like the adult subjects in the earlier study, discriminated between speech sounds having voice-onset times that differed by only 0.02 second. Even very early during postnatal development, the human auditory system is ready to make very fine discriminations.

Table 10.1 lists some of the responses infants make to various types of speech sounds. (See *Table 10.1.*)

The Prespeech Period and the First Words

Kaplan and Kaplan (1970) have outlined the progression of early vocalizations in infants. The first sound that a baby makes is crying. As we will see in Chapter 12, this aversive stimulus serves a useful function. It is important in obtaining behaviors from the baby's caregivers. At about one month of age, infants start making other sounds, including one that is called *cooing* because of the prevalence of the *oo* sound. Often during this period, babies also make a series of sounds that resemble a halfhearted attempt to mimic the sound of crying.

At around six months, a baby's sounds begin to resemble those that occur in speech. Even though their babbling does not contain words—and does not appear to involve attempts to communicate verbally—the sounds infants make, and the rhythm in which they are articulated, reflect the adult speech that babies hear. Mehler et al. (1988) found that four-day-old infants preferred to hear a voice speaking French, their parents' native language. And this ability to discriminate the sounds and rhythms of the language spoken around them manifested itself in the infants' own vocalizations very early. Boysson-Bardies, Sagart, and Durand (1984) had adult French speakers listen to recordings of the babbling of children from various cultures. The adults could easily distinguish the babbling of eight-month-old French infants from that of babies of different language backgrounds.

A study by Kuhl et al. (1992) provides further evidence of the effect of children's linguistic environment on their language development. Native speakers learn not to distinguish between slight variations of sounds present in their language. In fact, they do not even *hear* the differences between them. For example, Japanese contains a sound that comes midway between /l/ and /r/. Different native speakers pronounce the sound differently, but all pronunciations are recognized as examples of the same phoneme. When native speakers of Japanese learn English, they have great difficulty distinguishing the sounds /l/ and /r/; for example, *right* and *light* sound to them like the same word. Presumably, the speech sounds a child hears alter the brain mechanisms responsible for analyzing them so that minor variations are not even perceived. The question is, When does this alteration occur? Most researchers have supposed that it happens only after children begin to learn the meanings of words, which occurs at around ten to twelve months of age.

Kuhl and her colleagues found, however, that this learning takes place much earlier. They studied six-month-old infants in the United States and Sweden. The infants were seated in their mothers' laps, where they watched an experimenter sitting nearby, playing with a silent toy. Every two seconds, a loudspeaker located to the infant's left presented the sound of a vowel. From time to time, the sound was altered. If the infant noticed the change and looked at the loudspeaker, the experimenter reinforced the response by activating a toy bear that pounded on a miniature drum. Thus, the procedure provided a test of infants' ability to distinguish slight differences in vowel sounds. (See *Figure 10.18.*)

The experimenters presented two different vowel sounds, one found in English but not in Swedish and the other found in Swedish but not in English. From time to time, they varied the sound slightly. The reactions of the Swedish infants and the American infants were strikingly different. Swedish infants noticed when the English vowel changed but not when the Swedish vowel changed; and American infants did the opposite. In other words, by the age of six months, the infants had learned not to pay attention to slight differences in speech sounds of their own language, but they were still able to distinguish slight differences in speech sounds they had never heard. Even though they were too young to understand the

meaning of what they heard, the speech of people around them had affected the development of their perceptual mechanisms.

Even before infants learn to talk, they display clear intent to communicate. For example, consider the following episode (from Bates, Camaioni, and Volterra, 1975).

> Marta is unable to open a small purse, and places it in front of her father's hand. . . . F. does nothing, so Marta puts the purse in his hand and utters a series of small sounds, looking at F. F. still does not react, and M. insists, pointing to the purse and whining. . . . finally, F. touches the purse clasp and simultaneously says, "Should I open it?" M. nods sharply. (p. 219)

Clearly, Marta wanted her father to do something for her, and she managed to communicate her request. Most attempts of preverbal infants to communicate fall into three major categories: *rejection, request* (for social interaction, for an object, or for an action), and *comment* (Sachs, 1993). *Rejection* usually involves pushing the unwanted object away and using facial expression and characteristic vocalizations to indicate displeasure. A *request for social interaction* usually involves the use of gestures and vocalizations to attract the caregiver's attention. A *request for an object* usually involves reaching and pointing and particular vocalizations. A *request for an action* (such as the one described above) similarly involves particular sounds and movements. Finally, a *comment* usually involves pointing out an object or handing it to the caregiver, accompanied by some vocalization.

Infants babble before they talk. They often engage in serious "conversations" with their caregivers, taking turns "talking" with them. Infants' voices are modulated, and the stream of sounds they make sound as though they are using a secret language (Menn and Stoel-Gammon, 1993).

At about one year of age, a child begins to produce words. The first sounds children use to produce speech appear to be similar across all languages and cultures: The first vowel is usually the soft *a* sound of *father*, and the first consonant is a *stop consonant* produced with the lips—*p* or *b*. Thus, the first word is often *papa* or *baba*. The next feature to be added is *nasality*, which converts the consonants *p* or *b* into *m*. Thus, the next word is *mama*. Naturally, mothers and fathers all over the world recognize these sounds as their children's attempts to address them.

The first sounds of a child's true speech contain the same phonemes that are found in the babbling sounds that the child is already making; thus, speech emerges from prespeech sounds. In the course of learning words from their caregivers and from older children, infants often invent their own **protowords**, unique strings of phonemes that serve word-like functions. The infants use these protowords consistently in particular situations (Menn and Stoel-Gammon, 1993). For

Figure 10.18

An American child being tested in the experiment by Kuhl and her colleagues.

protoword A unique string of phonemes that an infant invents and uses as a word.

example, Halliday (1975) reported that when his son Nigel wanted something, he would reach for it with an intent facial expression and say, "Na! Na!" until the desired object was given to him.

The development of speech sounds continues for many years. Some sequences are added very late. For example, the *str* of *string* and the *bl* of *blink* are difficult for young children to produce; they usually say *tring* and *link,* omitting the first consonant. Most children recognize sounds in adult speech before they can produce them. Consider this conversation (Dale, 1976):

> *Adult:* Johnny, I'm going to say a word two times and you tell me which time I say it right and which time I say it wrong: *rabbit, wabbit.*
>
> *Child: Wabbit* is wight and *wabbit* is wong.

Although the child could not pronounce the *r* sound, he clearly could recognize it.

The Two-Word Stage

At around eighteen to twenty months of age, children start putting two words together, and their linguistic development takes a leap forward. It is at this stage that linguistic creativity really begins. Consider the creativity in *allgone outside,* said by a child when the door was closed.

Like first sounds, children's two-word utterances are remarkably consistent across all cultures that have been observed. Children use words in the same way, no matter what language their parents speak. Even deaf children who learn sign language from their parents put two words together in the same way as children who can hear (Bellugi and Klima, 1972). And deaf children whose parents do not know sign language invent their own signs and use them in orderly, "rule-governed" ways (Goldin-Meadow and Feldman, 1977). Thus, the grammar of children's language at the two-word stage appears to be universal (Owens, 1992).

For many years, investigators described the speech of young children in terms of adult grammar, but researchers now recognize that children's speech simply follows different rules. Young children are incapable of forming complex sentences—partly because their vocabulary is small, partly because their short-term "working" memory is limited (they cannot yet encode a long string of words), and partly because their cognitive development has not yet reached a stage at which they can learn complex rules of syntax (Locke, 1993).

How Adults Talk to Children

Parents do not talk to children the way they talk to adults; they use only short, simple, well-formed, repetitive sentences and phrases (Brown and Bellugi, 1964). In fact, such speech deserves its own label: **child-directed speech** (Snow, 1986). In a comprehensive review of the literature, deVilliers and

deVilliers (1978) found that adults' speech to children is characterized by clear pronunciation, exaggerated intonations, careful distinctions between similar-sounding phonemes, relatively few abstract words and function words, and a tendency to isolate constituents that undoubtedly enables young children to recognize them as units of speech.

Another important characteristic of child-directed speech is that it tends to refer to tangible objects the child can see, to what the child is doing, and to what is happening around the child (Snow et al., 1976). Words are paired with objects the child is familiar with, which is the easiest way to learn them. For example, caregivers make statements and ask questions about what things are called, what noises they make, what color they are, what actions they are engaging in, who they belong to, and where they are located. Their speech contains more content words, and fewer verbs, modifiers, and functions words (Newport, 1975; Snow, 1977).

Adults—particularly caregivers, who have a continuing relationship with a child—tend to act as tutors when talking with children. For example, Snow and Goldfield (1982) found that as a mother and child repeatedly read a book over a period of thirteen months, the mother's speech became more and more complex, especially when they were discussing a picture that they looked at again and again.

Adults often expand children's speech by imitating it but putting it into more complex forms, which undoubtedly helps the child learn about syntactical structure (Brown and Bellugi, 1964):

> *Child:* Baby highchair.
> *Adult:* Baby is in the highchair.
>
> *Child:* Eve lunch.
> *Adult:* Eve is having lunch.
>
> *Child:* Throw daddy.
> *Adult:* Throw it to daddy.

People make allowances for the age of the child with whom they are talking. Mothers talk differently to two-year-olds than to ten-year-olds (Snow, 1972a). Even four-year-old children talk differently to two-year-olds than they do to adults or other four-year-olds (Shatz and Gelman, 1973). It seems unlikely that these differentiated speech patterns are innately determined. Snow (1972a) compared the speech patterns of a mother talking to a child with her speech patterns when she only pretended to be talking to a child. The woman's speech when the child was absent was simpler than it would have been if addressed to an adult, but when the child was present, it was simpler still. Clearly, then, feedback from children is important.

child-directed speech The speech of an adult directed toward a child; differs in important features from adult-directed speech and tends to facilitate learning of language by children.

The most important factor controlling adults' speech to children is the child's attentiveness. Both adults and children are very sensitive to whether another person is paying attention to them. As Snow (1986) notes, people do not talk *at* children, they talk *with* them. When a child looks interested, we continue with what we are doing. When we notice signs of inattention, we advance or simplify our level of speech until we regain the child's attention. Stine and Bohannon (1983) found that when children give signs that they do not understand what an adult is saying, the adult adjusts his or her speech, making it simpler.

Infants also exert control over what their caregivers talk about. The topic of conversation usually involves what the infant is playing with or is guided by what the infant is gazing at (Bohannon, 1993). This practice means that infants hear speech that concerns what they are already paying attention to, which undoubtedly facilitates learning. In fact, Tomasello and Farrar (1986) found that infants of mothers who talked mostly about the objects of their infants' gazes uttered their first words earlier than other infants and also developed larger vocabularies early in life.

An experiment by Snow (1972b) showed that children pay more attention to a tape recording of speech directed to a child than to a recording of speech directed to an adult. Other researchers have found that children respond best to speech that is slightly more complex than their own (Shipley, Smith, and Gleitman, 1969). Interacting with someone who has achieved slightly greater competence appears to be an optimum strategy for most learning. For example, if you want to improve your tennis game, you should play with someone a bit better than you are. A poorer player is no challenge; and if you play with someone of professional quality, you will hardly get a chance to return the ball. Thus, children modify adults' speech, keeping it at the optimal level of complexity.

Acquisition of Adult Rules of Grammar

The first words children use tend to be content words, probably because these words are emphasized in adult speech and because they refer to objects and actions that children can directly observe (Brown and Fraser, 1964). As children develop past the two-word stage, they begin to learn and use more and more of the grammatical rules that adults use. The first form of sentence lengthening appears to be the expansion of object nouns into noun phrases (Bloom, 1970). For example, *That ball* becomes *That a big ball*. Next, verbs get used more often, articles are added, prepositional phrases are mastered, and sentences become more complex. These results involve the use of inflections and function words. Function words,

you recall, are the little words (*the, to, and,* and so on) that help shape the syntax of a sentence. **Inflections** are special suffixes we add to words to change their syntactical or semantic function. For example, the inflection *-ed* changes most verbs into the past tense (*change* becomes *changed*), *-ing* makes a verb into a noun (*make* becomes *making*), and *-'s* indicates possession (*Paul's truck*). Table 10.2 shows the approximate order in which children acquire some of these inflections and function words. (See *Table 10.2*.)

It is more difficult for children to add an inflection or function word to their vocabulary than to add a new content word because the rules that govern the use of inflections or function words are more complex than those that govern the use of most content words. In addition, content words usually refer to concrete objects or activities. The rules that govern the use of inflections or function words are rarely made explicit. A parent seldom says, "When you want to use the past tense, add *-ed* to the verb"—nor would a young child understand such a pronouncement. Instead, children must listen to speech and figure out how to express such concepts as the past tense. Studies of children's speech have told us something about this process.

Table 10.2

The Approximate Order in Which Children Acquire Inflections and Function Words

Item	Example
1. Present progressive: *ing*	He is *sitting* down.
2. Preposition: *in*	The mouse is *in* the box.
3. Preposition: *on*	The book is *on* the table.
4. Plural: *-s*	The *dogs* ran away.
5. Past irregular: e.g., *went*	The boy *went* home.
6. Possessive: *-'s*	The *girl's* dog is big.
7. Uncontractible copula *be*: e.g., *are, was*	*Are* they boys or girls? *Was* that a dog?
8. Articles: *the, a, an*	He has *a* book.
9. Past regular: *-ed*	He *jumped* the stream.
10. Third person regular: *-s*	She *runs* fast.
11. Third person irregular: e.g., *has, does*	*Does* the dog bark?
12. Uncontractible auxiliary *be*: e.g., *is, were*	*Is* he running? *Were* they at home?
13. Contractible copula *be*: e.g., *'s, -re*	*That's* a spaniel. *They're* pretty.
14. Contractible auxiliary *be*: e.g., *-'s, -'re*	*He's* doing it. *They're* running slowly.

Source: Adapted from Table 9-3 from *Psychology and Language: An Introduction to Psycholinguistics* by Herbert H. Clark and Eve V. Clark, copyright © 1977 by Harcourt Brace Jovanovich, Inc., reprinted by permission of the publisher. After Brown (1973).

inflection A change in the form of a word (usually by adding a suffix) to denote a grammatical feature such as tense or number.

Table 10.3

Some Overextensions That Children Make While Learning New Words

Word	Original Referent	Application
mooi	Moon	Cakes, round marks on windows, writing on windows and in books, round shapes in books, round postmarks, letter *o*
buti	ball	Toy, radish, stone sphere at park entrance
ticktock	watch	All clocks and watches, gas meter, firehose wound on spool, bath scale round dial
baw	ball	Apples, grapes, eggs, squash, bell clapper, anything round
mem	horse	Cow, calf, pig, moose, all four-legged animals
fly	fly	Specks of dirt, dust, all small insects, child's own toes, crumbs of bread, a toad
wau-wau	dog	All animals, toy dog, soft house slippers, picture of an old man dressed in furs

Source: Adapted from Table 13-2 from *Psychology and Language: An Introduction to Psycholinguistics* by Herbert H. Clark and Eve V. Clark, copyright © 1977 by Harcourt Brace Jovanovich, Inc., reprinted by permission of the publisher. After E. Clark (1975).

The most frequently used verbs in most languages are *irregular*. Forming the past tense of such verbs in English does *not* involve adding *-ed*. (Examples are *go/went, throw/threw, buy/bought, see/saw,* and *can/could*.) The past tense of such verbs must be learned individually. Because irregular verbs get more use than do regular ones, children learn them first, producing the past tense easily in sentences such as *I came, I fell down,* and *She hit me.* Soon afterward, they discover the regular past tense inflection and expand their vocabulary, producing sentences such as *He dropped the ball.* But they also begin to say *I comed, I falled down,* and *She hitted me.* Having learned a rule, they apply it to all verbs, including the irregular ones that they were previously using correctly. In fact, it takes children several years to learn to use the irregular past tense correctly again.

Acquisition of Meaning

How do children learn to use and understand words? The simplest explanation is that they hear a word spoken at the same time that they see (or hear, or touch) the object to which the word refers. After several such pairings, they add a word to their vocabulary. In fact, children first learn the names of things with which they interact, or things that change (and thus attract their attention). For example, they are quick to learn words like *cookie* or *blanket,* but are slow to learn words like *wall* or *window* (Ross et al., 1986; Pease, Gleason, and Pan, 1993).

Suppose that we give a boy a small red plastic ball and say "ball." After a while, the child says "ball" when he sees it. Yet we cannot conclude from this behavior that the child knows the meaning of *ball.* So far, he has encountered only one referent for the word: a small one made of red plastic. If he says "ball" when he sees an apple or an orange, or even the moon, we must conclude that he does not know the meaning of *ball.* This type of error is called **overextension**—the use of a word to denote a larger class of items than is appropriate. If he uses the word to refer only to the small red plastic ball, his error is called an **underextension**—the use of a word to denote a smaller class of items than is appropriate. *Table 10.3* lists some examples of children's overextensions while learning the meanings of new words.

Both overextensions and underextensions are normal; a single pairing of a word with the object does not provide enough information for accurate generalization. Suppose that someone is teaching you a foreign language. She points to a penny and says "pengar." Does the word mean "penny," "money," "coin," or "round"? You cannot decide from this one example. Without further information, you may overextend or underextend the meaning of the word if you try to use it. If your teacher then points to a dollar bill and again says "pengar," you will deduce (correctly) that the word means "money."

Caregivers often correct children's overextensions. The most effective type of instruction occurs when an adult provides the correct label and points out the features that distin-

overextension The use of a word to denote a larger class of items than is appropriate, for example, referring to the moon as a *ball.*

underextension The use of a word to denote a smaller class of items than is appropriate, for example, referring only to one particular animal as a *dog.*

guish the object from the one with which the child has confused it (Chapman, Leonard, and Mervis, 1986). For example, if a child calls a yo-yo a "ball," the caregiver might say, "That's a yo-yo. See? It goes up and down" (Pease, Gleason, and Pan, 1993, p. 130).

Many words, including function words, do not have physical referents. For example, prepositions such as *on, in,* and *toward* express relations or directions, and a child needs many examples to learn how to use them appropriately. Pronouns are also difficult; for example, it takes a child some time to grasp the notion that *I* means the speaker: *I* means "me" when I say it, but *I* means "you" when you say it. In fact, parents usually avoid personal pronouns in speaking with their children. Instead, they use sentences such as *Does baby want another one?* (meaning "Do you want another one?") and *Daddy will help you* (meaning "I will help you").

Abstract words such as *apparently, necessity, thorough,* and *method* have no direct referents and must be defined in terms of other words. Therefore, children cannot learn their meanings until after they have learned many other words. Explaining the meaning of *apparently* to a child having a limited vocabulary would be as hopeless a task as my using a Russian dictionary (not a *Russian-English* dictionary) to determine the meaning of a Russian word. Because I do not understand Russian, the definition would be just as meaningless to me as the word being defined.

Evaluating Scientific Issues

Is There a Language Acquisition Device?

The linguistic accomplishments of young children are remarkable. Even a child who later does poorly in school learns the rules of grammar and the meanings of thousands of words. Some children fail to work hard at school, but no normal child fails to learn to talk. What shapes this learning process, and what motivates it?

There is vigorous controversy about why children learn to speak and, especially, why they learn to speak grammatically. Chomsky (1965) observed that the recorded speech of adults is not as correct as the dialogue we read in a novel or hear in a play; often, it is ungrammatical, hesitating, and full of unfinished sentences. In fact, he characterized everyday adult speech as "defective" and "degenerate." If this speech is really what children hear when they learn to speak, it is amazing that they manage to acquire the rules of grammar.

The view that children learn regular rules from apparently haphazard samples of speech has led many lin-

guists to conclude that the ability to learn language is innate. All a child has to do is to be in the company of speakers of a language. Linguists have proposed that a child's brain contains a "language acquisition device," which embodies rules of "universal grammar"; because each language expresses these rules in slightly different ways, the child must learn the details, but the basics are already there in the brain (Chomsky, 1965; Lennenberg, 1967; McNeill, 1970).

■ Do We Have Special Cognitive Structures for Language?

The assertion that an innate language acquisition device guides children's acquisition of a language is part of a general theory about the cognitive structures responsible for language and its acquisitions (Pinker, 1990). The most important components are as follows:

1. Children who are learning a language make hypotheses about the grammatical rules they need to follow. These hypotheses are confirmed or disconfirmed by the speech that they hear.
2. An innate language acquisition device (a part of the brain) guides children's hypothesis formation. Because they have this device, there are certain types of hypothetical rules that they will never entertain and certain types of sentences that they will never utter.
3. The language acquisition device makes reinforcement unnecessary; the device provides the motivation for the child to learn a language.
4. There is a critical period for learning a language. The language acquisition device works best during childhood; after childhood, languages are difficult to learn and almost impossible to master.

■ Evidence Concerning the Language Acquisition Device Hypothesis

At present, we have no way to evaluate the first assertion—that children make and test hypotheses about grammatical rules. No serious investigator believes that these hypotheses are conscious and deliberate; thus, we cannot simply ask children why they say what they do. We should probably consider the belief in children's hypothesis testing as a convenient metaphor for the fact that their speech sometimes follows one rule or another. For example, as we saw earlier, children often apply the regular past-tense rule even to irregular verbs, saying "I catched it" or "She hitted me" during one stage of language acquisition. Some researchers would say that the children are testing the hypothesis that all events in the past are expressed by adding *-ed* to the word that denotes the action.

A more important—and testable—assertion is that the hypothesis testing is guided by the language acquisition device. The most important piece of evidence in favor of this assertion is the discovery of **language universals:** characteristics that can be found in all languages that lin-

language universal A characteristic feature found in all natural languages.

guists have studied. Some of the more important language universals include the existence of noun phrases (*The quick brown fox . . .*); verb phrases (*. . . ate the chicken*); grammatical categories of words such as nouns and adjectives; and syntactical rules that permit the expression of subject-verb-object relations (*John hit Andy*), plurality (*two birds*), and possession (*Rachel's pen*).

But the fact that all languages share certain characteristics does not mean that they are the products of innate brain mechanisms. For example, Hebb, Lambert, and Tucker (1973) observed that language universals may simply reflect realities of the world. When people deal with each other and with nature, their interactions often take the form of an agent acting on an object. Thus, the fact that all languages have ways of expressing these interactions is not surprising. Similarly, objects come in slightly different shapes, sizes, and colors, so we can expect the need for ways (such as adjectives) to distinguish among them. It is not unreasonable to suppose that the same kinds of linguistic devices have been independently invented at different times and in different places by different cultures. After all, archaeologists tell us that similar tools have been invented by different cultures all around the world. People need to cut, hammer, chisel, scrape, and wedge things apart, and different cultures have invented similar devices to perform these tasks. We need not conclude that these inventions are products of a "tool-making device" located in the brain.

But even if *some* language universals are dictated by reality, others could indeed be the result of a language acquisition device. For example, consider the following sentences (Pinker, 1990):

A1. *Irv drove the car* into the garage.
A2. Irv drove the car.

B1. *Irv put the car* into the garage.
B2. Irv put the car.

Someone (such as a child learning a language) who heard sentences A1 and A2 could reasonably infer that sentence B1 could be transformed into sentence B2. But the inference obviously is false; sentence B2 is ungrammatical. The linguistic rules that say that sentence A2 is acceptable but that sentence B2 is not are very complex; and their complexity is taken as evidence that they must be innate, not learned. As Pinker (1990) concludes, "The solution to the problem [that children do not utter sentence B2] must be that children's learning mechanisms ultimately do not allow them to make the generalization" (p. 206).

This conclusion rests on the assumption that children use rules similar to the ones that linguists use. How, the reasoning goes, could a child master such complicated rules at such an early stage of cognitive development unless the rules were already wired into the brain? But perhaps the children are *not* following such complex rules. Perhaps they learn that when you say *put*

(something) you must always go on to say *where* you put something. Linguists do not like rules that deal with particular words, such as *put (something) (somewhere);* they prefer abstract and general rules that deal with *categories:* clauses, prepositions, noun phrases, and the like. But children learn particular words and their meanings—why should they not also learn that certain words must be followed (or must never be followed) by certain others? Doing so is certainly simpler than learning the complex and subtle rules that linguists have devised. It would seem that both complex and simple rules (or innate or learned ones) could explain the fact that children do not utter sentence B2.

The third assertion is that language acquisition occurs without the need of reinforcement—or even of correction. Brown and Hanlon (1970) recorded dialogue between children and parents and found that adults generally did not show disapproval when the children's utterances were ungrammatical and approval when they were grammatical. Instead, approval appeared to be contingent on the truth or accuracy of the children's statements. If there is no differential reinforcement, how can we explain the fact that children eventually learn to speak grammatically?

It is undoubtedly true that adults seldom say, "Good, you said that right," or, "No, you said that wrong." However, adults do distinguish between grammatical and ungrammatical speech of children. A study by Bohannon and Stanowicz (1988) found that adults are likely to repeat children's grammatically correct sentences verbatim but to correct ungrammatical sentences. For example, if a child says, "That be monkey," an adult would say, "That is a monkey." Adults were also more likely to ask for clarifications of ungrammatical sentences. Thus, adults *do* tend to provide the information children need to correct their faulty speech.

As we saw in an earlier section, adults talk differently to children than they do to other adults; they speak in ways that would seem to be optimal for promoting learning. Chomsky's assertion about the defectiveness and degeneracy of adult speech is not true—at least as far as it applies to what children hear. In fact, according to Newport, Gleitman, and Gleitman (1977), almost all the speech that a young child hears (at least, in industrialized English-speaking societies) is grammatically correct. If that is so, why should we hypothesize that a language acquisition device exists? Because, say some researchers, not all children are exposed to child-directed speech. "In some societies people tacitly assume that children aren't worth speaking to and don't have anything to say that is worth listening to. Such children learn to speak by overhearing streams of adult-to-adult speech" (Pinker, 1990, p. 218).

Pinker's statement is very strong; it says that children in some cultures have no speech directed toward them until they have mastered the language. It implies that the children's mothers do not talk with them and ignores the fact that older children may not be quite so choosy about their conversational partners. To conclude that such an extreme statement is true would require extensive observation and documentation of child-rearing practices in other cultures. One of the strongest biological tendencies of our species is for a mother to cherish, play with, and communicate with her offspring. If there really is a culture in which mothers do *not* do so, we need better documentation.

In fact, children do *not* learn a language that they simply overhear. Bonvillian, Nelson, and Charrow (1976) studied children of deaf parents whose only exposure to spoken language was through television or radio. This exposure was not enough; although the children could hear and did watch television and listen to the radio, they did not learn to speak English. It takes more than "overhearing streams of adult-to-adult speech" to learn a language. The way that parents talk to their children is closely related to the children's language acquisition (Furrow, Nelson, and Benedict, 1979; Furrow and Nelson, 1986). Thus, the question is, Just how much instruction (in the form of child-directed speech) do children need?

The fact that parents do not often reward their children's speech behaviors with praise or tangible reinforcers (such as candy) does not prove that reinforcement plays no role in learning a language. We humans are social animals; our behavior is strongly affected by the behavior of others. It is readily apparent to anyone who has observed the behavior of children that the attention of other people is extremely important to them. Children will perform a variety of behaviors that get other people to pay attention to them. They will make faces, play games, and even misbehave in order to attract attention. And above all, they will talk. Put yourself in the child's place. Adults or other children are likely to pay attention to you if you start talking to them. If they cannot understand your speech, you are unlikely to maintain their attention.

The final assertion—that the language acquisition device works best during childhood—has received the most experimental support. For example, Newport and Supalla (1987) studied the ability of people who were deaf from birth to use sign language. They found that the earlier the training began, the better the person was able to communicate. Also, Johnson and Newport (1989) found that native Korean and Chinese speakers who moved to the United States learned English grammar better if they arrived during childhood. The advantage did not appear to be a result of differences in motivation to learn a second language. Such results are consistent with the hypothesis that something happens to the brain after childhood that makes it more difficult to learn a language.

As you learned in Chapter 2, observational studies such as these do not prove that a cause-and-effect relation exists between the variables in question. Johnson and Newport suggest that people's age (in particular, the age of their brain) affects their language learning ability. But other variables are also correlated with age. For example, the Korean and Chinese speakers who moved to the United States as children spent several years in school; and perhaps the school environment is a particularly good place to learn a second language. In addition, adults are generally more willing to correct the grammatical errors made by children than those made by adolescents or other adults; thus, children may get more tutoring. It is certainly possible that the investigators are correct, but their results cannot be taken as *proof* that the brain contains an innate language acquisition device.

■ Does a Language Acquisition Device Exist?

In one sense, a language acquisition device does exist. The *human brain* is a language acquisition device; without it, languages are not acquired. And regions such as Wernicke's area and Broca's area seem to play especially important roles in verbal communication. The real controversy is over the characteristics of this language acquisition device. Is it so specialized that it contains universal rules of grammar and provides innate motivation that makes reinforcement unnecessary?

The basic argument for innate rules of grammar is that the rules that guide a child's speech are so complicated that they could not possibly be learned by young children. But perhaps the rules are simpler than the ones that linguists have proposed. If that is the case, then the argument loses its force. And just because a phenomenon (in this case, the acquisition of the rules of grammar) is complex and difficult to explain, we should not hastily conclude that there is really nothing to explain—that an innate brain mechanism takes care of it for us.

What about the role of reinforcement? Certainly, we need not deliberately teach our children to speak. Some parents do, of course, but many do not; and their children still learn to talk. Does this fact make verbal behavior different from all other kinds of behavior? This issue will not be resolved until we know much more about the role of reinforcement in other types of behaviors that are learned through observation and imitation. Reinforcement need not be consciously and intentionally delivered; it can be provided by attention and other social stimuli, and it may even be provided by the satisfaction one gains by talking the way other people do.

In my opinion, the best strategy is to keep an open mind. The ease with which young children learn a language must be explained. The explanation will obviously involve some sort of interaction between the particular characteristics of the human brain and the information supplied by the environment. The precise nature of the brain mechanisms and the environmental contributions remain to be determined.

Biology and Culture

Communication with Other Primate Species

The members of most species can communicate with one another. Even insects communicate: A female moth that is ready to mate can release a chemical that will bring male moths from miles away. And a dog can tell its owner that it wants to go for a walk by bringing its leash in its mouth and whining at the door. But until recently, humans were the only species that had *languages*—flexible systems that use symbols to express many meanings.

In the 1960s, Beatrice and Roger Gardner, of the University of Nevada, began Project Washoe (Gardner and Gardner, 1969, 1978), a remarkably successful attempt to teach sign language to a female chimpanzee named Washoe. Previous attempts to teach chimps to learn and use human language focused on speech (Hayes, 1952). These attempts failed because chimps lack the control of tongue, lips, palate, and vocal cords that humans have and thus cannot produce the variety of complex sounds that characterize human speech.

Gardner and Gardner realized this limitation and decided to attempt to teach Washoe a *manual language*—one that makes use of hand movements. Chimps' hand and finger dexterity is excellent, so the only limitations in their ability would be cognitive ones. The manual language the Gardners chose was based on ASL, the American sign language used by deaf people. As we saw in Chapter 6, ASL is a true language. It contains function words and content words and has regular grammatical rules.

Washoe was one year old when she began learning sign language; by the time she was four, she had a vocabulary of over one hundred thirty signs. Like children, she used single signs at first; then, she began to produce two-word sentences such as *Washoe sorry, gimme flower, more fruit,* and *Roger tickle.* Sometimes, she strung three or more words together, using the concept of agent and object: *You tickle me.* She asked and answered questions, apologized, made assertions—in short, did the kinds of things that children would do while learning to talk. She showed overextensions and underextensions, just as human children do. Occasionally, she even made correct generalizations by herself. After learning the sign for the verb *open* (as in *open box, open cupboard*), she used it to say *open faucet,* when requesting a drink. She made signs to herself when she was alone and used them to "talk" to cats and dogs, just as children will do. Although it is difficult to compare her progress with that of human children (the fairest comparison would be with that of deaf children learning to sign), humans clearly learn language much more readily than Washoe did.

Inspired by Project Washoe's success, several other investigators have taught primate species to use sign language. For example, Patterson began to teach a gorilla (Patterson and Linden, 1981), and Miles (1983) began to teach an orangutan. Washoe's training started relatively late in her life, and her trainers were not, at the beginning of the project, fluent in sign language. Other chimpanzees, raised from birth by humans who are native speakers of ASL, have begun to use signs when they are three months old (Gardner and Gardner, 1975).

Many psychologists and linguists have questioned whether the behavior of these animals can really be classified as verbal behavior. For example, Terrace et al. (1979) argue that the apes simply learned to imitate the gestures made by their trainers and that sequences of signs such as *please milk please me like drink apple bottle* (produced by a young gorilla) are nothing like the sequences that human children produce. Others have challenged these criticisms (Fouts, 1983; Miles, 1983; Stokoe, 1983), blaming much of the controversy on the method Terrace and his colleagues used to train their chimpanzee.

Certainly, the verbal behavior of apes cannot be the same as that of humans. If apes could learn to communicate verbally as well as children can, then humans would not have been the only species to have developed language. The usefulness of these studies rests in what they can teach us about our own language and cognitive abilities. Through them, we may discover what abilities animals need to communicate as we do. They may also help us understand the evolution of these capacities.

These studies have already provided some useful information. For example, Premack (1976) taught chimpanzees to "read" and "write" by arranging plastic tokens into "sentences." Each token represents an object, action, or attribute such as color or shape, much the way words do. His first trainee, Sarah, whom he acquired when she was one year old, learned to understand complex sentences such as *Sarah insert banana in pail, apple in dish.* When she saw the disks arranged in this order, she obeyed the instructions.

Chimpanzees apparently can use symbols to represent real objects and can manipulate these symbols logically. These abilities are two of the most powerful features of language. For Premack's chimpanzees, a blue plastic triangle means "apple." If the chimpanzees are given a blue plastic triangle and asked to choose the appropriate symbols denoting its color and shape, they choose the ones that signify "red" and "round," not "blue" and "triangular." Thus, the blue triangle is not simply a token the animals can use to obtain apples; it *represents* an apple for them, just as the word *apple* represents it for us.

Even though humans are the only primates that can pronounce words, several other species can *recognize* them. Savage-Rumbaugh (1990) taught Kanzi, a pygmy chimpanzee, to communicate with humans by pressing

Table 10.4

Semantic Relations Comprehended by Kanzi, a Pygmy Chimpanzee

Semantic Relations	N	Examples (Spoken)
Action-object	107	*"Would you please carry the straw?"* Kanzi looks over a number of objects on the table, selects the straw, and takes it to the next room.
Object-action	13	*"Would you like to ball chase?"* Kanzi looks around for a ball, finds one in his swimming pool, takes it out, comes over to the keyboard, and answers "Chase."
Object-location	8	*"Would you put the grapes in the swimming pool?"* Kanzi selects some grapes from among several foods and tosses them into the swimming pool.
Action-location	23	*"Let's chase to the A-frame."* Kanzi is climbing in trees and has been ignoring things that are said to him. When he hears this he comes down rapidly and runs to the A-frame.
Action-object-location	36	*"I hid the surprise by my foot."* Kanzi has been told that a surprise is around somewhere, and he is looking for it. When he is given this clue, he immediately approaches the speaker and lifts up her foot.
Object-action	9	*"Kanzi, the pine cone goes in your shirt."* Kanzi picks up a pine cone and puts it in his shirt.
Action-location-object	8	*"Go the refrigerator and get out a tomato."* Kanzi is playing in the water in the sink. When he hears this he stops, goes to the refrigerator, and gets a tomato.
Agent-action-object	7	*"Jeannine hid the pine needles in her shirt."* Kanzi is busy making a nest of blankets, branches, and pine needles. When he hears this, he immediately walks over to Jeannine, lifts up her shirt, takes out the pine needles, and puts them in his nest.
Action-object-recipient	19	*"Kanzi, please carry the cooler to Penny."* Kanzi grabs the cooler and carries it over to Penny.
Other—object-action-recipient; action-recipient-location; etc.	69	

Source: From Savage-Rumbaugh, E. S. *Developmental Psychobiology,* 1990, *23,* 599–620. Reprinted by permission.

Researcher Sue Savage-Rumbaugh taught her chimp, Kanzi, to communicate using a special keyboard.

buttons that contained symbols for words. Kanzi's human companions talked with him, and he learned to understand them. Although the structure of his vocal apparatus prevented him from responding vocally, *he often tried to do so.* During a three-month period, Savage-Rumbaugh and her colleagues tested Kanzi with 310 sentences, 302 of which the chimpanzee had never heard before. Only situations in which Kanzi could not have been guided by non-

verbal cues from the human companions were counted; often, Kanzi's back was to the speaker. He responded correctly 298 times. *Table 10.4* presents specific examples of these sentences and the actions that Kanzi took.

One conclusion that has emerged from the studies of primates is that true verbal ability is a social behavior. It builds on attempts at nonverbal communication in a social situation. The most successful attempts at teaching a language to other primates are those in which the animal and the trainer have established a close relationship in which they can successfully communicate nonverbally by means of facial expressions, movements, and gestures. Apes and orangutans clearly perceive people as other beings who can be loved, trusted, or feared. Nonhuman primates (and humans, for that matter) learn a language best while interacting with others. Such interactions naturally lead to attempts at communication; and if signs (or spoken words) serve to make communication easier and more effective, they will most readily be learned.

One of the most interesting questions asked of researchers in this area is whether animals who learn to communicate by means of signs will teach those signs to their offspring. The answer appears to be, "Yes, they will." Fouts, Hirsch, and Fouts (1983) obtained a ten-month-old infant chimpanzee, Loulis, whom they gave to Washoe to "adopt." Within eight days, the infant began to imitate Washoe's signs. To be certain that Loulis was learning the signs from Washoe and not from humans, the investigators used only the signs for *who, what, want, which, where, sign,* and *name* in his presence. As Fouts (1983) reported:

> [A] sign, *food* [which he now uses], was . . . actively taught by Washoe. On this occasion Washoe was observed to sign *food* repeatedly in an excited fashion when a human was getting her some food. Loulis was sitting next to her watching. Washoe stopped signing and took Loulis' hand in hers, molded it into the *food* sign configuration, and touched it to his mouth several times. (pp. 71-72)

Interim Summary

Language Acquisition by Children

Studies using the habituation of a baby's sucking response have shown that the human auditory system is capable of discriminating among speech sounds soon after birth. Human vocalization begins with crying, then develops into cooing and babbling, and finally results in patterned speech. During the two-word stage, children begin to combine words creatively, saying things they have never heard.

Child-directed speech is very different from that directed toward adults; it is simpler, clearer, and generally refers to items and events in the present environment. As young children gain more experience with the world and with the speech of adults and older children, their vocabulary grows and they learn to use adult rules of grammar. Although the first verbs they learn tend to have irregular past tenses, once they learn the regular past tense rule (add *-ed*), they apply this rule even to irregular verbs they previously used correctly.

Some researchers believe that a child learns language by means of a brain mechanism called a language acquisition device, which contains universal grammatical rules and motivates language acquisition. Although children's verbal performance can be described by complex rules, it is possible that simpler rules—which children could reasonably be expected to learn—can also be devised. Everyone agrees that deliberate reinforcement is not necessary for language learning, but a controversy exists about just how important child-directed behavior is. A critical period for language learning may exist, but the evidence is not yet conclusive.

Studies of the ability of other primates to learn language enable us to analyze some of the types of experiences necessary for acquiring the skills involved in producing and understanding speech. To the extent that apes can be taught at least some of the rudiments of language, their behaviors provide some hints about the ways humans acquire these skills.

Our language provides us with a beautiful medium for thought and expression. We can appreciate fine prose and poetry, enjoy the sound of an actor's voice, converse with a loved one, listen to our children's first words, and think thoughts that could never occur without language. What we know about language so far is a pitifully small part of the entire picture. The quest for an understanding of verbal behavior, the most complex of all our activities, has just begun.

Thought Questions

- Can you think of any examples of child-directed speech that you may have overheard (or engaged in yourself while talking with a young child)? How would you feel if you were talking with a baby who suddenly lost interest in you? Would you be motivated to do something to regain the baby's attention? What would you do?

- Do you think it is easier for a young child to learn a language than it is for an adult? How could we make a fair comparison of the tutoring young children and adults receive from people with whom they talk? Do you think that a modified form of child-directed language could be developed as an effective way of tutoring adults who want to learn a second language?

- Would you like to talk with a chimpanzee? If so, what would you like to talk about? What would it take to convince you that the animal was using something like a simplified human language, as opposed to simply repeating words and phrases learned by rote? Some people seem to be uncomfortable with the idea that the difference in the ability of humans and other primates to communicate may be a matter of degree and not an all-or-none matter. How do you feel about this issue?

Suggestions for Further Reading

Osherson, D.N., and Lasnik, H. *An Invitation to Cognitive Science. Vol. 1: Language.* Cambridge, Mass.: MIT Press, 1990.

Tanenhaus, M.K. *Psycholinguistics: An Overview.* Cambridge, England: Cambridge University Press, 1988.

Just, M.A., and Carpenter, P.A. *The Psychology of Reading and Language Comprehension.* Boston: Allyn and Bacon, 1987.

Volume 1 of *An Invitation to Cognitive Science* contains chapters written by experts on various topics of language. The Tanenhaus book provides general information about psycholinguistics, and the book by Just and Carpenter focuses on written language.

Berko Gleason, J. *The Development of Language.* New York: Macmillan, 1993.

This book does an excellent job of describing language acquisition in infants and children.

de Luce, J., and Wilder, H.T. *Language in Primates: Perspectives and Implications.* New York: Springer-Verlag, 1983.

This book describes attempts to teach language to nonhuman primates. It also describes the controversies about the success and significance of these attempts.

Chapter 11

Intelligence and Thinking

Chapter Outline

Theories of Intelligence

Spearman's Two-Factor Theory • Evidence from Factor Analysis • An Information-Processing Theory of Intelligence • A Neuropsychological Theory of Intelligence • *Biology and Culture: Definitions of Intelligence*

Spearman's two-factor theory proposes that intelligence consists of a global general factor and specific task-related factors. Factor analysis suggests that one or two general factors of intelligence may exist. Sternberg's triarchic theory of intelligence is an application of the information-processing approach that emphasizes the importance of adaptive behavior in a natural environment. Gardner's theory emphasizes the categories of aptitudes and skills (physical as well as cognitive) that permit people to thrive in their cultures. Researchers are coming to recognize that different environments require different types of skills; thus, different cultures have different definitions of intelligence.

Intelligence Testing

From Mandarins to Galton • Intelligence Tests • Reliability and Validity of Intelligence Tests • The Use and Abuse of Intelligence Tests

Binet's attempts to identify schoolchildren who needed special attention led him to develop a series of tests that eventually became the Stanford-Binet Scale. Binet and his colleague Simon developed the concept of norms with which to compare a particular individual and formulated the concept of mental age. Wechsler developed an intelligence test that could be applied to adults (the WAIS) and another for children (the WISC). The reliability of modern intelligence tests is excellent. Their validity is difficult to assess because we have no single criterion of intelligence. One way intelligence tests may be used is to identify gifted students and students with special needs so that they may be enrolled in appropriate educational programs. Intelligence tests may be abused if teachers and administrators expect little from students labeled as "unintelligent" and so fail to encourage them to achieve the most that they can.

The Roles of Heredity and Environment

The Meaning of Heritability • Sources of Environmental and Genetic Effects During Development • Results of Heritability Studies • *Evaluating Scientific Issues: The Issue of Race and Intelligence*

Variability in people's intellectual abilities is produced by three sources: environmental variability, genetic variability, and an interaction between the two. Environmental variability has its origins even before birth; it is influenced by factors that affect prenatal development and physical development during childhood as well as sources of formal education and intellectual stimulation. Genetic variability affects the structure and development of the brain and also affects people's resistance to diseases and other environmental events that can affect the development and functioning of the brain. The topic of race and intelligence has been the subject of considerable passion and debate, much of which has been illogical and misinformed. Environmental factors appear to play a larger role than hereditary ones in racial differences in performance on intelligence tests.

Thinking

Classifying • Formal and Natural Concepts • Deductive Reasoning • Inductive Reasoning • Problem Solving

Psychologists interested in the process of thinking have studied the formation and recognition of concepts, deductive reasoning, inductive reasoning, and problem solving. Concepts exist at the basic, subordinate, and superordinate level, but we mostly think about basic-level concepts. Concepts are more than simple collections of essential features; they can involve complex relationships. Deductive reasoning consists of applying general principles to specific instances and requires the ability to construct and manipulate mental models that represent a problem. Inductive reasoning consists of inferring general principles from particular facts; people use various forms of hypothesis testing to infer general principles. Problem solving requires a concept of a goal and an evaluation of the ability of particular behaviors to bring us closer to that goal.

A few years ago, while I was on a sabbatical leave, a colleague stopped by my office and asked if I would like to see an interesting patient. The patient, a seventy-two-year-old man, had suffered a massive stroke in his right hemisphere that had paralyzed the left side of his body. Three of us went to see him: Dr. W., an undergraduate psychology student who was on a summer internship, and I.

Mr. V. was seated in a wheelchair equipped with a large tray on which his right arm was resting; his left arm was immobilized in a sling, to keep it out of the way. He greeted us politely, almost formally, articulating his words carefully with a slight European accent.

Mr. V. seemed intelligent, and this impression was confirmed when we gave him some of the subtests of the Wechsler Adult Intelligence Test (WAIS-R). He could define rather obscure words, provide the meanings of proverbs, supply information, and do mental arithmetic. In fact, his verbal intelligence appeared to be in the upper 5 percent of the population. The fact that English was not his native language made his performance even more remarkable. But as we expected, he did poorly on even simple tasks that required him to deal with shapes and geometry. He failed to solve even the sample problem for the block design subtest, in which colored blocks must be put together to duplicate a pattern shown in a drawing.

The most interesting aspect of Mr. V.'s behavior after his stroke was his lack of reaction to his symptoms. After we had finished with the testing, we asked him to tell us a little about himself and his life-style. What, for example, was his favorite pastime?

"I like to walk," he said. "I walk at least two hours each day around the city, but mostly I like to walk in the woods. I have maps of most of the National Forests in the state on the walls of my study, and I mark all the trails I've taken. I figure that in about six months I will have walked all the trails that are short enough to do in a day. I'm too old to camp out in the woods."

"You're going to finish up those trails in the next six months?" asked Dr. W.

"Yes, and then I'll start over again!" he replied.

"Mr. V., are you having any trouble?" asked Dr. W.

"Trouble? What do you mean?"

"I mean physical difficulty."

"No." Mr. V. gave him a slightly puzzled look.

"Well, what are you sitting in?"

Mr. V. gave him a look that indicated he thought that the question was rather stupid—or perhaps insulting. "A wheelchair, of course," he answered.

"Why are you in a wheelchair?"

Now Mr. V. looked frankly exasperated; he obviously did not like to answer foolish questions. "Because my left leg is paralyzed!" he snapped.

Afterward, as we were discussing the case, the student asked why Mr. V. talked about continuing his walking schedule when he obviously knew that he couldn't walk. Did he think that he would recover soon?

"No, that's not it," said Dr. W. "He *knows* what his problem is, but he doesn't really *understand* it. The people at the rehab center are having trouble with him because he keeps trying to go outside for a walk.

"Mr. V.'s problem is not that he can't verbally recognize what's going on; it's that he just can't grasp its significance. The right hemisphere is specialized in seeing many things at once: in seeing all the parts of a geometric shape and grasping its form or in seeing all the elements of a situation and understanding what they mean. That is what's wrong. He can tell you about his paralyzed leg, about the fact that he is in a wheelchair, and so on, but he does not put these facts together and realize that his days of walking are over. In some ways Mr. V. is very intelligent, but in other ways he shows extremely poor judgment."

What is intelligence? We acknowledge that some people are more intelligent than others, but just what do we mean by that? In general, if people do well academically or succeed at tasks that involve their heads rather than their hands, we consider them to be intelligent. Thus, a critic who writes a witty, articulate review of an artist's exhibition of paintings is said to demonstrate his or her intelligence, whereas the painter is said to show his or her *talent*. Most psychologists would define **intelligence** as a person's ability to learn and remember information, to recognize concepts and their relations, and to apply the information to their own behavior in an adaptive way. Recently, psychologists have pointed out that any definition of intelligence depends on cultural judgments. Study of the types of skills that enable people to survive and flourish suggests that we should broaden our definition to include a wider range of abilities.

Traditionally, psychologists have followed two major approaches in their study of the nature of intelligence. The **differential approach** tries to devise tests that identify and measure individual differences in people's abilities to solve problems—particularly those that utilize skills important in the classroom. For example, these tests ask people to define words, explain proverbs, solve arithmetic problems, discover similarities in shapes and patterns, and answer questions about a passage of prose. These tests (which will be described later) are important to all of us because they are used to screen applicants to schools and candidates for jobs.

The **developmental approach** studies the ways in which infants learn to perceive, manipulate, and think about the world. The most influential proponent of this approach was the Swiss psychologist Jean Piaget (1896–1980). We will consider Piaget's work in detail in Chapter 12, which focuses on development over the lifespan. In the past few years, cognitive psychologists have begun to use a third approach, the **information-processing approach,** which is based on research methods they developed to investigate the types of skills people use to think and to solve various types of problems.

Different cultures have different definitions of intelligence. Members of the Aitutaki tribe from the Cook Islands respect a person's ability to obtain food from the sea.

have people run, jump, throw and catch a ball, lift weights, balance on a narrow beam, and perform other athletic feats. We would measure their performance on each task and add these numbers up, yielding a total score that we would call the *AQ,* or *athletic quotient.* But would this single measure be useful in predicting who would be the best baseball player, or swimmer, or gymnast? Obviously not. Athletic ability consists of a vari-

Theories of Intelligence

Differential approaches to the study of intelligence assume that we can best investigate the nature of intelligence by studying the ways in which people differ in their performance on tests of intellectual abilities. There is no doubt that people vary widely in many ways, such as in their abilities to learn and use words, to solve arithmetic problems, and to perceive and remember spatial information. But is intelligence a global trait or a composite of separate, independent abilities?

Psychologists have devised intelligence tests that yield a single number, usually called an IQ score. But the fact that the tests provide a single score does not itself mean that intelligence is a single, general characteristic. For example, suppose that we wanted to devise a test of athletic ability. We would have people run, jump, throw and catch a ball, lift weights, that we wanted to devise a test of athletic ability. We would

intelligence A person's ability to learn and remember information, to recognize concepts and their relations, and to apply the information to their own behavior in an adaptive way.

differential approach An approach to the study of intelligence that tries to devise tests that identify and measure individual differences in people's knowledge and abilities to solve problems.

developmental approach An approach to the study of intelligence that studies the way infants and children learn to perceive, manipulate, and think about the world.

information-processing approach An approach to the study of intelligence based on research methods that cognitive psychologists developed to study the types of skills people use to think and solve problems.

ety of skills, and different sports require different combinations of skills. As the American basketball player Michael Jordan learned, an outstanding basketball player might be only a mediocre baseball player.

Some investigators have suggested that certain intellectual abilities are completely independent of one another. For example, a person can be excellent at spatial reasoning but poor at solving verbal analogies. Even investigators who believe that intelligence is a global trait acknowledge that people also have specific intellectual abilities and that these abilities are at least somewhat independent. But psychologists disagree over whether specific abilities are totally independent or whether one general factor influences all abilities. We are going to look at three theories of intelligence: Spearman's two-factor theory, an information-processing theory, and a neuropsychological theory.

Spearman's Two-Factor Theory

Charles Spearman (1927) proposed that a person's performance on a test of intellectual ability is determined by two factors: the *g* **factor,** which is a general factor, and the *s* **factor,** which is a factor specific to a particular test. Spearman did not call his *g* factor "intelligence"; he considered the term too vague. He defined the *g* factor as comprising three "qualitative principles of cognition": apprehension of experience, eduction of relations, and eduction of correlates. A common task on tests of intellectual abilities—solving analogies—requires all three principles (Sternberg, 1985). For example, consider the following analogy:

LAWYER:CLIENT::DOCTOR: _____

This problem should be read as "LAWYER is to CLIENT as DOCTOR is to _____." *Apprehension of experience* refers to people's ability to perceive and understand what they experience; thus, reading and understanding each of the words in the analogy requires apprehension of experience. *Eduction* (not "eduCation") is the process of drawing or bringing out—that is, of figuring out from given facts. In this case, *eduction of relations* refers to the ability to perceive the relation between LAWYER and CLIENT; namely, that the lawyer works for and is paid by the client. *Eduction of correlates* refers to the ability to apply a rule inferred from one case to a similar case. Thus, the person whom a doctor works for and is paid by is obviously a PATIENT. Because analogy problems require all

g **factor** According to Spearman, a factor of intelligence that is common to all intellectual tasks; includes apprehension of experience, eduction of relations, and eduction of correlates.

s **factor** According to Spearman, a factor of intelligence that is specific to a particular task.

factor analysis A statistical procedure that identifies common factors among groups of tests.

three of Spearman's principles of cognition, he advocated their use in intelligence testing.

Empirical evidence for Spearman's two-factor theory comes from correlations among various tests of particular intellectual abilities. The governing logic is as follows: Suppose that we administer ten different tests of intellectual abilities to a group of people. If each test measures a separate, independent ability, the scores these people make on any one test will be unrelated to their scores on any other; the correlations among the tests will be approximately zero. However, if the tests measure abilities that are simply different manifestations of a single trait, the scores will be perfectly related; the intercorrelations will be close to 1.0. In fact, the intercorrelations among a group of tests of intellectual abilities are neither zero nor 1.0. Instead, most of these tests are at least moderately correlated, so that a person who scores well on a vocabulary test also tends to score better than average on other tests, such as arithmetic or spatial reasoning. The correlations among various tests of intellectual ability usually range from .30 to .70, which means that they have between 30 percent and 70 percent of their variability in common (Ozer, 1985).

Spearman concluded that a general factor (*g*) accounted for the moderate correlations among different tests of ability. Thus, a person's score on a particular test depends on two things: the person's specific ability (*s*) on the particular test (such as spatial reasoning) and his or her level of the *g* factor, or general reasoning ability.

Evidence from Factor Analysis

Factor analysis is a statistical procedure developed by Spearman and Pearson that permits investigators to identify *common factors* among groups of tests. In the case of intelligence tests, these common factors would be particular abilities that affect people's performance on more than one test. Suppose that a group of people take several different tests of intellectual ability. If each person's scores on several of these tests correlate well with one another, we would conclude that the tests are (at least partly) measuring the same factor. A factor analysis determines which sets of tests form groups. For example, Birren and Morrison (1961) administered the Wechsler Adult Intelligence Scale (WAIS, described in the next section) to 933 people. This test consists of eleven different subtests. Birren and Morrison calculated the correlations each subtest had with every other subtest and then subjected these correlations to a factor analysis. The details of the procedure are not important to us here, but the results and their implications are.

Table 11.1 lists the results of a factor analysis on Birren and Morrison's data. The analysis revealed three factors, labeled A, B, and C. The numbers in the three columns in the table are called *factor loadings;* they are somewhat like correlation coefficients in that they express the degree to which a particular test is related to a particular factor. For the various subtests on factor A, the largest factor loading is for vocabulary, followed by information, comprehension, and similarities. (For detailed descriptions of the subtests, see Table 11.4.) In the middle range are picture completion, arithmetic, picture arrangement, and digit symbol. Digit span, object assembly, and block design are the smallest. (See *Table 11.1*.) Verbal subtests make the most important contribution to factor A, so we might be tempted to call this factor *verbal ability*. But almost all tests make at least a moderate contribution, so some people may prefer to call this factor *general intelligence*. Digit span has a heavy loading on factor B (.84), and arithmetic and digit symbol have moderate loadings. Perhaps factor B is related to *maintaining information in short-term memory* and *manipulating numbers*. Factor C appears to be determined mainly by block design, object assembly, picture completion, and picture arrangement. A good name for this factor might be *spatial ability.*

Although factor analysis can give hints about the nature of intelligence, it cannot provide definitive answers. The names given to the factors are up to the investigator and are not prescribed by the mathematical analysis. Furthermore, factor analysis can never be more meaningful than the individual tests on which it is performed. To identify the relevant factors in human intelligence, one must include an extensive variety of tests in the factor analysis. For example, experience has shown that the WAIS is a useful predictor of scholastic performance and (to a lesser extent) of vocational success. Thus, it appears to measure some important abilities. But a factor analysis of the subtests will never reveal other important abilities that may *not* be measured by the WAIS. For example, the WAIS does not contain a test of musical ability. If it did, a factor analysis would undoubtedly yield an additional factor. Whether musical ability is a component of intelligence depends on how we decide to define intelligence; this question cannot be answered by a factor analysis.

Many investigators have performed factor analyses on tests of intellectual abilities. For example, Louis Thurstone (1938) administered a battery of 56 tests to 218 college students and then performed a factor analysis and extracted 7 factors, which he labeled *verbal comprehension, verbal fluency, number, spatial visualization, memory, reasoning,* and *perceptual speed.* At first, Thurstone thought that his results contradicted Spearman's hypothesized g factor. However, Eysenck suggested a few years later that a *second* factor analysis could be performed on Thurstone's factors. If the analysis found one common factor, then Spearman's g factor would receive support. In other words, if Thurstone's seven factors themselves had a second-order factor in common, this factor might be conceived of as general intelligence.

Cattell performed a second-order factor analysis and found not one but two major factors. Horn and Cattell (1966) called these factors *fluid intelligence* (g_f) and *crystallized intelligence* (g_c). Fluid intelligence is defined by relatively culture-free tasks, such as those that measure the ability to see relations among objects or the ability to see patterns in a repeating series of items. Crystallized intelligence is defined by tasks that require people to have acquired information from their culture, such as vocabulary and the kind of information learned in schools. Cattell regards fluid intelligence as closely related to a person's native capacity for intellectual performance; in other words, it represents a potential ability to learn and solve problems. In contrast, he regards crystallized intelligence as what a person has accomplished through the use of his or her fluid intelligence—what he or she has learned. Horn differs with Cattell; he cites evidence suggesting that both factors are learned but are also based on heredity. He says that g_f is based on casual learning and g_c is based on cultural, school-type learning (Horn, 1978).

Figure 11.1 illustrates items from five subtests that load heavily on the fluid intelligence factor. Although verbalization can help solve these problems, they are essentially nonverbal in form. In addition, the items differ from the types of problems encountered in school, and they do not appear to be closely tied to cultural experience. (See *Figure 11.1*.)

Tests that load heavily on the crystallized intelligence factor include word analogies and tests of vocabulary, general information, and use of language. According to Cattell, g_c depends on g_f. Fluid intelligence supplies the native ability, whereas experience with language and exposure to books, school, and other learning opportunities develop crystallized intelligence. If two people have the same experiences, the one with the greater fluid intelligence will develop the greater crystallized intelligence. However, a person with a high fluid intelligence exposed to an intellectually impoverished environment will develop a poor or mediocre crystallized intelligence. Table 11.2 presents a summary of tests that load on g_f and g_c. (See *Table 11.2*.)

No two investigators agree about the nature of intelligence. However, most believe that a small number of common

Table 11.1

Three Factors Derived by Factor Analysis of Scores on WAIS Subtests

Subtest	Factors		
	A	B	C
Information	.70	.18	.25
Comprehension	.63	.12	.24
Arithmetic	.38	.35	.28
Similarities	.57	.12	.27
Digit span	.16	.84	.13
Vocabulary	.84	.16	.18
Digit symbol	.24	.22	.29
Picture completion	.41	.15	.53
Block design	.20	.14	.73
Picture arrangement	.35	.18	.41
Object assembly	.16	.06	.59

Source: Adapted from Morrison, D. F. *Multivariate Statistical Methods.* New York: McGraw-Hill, 1967.

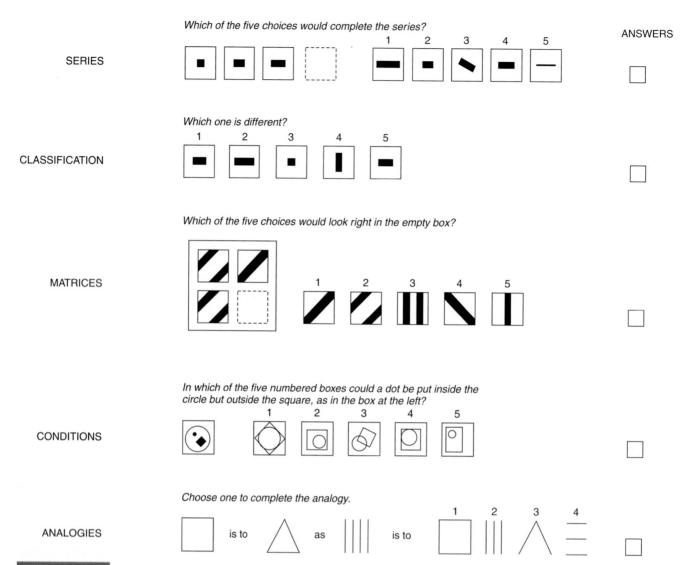

Figure 11.1

Five tests that correlate well with Cattell's g_f factor.

(First four tests taken from the Culture-Fair Intelligence Test, Scale 2, Form A test booklet. © 1949, 1960 R 1977, by the Institute for Personality and Ability Testing, Inc. Reproduced by permission of the copyright owner. Analogies test reproduced by permission of Raymond Cattell and of NFER-Nelson, Windsor, England.)

factors account for at least part of a person's performance on intellectual tasks.

An Information-Processing Theory of Intelligence

Sternberg (1985) has devised a theory of intelligence that derives from the information-processing approach used by many cognitive psychologists. Sternberg's theory has three

componential intelligence According to Sternberg, the mental mechanisms people use to plan and execute tasks; includes metacomponents, performance components, and knowledge acquisition components.

parts; he calls it a *triarchic* ("ruled by three") theory. The three parts of the theory deal with three aspects of intelligence: componential intelligence, experiential intelligence, and contextual intelligence. Taken together, these three components go beyond the abilities measured by most common tests of intelligence. They include practical aspects of behavior that enable a person to adapt successfully to his or her environment.

Componential intelligence consists of the mental mechanisms people use to plan and execute tasks. The components revealed by the factor analyses of verbal ability and deductive reasoning that I just described are facets of componential intelligence. Sternberg suggests that the components of intelligence serve three functions. *Metacomponents* (transcending components) are the processes by which people decide the nature of an intellectual problem, select a strategy for solving

Table 11.2

Summary of Tests with Large Factor Loadings on g_f or g_c

Test	Approximate Factor Loadings	
	g_f	g_c
Figural relations: Deduction of a relation when this is shown among common figures	.57	.01
Memory span: Reproduction of several numbers or letters presented briefly	.50	.00
Induction: Deduction of a correlate from relations shown in a series of letters, numbers, or figures, as in a letter series test	.41	.06
General reasoning: Solving problems of area, rate, finance, and the like, as in an arithmetic reasoning test	.31	.34
Semantic relations: Deduction of a relation when this is shown among words, as in an analogies test	.37	.43
Formal reasoning: Arriving at a conclusion in accordance with a formal reasoning process, as in a syllogistic reasoning test	.31	.41
Number facility: Quick and accurate use of arithmetic operations such as addition, subtraction, and multiplication	.21	.29
Experiential evaluation: Solving problems involving protocol and requiring diplomacy, as in a social relations test	.08	.43
Verbal comprehension: Advanced understanding of language, as measured in a vocabulary reading test	.08	.68

Source: Adapted from Horn, J. L. Organization of abilities and the development of intelligence. *Psychological Review,* 1968, *75,* 249. Copyright 1968 by the American Psychological Association. Adapted by permission of the author.

it, and allocate their resources. For example, good readers vary the amount of time they spend on a passage according to how much information they need to extract from it (Wagner and Sternberg, 1983). This decision is controlled by a meta-component of intelligence. *Performance components* are the processes actually used to perform the task—for example, word recognition and working memory. *Knowledge acquisition components* are those the person uses to gain new knowledge by sifting out relevant information and integrating it with what he or she already knows.

The second part of Sternberg's theory deals with experiential intelligence. **Experiential intelligence** is the ability to

deal effectively with novel situations and to automatically solve problems that have been encountered previously. According to Sternberg's theory, a person with good experiential intelligence is able to deal more effectively with novel situations than is a person with poor experiential intelligence. The person is better able to analyze the situation and to bring mental resources to bear on the problem, even if he or she has never encountered one like it before. After encountering a particular type of problem several times, the person with good experiential intelligence is also able to "automate" the procedure so that similar problems can be solved without much thought, freeing mental resources for other work. A person who has to reason out the solution to a problem every time it occurs will be left behind by people who can give the answer quickly and automatically. Sternberg suggests that this distinction is closely related to the distinction between fluid and crystallized intelligence (Horn and Cattell, 1966). According to Sternberg, tasks that use fluid intelligence are those that demand novel approaches, whereas tasks that use crystallized intelligence are those that demand mental processes that have become automatic.

The third part of Sternberg's theory deals with **contextual intelligence**—intelligence reflecting the behaviors that were subject to natural selection in our evolutionary history. Contextual intelligence takes three forms: adaptation, selection, and shaping. The first form, *adaptation,* consists of fitting oneself into one's environment by developing useful skills and behaviors. In different cultures, adaptation will take different forms. For example, knowing how to distinguish between poisonous and edible plants is an important skill for a member of a hunter-gatherer tribe. Knowing how to present oneself in a job interview is an important skill for a member of an industrialized society.

The second form of contextual intelligence, *selection,* refers to the ability to find one's own niche in the environment. For example, Feldman (1982) studied some of the child prodigies who appeared on the *Quiz Kids* radio and television shows in the United States during the 1940s and 1950s. These children were selected for their ability to answer factual-knowledge questions quickly, and they had very high IQ scores. Feldman's follow-up study indicated that the ones who went on to have the most distinguished careers were those who had found something that interested them and had stuck to it. Those who failed to do so accomplished very little, despite

experiential intelligence According to Sternberg, the ability to deal effectively with novel situations and to automatically solve problems that have been encountered previously.

contextual intelligence According to Sternberg, intelligence that reflects the behaviors that were subject to natural selection: *adaptation*—fitting oneself into one's environment by developing useful skills and behaviors; *selection*—finding one's own niche in the environment; and *shaping*—changing the environment.

Knowing how to distinguish between poisonous plants, edible plants, and plants with medicinal properties is an important skill. This woman, a member of the Sarawak tribe, is collecting medicinal herbs in a Malaysian rainforest.

Table 11.3
An Outline of Sternberg's Triarchic Theory of Intelligence

Componential Intelligence
   Metacomponents (e.g., planning)
   Performance components (e.g., lexical access)
   Knowledge acquisition components (e.g., ability to acquire vocabulary words)

Experiential Intelligence
   Novel tasks
   Automated tasks

Contextual Intelligence
   Adaptation (adapting to the environment)
   Selection (finding a suitable environment)
   Shaping (changing the environment)

---

their high IQs. According to Sternberg, the difference was a reflection of the selective aspect of contextual intelligence.

The third form of contextual intelligence is *shaping*. Sometimes, adapting to the environment or selecting a new one is not possible or profitable. In this case, intelligent behavior consists of shaping the environment itself. For example, a person whose talents are not appreciated by his or her employer may decide to start his or her own business.

The importance of Sternberg's emphasis on practical intelligence is supported by observations of people with damage to their frontal lobes. Even after sustaining massive damage to the frontal lobes (for example, after an automobile or motorcycle accident), people often continue to score well on standard intelligence tests. Thus, we are tempted to conclude that their intelligence is unimpaired. But such people lose the ability to plan their lives or even their daily activities. I became familiar with the case of a formerly successful physician who had received a head injury that severely damaged his frontal lobes. Even though he still had a high IQ as measured by intelligence tests, he could no longer perform his job as a physician. He became a delivery truck driver for his brother, who owned a business. He was able to carry out this job only be-

cause his brother did all the planning for him, carefully laying out his route and instructing him to call the brother if he encountered any trouble. The man's behavior lost its flexibility and insightfulness. For example, if he found the front door locked at a business to which he was supposed to deliver an order, it would not occur to him to go around to the back; his brother would have to suggest that by telephone. Clearly, the man's behavior lacked a very crucial component of intelligence. The fact that this component is not measured by most intelligence tests indicates that these tests are missing something important.

Table 11.3 provides a summary of the key concepts of Sternberg's triarchic theory.

A Neuropsychological Theory of Intelligence

As we saw in the example I just presented, neuropsychological observations have provided us with some important insights about the nature of intelligence. Gardner (1983) has suggested a theory of intelligence based on a neuropsychological analysis of human abilities. As you have seen in previous chapters, localized brain damage can impair specific types of abilities. For example, damage to various parts of the left hemisphere can impair verbal abilities, and damage to various parts of the right hemisphere can impair the ability to orient well in space. As we will see in Chapter 13, right-hemisphere damage can also impair people's ability to produce and recognize facial expressions of emotion.

Gardner concludes that intelligence falls into seven categories: *linguistic intelligence, musical intelligence, logical-mathematical intelligence, spatial intelligence, bodily-kines-*

thetic intelligence, and two types of *personal intelligence.* Bodily-kinesthetic intelligence includes the types of skills that athletes, typists, dancers, or mime artists exhibit. Personal intelligence includes awareness of one's own feelings (*intrapersonal intelligence*) and the ability to notice individual differences in other people and to respond appropriately to them—in other words, to be socially aware (*interpersonal intelligence*).

Three of Gardner's types of intelligence—verbal intelligence, logical-mathematical intelligence, and spatial intelligence—are not unusual, having been identified previously by many other researchers. But why include the others? According to Gardner, all seven abilities are well represented in the brain in that specific brain damage can impair some of them but leave others relatively intact. For example, people with damage to the left parietal lobe can sustain an *apraxia,* an inability to perform sequences of voluntary skilled movements. In contrast, people with damage to the right parietal lobe "lose touch with themselves." For one thing, they are likely to ignore the left sides of their bodies, failing to shave or apply makeup to the left sides of their faces or to put on the left sleeves of their shirts or coats. In addition, like Mr. V., the man described in the opening vignette, they tend to become unaware of the consequences of their physical condition. In another example of a neuropsychological relation, people with damage to the frontal or temporal lobes—especially of the right hemisphere—may have difficulty evaluating the significance of social situations. These examples illustrate bodily-kinesthetic intelligence and both intrapersonal and interpersonal intelligence.

Tests of intelligence emphasize the kinds of skills that can easily be tested at a desk or table with paper and pencil or small puzzles. In general, we have tended not to consider skill at moving one's body as a measure of intelligence, although this talent was undoubtedly selected for during the evolution of our species. Individuals who could more skillfully prepare tools, hunt animals, climb trees, scale cliffs, and perform other tasks requiring physical skills were more likely to survive and reproduce. Psychologists have developed mechanical aptitude tasks, primarily to help employers select skilled prospective employees, but such skills have generally been regarded as representing something less than intelligence. If a person has good verbal skills, most people in Western cultures will not regard the person as less intelligent if he or she is also clumsy. Similarly, they will not credit a person who has poor verbal skills with a measure of intelligence just because the person is physically skilled.

Gardner's theory has the advantage of being based on neuropsychological realities. It also accommodates the views of intelligence held by some non-Western cultures. For example, he would recognize the ability of a member of the Pu-

---

syllogism A logical construction that contains a major premise, a minor premise, and a conclusion. The major and minor premises are assumed to be true, and the truth of the conclusion is to be evaluated by deductive reasoning.

---

luwat culture of the Caroline Islands to navigate across the sea by the stars as an example of intelligence (Gladwin, 1970).

Biology and Culture

Definitions of Intelligence

The syllogism, a form of deductive logic invented by Aristotle, is often found in tests of intelligence. A **syllogism** is a logical construction that consists of a major premise (e.g., *All mammals have fur*), a minor premise (e.g., *A bat is a mammal*), and a conclusion (e.g., *A bat has fur*). The major and minor premises are assumed to be true. The problem is to decide whether the conclusion is true or false. Several studies suggested that illiterate, unschooled people in remote villages in various parts of the world were unable to solve syllogistic problems. Scribner (1977) visited two tribes of people in Liberia, West Africa, the Kpelle and the Vai. She found that, indeed, the tribespeople gave what Westerners would consider to be wrong answers.

But Scribner found that the people were not unable to reason logically. They simply approached problems differently. For example, she presented the following problem to a Kpelle farmer. At first glance, the problem appears to be a reasonable one even for an illiterate, unschooled person because it refers to his own tribe and to an occupation he is familiar with.

> All Kpelle men are rice farmers.
> Mr. Smith is not a rice farmer.
> Is he a Kpelle man?

The man replied:

> *Subject:* I don't know the man in person. I have not laid eyes on the man himself.
> *Experimenter:* Just think about the statement.
> *Subject:* If I know him in person, I can answer that question, but since I do not know him in person, I cannot answer that question.
> *Experimenter:* Try and answer from your Kpelle sense.
> *Subject:* If you know a person, if a question comes up about him you are able to answer. But if you do not know the person, if a question comes up about him it's hard for you to answer. (Scribner, 1977, p. 490)

The farmer's response did not show that he was unable to solve a problem in deductive logic. Instead, it indicated that as far as he was concerned, the question was unreasonable. In fact, his response contained an example of logical reasoning: "If you know a person . . . you are able to answer."

Luria (1977) received a similar answer from an illiterate Uzbekistanian woman, who was asked the following:

In the far north all bears are white.

Novaya Zemyla is in the far north.

What color are the bears there?

The woman replied, "You should ask the people who have been there and seen them. We always speak of only what we see; we don't talk about what we haven't seen."

Scribner found that sometimes illiterate people would reject the premises of her syllogism, replace them with what they knew to be true, and then solve the new problem, *as they had defined it.* For example, she presented the following problem to a Vai tribesperson.

All women who live in Monrovia are married.

Kemu is not married.

Does she live in Monrovia?

The answer was yes. The respondent said, "Monrovia is not for any one kind of people, so Kemu came to live there." The suggestion that only married women live in Monrovia was absurd, because the tribesperson knew otherwise. Thus, if Kemu wanted to live there, she could—and did.

Clearly, we cannot measure the intellectual ability of people in other cultures against our own standards. In the world of traditional tribal people, problems are solved by application of logical reasoning to facts gained through direct experience. Their deductive-reasoning ability is not necessarily inferior to ours; it is simply different.

Interim Summary

Theories of Intelligence

Although intelligence is often represented by a single score, IQ, modern investigators do not deny the existence of specific abilities. What is controversial is whether a general factor also exists. Spearman thought so; he named the factor *g* and demonstrated that people's scores on a variety of specific tests of ability were correlated. However, he believed that specific factors (*s* factors) also existed. Thurstone performed a factor analysis on fifty-six individual tests that revealed the existence of seven factors, not a single *g* factor. Eysenck reasoned that because these factors were themselves correlated, a factor analysis on *them* was justified. Cattell performed such an analysis and obtained two factors, and he confirmed this result with factor analyses of tests of his own. The nature of the tests that loaded heavily on these two factors suggested the names *fluid intelligence* (g_f) and *crystallized intelligence,* (g_c) with the former representing a person's native ability and the latter representing what a person learns.

Sternberg's triarchic theory of intelligence attempts to integrate laboratory research using the information-processing approach and an analysis of intelligent behavior in the natural environment. According to Sternberg, we use componential

intelligence to plan and execute tasks. We use experiential intelligence to apply past strategies to new problems. Finally, we use contextual intelligence to adapt to, select, or shape our environment. Gardner's neuropsychological theory of intelligence is based primarily on the types of skills that can be selectively lost due to brain damage. His definition of intelligence includes many abilities that are commonly regarded as "skills" or "talents." Like Sternberg's theory, Gardner's theory emphasizes the significance of behaviors to the culture in which they occur.

The concept of intelligence is determined by culture. Most Western societies include academic skills such as verbal ability and formal reasoning in their definitions of intelligence and regard nonacademic abilities as talents. People in preindustrial societies are less likely to approach a logical problem abstractly. Instead, they tend to base their conclusions on what they know to be true—and not on the hypothetical situations proposed by the person questioning them. In their societies, such an approach is more likely than an academic approach to solve the kinds of problems they encounter.

Thought Questions

- How would you define intelligence? Can you think of a definition that would work equally well for someone from a preliterate society and someone having many years of formal education?

- How do you rate your own fluid and crystallized intelligence? Can you think of instances of your own behavior (for example, answering questions, solving problems, working out a strategy) that illustrate each type of intelligence?

Intelligence Testing

Assessment of intellectual ability, or intelligence testing, is a controversial topic because of its importance in modern society. Unless people have special skills that suit them for a career in sports or entertainment, their economic success depends heavily on formal education. And admission to colleges and eligibility for scholarships are largely determined by the results of tests of intellectual ability. In addition, many employers use specialized aptitude tests to help them select among job candidates. Because the scores achieved on these tests have major implications for the quality of people's adult lives, testing has become one of the most important areas of applied psychology. Today there are hundreds of tests of specific abilities, such as manual dexterity, spatial reasoning, vocabulary, mathematical aptitude, musical ability, creativity, and memory. There are also general tests of scholastic aptitude, some of which you have probably taken yourself. All these tests vary widely in reliability, validity, and ease of administration.

From Mandarins to Galton

Undoubtedly, humans have been aware of individual differences in abilities since our species first evolved.

Some people were more efficient hunters, some were more skillful at constructing tools and weapons, and some were more daring and clever warriors. As early as 2200 B.C., Chinese administrators tested civil servants (mandarins) periodically to be sure that their abilities qualified them for their jobs. But in Western cultures, differences in social class were far more important than individual differences in ability until the Renaissance, when the modern concept of individualism came into being.

The term *intelligence* is an old one, deriving from the Latin *intellectus* (meaning "perception" or "comprehension"). However, its use in the English language dates only from the late nineteenth century, when it was revived by the philosopher Herbert Spencer (1820-1903) and by the biologist-statistician Sir Francis Galton (1822-1911). Galton was the most important early investigator of individual differences in ability. He was strongly influenced by his cousin Charles Darwin, who stressed the importance of inherited differences in physical and behavioral traits related to a species' survival. Galton observed that there were family differences in ability and concluded that intellectual abilities were heritable. Having noted that people with low ability were poor at making sensory discriminations, he decided that tests involving such discriminations would provide valid measures of intelligence.

In 1884, Galton established the Anthropometric ("human-measuring") Laboratory at the International Health Exhibition in London. His exhibit was so popular that afterward his laboratory became part of the South Kensington Museum. He tested over nine thousand people on seventeen variables, including height and weight, muscular strength, and the ability to perform sensory discriminations. One task involved detecting small differences in the weights of objects of the same size and shape. The use of simple tests of sensory discrimination fell into disfavor among subsequent researchers in the field of intelligence, so Galton's program was not continued after his death.

Nevertheless, Galton made some important contributions to science and mathematics. His systematic evaluation of various large numbers of people and the methods of population statistics he developed served as models for the statistical tests now used in all branches of science. His observation that the distribution of most human traits closely resembles the normal curve (developed by the Belgian statistician Lambert Quételet, 1796–1874) is the foundation for many modern tests of statistical significance. (See *Figure 11.2.*)

Galton also outlined the logic of a measure he called *correlation*: the degree to which variability in one measure is related to variability in another. From this analysis, Karl Pearson derived the correlation coefficient (*r*) used today to assess the degree of statistical relation between variables. (I discussed this measure in Chapter 2.) In addition, Galton de-

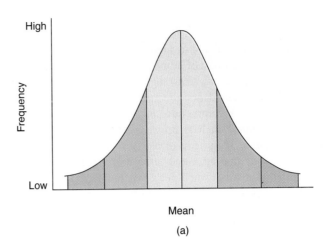

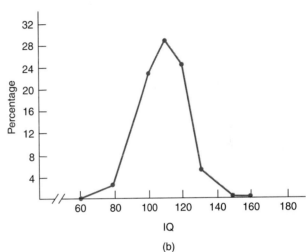

Figure 11.2

The normal curve and data from intelligence testing. (a) A mathematically derived normal curve. (b) A curve showing the distribution of IQ scores of 850 children 2 1/2 years of age.

(From Terman, L.M., and Merrill, M.A. Stanford-Binet Intelligence Scale. Boston: Houghton Mifflin, 1960; material cited pertains to the 1960 edition and not to the Fourth Edition, published in 1985. Reproduced by permission of The Riverside Publishing Company.)

veloped the logic of *twin studies* and *adoptive parent studies* to assess the heritability of a human trait. I will discuss these methods later in the chapter. (You also read about them in Chapter 3.)

Intelligence Tests

Modern intelligence tests began in France, with the work of Alfred Binet (1857–1911). His test, since adapted by American psychologists, is still used today. Another psychologist, David Wechsler, devised two intelligence tests, one for adults and another for children.

The Binet-Simon Scale

Alfred Binet (1857–1911), a French psychologist, disagreed with Galton's conception of human intelligence. He and a colleague (Binet and Henri, 1896) suggested that a group of simple sensory tests could not adequately determine a person's intelligence. They recommended measuring a variety of psychological abilities (such as imagery, attention, comprehension, imagination, judgments of visual space, and memory for various stimuli) that appeared to be more representative of the traits that distinguished people of high and low intelligence.

To identify children who were unable to profit from normal classroom instruction and needed special attention, Binet and a colleague, Theodore Simon, assembled a collection of tests, many of which had been developed by other investigators, and published the **Binet-Simon Scale** in 1905. The tests were arranged in order of difficulty, and the researchers obtained norms for each test. **Norms** are data concerning comparison groups that permit the score of an individual to be assessed relative to his or her peers. In this case, the norms consisted of distributions of scores obtained from children of various ages. Binet and Simon also provided a detailed description of the testing procedure, which was essential for obtaining reliable scores. Without a standardized procedure for administering a test, different testers can obtain different scores from the same child.

Binet revised the 1905 test in order to assess the intellectual abilities of both normal children and those with learning problems. The revised versions provided a procedure for estimating a child's **mental age**—the level of intellectual development that could be expected for an average child of a partic-

ular age. For example, if a child of eight scores as well as average ten-year-old children, his or her mental age is ten years. Binet did not develop the concept of IQ (intelligence quotient). Nor did he believe that the mental age derived from the test scores expressed a simple trait called "intelligence." Instead, he conceived of the overall score as the average of several different abilities.

The Stanford-Binet Scale

Lewis Terman, of Stanford University, translated and revised the Binet-Simon Scale in the United States. The revised group of tests, published in 1916, became known as the Stanford-Binet Scale. Revisions by Terman and Maud Merrill were published in 1937 and 1960. In 1985, an entirely new version was published. The **Stanford-Binet Scale** consists of various tasks grouped according to mental age. Simple tests include identifying parts of the body and remembering which of three small cardboard boxes contains a marble. Intermediate tests include tracing a simple maze with a pencil and repeating five digits orally. Advanced tests include explaining the difference between two abstract words that are close in meaning (such as *fame* and *notoriety*) and completing complex sentences.

The 1916 Stanford-Binet Scale contained a formula for computing the intelligence quotient (IQ), a measure devised by Stern (1914). The **intelligence quotient (IQ)** represents the idea that if test scores indicate that a child's mental age is equal to his or her chronological age (that is, calendar age), the child's intelligence is average; if the child's mental age is above or below his or her chronological age, the child is more or less intelligent than average. This relation is expressed as the quotient of mental age (MA) and chronological age (CA). The result is called the **ratio IQ**:

$$IQ = \frac{MA}{CA} \times 100$$

The quotient is multiplied by 100 to eliminate fractions. For example, if a child's mental age is ten and the child's chronological age is eight, then his or her IQ is $(10 \div 8) \times 100 = 125$.

The 1960 version of the Stanford-Binet Scale replaced the ratio IQ with the deviation IQ. Instead of using the ratio of mental age to chronological age, the **deviation IQ** compares a child's score with those received by other children of the same chronological age. (The deviation IQ was invented by David Wechsler, whose work is described in the next section.) Suppose that a child's score is one standard deviation above the mean for his or her age. The standard deviation of the ratio IQ scores is 16 points, and the score assigned to the average IQ is 100 points. (See Chapter 2 for a description of the standard deviation, a measure of variability.) If a child's score is one standard deviation above the mean for his or her age, the child's deviation IQ score is 100 + 16 (the standard deviation) = 116. A child who scores one standard deviation below the mean receives a deviation IQ of 84 (100 − 16). (See *Figure 11.3.*)

Binet-Simon Scale An intelligence test developed by Binet and Simon in 1905; the precursor of the Stanford-Binet Scale.

norm Data concerning comparison groups that permit the score of an individual to be assessed relative to his or her peers.

mental age A measure of a person's intellectual development; the level of intellectual development that could be expected for an average child of a particular age.

Stanford-Binet Scale An intelligence test that consists of various tasks grouped according to mental age; provides the standard measure of the intelligence quotient.

intelligence quotient (IQ) A simplified single measure of general intelligence; by definition, the ratio of a person's mental age to his or her chronological age, multiplied by 100; often derived by other formulas.

ratio IQ A formula for computing the intelligence quotient; mental age divided by chronological age, multiplied by 100.

deviation IQ A procedure for computing the intelligence quotient; compares a child's score with those received by other children of the same chronological age.

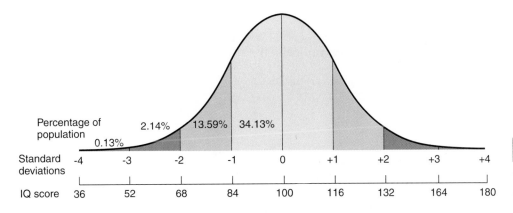

Percentage of
population
0.13% 2.14% 13.59% 34.13%

Standard
deviations   -4   -3   -2   -1   0   +1   +2   +3   +4

IQ score   36   52   68   84   100   116   132   164   180

Figure 11.3

Calculating the deviation IQ score.

Wechsler's Tests

When David Wechsler was chief psychologist at New York City's Bellevue Psychiatric Hospital, he developed several popular and well-respected tests of intelligence. The Wechsler-Bellevue Scale, published in 1939, was revised in 1942 for use in the armed forces and was superseded in 1955 by the Wechsler Adult Intelligence Scale (WAIS). This test was revised again in 1981 (the WAIS-R). The **Wechsler Intelligence Scale for Children (WISC),** first published in 1949 and revised in 1974 (the WISC-R), closely resembles the WAIS. Wechsler also devised an intelligence test for preschoolchildren, a memory scale, and other measures of ability.

The WAIS-R consists of eleven subtests, divided into two categories: verbal and performance. *Table 11.4* lists the subtests and a typical question or problem for each. The norms obtained for the WAIS-R permit the tester to calculate a deviation IQ score.

The WAIS-R has become the most popular individually administered adult intelligence test. An important advantage is that it tests verbal and performance abilities separately. Neuropsychologists often use it because people with brain damage tend to score very differently on the performance and verbal tests; thus, comparisons of performance and verbal test scores suggest the presence of undiagnosed brain damage. Because people who have had few educational and cultural opportunities often do worse on the verbal tests than on the performance tests, the WAIS-R is useful in estimating what their score might have been had they been raised in a more favorable environment.

Reliability and Validity of Intelligence Tests

As you will recall from Chapter 2, the adequacy of a measure is represented by its reliability and validity. In the case of intelligence testing, reliability is assessed by the correlation between the scores people receive on the same measurement on two

The block design subtest is part of both of Wechsler's Scales, the WISC-R for children and the WAIS-R for adults.

Wechsler Adult Intelligence Scale (WAIS) An intelligence test for adults devised by David Wechsler; contains eleven subtests divided into the categories of verbal and performance.

Wechsler Intelligence Scale for Children (WISC) An intelligence test for children devised by David Wechsler; similar in form to the Wechsler Adult Intelligence Scale.

Table 11.4

WAIS-R Subtests and Typical Questions or Problems

Subtest	Typical Question or Problem
Verbal	
Information	"What is the capital of France?"
Digit span	"Repeat these numbers back to me: 46239."
Vocabulary	"What does the word *conventional* mean?"
Arithmetic	"Suppose you bought six postcards for thirteen cents each and gave the clerk a dollar. How much change would you receive?" (Paper and pencil cannot be used.)
Comprehension	"Why are we tried by a jury of our peers?"
Similarities	"How are goldfish and canaries similar to each other?"
Performance	
Picture completion	The tester shows the subject a picture with a missing part (such as a mouse without its whiskers) and says, "Tell me what's missing."
Picture arrangement	The tester shows a series of cartoon pictures (without words) and instructs the subject to arrange them in the proper sequence.
Block design	The tester shows a picture and four or nine blocks divided diagonally into red and white sections, then instructs the subject to arrange the blocks so that they match the design in the picture.
Object assembly	The tester gives the subject pieces of cardboard cut like a jigsaw puzzle and instructs him or her to assemble it. (When properly assembled, the pieces form the shape of a common object.)
Digit symbol	The tester presents a set of ten designs paired with the ten numerals and instructs the subject to write the corresponding symbols beneath each of a long series of numerals.

different occasions; perfect reliability is 1.0. High reliability is achieved by means of standardized test administration and objective scoring: All test takers are exposed to the same situation during testing, and all test givers score responses in the same way. The acceptable reliability of a modern test of intellectual ability should be at least .85.

Validity is the correlation between test scores and the **criterion**—an independent measure of the variable that is being assessed. For example, suppose that you plan to estimate people's wealth by observing how many money-related words they use when describing a picture that illustrates a story. (This example is fictitious; no one has developed such a test—I think.) You can determine the validity of the test by seeing how accurately it estimates people's actual wealth (the criterion).

Because there is no single definition of intelligence, there is no single criterion measure. However, most tests of intelligence correlate reasonably well with measures like success in school (between .40 and .75). Thus, because intellectual ability plays at least some role in academic success, IQ appears to have some validity. *Table 11.5* illustrates the relation between students' scores on the verbal subtest of the Scholastic Apti-

tude Test (SAT) and the grades they subsequently earned during their first years in college.

The Use and Abuse of Intelligence Tests

Many kinds of institutions use intelligence tests and tests of specific abilities. Schools that group students according to ability usually do so on the basis of test scores. Schools also administer tests to students who appear to be slow learners in order to assess educational needs that may require them to participate in special programs. At selective academic institutions, test scores usually serve as an important criterion for admission. Similarly, many business organizations use ability tests to screen job candidates. Because test scores have such important consequences for people's opportunities, we must

criterion An independent measure of a variable being assessed. For example, college grades are the criterion measure for scores on the Scholastic Aptitude Test.

Table 11.5

Verbal Scores Received on the Scholastic Aptitude Test (SAT) and Freshman-Year Grade Point Averages of 250 American College Students

	Freshman-Year Grade Point Average							
	F	D		C		B		A
SAT Verbal Score	0.00–0.49	0.50–0.99	1.00–1.49	1.50–1.99	2.00–2.49	2.50–2.99	3.00–3.49	3.50–3.99
750–799						1		2
700–749					2		5	4
650–699				1	8	3	4	2
600–649				4	10	7	5	1
550–599			6	12	16	13	2	
500–549		4	7	25	21	5	3	
450–499		5	10	14	7	2		
400–449	1	6	8	5	4	1		
350–399	2	5	4	2				
300–349	1							

Source: Adapted from Lewis R. Aiken, *Psychological Testing and Assessment*, Sixth Edition. Copyright © 1988 by Allyn and Bacon. Used with permission.

know whether intelligence tests are valid and whether they are being used appropriately.

Possible Problems

Critics of intelligence testing have argued that intelligence tests do not measure people's abilities at all; rather, they measure what people have learned. Therefore, people's educational opportunities in the home, neighborhood, and school directly influence their performance on intelligence tests. Consider the effects of a person's family background and culture on his or her ability to answer questions such as "Who wrote *Romeo and Juliet?*" "What is a hieroglyph?" "What is the meaning of *catacomb*?" and "What is the thing to do if another boy (or girl) hits you without meaning to?" (Vernon, 1979, p. 22). Obviously, a child from a middle-class family is much more likely to be able to answer the first three questions than is an equally intelligent child from a deprived environment. The answer given to the fourth question is also likely to be culturally determined. Test constructors have responded to this criticism, and modern tests are much less likely to contain questions that are obviously culturally biased.

Unfortunately, the problem of cultural bias has not yet been solved. Even though questions having obvious cultural bias are no longer incorporated into intelligence tests, different experiences can lead to different test-taking strategies in nonobvious ways. For example, as we saw earlier, Kpelle tribespeople approach hypothetical logical problems very differently from people in literate societies. Their "failure" to solve such problems indicates cultural differences, not intellectual differences.

A potential abuse of intelligence tests is to deprive low-scoring children of opportunities to receive an education that will make them competitive later in life. Children who discover that they have scored poorly on an intelligence test are likely to suffer feelings of inferiority and may become disinclined to try to learn because they believe that they cannot. In addition, undue emphasis on testing may affect a school's curricula and methods of teaching. Teachers and administrators may try to teach information and skills that are measured by tests instead of basing their curricula on children's needs. Clearly, schools should use intelligence tests with great caution. If the results are not themselves used intelligently, such tests are actually harmful.

Identifying Specific Learning Needs

Intelligence testing has potential benefits when it is used in accordance with Binet's original purpose: to identify students who require special instruction. Children with severe learning problems are likely to develop a strong sense of inferiority if they are placed in classes with children whose academic progress is much faster than theirs; such children will probably benefit most from special teaching methods. These tests can also identify exceptionally bright students who are performing poorly because they are bored with the pace of instruction or who have been labeled as "troublemakers" by their teachers.

Many otherwise bright children suffer from various learning disabilities. Some have trouble learning to read or write; some perform poorly at arithmetic or motor skills. For example, some children have developmental dyslexias that make learning to read difficult for them. Dyslexic children are often frustrated by the contrast between their inability to read and their other abilities. They may act out this frustration through disruptive behavior at school and at home, or they may simply stop trying to excel at anything. As a result, they are sometimes stigmatized as mentally retarded and denied the opportunity for a good education. In this situation, tests of intellectual abilities are extremely useful. By identifying a specific learning disability in an otherwise bright child, testing helps ensure remedial action and prevents mislabeling.

Identifying Degrees of Mental Retardation

Binet's original use of intelligence tests—to identify children who learn more slowly than most others and who therefore need special training—is still important. Some children are so deficient in intellectual abilities that they require institutional care. Intelligence tests are an accepted means of evaluating the extent of a child's disabilities and, thus, of indicating the most appropriate remedial program.

The term **mental retardation** was originally applied to children with severe learning problems because they appeared to achieve intellectual skills and competencies at a significantly later age than most children. Their achievements came more slowly; thus, their developmental stages seemed to be retarded. Although most mentally retarded people were formerly relegated to a bleak and hopeless existence in institutions, many successful training programs have been initiated in recent years. I will discuss the causes of mental retardation later in this chapter.

Mental retardation is often accompanied by deficits in physical and social skills. The most severe classification, *profound mental retardation,* designates people with mental ages of under 3 years and with IQ scores under 20. These people usually have severe brain damage, and they almost always also have physical defects. The next category is *severe mental retardation,* which includes people with mental ages of 3 to 4 years and with IQ scores between 20 and 35. Few of these people learn to read and write unless they are trained by special methods. Both groups need custodial care.

Moderate mental retardation designates people with mental ages ranging from 4 to 7 1/2 years and with IQ scores of 36 to 51. Many of these people also require custodial care. *Mild mental retardation* designates people with mental ages of 7 1/2 to 11 years and with IQ scores of 52 to 67. With adequate training, most mildly mentally retarded people can lead independent lives and perform well at jobs that do not require a great deal of intellectual ability.

mental retardation   Mental development that is substantially below normal; often caused by some form of brain damage or abnormal brain development.

With adequate training, most mildly retarded people can lead independent lives and perform well at jobs.

Interim Summary

Intelligence Testing

Although the earliest known instance of ability testing was carried out by the ancient Chinese, modern intelligence testing dates from the efforts of Galton to measure individual differences. Galton made an important contribution to the field of measurement, but his tests of simple perceptual abilities were abandoned in favor of tests that attempt to assess more complex abilities, such as memory, logical reasoning, and vocabulary.

Binet developed a test that was designed to assess students' intellectual abilities in order to identify children with special educational needs. Although the test that superseded his, the Stanford-Binet Scale, provided for calculation of IQ, Binet believed that "intelligence" was actually a composite of several specific abilities. For him, the concept of mental age was a convenience, not a biological reality. Wechsler's two intelligence tests, the WAIS-R for adults and the WISC-R for children, are widely used today. The information provided by the verbal and performance scores helps neuropsychologists diagnose brain damage and can provide at least a rough estimate of the innate ability of poorly educated people.

The reliability of modern intelligence tests is excellent, but assessing their validity is still difficult. Because no single criterion measure of intelligence exists, intelligence tests are validated by comparing the scores with measures of achievement, such as scholastic success.

Intelligence tests can have both good and bad effects on the people who take them. The principal benefit is derived by identifying children with special needs (or special talents) who will profit from special programs. The principal danger lies in stigmatizing those who score poorly and depriving them of the opportunity for good jobs or further education.

Thought Questions

- Do you think it is a good idea for a person to know his or her IQ score? What would be some possible consequences of this knowledge? Would you like to know your own IQ score?
- Suppose you wanted to devise an intelligence test of your own. What kinds of problems would you want to include? What abilities would these problems measure?

The Roles of Heredity and Environment

Abilities of various kinds—intellectual, athletic, musical, and artistic—appear to run in families. Why? Are the similarities due to heredity, or are they solely the result of a common environment, which includes similar educational opportunities and exposure to people having similar kinds of interests? We considered this problem briefly in Chapter 3; now we will examine it in more detail. As we will see, the evidence suggests that both hereditary and environmental factors play a role.

The Meaning of Heritability

When we ask how much influence heredity has on a given trait, we are usually asking what the heritability of the trait is. **Heritability** is a statistical measure that expresses the proportion of the observed variability in a trait that is a direct result of genetic variability. The value of this measure can vary from 0 to 1.0. The heritability of many physical traits in most cultures is very high; for example, eye color is affected almost entirely by hereditary factors and little, if at all, by the environment. Thus, the heritability of eye color is close to 1.0.

Heritability is a concept that many people misunderstand. It does not describe the extent to which the inherited genes are responsible for producing a particular trait; it measures the relative contributions of differences in genes and differences in environmental factors to the overall observed variability of the trait in a particular population. An example may make this distinction clear. Consider the heritability of

hair color in the Eskimo culture. Almost all young Eskimos have black hair, whereas older Eskimos have gray or white hair. Because all members of this population possess the same versions of the genes that determine hair color, the genetic variability with respect to those genes is essentially zero. All the observed variability in hair color in this population is explained by an environmental factor: age. Therefore, the heritability of hair color in the Eskimo culture is zero.

As with hair color, we infer the heritability of a person's intelligence from his or her observed performance. Thus, looking at a person's IQ score is equivalent to looking at the color of a person's hair. By measuring the correlation between IQ score and various genetic and environmental factors, we can arrive at an estimate of heritability. Clearly, even if hereditary factors do influence intelligence, the heritability of this trait must be considerably less than 1.0 because so many environmental factors (such as the mother's prenatal health and nutrition, the child's nutrition, the educational level of the child's parents, and the quality of the child's school) can influence it.

When we consider studies that assess the heritability of intellectual abilities, we should be aware of the following considerations:

1. The heritability of a trait depends on the amount of variability of genetic factors in a given population. If there is little genetic variability, genetic factors will appear to be unimportant. Because the ancestors of people living in developed Western nations came from all over the world, genetic variability is likely to be much higher there than in an isolated tribe of people in a remote part of the world. Therefore, if a person's IQ score is at all affected by genetic factors, the measured heritability of IQ will be higher in, say, North American culture than in an isolated tribe.

2. The relative importance of environmental factors in intelligence depends on the amount of environmental variability (EV) that occurs in the population. If environmental variability is low, then environmental factors will appear to be unimportant. In a society with a low variability in environmental factors relevant to intellectual development—one in which all children are raised in the same way by equally skilled and conscientious caregivers, all schools are equally good, all teachers have equally effective personalities and teaching skills, and no one is discriminated against—the effects of EV would be small and those of GV (genetic variability) would be large. In contrast, in a society in which only a few privileged people receive a good education, environmental factors would be responsible for much of the variability in intelligence: The effects of EV would be large relative to those of GV.

3. Heritability is affected by the degree to which genetic inheritance and environment interact. Genetic factors and en-

heritability The degree to which the variability of a particular trait in a particular population of organisms is a result of genetic differences among those organisms.

vironmental factors often affect each other. For example, suppose that because of genetic differences some children are calm and others are excitable. Suppose that the excitable children will profit most from a classroom in which distractions are kept to a minimum and teachers are themselves calm and soothing. Further suppose that the calm students will profit most from an exciting classroom that motivates them to work their hardest. In this situation, the actual performance of the students would be based on an *interaction* between heredity and environment. If all students were taught in a calm classroom, the excitable children would perform best and hence learn more and obtain better IQ scores. If all students were taught in an exciting classroom, the calm children would do better and obtain the higher scores. (Ideally, a child's learning environment should match his or her hereditary predispositions.)

Sources of Environmental and Genetic Effects During Development

Both biological and environmental factors occurring before or after birth can affect intellectual abilities. Newborn infants cannot be said to possess any substantial intellectual abilities; rather, they are more or less capable of *developing* these abilities during their lives. Therefore, prenatal influences can be said to affect a child's *potential* intelligence by affecting the development of the brain. Factors that impair brain development will necessarily also impair the child's potential intelligence.

The factors that control the development of a human organism are incredibly complex. For example, the most complicated organ—the brain—consists of many billions of neurons, all of which are connected to other neurons. In addition, many of these neurons are connected to sensory receptors, muscles, or glands. During development, these billions of neurons must establish the proper connections so that the eyes send their information to the visual cortex, the ears send theirs to the auditory cortex, and the nerve cells controlling movement connect with the appropriate muscles.

Experiments have shown that as the axons of developing neurons grow, they thread their way through a tangle of other growing cells, responding to physical and chemical signals along the way, much as a salmon swims upriver to the tributary in which it was spawned. During this stage of prenatal development, differentiating cells can be misguided by false signals. For example, if a woman contracts German measles during early pregnancy, toxic chemicals produced by the disease virus may adversely affect the development of the fetus. Sometimes, these chemicals can misdirect the interconnec-

tions of brain cells and produce mental retardation. Thus, although development of a human organism is programmed genetically, environmental factors can affect development even before a person is born.

Harmful prenatal environmental factors include physical trauma (for instance, through injury to the mother in an automobile accident) and toxic effects. A developing fetus can be exposed to toxins from diseases contracted by the mother during pregnancy (such as German measles) or from other sources. A pregnant woman's intake of various drugs can have disastrous effects on fetal development. For example, alcohol, opiates, cocaine, and the chemicals present in cigarettes can harm fetuses. There is some evidence that even a single alcoholic "binge" during a critical stage of pregnancy can cause permanent damage to the fetus. One of the most common drug-induced abnormalities, the fetal alcohol syndrome, is seen in many offspring of women who are chronic alcoholics. Children with **fetal alcohol syndrome** are much smaller than average, have characteristic facial abnormalities, and, more significantly, are mentally retarded. *Figure 11.4* shows the face of a child with fetal alcohol syndrome as well as the faces of a normal rat fetus and of a rat fetus whose mother received alcohol during early pregnancy.

Development can also be harmed by genetic abnormalities. Some of these abnormalities cause brain damage and consequently produce mental retardation. The best-known example of these abnormalities is *Down syndrome*, which I described in Chapter 3. Although Down syndrome is a genetic disorder, it is not hereditary; it results from imperfect division of the twenty-three pairs of chromosomes during the development of an ovum or (rarely) a sperm. Chapter 3 also described *phenylketonuria* (PKU), an inherited metabolic disorder that disrupts normal brain development. If left untreated, PKU can result in severe mental retardation.

From birth onward, a child's brain continues to develop. Environmental factors can either promote or impede that development. Postnatal factors such as birth trauma, diseases that affect the brain, or toxic chemicals can prevent optimum development and thereby affect the child's potential intelligence. For example, encephalitis (inflammation of the brain), when contracted during childhood, can result in mental retardation. So can the ingestion of poisons such as mercury or lead.

Educational influences in the environment, including (but not limited to) schooling, enable a child to attain his or her potential intelligence. By contrast, a less-than-optimum environment prevents the fullest possible realization of potential intelligence. Experience with mentally retarded people demonstrates this point. Known causes account for only about 25 percent of observed cases of mental retardation. In addition, people whose mental retardation has no obvious physical cause are likely to have close relatives who are also mentally retarded. These findings strongly suggest that many of the remaining 75 percent of cases are hereditary. However, environmental causes (such as poor nutrition or the presence

fetal alcohol syndrome A disorder that adversely affects an offspring's brain development that is caused by the mother's alcohol intake during pregnancy.

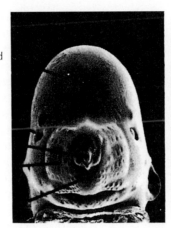
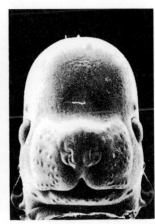

Narrow forehead

Short palpebral
fissures

Small nose

Long upper lip
with deficient
philtrum

Figure 11.4

A child with fetal alcohol syndrome, along with magnified views of a rat fetus whose mother received alcohol during pregnancy *(left)* and a normal rat fetus *(right)*.
(Photographs courtesy of Katherine K. Sulik.)

of environmental toxins) can produce brain damage in members of the same family; thus, not all cases of *familial* mental retardation are necessarily *hereditary*.

Clearly, the interactive effects of environmental and genetic factors are complex. The effects of hereditary factors on adult intellectual ability are necessarily indirect, and many environmental factors exert their effects throughout a person's life. Because an adult's intellectual abilities are the product of a long chain of events, we cannot isolate the effects of the earliest factors. The types of genetic and environmental factors that influence potential intelligence at each stage of development are summarized below.

Conception. A person's genetic endowment sets limits on his or her brain anatomy and thus on his or her potential intelligence.

Prenatal development. Good nutrition and a normal pregnancy result in optimum brain development and optimum potential intelligence. Drugs, toxic substances, poor nutrition, and physical accidents can impair brain development, thus lowering potential intelligence. Genetic disorders such as phenylketonuria and Down's syndrome can impair brain development, thus lowering potential intelligence.

Birth. Anoxia (lack of oxygen) or head trauma can cause brain damage, thus lowering potential intelligence.

Infancy. The brain continues to develop and grow. Good nutrition continues to be important. Sensory stimulation and interaction with a responsive environment are important for cognitive development. An infant's environment and brain structure jointly determine his or her intelligence.

Later life. A person's intelligence continues to be jointly determined by environmental factors and brain struc-

ture and chemistry. Aging brings with it an increased chance of developing senile dementia—a class of diseases characterized by the progressive loss of cortical tissue and a corresponding loss of mental functions. (*Senile* means "old"; *dementia* literally means "an undoing of the mind.") The most common causes of dementia are Alzheimer's disease (discussed in Chapter 12) and *multiple infarcts*—the occurrence of a large number of small strokes, each of which damages a small amount of brain tissue. In addition, as we will see in Chapter 12, mental deterioration can also be produced by depression, a psychological disorder. Unlike Alzheimer's disease or multiple infarcts, depression can be treated with drugs and with psychotherapy.

Results of Heritability Studies

Estimates of the degree to which heredity influences a person's intellectual ability come from several sources. As we saw in Chapter 3, the two most powerful methods are comparisons between identical and fraternal twins and comparisons between adoptive and biological relatives.

General Intelligence

Table 11.6 presents correlations in intelligence between people of varying kinships and estimates based on these data of the relative contributions of genetic and environmental factors. The data in the table were obtained from a summary of several studies by Henderson (1982). As you can see, the correlation between two people is indeed related to their genetic similarity. (See *Table 11.6, top.*) For example, the correlation between identical twins is larger than that between fraternal twins. In addition, the correlation between parent and child is approximately the same regardless of whether or not the child

Table 11.6

Correlations in Intelligence Between Pairs of People with Varying Kinships and Estimates of Relative Contributions of Genetic and Environmental Factors

Relationship	Rearing	Percentage of Genetic Similarity	Correlation
Same individual	—	100	.87
Identical twins	Together	100	.86
Fraternal twins	Together	50	.62
Siblings	Together	50	.41
Siblings	Apart	50	.24
Parent-child	Together	50	.35
Parent-child	Apart	50	.31
Adoptive parent–child	Together	?	.16

Estimates of Contributions of Genetics and Environment to Variability in Intelligence

Comparison	Genetics	Environment
Identical twins together versus fraternal twins together	.58	.28
Parent-offspring together versus parent-offspring apart	.50	.04
Siblings together versus siblings apart	.25	.25

Source: Adapted from Henderson N. D. A Human behavior genetics, pp. 403–440. Reproduced, with permission from the *Annual Review of Psychology*, Volume 33. © 1982 by Annual Reviews Inc.

is raised by the parent (.35 versus .31). This correlation, in turn, is higher than that between an adopted child and the parent who raises him or her (.16).

The bottom portion of Table 11.6 shows that estimates of the importance of common genetic and environmental factors vary considerably, depending on the type of comparison made. Estimates of genetic influence range from 25 to 58 percent. Thus, heredity contributes substantially to the observed differences in IQ scores. (See *Table 11.6, bottom.*)

We should be careful not to misinterpret the meaning of estimates of genetic or environmental influences on IQ scores. These estimates indicate only how much of the variability of that trait *in that population* appears to be related to genetic or environmental differences. Suppose that we were to raise some babies in stimulating, responsive environments, others

in mediocre environments, and still others in environments so impoverished that words were never spoken. The babies in the impoverished environments would never even learn to talk, and their IQs would be very low. In such a case, we would find that environmental factors accounted for nearly 100 percent of the observed variability in this population, with genetic factors being almost negligible in comparison.

The fact that, by most estimates, genetic factors account for approximately 50 percent of the variability in IQ scores means that the other half of the variability is accounted for by environmental factors. However, when the data presented in Table 11.6 are used to estimate the contribution of environmental factors, the results suggest that this contribution is less than 25 percent. Some estimates, based on comparisons of parents and their offspring raised together or apart, suggest a value of only *4 percent.* Why are these figures so low?

Plomin (1988) suggests that estimates of the importance of environmental factors tend to be low because the environment in a given family is not identical for all its members. Some environmental variables within a family are shared by all members of the family, such as the number of books the family has, the examples set by the parents, the places the family visits on vacation, the nosiness or quietness of the home, and so on. But not all of the environmental factors that affect a person's development and behavior are shared in this way. For example, no two children are treated identically, even by family members; differences in their appearances and personalities affect the way other people treat them. Different members of a family will probably have different friends and acquaintances, attend different classes in school, and, in general, be exposed to different influences. And once people leave home, their environments become even more different.

Estimates of the contribution of environmental variability to intelligence based on measurements made during childhood tend to be higher than similar estimates based on measurements made during adulthood. The reason for this difference may be that during childhood family members share a more similar environment, whereas during adulthood their environments become less similar. As Plomin notes, recent studies of genetically unrelated children (of a mean age of under ten years) adopted and raised in the same families, suggest that up to 30 percent of the variability in IQ scores is due to common environmental factors. However, when the comparison is made among young adults, the figure drops to less than 3 percent. Thus, once children leave home and are exposed to different environmental variables, the effect of a common family environment almost disappears. What is left, in the case of *related* individuals, is their common genetic heritage.

Specific Abilities

So far, I have discussed the effects of genetic and environmental factors on tests of general intelligence. Scarr and Weinberg (1978) compared some specific intellectual abilities of parents and their adopted and biological children and of

Although heredity plays an important role in intelligence, children's home environments can determine whether they achieve their full potential.

children and their biological and adopted siblings. To do so, they administered four of the subtests of the Wechsler Adult Intelligence Scale: arithmetic, vocabulary, block design, and picture arrangement. (*Table 11.4* showed the nature of these subtests.) Table 11.7 shows the results. As you can see, the correlations between biological relatives were considerably higher than those between adoptive relatives, indicating that genetic factors played a more significant role than shared environmental factors. In fact, with the exception of vocabulary,

adopted children showed little resemblance to other members of their family. (See *Table 11.7.*)

These results suggest that a person's vocabulary is more sensitive to his or her home environment than are other specific intellectual abilities. Presumably, such factors as the availability of books, parental interests in reading, and the complexity of vocabulary used by the parents have a significant effect on the verbal skills of all members of the household, whether or not they are biologically related.

Table 11.7

Correlations Between Parent and Adoptive or Biological Child for Four WAIS Subscales

	Relationship		
WAIS Subscale	Father-Offspring	Mother-Offspring	Sibling
Adoptive family correlations			
Arithmetic	.07	−.03	−.03
Vocabulary	.24	.23	.11
Block design	.02	.13	.09
Picture arrangement	−.04	−.01	.04
Biological family correlations			
Arithmetic	.30	.24	.24
Vocabulary	.39	.33	.22
Block design	.32	.29	.25
Picture arrangement	.06	.19	.16

Source: Adapted from Scarr, S., and Weinberg, R. A. *American Sociological Review,* 1978, *43,* 674–692. Adapted with permission.

Evaluating Scientific Issues

The Issue of Race and Intelligence

The fact that heredity appears to play an important role in people's innate intellectual capacities raises the question of whether people of some races are generally more intelligent than those of other races. Because of the harmful effects that racism has had on the lives of so many people, this question is not simply an academic one.

■ Are There Racial Differences in Intelligence?

Many studies have established the fact that there are racial differences in scores on various tests of intellectual abilities. For example, people who are identified as "black" generally score an average of 85 on IQ tests, whereas people who are identified as "white" score an average of 100 (Lynn, 1978; Jensen, 1985). Thus, although many blacks score better than many whites, on the average whites do better on these tests.

The issue is not the facts themselves but what these facts *mean*. Some authors say that the racial differences in scores on the tests are caused by heredity. *The Bell Curve*, a book written by a psychologist and a sociologist (Herrnstein and Murray, 1994), provoked a furor among psychologists and in the news media. The book asserted that psychologists agree that a general factor exists; that IQ tests measure what most people think of as intelligence; that IQ is almost impossible to modify through education and special training; that IQ is genetically determined; and that racial differences in IQ are the result of heredity.

■ What Is the Evidence for Racial Differences in Intelligence?

Needless to say, the assertions made in *The Bell Curve* have not gone unchallenged. Sternberg (1995) examined them and found that there is scientific evidence against all of them. First, as we have already seen in this chapter, most psychologists deny that intelligence can be accounted for by a single factor. And if you ask people what they mean by the word *intelligence*, three factors emerge from their responses: verbal ability, practical problem-solving ability, and social competence (Sternberg et al., 1981). Different cultures weight these factors differently; some think that social competence is more important, while others value competence on cognitive tasks (Berry, 1984; Okagaki and Sternberg, 1993).

What about the assertions that IQ is almost impossible to modify? In fact, special programs *have* been successful in raising children's IQ scores—on the order of 8 to 20 points (Ramey, 1994). The fact that our educational sys-

tem often fails to help children achieve their ultimate potential does not mean that we should abandon any attempts to raise the achievement level of children who have lower IQ scores. Perhaps we should try to improve our educational system instead.

And what about genetics? There are many reasons why we *cannot* conclude that the observed racial differences in average test scores are the result of heredity. I will examine the two most important ones here: the definition of race and the role of the environment. First, let us examine the concept of *race*. A biologist uses the term to identify a population of plants or animals that has some degree of reproductive isolation from other members of the species, with which it is perfectly capable of interbreeding. For example, collies, cocker spaniels, and beagles constitute different races of dogs (although we usually refer to them as *breeds*). In this case, reproductive isolation is imposed by humans; within obvious size limits, different breeds of dogs can readily mate with each other and produce viable offspring.

Any isolated group of organisms will, as a result of chance alterations in genetic factors and differences in local environment, become genetically different over time. Groups of humans whose ancestors mated only with other people who lived in a restricted geographical region tend to differ from other groups on a variety of hereditary traits, including stature, hair color, skin pigmentation, and blood type. However, subsequent migrations and conquests caused the interbreeding of many different groups of people. As a result, human racial groups are much more similar than, say, breeds of dogs, so that classifying people on the basis of race is a difficult and somewhat arbitrary matter.

Many researchers have used the trait of skin pigmentation to classify people by race. Two chemicals, melanin and keratin, cause skin to be black and yellow, respectively; a combination produces brown skin, while lighter-colored skin contains little of either substance. Evidence suggests that the selective value of differing amounts of skin pigmentation is related to its ability to protect against the effects of sunlight (Loomis, 1967). Such protection was important near the equator, where the sun is intense all year, but was less important in temperate zones. Because vitamin D is synthesized primarily through the action of sunlight on deep layers of the skin, *lack* of pigmentation was advantageous to residents of northern latitudes, except to those living in Arctic regions, where vitamin D was readily available from fish and seal meat.

The selective advantage of differences in skin pigmentation is obvious. But there is no plausible reason to expect these differences to be correlated either with other physical measures or with measures of intellectual ability. Both the tallest people in the world (the Masai) and the shortest (the Pygmy) have black skin. Nor are shape of nose and forehead, hair texture, blood groups, and many other physical features well correlated with skin pigmentation. We would never classify varieties of dogs by color, assigning golden retrievers and Chihuahuas to one group and black Labrador retrievers and Scotties to another. Why, then, should we do so with humans?

The second reason why we cannot conclude that racial differences in test scores are caused by heredity is the existence of environmental differences. In North America, racial membership is a cultural phenomenon, not a biological one. A man with three grandparents of European origin and one grandparent of African origin is defined as "black" unless he hides this fact and defines himself as "white." Black people and white people are treated differently: The average black family is poorer than the average white one; blacks usually attend schools of lesser academic quality than whites; pregnant black women typically receive poorer medical care than their white counterparts, and their diet tends to be not as well balanced; and so on. In these circumstances, we would expect people's IQ scores to differ in accordance with whether they had been *raised* as average blacks or as average whites—in other words, independently of their genetic backgrounds.

Some investigators have attempted to use statistical methods to remove the effects of environmental variables, such as socioeconomic status, that account for differences in performance between blacks and whites.

Former U.S. Armed Forces Chief of Staff Colin Powell. Knowing a person's race tells us very little about his or her intelligence.

However, these methods are controversial, and many statisticians question their validity. On the other hand, a study by Scarr and Weinberg (1976) provides unambiguous evidence that environmental factors can substantially increase the measured IQ of a black child. Scarr and Weinberg studied ninety-nine black children who were adopted while they were young into white families of higher-than-average educational and socioeconomic status. The expected average IQ of black children in the same area who were raised in black families was approximately 90. The average IQ of the adopted group was observed to be 105.

■ Race Tells Us Very Little about Intelligence

Some authors have flatly stated that there are no racial differences in biologically determined intellectual capacity. But this claim, like the one asserting that blacks are inherently less intelligent than whites, has not been proved scientifically. Although we know that blacks and whites have different environments and that a black child raised in an environment similar to that of a white child will receive a similar IQ score, the question of whether any racial hereditary differences exist has not been answered. However, given that there is at least as much variability in intelligence between two people selected at random as there is between the average black and the average white, knowing a person's race tells us very little about how intelligent he or she may be.

Although the issue of race and intelligence as presently conceived does not appear to be meaningful, it would be scientifically interesting to study the effects of different environments on inherited intellectual capacity. One such investigation might involve human populations whose ancestors came from desert regions, cold regions, humid regions, regions with widely fluctuating temperatures, regions with a high level of diseases, regions where food is difficult to obtain, regions where food is easily available, regions where the last ice age affected the native population, regions where trade has been important, and regions that have been isolated and self-sufficient. Direct comparisons of the innate intellectual abilities of these people could tell us which environmental factors have been important in the selection of intellectual abilities. However, these factors would not be synonymous with racial differences.

The interesting and more valid questions concerning race are those addressed by social psychologists and anthropologists—questions concerning issues such as the prevalence of prejudice, ethnic identification and cohesiveness, fear of strangers, and the tendency to judge something (or someone) that is different as inferior. In fact, Chapter 15 discusses the topic of prejudice from the perspective of social psychology.

Interim Summary

The Roles of Heredity and Environment

Variability in all physical traits is determined by a certain amount of genetic variability, environmental variability, and an interaction between genetic and environmental factors. The degree to which genetic variability is responsible for the observed variability of a particular trait in a particular population is called *heritability*. Heritability is not an indication of the degree to which the trait is determined by biological factors; rather, it reflects the relative proportions of genetic and environmental variability found in a particular population.

Intellectual development is affected by many factors, both prenatal and postnatal. A person's heredity, because of its effect on brain development, determines his or her potential intelligence. This potential intelligence can be permanently reduced during prenatal or postnatal development by injury, toxic chemicals, poor nutrition, or disease. And in order for a person to achieve his or her potential intelligence, the person must have an environment that will foster the learning of facts and skills needed to function well in society.

Twin studies and studies comparing biological and adoptive relatives indicate that both genetic and environmental factors affect intellectual ability, which is probably not surprising. These studies also point out that not all of a person's environment is shared by other members of the family; each person is an individual and is exposed to different environmental variables.

Some people have suggested that racial differences in intellectual ability are the result of differences in heredity. However, the available data do not support this conclusion. First, race is almost always defined culturally, not genetically. Second, we cannot rule out the effects of environmental differences. It is impossible to measure people's inherited intellectual ability directly; all we can do is measure their *performance*—on tests, in school, or on the job. Because performance is determined by what people have learned, it reflects environmental factors as well as genetic ones. Because members of different racial groups have unequal opportunities to use their innate biological capacities to develop intellectual skills, no conclusions can be made about whether the racial differences are hereditary. The little evidence we do have suggests that when educational opportunities are equalized, so are intelligence test scores.

Thought Questions

- Can you think of any types of environments that may have favored natural selection for particular kinds of abilities—for example, mathematical ability, spatial ability, perceptual ability, or ability to memorize stories?

- One of the most hotly contested issues in education today is that of "tracking"—assigning students having different levels of academic ability to different classes. Taking the point of view of students having high and low levels of ability, try to think of some arguments for and against this practice.

Thinking

One of the most important components of intelligence is thinking: categorizing, reasoning, and solving problems. Thinking is an activity that takes place where no one can see it—inside our heads. Because it is hidden, we can only infer its existence from people's behavior. When we think, we perceive, classify, manipulate, and combine information. When we are through, we know something we did not know before (although our "knowledge" may be incorrect).

The purpose of thinking is, in general, to solve problems. These problems may be simple classifications (*What is that, a bird or a bat?*). They may involve decisions about courses of actions (*Should I buy a new car or pay to fix the old one?*) Or they may require the construction, testing, and evaluations of complex plans of action (*How am I going to manage to earn money to support my family, help raise our children, and continue my education so that I can get out of this dead-end job—and still be able to enjoy life?*). Much, but not all, of our thinking involves language. We certainly think to ourselves in words, but we also think in shapes and images. And some of the mental processes that affect our decisions and plans take place without our being conscious of them. Thus, we will have to consider nonverbal processes as well as verbal ones (Reber, 1992; Holyoak and Spellman, 1993).

This section discusses the important elements and goals of thinking: classification and concept formation, logical reasoning, and problem solving.

Classifying

When we think, we do not consider each object or each event as a completely independent entity. Instead, we classify things—categorize them according to their characteristics. Then, when we have to solve a problem involving a particular object or situation, we can use information that we have already learned about similar objects or situations. To take a very simple example, when we enter someone's house for the first time, we recognize chairs, tables, sofas, lamps, and other pieces of furniture even though we may have never seen these particular items before. Because we recognize these categories of objects, we know where to sit, how to increase the level of illumination, and so on.

Concepts are categories of objects, actions, or states of being that share some attributes: cat, comet, team, destroying, playing, forgetting, happiness, truth, justice. Most thinking

concept A category of objects or situations that share some common attributes.

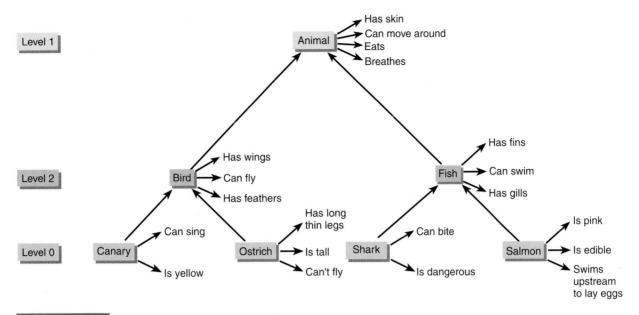

Figure 11.5

Collins and Quillian's model of the hierarchical organization of concepts in semantic memory.
(From Robert L. Solso, Cognitive Psychology, *Second Edition. Copyright © 1988 by Allyn and Bacon. After Collins and Quillian (1969). Reproduced with permission.)*

deals with the relations and interactions among concepts. For example, *The hawk caught the sparrow* describes an interaction between two birds; *Studying for an examination is fun* describes an attribute of a particular action; and *Youth is a carefree time of life* describes an attribute of a state of being. (There is no rule that says that thoughts have to be true!) Let us examine some features of concepts and concept formation.

Concepts exist because the characteristics of objects have consequences for us. For example, *mean dogs* may hurt us, whereas *friendly dogs* may give us pleasure. *Mean dogs* tend to growl, bare their teeth, and bite, whereas *friendly dogs* tend to prance around, wag their tails, and solicit our attention. Thus, when we see a dog that growls and bares its teeth, we avoid it because it may bite us; but if we see one prancing around and wagging its tail, we may try to pet it. We have learned to avoid or approach dogs who display different sorts of behavior through direct experience with dogs or through the vicarious experience of watching other people interact with them. The point is, we can learn the concepts of mean and friendly dogs from the behavior of one set of dogs while we are young and respond appropriately to other dogs later in life. Our experiences with particular dogs *generalize* to others.

Formal and Natural Concepts

Formal concepts are defined by listing their essential characteristics, as a dictionary definition does (or as this textbook does). For example, dogs have four legs, a tail, fur, and wet noses; are carnivores; can bark, growl, whine, and howl; pant when they are hot; bear live young; and so on. Thus, a formal

concept is a sort of category that has rules about membership and nonmembership.

Psychologists have studied the nature of formally defined concepts, such as species of animals. Collins and Quillian (1969) suggested that such concepts are organized hierarchically in semantic memory. Each concept has associated with it a set of characteristics. Consider the hierarchy of concepts relating to animals shown in Figure 11.5. At the top is the concept *animal,* with which are associated the characteristics common to all animals, such as *has skin, can move around, eats, breathes,* and so on. Linked to the concept *animal* are groups of animals, such as *birds, fish,* and *mammals,* along with their characteristics. (See *Figure 11.5.*)

Collins and Quillian assumed that the characteristics common to all members of a group of related concepts (such as all birds) were attached to the general concept (in this case *bird*) rather than to all the members. Such an arrangement would produce an efficient and economical organization of memory. For example, all birds have wings. Thus, we need not remember that a canary, a blue jay, a robin, and an ostrich all have wings; we need only remember that each of these concepts belong to the category of *bird* and that birds have wings.

Collins and Quillian tested the validity of their model by asking people questions about the characteristics of various concepts. Consider the concept *canary.* The investigators asked people to say "true" or "false" to statements such as *A canary*

formal concept A category of objects or situations defined by listing their common essential characteristics, as dictionary definitions do.

eats. When the question dealt with characteristics that were specific to the concept (such as *can sing,* or *is yellow*), the subjects responded quickly. If the question dealt with a characteristic that was common to a more general concept (such as *has skin* or *breathes*), the subjects took a longer time in answering. Presumably, when asked a question about a characteristic that applied to all birds or to all animals, the subjects had to "travel up the tree" from the entry for *canary* until they found the level that provided the answer. The farther they had to go, the longer the process took. (See *Figure 11.5.*)

The model just presented has an appealing simplicity and logic to it, but it turns out that people's brains do not follow such tidy, logical schemes in classifying concepts and their characteristics. For example, although people may indeed conceive of objects in terms of a hierarchy, a particular person's hierarchy of animals need not resemble that compiled by a zoologist. For example, Rips, Shoben, and Smith (1973) found that people said "yes" to *A collie is an animal* faster than they did to *A collie is a mammal.* According to Collins and Quillian's model, *animal* comes above *mammal* in the hierarchy, so the results should have been just the opposite.

Although some organization undoubtedly exists between categories and subcategories, it appears not to be perfectly logical and systematic. For example, Roth and Mervis (1983) found that people judged *Chablis* to be a better example of *wine* than of *drink,* but they judged *champagne* to be a better example of *drink* than of *wine.* This inconsistency clearly reflects people's experience with the concepts. Chablis is obviously a wine: It is sold in bottles that resemble those used for other wines, it looks and tastes similar to other white wines, the word *wine* is found on the label, and so on. By these standards, champagne appears to stand apart. A wine expert would categorize champagne as a particular type of wine. But the average person, not being particularly well acquainted with the fact that champagne is made of fermented grape juice, encounters champagne in the context of something to drink on a special occasion, something to christen ships with, and so on. Thus, its characteristics are perceived as being rather different from those of Chablis.

Rosch (1975; Mervis and Rosch, 1981) suggested that people do not look up the meanings of concepts in their heads the way they seek definitions in dictionaries. The concepts we use in everyday life are *natural concepts,* not formal ones discovered by experts who have examined characteristics we are not aware of. **Natural concepts** are based on our own perceptions and interactions with things in the world. For example, some things have wings, beaks, and feathers, and they fly, build nests, lay eggs, and make high-pitched noises. Other things are furry, have four legs and tails, and run around on the ground. Formal concepts consist of carefully defined sets of rules governing membership in a particular category; natural concepts are collections of memories of particular examples that share some similarities. Formal concepts are used primarily by experts (and by people studying to become experts), whereas natural concepts are used by ordinary people in their daily lives.

Rosch suggests that people's natural concepts consist of collections of memories of *particular examples,* called **exemplars,** that share some similarities. The boundaries between formal concepts are precise, whereas those between natural concepts are fuzzy—the distinction between a member and a nonmember is not always clear. Thus, to a nonexpert, not all members of a concept are equally good examples of that concept. A robin is a good example of *bird;* a penguin or ostrich is a poor one. We may acknowledge that a penguin is a bird because we have been taught that it is, but we often qualify the category membership by making statements such as "*Strictly speaking,* a penguin is a bird." Exemplars represent the important characteristics of a category—characteristics that we can easily perceive or that we encounter when we interact with its members.

According to Rosch et al. (1976), natural concepts vary in their level of precision and detail. They are arranged in a hierarchy from very detailed to very general. When we think about concepts and talk about them, we usually deal with **basic-level concepts**—those that make important distinctions between different categories—but do not waste time and effort with those that do not matter. For example, *chair* and *apple* are basic-level concepts. Concepts that refer to collections of basic-level concepts, such as *furniture* and *fruit,* are called **superordinate concepts.** Concepts that refer to types of items within a basic-level category, such *lawn chair* and *McIntosh apple,* are called **subordinate concepts.** (See *Figure 11.6.*) just a simple hierarchy of apples

The basic-level concept tends to be the one that people spontaneously name when they see a member of the category. That is, all types of chairs tend to be called "chair," unless there is a special reason to use a more precise label (for example, if you wanted to buy a particular kind of chair). People tend to use basic-level concepts for a very good reason: *cognitive economy.* The use of subordinate concepts wastes time and effort on meaningless distinctions, and the use of superordinate concepts loses important information. Rosch et al. (1976) presented people with various concepts and gave them 90 seconds to list as many attributes as they could for each of them. The subjects supplied few attributes for superordinate concepts but were able to think of many for basic-level concepts. Subordinate concepts evoked no more responses than basic-

natural concept A category of objects or situations based on people's perceptions and interactions with things in the world; based on exemplars.

exemplar A memory of particular examples of objects or situations that are used as the basis of classifying objects or situations into concepts.

basic-level concept A concept that makes important distinctions between different categories.

superordinate concept A concept that refers to collections of basic-level concepts.

subordinate concept A concept that refers to types of items within a basic-level category.

Level of Concept

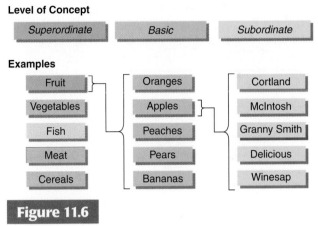

Figure 11.6

Examples of basic-level, subordinate, and superordinate concepts.

level concepts did. Thus, because they deal with a large number of individual items and their characteristics, basic-level concepts represent the most information in the most efficient manner. When people think about basic-level concepts, they do not have to travel up or down a tree to find the attributes that belong to the concept. The attributes are directly attached to the exemplars that constitute each concept.

It is important to recognize that concepts can represent something more complex than simple exemplars or collections of attributes. Goldstone, Medin, and Gentner (1991) showed subjects groups of figures and asked them to indicate which were most similar to each other. When they showed the subjects two triangles, two squares, and two circles, the

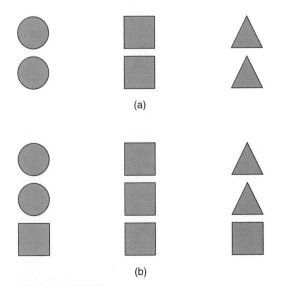

Figure 11.7

Concept formation. Subjects were asked which of the groups of shapes were most similar. (a) Three pairs of geometrical shapes. (b) The same shapes with the addition of squares.

subjects said that the squares and triangles were most similar, presumably because both contained straight lines and angles. However, when they added a square to each of the pairs, the subjects said that the two most similar groups were the triangles plus square and the circles plus square. (See *Figure 11.7*.) The concept this time was "two things and a square." If the subjects were simply counting attributes, then the addition of a square to the pairs should not have changed their decision. As this study shows very clearly, concepts can include relations among elements that cannot be described by counting attributes.

Concepts are the raw material of thinking; they are what we think about. But thinking itself involves the manipulation and combination of concepts. Such thinking can take several forms, but most the common forms are deductive reasoning and inductive reasoning.

Deductive Reasoning

Deductive reasoning consists of inferring specific instances from general principles or rules. For example, the following two series of sentences express deductive reasoning:

> John is taller than Phil.
>
> Sue is shorter than Phil.
>
> Therefore, John is taller than Sue.

> All mammals have fur.
>
> A bat is a mammal.
>
> Therefore, a bat has fur.

Deductions consist of two or more statements from which a conclusion is drawn. The first group of sentences presented above involve the application of a simple mathematical principle. The second group of sentences presents a syllogism, described earlier in this chapter.

People differ widely in their ability to solve syllogisms. For example, many people would agree with the conclusion of the following syllogism:

> All mammals have fur.
>
> A zilgid has fur.
>
> Therefore, a zilgid is a mammal.

These people would be wrong; the conclusion is not warranted. The major premise says only that all mammals have fur. It leaves open the possibility that some animals that have fur are not mammals.

Mental Models

Why are some people better than others at solving syllogisms? Johnson-Laird (1985) notes that syllogistic reasoning

deductive reasoning Inferring specific instances from general principles or rules.

is much more highly correlated with spatial ability than with verbal ability. Spatial ability includes the ability to visualize shapes and to manipulate them mentally. Why should skill at logical reasoning be related to this ability? Johnson-Laird and his colleagues (Johnson-Laird and Byrne, 1991; Johnson-Laird, Byrne, and Schaeken, 1992) suggest that people solve problems involving logical deduction by constructing **mental models,** mental constructions based on physical reality. For example, read the following problem and answer it: *A is less than C. B is greater than C. Is B greater than A?* In order to compare A with B, you must remember the order of the three elements. One kind of mental model is an imaginary line going from small to large in which you mentally place each item on the line as you encounter it. Then, with all three elements in a row, you can answer the question. (See *Figure 11.8.*)

In fact, when we solve problems concerning comparisons of a series of items, we tend to think about our own mental model that represents the information rather than about the particular facts given to us (Potts, 1972). For example, read the following passage:

> Although the four craftsmen were brothers, they varied enormously in height. The electrician was the very tallest, and the plumber was shorter than him. The plumber was taller than the carpenter, who, in turn, was taller than the painter. (Just and Carpenter, 1987, p. 202)

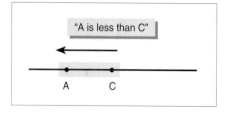

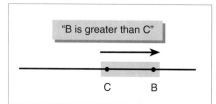

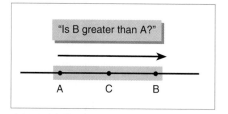

Figure 11.8

A mental model. Logical problems are often solved by imagining a physical representation of the facts.

After reading this passage, people can more easily answer questions about pairs of brothers who largely differ in height. For example, they are faster to answer the question "Who is taller, the electrician or the painter?" than the question "Who is taller, the plumber or the carpenter?" This finding is particularly important because the passage explicitly states that the plumber was taller than the carpenter, *but one must infer that the electrician was taller than the painter.* Just and Carpenter's study shows that the result of an inference can be more readily available than information explicitly given. How can this be? The most plausible explanation is that when people read the passage, they construct a mental model that represents the four brothers arranged in order of height. The painter is clearly the shortest and the electrician is clearly the tallest. Thus, a comparison between the extremes can be made very quickly. (See *Figure 11.9.*)

We use our spatial ability to construct models for representing and manipulating many types of information. For example, answer the following question and try to think about how you go about doing so: *What do you call your mother's sister's son?* Most people report that they answer the question

The late Nobel laureate Richard Feynman, who solved complex problems by inventing bizarre mental models.

mental model A mental construction based on physical reality that is used to solve problems of logical deduction.

Figure 11.9

A "mental model" of the craftsmen experiment. Subjects could judge the relative heights of the electrician and the painter faster than those of the plumber and the carpenter. Although the passage describing the craftsmen explicitly compared the heights of the plumber and carpenter, people had to infer that the electrician was taller than the painter.

by constructing a mental family tree, with their mother above them, their mother's sister to the side, and her son below her. Then, comparing that location with their own, they can easily see that the answer is "cousin." (See *Figure 11.10.*) Luria (1973) found that people with damage to the parietal lobes had difficulty answering such questions. As you learned in Chapter 4, the parietal lobes are involved with somatosensation and spatial abilities. Luria suggested that an impairment in spatial abilities makes it difficult for people with parietal lobe damage to construct a mental family tree.

Many creative scientists and engineers report that they use mental models to reason logically and solve practical and theoretical problems (Krueger, 1976). For example, the

American physicist and Nobel laureate Richard Feynman said that he used rather bizarre mental models to keep track of characteristics of complex mathematical theorems to see whether they were logical and consistent. Here is how Feynman described his thought processes:

> When I'm trying to understand . . . I keep making up examples. For instance, the mathematicians would come in with a . . . theorem. As they're telling me the conditions of the theorem, I construct something that fits all the conditions. You know, you have a set (one ball)—disjoint (two balls). Then the balls turn colors, grow hairs, or whatever, in my head as they [the mathematicians] put more conditions on. Finally, they state the theorem, which is some . . . thing about the ball which isn't true for my hairy green ball thing, so I say "False!" (Feynman, 1985, p. 70)

Such use of mental models by a talented and gifted scientist strengthens the conclusion that being able to convert abstract problems into tangible mental models is an important aspect of intelligent thinking.

Inductive Reasoning

As we saw, deductive reasoning involves applying the rules of logic to infer specific instances from general principles or rules. This type of reasoning works well when general principles or rules have already been worked out. But how do we accumulate new knowledge and formulate new general prin-

Figure 11.10

A spatial model of reasoning: "What do you call your mother's sister's son?"

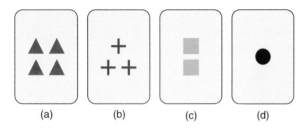

Figure 11.11

Examples of the type of cards used in a test of inductive reasoning.

ciples or rules? Having read Chapter 2 of this book, you already know the answer—by following the scientific method. But few people know the rules of the scientific method, and even those who do seldom follow them in their daily lives.

Inductive reasoning is just the opposite of deductive reasoning; it consists of inferring general principles or rules from specific facts. A well-known laboratory example of inductive reasoning works like a guessing game. The subjects are shown cards that contain figures differing in several dimensions, such as shape, number, and color. On each trial, they are given two cards and asked to choose the one that represents a particular concept. After they choose a card, the experimenter says "right" or "wrong." (See *Figure 11.11*.)

One trial is not enough to recognize the concept. For example, if the first trial reveals that card (a) is correct, then the concept could be *red*, or *four*, or *triangle*, or some combination of these, such as *red triangle*, *four red shapes*, or even *four red triangles*. Information gained from the second trial permits the subject to rule out some of these hypotheses—for example, now it appears that shape does not matter, but color and number do. The subject uses steps to solve the problem much the way a scientist does: Form a hypothesis on the basis of the available evidence and test that hypothesis on subsequent trials. If it is proven false, abandon it, try to think of a hypothesis consistent with what went before, and test the new hypothesis.

Logical Errors in Inductive Reasoning

Obviously, people can be trained to follow the rules of the scientific method. However, without special training, they follow commonsense rules, some of which work and some of which do not. Psychologists interested in people's inductive reasoning ability have identified several tendencies that lead them astray. It is precisely because of such tendencies that we need to learn specific rules (such as those of the scientific method) so that we can have confidence in our conclusions.

Psychologists have identified several tendencies that interfere with people's ability to reason inductively. These include the failure to select the information they need to test a hypothesis, the failure to seek information that would be provided by a comparison group, and the disinclination to seek evidence that would indicate whether a hypothesis is false.

Failure to Select Appropriate Information. When reasoning inductively, people often fail to select the information they need to test a hypothesis. For example, consider the following task, from an experiment by Wason and Johnson-Laird (1972).

> Your job is to determine which of the hidden parts of these cards you need to see in order to answer the following question decisively:
>
> **For these cards is it true that if there is a vowel on one side there is an even number on the other side?**
>
> You have only one opportunity to make this decision; you must not assume that you can inspect the cards one at a time. Name those cards which it is absolutely essential to see.

The subjects were shown four cards like those shown in Figure 11.12. Read the problem again, look at the cards, and decide which card (or cards) you would have to see. (See *Figure 11.12*.)

Most people say that they would need to see card (a), and they are correct. If there was *not* an even number on the back of card (a), then the rule is not correct. However, many subjects failed to realize that card (d) must also be inspected. True, there is no even number on this card, but what if there is a vowel on the other side? If there is, then the rule is (again) proved wrong. Many subjects also wanted to see card (c), but there is no need to do so. The hypothesis says nothing about whether an even number can be on one side of the card *without* there being a vowel on the other side.

So people do not always attack a problem logically or efficiently. As we know, people have to be taught the rules of logic; they do not automatically apply them when trying to solve a problem. But under certain circumstances, most people *do* reason logically. For example, Griggs and Cox (1982)

---

inductive reasoning Inferring general principles or rules from specific facts.

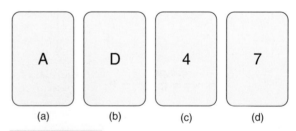

Figure 11.12

Cards used in a formal test of problem solving.

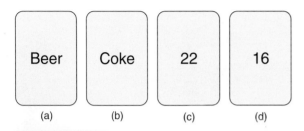

(a)   (b)   (c)   (d)

Figure 11.13

Cards used in a more realistic version of the problem-solving test.

presented a slightly different version of this test. They asked people to decide which cards should be checked to see whether the following statement was true: "If a person is drinking beer, she must be over age nineteen." The cards represented people; their age was on one side and their beverage (beer or Coke) was on the other. Which card(s) would you check? (See *Figure 11.13.*)

Most subjects correctly chose cards (a) and (d). They knew that if someone were drinking beer, she must be old enough. Similarly, if someone were sixteen years old, we must check to see what she was drinking. The subjects readily recognized the fact that we do not need to know the age of someone drinking Coke, and someone twenty-two years old can drink whatever beverage she prefers. This study shows that experiments using puzzles designed to test people's reasoning ability do not always assess their ability to apply a logical rule to a practical situation.

Failure to Consider a Comparison Group.   Another tendency that interferes with people's ability to reason inductively is their failure to consider a comparison group. Suppose that you learn that 79 percent of the people with a particular disease get well within a month after taking a new, experimental drug (Stich, 1990). What would you conclude? Is the drug effective? The correct answer to this question is, "We cannot conclude anything—we need more information." What we need to know is what happens to people with the disease if they do *not* take the drug. If we find that only 22 percent of these people recover within a month, then we would conclude that the drug is effective; 79 percent is much greater than 22 percent. On the other hand, if we find that 98 percent recover without taking the drug, then we would conclude that the drug is worse than useless—it actually interferes with recovery. In other words, we need a control group. But most people are perfectly willing to conclude that, because 79 percent seems like a high figure, the drug must work. Seeing the neces-

confirmation bias A tendency to seek evidence that might confirm a hypothesis rather than evidence that might disconfirm it; a logical error.

sity for a control group does not come naturally; unless people are deliberately taught about control groups, they will not realize the need for them.

Failure to seek or use information that would be provided by a control group has been called *ignoring the base rate.* As several researchers have suggested, the problem here may be that we engage in two types of reasoning (Reber, 1992). One type of reasoning is deliberate and conscious and involves explicit memories of roles that we can describe verbally. The other type of reasoning is unconscious and uses information we have learned implicitly. (The distinction between explicit and implicit memories and their relation to consciousness was discussed in Chapters 8 and 9.) Because the explicit and implicit memory systems involve at least some different brain mechanisms, information from one system cannot easily interact with information from the other system. In fact, if people are allowed to observe actual occurrences of certain events (that is, acquire the information about the base rate of occurrence automatically and implicitly), they *do* consider information about event frequency (Holyoak and Spellman, 1993).

Failure to Seek Disconfirming Evidence.   Yet another tendency that interferes with people's ability to reason inductively is a disinclination to seek evidence that would indicate whether a hypothesis is false. Instead, people tend to seek evidence that might confirm their hypothesis; they exhibit the **confirmation bias.** For example, Wason (1968) presented people with the series of numbers "two, four, six" and asked them to try to figure out the rule to which they conformed. The subject was to test his or her hypothesis by making up series of numbers and saying them to the experimenter, who would reply "yes" or "no." Then, whenever the subject decided that enough information had been gathered, he or she could say what the hypothesis was. If the answer was correct, the problem was solved. If it was not, the subject was to think of a new hypothesis and test that one.

Several rules could explain the series "two, four, six." The rule could be "even numbers," or "each number is two more than the preceding one," or "the middle number is the mean of the first and third number." When people tested their hypotheses, they almost always did so by presenting several sets of numbers, *all of which were consistent with their hypotheses.* For example, if they thought that each number was two more than the preceding one, they might say "ten, twelve, fourteen" or "sixty-one, sixty-three, sixty-five." *Very few* subjects tried to test their hypotheses by choosing a set of numbers that did *not* conform to the rules, such as "twelve, fifteen, twenty-two." In fact, the series "twelve, fifteen, twenty-two" does conform to the rule. The rule was so simple that few subjects figured it out: Each number must be larger than the preceding one.

The confirmation bias is very strong. Unless people are taught to do so, they tend not to think of possible nonexamples of their hypotheses and to see whether they might be true—the way that scientists do. But in fact, evidence that disconfirms a hypothesis is conclusive, whereas evidence that confirms it is not. Suppose that you thought that the answer to the problem I just described was "even numbers." You could give ascending lists of three even numbers hundreds of times, and each list would be correct. But, of course, your rule would still be wrong. If you gave just one nonexample—say, "five, six, seven," the experimenter would say "yes" and you would immediately know that the answer was not "even numbers."

The confirmation bias in inductive reasoning has a counterpart in deductive reasoning. For example, consider the following sentences (Johnson-Laird, 1985):

All the pilots are artists.

All the skiers are artists.

True or false: All the pilots are skiers.

Many people say "true." They test the truth of the conclusion by imagining a person who is a pilot and an artist and a skier—and that person complies with the rules. Therefore, they decide that the conclusion is true. But if they would try to *disconfirm* the conclusion—to look for an example that would fit the first two sentences but not the conclusion—they would easily find one. Could a person be a pilot but *not* a skier? Of course; the first two sentences say nothing to rule out that possibility. There are artist–pilots and there are artist–skiers, but nothing says that there must be artist–pilot–skiers.

The tendency to seek (and to pay more attention to) events that might confirm our beliefs is demonstrated by the way we have distorted the original meaning of the saying, "The exception proves the rule." Most people take this to mean that we can still consider a rule to be valid even if we encounter some exceptions. But that conclusion is illogical: If there is an exception, the rule is *wrong*. In fact, the original meaning of the phrase was, "The exception *tests* the rule," which it does. The word "prove" comes from the Latin *probare*, "to test."

Problem Solving

The ultimate function of thinking is to solve problems. We are faced with an enormous variety of them in our daily lives: fixing a television set, planning a picnic, choosing a spouse, navigating across the ocean, solving a math problem, tracking some game, designing a bridge, finding a job. The ability to solve problems is related to academic success, vocational success, and overall success in life, so trying to understand how we do so is an important undertaking.

The Spatial Metaphor

According to Holyoak (1990), a problem is a state of affairs in which we have a goal but do not have a clear understanding of how it can be attained. As he notes, when we talk about problems, we often use spatial metaphors to describe them (Lakoff and Turner, 1989). We think of the solving of a prob-

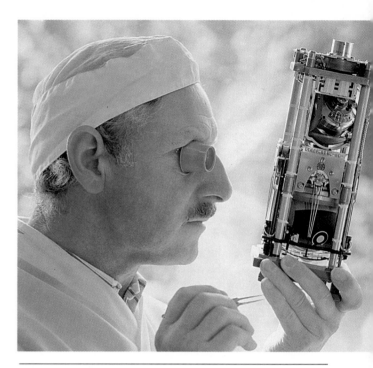

Problem solving takes many forms. An engineer examines a defective navigational instrument.

lem as *finding a path to the solution*. We may have to *get around roadblocks* that we encounter or *backtrack* when *we hit a dead end*. If we *get lost*, we may try to *approach the problem from a different angle*. If we have experience with particular types of problems, we may know some *shortcuts*.

In fact, Newell and Simon (1972) have used the spatial metaphor to characterize the problem-solving process. At the beginning of a person's attempt to solve a problem, the *initial state* is different from the *goal state*—if it were not, there would be no problem. The person solving the problem has a number of *operators* available. Operators are actions that can be taken to change the current state of the problem; metaphorically, operators move the current state from one position to another. Not all people will be aware of the operators that are available. Knowledge of operators depends on education and experience. In addition, there may be various costs associated with different operators; some may be more difficult, expensive, or time-consuming than others. The *problem space* consists of all the possible states that can be achieved if all the possible operators are applied. A *solution* is a sequence of operators (a "path") that moves from the initial state to the goal state.

Figure 11.14 illustrates this process schematically. The circles represent the current or possible states of affairs while the problem is being solved. The arrows represent the operators—the actions that can be taken. Some actions are reversible (double arrows); others are not. A solution follows a path from the initial state to the goal state. (See *Figure 11.14.*)

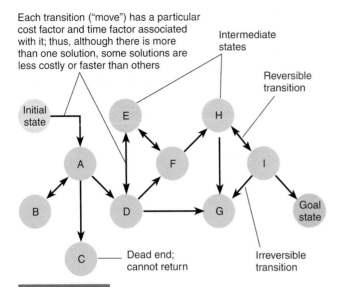

Each transition ("move") has a particular cost factor and time factor associated with it; thus, although there is more than one solution, some solutions are less costly or faster than others

Intermediate states

Reversible transition

Initial state

Dead end; cannot return

Irreversible transition

Goal state

Figure 11.14

Newell and Simon's spatial metaphor of the problem-solving process. Each transition ("move") has a particular cost factor and time factor associated with it; thus, although there is more than one solution, some solutions are less costly or faster than others.

(Adapted from Holyoak, K.J. In An Invitation to Cognitive Science, *Vol. 3: Thinking, edited by D.N. Osherson and E.E. Smith. Cambridge, Mass.: MIT Press, 1990.)*

Algorithms and Heuristics

Some kinds of problems can be solved by following a sequence of operators known as an algorithm. **Algorithms** are procedures that consist of series of steps that, if followed in the correct sequence, will provide a solution. For example, you are undoubtedly familiar with an algorithm known as "long division." If you properly apply the steps of this algorithm to divide one number by another, you will obtain the correct answer. But many problems are not as tidy as math problems, nor as easy to solve. When there is no algorithm to follow, we must follow a *heuristic* to guide our search for a path to the solution. **Heuristics** (pronounced *hyoo-ris-tiks,* derived from the Greek *heuriskein,* "to discover") are general rules that are useful in guiding our search for a path to the solution of a problem. Heuristics tell us what to pay attention to, what to ignore, and what strategy to take.

algorithm A procedure that consists of a series of steps that will solve a specific type of problem.

heuristic A general rule that guides decision making.

means-ends analysis A general heuristic method of problem solving that involves looking for differences between the current state and the goal state and seeking ways to reduce the differences.

Heuristic methods can be very specific, or they can be quite general, applying to large categories of problems. For example, management courses try to teach students problem-solving methods they can use in a wide variety of contexts. Newell and Simon (1972) suggest a general heuristic method that can be used to solve *any* problem: means-ends analysis. The principle behind **means-ends analysis** is that a person should look for differences between the current state and the goal state and seek ways to reduce these differences. The steps of this method are as follows (Holyoak, 1990, p. 121):

1. Compare the current state to the goal state and identify differences between the two. If there are none, the problem is solved; otherwise, proceed.
2. Select an operator that would reduce one of the differences.
3. If the operator can be applied, do so; if not, set a new *subgoal* of reaching a state at which the operator could be applied. Means-ends analysis is then applied to this new subgoal until the operator can be applied or the attempt to use it is abandoned.
4. Return to step 1.

Suppose that the problem is to clear snow off my driveway. Rejecting several possible operators because they are too time-consuming or too costly *(dig the snow off with my hands* or *melt the snow with a propane torch),* I decide to apply the operator *start the snowblower and run it up and down the driveway.* Unfortunately, I find that the snowblower will not start, which means that the operator I have chosen cannot be applied. Thus, I set up a subgoal: *Fix the snowblower.*

One possible operator that will get me toward that subgoal is *put the snowblower in the car and bring it to a mechanic,* but the snow on my driveway precludes that option. Therefore, I decide to fix it myself. In order to fix the snowblower, I have to know what the problem is. I consider some possible actions, including *take the engine apart to see whether something inside is broken,* but I decide to try some simpler ones, such as *see whether the wire is attached to the spark plug* or *see whether there is gasoline in the tank.* I find the wire attached but the gas tank empty. The only operator that will get me to my subgoal is *fill the tank with gasoline.* But I have no gasoline. Therefore, I construct another subgoal: *Get some gasoline.*

What are the possible sources of gasoline? A gas station? No, I can't move the car. A neighbor? The snow is so deep that I do not want to fight my way through the drifts. The tank of my car? That's it. New subgoal: *Remove some gasoline from the car's fuel tank.* How do I get it out? New subgoal: *Find rubber hose to siphon the gasoline into the tank of the snowblower.* I do so, I start the engine, and I clear the snow off the driveway. The problem is solved.

The example I have just cited is obviously not very challenging, but it does illustrate the use of means-ends analysis. At all times, the person's activity is oriented toward reducing the distance between the current state and the goal state. If problems are encountered along the way (that is, if operators cannot be applied), then subgoals are created and means-ends analysis is applied to solving *that* problem—and so on, until the goal is reached.

Of course, there may be more than one solution to a particular problem, and some solutions may be better than others. A good solution is one that uses the smallest number of actions while minimizing the associated costs. The relative importance of cost and speed determines which solution is best. For example, if the problem is to rescue a child who is up to her neck in quicksand, the best solution may be the most expensive one: Drive your $75,000 Mercedes into the pool of quicksand, climb onto the roof, jump down to the hood, reach over the front of the car, pull her out, and then climb back over the top of the car and get to dry land before the car sinks. Finding a large object other than your valuable car would be cheaper, but it would take too much time.

Intelligent problem solving involves more than trying out various actions (applying various operators) to see whether they bring me closer to the goal. It also involves *planning*. When we plan, we act vicariously, "trying out" various actions in our heads. Obviously, planning requires that we know something about the consequences of the actions we are considering. Experts are better at planning than novices are. If we do *not* know the consequences of particular actions, we will be obliged to try each action (apply each operator) and see what happens. Planning is especially important when many possible operators are present, when they are costly or time-consuming, or when they are irreversible. If we take an irreversible action that brings us to a dead end, we have failed to solve the problem.

Interim Summary

Thinking

Formal concepts are defined as lists of essential characteristics of objects and events. In everyday life, we use natural concepts—collections of memories of particular examples, called exemplars. Concepts exist at the basic, subordinate, and superordinate level. We do most of our thinking about concepts at the basic level.

Deductive reasoning consists of inferring specific instances from general principles. That is, we take information that is already known and see whether particular occurrences are consistent with that information. One of the most important skills in deductive reasoning is the ability to construct mental models that represent problems.

Inductive reasoning involves inferring general principles from particular facts. This form of thinking involves generating and testing hypotheses. Without special training (such as learning the rules of the scientific method), people often ignore relevant information, ignore the necessity of control groups, or show a confirmation bias—the tendency to look only for evidence that confirms one's hypothesis. However, performance on some puzzle-like tests of reasoning may not accurately reflect people's ability to apply the rules of logic in more realistic situations. In addition, not all information has equal effects on judgments; explicit and implicit memories appear to play different roles.

Problem solving is best represented spatially: We follow a path in the problem space from the initial state to the goal state, using operators to get to each intermediate state. Sometimes a problem fits a particular mold and can be solved with an algorithm—a cut-and-dried set of operations. However, in most cases, a problem must be attacked by following a heuristic—a general rule that helps guide our search for a path to the solution of a problem. The most general heuristic is means-ends analysis, which involves taking steps that reduce the distance from the current state to the goal. If obstacles are encountered, subgoals are created and attempts are made to reach them.

Thought Questions

- Try to think of a new concept you have learned recently. Can you describe its features, or is it easier to think of an exemplar?
- Chapter 2 described the scientific method. Some of the rules and procedures you learned there were designed to avoid the errors in logical thinking that were described in this chapter. Try to relate the scientific method to these errors.

Suggestions for Further Reading

Aiken, L. *Psychological Testing and Assessment,* 6th ed. Boston: Allyn and Bacon, 1988.

Gardner, H. *Frames of Mind: The Theory of Multiple Intelligences.* New York: Basic Books, 1983.

Kaplan, R.M., and Saccuzzo, D.P. *Psychological Testing: Principles and Issues.* Pacific Grove, CA.: Brooks/Cole, 1989.

Sternberg, R.J. *Beyond IQ: A Triarchic Theory of Human Intelligence.* Cambridge, England: Cambridge University Press, 1985.

Gardner's book describes his theory, which is based on the existence of specific brain functions related to talents often overlooked by traditional tests of intelligence. The books by Aiken and by Kaplan and Saccuzzo provide excellent discussions of the differential, or psychometric, approach to intelligence. Sternberg's book describes his information-processing theory of intelligence.

Kamin, L. *The Science and Politics of IQ.* New York: John Wiley & Sons, 1974.

Scarr, S. *Race, Social Class, and Individual Differences in IQ.* Hillsdale, N.J.: Lawrence Erlbaum Associates, 1981.

Vale, J.R. *Genes, Environment, and Behavior.* New York: Harper & Row, 1980.

Kamin's book examines the history of the scientific study of intelligence—in particular, its contamination by racism and ethnocentrism. The books by Scarr and by Vale provide excellent discussions of the interrelations between environmental and hereditary influences on intelligence.

Chapter 12

Life-Span Development

Chapter Outline

Prenatal Development

Stages of Prenatal Development • Threats to Normal Prenatal Development

During the prenatal period, the fertilized ovum develops into a fetus, a human in miniature. The crucial factors in the fetus's development are the mother's diet and physical health; the presence of toxins in the prenatal environment can cause the fetus to be born with physical and cognitive defects.

Physical and Perceptual Development in Infancy and Childhood

Motor Development • Perceptual Development

Timing and experience are two key elements in normal motor and perceptual development. For normal development to occur, a child must encounter stimulation from the environment during a specific time interval. If stimulation does not occur during this period, normal development is impeded, perhaps permanently.

Cognitive Development in Childhood

The Importance of a Responsive Environment • The Work of Jean Piaget • Vygotsky's Sociocultural Theory of Cognitive Development • Developmental Models of Information Processing in Cognitive Development • *Evaluating Scientific Issues: The Effects of Television Viewing on Children's Cognitive Development*

In Piaget's view, a child passes through four distinct intellectual changes, which coincide with changes in a child's nervous system and with a child's experience, on his or her way to becoming an adult. According to Vygotsky, a child's cognitive development is strongly influenced by sociocultural variables, especially language. Information-processing models of cognitive development center on how brain maturation influences the development of cognitive processes.

Social Development in Childhood

Behaviors of the Infant That Foster Attachment • The Nature and Quality of Attachment • Interactions with Peers • Approaches to Childrearing • Growing Up in a Single-Parent or Divorced Family

Attachment is the social and emotional bond that develops between an infant and caregiver during infancy. The quality of attachment depends largely on the nature of infants' relationships with their caregivers. Social development during childhood is influenced by both the child's interactions with peers and the parent's

style of childrearing. Children in single-parent families and divorced families appear to undergo normal social development when certain conditions are met.

Development of Gender Roles

The Nature of Gender Differences • *Biology and Culture: The Causes of Gender Role Differences*

Evolution appears to have shaped differences in brain development for males and females: Males tend to have better spatial abilities and females tend to have better communication skills. Socialization processes, such as parenting, are involved in shaping gender-appropriate behavior. However, most gender differences in behavior are small.

Moral Development

Piaget's Theory of Moral Development • Kohlberg's Theory of Moral Development • Evaluation of Piaget's and Kohlberg's Theories of Moral Development

Piaget concluded that people pass through two stages of moral development. The first is marked by egocentrism and adherence to rules and the second by empathy. Kohlberg argued that moral development ascends through three levels: externally defining morality, considering how the social system relates to morality, and, finally, understanding the principles on which moral principles are based.

Adolescence

Physical Development • Social Development • Identity and Self-Perception

Adolescence begins with sexual maturation, which brings with it marked changes in social behavior. Females tend to build relationships based on trust, while males tend to seek social support in becoming more independent. A key aspect of adolescent social development involves forming an identity.

Adulthood and Old Age

Physical Development • Cognitive Development • Social Development

Our physical abilities peak in early adulthood and decline gradually thereafter, although adopting a healthy life-style can retard loss of these abilities. Compared to young adults, older adults perform worse on tests of abstract reasoning but better on tests related to general knowledge and abilities related to experience. Success in love, family, and work is the yardstick by which most people measure their satisfaction in life.

One day, a colleague of mine, Dr. D., approached me in the hall and asked me how old my daughter was. When I said she was six months old, he asked whether my wife and I would mind if he used her for a demonstration in his child development class. I said it would be fine with me, and I was sure my wife would agree also.

The next week, my wife brought our daughter to the psychology building at the appointed time. Dr. D. ushered them into a small room that contained a large square table. Part of the surface of the table was a strip of plywood about a foot wide, which ran along one edge. It was painted in a bright red-and-black checkerboard pattern. The rest of the table was topped with an enormous piece of glass. The floor under the glass, about three feet below, was painted in the same checkerboard pattern.

Dr. D. asked my wife to place our daughter at one corner of the table, on the end of the plywood platform. After my wife had done so, and after she had reassured our daughter that everything was all right, he asked her to go to the opposite corner of the table and stand there. He glanced up at the one-way glass that separated the room from the adjoining classroom, which contained a small group of students who were watching the procedure.

"Now ask her to come to you," he said.

"Come here, Kerstin," said my wife in a cheerful tone.

Kerstin grinned, made a happy noise, and scampered across the glass, making slapping sounds with her hands as she crawled. She seemed heedless of the three-foot drop beneath the glass.

My wife picked her up, smiled at Dr. D., and realized from the expression on his face that something had gone wrong. He glanced at the one-way glass, cleared his throat, and said, "Let's try it again."

The second trial was like the first. In fact, this time Kerstin did not even wait for my wife to get to her corner before she started across the glass. Clearly, she knew how the game was played.

"Kerstin hasn't done this before, has she?" asked Dr. D.

"No, she hasn't," my wife replied. "But I think I know why she wasn't afraid of crawling onto the glass. That *was* what you expected, wasn't it?"

"Yes," he said.

"We have a glass-topped coffee table in the living room at home, and Kerstin likes to play there. She used to like to lie on the floor under it and look up through the glass, and the past couple of months we've put her on top of it and let her crawl around."

Dr. D. looked relieved. "That explains it," he said. "She has learned to trust her sense of touch, even though she undoubtedly could perceive that the floor under the glass was far away." He paused a few seconds. "Actually," he said, "this provides a nice demonstration of the interaction between experience and development. Although children change in predictable ways as they mature, their development is shaped by their encounters with their environment."

He thanked my wife and turned toward the classroom. He was obviously thinking about how he would take advantage of this unexpected happening in the rest of his lecture.

Human development is a series of changes that occurs to each of us during our lives. We can see different parts of the cycle by looking at our grandparents, our parents, our friends, and our children. At one time, psychologists studied development from birth through childhood. But we have learned that developmental processes do not stop there. Growing older is a matter not only of aging, but also of changing—personally, intellectually, and socially. (See *Table 12.1.*) *Life-span developmental psychology* studies these processes and the patterns of change that occur within an indi-

Table 12.1

Phases of the Life-Span

Phase	Approximate Age	Highlights
1. Prenatal	Conception through birth	Rapid physical development of both nervous system and body
2. Infancy	Birth to 2 years	Motor development; attachment to primary caregiver
3. Childhood	1½ years to 12 years	Increasing ability to think logically and reason abstractly; refinement of motor skills; peer influences
4. Adolescence	13 years to about 20 years	Thinking and reasoning becomes more adultlike; identity crisis; continued peer influences
5. Adulthood	20 years to 65 years	Love, marriage, career; stability and then decrease in physical abilities
6. Old age	65 years and older to death	Reflection on life's work and accomplishments; physical health deteriorates; prepare for death; death

vidual over life's course. Developmental psychologists study both the similarities and the differences among people as they develop and change over the course of their lives. In this chapter, we are interested in when and how these similarities and differences occur. You will learn explanations for many of the changes that you have experienced so far and will get a preview of changes yet to come. We will discuss each of the major developmental periods: prenatal development, infancy and childhood, adolescence, and adulthood and old age.

Prenatal Development

The nine months between conception and birth is called the **prenatal period**. The length of a normal pregnancy is 266 days, or 38 weeks. The prenatal period involves three developmental stages: the zygote, the embryo, and the fetal stages.

Stages of Prenatal Development

Conception, or the union of the ovum (egg) and sperm, is the starting point for prenatal development. During the **zygote stage**, which lasts about two weeks, the *zygote*, or the cell that is formed at conception, divides many times, and the internal organs begin to form. By the end of the first week, the zygote consists of about a hundred cells. Many of the cells are arranged in two layers, one for the skin, hair, nervous system, and sensory organs and the other for the digestive and respiratory systems and glands. Near the end of this stage, a third layer of cells appears, those that will eventually develop into the circulatory and excretory systems and muscles.

The second stage of prenatal development, the **embryo stage**, begins at about two weeks and ends about eight weeks after conception. During this stage, the zygote is transformed into an embryo and development occurs at an incredibly rapid pace. Within a month after conception, a heart has begun to beat, a tiny brain has started to function, and most of the major body structures are beginning to form. By the end of this stage, the major features that define the human body—the arms, hands, fingers, legs, toes, shoulders, head, and eyes—are discernible. Behaviorally, the embryo can react reflexively to stimulation. For example, if the mouth is stimulated, the embryo moves its upper body and neck. This stage is also noteworthy because it is now that the embryo is most susceptible to chemicals that can cause birth defects, including drugs such as alcohol or toxins produced by diseases such as German measles. These substances are called **teratogens** (from the Greek, *teras*, meaning monster).

Sexual development begins during the embryo stage. The determining factor for sex is the Y chromosome, which is contributed by the male parent at conception. If it is present, the embryo will become a male (XY); if it is not, it will become a female (XX). Early in prenatal development, the embryo develops a pair of gonads that will become either ovaries or testes. (The word *gonad* comes from the Greek *gonos*, "pro-

prenatal period The nine months between conception and birth. This period is divided into three developmental stages: the zygote, the embryo, and the fetal stages.

zygote stage The first stage of prenatal development, during which the zygote divides many times and the internal organs begin to form.

embryo stage The second stage of prenatal development, beginning two weeks and ending about eight weeks after conception, during which the heart begins to beat, the brain starts to function, and most of the major body structures begin to form.

teratogens Drugs or other substances that can cause birth defects.

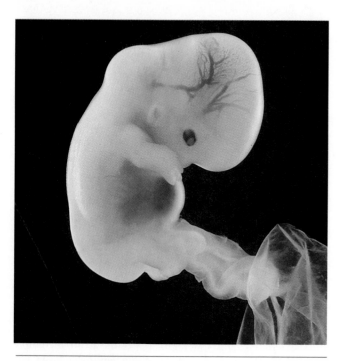

As this photograph of a six-week old fetus illustrates, most of the major features that define the human body are present near the end of the embryonic stage of development (which starts at about 2 weeks and ends about 8 weeks after conception).

creation.") If a Y chromosome is present, a gene located on it causes the production of a chemical signal that makes the gonads develop into testes. Otherwise, the gonads become ovaries.

The development of the other sex organs is determined by the presence or absence of testes. If testes are present, they begin secreting a class of sex hormones known as **androgens** (*andros* means "man"; *gennan* means "to produce"). The most important androgen is *testosterone*. Androgens bring about the development of the male internal sex organs, the penis, and the scrotum. Thus, these hormones are absolutely necessary for the development of a male. In contrast, the development of female sex organs (uterus, vagina, and labia) occurs naturally; it does not need to be stimulated by a hormone. If the gonads completely fail to develop, the fetus becomes female, with normal female sex organs. Of course, lacking ovaries, such a person cannot produce ova. (See *Figure 12.1.*)

The final stage of prenatal development is the **fetal stage**, which lasts about seven months. It officially begins with the appearance of bone cells and ends with birth. At the end of the

androgens The primary class of sex hormones in males. The most important androgen is testosterone.

fetal stage The third and final stage of prenatal development, which lasts for about seven months, beginning with the appearance of bone tissue and ending with birth.

second month of pregnancy, the fetus is about one and a half inches long and weighs about one ounce. By the end of the third month, the development of major organs is completed and the bones and muscles are beginning to develop. The fetus is now three inches long and weighs about three ounces. The fetus may show some movement, especially kicking.

By the end of the fourth month, the fetus is about six inches long and weighs about six ounces. It is also now sleeping and waking regularly. Fetal movements also become strong enough to be felt by the mother, and the heartbeat is strong enough to be heard through a stethoscope. During the sixth month, the fetus grows to over a foot long and weighs about one and a half pounds. The seventh month is a critical month because if the fetus is born prematurely at this point, it has a fair chance of surviving. However, fetuses mature at different rates, and some seven-month-old fetuses may be mature enough to survive while others may not.

During the last two months of prenatal development, the fetus gains weight at the rate of about half a pound per week. On average, the fetus is about twenty inches long and weighs about seven pounds at the end of this period. The fetus is now ready to be born.

Threats to Normal Prenatal Development

Under normal conditions, the prenatal environment provides just the right supply of nutrients to the fetus. Probably the single most important factor in the fetus's development is the mother's diet: The food she eats is the fetus's only source of nutrition. If the mother is extremely malnourished, the fetus's nervous system develops abnormally, and it may be born mentally retarded.

In addition to poor diet, teratogens can also cause birth defects. Psychologists who study birth defects are very interested in how drugs affect the fetus because taking drugs is a behavior that is directly under the control of the mother. Certain antibiotics, especially when taken in large quantities over long periods, can produce fetal defects. For example, tetracycline, a common antibiotic, can cause irregularities in the bones and discoloration of the teeth. Certain tranquilizers may produce a cleft palate. Heroin and cocaine produce more dramatic effects. If a pregnant woman is addicted to heroin, her baby is likely to be born addicted. The baby will show withdrawal symptoms, such as hyperactivity, irritability, and tremors. The symptoms make the baby harder to care for, which, in turn, makes attachment between mother and baby difficult.

A pregnant woman's cigarette smoking is another behavior that can affect the fetus. The carbon monoxide contained in cigarette smoke reduces the supply of oxygen to the fetus. Reduced oxygen levels are particularly harmful to the fetus during the last half of pregnancy when the fetus is developing most rapidly and its demand for oxygen is greatest. The main effects of mothers' smoking are increased rate of miscarriages,

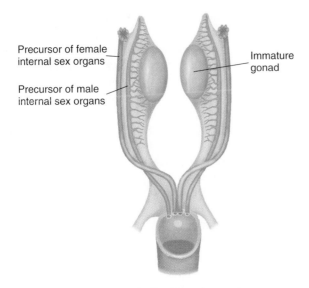

Precursor of female internal sex organs

Precursor of male internal sex organs

Immature gonad

Early in Fetal Development

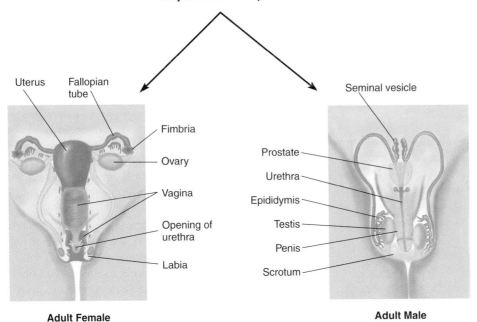

Uterus
Fallopian tube

Fimbria

Ovary

Vagina

Opening of urethra

Labia

Adult Female

Seminal vesicle

Prostate

Urethra

Epididymis

Testis

Penis

Scrotum

Adult Male

Figure 12.1

Differentiation and development of the sex organs.

low birthweight babies, and increased chance of premature birth.

Although a woman's regular use of any psychoactive drug during her pregnancy is likely to have harmful effects on the fetus, alcohol use during pregnancy has been most widely studied (Coles et al., 1992). Collectively, these effects, including both pre- and postnatal growth deficits, deformations of the eyes and mouth, brain and central nervous system abnormalities, and heart deformation, are known as *fetal alcohol syndrome (FAS)*, which we discussed in Chapter 11. The likelihood of stunted growth is doubled if a woman drinks. Drinking as little as two ounces of alcohol a day early in pregnancy can produce some symptoms of FAS (Astley et al., 1992). Even if children with FAS are reared in healthy environments with regular, nutritious meals, their physical and intellectual development still falls short of that of normal children (Hanson, Jones, and Smith, 1976).

Interim Summary

Prenatal Development

The three stages of prenatal development span the time between conception and birth. In just nine months, the zygote grows from a single cell, void of human resemblance, into a fully developed fetus, complete with physical features that look much like yours and mine, except in miniature. Gender is determined by the sex chromosomes. Male sex organs are produced by the action of a gene on the Y chromosome that causes the gonads to develop into testes. The testes secrete androgens, which stimulate the development of male sex organs. If testes are not present, the fetus develops as a female. The most important factor in normal fetal development is the mother's nutrition. Normal fetal development can be disrupted by the presence of teratogens, which can cause mental retardation and physical deformities. One well-studied teratogen is alcohol, which, when consumed by a pregnant woman, may lead to fetal alcohol syndrome.

Thought Questions

- Each of us experiences similar developmental stages and processes, so why do we end up so different from each other?
- Suppose that you are a psychologist working in a pediatric clinic. A woman, pregnant with her first child, asks you for advice on what she can do to care for her unborn child. Based on what you now know about prenatal development, what advice would you give her?

Physical and Perceptual Development in Infancy and Childhood

By general agreement, babies are called infants until two years of age. A newborn human infant is a helpless creature, absolutely dependent on adult care. But recent research has shown that newborns do not passively await the ministrations of their caregivers. They quickly develop skills that shape the behavior of the adults with whom they interact.

Motor Development

At birth, the infant's most important movements are reflexes—automatic movements in response to specific stimuli. The most important reflexes are the rooting, sucking, and swallowing responses. If a baby's cheek is lightly touched, he or she will turn the head toward the direction of the touch (the *rooting* response). If the object makes contact with the baby's lips, the baby will open the mouth and begin *sucking*. When milk or any other liquid enters the mouth, the baby will automatically make *swallowing* movements. Obviously, these reflexes are important for the baby's survival. As we will see later in this chapter, these behaviors are important for an infant's social development as well.

Normal motor development follows a distinct pattern, which appears to be dictated by maturation of the muscles

maturation Any relatively stable change in thought, behavior, or physical growth that is due to the aging process and not to experience.

and the nervous system. **Maturation** refers to any relatively stable change in thought, behavior, or physical growth that is due to the aging process and not to experience. Although individual children progress at different rates, their development follows the same basic maturational pattern. (See *Figure 12.2*.) Development of motor skills requires two ingredients: maturation of the child's nervous system and practice. Development of the nervous system is not complete at birth; considerable growth occurs during the first several months (Dekaban, 1970). In fact, some changes are still taking place in early adulthood.

Particular kinds of movements must await the development of the necessary neuromuscular systems. But motor development is not merely a matter of using these systems once they develop. Instead, physical development of the nervous system depends, to a large extent, on the baby's own movements while interacting with the environment. In turn, more complex movements depend on further development of the nervous system—different steps in motor development are both a cause of further development and an effect of previous development (Thelen, 1995).

Perceptual Development

If we want to study how older children or adults perceive the world, we can simply ask them about their experiences. We can determine how large an object must be for them to see it or how loud a sound must be for them to hear it. But we cannot talk to infants and expect to get any answers; we must use their nonverbal behavior as an indicator of what they can perceive.

We have known for a long time that a newborn's senses function at least to a certain extent. We know that the auditory system can detect sounds because the baby will show a startle reaction when presented with a sudden, loud noise. Similarly, a bright light will elicit eye closing and squinting. A cold object or a pinch will produce crying, so the sense of touch must be present. If held firmly and tilted backward, a baby will stiffen and flail his or her arms and legs, indicating that babies have a sense of balance.

Newborn infants indicate their taste preferences by facial expression and by choosing to swallow or not to swallow different liquids. When an infant is given a sweet liquid, the face relaxes in an expression rather like a smile; but when it is given a sour or bitter liquid, the face indicates displeasure. Newborn infants can even learn to recognize particular odors. Sullivan et al. (1991) presented one-day-old infants with a citrus odor and then gently stroked them. The next day, these infants (but not control infants) turned toward a cotton swab containing the odor that had been paired with the stroking.

Most investigations of the perceptual abilities of newborn infants have taken advantage of the fact that babies have good control of movements of their heads, eyes, and mouths. We will look at the results of some of these studies next.

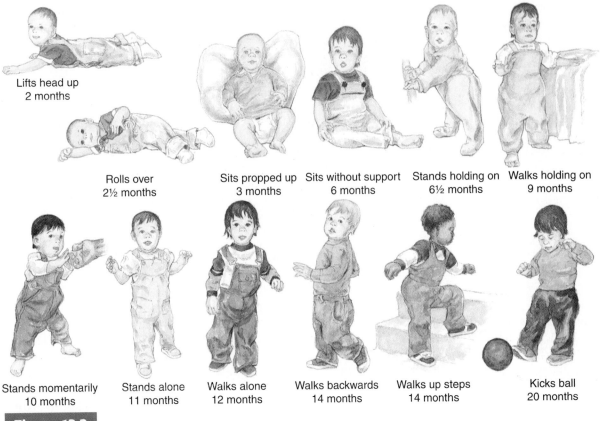

Lifts head up
2 months

Rolls over
2½ months

Sits propped up
3 months

Sits without support
6 months

Stands holding on
6½ months

Walks holding on
9 months

Stands momentarily
10 months

Stands alone
11 months

Walks alone
12 months

Walks backwards
14 months

Walks up steps
14 months

Kicks ball
20 months

Figure 12.2

Milestones in a child's motor development.
(Adapted from Shirley, M.M. The First Two Years. Vol. 2: Intellectual Development. *Minneapolis: University of Minnesota Press, 1933.)*

Perception of Patterns

The visual perceptual abilities of infants can be studied by observing their eye movements as visual stimuli are shown to them. A harmless spot of infrared light, invisible to humans, is directed onto the baby's eyes. A special television camera, sensitive to infrared light, records the spot and superimposes it on an image of the display that the baby is looking at. The technique is precise enough to determine which parts of a stimulus the baby is scanning. For example, Salapatek (1975) reported that a one-month-old infant tends not to look at the inside of a figure. Instead, the baby's gaze seems to be "trapped" by the edges. By the age of two months, the baby scans across the border to investigate the interior of a figure. Figure 12.3 shows a computer-drawn reconstruction of the paths followed by the eye scans of infants of these ages. (The babies were looking at real faces, not the drawings shown in the figure.) (See *Figure 12.3.*)

The work by Salapatek and his colleagues suggests that at the age of one or two months, babies are probably not perceiving complete shapes; their scanning strategy is limited to fixations on a few parts of the object at which they are looking. However, by three months, babies show clear signs of pattern recognition. For example, they prefer to look at stimuli that resemble the human face over stimuli that do not (Rosser, 1994).

Perception of Space

The ability to perceive three-dimensional space comes at an early age. Gibson and Walk (1960) placed six-month-old babies on what they called a visual cliff—a platform containing a checkerboard pattern. The platform adjoined a glass shelf mounted several feet over a floor that was also covered by the checkerboard pattern. Most babies who could crawl would not venture out onto the glass shelf. The infants acted as if they were afraid of falling. Recall, though, how, in the opening vignette, my daughter Kerstin was not afraid to crawl out onto the glass of the visual cliff during the demonstration with Dr. D. Her previous experience with our glass-topped coffee table had taught her that the glass would support her weight as she crawled around on top of it.

As you learned in Chapter 7, several different types of cues in the environment contribute to depth perception. One cue arises from the fact that each eye gets a slightly different view of the world (Poggio and Poggio, 1984). This form of

1-month old

2-month old

Finish

Start

Start

Finish

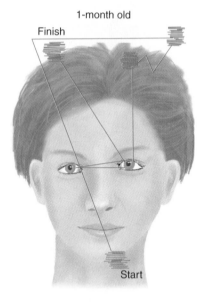

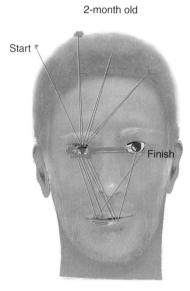

Figure 12.3

The scanning sequence used by infants viewing faces.

(From Salapatek, P. Pattern perception in early infancy. In Infant Perception: From Sensation to Cognition. Vol. 1: Basic Visual Processes, *edited by L.B. Cohen and P. Salapatek. New York: Academic Press, 1975. Reprinted with permission.)*

depth perception, *stereopsis* ("solid appearance"), is the kind obtained from a stereoscope or a three-dimensional movie. The brain mechanisms necessary for stereopsis will not develop unless animals have experience viewing objects with both eyes during a critical period early in life.

The term **critical period** refers to the specific time during which certain experiences *must* occur if an organism is to develop normally. Many behavioral, perceptual, and cognitive abilities are subject to critical periods. For example, as we shall see later in this chapter, if infants are not exposed to a stimulating environment and do not have the opportunity to interact with caregivers during the first two years of their lives, their cognitive development will be retarded. Human development is more than an unfolding of a genetically determined program. It consists of a continuous *interaction* between physical maturation and environmental stimulation.

The critical period in the development of stereopsis has important implications for the development of normal vision. If an infant's eyes do not move together properly—if they both are directed toward the same place in the environment (that is, if the eyes are "crossed")—the infant never develops stereoscopic vision, even if the eye movements are later corrected by surgery on the eye muscles. Banks, Aslin, and Letson (1975) studied infants whose eye movement deficits were later corrected surgically. Their results show that the critical period ends sometime between one and three years of age. If surgery occurs before this time, stereoscopic vision will develop. If the surgery occurs later, it will not.

Interim Summary

Physical and Perceptual Development in Infancy and Childhood

A newborn infant's first movements are actually reflexes that are crucial to its survival. For example, the rooting, sucking, and swallowing reflexes are important in finding and consuming food. More sophisticated movements, such as crawling and standing, develop and are refined through natural maturation and practice.

A newborn's senses appear to be at least partially functional at birth. However, normal development of the senses, like that of motor abilities, depends on experience. Genetically, an infant has the potential to develop motor and sensory abilities that coincide with the maturation of its nervous system. But in order for this potential to be realized, the infant's environment must supply the opportunity to test and practice these skills. If an infant is deprived of the opportunity to practice them during a critical period, these skills may fail to develop, which will affect his or her performance as an adult.

A visual cliff. The child does not cross the glass bridge.

critical period A specific time in development during which certain experiences must occur for normal development to occur.

Thought Question

■ Suppose you are expecting your first child. How might you design your child's room (or nursery) to facilitate his or her motor and perceptual development? What kinds of toys would you include in the room? What sorts of experiences might you wish to have with your child to promote normal motor and sensory development?

Cognitive Development in Childhood

As children grow, their nervous systems mature and they undergo new experiences. Perceptual and motor skills develop in complexity and competency. Children learn to recognize particular faces and voices, begin to talk and respond to the speech of others, and learn how to solve problems. Infants as young as thirteen months are even able to form memories of specific events (Bauer, 1996). In short, their cognitive capacities develop.

The Importance of a Responsive Environment

The cognitive development of infants is the process by which they get to know things about themselves and their world. Although cognitive development appears to involve both evolutionary and environmental variables (Geary, 1995), I will focus mainly on environmental factors in this section. I will discuss evolutionary contributions to development later in the chapter.

Evidence suggests that one of the first steps in cognitive development is learning that events in the environment are often dependent on one's own behavior. Thus, the environment that is most effective in promoting cognitive development is one in which the infant's behavior has tangible effects. In an experiment testing this hypothesis, Watson and Ramey (1972) presented three groups of infants with a mobile ten minutes per day for fourteen days. A pillow containing a pressure-sensitive switch was placed under the baby's head, and the mobile was suspended above the baby's face. For one group, the mobile automatically rotated whenever the infant moved his or her head and activated the switch. For another group, the mobile remained stationary. For a third group, the mobile intermittently moved on its own (not in response to head movement).

Several weeks later, the babies were tested again. Those who had learned the contingency between head turning and mobile movement continued to turn their heads. In contrast, when the babies in the second and third groups were given the opportunity to make the mobile move by turning their heads, they did *not* learn to control it. It was as if they had learned that nothing they could do would affect the movements of the mobile. (See *Figure 12.4*.)

These results may have implications for infant-rearing practices. In some tragic cases, babies have been raised in unresponsive, unstimulating institutions. In one institution, infants were cared for physically but were raised in cribs that visually isolated them from each other. Although their physical needs were fulfilled, they received no individual attention from their caregivers (Dennis, 1973). The children raised under these conditions were extremely retarded in cognitive, language, and motor development. Dennis found that when children were adopted from the nursery and raised in a normal home environment, they showed significant gains in physical and intellectual development. However, there was evidence for a critical period. Infants adopted before two years of age eventually achieved a normal level of development, whereas children who were adopted after the age of two years remained behind normally raised children. Thus, an unstimulating environment may produce permanent damage if it persists through the child's first two years of life.

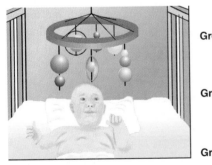

	First Condition	Later Condition
Group A	Head turning causes mobile to move. *Babies learn to move head.*	Head turning causes mobile to move. *Babies continue to move head.*
Group B	Mobile remains stationary.	Head turning causes mobile to move. *Babies do not learn to move head.*
Group C	Mobile intermittently moves on its own.	Head turning causes mobile to move. *Babies do not learn to move head.*

Figure 12.4

The importance of a responsive environment.
(Based on Watson, J.S., and Ramey, C.T. Reactions to responsive contingent stimulation in early infancy. Merrill-Palmer Quarterly, *1972, 18, 219–227.)*

The Work of Jean Piaget

The most influential student of child development has been Jean Piaget (1896–1980), a Swiss psychologist, who viewed cognitive development as a maturational process. Piaget formulated the most complete and detailed description of the process of cognitive development that we now have. His conclusions were based on his observations of the behavior of children—first, of his own children at home and, later, of other children at his Center of Genetic Epistemology in Geneva. He noticed that children of similar age tend to engage in similar behaviors and to make the same kinds of mistakes in problem solving. He concluded that these similarities are the result of a sequence of development that all normal children follow. Completion of each period, with its corresponding abilities, is the prerequisite for entering the next period.

According to Piaget, as children develop, they acquire **cognitive structures**, mental representations or rules that are used for understanding and dealing with the world and for thinking about and solving problems. The two principal types of cognitive structures are schemata and concepts. **Schemata** (*schema* is the singular form) are mental representations or sets of rules that define a particular category of behavior— how the behavior is executed and under what conditions. A

child is said to have a "grasping schema" when she is able to grasp a rattle in her hand. Once she has learned how to grasp a rattle, she can then use the same schema to grasp other objects. A child has acquired a "picking up schema" when he is able to lift the rattle from a surface.

Piaget suggested that as a child acquires knowledge of the environment, he or she develops mental structures called *concepts*—rules that describe properties of environmental events and their relations to other concepts. For example, concepts about the existence of various objects include what the objects do, how they relate to other objects, and what happens when they are touched or manipulated. Thus, an infant's cognitive structure includes concepts of such things as rattles, balls, crib slats, hands, and other people.

Infants acquire schemata and concepts by interacting with their environment. According to Piaget, two processes help a child adapt to its environment: assimilation and accommodation. **Assimilation** is the process by which new information is modified to fit existing schemata. For example, when a child moves a wooden block along a surface while making the rumbling sound of an engine, he has assimilated the wooden block into his schema of a car. **Accommodation** is the process by which old schemata are changed by new experiences. Accommodation produces either new schemata or changes in existing ones. For example, suppose that a young girl's concept of animal has three categories: doggies, kitties, and teddies. If she sees a picture of a deer and calls it a kitty, she has assimilated the new information into an existing concept. However, if she decides that a deer is a new kind of animal, she will accommodate her animal concept to include the new category. Now this concept consists of doggies, kitties, teddies, and deer.

Piaget's Four Periods of Cognitive Development

Although development is a continuous process, the cognitive structures of children vary from age to age. We can make inferences about the rules children of certain ages use to understand their environment and control their behavior. Thus Piaget divided cognitive development into four periods: sensorimotor, preoperational, concrete operational, and formal operational. (See *Table 12.2.*) What a child learns in one period enables him or her to progress to the next period.

According to Piaget, children develop schemes, such as grasping objects or putting them into their mouths, which become the basis for understanding current and future experiences.

cognitive structures According to Piaget, mental representations or rules, such as schemata or concepts, that are used for understanding and dealing with the world and for thinking about and solving problems.

schemata Mental representations or sets of rules that define a particular category of behavior. Schemata include rules that help us to understand current and future experiences.

assimilation The process by which new information about the world is modified to fit existing schemata.

accommodation The process by which existing schemata are modified or changed by new experiences.

	Table 12.2	
	The Four Periods of Piaget's Theory of Cognitive Development	

Period	Approximate Age	Major Features
Sensorimotor	Birth to 2 years	Object permanence; deferred imitation; rudimentary symbolic thinking
Preoperational	2 to 6 or 7 years	Increased ability to think symbolically and logically; egocentrism; cannot yet master conservation problems
Concrete operational	6 or 7 years to 11 years	Can master conservation problems; can understand categorization; cannot think abstractly
Formal operational	11 years upward	Can think abstractly and hypothetically

The Sensorimotor Period. The **sensorimotor period**, which lasts for approximately the first two years of life, is the first stage in Piaget's theory of cognitive development. It is marked by an orderly progression of increasingly complex cognitive development ranging from reflexes to symbolic thinking. During this period, cognition is closely tied to external stimulation. An important feature of the sensorimotor period is the development of **object permanence**, the idea that objects do not disappear when they are out of sight. Until about six months of age, children appear to lose all interest in an object that disappears from sight—the saying "out of sight, out of

mind" seems particularly appropriate. In addition, cognition consists entirely in behavior: Thinking is doing.

At first, infants do not appear to have a concept for objects. They can look at visual stimuli and will turn their heads and eyes toward the source of a sound, but hiding an object elicits no particular response. At around three months, they become able to follow moving objects with their eyes. If an object disappears behind a barrier, infants will continue to stare at the place where the object has disappeared but will not search for it.

At around five months, infants can grasp and hold objects and gain experience with manipulating and observing them. They can also anticipate the future position of a moving object. If a moving object passes behind a screen, infants turn their eyes toward the far side of the screen, seeming to anticipate the reappearance of the object on the other side.

During the last half of the first year, infants develop much more complex concepts concerning the nature of physical objects. They grasp objects, turn them over, and investigate their properties. By looking at an object from various angles, they learn that the object can change its visual shape and still be the same object. In addition, if an object is hidden, infants will actively search for it; their object concept now contains the rule of object permanence. For infants at this stage of development, a hidden object still exists. "Out of sight" is no longer "out of mind." For example, in the game of peekaboo, babies laugh because they know that after momentarily disappearing, you will suddenly reappear and say, "Peekaboo."

By early in the second year, object permanence is well-enough developed that infants will search for a hidden object in the last place they saw it hidden. However, at this stage, infants can only keep track of changes in the hiding place that they can see. For example, if an adult picks up an object, puts it under a cloth, drops the object while his or her hand is hidden, closes the hand again, and removes it from the cloth, infants will look for the object in the adult's hand. When they do not find the object there, they look puzzled or upset and do not search for the object under the cloth. (See *Figure 12.5.*)

Near the end of the sensorimotor period, two other interesting developments occur. First, children develop the ability to imitate actions that they have seen others perform, a behavior that Piaget called **deferred imitation**. This ability is

This infant has acquired the concept of object permanence: She understands that her mother is hiding behind the wooden object and will soon stand up and say "peekaboo."

sensorimotor period This first period in Piaget's theory of cognitive development, lasting from birth to two years. It is marked by an orderly progression of increasingly complex cognitive development: reflexes, permanence, a rough approximation of causality, imitation, and symbolic thinking.

object permanence The idea that objects do not disappear when they are out of sight.

deferred imitation A child's ability to imitate the actions he or she has observed others perform. Piaget believed deferred imitation to result from the child's increasing ability to form mental representations of behavior performed by others.

Object is in experimenter's hand.

Experimenter closes hand. . .

. . . puts hand under cloth. . .

. . . removes hand, leaving object under the cloth.

Infant looks in experimenter's hand.

Obviously upset, infant quits.

Figure 12.5

Object permanence. An infant will not realize that the object has been left under the cloth.
(Adapted from Bower, T.G.R. Perception in Infancy, *2nd ed. San Francisco: W.H. Freeman, 1972.)*

due to their increasing ability to form mental representations of actions that they have observed. These representations may then be recalled at a later time to direct particular imitative actions and symbolic play, such as pretending to feed a doll or taking a stuffed animal for a walk. Second, as having an imagination shows, two-year-old children begin to think symbolically. They can use words to represent objects such as balls and animals. This is a critical developmental step because this skill is crucial to language development.

The Preoperational Period. Piaget's second period of cognitive development, the **preoperational period**, lasts from approximately age two to age seven and involves the ability to think logically as well as symbolically. This period is characterized by rapid development of language ability and of the ability to represent things symbolically. The child arranges toys in new ways to represent other objects (for example, a row of blocks can represent a train), begins to classify and

preoperational period The second of Piaget's periods, which represents a four- to five-year transitional period between first being able to think symbolically and then being able to think logically. During this stage, children become increasingly capable of speaking meaningful sentences.

categorize objects, and starts learning to count and to manipulate numbers.

Piaget asserted that development of symbolism actually begins during the sensorimotor period, when a child starts imitating events in his or her environment. For example, a child might represent a horse by making galloping movements with the feet or a bicycle by making steering movements with the hands. Symbolic representations like these are called *signifiers*: The motor act represents (signifies) the concept because it resembles either the movements the object makes or the movements the child makes when interacting with the object.

Concepts can also be represented by words, which are symbols that have no physical resemblance to the concept; Piaget referred to such abstract symbols as *signs*. Signifiers are personal, derived from the child's own interactions with objects. Therefore, only the child and perhaps members of the immediate family will understand a child's signifiers. In contrast, signs are social conventions. They are understood by all members of a culture. A child who is able to use words to think about reality has made an important step in cognitive development.

Piaget's work demonstrated quite clearly that a child's representation of the world is different from that of an adult. For example, most adults realize that a volume of water re-

Figure 12.6

Conservation. Early in the preoperational period, a child does not have the ability to conserve a liquid quantity.

mains constant when poured into a taller, narrower container, even though its level is now higher. However, early in the preoperational period, children will fail to recognize this fact; they will say that the taller container contains more water. (See *Figure 12.6.*) The ability to realize that an object retains mass, number, or volume when it undergoes various transformations is called **conservation**; the transformed object conserves its original properties. (See *Figure 12.7.*)

Piaget concluded that the abilities to perceive the conservation of number, mass, weight, and volume are attributes of increasing cognitive development. His studies showed number to be conserved by age six, whereas conservation of volume did not occur until age eleven. Presumably, conservation of number comes first because children can verify the stability of number once they learn to count.

Another important characteristic of the preoperational period is **egocentrism**, or a child's belief that others see the world in precisely the way he or she does. For example, a preoperational child sees the world only from his or her own point of view. A three-year-old child may run to a corner, turn his back to you, and cover his eyes in an attempt to hide during a game of hide and seek, not realizing that he is still in plain view.

The Period of Concrete Operations. Piaget's third stage of cognitive development, the **period of concrete operations**, spans approximately ages seven to eleven and involves children's developing understanding of the conservation principle and other concepts, such as categorization. Its end marks the transition from childhood to adolescence. This period is characterized by the emergence of the ability to perform logical analysis, by an increased ability to empathize with the feelings and attitudes of others, and by an understanding of more

complex cause-and-effect relations. The child becomes much more skilled at the use of symbolic thought. For example, even before the period of concrete operations, children can arrange a series of objects in order of size and can compare any two objects and say which is larger. However, if they are shown that stick A is larger than stick B and that stick B is larger than stick C, they cannot infer that stick A is larger than stick C.

During the early part of this period, children become capable of making such inferences. However, although they can reason with respect to concrete objects, such as sticks that they have seen, they cannot do so with hypothetical objects. For example, they cannot solve the following problem: "Judy is taller than Frank and Frank is taller than Carl. Who is taller, Judy or Carl?" The ability to solve such problems awaits the next period of cognitive development.

The Period of Formal Operations. During the **period of formal operations**, which begins at about age eleven, children

conservation Understanding that specific properties of objects (height, weight, volume, length) remain the same despite apparent changes in the shape or arrangement of those objects.

egocentrism Self-centeredness; preoperational children can see the world only from their own perspective.

period of concrete operations The third period in Piaget's theory of cognitive development, during which children come to understand the conservation principle and other concepts, such as categorization.

period of formal operations The fourth period in Piaget's theory of cognitive development, during which individuals first become capable of more formal kinds of abstract thinking and hypothetical reasoning.

Conservation of Mass

The experimenter presents two balls of clay.

The experimenter rolls one ball into a "sausage" and asks the child whether they still contain the same amount of clay.

Figure 12.7

Various tests of conservation.

(Adapted from Of Children, An Introduction to Child Development, *4th ed. by Guy R. Lefrancois. [c] 1983, 1980 by Wadsworth, Inc. Reprinted by permission of Wadsworth Publishing Company, Belmont, California, 94002.)*

Conservation of Length

The experimenter presents two dowels.

The experimenter moves one dowel to the right and asks the child whether they are still the same length.

Conservation of Number

The experimenter presents two rows of poker chips.

The experimenter moves one row of chips apart and asks the child whether each row still contains the same number.

first become capable of abstract reasoning. They can now think and reason about hypothetical objects and events. They also begin to understand that under different conditions, their behavior can have different consequences. Formal operational thinking is not "culture free"—it is influenced by cultural variables, especially formal schooling (Piaget, 1972; Rogoff and Chavajay, 1995). Without exposure to the principles of scientific thinking, such as those taught in junior high school and high school science classes, people do not develop formal operational thinking.

As evidence that children think differently as they progress through the different periods of cognitive development, consider the answers that three of my children gave to the question "If you were to go to the moon today, what would it be like?"

> Caden (age seven, but still preoperational because he cannot solve the water conservation problem): "I don't know, what do you think?"

> Colin (age nine, concrete operational because he easily solves the water conservation problem): "I don't know because I've never been to the moon."

> Tara (age eleven, early formal operational): "It would be cold, dark, scary, and lonely if I were there by myself."

Notice the difference between Colin's and Tara's answers. Colin doesn't know the answer to the question because he's never been there before, a clear indication of concrete operational thinking. But Tara can *imagine* what it's like, partly because she has learned something about the moon in school (it's cold and dark) and partly because she can hypothetically place herself on the moon and imagine that it's also a lonely and scary place. At age eleven, Tara is at the beginning of the formal operations period.

Although Piaget held that there are four periods of cognitive development, not all people reach the formal opera-

tional period, even as physically mature adults. In some cases, adults show formal operational thought only in their areas of expertise. Thus, a mechanic may be able to think abstractly while repairing an engine but not while solving math or physics problems. A physicist may be able to reason abstractly when solving physics problems but not while reading poetry. However, once an individual reaches that level of thinking, he or she will always, except in the case of brain disease or injury, perform intellectually at that level.

Evaluation of Piaget's Contributions

Piaget's theory has had an enormously positive impact, stimulating interest and research in developmental psychology (Halford, 1989, 1990; Beilin, 1990). However, not all of Piaget's conclusions have been accepted uncritically. One criticism leveled at Piaget is that he did not always define his terms operationally. Consequently, it is difficult for others to interpret the significance of his generalizations. Many of his studies lack the proper controls that I discussed in Chapter 2. Thus, much of his work is not experimental, which means that cause-and-effect relations among variables cannot be identified with certainty.

Subsequent evidence has suggested that a child's ability to conserve various physical attributes occurs earlier than Piaget had supposed. For example, Gelman (1972) found that when the appropriate task is used, even three-year-old children are able to demonstrate conservation of number. We must recognize that an estimate of a child's cognitive ability can be substantially affected by the testing method.

Piaget also appears to have underestimated the ability of young children to understand another person's point of view. In other words, they are less egocentric than he thought. For example, Flavell et al. (1981) found that even a three-year-old child realizes that a person looking at the opposite side of a card the child is examining will not see the same thing. Clearly, the child recognizes the other person's point of view.

Despite the fact that Piaget's method of observation led him to underestimate some important abilities, his meticulous and detailed observations of child behavior have been extremely important in the field of child development and have had a great influence on educational practice. His theoretical framework has provided a basis for more scientific studies and will undoubtedly continue to do so for many years.

Vygotsky's Sociocultural Theory of Cognitive Development

Piaget's theory of cognitive development focuses on children's interactions with the physical world—they form internal representations of the world based on their experiences with physical objects. Another theorist, Lev Vygotsky, agreed that experience with physical objects is an important factor in cognitive development. But he disagreed that this is the whole story. Instead, he argued that the culture in which one lives also plays a significant role in cognitive development (Vygotsky, 1934/1987). Although Vygotsky's work was conducted during the 1920s and early 1930s (he died of tuberculosis in 1934), his writings have had a major impact on recent conceptualizations of cognitive development during childhood (Kozulin and Falik, 1995). In this section, we will briefly examine some of Vygotsky's ideas on how sociocultural variables influence cognitive development.

Vygotsky argued that children do not learn to think about the physical world in a vacuum. The cultural context—what they hear others say about the world and how they see others interact with physical aspects of the world—matters. Thus parents, teachers, friends, and many others help children acquire ideas about how the world works. We would expect, then, that children raised in nonstimulating environments devoid of stimulating interactions with others, with books, and, yes, with television would lag behind that of children raised in more stimulating environments. And this is exactly what has been found (Rymer, 1992). Consider, too, that culture significantly influences children's ability to solve math problems. For instance, Korean children, whose culture conceptualizes math problems differently from Western culture, appear to be better at solving multidigit addition and subtraction problems than are North American children (Fuson and Kwon, 1992).

Vygotsky further believed that children's use of speech also influences their cognitive development. Children up to about age seven can often be observed talking to themselves. While drawing in a coloring book, a child may say, "I'll color her arms and face green and her pants black." Piaget would interpret such talk as being egocentric and nonsocial because it is directed at the self, because it may not make sense to a listener, and because its purpose is not to communicate information. Vygotsky's interpretation would be different. He would argue that the child's talk actually reflects the formula-

tion of a plan that will serve as a guide to subsequent behavior. According to Vygotsky, language is the basis for cognitive development, including the ability to remember, solve problems, make decisions, and formulate plans.

After about age seven, children stop vocalizing their thoughts and instead carry on what Vygotsky labeled *inner speech*. Inner speech represents the internalization of words and the mental manipulation of them as symbols for objects in the environment. As children interact with their parents, teachers, and peers, they learn new words to represent new objects. As the "expertise" of the people they interact with increases, so does the children's cognitive skills. For example, Rogoff and her colleagues (1990) have shown that children become better problem-solvers if they practice solving problems with their parents or with more experienced children than if they practice the problems alone or with children of similar cognitive ability.

Thus, while Piaget argued for a purely maturational view of children's cognitive development, Vygotsky stressed the importance of sociocultural influences, such as language and interactions with other people, on cognitive development. As we have seen, research partially supports both theorists' ideas. Piaget's descriptions of the milestones involved in cognitive development have proved to be fairly accurate. However, Vygotsky's work has gone beyond Piaget's theory in explaining how cultural variables, especially language, influence cognitive development.

Developmental Models of Information Processing in Cognitive Development

Both Piaget and Vygotsky saw cognitive development as a process of forming internal representations of the external world. Piaget focused on the development of schemata, the processes of assimilation and accommodation, and abstract reasoning. Vygotsky focused on the role of language in the development of problem-solving skills, decision making, and formulating plans. An alternative approach is to view cognitive development in terms of *information processing*, which, as you will recall, involves the storage, encoding, and retrieval of information. Two developmental models of information processing have emerged in recent years: Case's M-Space Model and Fischer's Skill Model.

Case's M-Space Model

According to Case (1985, 1992), cognitive development is a matter of a child becoming more efficient in using mental strategies. The heart of Case's model is **mental space (M-space)**—a hypothetical construct, similar to short-term or

mental space (M-space) A hypothetical construct in Case's model of cognitive development similar to working memory, whose primary function is to process information from the external world.

working memory, whose chief function is the processing of information from the external world. Expansion of M-space, or increases in a child's information-processing capacity, is caused by a combination of three variables.

First, as the brain matures, so does its capacity to process greater amounts of information. Maturation of the brain, specifically the increasing number of networks of neural connections and increasing myelinization of neurons, also enhances more efficient processing of information. Second, as children become more practiced at using schemata, less demand is placed on cognitive resources, which can now be devoted to other, more complex cognitive tasks. For example, when children first learn to ride a bicycle, they must focus entirely on keeping their balance and steering the bike in a straight line. But after they have acquired these skills, they no longer have to devote so much attention to steering the bike and not falling off. Now they can look around, talk to other bike riders, and so on. Third, schemata for different objects and events become integrated so that children now think in novel ways about these objects and events. The net result of such integration is the acquisition of *central conceptual structures*—networks of schemata that allow children to understand the relationships among the objects and events represented by schemata. As increasingly complex central conceptual structures are formed, children advance to higher levels of cognitive development, as represented in Piaget's stages. Each of the milestones in Piaget's theory, such as deferred imitation and conservation, requires increasing amounts of M-space.

Fischer's Skill Model

In Fischer's skill model, cognitive development involves skill learning, or the acquisition of competencies on particular tasks, such as those found in each of Piaget's developmental periods. Fischer emphasizes the child's **optimal level of skill performance,** or the brain's maximal capacity for information processing. According to Fischer, as the brain matures, the child advances through stages of cognitive growth that parallel Piaget's periods of cognitive development (Fischer and Farrar, 1987; Fischer and Pipp, 1984). During each stage, the child's capacity to process information increases, as does the level of skill required for mastery of specific cognitive tasks, such as conservation tasks. As the child encounters different problems, new skills are acquired, practiced, and perfected. These skills become integrated, leading to increases in the child's ability to reason and think abstractly.

A child cannot progress from one Piagetian period to another until his or her brain has matured sufficiently to permit acquisition of the cognitive skills necessary to master tasks representative of the next period. For example, a preoperational child is not able to solve conservation tasks until his or

optimal level of skill performance According to Fischer's skill model, the brain's maximal capacity for information processing.

her brain has matured sufficiently to permit acquisition of the necessary skills. Even if a parent explains the task, the child's brain will not be able to encode, store, and later retrieve those instructions. When faced with the conservation problem later, the child will still be unable to solve it.

Both Case's M-space model and Fischer's skill model rely on brain maturation as the primary explanation for children's increasing ability to think logically and abstractly. And both models essentially rephrase Piaget's theory of cognitive development in information processing terms. The purpose of these models has not been to discredit Piaget's theory. On the contrary, one important function of these models has been to reinterpret the theory in the language of modern cognitive psychology. Perhaps by conceptualizing children's thought processes in terms of the interplay of Piaget's theory, brain-maturation processes, and the acquisition of novel and more complex information-processing abilities, further advances in understanding cognitive development will emerge.

Evaluating Scientific Issues

The Effects of Television Viewing on Children's Cognitive Development

A child's cognitive development is influenced by many factors, including parents' education and occupational status, number of siblings, social class of playmates, nature of the neighborhood, availability of educational resources such as books in the home, opportunity for travel, and quality of schooling. A child from a privileged social milieu is much more likely to be exposed to situations that promote cognitive development. But almost all children in industrialized societies, even those in the poorest households, are exposed for several hours a day to a near universal factor—television.

■ **What Are the Effects of Television Viewing on Children?**

There are two issues that concern us here—the *content* of television programs and the general effects of the *medium* itself. Let us consider content first. There is no question that television does not do the good it could, and it probably does some harm. One of the best examples of the good it can do is demonstrated by *Sesame Street*, a program that was devised to teach school-readiness skills, such as counting, letter recognition, and vocabulary. Research indicates that the program has succeeded in its goals; children who watch *Sesame Street* have better vocabularies, have better attitudes toward school, adapt better to the classroom, and have more positive attitudes toward children of other races (Bogatz and Ball, 1972). (*Sesame Street* emphasizes multiculturalism in its choice of characters and the activities and interests they display.) Rice et al. (1990) studied a large sample of three- to five-year-old children from a wide range of socioeconomic backgrounds and found that children of *all* backgrounds profited from watching *Sesame Street*—the advantages were not restricted to middle-class children.

On the other hand, many television programs are full of violence, and watching them may well promote aggressiveness and impatience with nonviolent resolution of disagreements in the children who watch such shows. (We will examine research on this issue in Chapter 13.) In addition, commercial television affects consumer behavior. Sponsors target many of their commercial messages at children (McNeal, 1990). Furthermore, sponsors produce commercials that encourage children to demand that their parents purchase particular snack foods, toys, and other items (Taras et al., 1989). However, commercials related to the purchase and consumption of alcoholic beverages and those containing antidrinking messages do not appear to influence children's expectancies about the positive or negative effects of alcohol (Lipsitz et al., 1993), perhaps because they are not specifically targeted toward very young audiences. Nonetheless, we can ask ourselves whether sponsors are likely to find it in their interests to educate children to be informed consumers.

■ Criticisms That Claim That Television Impairs Cognitive Development

The second issue that people have raised about children and television regards the nature of the medium itself, and it is this issue that I will examine in the rest of this section. Many people who have written about the potential effects of television *as a medium* on children's cognitive development have concluded that the medium is generally harmful. Anderson and Collins (1988) summarize some of the criticisms these people have made:

- Television has a mesmerizing power over children's attention; this power is exerted by the movement, color, and visual changes typical of television.
- Children do not think about television programs; that is, they do not engage in inferential and reflective thought while viewing television.
- Children get overstimulated by television; by some accounts, this leads to hyperactivity and by other accounts, this leads to passivity.
- Television viewing displaces valuable cognitive activities, especially reading and homework.
- Attention span is shortened, probably because of the rapid pace at which visual images are presented.
- Creativity and imagination are reduced; in general, the child becomes cognitively passive.
- Reading achievement is reduced. (Anderson and Collins, 1988, p. 4)

■ Does the Evidence Support these Criticisms of Television as a Medium?

In a review of their own research and of that of others, Anderson and Collins conclude that there is little evi-

Does television viewing promote or retard cognitive development in children?

dence to support these criticisms. In fact, the evidence directly contradicts some of them. Let us examine four of the most important criticisms: that television mesmerizes children, that it overstimulates them, that it displaces valuable cognitive activities, and that it reduces their reading achievement.

Before we look at the evidence concerning these issues, we should ask just how much of a child's time is dominated by the medium. Estimates vary according to the method used. Studies of two-year-olds have shown that they view up to two hours of television per day (Hollenbeck, 1978), and studies of older children have shown that they may watch a little over three hours of television per day (Neilsen, 1990). Boys tend to view more television than do girls and, across all ages, children with low IQs from low income families watch more television than do other children (Huston et al., 1990; Huston, Watkins, and Kunkel, 1989).

The most objective measures of the amount of time children spend watching television have been obtained by placing a time-lapse video camera and videotape machine in people's homes next to their television sets so that the viewers can be recorded. Anderson et al. (1985) used this method to measure television viewing by members of ninety-nine families in a New England city. They found that children watched television about sixteen hours per week.

According to Anderson and Collins (1988), while watching television, children are often engaged in other activities: They eat, play with toys, draw or color pictures, read, play games, sleep, talk with others, or do their homework. They often enter and leave the room while the television is on. Thus, although the children do watch television a substantial amount of the time, it is probably inaccurate to say that the average North American child spends more time watching television than attending school.

Mesmerization.   Some critics have said that television is "addictive" and "mesmerizing," that children who watch it have "glazed eyes" and are "spaced out" (Moody, 1980). Support for such terrible effects comes not from controlled experiments but from anecdotes and assertions of experts. In fact, studies that actually observe children who are watching television find no such effects. Children are rarely "glued" to the television set. They look away from it between 100 and 200 times each hour (Anderson and Field, 1983). They rarely look at the screen for much more than one minute at a stretch. Their viewing behavior is related to program content: They tend to pay attention when they hear other children's voices, interesting sound effects, and peculiar voices and when they see movement on the screen. They tend *not* to pay attention when they hear men's voices or see no signs of activity on the screen (Anderson and Lorch, 1983).

The selectivity shown by young viewers is certainly *not* consistent with the behavior of someone who has been "mesmerized." The fact that the sound track of a television program has so much effect on children's looking behavior suggests that children have learned to use auditory cues to help them decide whether to watch, especially when time sharing—alternating their attention between the television and another activity. If they hear certain kinds of sounds, they turn their attention away from the alternate activity and look at the screen to see whether something interesting is happening.

Overstimulation.   Moody (1980) states that "television is an intense kaleidoscope of moving light and sound. It can create extreme excitement in the brain and, after prolonged viewing, it can produce a 'drugged state'" (p. 18). Anderson and Collins found no evidence to support such claims. And the fact that children look away from television so often suggests that if they found television too stimulating they would have an easy means for reducing potential overarousal—simply looking away from the screen. Certainly, an exciting program can excite the viewer, but no evidence suggests that "kaleidoscopic images" act like drugs on the brains of young children.

Displacement of Activities That Stimulate Cognitive Development.   Perhaps television takes up time that would otherwise be spent on activities that would stimulate children's cognitive development (Singer and Singer, 1990). Some evidence with respect to this possibility comes from observations made before and after television was available in remote towns (Hornik, 1981). In fact, television viewing primarily displaced other entertainment activities, such as listening to the radio, reading comic books, or going to movies. It had little effect on time spent reading or doing homework. As most parents undoubtedly know, many children do their homework in front of the television set, switching their attention back and forth between the screen and their studies. In general, children are

more likely to use television as a backdrop for their math homework than for reading (Patton, Stinard, and Routh, 1983). Surprisingly, there is no evidence that the quality of the homework suffers.

Reduction in Children's Reading Achievement.   The fact that children are less likely to watch television while doing homework that involves reading suggests that reading and viewing are at least somewhat incompatible. Indeed, one criticism of television—that it retards children's reading achievement—has received some support. Measurements of children's reading skills before and after television became available suggested that television viewing decreased the reading skills of young children (Corteen and Williams, 1986). However, the effects were slight and were not seen in older children. Perhaps, then, television viewing does interfere with reading achievement in young children.

■ What Should We Conclude?

Although children spend a considerable amount of time watching television, the negative effects of their viewing appear to be negligible. Children do not appear to become mesmerized or overstimulated by television. Nor does television viewing appear to detract significantly from other activities that would stimulate children's cognitive development or substantially reduce their reading achievement.

However, the possibility exists that television programs could do more to stimulate children's cognitive development. I have focused on the potential *harm* that may be done by watching television, not on the potential *good* that could be achieved through this medium. Educational programs and other shows that take into account children's developmental needs would seem to be especially conducive to the stimulation of children's imagination, creativity, language skills, and prosocial behavior.

Interim Summary

Cognitive Development in Childhood

The first step in a child's cognitive development is learning that many events are contingent on his or her own behavior. This understanding occurs gradually and is controlled by the development of the nervous system and by increasingly complex interactions with the environment.

Piaget divided a child's cognitive development into four periods—a system that is widely, if not universally, accepted. The periods are determined by the joint influences of the child's experiences and the maturation of the child's nervous system. An infant's earliest cognitive abilities are closely tied to the external stimuli in the immediate environment; objects exist for the infant only when they are present. Gradually, infants learn that objects exist even when hidden. The development of object permanence leads to the ability to represent things symbolically, which is a prerequisite for the use of language. Next, the ability to perform logical analysis and to understand more complex cause-and-effect relations develops. Around the age of eleven, a child develops more adultlike cognitive abilities—abilities that may allow the child to solve difficult problems by means of abstract reasoning.

Piaget's critics point out that in some cases, his tests of cognitive development underestimate children's abilities. For example, if tested appropriately, it is evident that they conserve various properties earlier than he thought, and that their egocentrism is less pronounced than his tests indicated. Nevertheless, his conclusions continue to have a profound impact on the field of child development. Vygotsky's writings and the research they have stimulated have showed that the sociocultural context in which children are raised has a significant impact on their cognitive development. In particular, language appears to influence how children learn to think, solve problems, formulate plans, make decisions and contemplate ideas.

Two information-processing accounts of cognitive development have been developed recently. Case's M-space model argues that cognitive development proceeds according to expansion of mental space, or the brain's information-processing capacity. M-space expands due to three causes: brain maturation, practice using schemata, and the integration of schemata for different objects and events. Fischer's skill model focuses on the relation between brain maturation and a child's ability to learn new cognitive skills specific to particular tasks, such as conservation. Maturation of the brain permits the child to acquire new cognitive skills necessary to solve increasingly complex tasks. Both of these models essentially reinterpret Piaget's theory in the language of information processing.

The survey of the scientific literature by Anderson and Collins (1988) makes the medium of television look like less of a threat to children's cognitive development than many people believe. Studies that actually examine the viewing behavior of children rather than speculate about harmful effects show us that children are not passive recipients of whatever the medium offers them. They watch what interests them and look away at other times, and they engage in a variety of other behaviors while sitting in front of the set. Fortunately, children are more discerning in their watching than many people have believed.

Thought Questions

- An earlier thought question asked you to design a home environment that would facilitate your child's motor and perceptual development. How might you also construct that environment to facilitate your child's cognitive development? What types of toys would you give your child to play with and what kinds

of personal interactions would you want to have with him or her?
- How would you go about developing a test for determining which of Piaget's periods of cognitive development a child is in? What kinds of activities would you include in such a test and how would the child's behavior with respect to those activities indicate the child's stage of development?

Social Development in Childhood

Normally, the first adults with whom infants interact are their parents. In most cases, one parent serves as the primary caregiver. As many studies have shown, a close relationship called attachment is extremely important for infants' social development. **Attachment** is a social and emotional bond between infant and caregiver that spans both time and space. It involves both the warm feelings that the parent and child have for each other and the comfort and support they provide for each other, which becomes especially important during times of fear or stress. This interaction must work both ways, with each participant fulfilling certain needs of the other. Formation of a strong and durable bond depends on the behavior of both people in the relationship. According to theorist John Bowlby (1969), attachment is a part of many organisms' (such

---

Attachment is the cornerstone of an infant's social development and it has important implications on the parent's social behavior as well.

attachment A social and emotional bond between infant and caregiver that spans both time and space.

as waterfowl's, sheep's, cows', and monkeys') native endowment. He and Mary Ainsworth have developed an approach that has succeeded in discovering the variables that influence attachment in humans (Ainsworth and Bowlby, 1991). We are going to look at what Bowlby, Ainsworth, and other researchers have learned about human attachment.

Keep in mind that cultural variables strongly influence the development of attachment. Interactions between infant and parent produce different sorts of attachment behaviors that vary from culture to culture. For example, in an extensive comparison of cross-cultural attachment patterns, Harwood, Miller, and Irizarry (1995) found that white American mothers desire their children to be self-sustaining individuals and so emphasize independence, self-reliance, and self-confidence in their interactions with their children. In contrast, Puerto Rican mothers desire their children to be polite and law-abiding persons and thus stress the importance of respect, courtesy, and tact in interacting with their children.

Behaviors of the Infant That Foster Attachment

Newborn infants rely completely on their parents (or other caregivers) to supply them with nourishment, keep them warm and clean, and protect them from harm. To most parents, the role of primary caregiver is much more than a duty; it is a source of joy and satisfaction. Nearly all parents anticipate the birth of their children with the expectation that they will love and cherish them. And when a child is born, most of them do exactly that. As time goes on, and as parent and child interact, they become strongly attached to each other. What factors cause this attachment to occur? Evidence suggests that human infants are innately able to produce special behaviors that shape and control the behavior of their caregivers. As Bowlby (1969) noted, the most important of these behaviors are sucking, cuddling, looking, smiling, and crying.

Sucking

A baby must be able to suck in order to obtain milk. But not all sucking is related to nourishment. Piaget (1952) noted that infants often suck on objects even when they are not hungry. Nonnutritive sucking appears to be an innate behavioral tendency in infants that serves to inhibit a baby's distress. In modern society, most mothers cover their breasts between feedings or feed with a bottle, so a baby's nonnutritive sucking must involve inanimate objects or the baby's own thumb. But in Uganda, mothers were observed to give their babies access to a breast when they were fussy, just as mothers in other cultures would give them a pacifier (Ainsworth, 1967).

Cuddling

Infants of all species of primates have special reflexes that encourage front-to-front contact with their mothers. For example, a baby monkey clings to its mother shortly after birth.

This clinging leaves the mother free to use her hands and feet. Human infants are carried by their parents and do not hold on by themselves. However, infants do adjust their posture to mold themselves to the contours of the parent's body. This cuddling response plays an important role in reinforcing the behavior of the caregiver. Some infants, perhaps because of hereditary factors or slight brain damage, do not make the cuddling response and remain rigid in the adult's arms. Adults who hold such infants tend to refer to them as being not very lovable (Ainsworth, 1973).

Harry Harlow (1974) conducted a series of experiments on infant monkeys and showed that clinging to a soft, cuddly form appears to be an innate response. Harlow and his colleagues isolated baby monkeys from their mothers immediately after birth and raised them alone in cages containing two mechanical surrogate mothers. One surrogate mother was made of bare wire mesh but contained a bottle that provided milk. The other surrogate was padded and covered with terry cloth but provided no nourishment.

The babies preferred to cling to the cuddly surrogate and went to the wire model only to eat. If they were frightened, they would rush to the cloth-covered model for comfort. These results suggest that close physical contact with a cuddly object is a biological need for a baby monkey, just as food and drink are. A baby monkey clings to and cuddles with its mother because the contact is innately reinforcing, not simply because she provides it with food.

Undoubtedly, physical contact with soft objects is also inherently reinforcing for human infants. The term *security blanket* suggests that these objects are comforting during times of distress. Indeed, children are most likely to ask for their special blankets or stuffed animals before going to bed, when they are ill, or when they are in an unfamiliar situation.

Looking

For infants, looking serves as a signal to parents: even a very young infant seeks eye-to-eye contact with his or her parents. If a parent does not respond when eye contact is made, the baby usually shows signs of distress. Tronick et al. (1978) observed face-to-face interactions between mothers and their infants. When the mothers approached their babies, they typically smiled and began talking in a gentle, high-pitched voice. In return, infants smiled and stretched their arms and legs. The mothers poked and gently jiggled their babies, making faces at them. The babies responded with facial expressions, wiggles, and noises of their own.

To determine whether the interaction was really two-sided, the experimenters had each mother approach her baby while keeping her face expressionless or masklike. At first, the infant made the usual greetings, but when the mother did not respond, the infant turned away. (See *Figure 12.8.*) From time to time, the infant looked at her again, giving a brief smile, but again turned away when the mother continued to stare without changing her expression. These interactions were recorded on videotape and were scored by raters who did not know the purpose of the experiment, so the results were not biased by the experimenters' expectations.

Each mother found it difficult to resist her baby's invitation to interact. In fact, some of the mothers broke down and smiled back. Most of the mothers who managed to hold out (for three minutes) later apologized to their babies, saying something like, "I am real again. It's all right. You can trust me again. Come back to me" (Tronick et al., 1978, p. l0). This study clearly shows that the looking behavior of an infant is an invitation for the mother to respond.

Smiling

For almost any human, but especially for a parent, the smile of an infant is an exceedingly effective reinforcer. For example, the day after reading an article about imitation of facial expressions by newborn infants, I had a conversation with a woman who was holding her two-month-old daughter. The baby was alert, actively looking at the people around her. For approximately five minutes, she made no particular facial expression. Then I remembered the article and mentioned it to the baby's father, who was also present. He suggested that I see whether his daughter would imitate my facial expression. I stuck out my tongue, and immediately, the baby smiled, made a noise, and stuck out her tongue. I can still feel the delight that her smile gave me.

By the time an infant is five weeks old, visual stimuli begin to dominate as elicitors for smiling. A face (especially a moving one) is a more reliable elicitor of a smile than a voice

is; even a moving mask will cause an infant to smile. At approximately three months of age, specific faces—those of people to whom the infant has become attached—will elicit smiles. The significance of these observations should be obvious. An infant's smile is very rewarding. Almost every parent reports that parenting becomes a real joy when the baby starts smiling as the parent approaches—the infant is now a "person."

Crying

For almost any adult, the sound of an infant's crying is intensely distressing or irritating. An infant usually cries only when he or she is hungry, cold, or in pain (Wolff, 1969). In these situations, only the intervention of an adult can bring relief. The event that most effectively terminates crying is being picked up and cuddled, although unless the baby is fed and made more comfortable, he or she will soon begin crying again. Because picking up the baby stops the crying, the parent learns through negative reinforcement to pick up the infant when he or she cries. Thus, crying serves as a useful means for a cold, hungry, or wet child to obtain assistance.

Wolff (1969) suggested that babies have different patterns of crying. Konner (1972), who was studying a hunter-gatherer tribe in Africa, found that a pain cry caused all the people in earshot to turn toward the infant and induced several of them to run toward the child. However, a hunger cry was responded to only by the child's caregivers. More recent evidence suggests that babies' cries do not fall into need-

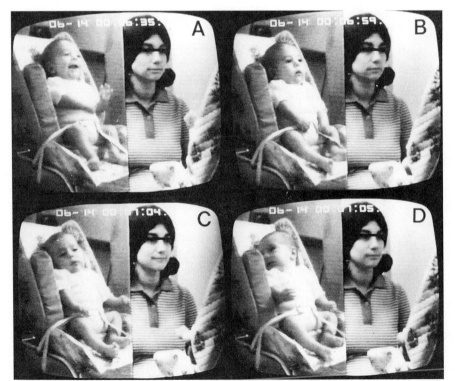

Figure 12.8

Reaction of an infant to its mother's expressionless face. Although each panel shows mother and infant side by side, they actually faced each other. The infant greets the mother with a smile and, getting no response, eventually turns away from her.

(From Tronick, E., Als, H., Adamson, L., Wise, S., and Brazelton, T.B. The infant's response to entrapment between contradictory messages in face-to-face interaction. Journal of the American Academy of Child Psychiatry, *1978, 17, 1–13. © 1978 American Academy of Child Psychiatry.)*

specific categories—there is no "hunger cry," no different cry for pain, and so on. Instead, cries simply vary in intensity, according to the level of the infant's distress. However, the *onset* of crying provides important information. If a baby suddenly begins crying intensely, mothers are more likely to assume that the baby is afraid or in pain. If the cry begins more gradually, mothers suspect hunger, sleepiness, or a need for a diaper change (Gustafson and Harris, 1990).

The Nature and Quality of Attachment

For an infant, the world can be a frightening place. The presence of a primary caregiver provides a baby with considerable reassurance when he or she first becomes able to explore the environment. Although the unfamiliar environment produces fear, the caregiver provides a secure base that the infant can leave from time to time to see what the world is like. Let's look at two issues that develop as infants explore their world: stranger and separation anxiety and reactions to strange situations.

Stranger Anxiety and Separation Anxiety

Babies are born prepared to become attached to their primary caregivers, which in most cases are their mothers. Attachment appears to be a behavior pattern that is necessary for normal development (Ainsworth, 1974; Bowlby, 1973). However, although attachment appears to be an inherited disposition, infants do not have a natural inclination to become attached to any one specific adult. Rather, the person to whom the baby becomes attached is determined through learning; the individual who serves as the infant's primary caregiver is usually the object of the attachment.

Attachment partially reveals itself in two specific forms of infant behavior: stranger anxiety and separation anxiety. **Stranger anxiety**, which usually appears in infants between the ages of six and twelve months, consists of wariness and

stranger anxiety The wariness and fearful responses, such as crying and clinging to their caregivers, that the infant exhibits in the presence of strangers.

separation anxiety A set of fearful responses, such as crying, arousal, and clinging to the caregiver, that the infant exhibits when the caregiver attempts to leave the infant.

Strange Situation A test of attachment in which an infant is exposed to different stimuli that may be distressful.

secure attachment A kind of attachment in which infants use their mothers as a base for exploring a new environment. They will venture out from their mothers to explore a Strange Situation but return periodically.

resistant attachment A kind of attachment in which infants show mixed reactions to their mothers. They may approach their mothers upon their return but, at the same time, continue to cry or even push their mothers away.

sometimes fearful responses, such as crying and clinging to their caregivers, that infants exhibit in the presence of strangers. Male strangers generate the most anxiety in infants. Child strangers generate the least anxiety, while female strangers generate an intermediate amount of anxiety (Skarin, 1977). Stranger anxiety can be reduced and even eliminated under certain conditions. For example, if the infant is in familiar surroundings with his or her mother, such as at home, and the mother acts friendly toward the stranger, the infant is likely to be less anxious in the presence of the stranger than he or she would if the surroundings were unfamiliar or if the mother was unfriendly toward the stranger (Rheingold and Eckerman, 1973).

Separation anxiety is a set of fearful responses, such as crying, arousal, and clinging to the caregiver, that an infant exhibits when the caregiver attempts to leave the infant. Separation anxiety differs from stranger anxiety in two ways: time of emergence and the conditions under which the fear responses occur. It first appears in infants when they are about six months old and generally peaks at about fifteen months—a finding consistent among many cultures (Kagan, Kearsley, and Zelazo, 1978). Like stranger anxiety, separation anxiety can occur under different conditions with different degrees of intensity. For example, if an infant is used to being left in a certain environment, say a day-care center, he or she may show little or no separation anxiety (Maccoby, 1980). The same holds true for situations in which the infant is left with a sibling or other familiar person (Bowlby, 1969). However, if the same infant is left in an unfamiliar setting with unfamiliar people, he or she is likely to show separation anxiety (Bowlby, 1982). Familiarity, then, at least for infants, breeds attachment.

Ainsworth's Strange Situation

Ainsworth and her colleagues (Ainsworth et al., 1978) have developed a test of attachment called the **Strange Situation** that consists of a series of eight episodes, during which the baby is exposed to various events that might cause some distress. The episodes involve the experimenter introducing the infant and the parent to a playroom and then leaving, the parent leaving and being reunited with the infant, or a stranger entering the playroom with and without the parent present. Each episode lasts for approximately three minutes. The Strange Situation is based on the idea that if the attachment process has been successful, an infant should use his or her mother as a secure base from which to explore an unfamiliar environment. By noting the infant's reactions to the Strange Situation, researchers can evaluate the nature of the attachment.

The use of the Strange Situation has led Ainsworth and her colleagues to identify three patterns of attachment. **Secure attachment** is the ideal pattern: Infants show a distinct preference for their mothers over the stranger. Infants may cry when their mothers leave, but they stop as soon as they return. Babies may also form two types of insecure attachments. Babies with **resistant attachment** show tension in their relations with their mothers. Infants stay close to their mothers before the mothers leave but show both approach and avoidance behaviors when the mothers return. Infants continue to cry for a while after their mothers return and may even push them away. **Avoidant attachment** is seen in about 20 percent of middle-class American infants. Infants who display this pattern generally do not cry when they are left alone. When their mothers return, the infants are likely to avoid or ignore them. These infants tend not to cling and cuddle when they are picked up.

Although infants' personalities certainly affect the nature of their interactions with their caregivers and hence the nature of their attachment, mothers' behavior appears to be the most important factor in establishing a secure or insecure attachment (Ainsworth et al., 1978; Isabella and Belsky, 1991). Mothers of *securely* attached infants tend to be those who respond promptly to their crying and who are adept at handling them and responding to their needs. The babies apparently learn that their mothers can be trusted to react sensitively and appropriately. Mothers who do not modulate their responses according to their infants' own behavior—who appear insensitive to their infants' changing needs—are most likely to foster *avoidant* attachment. Mothers who are impatient with their infants and who seem more interested in their own activities than in interacting with their offspring tend to foster *resistant* attachment.

The nature of the attachment between infants and caretakers appears to be related to children's later social behavior. For example, Waters, Wippman, and Sroufe (1979) found that children who were *securely* attached at fifteen months were among the most popular and the most sociable children in their nursery schools at three and one-half years of age. In contrast, *insecurely* attached infants had difficulties with social adjustment later in childhood; they had poor social skills and tended to be hostile, impulsive, and withdrawn (Erickson, Sroufe, and Egheland, 1985).

Of course, mothers are not the only people who can form close attachment with infants; so can fathers and other adults who interact with them. In fact, Parke and Tinsley (1981) observed that fathers are just as likely as mothers to touch, talk to, and kiss their babies. However, when the mother serves as the primary caregiver, fathers tend to play somewhat different roles. In general, they tend to engage in more physical games, lifting, tossing, and bouncing their babies. This difference may account for the fact that babies tend to seek out their mothers when they are distressed but look for their fathers when they want to play (Clarke-Stewart, 1978).

In our culture, secure attachment would seem to be more adaptive in terms of getting along with both peers and adults than would insecure attachment. What is becoming increasingly clear is that attachment plays an influential role in social relationships, including those found in adolescence and adulthood, such as romantic love (Feeney and Noller, 1991). Among women, insecure attachment seems to be correlated with clinical depression and difficulties in coping with stress (Barnas, Pollina, and Cummings, 1991).

Effects of Child Day Care

The importance of attachment inevitably leads to the question of whether child day care has deleterious effects on a child's development. In recent years, many families have entrusted their infants to day care because both parents work. In the United States, more than half of all mothers are employed outside the home (U.S. Bureau of the Census, 1990). Thus, because so many infants spend much of their waking hours away from their families, the question of the effects of day care is not simply academic.

Without question, the quality of care provided in a day-care center is critical. Studies conducted during the 1970s found that day care had no effect on attachment; however, most of these studies were carried out in excellent facilities attached to universities (Clarke-Stewart and Fein, 1983). High-quality day care is expensive. The day care available to low-income families is generally of lower quality than that available to middle- or upper-income families. Regrettably, infants who receive the poorest day care tend to be members of unstable households, often headed by single mothers. Thus, they receive a double dose of less-than-optimal care. Day care need not impair a child's development, but the realities are that it sometimes does.

The age at which an infant enters child care appears to play an important role in the development of attachment. Some studies (for example, Belsky and Rovine, 1988) have shown that infants, especially boys, whose mothers work outside the home during their first year of life are more likely to show insecure patterns of attachment on Ainsworth's Strange Situation. Other studies indicate that the children of both lower-class and middle-class families are more likely to develop insecure attachments if they enter day care during the first year of life (Shaffer, 1989). Entry after the first year is less likely to have negative effects.

Interactions with Peers

Although the attachment between an infant and his or her primary caregiver is the most important social interaction in early life, a child's social development also involves other people. A normal infant develops attachments with other adults and with older siblings if there are any. But interaction with peers—children of a similar age—is especially important to social development.

Studies by Harlow and his colleagues (Harlow, 1974) have shown that social contact with peers is essential to an infant monkey's social development. An infant monkey that is raised with only a cuddly surrogate mother can still develop into a reasonably normal adult. However, an isolated monkey that does not interact with other juveniles before puberty

avoidant attachment   A kind of attachment in which infants avoid or ignore their mothers and often do not cuddle when held.

shows severe deficits. When a previously isolated adolescent monkey is introduced to a colony of normally reared age mates, it will retreat with terror and huddle in a corner in a desperate attempt to hide.

Apparently, social interaction helps young monkeys learn how to respond to each other—how to cope with fear, when to be dominant, and when not to challenge a more powerful and aggressive playmate. Young monkeys, like human children, engage in play, and this play appears to teach them what they need to know in order to form adult relationships.

Other studies by Harlow and his colleagues have shown that the pathological fear shown by a monkey raised in isolation can be eliminated (Novak and Harlow, 1975). The crucial variable seems to be the abruptness with which a formerly isolated monkey is introduced to a social situation. If it is first placed with a younger, not-so-threatening "therapist" monkey, it gradually learns how to interact normally with older monkeys.

An experiment by Fuhrman, Rahe, and Hartup (1979) demonstrates that research using nonhuman primates can have important implications for understanding human development. These researchers used the "juvenile therapist" technique that Harlow and his associates discovered to improve peer interactions among socially withdrawn children aged two and one-half to six and one-half years. The children appeared to be relatively isolated from their peers, spending less than a normal amount of time with them. Each child was paired with a same-age or younger partner for a series of ten play sessions of twenty minutes each. Interactions with peers were observed before, during, and after the play session. The play sessions were successful—they increased the amount of time that the isolated children spent with their peers. Furthermore, the children who were paired with younger "therapists" showed the greatest change. Control subjects, who did not participate in play sessions with another child, showed no change over the four-to-six-week periods.

Approaches to Childrearing

What was your home life like when you were a child? Did your parents establish rules and expect you to obey them, or did they let you do as you pleased whenever you pleased? Psychologists have found that whether parents establish rules and how they enforce those rules affect the social development of their children (Baumrind, 1983; Buri et al., 1988).

In general, parents seem to adopt one of three approaches when raising their children: authoritarian, permissive, or authoritative (Baumrind, 1983). *Authoritarian parents* establish firm rules and expect them to be obeyed without question. Disobedience is met with punishment. *Permissive parents* adopt the opposite strategy: few rules are imposed, and parents do little to influence their children's behavior. *Authoritative parents* also establish rules and enforce them, but not merely through punishment. Instead, they seek to explain the

relationship between the rules and punishment. In authoritative homes, allowances are also made for exceptions to the rules. Rules are established not as absolute or inflexible laws, but rather as general behavioral guidelines.

Suppose that a 10-year-old boy has just broken a glass vase by accidentally hitting it with a ball. How would the three kinds of parents react to the child? Perhaps it would go something like this:

> *Authoritarian parents:* "You know better than that! Don't you ever play with a ball in the house again. Now go to your bedroom and don't come out until I tell you to."

> *Permissive parents:* "Well, don't worry about it. These things happen; it was an accident."

> *Authoritative parents:* "You know better than that—you agreed not to play with the ball in the house. Now you know why we made that rule. Go get the broom and the dust pan and clean up this mess. When you finish, go to your bedroom and wait for me. I want to talk to you some more about this."

Not surprisingly, authoritarian parents tend to have children who are more unhappy and distrustful than are children of permissive or authoritative parents. You may think that children of permissive parents are most likely to be self-reliant and curious. Not so. In fact, they appear to be the least so, probably because they never received parental encouragement and guidance for developing these sorts of behaviors. Rather, they are left on their own without benefit of learning directly from an adult's experience and without the guidance needed to learn self-control. Authoritative parents raise their children in an environment in which individuality and personal responsibility are encouraged, and so they tend to rear children who are self-controlled, independent, and socially competent. Psychologically, then, one important element in raising happy and independent children is an open line of communication between parent and child.

Growing Up in a Single-Parent or Divorced Family

Today, almost 25 percent of American children live in single-parent homes. In the period from 1970 to 1988, the number of single-parent homes doubled. There appear to be two primary reasons for the increase in single-parent households: an increased divorce rate and an increase in the number of unwed mothers, mostly teenagers, who keep their babies.

Many children of teenage mothers are raised under unfavorable circumstances, including poverty and limited educational opportunities. It seems that being raised by a teenager with limited education and experience in combination with poverty contributes to the development of both behavior problems and learning delays. If the mother finishes high school and has social support from her family and friends, her child is more likely to develop similarly to children who live with both parents (Osofsky, 1990; Sandven and Resnick, 1990).

The effects of divorce on children are a little different. Younger children seem to be affected more negatively than are older children (Allison and Furstenberg, 1989). Regardless of a child's age, though, if conflict still exists between the parents after the divorce or if the child has infrequent or no contact with one of the parents after the divorce, the child is likely to experience negative consequences from the divorce (for example, anxiety, self-control problems, aggression, or withdrawal). Decreased parental conflict and frequent interaction with both parents seem to reduce many of the adverse effects of divorce (Sroufe, Cooper, and DeHart, 1992). A lesson to be learned here is that it is the conflict between parents that seems most to interfere with a child's normal development and not the divorce itself. If the divorce brings with it increased cooperation between parents, the child's development is more likely to proceed normally.

Interim Summary

Social Development in Childhood

Because babies are totally dependent on their parents, the development of attachment between parent and infant is crucial to the infant's survival. A baby has the innate ability to shape and reinforce the behavior of the parent. To a large extent, the baby is the parent's teacher. In turn, parents reinforce the baby's behavior, which facilitates the development of a durable attachment between them.

Some of the behaviors that babies possess innately are sucking, cuddling, looking, smiling, and crying. These behaviors promote parental responses and are instrumental in satisfying physiological needs.

Infants are normally afraid of novel stimuli, but the presence of their caregivers provides a secure base from which they can explore new environments. Ainsworth's Strange Situation allows a researcher to determine the nature of the attachment between infant and caregiver. By using this test, several investigators have identified some of the variables—some involving infants and some involving mothers—that influence attachment. Fathers, as well as mothers, can form close attachments with infants. Excellent child care by outsiders will not harm a child's social development, but less-than-excellent child care, especially if it begins in the child's first year of life, can adversely affect attachment.

Development also involves the acquisition of social skills. Interaction with peers is probably the most important factor in social development among children and adolescents. However, a caregiver's style of parenting can also have strong effects on the social development of children and adolescents. Authoritative parents, compared to authoritarian and permissive parents, tend to rear competent, self-reliant, and independent children. In addition, social development is also influenced by other aspects of the home environment, such the presence or absence of either parent. The social development of children raised in single-parent (mother only) families appears to progress normally if the mother completes high school and enjoys strong social support from family and friends. Divorce marked by cooperation between the parents produces a similar result.

Thought Questions

- We know that attachment occurs in humans and other primates. Do you think it occurs in other species, especially other mammalian species, as well? What kind of evidence would you need to collect to say that it does, in fact, occur in another species? Could you develop a test like Harlow's for researching attachment in other species? Develop your answer with a specific species in mind, for example, cats or dogs.
- What sort of relationship might exist between the kind of attachment an infant experiences and how, later, as a child, he or she might react to his or her parents' divorce?

Development of Gender Roles

Physical development as a male or a female is only one aspect of sexual development. Social development is also important. A person's **gender identity** is one's private sense of being a male or female and consists primarily of the acceptance of membership in a particular group of people: males or females. Acceptance of this membership does not necessarily indicate acceptance of the gender roles or gender stereotypes that may accompany it. For example, a dedicated feminist may fight to change the role of women in her society but still clearly identify herself as a woman. **Gender roles** are cultural expectations about the ways in which men and women should think and behave. Closely related to them are **gender stereotypes**, beliefs about differences in the behaviors, abilities, and personality traits of males and females. Society's gender stereotypes have an important influence on the behavior of its members. In fact, many people unconsciously

gender identity One's private sense of being male or female.

gender role Cultural expectations about the ways in which men and women should think and behave.

gender stereotypes Beliefs about differences in the behaviors, abilities, and personality traits of males and females.

Many people acquire their gender identities and gender roles as a result of the gender stereotypes they learn as children.

develop their gender identity and gender roles based on gender stereotypes they learned as children. This section considers the role of gender stereotypes in influencing the nature and development of gender roles.

Berk (1994) notes that by age two children begin to perceive themselves as being a boy or a girl. In the process of learning what it means to be boys or girls, children associate, in a stereotypical manner, certain toys, games, attitudes, and behaviors, such as being aggressive or compliant, with one gender or the other (Huston, 1983; Jacklin and Maccoby, 1983; Picariello, Greenberg, Pillemer, 1990). For example, consider an experiment conducted by Montemayor (1974), who invited children between the ages of six and eight years to play a game that involved tossing marbles into a clown's body. Some of the children were told that they were playing a "girl's game," some were told it was a "boy's game," and others were told nothing. Boys and girls both said that the game was more fun when it had been described as appropriate to their gender, and they even attained better scores when it was.

Where do children learn gender stereotypes? Although a child's peer group and teachers are important, parents play an especially important role in the development of gender stereotypes. For example, parents tend to encourage and reward their sons for playing with "masculine" toys such as cars and trucks and objects such as baseballs and footballs (Fagot and Hagan, 1991). And parents tend to encourage and reward their daughters for engaging in "feminine" activities that promote dependency, warmth, and sensitivity, such as playing house or hosting a make-believe tea party (Dunn, Bretherton, and Munn, 1987; Lytton and Romney, 1991). Parents who do not encourage or reward these kinds of stereotypical activities tend to have children whose attitudes and behavior reflect fewer gender stereotypes (Weisner and Wilson-Mitchell, 1990).

The Nature of Gender Differences

The origin and nature of gender differences has been and is likely to continue to be a controversial topic in psychology (Eagly, 1995; Shibley Hyde and Plant, 1995). Part of the controversy stems from the way differences between males and females are measured and how large those differences seem to be, and part of it stems from the sociopolitical implications of these differences (for example, sexism). In this section, we will discuss only those differences that presently have strong empirical support.

Berk (1994) has reviewed recent research on gender differences and has concluded that the most reliable differences are the following: Girls show earlier verbal development, more effective expression and interpretation of emotional cues, and a higher tendency to comply with adults and peers. Boys show stronger spatial abilities, increased aggression, and greater tendency toward risk taking. Boys are also more likely to show developmental problems such as language disorders, behavior problems, or physical impairments.

These differences are unlikely to be wholly biologically determined. In fact, socialization undoubtedly has a strong influence. Also, most gender differences are small. For example, after reviewing scores obtained from the Wechsler Intelligence Scales and the California Achievement Tests between 1949 and 1985, Feingold (1993) concluded that cognitive gender differences were small or nonexistent in children and small in adolescents. Deaux (1985) reports that on average, only 5 percent of the variability in individual differences among children can be attributed to gender; the other 95 percent is due to individual genetic and environmental factors. Therefore, gender, by itself, is not a very good predictor of a person's talents, personality, or behavior.

Biology and Culture

The Causes of Gender Role Differences

As we have just seen, children readily learn gender stereotypes and adopt the roles deemed appropriate for their gender. Two causes—biology and culture—may be responsible for this acceptance.

■ Biological Causes

One possible explanation of gender roles focuses on biological differences. Perhaps some of the observed differences between males and females can be attributed to chromosomal differences or to the effects of sex hormones. After all, these factors produce differences in the bodies of males and females, so perhaps they could affect their behavior, too.

A likely site of biologically determined gender differences is the brain. Studies using laboratory animals have shown that the exposure of a developing brain to male sex hormones has long-term effects. The hormones alter the development of the brain and produce changes in the animals' behavior, even in adulthood (Carlson, 1995). In addition, the human brain shows some gender differences, which are probably also caused by exposure to different patterns of hormones during development (Hofman and Swaab, 1991). The precise effects of these differences on the behavior of males and females is not presently well understood.

Gender differences in two types of cognitive ability—verbal ability and spatial ability—may be at least partly caused by differences in the brain. Girls tend to learn to speak and to read sooner than boys, and boys tend to be better at tasks requiring spatial perception. Kimura (1987) suggests possible reasons for these sex differences. While the human brain was evolving into its present form, our ancestors were hunter-gatherers, and men and women probably had different roles. Women, due to restrictions on their movements imposed by childbearing, were more likely to work near the home, performing fine manual skills with small, nearby objects. Men were more likely to range farther from home, engaging in activities that involved coordination of body movements with respect to distant objects, such as throwing rocks or spears or launching darts toward animals. In addition, men had to be able to keep track of where they were so they could return home after following animals for long distances.

These specializations might favor the evolution of gender differences. In particular, women's movements might be expected to be better integrated with nearby objects, whereas men's movements might be expected to be better integrated with objects located at a distance. If Kimura's

(1987) reasoning is correct, it is easy to see why, on average, men's spatial abilities are better than those of women. But why do girls learn to speak and read sooner than boys? Many researchers believe that our ancestors used hand gestures long before verbal communication developed. Kimura suggests that fine motor control and speech production are closely related—that the neural circuits that control the muscles we use for speech may be closely related to those we use to move our hands.

More recently, Buss (1995) has argued that other differences in the adaptive problems that men and women have faced in the course of evolution have led to gender differences. As we learned in Chapter 3, chief among these adaptive problems are issues tied to reproduction. For women, these problems include identifying and attracting a mate who is willing to invest his resources (time, energy, property, food, and so on) in her and her children. For men, these problems include identifying and attracting a fertile female who is willing to copulate with him. Buss argues that over the course of evolution, men and women have come to differ because the problems posed by reproduction and childrearing require different strategies for their successful resolution.

Of course, Kimura and Buss's accounts are speculative. However, they provide a good example of the biological approach—in particular, the functional, evolutionary approach—to an understanding of human behavior.

■ Cultural Causes

Although evolutionary forces may have laid the groundwork for gender differences in brain mechanisms associated with verbal ability and spatial ability, practice at and training in tasks involving these abilities can improve people's performance at them (Hoyenga and Hoyenga, 1993). In fact, most psychologists believe that socialization plays the most significant role in the establishment of gender role differences. First adults and then peers teach, by direct instruction and by example, what is expected of boys and girls. These expectations are deeply ingrained in our culture and unconsciously affect our perceptions and our behavior. When someone announces the birth of a baby, most of us immediately ask, "Is it a boy or a girl?" Parents often dress their infants in clothing that makes it easy for strangers to recognize the infant's gender. And once we find out a baby's sex, we interact with the child in subtly (and not so subtly) different ways.

For example, Condry and Condry (1976) showed college students a videotape of a baby crying. The subjects tended to see the crying as "angry" if they believed that the baby was a boy and "fearful" if they thought the baby was a girl. Obviously, these judgments were the results of their gender stereotypes and not of their perceptions.

The effect of gender on an adult's *perception* of infants is clear and has been confirmed in many studies. What about differences in the behaviors directed toward boys and girls? The strongest difference in the way parents socialize their sons and daughters appears to be their encouragement of gender-typed play and the choice of "gender-appropriate" toys. Many parents encourage their boys to play with trucks, blocks, and other toys that can be manipulated and encourage their girls to play with dolls. However, a cross-cultural review of 172 studies conducted in North America, Australia, and Western Europe concluded that parents do not consistently treat their sons and daughters differently in any other important ways (Lytton and Romney, 1991).

Although parents do encourage "sex-appropriate" play, there is evidence that biological factors may play an initial role in children's preferences. Although fathers are less likely to give dolls to one-year-old boys than to one-year-old girls, the boys who do receive the dolls are less likely to play with them (Snow, Jacklin, and Maccoby, 1983). Perhaps, as Lytton and Romney (1991) suggest, adults' expectations and encouragement build on children's preferences, producing an amplifying effect. Then, because boys' toys provide more opportunity for developing motor skills, visuospatial skills, and inventiveness and girls' toys provide more opportunity for nurturance and social exchange, some important differences in sex roles may become established.

Once children begin to play with other children outside the home, peers have a significant influence on the development of their gender roles. In fact, Stern and Karraker (1989) found that the behavior of two-to-six-year-old children was even more influenced by the knowledge of a baby's gender than was the behavior of adults. By the time children are three years old, they reinforce gender-typed play by praising, imitating, or joining in the behavior. In contrast, they criticize gender-inappropriate behavior (Langlois and Downs, 1980). Parents indirectly encourage gender-stereotyped play by seeking out children of the same sex as playmates for their own children (Lewis et al., 1975).

Of course, all the research I have cited in this section describes *tendencies* of parents and children to act in a particular way. Some parents make a deliberate attempt to encourage their children's interest in both "masculine" and "feminine" activities, with the hope that doing so will help keep all opportunities for achievement and self-expression open to them, regardless of their gender. Almost everywhere, men and women are treated unequally. In most industrialized countries, laws prohibit overt sexual discrimination. But despite these laws, women have more difficulty obtaining prestigious jobs, and the higher levels of government and industry tend to be dominated by men. Our society may indeed be moving toward a time in which a person's gender neither hinders nor favors his or her aspirations, but clearly this time has not yet arrived.

Interim Summary

Development of Gender Roles

Children's gender roles tend to conform to their society's gender stereotypes. Very few real differences exist between the sexes and those that do are relatively small. Females tend to show earlier verbal development, are better at expressing emotion and interpreting emotional cues, and show more compliance with adults and peers. Males tend to have better spatial abilities, are more aggressive, and tend to take more risks.

Some of these differences may have biological roots. Kimura suggests that the different tasks performed by our ancestors shaped brain development and favored men with better spatial skills and women with better communication skills. Buss argues that problems related to reproduction and childrearing have caused gender differences in how these problems are solved. But most gender differences in abilities and behaviors are small, and socialization undoubtedly plays a significant part in gender role differences.

Research has shown that both parents and peers tend to encourage children to behave in gender-appropriate ways—especially with regard to play activities and toys. However, scientific studies have revealed few other reliable differences in the ways parents treat young boys and girls.

Thought Questions

- Can you imagine an alternative course of human evolution in which gender roles would have developed along different lines? What events in the course of human evolution could have happened (but did not, of course) that would have changed the nature of gender roles as we know them today?
- Imagine that you had been born the opposite gender—instead of being a male, you are a female, or vice versa. In what significant ways would your life be different? For example, in what important ways would your social, emotional, and intellectual experiences be different? (Be careful not to base you answer on stereotypes you have of the other gender.)

Moral Development

The word *morality* comes from a Latin word that means "custom." Moral behavior is behavior that conforms to a generally accepted set of rules. With very few exceptions, by the time a person reaches adulthood, he or she has accepted a set of rules about personal and social behavior. These rules vary in different cultures and may take the form of laws, taboos, and even sorcery (Chasdi, 1994). Let us begin by considering the way a child acquires a concept of morality. The pioneer in this field, as in cognitive development, was Jean Piaget.

Piaget's Theory of Moral Development

According to Piaget, the first stage of moral development (ages five to ten years) is **moral realism**, which is characterized by egocentrism, or "self-centeredness," and blind adherence to rules.

Egocentric children can evaluate events only in terms of their personal consequences. Their behavior is not guided by the effects it might have on someone else, because they are not capable of imagining themselves in the other person's place. Thus, young children do not consider whether an act is right or wrong but only whether it is likely to have good or bad consequences *personally*. Punishment is a bad consequence, and the fear of punishment is the only real moral force at this age. A young child also believes that rules come from parents (or other authority figures, such as older children or God) and that rules cannot be changed.

Older children and adults judge an act by the intentions of the actor as well as by the consequences of the act. A young child considers only an act's objective outcomes, not the subjective intent that lay behind the act. For example, Piaget told two stories, one about John, who accidentally broke fifteen cups, and Henry, who broke one cup while trying to do something that was forbidden to him. When a young child is asked which of the two children is the naughtiest, the child will say that John is, because he broke fifteen cups. He or she will not take into account the fact that the act was entirely accidental.

As children mature, they become less egocentric and more capable of empathy. Older children (older than age seven) can imagine how another person feels. This shift away from egocentrism means that children's behavior may be guided not merely by the effects acts have on themselves but also by the effects they have on others. At around ten years of age, children enter Piaget's second stage of moral development, **morality of cooperation**, during which rules become more flexible as the child learns that many of them (such as those that govern games) are social conventions that may be altered by mutual consent.

Kohlberg's Theory of Moral Development

Piaget's description of moral development has been considerably elaborated on by Lawrence Kohlberg (1927–1987). Kohlberg studied boys between ten and seventeen years of age, and he studied the same boys over the course of several years. He presented the children with stories involving moral dilemmas. For example, one story described a man called Heinz whose wife was dying of a cancer that could only be treated by a medication discovered by a druggist living in the same town. The man could not afford the price demanded by the druggist, so the distraught man broke into the druggist's store and stole enough of the drug to save his wife's life. The boys were asked what Heinz should have done and why he should have done it. On the basis of his research, Kohlberg decided that moral development consisted of three levels and seven stages. (See *Table 12.3.*) These stages are closely linked to children's cognitive development as outlined by Piaget.

The first two stages belong to the **preconventional level**, during which morality is externally defined. During stage 1, *morality of punishment and obedience*, children blindly obey authority and avoid punishment. When asked to decide what Heinz should do, children base their decisions on fears about being punished for letting one's wife die or for committing a crime. During stage 2, *morality of naive instrumental hedonism*, children's behavior is guided egocentrically by the pleasantness or unpleasantness of its consequences to them. The moral choice is reduced to a weighing of the probable risks and benefits of stealing the drug.

The next two stages belong to the **conventional level**, which includes an understanding that the social system has an interest in people's behavior. During stage 3, *morality of maintaining good relations*, children want to be regarded by people who know them as good, well-behaved children. Moral decisions are based on perceived social pressure. Either Heinz should steal the drug because people would otherwise regard him as heartless, or he should not steal it because they would regard him as a criminal. During stage 4, *morality of maintaining social order*, laws and moral rules are perceived as instruments used to maintain social order and, as such, must be obeyed. Thus, both protecting a life and respecting people's property are seen as rules that help maintain social order.

Kohlberg also described a final level of moral development—the **postconventional level**, during which people realize that moral rules have some underlying principles that apply to all situations and societies. During stage 5, *morality of social contracts*, people recognize that rules are social contracts, that not all authority figures are infallible, and that individual rights can sometimes take precedence over laws. During stage 6, *morality of universal ethical principles*, people

moral realism The first stage of Piaget's model of moral development, which includes egocentrism and blind adherence to rules.

morality of cooperation The second stage of Piaget's model of moral development, which involves the recognition of rules as social conventions.

preconventional level Kohlberg's first level of moral development, which bases moral behavior on external sanctions, such as authority and punishment.

conventional level Kohlberg's second level of moral development, in which people realize that society has instituted moral rules to maintain order and to serve the best interests of its citizenry.

postconventional level Kohlberg's third and final level of moral development, in which people come to understand that moral rules include principles that apply across all situations and societies.

Table 12.3

Levels and Stages of Kohlberg's Theory of Moral Development

Level and Stage	Highlights
Preconventional Level	
Stage 1: Morality of punishment and obedience	Avoidance of punishment
Stage 2: Morality of naive instrumental hedonism	Egocentric perspective; weighing of potential risks and benefits
Conventional Level	
Stage 3: Morality of maintaining good relations	Morality based on approval from others
Stage 4: Morality of maintaining social order	Rules and laws define morality
Postconventional Level	
Stage 5: Morality of social contracts	Obey societal rules for the common good, although individual rights sometimes outweigh laws
Stage 6: Morality of universal ethical principles	Societal laws and rules based on ethical values
Stage 7: Morality of cosmic orientation	Adoption of values that transcend societal norms

perceive rules and laws as being justified by abstract ethical values, such as the value of human life and the value of dignity. In stage 7, the *morality of cosmic orientation*, people adopt values that transcend societal norms. This stage represents the zenith of moral development. As Kohlberg noted, only a very few people, such as Eleanor Roosevelt and Albert Schweitzer, ever reach this state. In fact, Kohlberg believed that not all people reach the postconventional level of moral development.

Evaluation of Piaget's and Kohlberg's Theories of Moral Development

Piaget's and Kohlberg's theories have greatly influenced research on moral development, but they have received some criticism. For example, Piaget's research indicated that children in the first stage (moral realism) respond to the magnitude of a transgression rather than to the intent behind it. But even adults respond to the magnitude of a transgression and rightly so. The theft of a few postage stamps by an office worker is not treated the same way as the embezzlement of thousands of dollars.

Kohlberg's conclusions have also been challenged. For example, Sobesky (1983) found that changes in the wording of Heinz's dilemma would drastically change people's responses. If the possibility of imprisonment was underscored, people tended to make more responses belonging to the preconventional level. Many researchers agree with Rest (1979), who concluded that Kohlberg's "stages" are not coherent entities but do describe a progression in the ability of children to consider more and more complex reasons for moral rules.

A different type of criticism was leveled by Gilligan (1977, 1982), who suggested that Kohlberg's theory is gender-biased. According to her, these studies indicated that men (in general) adhered to universal ethical principles, whereas women (in general) preferred to base their moral judgments on the effects these judgments would have on the people involved. Men's judgments were based more on abstract ideas of *justice*, whereas women's judgments were based more on concrete considerations of *caring* and *concern for relationships*.

However, most researchers have *not* found that men's and women's moral judgments tend to be based on different types of values. For example, Donenberg and Hoffman (1988) found that boys and girls were equally likely to base their moral judgments on justice or caring and that the sex of the main character in the moral dilemma had no effect on their judgments. Walker (1989) tested 233 subjects ranging in ages from 5 to 63 years and found no reliable gender differences. Thus, the available evidence does not appear to support Gilligan's conclusion that such concern is related to a person's gender.

Interim Summary

Moral Development

Piaget suggested that moral development consists of two principal stages: moral realism, characterized by egocentrism and blind adherence to rules, and morality of cooperation, characterized by empathy and a realization that behavior is judged by the effects it has on others. Kohlberg suggested that moral development consists of three levels, each divided into two stages. During the preconventional level, morality is based on the personal consequences of an act. During the conventional level, morality is based on the need to be well regarded and on sharing a common interest in social order. During the postconventional level, which is achieved by only a few people, morality becomes an abstract, philosophical virtue.

Critics of Piaget and Kohlberg point out that the stages of moral development are, to a certain degree, products of the measuring instruments. Although it does not appear, as Gilligan originally suggested, that females follow different moral rules than males, her work has sensitized researchers to the importance of including both sexes in studies of human development. Subtle changes in the way that moral dilemmas are posed can produce very different answers.

Thought Questions

■ Karen's parents are going away for the weekend and ask her to go with them. Karen, who is fifteen years old, says that she can't go because she has a special gymnastics practice on Saturday. Disappointed, her parents accept her answer, and agree to let Karen stay home because they know how important gymnastics is to her. Later, after they return, they learn that Karen had lied to them about the practice. When they confront Karen, she tells them that she knows that she lied to them but that she did it so as not to hurt their feelings—she really did not want to go away with them for the weekend. Karen's parents say that they understand her dilemma but that they feel they must punish her anyway for breaking an important family rule. How do you suppose that Piaget and Kohlberg would explain Karen's level of morality? How would they explain her parents' level of morality?

Adolescence

After childhood comes adolescence, the threshold to adulthood. (In Latin, *adolescere* means "to grow up.") The transition between childhood and adulthood is as much social as it is biological. In some societies, people are considered to be adults as soon as they are sexually mature, at which time they may assume adult rights and responsibilities, including marriage. In most industrialized societies, where formal education often continues into the late teens and early twenties, adulthood officially comes several years later. The end of adolescence is difficult to judge because the line between adolescence and young adulthood is fuzzy: There are no distinct physical changes that mark this transition.

puberty The period during which people's reproductive systems mature, marking the beginning of the transition from childhood to adulthood.

Physical Development

Puberty (from the Latin *puber*, meaning "adult"), the period during which people's reproductive systems mature, marks the beginning of the transition from childhood to adulthood. Many physical changes occur during this stage: People reach their ultimate height, develop increased muscle size and body hair, and become capable of reproduction. There is also a change in social roles. As a child, a person is dependent on parents, teachers, and other adults. As an adolescent, he or she is expected to assume more responsibility. Relations with peers also suddenly change; members of one's own sex become potential rivals for the attention of members of the other sex.

Sexual Maturation

The internal sex organs and genitalia do not change much for several years after birth, but they begin to develop again at puberty. When boys and girls reach about eleven to fourteen years of age, their testes or ovaries secrete hormones that begin the process of sexual maturation. This activity of the gonads is initiated by the hypothalamus, the part of the brain to which the pituitary gland is attached. The hypothalamus instructs the pituitary gland to secrete hormones that stimulate the gonads to secrete sex hormones. These sex hormones act on various organs of the body and initiate the changes that accompany sexual maturation. (See *Figure 12.9.*)

The sex hormones secreted by the gonads cause growth and maturation of the external genitalia and of the gonads themselves. In addition, these hormones cause the maturation of ova and the production of sperm. All these developments are considered primary sex characteristics, because they are essential to the ability to reproduce. The sex hor-

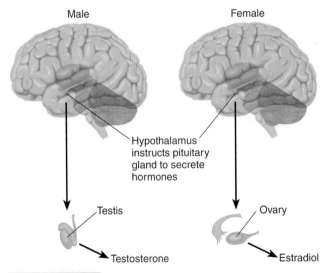

Figure 12.9

Sexual maturation. Puberty is initiated when the hypothalamus instructs the pituitary gland to secrete hormones that cause the gonads to secrete sex hormones.

mones also stimulate the development of secondary sex characteristics, the physical changes that distinguish males from females. Before puberty, boys and girls look much the same—except, perhaps, for their hairstyles and clothing. At puberty, young men's testes begin to secrete testosterone; this hormone causes their muscles to develop, their facial hair to grow, and their voices to deepen. Young women's ovaries secrete *estradiol*, the most important *estrogen*, or female sex hormone. Estradiol causes women's breasts to grow and their pelvises to widen, and it produces changes in the layer of fat beneath the skin and in the texture of the skin itself.

Development of the adult secondary sex characteristics takes several years, and not all characteristics develop at the same time. The process begins in girls at around age eleven. The first visible change is the accumulation of fatty tissue around the nipples, followed shortly by the growth of pubic hair. The spurt of growth in height commences, and the uterus and vagina begin to enlarge. The first menstrual period begins at around age thirteen, just about the time the rate of growth in height begins to decline. In boys, sexual maturation begins slightly later. The first visible event is the growth of the testes and scrotum, followed by the appearance of pubic hair. A few months later, the penis begins to grow, and the spurt of growth in height starts. The larynx grows larger, which causes the voice to become lower. Sexual maturity—the ability to father a child—occurs at around age fifteen. The growth of facial hair usually occurs later; often a full beard does not grow until the late teens or early twenties.

In industrialized societies, the average age at the onset of puberty has been declining. For example, the average age at the onset of menstruation was between fourteen and fifteen years in 1900 but is between twelve and thirteen years today. The most important reason for this decline is better childhood nutrition. It appears that this decline is leveling off in industrialized societies, but in many developing countries, the age of the onset of puberty is beginning to fall as these countries enjoy increasing prosperity.

Behavioral Effects of Puberty

The changes that accompany sexual maturation have a profound effect on young people's behavior and self-concept. They become more sensitive about their appearance. Many girls worry about their weight and the size of their breasts and hips. Many boys worry about their height, the size of their genitals, their muscular development, and the growth of their beards. In addition, most adolescents display a particular form of egocentrism that develops early in the transition into the stage of formal operations: *self-consciousness*. Some developmental psychologists believe that self-consciousness results from the difficulty in distinguishing their own self-perceptions from the views other people have of them.

Because the onset of puberty occurs at different times in different individuals, young adolescents can find themselves more or less mature than some of their friends, and this dif-

ference can have important social consequences. An early study by Jones and Bayley (1950) found that early-maturing boys tended also to become more socially mature and were most likely to be perceived as leaders by their peers. Late-maturing boys tended to become hostile and withdrawn and often engaged in negative attention-getting behavior. Later studies have generally confirmed these findings (Peterson, 1985; Brooks-Gunn, 1988). The effect of age of maturity in girls is less clear. Some studies indicate that early-maturing girls may benefit from higher status and prestige, but they are also more likely to engage in norm-breaking behaviors such as stealing, cheating on exams, staying out late, and using alcohol (Brooks-Gunn, 1989). Brooks-Gunn suggests that the primary cause of the norm-breaking behaviors is the fact that early-maturing girls are more likely to become friends with older girls.

Social Development

During adolescence, a person's behavior and social roles change dramatically. Adolescence is not simply a continuation of childhood; it marks a real transition from the dependency of childhood to the relative independence of adulthood. Adolescence is also a period during which many people seek out new experiences and engage in reckless behavior—behavior that involves psychological, physical, and legal risks for them as well as for others, as for example, speeding in a car, having sexual relations, and using illegal drugs (Arnett, 1995).

Forming an Identity

You have probably heard the term *identity crisis*, as in "She's having an identity crisis." The phrase was coined by Erik Erikson, a psychoanalyst who studied with Anna Freud, Sigmund Freud's daughter. Based on his observations of patients in his psychoanalytical practice and on research that he conducted with children, Erikson developed a theory of *psychosocial* development, which divides human development into eight stages. Erikson proposed that people encounter a series of crises in their social relations with other people and that the way these conflicts are resolved determines the nature of development. In fact, according to Erikson, the resolution of these conflicts *is* development. If the conflict is resolved positively, the outcome is a happy one; if it is not resolved or is resolved negatively, the outcome is unhealthy and impairs development. Because the nature of people's social relations changes throughout life, their psychosocial development does not end when they become adults. Table 12.4 lists Erikson's eight stages of development, the nature of the crises, the social relationships involved in these crises, and the possible consequences—favorable or unfavorable—of these crises. (See *Table 12.4*.)

Erikson argued that the primary crisis faced by adolescents is identity versus role confusion. If they are able to de-

Table 12.4

Erikson's Eight Stages of Psychosocial Development

Period	Conflict	Outcome	
		Positive Resolution	Negative Resolution
Childhood	Trust vs. mistrust Autonomy vs. self-doubt Initiative vs. guilt Competence vs. inferiority	Trust, security, confidence, independence, curiosity, competence, industry	Insecurity, doubt, guilt, low self-esteem, sense of failure
Adolescence	Identity vs. role confusion	Strong sense of self-identity	Weak sense of self
Adulthood	Intimacy vs. isolation Generativity vs. stagnation Integrity vs. despair	Capacity to develop deep and meaningful relationships and care for others; consideration for future generations; personal sense of worth and satisfaction	Isolation, unhappiness, Selfishness, stagnancy, sense of failure and regret

velop plans for accomplishing career and personal goals and to decide which social groups they belong to, they have formed a personal identity. Failure to form an identity leaves a teenager confused about his or her role in life.

Erikson's concept of the identity crisis has been researched extensively by Marcia (1967, 1980), who has asserted that developing an identity consists of two components, crisis and commitment. A *crisis* is a period during which an adolescent struggles intellectually to resolve issues related to personal values and goals. For example, a teenager who questions the religious and moral values of his or her parents is experiencing a crisis. *Commitment* is a decision based on consideration of alternative values and goals that leads to a specific course of action. For instance, a teenager who decides to go to a different church than his or her parents is said to make a commitment. In this case, he or she also is said to identify with the beliefs of that church.

Marcia hypothesized that adolescents experience different degrees of crisis and commitment. Some teenagers never experience crises, and others do but may never resolve them. In trying to make sense of the different ways in which adolescents experience identity crises, Marcia developed four possibilities, which he called *identity statuses.* (See *Figure 12.10.*)

Adolescents who experience a crisis, consider alternative solutions to it, and are committed to a course of action based on personal values are said to be *identity achievers.* Identity achievers are self-confident and have a high level of moral development (Dellas and Jernigan, 1990). Adolescents who experience a crisis but do not resolve it and therefore cannot become committed are said to be in *moratorium.* Teenagers who have not experienced a crisis but who are nonetheless committed to a course of action are said to be in *foreclosure.* Teenagers in foreclosure are typically adolescents who iden-

tify strongly with people such as their parents and as a result never consider alternatives to those identities. They can be dogmatic in their views and feel threatened by others who challenge their identities (Frank, Pirsch, and Wright, 1990). Adolescents who experience a crisis and who do not become committed are said to experience *identity diffusion.* Teenagers who are identity diffused, especially over a long time period, tend to be immature, to be impulsive, and to have a sense of hopelessness about the future (Archer and Waterman, 1990). Erikson would probably have considered these people as being identity confused.

Marcia's research has shown that adolescents move in and out of the different statuses as they experience new situa-

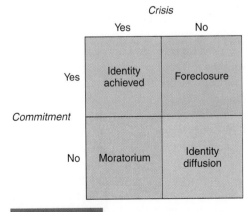

Figure 12.10

Marcia's four identity statuses. Different combinations of crises and commitment yield four different identity statuses.

tions and crises. A teenager does not necessarily move progressively from one status to another. For example, after thinking about whether to major in business or engineering, a college student may decide on engineering because she thinks that she will like the work and earn good money. In terms of this decision, she is an identity achiever. However, after taking several engineering courses, she may decide that she really doesn't like engineering after all. Now she must decide whether to keep her major or change it. She is now no longer committed; she is in moratorium.

Marcia's research is interesting for two reasons. First, it shows that most adolescents do indeed experience crises in their search for an identity. Second, it shows that a teenager's psychological reaction to a crisis depends on the point in time during which he or she is dealing with the crisis. That there are four possible avenues that can be involved in achieving an identity testifies to the complexity of "finding oneself."

Marcia's work, then, buttresses Erikson's view of adolescence. However, Erikson's theory would have us believe that teenagers are searching for an identity on their own, independent of parents and others. As Gilligan (1982) contends, this is more likely to be true for boys than for girls. Her point is that girls are more likely than boys to seek and develop close relationships with others. In her view, a girl's search for identity is strongly influenced by the desire to be involved in close relationships with others. Gilligan's hypothesis reinforces many researchers' belief in the social nature of identity development: The search for an identity is enmeshed in a social context that may strongly influence how a teenager responds to a crisis.

Identity and Self-Perception

The search for a personal identity brings with it changes in self-concept and self-esteem (Berk, 1993). During childhood, children tend to perceive themselves in terms of both physical traits, such as "I am a boy and have brown hair and blue eyes" and individual personality characteristics, such as "I am honest" or "I am smart" (Damon and Hart, 1992). During adolescence teenagers become more focused on their social relationships and tend to perceive themselves more in terms of their interactions with others. They may use phrases such as "I am outgoing" or "I am trustworthy" to describe themselves. In late adolescence, teenagers begin to perceive themselves more in terms of the values that they hold. They may now describe themselves in terms of their political, social, or philosophical views, such as "I am a conservative" or "I am an environmentalist."

As a teenager strives to develop an identity, earlier self-perceptions, including those held during childhood, are incorporated into his or her emerging self-concept. Newer self-perceptions do not merely replace older ones. Instead, the newer ones augment the older ones so that, for example, a teenager may perceive herself to be a blonde-haired young woman who is shy, trustworthy, and moderate in her political

views. An adolescent's identity, then, seems inextricably bound to his or her perceptions of self.

Sexuality

Sexuality has become a very evident component of modern culture in most industrialized societies. Displays of sexual attractiveness play an important role in advertisements in magazines and on television; sexual activities are portrayed in books and films; personal sexual practices are discussed in print and during talk shows on radio and television. Sexuality was always a part of life (after all, our species has managed to propagate during all periods of history), but during the latter part of this century, it has become much more open and evident than it was previously.

Sexual behavior occurring during adolescence has increased in frequency during the past few decades. Fifty years ago, approximately 20 percent of the females and 40 percent of the males in the United States said that they had engaged in sexual intercourse by age twenty. Now these figures are approximately 50 percent for both males and females (Brooks-Gunn and Furstenberg, 1989). These figures seem to have peaked in the late 1970s. Since then, they have declined slightly and expressions of guilt feelings about sexual behavior have increased (Gerrard, 1986, 1987).

Friendships and Relations with Parents

The nature of friendship changes during adolescence, and it changes in different ways for boys and girls. For girls, the most important function of childhood friendships is having someone with whom to do things—someone with whom to share activities and common interests. At around the age of fourteen years, girls begin to seek companions who can provide social and emotional support. As girls become aware of their growing sexuality and the changes in their relationships with boys, close friends serve as confidants—as sounding boards who help to define their behavior and social roles. Adolescent boys' friendships are likely to be less intense than those of girls. Boys are more concerned with establishing and asserting their independence and defining their relation to authority; thus, groups of friends serve as allies—as mutual-aid societies, so to speak.

As adolescents begin to define their new roles and to assert them, they almost inevitably come into conflict with their parents. Some writers have claimed that changes in modern society have given rise to a "youth culture" that is apart from the rest of society and a "generation gap" that separates young people from their elders. However, research indicates that most of the differences between people of different generations are in style rather than in substance. Adolescents and their parents tend to have similar values and attitudes toward important issues (Youniss and Smollar, 1985). Unless serious problems occur, family conflicts tend to be provoked by relatively minor issues, such as messy rooms, loud music, clothes, curfews, and household chores. These problems tend to begin around the time of puberty; if puberty occurs particularly early or late, so does the conflict (Paikoff and Brooks-Gunn, 1991).

Adolescence is said to be a time of turmoil, a period characterized by unhappiness, stress, and confusion. While a few adolescents are unhappy most of the time (and most are unhappy some of the time), studies have found that the vast majority of teenagers generally feel happy and self-confident (Offer and Sabshim, 1984; Peterson and Ebata, 1987). But mood states do seem to be more variable during the teenage years than during other times of life. Csikszentmihalyi and Larson (1984) randomly sampled the mood states of a group of high school students. They gave them electronic beepers that sounded at random intervals that were, on the average, two hours apart. Each time the beepers sounded, the students stopped what they were doing and filled out a questionnaire that asked what they were doing, how they felt, what they were thinking about, and so on. The investigators found that the students' moods could swing from high to low and back again in the course of a few hours. The questionnaires also revealed conflicts between the subjects and other family members. Although the subjects of the conflicts were usually trivial, they nevertheless concerned the teenagers deeply. As the authors noted,

> Asking a boy who has spent many days practicing a song on the guitar "Why are you playing that trash?" might not mean much to the father, but it can be a great blow to the son. The so-called "growth pains" of adolescence are no less real just because their causes appear to be without much substance to adults. In fact, this is exactly what the conflict is all about: What is to be taken seriously? (Csikszentmihalyi and Larson, 1984, p. 140)

Interim Summary

Adolescence

Adolescence is the transitional stage between childhood and adulthood. Puberty is initiated by the hypothalamus, which causes the pituitary gland to secrete hormones that stimulate maturation of the reproductive system.

Puberty marks a significant transition, both physically and socially. Early maturity appears to be socially beneficial to boys, because early maturers are more likely to be perceived as leaders. The effects of early maturity in girls is mixed; although their advanced physical development may help them acquire some prestige, early-maturing girls are more likely to engage in norm-breaking behavior.

A focal point in adolescent development is the formation of an identity. Both Erikson and Marcia argue that adolescents face identity crises, the outcome of which determines the nature and level of identity that teenagers will form. Marcia argues that forming an identity has two primary components—

the crisis itself and the commitment or decision regarding a specific course of action after consideration of possible alternatives. The extent to which a teenager experiences a crisis and how he or she resolves it leads to different kinds of identity status: identity achievement, moratorium, foreclosure, or identity diffusion. An adolescent's identity may also be influenced by gender issues, such as females' greater tendency to desire to form close relationships with others.

The nature of friendship changes during adolescence. Girls seek out confidants rather than playmates, and boys join groups that provide mutual support in their quests to assert their independence. Sexuality becomes important and many people engage in sexual intercourse in their teens.

Although adolescence brings conflicts between parents and children, these conflicts tend to be centered on relatively minor issues. Most adolescents hold the same values and attitudes concerning important issues as their parents do. Mood swings during adolescence can be dramatic, but on the whole, teenagers report that they are generally happy and self-confident.

Thought Questions

- Every term, I ask my introductory psychology students for a show of hands to indicate who among them consider themselves to be adults. When I first started this practice, I thought that the vast majority of my students would raise their hands. Much to my surprise, though, fewer than 1 percent did (as is true of all my introductory students since then). When I ask them for an explanation, I always get the same answer: Those who see themselves as adults are *financially independent* from their parents; those who still see themselves as adolescents are not. Do you consider yourself to be an adult? For what reasons?

- What important behavioral effects did you experience as a result of your own sexual maturation? In what ways did your social and emotional lives change? How does your experience compare to those of your friends who underwent puberty before or after you did?

Adulthood and Old Age

It is much easier to outline child or adolescent development than adult development; children and adolescents change faster, and the changes are closely related to age. Adult development is much more variable because physical changes in adults are more gradual. Mental and emotional changes during adulthood are more closely related to individual experience than to age. Some people achieve success and satisfaction with their careers, while some hate their jobs. Some marry and have happy family lives, while others never adjust to the roles of spouse and parent. No single description of adult development will fit everyone.

Physical Development

As we grow older, there is one set of changes that we can count on—physical ones. Our physical abilities peak at around age thirty and decline gradually thereafter. By maintaining a well-balanced diet, exercising regularly, and not smoking, drinking, or using drugs, we can, in large measure, help our bodies maintain some of their physical vigor even into old age. This is not to say that good diet and exercise habits can make a seventy-year-old look and feel like a twenty-five-year-old. But if we don't eat well and exercise regularly, we will have less physical energy and poorer muscle tone than if we do. And apparently, staying in shape as a younger adult pays off in one's later years. Older people who were physically fit as younger adults are generally in better health and feel better about themselves than do those who are not (Perlmutter and Hall, 1985).

Unfortunately, though, prudent diets and exercising are not panaceas for the physical changes that accompany aging. People in their later forties, fifties, and sixties often experience decreases in visual acuity and the ability to perceive depth, hearing, sensitivity to odors and flavors, reaction time, agility, physical mobility, and physical strength.

Some interesting research conducted by Daniel Rudman has shown that there may be a way of halting, if not reversing, the physical effects of aging (Rudman, cited in Darrach, 1992). He persuaded twenty-one elderly men to volunteer for a study in which half of them would be injected with human growth hormone (three times a week for six months) and the other half would just receive monthly health checkups. Males who received the hormone injections had a 10 percent increase in muscle mass, a 9 percent increase in skin thickness, sizable increases in the masses of the liver and spleen, and a 14 percent decrease of their body fat. Over the same time period, males in the control group showed decreases in muscle, bone, and organ mass. These results suggests that rate at which most people age is susceptible to manipulation, a positive sign that it can be slowed down.

Muscular strength peaks during the late twenties or early thirties and then declines slowly thereafter as muscle tissue gradually deteriorates. By age seventy, strength has declined by approximately 30 percent in both men and women (Young, Stokes, and Crowe, 1984). However, age has much less effect on *endurance* than on strength. Both laboratory tests and athletic records reveal that older people who remain physically fit show remarkably little decline in the ability to exercise for extended periods of time (Spirduso and MacRae, 1990).

Although it is easy to measure a decline in the sensory systems (such as vision or hearing), older people often show very little *functional* change in these systems. Most of them learn to make adjustments for their sensory losses, using ad-

ditional cues to help them decode sensory information. For example, people with a hearing loss can learn to attend more carefully to other people's gestures and lip movements; they can also profitably use their experience to infer what is said.

Functional changes with age are also minimal in highly developed skills. For example, Salthouse (1984, 1988) found that experienced older typists continued to perform as well as younger ones, despite the fact that they performed less well on standard laboratory tests of sensory and motor skills, including the types of skills that one would expect to be important in typing. The continuous practice they received enabled them to develop strategies to compensate for their physical decline. For example, they tended to read farther ahead in the text they were typing, which enabled them to plan in advance the patterns of finger movements they would have to make.

Loss of physical ability during adulthood can be minimized by following a program of regular exercise. The best results are obtained when people both exercise regularly and eat a low-fat, high-fiber diet.

With regular exercise and a flexible attitude, individuals can accommodate their interests and activities to the inevitable changes in physical abilities brought by aging. There is no reason why a reasonably healthy person of *any* age should stop enjoying life because of physical limitations.

Cognitive Development

Psychologists have studied the effects of education and experience on intellectual abilities and have questioned whether intelligence inevitably declines with age. Most of us can conceive of a future when we can no longer run as fast as we do now or perform well in a strenuous sport, but we do not like to think of being outperformed intellectually by younger people. And, in fact, research indicates that people can get old without losing their intellectual skills.

Cognitive Development and Brain Disease

Before I discuss the normal effects of aging in a healthy individual, I should discuss some changes caused by disease. As people get older, they have a greater risk of developing senile or presenile dementia—a class of diseases characterized by the progressive loss of cortical tissue and a corresponding loss of mental functions. (*Senile* means "old"; *dementia* literally means "an undoing of the mind.") The distinction between senile and presenile dementia is not important, because the disease process is the same in both cases. The most prevalent form of dementia is Alzheimer's disease, which occurs in approximately 5 percent of the population above the age of sixty-five. **Alzheimer's disease** is characterized by progressive loss of memory and other mental functions. At first, the patient may have difficulty remembering appointments and sometimes fail to think of words or people's names. As time passes, he or she shows increasing confusion and increasing difficulty with tasks such as balancing a checkbook. In the early stages of the disease, memory deficit involves recent events; but as the disease progresses, even old memories are affected. If the person ventures outside alone, he or she is likely to get lost. Eventually, the person becomes bedridden, becomes completely helpless, and, finally, dies (Terry and Davies, 1980; Khachaturian and Blass, 1992).

Geneticists have discovered that defects in the twenty-first chromosome cause at least one kind of Alzheimer's disease, which seems to reduce levels of brain acetylcholine (Gottfries, 1985; Selkoe, 1989). Alzheimer's disease produces severe degeneration of the hippocampus and cerebral cortex, especially the association cortex of the frontal and temporal lobes. Figure 12.11 shows a computer-enhanced photograph of a slice through a normal brain (right) and the brain of a patient who died of Alzheimer's disease (left). You can see that much of the tissue of the Alzheimer's brain has been lost; the grooves in the brain (sulci and fissures) are much wider. (See *Figure 12.11*.)

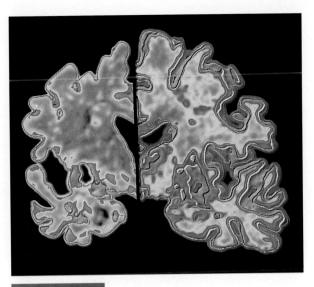

Figure 12.11

Alzheimer's disease. A computer-enhanced photograph of a slice through the brain of a person who died of Alzheimer's disease (left) and a normal brain (right). Note that the grooves (sulci and fissures) are especially wide in the Alzheimer's brain, indicating degeneration of the brain.

An even more common cause of mental deterioration in old age is depression, a psychological disorder. Some people find old age an unpleasant condition: They are declining physically, they no longer have jobs or family-related activities that confirm their usefulness to other people, and many old friends have died, are infirm, or have moved away. With this sense of loss or deprivation, some older people become depressed; they lose their appetite for food and for living in general, have trouble concentrating, and suffer losses in memory. Too often these symptoms of depression are diagnosed as dementia. Yet unlike dementia, depression is treatable with psychotherapy and drugs, as we will see in Chapters 17 and 18.

Cognitive Development and Normal Aging

Studies have shown clearly that aging affects different intellectual abilities to different degrees. Schaie (1990), describing the results of the Seattle Longitudinal Study, reports that on average, people's scores on five tests of intellectual abilities showed an increase until their late thirties or early forties, then a period of stability until their mid-fifties or early sixties, followed by a gradual decline. However, the decline was not uniform for all abilities. Figure 12.12 shows the percent-

Alzheimer's disease A fatal degenerative disease in which neurons of the brain progressively die, causing loss of memory and other cognitive processes.

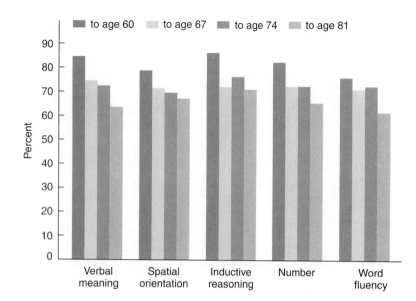

Figure 12.12

Results from the Seattle Longitudinal Study of Aging. Percentage of subjects of various age groups who maintained stable levels of performance on each of five tests of intellectual ability over a seven-year period.

(From Schaie, K.W. In Handbook of the Psychology of Aging, *3rd ed., edited by J.E. Birren and K.W. Schaie. San Diego: Academic Press, 1990. Reprinted by permission.)*

age of subjects who maintained stable levels of performance on each of the tests over a seven-year period. As you can see, the performance of most of the subjects—even the oldest—remained stable. (See *Figure 12.12.*)

In a twenty-one-year longitudinal study of changes in adult memory, Schaie (1980) investigated subjects' ability to recognize and recall words. He found that adult subjects' ability to *recognize* words actually increased slightly up to about age sixty and declined slightly thereafter. (See *Figure 12.13.*) (Note, too, that females at all ages outperformed males at word recognition.) In contrast, ability to *recall* words decreased at a moderate pace from age twenty-five onward. Schaie has suggested that older people benefit more from retrieval cues found in recognition tasks than do younger people (Schaie and Willis, 1991).

More recent research by Kirasic (1991) has shown that, at least for performance on spatial tasks, deficits in short-term memory may coincide with aging. For example, Kirasic and Bernicki (1990) showed young and older adults sixty-six slides of a walk through a real neighborhood. Sometimes the slides were in the correct order; at other times, they were mixed up. All subjects were then asked to make distance estimates between some of the scenes shown in the slides.

Both younger and older subjects performed equally well in estimating distances for the slides presented in logical order. But older subjects performed less well than younger subjects when the slides were scrambled. Kirasic and Bernick concluded that information from the slides presented in normal order was encoded into short-term memory similarly for both sets of subjects. However, the scrambled presentation of slides taxed available resources in the older subjects' short-term memory, resulting in performance decline.

If memory shows wear with age, one might reasonably suspect that intelligence, too, would show a similar decline. This was once thought to be true based on results from cross-

sectional studies (studies that compare different age groups on the same task). However, we now know that this is not the case, largely due to the work of Schaie and Strother (1968), who compared results from a cross-sectional approach with results from a longitudinal approach (a study in which a

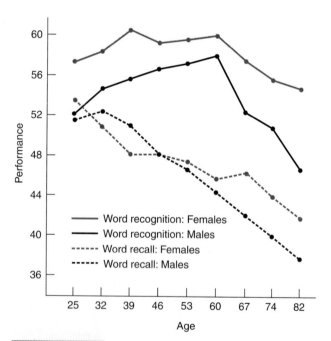

Figure 12.13

Changes in adult ability to recognize words and to recall them over time. With age, the ability to recall words declined faster than did word recognition.

(Based on Schaie, K.W. Cognitive development in aging. In Language and Communication, *edited by L.K. Obler and M.L. Albert. New York: D.C. Heath, 1980.)*

group of subjects is followed over some time period in order to identify developmental changes that occur over time). For example, look at Figure 12.14, which shows performance on a verbal abilities subsection of an intelligence test plotted as a function of age. (Here verbal abilities means the ability to understand ideas represented by words.) The cross-sectional data show that intelligence scores decrease—and rather precipitously so—after age fifty. The longitudinal data paint a different picture: Scores increase until about age fifty-five and then decline gradually. (See *Figure 12.14.*)

What accounts for these differences? Cross-sectional studies do not take into account the fact that the people being tested are not the same age and were reared in different time periods. Thus, one explanation for these disparate results is that older people did not have the same educational and career opportunities as their younger counterparts taking the test may have had. The longitudinal method takes this possibility into consideration by testing the same people at regular intervals spanning many years. In doing so, it gives a more accurate picture of the relationship between age and intelligence.

As we saw in Chapter 11, many investigators believe that intelligence can be divided into two broad categories. In general, older people in good health do well on tests of *crystallized intelligence*—abilities that depend on knowledge and experience, the "seat of the pants" learning that comes from everyday life. Vocabulary, the ability to see similarities between objects and situations, and general information are all aspects of crystallized intelligence. On the other hand, *fluid intelligence*—the capacity for abstract reasoning—appears to decline with age (Baltes and Schaie, 1974; Horn, 1982). The ability to solve puzzles, to memorize a series of arbitrary items such as unrelated words or letters, to classify figures into categories, and to change problem-solving strategies easily and flexibly are aspects of fluid intelligence.

The fact that older people excel in crystallized intelligence and younger people excel in fluid intelligence is reflected in the kinds of intellectual endeavors for which the two age groups seem to be best suited. For example, great mathematicians usually make their most important contributions during their twenties or early thirties; apparently the ability to break out of the traditional ways of thinking and to conceive new strategies is crucial in such achievements. In contrast, great contributions to literature and philosophy, in which success depends heavily on knowledge and experience, tend to be made by older people.

Another aspect of intellectual ability is speed. Older people have difficulty responding and performing quickly. When time pressures prevail, their performance is worse than that of younger people. However, when time requirements are relaxed, the performance of older people improves much more than does that of younger people (Arenberg, 1973; Botwinick and Storandt, 1974).

Part of the age-related decline in speed can be attributed to deterioration in sensory functions and to difficulty in changing strategies to meet new demands. But another im-

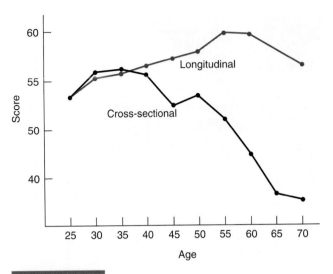

Figure 12.14

A comparison of cross-sectional and longitudinal data concerning changes in verbal ability with age. In contrast to the cross-sectional data, the longitudinal data show that verbal ability increased gradually to about age fifty-five and then decreased gradually.

(Based on Schaie, K.W. and Strother, C.R. A cross-sequential study of age changes in cognitive behavior, Psychological Bulletin, *1968, 70, p. 675.)*

portant reason for decreased speed is caution; older people appear to be less willing to make mistakes. In some endeavors, this caution is valuable. In fact, many societies reserve important decision-making functions for older people because they are less likely to act hastily. A study by Leech and Witte (1971) illustrates the effect of caution on performance. The investigators found that older people who were paid for each response they made—correct or incorrect—learned lists of pairs of words faster than did older people who were paid only for correct responses. The payment for incorrect responses increased their willingness to make a mistake, and this relaxation of their normal caution paid off in an increased speed of learning.

Social Development

Recall that Erikson believed that the adult years consist of three psychosocial stages: intimacy versus isolation, during which people succeed or fail in loving others; generativity versus stagnation, during which people either withdraw inwardly and focus on their problems or reach out to help others; and integrity versus despair, during which life is reviewed with either a sense of satisfaction or with despair.

Another attempt to understand stages of adult development is that of Daniel Levinson (Levinson et al., 1978). Levinson and his colleagues interviewed forty men—busi-

The culture in which one is raised exercises a profound influence on the kinds of social activities that one values and participates in as an adult.

ness executives, blue-collar workers, novelists, and biologists—and analyzed the biographies of famous men and examined stories of men's lives as portrayed in literature. They claimed to have discovered a pattern common to most men's lives. Instead of proceeding smoothly, their lives were characterized by several years of stability punctuated by crises. The crises were periods during which the men began to question their *life structures*: their occupations, their relations with their families, their religious beliefs and practices, their ethnic identities, and the ways they spent their leisure time. During times of transition—which caused considerable anxiety and turmoil—the men reevaluated the choices they had made and eventually settled on new patterns that guided them through another period of stability. Periods of transition lasted around four or five years, whereas the intervening periods of stability lasted six or seven years.

For Levinson, the most important crises occur early in adulthood, when choices must be made about career and marriage, and at mid-life (during the early to mid-forties), when realities about one's life structure must finally be faced. Although Levinson did not invent the notion of the mid-life crisis, he certainly helped bring it to the attention of the general public and helped make the term a part of everyone's vocabulary. Levinson concluded that the mid-life crisis happened to all men. Men whose life structures do not yet meet their prior goals and expectations realize that the future will probably not bring the success that up until then has eluded them. Men who *have* succeeded begin to question whether the goals they had set for themselves were meaningful and worthwhile. All men, successful or not, also begin to confront

the fact that they are getting older. They are starting to detect some signs of physical decline, and they are witnesses to the death of their parents or their parents' friends.

Several investigators have defined objective criteria for the presence of a mid-life crisis and have looked for its presence in representative samples of subjects. For example, Costa and McCrae (1980) administered a *Midlife Crisis Scale* to a total of 548 men aged 35 to 79 years. The scale contained items asking whether the subjects were experiencing any of the symptoms of a mid-life crisis, such as dissatisfaction with job and family, a sense of meaninglessness, or a feeling of turmoil. They found no evidence for a mid-life crisis. Some people did report some of the symptoms, but they were no more likely to occur during the early- to mid-forties than at any other age. A study of sixty women (Reinke, Holmes, and Harris, 1985) also found no evidence of a mid-life crisis. This finding does not mean that middle-aged people do not periodically contemplate or question the important issues in their lives; of course they do. But there appears to be no crisis—in the dramatic sense—to these reflective periods.

Adult development occurs against the backdrop of what many developmental psychologists consider to be the two most important aspects of life: love and work. For most of us, falling in love is more than just a compelling feeling of wanting to be with someone. It often brings with it major responsibilities, such as marriage and children. Work, too, is more than just a way to pass time. It involves setting and achieving goals related to income, status among peers, and accomplishments outside the family. For most adults, overall satisfaction with life reflects the degree to which they have been successful in marriage, raising a family, and achieving goals. With this in mind, let's look briefly at how love and work ebb and flow over the course of adult development.

Marriage and Family

For 95 percent of adults under forty falling in love with someone results in marriage. Newlyweds are generally happy with their marriages and seem to become happier when children enter the picture (Rollins and Feldman, 1970). However, as children begin to demand more of their parents' time and emotional resources, couples report increasing unhappiness in marriage. Generally speaking, mothers assume more responsibilities than fathers for the day-to-day care of children (Biernat and Wortman, 1991). As a result, they spend more time doing housework and less time talking to their husbands (Peskin, 1982), which can place strain on their marital happiness. However, if husband and wife can find time together in the evenings, and if the husband is able share in the parenting and household chores, the stress of adapting to family life is lessened considerably (Daniels and Weingarten, 1982).

As children grow older and become more self-sufficient in caring for themselves, the day-to-day burdens of raising a family taper off and husbands and wives are able to spend more time with each other. However, adolescents pose new problems for their parents: They may question parental authority, and their burgeoning social agenda may put a wrinkle in their parents' personal and social calendars. For many parents, rearing adolescents, particularly during the time just prior to their leaving home, represents the low point of marital happiness (Cavanaugh, 1990).

Generally speaking, once a family's youngest child has left home, marital happiness increases and continues to do so through the remainder of the couple's life together. It was once thought that the "empty nest" posed problems for the middle-aged couple, particularly for the mother, who was thought to define her role solely around her children. Although parents may miss daily contact with their children, they also feel happy (not to mention relieved) that a major responsibility of life—raising self-reliant children who become responsible members of society—has been completed successfully. Just as importantly, the parents now have time for each other and freedom to pursue their own interests. It may true that an empty nest is a happy nest. Research tends to support this statement. In one study, only 6 percent of empty nest couples reported that life prior to their last child leaving home was better than their empty nest experience. Over 50 percent of the couples interviewed said that their lives were better now than before their children had left home (Deutscher, 1968; Neugarten, 1974).

Work

The task of raising a family is balanced with one or both parents having a career. In fact, events that occur in the workplace often affect the quality of home life. A promotion and a raise can mean that the family can now do things that they couldn't before—they can now pursue a new hobby or travel together. Working long hours to get that raise, however, can decrease the amount of time that a couple can spend together with their children.

With the dramatic increase in the number of women entering the work force in the past twenty-five years, many psychologists have focused their research efforts on understanding *dual-earner marriages*—those in which both parents work full- or part-time. Compared to single-earner marriages, dual-earner families generally have a better standard of living in terms of material possessions and saving money for their children's college education and for retirement. Another important benefit accrues, especially to the wife: She is able to achieve recognition and independence outside the home (Crosby, 1991). Most husbands in dual-earner marriages support their wives' working. In addition, they find their wives more interesting, more essential, and more helpful mates (Schaie and Willis, 1992).

But all is not bliss in dual-earner marriages. If both partners are working, who manages the household and takes care of the children? In most cases, the woman still does, which often means that she has two roles, one as mother and one as wage earner. Apparently, a husband's support of his wife's working does not always go as far as actually pitching in at home. However, husbands who believe strongly in equality for women are likely to help out at home (Bird, Bird, and Scruggs, 1984).

Death

Death is the final event of life. It is a biological and social event—family and friends are emotionally affected by the death of a loved one. Although a death may claim a life at any time, most people die when they are old. One question that developmental psychologists have asked about death and dying among the elderly is, How do old people view the inevitability of their own deaths?

At one time or another, most of us contemplate our own deaths. Some of us may contemplate death more than others, but, to be sure, the thought of death crosses our minds at least occasionally. As you might expect, elderly people contemplate their deaths more often than do younger people. Generally speaking, they fear deaths less than their younger counterparts do (Kalish, 1976). Why? No one knows for sure, but a tentative explanation may be that older people have had more time to review the past and to plan for the future knowing that death is close at hand. Thus, they are able to prepare themselves psychologically (and financially) for death.

Contemplating and preparing for death, though, is not like knowing that you are actually dying. The changes in attitude that terminally ill people experience have been studied by Kübler–Ross (1969, 1981). After interviewing hundreds of dying people, she concluded that people undergo five distinct phases of psychologically coping with death. The first stage is *denial*. When terminally ill people learn of their condition, they generally try to deny it. *Anger* comes next—now they resent the certainty of death. In the third stage, *bargaining*, people attempt to negotiate their fate with God or others, pleading that their lives might be spared. While bargaining, they actually realize that they are, in fact, going to die. This leads to *depression*, the fourth stage, which is characterized by a sense of hopelessness and loss. The fifth and final stage, *acceptance*, is marked by a more peaceful resignation to the facts.

Kübler-Ross's work points up the psychological factors involved in dying and has provided an initial theory about how the dying come to grips with their fate. Her work, though, has not been accepted uncritically. Her research was not scientific—her method for interviewing people was not systematic, and her results are largely anecdotal. Moreover, of the five stages, denial is the only one that appears to be universal. Apparently, not all terminally ill people have the same psychological response to the fact that they are dying.

However, despite its flaws, Kübler-Ross's work is important because it has prompted an awareness, both scientific and public, of the plight of the terminally ill. The scientific response, as you might guess, has been to do more medical research in the hope of prolonging the lives of people with cancer and other terminal illnesses. The public response has involved the attempt to provide support for the dying and their families through *hospice* services (Aiken, 1994). In the past, hospices were places where strangers and pilgrims could find rest and shelter. Today, hospices are special places that provide medical and psychological support for the dying and their families. In cases in which the dying person wishes to die at home, hospice volunteers work in that setting. The primary functions of hospice services are twofold: to provide relief from pain and to allow the person to die with dignity. No attempt is made to prolong life through technology if doing so would diminish the self-respect of the dying person and his or her family. To die with dignity is perhaps the best death possible—for together, the dying and his or her loved ones are able to experience, for the last time together, reverence for the life experience.

Interim Summary

Adult Development

Up to the time of young adulthood, human development can reasonably be described as a series of stages: a regular sequence of changes that occur in most members of our species. However, development in adulthood is much more variable and few generalizations apply. Aging brings with it a gradual deterioration in people's sensory capacities and changes in physical appearance that many people regard as unattractive. The effects of these changes can be minimized by vigorous participation in life's activities.

Although older people are more likely to develop dementing illnesses such as Alzheimer's disease, severe intellectual deterioration is often caused by depression, which can usually be treated successfully. Rather than undergoing sudden intellectual deterioration, older people are more likely to exhibit gradual changes, especially in abilities that require flexibility and learning new behaviors. Intellectual abilities that depend heavily on crystallized intelligence—an accumulated body of knowledge—are much less likely to decline than are those based on fluid intelligence—the capacity for abstract reasoning.

Erikson and Levinson have both proposed that people encounter a series of crises that serve as turning points in development. Erikson's stages span the entire life cycle, from infancy to old age, whereas Levinson's stages concentrate on mid-life development. There appears to be no evidence that supports the idea that people experience a mid-life crisis. Adult social development occurs within the context of love, marriage, family, and work. Marriages seem to be happiest just after the birth of children and after the children have left home. It appears to be unhappiest just before the children leave home—possibly due to the emotional and time demands that adolescents place on their parents. Many families have parents who both work, which helps ease the financial burdens of raising a family and long-term financial obligations. And although the woman who works gains respect outside the home, she is often faced with also having to manage most of the household responsibilities.

Older people have less fear of death than younger people have, perhaps because they have had more time to contemplate and prepare for it. Kübler–Ross's interviews with terminally ill people have revealed that many of them seem to experience a five-stage process in facing the reality that they are, in fact, going to die. Although her research has been found to have some methodological flaws, it has drawn both scientific and public attention to the plight of the terminally ill and the necessity of properly caring for them.

Thought Questions

- Suppose that you have just been hired to direct a community mental health program for adults. The focus of this program is on prevention—minimizing the negative effects of the aging process on adults who participate in the program. Your first task is to design a comprehensive plan to maximize adults' physical, social, emotional, and intellectual capacities. What activities would you include in such a plan and why?

- How would you devise your own personal plan to grow old gracefully? What kinds of things would you include? What sorts of activities would you need to do in order to make the most of your physical and mental abilities?

Suggestions for Further Reading

Steinberg, L., and Belsky, J. *Infancy, Childhood, and Adolescence: Development in Context.* New York: McGraw-Hill, 1991.

Berk, L. E. *Infants, Children, and Adolescents.* Boston: Allyn and Bacon, 1993.

These two texts present excellent overviews of research and theory in the fields of infant, childhood, and adolescent development.

Schaie, W. K., and Willis, S. L. *Adult Development and Learning*, 3rd. ed. New York: HarperCollins, 1992.

A well-written and thorough introduction to the major issues involved in studying adult development.

Hoyenga, K. B., and Hoyenga, K. T. *Gender-Related Differences: Origins and Outcomes.* Boston: Allyn and Bacon, 1993.

This book examines gender differences from evolutionary, physiological, and cultural perspectives.

Harwood, R. L., Miller, J. G., and Irizarry, N. L. *Culture and Attachment: Perceptions of the Child in Context.* New York: Guilford, 1995.

As its title implies, this book considers cultural variables that influence the development of attachment between infants and their caregivers, including socioeconomic status, perceptions of different attachment behaviors, and perceptions of children themselves.

Chapter 13

Motivation
and Emotion

Chapter Outline

What Is Motivation?

Biological Needs • Physiology of Reinforcement • Optimum-Level Theory • Perseverance

Motivation refers to a group of phenomena that affect the nature, strength, and persistence of an individual's behavior. One important category of motivated behaviors involves internal regulation—the maintenance of homeostasis. Motivation is closely related to the processes of reinforcement and punishment. All reinforcing stimuli (including addictive drugs) appear to cause the release of dopamine in the brain. The optimum-level theory suggests that we are motivated to approach stimuli that bring our level of arousal closer to its optimum level. Self-produced conditioned reinforcers and experience with intermittent reinforcement affect an individual's perseverance.

Eating

What Starts a Meal? • What Stops a Meal? • Obesity • Anorexia Nervosa

Eating is caused by both social and physiological factors. The most important physiological factor is the detection of a fall in the level of nutrients available in the blood. Short-term control of eating involves detectors in the stomach that monitor the level of nutrients received during a meal. Long-term control appears to involve a chemical released by overnourished fat cells. Both genetic and environmental factors are responsible for obesity. Anorexia nervosa is a serious, often life–threatening disorder whose causes are not well understood.

Sexual Behavior

Effects of Sex Hormones on Behavior • Sexual Orientation

Hormones play an important role in motivating sexual behavior. Sex hormones have organizational effects that affect prenatal development and activational effects in adulthood. Although testosterone is the most important male sex hormone, it stimulates sexual desire in both men and women. The development of sexual orientation appears to have biological roots, both hormonal and genetic.

Aggressive Behavior

Ethological Studies of Aggression • Hormones and Aggression • Environmental Variables That Affect Human Aggression

Ethological studies show that aggression serves useful purposes in most species of animals. In males of most species, male sex hormones have both organizational and activational effects on aggressive behavior. Field

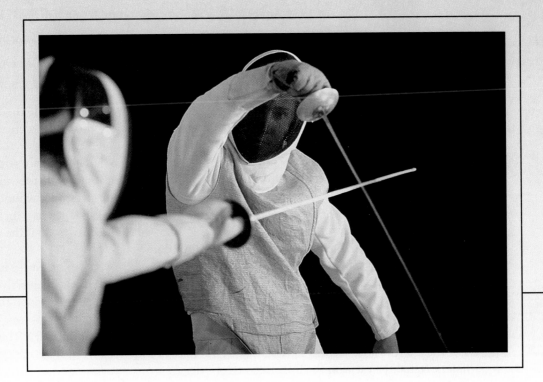

studies suggest that violence in the mass media may promote aggression, but these studies are not yet conclusive.

The Nature of Emotion

Emotions as Response Patterns • Social Judgments: Role of the Orbitofrontal Cortex • Measuring Emotional Responses: Lie Detection in Criminal Investigation

An emotion is a particular pattern of behaviors, physiological responses, and feelings evoked by a situation that has motivational relevance. Emotional response patterns have three components: behavioral, autonomic, and hormonal. Prefrontal lobotomies decrease people's emotional reactions by disconnecting the orbitofrontal cortex from the rest of the brain. This region is involved in social judgments and emotional reactions. Polygraphic lie detection attempts to identify emotional reactions associated with deception, but studies show that the technique gives unreliable results.

Expression and Recognition of Emotions

The Social Nature of Emotional Expressions in Humans • Situations That Produce Emotions: The Role of Cognition • *Biology and Culture: Are Emotional Expressions Innate?*

Expressions of emotion are largely innate social behaviors that communicate important information between individuals. Although emotional reactions are automatic responses that are seen in many species, cognition plays an important role in recognition of emotion-inducing situations. Cross-cultural studies show that people in all cultures show similar facial expressions, although cultural rules determine under what circumstances people should let their feelings show.

Feelings of Emotion

The James-Lange Theory • Effects of Spinal Cord Damage • *Evaluating Scientific Issues: Is Cognition Essential for Emotion?*

According to the James-Lange theory, feelings of emotion are caused by feedback from the body when a situation causes an emotional reaction. This feedback comes from behaviors and from responses controlled by the autonomic nervous system. The effects of spinal cord injury on feelings of emotion tend to support the James-Lange theory.

*I*n 1954, James Olds, a young assistant professor, designed an experiment to determine whether the reticular formation (located in the back part of the brain stem) might play a role in learning. Olds decided to place a small wire in the brains of rats in order to stimulate the reticular formation with electricity. Perhaps the stimulation would facilitate their learning of a maze. If the stimulated animals learned the task faster than those that were not stimulated, his hypothesis would have strong support.

Olds enlisted the aid of Peter Milner, a graduate student who had experience with the surgical procedure needed to implant the electrodes in the brain. Because the procedure had only recently been developed and was not very accurate, one of the electrodes wound up in the wrong place—near the opposite end of the brain, in fact. This accident was a lucky one, because Olds and Milner discovered a phenomenon they would not have seen if the electrode had been located where they had intended it to be.

Olds and Milner had heard a talk by another physiological psychologist, Neal Miller, who had discovered that electrical stimulation of some parts of the brain could be aversive. Animals would work to avoid having the current turned on. The investigators decided that before they began their study, they would make sure that aversive stimulation was not occurring, because it might interfere with the animals' performance in the maze. The behavior of most of the animals was unremarkable, but here is Olds's report of what happened when he tested the rat with the misplaced electrode:

> I applied a brief train of 60-cycle sine-wave electrical current whenever the animal entered one corner of the enclosure. The animal did not stay away from that corner, but rather came back quickly . . . By the time the third electrical stimulus had been applied the animal seemed indubitably to be "coming back for more." (Olds, 1973, p. 81)

Realizing that they had just seen something very important, Olds and Milner put more electrodes in rats' brains and allowed the rats to press a switch that controlled the current to the brain. The rats quickly learned to press the switch at a rate of over seven hundred times per hour. It turned out that the reinforcing effect of the electrical brain stimulation was very potent; when given a choice between pressing the lever and eating, drinking, or copulating, animals would choose the lever.

Olds and Milner's discovery probably had more impact on psychology than any other experiment performed by physiological psychologists. Articles in the popular press speculated on the nature of the "pleasure centers" in the brain. And some writers warned that a totalitarian society might someday control its population by putting electrodes in people's brains. Such speculations prompted Eliot Valenstein to write a book demystifying the phenomenon, putting it in perspective (Valenstein, 1973).

The interest in reinforcing brain stimulation has peaked, but because the circuits discovered by Olds and Milner are responsible for the powerful addictive potential of drugs such as cocaine, the research they began is still continuing. Many investigators are trying to understand the function these circuits play and how they relate to the effects of addictive drugs and the effectiveness of natural reinforcers. (By the way, it turns out that electrical stimulation of the reticular formation does *not* facilitate learning, but that is another story.)

When we investigate the causes of human behavior, we immediately encounter inconsistency. In a given situation, different people act differently, and even a single individual acts differently at different times. There are many reasons for inconsistent behavior. A person eats or does not eat, depending on how recent his or her last meal was and how tasty the available food is. A person who usually picks up hitchhikers does not do so if he learns that a convict has just escaped from a nearby penitentiary. A person who likes to play tennis will probably turn down a game if she is suffering from a severe headache.

All these reasons for inconsistent behavior are aspects of *motivation* (derived from a Latin word meaning "to move"). Of course, once the reasons are known, the behaviors are no longer considered "inconsistent." In common usage, motivation refers to a driving force that moves us to a particular action. More formally, **motivation** is a general term for a group of phenomena that affect the *nature* of an individual's behavior, the *strength* of the behavior, and the *persistence* of the behavior.

Motivation includes two types of phenomena. First, stimuli that were previously associated with pleasant or unpleasant events motivate approach or avoidance behaviors. For example, if something reminds you of an interesting person you met recently, you may try to meet that person again by consulting a telephone directory and making a telephone call. Second, being deprived of a particular reinforcer increases an organism's preference for a particular behavior. Besides obvious reinforcers such as food or water, this category includes more subtle ones. For example, after spending a lot of time performing routine tasks, we become motivated to go for a walk or meet with friends.

The first part of this chapter describes the nature of motivation and its relation to reinforcement. There are many approaches to motivation: physiological, behavioral, cognitive, and social. The emphasis here is on behavioral and physiological aspects of motivation—the external stimuli and internal changes that affect a person's behavior. Motivation affects all categories of behavior, so a complete discussion of motivation would have to consider everything we do. Rather than say too little about too many things, the first part of this chapter considers three important categories of motivated behaviors: eating, sexual behavior, and aggression. These behaviors are particularly important to the survival of the individual and of the species. The discussion of motivation will not end with this chapter. As you will see, motivation plays an especially important role in social behavior; thus, I will discuss some topics dealing with social motivation in Chapter 15.

The second part of this chapter describes research on emotion. Motivation and emotion are often discussed together and in that order. There is a good reason for this pairing. Our behavior is motivated by situations that we tend to approach or to avoid—situations that are important to us. Besides motivating us to do something, these situations evoke behaviors that other people can recognize, including facial expressions, changes in posture, and alterations in tone of voice. They also affect how we *feel*. In other words, situations that motivate our behavior also provoke emotions.

What Is Motivation?

Motivation cannot be separated from reinforcement and punishment. We are motivated to perform a behavior to gain (or avoid losing) a reinforcer or to avoid (or escape from) a punisher. Some reinforcers and punishers, such as food or pain, are obvious; others, such as smiles or frowns, are subtle. This section describes the attempts psychologists have made to identify the nature of reinforcement and to relate the process of reinforcement to motivation.

Biological Needs

Biological needs can be very potent motivators; starving people have killed others for food. And you can undoubtedly imagine how hard you would struggle to breathe if something obstructed your windpipe. To survive, we all need air, food, water, various vitamins and minerals, and protection from extremes in temperature. Complex organisms possess physiological mechanisms that detect deficits or imbalances associated with these needs and **regulatory behaviors** that bring physiological conditions back to normal. Examples of regulatory behaviors include eating, drinking, hunting, shivering, building a fire, and putting on a warm coat. This process of detection and correction, which maintains physiological systems at their optimum value, is called **homeostasis** ("stable state"). Deficits or imbalances motivate us because they cause us to perform the appropriate regulatory behaviors.

A regulatory system has four essential features: the **system variable** (the characteristic to be regulated), a **set point** (the optimum value of the system variable), a **detector** that monitors the value of the system variable, and a **correctional mechanism** that restores the system variable to the set point. A simple example of such a regulatory system is a room whose temperature is regulated by a thermostatically controlled heater. The system variable is the air temperature of the room,

motivation A general term for a group of phenomena that affect the nature, strength, or persistence of an individual's behavior.

regulatory behavior A behavior that tends to bring physiological conditions back to normal, thus restoring the condition of homeostasis.

homeostasis The process by which important physiological characteristics (such as body temperature and blood pressure) are regulated so that they remain at their optimum level.

system variable The variable controlled by a regulatory mechanism; for example, temperature in a heating system.

set point The optimum value of the system variable in a regulatory mechanism. The set point for human body temperature, recorded orally, is approximately 98.6°F.

detector In a regulatory process, a mechanism that signals when the system variable deviates from its set point.

correctional mechanism In a regulatory process, the mechanism that is capable of restoring the system variable to the set point.

and the detector for this variable is a thermostat. The thermostat can be adjusted so that contacts of a switch will close when the temperature falls below a preset value (the set point). Closure of the contacts turns on the correctional mechanism— the coils of the heater. (See *Figure 13.1*.)

If the room cools below the set point, the thermostat turns the heater on, which warms the room. The rise in room temperature causes the thermostat to turn the heater off. Because the activity of the correctional mechanism (heat production) feeds back to the thermostat and causes it to turn the heater off, this process is called **negative feedback**. Negative feedback is an essential characteristic of all regulatory systems.

The **drive reduction hypothesis** was the earliest attempt to explain the nature of motivation and reinforcement. This theory stated that biological needs, caused by deprivation of the necessities of life, are unpleasant. The physiological changes associated with, say, going without food for several hours produce an unpleasant state called *hunger*. Hunger serves as a **drive**, energizing an organism's behavior. The organism then engages in behaviors that in the past have obtained food. The act of eating reduces hunger, and this drive reduction is reinforcing. (See *Figure 13.2*.)

Not all drives are based on homeostasis—on biological needs like the ones for food and water. The most obvious example is the drive associated with sexual behavior. An individual can survive without sexual behavior; but the sex drive is certainly motivating, and sexual contact is certainly reinforcing. Similarly, most organisms placed in a featureless environment will soon become motivated to seek something new; they will work at a task that gives them a view of the world outside.

The drive reduction hypothesis of reinforcement has fallen into disfavor for two primary reasons. The first is that drive is almost always impossible to measure. For example, suppose you obtain pleasure from watching a set of color slides taken by a friend while on vacation. According to the drive reduction hypothesis, your "exploratory drive" or "curiosity drive" is high, and looking at vacation slides reduces it, providing reinforcement. Or consider a woman who very

much enjoys listening to music. What drive induces her to turn on her stereo system? What drive is reduced by this activity? There is no way to measure "drive" in either of these examples and confirm that it actually exists; thus, the hypothesis cannot be experimentally tested.

The second problem is that if we examine our own behavior, we find that most events we experience as reinforcing are also exciting, or drive *increasing*. The reason a roller coaster ride is fun is certainly not because it *reduces* drive. The same is true for skiing, surfing, or viewing a horror film. Likewise, an interesting, reinforcing conversation is one that is exciting, not one that puts you to sleep. And people who engage in prolonged foreplay and sexual intercourse do not view these activities as unpleasant because they are accompanied by such a high level of drive. In general, the experiences we really want to repeat (that is, the ones we find reinforcing) are those that increase, rather than decrease, our level of arousal.

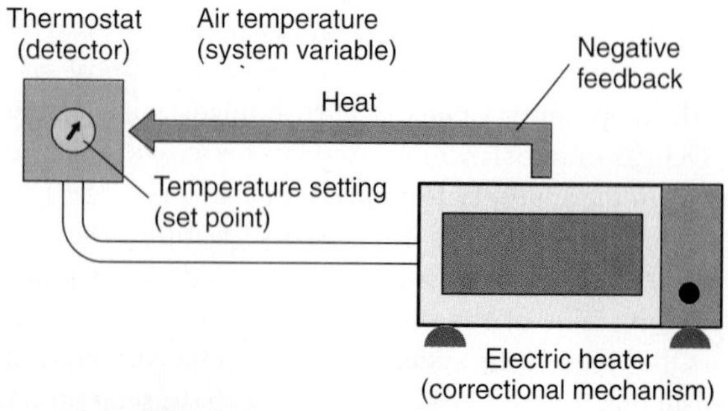

Physiology of Reinforcement

To understand the nature of reinforcement we must understand something about its physiological basis. As we saw in the opening vignette of this chapter, Olds and Milner discovered quite by accident that electrical stimulation of parts of the brain can reinforce an animal's behavior.

The neural circuits stimulated by the electricity are also responsible for the motivating effects of natural reinforcers such as food, water, or sexual contact, and of drugs such as heroin, alcohol, and cocaine. Almost all investigators believe that the electrical stimulation of the brain is reinforcing because it activates the same system that is activated by natural reinforcers and by drugs that people commonly abuse. The normal function of this system is to strengthen the connections between the neurons that detect the discriminative stimulus (such as the sight of a lever) and the neurons that produce the operant response (such as a lever press). The electrical brain stimulation activates this system directly. (See *Figure 13.3*.)

Researchers have discovered that an essential component of the reinforcement system consists of neurons that release dopamine as their transmitter substance. Thus, all reinforcing stimuli appear to trigger the release of dopamine in the

Thermostat (detector) Air temperature (system variable) Negative feedback

Heat

Temperature setting (set point)

Electric heater (correctional mechanism)

Figure 13.1

An example of a regulatory system.

negative feedback A process whereby the effect produced by an action serves to diminish or terminate that action. Regulatory systems are characterized by negative feedback loops.

drive reduction hypothesis The hypothesis that a drive (resulting from physiological need or deprivation) produces an unpleasant state that causes an organism to engage in motivated behaviors. Reduction of drive is assumed to be reinforcing.

drive A condition, often caused by physiological changes or homeostatic disequilibrium, that energizes an organism's behavior.

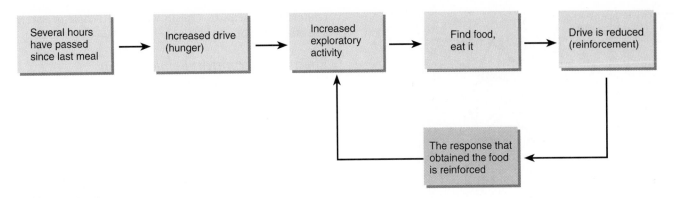

Figure 13.2

The drive reduction hypothesis of motivation and reinforcement.

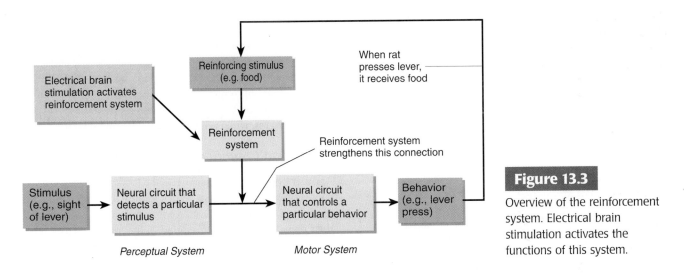

Figure 13.3

Overview of the reinforcement system. Electrical brain stimulation activates the functions of this system.

brain. For example, *Figure 13.4* illustrates the effects of sexually related stimuli and sexual activity on the release of dopamine in a part of the brain known to be associated with reinforcement.

Optimum-Level Theory

Although events that increase our level of arousal are often reinforcing, there are times when a person wants nothing more than some peace and quiet. In this case *avoidance* of exciting stimuli motivates our behavior. As we saw in Chapter 5, the removal (or avoidance) of an aversive stimulus produces *negative reinforcement*. In an attempt to find a common explanation for both positive and negative reinforcement, some psychologists have proposed the **optimum-level hypothesis** of reinforcement and punishment: When an individual's arousal level is too high, less stimulation is reinforcing; when

> **optimum-level hypothesis** The hypothesis that organisms will perform behavior that restores the level of arousal to an optimum level.

it is too low, more stimulation is desired (Berlyne, 1966; Hebb, 1955). Berlyne hypothesized two forms of exploration: *Diversive exploration* is a response to understimulation (boredom) that increases the diversity of the stimuli the organism tries to come in contact with; *specific exploration* is a response to overstimulation (usually because of a specific need, such as lack of food or water) that leads to the needed item, thereby decreasing the organism's drive level.

The hypothesis that organisms seek an optimum level of arousal is certainly plausible. Any kind of activity—even the most interesting and exciting one—eventually produces satiety; something that was once reinforcing becomes bothersome. (Even the most avid video game player eventually moves on to something else.) Presumably, participation in an exciting behavior gradually raises an organism's arousal above its optimum level. However, the logical problem that plagues the drive reduction hypothesis also applies to the optimum-level hypothesis. Because we cannot measure an organism's drive or arousal, we cannot say what its optimum level should be. Thus, the optimum-level hypothesis remains without much empirical support.

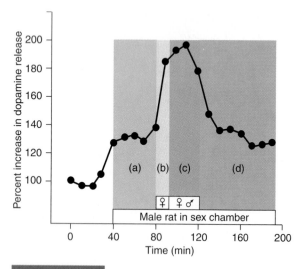

Figure 13.4

Release of dopamine produced by reinforcing stimuli. The graph indicates levels of dopamine in a region of a male rat's forebrain. (a) Rat is placed in apparatus in which it has mated before. (b) Receptive female is placed behind a wire-mesh partition. (c) Partition is removed; the animals copulate. (d) The female is removed.

Perseverance

Some people work hard even though the rewards for their work seem to occur very seldom; we refer to these people as well motivated. They exhibit **perseverance**. Their behavior shows persistence; they continue to perform even though their work is not regularly reinforced. Other people give up easily or perhaps never really try. Understanding the effects of

reinforcement helps us explain why some people persevere and others do not.

Effects of Intermittent Reinforcement

We saw in Chapter 5 that when an organism's behavior is no longer reinforced, the behavior eventually ceases, or extinguishes. If the behavior was previously reinforced every time it occurred, extinction is very rapid. However, if it was previously reinforced only intermittently, the behavior persists for a long time. Intermittent reinforcement leads to perseverance, even when the behavior is no longer reinforced.

Many human behaviors are reinforced on intermittent schedules that require the performance of long sequences of behaviors over long intervals of time. A person's previous experience with various schedules of reinforcement probably affects how long and how hard the person will work between occasions of reinforcement. If all attempts at a particular endeavor are reinforced (or if none are), the person is unlikely to pursue a long and difficult project that includes the endeavor. If we knew more about a person's previous history with various schedules of reinforcement, we would probably know more about his or her ability to persevere when the going gets difficult (that is, when reinforcements become scanty).

The Role of Conditioned Reinforcement

Another phenomenon that affects the tendency to persevere is conditioned reinforcement. When stimuli are associated with reinforcers, they eventually acquire reinforcing properties of their own. For example, the sound of the food dispenser reinforces the behavior of a rat being trained to press a lever.

Motivation is not merely a matter of wanting to do well and to work hard. It also involves the ability to be reinforced by the immediate products of the work being done. If a person has regularly been exposed to particular stimuli in association with reinforcers, that person's behavior can be reinforced by those stimuli. In addition, if the person has learned how to recognize self-produced stimuli as conditioned reinforcers, the performance of the behaviors that produce them will be "self–reinforcing." For example, you will recall the schoolgirl I mentioned in Chapter 5 who tirelessly practiced writing the letters of the alphabet. She did so because she had learned to recognize the letters and had previously been praised by her teacher (and perhaps by her parents, as well) for producing letters that looked the way they should. Thus, the production of properly formed letters provided a conditioned reinforcer, which kept her working. As you learned earlier, the usual name for this process is *satisfaction*.

Failure to Persist: Learned Helplessness

A large body of evidence suggests that organisms can learn that they are powerless to affect their own destinies. Maier

One meaning of motivation is perseverance—working steadily on projects that take much time and effort to complete.

perseverance The tendency to continue to perform a behavior even when it is not being reinforced.

and Seligman (1976) reported a series of experiments demonstrating that animals can learn that their own behavior has no effect on an environmental event. This result is exactly the opposite of what has been assumed to be the basis of learning. All the examples of learning and conditioning cited so far have been instances in which one event predicts the occurrence of another. **Learned helplessness** involves learning that an aversive event *cannot* be avoided or escaped.

Overmeier and Seligman (1967) conducted the basic experiment. They placed a dog in an apparatus in which it received electrical shocks that could not be avoided; nothing the animal did would prevent the shocks. Next, they placed the dog in another apparatus in which the animal received a series of trials in which a warning stimulus was followed by an electrical shock. In this case the animal could avoid the shocks simply by stepping over a small barrier to the other side of the apparatus. Dogs in the control group learned to step over the barrier and avoid the shock, but dogs that had previously received inescapable shocks in the other apparatus failed to learn. They just squatted in the corner and took the shock as if they had learned that it made no difference what they did. They had learned to be helpless.

Seligman (1975) has suggested that the phenomenon of learned helplessness has important implications for behavior. When people have experiences that lead to learned helplessness, they become depressed and their motivational level decreases. The change in motivation occurs because the helplessness training lowers their expectation that trying to perform a task will bring success. Seligman also suggested that learned helplessness has the characteristics of a personality trait; that is, people who have had major experiences with insolvable tasks will not try hard to succeed in other types of tasks, including ones they could otherwise have solved.

Seligman's theory of learned helplessness has been challenged by other investigators, who have explained the phenomenon in other ways. The issue is whether learning to be helpless in a particular situation generalizes only to similar situations or to a wide variety of them. For example, McReynolds (1980) observed that when people experience a situation in which reinforcements are not contingent on their responding, their responding extinguishes. If the situation then changes to one in which responding will be reinforced, the people will continue not to respond *unless they perceive that the schedule of reinforcement has changed.* The more similar the second situation is to the first, the more likely it is that the person will act helpless. This explanation describes the phenomenon of learned helplessness as a failure to discriminate between the condition under which responding is reinforced and the condition under which it is not. Further research will have to determine whether learned helplessness

is, as Seligman asserts, a stable personality trait or whether it can be explained by the principles of instrumental conditioning.

Interim Summary

What Is Motivation?

Motivation is a general term for a group of phenomena that affect the *nature, strength,* and *persistence* of an individual's behavior. It includes a tendency to perform behaviors that bring an individual in contact with an appetitive stimulus or that move it away from an aversive one. One important category of motivated behaviors involves internal regulation—the maintenance of homeostasis. Regulatory systems include four features: a system variable (the variable that is regulated), a set point (the optimum value of the system variable), a detector to measure the system variable, and a correctional mechanism to change it. Formerly, psychologists believed that aversive drives were produced by deprivation and that reinforcement was a result of drive reduction. However, the fact that we cannot directly measure an individual's drive level makes it impossible to test this hypothesis. In addition, many reinforcers increase drive rather than reduce it. Thus, most psychologists doubt the validity of the drive reduction hypothesis of reinforcement.

The discovery that electrical stimulation of parts of the brain could reinforce behavior led to the study of the role of brain mechanisms involved in reinforcement. Apparently, all reinforcing stimuli (including addictive drugs) cause the release of dopamine in the brain.

Because high levels of drive or arousal can be aversive, several investigators proposed the optimum-level theory of motivation and reinforcement. This theory suggests that organisms strive to attain optimum levels of arousal; thus, reinforcement and punishment are seen as two sides of the same coin. However, a problem remains: Because drive cannot be directly measured, we cannot determine whether an individual's drive is above or below its optimum level.

Perseverance is the tendency to continue performing a behavior that is no longer being externally reinforced. Two factors appear to control perseverance. One is the organism's previous history with intermittent reinforcement. The second factor is its opportunity to develop behaviors that produce conditioned reinforcers, such as the satisfaction we derive when we complete the little steps that constitute a long and difficult task.

Some experiences can diminish an organism's perseverance and its ability to cope with new situations. Learned helplessness involves learning that an aversive event cannot be avoided or escaped.

Psychologists still dispute whether learned helplessness is specific to a particular situation or generalizes to a wide variety of them. In any event, the phenomenon is of practical importance because it may well be a factor in psychological disorders such as depression.

learned helplessness A response to exposure to an inescapable aversive stimulus, characterized by reduced ability to learn a solvable avoidance task; thought to play a role in the development of some psychological disturbances.

Thought Questions

■ Have you ever been working hard on a problem and suddenly thought of a possible solution? Did the thought make you feel excited and happy? What do you think we would find if we could measure the release of dopamine in your brain?

■ Executives of tobacco companies insist that cigarettes are not addictive and assert that people smoke because of the pleasure the act gives them. Do you agree? In your opinion, what are the characteristics that indicate the presence of an addiction?

Eating

Eating is one of the most important things we do, and it can also be one of the most pleasurable. Much of what an animal learns to do is motivated by the constant struggle to obtain food. The need to eat certainly shaped the evolutionary development of our own species.

Simply put, motivation to eat is aroused when there is a deficit in the body's supply of stored nutrients, and it is satisfied by a meal that replenishes this supply. A person who exercises vigorously uses up the stored nutrients more rapidly and consequently must eat more food. Thus, the amount of food a person normally eats is regulated by physiological need. But what, exactly, causes a person to start eating, and what brings the meal to an end? These are simple questions, yet the answers are complex. There is no single physiological measure that can tell us reliably whether a person should be hungry; hunger is determined by a variety of conditions. So instead of asking what the *cause* of hunger is, we must ask what the *causes* are.

What Starts a Meal?

Although hunger and satiety appear to be two sides of the same coin, investigations have shown that the factors that cause a meal to begin are different from the ones that end it. Therefore, I will consider these two sets of factors separately.

Cultural and Social Factors

Most of us in Western society eat three times a day. When the time for a meal comes, we get hungry and eat, consuming a relatively constant amount of food. The regular pattern of eating is not determined solely by biological need; it is at least partially determined by habit. If you have ever had to miss a meal, you may have noticed that your hunger did not continue to grow indefinitely. Instead, it subsided some time after the meal would normally have been eaten only to grow again just before the scheduled time of the next one. Hunger, then, can wax and wane according to a learned schedule.

What we eat and how we eat is determined by cultural factors.

Besides learning *when* to eat, we learn *what* to eat. Most of us would refuse to eat fresh clotted seal blood, but many Eskimos consider it a delicacy. What we accept as food depends on our culture. Our tastes are also shaped by habits acquired early in life. A child whose family eats nothing but simple meat-and-potato dishes will probably not become a venturesome gastronome.

Our immediate environment also affects our hunger. We are much more likely to feel hungry, and to consume more food, in the presence of companions who are doing the same. Even a chicken that has finished its meal will start eating again if it is placed among other chickens who are busily eating. Similarly, you may sometimes join some friends at their table just after you have eaten. You say, no, you don't want to eat . . . well, perhaps just a bite to keep them company—and you eat almost as much as they do.

Physiological Factors

Cultural and social factors assuredly influence when and how much we eat. But everyone would also agree that the "real" reason for eating must be related to the fact that the body needs nourishment: If all other factors were eliminated, eating would be determined by some internal physiological state. What are the internal factors that cause us to eat?

Many years ago, Cannon and Washburn (1912) suggested that hunger resulted from an empty stomach. The walls of an empty stomach rubbed against each other, producing what we commonly identify as hunger pangs. (Cannon also suggested that thirst was produced by a dry mouth, because a loss of body fluid resulted in a decreased flow of saliva. Some skeptics called Cannon's explanation of hunger and thirst the "spit and rumble theory.") However, removal of the stomach does not abolish hunger pangs. Inglefinger (1944) interviewed patients whose stomachs had been removed because of cancer or large ulcers; their esophagi had been attached directly to their small intestines. Because they had no stomachs to catch and hold food, they had to eat small, frequent meals. Despite their lack of a stomach, these people reported the same feelings of hunger and satiety that they had had before the operation.

A more likely cause of hunger is depletion of the body's store of nutrients. The primary fuels for the cells of our body are glucose (a simple sugar) and fatty acids (chemicals produced when fat is broken down). If our digestive system contains food, these nutrients are absorbed into the blood and nourish our cells. But the digestive tract is sometimes empty; in fact, most of us wake up in the morning in that condition. So there has to be a reservoir that stores nutrients to keep the cells of the body nourished when the gut is empty. Indeed, there are two reservoirs—one short-term and the other long-term. The short-term reservoir stores carbohydrates, and the long-term reservoir stores fats.

The short-term reservoir is located in the cells of the muscles and the liver, and it is filled with a carbohydrate—a form of animal starch called **glycogen.** When glucose is received from a meal, some of it is used for fuel and some is converted into glycogen and stored in the liver. Our long-term reservoir consists of adipose tissue (fat tissue), which is found beneath the skin and in various locations in the abdomen. Adipose tissue consists of cells capable of absorbing nutrients from the blood, converting them to triglycerides (fats), and storing them. They can expand in size enormously; in fact, the primary physical difference between an obese person and a person of normal weight is the size of their fat cells, which is determined by the amount of triglycerides that these cells contain.

The long-term fat reservoir is obviously what keeps us alive during a prolonged fast. Once the level of glycogen in our short-term carbohydrate reservoir gets low, fat cells start breaking down fats and releasing fatty acids and a carbohy-

drate called *glycerol.* The brain primarily lives on glucose, and the rest of the body lives on fatty acids. Glycerol is converted into glucose, so the brain continues to be nourished even after the short-term reservoir is depleted. (See *Figure 13.5.*)

Because glucose is such an important fuel, Mayer (1955a) proposed the glucostatic hypothesis of hunger. According to the **glucostatic hypothesis,** hunger occurs when the level of glucose in the blood becomes low, presumably after the glycogen in the body's short-term reservoir has been used up. Mayer theorized that this decrease in blood sugar is detected by glucose-sensitive neurons in the brain called *glucostats.* (The term gluco*stat* is analogous to thermo*stat,* but it refers to the measurement of glucose rather than temperature.) Mayer suggested that these detectors activate neural circuits that make a person hungry, thus stimulating the correctional mechanism, eating.

Subsequent evidence suggests that there are two different types of nutrient detectors, which measure the blood level of the two primary nutrients, glucose and fatty acids (Friedman, Tordoff, and Ramirez, 1986; Friedman, Tordoff, and Kare, 1991). The glucose detectors appear to be located in the liver, but the location of the fatty acid detectors is not yet known (Ritter and Taylor, 1989; Ritter, Brenner, and Yox, 1992). Both sets of detectors send information to the brain, and activity of neural circuits there stimulates hunger.

What Stops a Meal?

Nutrient detectors sense the fact that the body's supplies of stored energy are getting low by measuring glucose and fatty acids in the blood. Through their connection with the brain these detectors are able to stimulate hunger. But what *ends* hunger? What brings a meal to its finish? Consider what happens when you eat. Your stomach fills with food, and the digestive process begins. However, about an hour passes before significant amounts of nutrients are absorbed from the intestines into the bloodstream. Therefore, the body's supply of fuel is not replenished until a rather long time after the meal begins. If you were to continue to eat until the nutrients actually entered the bloodstream, your stomach would burst. Therefore, some other detectors must be responsible for stopping the meal.

Although evidence suggests that the primary cause of hunger is not an empty stomach, the primary cause of satiety (that is, the cessation of hunger, caused by eating) seems to be a *full* stomach. Many studies have shown that satiety is caused by entry of a sufficient quantity of nourishing food into the stomach. Therefore, the stomach must contain detectors that sense the presence of food. We have known for a long time that hunger can be abolished by injecting food into an animal's stomach by means of a flexible tube. Even though the animal does not get to taste and smell the food, it will not subsequently eat. Davis and Campbell (1973) showed how precisely the stomach can measure its contents. The investigators allowed hungry rats to eat their fill and then removed

---

glycogen An insoluble carbohydrate that can be synthesized from glucose or converted to it; used to store nutrients.

glucostatic hypothesis The hypothesis that hunger is caused by a low level or availability of glucose, a condition that is monitored by specialized sensory neurons.

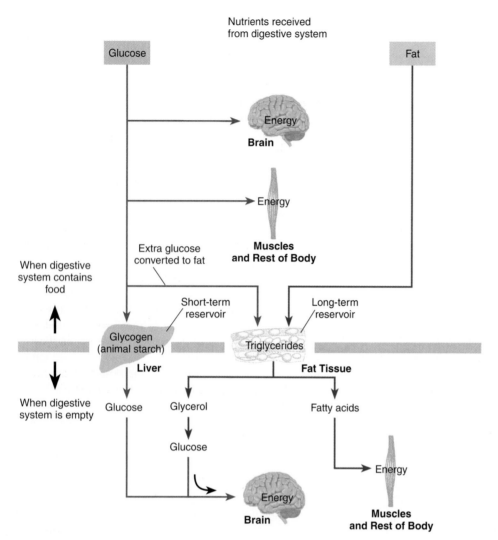

Figure 13.5

Overview of food metabolism. When the digestive system contains food, glucose nourishes the brain and muscles. Extra glucose is stored in the liver and converted to fat. When the digestive system is empty, glucose obtained from glycogen stored in the liver nourishes the brain until this short-term reservoir is used up. Fatty acids from fat tissue nourish the muscles and glycerol is converted to glucose to nourish the brain.

some food from their stomachs. When they let the rats eat again, they ate almost exactly as much as had been taken out.

The stomach appears to contain detectors that inform the brain about the chemical nature of its contents as well as the quantity. The ability to detect the chemical nature of food that has entered the stomach is important, because eating should stop relatively soon if the food is very nutritious but should continue for a longer time if it is not. Deutsch, Young, and Kalogeris (1978) injected either milk or a dilute salt solution into hungry rats' stomachs and thirty minutes later allowed them to eat. The rats that had received injections of milk ate less than the ones that had received the salt solution. Because the rats could not taste what was put in their stomachs, the effect had to come from detectors there. The nature of these detectors is not known, but they must respond to some chemicals present in food. You can try an experiment of your own: Drink two glasses of water when you are very hungry and see whether they satisfy your appetite.

I must note that the detectors that measure the amount and nutritive value of food in the stomach contribute only to short-term control of eating—the termination of a single meal. Long-term factors also control food intake. For example, when people eat especially nutritious food, they soon learn to eat less. When they begin to exercise more, and hence burn up their store of nutrients faster, they soon start eating more. For a long time, investigators believed that fat tissue provided some chemical signal that could be detected by the brain. When too much fat began accumulating, more of this chemical was secreted, and the person began eating less. If the amount of body fat began to decrease, the level of the chemical fell and the person began eating more.

After many years of searching for such a chemical signal, researchers have finally succeeded in finding one. The discovery came after years of study with a strain of genetically obese mice. The *ob mouse* (as this strain is called) has a low metabolism, overeats, and gets monstrously fat. It also develops diabetes in adulthood, just as many obese people do. Recently, researchers in several laboratories have discovered the cause of the obesity (Campfield et al., 1995; Halaas et al., 1995; Pelleymounter et al., 1995). A particular gene, called OB, normally produces a protein known as *leptin* (from the Greek word *leptos,* "thin"). Leptin is normally secreted by fat cells that have absorbed a large amount of triglyceride. Because of a genetic mutation, the fat cells of ob mice are unable to secrete leptin.

Leptin has profound effects on metabolism and eating, acting as an anti-obesity hormone. If ob mice are given daily injections of leptin, their metabolic rate increases, their body temperature rises, they become more active, and they eat less. As a result, their weight returns to normal. The treatment works even when the leptin is injected directly into the brain, indicating that the chemical acts directly on the neural circuits that control eating and metabolism. *Figure 13.6* shows a picture of an untreated ob mouse and an ob mouse that has received injections of leptin.

What about humans? Maffei et al. (1995) found that leptin is found in humans and that the level of leptin in the blood is correlated with obesity; thus, this chemical signal appears to be present in our species as well as in mice. But if leptin is produced by human fat cells, why do some people nevertheless overeat and become obese? As we will see in the next section, research has suggested a possible answer to this question.

Obesity

The mechanisms that control eating generally do a good job. However, some people do *not* control their eating habits and become too fat or too thin. Does what we have learned about the normal regulation of food intake help us understand these disorders?

Obesity is extremely difficult to treat. The enormous financial success of diet books, fat farms, and weight reduction programs attests to the trouble people have losing weight.

Figure 13.6

The effects of leptin on obesity in mice of the ob (obese) strain. The ob mouse on the left is untreated; the one on the right received daily injections of leptin.

(Photo courtesy of Dr. J. Sholtis, The Rockefeller University. Copyright © 1995 Amgen, Inc.)

Kramer et al. (1989) reported that four to five years after participating in a fifteen-week behavioral weight loss program, fewer than 3 percent of the participants managed to maintain the weight loss they had achieved during the program. Even drastic means such as gastric and intestinal surgery (designed to limit the amount of food that the stomach can hold or to prevent food from being fully digested before it is eliminated) are not the answer. These procedures have risks of their own, often produce unpleasant side effects, and have a failure rate of at least 40 percent (Kral, 1989).

Many psychological variables have been suggested as causes of obesity, including lack of impulse control, poor ability to delay gratification, and maladaptive eating styles (primarily eating too fast). However, in a review of the literature, Rodin, Schank, and Striegel-Moore (1989) found that none of these suggestions has received empirical support. Rodin and her colleagues also found that unhappiness and depression seem to be the *effects* of obesity, not its causes, and that dieting behavior seems to make the problem worse. (As we shall see later in this section, repeated bouts of weight loss and gain make subsequent weight loss more difficult to achieve.)

There is no single, all-inclusive explanation for obesity, but there are many partial ones. Habit plays an important role in the control of food intake. Early in life, when we are most active, we form our ideas about how much food constitutes a meal. Later in life, we become less active, but we do not always reduce our food intake accordingly. We fill our plates according to what we think is a proper-sized meal (or perhaps the plate is filled for us), and we eat everything, ignoring the satiety signals that might tell us to stop before the plate is empty.

One reason that many people have so much difficulty losing weight is that metabolic factors appear to play an important role in obesity. In fact, a good case can be made that obesity is most often not an *eating disorder* but rather a *metabolic disorder.* (*Metabolism* refers to the physiological processes—including the production of energy from nutrients—that take place within an organism.) Just as cars differ in their fuel efficiency, so do people. Rose and Williams (1961) studied pairs of people who were matched for weight, height, age, and activity. Some of these matched pairs differed by a factor of two in the number of calories they ate each day. People with an efficient metabolism have calories left over to deposit in the long-term nutrient reservoir; thus, they have difficulty keeping this reservoir from growing. In contrast, people with an inefficient metabolism can eat large meals without getting fat. Thus, whereas a fuel-efficient automobile is desirable, a fuel-efficient body runs the risk of becoming obese.

Differences in metabolism appear to have a hereditary basis. Griffiths and Payne (1976) found that the children of obese parents weighed more than other children even though they ate less. Stunkard et al. (1986) found that the body weight of a sample of people who had been adopted as infants was highly correlated with their *biological* parents but not with their *adoptive* parents. Thus, a person's weight (presumably closely related to his or her metabolic efficiency) is influenced by genetic factors.

Why are there genetic differences in metabolic efficiency? James and Trayhurn (1981) suggest that under some environmental conditions metabolic efficiency is advantageous. That is, in places where food is only intermittently available in sufficient quantities, being able to stay alive on small amounts of food and to store up extra nutrients in the form of fat when food becomes available for a while is a highly adaptive trait. Therefore, the variability in people's metabolisms may reflect the nature of the environment experienced by their ancestors. For example, physically active lactating women in Gambia manage to maintain their weight on only 1500 calories per day (Whitehead, et al., 1978). This high level of efficiency, which allows people to survive in environments in which food is scarce, can be a disadvantage when food is readily available because it promotes obesity.

Another factor—this one nonhereditary—can influence people's metabolism. Many obese people diet and then relapse, thus undergoing large changes in body weight. Some investigators have suggested that starvation causes the body's metabolism to become more efficient. For example, Brownell et al. (1986) fed rats a diet that made them become obese and then restricted their food intake until their body weights returned to normal. Then they made the rats fat again and reduced their food intake again. The second time, the rats became fat much faster and lost their weight much slower. Clearly, the experience of gaining and losing large amounts of body weight altered the animals' metabolic efficiency.

Steen, Oppliger, and Brownell (1988) obtained evidence that the same phenomenon (called the "yo-yo" effect) takes place in humans. They measured the resting metabolic rate in two groups of high school wrestlers: those who fasted just before a meet and binged afterwards and those who did not. (The motive for fasting just before a match is to qualify for a lower-weight group, in which the competition is presumably less challenging.) The investigators found that wrestlers who fasted and binged developed more efficient metabolisms. Possibly, these people will have difficulty maintaining a normal body weight as they get older.

As we saw in the previous subsection, overnourished fat cells secrete a protein known as leptin, which lowers weight by increasing metabolic rate (that is, by making the individual's metabolism become less efficient) and decreasing food intake. Why, then, do some people become fat? Are they like ob mice, with defective OB genes? The answer is no. The fat cells of most obese people do secrete leptin, but the people

nevertheless have efficient metabolisms and overeat (Maffei et al., 1995). A recent discovery suggests a possible answer to this puzzle. As you learned in Chapter 4, hormones act on their target cells by stimulating receptor molecules located on these cells. Using the techniques of molecular genetics, Tartaglia et al. (1995) discovered the leptin receptor. In order for leptin to reduce weight, the brain must contain functioning leptin receptors. Perhaps, researchers speculate, some people have leptin receptors that do not respond normally to the presence of leptin in the blood. The overgrown fat cells of these people secrete high levels of leptin, but the effect the hormone produces in the brain is less intense than normal. Hence, the people overeat.

These are exciting times for scientists studying the physiology of obesity, and they are promising times for people who would like to lose weight. Would it be possible to increase the blood level of leptin in obese people enough to compensate for the relative insensitivity of their leptin receptors? At present, this strategy would not be practical, because the leptin would have to be given in daily injections. And we do not yet know whether increasing the blood level of leptin would produce any unwanted side-effects. In any event, now that the basic mechanism of long-term regulation of fat tissue has apparently been discovered, researchers have a much better chance of finding ways to help obese people lose weight.

Anorexia Nervosa

Most people, if they have an eating problem, tend to overeat. However, some people, especially young adolescent women, have the opposite problem: They suffer from **anorexia nervosa,** a disorder characterized by a severe decrease in eating. The literal meaning of the word *anorexia* suggests a loss of appetite, but people with this disorder generally do *not* lose their appetites. Their limited intake of food occurs despite intense preoccupation with food and its preparation. They may enjoy preparing meals for others to consume, collect recipes, and even hoard food that they do not eat. They have an intense fear of becoming obese, and this fear continues even if they become dangerously thin. Many exercise by cycling, running, or almost constant walking and pacing.

Another eating disorder, **bulimia nervosa,** is characterized by a loss of control of food intake. (The term *bulimia* comes from the Greek *bous*, "ox," and *limos*, "hunger.") People with bulimia nervosa periodically gorge themselves with food, especially dessert or snack food, especially in the afternoon or evening. These binges are usually followed by self-induced vomiting or the use of laxatives, along with feelings of depression and guilt (Mawson, 1974; Halmi, 1978). With this combination of binging and purging, the net nutrient intake (and consequently, the body weight) of bulimics can vary; Weltzin et al. (1991) report that 44 percent of bulimics undereat, 37 percent eat a normal amount, and 44 percent overeat. Episodes of bulimia are seen in some patients with anorexia nervosa.

anorexia nervosa An eating disorder characterized by attempts to lose weight, sometimes to the point of starvation.

bulimia nervosa A loss of control over food intake characterized by gorging binges followed by self-induced vomiting or use of laxatives; also accompanied by feelings of guilt and depression.

Great Britain's Princess Diana revealed that she suffered from bulimia for several years.

The fact that anorexia nervosa is seen primarily in young women has prompted both biological and social explanations. There is good evidence, primarily from twin studies, that hereditary factors play a role in the development of anorexia (Russell and Treasure, 1989). The existence of hereditary factors suggests that abnormalities in physiological mechanisms may be involved. However, most psychologists believe that the emphasis our society places on slimness—especially in women—is largely responsible for this disorder. But the success rate of psychotherapy used to treat anorexia is not especially encouraging (Patton, 1989).

About one patient in thirty dies of the disorder. Many anorexics suffer from osteoporosis, and bone fractures are common. When the weight loss becomes severe enough, anorexic women cease menstruating. Two disturbing reports (Artmann et al., 1985; Lankenau et al., 1985) indicate that CT scans of anorexic patients show evidence of loss of brain tissue. Some of the lost tissue, but not all, apparently returns after recovery.

Another possible cause of anorexia and bulimia is that changes in a young woman's endocrine status alter her metabolism or the neural mechanisms involved in feeding. Indeed, the female sex hormones progesterone and estradiol have been shown to affect food intake and body weight of laboratory animals through their interactions with receptors for these hormones located in various organs, including the brain and adipose tissue (Wade and Gray, 1979). However, no evidence yet shows that anorexia nervosa in humans is related to this phenomenon. Many studies have found evidence of metabolic differences between anorexics and people of normal weight. But because prolonged fasting and the use of laxatives have many effects, interpreting these differences is difficult (Halmi, 1978).

Anorexia nervosa is a serious condition; understanding its causes is more than an academic matter. We can hope that research on the biological and social control of feeding and metabolism will help us understand this puzzling and dangerous disorder.

Interim Summary

Eating

Hunger is the feeling that precedes and accompanies an important regulatory behavior: eating. Eating begins for both social and physiological reasons. Physiologically, the most important event appears to be the detection of a lowered supply of nutrients available in the blood. Detectors in the liver measure glucose level, and detectors elsewhere in the body measure the level of fatty acids. Both sets of detectors inform the brain of the need for food and arouse hunger. We stop eating for different reasons. Detectors responsible for satiety, which appear to be located in the walls of the stomach, monitor both the quality and the quantity of the food that has just been eaten. Long-term control of eating appears to be regulated by a chemical known as leptin, which is released by overnourished fat tissue and detected by cells in the brain. The effects of this chemical are to decrease meal size and increase metabolic rate, thus helping the body burn up its supply of triglycerides.

Sometimes, normal control mechanisms fail, and people gain too much weight. For any individual, genetic and environmental factors may interact to cause the person's weight to deviate from the norm. People differ genetically in the efficiency of their metabolisms, and this efficiency can easily lead to obesity. Particular eating habits, especially those learned during infancy, can override the physiological signals that would otherwise produce satiety. Experiences such as repeated fasting and refeeding (the yo-yo effect) are often accompanied by overeating. More research on the causes of obesity may lead to ways of determining which factors are responsible for an individual's excessive weight. It is too soon to know how the discovery of leptin and the leptin receptor will aid in the treatment of obesity.

Anorexia nervosa is a serious, even life-threatening, disorder. Most anorexic patients are young women. Although they avoid eating, they often remain preoccupied with food. Studies have found metabolic differences in anorexic patients, but we cannot determine whether these differences are the causes or the effects of the disorder. Researchers are beginning to study possible abnormalities in the regulation of chemicals in the brain that seem to play a role in normal control of feeding to see whether medical treatments can be discovered.

Thought Questions

■ The drive reduction hypothesis of motivation and reinforcement says that drives are aversive and satiety is pleasurable. Clearly, *satisfying* hunger is pleasurable, but what about *satiety*? Which do you prefer, eating a meal while you are hungry or feeling full afterward?

- One of the last prejudices that people admit to publicly is a dislike of fat people. Is this fair, given that genetic differences in metabolism are such an important cause of obesity?

- Do you think that the fact that almost all anorexics are female is caused entirely by social factors (such as the emphasis on thinness in our society), or do you think that biological factors (such as hormonal differences) also play a role? Can you think of any ways to answer these questions experimentally?

Sexual Behavior

The motivation to engage in sexual behavior can be very strong (I doubt that most people need for me to tell them that). However, sexual behavior is not motivated by a physiological need, the way eating is. Because we must perform certain behaviors in order to reproduce, the process of natural selection has ensured that our brains are constructed in such a way as to cause enough of us to mate with each other that the species will survive.

Effects of Sex Hormones on Behavior

Sex hormones, hormones secreted by the testes and ovaries, have effects on cells throughout the body. In general, these effects promote reproduction. For example, they cause the production of sperms, build up the lining of the uterus, trigger ovulation, and stimulate the production of milk. Sex hormones also affect nerve cells in the brain, thereby affecting behavior.

Sex hormones do not *cause* behaviors. Behaviors are responses to particular situations and are affected by people's experiences in the past. What sex hormones do is affect people's *motivation* to perform particular classes of reproductive behaviors. We therefore start our exploration of sexual behavior with the motivational effects of sex hormones.

Effects of Androgens

As we saw in Chapter 12, androgens such as testosterone are necessary for male sexual development. During prenatal development, the testes of male fetuses secrete testosterone, which causes the male sex organs to develop. This hormone also affects the development of the brain. The prenatal effects of sex hormones are called **organizational effects** because they alter the organization of the sex organs and the brain. Studies using laboratory animals have shown that if the organizational effects of androgens on brain development are

prevented, the animal later fails to exhibit male sexual behavior. In addition, males cannot have an erection and engage in sexual intercourse unless testosterone is present in adulthood. These effects are called **activational effects** because the hormone activates sex organs and brain circuits that have already developed.

Davidson, Camargo, and Smith (1979) performed a carefully controlled double-blind study of the activational effects of testosterone on the sexual behavior of men whose testes failed to secrete normal amounts of androgens. The men were given monthly injections of a placebo or one of two different dosages of a long-lasting form of testosterone. When the men receiving testosterone were compared with the men in the control group, the effect of testosterone on total number of erections and attempts at intercourse during the month following the injection was found to be large and statistically significant, and the larger dosage produced more of an effect than did the smaller dosage. Thus, we may conclude that testosterone definitely affects male sexual performance.

If a man is castrated (has his testes removed, usually because of injury or disease), his sex drive will inevitably decline. Usually, he first loses the ability to ejaculate, and then he loses the ability to achieve an erection (Bermant and Davidson, 1974). But studies have shown that some men lose these abilities soon after castration, whereas others retain at least some level of sexual potency for many months. Injections or pills of testosterone quickly restore potency. Possibly, the amount of sexual experience prior to castration affects performance afterward. Rosenblatt and Aronson (1958) found that male cats who had copulated frequently before castration were able to perform sexually for much longer periods of time after the surgery. Perhaps the same is true for men.

Events taking place in the environment can affect testosterone levels: Sexual activity raises the level, and stress lowers it. Even the anticipation of sexual activity can affect testosterone secretion. A scientist stationed on a remote island (Anonymous, 1970) removed his beard with an electrical shaver each day and weighed the clippings. Just before he left for visits to the mainland (and to the company of a female companion), his beard began growing faster. Because rate of beard growth is related to androgen levels, the effect indicates that his anticipation of sexual activity stimulated testosterone production. Confirming these results, Hellhammer, Hubert, and Schurmeyer (1985) found that watching an erotic film increased men's testosterone levels.

organizational effect An effect of a hormone that usually occurs during prenatal development and produces permanent changes that alter the subsequent development of the organism. An example is androgenization.

activational effect The effect of a hormone on a physiological system that has already developed. If the effect involves the brain, it can influence behavior. An example is facilitation of sexual arousal and performance.

Testosterone affects sex drive, but it does not determine the *object* of sexual desire. A homosexual man who receives injections of testosterone will not suddenly become interested in women. If testosterone has any effect, it will be to increase his interest in sexual contact with other men. I will have more to say about sexual orientation in a later section.

Although evidence shows clearly that testosterone affects men's sexual performance, we humans are uniquely emancipated from the biological effects of hormones in a special way. Not all human sexual activity requires an erect penis. A man does not need testosterone to be able to kiss and caress his partner or to engage in other noncoital activities. Men who have had to be castrated and who cannot receive injections of testosterone for medical reasons report continued sexual activity with their partners. For humans, sexual activity is not limited to coitus.

Androgens appear to activate sex drive in women as well as in men. Salmon and Geist (1943) reported that testosterone has a stimulating effect on sexual desire and on the sensitivity of the clitoris to touch. Persky et al. (1978) studied the sexual activity of eleven married couples ranging in age from twenty-one to thirty-one. The subjects kept daily records of their sexual feelings and behavior, and the experimenters measured their blood levels of testosterone twice a week. Couples were more likely to engage in intercourse when the woman's testosterone level was at a peak. In addition, the women reported finding intercourse more gratifying during these times.

Effects of Progesterone and Estrogen

In most species of mammals, the hormones estradiol and progesterone have strong effects on female sexual behavior. The levels of these two sex hormones fluctuate during the menstrual cycle of primates and the **estrous cycle** of other female mammals. The difference between these two cycles is primarily that the lining of the primate uterus—but not that of other mammals—builds up during the first part of the cycle and sloughs off at the end. A female mammal of a nonprimate species—for example, a laboratory rat—will receive the advances of a male only when the levels of estradiol and progesterone in her blood are high. This condition occurs around the time of ovulation, when copulation is likely to make her become pregnant. During this time, the female will stand still while the male approaches her. If he attempts to mount her, she will arch her back and move her tail to the side, giving him access to her genitalia. In fact, an estrous female rat often does not wait for the male to take the initiative; she engages in seductive behaviors such as hopping around and wiggling her ears. These behaviors usually induce sexual activity by the male (McClintock and Adler, 1978).

A female rat whose ovaries have been removed is normally nonreceptive—even hostile—to the advances of an eager male. However, if she is given injections of estradiol and progesterone to duplicate the hormonal condition of the receptive part of her estrous cycle, she will receive the male or even pursue him. In contrast, women and other female primates are unique among mammals in their sexual activity: They are potentially willing to engage in sexual behavior at any time during their reproductive cycles. Some investigators have suggested that this phenomenon made monogamous relationships possible; because the male can look forward to his mate's receptivity at any time during her menstrual cycle, he is less likely to look for other partners.

In higher primates (including our own species), the ability to mate is not controlled by estradiol and progesterone. Most studies have reported that changes in the level of estradiol and progesterone have only a minor effect on women's sexual interest (Adams, Gold, and Burt, 1978; Morris et al., 1987). However, as Wallen (1990) points out, these studies have almost all involved married women who live with their husbands. In stable, monogamous relationships in which the partners are together on a daily basis, sexual activity can be instigated by either of them. Normally, a husband does not force his wife to have intercourse with him, but even if the woman is not physically interested in engaging in sexual activity at a particular moment, she may find that she wants to do so because of her affection for him. This fact poses an interesting question. If all of a woman's sexual encounters were initiated by her, without regard to her partner's desires, would we find that variations in estradiol and progesterone across the menstrual cycle would affect her behavior? Studies using monkeys suggest that this may be the case (Wallen et al., 1986). And as Alexander et al. (1990) showed, women taking oral contraceptives (which prevent the normal cycles in secretion of ovarian hormones) were less likely to show fluctuations in sexual interest during the menstrual cycle.

Sexual Orientation

When people reach puberty, the effects of sex hormones on their maturing bodies and on their brains increase their interest in sexual activity. As sexual interest increases, most people develop a special interest in members of the other sex—they develop a heterosexual orientation. Why does opposite-sex attraction occur? And why does same-sex attraction sometimes occur? As we shall see, research has not yet provided definite answers to these questions, but it has provided some hints.

Homosexual behavior (engaging in sexual activity with members of the same sex; from the Greek *homos,* meaning "the same") is seen in male and female animals of many different species. The widespread occurrence of homosexual behavior means that we should not refer to it as "unnatural." However, humans are apparently the only species in which some members regularly exhibit *exclusive* homosexuality. Other animals, if they are not exclusively heterosexual, are likely to be bisexual, engaging in sexual activity with members of both sexes. In contrast, the number of men and women

estrous cycle The ovulatory cycle in mammals other than primates; the sequence of physical and hormonal changes that accompany the ripening and disintegration of ova.

who describe themselves as exclusively homosexual exceeds the number who describe themselves as bisexual.

Traditional theories of sexual orientation have stressed the importance of a person's early environment. Earlier in this century, most mental health professionals regarded homosexuality as a disorder, caused by a faulty home environment—for example, as the result of having been raised by an overprotective mother and an indifferent father.

More recent research has refuted these conclusions. First, there is no evidence that homosexuality is a disorder. The adjustment problems that some homosexuals have occur because our society at large treats them differently. Therefore, even if we observe more neuroses in homosexuals than in heterosexuals, we cannot conclude that their maladjustment is directly related to their sexual orientation. In a society that was absolutely indifferent to a person's sexual orientation, homosexuals might be as well adjusted as heterosexuals. In fact, a large number of homosexuals are well adjusted and happy with themselves (Bell and Weinberg, 1978), suggesting that homosexuality is not necessarily associated with emotional difficulties.

As we saw, some studies suggested that homosexuality is an emotional disturbance caused by faulty child rearing. However, much of the data in these studies were gathered from people who went to a psychiatrist or clinical psychologist for help with emotional problems. Therefore, they were not necessarily typical of all homosexuals, and we cannot know whether their homosexuality was caused by an unhappy childhood, whether their unhappy childhood was caused by early manifestations of homosexual tendencies, or whether their emotional instability and homosexual orientation were purely coincidental.

An ambitious project reported by Bell, Weinberg, and Hammersmith (1981) studied a large number of male and female homosexuals, most of whom had not sought professional psychological assistance. The researchers obtained their subjects by placing advertisements in newspapers, approaching people in gay bars and bookstores, and asking homosexuals to recommend friends. The study took place in San Francisco, where homosexuals form a large part of the population.

The subjects were asked about their relationships with their parents, siblings, and peers and about their feelings, gender identification, and sexual activity. The results provided little or no support for traditional theories of homosexuality. The major conclusions of the study follow:

1. Sexual orientation appears to be determined prior to adolescence and prior to homosexual or heterosexual activity. The most important single predictor of adult homosexuality was a self-report of homosexual feelings, which usually occurred three years before first genital homosexual activity. This finding suggests that homosexuality is a deep-seated tendency. It also tends to rule out the suggestion that seduction by an older person of the same sex plays an important role in the development of homosexuality.

Homosexuality includes romantic attraction, as well as sexual attraction, to another person of the same sex.

2. Most homosexual men and women have engaged in some heterosexual experiences during childhood and adolescence, but in contrast to their heterosexual counterparts, they found these experiences unrewarding. This pattern is also consistent with the existence of a deep-seated predisposition prior to adulthood.

3. There is a strong relation between gender nonconformity in childhood and the development of homosexuality. Gender nonconformity is characterized by an aversion in boys to "masculine" behaviors and in girls to "feminine" behaviors.

As the researchers admit, the results of the study are consistent with the hypothesis that homosexuality is at least partly determined by biological factors. That is, biological variables may predispose a child to behavior that is more typical of the other sex and eventually to sexual arousal by members of his or her own sex.

Is there evidence of what these biological causes of homosexuality may be? We can immediately rule out the suggestion that male homosexuals have insufficient levels of testosterone in their blood; well-adjusted male homosexuals have normal levels of testosterone (Tourney, 1980).

A more likely cause of male homosexuality is the pattern of exposure of the developing brain to sex hormones. Some experiments suggest that if a female rat is subjected to stress during pregnancy, the pattern of secretion of sex hormones is altered, and the sexual development of the male offspring is affected (Ward, 1972; Anderson et al., 1986). Three laboratories have studied the brains of deceased heterosexual and homosexual men and have found differences in the size of two different subregions of the hypothalamus and in a bundle of axons that connects the right and left temporal lobes (Swaab and Hofman, 1990; LeVay, 1991; Allen and Gorski, 1992). We cannot necessarily conclude that any of these regions is directly involved in people's sexual orientation, but the results do suggest that the brains may have been exposed to different patterns of hormones prenatally.

As we saw, when the organizational effects of androgens are blocked in male laboratory animals, the animals fail to develop normal male sex behavior. Nature has performed the equivalent experiment in humans (Money and Ehrhardt, 1972; Ris-Stalpers et al., 1990). Some people are insensitive to androgens. They have **androgen insensitivity syndrome,** caused by a genetic mutation that prevents the formation of androgen receptors. Because the cells of the body cannot respond to the androgens, a genetic male with this syndrome develops female *external* genitalia instead of a penis and scrotum. The person does not develop ovaries or a uterus.

If an individual with this syndrome is raised as a girl, all is well. Normally, the testes (which remain in the abdomen) are removed because they often become cancerous. At the appropriate time, the person is given estrogen pills to induce puberty. Subsequently, the individual will function sexually as a woman. Women with this syndrome report average sex drives, including normal frequency of orgasm in intercourse. Most marry and lead normal sex lives. Of course, lacking a uterus and ovaries, they cannot have children.

Although little research has been done on the origins of female homosexuality, Money, Schwartz, and Lewis (1984) found that the incidence of homosexuality was several times higher than the national average in women who had been exposed to high levels of androgens prenatally. (The cause of the exposure was an abnormality of the adrenal glands, which usually secrete very low levels of these hormones.) Thus, sexual orientation in females may indeed be affected by biological factors.

There is also some evidence that genetics may play a role in sexual orientation. Twin studies take advantage of the fact that identical twins have identical genes, whereas the genetic similarity between fraternal twins is, on the average, 50 percent. Bailey and Pillard (1991) studied pairs of male twins in which at least one member identified himself as homosexual. If both twins are homosexual, they are said to be *concordant* for this trait. If only one is homosexual, the twins are said to be *discordant.* Thus, if homosexuality has a genetic basis, the percentage of identical twins concordant for homosexuality should be higher than that for fraternal twins. And this is exactly what Bailey and Pillard found; the concordance rate was 52 percent for identical twins and 22 percent for fraternal twins. In a subsequent study, Bailey et al. (1993) found evidence that heredity plays a role in female homosexuality, too. The concordance rates for female identical and fraternal twins were 48 percent and 16 percent, respectively.

As we have seen, there is evidence that two biological factors—prenatal hormonal exposure and heredity—can affect a person's sexual orientation. These research findings certainly contradict the suggestion that a person's sexual orientation is a moral issue. It appears that homosexuals are no more responsible for their sexual orientation than heterosexuals are. Ernulf, Innala, and Whitam (1989) found that people who believed that homosexuals were "born that way" expressed more positive attitudes toward them than did people who believed that they "chose to be" or "learned to be" that way. Thus, we can hope that research on the origins of homosexuality will reduce prejudice based on a person's sexual orientation.

Interim Summary

Sexual Behavior

Testosterone has two major effects on male sexual behavior: organizational and activational. In the fetus, testosterone organizes the development of male sex organs and of some neural circuits in the brain; in the adult, testosterone activates these structures and permits erection and ejaculation to occur. The sexual behavior of female mammals with estrous cycles depends on estradiol and progesterone, but these hormones have only a minor effect on women's sexual behavior. Women's sexual desire, like that of men, is much more dependent on androgens.

The development of sexual orientation appears to have biological roots. A large-scale study of homosexuals failed to find evidence that child-rearing practices fostered homosexuality. Studies have identified three regions of the brain that are of different sizes in homosexual and heterosexual males. These results suggest that the brains of these two groups may have been exposed to different patterns of hormones early in life. In addition, twin studies indicate that homosexuality has a genetic component, as well.

Although an individual's sex life is a personal, private matter, scientific investigation into its nature in no way diminishes its quality. A thorough understanding of the social and biological determinants of sexual behavior will enable us to help those who experience sexual dysfunctions, thus enhancing at least some people's sex lives.

Thought Questions

- Whatever the relative roles played by biological and environmental factors may be, most investigators believe that a person's sexual orientation is not a matter of choice. Why do you think so many people consider sexual orientation to be a moral issue?
- During the Summer Olympics of 1992, a heated controversy arose over the use of sex testing of female athletes. One of the effects of androgens is to increase the size and strength of skeletal muscles; thus, men generally have greater physical strength than women have. To prevent men from disguising themselves as women and unfairly competing in women's events, the officials decided to confirm women's sex by taking a sample of cells and examining their chromosomes. Thus, a woman with androgen insensitivity syndrome and an XY genotype would be disqualified from Olympic

androgen insensitivity syndrome An inherited condition caused by a lack of functioning androgen receptors. Because androgens cannot exert their effects, a person with XY sex chromosomes develops as a female, with female external genitalia.

competition in women's events—and, in fact, this occurred in 1992. In your opinion, is this practice fair? Why or why not?

Aggressive Behavior

Aggression is a serious problem in human society; every day, we hear or read about incidents involving violence and cruelty, and undoubtedly, thousands more go unreported. If we are to provide a safe environment for everyone, we must learn more about the causes of aggressive behavior. Many factors probably influence a person's tendency to commit acts of aggression, including childhood experiences, exposure to violence on television and in the movies, peer group pressures, hormones and drugs, and malfunctions of the brain. Various aspects of aggressive behavior have been studied by zoologists, physiological psychologists, sociologists, social psychologists, political scientists, and psychologists who specialize in the learning process. We will examine several of these aspects here.

Ethological Studies of Aggression

The utility of species-typical behaviors such as sexual activity, parental behavior, food gathering, and nest construction is obvious; we can easily understand their value to survival. But violence and aggression are also seen in many species, including our own. If aggression is harmful, one would not expect it to be so prevalent in nature. Ethologists—zoologists who study the behavior of animals in their natural environments—have analyzed the causes of aggression and have shown that it, too, often has value for the survival of a species.

The Social Relevance of Intraspecific Aggression

Intraspecific aggression involves an attack by one animal upon another member of its species. Ethologists have shown that intraspecific aggression has several biological advantages. First, it tends to disperse a population of animals, forcing some into new territories, where necessary environmental adaptations may increase the flexibility of the species. Second, when accompanied by rivalry among males for mating opportunities, intraspecific aggression tends to perpetuate the genes of the healthier, more vigorous animals.

Human cultures, however, are very different even from those of other species of primates. Perhaps intraspecific aggression has outlived its usefulness for humans and we would benefit from its elimination. Whatever the case may be, we must understand the causes of human aggression in order to eliminate it or direct it to more useful purposes.

Threat and Appeasement

Ethologists have discovered a related set of behaviors in many species: ritualized threat gestures and appeasement gestures.

Threat gestures enable an animal to communicate aggressive intent to another before engaging in actual violence. For example, if one dog intrudes on another's territory, the defender will growl and bare its teeth, raise the fur on its back (presumably making it look larger to its opponent), and stare at the intruder. Almost always, the dog defending its territory will drive the intruder away. Threat gestures are particularly important in species whose members are able to kill each other (Lorenz, 1966; Eibl-Eibesfeld, 1980). For example, wolves often threaten each other with growls and bared teeth but rarely bite each other. Because an all-out battle between two wolves would probably end in the death of one and the serious wounding of the other, the tendency to perform ritualized displays rather than engage in overt aggression has an obvious advantage to the survival of the species.

To forestall an impending attack, one of the animals must show that it does not want to fight—that it admits defeat. The submissive animal makes an **appeasement gesture.** If a pair of wolves gets into a fight, one animal usually submits to the other by lying down and exposing its throat. The sight of a helpless and vulnerable opponent presumably terminates the victor's hostility, and the fight ceases. The aggression of the dominant animal is *appeased.*

Appeasement gestures are even a part of human behavior. Suppose you are a male of average size standing at a bar next to a muscular, 280-pound male wearing a jacket with a skull and crossbones stenciled on the back. Would you stare directly at his face? And if he happened to stare at you, would you stand up tall and meet his gaze or slouch down a bit, displaying a diffident look on your face?

Hormones and Aggression

In birds and most mammals, androgens appear to exert a strong effect on aggressiveness. You will recall from the section on sexual behavior that testosterone has an *organizational* effect on the development of sex organs and the brain and an *activational* effect during adulthood. Testosterone also appears to exert the same effects on some forms of aggressive behavior. An adult male mouse will fiercely attack other male mice that intrude into its territory. But if a male mouse is castrated early in life, before its brain has matured, it will not attack another male when it grows up, even if it is given injections of testosterone (Conner and Levine, 1969). (See *Figure 13.7.*)

---

intraspecific aggression The attack by one animal upon another member of its species.

threat gesture A stereotyped gesture that signifies that one animal is likely to attack another member of the species.

appeasement gesture A stereotyped gesture made by a submissive animal in response to a threat gesture by a dominant animal; tends to inhibit an attack.

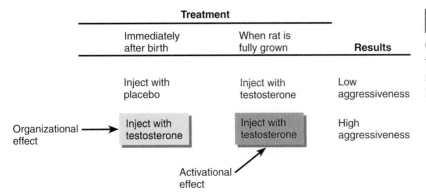

Figure 13.7

Organizational and activational effects of testosterone on aggressive behavior of male mice that were castrated immediately after birth.

Do hormones also influence aggressive behavior in humans? The fact that men are generally more aggressive than women (Maccoby and Jacklin, 1974) and the fact that a man's sexual behavior depends on the presence of testosterone suggest that this hormone also influences their aggressive behavior. Some cases of aggressiveness—especially sexual assault—have been treated with drugs that block androgen receptors and thus prevent androgens from exerting their normal effects. The rationale is based on animal research that indicates that androgens promote both sexual behavior and aggression in males. However, the efficacy of treatment with antiandrogens has yet to be established conclusively (Bain, 1987).

Another way to determine whether androgens affect aggressiveness in humans is to examine the testosterone levels of people who exhibit varying levels of aggressive behavior. However, even though this approach poses fewer ethical problems, it presents methodological ones. First, let me review some evidence. Dabbs et al. (1987) measured the testosterone levels of male prison inmates and found a significant correlation with several measures of violence, including the nature of the crime for which they were convicted, infractions of prison rules, and ratings of "toughness" by their peers. These relations are seen in female prison inmates, too. Dabbs et al. (1988) found that women prisoners who showed unprovoked violence and had several prior convictions also showed higher levels of testosterone.

But we must remember that *correlation* does not necessarily indicate *causation*. A person's environment can affect his or her testosterone level. For example, losing a tennis match or a wrestling competition causes a fall in blood levels of testosterone (Mazur and Lamb, 1980; Elias, 1981). In a very elaborate study, Jeffcoate et al. (1986) found that the blood levels of a group of five men confined on a boat for fourteen days changed as they established a dominance-aggression ranking among themselves: The higher the rank, the higher the testosterone level was. Thus, we cannot be sure in any correlational study that high testosterone levels *cause* people to become dominant or violent; perhaps their success in establishing a position of dominance increases their testosterone levels relative to those of the people they dominate.

As everyone knows, some athletes take anabolic steroids in order to increase their muscle mass and strength and, sup-

posedly, to increase their competitiveness. Anabolic steroids include natural androgens and synthetic hormones having androgenic effects. Thus, we might expect that these hormones would increase aggressiveness. Indeed, several studies have found exactly that. For example, Yates, Perry, and Murray (1992) found that male weightlifters who were taking anabolic steroids were more aggressive and hostile than those who were not. But as the authors note, we cannot be certain that the steroid is responsible for the increased aggressiveness; it could simply be that the men who were already more competitive and aggressive were the ones who chose to take the steroids. Taken together, the findings reviewed in this section suggest (but still do not prove) that androgens play a role in stimulating aggression in humans.

Environmental Variables That Affect Human Aggression

Imitation of Aggression

Consider the significance of a conversation like this one:

> *Parent:* I don't know what to do with Johnny. His teacher says he is simply impossible. He just can't keep from hitting and kicking other children.
>
> *Friend:* Perhaps he needs more discipline.
>
> *Parent:* But I spank him all the time!

Why does Johnny persist in being aggressive even though this behavior is regularly punished? Some psychologists suggest that, instead of suppressing his violent behavior, frequent spankings have *taught* him to be aggressive. When his parents become upset with his behavior, they resort to physical violence. And Johnny learns to imitate them.

A large percentage of nonviolent people may have been spanked at least once when they were children, with no obvious harm. But when parents habitually resort to aggression, their children are likely to do the same. In the extreme case of child abuse, parents who beat their children usually turn out to have been victims of child abuse themselves; this unfortunate trait seems to be passed along like an unwanted family heirloom (Parke and Collmer, 1975).

Most parents do not beat their children or even spank them frequently. But there is another opportunity for imitation that is of concern to society: examples of violence on television or in movies, comic books, and video games. All too often, the heroes disdain peaceful solutions to their problems and instead seek to resolve them through fighting. Most people agree that it would be unfortunate if real people were as violent as the ones we see on television. Does the continued observation of violence in the mass media lead children to choose aggressive means to solve their problems? Or are the television networks' representatives correct when they argue that children have no trouble separating fact from fantasy and that the mass media only give us what we want anyway?

Field studies suggest, but do not prove, that long-term viewing of violence on television causes children to be more violent. For example, Lefkowitz et al. (1977) observed a correlation of .31 between boys' viewing of violence and their later behavior. They reported that the greater the boys' preference for violent television at age eight, the greater their aggressiveness was both at that age and ten years later, at age eighteen. (Girls were found to be much less aggressive, and no relation was observed between television viewing and violence.)

Feshbach and Singer (1971) carried out a bold and interesting field study in an attempt to manipulate directly the amount of violence seen by boys on television—and thus to determine whether the viewing would affect their later aggressiveness. With the cooperation of directors of various private boarding schools and homes for neglected children, half the teenage boys were permitted to watch only violent television programs, the other half only nonviolent ones. Six months later, no effect was seen on the behavior of the boys in the private schools. The boys in the homes for neglected children who had watched violent programs tended to be slightly *less* aggressive than subjects who had watched the nonviolent ones.

Two factors prevent us from concluding from this study that violent television programs promote pacifism or at least have no effect. First, by the time people reach their teens, they may be too old to be affected by six months of television viewing; the critical period may come earlier. Second, some of the boys resented not being allowed to watch their favorite (in this case, violent) television programs, and this resentment may have made them more aggressive.

As with many other complex social issues, we lack definitive evidence that television violence makes members of our society more aggressive. However, the stakes in this particular issue are high enough that we should tolerate some uncertainty and choose what is clearly the lesser of two evils. Given both the possibility that violence on television has a harmful effect and the fact that no harm can come from reducing the amount of aggression on the airwaves, we should make every effort to present a more peaceful and constructive model of human behavior to our children.

Interim Summary

Aggressive Behavior

Aggression serves useful purposes in the majority of species. Ethological studies of other species reveal the presence of mechanisms to avert violence: Threat gestures warn of an impending attack, and appeasement gestures propitiate the potential aggressor. In males of most species of animals, androgens have both organizational and activational effects on aggressive behavior. The same is probably true for humans, but definitive studies are impossible for ethical reasons.

Field studies on the effects of televised violence are not conclusive. Observational studies have revealed a modest relation between preference for violent television shows and boys' aggressiveness, but we cannot be sure that watching the violence *causes* the aggressiveness. An attempt to manipulate aggression by forcing children to watch violent or nonviolent television shows was inconclusive because many children resented their loss of choice.

Thought Questions

- From the point of view of evolution, aggressive behavior and a tendency to establish dominance have useful functions. In particular, they increase the likelihood that only the most healthy and vigorous animals will reproduce. Can you think of examples of good and bad effects of these tendencies among members of our own species?

The Nature of Emotion

In a real sense, emotions are what life is all about. Life without emotion would be bland and empty. When important things happen to us, they change our feelings. They make us feel happy, sad, proud, fearful. But emotions consist of more than feelings. They are evoked by particular kinds of situations, they tend to occur in association with approach or avoidance behaviors, and they are accompanied by expressions such as smiles and frowns that convey our feelings to other people. Most psychologists who have studied emotions have focused on one or more of the following questions: What kinds of situations produce emotions? What kinds of feelings do people say they experience? What kinds of behaviors do people engage in? What physiological changes do people undergo in situations that produce strong emotions?

Although no general theory of emotion is available to give us a consistent definition, the term **emotion** is generally used by psychologists for a display of feelings that are evoked when important things happen to us. Emotions are relatively brief and occur in response to events having motivational rel-

emotion   A relatively brief display of a feeling made in response to environmental events having motivational significance or to memories of such events.

evance (or to their mental re-creation, as when we remember something embarrassing we did in the past and experience the feelings of embarrassment again). Emotions are the consequence of events that motivate us. When we encounter reinforcing or punishing stimuli, stimuli that motivate us to act, we express and experience positive or negative emotions. The nature of the emotions depends on the nature of the stimuli and on our prior experience with them.

The following discussion of emotion is divided into three sections: the response patterns that are elicited by emotional stimuli, the expression of emotions and their recognition by others, and feelings of emotions.

Emotions as Response Patterns

If you ask someone to define the word *emotion,* he or she will probably talk about feelings. But the ultimate reason for the existence of emotions is to provide patterns of behavior appropriate to particular situations. Evolution has selected for patterns of emotional responses that are useful to the individual making them.

All emotional responses contain three components: behavioral, autonomic, and hormonal. The *behavioral* component consists of muscular movements that are appropriate to the situation that elicits them. For example, a dog defending its territory against an intruder first adopts an aggressive posture, growls, and shows its teeth. If the intruder does not leave, the defender runs toward it and attacks. *Autonomic* responses—that is, changes in the activity of the autonomic nervous system—facilitate these behaviors and provide quick mobilization of energy for vigorous movement. As a consequence, the dog's heart rate increases, and changes in the size of blood vessels shunt the circulation of blood away from the digestive organs toward the muscles. *Hormonal* responses reinforce the autonomic responses. The hormones secreted by the adrenal glands further increase heart rate and blood flow to the muscles and also make more glucose available to them.

This section discusses research on the brain mechanisms that control overt emotional behaviors and the autonomic and hormonal responses that accompany them. Special behaviors that communicate emotional states to other animals, such as the threat gestures that precede an attack and the smiles and frowns used by humans, will be discussed in the next section.

Conditioned Emotional Responses

Emotional responses, like all other responses, can be modified by experience. For example, we can learn that a particular situation is dangerous or threatening. Once the learning has taken place, we will become frightened when we encounter that situation. This type of response, acquired through the process of classical conditioning, is called a conditioned emotional response.

A **conditioned emotional response** is produced by a neutral stimulus that has been paired with an emotion-pro-

ducing stimulus. For example, suppose you are helping a friend prepare a meal. You pick up an electric mixer to mix some batter for a cake. Before you can turn the mixer on, the device makes a sputtering noise and then gives you a painful electrical shock. Your first response would be a defensive reflex: You would let go of the mixer, which would end the shock. This response is *specific;* it is aimed at terminating the painful stimulus. The painful stimulus would also elicit *nonspecific* responses controlled by your autonomic nervous system: Your eyes would dilate, your heart rate and blood pressure would increase, you would breathe faster, and so on. The painful stimulus would also trigger the secretion of some stress-related hormones, another nonspecific response.

Suppose, now, that a while later you visit your friend again and once more agree to make a cake. Your friend tells you that the electric mixer is perfectly safe—it has been fixed. Just seeing the mixer and thinking of holding it again makes you a little nervous, but you accept your friend's assurance and pick it up. Just then, it makes the same sputtering noise that it did when it shocked you. What would your response be? Almost certainly, you would drop the mixer again, even if it did not give you a shock. And your pupils would dilate, your heart rate and blood pressure would increase, and your endocrine glands would secrete some stress-related hormones. In other words, the sputtering sound would trigger a conditioned emotional response.

If an organism learns to make a specific response that avoids contact with the aversive stimulus (or at least minimizes its painful effect), most of the nonspecific "emotional" responses will eventually disappear. That is, if the organism learns a successful **coping response**—a response that terminates, avoids, or minimizes an aversive stimulus—the emotional responses will no longer occur. For example, suppose you suspect that your friend's electric mixer is still defective but you are determined to make the cake anyway. You get your gloves from the pocket of your overcoat and put them on. Now you can safely handle the mixer; the gloves provide electrical insulation for your hands. This time the sputtering noise does not bother you because you are protected from electrical shocks. The noise does not activate your autonomic nervous system, nor does it cause your glands to secrete stress-related hormones.

Research by physiological psychologists indicates that a particular brain region plays an important role in the expression of conditioned emotional responses. This region is the *amygdala,* which is located in the temporal lobe, just in front of the hippocampus. (Refer to *Figure 4.33.*) It serves as a focal

conditioned emotional response A classically conditioned response produced by a stimulus that evokes an emotional response—in most cases, including behavioral and physiological components.

coping response A response that permits an animal to escape, avoid, or minimize the stressful (harmful or painful) effects of an aversive stimulus.

point between sensory systems and systems responsible for behavioral, autonomic, and hormonal components of conditioned emotional responses (Kapp et al., 1982; LeDoux, 1995).

Many studies have found that damage to the amygdala disrupts the behavioral, autonomic, and hormonal components of conditioned emotional responses. After this region has been destroyed, animals no longer show signs of fear when confronted with stimuli that have been paired with aversive events. They also act more tamely when handled by humans, their blood levels of stress hormones are lower, and they are less likely to develop ulcers or other forms of stress-induced illnesses (Coover, Murison, and Jellestad, 1992; Davis, 1992b; LeDoux, 1992). Conversely, when the amygdala is stimulated by means of electricity or by an injection of an excitatory drug, animals show physiological and behavioral signs of fear and agitation (Davis, 1992b). In fact, long-term stimulation of the amygdala produces gastric ulcers (Henke, 1982). These observations suggest that the autonomic and hormonal components of emotional responses controlled by the amygdala are among those responsible for the harmful effects of long-term stress. (I will discuss the topic of stress in Chapter 16.)

Social Judgments: Role of the Orbitofrontal Cortex

Although conditioned emotional responses can be elicited by very simple stimuli, our emotions are often reactions to very complex situations; those situations involving other people can be especially complex. Perceiving the meaning of social situations is obviously more complex than perceiving individual stimuli; it involves experiences and memories, inferences and judgments. In fact, the skills involved include some of the most complex we possess. These skills are not localized in any one part of the cerebral cortex, although research does suggest that the right hemisphere is more important than the left. But one region of the brain—the orbitofrontal cortex—plays a special role.

The **orbitofrontal cortex** is located at the base of the frontal lobes. It covers the part of the brain just above the *orbits*—the bones that form the eye sockets—hence the term *orbitofrontal*. (See *Figure 13.8.*) The orbitofrontal cortex receives information from the sensory system and from the regions of the frontal lobes that control behavior. Thus, it knows what is going on in the environment and what plans are being made to respond to these events. It also communicates extensively with the limbic system, which is known to play an important role in emotional reactions. In particular, its connections with the amygdala permit it to affect the activity of the amygdala, which, as we saw, plays a critical role in emotional responses.

The fact that the orbitofrontal cortex plays an important role in emotional behavior is shown by the effects of damage to this region. The first—and most famous—case comes from the mid–nineteenth century. Phineas Gage, a dynamite worker, was using a steel rod to ram a charge of dynamite into a hole drilled in solid rock. The charge exploded and sent the

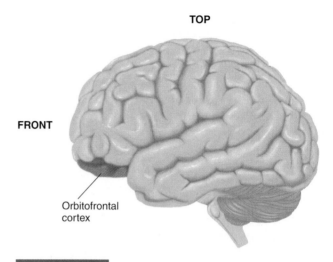

TOP

FRONT

Orbitofrontal cortex

Figure 13.8

The orbitofrontal cortex.

rod into his cheek, through his brain, and out the top of his head. (See *Figure 13.9.*) He survived, but he was a different man. Before his injury, he was serious, industrious, and energetic. Afterward, he became childish, irresponsible, and thoughtless of others. He was unable to make or carry out plans, and his actions appeared to be capricious and whimsical. His accident largely destroyed the orbitofrontal cortex.

Over the succeeding years, physicians reported several cases similar to that of Phineas Gage. In general, damage to the orbitofrontal cortex reduced people's inhibitions and self-concern; they became indifferent to the consequences of their actions. In addition, although they remained sensitive to noxious stimuli, the pain no longer bothered them—it no longer produced an emotional reaction. Then, in 1935, the report of an experiment on a chimpanzee triggered events whose repercussions are still felt today.

Jacobsen, Wolf, and Jackson (1935) tested some chimpanzees on a behavioral task that requires the animal to remain quiet and to remember the location of food that the experimenter has placed behind a screen. One animal, Becky, displayed a violent emotional reaction whenever she made an error while performing this task. "[When] the experimenter lowered . . . the opaque door to exclude the animal's view of the cups, she immediately flew into a temper tantrum. . . . After a few such reactions during the training period, the animal would make no further responses . . ." After the chimpanzee's frontal lobes were removed, she became a model of good comportment. "If the animal made a mistake, it showed no evidence of emotional disturbance but quietly awaited the loading of the cups for the next trial" (Jacobsen, Wolf, and Jackson, 1935, pp. 9–10).

orbitofrontal cortex   A region of the prefrontal cortex that plays an important role in recognition of situations that produce emotional responses.

Figure 13.9

A bust and the skull of Phineas Gage. The steel rod entered his left cheek and exited through his left forehead.
(Warren Museum, Harvard Medical School. Reprinted with permission.)

These findings were reported at a scientific meeting in 1935, which was attended by Egas Moniz, a Portuguese neuropsychiatrist. Another report presented at that meeting indicated that radical removal of the frontal lobes in a human patient (frontal lobotomy, performed because of a tumor) did not appear to produce intellectual impairment (Brickner, 1936). These two reports suggested that frontal lobotomy might reduce pathological emotional reactions and that the operation might not have serious consequences for the patient's intellect. One of Jacobsen's colleagues reported that "Dr. Moniz . . . asked if frontal-lobe removal . . . eliminates frustrational behavior, why would it not be feasible to relieve anxiety states in man by surgical means?" (Fulton, 1949, pp. 63–64). In fact, Moniz did persuade a neurosurgeon to do so, and approximately one hundred operations were eventually performed under his supervision. In 1949, Moniz received the Nobel Prize for the development of the prefrontal lobotomy procedure.

Earlier, I said that the repercussions of the 1935 meeting are still felt today. Since that time, tens of thousands of people have received prefrontal lobotomies, primarily to reduce symptoms of emotional distress, and many of these people are still alive. At first, the procedure was welcomed by the medical community because it provided their patients with relief from emotional anguish. Only after many years were careful studies performed on the side effects of the procedure. These studies showed that although patients did perform well on standard tests of intellectual ability, they showed serious changes in per-

sonality, becoming irresponsible and childish. They also lost the ability to carry out plans and most were unemployable. And although pathological emotional reactions were eliminated, so were normal ones. Because of these findings, and because of the discovery of drugs and therapeutic methods that relieve patients' symptoms without producing such drastic side effects, neurosurgeons eventually abandoned the prefrontal lobotomy procedure (Valenstein, 1986).

What, exactly, does the orbitofrontal cortex do? One possibility is that it is involved in assessing the personal significance of whatever is currently happening. However, this suggestion does not appear to be correct. A person whose orbitofrontal cortex has been damaged by disease or accident is still able to accurately assess the significance of particular situations, but only in a *theoretical* sense. For example, Eslinger and Damasio (1985) found that a patient with bilateral damage of the orbitofrontal cortex displayed excellent social judgment. When he was given hypothetical situations that required him to make decisions about what the people involved should do—situations involving moral, ethical, or practical dilemmas—he always gave sensible answers and justified them with carefully reasoned logic. However, his own life was a disaster. He frittered away his life savings on investments that his family and friends pointed out were bound to fail. He lost one job after another because of his irresponsibility. He became unable to distinguish between trivial decisions and important ones, spending hours trying to decide where to have dinner but failing to use good judgment in situations that concerned his occupation and family life. As the authors noted, "He had learned and used normal patterns of social behavior before his brain lesion, and although he could recall such patterns when he was questioned about their applicability, *real-life situations failed to evoke them*" (p. 1737). Thus, it appears that the orbitofrontal cortex is not directly involved in making judgments and conclusions about events (these occur elsewhere in the brain) but rather in *translating these judgments into appropriate feelings and behaviors.*

Measuring Emotional Responses: Lie Detection in Criminal Investigation

In a criminal investigation in which there is not enough physical evidence to indicate who is guilty and who is innocent, the authorities will interrogate witnesses and suspects and try to determine who is telling the truth. If we had a procedure that could tell when a person was lying, we could be sure that the guilty party would be convicted and that the innocent would go free. Professional polygraphers (people who operate "lie detector" machines) say that we *do* have a method to detect deception: They ask people questions about the crime and measure their emotional responses when they answer the questions. Are the polygraphers right? What does a careful scientific analysis say?

In 1986, an American television network, CBS, hired four different polygraphers to find out which of four employees of

Research indicates that the accuracy of lie-detector tests is not very high.

a photography magazine (which the network owns) had stolen an expensive camera (Lykken, 1988). Each of the polygraphers were told that one of the four employees was suspected but that definite proof was lacking. Sure enough, the polygraphers identified the suspect—a different person in each case—as guilty. Needless to say, no camera was stolen; all the employees were innocent.

The fact that some polygraphers will supply the desired results for a client is certainly contemptible and unethical, but it does not necessarily follow that the practice of lie detection is invalid. After all, there are good and bad practitioners in every profession. How good are careful, well-run polygraph tests at detecting deception?

Before looking at the evidence. we should examine the methods that are used. A polygraph used for a lie detector test is a machine that records physiological reactions associated with people's emotional reactions: heart rate, blood pressure, breathing, and skin conductance (a measure of sweating). The subject is hooked up to the machine, and the questioning begins. Polygraphers use two general methods of questioning: the *control question test* and the *guilty knowledge test.*

The control question test attempts to establish a pattern of physiological responding when the subject lies and when he or she tells the truth. In this test, the examiner may instruct the subject to say "no" to simple yes-or-no questions about the day of the week. Obviously, the examiner will know when the subject is lying and can compare the pattern of responses with truthful and untruthful statements. Then, when the important questions are asked, the examiner can, theoretically, tell when the subject is lying. For this method to work, the subject must show an emotional reaction when he or she lies. Obviously, if the subject truly believes that the polygraph can detect lies, the reaction will be that much stronger. In fact, sometimes the examiner will trick the subject into this belief by having him or her choose a playing card from a deck, look at it, and then say "no" to every question the examiner asks about its identity. The examiner looks at the polygraph record and says, "I can see from your reactions that it is the queen of

hearts." The subject is impressed; now he or she is convinced that the polygraph works and is more likely to display an emotional reaction during an attempt to lie. (Of course, the examiner does not tell the subject that the cards are marked.)

The problem with the control question test is that even innocent people may react more strongly to a relevant question (that is, a crime-related question) than to a control question. First of all, stress is inevitable during a lie detector test. As Lykken (1988) notes, "Only someone who has actually had the polygraph attachments applied to one's body, and then been asked a series of intrusive questions by a stranger, can fully appreciate how vulnerable one feels in that situation" (p. 112). Even an innocent person can react emotionally when asked whether he or she stole money or molested a little child.

Lykken (1988) reviewed the scientific literature on the validity of polygraph tests using the control question technique and found that although the studies correctly identified most of the cases of lying, the incidence of *false positives*—of incorrect indications that innocent people were lying—was almost 50 percent. And these studies were performed meticulously by well-trained examiners. You will understand why the laws of most countries do not permit polygraph tests to be used in court against people who are accused of crimes.

The second method of questioning—the guilty knowledge test—appears to be more reliable than the control question test. This method, developed by Lykken (1981), does not ask whether the subject committed a crime. Instead, it poses several multiple-choice questions about information that only the criminal could know. For example, suppose that a bank robber drops his hat in an alley after leaving the scene of a crime. The examiner will ask the following questions and note the reaction to each of the alternatives:

1. The robber in this case dropped something while escaping. If you are that robber, you will know what he dropped. Was it: a weapon? a face mask? a sack of money? his hat? his car keys?

2. Where did he drop his hat? Was it: in the bank? on the bank steps? on the sidewalk? in the parking lot? in an alley?

3. I'm going to show you five red hats or caps, one at a time. If one of them is your hat, you will recognize it. Which of these hats is yours? Is it: this one? this one? . . . etc. (Lykken, 1988, p. 121)

If the subject knows nothing about the loss of the hat, the chances of showing the strongest reaction to the critical item on any one of the three multiple-choice questions is one in five. The chances of accidentally showing the strongest reaction to *all three* of the questions is eight in a thousand. Of course, if the examiner accidentally (or deliberately) asks the questions in such a way that the answer is obvious (for example, by pausing dramatically before mentioning the critical item), then the test is invalid. The best situation, according to Lykken, is for the examiner not to know which alternatives indicate the guilty knowledge. And the alternatives themselves must be well chosen; as you have undoubtedly learned through your own experience, the alternatives to some poorly written multiple-choice examination questions are simply not plausible. Studies have shown that the guilty knowledge test is much more accurate than the control question test. Almost 90 percent of guilty subjects are correctly identified, and only about 3 or 4 percent of innocent people are incorrectly identified.

Not all criminal investigations can use the guilty knowledge test. For example, the test cannot use any of the information that has been presented to the public by the news media because the subject may have learned of it that way. And if information about the details of the crime are not known to the authorities, it will not be possible to construct any test questions.

As Lykken (1988) notes, unlike Pinocchio, whose nose grew every time he told a lie, we do not emit a distinctive physiological response every time we try to deceive. Given that the overwhelming majority of polygraph tests use the control question procedure, they will inevitably misidentify innocent people as deceptive. Although the test results cannot be used in court, they can misdirect a police investigation by focusing suspicion on innocent people. The guilty knowledge test shows promise, but more research will be needed to know whether it will find a useful place in criminal investigations.

Interim Summary

The Nature of Emotion

Emotion refers to behaviors, physiological responses, and feelings evoked by appetitive or aversive stimuli. Emotional response patterns consist of behaviors that deal with particular situations and physiological responses (both autonomic and hormonal) that support the behaviors. The amygdala organizes behavioral, autonomic, and hormonal responses to a variety of situations, including those that produce fear or anger. Stimulation of the amygdala leads to emotional responses, and its destruction disrupts them.

Between the late 1930s and the late 1950s, many people received prefrontal lobotomies. The most important region affected by the surgery was probably the orbitofrontal cortex. The operations often relieved emotional anguish and the suffering caused by pain. But it also made people become largely indifferent to the social consequences of their own behavior and to the feelings of others, and it interfered with their ability to make and execute plans. Prefrontal lobotomies are no longer performed.

The orbitofrontal cortex plays an important role in social judgments and emotional reactions. People with damage to this region are able to explain the implications of complex social situations but are unable to respond appropriately when these situations concern *them*. Thus, this region appears to be necessary for translating judgments about the personal significance of events into appropriate actions and emotional responses.

Polygraphic lie detection attempts to measure people's emotional reactions to answers they give to questions about a crime. Unfortunately, even innocent people may react to such questions. The rate of false positives (incorrect conclusions that innocent people are lying) is almost 50 percent. The guilty knowledge test appears to be a better method than the control question test. The suspect is asked about information only the criminal could know, and an emotional reaction to that information suggests the possession of such knowledge.

Thought Questions

- Phobias are dramatic examples of conditioned emotional responses. We can acquire these responses without direct experience with an aversive stimulus. For example, a child who sees a parent show signs of fright in the presence of a dog may also develop a fear reaction to the dog. Do you think that some prejudices might be learned in this way, too?
- If you were falsely accused of a crime, would you want to submit to a lie-detector test to try to prove your innocence? Why or why not?

Expression and Recognition of Emotions

The previous section described emotions as organized responses (behavioral, autonomic, and hormonal) that deal with the existing situation in the environment, such as events that pose a threat. For our earliest premammalian ancestors, that is undoubtedly all there was to emotions. But over time, other responses, having new functions, evolved. Many species of animals (including our own) communicate their emotions to others by means of postural changes and facial expressions. These expressions serve useful social functions. They tell other individuals how we feel and—more to the point—what we are likely to do. For example, they warn a rival that we are angry or tell friends that we are sad and would like some comfort and reassurance. This section reviews theories and research on the expression and recognition of emotions.

The Social Nature of Emotional Expressions in Humans

A good case can be made that emotions exist because expressions of emotion communicate important information to other members of the species. An interesting study by Kraut and Johnston (1979) showed that people are more likely to express signs of happiness in the presence of other people than when they are alone. The investigators unobtrusively observed whether people smiled in three situations: while bowling and making a strike or missing one, while watching a hockey game and seeing the home team score or be scored against, and while walking down a street on a beautiful day or a hot and humid one. They found that the happy situations (making a strike, seeing the home team score, or experiencing a beautiful day) produced only small signs of happiness when the people being observed were alone. However, when the people were interacting socially with other people, they were much more likely to smile. For example, bowlers who made a strike usually did not smile when the ball hit the pins. However, when the bowlers turned around to face their companions, they often smiled.

Of course, under some conditions, we suppress expressions of emotion, exaggerate them, or try to fake them, as we will see later in this chapter. But when we do express emotions, they tend to be displayed toward other people.

Situations That Produce Emotions: The Role of Cognition

Emotions do not occur spontaneously; they are provoked by particular stimuli, as we saw in the section on conditioned emotional responses. For humans, the eliciting stimuli and the emotions they produce can be far removed from each other in time, and they can involve cognitive processes. For example, we can experience emotions by remembering things that happened to us or things we did or by imagining events that *might* occur. In addition, emotions can be the products of cognitive processes. For example, suppose that someone says something to you that, on the surface, appears to be complimentary. This event would probably make you feel pleased. But suppose you later think about the remark and realize that it was actually a disguised insult. This realization—a product of your cognitive processes—leads you to become angry.

Most investigators believe that humans do not differ substantially from most other mammals in their expressions and feelings of emotion. There are differences, of course, but the differences appear to be less important than the similarities. If you have ever had a dog, you know that it can express fear, anger, happiness, sadness, surprise, shame, and other emotions in ways that we can recognize as similar to ours. However, we do differ substantially from other animals in the *types of stimuli* that can evoke these emotions. For example, an animal may become frightened and embarrassed by the presence of a large group of strangers, but only humans can become frightened and embarrassed by having to perform in front of a television camera, because only humans realize that they are confronting an unseen audience. Similarly, only humans can experience feelings of love and longing while looking at a picture of an absent loved one.

In humans, emotions are often produced by judging the significance of a particular situation. For example, after a performance, a pianist may perceive the applause as praise for an outstanding performance, judging it to be a positive evaluation of her own worth. She feels pride and satisfaction. In this case, her emotional state is produced by social reinforcement—the expression of approval and admiration by other people. However, if the pianist believes that she has performed poorly, she may judge the applause as the mindless enthusiasm of people who have no taste or appreciation for music, so that she feels only contempt. Furthermore, the person who turned the pages of the music is also present on the stage and thus also perceives the applause. However, because he does not evaluate the applause as praise for anything he did, he does not experience the emotions the pianist feels. The applause may even make him feel jealous. Clearly, a given set of stimuli does not always elicit the same emotion. Judgments made about the significance of the stimuli determine the emotion the person feels.

Biology and Culture

Are Emotional Expressions Innate?

Charles Darwin (1872/1965) suggested that human expressions of emotion have evolved from similar expressions in other animals. He said that emotional expressions are innate, unlearned responses consisting of a complex set of movements, principally of the facial muscles. Thus, a man's sneer and a wolf's snarl are biologically determined response patterns, both controlled by innate brain mechanisms, just as coughing and sneezing are. (Of course, men can sneer and wolves can snarl for quite different reasons.) Some of these movements resemble the behaviors themselves and may have evolved from them. For example, a snarl shows one's teeth and can be seen as an anticipation of biting.

■ Cross-Cultural Expression and Recognition of Emotions

Darwin performed what was probably the first cross-cultural study of behavior. He obtained evidence for his conclusion that emotional expressions were innate by observing his own children and by corresponding with people living in various isolated cultures around the world. He reasoned that if people all over the world, no matter how isolated, show the same facial expressions of emotion, these expressions must be inherited instead of learned. The logical argument goes like this: When groups of people are isolated for many years, they develop different languages. Thus, we can say that the words people use are arbitrary; there is no biological basis for using particular words to represent particular concepts. However, if facial expressions are inherited, they should take approximately the same form in people from all cultures, despite their isolation from one another. And Darwin did, indeed, find that people in different cultures used the same patterns of movement of facial muscles to express a particular emotional state.

In 1967 and 1968, Ekman and Friesen carried out some interesting cross-cultural observations that validated those of Darwin (Ekman, 1980). They visited an isolated tribe in a remote area of New Guinea—the South Fore tribe. This group of 319 adults and children had never been exposed to Western culture. They had never seen a movie, lived in a Western town, or worked for someone from outside their culture. If they were able to identify accurately the emotional expressions of Westerners as well as they could identify those of members of their own tribe, and if their own facial expressions were the same as those of Westerners, then the researchers could conclude that these expressions were not culturally determined.

Because translations of single words from one language to another are not always accurate, Ekman and Friesen told little stories to describe an emotion instead of presenting a single word. They told the story to a subject, presented three photographs of Westerners depicting three different emotions, and asked the subject to choose the appropriate one. Read the captions of Figure 13.10 and see whether you would have any trouble matching each of these stories with one of the photographs shown there. (See *Figure 13.10.*)

I am sure that you did not have any trouble—and neither did the members of the Fore tribe. In a second study, Ekman and Friesen asked Fore tribespeople to imagine how they would feel in situations that would produce various emotions, and the researchers videotaped their facial expressions. They showed photographs of the videotapes to American college students, who had no trouble identifying the emotions. Four of them are shown in Figure 13.11. The caption describes the story that was used to elicit each expression. (See *Figure 13.11.*)

Darwin suggested that a man's sneer and a wolf's snarl are both biologically determined response patterns.

Other researchers have compared the facial expressions of blind and normally sighted children. They reasoned that if the facial expressions of both groups were similar, the expressions would be natural for our species and would not require learning by imitation. (Studies of

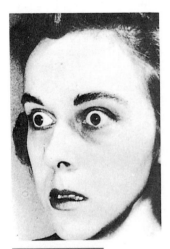  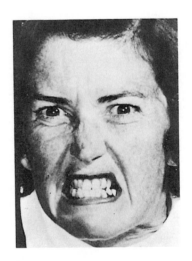

Figure 13.10

Recognizing emotional expressions. Ekman and Friesen asked members of the South Fore tribe of New Guinea to match the following stories with the appropriate photographs. *Fear*—She is sitting in her house all alone and there is no one else in the village; and there is no knife, ax, or bow and arrow in the house. A wild pig is standing in the door of the house and . . . she is afraid the pig will bite her. *Happy*—Her friends have come and she is happy. *Anger*—She is angry and is about to fight.

(Ekman, 1980, p. 130. Photographs from Ekman, P. The Face of Man: Expressions of Universal Emotions in a New Guinea Village. *New York: Garland STPM Press, 1980. By permission of Silvan Tomkins. Photo by Ed. Gallob.)*

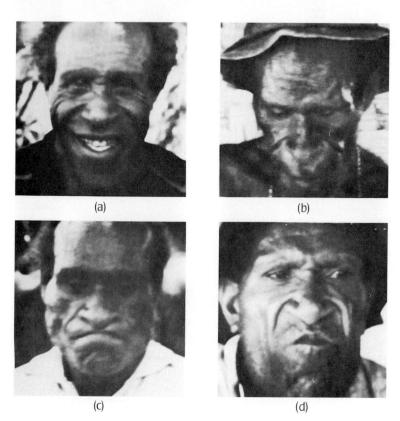

(a)

(b)

(c)

(d)

Figure 13.11

Portraying emotions. Ekman and Friesen asked South Fore tribesmen to make faces (shown in the photographs) when they were told stories. (a) "Your friend has come and you are happy." (b) "Your child had died." (c) "You are angry and about to fight." (d) "You see a dead pig that has been lying there a long time."

(From Ekman, P. The Face of Man: Expressions of Universal Emotions in a New Guinea Village. New York: Garland STPM Press, 1980. Reprinted with permission.)

blind adults would not be conclusive because adults would have heard enough descriptions of facial expressions to be able to pose them.)

In fact, the facial expressions of young blind and sighted children are very similar. However, as blind children grow older, their facial gestures tend to become somewhat less expressive (Woodworth and Schlosberg, 1954; Izard, 1971). This finding suggests that social reinforcement is important in maintaining our displays of emotion. However, the evidence clearly shows that we do not have to learn to smile, frown, or show other feelings with our facial gestures. Both the cross-cultural studies and the investigations of blind children confirm the naturalness of these expressions.

The results of cross-cultural studies and studies of blind people suggest strongly that situations expected to have emotional relevance produce consistent patterns of contraction in the facial muscles. The patterns of movement are apparently inherited—wired into the brain, so to speak. The consistency of facial movements suggests an underlying consistency of emotional feeling throughout our species.

■ Cultural Control of Emotional Expression: Display Rules

We all realize that other people can recognize our expressions of emotions. Consequently, we sometimes try to hide our true feelings, attempting to appear impassive or even to display an emotion different from what we feel. At other times, we may exaggerate our emotional response to make

sure that others see how we feel. For example, if a friend tells us about a devastating experience, we make sure that our facial expression conveys sadness and sympathy. Researchers have studied all these phenomena.

Attempting to hide an emotion is called **masking.** An attempt to exaggerate or minimize the expression of an emotion is called **modulation.** And an attempt to express an emotion we do not actually feel is called **simulation.** According to Ekman and Friesen (1975), the expression of emotions often follows culturally determined **display rules**—rules that prescribe under what situations we should or should not display signs of particular emotions. Although the patterns of muscular movements that accompany particular feelings are biologically determined, these movements can, to a certain extent, be controlled by display rules. (See *Figure 13.12.*)

Each culture has a particular set of display rules. For example, in Western society, it is impolite for a winner to show too much pleasure and for a loser to show too much disappointment. The expression of these emotions is supposed to be modulated downward. Also, in many soci-

masking Attempting to hide the expression of an emotion.

modulation An attempt to exaggerate or minimize the expression of an emotion.

simulation An attempt to express an emotion that one does not actually feel.

display rule A culturally determined rule that prescribes the expression of emotions in particular situations.

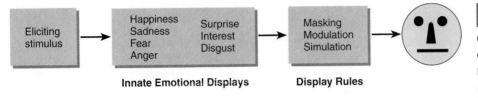

Figure 13.12

Controlled facial displays. Innate emotional displays can be modified by display rules.
(Adapted from Ekman, P., and Friesen, W. Semiotica, 1969, 1, 49–98.)

eties, it is unmanly to cry or to show fear and unfeminine to show anger.

Several studies have found that North American boys and girls differ in their facial expressions of emotion as they get older, presumably because they learn about their society's gender-specific display rules. Very young infants show no sex differences in facial expression (Field, 1982). However, by the time they are in nursery school, boys and girls begin to differ: Girls are more likely to show facial expressions of emotion. Buck (1975, 1977) showed various types of color slides to nursery–schoolchildren and unobtrusively videotaped their faces as they watched. Some slides were pleasant, some puzzling, and some unpleasant. He showed the videotapes of the children to adults (university students) and asked them to try to guess the nature of the children's emotional expressions. Buck assumed that the accuracy of the ratings would indicate the degree of emotional expression. The adults could guess the girls' emotions more accurately than the boys'.

Ekman and his colleagues (Ekman, Friesen, and Ellsworth, 1972; Friesen, 1972) attempted to assess a different kind of culturally determined display rule. They showed a distressing film to Japanese and American college students, singly and in the presence of a visitor, who was described to the subjects as a scientist. Because the Japanese culture discourages public display of emotion, the researchers expected that the Japanese students would show fewer facial expressions of emotion when in public than when alone.

The researchers recorded the facial expressions of their subjects with hidden cameras while the subjects viewed a film showing a gruesome and bloody coming-of-age rite in a preliterate tribe. The results were as predicted. When the subjects were alone, American and Japanese subjects showed the same facial expressions. When they were with another person, the Japanese students were less likely to express negative emotions and more likely to mask these expressions with polite smiles. Thus, people from both societies used the same facial expressions of emotion but were subject to different social display rules.

When people attempt to mask the expression of a strongly felt emotion, they usually are not completely able to do so. That is, there is some **leakage,** or subtle sign of the emotion (Ekman and Friesen, 1969). Ekman and Friesen (1974) investigated this phenomenon. They showed an unpleasant film of burns and amputations to female nursing students. After watching the film, the subjects were interviewed by an experimenter, who asked them about the film. Some of the subjects were asked to pretend to the interviewer that they had seen a pleasant film. The experimenters videotaped the subjects during the interviews and showed these tapes to a separate group of raters, asking them to try to determine whether the people they were watching were being honest or deceptive. The raters were shown videotapes of the subjects' faces or bodies. The results indicated that the raters could detect the deception better when they saw the subjects' bodies than when they saw their faces. Apparently, people are better at masking signs of emotion shown by their facial muscles than those shown by muscles in other parts of their body. Presumably, people recognize the attention paid to the face and learn to control their facial expressions better than they do the movements of the rest of the body.

Interim Summary

Expression and Recognition of Emotions

Expressions of emotion communicate important information among people. An observational study of humans indicated that smiles appear to occur most often when someone is interacting socially with other people. This finding supports the social nature of emotional expression.

Emotions are provoked by particular stimuli, and in humans these stimuli can involve cognitive processes as well as external events. For example, emotions can result from our judgments about complex social situations.

Darwin believed that expression of emotion by facial gestures was innate and that muscular movements were inherited behavioral patterns. Ekman and his colleagues showed that members of the South Fore tribe recognized facial expressions of Westerners and made facial gestures that were clear to Westerners. These results, along with observations of blind children, strongly suggest that emotional expressions are innate behavior patterns and that Darwin was correct.

Expressions of emotion are not always frank and honest indications of a person's emotional state. They can be masked, modulated, or simulated according to culturally determined display rules. For example, although male and female infants

leakage A sign of expression of an emotion that is being masked.

do not differ in their degree of emotional expression, boys and girls begin to acquire different patterns of responding during early childhood. Cultural differences also exist, as the study comparing Japanese and American people observed. Even when a person attempts to mask his or her expression of emotion, some leakage occurs, particularly in movements of the body. Presumably, we learn to control our facial expressions better because we are aware of the attention other people pay to these expressions.

Thought Questions

■ We can move our facial muscles to simulate expressions of emotions, but these expressions are usually less convincing than spontaneous ones. Have you ever found yourself trying to suppress a smile when you wanted to seem serious or to look happy when you were really feeling sad? If you wanted to be an actor or a model, how would you try to develop realistic expressions of emotions?

Feelings of Emotion

So far, we have examined two aspects of emotions: the patterns of behavioral, autonomic, and hormonal responses that are produced by a situation that provokes an emotion and the communication of emotional states among people. The next aspect of emotion we will examine in this chapter is the subjective component—feelings of emotion.

From very early times, people have associated emotions with physiological responses. We can easily understand why. Strong emotions can cause increased heart rate, irregular breathing, queasy feelings in the internal organs, trembling, sweating, reddening of the face, or even fainting. The question is whether these physiological changes *constitute* emotions or are merely symptoms of some other underlying process. That is, do we feel frightened because we tremble, or do we tremble because we feel frightened? In this section, we will look at some theories that attempt to answer these questions.

The James–Lange Theory

William James (1842–1910), an American psychologist, and Carl Lange (1834–1900), a Danish physiologist, independently suggested similar explanations for emotion, which most people refer to collectively as the James-Lange theory (James, 1884; Lange, 1887). Basically, the **James–Lange theory** states that emotion-producing situations elicit an appropriate set of physiological responses, such as trembling,

James-Lange theory A theory of emotion that suggests that behaviors and physiological responses are directly elicited by situations and that feelings of emotions are produced by feedback from these behaviors and responses.

sweating, and increased heart rate. The situations also elicit behaviors, such as clenching of the fists or fighting. The brain receives sensory feedback from the muscles and from the organs that produce these responses, and it is this feedback that constitutes our feelings of emotion. As James put it:

> *The bodily changes follow directly the perception of the exciting fact, and . . . our feelings of the same changes as they occur is the emotion.* Common sense says we lose our fortune, are sorry, and weep; we meet a bear, are frightened, and run. . . . The hypothesis here to be defended says that this order of sequence is incorrect. . . . The more rational statement is that we feel sorry because we cry, angry because we strike, afraid because we tremble, and not that we cry, strike, or tremble because we are sorry, angry or fearful, as the case may be. (James, 1890, p. 449)

Chapter 15 describes a topic of research called *attribution,* by which process we make conclusions about the causes of other people's behavior. James's approach is closely related to the process of attribution. He suggests that our own emotional feelings are based on what we find ourselves doing and on the sensory feedback we receive from the activity of our muscles and internal organs. Where feelings of emotions are concerned, we are self-observers. Thus, patterns of emotional responses and expressions of emotions give rise to feelings of emotion. By this reasoning, feelings of emotions are simply by-products of emotional responses. (See *Figure 13.13.*)

James's description of the process of emotion may strike you as being at odds with your own experience. Many people think that they experience emotions directly, internally. They

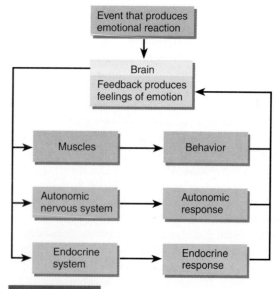

Figure 13.13

A diagrammatic representation of the James–Lange theory of emotion. An event in the environment triggers behavioral, autonomic, and endocrine responses. Feedback from these responses produces feelings of emotions.

consider the outward manifestations of emotions to be secondary events. But have you ever found yourself in an unpleasant confrontation with someone else and discovered that you were trembling, even though you did not think that you were so bothered by the encounter? Or did you ever find yourself blushing in response to some public remark that was made about you? Or did you ever find tears coming to your eyes while watching a film that you did not think was affecting you? What would you conclude about your emotional states in situations like these? Would you ignore the evidence from your own physiological reactions?

Effects of Spinal Cord Damage

Hohman (1966) collected data from humans that directly tested James's hypothesis. He questioned people who had suffered damage to the spinal cord about how intense their emotional feelings were. If feedback from the body is important, one would expect that emotional feelings would be less intense if the injury were high (that is, close to the brain) than if it were low, because a high spinal cord injury would make the person become insensitive to a larger part of the body. In fact, this result is precisely what Hohman found: The higher the injury, the less intense the feeling was. (See *Figure 13.14.*)

The comments of patients with high spinal cord injuries suggest that the severely diminished feedback does change their feelings but not necessarily their behavior.

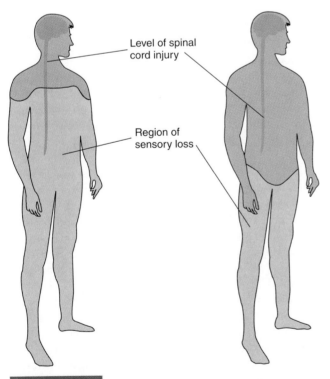

Figure 13.14

Hohman's investigation of emotion in people with spinal cord damage. The higher the spinal cord damage, the less intense was the person's feeling.

I was at home alone in bed one day and dropped a cigarette where I couldn't reach it. I finally managed to . . . put it out. I could have burned up right there, but the funny thing is, I didn't get all shook up about it. I just didn't feel afraid at all. . . .

Sometimes I act angry when I see some injustice. I yell and cuss and raise hell, because if you don't . . . I've learned people will take advantage of you, but it doesn't have the heat to it that it used to. It's a mental kind of anger. (Hohman, 1966, pp. 150–151)

These comments suggest that people do not necessarily engage in emotional behavior *because of* their feelings; lacking these feelings, people still engage in the same behaviors for "rational" reasons.

Evaluating Scientific Issues

Is Cognition Essential for Emotion?

One of the current controversies among psychologists interested in feelings of emotion is the relative importance of automatic processes (such as classical conditioning) and cognitive processes (especially those involving conscious thought). Some psychologists, such as Richard Lazarus (1984), believe that emotions are produced only by cognitive processes—by anticipating, experiencing, or imagining the outcomes of important interactions with the environment. Others, such as Robert Zajonc (1984), insist that cognitive appraisal is not *necessary and that emotions are automatic, species-typical responses heavily influenced by classical conditioning.*

■ **Classical Conditioning or Cognitive Processes?** Although the two sides of the debate appear to have been drawn sharply, it seems clear that both automatic processes and conscious deliberation play a role in the expression and feelings of emotion. Some examples of emotions clearly involve cognitive processes. For instance, as we saw earlier in this chapter, a person can become angry after realizing that someone's "kind words" actually contained a subtle insult. This anger is a result of cognition. But sometimes, emotional reactions and their associated feelings seem to occur automatically. As we saw, through the process of classical conditioning, stimuli can evoke emotional reactions before we have time to realize what is happening. In some cases, we may be acting in a hostile and angry manner without realizing what we are doing. If cognitive processes are responsible for our anger, they are certainly not conscious, deliberate ones.

One of the problems with this debate (as with many other debates) is that the opponents sometimes define the same terms in different ways. For example, not everyone agrees which operations of the brain should be regarded as cognitive and which should not. According to Lazarus, many cognitive processes are unconscious and relatively automatic. But if cognitive processes need not be conscious, how can we tell whether a given process is cognitive? And if we cannot tell, how can we hope to decide whether cognition is necessary for all emotions? If our definition of cognition is too general, we would have to conclude that *all* responses require cognition.

Let's look at some of the evidence. The person most responsible for directing researchers' attention to the possible interaction between cognition and physiological reactions in feelings of emotions is Stanley Schachter. Schachter (1964) proposed that feelings of emotions are determined *jointly* by perception of physiological responses and by cognitive assessment of a specific situation. Thus, to Schachter, emotion is cognition plus perception of physiological arousal. Both are necessary.

Schachter and Singer (1962) tested this hypothesis by arranging to induce physiological arousal in groups of subjects placed in various situations. All subjects were told that they were part of an investigation on the effects of a vitamin called "suproxin" on visual perception. No such vitamin exists. The investigators gave some subjects injections of adrenaline, a hormone that stimulates a variety of autonomic nervous system effects associated with arousal, such as increased heart rate and blood pressure, irregular breathing, warming of the face, and mild trembling. Other subjects received a control injection of a salt solution, which has no physiological effects.

Next, the researchers placed some subjects in an anger-provoking situation in which they were treated rudely and subjected to obnoxious test questions such as the following: "How many men, besides your father, has your mother slept with? (a) one, (b) two, (c) three, (d) four or more." Others were treated politely and saw the antics of another "subject" (a confederate who was hired by the experimenters) who acted silly and euphoric. The experimenters hoped that these two situations, together with the physiological reactions produced by the injections of adrenaline, would promote either negative or positive emotional states.

Finally, some subjects were correctly informed that the injections they received would produce side effects such as trembling and a pounding heart. Others were told to expect irrelevant side effects or none at all. Schachter and Singer predicted that the subjects who knew what side effects to expect would correctly attribute their physiological reactions to the drug and would not experience a change in emotion. Those who were misinformed would note their physiological arousal and conclude that they were feeling especially angry or happy, as the circumstance dictated. All subjects reported their emotional states in a questionnaire.

The results were not as clear-cut as the experimenters had hoped. The adrenaline did not increase the intensity of the subjects' emotional states. However, subjects who expected to experience physiological arousal as a result of the injection reported much less of a change in their emotional states than did those who did not expect it, *regardless of whether they had received the adrenaline or the placebo*. In other words, no matter what their physiological state was, they felt less angry or happy after having been exposed to one of the emotional situations. These results suggest that we *interpret* the significance of our physiological reactions rather than simply experience them as emotions.

Nisbett and Schachter (1966) provided further evidence that subjects can be fooled into attributing their own naturally occurring physiological responses to a drug and thus into feeling less "emotional." First, they gave all subjects a placebo pill (one having no physiological effects). Half the subjects were told that the pill would make their hearts pound, their breathing increase, and their hands tremble; the other half (the control subjects) were told nothing about possible side effects. Then, the researchers strapped on electrodes and gave the subjects electrical shocks. All subjects presumably experienced pain and fear, and, consequently, their heart rates and breathing increased, they trembled, and so on. Yet the subjects who perceived their reactions as drug-induced were able to tolerate stronger shocks than were the control subjects, and they reported less pain and fear. Thus, cognition can affect people's judgments about their own emotional states and even their tolerance of pain.

The precise nature of the interaction between cognition and physiological arousal has not been determined. For example, in the Nisbett and Schachter experiment, although the verbal instructions about effects of the placebo affected the subjects' reactions to pain, it did not seem to do so through a logical, reasoned process. In fact, Nisbett and Wilson (1977) later reported that subjects did *not* consciously attribute their increased tolerance of pain to the effects of the pill. When subjects were asked whether they had thought about the pill while receiving the shocks or whether it had occurred to them that the pill was causing some physical effects, subjects typically gave answers such as "No, I was too worried about the shock." Even after the experimenters explained the experiment and its rationale in detail, subjects typically reported "that the hypothesis was very interesting and that many people probably would go through the process that the experimenter described, but so far as they could tell, they themselves had not" (Nisbett and Wilson, 1977, p. 237).

Schachter's major contribution to the study of emotion was to make other psychologists consider the complex interactions between the automatic and conscious processes that are responsible for producing and perceiving emotional responses. As I said in the beginning of the chapter, emotions are what life itself is all about, so we should not be surprised that emotions are influenced by—and in turn have an influence on—so many different types of variables.

■ What Should We Conclude?

Too often, scientists—like the rest of us—tend to see complex interactions as simple dichotomies. For example, behavior is not the result of nature *or* nurture. Similarly, if we find that emotions can be affected by cognitive factors, we need not conclude that emotions can never be automatic reactions. Nor should we conclude that cognitive processes are irrelevant just because we find that some emotions are classically conditioned responses. Perhaps the best way to understand emotions is to remember that they are *responses* to events that are important to us. Some events are important to us for complicated reasons. In such cases, the emotional reactions these events produce must involve complex cognitive processes. Other events have a simple, direct relation to our well-being. In these cases, very simple brain processes can produce the emotional reactions.

Interim Summary

Feelings of Emotion

From the earliest times, people recognized that emotions were accompanied by feelings that seemed to come from inside the body. James and Lange suggested that the physiological and behavioral reactions to emotion-producing situations were perceived by people as states of emotion and that emotional states were not the *causes* of these reactions. Hohman's study of people with spinal cord damage supported the James-Lange theory. People who could no longer feel the reactions from most of their body reported that they no longer experienced intense emotional states. However, the loss of feelings did not necessarily affect their behavior; thus, emotional feelings and behaviors may be at least somewhat independent.

Although emotional states are sometimes produced by automatic, classically conditioned responses, some psychologists have suggested that the perception of our own emotional state is not determined solely by feedback from our behavior and the organs controlled by the autonomic nervous system. It is also determined by cognitive assessment of the situation in which we find ourselves. Schachter and his colleagues found that information about the expected physiological effects of drugs (or placebos) influenced subjects' reports about their emotional state. In one study, subjects even tolerated more intense electrical shocks, apparently discounting their own fear. Although these results do not support any single comprehensive theory of emotion, they do underscore the importance of cognitive factors in emotion and the complexity of this phenomenon. Emotions are undoubtedly not the products of automatic processes *or* of cognitive processes but rather involve both factors.

Thought Questions

- As you know, we tend to become accustomed to our present circumstances. If we finally achieve a goal we have been striving for—a car, a well–paying job, a romantic attachment with a wonderful person—we find that the happiness it brings us is not permanent. But if we then lose what we have gained, we are even less happy than we were in the first place. Is it ever possible for a person to be happy all the time?
- We can control the *display* of our emotions, but can we control our feelings? Can you think of any ways to make yourself feel happy or stop feeling angry?

Suggestions for Further Reading

Beck, R.C. *Motivation: Theories and Principles,* 3rd ed. Englewood Cliffs, NJ: Prentice-Hall, 1989.

Franken, R.E. *Human Motivation,* 3rd ed. Pacific Grove, CA: Brooks/Cole Publishing, 1994.

These texts describe the general principles of motivation as well as specific types of motivated behavior.

Stellar, J.R., and Stellar, E. *The Neurobiology of Motivation and Reward.* New York: Springer-Verlag, 1985.

This book discusses the biology of reinforcement.

Logue, A.W. *The Psychology of Eating and Drinking,* 2nd ed. New York: W.H. Freeman, 1992.

This book covers alcohol abuse as well as eating and eating disorders.

Kelley, K., and Byrne, D. *Human Sexual Behavior.* Englewood Cliffs, NJ: Prentice-Hall, 1991.

This book is well written and describes sexual behavior and the social and biological variables that affect it.

Carlson, J.G., and Hatfield, E. *Psychology of Emotion.* Belmont, CA: Wadsworth, 1989.

James, W. *Principles of Psychology.* New York: Henry Holt, 1890.

Stein, N.L., Leventhal, B., and Trabasso, T. (eds.). *Psychological and Biological Approaches to Emotion.* Hillsdale, NJ: Lawrence Erlbaum Associates, 1990.

The book by Carlson and Hatfield covers the field of emotion. James's book provides insights into the history of our thinking about emotion. The book edited by Stein, Leventhal, and Trabasso contains chapters by experts in the field of emotion.

Ben-Shakhar, G., and Furedy, J.J. *Theories and Applications in the Detection of Deception.* New York: Springer-Verlag, 1990.

Lykken, D.T. *A Tremor in the Blood: Uses and Abuses of the Lie Detector.* New York: McGraw-Hill, 1981.

Both books provide a good review of the methods of lie detection and research on its reliability and validity. I particularly recommend the one by Lykken because of its informal style and its wealth of interesting details and vivid examples.

Chapter 14

Personality

Chapter Outline

Trait Theories of Personality

Personality Types and Traits • Identification of Personality Traits

Trait theories of personality stress that personality consists of enduring characteristics evident in behavior in many situations. Several researchers have identified traits that appear to form the core of personality including extraversion, neuroticism, psychoticism, openness, agreeableness, and conscientiousness.

Psychobiological Approaches

Heritability of Personality Traits • Brain Mechanisms in Personality

Psychobiological approaches to the study of personality focus on the role of inherited factors and brain mechanisms in personality development. Although most of the variability in personality traits is due to heredity, a substantial portion is also due to the interaction of heredity and environment. The neural systems responsible for reinforcement, punishment, and arousal appear to underlie the personality traits of extraversion, neuroticism, and psychoticism. Other research shows that shyness may have its roots in a neural mechanism that includes the amygdala.

The Social Learning Approach

Expectancies and Observational Learning • Reciprocal Determinism and Self-Efficacy • Person Variables • Locus of Control • *Evaluating Scientific Issues: Traits versus Situations as Predictors of Behavior*

The social learning approach to the study of personality represents a mixture of behavior-analytic and cognitive concepts. Bandura asserts that personality development involves the imitation of others' behavior and expectations about potential reinforcing and punishing contingencies. Bandura also argues that the interaction of behavioral, environmental, and personal (cognitive) variables ultimately determines personality. Prominent among these variables is self-efficacy, or one's expectations of success in a given situation. Mischel extended Bandura's emphasis on personal variables to include five other factors: competencies, encoding strategies and personal constructs, expectancies, subjective values, and self-regulatory systems and plans. Rotter's work has shown that the extent to which people perceive their behavior to be controlled by internal variables or external variables also plays an important role in personality. Current thinking in psychology stresses that behavior results from the interaction of dispositional and situational variables.

The Psychodynamic Approach

The Development of Freud's Theory • Structures of the Mind: Id, Ego, and Superego • Defense Mechanisms • Freud's Psychosexual Theory of Personality Development • Further Development of Freud's Theory: The Neo-Freudians • Some Observations on Psychodynamic Theory and Research

The psychodynamic approach to the study of personality began with the work of Freud, who proposed that personality development is based on psychosexual tensions that are present from birth. Freud theorized that personality develops as psychosexual tensions express themselves during different stages of development. Defense mechanisms reduce the anxiety produced by conflicts among the id, ego, and superego. The neo-Freudians accepted parts of Freud's theory but rejected others. Although Freud's theory influenced many Western conceptions of human nature, it has not been supported by scientific research, largely because the theory itself is ambiguous and its tenets are untestable.

The Humanistic Approach

Maslow and Self-Actualization • Rogers and Conditions of Worth • Some Observations on the Humanistic Approach

Humanistic psychologists are interested in personal growth, satisfaction with life, and positive human values. Maslow argued that reaching one's potential first requires satisfaction of basic needs, such as food, safety, love, and esteem. Rogers maintained that self-actualization is best realized in circumstances characterized by unconditional positive regard. The humanistic approach remains empirically unsubstantiated.

Assessment of Personality

Objective Tests of Personality • Projective Tests of Personality • Evaluation of Projective Tests • *Biology and Culture: Gender Differences in Personality*

Specific tests have been devised to study personality. Objective tests, such as the MMPI and the NEO-PI, contain multiple-choice and true-false questions that are aimed at revealing the extent to which the test-taker possesses specific traits. Projective tests, such as the Rorschach Inkblot Test and the Thematic Apperception Test, present the test-taker with ambiguous stimuli; it is assumed that test-takers will "project" aspects of their personality into their responses to these stimuli. Although projective tests are still widely used, they have low reliability and validity. Although gender differences in personality have been found to have high heritability, they are also strongly influenced by cultural variables and survival needs.

*T*he identical twin boys were separated at the age of thirty-seven days and were adopted by two different working-class families in Ohio. Coincidentally, both were named Jim by their adoptive families. They did not meet each other again until the late 1970s.

Both Jims liked math in school, but neither liked spelling. At ten years of age, they both developed sinus headaches and a few years later developed migraine headaches. They both used the same words to describe their head pain. The twins had identical pulse rates and blood pressures, and both put on ten pounds of weight at the same time in their lives. Both Jims were clerical workers who enjoyed woodworking, served as volunteers for police agencies, enjoyed spending their vacations in Florida, had married and divorced women named Linda, chewed their nails, owned dogs named Toy, and drove Chevrolets.

Bridget and Dorothy, also identical twins, were thirty-nine years old when they were reunited. Each came to their meeting wearing seven rings on her fingers, two bracelets on one wrist, and a watch and a bracelet on the other. Although the two women were raised by families of very different socioeconomic levels, their personalities were very similar. The most striking difference between them was that the twin raised by the family of modest means had problems with her teeth.

Oskar and Jack were born in Trinidad. Their mother, a German, took Oskar back to Germany, where he was raised as a Catholic. He became a member of a Nazi youth group. His brother Jack was raised by his father in the Caribbean as a Jew. He spent part of his adolescence on a kibbutz in Israel. At the time of their reunion, Oskar lived in Germany and Jack in southern California. When the twins met at the airport, both were wearing wire-rimmed glasses and two-pocket shirts with epaulets. Both had mustaches. They both liked spicy foods and sweet liqueurs, tended to fall asleep while watching television, kept rubber bands on their wrists, thought it funny to sneeze in a crowd of people, flushed the toilet before using it, and read magazines from back to front. Although their backgrounds were very different, their scores on a widely used personality test were very similar.

These striking cases of identical twins reunited in adulthood suggest that heredity plays an important role in shaping personality. However, like all pieces of anecdotal evidence, they must be regarded as clues, subject to the confirmation by careful scientific evaluation. The Minnesota Study of Twins Reared Apart is one of several research projects designed to determine the roles of heredity and environment in the development of personality.

The reunion of this pair of twins prompted Dr. Thomas Bouchard to initiate the Minnesota Study of Twins Reared Apart.

Each semester, I ask students in my introductory psychology class to respond, anonymously and in writing, to different psychological questions. One question I recently asked was "Are you a happy person and why or why not?" Consider two answers that I received:

> . . . I have always been a happy person. I don't really remember ever not being happy. Even as a kid I had lots of friends, nobody ever seemed to get mad at me. I like other people a lot. It seems the more I like people, the more I try to help them, the more they like me, and the happier I am.

> . . . I wouldn't say that I am not happy. It's just that what makes me happy doesn't usually seem to be the same kinds of things that make my parents or even some of my friends happy. I would rather stay at home and read a novel or watch a movie by myself than go to a party . . . I like people but I don't necessarily find my happiness in them.

How would you respond to this question? Would your own response be the same as one of the answers given above? Probably not. After all, people differ so much. People have different styles of thinking, of relating to others, and of working, all of which reflect differences in personality—differences crucial to defining us as individuals. Common experience tells us that there is no one else just like us. There may even be significant differences in the personal characteristics of identical twins.

Such everyday observations provide a starting point for psychology's study of personality. But unlike such informal observations, psychology's approach to studying personality is considerably more calculated. For example, to many people, personality is nothing more than "what makes people different from one another." But to psychologists, the concept is generally defined much more narrowly. **Personality** is a particular pattern of behavior and thinking that prevails across time and situations and differentiates one person from another.

Psychologists do not draw inferences about personality from casual observations of people's behavior. Rather, their assessment of personality is derived from results of special tests designed to identify particular personality characteristics. The goal of psychologists who study personality is to discover the causes of individual differences in behavior.

This goal has led to two specific developments in the field of personality psychology: the development of theories that attempt to explain such individual differences and the development of methods by which individual patterns of behavior can be studied, and classified. In this chapter, we will discuss what is currently known about personality. First, I will present an overview of the major theories of personality. Next, I will describe the methods used by psychologists to study individual differences in personality.

Before I begin our discussion, though, I would like to offer a caveat about our study of personality. We must be careful to avoid the nominal fallacy: Merely *identifying* and *describing* a personality characteristic is not the same as *explaining* it. However, identification is the first step on the way to explanation. What types of research efforts are necessary to study personality? Some psychologists devote their efforts to the development of tests that can reliably measure differences in personality. Others try to determine the events—biological and environmental—that cause people to behave as they do. Thus, research on human personality requires two kinds of effort: identifying personality characteristics and determining the variables that produce and control them (Buss, 1995).

Trait Theories of Personality

As you will see in this chapter, the word *personality* means different things to different people. The way in which personality is used by trait theorists is similar to the way in which we often think of personality in everyday life: a set of personal characteristics that determines the different ways we act and react in a variety of situations.

Personality Types and Traits

It has long been apparent that people differ in personality. The earliest known explanation for these individual differences is the humoral theory, proposed by the Greek physician Galen in the second century and based on then-common medical beliefs that had originated with the ancient Greeks. The body was thought to contain four humors, or fluids: yellow bile, black bile, phlegm, and blood. People were classified according to the disposition supposedly produced by the predominance of one of these humors in their systems. Choleric people, who had an excess of yellow bile, were bad-tempered and irritable. Melancholic people, who had an excess of black bile, had gloomy and pessimistic temperaments. Phlegmatic people, whose bodies contained an excessive amount of phlegm, were sluggish, calm, and unexcitable. Sanguine people had a preponderance of blood (*sanguis*), which made them cheerful and passionate. (See *Figure 14.1*.)

Although later biological investigations discredited the humoral theory, the notion that people could be divided into different **personality types**—different categories into which personality characteristics can be assigned based on factors such as developmental experiences—persisted long afterward. For example, Freud's theory, which maintains that people go through several stages of psychosexual development,

personality A particular pattern of behavior and thinking prevailing across time and situations that differentiates one person from another.

personality types Different categories into which personality characteristics can be assigned based on factors such as developmental experiences or physical characteristics.

Figure 14.1

Characteristics of the four humors, according to a medieval artist: (a) choleric—violent and aggressive temperament; (b) melancholic—gloomy and pessimistic temperament; (c) phlegmatic—sluggish, relaxed, and dull temperament; and (d) sanguine—outgoing, passionate, and fun-loving temperament.

predicts the existence of different types of people, each type having problems associated with one of these stages. We will discuss some of these problems later in this chapter.

Personality types are useful in formulating hypotheses because when a theorist is thinking about personality variables, extreme cases are easily brought to mind. But after identifying and defining personality types, one must determine whether these types actually exist and whether knowing a person's personality type can lead to valid predictions about his or her behavior in different situations.

Most modern investigators reject the idea that individuals can be assigned to discrete categories. Instead, they generally conceive of individual differences in personality as being in degree, not kind. Tooby and Cosmides (1990) also argue that the nature of human reproduction makes the evolution of specific personality types unlikely—sex produces a reshuffling of the genes in each generation, making it highly unlikely that a single, unified set of genes related to personality type would be passed from one generation to the next.

Rather than classify people by categories, or types, many investigators prefer to measure the degree to which an individual expresses a particular personality trait. A **personality trait** is an enduring personal characteristic that reveals itself in a particular pattern of behavior in different situations. A simple example illustrates the difference between types and traits. We could classify people into two different *types*: tall people and short people. Indeed, we use these terms in everyday language. But we all recognize that height is best conceived of as a *trait*—a dimension on which people differ along a wide range of values. If we measure the height of a

large sample of people, we will find instances all along the distribution, from very short to very tall. (See *Figure 14.2*.) It is not that people are only either tall or short (analogous to a personality type) but that people vary in the extent to which they are one or the other (analogous to a personality trait).

We assume that people tend to behave in particular ways: some are friendly, some are aggressive, some are lazy, some are timid, some are reckless. Trait theories of personality fit this common-sense view. However, personality traits are not simply patterns of behavior: They are factors that underlie these patterns and are responsible for them. Once our personality traits are developed, they reside in our brains. I am not saying that the acquisition of personality traits is strictly biological and that learning is not involved. But if our personality traits are changed through learning, those changes must occur in our brains. In other words, we carry our per-

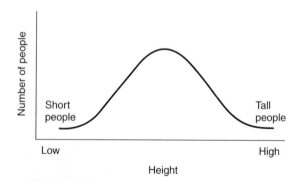

Figure 14.2

The distribution of height. We can measure people's heights, a trait, on a continuous scale. We can also look at the extremes and divide people into the categories of short- and tall-types.

personality trait An enduring personal characteristic that reveals itself in a particular pattern of behavior in a variety of situations.

sonality traits around with us in our heads—or more exactly, in our brains.

Identification of Personality Traits

Trait theories of personality do not pretend to be all-encompassing explanations of behavior—at least not yet. Instead, they are still at the stage of discovering, describing, and naming the regular patterns of behavior that people exhibit (Goldberg, 1993). In all science, categorization must come before explanation; we must know what we are dealing with before we can go about providing explanations. The ultimate goal of the personality psychologist is to explain what determines people's behavior—which is the ultimate goal of all branches of psychology.

Allport's Search for Traits

Gordon Allport (1897–1967), one of the first psychologists to search systematically for a basic core of personality traits, began his work by identifying all the words in an unabridged dictionary of the English language that described aspects of personality (Allport and Odbert, 1936). He found approximately 18,000 words, which he then further analyzed for those that described only stable personality characteristics. He eliminated words that represented temporary states, such as *flustered,* or evaluations, such as *admirable.* This still left him with over 4000 words.

Allport was interested in learning how many traits are needed to describe personality and exactly what these traits may be. For example, many of those 4000 words, such as *shy* and *bashful,* are synonyms. Although each synonym presumably makes some sort of distinction about a trait, a group of synonyms together might be used to describe the same underlying trait. Many trait theorists believe that the most basic set of personality traits ranges from 3 to 16 traits.

Allport's research stimulated other psychologists to think about personality in terms of traits or dispositions. In fact, most modern trait theories can be traced to Allport's earlier theoretical work. Like Allport, modern trait theorists maintain that only when we know how to describe an individual's personality will we be able to explain it.

Cattell: Sixteen Personality Factors

You may recall from Chapter 11 that factor analysis identifies variables that tend to be correlated. To use factor analysis to study personality, researchers must observe the behavior of a large number of people. Usually, the observations are limited to responses to questions on paper-and-pencil tests, but occasionally, investigators observe people's behavior in seminatural situations. Statistical procedures then permit investigators to determine which items a given person tends to answer in the same way; they can then infer the existence of common factors. For example, a shy person would tend to say "no" to

Surface traits, such as friendliness, are those traits that are obvious to others.

statements such as "I attend parties as frequently as I can" or "When I enter a room full of people, I like to be noticed." In contrast, outgoing people would tend to say "yes" to these statements.

To the degree that people possess orderly personality traits, they tend to answer certain clusters of questions in particular ways. Raymond Cattell (b. 1905) began his search for a relatively small number of basic personality traits with Allport and Odbert's (1936) list of adjectives. In addition, he collected data on people's personality characteristics from interviews, records describing their life histories, and from observing how people behave in particular situations. From this list, Cattell began to construct preliminary versions of a questionnaire called the 16PF. Then, using factor analysis, he analyzed responses from thousands of people to whom the inventory had been administered. Eventually, he identified sixteen personality factors.

Cattell referred to these sixteen traits as *source traits* because, in his view, they are the cornerstones upon which personality is built: They are the primary factors underlying observable behavior. He called groups of similar types of observable behavior *surface traits;* he included such traits as kindness, honesty, and friendliness because they are visible to others. They represent the surface of personality and spring forth from source traits, which lie deeper within the personality. Figure 14.3 illustrates a personality profile of a hypothetical individual rated on Cattell's sixteen factors. The factors are listed in order of importance, from top to bottom. Look at the ratings to see whether you think they would help you predict the person's behavior. (See *Figure 14.3.*)

Eysenck: Three Factors

Hans Eysenck (b. 1916) also used factor analysis to devise his theory of personality (Eysenck, 1970; Eysenck and Eysenck, 1985). His research identified three important factors: extra-

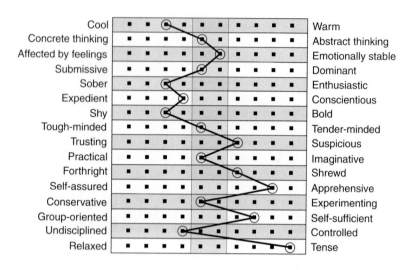

Figure 14.3

A hypothetical personality profile using Cattell's sixteen personality factors.

(Copyright © 1956, 1973, 1982, 1986 by the Institute for Personality and Ability Testing, Inc., P.O. Box 188, Champaign, Illinois, USA 61824–0188. Adapted and reproduced by permission.)

version, neuroticism, and psychoticism. These factors are bipolar dimensions. Extraversion is the opposite of introversion, neuroticism is the opposite of emotional stability, and psychoticism is the opposite of self-control. **Extraversion** refers to an outgoing nature and a high level of activity; **introversion** refers to a nature that shuns crowds and prefers solitary activities. **Neuroticism** refers to a nature full of anxiety, worries, and guilt; **emotional stability** refers to a nature that is relaxed and at peace with itself. **Psychoticism** refers to an aggressive, egocentric, and antisocial nature; **self-control** refers to a kind and considerate nature, obedient of rules and laws. Eysenck's use of the term *psychoticism* is different from its use by most clinical psychologists; his term refers to antisocial tendencies and not to a mental illness. A person at the extreme end of the distribution of psychoticism would receive the diagnosis of antisocial personality disorder. (I will discuss this disorder in more detail in Chapter 17.)

Table 14.1 lists some questions that have high correlations or factor loadings on Eysenck's three factors. The best way to understand the meaning of these traits is to read the questions and to imagine the kinds of people who would answer "yes" or "no" to each group. If a factor loading is preceded by a minus sign, it means that people who say "no"

receive high scores on the trait; otherwise, high scores are obtained by those who answer "yes." (See *Table 14.1.*)

According to Eysenck, the most important aspects of a person's temperament are determined by the combination of the three dimensions of extraversion, neuroticism, and psychoticism—just as colors are produced by the combinations of the three dimensions of hue, saturation, and brightness.

extraversion The tendency to seek the company of other people, to be lively, and to engage in conversation and other social behaviors with them.

introversion The tendency to avoid the company of other people, especially large groups of people; shyness.

neuroticism The tendency to be anxious, worried, and full of guilt.

emotional stability The tendency to be relaxed and at peace with oneself.

psychoticism The tendency to be aggressive, egocentric, and antisocial.

self-control The tendency to be kind, considerate, and obedient of laws and rules.

Table 14.1

Some Items from Eysenck's Tests of Extraversion, Neuroticism, and Psychoticism

Factor	Loading
Extraversion	
Do you like mixing with people?	.70
Do you like plenty of bustle and excitement around you?	.65
Are you rather lively?	.63
Neuroticism	
Do you often feel "fed-up"?	.67
Do you often feel lonely?	.60
Does your mood often go up and down?	.59
Psychoticism	
Do good manners and cleanliness matter much to you?	-.55
Does it worry you if you know there are mistakes in your work?	-.53
Do you like taking risks for fun?	.51

Source: Adapted from Eysenck, H.J., and Eysenck, M.W. *Personality and Individual Differences: A Natural Science Approach.* New York: Plenum Press, 1985.

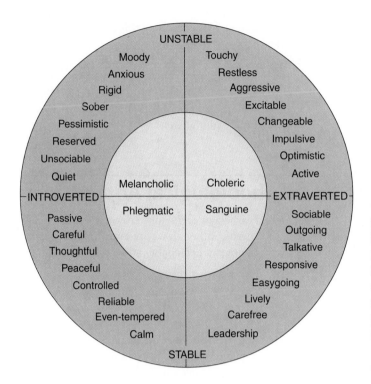

Figure 14.4

Eysenck's theory illustrated for two factors. According to Eysenck, the two dimensions of neuroticism (stable versus unstable) and introversion–extraversion combine to form a variety of personality characteristics. The four personality types based on the Greek theory of humors are shown in the center.

(From Eysenck, H.J. The Inequality of Man. London: Temple Smith, 1973. Reprinted with permission.)

Figure 14.4 illustrates the effects of various combinations of the first two of these dimensions—extraversion and neuroticism—and relates them to the four temperaments described by Galen. (See *Figure 14.4.*)

More than most other trait theorists, Eysenck emphasizes the biological nature of personality (Eysenck, 1991). For example, consider the introversion-extraversion dimension, which is biologically based, according to Eysenck, on an optimum arousal level of the brain. Eysenck believes that the functioning of a neural system located in the brain stem produces different levels of arousal of the cerebral cortex. Introverts have relatively high levels of cortical excitation, while extraverts have relatively low levels. Thus, in order to maintain the optimum arousal level, the extravert requires more external stimulation than does the introvert. The extravert seeks stimulation from external sources by interacting with others or by pursuing novel and highly stimulating experiences. The introvert avoids external stimulation in order to maintain his or her lower arousal level at an optimum state. Different states of arousal are hypothesized to lead to different values of the extraversion trait for different people.

Eysenck's theory has received considerable support, especially from his own laboratory, which has been highly productive. Most trait theorists accept the existence of his three factors because they have emerged in factor analyses performed by many different researchers.

The Five–Factor Model

As we saw earlier, Allport attempted to discover personality traits through an analysis of the words we use to describe differences in personality. Languages reflect the observations of a culture; that is, people invent words to describe distinctions they notice. An analysis of such distinctions by Tupes and Christal (1961), replicated by Norman (1963), has led to the five-factor model (McCrae and Costa, 1985, 1987, 1990). The **five-factor model** proposes that personality is composed of five primary dimensions: neuroticism, extraversion, openness, agreeableness, and conscientiousness. These factors are measured by the **Neuroticism, Extraversion, and Openness Personality Inventory,** or **NEO-PI.** (The name was chosen before the factors of agreeableness and conscientiousness were added.)

The NEO-PI consists of 181 items that potentially describe the person being evaluated, which can be the person answering the questions or someone he or she knows well (McCrae and Costa, 1990). (Studies have shown that self-ratings agree well with ratings of spouses and other people who know a person well.) The test items are brief sentences, such as "I really like most people I meet" or (for ratings by someone else) "She has a very active imagination." The person taking the test rates the accuracy of each item on a scale of 1 to 5,

five-factor model   A theory stating that personality is composed of five primary dimensions: neuroticism, extraversion, openness, agreeableness, and conscientiousness. This theory was developed using factor analyses of ratings of the words people use to describe personality characteristics.

Neuroticism, Extraversion, and Openness Personality Inventory (NEO-PI)   The instrument used to measure the elements described in the five-factor model (neuroticism, extraversion, openness, agreeableness, and conscientiousness).

from strong disagreement to strong agreement. The scores on each of the five factors consist of the sums of the answers to different sets of items.

McCrae, Costa, and Busch (1986) attempted to validate the five-factor model by performing a factor analysis on a list of adjectives contained in a test called the California Q-Set. This test consists of one-hundred brief descriptions (such as "irritable," "cheerful," "arouses liking," and "productive"). The items were provided by many psychologists and psychiatrists who found the words useful in describing people's personality characteristics. Thus, the words are not restricted to a particular theoretical orientation. McCrae and his colleagues found that factor analysis yielded the same five factors as the analysis based on everyday language: neuroticism, extraversion, openness, agreeableness, and conscientiousness. Indeed, the five-factor model is regarded by personality psychologists as a robust model of personality (Magai and McFadden, 1995).

Does there seem to be a biological basis for these five factors? Preliminary research suggests that the answer to this question is a qualified yes. Neuroticism, extraversion, openness, agreeableness, and conscientiousness seem to be strongly heritable, although the evidence supporting the heritability of neuroticism and extraversion is stronger than that for the other factors (Loehlin, 1992).

Interim Summary

Trait Theories of Personality

We can conceive of personality characteristics as types or traits. The earliest theory of personality classified people into types according to their predominant humor, or body fluid. Today, most psychologists conceive of personality differences as being represented by degree, not kind.

Personality traits are the factors that underlie patterns of behavior. Presumably, these factors are biological in nature, although they may be the products of learning as well as heredity. The search for core personality traits began with Allport, who studied how everyday words are used to describe personality characteristics. Although he never isolated a core set of traits, his work inspired others to continue the search for such traits. Several researchers developed their theories of personality through factor analysis. Cattell's analyses indicated the existence of sixteen personality factors and Eysenck's research suggested that personality is determined by three dimensions: extraversion (versus introversion), neuroticism (versus emotional stability), and psychoticism (versus self-control). McCrae and Costa's five-factor model, based on an analysis of words used to describe people's behavioral traits, includes extraversion, neuroticism, agreeableness, openness, and conscientiousness.

Thought Questions

- Think of one personality trait that you are sure that you possess. How did you come to possess this trait?

To what extent does possessing this trait *explain* the kind of person you are?
- Make a list of all the personality traits that you feel describe you. Which approach to personality—Cattell's, Eysenck's, or the five-factor model—do you feel best represents the personality traits you possess? What are the reasons for your answer?

Psychobiological Approaches

As I noted earlier, we carry our personality traits around with us in our heads. Although we are far from understanding the psychobiology of personality, some progress has been made.

Heritability of Personality Traits

Several trait theorists, including Cattell and Eysenck, have asserted that a person's genetic history has a strong influence on his or her personality. Many studies have shown that some personality traits are strongly heritable (Emde et al., 1992; McCue, Bacon, and Lykken, 1993).

As we saw in Chapter 3, the heritability of a trait can be assessed by comparing identical with fraternal twins, comparing twins raised together with twins raised apart, and comparing biological with adoptive relatives. Many studies

Research into the genetic basis of personality suggests that traits such as extraversion may be inherited.

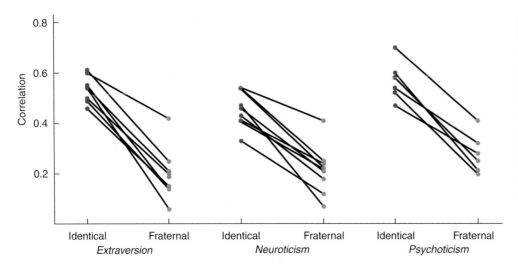

Figure 14.5

Correlations between members of pairs of identical and fraternal twins on tests of extraversion, neuroticism, and psychoticism. Individual pairs of data points, connected by straight lines, come from different experiments.

(Based on data from Zuckerman, M. Psychobiology of Personality. Cambridge: Cambridge University Press, 1991.)

have found that identical twins are more similar to each other than are fraternal twins on a variety of personality measures, which indicates that these characteristics are heritable (Loehlin, 1992). The three sets of identical twins described at the beginning of this chapter—Jim and Jim, Bridget and Dorothy, and Oskar and Jack—who were separated early in life and united many years later, attest to the strength of genetic factors in influencing personality. Although each member of each set of twins was reared in a separate—indeed, a very different—environment, his or her personality was found to be incredibly similar to his or her twin's.

Figure 14.5 shows the results of eleven studies using various tests of Eysenck's factors of extraversion, neuroticism, and psychoticism compiled by Zuckerman (1991). The results of each study are shown as data points connected by straight lines. Every study found that identical twins were more similar than fraternal twins on every measure. (See *Figure 14.5.*) According to Zuckerman's calculations, the best estimates of the heritability of these three traits are extraversion, 70 percent; psychoticism, 59 percent; and neuroticism, 48 percent.

The results of these studies suggest that heredity is responsible for between 50 and 70 percent of the variability in these three personality traits. Thus, it would appear that the remaining 30 to 50 percent of the variability would be caused by differences in environment. In other words, some family environments should tend to produce extraverts, others should tend to produce introverts, and so on. But research indicates that the matter is not so simple.

Zuckerman (1991) reviewed several studies that measured the correlation in personality traits of pairs of identical twins raised together and raised apart. If family environment has a significant effect on personality characteristics, then the twins raised together should be more similar than those raised apart. But they were not. Taken as a group, these studies found no differences, indicating that differences in family

environment account for none of the variability of personality traits in the twins who were tested. Another approach, comparing the personality traits of parents with those of their adopted children, suggests that family environment may account for approximately 7 percent of the variability (Scarr et al., 1981). If 50 to 70 percent of the variability in personality traits is caused by heredity and zero to 7 percent is caused by family environment, what is responsible for the remaining 23 to 50 percent of the variability? The answer is this: Heredity and environment interact.

As we saw in Chapter 3, heredity and environment can interact. In fact, the major source of the interaction seems to be the effect that people's heredity has on their family environments (Plomin and Bergeman, 1991). That is, people's genetic endowment plays an important role in determining how family members interact with them. **Figure 14.6** shows the correlations between the ratings of various characteristics of the family environment made by pairs of identical and fraternal twins. (See *Figure 14.6.*) The family characteristics that they rated included cohesion, expressiveness, conflict, achievement, culture, activity, organization, and control. The identical twins agreed on their ratings much more than the fraternal twins did; that is, identical twins were much more likely to have experienced similar family environments.

There are two possible explanations for these results: The family environments could have been more similar for identical twins than for fraternal twins, or the family environments could have really been the same in all cases but were simply *perceived* as different by the fraternal twins. Evidence suggests that the first possibility is correct. That is, the family environments really were more similar for identical twins (Loehlin, 1992). How can this be? One might think that each family has a certain environment and that everyone in the household comes under its influence.

Although there are aspects of a family that are shared by the entire household, the factors that play the largest role in

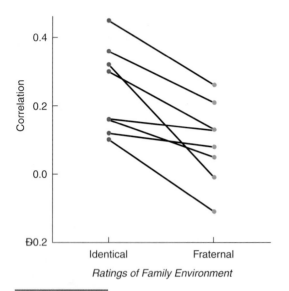

Figure 14.6

Correlations between members of pairs of twins on ratings of characteristics of their family environments. Individual pairs of data points represent ratings of cohesion, expressiveness, conflict, achievement, culture, activity, organization, and control.

(Based on data from Plomin, R., and Bergemen, C.S. Behavioral and Brain Sciences, 1991, 14, 373–427.)

shaping personality development appear to come from social interactions between an individual and other family members. And these social interactions are different for different people. Because of hereditary differences, one child may be more sociable; this child will be the recipient of more social interactions. Another child may be abrasive and disagreeable; this child will be treated more coldly. In the case of identical twins, who have no hereditary differences, the amount of social interactions with each twin is likely to be similar.

Even physical attributes (which are largely hereditary) will affect a child's environment. A physically attractive child will receive more favorable attention than will an unattractive child. In fact, studies that examined videotaped interactions between mothers and their children confirm that heredity does have an important influence on the nature of these interactions (Plomin and Bergeman, 1991). Thus, although a child's environment plays an important part in his or her personality development, hereditary factors play a large role in determining the nature of this environment.

One caution about this interpretation is in order. Although the studies I have cited have been replicated in several cultures, none of them have investigated the effects of the full range of cultural differences in family lives. That is, when comparisons have been made between twins raised together and those raised apart, almost all have involved family environments *within* the same culture. It is possible that cultural differences in family environments could be even more important than the differences produced by a person's heredity; only cross-cultural studies will be able to test this possibility.

Are all personality traits a product, direct or indirect, of a person's heredity? The answer is no. Some personality characteristics show a strong effect of shared environment but almost no effect of genetics. For example, twin studies have found a strong influence of family environment, but not of heredity, belief in God, involvement in religion, masculinity/femininity, attitudes toward racial integration, and intellectual interests (Loehlin and Nichols, 1976; Rose, 1988). Thus, people tend to *learn* some important social attitudes from their family environments.

Brain Mechanisms in Personality

There is no doubt that brain mechanisms are involved in personality traits. For example, brain damage can produce permanent changes in personality, and drugs that affect particular neurotransmitters can alter people's moods and anxiety levels. But what particular brain mechanisms are involved in personality, and what personality traits do they affect? Several psychologists have attempted to relate extraversion, neuroticism, and psychoticism to underlying physiological mechanisms (Eysenck and Eysenck, 1985; Gray, 1987; Zuckerman, 1991).

Zuckerman (1991) suggests that the personality dimensions of extraversion, neuroticism, and psychoticism are determined by the neural systems responsible for reinforcement, punishment, and arousal. People who score high on extraversion are particularly sensitive to reinforcement—perhaps their neural reinforcement systems are especially active.

Infants who later become extraverts show higher activity levels, whereas adult extraverts show more reinforcement-seeking behavior. Adult extraverts participate in more social activities and tend to shift from one type of activity to another. They are optimistic; they expect that their pursuits will result in reinforcing outcomes. However, unlike people who score high on psychoticism, they are sensitive to the effects of punishment and can learn to act prudently.

People who score high on neuroticism are anxious and fearful. If they also score high on psychoticism, they are hostile as well. These people are particularly sensitive to the punishing effects of aversive stimuli. Zuckerman therefore suggests that the personality dimension of neuroticism is controlled by the sensitivity of the neural system responsible for punishment, which appears to involve the amygdala. As we saw in Chapter 13, an important function of the amygdala is to organize the behavioral, autonomic, and hormonal components of conditional emotional responses. If this system was oversensitive, a person would be expected to be especially fearful of situations in which he or she might encounter aversive stimuli. The amygdala is also involved in aggression. Thus, neurotics who also score high on psychoticism will tend to express their fear in the form of aggression.

People who score high on psychoticism have difficulty learning when *not* to do something. As Zuckerman suggests, they have a low sensitivity to punishment. They also have a high tolerance for arousal and excitation; in other words, we could say that their optimum level of arousal is abnormally high. As we saw in Chapter 13, some theorists hypothesize that people seek situations that provide an optimum level of arousal: Too much or too little arousal is aversive. Therefore, a person with a high optimum level of arousal (a high tolerance for excitement) seeks out exciting situations and performs well in them. (A neurotic would find these situations aversive, and his or her behavior would become disorganized and inefficient.) A person with a high tolerance for excitement makes a good warrior but does not fit in well in civilized society. Table 14.2 summarizes Zuckerman's hypothetical explanations for the three major personality dimensions. (See *Table 14.2.*)

Research using laboratory animals has provided support for Zuckerman's suggestions concerning neuroticism. A neurotic person avoids unfamiliar situations because he or she fears encountering aversive stimuli, whereas an emotionally stable person is likely to investigate the situation to see whether anything interesting will happen. The same is true for other species. For example, about 15 percent of kittens avoid novel objects, and this tendency persists when they become adults; some cats are "timid," while others are "bold." When a timid cat encounters a novel stimulus (such as a rat), the activity of the neural circuits in its amygdala responsible for defensive responses becomes more active (Adamec and Stark-Adamec, 1986). (Yes, some cats are afraid of rats.)

Kagan, Reznick, and Snidman (1988) investigated the possibility that timidity in social situations (shyness) has a biological basis in humans. They noted that about 10 to 15 percent of normal children between the ages of two and three become quiet, watchful, and subdued when they encounter an unfamiliar situation. In other words, like the kittens, they are shy and cautious in approaching novel stimuli. Childhood shyness seems to be related to two personality dimensions: a low level of extraversion and a high level of neuroticism (Briggs, 1988).

Kagan and his colleagues selected two groups of twenty-one-month-old and thirty-one-month-old children according to their reactions to unfamiliar people and situations. The shy group consisted of children who showed signs of inhibition, such as clinging to their mothers or remaining close to them, remaining silent, and failing to approach strangers or other novel stimuli. The nonshy group showed no such inhibition; these children approached the strangers and explored the novel environment. The children were similarly tested for shyness several more times, up to the age of seven and a half years.

The investigators found shyness to be an enduring trait; children who were shy at the ages of twenty-one or thirty-one months continued to be shy at the age of seven and a half years. In addition, the two groups of children showed differences in their physiological reactions to the test situation. Shy children were more likely to show increases in heart rate, their pupils tended to be more dilated, their urine contained more norepinephrine, and their saliva contained more cortisol. (Norepinephrine and cortisol are two hormones secreted during times of stress. Furthermore, their secretion in fearful situations is controlled by the amygdala.) Obviously, the shy children found the situation to be stressful, whereas the nonshy children did not.

This study suggests that the biological basis of an important personality characteristic during childhood—shyness—may be the excitability of neural circuits that control avoidance behaviors. Of course, the experimenters did not observe differences in the children's brains, so we cannot be sure about the nature of the brain differences between the two groups of children. Further research with both humans and laboratory animals may help us understand the biological differences responsible for personality characteristics.

Interim Summary

Psychobiological Approaches

Studies of twins and adopted children indicate that personality factors, especially extraversion, neuroticism, and psychoticism, are affected strongly by genetic factors. However, there is little evidence for an effect of common family environment, largely because an individual's environment is strongly affected by heredity factors, such as personality and physical attributes.

Important personality traits are likely to be the products of neural systems responsible for reinforcement, punishment, and arousal. Zuckerman believes that extraversion is caused by a sensitive reinforcement system, neuroticism is caused by a sensitive punishment system (which includes the amygdala), and psychoticism is caused by the combination of a deficient punishment system and an abnormally high optimum level of arousal.

Few studies have directly tested the hypothesis that personality differences can be accounted for by biological differences. One experiment, however, indicates that childhood shyness is a relatively stable trait that can be seen in the way children react to strangers and strange situations. The differ-

Table 14.2

Zuckerman's (1991) Hypothetical Biological Characteristics That Correspond to Personality Dimensions

Personality Trait	Biological Characteristics
Extraversion	High sensitivity to reinforcement
Neuroticism	High sensitivity to punishment
Psychoticism	Low sensitivity to punishment; high optimal level of arousal

ences between shy and nonshy children manifest themselves in physiological responses controlled by the amygdala that indicate the presence of stress.

Thought Questions

- I have identical twin boys. One is much more outgoing than the other. If personality traits are heritable, how would you explain this difference—how can they share 100 percent of their genes yet have different "personalities"?

- Are you a thrill seeker? To what extent do you seek out situations that might be termed risky or at least mildly exciting? Depending on your answers to these questions, what might Zuckerman say about your personality (in terms of psychoticism)?

The Social Learning Approach

Some psychologists, such as Cattell and Eysenck, are interested in the ways people differ with respect to their personality traits. Other psychologists are more interested in the ways a person's personality is affected by environmental and cognitive variables. These psychologists view personality and its development as a process in which behavioral, cognitive, and environmental variables interact to produce a person's personality. **Social learning theory** embodies the idea that both the consequences of behavior and an individual's beliefs about those consequences determine personality.

Social learning theory stems partially from B. F. Skinner's experimental analysis of behavior. Although Skinner's work has influenced contemporary personality theory, he should not be mistaken for a personality theorist. He was definitely not one.

For Skinner, behavior is explained *entirely* in terms of its consequences. Behavior is consistent from one situation to the next because it is maintained by similar kinds of consequences across those situations. Behavior changes only when the consequences for behaving change. Skinner's ideas have attracted the attention of some personality researchers because they are experimentally based and provide testable hypotheses for predicting an individual's behavior within and across situations. Social learning theorists have modified and applied Skinner's ideas to their own work. One such researcher is Albert Bandura (b. 1925), who blended Skinner's ideas with his own ideas about how cognitive factors may influence behavior.

social learning theory The idea that both consequences of behavior and an individual's beliefs about those consequences determine personality.

expectancy The belief that a certain consequence will follow a certain action.

Expectancies and Observational Learning

Cognitive processing, including the individual's interpretation of the situation, is central to social learning theory (Bandura, 1973, 1986). An important aspect of cognition for Bandura and other social learning theorists is **expectancy**, the individual's belief that a specific consequence will follow a specific action. Expectancy refers to how someone perceives the contingencies of reinforcement for his or her own behavior. If a person does something, it may be because he or she expects to be rewarded or punished. In different situations, expectancies may vary. For example, a child may learn that he can get what he wants from his younger sister by hitting her. However, on one occasion, his parents may catch him hitting his sister and punish him. His expectancy may now change: He may still get what he wants by behaving aggressively, but if he is caught, he'll be punished. This new expectancy may influence how he behaves toward his sister in the future (especially around his parents).

At the heart of the social learning theory account of personality is the idea that personality is the result of observing and imitating the actions of others. Observing a model perform a behavior leads to an expectancy that our performance of the same behavior will produce a favorable result.

Expectancies also permit people to learn actions vicariously, that is, without those actions being directly reinforced. The vicarious nature of some learning experiences is obvious in children as they imitate the actions of others. A three-year-old who applies deodorant to herself does so not because this behavior has been reinforced in the past, but rather because after watching her mother do it, she expects it would be "fun" for her to do so, too.

Vicarious learning is better known as **observational learning**, which is learning through observing the kinds of consequences others (called *models*) experience as a result of their behavior. Observational learning is a form of learning in which an expectancy about reinforcement is formed merely by observing another's behavior and the consequences it produces. Your own experience is no doubt filled with examples of observational learning—learning to dance, to make a paper airplane, to write in cursive, and to engage in many other activities. The more complex the behavior, *the more times we must observe it being executed, and practice what we have observed*, before we can learn it well. Learning to tie a shoe lace requires more attention to details than learning to roll a ball across the floor.

Reciprocal Determinism and Self-Efficacy

Unlike many personality researchers, Bandura does not believe that either personal characteristics (traits) or the environment alone determines personality (Bandura, 1978). Rather, he argues for **reciprocal determinism**, the idea that behavior, environmental variables, and person variables, such as perception, interact to determine personality (See *Figure 14.7*). We know that our actions can affect the environment. We also know that the environment can affect our behavior. Likewise, our thoughts may affect the ways in which we behave to change the environment, and in turn, those changes can influence our thoughts. When our acts of kindness are met with kindness in return, we perceive the environment as friendly and are apt to show kindness under other, similar circumstances. Likewise, when we are treated rudely, we perceive the environment as unfriendly (perhaps hostile) and will likely attempt to avoid or change similar environments in the future.

According to Bandura (1982), **self-efficacy**, or one's expectations of success in a given situation, is an important determinant of whether one will attempt to make changes in one's environment. Each day, we make many decisions based on our perceptions of the extent to which our actions will produce reinforcement. Our actions are based on our evaluation of our competency. Moreover, self-efficacy not only determines whether we will engage in a particular behavior, it also determines the extent to which we will maintain that behavior in the face of adversity. For example, if you believe that you are unqualified for a job even though you really desire it, you are apt not to apply for an interview for that job. However, if you are confident of your qualifications for the job, you will surely attempt the interview. Even if you are turned down for that job, you may interview for a similar position because you are sure of your abilities. Low self-efficacy can hamper both the frequency and the quality of behavior-environment interactions, and high self-efficacy can facilitate both.

Related to self-efficacy is the extent to which an individual feels optimistic or pessimistic about his or her life's circumstances. Seligman and Schulman (1986) have found that people (in the case of their study, life insurance agents) who can find something positive in less-than-desirable circumstances are generally more successful than are people who view those circumstances negatively. It seems that otherwise cheerless circumstances stimulate optimists to seek creative means of "putting the circumstances right." Pessimists are more likely to throw up their arms in despair and to give up. Thus, if there is a solution to be found for a problem, the optimist has the better chance of finding it.

Person Variables

Like Bandura, Walter Mischel (b. 1930) believes that much of one's personality is learned through interaction with the environment. Also like Bandura, Mischel emphasizes the role of cognition in determining how one learns the relationship between one's behavior and its consequences. In addition, though, Mischel argues that individual differences in cogni-

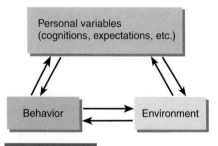

Figure 14.7

Patterns of interaction in reciprocal determinism. According to Bandura, behavior, environment, and personal variables, such as cognitions and expectations, interact to determine personality.

observational learning Learning through observing the kinds of consequences others (called *models*) experience as a result of their behavior.

reciprocal determinism The idea that behavior, environment, and personal variables, such as perception, interact to determine personality.

self-efficacy The expectations of success; the belief in one's own competencies.

tion, or **person variables** as he calls them, account for differences in personality. Mischel (1984) proposed five person variables that figure significantly in social learning:

- *Competencies*. We each have different skills, abilities, and capacities. What we know and the kinds of behaviors that have been reinforced in the past influence the kinds of actions in which we will likely engage in the future.

- *Encoding strategies and personal constructs*. We also differ in our ability to process information. The way we process information determines how we perceive different situations. One person may perceive going on a date as fun, and so look forward to it; another person may perceive going on a date as potentially boring, and so dread it.

- *Expectancies*. On the basis of our past behavior and our knowledge of current situations, we form expectancies about the effects of our behavior on the environment. Expecting our behavior to affect the environment positively leads to one course of action; expecting our behavior to affect it negatively leads to another.

- *Subjective values*. The degree to which we value certain reinforcers over others influences our behavior. We seek those outcomes that we value most.

- *Self-regulatory systems and plans*. We monitor our progress toward achieving goals and subject ourselves to either self-punishment or self-reinforcement, depending on our progress. We also modify and formulate plans regarding how we feel a goal can best be achieved.

Mischel's view is a dynamic one—people's thoughts and behaviors are undergoing constant change as they interact with the environment. New plans are made and old ones reformulated; people adjust their actions in accordance with their competencies, subjective values, and expectancies of behavior—environment interactions.

Locus of Control

Other social learning theorists, such as Julian Rotter (b. 1916), have argued that the extent to which one perceives oneself to be in control of particular situations is also an important element of personality. **Locus of control** refers to whether one believes that the consequences of one's actions are controlled by internal, person variables or by external, environmental variables (Rotter, 1954, 1966). A person who ex-

person variables　Individual differences in cognition, which, according to Mischel, include competencies, encoding strategies and personal constructs, expectancies, subjective values, and self-regulatory systems and plans.

locus of control　An individual's beliefs that the consequences of his or her actions are controlled by internal person variables or by external environmental variables.

People with an internal locus of control believe that achievement of their goals depends upon their personal efforts toward accomplishing those goals.

pects to control his or her own fate—or, more technically, who perceives that rewards are dependent upon his or her own behavior—has an internal locus of control. A person who sees his or her life as being controlled by external forces unaffected by his or her own behavior has an external locus of control (See *Figure 14.8.*)

Rotter developed the *I-E Scale*, which assesses the degree to which people perceive the consequences of their behavior to be under the control of internal or external variables. The I-E Scale contains twenty-nine pairs of statements to which a person indicates his or her degree of agreement. A typical item on the scale might look something like this:

> The grades that I get depend on my abilities and how hard I work to get them.

> The grades that I get depend mostly on my teacher and his or her tests.

The scale is scored by counting the number of choices consistent with either the internal or the external locus of control orientation. Scores may range from 0 to 23, with lower scores indicative of greater internal locus of control. Of all the populations Rotter has assessed with the I-E Scale, the highest level of internal locus of control was obtained from a group of Peace Corps volunteers (Rotter, 1966).

Rotter's scale has been used in hundreds of studies of social behavior in a wide variety of situations. Consider some of the findings obtained from research using the I-E Scale:

- People having internal locus of control orientations will work harder to obtain a goal if they believe that they can control the outcome in a specific situation. Even when told that a goal could be obtained with their own skill and effort, those having external orientations tended not to try as hard as those having internal orientations (Davis and Phares, 1967).

Internal Locus of Control

Poor performance on test	Good performance on test

It's my own fault. I should have spent more time studying.

Great! I knew all that studying would pay off.

External Locus of Control

Poor performance on test	Good performance on test

These tests are just too hard. The questions are impossible.

Did I get lucky or what? The teacher must really have gone easy on the grading.

Figure 14.8

Internal and external loci of control. People having internal loci of control perceive themselves as being able to determine the outcomes of the events in their lives. People having external loci of control perceive the events in their lives to be determined by environmental variables.

- People having internal orientations are also more likely to be aware of and to use good health practices. They are more apt to take preventive medicines, to exercise regularly, and to quit smoking than are people having external orientations (Strickland, 1979). They are, however, also more likely to blame themselves when they fail, even when failure is not their fault (Phares, 1984).

Evaluating Scientific Issues

Traits Versus Situations as Predictors of Behavior

Social learning theorists stress the importance of the environment as an influence on behavior and tend to place less emphasis on the role of personality traits. They argue that the situation often plays a strong role in determining behavior. In contrast, trait theorists argue that personality traits are stable characteristics of individuals and that knowing something about these traits permits us to predict an individual's behavior.

■ The Case for Situationism

Mischel (1968, 1976) has suggested that stable personality traits do not exist—or if they do, they are of little importance. Situations, not traits, best predict behavior. He asks us to consider two situations: a party to celebrate someone's winning a large sum of money in a lottery and a funeral. People will be much more talkative, cheerful, and outgoing at the party than at the funeral. How much will knowing a person's score on a test of introversion-extra-

version enable you to predict whether he or she will be talkative and outgoing? In this case, knowing the situation has much more predictive value than knowing the test score.

Mischel cites several studies in support of his position. One of the first of these studies was performed over sixty years ago. Hartshorne and May (1928) designed a set of behavioral tests to measure the traits of honesty and self-control and administered them to over ten thousand students in elementary school and high school. The tests gave the children the opportunity to be dishonest—for example, to cheat on a test, lie about the amount of homework they had done, or keep money with which they had been entrusted. In all cases, the experimenters had access to what the children actually did, so they could determine whether the child acted honestly or dishonestly. They found that a child who acted honestly (or dishonestly) in one situation did not necessarily act the same way in a different situation. The average correlation of a child's honesty from situation to situation—the cross-situational consistency—was below .30. The authors concluded that "honesty or dishonesty is not a unified character trait in children of the ages studied, but a series of specific responses to specific situations" (p. 243).

Mischel (1968) reviewed evidence from research performed after the Hartshorne and May study and found that most personal characteristics showed the same low cross-situational consistency—.30 or lower. He concluded that the concept of personality trait was not useful. People's behavior was determined by the situations in which they found themselves, not by any intrinsic personality traits.

■ The Case for Personality Traits

Other psychologists disagree with Mischel. For example, Epstein (1979) noted that personality traits are more stable than some of these measures had suggested. He noted that assessments of cross-situational consistency usually test a group of people on two occasions and correlate their behavior in one situation with their behavior in the other. He showed that repeated measurements across *several* days yielded much higher correlations. In a study of his own, a group of twenty-eight undergraduates kept daily records of their most pleasant and most unpleasant experiences for a month. For each experience, they recorded the emotions they felt, their impulses to action, and their actual behavior. The correlation between a person's emotions, impulses, or behavior on any two days was rather low—on the order of .30. However, when he grouped measurements (that is, correlated the ratings obtained on odd-numbered days with those obtained on even-numbered days), the correlation rose dramatically—up to around .80.

Although Mischel is skeptical about the value of the concept of personality trait, he has acknowledged that particular personality traits may be important as predictors of behavior (Mischel, 1977, 1979). He also points out that some situations by their very nature severely constrain a person's behavior, whereas others permit a wide variety of responses. For example, red lights cause almost all motorists to stop their cars. In this case, knowing the particular situation (the color of the traffic light) predicts behavior better than knowing something about the personality characteristics of the drivers. Conversely, some situations are weak and have little control over people's behavior. As Zuckerman (1991) points out, a yellow light is such a situation; when drivers see a yellow light, some will stop if they possibly can and others will accelerate and rush through the intersection. The difference between the two behaviors is likely determined by individual personality traits.

Personality and situations are usually conceived of as independent variables, but they are not always independent. In laboratory settings, experimenters assign people to various situations. Here, situation and personality are truly independent. However, as Bem and Allen (1974) pointed out, people in life outside the laboratory are able to exert some choice over the situations they enter. For instance, a party is a moderately powerful situation and tends to produce extraverted behaviors. Introverted people may stay away from parties to avoid situations that encourage behaviors with which they are not comfortable. Similarly, extraverts may avoid situations in which they are alone. The fact that people choose their own situations means that personality traits interact with situations. Emmons, Diener, and Larsen (1986) found that people do, indeed, show consistent patterns in the types of situations they choose; and when circumstances force

them to be in situations they do not normally choose, they feel uncomfortable.

■ What Should We Conclude?

Acknowledging the stability of personality over many situations and the interaction between personality and situations, most psychologists agree that the original question, "Which is more important in determining a person's behavior, the situation or personality traits?" has proved too simplistic. Some types of personality traits will prevail in most situations; some situations will dictate the behavior of most people. But some interactions between situation and personality require the analysis of both variables.

Figure 14.9 illustrates some of the most important factors that control the development of an individual's personality traits. It also shows the interactions between these traits and situational factors in determining behavior. (See *Figure 14.9.*)

Interim Summary

The Social Learning Approach

Social learning theory blends Skinner's notion of reinforcement with cognitive concepts such as expectancy to explain social interaction and personality. According to Bandura, people learn the relation between their behavior and its consequences by observing how others' behavior is rewarded and punished. In this way, people learn to expect that certain consequences will follow certain behaviors. Bandura also believes that personality is the result of reciprocal determinism—the interaction of behavior, environment, and person variables, such as perception. The extent to which a person is likely to attempt to change his or her environment is related to self-efficacy, the expectation that he or she will be successful in producing the change. People with low self-efficacy tend not to try to alter their environments; just the opposite is true for people with high self-efficacy.

Mischel has argued that personality differences are due largely to person variables—individual differences in cognition. These variables include competencies, encoding strategies and personal constructs, expectancies, subjective values, and self-regulatory systems and plans. Rotter's research has shown that locus of control—the extent to which people believe that their behavior is controlled by person variables or by environmental variables—is also an important determinant of personality.

In the past, psychologists disagreed about the relative importance of situations and personality traits in determining a person's behavior. It now appears that personality traits are correlated with behavior, especially when multiple observations of particular behaviors are made. In addition, some situations (such as a funeral or a stoplight) are more powerful

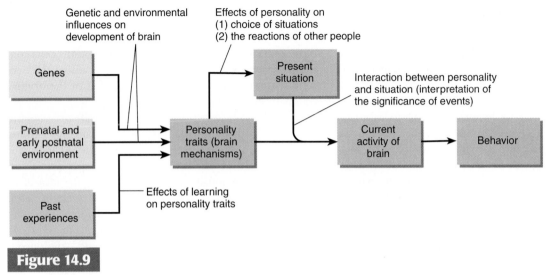

Figure 14.9

Personality traits and the interactions between traits and situations determine behavior.

than others, exerting more control on people's behavior. Traits and situations interact: Some people are affected more than others by a particular situation, and people tend to choose the types of situations in which they find themselves. People's personality traits directly affect situational variables.

Thought Questions

- Think of a situation in which you modeled your behavior after someone else's. What factors led you to imitate this behavior? To what extent did you form an expectancy that imitating this behavior would lead to a particular consequence?
- Provide a personal example of reciprocal determinism. Explain the interaction of behavior, environmental variables, and person variables in this example.
- Do you feel that you have an internal or external locus of control? Describe a recent decision that you made or a social interaction that you had to use as an example. How would your life be different if you adopted the opposite form of locus of control?

The Psychodynamic Approach

The work of Sigmund Freud has had a profound and lasting effect on twentieth-century society. Terms such as *ego, libido, repression, rationalization,* and *fixation* are as familiar to many Western laypeople as to clinicians. Before Freud formulated his theory, people believed that most behavior was determined by rational, conscious processes. Freud was the first to

psychodynamic A term used to describe the Freudian notion that the mind is in a state of conflict among instincts, reasons, and conscience.

claim that what we do is often irrational and that the reasons for our behavior are seldom conscious. The mind, to Freud, was a battleground for the warring factions of instinct, reason, and conscience; the term **psychodynamic** refers to this struggle.

The Development of Freud's Theory

Sigmund Freud (1856–1939) was a Viennese physician who acquired his early training in neurology in the laboratory of Ernst Wilhelm von Brücke, an eminent physiologist and neuroanatomist. Freud's work in the laboratory consisted mostly of careful anatomical observation rather than experimentation. Careful observation also characterized his later work with human behavior; he made detailed observations of individual patients and attempted to draw inferences about the structure of the human psyche from these cases. (As we saw in Chapter 1, *psyche,* from the Greek word for "breath" or "soul," refers to the mind.)

Freud left Vienna briefly and studied in Paris with Jean Martin Charcot, who was investigating the usefulness of hypnosis as a treatment for hysteria. Patients with hysteria often experience paralysis of some part of the body or loss of one of the senses, and no physiological cause can be detected. The fact that hypnosis could be used either to produce or to alleviate these symptoms suggested that they were of psychological origin. Charcot proposed that hysterical symptoms were caused by some kind of psychological trauma. Freud was greatly impressed by Charcot's work and became even more interested in problems of the mind.

Freud returned home to Vienna, opened his medical practice and began an association with Josef Breuer, a prominent physician. Freud and Breuer together published a book called *Studies on Hysteria,* and one of the cases cited in it, that of Anna O., provided the evidence that led to some of the most important tenets of Freud's theory.

Breuer had treated Anna O. twelve years before he and Freud published their book. She suffered from an incredible number of hysterical symptoms, including loss of speech, disturbances in vision, headaches, and paralysis and loss of feeling in her right arm. Under hypnosis, Anna was asked to think about the time when her symptoms had started. Each of her symptoms appeared to have begun just when she was unable to express a strongly felt emotion. While under hypnosis, she experienced these emotions again, and the experience gave her relief from her hysterical symptoms. It was as if the emotions had been bottled up, and reliving the original experiences uncorked them. This release of energy (which Breuer and Freud called *catharsis*) presumably eliminated the hysterical symptoms.

The case of Anna O. is one of the most frequently reported cases in the annals of psychotherapy. However, Breuer's original description appears to be inaccurate in some of its most important respects (Ellenberger, 1972). Apparently, the woman was not cured at all by Breuer's hypnosis and psychotherapy. Ellenberger discovered hospital records indicating that Anna O. continued to take morphine for the distress caused by the disorders Breuer had allegedly cured. Freud appears to have learned later that the cure was a fabrication, but this fact did not become generally known until recently. However, Breuer's failure to help Anna O. with her problems does not mean that we must reject psychoanalysis. Although Breuer's apparent success inspired Freud to examine the unconscious, Freud's theory of personality must stand or fall on its own merits when evaluated by modern evidence.

The case of Anna O., along with evidence obtained from his own clinical practice, led Freud to reason that human behavior is motivated by instinctual drives, which, when activated, supply "psychic energy." This energy is aversive, because the nervous system seeks a state of quiet equilibrium. According to Freud, if something prevents the psychic energy caused by activation of a drive from being discharged, psychological disturbances will result.

Freud believed that instinctual drives were triggered by traumatic events in a person's life. During such an event, the individual is forced to hide strong emotion. And because it cannot be expressed normally, the emotion is expressed neurotically—that is, with excessive anxiety. The individual cannot recall the emotions or the events that produced it because they are embedded in the **unconscious**, the inaccessible part

of the mind. Unconscious memories and emotions exert control over conscious thoughts and actions, causing the neurotic symptoms to linger and the emotions of the original traumatic event to stay secret.

Freud also believed that the mind actively prevents unconscious traumatic events from reaching conscious awareness. That is, the mind *represses* the memories of traumatic events, most of which are potentially anxiety-provoking, from being consciously discovered. He used the idea of an iceberg as a metaphor to describe the mind. Only the tip is visible above water; the much larger and more important part of it is submerged. Likewise, the conscious mind hides a larger and more important part of the mind—the unconscious. To understand a person's personality, we must tap his or her unconscious.

Freud, then, argued that our personalities are determined by both conscious and unconscious powers, with the unconscious exerting considerable influence on the conscious. To understand how the unconscious exerts its control over conscious thought and action, we need to explore Freud's view of the structure of personality.

Structures of the Mind: Id, Ego, and Superego

Freud was struck by the fact that psychological disturbances could stem from events that a person apparently could no longer consciously recall, although they could be revealed during hypnosis. This phenomenon led him to conclude that the mind consists of unconscious, preconscious, and conscious elements. The *unconscious* includes mental events of which we are not aware, the *conscious* entails mental events of which we are aware, and the *preconscious* involves mental events that may become conscious through effort.

Freud divided the mind into three structures: the id, the ego, and the superego. (See *Figure 14.10.*) The operations of the **id** are completely unconscious. The id contains the **libido**, which is the primary source of instinctual motivation for all psychic forces; this force is insistent and is unresponsive to the demands of reality. The id obeys only one rule—to obtain immediate gratification in whatever form it may take—called the **pleasure principle**. If you are hungry, the id compels you to eat; if you are angry, the id prompts you to strike out or to seek revenge or to destroy something. Freud (1933) conceived of the id as

> . . . the dark, inaccessible part of our personality. . . . We approach the id with analogies: we call it a chaos, a cauldron full of seething excitations. . . . It is filled with energy reaching it from the instincts, but it has no organization, produces no collective will, but only a striving to bring about the satisfaction of the instinctual needs subject to the observance of the pleasure principle. (p. 65)

unconscious The inaccessible part of the mind.

id The unconscious reservoir of libido, the psychic energy that fuels instincts and psychic processes.

libido An insistent, instinctual force that is unresponsive to the demands of reality; the primary source of motivation.

pleasure principle The rule that the id obeys: Obtain immediate gratification, whatever form it may take.

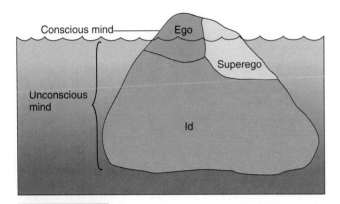

Figure 14.10

Freud's conception of the structure of the mind. Freud compared the conscious portion of the mind to the tip of an iceberg and the unconscious portion to the larger part of the iceberg below the water's surface. While the id is completely unconscious, both the ego and superego may be partially conscious and partially unconscious. In addition, Freud argued that part of the mind is preconscious (not shown in this figure), or contains information that may be brought into consciousness through effort.

The **ego** is the self; it controls and integrates behavior. It acts as a mediator, negotiating a compromise among the pressures of the id, the counterpressures of the superego, and the demands of reality. The ego's functions of perception, cognition, and memory perform this mediation. The ego is driven by the **reality principle**, the tendency to satisfy the id's demands realistically, which almost always involves compromising the demands of the id and superego. It involves the ability to delay gratification of a drive until an appropriate goal is located. To ward off the demands of the id when these demands cannot be gratified, the ego uses defense mechanisms (described later). Some of the functions of the ego are unconscious.

The **superego** is subdivided into the conscience and the ego-ideal. The **conscience** is the internalization of the rules and restrictions of society. It determines which behaviors are permissible and punishes wrongdoing with feelings of guilt. The **ego-ideal** is the internalization of what a person would like to be—his or her goals.

Freud believed the mind to be full of conflicts. A conflict might begin when one of the two primary drives, the sexual instinctual drive or the aggressive instinctual drive, is aroused. The id demands gratification of these drives but is often held in check by the superego's internalized prohibitions against the behaviors the drives tend to produce. *Internalized prohibitions* are rules of behavior learned in childhood that protect the person from the guilt he or she would feel if the instinctual drives were allowed to express themselves.

The result of the conflict is *compromise formation*, in which a compromise is reached between the demands of the

id and the suppressive effects of the superego. According to Freud, phenomena such as dreams, artistic creations, and slips of the tongue (we now call them Freudian slips) are examples of compromise formation.

In what many consider to be his greatest work, *The Interpretation of Dreams,* Freud wrote, "The interpretation of dreams is the royal road to a knowledge of the unconscious activities of the mind" (Freud, 1900, p. 647). To Freud, dreams were motivated by repressed wishes and urges. By analyzing dreams, Freud thought repressed wishes and memories could be rediscovered. For example, Freud believed that the **manifest content** of a dream—its actual story line—is only a disguised version of its **latent content**—its hidden message, which is produced by the unconscious. The latent content might be an unexpressed wish related to the aggressive instinctual drive.

For example, a person may desire to hurt or injure another person, perhaps a coworker with whom he or she is competing for a promotion. However, if the person acted out this scenario in a dream, he or she would experience guilt and anxiety. Therefore, the aggressive wishes of the unconscious are transformed into a more palatable form—the manifest content of the dream might be that the coworker accepts a job offer from a different company, removing any competition for the promotion. The manifest content of this dream manages to express, at least partly, the latent content supplied by the unconscious.

In addition to analyzing his patient's dreams, Freud also developed the technique of free association to probe the unconscious mind for clues of intrapsychic conflict. **Free association** is a method of analysis in which an individual is asked to relax, clear his or her mind of what he or she is currently thinking, and then report all thoughts, images, perceptions,

ego The self. The ego also serves as the general manager of personality, making decisions regarding the pleasures that will be pursued at the id's request and the moral dictates of the superego that will be followed.

reality principle The tendency to satisfy the id's demands realistically, which almost always involves compromising the demands of the id and superego.

superego The repository of an individual's moral values, divided into the conscience—the internalization of a society's rules and regulations—and the ego-ideal—the internalization of one's goals.

conscience The internalization of the rules and restrictions of society; it determines which behaviors are permissible and punishes wrongdoing with feelings of guilt.

ego-ideal The internalization of what a person would like to be—his or her goals and ambitions.

manifest content The apparent story line of a dream.

latent content The hidden message of a dream, produced by the unconscious.

free association A method of Freudian analysis in which an individual is asked to relax, clear his or her mind of current thoughts, and then report all thoughts, images, perceptions, and feelings that come to mind.

and feelings that come to mind. During free association, Freud looked for particular patterns in his patient's report that might reveal wishes, fears, and worries that the patient's mind might be keeping hidden. For example, free association might reveal, among other things, the thought of beating someone up, an image of a knife, and perhaps a feeling of relief. Recognizing a pattern in his patient's report, he then may draw conclusions about the client's hidden desire to harm someone and about the reasons motivating both that desire and the relief experienced once the aggressive urge is satisfied.

Defense Mechanisms

According to Freud, the ego contains **defense mechanisms**—mental systems that become active whenever unconscious instinctual drives of the id come into conflict with internalized prohibitions of the superego. The signal for the ego to utilize one of its defenses is the state of anxiety produced by an intrapsychic conflict. This unpleasant condition motivates the ego to apply a defense mechanism and thus reduce the anxiety. Let's look at six important defense mechanisms (*See Table 14.3.*)

Repression is responsible for actively keeping threatening or anxiety-provoking memories from our conscious aware-

Freud argued that creativity was often the result of sublimation—the redirection of psychic energy from an unacceptable outlet, such as sexual behavior, to an acceptable outlet, such as a work of art.

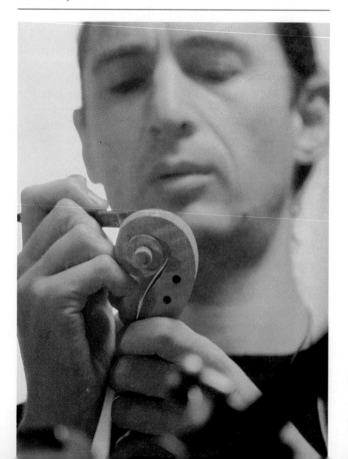

ness. For example, a person may have witnessed a brutal murder but cannot recall it later because of the uncomfortable emotions it would arouse. Freud believed that repression was perhaps the most powerful of the defense mechanisms.

Reaction formation involves replacing an anxiety-provoking idea with its opposite. An often-cited example of a reaction formation is that of a person who is aroused and fascinated by pornographic material but whose superego will not permit this enjoyment. He or she becomes a militant crusader against pornography. Reaction formation can be a very useful defense mechanism in this situation, permitting acceptable interaction with the forbidden sexual object. The crusader against pornography often studies the salacious material to see just how vile it is so that he or she can better educate others about its harmful nature. Thus, enjoyment becomes possible without feelings of guilt.

Projection involves denial of one's own unacceptable desires and the discovery of evidence of these desires in the behavior of other people. For example, a man who is experiencing a great deal of repressed hostility may perceive the world as being full of people who are hostile to him. In this way, he can blame someone else for any conflicts in which he engages.

Sublimation is the diversion of psychic energy from an unacceptable drive to an acceptable one. For example, a person may feel strong sexual desire but find its outlet unacceptable because of internalized prohibitions. Despite repression of the drive, its energy remains and finds another outlet, such as artistic or other creative activities. Freud considered sublimation to be an important factor in artistic and intellectual creativity. He believed that people have a fixed amount of drive available for motivating all activities; therefore, surplus sexual instinctual drive that is not expended in its normal way can be used to increase a person's potential for creative achievement.

Rationalization is the process of inventing an acceptable reason for a behavior that is really being performed for another, less acceptable reason. For example, a man who feels guilty about his real reasons for purchasing a magazine con-

defense mechanisms Mental systems that become active whenever unconscious instinctual drives of the id come into conflict with internalized prohibitions of the superego.

repression The mental force responsible for actively keeping memories, most of which are potentially threatening or anxiety-provoking, from being consciously discovered.

reaction formation A defense mechanism that involves behaving in a way that is the opposite of how one really feels because the true feelings produce anxiety.

projection A defense mechanism in which one's unacceptable behaviors or thoughts are attributed to someone else.

sublimation A defense mechanism that involves redirecting pleasure-seeking or aggressive instincts toward socially acceptable goals.

rationalization A defense mechanism that justifies an unacceptable action with a more acceptable, but false, excuse.

Table 14.3

Freudian Defense Mechanisms

Defense Mechanism	Description	Example
Repression	The mind's active attempt to prevent memories of traumatic experiences from reaching conscious awareness.	Failure to remember the death of a loved one or other highly upsetting events that occurred earlier in your life.
Reaction Formation	Replacing an anxiety-provoking idea with its opposite.	Having intense feelings of dislike for a person, but acting friendly and kind toward him or her.
Projection	Denial of one's unacceptable feelings and desires and finding them in others.	Denying that you have negative feelings toward someone, but asserting that person to have negative feelings toward you.
Sublimation	Channeling psychic energy from an unacceptable drive into a more acceptable one.	Diverting energy from the sex drive to produce a work of art.
Rationalization	Creating an acceptable reason for a behavior that is actually performed for a less acceptable reason.	Asserting that you donate money to charities because you truly are a generous person when really you want the tax break for the donation.
Conversion	The manifestation of a psychic conflict in terms of physical symptoms.	A psychic conflict, perhaps aroused by a particular person, causes you to develop symptoms of deafness or blindness to avoid contact with him or her.

This table shows several of the most frequently used defense mechanisms.

taining pictures of naked men or women may say, "I don't buy the magazine for the pictures. I buy it to read the interesting and enlightening articles it contains."

Conversion is the provision of an outlet for intrapsychic conflict in the form of a physical symptom. The conflict is transformed into blindness, deafness, paralysis, or numbness. (This phenomenon has also been called *hysteria*, which should not be confused with the common use of the term to mean "running around and shouting and generally acting out of control.") For example, a person might develop blindness so that he or she will no longer be able to see a situation that arouses a strong, painful intrapsychic conflict. Anna O.'s problem would be described as a conversion reaction.

Freud's Psychosexual Theory of Personality Development

Freud believed that personality development involves passing through several *psychosexual stages* of development—stages that involve seeking pleasure from specific parts of the body called *erogenous zones*. As we will see, each stage of personality development involves deriving physical pleasure from a different erogenous zone. (Freud used the term *sexual* to refer

to physical pleasures and the many ways an individual might seek to gratify an urge for such pleasure. He did not generally use the term to refer to orgasmic pleasure.)

Freud's theory of personality development has been extremely influential because of its ability to explain personality disorders in terms of whole or partial **fixation**—arrested development due to failure to pass through an earlier stage of development. Freud believed that a person becomes fixated at a particular stage of development when he or she becomes strongly attached to the erogenous zone involved in that stage. Although normal personality development involves passing successfully through all the psychosexual stages, Freud maintained that most people become more or less fixated at some point in their development. Let's take a closer look at Freud's psychosexual stages and the kinds of fixation that may develop in them.

conversion A defense mechanism that involves converting an intrapsychic conflict into a physical form, such as blindness, deafness, paralysis, or numbness.

fixation An unconscious obsession with an erogenous zone resulting from failure to resolve the crisis associated with the corresponding stage of psychosexual development.

Because newborn babies can do little more than suck and swallow, their sexual instinctual drive finds an outlet in these activities. Even as babies become able to engage in more complex behaviors, they continue to receive most of their sexual gratification orally. The early period of the **oral stage** of personality development is characterized by sucking and is passive. Later, as babies become more aggressive, they derive their pleasure from biting and chewing.

Fixation at the oral stage may result from early (or delayed) weaning from breast to bottle to cup. Someone whose personality is fixated at the early oral stage might be excessively passive. "Biting" sarcasm or compulsive talking can represent fixation at the later, more aggressive phase of the oral stage. Other oral stage fixation activities include habits such as smoking and excessive eating.

The **anal stage** of personality development begins during the second year of life; now babies begin to enjoy emptying their bowels (*anal* is derived from *anus*, the opening of the large intestine). During the early part of this stage, called the expressive period, babies enjoy expelling their feces. Later, in the retentive period, they derive pleasure from retaining them. Improper toilet training can result in fixation at the anal stage. People fixated at the anal expressive period are characterized as destructive and cruel; anal retentives are seen as stingy and miserly.

At around age three, a child discovers that it is pleasurable to play with his penis or her clitoris, and enters the **phallic stage**. (*Phallus* means "penis," but Freud used the term bisexually in this context.) Children also begin to discover the sex roles of their parents, and they unconsciously attach themselves to the parent of the opposite sex. A boy's attachment to his mother is called the *Oedipus complex*, after the Greek king of mythology who unknowingly married his mother after killing his father. For a time, Freud believed that a girl formed a similar attachment with her father, called the *Electra complex*, but he later rejected this concept. (In Greek mythology, Electra aided by her brother killed her mother and her mother's lover to avenge her father's death.)

In boys, the Oedipus complex normally becomes repressed by age five, although the conflicts that occur during the phallic stage continue to affect their personalities through-

Does toilet training affect personality development? Freud thought so: He asserted that improper toilet training caused personality development to become fixated during the anal stage of psychosexual development.

out life. A boy's unconscious wish to take his father's place is suppressed by his fear that his father will castrate him as punishment. (In fact, Freud believed that young boys regarded females as castrated males.) The conflict is finally resolved when the boy begins to model his behavior after that of his father so that he achieves identification with the father. Failure to resolve this conflict causes the boy to become fixated at this stage. The boy then becomes preoccupied with demonstrations of his manhood, continually acting "macho."

Girls supposedly experience fewer conflicts than boys do during the phallic stage. According to Freud, the chief reason for their transfer of love from their mothers (who provided primary gratification during early life) to their fathers is penis envy. A girl discovers that she and her mother lack this organ, so she becomes attached to her father, who has one. This attachment persists longer than the Oedipus complex, because the girl does not have to fear castration as revenge for usurping her mother's role. Freud believed that penis envy eventually becomes transformed into a need to bear children. The missing penis is replaced by a baby. A girl who becomes fixated during the phallic stage develops strong feelings of being inferior to men, which are expressed in seductive or otherwise flirtatious behavior. For example, she may become attracted to older men ("father figures") and attempt to se-

---

oral stage   The first of Freud's psychosexual stages, during which the mouth is the major erogenous zone—the major source of physical pleasure. Early in this stage, the mouth is used for sucking; later in the stage it is used for biting and chewing.

anal stage   The second of Freud's psychosexual stages, during which the primary erogenous zone is the anal region. Freud argued that during this time, children take pleasure in retaining or expelling feces.

phallic stage   The third psychosexual stage. During this stage, the primary erogenous zone is the genital area. At this time, children not only wish to stimulate their genitalia, but also become attached to the opposite-sex parent.

duce them to demonstrate her power over them and thereby relieve her feelings of inferiority.

After the phallic stage comes a **latency period** of several years, during which the child's sexual instinctual drive is mostly submerged. Following this period, the onset of puberty, the child, now an adolescent, begins to form adult sexual attachments to age mates of the other sex. Because the sexual instinctual drive now finds its outlet in heterosexual genital contact, this stage is known as the **genital stage**.

Further Development of Freud's Theory: The Neo-Freudians

As you might imagine, Freud's theory created quite a controversy in the Victorian era in which it was unveiled. Its emphasis on childhood sexuality and seething internal conflicts seemed preposterous and offensive to many. Yet, the theory's proposal that our thoughts and behavior as adults stem from unconscious forces as well as from our early childhood experiences were revolutionary and recognized by many scholars as genuinely original ideas. Freud attracted a number of followers who studied his work closely but who did not accept it completely. Each of these people agreed with Freud's view on the dynamic forces operating within the psyche. Each of them disagreed with Freud, though, on how much importance to place on the role of unconscious sexual and aggressive instincts in shaping personality. Four psychodynamic theorists, Carl Jung, Alfred Adler, Karen Horney, and Erik Erikson, have been particularly influential in elaborating psychodynamic theory.

Carl Jung

Early in the twentieth century, several students of psychoanalysis met with Freud to further the development of psychoanalysis. One of these people was Carl Jung (1875–1961). Freud called Jung "his adopted eldest son, his crown prince and successor" (Hall and Nordby, 1973, p. 23). However, Jung developed his own version of psychodynamic theory that deemphasized the importance of sexuality. He also disagreed with his mentor on the structure of the unconscious. Unfortunately, Freud had little tolerance of others' opinions. After 1913, he and Jung never saw each other again. Jung continued to develop his theory after the split by drawing ideas from mythology, anthropology, history, and religion, as well as from an active clinical practice in which he saw people with psychological disorders.

To Jung, libido was a positive creative force that propels people toward personal growth. He also believed that forces other than the id, ego, and superego, such as the collective unconscious, form the core of personality. To Jung, the ego was totally conscious, and contained the ideas, perceptions, emotions, thoughts, and memories of which we are aware. One of Jung's more important contributions to psychodynamic theory was his idea of the **collective unconscious**, which contains memories and ideas inherited from our ancestors. Stored in the collective unconscious are **archetypes**, inherited and universal thought forms and patterns that allow us to notice particular aspects of our world (Carver and Scheier, 1992). From the dawn of our species, all humans have had roughly similar experiences with things such as mothers, evilness, masculinity, and femininity. Each one of these is represented by an archetype. For example, the *shadow* is the archetype containing basic instincts that allow us to recognize aspects of the world such as evil, sin, and carnality. Archetypes are not stored images or ideas—we are not born with a picture of evil stored somewhere in our brains—but we are born with an inherited disposition to behave, perceive, and think in certain ways.

Alfred Adler

Like Jung, Alfred Adler (1870–1937) studied with Freud. Also like Jung, Adler felt that Freud overemphasized the role of sexuality in personality development. Adler argued that feelings of inferiority play the key role. Upon birth, we are dependent on others for survival. As we mature, we encounter people who are more gifted than we are in almost every aspect of life. The inferiority we feel may be social, intellectual, physical, or athletic. These feelings create tension that motivates us to compensate for the deficiency. Emerging from this need to compensate is a **striving for superiority**, which Adler believed to be the major motivational force in life.

According to Adler (1939), striving for superiority is affected by another force, *social interest*, which is an innate desire to contribute to society. Social interest is not wholly instinctual, though, because it can be influenced by experience. Although individuals have a need to seek personal superiority, they have a greater desire to sacrifice for causes that benefit the society as a whole. Thus, while Freud believed that people act in their own self-interests, motivated by the id, Adler believed that people desire to help others, directed by social interest.

---

latency period The period between the phallic stage and the genital stage during which there are no unconscious sexual urges or intrapsychic conflicts.

genital stage The final of Freud's psychosexual stages (from puberty through adolescence). During this stage, the adolescent develops adult sexual desires.

collective unconscious According to Jung, the part of the unconscious that contains memories and ideas inherited from our ancestors over the course of evolution.

archetypes Universal thought forms and patterns that Jung believed resided in the collective unconscious.

striving for superiority The motivation to seek superiority. Adler argued that striving for superiority is born from our need to compensate for our inferiorities.

Karen Horney

Karen Horney (pronounced "Horn-eye"; 1885–1952), like other Freudian dissenters, did not believe that sex and aggression are the primary themes of personality. She did agree with Freud, though, that anxiety is a basic problem that people must address and overcome.

According to Horney, individuals suffer from basic anxiety caused by insecurities in relationships. People often feel alone, helpless, or uncomfortable in their interactions with others. For example, a person who begins a new job is often unsure of how to perform his or her duties, whom to ask for help, and how to approach his or her new coworkers. Horney theorized that to deal with basic anxiety, the individual has three options (Horney, 1950):

- *Moving toward others.* Accept the situation and become dependent on others. This strategy may entail an exaggerated desire for approval or affection.

- *Moving against others.* Resist the situation and become aggressive. This strategy may involve an exaggerated need for power, exploitation of others, recognition, or achievement.

- *Moving away from others.* Withdraw from others and become isolated. This strategy may involve an exaggerated need for self-sufficiency, privacy, or independence.

Horney believed that these three strategies corresponded to three **basic orientations** with which people approach their lives. These basic orientations reflect different personality characteristics. The *self-effacing solution* corresponds to the moving toward others strategy and involves the desire to be loved. The *self-expansive solution* corresponds to the moving against others strategy and involves the desire to master oneself. The *resignation solution* corresponds to the moving away strategy and involves striving to be independent of others.

Horney maintained that personality is a mixture of the three strategies and basic orientations. As the source of anxiety varies from one situation to the next, so may the strategy and basic orientation that is used to cope with it. Like Adler, Horney thought environmental variables influenced personality development. From her view, to understand personality, one must consider not only psychodynamic forces within the mind, but also the environmental conditions to which those forces are reacting.

Erik Erikson

Erik Erikson (1902–1994) studied with Anna Freud, Sigmund Freud's daughter. He emphasized social aspects of personality development rather than biological factors. He also differed with Freud about the timing of personality development. For Freud, the most important development occurs during early childhood. Erikson emphasized the ongoing process of development throughout the life span. As we saw in Chapter 12, Erikson proposed that people's personality traits develop as a result of a series of crises they encounter in their social relations with other people. Because these crises continue throughout life, psychosocial development does not end when people become adults.

Erikson's theory of lifelong development has been very influential, and his term *identity crisis* has become a familiar one. However, because his theory does not make many empirically testable predictions, it has received little empirical support.

Some Observations on Psychodynamic Theory and Research

Freud's psychodynamic theory has had a profound effect on psychological theory, psychotherapy, and literature. His writing, although nowadays regarded as sexist, is lively and stimulating, and his ideas have provided many people with food for thought. However, his theory has received little empirical support, mainly because he used concepts that are poorly defined and that cannot be observed directly. How is one to study the ego, the superego, or the id? How can one prove (or disprove) that an artist's creativity is the result of a displaced aggressive or sexual instinctual drive? The writings of the neo-Freudians have had even less influence on modern research. Although the theories of Jung, Adler, Horney, and Erikson have their followers, scientific research on personality has largely ignored them.

The emphasis by Freud and his followers on the potentially harmful effects of particular types of childhood environments has led some psychotherapists to conclude that their patients' maladjustments and mental disorders are, by and large, caused by their parents. Many parents have blamed themselves for their children's disorders and have suffered severe feelings of guilt. But many forms of mental disorders—particularly the most serious ones—are largely a result of heredity and are not affected much by family environment. Hence, the teachings of Freud and his followers have compounded the tragedy of mental illness by causing parents to be accused unjustly of poor parenting practices.

The one Freudian phenomenon that has undergone experimental testing is repression. This phenomenon is very important to Freud's theory because it is one of the primary ego defenses and because it operates by pushing memories (or newly perceived stimuli) into the unconscious. Thus, experimental verification of repression would lend some support to Freud's notions of intrapsychic conflict and the existence of the unconscious.

The results of research on repression have not been conclusive. Typically, the researchers in repression experiments

---

basic orientations Horney's sets of personality characteristics that correspond to the strategies of moving toward others, moving against others, and moving away from others.

ask subjects to learn some material associated with an un-pleasant, ego-threatening situation, and they then compare their memory for the information with that of subjects who learned the material under nonthreatening conditions. If repression occurs, the threatened subjects should remember less of the material than the nonthreatened subjects will. Some studies have reported positive results, but later experiments have shown that other, non-Freudian phenomena could explain them more easily (D'Zurilla, 1965). Perhaps the most important point here is that none of the experiments can really be said to have threatened the subjects' egos, producing the level of anxiety that would lead to the activation of a defense mechanism. Any experimental procedure that did so would probably be unethical.

Thus, it is difficult to test even the most specific prediction of Freud's theory. It is very hard, perhaps impossible, to prove that a person's behavior and personality are products of unconscious conflicts.

Interim Summary

The Psychodynamic Approach

Freud believed that the mind is full of conflicts between the primitive urges of the id and the internalized prohibitions of the superego. According to Freud, these conflicts tend to be resolved through compromise formation and through ego defenses such as repression, sublimation, and reaction formation. His theory of psychosexual development, a progression through the oral, anal, phallic, and genital stages, provided the basis for a theory of personality and personality disorders.

Freud's followers, most notably Jung, Adler, Horney, and Erikson, embraced different aspects of Freud's theory, disagreed with other aspects, and embellished still other aspects. Jung disagreed with Freud about the structure of the unconscious and the role of sexuality in personality development, and saw libido as a positive life force. Adler also disagreed with Freud on the importance of sexuality. Instead, Adler emphasized the need to compensate for our inferiorities and our innate desire to help others as the major forces in personality development. Horney argued that personality is the result of the strategies and behaviors people use to cope with anxiety, which she believed is the fundamental problem that all people must overcome in the course of normal personality development. Erikson maintained that personality development is more a matter of psychosocial processes than of psychosexual processes. He viewed personality development as involving eight stages, each of which involves coping with a major conflict or crises. Resolution of the conflict allows the person to pass to the next stage; failure to resolve it inhibits normal personality development.

Although Freud was a brilliant and insightful thinker, his theory has not been experimentally verified, primarily because most of his concepts are unobservable and, therefore, untestable. Even though many modern psychologists do not believe his psychodynamic theory to be correct, Freud made an important contribution to psychology with his realization that not all causes of our behavior are available to consciousness; many are unknown to us. In Chapter 18, we will examine psychoanalysis, the therapeutic technique based on his theory of personality.

Thought Questions

- Have you ever found yourself using any of the Freudian defense mechanisms discussed in this chapter? If so, under what circumstances do you tend to use them, and what unconscious conflict do you suppose you might be protecting yourself from?
- Do you possess any behaviors that may represent a fixation? If so, what are they and what fixations do they represent?
- Which neo-Freudian view on personality development makes the most sense to you? Why do you feel this way—what is your rationale for concluding that one view is more sensible than the others? Which of the theories best explains your own personality development? Provide an example.

The Humanistic Approach

The **humanistic approach** to the study of personality seeks to emphasize the positive, fulfilling elements of life. Humanistic psychologists are interested in nurturing personal growth, life satisfaction, and positive human values. They believe that people are innately good and have an internal drive for **self-actualization**—the realization of one's true intellectual and emotional potential. The two most influential humanistic theorists have been Abraham Maslow and Carl Rogers.

Maslow and Self-Actualization

For both Freud and Abraham Maslow (1908–1970), motivation is one of the central aspects of personality. However, where Freud saw strong instinctual urges generating tensions that could not be completely resolved, Maslow saw positive impulses that could be easily overwhelmed by the negative forces within one's culture. According to Maslow (1970), human motivation is based on a hierarchy of needs. Our motivation for different activities passes through several levels,

humanistic approach An approach to the study of personality in which the emphasis is placed on the positive, fulfilling aspects of life.

self-actualization The realization of one's true intellectual and emotional potential.

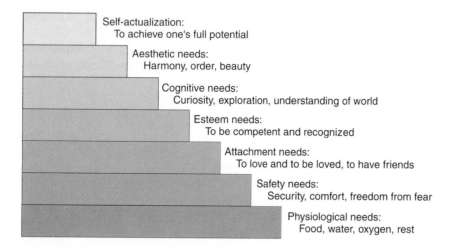

Self-actualization:
To achieve one's full potential

Aesthetic needs:
Harmony, order, beauty

Cognitive needs:
Curiosity, exploration, understanding of world

Esteem needs:
To be competent and recognized

Attachment needs:
To love and to be loved, to have friends

Safety needs:
Security, comfort, freedom from fear

Physiological needs:
Food, water, oxygen, rest

Figure 14.11

Maslow's hierarchy of needs. According to Maslow, every person's goal is to become self-actualized. In order to achieve this goal, individuals must first satisfy several basic needs.

with entrance to subsequent levels depending on first satisfying needs in previous levels. (*See Figure 14.11.*) If an individual's needs are not met, he or she cannot scale the hierarchy and so will fail to attain his or her true potential.

Abraham Maslow considered Albert Einstein to possess those qualities representative of self-actualization, including self-acceptance, a focus on finding solutions to cultural problems, open-mindedness, and spontaneity.

In Maslow's view, understanding personality requires understanding this hierarchy. Our most basic needs are *physiological needs*, including the need for food, water, oxygen, rest, and so on. Until these needs are met, we cannot be motivated by needs found in the next level (or any other level). If our physiological needs are met, we find ourselves motivated by *safety needs*, including the need for security and comfort, as well as for peace and freedom from fear. Once the basic survival and safety needs are met, we can become motivated by *attachment needs*, the need to love and to be loved, to have friends and to be a friend. Next, we seek to satisfy esteem needs—to be competent and recognized as such. You are probably beginning to get the picture: We are motivated to achieve needs higher in the hierarchy only after first satisfying lower needs. If we are able to lead a life in which we have been able to provide ourselves food and shelter and to surround ourselves with love, we are free to pursue self-actualization.

Maslow based his theory partially on his own assumptions about human potential and partially on his case studies of historical figures whom he believed to be self-actualized, including Albert Einstein, Eleanor Roosevelt, Henry David Thoreau, and Abraham Lincoln. Maslow examined the lives of each of these people in order to assess the common qualities that led each to become self-actualized. In general, he found that these individuals were very self-accepting of themselves and of their lives' circumstances, were focused on finding solutions to pressing cultural problems rather than to personal problems, were open to others' opinions and ideas, were spontaneous in their emotional reactions to events in their lives, had strong senses of privacy, autonomy, human values, and appreciation of life, and had a few intimate friendships rather than many superficial ones.

Maslow (1964) believed that the innate drive for self-actualization is not specific to any particular culture. He viewed it as being a fundamental part of human nature. In his words, "Man has a higher and transcendent nature, and this is part of his essence. . . his biological nature of a species which has evolved" (p. xvi).

Rogers and Conditions of Worth

Carl Rogers (1902–1987) also believed that people are motivated to grow psychologically, aspiring to higher levels of fulfillment as they progress toward self-actualization (Rogers, 1961). Like Maslow, Rogers believed that people are inherently good and have an innate desire for becoming better. Rogers, though, did not view personality development in terms of satisfying a hierarchy of needs. Instead, he believed that personality development centers on one's *self-concept*, or one's opinion of oneself, and on the way one is treated by others.

Rogers argued that all people have a need for *positive regard*, or approval, warmth, love, respect, and affection flowing from others. Young children, in particular, show this need when they seek approval for their actions from parents and siblings. In Rogers's view, children often want others to like them to the extent that gaining positive regard is a major focus of their lives. The key to developing a psychologically healthy personality, though, is to develop a positive self-concept or image of oneself. How does one do this? Rogers's answer is that we are happy if we feel that others are happy with us. Likewise, we are also unhappy with ourselves when others are disappointed in or unsatisfied with us.

Thus, our feelings toward ourselves depend to a large extent on what others think of us. As children, we learn that there exist certain conditions or criteria that must be met before others give us positive regard. Rogers called these criteria **conditions of worth.**

Positive regard is often conditional. For example, parents may act approvingly toward their young child when he helps in the kitchen or in the yard but not when he pinches his younger sister or tells a fib about how many cookies he has taken from the cookie jar. The boy learns that what others think of him depends on his actions. Soon, too, he may come to view himself as others view him and his behavior: "People like me when I do something good and they don't like me when I do something bad."

Although conditions of worth are a necessary part of the socialization process, they can have negative effects on personality development if satisfying them becomes the individual's major ambition. So long as the individual focuses chiefly on seeking positive regard from others, he or she may ignore other aspects of life, especially those that lead to positive personality growth. In Rogers's view, then, conditions of worth may stand in the way of self-actualization. An individual may devote her life to satisfying the expectations and demands of others in lieu of working toward realizing her potential. In this sense, the need for positive regard may smother an individual's progress toward self-actualization.

According to Rogers, the solution to this problem is **unconditional positive regard**, or love and acceptance that has no strings attached. In a family setting, this means that parents may establish rules and expect their children to obey them, but not if doing so compromises the children's feelings of worth and self-respect. For example, if a child misbehaves,

According to Rogers, all people have a basic need for approval, warmth, and love from others. This need is best met through unconditional positive regard: love and acceptance with no strings attached.

the parents should focus on the child's behavior and not the child. (As many a parent will attest, this is easier said than done.) In this way, the child learns that her behavior is wrong but that her parents still love her. Unconditional positive regard allows people to work toward realizing their potential unfettered by what others think of them.

In developing his theory, Rogers used unstructured interviews in which the client, not the therapist, directed the course of the conversation. He believed that if the therapist provided an atmosphere of unconditional positive regard, a client would eventually reveal her *true self*, the kind of person she now is, as well as her *ideal self*, the kind of person that she would like to become. Rogers also gave the Q sort test to many of his clients. This test consists of a variety of cards, each of which contains a statement such as "I am generally an optimistic person" or "I am generally an intolerant person." The client's task is to sort the cards into several piles that vary in degree from "least like me" to "most like me." The client sorts the cards twice, first on the basis of his real self and next in terms of his ideal self. The difference between the arrangement of the cards in the piles is taken as an index of how close the client is to reaching his ideal self. Rogers's goal as a therapist was to facilitate the client becoming his ideal self. I will discuss Rogers's approach to therapy in more detail in Chapter 18.

conditions of worth Conditions that others place on us for receiving their positive regard.

unconditional positive regard Unconditional love and acceptance of an individual by another person.

Some Observations on the Humanistic Approach

The humanistic approach is impressive because of its emphasis on people seeking a healthy well-being. Indeed, the approach has wide appeal to those who seek an alternative to the more mechanistic and strictly biologically or environmentally determined views of human nature. However, critics point up two closely related problems with this approach.

First, many of the concepts used by humanistic psychologists are defined subjectively and so are difficult to test empirically. For example, how might we empirically examine the nature of self-actualization? Few published studies have even attempted to answer this question. By now, you know the hallmark of a good theory—the amount of research it generates. On this count, the humanistic approach comes up short.

A second criticism of the humanistic approach is that it cannot account for the origins of personality. It is subject to the nominal fallacy; it describes personality, but it does not explain it. Humanistic psychologists believe that self-actualization is an innate tendency, but there is no research that shows it to be so. Conditions of worth are said to hamper a child's quest for self-actualization and thus alter the course of personality development away from positive psychological growth. However, the humanistic approach provides no objective explanation of this process. Although the humanistic approach may offer a positive view of human nature and give apparent purpose to life, this view is largely unsubstantiated.

Before moving on to the next section, take a few moments to examine Table 14.4, which reviews each of the major theories of personality we have discussed. (See *Table 14.4.*)

Interim Summary

The Humanistic Approach

The humanistic approach attempts to understand personality and its development by focusing on the positive side of human nature and people's attempts to reach their full potential: self-actualization.

Maslow argued that self-actualization is achieved only after the satisfaction of several other important but lesser needs, for example, physiological, safety, and attachment needs. Maslow's case study analysis of people whom he believed to be self-actualized revealed several common personality characteristics including self-acceptance, a focus on addressing cultural problems and not personal ones, spontaneity, preservation of privacy, an appreciation for life, and possession of a few very close, intimate friendships.

According to Rogers, the key to becoming self-actualized is developing a healthy self-concept. The primary roadblocks in this quest are conditions of worth—criteria that we must meet to win the positive regard of others. Rogers maintained

---

Table 14.4

A Summary of the Major Personality Theories

Theory	Primary Figures	Primary Emphases	Primary Strengths	Primary Limitations
Trait	Allport, Cattell, Eysenck	An individual's traits determines personality.	Focuses on stability of behavior over long periods. Attempts to measure traits objectively.	Largely descriptive; ignores situational variables that may affect behavior.
Psychobiological	Eysenck, Zuckerman	The role of genetics and the brain and nervous system in personality development.	Emphasis on the interaction of biological and environmental in determining personality; rigorous empirical approach.	Reliance on correlational methods in determining the role of genetics in personality.
Social Learning	Bandura, Mischel, Rotter	Personality is determined by both the consequences of behavior and our perception of them.	Focuses on direct study of behavior and stresses rigorous experimentation.	Ignores biological influences on personality development. Often more descriptive than explanatory.
Psychodynamic	Freud, Jung, Adler, Horney, Erikson	Unconscious psychic conflicts; repression of anxiety-provoking ideas and desires.	The idea that behavior may be influenced by forces outside of conscious awareness.	Basic concepts are not empirically testable.
Humanistic	Maslow, Rogers	Stresses the positive aspects of human nature and how to become a better person.	Useful in therapeutic settings.	Contains vague and untestable concepts; primarily descriptive.

that too often people value themselves only to the extent that they believe other people do. As a result, they spend their lives seeking the acceptance of others instead of striving to become self-actualized. Rogers proposed that only by treating others with unconditional positive regard could we help people to realize their true potentials.

Although the humanistic approach emphasizes the positive dimensions of human experience and the potential that each of us has for personal growth, it has been faulted for being unscientific. Critics argue that its concepts are vague and untestable and that it is more descriptive than explanatory.

Thought Questions

- Are you a self-actualized person? If not, what obstacles might be standing in the way of your reaching your true potential?
- Describe some of the conditions of worth that others have placed on you as you have developed into an adult. Explain how your experience confirms or disconfirms Rogers's idea that conditions of worth are impediments to personal growth and to the development of a healthy self-concept.

Assessment of Personality

Think for a moment of your best friend. What is he or she like? Outgoing? Impulsive? Thoughtful? Moody? You can easily respond "yes" or "no" to these alternatives because you have spent enough time with your friend to know him or her quite well. After all, one of the best ways to get to know people—what they are like and how they react in certain situations—is to spend time with them. Obviously, psychologists do not have the luxury of spending large amounts of time with people in order to learn about their personalities. Generally, they only have a short period to accomplish this goal. From this necessity, personality tests were first developed. The underlying assumption of any personality test is that personality characteristics can be measured. This final section of the chapter describes the two primary types of personality tests—objective tests and projective tests.

---

objective personality tests Tests for measuring personality that can be scored objectively, such as a multiple-choice or true-false test.

Minnesota Multiphasic Personality Inventory (MMPI) An objective test originally designed to distinguish individuals with different psychological problems from normal individuals. It has since become popular as a means of attempting to identify personality characteristics of people in many everyday settings.

Objective Tests of Personality

Objective personality tests are similar in structure to classroom tests. Most contain multiple-choice and true-false items, although some allow the person taking the test to indicate the extent to which he or she agrees or disagrees with an item. The responses that subjects can make on objective tests are constrained by the test design. The questions asked are unambiguous, and explicit rules for scoring the subjects' responses can be specified in advance.

One of the oldest and most widely used objective tests of personality is the **Minnesota Multiphasic Personality Inventory (MMPI)**, devised by Hathaway and McKinley in 1939. The original purpose for developing the test was to produce an objective, reliable method for identifying various personality traits that were related to a person's mental health. The developers believed that this test would be valuable in assessing people for a variety of purposes. For instance, it would provide a specific means of determining how effective psychotherapy was. Improvement in people's scores over the course of treatment would indicate that the treatment was successful.

In devising this test, Hathaway and McKinley wrote 504 true-false items and administered the test to several groups of people in mental institutions in Minnesota who had been diagnosed as having certain psychological disorders. These diagnoses had been arrived at through psychiatric interviews with the patients. Such interviews are expensive, so a simple paper-and-pencil test that accomplished the same result would be valuable. The control group consisted of relatives and friends of the patients, who were tested when they came to visit them. (Whether these people constituted the best possible group of normal subjects is questionable.) The responses were analyzed empirically, and the questions that correlated with various diagnostic labels were included in various scales. For example, if people who had been diagnosed as paranoid tended to say true to "I believe I am being plotted against," this statement would become part of the paranoia scale.

The current revised version of the MMPI, the MMPI-2, has norms based on a sample of people that is much more representative ethnically and geographically than the original sample (Graham, 1990). It includes 550 questions, grouped into 10 clinical scales and 4 validity scales. A particular item can be used on more than one scale. For example, both people who are depressed and those who are hypochondriacal tend to agree that they have gastrointestinal problems. The clinical scales include a number of diagnostic terms traditionally used to label psychiatric patients, such as hypochondriasis, depression, or paranoia.

The four validity scales were devised to provide the tester with some assurance that subjects are answering questions reliably and accurately and that they can read the questions and pay attention to them. The ? scale (cannot say) is simply the number of questions not answered. A high score on this scale indicates either that the person finds some questions irrelevant or that the person is evading issues that he or she finds painful.

The L scale (lie) contains items such as "I do not read every editorial in the newspaper every day" and "My table manners are not quite as good at home as when I am out in company." A person who disagrees with questions like these is almost certainly not telling the truth. A high score on the L scale suggests the need for caution in interpreting other scales and also reveals something about the subject's personality. In particular, people who score high on this scale tend to be rather naive; more sophisticated people realize that no one is perfect and do not try to make themselves appear to be so.

The F scale (frequency) consists of items that are answered one way by at least 90 percent of the normal population. The usual responses are "false" to items such as "I can easily make other people afraid of me, and sometimes do it for the fun of it" and "true" to items such as "I am liked by most people who know me." A high score on this scale indicates carelessness, poor reading ability, or very unusual personality traits.

The K scale (defensiveness) was devised to identify people who are trying to hide their feelings to guard against internal conflicts that might cause them emotional distress. A person receives a high value on the K scale by answering "false" to statements such as "Criticism or scolding hurts me terribly" and "At periods, my mind seems to work more slowly than usual." People who score very low on this scale tend to be in need of help or to be unusually immune to criticism and social influences.

Some psychologists argue that validity scales are useless or even harmful in most testing situations. For example, consider the following item: "Before voting, I thoroughly investigate the qualifications of all candidates." According to Crowne and Marlowe (1964), anyone who answers "yes" to such a question has to be lying. But as McCrae and Costa (1990) note, people taking tests do not necessarily respond passively to each item, taking it at face value. Instead, their response is based on their interpretation of what they think the question means. They suggest that most people will say to themselves, " 'Surely these psychologists didn't mean to ask if I actually study the voting records of every single political candidate, from President to dogcatcher. No one does, so that would be a stupid question to ask. What they must have meant to ask was whether I am a concerned citizen who takes voting seriously. Since I am and I do, I guess I should answer yes' " (McCrae and Costa, 1990, p. 40).

projective tests Unstructured personality measures in which a person is shown a series of ambiguous stimuli, such as pictures, inkblots, or incomplete drawings. The person is asked to describe what he or she "sees" in each stimulus or to create stories that reflect the theme of the drawing or picture.

Rorschach Inkblot Test A projective test in which a person is shown a series of symmetrical inkblots and asked to describe what he or she thinks they represent.

There is evidence to support McCrae and Costa's suggestion. When psychologists calculate a person's score on the MMPI, they usually apply a correction factor derived from the validity scales. Several studies have shown that the application of the correction factors to the scores of normal subjects actually reduces the validity of these scores. McCrae and Costa suggest that when the MMPI is administered to normal subjects for research purposes, such corrections should not be made. However, validity scales may be useful in situations in which subjects may be motivated to lie (for example, when a personality test is used to screen job applicants) or in cases in which the test is being used clinically to evaluate the possibility of mental illness or personality disorder.

As well as being used in clinical assessment, the MMPI has been employed extensively in personality research, and a number of other tests, including the California Psychological Inventory and the Taylor Manifest Anxiety Scale, are based on it. However, the MMPI has its critics. As we saw earlier, the five-factor model of personality has received considerable support. Some of its advocates have noted that the MMPI misses some of the dimensions measured by the NEO-PI, which includes tests of neuroticism, extraversion, openness, agreeableness, and conscientiousness (Johnson et al., 1984). Thus, these factors will be missed by a clinician or researcher who relies only on the MMPI. For this reason, many researchers—especially those interested in the psychobiology of personality—no longer use the MMPI.

Projective Tests of Personality

Projective tests of personality are different in form from objective ones and are derived from psychodynamic theories of personality. Psychoanalytically oriented psychologists believe that behavior is determined by unconscious processes more than by conscious ones. Thus, they believe that a test that asks straightforward questions is unlikely to tap the real roots of an individual's personality characteristics. **Projective tests** are designed to be ambiguous so that the person's answers will be more revealing than simple agreement or disagreement with statements provided by objective tests. The assumption of projective tests is that an individual will "project" his or her personality into the ambiguous situation and thus make responses that give clues to this personality. In addition, the ambiguity of the test makes it unlikely that subjects will have preconceived notions about which answers are socially desirable. Thus, it will be difficult for a subject to give biased answers in an attempt to look better (or worse) than he or she actually is.

The Rorschach Inkblot Test

One of the oldest projective tests of personality is the Rorschach Inkblot Test, published in 1921 by Hermann Rorschach, a Swiss psychiatrist. The **Rorschach Inkblot Test**

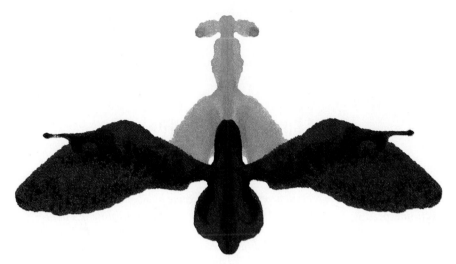

Figure 14.12

An inkblot similar to one that appears in the Rorschach Inkblot Test.

consists of ten pictures of inkblots, originally made by spilling ink on a piece of paper that was subsequently folded in half, producing an image that is symmetrical in relation to the line of the fold. Five of the inkblots are black and white, and five are color. (See *Figure 14.12*.) The subject is shown each card and asked to describe what it looks like. Then the cards are shown again, and the subject is asked to point out the features he or she used to determine what was seen. The responses and the nature of the features the subject uses to make them are scored on several dimensions.

In the following example described by Pervin (1975), a person's response to a particular inkblot (a real one, not the one shown in Figure 14.12) might be "Two bears with their paws touching one another playing pattycake or could be they are fighting and the red is the blood from the fighting." The classification of this response, also described by Pervin, would be: large detail of the blot was used, good form was used, movement was noted, color was used in the response about blood, an animal was seen, and a popular response (two bears) was made. A possible interpretation of the response might be:

> Subject starts off with popular response and animals expressing playful, "childish" behavior. Response is then given in terms of hostile act with accompanying inquiry. Pure color response and blood content suggest he may have difficulty controlling his response to the environment. Is a playful, childlike exterior used by him to disguise hostile, destructive feelings that threaten to break out in his dealings with the environment? (Pervin, 1975, p. 37)

Although the interpretation of people's responses to the Rorschach Inkblot Test was originally based on psychoanalytical theory, many investigators have used it in an empirical fashion. That is, a variety of different scoring methods have been devised, and the scores obtained by these methods have been correlated with clinical diagnoses, just as investigators have done with people's scores on the MMPI. When this test

is used empirically, the style and content of the responses are not interpreted in terms of a theory (as Rorschach interpreted them) but are simply correlated with other measures of personality.

The Thematic Apperception Test

Another popular projective test, the **Thematic Apperception Test (TAT)**, was developed in 1938 by the American psychologists Henry Murray and C.D. Morgan to measure various psychological needs. People are shown a picture of a very ambiguous situation and are asked to tell a story about what is happening in the picture, explaining the situation, what led up to it, what the characters are thinking and saying, and what the final outcome will be. Presumably, the subjects will "project" themselves into the scene, and their stories will reflect their own needs. As you might imagine, scoring is difficult and requires a great deal of practice and skill. The tester attempts to infer the psychological needs expressed in the stories.

Consider the responses of one woman to several TAT cards, along with a clinician's interpretation of these responses (Phares, 1979). The questions asked by the examiner are in parentheses.

> Card 3BM. Looks like a little boy crying for something he can't have. (Why is he crying?) Probably because he can't go somewhere. (How will it turn out?) Probably sit there and sob hisself to sleep. Card 3GF. Looks like her boyfriend might have let her down. She hurt his feelings. He's closed the door on her. (What did he

Thematic Apperception Test (TAT) A projective test in which a person is shown a series of ambiguous pictures that involve people. The person is asked to make up a story about what the people are doing or thinking. The person's responses are believed to reflect aspects of his or her personality.

say?) I don't know. Card 10. Looks like there's sorrow here. Grieving about something. (About what?) Looks like maybe one of the children's passed away.

Interpretation: The TAT produced responses that were uniformly indicative of unhappiness, threat, misfortune, a lack of control over environmental forces. None of the test responses were indicative of satisfaction, happy endings, etc. . . . In summary, the test results point to an individual who is anxious and, at the same time, depressed. (Phares, 1979, p. 273)

The pattern of responses in this case is quite consistent; few people would disagree with the conclusion that the woman is sad and depressed. However, not all people provide such clear-cut responses. As you might expect, interpreting differences in the stories of people who are relatively well-adjusted is much more difficult. As a result, distinguishing among people with different but normal personality traits is hard.

Evaluation of Projective Tests

Most empirical studies have found that projective tests such as the Rorschach Inkblot Test and the TAT have poor reliability and little validity. For example, Eron (1950) found no differences between the scores of people who were in mental hospitals and college students. (No, I'm not going to make a joke about that.) Entwisle (1972) reported that "recent studies . . . yield few positive relationships between need achievement [measured by the TAT] and other variables" (p. 179). In a review of over three hundred studies, Lundy (1984) found that the validity of the TAT appears to be lower when it is administered by an authority figure, in a classroom setting, or when it is represented as a test. Lundy (1988) suggests that in such situations, the subjects are likely to realize that they are talking about themselves when they tell a story about the cards and may be careful about what they say.

Even if people taking the TAT are not on their guards, their scores are especially sensitive to their moods (Masling, 1960). So the scores they receive on one day are often very different from those they receive on another day. But a test of personality is supposed to measure enduring traits that persist over time and in a variety of situations. The TAT has also been criticized for potential gender bias, mostly because of male-dominated themes, such as power, ambition, and status, used to score the test (Worchel, Aaron, and Yates, 1990).

The reliability and validity of the Rorschach Inkblot Test are also rather low. One study that used the most reliable scoring method found little or no correlation between subjects' scores on the Rorschach and their scores on six objective tests of personality (Greenwald, 1990).

If projective tests such as the Rorschach and the TAT have been found to be of low reliability and validity, why do many clinical psychologists and psychiatrists continue to use them? The primary reason seems to be tradition. The use of these tests has a long history and the rationale for the tests is

consistent with psychodynamic explanations of personality. Many psychodynamic and clinical psychologists still argue that the tests are valuable for discovering and evaluating inner determinants of personality (Watkins, 1991).

Biology and Culture

Gender Differences in Personality

From a very early age, people in all cultures learn that boys and girls and men and women are different in at least two ways—physically and psychologically. The psychological differences often are more difficult to detect than the physical differences, but, nonetheless, males and females tend not only to perceive aspects of their environments differently, but also to behave differently under some circumstances.

■ What Gender Differences in Personality Actually Exist?

People in all cultures hold certain beliefs, called *stereotypes*, about differences between males and females. A stereotype is a belief that people possess certain qualities because of their membership in a particular group, in this case, a gender. (I will discuss stereotypes and their origins in Chapter 15.) In general, stereotypes are more flattering about men than women: Men are stereotyped to be more competent, independent, decisive, and logical and women are stereotyped to be less competent, competitive, ambitious, independent, and active (Broverman et al., 1972; Pearson, Turner, and Todd-Mancillas, 1991).

Thousands of psychological studies of gender differences do not confirm most of these stereotypes. In terms of personality, males and females are actually more alike than different. For instance, there seem to be few significant differences between the genders in terms of the personality variables, such as introversion and extraversion, associated with intelligence (Snow and Weinstock, 1990), friendships (Jones, 1991), or perceived career success (Poole, Langan-Fox, and Omodei, 1991).

Research has revealed some gender differences in personality characteristics related to social behavior. One social behavior that shows large gender differences is aggression. During play, young boys often display more aggression than do young girls (Fabes and Eisenberg, 1992). In a recent longitudinal study of elementary and high school students, males where shown to be more aggressive than were females and patterns of aggression were found to be less stable for males than for females (Woodall and Matthews, 1993).

However, gender differences in aggression may vary in different cultures. For example, in one study of preschoolers, American and Israeli girls were shown to

Higher levels of aggressive behavior in males is one of the few important psychological differences between males and females.

start fewer fights than did their respective male counterparts, but Israeli girls started more fights than did American boys (Lauer, cited in Bower, 1991). The higher levels of aggression among Israeli children may be due, in part, to their country's constant preparation for and frequent participation in military conflicts. In addition, in some cultures and subcultures, girls may join gangs that are involved in aggressive activities. For example, in Chihuahua, Mexico, a girl being initiated into a gang must fistfight a gang member (Bower, 1991). Girl gangs often join their "brother" gangs in defending their turf against other male gangs. Girl gangs also fight other girl gangs, and such fights may involve knifefighting and rockthrowing as well as fistfighting.

Several other gender differences related to personality and social behavior have been recently documented. Males tend to emerge as leaders when the group to which they belong needs to accomplish a specific task. Females tend to emerge as leaders when the groups to which they belong stress interpersonal relationships (Eagly and Karau, 1991). Females tend to be more empathetic and tend to offer assistance to others when the situation demands comforting others. Men are more likely to offer assistance when the situation demands physical aid (Eisenberg et al., 1991). Likewise, females tend to be more empathetic and expressive in their relationships while males tend to be less intimate (Buss, 1995).

■ Biological Origins of Personality Differences

As I noted earlier in this chapter, personality traits appear to have a strong heritable component. For example, in a review of recent advances in behavior genetic research related to personality, Rose (1995) concluded that heredity accounts for a large segment of the variability in personality traits among individuals and may also explain continuity and changes in personality over the lifespan.

Unfortunately, not much is known about how genes influence gender differences in personality and behavior. The only thing we can say with any certainty is that personality differences between the sexes seem likely to have evolved as a direct result of the *biological* differences between males and females with respect to the division of labor required by sexual reproduction, as described in Chapter 3 (Loehlin, 1992; Tooby and Cosmides, 1990). For example, because of their greater physical and biological investment in reproduction, females may have developed tendencies to become more empathetic and interpersonally skilled. These traits would appear to be advantageous with respect to soliciting support from the father and others during pregnancy and childrearing (Buss, 1995). And because of their larger size and greater strength, males may have evolved tendencies toward hunting, fighting, and protecting their families and social unit. In modern times, these behaviors may translate into aggression and leadership tendencies. Females still have strong tendencies to be empathetic and skilled interpersonal communicators, most likely because cultural evolution has favored these behaviors.

■ Cultural Origins of Personality Differences

While the genetic and evolutionary contributions to gender differences in personality remain matters of speculation, the cultural origins of such differences seem clearer and would appear to center on the histories, environmental conditions, economic structures, and survival needs of different cultures (Wade and Tavris, 1994). That is, the behavioral tendencies and personality traits of males and females vary from culture to culture, depending on the specific conditions under which members of each culture live.

For example, consider how males and females in three different New Guinea tribes are expected to act (Harris, 1991). Among the Arapesh, both men and women are ex-

To a large extent, the specific culture in which people live influences the behavioral tendencies and personality traits of males and females.

pected to be cooperative and sympathetic, much as we expect the ideal American "mom" to be. Among the Mundugumor, both men and women are expected to be fierce and aggressive, similar to what we might expect of the men in our culture whom we call "macho." Finally, among the Tchambuli, women shave their heads, are boisterous, and provide food; the men tend to focus on art, their hairstyles, and gossiping about women.

As living conditions change, so does a culture's conception of the behaviors and personality traits appropriate to gender. For instance, as Wade and Tavris (1994) point out, the twentieth century has witnessed two unprecedented advances in technology, both of which have important implications for what most Western cultures consider to be gender-appropriate traits. First, because of advances in contraceptive technology, women may choose to limit the number of children they bear and make plans for when they bear them. Second, in today's job market, less emphasis is placed on physical skills and more on intellectual skills.

Combined, these two factors allow women to compete head-to-head with men not only for employment but also for leadership positions in today's global economy. And, as a result, we are finding that the stereotypes we once held of both men and women are breaking down. Many women have personality characteristics that were once thought to be exclusively male traits, such as extraversion, assertiveness, competitiveness, and ambitiousness. In fact, in the not-too-distant future, personality psychologists may discover that gender dif-

ferences in aggression, empathy, and other personality characteristics related to social behavior will no longer exist.

Interim Summary

Assessment of Personality Traits

Objective tests contain items that can be answered and scored objectively, such as true-false or multiple-choice questions. One of the most important objective personality tests is the Minnesota Multiphasic Personality Inventory, which was empirically devised to discriminate among people who had been assigned various psychiatric diagnoses. It has since been used widely in research on personality. Its validity scales have been challenged by researchers who suggest that most people's responses can be taken at face value. More recently, researchers interested in personality have turned to tests not based on people with mental disorders, such as the NEO-PI.

Projective tests, such as the Rorschach Inkblot Test and the Thematic Apperception Test, contain ambiguous items that elicit answers that presumably reveal aspects of the subjects' personalities. Because answers can vary widely, test administrators must receive special training to interpret them. Unfortunately, evidence suggests that the reliability and validity of such tests is not particularly high.

What few gender differences exist in personality seem to be related to social interaction. Although personality traits have been shown to have high heritability, cultural variables—living conditions related to a specific culture's traditions, economy, environmental conditions, and survival needs—play a powerful role in shaping personality and behavior. As these conditions change, so do the types of personality traits and behaviors necessary for survival during culture change. Thus, we should not be surprised when both males and females behave in ways that are contrary to the common stereotypes we hold regarding gender-specific personality characteristics.

Thought Questions

- Which kind of personality inventory—objective tests or projective tests—do you suppose would be more effective in revealing the more important aspects of your personality? Why?
- If your results on a personality inventory revealed that you possess a personality trait that you didn't think you had (especially if it is a negative trait), how would you react? Would you tend to disparage the test, or would you admit that, in fact, this trait is part of your personality?
- What kinds of personality differences between males and females have you noticed? Are these differences genuine or are they a product of the stereotypes you hold of the sexes? How do you know?

Suggestions for Further Reading

Buss, A. H. *Personality: Temperament, Social Behavior, and the Self.* Boston: Allyn and Bacon, 1995.

Carver, C.S., and Scheier, M.F. *Perspectives on Personality,* Second Edition. Boston: Allyn and Bacon, 1992.

Theories of personality, personality testing, and research on the determinants of personality receive thorough coverage in these texts.

Loehlin, J. C. *Genes and Environment in Personality Development.* London: Sage, 1992.

This brief book explains what is known about the heritability of personality traits. Topics covered include behavior genetic research, the relation of genes and environment to the personality traits described in the five-factor model of personality, and how evolution has influenced personality development.

Bandura, A. *Social Foundations of Thought and Action: A Social Cognitive Theory.* Englewood Cliffs, NJ: Prentice-Hall, 1986.

In this book, Bandura presents his account of social cognition and social behavior, which is derived from the behavior-analytic tradition and cognitive psychology.

Freud, S. *General Introduction to Psychoanalysis,* trans. J. Riviere. New York: Permabooks, 1957.

Jones, E. *The Life and Work of Sigmund Freud.* New York: Basic Books, 1953.

The best resource on Freud's theories of personality is Freud himself. Jones provides an interesting discussion of Freud's life as well as of his writings.

Chapter 15

Social Psychology

Chapter Outline

Social Cognition

Schemata and Social Cognition • The Self • Attribution • Attributional Biases • Attribution, Heuristics, and Social Cognition

Our thoughts, feelings, perceptions, and beliefs about the world are organized in mental frameworks, or schemata, which help us manage and synthesize information about our social world. Our self-concept is based on schemata that organize and synthesize personal knowledge and feelings we have about ourselves. In making attributions about the causes of another person's behavior, we consider the relative contributions of dispositional and situational factors. However, we tend to overestimate the role of dispositional factors and underestimate the role of situational factors—a phenomenon called the fundamental attribution error. We also often misapply heuristics or mental shortcuts when making attributions.

Attitudes and Their Formation

Formation of Attitudes • Attitude Change and Persuasion • Cognitive Dissonance • Self-Perception

Attitudes have affective, behavioral, and cognitive components and may be learned through mere exposure to the object of the attitude, classical conditioning processes, and imitation. To understand explicit attempts to change a person's attitude, we must consider both the source of the intended persuasive message and the message itself. A message tends to be persuasive if its source is credible or attractive and if it is pitched correctly at its intended audience. Cognitive dissonance is an aversive state that occurs when our attitudes and behavior are inconsistent. Our own observations of our behavior and situation also influence attitude development.

Prejudice

The Origins of Prejudice • Self-Fulfilling Prophecies • Hope for Change

A prejudice is an attitude toward a particular group based on characteristics of that group. A self-fulfilling prophecy is a stereotype that influences a person to act in ways congruent with that stereotype. Teaching people to think about members of other groups as individuals and to consider them in terms of their personal situations and characteristics can reduce prejudices and tendencies toward stereotyping.

Social Influences and Group Behavior

Imitation • Social Facilitation • Social Loafing • Reciprocity • Commitment • Attractive People • Authority • Deindividuation • Group Decision Making • Resisting Social Influences

Conformity and bystander intervention are two instances in which we tend to imitate the actions of others. The presence of others enhances the performance of a well-learned behavior but interferes with the performance of complex or not well-learned behavior. When a group of people must collectively perform a task, the effort of any one individual is usually less than we would predict had the individual attempted the task alone, a behavior known as social loafing. We tend to reciprocate favors that others do for us, honor commitments we make to others, respond positively to requests made of us by attractive people and authority figures, and identify with group values and goals. Unscrupulous persons often exploit these tendencies for their own gain. Effective group decision making can be hampered by elements of the discussion leading to the decision. Recognizing how people may try to exploit the rules of social influence is helpful in reducing the effectiveness of such exploitation.

Interpersonal Attraction and Loving

Interpersonal Attraction • *Evaluating Scientific Issues: Does Love Thrive on Adversity?* • Loving • *Biology and Culture: Evolution, Interpersonal Attraction, and Love*

We tend to be attracted to others who think positively of us, who are similar to us, who are physically attractive, and who live, work, or play near us. Sternberg's theory of love describes how the elements of intimacy, passion, and commitment are involved in the different kinds of love. Interpersonal attractions occur under many conditions—not just those that are ideal. From an evolutionary perspective, love plays an important role in reproduction and childrearing.

*S*everal years ago, my family and I were visiting my father. He had decided to buy a new car and asked if I would visit some dealers with him.

We took test drives in two cars and he made his decision. Now it was time to settle on the options and the price. The first task was easy. The salesperson read off a list of options and my father said yes or no to each one.

The second task was a bit more difficult. As you know, cars usually sell for less than the sticker price. The question for my father was, how much less?

My father had been studying advertisements in the newspaper and had a rough idea of the price he would have to pay. He proposed a price to the salesperson and said that he wanted it to include the taxes.

The salesperson said that he would have to get his sales manager's approval on the price. He left the office. We waited. Ten minutes later he returned and said, "I'm sorry it took so long. I need a deposit to show the sales manager that you are serious. Do you have twenty dollars?"

"Of course," said my father. He took out his wallet and handed the salesperson a twenty-dollar bill. The sales person took it and then pointed to a piece of paper on his desk. "Write a note that I can show my sales manager. Say 'I agree to purchase the car at the stated price.'"

"What for?" my father asked.

"I need to show him that you're serious and that I'm not wasting his time."

My father gave the salesperson a sharp look but wrote the note.

We waited—this time longer. The salesperson returned, looking pleased. "I got him to agree to your price," he said.

"Fine," said my father, who then repeated the price.

"Let's draw up the contract," replied the salesperson.

"That includes the taxes," my father reminded him.

The salesman laughed. "If we sold you the car for that price, we'd be losing money." He then quoted us a figure that was several hundred dollars higher than the one my father had originally proposed.

My father and I looked at each other. "Shall we go?" I asked.

"Yes." He turned to the salesperson. "I'd like my twenty dollars." The salesperson protested, but we left.

"What was all that about?" he asked me as we drove away. "That foolishness with the twenty dollars, I mean."

Having just read a book on social influence, I was ready with an answer. "He was hoping that once you made a commitment—gave him some money and put your offer in writing—that you would find it difficult to say no when he came back with the higher price. He obviously had no intention of accepting your offer."

"I could see that. If he had just been straightforward about it, maybe we could have made a deal, but I don't like it when someone tries to make a fool out of me."

"You're right," I said. "But if that trick didn't work most of the time, they wouldn't use it."

---

*M*ost human activities are social: We spend most of our waking hours interacting with other people. Our behavior affects the way others act and, in turn, their behavior affects our actions. The field of psychology that studies our social nature is called **social psychology**. It is, in the words of Gordon Allport (1968), the examination of "how the thoughts, feelings, and behavior of individuals are influenced by the actual, imagined, or implied presence of others" (p. 3).

This chapter examines the effects that people have on each other's behavior. Interactions with other people affect all aspects of human behavior from infancy through old age. The important people in our lives shape our emotions, thoughts, and personalities. Our perceptions—which we think of as private, solitary events—are affected by our interactions with others. Social psychologists have found that even the most personal and supposedly subjective aspects of human life, such as interpersonal attraction, can be studied objectively. We should not be disappointed that phenomena such as reinforcement play a role in determining with whom we fall in love. Instead, we should appreciate the intricate interplay of biological and social factors that control behaviors that are important both to the survival of our species and to our individual happiness.

Social Cognition

Understanding social behavior requires considerable attention to a person's environment, both physical and social. Sizing up a social situation depends on many cognitive processes, including memory for people, places, and events; concept formation skills; and, more fundamentally, sensory and perceptual abilities (Schneider, 1991). In recent years, social psychologists have begun to apply our knowledge of these basic processes to understanding **social cognition**—how people attend to, perceive, interpret, and respond to social information.

Schemata and Social Cognition

All of us form impressions of others: friends, neighbors, supervisors, or teachers—virtually everyone we meet. We assign all sorts of characteristics to them. We may, for example, think of someone as friendly or hostile, helpful or selfish. A major task of social psychology is to understand how we form these impressions. In Solomon Asch's (1952) words, "How do the perceptions, thoughts, and motives of one person become known to other persons?" (p. 143). To answer questions like this, psychologists study **impression formation**, the way in which we form impressions of others and attribute specific characteristics to them. As noted by Asch over four decades ago, our impressions of others are formed by more complex rules than just a simple sum of the characteristics that we use to describe people.

Schema

A central theme of cognitive psychology is the concept of schema (*schemata* is the plural form), a mental framework or body of knowledge that organizes and synthesizes information about a person, place, or thing. Schemata aid us in interpreting the world. The first time you visited your psychology professor in his or her office, for example, there were probably few surprises. The schema that you have of "professor" guided your interactions with him or her. However, you would probably be surprised if you saw that your professor's office was filled with bowling trophies, autographed photos of rock stars, or rare posters of Elvis. Such possessions are probably inconsistent with your impression of professors.

As an example of how schemata guide our interpretations, try to understand the following passage:

> The procedure is actually quite simple. First you arrange things into different groups. Of course, one pile may be sufficient depending on how much there is to do. . . . It is important not to overdo things. That is, it is better to do too few things at once than too many. In the short run this may not seem important, but complications can easily arise. A mistake can be expensive as well. At first the whole procedure will seem complicated. Soon, however, it will become just another facet of life. (Bransford and Johnson, 1972, p. 722)

Does this passage make sense to you? What if I tell you that the title of the passage is "Washing Clothes"? Now you can interpret the passage easily, for the sentences make perfect sense within the context of your schemata for washing clothes. Not surprisingly, research has demonstrated that understanding is greater when people know the title of the passage before it is read (Bransford and Johnson, 1972).

Central Traits

If you were asked to describe a friend, you would probably list a few general attributes that, in your opinion, best portray what he or she is like. You might, for example, use the terms *caring* or *warm* to refer to those features that seem most representative of your friend's personality. Personality characteristics that seem to be the most characteristic of people are called **central traits**. The more distinctive your friend's traits are, the more you will tend to use information about those traits to categorize him or her into particular social classes, such as religion, career, hobbies, and so on (Nelson and Miller, 1995). In other words, a person's distinctive characteristics help us distinguish one individual from others—a person's central traits make him or her stand out from the crowd.

social psychology The branch of psychology that studies our social nature—how the actual, imagined, or implied presence of others influences our thoughts, feelings, and behaviors.

social cognition The processes involved in perceiving, interpreting, and acting on social information.

impression formation The way in which we form impressions of others and attribute specific characteristics and traits to them.

schema A mental framework or body of knowledge that organizes and synthesizes information about a person, place, or thing.

central traits Personality attributes that seem to be the most typical of a particular individual.

Using central traits to describe your friend helps you to summarize a large amount of information gathered through your interactions with him or her. Asch (1946) demonstrated that central traits could be powerful tools for forming impressions of others. He provided subjects with a list of traits describing a hypothetical person. Some received a list that included the trait "warm," while others received an identical list, except that the trait "warm" was replaced by "cold." Subjects given the list including "warm" were more likely to see the person as generous, happy, and altruistic. But not all traits seemed to be so important. When the words "polite" and "blunt" were substituted for "warm" and "cold," no differences were observed in subjects' impressions. Our perception of others, then, seems to be based partially on the schemata we have of people's central traits.

The Primacy Effect

Getting to know someone takes time and usually requires many interactions. Perhaps the first time you saw someone was at a party when he was loud and boisterous, having a good time with his friends. But later, you learn that he is a math major with excellent grades who is actually generally reserved. What is your general impression of this person: Loud and boisterous, or bright and shy? To determine whether first impressions might overpower later impressions, Asch (1946) presented one of the following lists of words to each of two groups of subjects:

Intelligent, industrious, impulsive, critical, stubborn, envious

Envious, stubborn, critical, impulsive, industrious, intelligent

Notice that these lists contain the same words but in reverse order. After they saw the list, Asch asked the subjects to describe the personality of the person having these characteristics. People who heard the first list thought of the person as someone who was able and productive but who possessed some shortcomings. The person described by the second list, however, was seen as someone who had serious problems. The tendency to form an impression of a person based on the initial information we learn about him or her is called the **primacy effect**. The first impression we receive of a person seems to be resilient.

The Self

If I asked you who you are, how would you respond? You might tell me your name, that you are a student, and perhaps that you are also an athlete or have a part-time job. Alternatively, you could tell me about your family, your nationality, ethnicity, or religion. There are many ways you could potentially describe yourself to me, all of which would reflect your **self-concept**—your knowledge, feelings, and ideas about yourself. The **self** is a person's distinct individuality. Your self-concept, then, is your self-identity—how you perceive your-

self and interpret events that are relevant to defining who you are. At the core of the self-concept is the **self-schema**—a mental framework that represents and synthesizes information about oneself. The self-schema, then, is a cognitive structure that organizes the knowledge, feelings, and ideas that constitute the self-concept.

The self-concept is dynamic; it changes with experience. Some researchers, such as Markus and Nurius (1986), argue that we should think of ourselves in terms of a working self-concept that changes as we have new experiences or receive feedback about our behavior. That is, each of us has many potential selves that we might become depending on experience. Can you imagine the different twists and turns that your life might take and how your self-concept might be affected as a result? Can you imagine the circumstances that might lead you to change your major, drop out of school, or get married or divorced, and how your self-concept might be affected? Consider how people who had experienced a traumatic life event (for example, the death of a family member or friend) responded when they were asked to describe their current and possible future selves (Porter, Markus, and Nurius, 1984, cited in Baron and Byrne, 1994). They all reported that they were worried, upset, depressed, and lacked control over their lives. That is, everyone described similar *current* selves. Nonetheless, some people described different sorts of possible *future* selves. The people who had not yet recovered from the traumatic event predicted that they would be unhappy and lonely. The people in the recovered group predicted just the opposite: They saw themselves as being happy, being self-confident, and having many friends. Thus, thinking of ourselves only in terms of who we are at present does not accurately reflect the kind of person we might become.

Culture plays a powerful role in the formation of the self-concept, the perceptions one forms of others, and the extent to which others may influence the development of one's self-concept. For example, in North America, parents sometimes encourage their children to eat all their dinner by admonishing them to "think about all the starving children in China and how lucky you are not to be in their situation," while in Japan, parents often urge their finicky children to "think of the farmer who worked so hard to produce this rice for you; if you don't eat it he will feel bad, for his efforts will have been in vain" (Markus and Kitayama, 1991). American and other Western cultures often emphasize the uniqueness of the individual and an appreciation of being different from

primacy effect The tendency to form impressions of people based on the first information we receive about them.

self-concept Self-identity. One's knowledge, feelings, and ideas about oneself.

self A person's distinct individuality.

self-schema A mental framework that represents and synthesizes information about oneself; a cognitive structure that organizes the knowledge, feelings, and ideas that constitute the self-concept.

People in many Eastern cultures are more likely to construe their self-concepts in terms of the social interactions they have with others than are people in Western cultures.

others. In contrast, Japanese and other Eastern cultures often emphasize paying attention to others and the relatedness of the individual and others.

Markus and Kitayama (1991) have conceptualized two construals of the self that reflect such cultural differences. (To *construe* something is to interpret it or explain its meaning.) The *independent construal* emphasizes the uniqueness of the self, its autonomy from others, and self-reliance. Although other people have an influence on a person's behavior, a person's self-concept is largely defined independently of others. The *interdependent construal* emphasizes the interconnectedness of people and the role that others play in developing an individual's self-concept. In the interdependent construal, what others think of the individual or do to the individual matter—the person is extremely sensitive to others and strives to form strong social bonds with them.

Markus and Kitayama's own research supports their model. For example, they have shown that students from India (an Eastern culture) judge the self to be more similar to others, whereas American students judge the self to be more dissimilar to others (Markus and Kitayama, 1991). Markus and Kitayama have also shown that Japanese students tend to associate positive feelings with interpersonal behaviors and tend not to associate such feelings with personal achievements. In contrast, American students tend to feel satisfaction in their accomplishments (Kitayama and Markus, 1992).

Attribution

In some ways, we are all practicing social psychologists (Jones, 1990). Each of us uses certain principles to construct theories about the nature and causes of other people's behavior. We are confronted each day by many thousands of individual acts performed by other people. Some acts are important to us because they provide clues about people's

personality characteristics, how they are likely to interact with us, and how they are perceiving us. If we had to pay careful attention to each of these acts—to classify them, to think about their significance, and to compare them with other observations—we would be immobilized in thought. Instead, we use schemata that often lead us to the correct conclusions. In doing so, we save much time and effort.

However, as useful as these strategies may be, they sometimes lead us astray. We may unfairly categorize other people on the basis of superficial characteristics. We may uncritically adopt attitudes we were taught, to the detriment of other people and of ourselves. The process by which people infer the causes of other people's behavior is called **attribution**.

Disposition versus Situation

The primary classification that we make concerning the causes of a person's behavior is the relative importance of situational and dispositional factors (Heider, 1958). **Situational factors** are stimuli in the environment. **Dispositional factors** are individual personality characteristics. One of the tasks of socialization is to learn what behaviors are expected in various kinds of situations. Once we learn that in certain situations most people act in a specific way, we develop schemata for how we expect people to act in those situations. For example, when people are introduced, they are expected to look at each other, smile, say something like "How do you do?" or "It's nice to meet you," and perhaps offer to shake the other person's hand. If people act in conventional ways in given situations, we are not surprised. Their behavior appears to be dictated by social custom—by the characteristics of the situation.

As we get to know other people, we also learn what to expect from them as individuals. We learn about their dispositions—the kinds of behaviors in which they tend to engage. We learn to characterize people as friendly, generous, suspicious, pessimistic, or greedy by observing their behavior in a variety of situations. Sometimes, we even make inferences from a single observation (Krull and Erickson, 1995). If someone's behavior is very different from the way most people would act in a particular situation, we attribute his or her behavior to internal or dispositional causes. For example, if we see a person refuse to hold a door open for someone in a wheelchair, we assign that person some negative dispositional characteristics.

Kelley's Theory of Attribution

Kelley (1967) has suggested that we attribute the behavior of other people to external (situational) or internal (disposi-

---

attribution The process by which people infer the causes of other people's behavior.

situational factors Environmental stimuli that affect a person's behavior.

dispositional factors Individual personality characteristics that affect a person's behavior.

tional) causes on the basis of three factors: consensus, consistency, and distinctiveness (Kelley, 1967; Kelley and Michela, 1980).

Consensual behavior—a behavior shared by a large number of people—is usually attributed to external causes. The behavior is assumed to be demanded by the situation. For example, if someone asks an acquaintance for the loan of a coin to make a telephone call, we do not conclude that the person is especially generous if he or she complies. The request is reasonable and costs little; lending the money is a consensual behavior. However, if a person has some change but refuses to lend it, we readily attribute dispositional factors such as stinginess or meanness to that person.

We also base our attributions on **consistency**—on whether a person's behavior occurs reliably over time and across situations. For example, if you meet someone for the first time and notice that she speaks slowly and without much expression, stands in a slouching posture, and sighs occasionally, you will probably conclude that she has a sad disposition. Now, suppose that after she has left, you mention to a friend that the young woman seems very passive. Your friend says, "No, I know her well, and she's usually very cheerful." With this new evidence about her behavior you may reassess and wonder what happened to make her act so sad. If a person's pattern of behavior is consistent, we attribute the behavior to internal causes. Inconsistent behaviors lead us to seek external causes.

Finally, we base our attributions on **distinctiveness**—the extent to which a person performs a particular behavior only in a particular situation. Behaviors that are distinctively associated with a particular situation are attributed to situational factors; those that occur in a variety of situations are attributed to dispositional factors. For example, suppose that a mother observes that her little boy is generally polite but also that whenever he plays with the child next door, he acts sassy toward her. She does not conclude that her son has a rude disposition; she probably concludes that the child next door has a bad influence on him. Because her child's rude behavior occurs only under a distinctive circumstance (the presence of the child next door), she attributes it to external causes. Table 15.1 summarizes Kelley's ideas about the factors that determine internal or external attributions. (See *Table 15.1.*)

consensual behavior Behavior that is shared by many people; behavior that is similar from one person to the next. To the extent that people engage in the same behavior, their behavior is consensual.

consistency The extent to which a person's behavior is consistent across time.

distinctiveness The extent to which a person engages in a particular behavior in one situation but not in others.

fundamental attribution error The tendency to overestimate the significance of dispositional factors and underestimate the significance of situational factors in explaining other people's behavior.

Table 15.1

Kelley's Theory of Attribution.
Kelley's Theory Is Based on the Principles of Consensus, Consistency, and Distinctiveness

	Attribution of External Causality	Attribution of Internal Causality
Consensus	High. Person lends coin for telephone call, performing a socially acceptable behavior.	Low. Person refuses to lend coin and seems stingy or mean.
Consistency	Low. Usually cheerful person acts sad and dejected; we wonder what event has caused the sadness.	High. We meet a person who speaks slowly, slouches, and conclude that we have met a person who is sad by nature.
Distinctiveness	High. A child is rude only when playing with a certain friend; we conclude that the friend is a bad influence.	Low. A child acts sassy, says mean and nasty things to everyone he or she meets. We conclude that the child is rude.

Attributional Biases

When we make attributions, we do not function as impartial, dispassionate observers. Our biases affect our conclusions about the actor (the person performing the behavior). Let's look at two kinds of bias: the fundamental attribution error and false consensus.

The Fundamental Attribution Error

When attributing an actor's behavior to possible causes, an observer tends to *overestimate* the significance of dispositional factors and *underestimate* the significance of situational factors. This kind of bias is called the **fundamental attribution error**. For example, if we see a driver make a mistake, we are more likely to conclude that the driver is careless than to consider that external factors may have temporarily distracted him.

The fundamental attribution error is remarkably potent. Even when evidence indicates otherwise, people seem to prefer dispositional explanations to situational ones. For example, consider a study by Ross, Amabile, and Steinmetz (1977). Pairs of students played a contrived quiz game in which the questioner asked any question he or she wanted to, no matter how obscure. In this situation, a person can easily stump someone else by choosing some topic that he or she knows more about than the average person. After the game, the sub-

Holding the view that a gay person, such as this man, deserves to die from AIDS is an example of a specific form of the fundamental attribution error in which a person believes that life "justly" rewards or punishes people for their actions.

jects were asked to rate both their own levels of general knowledge and that of their opponents. Subjects who played the role of contestant tended to rate the questioners as much more knowledgeable than themselves. Apparently, they attributed the difficult questions to factors internal to their opponents rather than to the situation. When the subjects served as questioners, they did not make an internal attribution; they rated themselves as only slightly more knowledgeable than the people they had questioned. Thus, a person is less likely to make the fundamental attribution error when he or she is the actor (in this case, the questioner).

Another example of the fundamental attribution error—called the **belief in a just world**—is the belief that people get what they deserve in life (Lerner, 1966). According to this idea, when misfortune or tragedy strikes, people tend to blame the victim instead of attributing the source of the problem to situational factors outside the victim's control. As a result, an innocent victim may be blamed for circumstances over which he or she had no control and any suffering is seen as being deserved. In a study of people from twelve different countries, Furnham (1992) discovered that the susceptibility to the belief in a just world attribution error was positively correlated with wealth and social status. That is, across many countries (which included countries from both Eastern and Western cultures), a person was more likely to commit this

kind of fundamental attribution error if he or she was wealthy and had high social status.

We see the belief in a just world effect occurring each day, especially as expressed in negative statements about others. For example, consider the statement "gays deserve AIDS." This belief ignores the fact that AIDS kills heterosexuals and children as well. Among college students, negative attitudes toward homosexuals is positively correlated with negative attitudes toward AIDS patients, although the more students knew about AIDS, the more positive they were about AIDS patients (Ambrosio and Sheehan, 1991).

When trying to explain our own behavior, we are much more likely to attribute it to characteristics of the situation than to our own disposition, a phenomenon called the **actor-observer effect**. In other words, we tend to see our own behavior as relatively variable and strongly influenced by the situation, while we see the behavior of others as more stable and due to personal dispositions. When we try to explain our own behavior, we are *not* likely to make the fundamental attribution error (Sande, Goethals, and Radloff, 1988).

A study of college-age male-female couples demonstrates the actor-observer effect (Orvis, Kelley, and Butler, 1976). Each partner was asked separately to describe disagreements in the relationship, such as arguments and criticism. Each partner was also asked to explain his or her attribution of the underlying causes of the disagreements. When describing his or her own behavior, each person tended to refer to environmental circumstances, such as financial problems or not getting enough sleep. However, when describing their partners' behavior, subjects often referred to specific negative personality characteristics, such as selfishness or low commitment to the relationship.

Why do we tend to commit the fundamental attribution error when we observe the behavior of others but not when we explain the causes of our own behavior? Jones and Nisbett (1971) suggested two possible reasons. First, we have a different focus of attention when we view ourselves. When we ourselves are doing something, we see the world around us more clearly than we see our own behavior. However, when we observe someone else doing something, we focus our attention on what is most salient and relevant: that person's behavior, not the situation in which he or she is placed.

A second possible reason for these differences in attribution is that different types of information are available to us about our own behavior and that of other people. We have more information about our own behavior and we are thus more likely to realize that our own behavior is often inconsistent. We also have a better notion of which stimuli we are attending to in a given situation. This difference in informa-

belief in a just world　The belief that people get what they deserve in life; a fundamental attribution error.

actor-observer effect　The tendency to attribute one's own behavior to situational factors but others' behavior to dispositional factors.

tion leads us to conclude that the behavior of other people is consistent and thus is a product of their personalities, whereas ours is affected by the situation in which we find ourselves.

When we attempt to attribute causes to our own behavior—to explain the reasons for our actions—we tend to attribute our accomplishments and successes to internal causes and our failures and mistakes to external causes, a phenomenon called the **self-serving bias**. For example, suppose that you receive an outstanding score on a test. If you are like most people, you will feel the high score is well deserved. After all, you are a smart individual who studied hard for the test. Your attributions reflect internal causes for the test score: You are bright and a hard worker. Now suppose that you receive an F on the test—now what sorts of attributions do you tend to make? Again, if you are like most people, you may blame your low score on the fact that it was a difficult, even "unfair," test or on the teacher for being so picky about the answers he or she counted as wrong. Your attributions in this case blame external causes for the low score—the test's difficulty and the pickiness of your teacher in grading it. One possible explanation for the self-serving bias is that people are motivated to protect and enhance their self-esteem (Brown and Rogers, 1991; Baron and Byrne, 1994). Simply put, we protect our self-esteem when we blame failure on the environment and we enhance it when we give ourselves credit for our successes.

False Consensus

Another attribution error is the tendency of an observer to perceive his or her own response as representative of a general consensus—an error called **false consensus**. For example, Sherman, Presson, and Chassin (1984) found that male high school students who smoke believe that a majority of their peers do so, too, whereas nonsmokers believe that a majority do not smoke. Obviously, both groups cannot be correct.

One explanation accounts for false consensus in terms of self-esteem. Presumably, people do not like to think of themselves as being too different from other people, so they prefer to think that most other people will act the way they do. Another possible explanation is that people tend to place themselves in the company of others who are similar to themselves (Ross, 1977). As we will see later, an important variable in interpersonal attraction is similarity in behavior and attitudes. Thus, when people conclude that other people are more similar to themselves than they actually are, the error may be a result of a bias in selecting people to meet and become friends with rather than of a need to minimize damage to their self-esteem.

Attribution, Heuristics, and Social Cognition

We tend to follow general rules, or heuristics, when making decisions. This tendency is especially evident when we make social judgments. Most of the time, these rules serve us well. However, they sometimes lead us astray. When they do, we refer to them as biases or fallacies. The two most important kinds of heuristics are representativeness and availability.

The Representativeness Heuristic

When we meet someone for the first time, we notice his or her clothes, hairstyle, posture, manner of speaking, hand gestures, and many other characteristics. Based on our previous experience, we use this information to make tentative conclusions about other characteristics that we cannot immediately discover. In doing so, we attempt to match the characteristics we can observe with stereotypes we have of different types of people. If the person seems representative of one of these stereotypes, we conclude that he or she fits that particular category (Lupfer, Clark, and Hutcherson, 1990). In making this conclusion, we use the **representativeness heuristic**—we classify an object into the category to which it appears to be the most similar.

The representativeness heuristic is based on our ability to categorize information. We observe that some characteristics tend to go together (or we are taught that they do). When we observe some of these characteristics, we conclude that the others are also present. Most of the time this strategy works; we are able to predict people's behavior fairly accurately.

Sometimes, the representativeness heuristic can mislead us. Consider the following example. I (a professor of psychology) have a friend who is also a professor. He likes to swim laps in the pool every lunch hour. He also likes to play tennis; if he can find a willing opponent, he will even play in the dead of winter if the court can be swept clear of snow. Which of the following is his field: (a) sports medicine or (b) psychology?

If you said "psychology," you were most likely to be right, because I am a professor of psychology and am therefore likely to have friends who are also professors of psychology. In addition, there are many more professors of psychology than professors of sports medicine. Yet you may have chosen alternative (a) or at least seriously considered it. The image of an athletic, tennis-playing person seems to be such a distinctive cue that it is difficult *not* to conclude that my friend works in sports medicine. The image seems to be more representative of a person professionally involved in sports than of one involved in psychology. Paying too much attention to

---

self-serving bias The tendency to attribute our accomplishments and successes to internal causes and our failures and mistakes to external causes.

false consensus The tendency of a person to perceive his or her own response as representative of a general consensus.

representativeness heuristic A general rule for decision making through which people classify a person, place, or thing into the category to which it appears to be the most similar.

the image is an example of the **base-rate fallacy**—the failure to consider the likelihood that a person is a member of a particular category. In this case, the strong athletic image tends to make us ignore the relative numbers of professors of psychology and of sports medicine.

Learning to play the odds, so to speak, and so to avoid being misled by distinctive characteristics is particularly important in certain intellectual endeavors. For example, physicians who are experienced in making diagnoses of diseases teach their students to learn and make use of the probabilities of particular diseases and not to be fooled by especially distinctive symptoms. In fact, Zukier and Pepitone (1984) posed a problem to first-year medical students and to residents who had completed their clinical training. The inexperienced students were tricked by the base-rate fallacy but the residents played the odds, as they had been taught to do.

The Availability Heuristic

When people attempt to assess the importance or the frequency of an event, they tend to be guided by the ease with which examples of that event come to mind—by how available these examples are to the imagination. This mental shortcut is called the **availability heuristic**. In general, the things we are able to think of most easily are more important and occur more frequently than things that are difficult to imagine. Thus, the availability heuristic works well—most of the time.

Some events are so vivid that we can easily picture them happening. We can easily picture getting mugged while walking through the heart of a large city at night or being involved in an airplane crash, probably because such events are often reported in the news and because they are so frightening. Thus, people tend to *overestimate* the likelihood of such misfortunes happening to them. Tversky and Kahneman (1982) demonstrated the effect of availability by asking people to estimate whether English words starting with *k* were more or less common than words with *k* in the third position (for example, *kiss* versus *lake*). Most people said that there were more words starting with *k*. In fact, there are more than twice as many words having *k* in the third position as those having *k* in the first. But because thinking of words that start with a particular letter is easier than thinking of words that contain the letter in another position, people are misled in their judgment.

Many variables can affect the availability of an event or a concept and thus increase its effect on our decision making. For example, having recently seen a particular type of event makes it easier for us to think of other examples of that event. This phenomenon is called *priming*. Many first-year medical students demonstrate this phenomenon when, after learning the symptoms of various diseases, they start "discovering" these very symptoms in their own bodies.

Higgins, Rholes, and Jones (1977) demonstrated the effects of priming on judging the personality characteristics of strangers. They had subjects work on a task that introduced various descriptive adjectives. Next, the experimenters de-scribed an imaginary person, saying that he had performed such feats as climbing mountains and crossing the Atlantic Ocean in a sailboat. Finally, they asked the subjects to give their impressions of this person. Those subjects who had previously been exposed to words such as *adventurous* reported favorable impressions, whereas those who had been exposed to words such as *reckless* reported unfavorable ones. The priming effect of the descriptive adjectives had biased their interpretation of the facts.

The availability heuristic also explains why personal encounters tend to have an especially strong effect on our decision making. For example, suppose that you have decided to purchase a new car. You have narrowed your choice down to two models, both available for about the same price. You read an article in a consumer magazine that summarizes the experiences of thousands of people who have purchased these cars, and their testimony shows clearly that one of them has a much better repair record. You decide to purchase that brand and mention the fact to a friend you happen to meet later that day. She says, "Oh, no! Don't buy one of those! I bought one last year, and it has been nothing but trouble. I had it for only two weeks when it first broke down. I was in the middle of nowhere and had to walk five miles to the nearest phone. I got it towed to a garage, and they had to order a part from the manufacturer. I ended up staying in that town for two days before it was fixed. Since then, I've had trouble with the air conditioner and the transmission." Would this experience affect your decision to buy that brand of automobile?

Most people would take this personal encounter very seriously. Even though it consists of the experience of only one person, whereas the survey in the consumer magazine represents the experience of thousands of people, a vivid personal encounter is much more available and memorable than a set of statistics and tends to have a disproportionate effect on our own behavior (Borgida and Nisbett, 1977).

Interim Summary

Social Cognition

Social cognition involves our perception and interpretation of information about our social environment and our behavior with respect to changes in that environment. Our experiences give rise to schemata, the mental frameworks with which we organize and synthesize information about our interactions with others. Central traits, or representative characteristics of people, function as schemata and help us to form impressions of others. The initial information we learn

base-rate fallacy The failure to consider the likelihood that a person, place, or thing is a member of a particular category.

availability heuristic A general rule for decision making through which a person judges the likelihood or importance of an event by the ease with which examples of that event come to mind.

about someone figures prominently in forming an impression about that person—a tendency called the primacy effect.

A person's self-concept represents his or her knowledge, feelings, and ideas about himself or herself. At the center of the self-concept is the self-schema, a mental framework for processing and interpreting information about the self. Our self-concepts change with our personal experiences and are influenced by the culture in which we live. In fact, different cultures often have different ways of conceptualizing the self. Western cultures, such as ours, emphasize the uniqueness of the self. In contrast, Eastern cultures, such as Japan and India, emphasize the interdependence of the self and others.

We attribute particular instances of behavior to two types of causes: situational and dispositional. If a behavior is consensual (many people are acting the same way), we attribute it to situational factors. If a behavior is consistent (a person acts the same way in a variety of situations), we attribute it to dispositional factors. If a behavior is distinctive (occurring only under certain circumstances), we attribute it to situational factors.

The fundamental attribution error is an overreliance on dispositional factors and underreliance on situational factors in the making of judgments about the causes of someone else's behavior. We are most likely to make the fundamental attribution error when trying to understand the causes of other people's behavior because we are more aware of the environmental factors that affect our own behavior. One example of the fundamental attribution error is the belief that people get exactly what they deserve in life, a phenomenon called belief in a just world. When comparing our behavior to that of others, we tend to see our own behavior as being more influenced by situational than dispositional factors and others' behavior as being more due to dispositional factors than to situational factors—a phenomenon called the actor-observer effect. However, when it comes to accepting credit for our successes or blame for our failures, we tend to show the self-serving bias: We tend to attribute our successes to internal or dispositional causes and failures to external or situational causes. False consensus refers to the tendency to believe that others act and believe much as we do.

We use mental shortcuts called heuristics in perceiving, in making decisions, and in determining what is going on around us. The representativeness heuristic describes our tendency to seize upon a few especially salient characteristics of a person or situation. Thus, we sometimes ignore other evidence and commit the base-rate error. The availability heuristic describes our tendency to judge the importance or the frequency of events by the ease with which examples come to mind. If we have recently been exposed to a particular concept, that concept becomes more available (through the phenomenon of priming) and thus biases our decisions. Personal encounters give rise to vivid memories of particular episodes, and the availability of these episodes, too, tends to outweigh less vivid—but more representative—evidence.

Thought Questions

- What factors do you feel have been most influential in the development of your self-concept? What sorts of experiences do you think will influence continued development of your self-concept during your college career? How do you envision your working self-concept changing with these experiences?

- How much of our social behavior do we engage in unconsciously—that is, without our awareness? What effect do you suppose being more conscious of our social interaction would have on that interaction? Might we be less prone to using heuristics incorrectly?

- Imagine yourself to be the first person on the scene of an auto accident in which several people have been injured badly. What factors—situational, dispositional, or some combination of them—would guide your behavior?

Attitudes and Their Formation

The study of **attitudes**—evaluations of persons, places, and things—and their formation constitutes an important part of the field of social psychology (Pratkanis, Breckler, and Greenwald, 1989).

Formation of Attitudes

Attitudes have three different components: affect, behavior, and cognition. (See *Figure 15.1*.) The affective component consists of the kinds of feelings that a particular topic arouses. The behavioral component consists of a tendency to act in a particular way with respect to a particular topic. The cognitive component consists of a set of beliefs about a topic. Social psychologists have studied all three aspects of attitudes, and we will examine their findings in this section.

Affective Components of Attitudes

Affective components of attitudes can be very strong and pervasive. The bigot feels uneasy in the presence of people from a certain religious, racial, or ethnic group; the nature lover feels exhilaration from a pleasant walk through the woods. Like other emotional reactions, these feelings are strongly influenced by direct or vicarious classical conditioning (Rajecki, 1989).

Direct classical conditioning is straightforward. Suppose that you meet someone who seems to take delight in embar-

attitude An evaluation of persons, places, and things.

 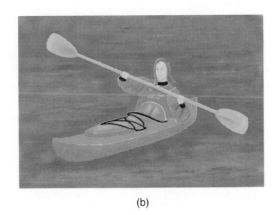 

(a)   (b)   (c)

Figure 15.1

The three components of attitude: affect, behavior, and cognition. (a) Affective component (feelings): Enjoys kayaking. (b) Behavioral component (actions): Pursues kayaking as a hobby. (c) Cognitive component (beliefs): Believes that kayaking has an element of risk but is fun.

rassing you. She makes clever, sarcastic remarks that disparage your intelligence, looks, and personality. Unfortunately, her remarks are so clever that your attempts to defend yourself make you appear even more foolish. After a few encounters with this person, the sight of her or the sound of her voice is likely to elicit feelings of dislike and fear. Your attitude toward her will be negative.

Vicarious classical conditioning undoubtedly plays a major role in transmitting parents' attitudes to their children. People are skilled at detecting even subtle signs of fear, hatred, and other negative emotional states in other people, especially when they know them well. Thus, children often perceive their parents' prejudices and fears even if these feelings are unspoken. Children who see their parents recoil in disgust at the sight of members of some ethnic group are likely to learn to react in the same way. We have a strong tendency to acquire classically conditioned behaviors when we observe them being elicited in other people by the conditional stimulus.

Simply being exposed repeatedly to an otherwise neutral object or issue over time may influence our attitude toward it. This attraction for the familiar is called the **mere exposure effect.** One of the first studies to demonstrate this effect used several neutral stimuli—toward which there were no positive or negative feelings—such as nonsense words, photographs of the faces of unknown people, and Chinese characters (Zajonc, 1968). The more the subjects saw the stimuli, the more they liked the stimuli later. Stimuli that were seen only once were liked more than ones never seen before. Even when the stimuli were flashed so briefly that they could not be recognized, subjects usually preferred a stimulus that had been previously presented to a novel one that they could recognize (Kunst-Wilson and Zajonc, 1980).

Cognitive Components of Attitudes

We acquire most beliefs about a particular topic quite directly: We hear or read a fact or opinion, or other people reinforce our statements expressing a particular attitude. Someone may say to a child, "Latinos are not very smart," or, "Whites will take advantage of you." A group of racially prejudiced people will probably ostracize a person who makes positive statements about the group or groups against which they are prejudiced. Conversely, conscientious parents may applaud their

A protest is one example of a situation in which a person's attitude on an issue corresponds to his or her behavior, in this case, demonstrating against legalized gambling.

mere exposure effect The formation of a positive attitude toward a person, place, or thing based solely on repeated exposure to that person, place, or thing.

child's positive statements about other ethnic groups or about social issues such as environmental conservation.

Children, in particular, form attitudes by imitating the behavior of people who play an important role in their lives. Children usually repeat opinions expressed by their parents. In the United States, many children label themselves as Democrats or Republicans long before they know the values for which these political parties stand. Often they ask their parents, "Are we Republicans or Democrats?" without considering whether they might have any choice in the matter. The tendency to identify with the family unit (and, later with peer groups) provides a strong incentive to adopt the group's attitudes.

Behavioral Components of Attitudes

People do not always behave as their expressed attitudes and beliefs would lead us to expect. In a classic example, LaPiere (1934) drove through the United States with a Chinese couple. They stopped at over 250 restaurants and lodging places and were refused service only once. Several months after their trip, LaPiere wrote to the owners of the places they had visited and asked whether they would serve Chinese people. The response was overwhelmingly negative; 92 percent of those who responded said that they would not. Clearly, their behavior gave less evidence of racial bias than their expressed attitudes did. This study has been cited as proof that attitudes do not always influence behavior. However, more recent research indicates that there is a relation between attitudes and behavior but that the relation is influenced by several factors.

Degree of Specificity.   If you measure a person's general attitude toward a topic, you will be less likely to be able to predict his or her behavior. Behaviors, unlike attitudes, are specific events. As the attitude being measured becomes more specific, the person's behavior becomes more predictable. For example, Weigel, Vernon, and Tognacci (1974) measured people's attitudes toward a series of topics that increased in specificity from "a pure environment" to "the Sierra Club" (an American organization that supports environmental causes). They used the subjects' attitudes to predict whether they would volunteer for various activities to benefit the Sierra Club. A person's attitude toward environmentalism was a poor predictor of whether he or she would volunteer; his or her attitude toward the Sierra Club itself was a much better predictor. (See *Table 15.2*.) For example, a person might favor a pure environment but also dislike organized clubs or have little time to spare for meetings. This person would express a positive attitude toward a pure environment but would not join the club or volunteer for any activities to support it.

self-attribution Attributions made about the causes of our behavior based on our self-observations of the way we act in different situations.

Table 15.2

Correlation Between Willingness to Join or Work for the Sierra Club and Various Measures of Related Attitudes

Attitude Scale	Correlation
Importance of a pure environment	.06
Pollution	.32
Conservation	.24
Attitude toward the Sierra Club	.68

(*Source:* Based on Weigel, R.H., Vernon, D.T.A., and Tognacci, L.N. Specificity of the attitude as a determinant of attitude-behavior congruence. *Journal of Personality and Social Psychology*, 1974, *30*, 724–728.)

Motivational Relevance.   Expressing a particular attitude toward a topic takes less effort than demonstrating that commitment with a time-consuming behavior. As the old saying puts it, "Talk is cheap." Sivacek and Crano (1982) demonstrated this phenomenon by asking students to volunteer their time to help campaign against a law pending in the state legislature that would raise the drinking age from eighteen to twenty. Although almost all of the students were opposed to the new drinking law, younger students, who would be affected by its passage, were much more likely to volunteer their time and effort. Thus, attitudes are more likely to be accompanied by behaviors if the effects of the behaviors have motivational relevance for the individual.

Self-Attribution.   Another variable that affects the relation between attitude and behavior is the way a person formed his or her attitude. If a person has developed an attitude from the opinions or persuasive arguments of other people, the attitude will usually be a poor predictor of behavior. In contrast, an attitude formed through self-attribution is likely to be an excellent predictor of behavior.

Self-attribution occurs because we are all self-observers: We see how we behave in various situations and make attributions about our own dispositions, just as we make them about other people's. If we observe that someone else habitually avoids talking with people who smoke, we can conclude that the person has a negative attitude toward smokers. If we find ourselves avoiding people who smoke, we can make a similar self-attribution.

Constraints on Behavior.   Other more obvious factors, such as existing circumstances, also produce discrepancies between attitudes and behaviors. For example, a young man might have a very positive attitude toward a certain young woman. If he were asked, he might express a very positive attitude toward kissing her. However, he never kisses her because she has plainly shown that she is not interested in him. No matter how carefully we measure the young man's attitudes, we cannot predict his behavior without additional information (in this case, from the young woman).

Attitude Change and Persuasion

People often attempt to persuade us to change our attitudes. Two aspects of the persuasion process have received special attention, the *source* of the message and the *message* itself.

A message tends to be more persuasive if its source is credible. Source credibility is high when the source is perceived as knowledgeable and is trusted to communicate this knowledge accurately. For example, in one study, people developed a more favorable attitude toward different types of medicine when the information appeared in the prestigious medical journal *New England Journal of Medicine* than when it appeared in a mass-circulation tabloid (Hovland and Weiss, 1951).

Messages also seem to have more impact when the source is physically attractive. For example, physically attractive people are more likely than physically unattractive people to persuade others to sign a petition (Chaiken, 1979). Individuals who are asked to endorse products for advertisers are almost always physically attractive or appealing in other ways.

As you would expect, aspects of the message itself are important in determining its persuasive appeal. For example, is an argument that provides only one side of an issue more effective than one that presents both sides? The answer depends on the audience. If the audience either knows very little about the issue or already holds a strong position with respect to it, one-sided arguments tend to be more effective. If the audience is well informed about the issue, however, a two-sided argument tends to be more persuasive (McAlister et al., 1980).

How effective are scare tactics embedded in the message in changing someone's attitude? This question was addressed when a program called Scared Straight was implemented in New Jersey to persuade youthful offenders to abandon their delinquent lifestyles. The program entailed an afternoon visit to Rahway State Prison and a very distressing, intimidating encounter with some prison inmates. Although the program initially appeared successful, the majority of the offenders exposed to the program eventually returned to delinquent activities (Hagan, 1982). Other research has shown that scare tactics may be effective in bringing about change, but only when combined with instructive information about *how* to change one's behavior (Cialdini, Petty, and Cacioppo, 1981). Messages appear most effective in changing attitudes when they contain both emotional and informative (cognitive) components.

Petty and Cacioppo (1986, 1993) have proposed the **elaboration likelihood model** to account for attitude change through persuasion. (See *Figure 15.2*.) According to this model, persuasion can take either a central or a peripheral route. The central route requires a person to think critically about the argument or arguments being presented, to weigh their relative strengths and weaknesses, and to elaborate on

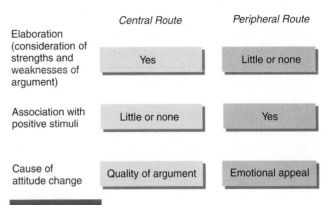

Persuasive Message

	Central Route	*Peripheral Route*
Elaboration (consideration of strengths and weaknesses of argument)	Yes	Little or none
Association with positive stimuli	Little or none	Yes
Cause of attitude change	Quality of argument	Emotional appeal

Figure 15.2

The elaboration likelihood model of attitude change. Persuasive messages may center either on a substantive argument that requires an individual to think critically about its strengths and weaknesses (the central route) or on a superficial argument that is associated with positive stimuli (the peripheral route).

the relevant themes. At issue is the actual substance of the argument, not its emotional or superficial appeal. The peripheral route, on the other hand, refers to attempts at persuasion in which the change is associated with positive stimuli—a professional athlete, a millionaire, or an attractive model—that actually may have nothing to do with the substance of the argument. Selling products by associating them with attractive people or implying that buying the product will result in emotional, social, or financial benefits are examples of the use of peripheral attitude change techniques.

Cognitive Dissonance

Although we usually regard our attitudes as causes of our behavior, our behavior also affects our attitudes. Two major theories attempt to explain the effects of behavior on attitude formation. The oldest theory is cognitive dissonance theory, developed by Leon Festinger (1957). According to **cognitive dissonance theory**, when we perceive a discrepancy between our attitudes and behavior, between our behavior and self-

elaboration likelihood model A model that explains the effectiveness of persuasion. The *central route* requires the person to think critically about an argument and the *peripheral route* entails the association of the argument with something positive.

cognitive dissonance theory The theory that changes in attitude can be motivated by an unpleasant state of tension caused by a disparity between a person's beliefs or attitudes and behavior, especially beliefs or attitudes that are related to the person's self-esteem.

image, or between one attitude and another, an unpleasant state of anxiety, or dissonance, results. For example, a person may successfully overcome a childhood racial prejudice but may experience unpleasant emotional arousal at the sight of a racially mixed couple. The person experiences a conflict between the belief in his own lack of prejudice and the evidence of prejudice from his behavior. This conflict produces dissonance, which is aversive.

In Festinger's view, an important source of human motivation is *dissonance reduction*: The aversive state of dissonance motivates a person to reduce it. Because dissonance reduction involves the removal of an aversive stimulus, it serves as a negative reinforcer. A person can achieve dissonance reduction by (1) reducing the importance of one of the dissonant elements, (2) adding consonant elements, or (3) changing one of the dissonant elements.

Suppose that a student believes that he is very intelligent but he invariably receives bad grades in his courses. Because the obvious prediction is that intelligent people get good grades, the discrepancy causes the student to experience dissonance. To reduce this dissonance, he may decide that grades are not important and that intelligence is not very closely related to grades. He is using strategy 1, reducing the importance of one of the dissonant elements—the fact that he received bad grades in his courses. Or he can dwell on the belief that his professors were unfair or that his job leaves him little time to study. In this case, he is using strategy 2, reducing dissonance by adding consonant elements—those factors that can account for his poor grades and hence explain the discrepancy between his perceived intelligence and grades. Finally, he can use strategy 3 to change one of the dissonant elements. He can either start getting good grades or revise his opinion of his own intelligence.

Induced Compliance

Most of us believe that although we can induce someone to do something, getting someone to change an opinion is much harder. However, Festinger's theory of cognitive dissonance and supporting experimental evidence indicate otherwise. Under the right conditions, when people are coerced into doing something or are paid to do something, the act of **compliance**—engaging in a particular behavior at someone else's request—causes a change in their attitudes.

Cognitive dissonance theory predicts that dissonance occurs when a person's behavior has outcomes harmful to self-esteem; there is a conflict between the person's belief in his or her own worth and the fact that he or she has done something that damages this belief. The person will then seek to justify the behavior. For example, a poorly paid vacuum cleaner sales representative is likely to convince himself that the shoddy merchandise he sells is actually good. Otherwise, he must question why he works for a company that pays him

poorly and requires him to lie to prospective customers about the quality of the product in order to make a sale. Conversely, an executive of one of the commercial television networks may know that the programs she produces are sleazy, mindless drivel, but she is so well paid that she does not feel bad about producing them. Her high salary justifies her job and probably also provides her with enough self-esteem that she has decided that the public gets what it deserves anyway.

Festinger and Carlsmith (1959) verified this observation by having subjects perform very boring tasks, such as putting spools on a tray, dumping them out, putting them on the tray again, dumping them out again, and so on. After the subjects had spent an hour on exercises like this, the experimenter asked each subject whether he or she would help out in the study by trying to convince the next subject that the task was interesting and enjoyable. Some subjects received one dollar for helping out; others received twenty dollars. Control subjects were paid nothing. The experimenters predicted that subjects who were paid only one dollar would perceive the task as being relatively interesting. They had been induced to lie to a "fellow student" (actually, a confederate of the experimenters) for a paltry sum. Like the vacuum cleaner sales representative, they should convince themselves of the worth of the experiment to maintain their self-esteem. Poorly paid subjects did in fact rate the task better than did those who were well paid. (See *Figure 15.3*.) Clearly, our actions have an effect on our attitudes. When faced with inconsistency between our behavior and our attitudes, we often change our attitudes to suit our behavior.

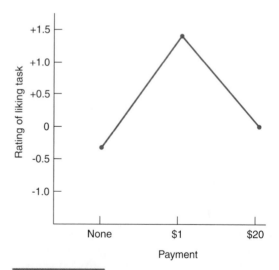

Figure 15.3

Effects of induced compliance. People who received $1 to lie about a boring task later indicated that they liked the task more than did people who received $20.

(Based on data from Festinger, L., and Carlsmith, J.M. Cognitive consequences of forced compliance. Journal of Abnormal and Social Psychology, *1959, 58, 203–210.)*

compliance Engaging in a particular behavior at another person's request.

Arousal and Attitude Change

Festinger's theory hypothesizes that dissonance reduction is motivated by an aversive drive. A study by Croyle and Cooper (1983) obtained physiological evidence to support this hypothesis. The experimenters chose as their subjects Princeton University students who disagreed with the assertion "Alcohol use should be totally banned from the Princeton campus and eating clubs." Each subject was induced to write an essay containing strong and forceful arguments in favor of the assertion or in opposition to it. While the subjects were writing the essay, the experimenters measured the electrical conductance of their skin, which is known to be a good indicator of the physiological arousal that accompanies stress. Some subjects were simply told to write the essay. Other subjects were told that their participation was completely voluntary and that they were free to leave at any time; they even signed a form emphasizing the voluntary nature of the task. Of course, all subjects felt social pressure to continue the study, and all of them did. Those who were simply told to write the essay should have felt less personal responsibility for what they wrote and would therefore be expected to experience less cognitive dissonance than those who believed that they had exercised free choice in deciding to participate.

Subjects in the "free choice" condition who had written essays contradicting their original opinions showed both a change in opinion and evidence of physiological arousal. Those subjects who were simply told to write the essay or who wrote arguments that they had originally agreed with showed little sign of arousal or attitude change. (See *Figure 15.4.*)

Attitudes and Expenditures

Festinger's theory of cognitive dissonance accounts for another relation between behavior and attitudes: our tendency to value an item more if it costs us something. For example, some people buy extremely expensive brands of cosmetics even though the same ingredients are used in much cheaper brands. Presumably, they believe that if an item costs more, it must work better. Following the same rationale, most animal shelters sell their stray animals to prospective pet owners, not only because the money helps defray their operating costs, but also because they assume that a purchased pet will be treated better than a free pet.

Aronson and Mills (1959) verified this phenomenon. The experimenters subjected female college students to varying degrees of embarrassment as a prerequisite for joining what was promised to be an interesting discussion about sexual behavior. To produce slight embarrassment, they had the subjects read aloud five sex-related words (such as *prostitute*, *virgin*, and *petting*) to the experimenter, who was male. To produce more severe embarrassment, they had the women read aloud twelve obscene four-letter words and two sexually explicit passages of prose. The control group read nothing at all. The "interesting group discussion" turned out to be a tape recording of a very dull conversation.

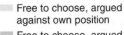
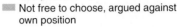
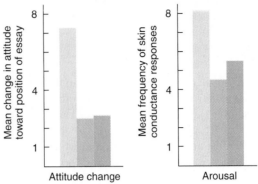

Figure 15.4

Physiological evidence for cognitive dissonance. Mean change in attitude toward the position advocated by the essay and mean frequency of skin conductance responses (a physiological index of arousal) in subjects who argued for or against their own positions.
(Based on data from Croyle, R.T., and Cooper, J. Dissonance arousal: Physical evidence. Journal of Personality and Social Psychology, *1983, 45, 782–791.)*

Festinger's theory predicts that the women who had to go through an embarrassing ordeal in order to join the group would experience some cognitive dissonance. They gave up something—some pride or self-esteem—to obtain a goal that they initially perceived to be worthwhile: the privilege of participating in an interesting discussion. This investment should make them view the "discussion" more favorably so that their effort would not be perceived as having been completely without value. The results were as predicted: The subjects who had been embarrassed the most rated the discussion higher than did the control subjects or the subjects who had experienced only slight embarrassment. We value things at least partly by how much they cost us.

Self-Perception

Daryl Bem (1972) proposed an alternative to the theory of cognitive dissonance. He defined **self-perception theory** in the following way:

self-perception theory The theory that we come to understand our attitudes and emotions by observing our own behavior and the circumstances under which it occurs.

Individuals come to "know" their own attitudes, emotions, and other internal states partially by inferring them from observations of their own overt behavior and/or the circumstances in which this behavior occurs. Thus, to the extent that internal cues are weak, ambiguous, or uninterpretable, the individual is functionally in the same position as an outside observer, an observer who must necessarily rely on those same external cues to infer the individual's inner states. (Bem, 1972, p. 2)

Bem noted that an observer who attempts to make judgments about someone's attitudes, emotions, or other internal states must examine the person's behavior for clues. For example, if you cannot ask someone why he or she is doing something, you must analyze the situation in which the behavior occurs to try to determine the motivation. Bem suggested that people analyze their own internal states in a similar way, making attributions about the causes of their own behavior.

You will recall the experiment by Festinger and Carlsmith (1959) in which students who were paid only $1 later rated a boring task as more interesting than did those who were paid $20. How does self-perception theory explain these results? Suppose that an observer watches a subject who has been paid $1 to deliver a convincing speech to another student about how interesting a task was. Because being paid such a small sum is not a sufficient reason for calling a dull task interesting, the observer will probably conclude that the student actually enjoyed the task. Lacking good evidence for external causes, the observer will attribute the behavior to a dispositional factor: interest in the task. Bem argued that the subject makes the same inference about himself or herself. Because the subject was not paid enough to tell a lie, he or she must have enjoyed the task. The principal advantage of self-perception theory is that it makes fewer assumptions than does dissonance theory; it does not postulate a motivating aversive-drive state. But as Croyle and Cooper's (1983) experiment on essay writing showed, some conflict situations do produce arousal. Perhaps self-perception and cognitive dissonance occur under different situations, producing attitude changes for different reasons. Further evidence will be needed to determine whether the theories are competing or complementary.

Interim Summary

Attitudes and Their Formation

Attitudes have affective components, primarily formed through direct or vicarious classical conditioning, and cognitive components, formed through direct instruction, reinforcement, imitation, or mere exposure.

We now understand the principal reasons for poor correspondence between attitudes and behavior: differences in degree of specificity of the attitude and behavior, motivational relevance, the opportunity a person has had to observe his or her own attitude-related behavior, and external constraints that prevent a person's acting on his or her attitudes.

Explicit attempts at changing our attitudes often involve persuasion. We tend to be persuaded by arguments that have a credible source, such as an expert on a particular topic, or an attractive source, such as a handsome or beautiful model. Aspects of the message being delivered in a persuasive appeal are also important. If you know little about an issue or hold a strong opinion about it, then you are likely to be persuaded by a one-sided appeal. However, if you are already well informed about the issue, then you are likely to find a two-sided appeal more persuasive. Scare tactics appear to work best when they include information that is instructive (that is, that explains how to change one's behavior) as well as emotional.

Festinger's theory of cognitive dissonance suggests reasons for interactions between attitudes and behavior. It proposes that discrepancies between attitudes and behavior, between behavior and self-image, or between one attitude and another lead to the unpleasant state of cognitive dissonance. Reduction of this dissonance by changing the importance of dissonant elements, adding consonant ones, or changing one of the dissonant elements provides negative reinforcement. This theory explains why we place a higher value on things that cost us something; it also predicts that behaviors can lead to attitude changes.

Bem's alternative to cognitive dissonance—self-perception theory—suggests that many of our attitudes are based on self-observation. When our motives are unclear, we look to the situation for the stimuli and probable reinforcers and punishers that cause us to act as we do.

Thought Questions

- Attitudes have sometimes been described as "predispositions to act." What might this phrase mean? Do you believe this statement to be an accurate description of attitudes? Why or why not?
- What kinds of arguments would be effective in persuading you to change your attitude toward a prominent political figure? How would you describe these arguments in psychological terms?
- Have you ever experienced cognitive dissonance? If so, what factors made you feel this way and how did you eventually reduce the dissonance?

prejudice An attitude or evaluation, usually negative, toward a group of people defined by their racial, ethnic, or religious heritage or by their gender, occupation, sexual orientation, level of education, place of residence, or membership in a particular group.

Prejudice

A **prejudice** is a particular form of attitude—an evaluation of a group of people defined by their racial, ethnic, or religious heritage or by their gender, occupation, sexual orientation, level of education, or place of residence. A prejudice (literally, a "prejudgment") is a sort of mental shortcut through which people focus on a few salient features of a person (such as skin color, accent, family name, or manner of dressing) and then assume that the person possesses other, mainly negative, characteristics, too. As you can see, a prejudice is an insidious example of the representativeness heuristic.

Stereotypes are an important component of prejudice. In fact, the meanings of the two terms overlap somewhat. But strictly speaking, a prejudice describes a negative attitude toward members of a particular group, whereas a **stereotype** describes a false belief about their characteristics. (Occasionally, stereotypes can include favorable beliefs.) In addition, stereotypes refer to false beliefs generally accepted within a particular culture, whereas prejudices can be acquired by an individual through his or her experience. Stereotypes may be used to exert control over others and to justify and maintain others in their present social standings (Fiske, 1993). For example, a male employer who holds a stereotype of women as "followers" rather than "leaders" effectively insures that women in his business will not be promoted into management positions.

Prejudice often leads to discrimination. *Discrimination* refers to behaviors, not to attitudes. In other contexts, the word *discrimination* simply means "to distinguish." In the present context, **discrimination** means treating people differently because of their membership in a particular group. Thus, we can discriminate favorably or unfavorably according to the nature of our attitudes and beliefs about the relative value of a particular group. Prejudice occurs any time members in one group, the *ingroup*, exhibit negative attitudes toward members of another group, called the *outgroup*. Discrimination occurs any time members of the ingroup display behavior intended to prevent members of the outgroup from having or getting something, such as a promotion, a raise, or a home in a particular neighborhood.

We tend to perceive members of our own ingroup more favorably than we perceive members of the outgroup. Likewise, we see members of our own ingroup as being more similar to each other than we do members of the outgroup. For example, Lee (1993) surveyed Chinese American and African American students concerning their perceptions of members of their own racial groups as well as their perceptions of the other racial group. Lee found that Chinese American students rated members of their own ingroup more favorably than they did members of the African American outgroup. Similarly, African American students rated members their own ingroup more favorably than they did members of the Chinese American outgroup. In addition, each ingroup perceived its own members to be more similar to each other than members

stereotype An overgeneralized and false belief about the characteristics of members of a particular group.

discrimination The differential treatment of people based on their membership in a particular group.

of the outgroup were to each other. It is easy to see how dividing the world into ingroups and outgroups—"us" and "them"—could lead to prejudice, stereotyping, and discrimination.

Although we most often think of prejudice, stereotypes, and discrimination occurring at the level of the individual, we often see these phenomena operating at the level of groups, even nations. At this level, they give rise to *ethnocentrism*, which, as you recall from Chapter 3, is the notion that one's own cultural, national, racial, or religious group is superior to or more deserving than others. Conflict—international conflict, civil war or unrest, and gang violence—often results from particular ethnocentric beliefs and behaviors. Understanding prejudice, stereotyping, and discrimination, then, are important aspects of understanding social interactions, especially conflict, across all levels of culture (Hymes et al., 1993).

The Origins of Prejudice

Unfortunately, prejudice seems to be an enduring characteristic of the human species and may be observed in education, business, athletics, and politics. History has shown that even groups of people who have been oppressed go on to commit their own type of ethnocentric exploitation if they manage to overthrow their oppressors. Why is prejudice such a widespread trait?

The Roots of Prejudice in Competition

Apparently, affiliation and prejudice are two sides of the same coin. That is, along with the tendency to identify with and feel close to members of our own group or clan goes the tendency to be suspicious of others. A classic experiment by Sherif et al. (1961) demonstrated just how easily intergroup mistrust and conflict can arise. The study took place at a remote summer camp. The subjects, eleven-year-old boys, were assigned to one of two cabins, isolated from each other. During the first week, the boys in each cabin spent their time together as a group, fishing, hiking, swimming, and otherwise enjoying themselves. The boys formed two cohesive groups, which they named the Rattlers and the Eagles. They became attached to their groups and strongly identified with them.

Next, the experimenters sowed the seeds of dissension. They set up a series of competition events between the two groups. The best team was to win a trophy for the group and individual prizes for its members. As the competition progressed, the boys began taunting and insulting each other. Then the Eagles burned the Rattlers' flag, and in retaliation, the Rattlers broke into the Eagles' cabin and scattered or stole their rivals' belongings. Although further physical conflict was prevented by the experimenters, the two groups continued to abuse each other verbally and seemed to have developed a genuine hatred for each other.

Finally, the experimenters arranged for the boys to work together. They sabotaged the water supply for the camp and had the boys fix it; they had the boys repair a truck that had broken down; and they induced the boys to pool their money to rent a movie. After the boys worked on cooperative ventures, rather than competitive ones, the intergroup conflicts diminished.

The findings of this experiment suggest that when groups of people compete with each other, they tend to view their rivals negatively. Note that the boys at the summer camp were racially and ethnically mixed; the assignment to one cabin or the other was arbitrary. Thus, a particular boy could have been either a Rattler-hating Eagle or an Eagle-hating Rattler, depending on chance assignment to one group or the other.

The Role of Self-Esteem in Prejudice

Most social psychologists believe that competition is an important factor in the development of prejudice. The competition need not be for tangible goods; it can be motivated by a desire for social superiority. As we have seen many times in this book, the concept of self-esteem helps explain many different types of behavior. The tendency to perceive one's own group (the ingroup) as superior and that of others (the outgroup) as inferior may be based on a need to enhance one's own self-esteem. Thus, people who belong to groups that preach racial hatred tend to be those whose own social status is rather low.

An experiment by Meindl and Lerner (1985) supports this conclusion. The experimenters exposed English-speaking Canadians to a situation designed to threaten their self-esteem. They asked the subjects to walk across the room to get a chair. For members of the experimental group, the chair was rigged in such a way that a pile of computer cards would be knocked over and scattered on the floor. In a situation like this, most people feel clumsy and foolish—and also a bit guilty about making trouble for the person who has to put the cards back in order. After this experience, the subjects were asked to describe their attitudes toward French-speaking Canadians. Subjects in the experimental group, who had toppled the cards, rated the "others" more negatively than did those in the control group, who had not toppled the cards in retrieving the chair. Presumably, by viewing the French-speaking Canadians as members of a group inferior to their own, the subjects partially compensated for the loss of their own self-esteem. However, levels of self-esteem have been shown to vary from culture to culture (Feather and McKee, 1993), and we should not expect that self-esteem would contribute equally to prejudice across cultures.

The Role of Social Cognition in Prejudice

Research on social cognition has also provided us with information about the origins of prejudice. When we follow heuristics or mental shortcuts, we sometimes make errors of judgment. These mental shortcuts also play a role in the development of prejudice.

As we saw, stereotypes are false beliefs about the members of an outgroup. These beliefs are convenient to the user

Members of ingroups often demonstrate similarities that distinguish them from members of outgroups.

because they provide a way for a person to classify other individuals quickly. The problem is that these beliefs are false. Stereotypes are learned from family members, from friends, and from the mass media. The latter source is particularly dangerous because it is both insidious and widespread. When members of minority groups are portrayed in television shows or in movies as criminals, as having low-status jobs, or as being rather comic and stupid, people acquire stereotypes without becoming aware that they have done so.

Recall that the availability heuristic involves our assuming that distinctive, easily imagined items occur more frequently. This phenomenon probably explains why people overestimate the rate of violent crime (because an act of violence is a frightening, distinctive event) and overestimate the relative numbers of violent crimes committed by members of minority groups (because members of minority groups tend to be more conspicuous). This tendency is an example of an **illusory correlation**—an apparent relation between two distinctive elements that does not actually exist (Spears, van der Pligt, and Eiser, 1985).

Another fallacy that promotes the formation of stereotypes is the **illusion of outgroup homogeneity**: People tend to assume that members of other groups are much more similar than are members of their own group (Linville, 1982). This tendency is even seen between the sexes: Men tend to perceive women as being more alike than men are, and women do the opposite (Park and Rothbart, 1982). The same is true for young and old people (Linville, Fischer, and Salovey, 1989). Most of us resist being stereotyped but never-

illusory correlation An apparent correlation between two distinctive elements that does not actually exist.

illusion of outgroup homogeneity A belief that members of groups to which one does not belong are very similar to one another.

theless practice this activity when thinking about members of other groups.

Self-Fulfilling Prophecies

A **self-fulfilling prophecy** is a stereotype that induces a person to act in a manner consistent with that stereotype. Such a tendency is especially insidious because the behavior of the person who is the target of the stereotype then tends to confirm the stereotype.

One of the most memorable examples of the self-fulfilling prophecy was demonstrated in an experiment by Snyder, Tanke, and Berscheid (1977). The experimenters had male subjects carry on telephone conversations with female subjects. Just before each conversation took place, the male subjects were shown a photograph of the young woman to whom they were to talk. In fact, the pictures were not those of the partner but were photographs of attractive or unattractive women chosen by the experimenters. The conversations that took place were recorded, and the voices of the female subjects were played to independent observers, who rated their impressions of the young women.

Based on the sound of the female subjects' voices and what they said, the independent observers rated the women whose partners believed them to be attractive as being more friendly, likable, and sociable. Obviously, the male subjects talked differently to women they thought to be attractive or unattractive. Their words had either a positive or negative effect on the young women, which could be detected by the observers.

Sometimes, people misperceive the evidence presented to them by the behavior of the target of a stereotype. In such cases, the perceiver considers the prophecy to be fulfilled even when the evidence says otherwise. For example, Ickes, Patterson, Rajecki, and Tanford (1982) had subjects interact with partners they expected to be friendly or unfriendly. If the subjects expected the partners to be unfriendly, they rated them as being that way even when the partners actually acted in a friendly manner.

Hope for Change

One of the primary reasons for prejudice is that it can serve to justify exploitation of the outgroup by the ingroup. If the outgroup can be portrayed as "stupid," "dependent," and "irresponsible," the ingroup can justify the exploitation of that outgroup as being in the outgroup's own best interest or at least conclude that its treatment of the outgroup is the best that the outgroup can reasonably expect. When ethnocentric practices lead to material advantages in the form of cheap labor or unequal sharing of resources, the injustices will tend to persist. Such situations are not easily altered by the discoveries of social psychologists.

However, many instances of personal prejudice are inadvertent. Many people are unaware of their stereotypes and

preconceptions about members of other groups; or, if they are aware of them, they can be persuaded that their beliefs are unjustified. The best solution in these cases is to teach people to become cognitively less lazy and to take the time to reflect about their biases. For example, Langer, Bashner, and Chanowitz (1985) gave a group of sixth-grade children specific training in thinking about the problems of people with disabilities. They thought about such problems as the ways that a person with disabilities might drive a car and the reasons a blind person might make a good newscaster. After this training, they were found to be more willing to go on a picnic with a person with disabilities than were children who did not receive the training. They were also more likely to see the specific consequences of particular disabilities rather than to view people with disabilities as "less fit." For example, they were likely to choose a blind child as a partner in a game of pin the tail on the donkey because they realized that the child would be likely to perform even better than a sighted child. Thus, at the individual level, people can learn to recognize their biases and to overcome their prejudices.

Interim Summary

Prejudice

Prejudice is a negative evaluation of a group of people defined by such characteristics as race, ethnicity, religion, gender, socioeconomic status, or sexual orientation. An important component of prejudice is the existence of a stereotype— a false belief about the characteristics possessed by members of a particular group. Prejudices often lead to discrimination—actual behaviors injurious to the members of the group. Intergroup conflict, such as war or gang violence, often has at its core ethnocentrism, or the belief that one's own group is superior to or more deserving than another group.

Prejudice seems to be an enduring human trait, and it is found in all cultures. One of its important causes appears to be competition between groups for limited resources and the increased self-esteem that results from affiliating with a group perceived to be better than other groups. The study at the boy's camp by Sherif and his colleagues indicates just how easily prejudices can form, even when the groups consist of similar types of individuals.

Stereotypes are examples of the heuristics that guide us through many of our social encounters. One reason we tend to view outgroup members negatively is our use of the availability heuristic: Negative behaviors are often more vivid than positive ones, and outgroup members are more noticeable. Thus, when outgroup members commit an illegal act, we are more likely to notice it and to remember it. We then incorrectly conclude that the behavior is a characteristic of the outgroup as a whole.

self-fulfilling prophecy A stereotype that causes a person to act in a manner consistent with that stereotype.

People also tend to apply the illusion of outgroup homogeneity. Although they realize that their own group contains members who are very different from each other, they tend to view members of other groups as rather similar. Obviously, this tendency contributes to the formation of stereotypes.

Prejudices have many harmful effects, such as the self-fulfilling prophecy, in which being perceived as inferior leads the target of the prejudice to act that way. And even when the person does not, the observer may misperceive—or at least selectively perceive—the behavior. However, there is hope for the future. Many instances of prejudices are inadvertent. And when people are taught to think about members of other groups as individuals having specific characteristics, they can learn to avoid relying on some of their injurious mental shortcuts.

Thought Questions

- Think about a prejudice that you have. (It could be toward a place or a thing; it doesn't have to be directed toward a particular group of people.) What factors have caused this prejudice? To what extent are stereotypes involved in this prejudice?
- How different are the members of your family compared to those of another family that you know? Describe how the illusion of outgroup homogeneity may or may not apply in this instance.

Social Influences and Group Behavior

Human beings are unmistakably social creatures: A great deal of our lives is spent in the company of others. By itself, this is not an especially profound observation, but it leads to some interesting implications, particularly for social psychologists. We do not merely occupy physical space with other people. We affiliate and form groups with each other. A **group** is a collection of individuals who generally have common interests and goals. For example, the members of the American Association of Retired Persons (AARP) have a different set of interests and goals than do members of the American Disabled Veterans Association (ADVA), although some interests and goals may overlap.

The emotions, cognitions, and behaviors that define each of us as individuals are strongly influenced, often without our awareness, by those with whom we interact. Frequently, this influence is unintentional: Other people may be equally unaware of how they are influencing us. At other

group A collection of individuals who generally have common interests and goals.

social norms Informal rules defining the expected and appropriate behavior in specific situations.

times, this influence is intended to manipulate us in some way (Santos, Leve, and Pratkanis, 1994). In this section we will consider the means by which we influence, and are influenced by, others.

Imitation

Probably the most powerful social influence on our behavior and attitudes is the behavior of other people. If we see people act in a particular way, we tend to act in that way, too. Sometimes, we observe that people are not performing a particular behavior; if so, we, too, tend not to perform that behavior.

Conformity

Most of us cherish our independence and like to think that we do what we do because we want to do it, not because others decree that we should. But none of us is immune to social influences, and most instances of conformity benefit us all. If we see someone whose face has been disfigured by an accident or disease, we do not stare at the person or comment about his or her appearance. If someone drops a valuable item, we do not try to pick it up and keep it for ourselves.

Many of the rules that govern our social behavior are formally codified as laws that we are legally obligated to follow. However, many other rules that influence our behavior are not formal laws but are, instead, unwritten agreements. These informal rules that define the expected and appropriate behavior in specific situations are called **social norms**, or, when applied to members of a particular group, *group norms*. How we look at strangers, the way we talk to our friends or our supervisors at work, and the kind of food that we eat are all influenced by the norms of the society in which we live. Despite the fact that they do not develop from a conspicuous formal or legal process, norms are very powerful sources of social influence, as we will see next.

A study Sherif (1936) conducted provided an empirical demonstration of the power of social influence in establishing group norms. Sherif's study was based on a perceptual illusion, originally discovered by astronomers, called the *autokinetic effect*: A small stationary light, when projected in an otherwise completely darkened room, appears to move. The illusion is so strong that even if someone is aware of the effect, the apparent movement often still persists.

Sherif first placed subjects in the room individually and asked each of them how far the light was moving at different times. The answers were quite variable; one subject might see the light move 6 cm on average, while another might see it move an average of 300 cm. Next, Sherif had groups of three people observe the light together and make a joint decision about the extent of the movement. Finally, the subjects would again observe the light individually. The most interesting result of the study was that once people had taken part in the group decision, their individual judgments tended to resemble those that the group had made. That is, the group estab-

Our manner of dress and grooming often reflect the prevailing norms of the group or groups with which we most strongly identify ourselves.

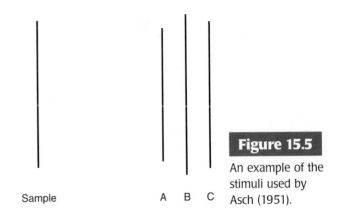

Figure 15.5

An example of the stimuli used by Asch (1951).

Sample   A   B   C

lished what Sherif called a *collective frame of reference*. The changing of one's thoughts or behavior to be similar to those of a social group is called **conformity**. Even when tested by themselves on a different day, the group members still conformed to this frame of reference.

Sherif's findings are not too surprising if we consider that the subjects found themselves in an uncertain situation. It makes sense to use other's opinions or judgments as a frame of reference when you are not sure what is going on. But just how strongly do group norms influence individual behavior when the situation is unambiguous—when we are certain that we perceive things as they really are? The answer to this question was provided in a series of elegant studies conducted by Solomon Asch (1951, 1952, 1955).

Asch asked several groups of seven to nine students to estimate the lengths of lines presented on a screen. A sample line was shown at the left, and the subjects were to choose which of the three lines to the right matched it. (See *Figure 15.5.*) The subjects gave their answers orally.

In fact, there was only one subject in each group; all the others were confederates of the experimenter. The seating was arranged so that the subject answered last. Under some conditions, the confederates made incorrect responses. When they made incorrect responses on six of the twelve trials in an experiment, 76 percent of the subjects went along with the group on at least one trial. Under control conditions, when the confederates responded accurately, only 5 percent of the subjects made an error.

Group pressure did not affect the subjects' perceptions; it affected their behavior. That is, the subjects went along with the group decision even though the choice still looked wrong to them—and even though the other people were complete strangers. When they were questioned later, they said that they had started doubting their own eyesight or had thought that perhaps they had misunderstood the instructions. The subjects who did not conform felt uncomfortable about disagreeing with the other members of the group. The Asch effect shows how strong the tendency to conform can be. Faced with a simple, unambiguous task while in a group of strangers who showed no signs of disapproval when the subject disagreed with them, the vast majority of subjects nevertheless ignored their own judgments and agreed with the obviously incorrect choice made by the other people.

We might ask why people so readily conform. Baron and Byrne (1994) suggest that the two most important reasons are the desire to be liked and the desire to be right. As we will see later, people tend to like other people who are similar to themselves, especially those who act like them and share their attitudes and opinions. Because most of us prefer to be liked, we tend to conform to the expectations of others. In addition, most of us prefer to be right rather than wrong.

Bystander Intervention

Conformity can sometimes have disastrous consequences. In 1964 in New York City, a woman named Kitty Genovese was chased and repeatedly stabbed by an assailant, who took thirty-five minutes to kill her. The woman's screams went unheeded by at least thirty-eight people who watched from their windows. No one tried to stop the attacker; no one even

conformity The adoption of attitudes and behaviors shared by a particular group of people.

made a quick, anonymous telephone call to the police. When the bystanders were questioned later, they could not explain their inaction. "I just don't know," they said.

As you can imagine, people were appalled and shocked by the bystanders' response to the Genovese murder. Commentators said that the apparent indifference of the bystanders demonstrated that American society, especially in urban areas, had become cold and apathetic. Experiments performed by social psychologists suggest that this explanation is wrong—people in cities are not generally indifferent to the needs of other people. The fact that Kitty Genovese's attack went unreported is not remarkable because thirty-eight people were present; it is precisely *because* so many people were present that the attack was not reported.

Darley and Latané have extensively studied the phenomenon of **bystander intervention**—the actions of people witnessing a situation in which someone appears to require assistance. Their experiments have shown that in such situations, the presence of other people who are doing nothing inhibits others from giving aid. For example, Darley and Latané (1968) staged an "emergency" during a psychology experiment. Each subject participated in a discussion about personal problems associated with college life with one, two, or five other people by means of an intercom. The experimenter explained that the participants would sit in individual rooms so that they would be anonymous and hence would be more likely to speak frankly. The experimenter would not listen in but would get their reactions later in a questionnaire. Actually, only one subject was present; the other voices were simply tape recordings. During the discussion, one of the people, who had previously said that he sometimes had seizures, apparently had one. His speech became incoherent, and he stammered out a request for help.

Almost all subjects left the room to help the victim when they were the only witness to the seizure. However, when there appeared to be other witnesses, the subjects were much less likely to try to help. In addition, those who did try to help reacted more slowly if other people were thought to be present. (See *Figure 15.6.*)

Darley and Latané reported that the subjects who did not respond were not indifferent to the plight of their fellow student. Indeed, when the experimenter entered the room, they usually appeared nervous and emotionally aroused, and they asked whether someone was helping the victim. The experimenters did not receive the impression that the subjects had decided not to act; rather, they were still in conflict, trying to decide whether they should do something.

bystander intervention The intervention of a person in a situation that appears to require his or her aid.

diffusion of responsibility An explanation of the failure of bystander intervention stating that when several bystanders are present, no one person assumes responsibility for helping.

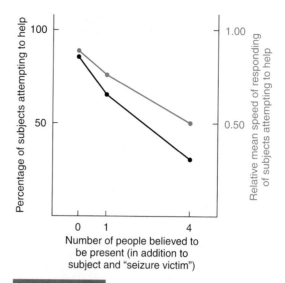

Figure 15.6

Bystander intervention. Percentage of subjects attempting to help as a function of the number of other people the subject believed to be present.

(Based on data from Darley, J.M., and Latané, B. Bystander intervention in emergencies: Diffusion of responsibility. Journal of Personality and Social Psychology, *1968, 8, 377–383.)*

Thus, it seems that whether bystanders will intervene in a particular circumstance depends, at least in part, on how they perceive the situation. Latané and Darley (1970) have proposed a model describing a sequence of steps bystanders face when confronted with a potential emergency:

The event must come to their attention or be noticed.

They must assume some responsibility for helping the victim.

The possible courses of action must be considered and compared.

Finally, they must actually implement the chosen course of action.

Of course, this sequence takes place rapidly and without much awareness on the bystander's part, as is true of many situations to which we respond daily.

Unfortunately, at least from the perspective of the victim, obstacles may arise at any one stage in this decision-making process that make it unlikely that a bystander will intervene. In many cases, the bystander who is aware that others are available to help may not feel any personal responsibility to do so, a phenomenon called **diffusion of responsibility**. This factor is considered to be responsible for the finding that help is less likely to be offered when there are several bystanders present. In addition, the bystander may not feel competent to intervene or may be fearful of doing so; consequently, no action is taken. Shotland and Heinold (1985) staged an accident

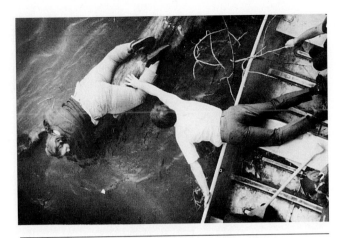

Not all bystanders are indifferent to the plight of people in danger. The man shown in this photograph rescued a woman who had been stranded on a floating log for forty minutes in the Mississippi River.

in which a person seemed to be bleeding. Bystanders who had received training in first-aid treatment were much more likely to come to the victim's aid, and they did so whether or not bystanders were present. Because they knew how to recognize an emergency and knew what to do, they were less likely to fear doing the wrong thing.

Social Facilitation

As we just saw, the behavior of other people has a powerful effect on our own. Studies have shown that even the mere presence of other people can affect a person's behavior. Triplett (1897) published the first experimental study on **social facilitation**—the enhancement of a person's performance by the presence of other people. He had people perform simple tasks, such as turning the crank of a fishing reel. He found that his subjects turned the crank faster and for a longer time if other people were present. Although many other studies found the same effect, some investigators reported just the opposite phenomenon: If the task was difficult and complex, the presence of an audience impaired the subjects' performance. You yourself have probably noticed that you have difficulty performing certain tasks if someone is watching you.

Robert Zajonc (pronounced "zi-onze";1965) has suggested an explanation for social facilitation. He claims that the presence of people who are watching a performer (or of people whom the performer perceives as watching) raises that person's arousal level. Presumably, the increase in arousal has the effect of increasing the probability of performing dominant responses: responses that are most likely to occur in a particular situation. When the task is simple, the dominant response is generally the correct one, so an audience improves performance. When the task is complex, a person can perform

many different responses and must decide which one is appropriate. The presence of the audience makes the selection of the appropriate behavior more difficult because the increased arousal tends to cause the person to perform the dominant response, which may not be the correct one.

Subsequent experiments have supported Zajonc's explanation. For example, Martens (1969) tested the prediction that the presence of a group increases a person's level of arousal. While subjects performed a complex motor task alone or in the presence of ten people, the experimenter determined physiological arousal by measuring the amount of sweat present on the subjects' palms. The presence of an audience produced a clear-cut effect: The subjects who performed in front of other people had sweatier palms.

Such arousal may contribute to the making of costly mistakes—at least from the perspective of the aroused person. For example, in their study of residential burglars, Cromwell et al. (1991) found that burglars who work in groups are five times more likely to get caught than are burglars who work alone. The researchers argue that burglary is a complex task that cannot be "well-learned" because each burglary is different and that in group burglaries, the burglars often report having to motivate each other in order to do the job. For example, consider the words of one burglar: "Man, you gotta get a bunch of people together and build up your nerve to do a house in this part of town. You get a bunch of guys together and you psych each other up to do the job." The complexity of the burglary combined with high levels of arousal may contribute to errors in "professional" judgment in both planning and carrying out the crime, which results in higher apprehension rates.

One factor that affects an individual's arousal level and, in turn, social facilitation, is the actor's perception of the audience. Sanna and Shotland (1990) found that subjects who believed that an audience would evaluate them positively performed better when the audience was present. Those who anticipated a negative evaluation performed worse.

Social Loafing

As we just saw, people usually try harder when other people are watching them. However, when the other people are coworkers rather than observers, the presence of a group sometimes results in a decrease in effort, or **social loafing**. Thus, a group is often *less* than the sum of its individual members. Many years ago, Ringelmann (cited by Dashiell, 1935) measured the effort that people made when pulling a rope in a mock tug-of-war contest against a device that measured the exerted force. Presumably, the force exerted by eight

social facilitation　The enhancement of task performance caused by the mere presence of others.

social loafing　The decreased effort put forth by individuals when performing a task with other people.

people pulling together in a simple task would be at least the sum of their individual efforts or even somewhat greater than the sum because of social facilitation. However, Ringelmann found that the total force exerted was only about half what would be predicted by the simple combination of individual efforts. The subjects exerted less force when they worked in a group.

More recent studies have confirmed these results and have extended them to other behaviors. Several variables have been found to determine whether the presence of a group will produce social facilitation or social loafing. One of the most important of them is identifiability. Williams, Harkins, and Latané (1981) asked subjects to shout as loud as they could individually or in groups. Subjects who were told that the equipment could measure only the total group effort shouted less loudly than those who were told that the equipment could measure individual efforts. The latter shouted just as loudly in groups as they did alone. These results suggest that a person's efforts in a group activity are affected by whether other people can observe his or her individual efforts. If they can, social facilitation is likely to occur; if they cannot, then social loafing is more likely.

Another variable that determines whether social facilitation or social loafing occurs is *individual responsibility*. If a person's efforts are duplicated by those of another person (and if his or her individual efforts are not identifiable), the person is likely to exert less-than-maximum effort. Harkins and Petty (1982) had subjects work in groups of four on a task that required them to report whenever a dot appeared in a particular quadrant of a video screen. In one condition, each subject watched an individual quadrant and was solely responsible for detecting dots that appeared there. In the other condition, all four subjects watched the same quadrant; thus, the responsibility for detecting dots was shared. Subjects did not loaf when they were responsible for their own quadrants.

In a recent review of the social loafing literature, Karau and Williams (1995) noted that two variables—gender and culture—appear to moderate people's tendency to become social loafers. Although all people in different cultures are susceptible to social loafing, the effect is smaller for women than for men and for people living in Eastern cultures than for those living in Western cultures. Karau and Williams offer a reasonable explanation for this finding—both women and people living in Eastern cultures tend to be more group- or collectively-oriented in their thinking and behaving than do men and people living in Western cultures. That is, women and people living in Eastern cultures tend to place greater importance on participating in group activities, which partially buffers them from social loafing effects.

Reciprocity

Another very strong social influence is **reciprocity**, the tendency to pay back favors others have done for us. When

The principle of reciprocity is at the heart of almost all social interaction, including the exchanging of gifts on special occasions.

someone does something for us, we feel uncomfortable until the debt is discharged. For example, if people invite us to their house for dinner, we feel obliged to return the favor in the near future. And owing a social debt to someone we do not like is especially distasteful. Often people will suffer in silence rather than ask for help from someone they dislike. Reciprocity is pervasive—every culture is known to have some form of the "golden rule" (Cialdini, 1993). It establishes a basic guideline for behavior in a wide range of situations, and its emergence in evolutionary history is considered to be crucial to the development of social life.

Reciprocity does not require that the "favor" be initially requested or even wanted. The debt of obligation can be so strong that reciprocity can be exploited by those who want us to comply with their requests when we would otherwise not do so. For example, people trying to sell something often try to capitalize on the reciprocity rule by giving the potential customer a free sample. Once the person has accepted the "gift," the sales representative tries to get him or her to return the favor by making a purchase. If you have ever accepted a piece of food from a friendly person handing out samples in a supermarket, you realize how hard it is to walk away without purchasing something. I know that I avoid accepting free samples because I dislike being manipulated into buying something I do not want.

Experiments conducted by social psychologists have confirmed the strength of reciprocity in human interactions. For example, Regan (1971) enlisted the participation of college students in an experiment that supposedly involved art appreciation. During a break, some subjects were treated to a soft drink by another "subject" (a confederate) or by the experimenter; others received nothing. After the experiment,

reciprocity The tendency to return, in kind, favors that others have done for us.

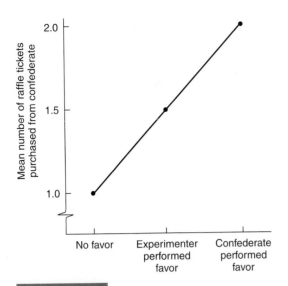

Figure 15.7

The strength of reciprocity. Mean number of raffle tickets purchased from a confederate when subjects received a favor or no favor from the experimenter or confederate.
(Based on data from Regan, D.T. Effects of favor and liking on compliance. Journal of Experimental Social Psychology, *1971, 7, 627–639.)*

the confederate asked each subject to purchase some raffle tickets he was selling. Compliance with the request was measured by the number of tickets each subject bought. (See *Figure 15.7*.) The subjects treated to a soft drink by the confederate purchased the most raffle tickets.

Commitment

Once people commit themselves by making a decision and acting on it, they are reluctant to renounce their commitment. For example, have you ever joined one side of an argument on an issue that you do not really care about only to find yourself vehemently defending a position that just a few minutes ago meant almost nothing to you? I certainly know I have. This phenomenon was demonstrated in a clever study by Knox and Inkster (1968). The experimenters asked people at the betting windows of a racetrack how confident they were that their horses would win. They questioned half the people just before they had made their bets, the other half just afterward. The people who had already made their bets were more confident than were those who had not yet paid. Their commitment increased the perceived value of their decision.

An experiment by Freedman and Fraser (1966) showed that commitment has a long-lasting effect on people's tendency to comply with requests. They sent a person posing as a volunteer worker to call on homeowners in a residential

California neighborhood and to ask them to perform a small task: to accept a 3-inch-square sign saying "Keep California Beautiful" or "Be a Safe Driver" or to sign a petition supporting legislation favoring one of these goals. Almost everyone agreed. Two weeks later, the experimenters sent another person to ask these people whether they would be willing to have public service billboards erected in front of their houses. To give them an idea of precisely what was being requested, the "volunteer worker" showed the homeowners a photograph of a house almost completely hidden by a huge, ugly, poorly lettered sign saying "DRIVE CAREFULLY." Over 55 percent of the people agreed to this obnoxious request! In contrast, only 17 percent of householders who had not been contacted previously (and asked to accept the smaller sign) agreed to have such a billboard placed on their property. Freedman and Fraser referred to their procedure as the *foot-in-the-door technique.*

Commitment increases people's compliance even when the reason for the original commitment is removed. For example, recall the opening vignette in which I described my father's experience when he tried to buy a new car. When the salesperson returned from talking to his sales manager, we assumed that my father would pay the price he had proposed for the car. In fact, he had made an earlier commitment for the car—he had signed a piece of paper describing the proposed price and handed the salesperson twenty dollars as a gesture of his good-faith intention to buy the car. However, the salesperson said that the dealership would lose money on the car if he sold it to my father at that price and then countered with a price several hundred dollars higher. My father refused the offer. All too often, though, the customer agrees to the higher price, even though it is not one he or she agreed to in the first place. This technique is called *low-balling.*

Commitment probably increases compliance for several reasons. First, the act of complying with a request in a particular category may change a person's self-image. Through the process of self-attribution, people who accept a small sign to support safe driving may come to regard themselves as public-spirited individuals—what sensible person is not for safe driving? Thus, when they hear the billboard request, they find it difficult to refuse. After all, they are public-spirited, so how can they say no? Saying no would imply that they did not have the courage of their convictions. Thus, this reason has at its root self-esteem; to maintain good self-esteem, the person must say yes to the larger request.

Commitment may also increase compliance because the initial, smaller request changes people's perception of compliance in general. Evidence supporting this suggestion was provided by Rittle (1981). While sitting in a waiting room before participating in an experiment, some adult subjects were approached by an eight-year-old child who was having trouble operating a vending machine. Later, while answering a series of questions designed to disguise the true nature of the experiment, they were asked to rate their perceptions of how unpleasant it might be to provide help to other people. After

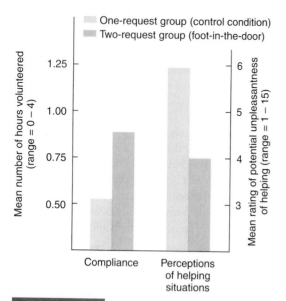

Figure 15.8

The effect of commitment on compliance and perceptions of the potential unpleasantness of helping situations. Mean number of hours volunteered (compliance) and mean rating of potential unpleasantness of volunteering for control subjects and subjects who first helped a child.

(Based on data from Rittle, R.H. Changes in helping behavior: Self versus situational perceptions as mediators of the foot-in-the-door technique. Personality and Social Psychology Bulletin, 1981, 7, 431–437.)

the subjects had answered all the questions and the study was apparently over, the interviewer asked them whether they would volunteer between thirty minutes and four hours of their time to participate in a research project. Subjects who had helped the child rated helping as less unpleasant and were more willing to participate in the research project than were people who had not helped the child. (See *Figure 15.8.*)

Attractive People

People also tend to be influenced by requests or persuasive messages from attractive people. As we will see in a later section, physical good looks are one of the most important factors in determining whether we find someone likable.

Kulka and Kessler (1978) demonstrated the effect of good looks on people's behavior in a controlled experiment. They staged mock trials of a negligence suit in which someone was suing another person for damages. The subjects served as jury members and decided how much money the plaintiffs should be awarded. Physically attractive plaintiffs received an average of $10,051, but physically unattractive plaintiffs received only $5,623. Justice may not be so blind after all.

Why is attractiveness such a potent influence on people's behavior? The most likely explanation involves classical conditioning and—again—self-esteem. Classical conditioning holds that when people have positive or negative reactions to some stimuli, they begin to have positive or negative reactions to other stimuli associated with those stimuli. Thus, as Cialdini (1993) notes, some people irrationally blame the weather forecaster for bad weather. Similarly, in ancient times, a messenger bringing news about a battle to the ruler of Persia was treated to a banquet if the news was good and beheaded if it was bad.

Advertisers regularly pay tribute to the effectiveness of association when they use attractive models and celebrities to endorse their products. For example, Smith and Engel (1968) showed two versions of an advertisement for a new car. One version included an attractive young woman and the other did not. When the subjects subsequently rated the car, those who saw the advertisement with the attractive young woman rated the car as faster, more appealing, more expensive looking, and better designed.

Besides making products or opinions more attractive by being associated with them, attractive people are better able to get others to comply with their requests. This phenomenon, like so many others, probably has self-esteem at its root. One of the reasons people tend to comply with the requests of attractive people is that they want to be liked by attractive people; in their minds, being liked by attractive people makes them more desirable, too. People tend to emphasize their associations with attractive and important people. We have all encountered name-droppers who want us to think that they are part of a privileged circle of friends. This phenomenon is even demonstrated by fans of sports teams. Cialdini et al. (1976) found that university students were more likely to wear sweatshirts featuring the university name on Mondays after the football team had won a game than after the team had lost. And Wann and Dolan (1994) have shown that spectators identify with, and are biased in favor of, fellow spectators who root for the same team.

Authority

People tend to comply with the requests of people in authority and to be swayed by their persuasive arguments, and such obedience is generally approved by society. For example, the Bible describes God's test of Abraham, who is ordered to sacrifice his beloved son Isaac. Just as he is about to plunge the knife, an angel tells him to stop; he has proved his obedience. Cohen and Davis (1981) cite a more recent, if less dramatic, example of unthinking obedience. A physician prescribed eardrops for a hospitalized patient with an ear infection. His order read "place in R ear." Unfortunately, he apparently did not put enough space between the abbreviation for right (R) and the word *ear*, because the nurse delivered the ear drops rectally. Neither she nor the patient thought to question such treatment for an earache.

A disturbing example of mindless obedience was obtained in a series of experiments performed by Milgram (1963), who advertised for subjects in local newspapers in order to obtain as representative a sample as possible. The subjects served as "teachers" in what they were told was a learning experiment. A confederate (a middle-aged accountant) serving as the "learner" was strapped into a chair "to prevent excessive movements when he was shocked," and electrodes were attached to his wrist. The subjects were told that "although the shocks can be extremely painful, they cause no permanent tissue damage."

The subject was then brought to a separate room housing an apparatus having dials, buttons, and a series of switches that supposedly delivered shocks ranging from 15 to 450 volts. The subject was instructed to use this apparatus to deliver shocks, in increments of 15 volts for each "mistake," to the learner in the other room. Beneath the switches were descriptive labels ranging from "Slight Shock" to "Danger: Severe Shock."

The learner gave his answers by pressing the appropriate lever on the table in front of him. Each time he made an incorrect response, the experimenter told the subject to throw another switch and give a larger shock. At the 300-volt level, the learner pounded on the wall and then stopped responding to questions. The experimenter told the subject to consider a "no answer" as an incorrect answer. At the 315-volt level, the learner pounded on the wall again. If the subject hesitated in delivering a shock, the experimenter said, "Please go on." If this admonition was not enough, the experimenter said, "The experiment requires that you continue," then, "It is absolutely essential that you continue," and finally, "You have no other choice; you must go on." The factor of interest was how long the subjects would continue to administer shocks to the hapless victim. A majority of subjects gave the learner what they believed to be the 450-volt shock, despite the fact that he pounded on the wall twice and then stopped responding altogether. (See *Figure 15.9.*)

In a later experiment, when the confederate was placed in the same room as the subject and his struggling and apparent pain could be observed, 37.5 percent of the participants—over a third—obeyed the order to administer further shocks (Milgram, 1974). Thirty percent were even willing to hold his hand against a metal plate to force him to receive the shock.

Milgram's experiments indicate that a significant percentage of people will blindly follow the orders of authority figures, no matter what the effects are on other people. Milgram had originally designed his experimental procedure to understand why ordinary people in Germany had participated in the murders of millions of innocent people during World War II. He had planned to perfect the technique in the United States and then travel to Germany to continue his studies. The results he obtained made it clear that he did not have to leave home. (However, as Lutsky (1995) has pointed out, other factors, including voluntary actions on the part of many Germans, contributed to the atrocities committed by the Germans during World War II.)

Most people find the results of Milgram's studies surprising. They can't believe that for such a large proportion of people the social pressure to conform to the experimenter's orders is stronger than the subject's own desire not to hurt someone else. As Ross (1977) points out, this misperception is an example of the fundamental attribution error. People tend to *underestimate* the effectiveness of situational factors and to *overestimate* the effectiveness of dispositional ones. Clearly, the tendency to obey an authority figure is amazingly strong. Perhaps we should emphasize to our children the importance of doing no harm to others at least as much as we emphasize obedience to authority.

Understandably, much of the attention given to Milgram's research focused on its considerable ethical implica-

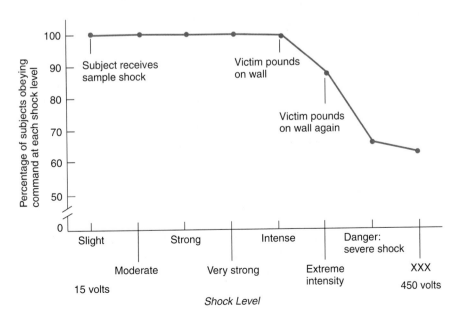

Figure 15.9

Data from one of Milgram's studies of obedience.

(From Baron, R.A., and Byrne, D. Social Psychology: Understanding Human Interaction, 7th ed. Boston: Allyn and Bacon, 1994. Reprinted with permission. After Milgram, 1963.)

tions (Elms, 1995). Many people, psychologists and nonpsychologists alike, have attacked his research on the grounds that it involved deception and too much emotional strain on the subjects. Indeed, Milgram's research helped prompt psychologists to strengthen ethical guidelines for conducting research with humans.

In his defense, however, it should be stressed that Milgram conducted an extensive debriefing at the end of each experimental session in which the true purpose of the experiment was explained to the subjects. The subjects were told that their behavior was quite typical of the way most people responded to the situation posed by the experiment. In addition, the subjects were later sent a detailed written report of the experimental procedure and a follow-up questionnaire asking them about their feelings regarding their participation. Eighty-four percent of the subjects said that they were glad to have participated in the experiment, and only 1.3 percent indicated that they wished they had not participated.

An additional objection to Milgram's research is that people may have had to confront a disturbing aspect of their own behavior—the self-realization that they were capable of actions that they find reprehensible. Milgram replied that at least some of his subjects considered their enhanced insight into their own behavior to have been enough to justify their participation. Of course, Milgram could not guarantee that somebody, somewhere, who had participated in his research might be deeply troubled by his participation. And therein lies another moral dilemma: To what extent is knowledge about behavior, in general, and insight about one's own behavior, in particular, to be avoided in case some people think that others might find this knowledge disturbing? That is not an easy question to answer and one that psychologists must grapple with each time they perform research such as that conducted by Milgram.

Deindividuation

Blindly obeying the commands of an authority figure is not the only situation in which we might find ourselves behaving in less-than-admirable ways. Sometimes, just being part of a crowd in which we lose our sense of identity can be sufficient to transform our otherwise normal behavior into unruly, sometimes violent acts. Not too long ago, several people were killed and many others injured when an impatient crowd charged the doors of an auditorium at a rock concert. Also not long ago, a large group of soccer fans, angry at their team's defeat, charged fans supporting the other team. Several people were trampled to death. And in the early part of this century, innocent people were lynched by mobs demanding that immediate justice be served for heinous crimes they had allegedly committed. No trial was held—the mob

deindividuation The replacement of one's personal identity by identification with the group's values and goals.

served as judge, jury, and executioner. What leads groups of people to behave in this manner?

Many social psychologists explain these acts in terms of **deindividuation**, in which one's personal identity—one's sense of self—is replaced by identification with the group's values and goals (Taylor, Peplau, and Sears, 1994). As a result, members "blend" into the group, achieving a sense of anonymity that causes them to assume less responsibility for their actions (Diener, 1980; Forsyth, 1990). Consider a study of empathy toward strangers conducted by Zimbardo (1970). In one condition, young women were easily identifiable: They wore name tags and were called by their names. In another condition, a different group of young women were not so easily identifiable: They wore large coats and hoods without name tags and were never referred to by their names. The two groups of women were given chances to administer electric shocks to a stranger, who was in actuality a confederate of Zimbardo's. The young women who were more or less unidentifiable gave nearly twice as many electric shocks to the stranger as did the young women whose identities were known. Thus, the amount of aggression Zimbardo observed in his subjects was strongly correlated with the extent to which their identities were known, reinforcing the idea that antisocial behavior observed in some groups is due to the loss of personal identity of its individual members.

Keep in mind, though, that deindividuation does not always produce negative effects. For instance, in the aftermath of natural disasters or personal calamities, people often form groups that, among other things, work to restore order, rebuild homes and businesses, distribute food and other supplies, and, in extraordinary cases, perform heroic rescues. During the weeks that followed the destruction wrought by Hurricane Opal in the city in which one of the authors lives (Auburn, Alabama), many people formed small groups and worked together to clear debris from streets, yards, and houses as well as to deliver food and water to those in need. People were heard to remark afterward that the hurricane actually helped bring the community closer together and that, at least for a while, they "lost themselves" in becoming part of a group whose only goal was to get things back to normal.

Group Decision Making

The process by which members of a group reach a decision is different from the process involved in individual decision making if only because decisions in groups are usually preceded by discussion. However, discussing issues relevant to a decision does not always guarantee that the best decision will be made. Two examples of problems associated with group decision making are group polarization and groupthink.

Group Polarization

In some group decision making situations, discussion of alternative choices leads to decisions that are either riskier or more conservative than the group's initial position on the issue at hand. In general, if the initial position of group members is to make a risky decision, group discussion will lead to making an even riskier decision. In contrast, if the initial position of group members is to make a conservative decision, group discussion will usually lead to an even more conservative decision. The tendency for the initial position of a group to become exaggerated during the discussion preceding a decision is called **group polarization**.

One important consequence of group polarization is attitude change. For example, suppose that you join a local environmental group because you have a desire to protect the environment. After attending several meetings and discussing environmental issues with other group members, you may find that your proenvironment attitude has become even stronger: You are more of an environmentalist than you thought you were! That group discussion can affect attitude change so powerfully has been documented in many psychology experiments. For example, Myers and Bishop (1970) found that the initial levels of racial prejudice voiced by groups was altered through group discussion. Discussion caused the group with an initially low level of prejudice to become even less prejudiced and discussion caused the group with an initially high level of prejudice to become even more prejudiced.

What causes group discussion to lead to polarization? Although several explanations have been offered, two seem the most plausible: those concerning informational and normative influence (Isenberg, 1986). *Informational influence* involves learning new information germane to the decision to be made. Information that favors a particular decision is often repeated; thus, the discussion becomes slanted toward that decision, increasing the likelihood that more and more members of the group will become convinced that this is the best decision. In addition, people also learn of information of which they were previously unaware, which makes them even more convinced that moving to a more extreme position is the best thing to do.

Normative influence involves comparison of one's individual views with the group norm. People in groups receive social reinforcement for agreeing with the views of others. The more that group members wish to achieve group cohesion in decision making, the greater the tendency for individual group members to embrace the logic underlying the group's decisions—no matter how extreme those decisions might be. Thus, the more that groups of people square off to debate important issues, such as abortion, gun control, welfare, and so on, the more likely it is that they will become convinced of the credibility of their *own* positions—not because they are the correct positions but because of the mutual support that group members give each other for holding those positions.

Groupthink

Irving Janis has studied a related phenomenon that sometimes occurs in group decision making—**groupthink**, the tendency to avoid dissent in the attempt to achieve group consensus (Janis, 1972, 1982). Janis developed the notion of groupthink after studying the ineffective decision making that led President John F. Kennedy to order the ill-fated attempt to overthrow the Castro regime in Cuba in 1961. The decision to embark on the Bay of Pigs invasion was made by Kennedy and a small group of advisors. After studying the conditions that led to this decision as well as other important group decisions that altered the course of twentieth-century history (such as the Japanese attack on Pearl Harbor), Janis proposed his theory of groupthink.

The theory specifies the conditions necessary for groupthink as well as its symptoms and consequences. (See *Figure 15.10.*) The conditions that foster groupthink include a stressful situation in which the stakes are very high, a group of people who already tend to think alike and who are isolated from others who could offer criticism of the decision, and a strong group leader who makes his or her position well known to the group. In the Bay of Pigs example, the overthrow of one of America's archenemies was at stake, Kennedy's advisors were like-minded regarding the invasion and met in secret, and Kennedy was a forceful and charismatic leader who made his intentions to invade Cuba known to the group.

group polarization The tendency for the initial position of a group to become exaggerated during the discussion preceding a decision.

groupthink The tendency to avoid dissent in the attempt to achieve group consensus in the course of decision making.

What group decision-making processes do you suppose led to the escalation of violence in the standoff that took place between the Branch Davidians and the U.S. government?

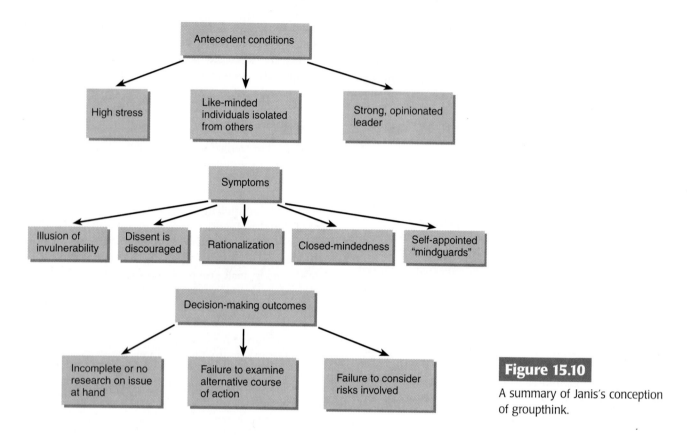

Figure 15.10

A summary of Janis's conception of groupthink.

Janis also notes five symptoms of groupthink, all of which were present during the decision to invade Cuba. First, group members share the illusion that their decision is sound, moral, and right—in a word, invulnerable. Second, dissent from the leader's views are discouraged, further supporting the illusion that the group's decision is the right one. Third, instead of assessing the strengths and weaknesses of the decision, group members rationalize their decision, looking only for reasons that support it. Fourth, group members are closed-minded—they are not willing to listen to alternative suggestions and ideas. And fifth, self-appointed "mindguards" exist within the group who actively discourage dissent from the group norm.

Combined, these symptoms lead to flawed decision making. They contribute to the tendency to conduct only incomplete or no research on the issue about which a decision is being made, to fail to examine alternative courses of action specified by the decision, and finally, to fail to consider potential risks inherent in the decision.

Janis argues that groupthink may be avoided by taking several precautions. First, criticism by group members should be encouraged. Second, relevant input should be sought from appropriate people who are not members of the group. Third, the group should be broken down into smaller subgroups in which different ideas and opinions are generated and developed. And fourth, the group leader should not overstate his or her position on the matter and should be on

guard for rationalization, closed-mindedness, and illusions of invulnerability.

Resisting Social Influences

At first glance, social influence may appear to be negative; perhaps we would be better off if all our behavior was under rational, conscious control. But as Cialdini (1993) points out, this conclusion is not warranted. Most of the time, our species profits from our tendencies to be fair in our interactions with others, to take our cues for acting from each other, to honor our commitments and to obey authority figures. If we had to expend time and effort in consciously deciding what to do in every situation we encountered in our lives, we would be exhausted at the end of each day and get hardly anything done. For most normal people in most situations, the automatic, unconscious reaction is the best and most efficient one. We should save our cognitive efforts for the times when they count the most. However, no general rule works all the time; exceptions can occur that have bad effects. For example, an authority figure can order us to do things that hurt ourselves or others, and advertisers and sales representatives who know the rules of social influence can induce us to purchase items we do not need.

Cialdini suggests that the best way to defend ourselves from the unscrupulous use of social influences is to be sensitive to ourselves and to the situation. Whenever we are spending money or committing ourselves to do something that will cost us time and effort, we should ask ourselves whether we feel any discomfort. Do we feel pressured? Do we feel tense? Do we wish we were somewhere else? If so, someone is probably trying to manipulate us. We should try to relax and step back from the situation. Does the other person stand to profit from what he or she is trying to get us to do? If we could go back to the time just before we got into this situation, would we put ourselves where we are now or would we avoid this situation? If we would avoid it, then now is the time to leave. The feeling that we have to keep going, that we have to live up to our commitment, is exactly what the other person is counting on.

We must realize that when someone is trying to manipulate us, the rules that govern normal social interchanges are off. Of course, we should be polite and honest—just as we want other people to be with us—but we are not obliged to return "favors" from someone trying to sell us something. If he or she tricks us into making a commitment, we should feel no compunction about breaking it. If someone tries to abuse our natural tendencies to be fair in our interactions with others, we should fight back. Otherwise, we run the risk of becoming cynical in our dealings of other people who are *not* trying to take advantage of us. Forewarned is forearmed.

Interim Summary

Social Influences and Group Behavior

You probably did not need to be told that one of the most important influences on our behavior is provided by other humans, but the experiments of social psychologists have shown us just how potent these social influences are. We tend to imitate the behavior of other people, conforming to social norms and preferring not to disagree with attitudes and judgments expressed by others. This tendency undoubtedly serves us well most of the time, but the fact that people are less likely to assist someone if other bystanders are present shows that imitation can also have unfortunate effects.

When they are part of a group or are observed by others, people act differently than when alone. In general, the presence of observers increases the likelihood that the performer will make the dominant response; depending on the complexity of the task, this effect can either facilitate or inhibit performance. When performing as part of a group, a person's efforts will usually be less vigorous if individual contribution cannot be measured. The most important variables that affect social loafing are identifiability and responsibility. If our efforts can be detected by others, the contingencies of social reinforcement and punishment come into play, and we tend not to loaf. Also, if we have a particular responsibility that is not duplicated by other people—if our contribution is a unique and important one—we tend to continue to work hard in support of the group effort.

When someone does us a favor, we tend to reciprocate, doing something for them when we have the opportunity. This tendency facilitates many types of social interactions, but an individual can sometimes be tricked into returning a small favor with a big one. When we commit ourselves to a course of action, we tend to honor this commitment. As the study with the billboards showed, we even act consistently with prior commitments when we are not conscious of having made them. And not everyone is treated equally by other people. Attractive people tend to get what they want from others; we find it difficult to say no to them. And, as Milgram's research showed, people will obey outlandish, even inhumane, requests from those perceived as authority figures. When we become absorbed in the values and goals of the group to which we belong, we lose our sense of personal identity, which may cause us to assume less responsibility for our actions and lead to antisocial behavior.

Effective group decision making may be hampered by both group polarization and groupthink. In group polarization, the initial position of the group is exaggerated to one extreme or the other for two reasons—informational influence and normative influence. Informational influence involves the repeated presentation of new and specific information that slants the opinion of the group toward either a riskier or a more conservative decision. Normative influence involves group members acting to obtain mutual reinforcement—they make the decision that is most likely to contribute to group cohesiveness. Groupthink develops in situations that are highly stressful when the group making a decision involves an opinionated group leader and like-minded individuals who are isolated from others. It is characterized by feelings that the group's decision is invulnerable, by lack of dissent, by rationalization, by closed-mindedness, and by "mindguards" who actively discourage differences of opinion. When steps are taken to avoid these symptoms, better, more effective decisions become possible.

Although our tendency to be influenced socially is generally in our best interests, sometimes unscrupulous persons take advantage of this tendency in attempts to exploit others. The best way to protect ourselves from such persons is to become more aware of situations in which such exploitation is likely to occur.

Thought Questions

■ How would social life be different if people tended *not* to conform to certain social norms? Think of an instance in which your behavior conformed to a social norm. How might the outcome of this social interaction have been different had you *not* conformed?

■ In lifesaving and CPR classes, students are taught to take control in emergency situations. For example, in a situation in which a person appears to be drowning, they assign onlookers specific responsibilities, such as calling 911, fetching rescue equipment, and so on. To what extent does taking control in this manner enhance bystander intervention? What effect might it have on the onlookers' tendency toward diffusion of responsibility?

- Suppose that you have been asked by your psychology professor to organize a small group of class members to prepare a presentation. As the leader of the group, what steps might you take to prevent the individual members of your group from becoming social loafers?

- How might the norm of reciprocity apply to social interactions on an international basis, for instance, negotiating trade agreements, peace treaties, or cultural exchanges?

Interpersonal Attraction and Loving

When an individual conforms to a group norm, it is the individual, not the group, who is being influenced. When you comply with the request of a car salesperson or obey the dictates of an authority figure, the influence flows in one direction; it is *your* behavior that is being influenced. However, many cases of social influence are reciprocal. As we shall see in this section, the behavior of two individuals may have mutual, although not necessarily equal, influences on each other.

Interpersonal Attraction

Many factors determine **interpersonal attraction,** or people's tendency to approach each other and evaluate each other positively. Some factors are characteristics of the individuals themselves; others are determined by the socially reinforcing aspects of the environment.

Positive Evaluation

Humans like to be evaluated positively—to be held in high regard by other people. This tendency is expressed in interpersonal attraction. Consider the following study. Geller et al. (1974) had female college students individually join group discussions with two other women, confederates of the experimenter. During the discussion, the confederates either treated the subject normally or ignored her, showing a lack of interest in what she said and changing the subject whenever she spoke. The subjects who were ignored found the conversations distressing; they felt very unhappy and even gave themselves poor ratings. Being ignored is a form of negative evaluation by other people, and it exerts a powerful effect.

Familiarity

We have learned that attractiveness plays an important role in social influence. Fortunately for the majority of us who are not especially beautiful or handsome, the variable of exposure also influences people's attitudes toward others. The more frequent the exposure, the more positive the attitude is.

In order for an attachment to form between people, they must meet each other. Festinger, Schachter, and Back (1950) found that the likelihood of friendships between people who lived in an apartment house was related to the distance between the apartments in which they lived; the closer the apartments, the more likely the friendship was. People were also unlikely to have friends who lived on a different floor unless their apartments were next to a stairway, where they would meet people going up or down the stairs.

Repetition generally increases our preference for a stimulus. This phenomenon applies to people as well. Even in the brief time it takes to participate in an experiment, familiarity affects interpersonal attraction. Saegert, Swap, and Zajonc (1973) had college women participate in an experiment supposedly involving the sense of taste. Groups of two students (all were subjects; no confederates this time) entered booths, where they tasted and rated various liquids. The movements of the subjects from booth to booth were choreographed so that pairs of women were together from zero to ten times. Afterward, the subjects rated their attraction to each of the other people in the experiment. The amount of attraction the subjects felt toward a given person was directly related to the number of interactions they had had—the more interactions they had had with others, the more attracted they were to those persons. (See *Figure 15.11.*)

Similarity

Another factor that influences interpersonal attraction is similarity—similarity in looks, interests, and attitudes. Couples tend to be similar in attractiveness. In fact, couples who are mismatched in this respect are the most likely to break up (White, 1980). Although we might think that people would seek the most attractive partners that they could find, people tend to fear rejection and ridicule. Men especially tend to be afraid of approaching attractive women (Bernstein et al., 1983).

Couples (and groups of friends) also tend to hold similar opinions. Presumably, a person who shares our opinions is likely to approve of us when we express them. Also, having friends who have similar opinions guarantees that our opinions are likely to find a consensus; we will not often find ourselves in the unpleasant position of saying something that brings disapproval from other people.

interpersonal attraction People's tendency to approach each other and to evaluate each other positively.

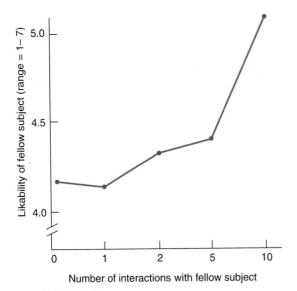

Figure 15.11

Familiarity, exposure, and attraction. The rated likability of a fellow subject as a function of number of interactions.

(Based on data from Saegert, S.C., Swap, W., and Zajonc, R.B. Exposure, context, and interpersonal attraction. Journal of Personality and Social Psychology, *1973, 25, 234–242.)*

Similarity of attitudes is not the only factor determining the strength of interpersonal attraction. Other kinds of similarities are also important, such as age, occupational status, and ethnic background. Friends tend to have similar backgrounds as well as similar attitudes.

Physical Appearance

We judge people by the characteristic that is supposed to be only skin deep—in general, we are more attracted to good-looking people than to unattractive people (Albright, Kenny, and Malloy, 1988). Social reinforcement provides a likely explanation for this phenomenon. Someone who is seen in the company of an attractive person and is obviously favored by this person is likely to be well regarded by other people.

Walster et al. (1966) studied the effects of physical appearance at a dance at which college students were paired by a computer. Midway through the evening, the experimenters asked the subjects to rate the attraction they felt toward their partners and to say whether they thought they would like to see them in the future. For both sexes, the only characteristic that correlated with attraction was physical appearance. Intelligence, grades, and personality variables seemed to have no significant effect.

When people first meet someone who is good looking, they rate the person as probably holding attitudes similar to their own and tend to assume that he or she has a good personality, a successful marriage, and high occupational status (Dion, Berscheid, and Walster, 1972). In fact, physically attractive people usually *do* possess many of these characteristics, probably because they receive favorable treatment from society (Hatfield and Sprecher, 1986).

However, among same-sex individuals, physical appearance may have its drawbacks—especially if members of the other sex are involved. For example, consider a study in which females were shown photos of the same woman dressed either casually or provocatively and either talking or not talking to a man in the presence of his female companion (Baenninger, Baenninger, and Houle, 1993). The female subjects rated the "other woman" in the photos more negatively when she was provocatively dressed than when she was casually dressed. Thus, we seem to take into account the particular circumstances under which we meet another person—his or her gender and the other people who may be present—when making judgments about that person and his or her attractiveness.

Evaluating Scientific Issues

Does Love Thrive on Adversity?

People may become attracted to one another under almost any circumstances. Hollywood often idealizes romantic relationships by showing us how they unfold under optimal conditions—two people in an idyllic setting, they hit it off, and end up in a relationship. But we all know that in real life, attraction between people isn't quite this easy. Sometimes this sort of interpersonal attraction occurs under just the opposite conditions. As Walster and Berscheid (1971) have put it, "Passion sometimes develops in conditions that would seem more likely to provoke aggression and hatred" (p. 47). How is it that love can spring forth from a less-than-optimal beginning?

■ Anxiety, Reinforcement, and Interpersonal Attraction

Consider a study conducted by Dutton and Aron (1974), who had an attractive young woman interview male college students as they walked across a suspension bridge spanning a gorge 280 feet deep. The bridge was 5 feet wide and 450 feet long and swayed and wobbled as they walked across it. The same woman interviewed control subjects on a more conventional, sturdy bridge spanning a ten-foot drop. The interviewer gave her telephone number to all subjects with the suggestion that they call her if they wanted to discuss the experiment further.

The men who were interviewed on the suspension bridge appeared to find the woman more attractive than did those who were interviewed on the ordinary bridge—they were much more likely to telephone her later. These results suggest that the anxiety produced by walking across the suspension bridge increased the men's attraction toward the woman. Dutton and Aron (1974) explained their findings using attribution theory: A man experiences increased arousal in the presence of a woman; he attributes it to the most obvious stimulus—the woman—and concludes that he is attracted to her. Later, he acts on this conclusion by telephoning her.

Arousal—pleasant or aversive—tends to increase interpersonal attraction between men and women, even if they hold dissimilar attitudes (McClanahan et al., 1990). For example, Rubin (1973) noted that couples of mixed religious background reported stronger degrees of romantic love. Presumably, the conflict that followed their choice of each other (especially with other family members) provided arousal that strengthened their mutual attraction. Similarly, an ancient Roman expert advised men to take their women to the Coliseum to see the gladiators fight because the experience would increase their romantic ardor.

■ An Alternative Explanation

Kenrick and Cialdini (1977) suggested that misattributed arousal was not the best explanation for why anxiety and fear increase interpersonal attraction. A person who is standing on a swaying suspension bridge most likely can identify the source of his or her arousal. Most people have better insight into the source of their emotions than Dutton and Aron assumed. If the subjects had correctly attributed their arousal to the bridge, they would not have needed to attribute it to the woman standing on it. Furthermore, a person who is present in an aversive situation does not inevitably become an aversive stimulus by association.

Consider what happened to the subjects. They started walking across the swaying bridge and met a calm, attractive young woman who stopped them and asked them to participate in an experiment. They spent several minutes talking with her, then continued on their way. Probably, this encounter *reduced* rather than increased their fear. The woman seemed calm and reassuring and accustomed to standing on the bridge. Because a stimulus that reduces anxiety becomes a reinforcer, the men's increased attraction toward the woman can be accounted for in terms of social reinforcement, not misattribution. The woman's presence

was noteworthy because it was associated with reduction of fear. You will remember from Chapter 5 that the reduction of an aversive stimulus, such as anxiety, serves as a negative reinforcer.

A further study by Dutton and Aron (1974) demonstrated that the presence of another person can, indeed, reduce anxiety. The experimenters led male subjects to expect to receive a weak electrical shock, a strong and painful electrical shock, or no shock. During a delay period, some subjects waited alone; others waited with a young woman. The subjects who were expecting a shock reported more attraction to the woman than did those who were not expecting a shock. Subjects who waited with the woman also reported less anxiety than did the subjects who had waited alone. That the woman's presence decreased the subjects' arousal provides support for the negative reinforcement hypothesis.

Interpersonal attraction is very complex. It develops under many different conditions—not always under ideal conditions and not just when one person helps reduce the other's fear or anxiety. In between these two extremes lies a vast middle ground, which awaits more research. As we will see next, there is also much to learn about how interpersonal attraction is transformed into love.

Loving

The relationships we have with others are generally marked by two different kinds of emotion: **liking**, a feeling of personal regard, intimacy, and esteem toward another person, and **loving**, a combination of liking and a deep sense of at-

Growing older need not be a barrier to interpersonal attraction.

liking   A feeling of personal regard, intimacy, and esteem toward another person.

loving   A combination of liking and a deep sense of attachment to, intimacy with, and caring for another person.

Table 15.3

Sternberg's Theory of Love

According to Sternberg, love is based on different combinations of intimacy, passion, and commitment. These elements may combine to form eight different kinds of relationships.

	Intimacy	Passion	Commitment
Nonlove			
Liking	*****		
Infatuated love		*****	
Empty love			*****
Romantic love	*****	*****	
Compassionate love	*****		*****
Fatuous love		*****	*****
Consummate love	*****	*****	*****

(*Source:* After Sternberg, R.J. A triangular theory of love. *Psychological Bulletin*, 1986, *93*, 119–135.)

*****indicates that element is present in the relationship; a blank space (   ) indicates that element is not present or present in low quantities in the relationship.

tachment to another person. Loving someone does not necessarily entail romance. You may have several close friends whom you love dearly yet have no desire to be involved with romantically.

Romantic love, also called **passionate love**, is an emotionally intense desire for sexual union with another person (Hatfield, 1988). Feeling romantic love generally involves experiencing five closely intertwined elements: a desire for intimacy with another, feeling passion for that person, being preoccupied with thoughts of that person, developing feelings of emotional dependence on that person, and feeling wonderful if that person feels romantic love toward you and dejected if not.

"Falling in love" and "being in love" are common expressions that people use to describe their passionate desires for one another. Passionate love may occur at almost any time during the life cycle, although people involved in long-term cohabitation or marriages seem to experience a qualitatively different kind of love. The partners may still make passionate love to one another, but passion is no longer the defining characteristic of the relationship. This kind of love is called **companionate love** and is characterized by a deep, enduring affection and caring for another. Companionate love is also marked by a mutual sense of *commitment*, or a strong desire to maintain the relationship. How passionate love develops into companionate love is presently an unanswered question,

although odds are that the sort of intimacy that punctuates romantic love is still a major force in the relationship. An important feature of intimacy is *self-disclosure*, or the ability to share deeply private feelings and thoughts with another. Indeed, part of loving another is feeling comfortable sharing deeply personal aspects of yourself with that person.

Robert Sternberg (1988) has developed a theory of how intimacy, passion, and commitment may combine to produce liking and several different forms of love. (See *Table 15.3.*) According to this theory, liking involves only intimacy, infatuation involves only passion, and empty love involves only commitment. Combining any two of these elements produces still other kinds of love. Romantic love entails both intimacy and passion but no commitment. Companionate love entails both intimacy and commitment but no passion. Fatuous love (a kind of loved marked by complacency in the relationship) entails both passion and commitment but no intimacy. The highest form of love, consummate love, contains all three elements.

passionate love (also called romantic love) An emotional, intense desire for sexual union with another person.

companionate love Love that is characterized by a deep, enduring affection and caring for another person, accompanied by a strong desire to maintain the relationship.

As this Rajasthani woman from India and Samburu tribesman from Kenya clearly demonstrate, the norms for attractiveness vary from culture to culture.

Sternberg's theory, of course, is descriptive. It characterizes different kinds of love, but it does not explain the origins of love. What function has love served in the evolution of our species? The answer can be summed up very succinctly: procreation and childrearing. Although love of any kind for another person is not a necessary requirement for sexual intercourse, a man and a woman who passionately love each other are more likely to have sex than are a man and a woman who do not. And if their union produces a child, then love serves another function—it increases the likelihood that both parents will share in the responsibilities of childrearing. Our capacity for loving, then, contributes in very practical ways to the continued existence of our species.

Biology and Culture

Evolution, Interpersonal Attraction, and Love

Are you married? If not, are you interested in marriage? You may not be married now, and you may not be interested in getting married, at least right away. But chances are that one day the "right" person will come along, you will fall in love with that person, get married, and perhaps have children. What will that person be like—what makes this person right for you?

An answer to this question may be found in sociobiological research, which, as you may recall from Chapter 3, is the study of the biological basis of social behavior. Sociobiological theory predicts that gender makes a difference in what people find attractive in their potential mates. Gender matters because males and females differ in their "investments" in reproduction and childrearing.

As we learned in Chapter 3, the costs of sexual behavior and reproduction are higher for women than for men (Kenrick et al., 1993). Sociobiologists argue that due to this difference, natural selection has favored different mating strategies for men and for women. Because male reproductive success rests on mating with fertile females, men seek potential mates who are reproductively capable (Buss, 1992). But there is a problem here—how can males tell if a female is fertile? As Buss (1989) and Symons (1979) have argued, males should prefer younger females to older ones because age is highly correlated with female fertility. And a clue to a woman's age is her physical attractiveness: smooth skin, absence of gray hair, girlish figure, white teeth, and high energy level (Buss, 1992). Thus, in their quest to find a mate, males place a premium on physical attractiveness.

In contrast, because female reproductive success is dependent on her investment of biological resources, women seek potential mates who can provide other types of resources, such as food, shelter, protection, and, in general, social and economic resources. And how can a female tell if a potential mate has and is willing to provide these resources? Sociobiologists assert that her best clues will be primarily the man's socioeconomic status and, to a lesser extent, his ability to work hard, his intelligence, and his kindness (Buss, 1992; Kenrick et al., 1994).

Research has shown that men do place a greater emphasis on physical attractiveness than do females and that women stress social status more than do men in evaluating potential mates. For example, in a cross-cultural study, Buss (1990) asked people from thirty-seven different cultures to assess which characteristics they found most desirable in a mate. Males from all cultures ranked physical attractiveness higher than females did, and females in thirty-six of the thirty-seven cultures placed a greater emphasis on socioeconomic status than males did. These results confirm earlier findings showing that the physical attractiveness of a woman is a better predictor of the socioeconomic status of her husband than is her intelligence, education, or wealth (Elder, 1969). Buss's cross-cultural data also support the sociobiological prediction that males will prefer younger women: The mean age difference between males and females on their wedding days was 2.99 years—with the bride being younger.

Buss has also shown that these tendencies translate into actual differences in the judgments people make about the effectiveness of the tactics men and women use to attract potential mates (Buss, 1988, 1992). Males use tactics involving displays of their resources—flashing money, taking their dates to fancy restaurants for dinner, and driving expensive cars—whereas females use tactics that enhance their physical attractiveness—dieting, wearing makeup, and wearing flattering clothing.

These differences in the importance assigned to physical attractiveness and socioeconomic status between men and women in mate selection also turn out to have an important effect on how people evaluate their partners in existing relationships. Consider a recent study conducted by Kenrick et al. (1994). Nearly 400 male and female college students involved in heterosexual dating relationships viewed photographs and read accompanying descriptions of people of the other sex. The subjects were told that they were helping the researchers improve the format for a university-sponsored dating service. In actuality, the researchers wished to learn how viewing the photographs of the members of the opposite sex and reading the accompanying descriptions of these persons would influence the subjects' perceptions of their current dating partners.

The persons depicted in the photographs were either highly attractive professional models or rather average-looking college students. The descriptions accompanying

the photographs were similar; they varied only according to a score on a personality test of dominance, defined by the experimenters as representing the person's natural leadership abilities. Subjects were told that a high dominance score meant that the person in the photograph was "authoritative and masterful" and that a low score meant that the person was "obedient and submissive." The photographs and descriptions were ordered to produce four combinations: physically attractive and high in dominance; physically attractive and low in dominance; average-looking and high in dominance; and average-looking and low in dominance.

Kenrick and his colleagues found clear gender differences in how their subjects evaluated their current dating relationships. (See *Figure 15.12*.) Compared to males who saw the photographs of average-looking women, males shown the photographs of physically attractive women rated their current dating relationships less favorably when the women were described as being low in dominance. (Physically attractive, dominant women had no effect on the males' evaluations of their current dating relationships.) In contrast, females who viewed photographs of dominant men—be they average-looking or handsome—tended to rate their current dating relationships as being less satisfactory than did women who viewed photographs of the men described as being low in dominance. Recall, though, that females are not totally insensitive to the influence of physical attractiveness on their social behavior. In some cases, females tend to evaluate physically attractive females negatively because those women appear to pose a threat to a heterosexual relationship (Baenninger et al., 1993).

Evolution, then, has selectively shaped social cognition—how we attend to, perceive, interpret, and respond to information in our social environment. The shaping process has been influenced by whether one is a male or a female because each gender makes different contributions to courtship and childrearing. Our attraction to members of the opposite sex and our choice of a mate do not occur by chance. Although chance and circumstance may determine where we live and the people we meet, our evolutionary history has provided the social and cognitive mechanisms for being attracted to, and falling in love with, the "right" person.

Interim Summary

Interpersonal Attraction and Loving

Although the factors that influence interpersonal attraction are complex and not yet fully understood, they all appear to involve social reinforcement. People learn to act in ways that reinforce friends and lovers in order to maintain

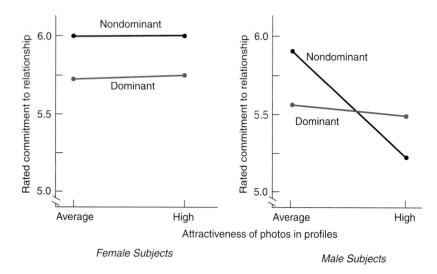

Figure 15.12

Results of Kenrick et al.'s study of sex, dominance, and physical attractiveness on evaluations of current dating relationships. Males shown photographs of physically attractive, nondominant women rated their commitments to their current dating relationships low. Women who viewed photographs of dominant men, regardless of the men's physical attractiveness, rated their commitments to their current dating relationships low.

(From Kenrick, D.T., Neuberg, S.L., Zierk, K. L., and Krones, J.M. Evolution and social cognition: Contrast effects as a function of sex, dominance, and physical attractiveness. Personality and Social Psychology Bulletin, *1994, 20, 210–217.)*

and strengthen their ties with them. Attraction is increased by positive evaluation of oneself by the other person, familiarity, similarity, shared opinions, and physical good looks.

Attribution also undoubtedly plays an important role in interpersonal attraction. For example, our beliefs about why other people act as they do affect how much we like them and are attracted to them. Early research seemed to indicate that anxiety could influence interpersonal attraction through the attribution process. Yet a careful analysis suggests that the reason romantic bonds can be strengthened by adversity involves negative reinforcement. The presence of another person makes an unpleasant situation more tolerable, and this reduction in strength of an aversive stimulus is reinforcing.

Loving someone entails a combination of liking and strong feelings of attachment. Sternberg's theory of love describes how different combinations of intimacy, passion, and commitment give rise to liking and to different kinds of love. For example, romantic love involves both intimacy and passion, but infatuation involves only passion.

From an evolutionary standpoint, love serves both procreative and childrearing functions. Sociobiologists have observed that men and women differ with respect to the social-cognitive cues they use when selecting potential mates. Men prefer potential mates to be young and physically attractive because young, attractive women tend to be fertile. Women prefer potential mates to control socioeconomic resources because these resources are important to supporting the family unit.

Thought Questions

- To what kinds of persons are you most attracted? What factors, dispositional or situational, appear to be the most important in the relationships you have?

- Is Sternberg's theory of love an accurate account of your own experience with different kinds of love? Are there kinds of love that you have experienced that are not included in his theory?

Suggestions for Further Reading

Baron, R.A., and Byrne, D. *Social Psychology: Understanding Human Interaction,* 7th ed. Boston: Allyn and Bacon, 1994.

This excellent and very readable text describes all aspects of social psychology.

Ross, L., and Nisbett, R.E. *The Person and the Situation: Perspectives of Social Psychology.* New York: McGraw-Hill, 1991.

This book describes the variables that influence our causal attributions and the interaction between persons and situations.

Smith, P.B., and Bond, M.H. *Social Psychology Across Cultures: Analysis and Perspectives.* Boston: Allyn and Bacon, 1994.

This short paperback presents cross-cultural perspectives on many of the topics discussed in the chapter. The book is written clearly and contains interesting insights into how cultural variables influence social behavior.

Cialdini, R.B. *Influence: Science and Practice,* 3rd ed. New York: Harper-Collins, 1993.

Cialdini's book is written for a general audience. It provides a fascinating, well-written, and often humorous account of the ways people influence each other.

Milgram, S. *Obedience to Authority.* New York: Harper & Row, 1974.

In this book, Milgram explains his rationale for conducting his controversial obedience research, describes in detail the research itself, and, finally, ponders its significance in light of moral and ethical considerations.

Barkow, J. H., Cosmides, L., and Tooby, J. (eds.). *The Adapted Mind: Evolutionary Psychology and the Generation of Culture.* New York: Oxford University Press, 1992.

This graduate-level text presents the case for the role of evolution in shaping cultural practices. Topics discussed include cooperation, mate selection, child-care, and language use.

Chapter 16

Life-Style, Stress, and Health

Chapter Outline

Cultural Evolution: Life-Style Choices and Consequences

Our life-styles have been shaped by environmental changes influenced by cultural evolution and our biology. Life-styles significantly affect individual survival.

Healthy and Unhealthy Life-Styles

Nutrition • Physical Fitness • Cigarette Smoking • Drinking Alcoholic Beverages • Sexually Transmitted Diseases and AIDS • *Biology and Culture: Cultural Reactions to Contagious Diseases* • Personal Safety: Using Seat Belts

In the long run, healthy behaviors enhance longevity and quality of life. Unhealthy behaviors, such as eating poorly, smoking, excessive use of alcohol, practicing unsafe sex, and not wearing seat belts while riding in a vehicle tend to affect our lives negatively in the long run but can affect them "positively" in the short run. Unhealthy behaviors are acquired and maintained because of their immediately reinforcing effects. Cultural reactions to persons with life-threatening contagious diseases are the result of powerful societal and psychological variables.

Unhealthy Life-Styles Are Preventable: Self-Control

We are often faced with a choice between an immediate, small reward and a delayed, but larger reward. Prior commitment to a course of action that allows us to obtain the delayed but larger reward constitutes self-control.

Stress and Health

The Biological Basis of Stress • Cognitive Appraisal and Stress • Stressful Life-Styles and Impaired Health • *Evaluating Scientific Issues: Is There a Cancer-Prone Personality?*

Our responses to stressful stimuli are governed by the autonomic nervous system, which produces changes in the activity of many organs, and by our perception of the extent to which a stimulus poses a threat to our physical or psychological well-being. Prolonged stress can lead to chronic heart disease, a breakdown of the immune system, which increases our susceptibility to infectious diseases, and, in some cases, an anxiety disorder called posttraumatic stress disorder. Personality variables, especially those involved in coping with stress, appear to be related to the development of cancer.

Coping with Everyday Stress

Sources of Stress • Coping Styles and Strategies • Stress Inoculation Training

Stress can be caused by a wide variety of sources—positive experiences as well as negative ones. The levels of stress that we experience can be controlled by the use of specific coping strategies. Stress inoculation training is a form of stress management that teaches people how to develop and implement effective coping strategies for handling stressful situations before they occur.

I spotted his pickup out of the corner of my eye. I hit the brakes and took a quick turn into the undeveloped cul-de-sac and pulled up alongside it.

There he was—asleep in the cab, a cooler full of beer beside him, several empties on the floor, and a half-drunk bottle propped between his legs. I woke him up. He was not happy to see me.

He looked at me through glazed-over eyes and told me, in colorful language, to leave and get out of his life. He clumsily opened the door and stumbled out of the truck. He reached behind him, grabbed the cooler of beer, turned around, and flung it to the ground. The cooler exploded and beer, ice, glass, and chunks of Styrofoam ricocheted onto both of us.

He stood there staring at me. I could see the tears welling up in his eyes. He started to cry. "Why do I do this—what makes me keep doing this?"

"That's a good question, Rick. C'mon, let's get you home," I replied.

I helped him into my car. He was asleep again before I could finish buckling him in.

As I drove him home, I thought about the question he had asked me—why does he keep getting drunk? It was hard for me to believe that this was the same person I had met only two years before. He had shown up in the doorway of a house I was building, paint roller in hand. He introduced himself to me and told me to put him to work. I did, and ever since then we had been close friends. In fact, our families became close—for a while we did almost everything together—eating dinner, camping, going to ball games, and spending holidays with each other.

But Rick's drinking soon ended all this. He began getting drunk on the job and in front of his children. For several months, he seemed to be drunk all the time. Up to this point, Rick had been one of the most successful residential building contractors in town. But a string of missed appointments, poor financial decisions, and unsupervised work crews took their inevitable toll. His wife tried desperately to save the business, but it was too late. He was forced to file for bankruptcy—he was nearly 3 million dollars in the red. He and his family lost their house, their car, and many friends. Rick was eventually forced to leave town, humiliated and broke.

As I look back on it now, I can see that he had become trapped in a vicious circle. When the pressure mounted at work, he would drink. As he drank more, the pressure intensified. Soon he was drinking every day, all day. He drank to relieve stress, not realizing that his drinking created more stress, until that's all he experienced—stress and drunkenness.

Time and again throughout this book, we have seen that human behavior and thought are the result of the *interaction* of biological and environmental variables. Psychology encompasses the study of this interaction and the application of the resulting knowledge to improving our lives. In this chapter, I wish to emphasize these points again with issues that may be closer to home for you—personal behaviors that have serious implications for your long-term physical health and your psychological well-being. The central theme of this chapter is that the particular behaviors that make up an individual's *life-style* have important consequences for that person's *quality of life*. As we saw in the story of Rick in the opening vignette, these consequences go beyond the individual; they also affect the lives and life-styles of others by changing the environment in which they live.

We will look first at how cultural evolution shapes our lives, especially in terms of the sorts of life-style choices we make. Next, we will study these choices as they relate to our personal health and safety. We will also discuss stress, its biological and psychological effects, and how to cope with it.

Cultural Evolution: Life-Style Choices and Consequences

Cultural evolution is a culture's adaptive change to recurrent environmental pressures. Unlike biological evolution, which is driven by biological forces, cultural evolution is driven mainly by psychological forces. Cultural evolution is a product of human intellect and physical capacity, both of which have strong genetic components. As you may recall from Chapter 3, cultural evolution has been the guiding force behind social, cultural, and technical innovation in such areas as law, the arts, science, medicine, and engineering. As a culture faces new problems, solutions are proposed and tested. Solutions that work are passed from generation to generation through imitation, books, oral histories, and, most recently, in electronic forms—bits of information stored on computer chips. Some solutions are modified by future generations so they work more effectively. Those that don't work are abandoned.

Consider the evolution of the computer over the past forty years. The first computers were cumbersome machines about the size of a large room and used mostly for the purpose of "crunching numbers"—literally computing. Today's computers are sleek machines many times smaller with numerous applications for solving problems in any field of endeavor and are central to the recording and transmission of information throughout the world. Computers are so prevalent because they are useful in helping people work more efficiently and productively. Early computer systems that were less efficient are no longer present; they have been replaced with more functional ones.

For our species, cultural evolution has been the primary agent involved in shaping **life-style**, the aggregate behavior of a person, or the way a person leads his or her life. The ways that we interact with others, the kinds of work we pursue, the hobbies and personal interests we enjoy, the habits we develop, and the decision to marry and raise a family or remain single are characteristics of our life-styles.

For our prehistoric ancestors, life-style was pretty much the same for everyone. When they were hungry, they hunted and gathered food; they walked or ran to get from one place to another; they worked hard to stay alive. Options about how to accomplish these tasks arose only as the pace of cultural evolution increased. That is, our ancestors learned more about creating more effective means of transportation, growing and storing food, and building homes from durable materials. Today, there is no predominant life-style; cultural evolution has afforded us the luxury of choosing from among many alternatives. We can hunt or gather food if we want, but we can also buy it in grocery stores or go to restaurants. When we want to go somewhere, we can walk or run, but more often we ride on planes, trains, and automobiles. Most of us in Western cultures no longer worry only about how to stay alive; we now worry about how to spend our spare time. Grocery stores, transportation, medicine, and leisure time are innovations spawned through cultural evolution.

The net result of cultural evolution is that we enjoy a much higher standard of living than did our prehistoric or even our relatively modern ancestors. However, cultural evolution has also produced threats to our health and safety. People can be hit and killed by cars and trucks. The manufacture of foods and other goods contributes to pollution, which may

Cultural evolution affords us many choices in matters related to our survival. Although most of us prefer to buy our food at the supermarket, some people prefer to pick their food fresh from the field.

cause disease. Chemical agents we use for lubrication and cleaning are poisonous. We must personally avoid these threats or risk injury or death.

Often the consequences of particular aspects of contemporary life-styles can threaten an individual's survival. For example, the amount and kinds of food we eat and excessive use of alcohol can lead to illness and, in some cases, premature death. In contrast, a healthy life-style can be viewed as one that ensures an individual's physical and psychological well-being. Typically, it includes, among other things, a nutritious diet, regular exercise, no use of tobacco, moderate use of alcohol, practice of safe sex, and even using seat belts in automobiles.

An unhealthy life-style tends to diminish an individual's physical and psychological well-being. An important question to raise, then, is, How and why are unhealthy life-styles acquired and maintained? After all, they appear to work against the process of natural selection. The answer to this question is a complicated one, so I will offer only a general response here. Although the consequences of life-style behaviors have obvious negative *biological* implications, the behaviors themselves are acquired and maintained by both *biological* and *psychological* factors.

It is easy to misinterpret biological evolutionary theory and argue that genes that give rise to unhealthy life-styles should eventually become extinct. Remember that natural selection operates on traits that affect the ability to reproduce. Most adaptations resulting from biological evolution concern only those relevant to surviving to sexual maturity, reproduc-

cultural evolution The adaptive change of a culture to recurrent environmental pressures.

life-style The aggregate behavior of a person; the way a person leads his or her life.

ing, and rearing offspring until they become self-sufficient. Many, if not most, of the consequences of unhealthy life-styles—heart disease, cancer, and the other negative effects of poor nutrition, alcoholism, and smoking—do not appear until people are well beyond reproductive age. Thus, there cannot be much selection against genes that promote unhealthy life-styles in biological evolution.

In addition, the law of effect (see Chapter 5) plays a powerful role in cultural evolution. In fact, its role in cultural evolution appears to be analogous to the role of natural selection in biological evolution. The law of effect states that behaviors that produce favorable consequences tend to be repeated and those that produce unfavorable consequences tend not to be repeated. Cultural practices and customs that result in reinforcement tend to be maintained, if not elaborated. Exercising, eating nutritious foods, getting sufficient rest, and other healthy behaviors are acquired and maintained because of the reinforcing consequences enjoyed by the people who practice them. But if unhealthy life-styles have negative consequences, how does the law of effect come into play?

The problem is that many of the behaviors involved in unhealthy life-styles have *reinforcing consequences in the short run* and *damaging consequences in the long run*. Many unhealthy behaviors are maintained because they tend to be available on a phony version of revolving credit—instead of "buy now, pay later," it takes the form of "enjoy now, suffer later." The teenager who puffs on a cigarette is receiving immediate rewards—physiological and psychological pleasure and perhaps the perception that he is cool. It is only many years later, when he is in his forties or fifties, that the life-threatening effects of smoking may appear. In the meantime, he has become physiologically addicted to the nicotine contained in the cigarette smoke. The law of effect actually works to our disadvantage in this case and partially accounts for why cultural evolution is tolerant of those who adopt unhealthy life-styles.

Interim Summary

Cultural Evolution: Life-Style Choices and Consequences

Our life-styles—the ways we interact with others; the kinds of work, hobbies, habits, and personal interests we pursue; and our decision to marry or remain single—are the results of the cumulative effects of cultural evolution on our society. Cultural evolution includes advances in technology and medicine and changes in social and cultural customs that are passed from one generation to the next. Although cultural evolution has improved our standard of living relative to that of our ancestors, it has also produced threats to our health and safety. These threats manifest themselves in particular life-style choices we make regarding our diet, physical activ-

> **coronary heart disease (CHD)**   The narrowing of blood vessels that supply nutrients to the heart.

ity, use of tobacco, alcohol and other drugs, sexual behavior, and personal safety.

Biological evolution cannot weed out individuals who adopt unhealthy life-styles because the consequences of living these life-styles are not usually felt until after people have passed their childbearing years. Many of the consequences of unhealthy behaviors are reinforcing in the short run but life-threatening in the long run. Thus, unhealthy behaviors are acquired and maintained because of their immediately reinforcing effects. It is usually only after many years that the cumulative negative effects of these life-styles threaten one's health.

Thought Questions

- What kinds of life-style choices have you made? Have they been generally healthy ones or unhealthy ones? What personal, social, and cultural factors influenced you to make the decisions you have?
- How has the law of effect operated in life-style decisions you have made? Can you explain some of your habits—good, bad, or otherwise—in terms of their immediately reinforcing effects? If you have an unhealthy habit, and you know it is unhealthy, why do you continue to engage in it? What steps might you take to break this habit?

Healthy and Unhealthy Life-Styles

A healthy life-style, you will recall, is one that enhances an individual's well-being—both physical and psychological—and an unhealthy life-style is one that diminishes physical and psychological well-being. Let's look at several elements that affect well-being: nutrition, physical fitness, tobacco use, alcohol abuse, sexual practices, and personal safety.

Nutrition

Until very recently, our species lived on a low-fat, high-fiber diet. Our ancestors lived mainly on fruits, vegetables, nuts, and lean meats. In the last 150 years or so, though, our diets have changed; they are now considerably higher in fats and lower in fiber, largely because of the consumption of processed foods, fried foods, and sweets. Although we eat foods like bananas, broccoli, and lean beef, we also consume foods like hot fudge sundaes, doughnuts, and fried chicken. Diets too high in saturated fats (those fats found in animal products and a few vegetable oils) and too low in fiber have been linked with specific health disorders, such as **coronary heart disease (CHD)**, the narrowing of blood vessels that

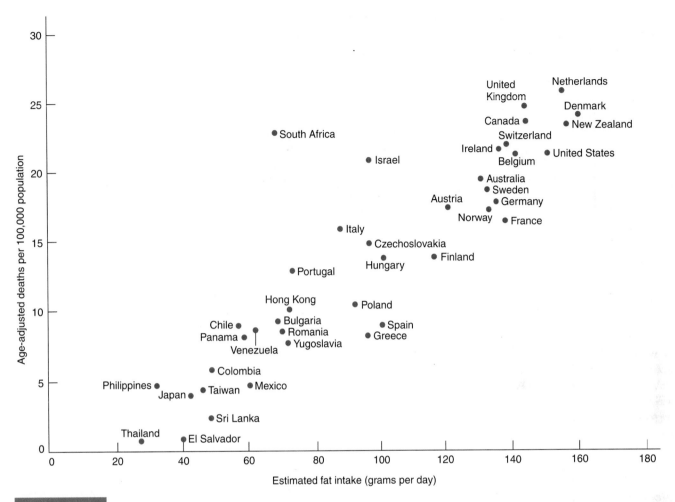

Figure 16.1

The correlation between diet and breast cancer. Nations whose citizens live on diets rich in fats face increased risk of death due to breast cancer.

(Adapted from Cohen, L.A. Diet and cancer. Scientific American, *1987, 42–48.)*

supply nutrients to the heart, and **cancer**, a malignant and intrusive tumor that destroys body organs and tissue (Cohen, 1987). CHD is the leading cause of death among people living in Western nations (Light and Girdler, 1993), and cancer is not far behind.

The chief culprit in CHD is **serum cholesterol**, a chemical that occurs naturally in the bloodstream, where it serves as a detoxifier. Cholesterol is also the source of lipid membranes of cells and steroid hormones. Thus, it is a vital substance; we would die without it. Cholesterol has two important forms: *HDL* (high-density lipoprotein) and *LDL* (low-density lipoprotein). HDL is sometimes called "good" cholesterol because high levels of it are inversely associated with CHD; it seems to play a protective role in the bloodstream. LDL is often called "bad" cholesterol because high levels of it are associated with the formation of atherosclerotic plaques, which clog arteries. Fiber is an important dietary component because it helps reduce LDL cholesterol levels (fiber also aids in digestion).

L. A. Cohen (1987) has shown that cultures having the highest death rates due to breast cancer are those whose citizens tend to consume relatively large amounts of fats. Figure 16.1 shows the correlation between death due to breast cancer and daily fat consumption for forty countries. As you can see, people in countries such as Canada and the United States have both a relatively high fat intake and relatively high death rates due to breast cancer. (See *Figure 16.1.*) In contrast, people in countries such as Japan and Thailand have both relatively low fat intake and relatively low death rates due to breast cancer. These data are correlational, however. They do

cancer A malignant, uncontrolled growth of cells that destroys surrounding tissue.

serum cholesterol A fat-like chemical found in the blood. One form (LDL) promotes the formation of atherosclerotic plaques. Another form (HDL) may protect against coronary heart disease.

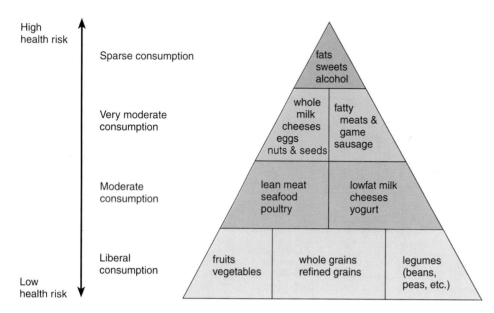

Figure 16.2

Fat, fiber, and health. Consuming foods low in fat but high in fiber contributes to a healthy life-style by reducing the risk of CHD and cancer.

(From Pennington, A.T. Considerations for a new food guide. Journal of Nutrition Education, *1981,* 12, *p. 53. Reprinted by permission.)*

not prove that high fat intake causes breast cancer, but they certainly suggest that such a possibility exists.

Nutrition plays an important role in good health and is pivotal to a healthy life-style. Based on Cohen's work, we would seem likely to decrease our risk for both CHD and cancer by *choosing* to eat low-fat, high-fiber foods. Which foods are low in fat but high in fiber? Figure 16.2 provides the answer by showing the classes of foods in increasing order of the health risk they pose. (See *Figure 16.2.*)

But many of our favorite foods are high-fat, low-fiber foods. The immediate effect of eating these foods is to delight the palate, but in the long run, a more serious consequence may occur: poor health, obesity, and possibly even death. Why might we prefer high-fat foods and sweets? In the past, our ancestors who faced starvation would be best served by eating fat, which provides the highest caloric values. In addition, sweet tastes usually indicate that food is safe, not poisonous. Thus, preferences for high-fat foods and for sweets was adaptive. These preferences have been passed genetically along to us, although because our living conditions differ from those of our ancestors, they are not always adaptive. For example, to many people, the appeal of glazed doughnuts and other sweet fatty foods is greater than that of more nutritious foods. And in the long run, a diet centered on sweet fatty foods is unhealthy.

Physical Fitness

Not only did our ancestors generally have healthier diets, they were probably also in better physical shape than most of us today. Hunting, gathering, and a nomadic existence ensured plenty of exercise. Most people today lead more sedentary lives. What exercise they get may consist of little more than walking to and from their car several times a day. Like high-

fat, low-fiber diets, lack of exercise is correlated with increased risk of CHD (Peters et al., 1983; Powell et al., 1987). People who exercise regularly appear to accumulate less body fat and to be less vulnerable to the negative effects of stress than are people who do not exercise regularly (Brown, 1991).

According to Ralph Paffenbarger, a noted epidemiologist who has devoted his career to studying CHD and cancer, people who exercise regularly are likely to live longer (Paffenbarger et al., 1986). His evidence comes from a long-term longitudinal study of the life-styles of 17,000 Harvard University alumni. He periodically questioned his subjects, inquiring about their exercise patterns (type of exercise, frequency, and so on) and physical health. Here is a sample of his results:

1. Between 1962 and 1978, 1,413 of the original 17,000 subjects died, 45 percent from CHD and 32 percent from cancer. Significantly more of these deaths occurred in subjects who had led sedentary lives.

2. Alumni who reported that they exercised the equivalent of thirty to thirty-five miles of running or walking per week faced *half* the risk of dying prematurely as that faced by those who reported exercising the equivalent of five or fewer miles per week.

3. On average, those who exercised moderately (an equivalent of twenty miles running or walking per week) lived about two years longer than those who exercised less than the equivalent of five miles.

Of course, these results do not mean that everyone who exercises regularly will live an extra two years. However, because regular exercise reduces high blood pressure, increases lung capacity, and decreases the ratio of bad (LDL) cholesterol to good (HDL) cholesterol, Paffenbarger's results suggest that regular exercise engenders good health.

According to Kenneth Cooper, aerobic exercises such as running, walking, bicycling, and swimming are superior to other forms of exercise for improving cardiovascular health (Cooper, 1968, 1970, 1985). **Aerobic exercises** are those which expend considerable energy, increase blood flow and respiration and thereby stimulate and strengthen the heart and lungs and increase the body's efficiency in using oxygen. According to Cooper (1985), running at least two miles in less than twenty minutes four times a week (or any equivalent aerobic exercise) significantly increases cardiovascular health. One study showed that aerobic exercise had an additional benefit: reduced heart response to mental stress (Kubitz and Landers, 1993). Two groups of students who had not exercised for at least three months prior to the study were divided into two groups. One group rode an exercycle three times a week for forty minutes for eight weeks; the other group did not perform any aerobic exercises. At the end of the eight-week period, both groups were given timed color perception and math tests. Subjects who participated in the aerobic exercise program showed lower absolute heart rates in response to the tests than did the subjects who did not exercise.

Thanks in large part to Cooper's pioneering research, aerobic exercise has become a common activity for millions of people throughout the world. During the early 1970s, jogging and swimming were favorite aerobic exercises for many; during the 1980s and 1990s, bicycling, walking, and aerobic dance became popular. The fact that Cooper's work could have such a profound effect on the everyday activities of people testifies to the power of scientific research in producing positive changes in life-style. In the next section, we will see similar results: Recent research on the hazards of cigarette smoking has helped to reduce the number of people who smoke.

Cigarette Smoking

Although tobacco products have been used in one form or another for many years, we have only recently discovered how harmful they can be to one's health. The Center for Disease Control (1987) reports that about 350,000 premature deaths in the United States each year are related to the use of tobacco. In addition to these health risks, people who use tobacco also face increased risks of bronchitis, emphysema, strokes, and ulcers. We know that the severity of these risks is directly correlated with the amount of carbon monoxide and tars contained in cigarette smoke. We also know that non-smokers who are exposed to air contaminated with cigarette smoke (second-hand smoke) also face increased risks of CHD and cancer (Janerich et al., 1991). Many jurisdictions have reacted to these findings by banning smoking in public places, such as offices, hospitals, grocery stores, restaurants, and classrooms.

Given the strong link between cigarette smoking and increased health risks plus the fact that people today are more knowledgeable about these risks, it is surprising that smoking is still as popular as it is. Table 16.1 shows the prevalence of

In the attempt to influence young people not to use tobacco, some anti-smoking activists have attacked popular cigarette advertisements.

cigarette smoking by age and gender in the United States and Canada. (See *Table 16.1.*) Tobacco use is especially high among families that are employed by the tobacco industry (Noland et al., 1990). Tobacco use is also increasing in Third World countries, such as in Africa and South America—apparently, as the North American market dwindles, tobacco manufacturers are seeking new markets less familiar with the hazards of smoking (McKim, 1991; Ray and Ksir, 1990).

What causes people—especially adolescents—to begin smoking? Psychologists know that both imitation and peer pressure contribute to the acquisition of the smoking habit (Taylor, 1991). For instance, adolescents who have favorable impressions of a smoker are likely to imitate that person's actions, including smoking. Cigarette manufacturers use this knowledge to advertise their products: They portray smoking as a glamorous, mature, independent, and sometimes rebellious behavior. Billboard and magazine advertisements generally portray cigarette smokers as young, healthy, attractive, and exciting persons. Adolescents who try smoking are twice as likely to smoke when they become adults, and seven of ten adolescents who smoke regularly maintain the habit into adulthood (Chassin et al., 1990).

Cigarette smoking, like other forms of drug use, is addictive. To say that a person is addicted to a drug means two things. First, it means that his or her nervous system may have developed a tolerance to the drug (for some drugs, such as cocaine, sensitization, not tolerance, occurs). And second, it means that he or she has become physically dependent on the drug. *Tolerance* simply means that the neurons in the central

aerobic exercises Physical activity that expends considerable energy, increases blood flow and respiration and thereby stimulates and strengthens the heart and lungs and increases the body's efficient use of oxygen.

<table>
<tr><td colspan="5" align="center">**Table 16.1**</td></tr>
</table>

Prevalence of Smoking by Age and Gender According to Percentage of the Population in Canada and the United States

	Canada		United States	
Age Range	Males	Females	Males	Females
20–24	31.4	32.0	31.3	31.9
25–44	35.4	31.4	39.9	32.2
45–64	33.6	25.6	35.7	31.4
Over 65	18.6	11.3	19.8	13.5

Source: Canadian data from McKim, W. *Drugs and Behavior: An Introduction to Behavioral Pharmacology* (2nd Ed.) Englewood Cliffs, NJ: Prentice-Hall, 1991. United States data from Taylor, S.E. *Introduction to Health Psychology.* New York: McGraw-Hill, 1991. Percentages for the 25–44 age range of Americans was derived by averaging over the age ranges 25–34 and 35–44 as provided by Taylor (1991).

nervous system (CNS) respond progressively less and less to the presence of the drug; larger doses of the drug are required to produce the same CNS effects that smaller doses produced earlier. *Physical dependence* means that CNS neurons now require the presence of the drug to function normally. Without the drug in the CNS, the individual will experience *withdrawal symptoms,* or uncomfortable physical conditions, such as sweating, tremors, and anxiety. In addition to tolerance and physical dependence, many drugs, including the nicotine in cigarette smoke, produce *psychological dependence,* a craving to use the drug for its pleasurable effects. In other words, obtaining and using the drug become focal points of an individual's life. You may have been around people who have "needed" a cigarette but were unable to get one at that moment. You likely noticed how getting a cigarette or thoughts of smoking preoccupied their attention. Another, perhaps more objective, way of describing psychological dependence is to say that it involves behavior that is acquired and maintained through positive reinforcement. A reinforcing drug is one that strengthens or maintains the behavior that constitutes seeking, acquiring, and using the drug.

The nicotine contained in cigarette smoke exerts powerful effects on the central nervous system and heart by stimulating postsynaptic receptors sensitive to acetylcholine, a neurotransmitter. This stimulation produces temporary increases in heart rate and blood pressure, decreases in body temperature, changes in hormones released by the pituitary gland, and the release of adrenaline from the adrenal glands. And, in common with all reinforcers, natural and artificial, it also causes dopamine to be secreted in the brain. As we saw in Chapters 4 and 13, the release of dopamine in the brain is reinforcing, so this effect contributes to the maintenance of cigarette smoking. Cigarette smoking may also be maintained by *negative reinforcement.* People who try to quit smoking usu-

ally suffer from withdrawal symptoms, including headaches, insomnia, anxiety, and irritability. These symptoms are relieved by smoking another cigarette. Such negative reinforcement appears to be extremely powerful. Over 60 percent of all smokers have tried to quit smoking at least once, but have lit up again to escape the unpleasant withdrawal symptoms.

Nicotine alone cannot be blamed for the health risks posed by cigarette smoking. These risks are caused by the combination of nicotine with other toxic substances, such as the carbon monoxide and tars found in cigarette smoke. For example, while nicotine causes an increase in heart rate, the carbon monoxide in smoke deprives the heart of the oxygen needed to perform its work properly. The smoker's heart undergoes stress because it is working harder with fewer nutrients than normal. Over a period of years, this continued stress weakens the heart, making it more susceptible to disease than is the heart of a nonsmoker.

Many smokers believe that they can diminish the health risks posed by their habit by switching to low-nicotine cigarettes. Unfortunately, this strategy is undermined by the fact that smokers develop a tolerance to nicotine and typically smoke more low-nicotine cigarettes to make up for the decreased nicotine content of their new brand.

New treatment programs for cigarette smokers have used the "transdermal patch," a round Band-Aid-like patch that allows nicotine to be absorbed through the skin. The patch was developed by a behavioral psychologist, Frank Etscorn. Over several months, the nicotine levels of the patches are reduced, and the individual is weaned from nicotine altogether. So far, success rates are quite high (about 60 percent), and 20 to 30 percent of those who quit still do not smoke after six months. You may think this rate low until you consider that the success rate of helping people quit smoking using other treatment approaches is only about 12 percent (Pomerleau, 1992).

Quitting smoking has both immediate and long-term positive effects, even if the individual has been smoking for a long time. Table 16.2 shows the time frame of the body's recovery from cigarette smoking. (See *Table 16.2.*) Even after as few as twenty minutes have passed since smoking a cigarette, the body begins showing recovery, including a return to normal blood pressure, pulse rate, and body temperature in the extremities. After seventy-two hours, breathing becomes easier, partially because of increased lung capacity. After five years, the risk of death by lung cancer is reduced by almost 50 percent.

Although quitting smoking is a positive change in life-style, it is better never to have started in the first place. (Every year, about 17 million of the 51 million smokers in the United States try to quit.) Psychologists and other health researchers are therefore not only interested in designing treatment programs to help people quit smoking, but also interested in developing prevention programs to help people, especially adolescents, resist the temptation to start smoking. Prevention programs are generally aimed at mitigating social factors such as imitation, peer pressure, and influence from advertisements that can initially induce people to light up (Evans, Raines, and Hanselka, 1984). Such programs involve educating adolescents about the health risks related to cigarette smoking and teaching them how to respond negatively to people who encourage them to smoke.

One Canadian anti-smoking program, the Waterloo Smoking Prevention Project (Flay et al., 1985), has been especially effective in reducing the number of young adolescents who experiment with smoking. Sixth-grade students were first asked to seek out information about smoking and to think about their beliefs regarding smoking. Next, the students were taught about the social pressures involved in smoking and were given explicit training in how to resist those pressures—for example, politely turning down a cigarette when one is offered. This training also included role playing such resistance strategies and asking each student to make a commitment regarding whether they would start smoking or not. The students were monitored five times over the next two years to see how many of them had experimented with smoking. By the end of the two-year period, fewer than 8 percent of the students who had been involved in the prevention program were experimenting with smoking. In contrast, almost 19 percent of the students who had not gone through the program had experimented with smoking. While these results are encouraging, keep in mind that these students were only monitored through seventh grade. Long-term prevention programs have shown that many participants begin experimenting with smoking later on, hinting that occasional "booster" sessions may be necessary to maintain the effects of the initial training (Murray et al., 1989).

Drinking Alcoholic Beverages

The psychological effects of alcohol (and other drugs) have been known to humanity longer than have those of nicotine. Alcohol, for example, has been used for thousands of years for its euphoria-inducing properties.

Alcohol is widely abused today. To abuse a substance means to use it in a way that poses a threat to the safety and well-being of the user, society, or both. Most people who use alcohol do not abuse it, and not all people who abuse alcohol are alcoholics. For example, people who drive under the influence of alcohol pose a serious threat to both themselves and others, but they may not be alcoholics.

Alcoholism is an addiction to ethanol, the psychoactive agent in alcoholic beverages. A psychoactive substance is any substance that affects brain and CNS functioning. In the United States today, there are about 6 million alcoholics and another 14 million people who are considered to be problem drinkers. About two-thirds of the U.S. population consumes alcohol, and about half of all alcohol is consumed by about a tenth of all drinkers (McKim, 1991). Male alcoholics outnumber female alcoholics by a ratio of about four or five to one (Lauer, 1989). Table 16.3 describes some of the physical, psychological, and social consequences of alcohol abuse. (See

---

Table 16.2

The Body's Response to Stopping Cigarette Smoking

Within 20 minutes of last puff
Blood pressure and pulse decrease to normal levels.
Body temperature of extremities increases to normal levels.

Within 1 day
Risk of heart attacks decreases.

Within 2 days
Nerve endings begin regenerating.
Taste and smell acuity increases.

Within 3 days
Breathing becomes easier due to relaxing of bronchial tubes.
Lung capacity increases.

From 2 weeks to 3 months
Blood circulation improves.
Walking and other exercises begin to seem easier.
Lung efficiency increases as much as 30 percent.

After 5 years
Risk of death due to lung cancer decreases by 47 percent.

Source: It's never too late to quit. *Living Well*, 1989, *Vol. IX*, No. 4. Kalamazoo, MI: Bob Hope International Heart Research Institute.

---

alcoholism An addiction to ethanol, the psychoactive agent in alcoholic beverages.

Table 16.3

The Negative Physical, Psychological, and Cultural Consequences of Alcohol Abuse

Physical
Cirrhosis of the liver, which results in death.
Poor nutrition.
Impaired sexual functioning.

Psychological
Gradual deterioration of cognitive functioning.
Increased feelings of anxiety and irritability.
Aggressive behavior.

Cultural
Impaired social skills and interpersonal functioning.
Divorce.
Employee absenteeism and decreased productivity.
Death of approximately 25,000 people a year in alcohol-related traffic accidents.

Table 16.3.) Abusing other drugs, such as cocaine or heroin, produces similar effects.

Because neuronal activity of the brain becomes suppressed and reduces inhibitory controls on behavior when moderate to heavy amounts of alcohol are consumed, individuals become more relaxed and more outgoing, show impaired motor coordination, and have difficulty thinking clearly. As more alcohol is consumed, neuronal activity in the brain is depressed further, producing distortions in perception, slurred speech, memory loss, impaired judgment, and poor control of movement. Unconsciousness and death may result from ingesting large amounts of alcohol over a relatively short period of time.

Once ingested, alcohol is rapidly absorbed from the stomach and intestinal tract. Because alcohol is a small fat- and water-soluble molecule, it is quickly and evenly distributed throughout the body via the circulatory system. Blood alcohol levels are affected by body weight and muscularity. Generally speaking, an obese or muscular individual would have to consume more alcohol than a slender person to attain the same level of intoxication. In addition, regardless of body characteristics, blood levels of alcohol increase more slowly in people who drink on a full stomach than in those having little or no food in their stomachs. Food in the stomach impairs absorption of substances through the gastrointestinal tract.

Inebriation is related to the manner in which alcohol is metabolized by the body. Unlike most other drugs, alcohol is metabolized by the liver at a constant rate, regardless of how much alcohol has been consumed. For example, in one hour, the body will metabolize the alcohol in 12 ounces of beer or 1 ounce of 80 to 100 proof liquor. Hence, if a person consumes more than 12 ounces of beer or 1 ounce of liquor per hour,

his or her blood alcohol level rises beyond that level caused by the first drink, and he or she may begin to become intoxicated. When blood alcohol levels reach 0.3 to 0.4 percent, people lose consciousness, and at 0.5 percent, neurons in the brain that control the respiratory and circulatory systems stop functioning, causing death. Driving under the influence of alcohol is defined in most jurisdictions as a blood alcohol level greater than 0.1 percent.

Although moderate drinkers develop little or no tolerance to alcohol, people who regularly consume large quantities of alcohol usually develop a tolerance. Heavy drinkers often suffer *delirium tremens*—the DTs—a pattern of withdrawal symptoms that includes trembling, irritability, hallucinations, sleeplessness, and confusion when they attempt to quit drinking. In many cases, alcoholics become so physically dependent on the drug that abrupt cessation of drinking produces convulsions and sometimes death.

Although you have probably heard the oft-quoted phrase that "drinking and driving don't mix," you have probably not heard that "drinking and using other drugs don't mix." Drinking and using other drugs can be deadly. Table 16.4 describes some of the dangerous consequences of mixing alcohol with other drugs, including over-the-counter medications. (See *Table 16.4*.)

As you learned in Chapter 3, an individual's tendency to become an alcoholic may have a genetic basis (McKim, 1991). Vaillant and Milofsky (1982), in a long-term study of adopted boys, found that sons of chronic alcoholics had a greater tendency to become alcoholics themselves, despite the fact that their adoptive parents were nonalcoholics. In a more recent study, Cloninger (1987) found that children of alcoholic parents adopted at birth into normal (nonalcoholic) homes were about four times more likely to abuse alcohol than were other adopted children whose biological parents were nonalcoholics. However, although we know that genetics are involved in alcoholism, we are far from understanding its precise role.

As Chapter 12 pointed out, women who drink moderate to heavy quantities of alcohol during pregnancy risk giving birth to children who suffer from symptoms of *fetal alcohol syndrome*. Alcohol crosses the placental barrier and enters the fetal blood supply, where it retards the development of the fetus's nervous system. Fetal alcohol syndrome is characterized by decreased birth weight and physical malformations. It is the third leading cause of birth defects involving mental retardation, but it is also preventable: If a woman does not drink alcohol during her pregnancy, she will not give birth to a child with fetal alcohol syndrome.

The use of alcohol is prompted by the same factors that contribute to a person's starting smoking: imitation and peer pressure. Many young people see drinking as the thing to do because it seemingly represents maturity, independence, and rebelliousness and because it is associated with having fun. For example, in their advertisements, brewers portray people using their products at the end of a hard day's work, at festive parties, and to celebrate special occasions. To their credit,

Table 16.4

The Effects of Mixing Alcohol with Other Drugs

Drug	Example	Possible Consequences of Using Simultaneously with Alcohol
Narcotics	Codeine or Percodan	Increased suppression of CNS functions and possible death due to respiratory failure
Minor pain relievers	Aspirin or Tylenol	Stomach irritation and bleeding; increased likelihood of liver damage from acetaminophen
Antidepressants	Tofranil, Triavil	Increased suppression of CNS functions; drinking some red wines (e.g., Chianti) while using some kinds of antidepressants may produce extremely high blood pressure. May also lead to death due to respiratory failure
Antihistamines	Actifed	Increased drowsiness, making operation of motor vehicles and power equipment more dangerous
CNS stimulants	Caffeine, Dexedrine	Reverses some of the depressive effects of alcohol; however, they do not produce increases in sobriety if consumed while one is drunk
Antipsychotics	Thorazine	Impaired control of motor movements and possible death due to respiratory failure
Antianxiety drugs	Valium	Decreased arousal; impaired judgment, which can lead to accidents in the home or on the road

Source: Based on Palfai, T., & Jankiewicz, H. *Drugs and Human Behavior.* Dubuque, IA: Wm. C. Brown, 1991 and data from the National Institute for Alcohol Abuse and Alcoholism Clearinghouse for Alcohol Information (1982).

some brewers are now using their advertisements also to inform consumers of the potential dangers of alcohol abuse.

Treatment programs for drug abuse, including smoking and drinking, may take several forms. In some cases, aversion therapy (see Chapter 18) is used; in others, less intrusive forms of therapy involving extensive counseling are used. In the latter case, the psychologist or counselor's general aim is to teach the individual to

1. identify environmental cues or circumstances that may cause the addictive behavior to occur or recur;

2. learn to behave in ways that are incompatible with the undesired behavior;

3. have confidence that he or she can overcome the addiction; and

4. view setbacks in overcoming the addiction as temporary and to see them as learning experiences in which new coping skills can be acquired.

Prevention programs for people with addictive behaviors are only moderately successful. For example, many alcohol management programs have about a 30 to 50 percent success rate (Marlatt et al., 1989). Recall that smoking cessation programs (not including those that use the nicotine patch) fare even worse: They have about a 12 percent success rate (Pomerleau, 1992). As you might guess, an important goal for psychologists in the twenty-first century is to develop more effective programs for treating addictive behaviors.

Sexually Transmitted Diseases and AIDS

In the context of a loving relationship, sexual activity would seem to represent the most emotionally intense form of intimacy. In other contexts, though, especially in casual sexual relationships, sexual activity may have severely negative consequences: It may result in contracting a sexually transmitted disease (STD). Individuals who contract an STD may find that their life-styles are drastically affected. Typically, these individuals experience a loss of self-esteem, and often they lose their ability to initiate or maintain sexual relationships. (See *Table 16.5.*)

Without a doubt, the most life-threatening illness that may be transmitted sexually is acquired immune deficiency syndrome (AIDS), which can also be transmitted through blood transfusions and the sharing of hypodermic needles among intravenous drug users. AIDS is the last stage of the illness triggered by the human immunodeficiency virus (HIV). Once prevalent mainly among homosexuals in the western hemisphere, AIDS quickly spread among heterosexuals as well. Up through early 1991, nearly 70 percent of the *world's* HIV infections were believed to be spread through heterosexual intercourse (Populi, 1991). The World Health Organization notes that 14 million people are known to be infected with HIV and predicts that by the beginning of the next century, 30 to 40 million people will be infected with the HIV virus that causes AIDS (O'Hare, 1994).

Table 16.5

Four STDs, Their Causes, Symptomology, and Treatment

STD	Cause	Symptoms	Treatment
Gonorrhea	Gonococcus bacterium	Appear 3 to 5 days after sexual contact with afflicted person. In both sexes, discharges of pus. Urination accompanied by a burning sensation. In female, pelvic inflammatory disease. If untreated, fevers, headaches, backaches, and abdominal pain develop.	Penicillin or other antibiotics.
Genital herpes	Herpes simplex type I and II virus	Small blisters around point of sexual contact. Blisters burst, causing pain. Symptoms recur every 1 to 2 weeks.	No cure, but an ointment called acyclovir speeds the healing process if applied early in the first episode of the disease.
Syphilis	Treponema pallidum bacterium	Chancre or lesion where bacteria first entered body. If untreated, the bacteria penetrate body tissue, including the brain. May result in death.	Penicillin or other antibiotics.
AIDS	Human immunodeficiency virus (HIV)	Destruction of body's immune system allowing diseases like cancer and pneumonia to infect the body.	Still in experimental stages. Several drugs are currently being tested. So far, results are mixed—none are successful in curing AIDS, but some appear promising in lessening the symptoms.

Certain changes in life-style, called *safe sex practices*, can reduce one's risk of contracting an STD or AIDS. These practices include limiting the number of one's sexual partners, finding out the sexual history of partners before engaging in sexual relations, using a condom during sex, and abstinence from sexual intercourse. In the case of AIDS, these life-style changes must involve not only safe sex practices, but also behaviors that will prevent nonsexual transmission of the AIDS virus, such as refusal to share hypodermic needles.

If everyone engaged in safe sex practices, and if intravenous drug users refused to share hypodermic needles, the AIDS threat would be reduced significantly. The problem, of course, is that it is one thing to talk about safe sex but another thing actually to practice it. Why is this so? For the intravenous drug user, the answer is clear: The most important thing in life is getting high. Nothing else really matters. For the couple about to engage in casual sex, the issue is less clear. Although each individual's behavior is motivated by sexual gratification, the social awkwardness involved in discussing each other's sexual history may lead to a failure to engage in safe sex behaviors.

One way to reduce this problem may be to establish prevention programs in which people *role-play* safe sex practices in an attempt to help them overcome the feelings of uneasiness involved in asking another about his or her sexual history (Bosarge, 1989). Prevention programs attempt to accomplish four main goals:

1. teach people the relationship between their behavior and getting STDs and AIDS;
2. familiarize people with safe sex practices, such as the proper way to use a condom;
3. break down barriers to using safe sex practices, such as refusal to inquire about a partner's sexual history, the idea that one is invulnerable to STD or AIDS infection, and myths about using condoms (such as only wimps use them);
4. provide encouragement and support for changes in behavior that reduce STD and AIDS risks.

Although prevention programs have been successful in reducing high-risk sexual behaviors, they are least successful in situations in which a person's personal or cultural values prevent him or her from engaging in safe sex practices (Herdt and Lindenbaum, 1992). These values generally involve misperceptions of what practicing safe sex means. Some males refuse to wear condoms because doing so would detract from their conception of what it means to be a man. These individuals perceive that practicing safe sex robs them of their masculinity. Many people, especially young people, have the mistaken belief that they are invulnerable to any type of misfortune, including contracting an STD or AIDS. They believe, in essence, that these things "happen to other people, not me." The challenge for psychologists and counselors is to reorient these types of thinking so that people learn the connection between their sexual behavior and its possible negative consequences.

Biology and Culture

Cultural Reactions to Contagious Diseases

Imagine that you are at a shopping mall in which everybody who is physically ill or unhealthy must wear a sign around his or her neck that identifies his or her illness. You have been shopping for a while and wish to rest for a few minutes. You approach a sitting area that has two benches, each of which is just wide enough for two people. Each bench is already occupied by one person. The person sitting on one bench is wearing sign that says "I have heart disease." The person sitting on the other bench is wearing a sign that says "I have AIDS." At which bench will you choose to sit?

If you are like many people, you are likely *not* to sit next to the person wearing the sign declaring that he or she has AIDS (Bishop, 1994; Rushing, 1995). But why? Perhaps you know that AIDS is a contagious disease and that heart disease is not. If you know that, perhaps you also know that there is absolutely no evidence that AIDS can be transmitted through casual contact, such as sitting next to an AIDS-infected person on a bench at the mall. Yet many people would not feel comfortable sitting next to the person with AIDS for fear that somehow they could catch the disease.

It is true that some segments of our culture have reacted sympathetically to people with AIDS—they have learned about the disease, what causes it, and how it spreads. These people would not feel particularly uncomfortable sitting on the bench next to the person with AIDS. It is also true that other segments of our culture have reacted with disdain, calling for quarantines (for example, refusing to let children with AIDS attend public school), ostracizing people with AIDS, or physically assaulting them and others who belong to high-risk groups (such as gay people). These people would surely have problems sitting on the bench next to the person with AIDS.

In fact, despite widespread media coverage of the AIDS epidemic throughout the world and instructional programs designed to educate the general public about AIDS, it remains the most feared, stigmatized, and publicly misunderstood contagious disease of our time (Rushing, 1995). When negative behavior of this sort occurs, especially on a collective, widespread social basis, it is referred to as *fear of contagion*. Historical analyses of previous epidemics, such as the Black Death, or bubonic

Some collective social reactions to AIDS, such as this one, are representative of fear of contagion.

plague, that struck Europe during the fourteenth century and the outbreak of cholera in Europe and the United States in the seventeenth century, have shown that fear of contagion is only likely to occur when four conditions are met. The disease must be deadly, it must appear suddenly, it must have no apparent explanation, and people must believe that many people are at risk of contracting it (Rushing, 1995).

The AIDS epidemic meets these four conditions. It is deadly and it appeared suddenly: The first cases of AIDS were reported in 1981, a year in which 295 diagnoses of AIDS were made and 126 people died from it. Only 10 years later, in 1991, 41,871 new cases were reported and 31,381 people had died from AIDS. In the 9 intervening years, 179,000 new cases were reported and 114,703 people died from it. AIDS still has no hard and fast explanation. We know that it is a virus, but we don't know how to kill it—there is no equivalent of penicillin to eradicate it. And, finally, as AIDS makes strong inroads into heterosexual populations, more and more people now see themselves and others like them to be at risk of contracting the disease. Many of these people hold the false belief that AIDS is transmitted through casual contact (Bishop, 1991a, 1991b).

It is relatively easy to explain fear of contagion during the periods of the bubonic plague and cholera. At that time, medical science was unsophisticated and lacked the technology needed to understand basic physiology. Fear of contagion in the time of AIDS is not so easily explained. After all, we live in a period marked by incredible advances in medicine and medical technology. Why don't more people accept the advice of medical experts who insist that AIDS cannot be contracted casually?

Bishop (1994) offers three possible answers to this question. First, some people may reason that just because no evidence currently exists that AIDS is spread through casual contact, it doesn't mean that such evidence may not be discovered. Medical experts tend to describe the transmission of AIDS through casual contact as being "near impossible" or "very unlikely," which leaves room for doubt in many people's minds.

Second, some people may mistake AIDS as having the same general characteristics of more typical contagious diseases such as chicken pox or the flu. As we learned in Chapter 11, people often use prototypes to represent concepts. You may recall that a prototype represents the typical member of a class of things and that people organize information about other members in that class around the prototype. For example, if you think of the flu as a prototypical contagious disease, you may then apply the characteristics of this disease to other members of the same category, such as AIDS. Thus, because you know that the flu is a contagious disease that is spread by casual contact, you extend this same characteristic to AIDS and believe that it, too, is spread by casual contact.

Finally, the availability heuristic may also play a role in people's thinking about the transmission of AIDS. Recall from the discussion of the availability heuristic in Chapter 15 that when people attempt to assess the importance or the frequency of an event, they tend to be guided by the ease with which examples of that event come to mind—by how available these examples are in their memories. In the case of contagious diseases, AIDS has captured the world's attention. Television, newspaper, and radio reports involving AIDS have dominated coverage of medical, life-style, and societal issues for the past fifteen years. No doubt this coverage has kept the public informed about many aspects of the disease, including the failure of attempts to find a cure. No doubt, too, that some of the coverage has increased concern over the likelihood of contracting AIDS. In fact, Bishop and his colleagues (1992) have found a strong correlation between how many news reports on AIDS people have been exposed to and the number of lives they believe have been lost to AIDS.

Fear of contagious diseases such as AIDS and the people who have them, then, is not merely the result of the actual threat to health that those diseases pose. Our *perception* of the likelihood of contracting a contagious disease and our tendency to misapply both prototypical thinking and the availability heuristic in drawing conclusions from the evidence appear also to contribute significantly to fear of contagion.

Personal Safety: Using Seat Belts

To our prehistoric ancestors, personal safety likely involved such behaviors as avoiding toxic plants, dangerous animals, and burning themselves with fire. Although successfully avoiding these dangers is in our own best interest, too, our present culture represents a much more complex environment posing far more threats to personal safety than our prehistoric ancestors experienced. A good example is traffic: Only our very recent ancestors faced the possibility of being killed in an automobile accident. Today, traffic accidents result in hundreds of thousands of injuries and deaths each year.

About thirty years ago, automobile manufacturers began installing seat belts in vehicles. The rationale was that staying put in a crash—as opposed to being tossed about in or from the vehicle—would reduce a person's risk of death and injury. The logic, of course, was sound, but there was a hitch in implementing the seat belt program: getting people to buckle up in the first place. Many jurisdictions have passed mandatory seat belt laws requiring that both driver and passengers wear seat belts at all times while riding in a vehicle. How effective these laws will be in promoting seat belt usage remains to be seen, although we can safely say that compliance with the law is presently less than 100 percent.

Why don't more people use seat belts? According to E. Scott Geller (1985), a behavior analyst, the reasons are twofold: First, people often travel safely in their vehicles without wearing seat belts, which leads them to believe that riding in a car is *not* dangerous and that there is no need to wear a seat belt. Second, as we have seen, children and adolescents often imitate the behaviors of their parents. Young people may learn whether to wear seat belts or not simply by observing whether their parents wear seat belts.

In an effort to change "seat belt behavior," Geller has tried to alter environmental influences by developing community programs to promote seat belt usage. One of his approaches has been to reward individuals with inexpensive items such as food coupons and lottery tickets for wearing their seat belts. The rewards are delivered to seat belt wearers by police officers and people staffing drive-up windows of banks and fast-food restaurants. His results: more than a doubling of seat belt usage rates. Although usage rates drop when the reward program is removed, they do not generally reach previous levels of nonusage. When seat belt programs are reinstituted from time to time, rates of usage increase.

Interim Summary

Healthy and Unhealthy Life-Styles

The kinds of food we eat, how much exercise we get, and the extent to which we use tobacco and alcohol, practice safe sex, and wear seat belts have profound implications for our health and longevity. Eating right, exercising regularly, not smoking, consuming alcohol moderately, practicing safe sex, and wearing a seat belt do not *guarantee* that one will live a long life, but they do improve one's chances.

People who have high-fat, low-fiber diets tend to be more susceptible to CHD and cancer than are people who have low-fat, high-fiber diets. But many of the foods we like the most are high in fat and low in fiber. In the short run, eating these foods may delight our palate, but over the long run, eating these foods may lead to weight gain and increased LDL cholesterol levels, both risk factors for CHD and cancer. A well-balanced diet in combination with exercising regularly reduces the risk of CHD and cancer.

Eating poorly and sedentary living are not the only aspects of life-style that put people at risk for developing CHD and cancer. Cigarette smoking and consuming alcohol have similar effects. Although today we now know much about how cigarette smoking and alcohol consumption negatively affect the body and lead to disease, many people continue to smoke and drink. Why do people start and continue to do these things? Once again, the answer is to be found in the immediate pleasure derived from engaging in these behaviors. In everyday language, these behaviors can make people feel good. In addition to being reinforcing, these behaviors are addictive—the body may become dependent on the chemicals contained in cigarette smoke and alcohol for normal, day-to-day functioning.

Another threat to health and longevity are sexually transmitted diseases. People have been advised to take precautionary measures against contracting any STD by practicing safe sex. In the case of AIDS, people who inject themselves with drugs are also advised not to share hypodermic needles. Programs aimed at preventing the spread of STDs and AIDS focus on teaching people the relationship between their behavior and the likelihood of contracting one or more of these diseases and how to use safe sex strategies.

Fear of contagion is influenced by four factors: The disease must be deadly, it must appear suddenly, it must have no apparent explanation, and people must believe that many people are at risk of contracting it. Despite educational efforts to inform the public about AIDS, fear of contagion with respect to AIDS remains a serious problem.

Psychologists have also studied variables that affect behaviors that contribute to personal safety, such as wearing seat belts. Geller has proposed that people do not wear seat belts for two reasons: They hold the false belief that riding in a car is not dangerous and they (especially children) imitate others who do not wear seat belts. However, Geller has found that community programs that reward the wearing of seat belts have positive effects.

Thought Questions

- In what kinds of unhealthy life-style behaviors do you engage? What psychological processes influenced how these behaviors developed? Why do you keep engaging in them?
- Have you thought much about changing your life-style behaviors? Do you have any bad habits that you would like to break or any good habits (like exercising more) that you would like to begin? If so, why haven't you

done so—what is preventing you from altering your behavior?

Unhealthy Life-Styles Are Preventable: Self-Control

Behaviors that make up our life-styles are partially the consequence of the environmental conditions created by cultural evolution and partially the result of our genetic and physiological constitution. Life-styles are not always wholly adaptive; some aspects of our life-styles are detrimental to both our longevity and our quality of life. We have seen that unhealthy aspects of our life-styles include poor nutrition, physical inactivity, cigarette smoking, alcohol abuse, failure to use safe sex practices, and failure to use seat belts while riding in automobiles.

Unhealthy life-styles can be avoided. The problem, of course, is getting people to substitute healthy behaviors for unhealthy ones and to make positive life-style changes. Cultural evolution, or, more specifically, advances in technology, have afforded us choices: to use a condom or not, to eat foods rich in vitamins and minerals or to follow a poor diet, to smoke or not, to wear seat belts or not, and so forth.

The essence of each of these choices is whether to opt for the *small, short-term reward* produced by one action or the *larger, longer-term reward* produced by another, necessarily incompatible action. You can eat fattening and unhealthy foods now or follow a prudent diet and lose weight and become healthier over the long run—but you cannot do both at the same time. You can have unprotected sex now with a partner you do not know very well and run the risk of getting an STD or AIDS or practice safe sex and enhance the likelihood that you will remain healthy. What really is at issue here is **self-control**, behavior that produces a larger, long-term reward when one is faced with the choice between it and a small, short-term reward.

Psychologists Howard Rachlin (1970) and George Ainslie (1975) proposed a clear and conceptually useful model of self-control. This model, based on laboratory research using animals, captures well the essence of most self-control decisions that we face. Look at Figure 16.3(a). The vertical axis represents the value of a reward to us; the horizontal axis represents the passage of time. The curve represents a large, long-term reward, for example, acquiring and maintaining good physical health. (See *Figure 16.3(a).*) Let us assume either that we are not in very good physical health (we have a high level of blood cholesterol because we eat a lot of high-

self-control Behavior that produces the larger, longer-term reward when people are faced with the choice between it and the smaller, short-term reward.

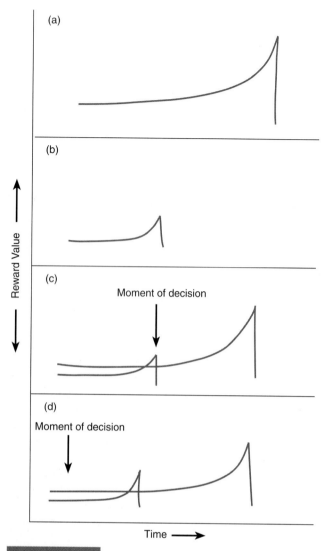

Figure 16.3

The relationship between commitment and self-control. (a) Value of the long-term, delayed reward. (b) Value of short-term, immediate reward. (c) No commitment, no self-control. (d) Self-control and commitment.

There comes a point in time at which the value of the small, short-term reward becomes greater than that of the larger, longer-term reward. (See *Figure 16.3(c)*.)

How can that be? Suppose that you are dieting. Further suppose that your roommate or spouse is baking cookies (imagine your favorite kind of cookie to make this example more realistic). You are drawn to the kitchen, where a dozen freshly baked cookies, giving off a tantalizing aroma, are sitting on the counter. Your roommate (or spouse) says, "Have one." Now you are faced with a choice: Do you eat a cookie or two (or perhaps more) and consume more calories than your diet calls for, or do you say, "No, thanks"? The temptation you face here is captured in Figure 16.3(c). At this moment, the value of the small, short-term reward, the cookies, exceeds that of the larger, longer-term reward, maintaining or losing weight. You can't regularly consume more calories than your diet calls for *and* maintain or lose weight. (See *Figure 16.3(c)*.)

Many psychologists argue that if you wait until you are faced with the choice between the small short-term reward and the larger, longer-term reward (*the moment of decision*), you will most likely opt for the small, short-term reward. The most effective way to exercise self-control is to somehow avoid having to make that choice in the first place. (See *Figure 16.3(d)*.) Self-control is a *prior commitment to a course of action that precludes making this decision*. According to this model, the best way to exercise self-control is to move the moment of decision to some time *before* you are confronted with the choice between the two rewards. That way, the value of the long-term reward is higher than the value of the shorter-term reward at the moment of decision. Setting your alarm clock the night before you have to get up early (as opposed to making the decision to get up the next morning when you are groggy) and enrolling in a payroll savings plan (as opposed to getting your paycheck and deciding then to put some of it in savings) are forms of prior commitment.

These three men have learned the benefits of self-control—in this case, choosing the long-term benefits of weight loss over the short-term rewards of eating.

fat, low-fiber foods, we smoke and drink more than we would like, and we don't get much exercise) or that we are in good condition and wish to remain that way. That is, the curve in Figure 16.3(a) represents a goal we wish to achieve or a condition we wish to maintain *in the long run*. Now look at Figure 16.3(b). This curve represents a smaller, shorter term reward, for example, the pleasure derived from eating a hot fudge sundae or fried chicken, smoking a cigarette, drinking a beer, or being sedentary. (See *Figure 16.3(b)*.) The curve representing the value of the short-term reward in (b) looks smaller than the curve representing the long-term reward in (a), and it is—some of the time. But now look at what happens when the two curves are placed in the same graph (c):

Without setting your alarm clock or enrolling in the savings plan, future events (the larger, longer-term reward) may have little influence on your behavior. In the case of dieting, prior commitment may include avoiding being home at times when your roommate or spouse is baking cookies or entering a contract with that person stating that he or she will not offer you any goodies. Other possible self-control strategies also exist for coping with situations like this. For example, you might imagine yourself saying "no" over and over again to such a temptation and feeling happy about your answer, and then following this model when actually faced with the temptation.

What is sorely needed is the development of effective commitment strategies that encourage people to make choices that benefit their life-styles. As we have seen, many treatment programs are unsuccessful at getting people to make lasting commitments to changes in their life-styles. Developing effective commitment strategies is a preeminent goal of **health psychology**, the branch of psychology concerned with the promotion and maintenance of sound health practices such as eating well, exercising regularly, not smoking or drinking, and engaging in safe sex practices.

Interim Summary

Unhealthy Life-Styles Are Preventable: Self-Control

The negative consequences of unhealthy behaviors can be avoided by exercising self-control—by opting to engage in behavior that produces the larger, but often delayed, reward when one is confronted with the choice between it and the smaller, more immediate reward. For example, you may opt to turn down dessert tonight (the smaller, more immediate reward) in the attempt to lose weight (the larger, less immediate reward). According to the model of self-control developed by Rachlin and Ainslie, self-control is most likely when you make a prior commitment to a course of action that leads only to the larger, longer-term reward. For example, you may turn down a dinner invitation tonight because you know that when the server brings the dessert tray to your table you will be unable to resist ordering dessert. Not placing yourself in that situation by declining the dinner invitation is a commitment to the larger, longer-term reward of losing weight.

Once you begin viewing life as consisting of a series of choices between small, short-term rewards, and larger, longer-term rewards, you can begin to see clearly how the choices you make now influence the consequences that you will face later.

Thought Questions

■ Think of an aspect of your life in which you would like to exercise more self-control. Explain how you might implement the model of self-control described in this section to help you with this aspect of your life. What

barriers might prevent you from implementing this model in your life?

■ Many people believe that exercising self-control is a matter of "will-power." What is will power, and how does it differ from the model of self-control about which you have just finished reading? From your point of view, is self-control due to will power? Why or why not?

Stress and Health

Stress is a pattern of physiological, behavioral, emotional and cognitive responses to real or imagined stimuli that are perceived as blocking a goal or endangering or otherwise threatening our well-being. These stimuli are generally aversive and are called **stressors**. Stress is not a direct product of cultural evolution, although the changes in the environment wrought by cultural evolution have helped make stress commonplace. Rather, stress is a product of natural selection. It is a behavioral adaptation that helped our ancestors fight or flee from wild animals and enemies. Likewise, stress often helps us confront or escape threatening situations (Linsky, Bachman, and Straus, 1995).

Stressors come in many forms. They may be catastrophic—such as hurricanes and tornadoes—or they may be relatively trivial, such as being stuck in traffic when you are already late for an appointment. Stressors are not always bad. Some stressors, such as athletic competition and class exams, can affect behavior in positive ways. However, when stress is extended over long periods, it can have negative effects on both a person's psychological health and a person's physical health (Selye, 1991).

The Biological Basis of Stress

Our physical response to stressors is governed by the autonomic nervous system, which, is controlled by the hypothalamus. Stress is a biological response that is experienced as an *emotion*, although the form it takes varies depending on the nature of the stressor. In some situations, we may feel frightened, and in others we may feel inspired or exhilarated.

When an individual senses a stressor, the hypothalamus sends signals to the autonomic nervous system and to the pi-

health psychology   The branch of psychology involved in the promotion and maintenance of sound health practices.

stress   A pattern of physiological, behavioral, and cognitive responses to stimuli (real or imagined) that are perceived as endangering one's well-being.

stressors   Stimuli that are perceived as endangering one's well-being.

Stressors, such as the inundation of one's home by flood waters, threatens one's normal life routine and well-being.

tuitary gland, both of which respond by stimulating body organs to change their normal activities:

1. Heart rate increases, blood pressure rises, blood vessels constrict, blood sugar levels rise, and blood flow is directed away from extremities and toward major organs.

2. Breathing becomes deeper and faster and air passages dilate, which permits more air to enter the lungs.

3. Digestion stops and perspiration increases.

4. The adrenal glands secrete adrenaline (epinephrine), which stimulates the heart and other organs.

It is easy to see why these changes are adaptive. They each prepare the body to deal with the stressor—collectively, these physiological responses produce a heightened psychological and physical state of alertness and readiness for action. Whether we confront the stressor or run from it, the biological response is generally the same. Likewise, regardless of the nature of the stressor, the biological response is the same. Whether you find yourself in a dark alley confronted by a man with a gun or facing your next psychology exam, the autonomic nervous system and the pituitary gland stimulate the body to respond to the stressor.

There are two cases in which such responses can be maladaptive. First, stress can produce anxiety, which may impair one's ability to perform a task. As you may have experienced yourself, anxiety can hinder performance on class tests, speaking in public, competition during athletic events, and remembering lines in a play.

The second case involves the effects of prolonged and severe stress. Many people's life-styles place them in situations in which they are confronted with stressors daily. As we will

general adaptation syndrome (GAS) The model proposed by Selye to describe the body's adaptation to chronic exposure to severe stressors. The body passes through an orderly sequence of three physiological stages: alarm, resistance, and exhaustion.

see shortly, such life-styles place these people at increased risk of illness.

Selye's General Adaptation Syndrome

Much of what we know about the effects of dealing with prolonged and severe stressors on the body stems from the work of Canadian endocrinologist Hans Selye. Through his work with laboratory animals, he found that chronic exposure to severe stressors produces a sequence of three physiological stages: *alarm, resistance,* and *exhaustion.* (See *Figure 16.4.*) Selye (1956) referred to these stages collectively as the **general adaptation syndrome (GAS).**

The responses in the *alarm stage* involve arousal of the autonomic nervous system and occur when the organism is first confronted with a stressor. During this stage, the organism's resistance to the stressor temporarily drops below normal, and the organism may experience shock—impairment of normal physiological functioning. With continued exposure to the stressor, the organism enters the *stage of resistance,* during which its autonomic nervous system returns to normal functioning. Resistance to the stressor increases and eventually plateaus at above normal levels. The stage of resistance, then, reflects the organism's adaptation to environmental stressors. However, with continued exposure to the stressor, the organism enters the *stage of exhaustion.* During this stage, the organism loses its ability to adapt, and resistance plummets to below normal levels, leaving the organism susceptible to illness and even death.

Biologically speaking, we are able to adapt to the presence of environmental stressors for only so long before we become susceptible to exhaustion and illness. The extent to which people can adapt varies across individuals and depends on how the stressor is perceived.

Chapter 13 pointed out that emotional responses evolved because they are useful and adaptive. Why, then, can they harm our health? The answer appears to be that our emotional responses are designed primarily to cope with short-term events. The physiological responses that accompany the negative emotions prepare us to threaten or fight rivals or to

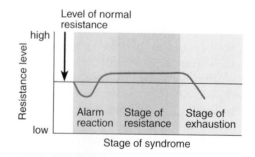

Figure 16.4

The general adaptation syndrome as proposed by Hans Selye.

(Selye, H. Stress without distress. New York: Harper & Row, 1974. Reprinted by permission.)

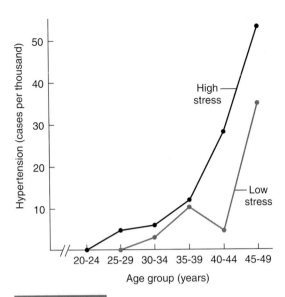

Figure 16.5

Stress and hypertension in air traffic controllers. Incidence of hypertension in various age groups of air traffic controllers at high-stress and low-stress airports.

(Based on data from Cobb, S., and Rose, R. M. Hypertension, peptic ulcer, and diabetes in air traffic controllers. Journal of the American Medical Association, 1973, 82, 476–482.)

run away from dangerous situations. Walter Cannon coined the phrase **fight-or-flight response**, which refers to the physiological reactions that prepare us for the strenuous efforts required by fighting or running away. Normally, once we have bluffed or fought with an adversary or run away from a dangerous situation, the threat is over and our physiological condition can return to normal. The fact that the physiological responses may have adverse long-term effects on our health is unimportant as long as the responses are brief. But when the threatening situations are continuous rather than episodic, they produce a more or less continuous stress response. This continued state of arousal can lead to CHD and other physical problems.

Several studies have demonstrated the deleterious effects of stress on health. For example, survivors of concentration camps, who were obviously subjected to long-term stress, have generally poorer health later in life than do other people of the same age (Cohen, 1953). Air traffic controllers—especially those who work at busy airports where the danger of collisions is greatest—show a greater incidence of high blood pressure, which gets worse as they grow older (Cobb and Rose, 1973). (See *Figure 16.5.*) They also are more likely to suffer from ulcers or diabetes.

Physiological Mechanisms Involved in Stress

As we saw in Chapter 13, emotions consist of behavioral, autonomic, and hormonal responses. The latter two compo-

nents—autonomic and hormonal responses—are the ones that can have adverse effects on health. (Well, I guess the behavioral components can, too, if a person rashly gets into a fight with someone much bigger and stronger.) Because threatening situations generally call for vigorous activity, the autonomic and hormonal responses that accompany them help make the body's energy resources available. The sympathetic branch of the autonomic nervous system is active, and the adrenal glands secrete epinephrine, norepinephrine, and steroid stress hormones. Because the effects of sympathetic activity are similar to those of the adrenal hormones, I will limit my discussion to the hormonal responses.

Epinephrine releases the stored form of glucose that is present in the muscles, thus providing energy for strenuous exercise. Along with norepinephrine, it also increases blood flow to the muscles by increasing the output of the heart, which also increases blood pressure. Over the long term, these changes contribute to CHD. The other stress-related hormone is *cortisol*, a steroid secreted by the cortex of the adrenal gland. Cortisol is called a **glucocorticoid** because it has profound effects on glucose metabolism, effects similar to those of epinephrine. In addition, glucocorticoids help break down protein and convert it to glucose, help make fats available for energy, increase blood flow, and stimulate behavioral responsiveness, presumably by affecting the brain. They have other physiological effects, too, some of which are only poorly understood. Almost every cell in the body contains glucocorticoid receptors, which means that few parts of the body are unaffected by these hormones. (See *Figure 16.6.*)

The secretion of glucocorticoids does more than help an animal react to a stressful situation—it helps it survive. If a rat's adrenal glands are removed, it becomes much more susceptible to the negative effects of stress. In fact, a stressful situation that a normal rat would take in its stride may kill one whose adrenal glands have been removed. And physicians treating people whose adrenal glands have been damaged or removed know that if these individuals are subjected to stress, they must be given additional amounts of glucocorticoid (Tyrell and Baxter, 1981).

Selye (1976) suggested that most of the harmful effects of stress were produced by the prolonged secretion of glucocorticoids. Although the short-term effects of glucocorticoids are essential, the long-term effects are damaging. These effects include increased blood pressure, damage to muscle tissue, a particular form of diabetes, infertility, stunted growth, inhibition of the inflammatory responses, and suppression of the immune system. High blood pressure can lead to heart attacks and stroke. Inhibition of growth in children subjected to prolonged stress prevents them from attaining their full

fight-or-flight response Physiological reactions that help ready us to fight or to flee a dangerous situation.

glucocorticoid A chemical, such as cortisol, that influences the metabolism of glucose, the main energy source of the body.

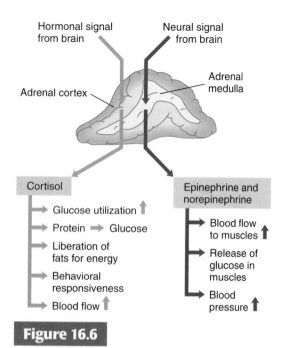

Figure 16.6

Control and the effects of secretion of epinephrine, norepinephrine, and cortisol by the adrenal gland.

height. Inhibition of the inflammatory response makes it more difficult for the body to heal itself after an injury, and suppression of the immune system makes an individual vulnerable to infections and (perhaps) cancer.

Several lines of research suggest that stress is related to aging in at least two ways. First, older people, even when they are perfectly healthy, do not tolerate stress as well as younger people do (Shock, 1977). Second, stress may accelerate the aging process (Selye and Tuchweber, 1976). Sapolsky and his colleagues have investigated one rather serious long-term effect of stress: brain damage. As you learned in Chapter 8, the hippocampal formation plays a crucial role in learning and memory. Evidence suggests that one of the causes of memory loss that occurs with aging is degeneration of this brain structure. Research conducted on animals has shown that long-term exposure to glucocorticoids destroys neurons located in a particular zone of the hippocampal formation. The hormone appears to destroy the neurons by making them more susceptible to the normal wear and tear that accompanies the aging process (Sapolsky, 1986; Sapolsky, Krey, and McEwen, 1986). Perhaps, then, the stress to which people are subjected throughout their lives increases the likelihood that they will have memory problems as they grow older.

Uno et al. (1989) found that if stress is intense enough, it can even cause brain damage in young primates. The investigators studied a colony of vervet monkeys housed in a primate center in Kenya. They found that some monkeys died, apparently as a result of stress. Vervet monkeys have a hierar-

chical society, and monkeys near the bottom of the hierarchy are picked on by the others; thus, they are almost continuously subjected to stress. (Ours is not the only species with social structures that cause stress in some of its members.) The deceased monkeys had gastric ulcers and enlarged adrenal glands, which are signs of chronic stress. In addition, neurons in a particular region of their hippocampal formations were completely destroyed. Severe stress appears to cause brain damage in humans as well. Jensen, Genefke, and Hyldebrandt (1982) found evidence of brain degeneration in CT scans of people who had been subjected to torture.

Cognitive Appraisal and Stress

As we have seen, many of the harmful effects of long-term stress are caused by our own reactions—primarily the secretion of stress hormones. Some events that cause stress, such as prolonged exertion or extreme cold, cause damage directly. These stressors will affect everyone; their severity will depend on each person's physical capacity. Selye's model has been useful for understanding the biological components involved in stress, but it does not explain the role of psychological components in stress. The effects of other stressors, such as situations that cause fear or anxiety, depend on people's perceptions and emotional reactivity. That is, because of individual differences in temperament or experience with a particular situation, some people may find a situation stressful and others may not. In these cases, it is the *perception* that counts.

One of the most important variables that determines whether an aversive stimulus will cause a stress reaction is the degree to which the situation can be controlled. When an animal can learn a coping response that allows it to avoid contact with an aversive stimulus, its emotional response will disappear. Weiss (1968) found that rats that learned to minimize (but not completely avoid) shocks by making a response whenever they heard a warning tone developed fewer stomach ulcers than did rats that had no control over the shocks. The effect was not caused by the pain itself, because both groups of animals received exactly the same number of shocks. Thus, being able to exert some *control* over an aversive situation reduces an animal's stress. Humans react similarly. Situations that permit some control are less likely to produce signs of stress than are those in which other people (or machines) control the situation (Gatchel, Baum, and Krantz, 1989). Perhaps this phenomenon explains why some people like to have a magic charm or other "security blanket" with them in stressful situations. Perhaps even *the illusion of control* can be reassuring.

Some psychologists argue that the psychological components in stress may influence the degree to which stressors arouse the autonomic nervous system. One such psychologist is Richard Lazarus, who argues that our *perception* of the stressor does, to a large extent, determine the stress we experience (Lazarus and Folkman, 1984). According to Lazarus, an individual's stress levels are affected by his or her **cognitive appraisal**, or perception, of the stressful situation. Cognitive appraisal is a two-stage process. In the first stage, we evaluate the threat: We attempt to judge the seriousness of the perceived threat posed by the stressor. If we decide that the threat is real, we pass to the second stage, during which we assess whether we have the resources necessary to cope adequately with the threat. The extent to which we believe both that the stressor is a serious one and that we *do not* have the resources necessary to deal with it determines the level of stress we will experience. The belief that we cannot deal effectively with a stressor perceived as being extremely dangerous leads to the highest levels of stress. Because different people may evaluate differently both the stressor and their ability to cope with it, they are likely to show different levels of stress when faced with the same stressor. We know from common experience that this is true. For example, people vary tremendously in their reactions to snakes: A harmless garter snake will arouse intense fear in some people and none in others.

Selye's findings, then, do not apply to all people; there are individual differences in how people react to prolonged exposure to stress. Some people, in fact, show little, if any, risk of becoming ill during or after chronic stress. Psychologist Susan Kobasa (1979) refers to these people as *hardy* individuals. In a study of how business executives coped with long-term stress, she found that some of her subjects became ill and some did not. What she wanted to know is what caused this difference. Through detailed analyses of her subjects' responses to different psychological inventories, she found that the hardy subjects viewed the stressors in their lives as challenges and that they met these challenges head-on—they did not avoid them or become anxious about them. They also felt that they had control over the challenges (stressors) rather than that the challenges had control over them.

In other words, Kobasa's findings support Lazarus's idea of the importance of cognitive appraisal in dealing with stress: How we initially size up the stressor, how we tackle it, and the extent to which we believe that we can control the stressor seem to influence whether we become at risk for illnesses related to being chronically stressed.

In a review of the factors that contribute to the development of hardiness, Kobasa and her colleague, Salvatore Maddi (1991), argue that the nature of early family home life is the cornerstone of hardiness. The combination of parental warmth, stimulating home environment, and family support in attempting to solve problems of moderate difficulty is correlated with the development of a hardy personality.

Stressful Life-Styles and Impaired Health

Selye's research involved exposing laboratory animals to chronic and intense stressors under controlled laboratory conditions. In addition to showing that resistance to stressors

appears to involve three stages, his results also showed that animals became seriously ill during the stage of exhaustion. Can prolonged exposure to severe stressors produce similar risks for humans? Many studies investigating the relationship of life-style to health have shown that the answer to this question is yes. Specifically, stressful life-styles have been shown to be related to increased risk of CHD, cancer, impaired immune system functioning, ulcers, and high blood pressure.

Stress and CHD

One of the leading causes of death in Western societies is CHD—diseases of the heart and the blood vessels. CHDs can cause heart attacks and strokes. Heart attacks occur when the blood vessels that serve the heart become blocked, while strokes involve the blood vessels in the brain. The two most important risk factors in CHD are high blood pressure and, as we learned earlier, a high level of cholesterol in the blood.

The degree to which people react to stress may affect the likelihood that they will suffer from CHD. For example, Wood et al. (1984) examined the blood pressure of people who had been subjected to a cold pressor test when they were children. The cold pressor test reveals how people's blood pressure reacts to the stress caused when their hand is placed in a container of ice water for one minute. Wood and his colleagues found that 70 percent of the subjects who hyperreacted to the stress when they were children had high blood pressure as adults, compared with 19 percent of those who showed little reaction to the stress.

A study of monkeys showed that individual differences in emotional reactivity are a risk factor for CHD. Manuck et al. (1983, 1986) fed a high-cholesterol diet to a group of monkeys, which increases the likelihood of their developing coronary artery disease. They measured the animals' emotional reactivity by threatening to capture the animals. (Monkeys avoid contact with humans, and they perceive being captured as a stressful situation.) Those animals who showed the strongest negative reactions eventually developed the highest rates of CHD. Presumably, these animals reacted more strongly to all types of stress, and their reactions had detrimental effects on their health.

Friedman and Rosenman (1959) identified a behavior pattern that appeared to be related to a person's susceptibility to CHD. They characterized the disease-prone **type A pattern** as one of excessive competitive drive, an intense disposition, impatience, hostility, fast movements, and rapid speech. Peo-

cognitive appraisal One's perception of a stressful situation.

type A pattern A behavior pattern characterized by high levels of competitiveness and hostility, impatience, and an intense disposition; supposedly associated with an increased risk of CHD.

ple with the **type B pattern** were less competitive; less hostile; more patient, easygoing, and tolerant; and they moved and talked more slowly; they were also *less* likely to suffer from CHD. Friedman and Rosenman developed a questionnaire that distinguished between these two types of people. The test is rather interesting, because the person who administers it is not a passive participant. The interviewer asks questions in an abrupt, impatient manner, interrupting the subject if he or she takes too much time to answer a question. The point of such behavior is to try to elicit type A behavior from the subject.

Researchers have devoted much attention to the relation between type A personality and CHD. The Western Collaborative Group Study (Rosenman et al., 1975), which studied 3,154 healthy men for eight and one-half years, found that the type A behavior pattern was associated with twice the rate of CHD relative to non-type A behavior patterns. Results such as these led an independent review panel to classify the type A behavior pattern as a risk factor for CHD (Review Panel, 1981). However, since then, many contradictory results have been obtained. For example, one large study found that although people classified as type A were more likely to have heart attacks, the long-term survival rate after having a heart attack was higher for type A patients than for type B patients (Ragland and Brand, 1988). In this case, it would seem better to be type A, at least after having a nonfatal heart attack. Other studies have failed to find a difference in the likelihood of CHD in people with type A and type B personalities (Dimsdale, 1988).

Williams et al. (1980) suggested that one aspect of the type A personality—hostility—is of particular importance in CHD. Several studies carried out in the early to mid-1980s confirmed that hostility was an important risk factor, but more recent studies have not. For example, Helmer, Ragland, and Syme (1991) studied 118 men who underwent angiography (X-ray inspection of the buildup of atherosclerotic plaque in the arteries of the heart that can ultimately cause a heart attack). They found no relation between either of two measures of hostility and the degree of coronary artery disease.

Although the relation between CHD and hostility or the type A behavior pattern is unclear, several studies have found that personality variables are related to particular risk factors. For example, Howard, Cunningham, and Rechnitzer (1976) found that people who exhibited extreme type A behavior were more likely to smoke and to have high blood pressure and high blood levels of cholesterol. Weidner et al. (1987) confirmed the high level of cholesterol in a sample of men

and women with the type A behavior pattern, and Irvine et al. (1991) confirmed the association between type A behavior and high blood pressure. And Lombardo and Carreno (1987) found that type A smokers held the smoke in their lungs longer, leading to a high level of carbon monoxide in their blood.

What are we to conclude? Most investigators believe that personality variables are involved in susceptibility to heart attack but that we need a better definition of just what these variables are. In addition, it is possible that different personality variables are associated with different risk factors, which make it difficult to tease out the relevant variables. Personality factors certainly play an important role in CHD, but at present, the precise nature of this role is uncertain. This topic is important and clearly merits further research.

Posttraumatic Stress Disorder

The aftermath of tragic and traumatic events such as those that accompany wars and natural disasters often includes psychological symptoms that persist long after the stressful events are over. **Posttraumatic stress disorder** is an anxiety disorder in which the individual has feelings of social withdrawal accompanied by untypically low levels of emotion caused by prolonged exposure to a stressor, such as a catastrophe. The symptoms produced by such exposure include recurrent dreams or recollections of the event, feelings that the traumatic event is recurring ("flashback" episodes), and intense psychological distress. These dreams, recollections, or flashback episodes lead the person to avoid thinking about the traumatic event, which often results in diminished interest in social activities, feelings of detachment from others, suppressed emotional feelings, and a sense that the future is bleak and empty. Particular psychological symptoms include

Soldiers, such as these prisoners being held in a Croatian concentration camp, are susceptible to experiencing posttraumatic stress disorder after they return to their civilian lives.

type B pattern A behavior pattern characterized by lower levels of competitiveness and hostility, patience, and an easygoing disposition; supposedly associated with a decreased risk of CHD.

posttraumatic stress disorder An anxiety disorder in which the individual has feelings of social withdrawal accompanied by untypically low levels of emotion caused by prolonged exposure to a stressor, such as a catastrophe.

difficulty falling or staying asleep, irritability, outbursts of anger, difficulty in concentrating, and heightened reactions to sudden noises or movements.

Posttraumatic stress disorder can strike people at any age. Children may show particular symptoms not usually seen in adulthood, including loss of recently acquired language skills or toilet training and somatic complaints such as stomachaches and headaches. Usually, the symptoms begin immediately after the traumatic event, but they are sometimes delayed for several months or years.

Some studies suggest that preexisting personality factors may play a role in the development of posttraumatic stress disorder. For example, Mikulincer and Solomon (1988) studied Israeli soldiers who suffered a combat stress reaction during the 1982 Lebanon war and found that those who tended to brood about their feelings were more likely to go on to develop posttraumatic stress disorder. The National Vietnam Veterans Readjustment Study carried out by the U.S. government found that four factors increased the likelihood that a soldier subjected to combat stress would develop posttraumatic stress disorder: being raised in a household with financial difficulty, having a history of drug abuse or dependency, having a history of affective disorders, and having a history of childhood behavior problems (Kulka et al., 1990).

The social support that people receive (or do not receive) after being exposed to an unusually stressful situation can affect the likelihood of their developing posttraumatic stress disorder. As a result, mental health professionals try to seek out victims of natural disasters and crimes such as rapes or shooting sprees to provide them with treatment that might prevent future psychological disorders.

Psychoneuroimmunology

As we have seen, long-term stress can be harmful to one's health and can even result in brain damage. The most important causes are elevated levels of glucocorticoids, epinephrine, and norepinephrine. But in addition, stress can impair the functions of the immune system, which protects us from assault by viruses, microbes, fungi, and other types of parasites. Study of the interactions between the immune system and behavior (mediated by the nervous system, of course) is called **psychoneuroimmunology**. I describe this new field in the following section.

The Immune System. The **immune system,** a network of organs and cells that protects the body from invading bacteria, viruses, and other foreign substances, is one of the most complex systems of the body. Its function is to protect us from infection. Because infectious organisms have developed devious tricks through the process of evolution, our immune system has evolved devious tricks of its own. The description I provide here is abbreviated and simplified, but it presents some of the important elements of the system.

The immune system derives from white blood cells that develop in the bone marrow and in the thymus gland. Some of

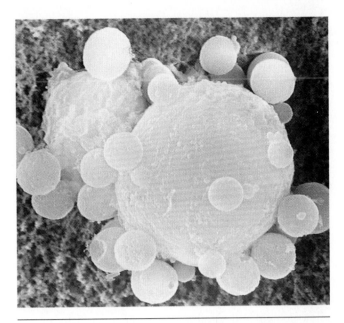

A T-lymphocyte at work destroying tumor cells.

the cells roam through the blood or lymph glands and sinuses; others reside permanently in one place. The immune reaction occurs when the body is invaded by foreign organisms.

There are two types of specific immune reactions: chemically mediated and cell-mediated. Chemically mediated immune reactions involve antibodies. All bacteria have unique proteins on their surfaces, called **antigens**. These proteins serve as the invaders' calling cards, identifying them to the immune system. Through exposure to the bacteria, the immune system learns to recognize these proteins. The result of this learning is the development of special lines of cells that produce specific **antibodies**—proteins that recognize antigens and help kill the invading microorganism. One type of antibody is released into the circulation by **B lymphocytes**, which receive their name from the fact that they develop in bone marrow. These antibodies, called **immunoglobulins**, are

psychoneuroimmunology Study of the interactions between the immune system and behavior as mediated by the nervous system.

immune system A network of organs and cells that protects the body from invading bacteria, viruses, and other foreign substances.

antigen The unique proteins found on the surface of bacteria; these proteins are what enable the immune system to recognize the bacteria as foreign substances.

antibodies Proteins in the immune system that recognize antigens and help kill invading microorganisms.

B lymphocytes Cells that develop in bone marrow and release immunoglobulins to defend the body against antigens.

immunoglobulins The antibodies that are released by B lymphocytes.

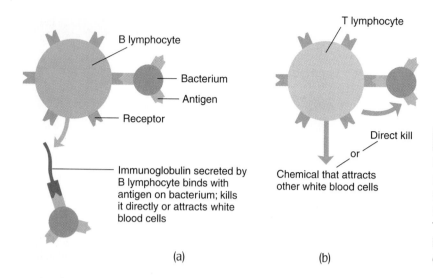

Figure 16.7

Immune reactions. (a) Chemically mediated reaction. The B lymphocyte detects an antigen on a bacterium and releases a specific immunoglobulin. (b) Cell-mediated reaction. The T lymphocyte detects an antigen on a bacterium and kills it directly or releases a chemical that attracts other white blood cells.

chains of protein. Each of five different types of immunoglobulin is identical except for one end, which contains a unique receptor. A particular receptor binds with a particular antigen, just as a molecule of a hormone or a transmitter substance binds with its receptor. When the appropriate line of B lymphocytes detects the presence of an invading bacterium, the cells release their antibodies, which bind with the bacterial antigens. The antibodies either kill the invaders directly or attract other white blood cells, which then destroy the invaders. (See *Figure 16.7(a).*)

The other type of defense mounted by the immune system, cell-mediated immune reactions, is produced by **T lymphocytes,** which originally develop in the thymus gland. These cells also produce antibodies, but the antibodies remain attached to the outside of their membranes. T lymphocytes primarily defend the body against fungi, viruses, and multicellular parasites. When antigens bind with their surface antibodies, the cells either directly kill the invaders or signal other white blood cells to come and kill them. (See *Figure 16.7(b).*)

In addition to the immune reactions produced by lymphocytes, natural killer cells continuously prowl through tissue. When they encounter a cell that has been infected by a virus or that has become transformed into a cancer cell, they engulf and destroy it. Thus, natural killer cells constitute an important defense against viral infections and the development of malignant tumors.

Although the immune system normally protects us, it can cause us harm, too. Allergic reactions occur when an antigen causes cells of the immune system to overreact, releasing a particular immunoglobulin that produces a localized inflammatory response. The chemicals released during

this reaction can enter the general circulation and cause life-threatening complications. Allergic responses are harmful, and why they occur is unknown.

The immune system can do something else that harms the body—it can attack its own cells. **Autoimmune diseases** occur when the immune system becomes sensitized to a protein present in the body and attacks the tissue that contains this protein. Exactly what causes the protein to be so targeted is not known. What is known is that autoimmune diseases often follow viral or bacterial infections. Presumably, in learning to recognize antigens that belong to the infectious agent, the immune system develops a line of cells that treat one of the body's own proteins as foreign. Some common autoimmune diseases include rheumatoid arthritis, diabetes, lupus, and multiple sclerosis.

Neural Control of the Immune System. Stress can suppress the immune system, resulting in a greater likelihood of infectious diseases, and it can also aggravate autoimmune diseases. It may even affect the growth of cancers. What is the physiological explanation for these effects? One answer, and probably the most important one, is that stress increases the secretion of glucocorticoids, and these hormones directly suppress the activity of the immune system. All types of white blood cells have glucocorticoid receptors, and suppression of the immune system is presumably mediated by these receptors (Solomon, 1987).

Because the secretion of glucocorticoids is controlled by the brain, the brain is obviously responsible for the suppressing effect of these hormones on the immune system. For example, in a study of rats, Keller et al. (1983) found that the stress of inescapable shock decreased the number of lymphocytes found in the blood. This effect was abolished by removal of the adrenal gland. Thus, the decrease in lymphocytes appears to have been caused by the release of glucocorticoids triggered by the stress. (See *Figure 16.8(a).*) However, the same authors found that removal of the adrenal glands did not abolish the effects of stress on another type of immune response: stimulation of lymphocytes by an antigen. (See *Figure*

T lymphocytes Cells that develop in the thymus gland that produce antibodies, which defend the body against fungi, viruses, and multicellular parasites.

autoimmune diseases Diseases such as rheumatoid arthritis, diabetes, lupus, and multiple sclerosis, in which the immune system attacks and destroys some of the body's own tissue.

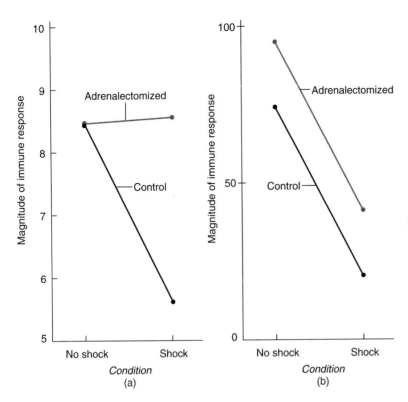

Figure 16.8

Effects of the removal of rats' adrenal glands on suppression of the immune system produced by inescapable shocks. (a) Number of white blood cells (lymphocytes) found in the blood. (b) Stimulation of lymphocyte production after exposure to an antigen.

(Based on data from Keller, S.E., Weiss, J.M., Schleifer, S.J., Miller, N.E., and Stein, M. Stress-induced suppression of immunity in adrenalectomized rats. Science, *1983, 221, 1301–1304.)*

16.8(b).) Thus, not all the effects of stress on the immune system are mediated by glucocorticoids; there must be other mechanisms as well.

These additional mechanisms may involve direct neural control. The bone marrow, the thymus gland, and the lymph nodes all receive neural input. Although researchers have not yet obtained direct proof that this input modulates immune function, it would be surprising if it did not.

In addition, the immune system appears to be sensitive to chemicals produced by the nervous system. The best evidence comes from studies of the opioids produced by the brain. Shavit et al. (1984) found that inescapable intermittent shock produced both analgesia (decreased sensitivity to pain) and suppression of the production of natural killer cells. These effects both seem to have been mediated by brain opioids, because both effects were abolished when the experimenters administered a drug that blocks opiate receptors. Shavit et al. (1986) found that natural killer cell activity could be suppressed by injecting morphine directly into the brain; thus, the effect of the opiates appears to take place in the brain. The mechanism by which the brain affects the natural killer cells is not yet known.

Infectious Diseases

When a married person dies, his or her spouse often dies soon afterward, frequently of an infection. In fact, a wide variety of stress-producing events in a person's life can increase the susceptibility to infectious diseases. For example, Glaser et al. (1987) found that medical students were more likely to contract acute infections—and to show evidence of suppres-

sion of the immune system—during the time that final examinations were given. In addition, autoimmune diseases often get worse when a person is subjected to stress, as Feigenbaum, Masi, and Kaplan (1979) found for rheumatoid arthritis. In a laboratory study, Rogers et al. (1980) found that when rats were stressed by handling them or exposing them to a cat, they developed a more severe case of an artificially induced autoimmune disease.

Stone, Reed, and Neale (1987) attempted to see whether stressful events in people's daily lives might predispose them to upper respiratory infection. If a person is exposed to a microorganism that might cause such a disease, the symptoms do not occur for several days; that is, there is an incubation period between exposure and signs of the actual illness. The authors therefore reasoned that if stressful events suppressed the immune system, one might expect to see a higher likelihood of respiratory infections several days after such stress. To test their hypothesis, they asked volunteers to keep a daily record of desirable and undesirable events in their lives over a twelve-week period. The volunteers also kept a daily record of any discomfort or symptoms of illness.

The results were as predicted: During the three-to-five-day period just before showing symptoms of an upper respiratory infection, people experienced an increased number of undesirable events and a decreased number of desirable events in their lives. (See *Figure 16.9.*) Stone et al. (1987) suggest that the effect is caused by decreased production of a particular immunoglobulin that is present in the secretions of mucous membranes, including those in the nose, mouth, throat, and lungs. This immunoglobulin serves as the first defense against infectious microorganisms that enter the nose

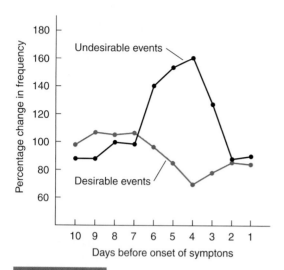

Figure 16.9

Mean percentage change in frequency of undesirable and desirable events during the ten-day period preceding the onset of symptoms of upper respiratory infections.

(Based on data from Stone, A.A., Reed, B.R., and Neale, J.M. Changes in daily event frequency precede episodes of physical symptoms. Journal of Human Stress, *1987, 13, 70–74.)*

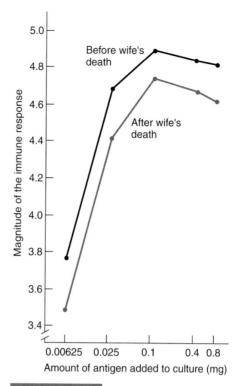

Figure 16.10

Stimulation of white blood cell (lymphocyte) production by an antigen in the blood of husbands before and after their wives' deaths.

(Adapted from Schleifer, S.J., Keller, S.E., Camerino, M., Thornton, J.C., and Stein, M. Suppression of lymphocyte stimulation following bereavement. Journal of the American Medical Association, *1983, 250, 374–377.)*

or mouth. They found that this immunoglobulin (known as IgA) is associated with mood. When a subject is unhappy or depressed, IgA levels are lower than normal. The results suggest that the stress caused by undesirable events may, by suppressing the production of IgA, lead to a rise in the likelihood of upper respiratory infections.

A direct relation between stress and the immune system was demonstrated by Kiecolt-Glaser et al. (1987). These investigators found that caregivers of family members with Alzheimer's disease—who certainly underwent considerable stress—showed weaker immune systems, based on several different laboratory tests.

Bereavement, another source of stress, also suppresses the immune system. Cancer and other illnesses have been observed to occur at higher-than-average rates among people who are widowed. To investigate the possibility that bereavement suppresses the immune system, Schleifer and several other researchers (1983) drew blood samples from fifteen men whose wives were dying of terminal breast cancer. Two blood samples were drawn, the first before the spouse's death and the second within two months afterward. Both times, an agent that normally stimulates blood lymphocyte activity was mixed with the lymphocytes, and the resultant level of activity was measured. On average, the activity level of blood lymphocytes after the spouse's death was less than before her death, which meant that the bereaved spouses were more susceptible to illness. (See *Figure 16.10.*) Taken together, the results of these studies (and many other similar studies) suggest a strong link between stress and weakening of the immune system.

Evaluating Scientific Issues

Is There a Cancer-Prone Personality?

Many people—both professionals and laypeople—believe that psychological factors play a role in determining whether people develop cancers or, if they do, whether the cancers can be "beaten." Some professionals have even suggested that having a "cancer-prone personality" is a risk factor for the disease. Is there any truth to this assertion?

■ Do Personality Characteristics Increase Susceptibility to Cancer?

The idea that personality is related to the development of cancer is not a new one. During the second century A.D., Galen, the Greek anatomist and physician, concluded that melancholic women were more likely than optimistic women to develop cancer (Bastiaans, 1985). Physicians in more recent times have reported similar relations between cancer-proneness and personality, but it was not until the 1950s that investigators attempted to do systematic studies (Gil, 1989). Several studies (for example, Le-Shan and Worthington, 1956a, 1956b; Kissen, 1963) suggested that cancer-prone people had difficulty expressing emotions (especially anger and hostility) and had low self-esteem.

The concept of the **type C (cancer-prone) personality** was introduced in the 1980s (Morris, 1980). According to Temoshok et al. (1985), the type C pattern is shown by a person "who is cooperative, unassertive, patient, who suppresses negative emotions (particularly anger), and who accepts/complies with external authorities" (p. 141). Temoshok and her colleagues conceive of the type C personality as the polar opposite of the type A pattern.

Investigators who believe in the existence of a cancer-prone personality assert that there is a direct physiological connection between personality characteristics and cancer. That is, the maladaptive coping styles of people with the type C personality cause physiological events that favor the development of cancer. For example, Temoshok (1987) suggests that the chronically blocked expressions of emotions in people with the type C personality cause the release of certain chemicals in the brain (neuropeptides) that disrupt the body's homeostatic mechanisms and impair the body's ability to defend itself against the growth of cancer cells. Eysenck (1988) suggested that the negative emotions cause the release of glucocorticoids, which (as you know) suppress the immune system and interfere with its ability to destroy cancer cells.

■ What Is the Evidence for the Cancer-Prone Personality?

Several studies have found a relation between personality variables and the presence or severity of cancer. For example, Temoshok et al. (1985) administered personality tests designed to measure type C personality characteristics to a group of patients who had been referred to a hospital for assessment and treatment of a malignant melanoma—a form of skin cancer that has a tendency to metastasize (spread to other parts of the body). They found that two personality variables were related to the thickness of the tumor: faith and nonverbal type C. People who scored high on faith agreed with statements such as "I'm placing my faith in God" (or "my doctor") and "Prayer can work miracles." People who scored high on nonverbal type C tended to be slow, lethargic, passive, and sad. Presumably, the existence of these personality variables favored the growth of the melanoma.

Most of the studies investigating the role of personality variables in cancer-proneness have assessed the personality characteristics of people who have already been identified as cancer patients. Some studies, like the one by Temoshok et al., have related the personality characteris-

tics to severity of the disease; others have compared the personality variables of cancer patients with those of people without cancer. As we shall see in the next section, all such studies share some methodological problems. A more clear-cut approach is to administer personality tests to a large group of people and then follow them for several years, seeing who gets cancer and who does not. Grossarth-Maticek and his colleagues carried out an ambitious study on 1353 residents of a small town in the former Yugoslavia (Grossarth-Maticek, Bastiaans, and Kanazir, 1985). They administered psychological tests and questionnaires about current health status and habits such as smoking and drinking in 1966 and then followed the subjects for ten years. Their results showed that people with type C personality characteristics were most likely to develop cancer—especially lung cancer.

Grossarth-Maticek and his colleagues began an even more ambitious follow-up study in 1974, when they administered personality tests to 19,000 residents of Heidelberg, Germany. The study is still under way, and so far only a few small samples of the original group have been examined. However, the results so far indicate that the test successfully identifies people who are likely to develop cancer (Grossarth-Maticek and Eysenck, 1990). Examples of the questions that tend to be answered "yes" by people who later develop cancer include "I prefer to agree with others rather than assert my own views," "I am unable to express my feelings and needs openly to other people," and "I often feel inhibited when it comes to openly showing negative feelings such as hatred, aggression, or anger."

■ Evaluating Evidence for the Cancer-Prone Personality

Many of the studies that reported an association between personality variables and cancer can be criticized on methodological grounds. First, evidence from studies that test people who already have cancer cannot prove that personality variables play a role in the onset or progression of the disease. Physicians have known for a long time that malignancies can have physiological effects that alter people's emotions and personality, and these changes can occur even before the cancer is detected (Borysenko, 1982; Shakin and Holland, 1988). Thus, what may look like a cause of the disease may actually be an effect.

Because Grossarth-Maticek and his colleagues administered personality tests to healthy people and looked for the subsequent development of cancer, their studies are not subject to this criticism. Indeed, this approach is the very best way to see whether a cause-and-effect link exists between personality and cancer. However, even if the link

type C personality A behavior pattern marked by cooperativeness, unassertiveness, patience, suppression of negative emotions, and acceptance of external authority; supposedly associated with an increased likelihood of cancer.

exists, we cannot be sure that cancer-proneness is a direct result of people's emotional reactions—that it is produced by suppression of the immune system, for instance. Instead, the effect could be caused by differences in people's behavior. For example, people who are passive and who have faith that God or their doctors will take care of them might not take responsibility for their own health. Believing that someone else is responsible for their health, they might not bother to try to maintain a healthy lifestyle. They might not be alert for warning signs of cancer or might even disregard them until they become so blatant that they cannot be ignored. They might be less likely to comply with the treatments prescribed by their physicians; after all, it is the doctor's responsibility to take care of them, not their own.

In any event, most investigators believe that if the immune system plays a role in the possible link between personality variables and cancer, it affects the *growth* of tumors, not their *formation*. Most of the studies using laboratory animals that have shown that stress can promote the growth of cancer have investigated tumors induced by viruses—and viruses do not appear to play a significant role in human tumors (Justice, 1987). Thus, this research may not be directly relevant to cancer in humans. The most important defense against the formation of tumors in humans appears to be carried out by mechanisms that help repair damaged DNA, and no one has yet shown a connection between stress and these mechanisms.

■ What Should We Conclude?

The weight of the evidence suggests that personality variables, particularly those relevant to people's coping styles in dealing with unpleasant and stressful situations, can affect the development of cancer. What we do not know is whether these variables do so *directly*, by altering the activity of the immune system, or *indirectly*, by affecting people's health-related behavior.

If personality traits play a role in the development of cancer, perhaps it would be possible to develop a form of psychotherapy that would alter these traits and help prevent or combat cancer. In fact, one careful study did find that psychotherapy can increase the survival rate of cancer patients. Spiegel, Bloom, and Yalom (1982) designed an experiment to see whether psychotherapy could help people cope with the anxiety, fear, and pain produced by their disease. (They did not intend the therapy to help the patients survive their disease.) The investigators randomly selected two groups of women with advanced breast cancer; one received psychotherapy and the other did not. All patients received standard medical treatment, including surgery, radiation, and chemotherapy. The psychotherapy did indeed help the woman in the experimental group cope with their cancer—they became less anxious and depressed and learned to reduce their pain. Thirteen years later, Spiegel and his colleagues decided to examine the medical records of the eighty-six subjects to

Cancer patients participate in a psychotherapy group to help them cope with their disease.

see whether the psychotherapy had affected the course of their disease (Spiegel, Bloom, Kraemer, and Gottheil, 1989). They expected to find that it had not. But it had; those who received a year of therapy lived an average of thirty-seven months, compared with nineteen months for the control subjects. Three women were still alive, and all of them had received the psychotherapy.

According to Spiegel, we cannot necessarily conclude that the psychotherapy prolonged the patients' survival time simply because it reduced stress. Instead, the psychotherapy could have encouraged them to comply better with their physicians' orders concerning medication and diet, and the reduction in pain may have made it possible for them to exercise more and maintain their general health. But clearly, these findings are important. Identifying the factors that helped retard the course of the illness could lead to the development of even more effective therapies.

Although Spiegel's report is encouraging, advocating and publicizing the belief that thinking negatively causes illnesses and thinking positively cures them has some harmful side effects. Even if the belief is true, variables such as heredity and exposure to carcinogens are by far the most important risk factors in tumor formation, and standard medical treatments provide by far the most effective forms of therapy. Some people may be tempted to forgo medical treatment, hoping that they can make their tumors wither away by thinking positively. Some therapists have advocated guided imagery, in which the patients visualize their white blood cells attacking their cancer cells. Such exercises may be harmless, but they seem to owe more to a belief in magic than an understanding of scientific evidence. Because early medical treatment is important, any delays in receiving such treatment may reduce the likelihood of a cure. If they cause a delay, even "harmless" exercises may threaten a patient's survival. In addition, a belief in the power of positive thinking can too easily turn into a game of "blame the victim." If someone tries to beat his or her cancer and fails to do so, then the implication is that the person simply did not try hard enough or had the wrong attitude. People dying of cancer should certainly not be led to believe that they are responsible for being unable to cure themselves; they do not need to be given an additional burden of guilt.

Interim Summary

Stress and Health

Stress is defined in terms of our physiological and psychological response to stimuli that either prevent us from obtaining a goal or endanger our well-being. People's emotional reactions to aversive stimuli can harm their health. Selye's well-known model describes how prolonged exposure to stress leads to illness and sometimes death. The stress response, which Cannon called the fight-or-flight response, is useful as a short-term response to threatening stimuli but is harmful in the long term. This response includes increased activity of the sympathetic branch of the autonomic nervous system and increased secretion of epinephrine, norepinephrine, and glucocorticoids by the adrenal gland.

Although increased levels of epinephrine and norepinephrine can raise blood pressure, most of the harm to health comes from glucocorticoids. Prolonged exposure to high levels of these hormones can increase blood pressure, damage muscle tissue, lead to infertility, inhibit growth, inhibit the inflammatory response, and suppress the immune system. It can also damage the hippocampus, and some investigators believe that glucocorticoids accelerate the aging process.

Because the harm of most forms of stress comes from our own response to it, individual differences in personality variables can alter the effects of stressful situations. The most important variable is the nature of a person's coping response. Research on the type A behavior pattern suggests that some of these variables—in particular, hostility—can predict the likelihood of CHD. However, the research findings are mixed, and some suggest that health-related behaviors may be more important than patterns of emotional reactions.

Posttraumatic stress disorder is a serious reaction to unusually intense stress that sometimes does not occur until several months after the stressful event. Personality factors appear to affect an individual's susceptibility to this disorder. Research has demonstrated the beneficial effects of social support after the stressful event.

Psychoneuroimmunology is a new field of study that investigates interactions between behavior and the immune system as mediated by the nervous system. The immune system consists of several types of white blood cells that produce chemically mediated and cell-mediated responses. The immune system can produce harm when it triggers an allergic reaction or when it attacks the body's own tissues in autoimmune diseases.

The most important mechanism by which stress impairs immune function is increased blood levels of glucocorticoids. In addition, neural input to the bone marrow, lymph nodes, and thymus gland may also play a role; and naturally occurring opioids appear to suppress the activity of internal killer cells.

A wide variety of stressful situations have been shown to increase people's susceptibility to infectious diseases. For example, the stress associated with the loss of a spouse appears to contribute to upper respiratory infections in some people.

Several investigators have suggested that a type C (cancer-prone) personality exists. Although the evidence is mixed, some careful, long-term studies suggest that cancerous tumors may develop faster in passive people who suppress the expression of negative emotions. A study on the effects of psychotherapy suggests that learning to cope with the pain and stress of cancer can increase survival rates. We do not know whether personality variables affect the growth of cancer directly, through internal physiological processes, or whether they affect people's health-related behavior, such as exercise, avoidance of smoking, and compliance with medical treatment.

Thought Questions

- What kinds of stressors do you face in your life? When confronted with a stressor, what kinds of physiological, emotional, cognitive, and behavioral reactions do you experience? What makes some stressors more aversive to you than others?
- Has the stress response outlived its usefulness to our species? It seems as though this response was more useful to our prehistoric ancestors in avoiding predators and finding food than it is to us in our work and play. In your opinion, would our lives be better off without this response? Explain.

Coping with Everyday Stress

Stress is a fact of everyday life, regardless of one's lifestyle. The degree to which we experience stress and the degree to which stress impairs our health depends to a large extent on our perception of the threat posed by the stressor. The number of potential stressors is very large. Depending on the individual, almost any aspect of the environment can be perceived as a stressor.

Sources of Stress

Stress can be induced by changes that threaten or otherwise complicate life. The death of a spouse, being promoted at work, changes in social activities, getting married, and sustaining a personal injury or illness are significant life changes that cause stress and disrupt everyday life (Holmes and Rahe, 1967). Some evidence has accumulated that suggests that if an individual experiences enough changes in life-style over a short time period, he or she is likely to develop a physical illness within the next two years (Rahe and Arthur, 1978). Other research suggests that not all people who encounter a series of significant stressors over a short period are at risk for illness (DuPue and Monroe, 1986). Why? Once again, the answer is because of the way in which people perceive stressors. Recall Lazarus's idea of cognitive appraisal: The amount of stress induced by a stimulus perceived to be a stressor is determined by how significant we *believe* its threat to be and whether we feel competent to cope with that threat.

Stressors do not have to be catastrophic or cause significant changes in life-style to induce stress. Often the everyday hassles we experience are enough to leave us feeling stressed out. Locking our keys in the car, being late for an appointment, or having a disagreement with a friend are examples of stressful everyday events.

A common source of daily stress comes simply from making routine choices about what to do, how to do it, or when to do it. Consider, for example, a choice between studying tonight for a test you have tomorrow or going to a party with some friends. You want to do both, but you can only do one (you are back into the classic self-control situation again—the choice between a small, short-term reward and a larger, long-term reward). Psychologists refer to this as an *approach-approach conflict* because the choice involves two desirable outcomes. Other choices involve *approach-avoidance conflicts*—one outcome is desirable and the other is not. For example, you want to visit England and decide to travel by ship because you are afraid of flying. Still other choices involve *avoidance-avoidance conflicts* in which both outcomes are undesirable. For instance, choosing between having a root canal procedure or having a tooth extracted creates stress because you do not want to have either one of them, yet one needs to be done.

Several different tests have been developed to measure the severity of various stressors on people. Among the first measures to be developed was Holmes and Rahe's (1967) Social Readjustment Rating Scale (SRRS), which was devised on the assumption that any *change* in a person's life—for better or worse—is a stressor. The test asks people to rate the amount of change or adjustment caused by recent events in their lives,

such as getting married or divorced, getting a new job or being fired, moving to a new location, and losing a loved one. Responses are given in terms of life-change units (LCUs)—how much change or adjustment is caused by specific events. Once a person completes the SRRS, the LCUs are summed, resulting in a single score. High scores indicate high levels of stress and low scores represent low levels of stress. People who get high scores have been shown to have more health-related illness and adjustment problems than have people who get lower scores (Holmes and Rahe, 1967; Monroe, Thase, and Simons, 1992).

Another commonly used scale, the Daily Hassles and Uplifts Scale, measures daily events that are either troublesome (hassles) or pleasant (uplifts) (DeLongis, Folkman, and Lazarus, 1988). This scale has people rate, at each day's end, the extent to which an event—such as the weather, deadlines, family, and physical appearance—served as a hassle or uplift for them on that day. This scale may be filled out daily over extended periods to provide a picture of how the routine events of everyday life create stress for people. Daily hassles yield a more accurate prediction of physical illness and adjustment problems than do daily uplifts (DeLongis et al., 1988) and major life events (Garrett et al., 1991).

Coping Styles and Strategies

So far, we have concentrated on discussing the bad news about stress: its damaging effects on the body and mind. Now, for the good news: Each of us can learn to control stress. We may not always be able to predict when and where we will encounter stressors or to control their intensity, but we can mitigate their damaging effects by adopting coping strategies that are consistent with our life-styles. A **coping strategy** is simply a plan of action that we follow, either in anticipation of encountering a stressor or as a direct response to stress as it occurs, which is effective in reducing the level of stress we experience.

According to Lazarus and Folkman (1984; Folkman and Lazarus, 1991), there are two types of coping responses: problem-focused and emotion-focused. **Problem-focused coping** is directed toward the source of the stress. For example, if the stress is job-related, a person might try to change conditions at the job site or take courses to acquire skills that will enable him or her to obtain a different job. **Emotion-focused coping** is directed toward a person's own personal reaction to the stressor. For example, a person might try to relax and forget about the problem or find solace in the company of friends. Obviously, if the source of a stress-producing problem has a potential solution, problem-focused coping is the best strategy. If it does not, then emotion-focused coping is the only option.

We each have our own idiosyncratic ways of dealing with stress that can be categorized as being emotion-focused. In fact, health psychologists have shown several of these methods to be effective in controlling stress, namely, aerobic exercise, cognitive reappraisal, progressive relaxation training, and social support.

---

coping strategy   A plan of action that a person follows to reduce the perceived level of stress, either in anticipation of encountering a stressor or in response to its occurrence.

problem-focused coping   Any coping behavior that is directed at reducing or eliminating a stressor.

emotion-focused coping   Any coping behavior that is directed toward changing one's own emotional reaction to a stressor.

Aerobic exercise, such as bicycling and rowing, not only has positive effects on physical health but also reduces stress. Being in good physical condition may simply make people feel better about themselves.

Aerobic Exercise

We have already seen that people who engage regularly in aerobic exercise are likely to live longer than people who do not exercise regularly (Paffenbarger et al., 1986). Another important benefit also accrues to those who consistently take time for aerobic workouts and that is stress reduction. Consider the results of an experiment involving mildly depressed female college students (McCann and Holmes, 1984). The students were assigned to one of three groups: a control group receiving no treatment for depression, a group who received relaxation training, and a group who engaged in aerobic exercises (jogging and dancing). The students rated their depression levels at the beginning of the experiment and then again ten weeks later. As expected, self-reported levels of depression for control subjects showed no change. Subjects given relaxation training showed a slight decrease in depression. Those who participated in aerobic exercises showed a large decrease in depression.

Although we know that aerobic exercise is effective in reducing stress, we do not yet know exactly how it reduces stress. One possibility is that increased heart and lung efficiency coupled with the lower blood pressure that results from aerobic exercise simply makes people feel better. Another possibility is that people who can adjust their schedules to make room for regular workouts have a sense of control that those who cannot find the time for exercise do not have. People who make exercise a priority in their schedules have to *control* other aspects of their lives to ensure that they do, indeed, exercise. As we saw in Chapter 14, people who have an internal locus of control take responsibility for the course of their lives, which means that they enjoy taking credit for their successes. And earning credit and achieving success can make for a happier life.

Cognitive Reappraisal

Aerobic exercise is not the coping strategy of choice for everyone. Some people find that simply altering their perceptions of the threat posed by stressors reduces stress. This coping strategy is called **cognitive reappraisal** (or *cognitive restructuring*) and is an extension of Lazarus and Folkman's idea of cognitive appraisal. The rationale underlying this strategy is easy to grasp: If our cognitive appraisal of a stressor is a determining factor in producing stress, then by *reappraising* that stressor as being less threatening, stress should be reduced. Sometimes simply learning to substitute an incompatible response, such as replacing a negative statement with a positive one, is sufficient to reduce stress (Lazarus, 1971; Meichenbaum, 1977). For example, students who suffer from test anxiety perceive tests as extremely threatening. They may say to themselves, "I am going to flunk the test tomorrow," or, "That test is going to be so hard." To reappraise the stressor in this case would involve replacing these statements with ones such as "I'm going to pass that test tomorrow" or "Sure, that test will be hard, but I'm ready for it."

Cognitive reappraisal is an effective coping strategy because it is often a more realistic approach to interpreting the threat posed by stressors than is the original appraisal. We have good reason to appraise a charging bear as a real threat, but not a college examination. After all, we may not be able to deal well with the bear, but we can always learn how to take tests and improve our study habits. An additional benefit of cognitive reappraisal is that it teaches the individual that he or she can take control of stressful situations.

Relaxation Training

A third coping strategy is simply learning to relax when confronted with a stressor. Relaxing is based on the same principle as cognitive reappraisal: Substitute an incompatible response for the stress reaction. Consider the following example. You are anxious to get home, but you are caught in rush hour traffic. Your blood pressure rises, you begin to perspire, and you feel a knot in your stomach. What would happen if you were to relax? First, these physical responses would gradually recede, and second, you would feel less stress.

One procedure for producing relaxation is the **progressive relaxation technique**. It involves three steps: (1) recognizing your body's signals informing you that you are experiencing stress; (2) using those signals as a cue to begin relaxing; and (3) relaxing by focusing your attention on dif-

cognitive reappraisal   Any coping strategy in which one alters one's perception of the threat posed by a stressor to reduce stress.

progressive relaxation technique.   A relaxation technique involving three steps: (1) recognizing the body's signals that indicate the presence of stress; (2) using those signals as a cue to begin relaxing; and (3) relaxing groups of muscles, beginning with those in the head and neck and then those in the arms and legs.

ferent groups of muscles, beginning with those in the head and neck and then those in the arms and legs. Here is an example of how relaxation may be used to reduce feelings of stress. Suppose that when confronted by a stressor—for example, a test—you respond by tensing certain muscles: those in your hand and fingers that you use to hold your pen or pencil and those around your mouth that you use to clench your teeth. Once you become aware of these responses, you can use them as cues to relax the muscle groups involved.

Social Support

Although all of us experience stress, the experience is a subjective and private matter. Nobody else can truly know what we feel inside. However, being confronted by a stressor and coping with stress are often social matters. We learn as children to seek others—parents, siblings, and friends—when we need help. This is a pattern of coping that continues over the lifespan. *Social support*, the help that we receive from others in times of stress, is an important coping strategy for many people for two reasons. First, we can benefit from the experience of others in dealing with the same or similar stressors. Other people can show us how to cope, perhaps by teaching us how to reappraise the situation. Second, other people can provide encouragement and incentives to overcome the stressor when we may otherwise fail to cope with the stressful situation.

Stress Inoculation Training

According to psychologist Donald Meichenbaum, the best way to cope with stress is to take the offensive—to have a plan in mind for dealing with stressors before you are actually confronted by them. In other words, people should not wait until they are faced with a stressor to cope with it. Instead, they should anticipate the kinds of stressors most likely to affect them and develop the most effective *coping plan* for dealing with specific stressors. Meichenbaum (1985), in fact, has devised a problem-focused coping method, called **stress inoculation training**, which focuses on helping people to develop coping skills that will decrease their susceptibility to the negative effects of stress. Stress inoculation training has been found to be effective in reducing stress levels among people working in a variety of settings, including nurses, teachers, police trainees (Bishop, 1994), and professional athletes (Cox, 1991).

In Meichenbaum's words, stress inoculation training

> . . . is analogous to the concept of medical inoculation against biological diseases. . . . Analogous to medical inoculation, [stress inoculation training] is designed to build "psychological antibodies," or coping skills, and to enhance resistance through exposure to stimuli that

stress inoculation training The stress management program developed by Meichenbaum for teaching people to develop coping skills that increase their resistance to the negative effects of stress.

are strong enough to arouse defenses without being so powerful as to overcome them. (1985, p. 21)

Stress inoculation training usually occurs in a clinical setting involving a therapist and a client and takes place over three phases aimed at achieving seven goals. (See *Table 16.6*.)

The first phase is called the *conceptualization phase* and involves two basic goals. Goal 1 involves learning about the *transactional* nature of stress and coping. Stress and coping are strongly influenced by the interaction of cognitive and environmental variables. A person experiences stress to the extent that he or she appraises the stressor—an environmental variable—as taxing or overwhelming his or her ability to cope with it—a cognitive variable. In Meichenbaum's view, coping is any behavioral-cognitive attempt to overcome, eliminate, or otherwise control the negative effects caused by the stressor (see also Lazarus and Folkman, 1984).

Goal 2 involves becoming better at realistically appraising stressful situations by taking stock of, or self-monitoring, patterns in maladaptive thinking, feeling, and behaving. A person may keep a diary, or a "stress log," to record stressful events, the conditions under which these events occur, and their reactions to these events.

The second phase is called the *skills acquisition and rehearsal phase* and involves Goals 3 through 5. Goal 3 involves learning specific problem-solving skills aimed at reducing stress. For example, a person may learn to identify and define a specific stressor and outline a plan for dealing with it in behavioral terms. The plan should include developing alternative ideas for dealing with the stressor and considering the possible consequences that correspond to each alternative. At this point, a person may find relaxation training and self-instructional training, in which he or she learns to make positive self-statements when confronted by a stressor, helpful.

Goal 4 involves learning and rehearsing emotion-regulation and self-control skills. These skills help people to remain calm and rational when confronted with a stressor. Goal 5 involves learning how to use maladaptive responses as a cue to invoke the new coping strategy. For example, when faced with a stressor, you may feel yourself getting tense. This feeling of tension is your cue to implement specific aspects of your inoculation training, which presumably would reduce your level of stress.

The third and final phase of Meichenbaum's program is called the *application and follow-through phase* and includes Goals 6 and 7. Goal 6 involves *imagery rehearsal*, in which a person practices coping with the stressor by imagining being confronted by that stressor in progressively more difficult situations. The purpose of rehearsing the coping skills is to build confidence in the ability to use the new coping strategy. Goal 7 involves learning to apply new coping abilities to both expected and unexpected stressors. This might be accomplished by imagining several situations in which you feel anxious, imagining implementing the coping strategy in response to the anxiety, and, finally, imagining feeling relieved as a result of coping with the stressor.

Table 16.6

Summary of the Phases and Goals of Meichenbaum's (1985) Stress Inoculation Training Program

Conceptualization Phase
Goal 1:   Learning the transactional nature of stress and coping.
Goal 2:   Learning to become better at realistically appraising stressful situations by learning self-monitoring skills with respect to negative or maladaptive thoughts, emotions, and behaviors.

Skills Acquisition and Rehearsal Phase
Goal 3:   Learning problem-solving skills specific to the stressor.
Goal 4:   Learning and rehearsing emotion-regulation and self-control skills.
Goal 5:   Learning how to use maladaptive responses as cues to implement the new coping strategy.

Application and Follow-Through Phase
Goal 6:   Learning to practice imagery rehearsal using progressively more difficult or stressful situations.
Goal 7:   Learning to apply new coping skills to other, perhaps unexpected, stressors.

Source: Adapted from Meichenbaum, D. *Stress Inoculation Training.* New York: Pergamon Press, 1985, pp.21–26.

How might we use Meichenbaum's system to deal with everyday stressors? Suppose that, like many people, you are uncomfortable in new social situations. You feel comfortable around friends and people that you know well, but you become anxious or nervous when you meet people for the first time. In fact, you become so nervous that it interferes with your ability to function socially—you may even begin to avoid social situations where you would meet new people.

Goal 1: Understanding the transactional nature of stress. In this case, you perceive meeting new people as stressful. You may avoid going to parties and other social functions, which makes you feel better because the anxiety goes away. Although you really want to become more outgoing, you become anxious when you find yourself in such social situations: Your stomach tenses, your palms sweat, and you worry about what to say and how to act. In other words, specific environmental variables—social functions, meeting new people, and so on—cause cognitive and emotional discomfort, such as anxiety and nervousness. You feel inadequate in coping with these types of social situations.

Goal 2: Learning to appraise these social situations realistically through self-monitoring. Which social situations make you feel the most nervous? Do you feel more anxious meeting same-sex or opposite-sex people? Are there instances when meeting new people is not anxiety-provoking? Do you feel less anxious when you are forced to meet people on your own or when a friend introduces you to others? By answering questions such as these, you learn more about the specific elements of the social situation that are stressful. And, through such self-monitoring (which also includes keeping a record of specific social situations and how you respond to them), you become more likely to look at the situation more objectively, which facilitates your ability to appraise the situation realistically. You may find, in fact, that only specific social situations, such as meeting people of the opposite sex, make you nervous.

Goal 3: Acquiring specific problem-solving behaviors targeted at reducing stress. What advice might you offer someone who experiences anxiety in social situations? What behaviors might you engage in that would be effective in reducing the amount of stress that you experience when meeting new people? What are the drawbacks to these different behaviors? By exploring these sorts of questions, you begin to think about which actions on your part might be effective at reducing stress in social situations. Let us assume that you have identified the stressor as being meeting people of the opposite sex. The next step is to outline a plan of action for coping with this stressor. You decide that you will tackle your problem by first thinking about how you might best engage in the following behaviors and then actually implementing them (questions in parentheses are examples of questions you might ask yourself while thinking about how you will implement a course of action):

1. You will go to a party a friend of yours is throwing next Friday night. (Should you go alone or with another friend for moral support? Should you arrive early or late?)

2. You will introduce yourself to the first member of the opposite sex that you meet by stating your name and asking the other person his or her name—"Hi, My name is _____; what's yours?" You will then ask this person where he or she is from, who he or she knows at the party, and what he or she is studying or does for a living. (What should I do if this person turns away at some point? Should I take it as a rejection or should I just forget about it and introduce myself to someone else?)

3. If the person responds to your questions, you will attempt to extend the conversation for at least another minute before you politely excuse yourself to talk with people that you know well. (If the conversation is going well, should I keep it going for as long as I can?)

4. You will meet at least three new people using this strategy before the party ends.

Outlining the problem and the steps toward resolving the problem in this fashion will allow you to develop a plan of action, to critique it (for example, what should I do if the person I have introduced myself to won't respond to my questions or is just as nervous about meeting people as I am?), and to reconsider the problem in light of your strategy.

Goal 4: Learning to control emotions and developing self-control in the face of the stressor. You may feel extremely anxious when meeting new people, even to the point that you feel as though you cannot control your anxiety—you want to run away from the situation. To overcome the stressor, though, you must learn to subordinate these feelings to more rational thinking. For example, when meeting new people, try to focus on what you must do to meet people rather than on your own anxiety. That is, concentrate on what it is you must do—the specific behaviors you need to execute in order to meet someone and carry on a conversation with him or her—rather than on feeling nervous. It is with this goal, more than any of the others, that a therapist is likely to be of help. A therapist would offer you advice on the step-by-step behaviors you would engage in to replace maladaptive emotions and responses with adaptive ones.

Goal 5: Using maladaptive responses as cues to implement the plan of action. The key to confronting stressors using stress inoculation training is to change how you respond to the symptoms of stress that the stressors elicit from you. Rather than panicking when you feel stressed, you use the symptoms of stress as a cue to implement what you have learned in your inoculation training. You may, for example, tell yourself, "I can handle the situation," or "I'll relax and just be myself," or, "Now is the time for me to introduce myself and ask this person his or her name," when you feel that first tinge of butterflies in your stomach. Goal 6 prepares you mentally for taking this step in reality.

Goal 6: Practicing the plan of action. Once you have decided the behaviors you need to adopt to reduce your stress, practice them mentally and with someone else. Picture yourself meeting someone that you have seen before but do not know. Imagine how you will respond if he or she asks you a particular question. Do a dress rehearsal as well. Ask one of your close friends to pretend that he or she is someone to whom you will introduce yourself. Ask your friend to respond to your questions the way he or she would if meeting you for the first time.

Goal 7: Applying new coping abilities in expected and unexpected socially stressful situations. Because you now better understand the nature of your stress and have acquired and practiced problem-solving skills and coping strategies, you are ready to imagine confronting the stressor in real-life situations. For example, imagine going to a party and meeting new people. Imagine the conversation you may carry on with the people you imagine to be there. After such imagery rehearsal, going to a real party and meeting new people should be less stressful. You may not become the life of the party, but you should be more comfortable mingling with your fellow partygoers.

Stress is an inevitable consequence of environmental change. Both large changes, such as a natural disaster or changing jobs, and small changes, such as remembering that we have a quiz tomorrow, contribute to the overall level of stress that we experience at any one time. Whether stress impairs our health depends on three variables: the extent to which we appraise the stressor as threatening, whether we engage in good health practices, and the extent to which we use coping strategies effectively. The combined effects of these variables on the relationship between stress and health are summarized in Figure 16.11. (See *Figure 16.11.*)

Interim Summary

Coping with Everyday Stress

Stress may stem from a wide variety of sources. Even positive events, such as the birth of a child or the marriage of a son or daughter can produce stress. Stress may lead to physical illness when a person undergoes several stressful events over a short period of time. However, the extent to which people become ill appears to depend on the extent to which they perceive a stressor as being a threat to their well-being and the extent to which they believe they can cope with that threat.

Lazarus and Folkman (1984) have identified two types of coping. Problem-focused coping represents any attempt to reduce stress by attempting to change the event or situation producing the stress. Emotion-focused coping centers on changing one's personal reaction to the stressful event or situation. Emotion-focused coping may involve activities such as aerobic exercise, cognitive reappraisal, relaxation training, and seeking social support.

Meichenbaum's stress inoculation training program is a problem-focused coping strategy that prepares people to cope with anticipated stressors. The program involves three phases and seven goals. The first phase involves learning how to conceptualize the transactional nature of stress. The second phase entails learning coping skills specific to the stressors in their lives and practicing or rehearsing these skills in hypothetical situations. The third phase involves preparing people to implement these coping skills in real-life situations. The seven goals of stress inoculation training focus on specific kinds of knowledge, behavior, and coping strategies central to preparing people to anticipate, confront, and reduce the threat posed by stressful situations.

Thought Questions

■ Which general approach do you take to coping with the stress in your life, problem-focused or emotion-focused? What led you to develop this style of coping? How effective are you at coping with stress?

■ What stressors do you seem to be able to handle better than your friends? What stressors are some of your

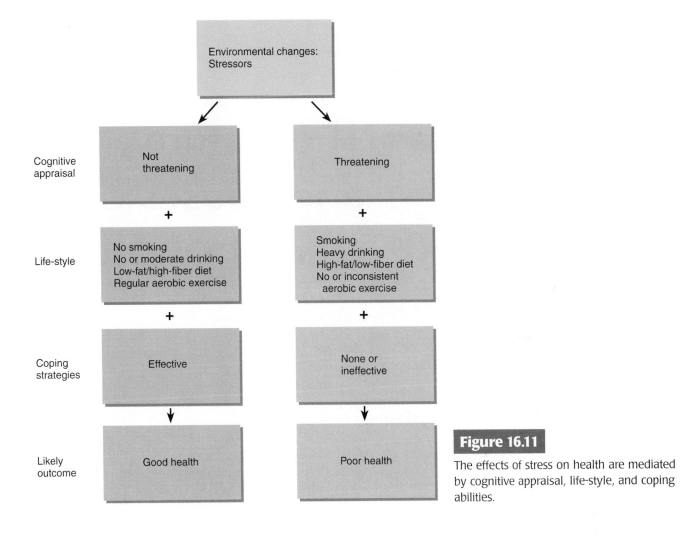

Figure 16.11

The effects of stress on health are mediated by cognitive appraisal, life-style, and coping abilities.

friends better at handling than you? To what extent do differences in perception of the threat posed by these stressors account for these differences in being able to cope with them?

- Think of a stressor that is especially difficult for you to deal with. Develop an outline based on Meichen-baum's stress inoculation training program for coping with this stressor. Explain the reasons why your program may or may not be effective in helping you cope with this stressor.

Suggestions for Further Reading

Bishop, G.D. *Health Psychology: Integrating Mind and Body.* Boston: Allyn and Bacon, 1994.

This book covers all aspects of health psychology. It contains specific chapters devoted to health promotion, stress, illness, and coping with stress and illness.

Meichenbaum, D. *Stress Inoculation Training.* New York: Pergamon Press, 1985.

This brief book outlines Meichenbaum's program for managing stress. Although the book was originally written for practitioners, it is written plainly enough for everyone to understand its contents.

Monat, A., and Lazarus, R.S. (eds.). *Stress and Coping: An Anthology.* New York: Columbia University Press, 1991.

This book is a collection of highly readable articles written by the foremost experts on stress and coping. The articles focus on both the biological and psychological components of stress and methods of coping with a variety of stressors.

Rushing, W.A. *The AIDS Epidemic: Social Dimensions of an Infectious Disease.* Boulder, CO: Westview Press, 1995.

This book provides an overview of the impact of AIDS on social behavior. It explores both the social causes of the disease as well as cultural reactions to it.

Chapter 17

The Nature and Causes of Mental Disorders

Chapter Outline

Classification and Diagnosis of Mental Disorders

What Is "Abnormal"? • Perspectives on the Causes of Mental Disorders • The DSM-IV Classification Scheme • Some Problems with DSM-IV Classification • The Need for Classification • Prevalence of Mental Disorders • *Evaluating Scientific Issues: Clinical Versus Actuarial Diagnosis*

Abnormal behavior is any behavior that departs from the norm. Several perspectives on the causes of mental disorders exist. The DSM-IV is a classification system that describes an individual's psychological condition on the basis of criteria that must be met before he or she should be diagnosed as having a mental disorder. Because it is based on the medical model of abnormal behavior, the DSM-IV may overlook environmental and cognitive causes of abnormal behavior. However, some form of classification of abnormal behavior is necessary to diagnose mental disorders accurately and to treat them effectively. Although researchers have developed statistical methods for diagnosing mental disorders, many clinical psychologists still prefer to rely on their clinical experiences to make such diagnoses.

Anxiety, Somatoform, and Dissociative Mental Disorders

Anxiety Disorders • Somatoform Disorders • Dissociative Disorders • *Biology and Culture: Culture-Bound Syndromes*

Several mental disorders involve unrealistic and excessive anxiety, fear, or guilt. These disorders may involve anxiety that has no apparent cause, intense fear of specific objects, intrusive thoughts, compelling urges to engage in ritual-like behavior, physical problems with no organic basis, and sudden disruptions in consciousness that affect one's sense of identity. Culture-bound syndromes are mental disorders that are present in only one or a few cultures.

Personality Disorders

Antisocial Personality Disorder

Personality disorders are marked by rigid traits that impair normal functioning. The most serious of these disorders is the antisocial personality disorder. Persons with this disorder are dishonest, irresponsible, incapable of feeling empathy or sympathy for others, mean-spirited, and feel no remorse for their misdeeds.

Psychoactive Substance Use Disorders

Description • Possible Causes

Psychoactive substance use disorders include both drug abuse and drug addiction. Both heredity and brain chemistry play prominent roles in these disorders.

Schizophrenic Disorders

Description • Types of Schizophrenia • Early Signs of Schizophrenia • Possible Causes

Schizophrenic symptoms include disorganized thought, disturbances of affect, distorted perception, and disturbances of motor activity. Each of the four types of schizophrenia is diagnosed according to specific criteria based on these symptoms. Signs or characteristics of schizophrenia may appear during childhood. Researchers have found that heredity, environmental stressors, brain damage, and biochemical factors play crucial roles in the different forms of schizophrenia.

Mood Disorders

Description • Possible Causes

Mood disorders involve extreme depression or swings between depression and extreme happiness and high energy levels. Mood disorders appear to involve one or more of the following causes: faulty cognition, heredity, brain biochemistry, and sleep/wake cycles.

t happened when I was about seven years old. It was a Sunday after-noon and I was watching television. I heard a lot of yelling and screaming in the kitchen. I ran to see what was the matter. They were in the midst of a fight. When they saw me, I turned and ran into the bedroom.

That was the last time I really remember seeing my father until I was about twenty-one. I'm told that my sister and I visited him after the divorce, but it's all pretty fuzzy to me. I know that shortly after my parents' big fight, my dad was institutionalized for the first time. His diagnosis: paranoid schizophrenia. My father has been in and out of mental institutions over the past thirty years. He is currently treated on an outpatient basis with chlorpro-mazine, a drug that reduces the symptoms of his disorder. He manages pretty well as long as he takes his medication.

I didn't go looking to reestablish a relationship with my father; it was all his doing. I was in college out west at the time. Somehow, he got my address and wrote me. He told me very little about the past fourteen years. He simply wanted to start with me anew. When I re-turned home for the Christmas holidays, I went to see him. He was in the intensive care unit of the local hospital. He had attempted suicide. His first words to me, after not seeing me for nearly a decade and a half, were, "I can't do anything right—not even kill myself."

Despite the situation, we managed to get reacquainted. He wanted to take the relation-ship a little faster than I did, which brings me to the point I wish to make. About a year after I saw him at the hospital, I received a phone call from him (I was then back at school 2000 miles away). He said he had saved some money and wanted to come to visit me. I was stunned: I thought to myself, "What would my friends think of me having a crazy father? I can't let him come out here." So I told him that this was a really bad time for me, that I was overloaded with school work, and that I had several exams coming up—all lies. I was simply embarrassed about having a father with a mental disorder. Disappointed, he said he under-stood about my heavy workload at school and that he would make other plans.

About two weeks later, I received another call from him. He told me that he had just got-ten home from visiting the city in which I was living, where he had spent the previous week. He said that he knew how busy I was, but that he just wanted to learn a little more about me and my life. He told me that after spending time in the town where I lived—walking the same streets that I walked and seeing the same mountains that I saw every day—he felt closer to me and could identify with me much more. And I had told him not to come. I now look back at the situation with a deep sense of humiliation and regret.

My sharing of such a personal experience with you might have made you feel at least a bit uncomfortable. That was part of my intention. If I had told you about my father's experi-ence with surgery for, say, a back problem, would you have felt uncomfortable? Probably not. Yet, when I tell you about my father's mental disorder you do. Why? That's a question I will leave for you to answer.

Life is complex, and things do not always go smoothly. We are all beset by major and minor tragedies, but we usually manage to cope with them. Occasionally, we find ourselves behaving irrationally, having trouble concentrating on a sin-gle topic, or experiencing feelings that do not seem appropri-ate for the circumstances. Sometimes, we brood about imaginary disasters or harbor hurtful thoughts about people we love. For most of us, however, these problems remain oc-casional and do not cause much concern.

But the lives of some people, like my father's, are domi-nated by disordered thoughts, disturbed feelings, or inappro-priate behaviors. Their problems become so severe that they cannot cope with life. Consequently, they either withdraw from it, seek the help of others, or are judged unfit by society and are placed in an institution. What goes wrong?

Some mental disorders—especially the less severe ones—appear to be caused by environmental factors or by a person's perception of these factors, such as stress or unhealthy family interactions. For example, a boy who is constantly criticized by an overbearing, demanding parent may learn to be passive and nonresponding so that the attacks will cease as soon as possible. This strategy may be adaptive in interactions with his parent, but it would be maladaptive if he were to use it too readily when stressed by other social situations. In contrast, many of the more severe mental disorders appear to be caused by hereditary and other biological factors that disrupt normal thought processes or produce inappropriate emotional reactions.

This chapter describes the nature of some of the more important mental disorders and discusses research on their causes; Chapter 18 discusses the treatment of mental disorders and the efforts of clinical psychologists to help people with problems of daily living. The descriptions of mental disorders in this chapter necessarily make distinctions that are not always easy to make in real life; the essential features of the more important mental disorders are simplified here for the sake of clarity. In addition, many of the cases that clinicians encounter are less clear-cut than the ones included here and are thus not so easily classified (Carson, Butcher, and Mineka, 1996). Space does not permit coverage of features in our society—such as problems of marriage and family life, social inequities, war, and personal adjustment—that cause mental stress but do not lead to diagnosis of a specific mental disorder. Fortunately, more and more people are coming to realize that the line dividing normal and abnormal behavior is not sharp and that they need not be "sick" to profit from professional advice concerning their feelings and behavior.

Classification and Diagnosis of Mental Disorders

To understand, diagnose, and treat psychological disorders, some sort of classification system is needed. The need for a comprehensive classification system of psychological disorders was first recognized by Emil Kraepelin (1856-1926), who provided his version in a textbook of psychiatry published in 1883. The Association of Medical Superintendents of American Institutions for the Insane, a forerunner of the American Psychiatric Association, later incorporated Kraepelin's ideas into a classification system of its own. The classification most widely used today still retains a number of Kraepelin's original categories.

What Is "Abnormal"?

Mental disorders are characterized by abnormal behavior, thoughts, and feelings. The term *abnormal* literally refers to any departure from the norm. Thus, a short or tall person is "abnormal" and so is someone who is especially intelligent or talented. Albert Einstein was "abnormal," and so were composer George Gershwin and baseball player Babe Ruth. But as

you know, the term *abnormal* has taken on a pejorative connotation: We use it to refer to characteristics that we dislike or fear.

The most important feature of a mental disorder is not whether a person's behavior is "abnormal"—different from that of most other people—but whether it is *maladaptive*. Mental disorders cause distress or discomfort and often interfere with people's ability to lead useful, productive lives. They often make it impossible for people to hold jobs, raise families, or relate to others socially. But then a person who holds an unpopular religious or political belief that violates a social norm may be ostracized by the community and find it impossible to find employment or to make friends. Certainly, in that society, the person's behavior is maladaptive. But should we say that the person has a mental disorder? Of course not. Depending on our own point of view, we might be tempted to label the behavior as courageous and wise or as misguided and foolish. But simply disagreeing with the government, with established religious practices, or with popular beliefs is not sufficient evidence for a diagnosis of mental illness.

Although the diagnosis of mental disorders should be as objective as possible, it may never be completely free from social and political judgments. In societies like ours, receiving direct messages from God and being transported on mystical voyages to heaven would probably be labeled as being hallucinatory or delusional, whereas in other times and places they might be taken as signs of holiness and devotion. If historical records are accurate, the behavior of many people who are now venerated as prophets or saints would be regarded quite differently if they were alive today. But the fact that diagnoses are affected by the social context does not mean that they are invalid. People *do* have mental disorders: They *do* have delusions and hallucinations, they *do* have thought disorders, they *do* experience inappropriate emotions. And mental disorders bring pain and discomfort to these people and to their friends and families.

The dividing line between normal behavior and abnormal behavior is not always clear.

Perspectives on the Causes of Mental Disorders

What causes mental disorders? In general, they are caused by an interaction among hereditary, cognitive, and environmental factors. In some cases, the genetic component is strong and the person is likely to develop a mental disorder even in a very supportive environment. In other cases, the cognitive and environmental components are strong. A complete understanding of mental disorders requires that scientists investigate genetic, cognitive, and environmental factors. Once genetic factors are identified, the scientist faces the task of determining the physiological effects of the relevant genes and the consequences of these effects on a person's susceptibility to a mental disorder. Understanding the cognitive factors involved in mental disorders requires identification of the origins of distorted perceptions and maladaptive thought patterns. And environmental factors encompass more than simply a person's family history or present social interactions; they also include the effects of prenatal health and nutrition, childhood diseases, and exposure to drugs and environmental toxins.

Different psychologists and other mental health professionals approach the study of mental disorders from different perspectives, each of which places more or less emphasis on these factors. The perspectives differ primarily in their explanation of the *etiology*, or origin, of mental disorders. Because several of these perspectives were discussed in Chapters 1 and 14, I will only briefly discuss them here as they pertain to mental disorders.

The Psychodynamic Perspective

According to the psychodynamic perspective, which is based on Freud's early work, mental disorders originate in intrapsychic conflict produced by the three warring factions of the mind—the id, ego, and superego. For some people, the conflict becomes so severe that the mind's defense mechanisms are ineffective, resulting in mental disorders that may involve, among other symptoms, extreme anxiety, obsessive thoughts and compulsive behavior, depression, distorted perceptions and patterns of thinking, and paralysis or blindness for which there is no physical cause.

As we saw in Chapter 14, the id, ego, and superego are hypothetical constructs—they are not physical structures of the brain. But Freud and his followers often spoke as if these structures were real, at least in their functions. Even today, psychodynamic theorists and practitioners approach mental disorders by emphasizing the role of intrapsychic conflict in creating psychological distress and maladaptive behavior. As we will see in Chapter 18, psychodynamic therapists attempt to make their clients more aware of these intrapsychic conflicts in an effort to resolve them.

The Medical Perspective

The medical perspective has its origins in the work of the ancient Greek physician Hippocrates. Recall from Chapter 14 that Hippocrates formulated the idea that excesses in the four humors (black bile, yellow bile, blood, and phlegm) led to emotional problems. Other physicians, Greek and Roman alike, extended Hippocrates' ideas and developed the concept of mental illness—illnesses of the mind. Eventually, specialized institutions or asylums were established where persons with mental disorders were confined. Early asylums were ill-run and the patients' problems were poorly understood and often mistreated. During the eighteenth and nineteenth centuries, massive reforms in the institutional care of people with mental disorders took place. The quality of the facilities and the amount of compassion for patients improved, and physicians, including neurosurgeons and psychiatrists, who were specifically trained in the medical treatment of mental disorders were hired to care for these patients.

Today the medical perspective is the dominant perspective in the treatment of mental disorders. As we will see in Chapter 18, many persons with mental disorders are no longer confined to mental institutions. Instead, they are treated on an out-patient basis with drugs that are effective in abating the

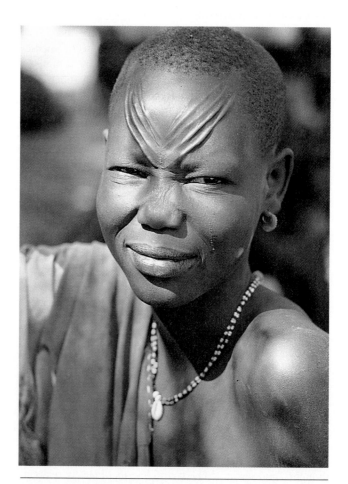

Cultural norms dictate what is appropriate in any given culture. For example, in the Sudan, the scars on this boy's forehead are considered normal. However, in North America such markings are apt to draw stares.

symptoms of mental disorders. Usually, only those people with very severe mental problems are institutionalized.

The medical model is based on the ideas that mental disorders are caused by specific abnormalities of the brain and nervous system and that, in principle, they should be approached the same way that physical illnesses are approached. As we shall see, several mental disorders, including schizophrenia, depression, and bipolar disorder, are known to have specific biological causes and can be treated to some extent with drugs. We shall also see that genetics play a pivotal role in some of these disorders.

However, not all mental disorders can be traced so directly to physical causes. For that reason, other perspectives, which focus on the cognitive and environmental factors involved in mental disorders, have emerged.

The Cognitive-Behavioral Perspective

In contrast to the medical perspective, the cognitive-behavioral perspective holds that mental disorders are *learned* maladaptive behavior patterns that can best be understood by focusing on environmental factors and a person's perception of those factors. In this view, a mental disorder is not something that arises spontaneously within a person. Instead, it is caused by the person's interaction with his or her environment. For example, a person's excessive use of alcohol or other drugs may be negatively reinforced by the relief from tension or anxiety that often accompanies intoxication.

As we saw in Chapters 1 and 5, behavior-analytic and cognitive approaches have different historical roots and behavior analysts and cognitive psychologists have different, often opposing, views on the causes of behavior. Still, these approaches have become intertwined in the treatment of mental disorders. According to the cognitive-behavioral perspective, it is not merely the environment that matters—what also counts is a person's ongoing subjective interpretation of the events taking place in his or her environment. Therapists operating from the cognitive-behavioral perspective therefore encourage their clients to replace or substitute maladaptive thoughts and behaviors with more adaptive ones.

The Humanistic Perspective

As we saw in Chapter 14, proponents of the humanistic perspective argue that proper personality development occurs when people experience unconditional positive regard. According to this view, mental disorders arise when people perceive that they must earn the positive regard of others. Thus, they become overly sensitive to the demands and criticisms of others. They lack confidence in their abilities and are unhappy with the kind of people they are. They may come to feel that they may have no control over the outcomes of the important (and even not so important) events in their lives. Such feelings often accompany depression. And as we will see in Chapter 18, the goal of humanistic therapy is to persuade people, often gently, to strive to achieve their own potential as human beings, whatever that may be.

Mental institutions strive to provide a safe haven for persons with mental disorders who are unable to cope with their situation on their own.

The Sociocultural Perspective

As you have seen time and again throughout this book, psychologists are paying more attention to the role of sociocultural factors in their attempts to understand how people think and behave. The development of mental disorders is no exception; pychologists are finding that the cultures in which people live play a significant role in the development of mental disorders. Cultural variables influence the nature and extent to which people interpret their own behaviors as normal or abnormal. What is considered perfectly normal in one culture may be considered abnormal in another. Moreover, mental disorders exist that appear to occur only in certain cultures—a phenomenon called *culture-bound syndromes*. We will examine this topic in depth later in "Biology and Culture: Culture-Bound Syndromes."

The sociocultural perspective is important not just because of the existence of culture-bound syndromes. Sociocultural factors also play a significant function in how different cultures label and interpret mental disorders and how people with mental disorders react to their culture's treatment of them. For example, in a Western culture like ours, people are often encouraged to get better. However, there are segments within our culture in which this positive attitude may not be present, and as a result, people with mental disorders in these parts of our culture never seek treatment or learn how to cope with their problems.

Table 17.1

Summary of the DSM-IV Classification Scheme for Axes I and II

Axis I—Major Clinical Syndromes

Disorders usually first appearing in infancy, childhood, or adolescence. Any deviation from normal development, including mental retardation, autism, attention deficit disorder with hyperactivity, excessive fears, speech problems, and highly aggressive behavior.

Delirium, dementia, amnestic, and other cognitive disorders. Disorders due to deterioration of the brain because of aging, disease (such as Alzheimer's disease, which was discussed in Chapter 12), or ingestion or exposure to drugs or toxic substances (such as lead).

* *Psychoactive substance abuse disorders.* Psychological, social, or physical problems related to abuse of alcohol or other drugs. (Psychoactive substance use and abuse was discussed in Chapters 1, 3, 4, and 16 and is also discussed in this chapter.)

* *Schizophrenia and other psychotic disorders.* A group of disorders marked by loss of contact with reality, illogical thought, inappropriate displays of emotion, bizarre perceptions, and usually some form of hallucinations or delusions.

* *Mood disorders.* Disorders involving extreme deviations from normal mood including severe depression (major depression), excessive elation (mania), or alternation between severe depression and excessive elation (bipolar disorder).

* *Anxiety disorders.* Excessive fear of specific objects (phobia); repetitive, persistent thoughts accompanied by ritualistic-like behavior that reduces anxiety (obsessive-compulsive behavior); panic attacks; generalized and intense feelings of anxiety; and feelings of dread caused by experiencing traumatic events such as natural disasters or combat.

* *Somatoform disorders.* Disorders involving pain, paralysis, or blindness for which no physical cause can be found. Excessive concern for one's health, as is typical in persons with hypochondriasis.

Factitious disorders. Fake mental disorders, such as Munchausen syndrome, in which the individual is frequently hospitalized because of his or her claims of illness.

* *Dissociative disorders.* Loss of personal identity and changes in normal consciousness, including amnesia and multiple personality disorder, in which there exists two or more independently functioning personality systems.

Sexual and gender identity disorders. Disorders involving fetishes, sexual dysfunction (such as impotence or orgasmic dysfunctions), and problems of sexual identity (such as transsexualism).

Eating disorders. Disorders related to excessive concern about one's body weight, such as anorexia nervosa (self-starvation) and bulimia (alternating periods of eating large amounts of food and vomiting). (Eating disorders were discussed in Chapter 13.)

Sleep disorders. Disorders including severe insomnia, chronic sleepiness, sleep walking, narcolepsy (suddenly falling to sleep), and sleep apnea. (Sleep disorders were discussed in Chapter 9.)

Impulse control disorders. Disorders involving compulsive behaviors such as stealing, fire setting, or gambling.

Adjustment disorders. Disorders stemming from difficulties adjusting to significant life stressors, such as death of a loved one, loss of a job or financial difficulties, and family problems, including divorce. (Some adjustment disorders, as they pertain to difficulty in coping with life stressors, were discussed in Chapter 16.)

Axis II—Personality Disorders

* Personality disorders are long-term, maladaptive, and rigid personality traits that impair normal functioning and involve psychological stress. Two examples are antisocial personality disorder (lack of empathy or care for others, lack of guilt for misdeeds, antisocial behavior, and persistent lying, cheating, and stealing) and narcissistic personality disorder (inflated sense of self-worth and importance and persistent seeking of attention).

The Diathesis-Stress Model of Mental Disorders

How should we make sense of these different perspectives—how should we think about the *causes* of mental disorders? Are they caused by conflict within the individual? Are they caused by genetic factors or abnormalities of the brain and nervous system? Are they caused by learning, by faulty interpretations of environmental events, or by the way a particular culture says that we should think and behave?

None of these perspectives by themselves is completely accurate in accounting for the origins of mental disorders. But elements of these perspectives may be combined to form a different, perhaps more comprehensive, perspective on mental disorders. The **diathesis-stress model** says that the combination of a person's genetics and early learning experiences yields a predisposition (a diathesis) for a particular mental disorder. However, the mental disorder will develop only if that person is confronted with stressors that exceed his or her coping abilities. In other words, a person may be predisposed toward a mental disorder yet not develop it either because he or she has not encountered sufficient stressors to trigger its development or because he or she possesses the cognitive-behavioral coping skills needed to limit the negative effects of the stressor.

For example, my father has schizophrenia, but I do not. He had polio as a child and faced many other severe stressors as an adolescent and adult. He was in his early thirties when he was diagnosed as having schizophrenia. Perhaps I have inherited the gene or set of genes that predisposes me toward this disorder. However, perhaps my life has not been sufficiently stressful for the disorder to develop, or perhaps I have acquired, through learning, the coping skills needed to prevent its development. As we will see, the diathesis-stress model has been shown to be an especially accurate model for understanding the causes of schizophrenia.

The DSM-IV Classification Scheme

Mental disorders can be classified in many ways, but the system most commonly used in North America today is the one presented in the American Psychiatric Association's **Diagnostic and Statistical Manual IV (DSM-IV)**. (Psychiatry is a medical specialty devoted to the treatment of mental disorders. The corresponding specialty within psychology is called clinical psychology.) Table 17.1 lists these classifications, with several subclassifications omitted for the sake of simplicity. The disorders described in this chapter are preceded by a colored dot. (See *Table 17.1.*)

The DSM-IV (1994) is the latest version of a classification scheme that was devised to provide a reliable, universal set of diagnostic categories having criteria specified as explicitly as possible. The DSM-IV describes an individual's psychological condition using five different criteria, called *axes*. Individuals undergoing evaluation are assessed on each of the axes. Axis I contains information on major psychological disorders that require clinical attention, including disorders that may develop during childhood. Personality disorders are found on Axis II. Diagnoses can be made that include both Axis I and Axis II disorders, and multiple diagnoses can occur on either axis alone. For example, major depression and alcohol dependence are both Axis I disorders, and both disorders may characterize one individual at any one period of time. A person's psychological condition may be due to several different psychological disorders described in the DSM-IV, just as one person may suffer simultaneously from several different physical disorders.

Axes III through V provide information about the life of the individual in addition to the basic classification provided by Axes I and II. Axis III is used to describe any physical disorders, such as skin rashes or heightened blood pressure, accompanying the psychological disorder. Axis IV specifies the severity of stress that the person has experienced (usually within the last year). This axis details the source of stress (for example, family or work) and indicates its severity and approximate duration. Axis V describes the person's overall level of psychological, social, or occupational functioning. The purpose of Axis V is to estimate the extent to which a person's quality of life has been diminished by the disorder. Ratings are made on a 100-point "Global Assessment of Functioning" (GAF) scale with 100 representing the absence or near absence of impaired functioning, 50 representing serious problems in functioning, and 10 representing impairment that may result in injury to the individual or to others.

The DSM-IV provides a systematic means of providing and evaluating a variety of personal and psychological information about any one specific individual. Let's consider an example to demonstrate the interrelationship among the five axes. Alcohol dependence (Axis I) often leads to marital problems, which may also be partially associated with an antisocial personality disorder (Axis II). Marital problems may lead to a divorce and these problems and the divorce are themselves stressors (Axis IV) that subsequently may contribute to an episode of major depression (Axis I). Alcohol dependence may eventually lead to physical problems, such as cirrhosis of the liver (Axis III). These problems, now acting in concert, are likely to lead to an increased impairment in overall life functioning (Axis V) so that the individual has only a few friends, none of them close, and is unable to keep a job. The evaluation of this person might be summarized as follows:

diathesis-stress model A causal account of mental disorders based on the idea that mental disorders develop when a person possesses a predisposition for a disorder and faces stressors that exceed his or her abilities to cope with them.

Diagnostic and Statistical Manual IV (DSM-IV) A widely used manual for classifying psychological disorders.

Axis I: Alcohol Dependence

Axis II: Antisocial Personality Disorder

Axis III: Alcoholic cirrhosis of the liver

Axis IV: Severe—divorce, loss of job

Axis V: GAF evaluation = 30, which represents a very serious impairment of functioning

Some Problems with DSM-IV Classification

Although the DSM-IV is the most widely used classification system for mental disorders, it is not without its problems. Reflecting the fact that the DSM-IV has been strongly influenced by psychiatrists, the DSM-IV tends to be more consistent with the medical perspective on mental disorders. This means that diagnosis and treatment based on the DSM-IV emphasizes biological factors, which, in turn, means that potential cognitive and environmental determinants may be overlooked.

Another potential problem with the DSM-IV (and perhaps with any classification scheme) is its questionable reliability. *Reliability* in this context means what it did in the context of psychological testing—consistency across applications. If the DSM-IV was perfectly reliable, users would be able to diagnose each case in the same way. But evaluating psychological disorders is not so easy. Using the DSM-IV is not like using a recipe; it is more like navigating your way through an unfamiliar city using only a crude map. Using this map, you may or may not reach your ultimate destination. Mental disorders do not have distinct borders that allow a mental health professional to diagnose a disorder in a person with 100 percent accuracy all of the time.

There will probably always be dangers in classifying mental disorders. No classification scheme is likely to be perfect, and no two people with the same diagnosis will behave in exactly the same way. Yet once people are labeled, they are likely to be perceived as having all the characteristics assumed to accompany that label; their behavior will probably be perceived selectively and interpreted in terms of the diagnosis. Mental health professionals, like other humans, tend to simplify things by pigeonholing people.

An experiment by Langer and Abelson (1974) illustrated how labeling someone can affect clinical judgments. A group of psychoanalysts were shown a videotape of a young man who was being interviewed. Half of the psychoanalysts were told that the man was a job applicant, while the other half were told that he was a patient. Although both groups of clinicians watched the same man exhibiting the same behavior, those who were told that he was a patient rated him as being more disturbed—that is, less well-adjusted. (See *Figure 17.1*.)

You should recognize the potential problems that are inherent in any system that labels human beings. It is easy to lapse into the mistaken belief that, somehow or other, label-

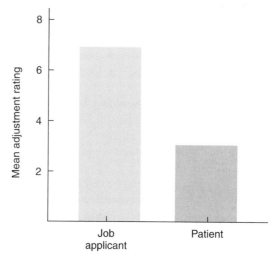

Figure 17.1

The dangers of diagnosis. Adjustment ratings of the same person by psychoanalysts who were told that he was either a "job applicant" or a "patient."

(Based on data from Langer, E.J., and Abelson, R.P. A patient by any other name. . . . : Clinician group difference in labeling bias. Journal of Consulting and Clinical Psychology, *1974, 42, 4–9.)*

ing disorders *explains* why people are like they are. Diagnosing a psychological disorder only *describes* the symptoms of the disorder; it does not explain its origins. To say that someone did something "because he's schizophrenic" does not explain his behavior at all. We need to be on guard against associating the names of disorders with people rather than with their symptoms. It is more appropriate to talk about "someone who displays the characteristics of schizophrenia" than to say that "he's a schizophrenic."

The Need for Classification

Because labeling can have negative effects, some people, such as Thomas Szasz (1960, 1987), have suggested that we should abandon all attempts to classify and diagnose mental disorders. In fact, Szasz (pronounced "zaws") has argued that the concept of mental illness has done more harm than good because of the negative effects it has on those people who are said to be mentally ill. For example, Szasz notes that labeling people as mentally ill places the responsibility for their care with the medical establishment, thereby relieving such people of responsibility for their mental states and for taking personal steps toward improvement.

However, proper classification has advantages for a patient. One advantage is that, with few exceptions, the recognition of a specific diagnostic category precedes the development of successful treatment for that disorder. Treatments for diseases such as diabetes, syphilis, tetanus, and malaria were found only *after* the disorders could be reliably diagnosed. A patient may have a multitude of symptoms, but before the cause of the disorder (and hence its treatment) can be discovered, the primary symptoms must be identified. For example, Graves' disease is characterized by irritability, restlessness, confused and rapid thought processes, and, occasionally, delusions and hallucinations. Little was known about the endocrine system during the nineteenth century when Robert Graves identified the disease, but we now know that this syndrome results from oversecretion of thyroxine, a hormone produced by the thyroid gland. Treatment involves prescription of antithyroid drugs or surgical removal of the thyroid gland, followed by administration of appropriate doses of thyroxine. Graves's classification scheme for the symptoms was devised many years before the physiological basis of the disease could be understood. But once enough was known about the effects of thyroxine, physicians were able to treat Graves' disease and strike it off the roll of mental disorders.

On a less dramatic scale, different kinds of mental disorders have different causes, and they respond to different types of psychological treatments or drugs. If future research is to reveal more about causes and treatments of these disorders, we must be able to classify specific mental disorders reliably and accurately.

Another important reason for properly classifying mental disorders relates to their prognosis. Some disorders have good prognoses; the patients are likely to improve soon and are unlikely to have a recurrence of their problems. Other disorders have progressive courses; patients are less likely to recover from these disorders. In the first case, patients can obtain reassurance about their futures; in the second case, patients' families can obtain assistance in making realistic plans.

Table 17.2

Prevalence Rates of Several Mental Disorders in the United States

Type of Disorder	Prevalence Rate*
Substance use disorder	26.6
Anxiety disorders	24.9
Mood disorders	19.3
Antisocial personality disorder	3.5
Schizophrenia and other psychotic disorders	0.7

Source: Adapted from Kessler, R.C., McGonagle, K.A., Zhao, S., Nelson, C., Hughes, M., Eshleman, S., Wittchen, H., and Kendler, K. Lifetime and 12-month prevalence of DSM-III-R psychiatric disorders in the United States. *Archives of General Psychiatry*, 1994, *51*, 8–19.

*Numbers represent the percentage of people who reported having experienced one of these mental disorders at some time during their lives.

Prevalence of Mental Disorders

To ascertain the prevalence of mental disorders in the United States, Kessler et al. (1994) interviewed nearly 8100 people, ages 18 to 54, living in major cities across the country. (See *Table 17.2*.) Substance use disorders, anxiety disorders, and mood disorders were found to be the most common types of mental disorders, followed by antisocial personality disorder and schizophrenia and other psychotic disorders. The findings of Kessler et al. suggest that mental disorders occur at a fairly high frequency in our culture. The investigators also found that men are about twice as likely as women to suffer from substance use disorders and about four times as likely to suffer from antisocial personality disorder. However, mood and anxiety disorders were found to be more common among women.

Evaluating Scientific Issues

Clinical Versus Actuarial Diagnosis

Clinical psychologists and other health professionals are often asked to make diagnoses and predictions of people's future behavior. These decisions are important; for example, they can determine whether someone receives a treatment that has significant side effects, whether someone receives parole, whether someone stands trial for a crime, or whether someone is placed in a hospital. Two activities contribute to diagnoses and predictions: collection of data and interpretation of data. Both activities are essential; unreliable or irrelevant data cannot be interpreted, and good data can be spoiled through misinterpretation.

Mental health professionals have many ways to collect data. They can observe people and note the presence or absence of particular behaviors. They can order medical tests such as EEGs, X rays, or CT scans. They can interview people and make note of their facial expressions and their responses to questions. They can administer objective and projective personality tests. They can examine documents that already exist, such as medical records, criminal records, or reports of behavior from mental or penal institutions.

Once data are gathered, they can be interpreted in two ways: using the clinical method or using the actuarial method. Although a considerable amount of scientific research indicates that the actuarial method is superior, many mental health professionals still prefer to use the clinical method. In this section, I will explain the difference between the two methods, summarize research that compares them, and discuss why use of the actuarial method is not more widespread.

■ How Do These Methods Differ?

Clinical judgments are those based on an expert's experience. The information that is collected may come from many sources, but it is not the *source* of information that distinguishes the clinical method from the actuarial method—it is the *processing* of that information. **Clinical judgments** are based on experts' memories of similar cases and, of course, on their knowledge of the symptoms that predict particular types of outcomes.

Actuarial judgments are made by applying empirically derived rules that relate particular indications (symptoms, test scores, or personal characteristics such as age, gender, and medical history) with particular outcomes. The actuarial method was first devised for setting the rates for insurance policies. For example, an insurer can estimate a person's longevity by knowing his or her age, height, weight, sex, and health-related habits such as smoking. Although the insurer may be wrong about a particular person (for example, a person may be killed in a traffic accident or may stop smoking), the predictions work very well when applied to groups of people.

■ Comparing the Clinical and Actuarial Methods

Mental health professionals are asked to make predictions about *individuals*, not groups of people. Does the actuarial method work well in such cases? According to scientific research on the subject, the answer is yes.

For a fair comparison of clinical and actuarial judgments, both methods should be applied to the same data. In addition, the eventual outcomes must be known—there must be a way to determine which judgments are right and which are wrong (Meehl, 1954). Goldberg (1970) performed one of the first studies to make such a comparison in the realm of clinical psychology. He analyzed the relation between patients' scores on the MMPI and the diagnoses they finally received when they were

Most psychotherapists prefer the clinical method for diagnosing mental disorders even though the actuarial method has been shown to be more accurate.

discharged from mental institutions. (You will recall from Chapter 14 that the MMPI, or Minnesota Multiphasic Personality Inventory, is extensively used in the diagnosis of mental disorders.) Goldberg found that a single actuarial rule effectively discriminated between people who were judged psychotic and those who were judged neurotic: Add the scores from three of the scales of the MMPI (L, Pa, and Sc) and subtract the scores from two others (Hy and Pt). If the score exceeds forty-five points, the person is diagnosed as psychotic.

Goldberg obtained the MMPI scores of 861 patients and sent them to 239 clinicians (experts and novices) who made diagnoses based on the information. On average, the judges were correct concerning 62 percent of the patients. The best judge was correct about 67 percent of the cases. The simple actuarial rule was superior; it was correct 70 percent of the time, which was better than the best of the expert clinical judges.

Leli and Filskov (1984) compared clinical and actuarial judgments on an important diagnosis—the presence of a progressive brain dysfunction such as Alzheimer's disease. As you can imagine, telling a family that one of its members does or does not have such a disorder has important consequences. The investigators used statistical methods to predict the presence of the disorder from scores on tests of intellectual abilities and were able to correctly identify 83 percent of the cases. Experienced clinicians who used the same information to make clinical judgments were correct only 58 percent of the time.

According to Dawes, Faust, and Meehl (1989), over a hundred studies have compared actuarial and clinical judgments in the social sciences, and almost every one has shown actuarial judgment to be superior. The criterion measures predicted in these studies include college grades, parole violations, responses to particular forms of therapy, length of psychiatric hospitalization, and violent behavior. As Meehl (1986) notes, "There is no controversy in social science that shows such a large body of qualitatively diverse studies coming out so uniformly . . . as this one" (p. 373).

■ Why Is the Actuarial Method More Accurate?

There are several reasons why actuarial judgments tend to be more accurate than clinical judgments. First, their reliability is always higher. Because a decision is based on a precise formula, the actuarial method always produces the same judgment for a particular set of data. On the other hand, an expert making a clinical judgment may

clinical judgments Diagnoses of mental disorders or predictions of future behavior based largely on experts' experience and knowledge.

actuarial judgments Diagnoses of mental disorders or predictions of future behavior based on numerical formulas derived from analyses of prior outcomes.

make different decisions about the same set of data on different occasions (Fries et al., 1986). Experts may become tired, their judgment may be influenced by some recent cases in which they were involved, or the order in which the information is presented to them may affect which items they consider in making their decisions.

Another reason for inaccuracy in clinical judgment is the fact that the human brain has difficulty sifting through a mass of data and retaining useful information while discarding useless or unreliable information. Clinicians often do not receive feedback about the accuracy of their judgments; if they do receive it, the feedback comes after a long time. Thus, they do not receive the information they need to decide which pieces of evidence they should consider in making their decisions. It is difficult for them to update their decision rules.

In Chapter 11, we saw that when people make decisions, they usually follow heuristic rules. And as we saw in Chapter 15, these rules can lead people astray. For example, we tend to pay too much attention to particularly striking cases and to underutilize valuable information about the incidence of particular pieces of evidence. Also, we all have a natural tendency to pay too much attention to information that is consistent with our own hypotheses and to ignore or minimize contradictory information (Greenwald et al., 1986). These tendencies interfere with experts' ability to make appropriate judgments.

■ Why Do Some Practitioners Prefer the Clinical Method?

More and more mental health professionals are using the actuarial method for diagnosis. For example, consulting firms have developed actuarial methods for scoring tests such as the MMPI or the Rorschach. Clinicians can send the raw scores to these firms and receive a report, or they can purchase programs for their own computers that will analyze the data on the spot.

However, most mental health professionals still use clinical methods of prediction more than actuarial methods. According to a survey of psychologists involved in assessing the possibility that patients have brain damage (Guilmette et al., 1989), most of the respondents preferred using tests and diagnostic procedures for which actuarial methods have *not* been developed. These findings suggest that some clinicians *avoid* the actuarial method. According to Dawes et al. (1989), some clinicians simply do not know about the research showing the superiority of the actuarial method. Others consider it dehumanizing; they believe that the method ignores the fact that each person is unique. (Of course, if each person were absolutely unique, even the clinical method would not work; an expert could make *no* predictions about a unique individual.) And perhaps experts prefer to use their own judgment for a perfectly understandable (and very human) reason: They find it difficult to believe that their diagnostic skills, developed over a long period of

training and practice, can be duplicated by a formula or by a computer program.

■ What Should We Conclude?

Scientific studies have shown that clinical judgments are consistently inferior to actuarial judgments. What do these results say about the role clinicians should play in trying to make predictions? First, it is clear that clinicians play an essential role in collecting data and in identifying new variables that may be important predictors. After all, the actuarial approach must have useful data if it is to work. For example, we humans are unexcelled in our ability to recognize complex visual patterns such as facial expressions, subtle indications of emotion in tones of voice and choice of words, and alterations in posture, gestures, or style of walking. Only humans are able to see these features, which often provide useful information for diagnostic purposes.

But perhaps experts should concentrate their efforts on what they do best and what a formula cannot do: observing people's behavior, developing new and useful measurements, and providing therapy. After all, helping people is a clinician's most important role. Perhaps routine diagnosis—a time-consuming activity—should be left to the actuarial method in those cases in which it has been shown to be superior.

Interim Summary

Classification and Diagnosis of Mental Disorders

Psychologists and other mental health professionals view the causes of mental disorders from several different perspectives. The psychodynamic perspective holds that mental disorders arise from intrapsychic conflict that overwhelms the mind's defense mechanisms. The medical perspective asserts that mental disorders have an organic basis, just as physical illnesses do. The cognitive-behavioral perspective maintains that mental disorders are learned patterns of maladaptive thinking and behaving. The humanistic perspective suggests that mental disorders arise from an oversensitivity to the demands of others and because positive regard from others is conditional on meeting those demands. The sociocultural perspective focuses on how cultural variables influence the development of mental disorders and people's subjective reactions to them. Many elements of these perspectives are integrated into the diathesis-stress model of mental disorders. This model is based on the idea that people's biological inheritance and early learning experiences predispose them to develop mental disorders. However, these disorders are only expressed if these people encounter stressors that overwhelm their capacities to cope with them. Thus, even though some people may be predisposed toward a disorder, the coping skills they have acquired through experience may be sufficient to prevent a disorder from manifesting itself.

Although clinical diagnosis is influenced by social norms, we should not abandon the attempt. The value of classification and diagnosis lies in the potential identification of disorders with common causes. Once disorders are classified, research can be carried out with the goal of finding useful therapies. The principal classification scheme in North America for mental disorders is the DSM-IV, which provides explicit criteria along five dimensions called axes. Axis I describes the major psychological disorders of clinical significance and Axis II contains personality disorders. The three remaining axes provide information about the individual, such as the presence of physical disorders, the level of stress, and the overall level of functioning.

Clinical judgments, such as diagnoses and predictions about a person's behavior, require the collection and interpretation of information. The interpretation can use the clinical method or the actuarial method. In the clinical method, an expert uses his or her experience and judgment to make a diagnosis. The actuarial method is based on a statistical analysis of the relation between different items of information and clinical outcomes. Although research has consistently found the actuarial method to be superior, many clinicians do not use it. Some psychologists believe that clinicians should concentrate on developing new measures and making observations of behavior that only humans can make and then employ actuarial methods to find the best ways to use the data they collect.

Thought Questions

■ The "Evaluating Scientific Issues" section discussed diagnoses of mental disorders and the pros and cons of basing such diagnoses on clinical versus actuarial methods. This discussion was written from the perspective of the psychologist. Let us turn the tables and consider the matter from the client's perspective. Suppose you were the client whose mental health was in question. Which method would you prefer your therapist to use in rendering a judgment about you? Why?

Anxiety, Somatoform, and Dissociative Mental Disorders

Anxiety, somatoform, and dissociative mental disorders used to be called *neuroses* and often still are. Most neuroses are strategies of perception and behavior that have gotten out of hand. They are characterized by pathological increases in anxiety or by defense mechanisms applied too rigidly, so that they have become maladaptive. Neurotic people are anxious, fearful, depressed, and generally unhappy. However, unlike people who are afflicted with *psychoses*, they do not suffer from delusions or severely disordered thought processes. Fur-

thermore, *they almost universally realize that they have a problem*. Most neurotics are only too aware that their strategies for coping with the world are not working. Neurotic behavior is usually characterized by avoidance rather than confrontation of problems. People with neuroses turn to imaginary illnesses, oversleeping, or convenient forgetfulness to avoid having to confront stressful situations.

Anxiety Disorders

Several important types of mental disorders are classified as anxiety disorders, which have fear and anxiety as their most prominent symptoms. **Anxiety** is a sense of apprehension or doom that is accompanied by certain physiological reactions, such as accelerated heart rate, sweaty palms, and tightness in the stomach. Anxiety disorders are the most common psychological disorders and appear to occur with greater frequency, for some unknown reason, among African Americans than among other Americans (Neal and Turner, 1991). This section examines three important anxiety disorders: panic disorder, phobic disorders, and obsessive compulsive disorder.

Panic Disorder: Description

Panic is a feeling of fear mixed with hopelessness or helplessness. We sometimes feel this way when we are trapped suddenly in an elevator or are in a car accident. I often feel a tinge of panic when I'm in a jet plane flying through rough air. For most people, panic can be linked to specific environmental events, such as those I have just mentioned.

People with **panic disorder** suffer from episodic attacks of acute anxiety—periods of acute and unremitting terror that grip them for lengths of time lasting from a few seconds to a few hours. The lifetime prevalence rate for panic disorder is estimated to be about 4 percent (Katerndahl and Realini, 1993). Women are approximately twice as likely as men to suffer from panic disorder. The disorder usually has its onset in young adulthood; it rarely begins after age thirty-five (Woodruff, Guze, and Clayton, 1972).

Panic attacks include many physical symptoms, such as shortness of breath, clammy sweat, irregularities in heartbeat, dizziness, faintness, and feelings of unreality. The victim of a panic attack often feels that he or she is going to die. Leon (1977) described a 38-year-old man who suffered from frequent panic attacks.

anxiety A sense of apprehension or doom that is accompanied by many physiological reactions, such as accelerated heart rate, sweaty palms, and tightness in the stomach.

panic A feeling of fear mixed with hopelessness or helplessness.

panic disorder Unpredictable attacks of acute anxiety that are accompanied by high levels of physiological arousal and that last from a few seconds to a few hours.

For most people, anxiety is a typical reaction to circumstances that are perceived to be dangerous—for example, walking along a narrow ledge several hundred feet above the ground—and is not considered to be abnormal. However, when anxiety interferes with carrying out day-to-day activities, it is considered to be a type of mental disorder.

During the times when he was experiencing intense anxiety, it often seemed as if he were having a heart seizure. He experienced chest pains and heart palpitations, numbness, shortness of breath, and he felt a strong need to breathe. He reported that in the midst of the anxiety attack, he developed a feeling of tightness over his eyes and he could only see objects directly in front of him (tunnel vision). He further stated that he feared that he would not be able to swallow.

. . . The intensity of the anxiety symptoms was very frightening to him and on two occasions his wife had rushed him to a local hospital because he was in a state of panic, sure that his heart was going to stop beating and he would die. His symptoms were relieved after he was given an injection of tranquilizer medication. . . . He began to note the location of doctor's offices and hospitals in whatever vicinity he happened to be . . . and he became extremely anxious if medical help was not close by. (Leon, pp. 112, 117)

Between panic attacks, people with panic disorder tend to suffer from **anticipatory anxiety**—a fear of having a panic attack. Because attacks can occur without apparent cause, these people anxiously worry about when the next one might strike them. Sometimes, a panic attack that occurs in a particular situation can cause the person to fear that situation; that is, a panic attack can cause a phobia, presumably through classical conditioning. Anxiety is a normal reaction to many stresses of life, and none of us is completely free from it. In fact, anxiety is undoubtedly useful in causing us to be more alert and to take important things seriously. However, the anxiety we all feel from time to time is significantly different from the intense fear and terror experienced by a person gripped by a panic attack.

Panic Disorder: Possible Causes

Panic disorders are extremely maladaptive, which makes it difficult to explain them. Researchers believe that such disorders are caused either by physical or cognitive factors or by interactions between the two.

Genetic and Physiological Causes.   Because the physical symptoms of panic attacks are so overwhelming, many patients reject the suggestion that they have a mental disorder, insisting that their problem is medical. In fact, they may be correct: A considerable amount of evidence suggests that panic disorder may have biological origins. First, the disorder appears to be hereditary; there is a higher concordance rate for the disorder between identical twins than between fraternal twins (Torgerson, 1983), and almost 30 percent of the first-degree relatives of a person with panic disorder also have panic disorder (Crowe et al., 1983). (*First-degree relatives* are a person's parents, children, and siblings.) According to Crowe et al. (1983), the pattern of panic disorder within a family tree suggests that the disorder is caused by a single, dominant gene.

Panic attacks can be triggered in people with histories of panic disorder by giving them injections of lactic acid (a byproduct of muscular activity) or by having them breathe air containing an elevated amount of carbon dioxide (Woods et al., 1988; Cowley and Arana, 1990). People with family histories of panic attack are more likely to react to sodium lactate, even if they have never had a panic attack previously (Balon et al., 1989). Some researchers believe that what is inherited is a tendency to react with alarm to bodily sensations that would not disturb most other people. In any event, as we shall see in Chapter 18, panic disorder is often treated successfully with drugs.

Cognitive Causes.   People who suffer from panic attacks also appear to be extremely sensitive to any element of risk or danger in their environments: These people *expect* to be threatened by environmental stressors and downplay or underestimate their abilities to cope with them (Mogg et al., 1993; Telch et al., 1989). The expectation of having to face stressors that they fear may overwhelm their coping abilities leads these people to develop a sense of dread. Soon, a full-blown panic attack results. Thus, merely anticipating that something bad is about to happen can precipitate a panic attack.

Phobic Disorders: Description

Phobias—named after the Greek god Phobos, who frightened one's enemies—are irrational fears of specific objects or situations. Because phobias can be so specific, clinicians have coined a variety of inventive names. (See *Table 17.3.*)

Almost all of us have one or more irrational fears of specific objects or situations, and it is difficult to draw a line be-

anticipatory anxiety A fear of having a panic attack; may lead to the development of agoraphobia.

Table 17.3

Names and Descriptions of Some Common Phobias

Name	Object or Situation Feared
Acrophobia	Heights
Agoraphobia	Open spaces
Ailurophobia	Cats
Algophobia	Pain
Astraphobia	Storms, thunder, lightning
Belonophobia	Needles
Claustrophobia	Enclosed spaces
Hematophobia	Blood
Monophobia	Being alone
Mysophobia	Contamination or germs
Nyctophobia	Darkness
Ochlophobia	Crowds
Pathophobia	Disease
Pyrophobia	Fire
Siderophobia	Railways
Syphilophobia	Syphilis
Taphophobia	Being buried alive
Triskaidekaphobia	Thirteen
Zoophobia	Animals, or a specific animal

tween these fears and phobic disorders. If someone is afraid of spiders but manages to lead a normal life by avoiding them, it would seem inappropriate to say that the person has a mental disorder. Similarly, many otherwise normal people are afraid of speaking in public. The term **phobic disorder** should be reserved for people whose fear makes their life difficult.

The DSM-IV recognizes three types of phobic disorder: agoraphobia, social phobia, and simple phobia. Agoraphobia (*agora* means "open space") is the most serious of these disorders. Most cases of agoraphobia are considered to be caused by panic attacks and are classified with them. **Agoraphobia** associated with panic attacks is defined as a fear of "being in places or situations from which escape might be difficult (or embarrassing) or in which help might not be available in the event of a panic attack. . . . As a result of this fear, the person either restricts travel or needs a companion when away from home." Agoraphobia can be severely disabling. Some people with this disorder have stayed inside their houses or apartments for years, afraid to venture outside.

Social phobia is an exaggerated "fear of one or more situations . . . in which the person is exposed to possible scrutiny by others and fears that he or she may do something or act in a way that will be humiliating or embarrassing." Most people with social phobia are only mildly impaired. **Specific phobia** includes all other phobias, such as fear of snakes, darkness, or heights. These phobias are often caused by a specific traumatic experience. Simple phobias are the easiest of all types of phobia to treat.

The lifetime prevalence rate for simple phobia is estimated to be about 14 percent for women and about 8 percent for men (Robins and Regier, 1991), but approximately a third of the population sometimes exhibit phobic symptoms (Goodwin and Guze, 1984). Both males and females are equally likely to exhibit social phobia, but females are more likely to develop agoraphobia. Phobias that begin to develop in childhood or early adolescence (primarily simple phobias) are likely to disappear, whereas those that begin to develop after adolescence are likely to endure. Social phobia tends to begin during the teenage years, whereas agoraphobia tends to begin during a person's middle or late twenties. These disorders rarely make their first appearance after age thirty.

Phobic Disorder: Possible Causes

Psychoanalytical theory attributes phobias to distress caused by intolerable unconscious impulses, such as an unresolved Oedipus complex. Almost all clinical psychologists and behavior analysts believe that phobias are learned by means of classical conditioning—whether direct or vicarious. *Direct classical conditioning* occurs when a particular animal or object is present in an especially unpleasant situation. *Vicarious classical conditioning* occurs when a person observes another person (especially a parent or someone else to whom the person is closely attached) show fright in the presence of a particular animal or object.

Environmental Causes—Learning. To say that phobias are learned through classical conditioning does not explain this disorder completely. Many people have traumatic, frightening experiences, but few of them go on to develop phobic disorders; thus, it appears that not all people are likely to develop phobias. Also, many people with phobias do not remember having had specific, early life experiences with the objects they fear. (Of course, they may have simply forgotten the experiences.)

In addition, some objects are more likely to be feared than others. People tend to fear animals (especially snakes, spiders, dogs, or rodents), blood, heights, and closed spaces. They are less likely to fear automobiles or electrical outlets, which are potentially more dangerous than some of the common objects of phobias, such as snakes or spiders.

phobic disorder An unrealistic, excessive fear of a specific class of stimuli that interferes with normal activities. The object of the anxiety is readily identifiable: It may be a snake, an insect, the out-of-doors, or closed spaces.

agoraphobia A mental disorder characterized by fear of and avoidance of being alone in public places; this disorder is often accompanied by panic attacks.

social phobia A mental disorder characterized by an excessive and irrational fear of situations in which the person is observed by others.

specific phobia An excessive and irrational fear of specific things, such as snakes, darkness, or heights.

As we will see in Chapter 18, the same classes of drugs useful in treating panic attacks also reduce the symptoms of agoraphobia. However, the most long-lasting results are obtained from behavior therapy.

Genetic Causes.   Some investigators suggest that a tendency to develop a fear of certain kinds of stimuli may have a biological basis that reflects the evolution of our species (Seligman, 1971). For example, chimpanzees raised in captivity will show signs of fear when they are shown a snake, even though they have had no previous experience with this animal. Öhman, Erixon, and Löfberg (1975) obtained results that support this suggestion. They showed subjects pictures of snakes, houses, and people's faces and gave them a painful electric shock after seeing one of the categories of pictures. All subjects showed a conditional emotional response (change in skin resistance) when tested with the stimuli afterward. Next, they presented the pictures several times without the shock. The emotional responses conditioned to the houses or the faces quickly extinguished, but those conditioned to the snakes were relatively long lasting.

As we saw in the preceding section, panic disorder, which often causes agoraphobia, appears to be a heritable trait. In contrast, simple or social phobias do not appear to run in families (Goodwin, 1983). The most important predisposing factor for developing these phobic disorders may be environmental. People who develop them tend to be from stable families and to have overprotective mothers (Goodwin and Guze, 1984).

Obsessive-Compulsive Disorder: Description

As the name implies, people with an **obsessive-compulsive disorder** suffer from **obsessions**—thoughts that will not leave them—and **compulsions**—behaviors that they cannot keep from performing. In one study, impaired control of mental activities, checking, urges involving loss of motor control, and feeling contaminated were found to be the major classes of obsessions and compulsions among a large sample of American college students (Sternberger and Burns, 1990). The lifetime prevalence rate is estimated to be about 2.5 percent (Robins and Regier, 1991).

Unlike people with panic disorder, people with obsessive compulsive disorder have a defense against anxiety—their compulsive behavior. Unfortunately, the need to perform this compulsive behavior often becomes more and more demanding of their time until it interferes with their careers

---

obsessive-compulsive disorder   Recurrent, unwanted thoughts or ideas and compelling urges to engage in repetitive ritual-like behavior.

obsession   An involuntary recurring thought, idea, or image.

compulsion   An irresistible impulse to repeat some action over and over even though it serves no useful purpose.

---

and daily lives. Obsessions are seen in many mental disorders, including schizophrenia. However, unlike persons with schizophrenia, people with obsessive-compulsive disorder recognize that their thoughts and behaviors are senseless and wish that they would go away.

Consider the case of Beth, a young woman who had become obsessed with cleanliness.

> Beth's concern for cleanliness gradually evolved into a thorough cleansing ritual, which was usually set off by her touching of her genital or anal area. In this ritual, Beth would first remove all of her clothing in a pre-established sequence. She would lay out each article of clothing at specific spots on her bed and examine each for any evidence of "contamination." She would thoroughly scrub her body, starting at her feet and working meticulously up to the top of her head, using certain washcloths for certain areas of her body. Any articles of clothing that appeared to have been "contaminated" were thrown into the laundry. Clean clothing was put on spots that were vacant. She would then dress herself in the opposite order from which she took the clothes off. If there were any deviations from this order, or if Beth began to wonder if she might have missed some contamination, she would go through the entire sequence again. It was not rare for her to do this four or five times in a row on certain evenings. (Meyer and Osborne, 1982, p. 158)

Females are slightly more likely than males to have this diagnosis. Like panic disorder, obsessive-compulsive disorder most commonly begins in young adulthood (Robbins et al., 1984). People with this disorder are unlikely to marry, perhaps because of the common obsessional fear of dirt and contamination or because the shame associated with the rituals they are compelled to perform causes them to avoid social contact (Turner, Beidel, and Nathan, 1985).

There are two principal kinds of obsessions: obsessive *doubt or uncertainty*, and obsessive *fear of doing something prohibited*. We all experience doubts about future activities (such as whether to look for a new job, eat at one restaurant or another, wear a raincoat or take an umbrella) and about past activities (such as whether one has turned off the coffeepot and whether one should have worn dressier clothes). But these uncertainties, both trivial and important, preoccupy some people with obsessive-compulsive disorder almost completely. Others are plagued with the fear that they will do something terrible—swear aloud in church, urinate in someone's living room, kill themselves or a loved one, or jump off a bridge—although they seldom actually do anything antisocial. And even though they are often obsessed with thoughts of killing themselves, fewer than 1 percent of them actually attempt suicide.

Most compulsions fall into one of four categories: *counting, checking, cleaning,* and *avoidance*. For example, people might repeatedly check burners on the stove to see that they are off and windows and doors to be sure that they are locked. Some people wash their hands hundreds of times a day, even when they become covered with painful sores. Other people meticulously clean their homes or endlessly wash, dry, and fold their clothes. Some become afraid to leave home because they fear contamination and refuse to touch other members of their families. If they do accidentally become "contaminated," they usually have lengthy purification rituals.

Obsessive-Compulsive Disorder: Possible Causes

Several possible causes have been suggested for obsessive-compulsive disorder. Unlike simple anxiety states, this disorder can be understood in terms of defense mechanisms. Some cognitive investigators have suggested that obsessions serve as devices to occupy the mind and displace painful thoughts. This strategy is seen in normal behavior: A person who "psyches himself up" before a competitive event by telling himself about his skill and stamina is also keeping out self-defeating doubts and fears. Like Scarlett O'Hara in *Gone with the Wind*, who repeatedly told herself, "I'll think about it tomorrow," we all say, at one time or another, "Oh, I'll think about something else," when our thoughts become painful.

Cognitive Causes.   Cognitive researchers also point out that persons with obsessive-compulsive disorder believe that they should be competent at all times, avoid any kind of criticism at all costs, and worry about being punished by others for behavior that is less than perfect (Sarason and Sarason, 1993). Thus, one reason people who have obsessive-compulsive disorder may engage in checking behavior is to reduce the anxiety caused by fear of being perceived by others as incompetent or to avoid others' criticism that they have done something less than perfectly.

If painful, anxiety-producing thoughts become frequent, and if turning to alternative patterns of thought reduces anxiety, then the principle of reinforcement predicts that the person will turn to these patterns more frequently. Just as an animal learns to jump a hurdle to escape a painful foot shock, a person can learn to think about a "safe topic" in order to avoid painful thoughts. If the habit becomes firmly established, the obsessive thoughts may persist even after the original reason for turning to them—the situation that produced the anxiety-arousing thoughts—no longer exists. A habit can thus outlast its original causes. As we will see in Chapter 18,

one effective approach to treating people with this disorder is to change their patterns of thinking.

Genetic Causes.   Evidence is beginning to accumulate suggesting that obsessive-compulsive disorder may have a genetic origin. Family studies have found that this disorder is associated with a neurological disorder called Tourette's syndrome, which appears during childhood (Pauls et al., 1986). **Tourette's syndrome** is characterized by muscular and vocal tics, including making facial grimaces, squatting, pacing, twirling, barking, sniffing, coughing, grunting, or repeating specific words (especially vulgarities). Pauls and his colleagues believe that the two disorders are produced by the same single, dominant gene. It is not clear why some people with the faulty gene develop Tourette's syndrome early in childhood and others develop obsessive-compulsive disorder later in life.

Not all cases of obsessive-compulsive disorder have a genetic origin. The disorder sometimes occurs after brain damage caused by various means, such as birth trauma, encephalitis, and head trauma (Hollander et al., 1990). As we shall see in Chapter 18, obsessive-compulsive disorder has been treated by psychosurgery, by drugs, and by behavior therapy. These treatments are sometimes effective, but the disorder often persists despite the efforts of experienced therapists.

Somatoform Disorders

The primary symptoms of a **somatoform disorder** are a bodily or physical (*sōma* means "body") problem for which there is no physiological basis. The two most important somatoform disorders are somatization disorder and conversion disorder.

Somatization Disorder: Description

Somatization disorder occurs mostly among women and involves complaints of wide-ranging physical ailments for which there is no apparent biological basis. This disorder used to be called *hysteria*. The older term derives from the Greek word *hystera*, meaning "uterus," because of the ancient belief that various emotional and physical ailments in women could be caused by the uterus wandering around inside the body, searching for a baby. (As a remedy, Hippocrates recommended marriage.) It is true that somatization disorder is seen almost exclusively in women; however, modern use of the term *hysteria* does not imply any gynecological problems. Moreover, this disorder is rare even among women: Regier et al. (1988) found that the incidence of somatization disorder in a sample of over eighteen thousand people was less than 1 percent in women and nonexistent in men. Somatization disorder is often chronic, lasting for decades.

Somatization disorder is characterized by complaints of symptoms for which no physiological cause can be found. Obviously, a proper diagnosis can be made only after medical examination and laboratory tests indicate the lack of disease. The DSM-IV requires that the person have a history of complaining of physical symptoms for several years. The com-

Tourette's syndrome   A neurological disorder characterized by tics and involuntary utterances, some of which may involve obscenities and the repetition of others' utterances.

somatoform disorder   A mental disorder involving a bodily or physical problem for which there is no physiological basis.

somatization disorder   A class of somatoform disorder, occurring mostly among women, that involves complaints of wide-ranging physical ailments for which there is no apparent biological cause.

plaints must include at least thirteen symptoms from a list of thirty-five, which fall into the following categories: gastrointestinal symptoms, pain symptoms, cardiopulmonary symptoms, pseudoneurological symptoms, sexual symptoms, and female reproductive symptoms. These symptoms must also have led the person to take medication, see a physician, or substantially alter her life. Almost every woman who receives the diagnosis of somatization disorder reports that she does not experience pleasure from sexual intercourse. Obviously, everyone has one or more physical symptoms from time to time that cannot be explained through a medical examination, but few people chronically complain of at least thirteen of them. Although people with somatization disorder often make suicide attempts, they rarely actually kill themselves.

Somatization disorder resembles another somatoform disorder, **hypochondriasis** (*hypochondria* means "under the cartilage"; the ancients believed that the disorder occurred when black bile collected in the upper abdomen, under the cartilage of the breastbone), the persistent and excessive worry about developing a serious illness. Unlike people with somatization disorder, who complain of specific physical symptoms, hypochondriacs demonstrate an excessive fear of illness. They interpret minor physical sensations as indications that they may have a serious disease. They spend a lot of time in physicians' offices and in hospitals.

Somatization Disorder: Possible Causes

Somatization disorder is most common in poorly educated women of low socioeconomic status (Guze, Woodruff, and Clayton, 1971). The disorder also runs in families. Coryell (1980) found that approximately 20 percent of first-degree female relatives of people with somatization disorder also had the disorder. In addition, many studies have shown that somatization disorder is closely associated with antisocial personality disorder (which I will describe in a later section). First-degree male relatives of women with somatization disorder have an increased incidence of alcoholism or antisocial behavior, and first-degree female relatives of convicted male criminals have an increased incidence of somatization disorder (Guze et al., 1967; Woerner and Guze, 1968). These findings suggest that a particular environmental or genetic history leads to different pathological manifestations in men and women.

Conversion Disorder: Description

Conversion disorder is characterized by physical complaints that resemble neurological disorders but have no underlying organic pathological basis. The symptoms include blindness, deafness, loss of feeling, and paralysis. According to the DSM-IV, a conversion disorder must have some apparent psychological reason for the symptoms; they must occur in response to an environmental stimulus that produces a psychological conflict, or they must permit the person to avoid an unpleasant activity or to receive support and sympathy. Unlike somatization disorder, conversion disorder can afflict both men and women.

The term *conversion*, when applied to a mental disorder, derives from psychoanalytical theory, which states that the energy of an unresolved intrapsychic conflict is converted into a physical symptom. Hofling (1963) described one such case:

> The patient had taken the day off from work to be at home with his wife and [newborn] baby. During the afternoon, he had felt somewhat nervous and tense, but had passed off these feelings as normal for a new father....
>
> ....The baby awoke and cried. Mrs. L. said that she would nurse him....As she put the baby to her breast, the patient became aware of a smarting sensation in his eyes. He had been smoking heavily and attributed the irritation to the room's being filled with smoke. He got up and opened a window. When the smarting sensation became worse he went to the washstand and applied a cold cloth to his eyes. On removing the cloth, he found that he was completely blind.
>
> ....Psychotherapy was instituted....The visual symptoms disappeared rather promptly, with only very mild and fleeting exacerbations during the next several months....
>
> ....He had been jealous of the baby—this was a difficult admission to make—and jealous on two distinct counts. One feeling was, in essence, a sexual jealousy, accentuated by his own sexual deprivation during the last weeks of the pregnancy. The other was...a jealousy of the maternal solicitude shown the infant by its mother. (Hofling, 1963, pp. 315–316)

Although the sensory deficits or paralyses of people with conversion disorders are not caused by damage to the nervous system, these people are not faking their illnesses. People who deliberately pretend they are sick in order to gain some advantage (such as avoiding work) are said to be *malingering*. Malingering is not defined as a mental disorder by the DSM-IV. Although it is not always easy to distinguish malingering from a conversion disorder, two criteria are useful. First, people with conversion disorders are usually delighted to talk about their symptoms in great detail, whereas malingerers are reluctant to do so for fear of having their deception discovered. Second, people with conversion disorders usually describe the symptoms with great drama and flair but do not appear to be upset about them.

As we just saw, somatization disorder consists of complaints of medical problems, but the examining physician is unable to see any signs that would indicate physical illness. In contrast, a patient with conversion disorder gives the appearance of having a neurological disorder such as blindness or

hypochondriasis A somatoform disorder involving persistent and excessive worry about developing a serious illness. People with this disorder often misinterpret the appearance of normal physical aches and pains.

conversion disorder A somatoform disorder involving the actual loss of bodily function, such as blindness, paralysis, and numbness, due to excessive anxiety.

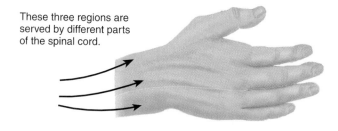

These three regions are served by different parts of the spinal cord.

Anesthesia of only the hand is not anatomically possible.

Figure 17.2

Glove anesthesia, a conversion disorder that was common at the turn of the century.

paralysis. *Psychophysiological disorders* (also called *psychosomatic disorders*) are not the result of fictitious or imaginary symptoms; they are real, organic illnesses caused or made worse by psychological factors. For example, stress can cause gastric ulcers, asthma, or other physical symptoms; ulcers caused by stress are real, not imaginary. Successful therapy would thus require reduction of the person's level of stress as well as surgical or medical treatment of the lesions in the stomach.

The particular physical symptoms of people with conversion disorders change with the times and with people's general sophistication. For example, around the turn of the century, patients commonly developed "glove" or "stocking" anesthesias, in which the skin over their hands or feet would become perfectly numb. It is physiologically impossible for these anesthesias to occur as a result of nerve damage; the patterns of anesthesia produced by organic means would be very different. Today people seldom suffer such a naive disorder. (See *Figure 17.2.*)

Conversion Disorder: Possible Causes

Psychoanalytical theory suggests that the psychic energy of unresolved conflicts (especially those involving sexual desires

dissociative disorders A class of disorders in which anxiety is reduced by a sudden disruption in consciousness, which in turn produces changes in one's sense of identity.

psychogenic amnesia A dissociative disorder characterized by the inability to remember important events or personal information.

the patient is unwilling or unable to admit to having) becomes displaced into physical symptoms. In other words, psychoanalysts regard conversion disorders as primarily sexual in origin.

In contrast, behavior analysts have suggested that conversion disorders can be learned for many reasons. This assertion gains support from the finding that people with these disorders usually suffer from physical symptoms of diseases with which they are already familiar (Ullman and Krasner, 1969). A patient often mimics the symptoms of a friend. Furthermore, the patient must receive some kind of reinforcement for having the disability; he or she must derive some benefit from it.

Ullman and Krasner cited a case that was originally reported by Brady and Lind (1961). A soldier developed an eye problem that led to his discharge and his receipt of a small disability pension. He worked at a series of menial jobs, returning periodically to the hospital for treatment of his eye condition. He applied for a larger disability pension several times but was turned down because his vision had not become worse. After twelve years, the man, who was currently being forced by his wife and mother-in-law to spend his spare evenings and weekends doing chores around the house, suddenly became "blind." Because of his total disability, he was given special training for the blind and received a larger pension. He also received a family allowance from the community and no longer had to work around the house. In this case, both criteria described by Ullman and Krasner were fulfilled: The patient was familiar with the disorder (indeed, he had a real eye disorder) and his symptoms were reinforced.

Dissociative Disorders

In somatoform disorders, anxiety is avoided by the appearance of the symptoms of serious physical disorders. In **dissociative disorders**, anxiety is reduced by a sudden disruption in consciousness, which in turn, produces changes in one's sense of identity.

Description

Like *conversion disorder*, the term *dissociative disorder* comes from Freud. According to psychoanalytical theory, a person develops a dissociative disorder when a massive repression fails to keep a strong sexual desire from consciousness. As a result, the person resorts to dissociating one part of his or her mind from the rest.

The most common dissociative disorder is **psychogenic amnesia,** in which a person "forgets" all his or her past life, along with the conflicts that were present, and begins a new one. The term *psychogenic* means "produced by the mind." Because amnesia can also be produced by physical means— such as epilepsy, drug or alcohol intoxication, and brain damage—clinicians must be careful to distinguish between amnesias of organic and psychogenic origin.

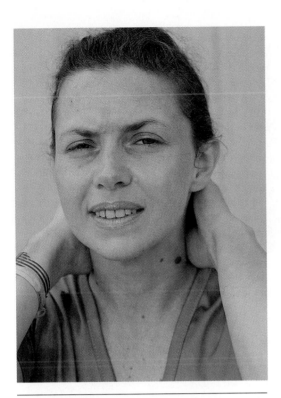

This woman, dubbed "Jane Doe," was found near death in Florida in 1980. She couldn't remember anything about herself, her past, or even how to read and write. Although a couple recognized Jane Doe as their daughter, she was never able to remember her past.

A **psychogenic fugue** (pronounced "*fyoog*") is a special form of amnesia in which a person deliberately leaves home and starts a new life elsewhere (*fugue* means "flight"). Consider the following example:

> Burt Tate was questioned by the police following an argument he had had with a customer in the diner where he worked as a short order cook. He had no identification, could not recall where he had lived prior to his arrival in town several weeks earlier, and could not describe his previous job. However, he did know the name of the town in which he now lived and the date. The police later identified Burt Tate as Gene Smith, who had been reported as a missing person in a city 200 miles away about a month earlier. He was identified positively by his wife, although he did not recognize her. His wife explained that he had been experiencing problems at work (as a manager in a manufacturing company), including being overlooked for a promotion, and that 2 days before his disappearance he had an argument with his son who referred to him as a "failure." (Spitzer et al., 1981, pp. 100–101)

Multiple personality disorder is a very rare, but very striking, dissociative disorder that is marked by the presence of two or more separate personalities within the individual,

either of which may be dominant at any given time. Only about a hundred cases of multiple personality have been documented, and some investigators believe that many, if not most of them, are simulations, not actual mental disorders.

An interesting instance of multiple personality is the case of Billy Milligan as told in the book, *The Minds of Billy Milligan* (Keyes, 1981). Milligan was accused of rape and kidnapping but was deemed not guilty by reason of insanity. His psychiatric examination showed him to have twenty-four different personalities. Two were women and one was a young girl. There was a Briton, an Australian, and a Yugoslavian. One woman, a lesbian, was a poet, while the Yugoslav was an expert on weapons and munitions and the Briton and Australian were minor criminals.

Multiple personality disorder has received much attention; people find it fascinating to contemplate several different personalities, most of whom are unaware of each other, existing within the same individual. Bliss (1980) suggests that multiple personality disorder is a form of self-hypnosis, established early in life that is motivated by painful experiences. In fact, the overwhelming majority of people diagnosed as having multiple personality disorder report having been physically abused when they were children (Kluft, 1984).

As we saw in Chapter 9, some psychologists believe that hypnosis is not a state but, rather, a form of social role playing. The same has been said for multiple personality disorder. Spanos, Weekes, and Bertrand (1985) found that when normal subjects were given appropriate instructions, they could easily simulate two different personalities. They adopted a new name for the new personality, and they gave different patterns of answers on a personality test when the second personality was "in control." Although people are often impressed by the remarkable differences between the various personalities of someone with multiple personality disorder, the acting required for this task is within the ability of most people. That is not to say that everyone with multiple personality disorder is faking, but the results of research do suggest that such patients be approached with skepticism.

Possible Causes

Dissociative disorders are usually explained as responses to severe conflicts resulting from intolerable impulses or as responses to guilt stemming from an actual misdeed. Partly because they are rare, dissociative disorders are among the least understood of the mental disorders. In general, the dissociation is advantageous to the person. Amnesia enables the person to forget about a painful or unpleasant life. A person with fugue not only forgets but also leaves the area to start a new existence. And multiple personalities allow a person to do

psychogenic fugue Amnesia with no apparent organic cause accompanied by a flight away from home.

multiple personality disorder A rarely seen dissociative disorder in which two or more distinct personalities exist within the same person; each personality dominates in turn.

things that he or she would really like to do but cannot because of the strong guilt feelings that would ensue. The alternate personality can be one with a very weak conscience.

Biology and Culture

Culture-Bound Syndromes

People in all societies have specific rules for categorizing behavior, and these rules can differ, often considerably, from culture to culture (Simons and Hughes, 1993). How behavior is categorized and whether any instance of behavior is considered to be appropriate is strongly influenced by social norms and values that exist at any moment in time (Bohannan, 1995). Many kinds of aberrant behavior—behavior that deviates from cultural norms—are not "officially" included in diagnostic manuals, such as the DSM-IV, yet are considered pathological within a given culture. That is, there seem to exist highly idiosyncratic mental disorders called **culture-bound syndromes**, which are found only within one or a few cultures. They do not exist across cultures, as schizophrenia and several other mental disorders appear to (Al-Issa, 1995). For example, consider the following two individual cases:

> I.A. is a young Nigerian man. He recently met a stranger, whom he greeted with a handshake. He now claims that his genitals have fallen off. After a medical examination, the physician tells I.A. that his genitals are, in fact, still where they are supposed to be. But I.A. is unconvinced. He reports that his genitals are not the same since shaking hands with the stranger.

> I. L. was an Inuit (Eskimo) hunter living in western Greenland. He hunted in the open sea from his kayak. He stopped because of *nangiarpok* (nong-ee-r-pok), or an intense fear of capsizing and drowning in a kayak. He withdrew socially from his people and eventually committed suicide. Although once common among western Greenlanders, this disorder is now rare because of changes in Greenlandic culture, especially with respect to hunting and fishing, introduced through exposure to Western civilization.

Many other such culture-bound syndromes appear to exist. Some Polynesian Islanders suffer from *cafard* (ka-fawr), a sudden display of homicidal behavior followed by exhaustion; some male Southeast Asians develop *koro*, an intense fear that the penis will retract into the body, resulting in death (they will often hold their penises firmly to prevent such from happening); some Japanese develop

This man and his son show no signs of nangiarpok, a culture-bound syndrome that is today observed only rarely.

an intense fear that their appearance, body odors, or behaviors are offensive to others, a condition called *Taijin kyofusho* (ta-ee-jeen ki-yo-foo-sho) (Simons and Hughes, 1993).

Likewise, immigrants to the United States often display culture-bound syndromes with which most U.S.-trained clinical psychologists and psychiatrists are unfamiliar. Many Puerto Ricans living in New York City complain of *ataque de nervious*, which is characterized by extreme anxiety, trembling, dizziness, shouting, aggression, and eventually unconsciousness. Nigerian students studying in the United States sometimes develop *brain fag*—difficulty studying, remembering, and concentrating. Occasionally, the student says that something is crawling around in his or her head. Among Bahamians and Haitians living in Miami, *falling-out* is not uncommon. Falling-out is essentially fainting—first the person becomes dizzy and then collapses as if paralyzed.

What causes culture-bound syndromes? That is a very difficult question to answer for several reasons. First, a worldwide classification scheme of mental disorders does not exist, which means that an exhaustive taxonomy of mental disorders also does not yet exist. Second, many culture-bound syndromes have only recently been discovered, and only a few have received much empirical scrutiny. Third, we do not yet have a complete explanation for major mental disorders, which affect millions of people, such as schizophrenia and depression, so it is not unreasonable to expect that the study of mental disorders that afflict fewer people, such as culture-bound syndromes, will be neglected. And fourth, and perhaps most important, many culture-bound syndromes are often described—and treated—using folklore. For example, in Japan, *Taijin kyofusho* is treated in a ritual that involves, among other things, massage and sweating. And in Nigeria, *brain fag* is believed to be related to *ori ode* (or

culture-bound syndromes   Highly unusual mental disorders, similar in nature to nonpsychotic mental disorders, that appear to be specific to only one or a few cultures.

"hunter in the head"), which is a condition believed to involve the individual's spiritual destiny (Simons and Hughes, 1993). Because practices based on folklore are widely accepted by members of the culture, alternative explanations, based on scientific methods, are neither sought nor readily accepted when offered.

Nonetheless, we may speculate about the origins of culture-bound syndromes. Most of those I have described are *specific* to certain environmental events or situations and appear similar in nature to simple and social phobias. Thus, it appears unlikely that these problems have either a strong heritability component or an organic (physiological) basis. Syndromes such as *nangiarpok, koro,* and *Taijin kyofusho* seem similar to what is described by the DSM-IV as a simple phobia, suggesting that they are learned responses to fear-eliciting stimuli. Other syndromes, such as *brain fag* and *falling-out,* may be learned escape responses—behaviors that remove the individual from a stressful or anxiety-provoking situation.

Certainly, culture-bound syndromes are interesting phenomena worthy of investigation. Understanding the development of these disorders may represent an important means of learning more about how cultures influence the course of an individual's life (Bohannan, 1995).

Interim Summary

Anxiety, Somatoform, and Dissociative Mental Disorders

People with anxiety, somatoform, and dissociative mental disorders have adopted strategies that have a certain amount of immediate payoff but in the long run are maladaptive. We can understand most of their problems as exaggerations of our own. Although their fears and doubts may be unrealistic, they do not seem bizarre and illogical.

Anxiety disorders include panic disorder, phobias, and obsessive-compulsive disorder. All of them (except simple phobia and social phobia) appear to have a genetic component. Panic disorder is the least adaptive of all these disorders; the person has no defense against his or her discomfort. In contrast, obsessive-compulsive disorder provides thoughts or behaviors that prevent the person from thinking about painful subjects or that ward off feelings of guilt and anxiety.

Simple phobias can probably be explained by classical conditioning; some experience (usually early in life) causes a particular object or situation to become a conditioned aversive stimulus. The fear associated with this stimulus leads to escape behaviors, which are reinforced because they reduce the person's fear. Agoraphobia is a much more serious disorder, and it is apparently not caused by a specific traumatic experience. Social phobia is a fear of being observed or judged by others; in its mildest form it involves a fear of speaking in public.

Somatoform disorders include somatization disorder and conversion disorder. Somatization disorder involves complaints of symptoms of illness without underlying physiological causes. Almost all people with this disorder are women. Conversion disorder involves specific neurological symptoms, such as paralysis or sensory disturbance, that are not produced by a physiological disorder. In most cases, the patient derives some gain from his or her disability.

Dissociative disorders are rare but interesting. Psychogenic amnesia (with or without fugue) appears to be a withdrawal from a painful situation or from intolerable guilt. Because amnesia is a common symptom of brain injury or neurological disease, physical factors must be ruled out before accepting a diagnosis of psychogenic amnesia. Multiple personalities are even more rare and presumably occur because they permit a person to engage in behaviors contrary to his or her code of conduct.

Culture-bound syndromes are mental disorders, similar in nature, which appear to be idiosyncratic to only one or a few cultures. These disorders frequently involve fear of specific objects or situations, such as *nangiarpok*—being unable to extricate oneself from a kayak if it capsizes—or *Taijin kyofusho*—social embarrassment. The precise origins of culture-bound syndromes is unknown, but it seems likely that they involve learned responses that reduce or eliminate anxiety or stress.

Thought Questions

- When was the last time you felt particularly anxious about something? Was the anxiety strong enough to disrupt your behavior, even momentarily? In what ways was your anxiety similar to or different from that which might be experienced by a person with an anxiety disorder, such as panic disorder or phobic disorder?
- Do you have a fear of anything—of heights, of dark places, of insects, of snakes, or of other things or situations? If you do, is it severe enough to be considered a phobia? How do you know?
- Reflect for a minute or two upon Beth, the woman who had an obsessive-compulsive cleaning ritual. How would you explain her behavior, given what you now know about the causes of obsessive-compulsive behavior?

Personality Disorders

The DSM-IV also classifies abnormalities in behavior that impair social or occupational functioning—personality disorders. Although there are several types of personality disorders, the only personality disorder I will specifically discuss here is the one that has the most impact on society: *antisocial personality disorder.* Table 17.4 provides a description of several other personality disorders. (See *Table 17.4.*)

Table 17.4

Descriptions of Various Personality Disorders*

Personality Disorder	Description
Paranoid	Suspiciousness and extreme mistrust of others; enhanced perception of being under attack by others.
Schizoid	Difficulty in social functioning—poor ability and little desire to become attached to others.
Schizotypal	Unusual thought patterns and perceptions; poor communication and social skills.
Histrionic	Attention-seeking; preoccupation with personal attractiveness; prone to anger when attempts at attracting attention fail.
Narcissistic	Self-promoting; lack of empathy for others; attention seeking; grandiosity.
Borderline	Lack of impulse control; drastic mood swings; inappropriate anger; becomes bored easily and for prolonged periods; suicidal.
Avoidant	Oversensitivity to rejection; little confidence in initiating or maintaining social relationships.
Dependent	Uncomfortable being alone or in terminating relationships; places others' needs above one's own in order to preserve the relationship; indecisive.
Obsessive-compulsive	Preoccupation with rules and order; tendency toward perfectionism; difficulty relaxing or enjoying life.
Passive-aggressive	Negative attitudes; negativity is expressed through passive means: complaining, expressing envy and resentment toward others who are more fortunate.
Depressive	Pervasive depressive cognitions and self-criticism; persistent unhappiness; feelings of guilt and inadequacy.

Source: Adapted from Carson, R. C., Butcher, J. N., and Mineka, S. *Abnormal Psychology and Modern Life,* 10th ed. New York: HarperCollins, 1996, p. 317.

*The antisocial personality disorder, not listed here, is described in detail in the text.

Antisocial Personality Disorder

People have used many different terms to label what we now call **antisocial personality disorder,** which is characterized by a failure to conform to standards of decency, repeated lying and stealing, a failure to sustain long-lasting and loving relationships, low tolerance of boredom, and a complete lack of guilt. Prichard (1835) used the term *moral insanity* to describe people whose intellect was normal but in whom the "moral and active principles of the mind are strongly perverted and depraved . . . and the individual is found to be incapable . . . of conducting himself with decency and propriety." Koch (1889) introduced the term *psychopathic inferiority,* which soon became simply *psychopathy* (pronounced *sy-kop-a-thee*); a person who displayed the disorder was called a *psychopath.* The first version of the DSM (the DSM-I) used the term *socio-*

pathic personality disturbance, which was subsequently replaced by the present term, *antisocial personality disorder.* Most clinicians still refer to such people as *psychopaths* or *sociopaths,* and I will, too, in this section.

Description

People with antisocial personality disorder cause a considerable amount of distress in society. Many criminals can be diagnosed as psychopaths, and most psychopaths have a record of criminal behavior. The diagnostic criteria of the DSM-IV include evidence of at least three types of antisocial behavior before age fifteen and at least four after age eighteen. The adult forms of antisocial behavior include inability to sustain consistent work behavior; lack of ability to function as a responsible parent; repeated criminal activity, such as theft, pimping, or prostitution; inability to maintain enduring attachment to a sexual partner; irritability and aggressiveness, including fights or assault; failure to honor financial obligations; impulsiveness and failure to plan ahead; habitual lying or use of aliases; and consistently reckless or drunken driving. In addition to meeting at least four of these criteria, the person must have displayed a "pattern of continuous antisocial

antisocial personality disorder A disorder characterized by a failure to conform to standards of decency; repeated lying and stealing; a failure to sustain lasting, loving relationships; low tolerance of boredom; and a complete lack of guilt.

behavior in which the rights of others are violated, with no intervening period of at least five years without antisocial behavior." Clearly, these are people most of us do not want to be around.

The lifetime prevalence rate for antisocial personality disorder is estimated to be about 3.5 percent (Robins and Regier, 1991), although estimates of prevalence reported in the DSM-IV are lower: about 3 percent for men and less than 1 percent for women. However, we cannot be sure that any of these figures are accurate because psychopaths do not voluntarily visit mental health professionals for help with their "problem." Indeed, most of them feel no need to change their ways. Psychopaths who are indicted for serious crimes will often be seen by psychiatrists in order to determine whether they are "sane," and some will feign some other mental illness so that they will be committed to a mental institution rather than to a prison. Once they reach the institution, they will quickly "recover" so that they can be released.

Cleckley (1976), one of the most prominent experts on psychopathy, has listed sixteen characteristics of antisocial personality disorder. (See *Table 17.5.*) Cleckley's list of features provides a good picture of what most psychopaths are like. They are unconcerned for other people's feelings and suffer no remorse or guilt if their actions hurt others. Although they may be superficially charming, they do not form real friendships; thus, they often become swindlers or confidence artists. Both male and female psychopaths are sexually promiscuous from an early age, but these encounters do not seem to mean much to them. Female psychopaths tend to marry early, to be unfaithful to their husbands, and to soon

Theodore Bundy, who died in the electric chair after being convicted of the brutal murders of two college women, is considered by many psychologists to be a classic example of the antisocial personality disorder.

become separated or divorced. They tend to marry other psychopaths, so their husbands' behavior is often similar to their own. Psychopaths habitually tell lies, even when there is no apparent reason for doing so and even when the lie is likely to be discovered. They steal things they do not need or even appear to want. When confronted with evidence of having lied or cheated, psychopaths do not act ashamed or embarrassed and usually shrug the incident off as a joke.

Psychopaths do not easily learn from experience; they tend to continue committing behaviors that get them into trouble. They also do not appear to be *driven* to perform their antisocial behaviors; instead, they usually give the impression that they are acting on whims. When someone commits a heinous crime such as a brutal murder, normal people expect that the criminal had a reason for doing so. However, criminal psychopaths are typically unable to supply a reason more compelling than "I just felt like it." They do not show much excitement or enthusiasm about what they are doing and do not appear to derive much pleasure from life.

Psychopaths tend not to become emotionally involved with other people. The following report illustrates this lack of attachment:

> I can remember the first time in my life when I began to suspect I was a little different from most people. When I was in high school my best friend got leukemia and died and I went to his funeral. Everybody else was crying and feeling sorry for themselves and as they were praying to get him into heaven I suddenly realized that I wasn't feeling anything at all. He was a nice guy but what the hell. That night I thought about it some more and found that I wouldn't miss my mother and father if they died and that I wasn't too nuts about my brothers and sisters for that matter. I figured there wasn't anybody I really cared for but, then, I didn't need any of them anyway so I rolled over and went to sleep. (McNeil, 1967, p. 87)

Table 17.5

Cleckley's Primary Characteristics of Antisocial Personality Disorder

1. Superficial charm and good "intelligence"
2. Absence of delusions and other signs of irrational thinking
3. Absence of "nervousness"
4. Unreliability
5. Untruthfulness and insincerity
6. Lack of remorse or shame
7. Inadequately motivated antisocial behavior
8. Poor judgment and failure to learn by experience
9. Pathologic egocentricity and incapacity for love
10. General poverty in major affective reactions
11. Specific loss of insight
12. Unresponsiveness in general interpersonal relations
13. Fantastic and uninviting behavior. . .
14. Suicide rarely carried out
15. Sex life impersonal, trivial, and poorly integrated
16. Failure to follow any life plan

Source: From Cleckley, H. *The Mask of Insanity,* 5th edition. St. Louis: C. V. Mosby, 1976, pp. 337–338. Reprinted with permission.

Possible Causes

Cleckley (1976) suggested that the psychopath's defect "consists of an unawareness and a persistent lack of ability to become aware of what the most important experiences of life mean to others. . . . The major emotional accompaniments are absent or so attenuated as to count for little" (p. 371). Some investigators have hypothesized that this lack of involvement is caused by an unresponsive autonomic nervous system. If a person feels no anticipatory fear of punishment, he or she is perhaps more likely to commit acts that normal people would be afraid to commit. Similarly, if a person feels little or no emotional response to other people and to their joys and sorrows, he or she is unlikely to establish close relationships with them.

Physiological Causes and Learning.   Many experiments have found that psychopaths do show less reactivity in situations involving punishment. For example, Hare (1965) demonstrated that psychopaths show fewer signs of anticipatory fear. All subjects in Hare's study watched the numerals 1 through 12 appear in sequential order in the window of a device used to present visual stimuli. They were told that they would receive a very painful shock when the numeral 8 appeared. Psychopathic subjects showed much less anticipatory responsiveness than did normal control subjects or nonpsychopathic criminals.

A study by Schmauk (1970) showed that although psychopaths are poor at learning to avoid aversive stimuli, they readily learn to avoid a loss of an appetitive stimulus. Schmauk trained subjects on an avoidance task, using three types of aversive stimuli: a physical stimulus (a painful electrical shock), a social stimulus (the experimenter's saying, "Wrong"), and loss of money (the experimenter took a quarter from a pile of quarters that he had given to the subject). Control subjects, who were neither psychopaths nor criminals, readily learned the task in response to all three types of aversive stimuli. Nonpsychopathic criminals also learned the task well, except when the motive was avoiding the aversive social stimulus; apparently, they were not very disturbed when the experimenter said, "Wrong." The psychopathic prisoners learned the task *only* when the motive was avoiding loss of money; they did not learn to avoid a painful electrical shock or hearing the experimenter say, "Wrong." Thus, we can conclude that psychopaths are perfectly capable of learning an avoidance task but that social stimuli or the fear of physical pain have little effect on their behavior.

Genetic Causes.   We do not yet know what causes the deficits in emotion and empathy displayed by psychopaths. These people often (but not always) come from grossly disturbed families that contain alcoholics and other psychopaths. Christiansen (1970) found that the concordance rate for psychopathy was 36 percent for identical twins and only 12 percent for fraternal twins, which suggests a heritability of nearly 50 percent. Mednick, Gabrielli, and Hutchings (1983) examined the

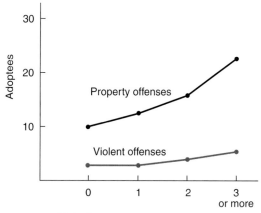

Figure 17.3

Heritability of psychopathy. Percentage of male adoptees convicted of violent crimes or crimes against property as a function of the number of convictions of their biological fathers.
(From Mednick, S.A., Gabrielli, W.F., and Hutchings, B. Genetic influences in criminal behavior: Some evidence from an adoptive cohort. In Prospective Studies of Crime and Delinquency, edited by K.T. Van Dusen and S.A. Mednick. Hingham, MA: Martinus Nijhoff, 1983. Reprinted

criminal records of men who had been adopted early in life and found that the likelihood of their being convicted of a crime was directly related to the number of convictions of their biological fathers. (See *Figure 17.3.*)

Environmental Causes—Parenting.   Another factor, parenting, also appears to play a role in antisocial personality disorder. The quality of parenting, especially as it relates to providing supervision for children, is strongly related to the development of antisocial personality disorder. In particular, children whose parents ignore them or who leave them unsupervised for prolonged periods, often develop patterns of misconduct and delinquency. When the parents do pay attention to their children, it tends to be in the form of harsh punishment or verbal abuse in response to their misdeeds. Thus, the children of these parents live in an environment that ranges from no attention at all to attention in the form of physical punishment and tongue lashings. In response, the children develop a pattern of behavior that is characterized by increased aggression, distrust of others, concern only for themselves, and virtually no sense of right and wrong.

Cognitive Causes.   Children who have conduct problems tend to view their environments differently from well-behaved children. They perceive the world as being hostile and interpret others' actions, even those of other children, as being aggressive and threatening. They may then strike out at someone else (whoever may be the object of their misperception) to avoid being attacked first. Their attack leads to a retaliation, either in the form of punishment by a parent or a teacher or in the form of a counterattack by other children. These children soon develop reputations for being aggressive and unlikable, which further contributes to the strengthening of their antisocial attitudes and behaviors.

Thus, a child may be biologically predisposed to behave aggressively and to have conduct problems. The key people in the child's environment may attempt to punish these actions with a commensurate level of physical or verbal punishment. The child, in turn, perceives his or her environment as hostile and reacts even more aggressively, perhaps due to a maladaptive perception of what is necessary for his or her personal survival. Eventually, a cycle may be established that is marked by behaviors and thoughts characteristic of antisocial personality disorder.

Interim Summary

Personality Disorders

Antisocial personality disorder, also called *psychopathy* or *sociopathy*, is a serious problem for society. Many criminals are psychopaths, and many psychopaths become criminals. The hallmarks of psychopathy are an apparent indifference to the effects of one's behavior on other people, impulsiveness, failure to learn from experience, sexual promiscuity and lack of commitment to a partner, and habitual lying. Some psychopaths are superficially charming, and many make a living cheating others out of their money.

Psychopathy tends to run in families, and there is evidence from twin studies that heredity, as well as a poor environment, may contribute to its development. The disorder is difficult to treat because psychopaths do not see any reason for changing; they do not perceive themselves as being in need of improvement.

Thought Questions

- Suppose that you have been hired as a screenwriter for a Hollywood movie about a psychopath. Before you start work in earnest, the head of the film company wants to see a sample of what you have in mind for this character and asks you to write a few paragraphs describing the opening scene of the movie. What would you write? What would your character be *doing* in this scene?

Psychoactive Substance Use Disorders

Psychoactive substance use disorders are closely related to personality disorders. In fact, many people who abuse alcohol and other drugs also have personality disorders. According to the DSM-IV, **psychoactive substance use disorders** include *psychoactive substance dependence*, or what is usually called "addiction," and *psychoactive substance abuse*, which is less severe but which still causes social, occupational, or medical problems.

Description

Drug addiction is one of the most serious problems that presently faces us. The lifetime prevalence rate for substance abuse disorder is estimated to be about 26.6 percent (Kessler et al., 1994). The lifetime prevalence rate for alcoholism is estimated to be about 13.8 percent (Carson et al., 1996).

Consider some of the disastrous effects caused by the abuse of humankind's oldest drug, alcohol: automobile accidents, fetal alcohol syndrome, cirrhosis of the liver, increased rate of heart disease, and increased rate of cerebral hemorrhage. Smoking (nicotine addiction) greatly increases the chances of dying of lung cancer, heart attack, and stroke; and women who smoke give birth to smaller, less healthy babies. Cocaine addiction often causes psychosis, brain damage, and death from overdose; it produces babies born with brain damage and consequent psychological problems. Competition for lucrative drug markets terrorizes neighborhoods, subverts political and judicial systems, and causes many deaths. Addicts who take their drugs intravenously run a serious risk of contracting AIDS. Why do people use these drugs and subject themselves to these dangers?

Possible Causes

People abuse certain drugs because the drugs activate the reinforcement system of the brain, which is normally activated only by natural reinforcers such as food, warmth, and sexual contact. Dopamine-secreting neurons are an important component of this system. Some drugs, such as crack cocaine, activate the reinforcement system rapidly and intensely, providing immediate and potent reinforcement. For many people, the immediate effects of drug use outweigh the prospect of dangers that lie in the future. As we saw in Chapter 4, although withdrawal symptoms make it more difficult for an addict to break his or her habit, these unpleasant symptoms are not responsible for the addiction itself.

Genetic and Physiological Causes

Not everyone is equally likely to become addicted to a drug. Many people manage to drink alcohol moderately, and even many users of potent drugs such as cocaine and heroin use them "recreationally," without becoming dependent on them.

psychoactive substance use disorders Mental disorders that are characterized by addiction to drugs or by abuse of drugs.

There are only two possible sources of individual differences in any characteristic: heredity and environment. Obviously, environmental effects are important; people raised in a squalid environment without any real hope for a better life are more likely than other people to turn to drugs to escape from the unpleasant world that surrounds them. But even in a given environment, poor or privileged, some people become addicts and some do not. Some of these behavioral differences are a result of genetic differences.

Most of the research on the effects of heredity on addiction have been devoted to alcoholism. As we learned in Chapter 3, most people drink alcohol sometime in their lives and thus receive firsthand experience of its reinforcing effects. The same is not true for cocaine, heroin, and other drugs that have even more potent effects. In most countries, alcohol is freely and legally available, whereas cocaine and heroin must be purchased illegally. From what we now know about the effects of addictive drugs on the nervous system, it seems likely that the results of studies on the genetics of alcoholism will apply to other types of drug addiction as well.

Alcohol consumption is not distributed equally across the population. In the United States, 10 percent of the population drink 50 percent of the alcohol (Heckler, 1983). As we also learned in Chapter 3, both twin studies and adoption studies have shown that susceptibility to alcoholism is heritable. In a review of the literature on alcohol abuse, Cloninger (1987) notes that there appear to be two principal types of alcoholics: those who have antisocial and pleasure-seeking tendencies—people who cannot abstain but drink consistently—and those who are anxiety-ridden—people who are able to go without drinking for long periods of time but are unable to control themselves once they start. (For convenience, I will refer to these two groups as *steady drinkers* and *bingers.*) Binge drinking is also associated with emotional dependence, be-

Table 17.6

Characteristic Features of Two Types of Alcoholism

| | *Types of Alcoholism* | |
Feature	Steady	Binge
Usual age of onset (years)	Before 25	After 25
Spontaneous alcohol seeking (inability to abstain)	Frequent	Infrequent
Fighting and arrests when drinking	Frequent	Infrequent
Psychological dependence (loss of control)	Infrequent	Frequent
Guilt and fear about alcohol dependence	Infrequent	Frequent
Novelty seeking	High	Low
Harm avoidance	Low	High
Reward dependence	Low	High

Source: From Cloninger, C.R. *Science,* 1987, *236,* 410–416. Copyright 1987 by the American Association for the Advancement of Science.

havioral rigidity, perfectionism, introversion, and guilt feelings about one's drinking behavior. Steady drinkers usually begin their alcohol consumption early in life, whereas binge drinkers begin much later. (See *Table 17.6.*)

An adoption study carried out in Sweden (Cloninger et al., 1985) found that men with fathers who were steady drinkers were almost seven times more likely to become steady drinkers themselves than were men whose fathers did not abuse alcohol. Family environment had no measurable effect; the boys began drinking whether or not the members of their adoptive families drank heavily. Very few women become steady drinkers; the daughters of steady-drinking fathers instead tend to develop somatization disorder. Thus, genes that predispose a man to become a steady-drinking alcoholic (antisocial type) predispose a woman to develop somatization disorder. The reason for this interaction with gender is not known.

Binge drinking is influenced both by heredity and by environment. The Swedish adoption study found that having a biological parent who was a binge drinker had little effect on the development of binge drinking unless the child was exposed to a family environment in which there was heavy drinking. The effect was seen in both males and females.

When we find an effect of heredity on behavior, we have good reason to suspect the existence of a biological difference. That is, genes affect behavior only by affecting the body. A susceptibility to alcoholism could conceivably be caused by differences in the ability to digest or metabolize alcohol or by differences in the structure or biochemistry of the brain.

Pregnant woman who are addicted to drugs often give birth to children who are also addicted, such as the child shown here in the arms of Mother Hale, a woman who has devoted her life to caring for others less fortunate than herself.

Most investigators believe that differences in brain physiology are more likely to play a role than are other biological symptoms. Cloninger (1987) notes that many studies have shown that people with antisocial tendencies, which includes steady drinkers, show a strong tendency to seek novelty and excitement. These people are disorderly and distractible (many have a history of hyperactivity as children) and show little restraint in their behavior. They tend not to fear dangerous situations or social disapproval and they are easily bored. On the other hand, binge drinkers tend to be anxious, emotionally dependent, sentimental, sensitive to social cues, cautious and apprehensive, fearful of novelty or change, rigid, and attentive to details. Their EEGs show little slow alpha activity, which suggests that they are aroused and anxious (Propping, Kruger, and Mark, 1981). When they take alcohol, they report a pleasant relief of tension (Propping, Kruger, and Janah, 1980).

The brains of steady drinkers may contain an undersensitive punishment mechanism, which makes them unresponsive to danger and to social disapproval. They may also have an undersensitive reinforcement system, which leads them to seek more intense thrills (including those provided by alcohol) in order to experience pleasurable sensations. Thus, they seek the euphoric effects of alcohol. On the other hand, binge drinkers may have an oversensitive punishment system. Normally, they avoid drinking because of the guilt they experience afterward; but once they begin, and once the sedative effect begins, the alcohol-induced suppression of the punishment system makes it impossible for them to stop.

Another approach to the study of the physiology of addiction is through the use of animal models. At least two different strains of alcohol-preferring rats have been developed through selective breeding, and studies have shown that these animals differ in interesting ways. Alcohol-preferring rats do just what their name implies: If given a drinking tube containing a solution of alcohol along with their water and food, they become heavy drinkers. The alcohol-nonpreferring rats abstain. Fadda et al. (1990) found that alcohol appeared to produce a larger release of dopamine in the brains of alcohol-preferring rats than in the brains of alcohol-nonpreferring rats. This result suggests that the reinforcing effect of alcohol is stronger in alcohol-preferring rats.

Cognitive Causes

Cooper, Russell, and George (1988) have argued that people develop patterns of heavy drug use because of what they believe about the personal benefits of using drugs. For example, people who believe that alcohol will help them to cope with negative emotions and who also expect that alcohol will make them more likable, sociable, or attractive, may use alcohol to obtain these *perceived positive* effects. In this view, drug abuse or dependence is seen as a way of coping with what are perceived to be personal shortcomings—having negative emotions, not being outgoing enough, feeling uncomfortable around others, and so on. Under the influence of alcohol or other drugs, these feelings are replaced with a false sense that these perceived shortcomings no longer exist. Thus, the use of drugs is negatively reinforced by the escape it provides from negative feelings. But the effect is temporary. The negative feelings return when the person is sober, which leads to further drug use. Soon, the person is intoxicated or high most or all of the time.

Interim Summary

Psychoactive Substance Abuse Disorders

Drug addiction is one of the most serious problems our society faces today. Apparently, all substances that produce addiction do so by activating the reinforcement system of the brain, which involves the release of dopamine. Most people who are exposed to addictive drugs—even those with high abuse potentials—do not become addicts. Evidence suggests that the likelihood of addiction, especially to alcohol, is strongly affected by heredity. There may be two types of alcoholism: one related to an antisocial, pleasure-seeking personality (steady drinkers), and another related to a repressed, anxiety-ridden personality (binge drinkers). Some investigators believe that a better understanding of the physiological basis of reinforcement and punishment will help us understand the effects of heredity on susceptibility to addiction. Inbreeding has produced strains of laboratory animals that prefer to drink alcohol, and evidence suggests that this preference may be related to differences in dopamine metabolism.

Thought Question

- Steady and binge drinkers appear to have different kinds of personality characteristics. Do you think these characteristics might be used as predictors of which kind of alcoholic a presently nonalcoholic person might become should he or she develop a tendency toward drinking?

Schizophrenic Disorders

Schizophrenia, the most common psychosis, includes several types, each having a distinctive set of symptoms. For many years, a controversy has been brewing over whether schizophrenia is one disorder with various subtypes or whether each subtype constitutes a distinct disorder. Because the prognosis differs for the various subtypes of schizophrenia, they appear to differ at least in severity. However, a particular individual may, at different times, meet the criteria for different subtypes. As we will see, recent biological evidence suggests that there are two basic types of schizophrenia.

Description

Schizophrenia—a group of psychological disorders involving distortions of thought, perception, and emotion; bizarre behavior; and social withdrawal—is a problem of enormous proportions. It afflicts an estimated 0.7 percent of the U.S. population, which means that at any one time, over 2 million Americans may be experiencing symptoms of schizophrenia (Kessler et al., 1994). In terms of the seriousness and prevalence of the disorder, schizophrenia is considered the "cancer" of psychological disorders.

Descriptions of symptoms in ancient writings indicate that the disorder has been around for thousands of years (Jeste et al., 1985). *Schizophrenia* is probably the most misused psychological term in existence. The word literally means "split mind," but it does *not* imply a split or multiple personality. People often say that they "feel schizophrenic" about an issue when they really mean that they have mixed feelings about it. A person who sometimes wants to build a cabin in Alaska and live off the land and at other times wants to take over the family insurance business may be undecided, but he or she is not schizophrenic. The man who invented the term, Eugen Bleuler, intended it to refer to a break with reality caused by such disorganization of the various functions of the mind that thoughts and feelings no longer worked together normally.

The prognosis for schizophrenia is described by the "law of thirds." Approximately one-third of the people who are diagnosed as having it will require institutionalization for the rest of their lives. About one-third show remission of symptoms and may be said to be cured of the disorder. And the final third are occasionally symptom-free (sometimes for many years) only to have the symptoms return, requiring more treatment and perhaps even institutionalization.

Schizophrenia is characterized by two categories of symptoms, positive and negative. **Positive symptoms** are those that make themselves known by their *presence*. These symptoms include thought disorders, hallucinations, and delusions. A **thought disorder**—a pattern of disorganized, irrational thinking—is probably the most important symptom of schizophrenia. People with schizophrenia have great difficulty arranging their thoughts logically and sorting out plausible conclusions from absurd ones. In conversation, they jump from one topic to another as new associations come up. Sometimes, they utter meaningless words or choose words for their rhyme rather than for their meaning. *Delusions* are beliefs that are obviously contrary to fact. **Delusions of persecution** are false beliefs that others are plotting and conspiring against oneself. **Delusions of grandeur** are false beliefs in one's power and importance, such as a conviction that one has godlike powers or has special knowledge that no one else possesses. **Delusions of control** are related to delusions of persecution; the person believes, for example, that he or she is being controlled by others through such means as radar or tiny radio receivers implanted in his or her brain.

The third positive symptom of schizophrenia is **hallucinations**, which are perceptions of stimuli that are not actually present. Consider a description by Carol North (1987), a former schizophrenic, of one of her perceptual experiences while she was a student:

> I began to notice things in a more sensitive way than I ever had before. Campus evergreens burst into the most intense contrasts of lights and darks and shades of greens that I had ever seen. I wandered around campus looking at everything I possibly could with great wonderment, as if I were seeing it all for the first time. . . . Weighted down with the burden of Pure Perception, I had to move slowly and carefully. I spent hours marveling at the texture of the bricks on the buildings, at the intricate moving patterns of the moonlight on the river. . . . I became so immersed in what I was doing that I didn't realize how ridiculous I must have looked bending down to examine and touch ordinary sidewalk cement. What no one else knew was that the cement had been secretly transformed into a wondrous substance, full of grains and lines, hieroglyphics, messages from worlds beyond, messages that I felt compelled to try to understand. (p. 84)

The most common schizophrenic hallucinations are auditory, but such hallucinations can also involve any of the other senses. The typical schizophrenic hallucination consists of voices talking to the person. Sometimes, they order the person to do something; sometimes, they scold the person for his or her unworthiness; sometimes, they just utter meaningless phrases. Sometimes, those with schizophrenia may also hear a voice that keeps a running commentary on their behavior, or they hear two or more voices. Here is how my father described these voices in a letter he wrote to me several years ago:

> The voices are silent when I'm talking and so far they are silent while writing you. They take a type of being another person and sometimes two or three. The voices are rapid and are almost instantly forgotten by me. The other characteristic of them is that they are

---

schizophrenia A serious mental disorder characterized by thought disturbances, hallucinations, anxiety, emotional withdrawal, and delusions.

positive symptoms Symptoms of schizophrenia that may include thought disorder, hallucinations, or delusions.

thought disorder A pattern of disorganized, illogical, and irrational thought that often accompanies schizophrenia.

delusions of persecution The false belief that other people are plotting against one.

delusions of grandeur The false belief that one is famous, powerful, or important.

delusions of control The false belief that one's thoughts and actions are being controlled by other people or forces.

hallucinations Perceptual experiences that occur in the absence of external stimulation of the corresponding sensory organ.

mostly constant. What they do is interrupt the train of thought—block some memory—fatigue—that's it.

In contrast to the positive symptoms, the **negative symptoms** of schizophrenia are known by the *absence* of normal behaviors: flattened emotional response, poverty of speech, lack of initiative and persistence, inability to experience pleasure, and social withdrawal (Crow, 1980; Andreasen and Olsen, 1982). Negative symptoms are not specific to schizophrenia; they are seen in many neurological disorders that involve brain damage, especially to the frontal lobes.

As we will see later in this chapter, evidence suggests that positive and negative symptoms result from different physiological disorders. Positive symptoms appear to involve excessive activity in some neural circuits that include dopamine as a transmitter substance. Negative symptoms appear to be caused by brain damage. Many researchers suspect that these two sets of symptoms involve a common set of underlying causes, but these causes have yet to be discovered.

Types of Schizophrenia

There are four types of schizophrenia: undifferentiated, catatonic, paranoid, and disorganized. Most cases of schizophrenia do not fit neatly into one of these categories, which I describe below. Many are diagnosed as **undifferentiated schizophrenia**; that is, the patients have delusions, hallucinations, and disorganized behavior but do not meet the criteria for catatonic, paranoid, or disorganized schizophrenia. In addition, some patients' symptoms change after an initial diagnosis, and their classification changes accordingly.

Catatonic schizophrenia (from the Greek *katateinein*, meaning "to stretch or draw tight") is characterized by various motor disturbances, including *catatonic postures*—bizarre, stationary poses maintained for many hours—and *waxy flexibility*, in which the person's limbs can be molded into new positions, which are then maintained. Contrary to popular assumptions, catatonic schizophrenics are often aware of all that

Catatonic schizophrenia is marked by a disturbance in motor functioning, including the tendency to assume a stationary pose, such as the one illustrated by the person shown here, for several hours at a time.

goes on about them and will talk about what happened after the episode of catatonia subsides.

The preeminent symptoms of **paranoid schizophrenia** are delusions of persecution, grandeur, or control. The word *paranoid* has become so widely used in ordinary language that it has come to mean "suspicious." However, not all paranoid schizophrenics believe that they are being persecuted. Some believe that they hold special powers that can save the world or that they are Christ, or Napoleon, or the president of the United States.

Paranoid schizophrenics are among the most intelligent of psychotic patients, so, not surprisingly, they often build up delusional structures incorporating a wealth of detail. Even the most trivial event is interpreted in terms of a grand scheme, whether it is a delusion of persecution or one of grandeur. The way a person walks, a particular facial expression or movement, or even the shapes of clouds can acquire special significance.

Disorganized schizophrenia is a serious progressive and irreversible disorder characterized primarily by disturbances of thought. People with disorganized schizophrenia often display signs of emotion, especially silly laughter, that are inappropriate to the circumstances. Also, their speech tends to be a jumble of words: "I came to the hospital to play, gay, way, lay, day, bray, donkey, monkey" (Snyder, 1974, p. 132). This sort of speech is often referred to as a *word salad*.

Early Signs of Schizophrenia

Eugen Bleuler (1911/1950), one of the pioneers in the diagnosis and study of schizophrenia, divided the disorder into *reactive* and *process* forms. Patients with a general history of

---

negative symptoms Symptoms of schizophrenia that may include the absence of normal behavior, flattened emotion, poverty of speech, lack of initiative and persistence, and social withdrawal.

undifferentiated schizophrenia A type of schizophrenia characterized by fragments of the symptoms of different types of schizophrenia.

catatonic schizophrenia A form of schizophrenia characterized primarily by various motor disturbances, including catatonic postures and waxy flexibility.

paranoid schizophrenia A form of schizophrenia in which the person suffers from delusions of persecution, grandeur, or control.

disorganized schizophrenia A type of schizophrenia characterized primarily by disturbances of thought and a flattened or silly affect.

good mental health were designated as having **reactive schizophrenia,** on the assumption that their disorder was a reaction to stressful life situations. Typically, these patients soon recovered, and few experienced another episode. Patients with indications of mental illness early in life were designated as having **process schizophrenia** and were considered to have a chronic disorder.

If process schizophrenia does have its roots in early life, an important task is to determine what the early predictors are. The ability to identify people with a high risk of schizophrenia while they are still young will allow clinicians to institute some form of therapy before the disorder becomes advanced. The early signs may also indicate whether the causes of schizophrenia are biological, environmental, or both.

In fact, many studies of people who become schizophrenics in adulthood have found that they were different from others even in childhood. However, these studies do not tell us whether these differences resulted from physiological disorders or from the behavior of other family members during the schizophrenics' infancies and early childhoods. One remarkable study obtained home movies of people with adult-onset schizophrenia that showed them and their siblings when they were children (Walker and Lewine, 1990). Although the schizophrenia did not manifest itself until adulthood, viewers of the films (six graduate students and one professional clinical psychologist) did an excellent job of identifying the children who were to become schizophrenics. The viewers commented on the children's poor eye contact, relative lack of responsiveness and positive affect, and generally poor motor coordination. Clearly, something was different about the behavior of the schizophrenics even early in life.

Possible Causes

Research into the causes of all kinds and forms of schizophrenia throughout this century reflects the challenge that psychologists face in attempting to understand how psychological and biological factors interact to influence behavior. The diathesis-stress model of mental disorders, discussed earlier in the chapter, appears to describe accurately the causes of schizophrenia: Schizophrenia appears to result from one or more inherited, biological predispositions that are activated by environmental stress. In fact, this is currently the predominant view of schizophrenia.

Genetic Causes

The heritability of schizophrenia—or more precisely, the heritability of a *tendency* toward schizophrenia—has now been firmly established by both twin studies and adoption studies. Identical twins are much more likely to be concordant for schizophrenia than are fraternal twins, and the children of parents with schizophrenia are more likely themselves to become schizophrenic, even if they were adopted and raised by nonschizophrenic parents (Kety et al., 1968; Farmer, McGuf-

Table 17.7

Summary of Major European Family and Twin Studies of the Genetics of Schizophrenia

Relation to Person Identified as Schizophrenic	Percentage with Schizophrenia
Spouse	1.0
Grandchild	2.8
Niece/nephew	2.6
Child	9.3
Sibling	7.3
Fraternal twin	12.1
Identical twin	44.3

Source: Davison, G.C., and Neale, J.M. *Abnormal Psychology.* New York: John Wiley & Sons, 1990, after Gottesman, McGuffin, and Farmer (1987).

fin, and Gottesman, 1987). Twin studies of schizophrenia compare the concordance rates of MZ twins with the concordance rates of siblings of different genetic relatedness who were reared either together or apart. (Recall from Chapter 3 that twins are concordant for a trait if neither or both express it and discordant if only one expresses it.) According to Gottesman and Shields (1982) and Gottesman (1991), concordance rates for MZ twins are about 50 percent, but they are less than about 20 percent for DZ twins.

If a person has been diagnosed with schizophrenia, there exists the possibility that other family members have the disorder, too. (See *Table 17.7.*) It is important to note that although the likelihood of developing schizophrenia increases if a person has schizophrenic relatives, this disorder is not a simple trait, like eye color, that is inherited. Even if both parents are schizophrenic, the probability that their child will develop schizophrenia is 30 percent or less.

Most investigators believe that a person inherits a *predisposition* to become schizophrenic. In their view, most environments will foster normal development, whereas certain other environments will trigger various disorders, including schizophrenia. If the diathesis-stress model is valid as it applies to schizophrenia, we would expect that some people carry a "schizophrenia gene" but do not express it. That is, their environments are such that schizophrenia is never triggered or they have acquired the coping skills needed to deal successfully with the environmental stressors that would oth-

reactive schizophrenia According to Bleuler, a form of schizophrenia characterized by rapid onset and brief duration; he assumed the cause was stressful life situations.

process schizophrenia According to Bleuler, a form of schizophrenia characterized by a gradual onset and a poor prognosis.

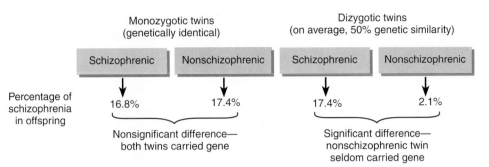

Figure 17.4

Heritability of schizophrenia. An explanation for evidence that people can have an unexpressed "schizophrenia gene."

erwise trigger the disorder. Such a person might be the non-schizophrenic member of a pair of monozygotic twins discordant for schizophrenia.

The logical way to test this model is to examine the children of both members of discordant pairs. Gottesman and Bertelsen (1989) found that the percentage of schizophrenic children was nearly identical for both members of such pairs: 16.8 percent for the schizophrenic parents and 17.4 percent for the nonschizophrenic parents. For the dizygotic twins, the percentages were 17.4 and 2.1, respectively. These results provide strong evidence that schizophrenia is heritable, and they also support the conclusion that carrying a "schizophrenia gene" does not mean that a person will necessarily become schizophrenic. (See *Figure 17.4.*) In other words, as suggested by the diathesis-stress model, environmental factors are also likely to be involved.

Physiological Causes—The Dopamine Hypothesis

Two classes of drugs have been found to affect the symptoms of schizophrenia. Cocaine and amphetamine cause these symptoms, both in schizophrenics and in nonschizophrenics; antipsychotic drugs reduce them. Because both types of drugs affect neural communication in which dopamine serves as a transmitter substance, investigators have hypothesized that abnormal activity of these neurons is the primary cause of schizophrenia. That is, the **dopamine hypothesis** states that the positive symptoms of schizophrenia are produced by over-activity of synapses that use dopamine as a transmitter substance.

Earlier in this century, when cocaine was cheap and freely available without prescription, there was an epidemic of cocaine psychosis. Cocaine was outlawed, and its use became much more rare. Now that a particularly potent form of cocaine ("crack") is available on the illegal market, health-care professionals are again encountering increasing numbers of cocaine-induced psychoses. Heavy users of cocaine develop a syndrome that closely resembles paranoid schizophrenia. They become suspicious and think that others are

plotting against them, they hear voices talking to them, and they often have tactile hallucinations, such as the feeling that small insects have burrowed under their skin.

Amphetamine and related substances also make all kinds of naturally occurring schizophrenia worse: Paranoids become more suspicious, disorganized schizophrenics become sillier, and catatonics become more rigid or hyperactive. Davis (1974) injected an amphetamine-like drug into schizophrenic patients whose symptoms had abated. Within one minute, each patient's condition changed "from a mild schizophrenia into a wild and very florid schizophrenia."

People with a diagnosis of schizophrenia constitute the largest proportion of patients in mental hospitals. Until around 1955, the number of patients in mental hospitals grew steadily every year; then the number of patients began to decline. Several factors led to this decrease, including a growing tendency to treat patients in community-based facilities. But one of the most important factors was the introduction of *chlorpromazine* (the trade name is Thorazine). Chlorpromazine and other antipsychotic drugs are remarkably effective in alleviating the positive symptoms of schizophrenia. Hallucinations diminish or disappear, delusions become less striking or cease altogether, and the patient's thought processes become more coherent. These drugs are not merely tranquilizers; for example, they cause a patient with catatonic immobility to begin moving again as well as cause an excited patient to quiet down. In contrast, true tranquilizers such as Librium or Valium only make a schizophrenic patient slow moving and groggy.

Amphetamine, cocaine, and the antipsychotic drugs act on synapses—the junctions between nerve cells—in the brain. As you may recall from Chapter 4, one neuron passes on excitatory or inhibitory messages to another by releasing a small amount of transmitter substance from its terminal button into the synaptic cleft. The chemical activates receptors on the surface of the receiving neuron, and the activated receptors either excite or inhibit the receiving neuron. Drugs such as amphetamine and cocaine cause the *stimulation* of receptors for dopamine. In contrast, antipsychotic drugs block dopamine receptors and *prevent* them from becoming stimulated. You can see why these findings from different drug studies led investigators to propose the dopamine hypothesis of schizophrenia.

dopamine hypothesis   The hypothesis that the positive symptoms of schizophrenia are caused by overactivity of synapses in the brain that use dopamine.

Physiological Causes—Neurological Disorders

Although the dopamine hypothesis has for several years been the dominant biological explanation for schizophrenia, other evidence suggests that it can offer only a partial explanation. Because antipsychotic drugs alleviate positive, but not negative, symptoms of schizophrenia (Angrist, Rotrosen, and Gershon, 1980), perhaps those patients who do not get better with medication have primarily negative symptoms.

Once investigators began paying more attention to negative symptoms, they discovered evidence for brain damage in patients exhibiting these symptoms. Several investigators have examined CT or MRI scans of patients with schizophrenia. For example, Weinberger and Wyatt (1982) found that the ventricles in the brains of schizophrenic patients were, on average, twice as large as those of normal subjects. Similarly, Pfefferbaum et al. (1988) found evidence that the sulci (the wrinkles in the brain) were wider in the brains of schizophrenic patients. Enlargement of the hollow ventricles of the brain and widening of the sulci indicates the loss of brain tissue—thus, the evidence implied the existence of some kind of neurological disease.

Loss of brain tissue, as assessed by CT scans, appears to be related to negative symptoms of schizophrenia but not to positive ones (Johnstone et al., 1978). In addition, patients with loss of brain tissue respond poorly to antipsychotic drugs (Weinberger et al., 1980). These studies suggest that positive and negative symptoms of schizophrenia have different causes: Positive symptoms are a result of overactivity of dopamine synapses, whereas negative symptoms are produced by actual loss of brain tissue.

A study by Suddath et al. (1990) provided further evidence for the relationship between brain damage and schizophrenia. The investigators examined MRI scans of monozygotic twins discordant for schizophrenia and found that in almost every case, the twin with schizophrenia had larger lateral and third ventricles. In addition, the hippocampus was smaller in the schizophrenic twin, and the total volume of the gray matter in the left temporal lobe was reduced. Figure 17.5 shows a set of MRI scans from a pair of twins. As you can see, the lateral ventricles are larger in the brain of the twin with schizophrenia. (See *Figure 17.5.*)

Several studies have indicated that the cause of brain damage in schizophrenia may be a viral infection. No direct evidence for virally induced schizophrenia exists, but evidence reveals similarities between schizophrenia and known viral disorders. Stevens (1988) notes some interesting similarities between schizophrenia and *multiple sclerosis*, a neurological disorder. Multiple sclerosis appears to be an autoimmune disease—triggered by a virus—in which the patient's own immune system attacks the myelin sheathe that cover most axons in the central nervous system. The natural histories of multiple sclerosis and schizophrenia are similar in several ways. Both diseases are more prevalent and more severe in people who spent their childhood in latitudes far from the equator. Both diseases are more common in people with low

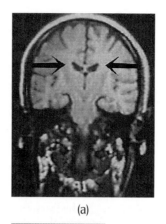 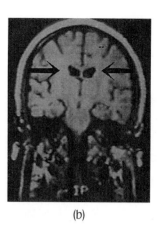

(a)   (b)

Figure 17.5

MRI scans of the brains of twins discordant for schizophrenia. (a) Normal twin. (b) Twin with schizophrenia.
(Courtesy of D.R. Weinberger, National Institute of Mental Health, Saint Elizabeth's Hospital, Washington, DC)

socioeconomic status, who live in crowded, deprived conditions. Both diseases are characterized by one of three general courses: (1) attacks followed by remissions, many of which produce no residual deficits; (2) recurrent attacks with only partial remissions, causing an increasingly major deficit; or (3) an insidious onset with a steady and relentless progression, leading to permanent and severe deficits. These similarities suggest that schizophrenia, like multiple sclerosis, could be a virally induced autoimmune disease.

A second possible neurological cause of schizophrenia is interference with normal prenatal brain development. Several studies show that people born during the winter months are more likely to develop schizophrenia later in life. Torrey, Torrey, and Peterson (1977) suggest that the causal factor could be seasonal variations in nutritional factors, or, more likely, variations in toxins or infectious agents in air, water, or food. Several diseases known to be caused by viruses, such as measles, German measles, and chicken pox, show a similar *seasonality effect*. The seasonality effect is seen most strongly in poor, urban locations, where people are at greater risk for viral infections (Machon, Mednick, and Schulsinger, 1983).

A seasonally related virus could affect either a pregnant woman or her newborn infant. Two pieces of evidence suggest that the damage is done prenatally. First, brain development is more susceptible to disruption prenatally than postnatally. Second, a study of the offspring of women who were pregnant during an epidemic of type A2 influenza in Finland occurring in 1957 showed an elevated incidence of schizophrenia (Mednick, Machon, and Huttunen, 1990). The increased incidence was seen only in the children of women who were in the second trimester of their pregnancies when the epidemic occurred. (See *Figure 17.6.*) Presumably, the viral infection produced toxins that interfered with the brain development of

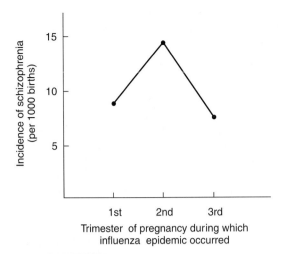

Figure 17.6

Schizophrenia and illness. Incidence of schizophrenia in the offspring of women who were pregnant during the 1957 influenza epidemic in Finland.

(Based on data of Mednick, S.A., Machon, R.A., and Huttunen, M.O. Archives of General Psychiatry, *1990, 47, 292.)*

some of the fetuses, resulting in the development of schizophrenia later in life.

A third possible neurological cause of schizophrenia is birth trauma. Schwarzkopf et al. (1989) found that if a schizophrenic person does not have relatives with a schizophrenic disorder—that is, if there is no evidence that the disease is a result of heredity—he or she is more likely to have had a history of complications at or around the time of childbirth. Thus, brain damage not related to heredity may also be a cause of schizophrenia.

Much more research will be necessary before investigators can determine whether, in fact, overactivity of dopamine synapses produces positive symptoms of schizophrenia and whether a viral infection produces the brain damage that results in negative symptoms. But such biological explanations for schizophrenia will not lessen the usefulness of psychotherapy (discussed in the next chapter) in the treatment of this disorder. Experience has shown that it is not enough merely to medicate a schizophrenic patient with drugs like chlorpromazine. It is also important to teach the person how to structure a new life and how to cope with the many problems he or she will encounter in reentering society. Psychotherapy is at present the only hope for patients with predominantly negative symptoms, who are not helped by antipsychotic drugs.

Cognitive and Environmental Causes— The Family and Expressed Emotion

Many researchers have tried to discover the cognitive and environmental factors that are responsible for triggering schizo-

phrenia in a person with a hereditary predisposition for it. Unfortunately, these attempts have not met with much success. Several studies have found that the likelihood of becoming schizophrenic is related only to a person's *biological* family history; it makes no difference whether a person is raised by schizophrenic or nonschizophrenic foster parents. One study carried out in Finland obtained different results. It found evidence that suggests that being raised by a "mentally healthy" family helps protect against the development of schizophrenia (Tienari et al., 1987). The researchers examined the children of schizophrenic mothers who had been adopted away early in life. Following interviews and psychological tests, the families who adopted the children were classified as well-adjusted, moderately maladjusted, or severely maladjusted. The children adopted by the well-adjusted families were least likely to show signs of mental disturbance, including schizophrenia. These results are encouraging. But because several other studies found no such protective influence, more evidence is needed to be sure that the effects are real.

The personality and communicative abilities of either or both parents appear to play an influential role in the development of schizophrenic symptoms in children. Several studies have shown that children raised by parents who are dominating, overprotective, rigid, and insensitive to the needs of others later develop schizophrenia (Roff and Knight, 1981). In many cases, a parent may be verbally accepting of the child yet in other ways reject him or her, which establishes a conflict for the child called a **double-bind**. For example, a mother may encourage her son to become emotionally dependent on her yet continually reject him when he tries to hug her or sit on her lap or play with her.

Schizophrenia also seems to occur at a higher than average rate among children who were reared in families wrought with discord. For example, in a study of fourteen schizophrenic individuals, Lidz and his colleagues (1965) found that each of these individuals had a family that underwent either chronic discord in which the integrity of the parents' marriage was perpetually threatened or marital problems in which the bizarre behavior of one family member was tolerated by the other members. Children in families in which parents treat them with hostility or in which parents present confusing communication to them are at risk for developing schizophrenia (Goldstein, 1987). However, researchers are still not sure whether marital discord, family hostility, and confusing communications are a cause or an effect of childrens' schizophrenia. More research is needed to address this issue.

Researchers also have identified a social variable that affects the likelihood that a person with schizophrenia will recover. Brown and his colleagues (Brown et al., 1966; Brown, 1985) identified a category of behaviors of families of individuals recovering from schizophrenia that seemed to be related to the patients' rates of recovery. They labeled this

double-bind   The conflict caused for a child when he or she is given inconsistent messages or cues from a parent.

variable **expressed emotion**, which consists of expressions of criticism, hostility, and emotional overinvolvement by the family members toward the patient. Patients living in family environments in which the level of expressed emotion was low were more likely to recover, whereas those in families in which it was high were likely to continue to exhibit schizophrenic symptoms.

Jenkins and Karno (1992) report that in the past decade, over one hundred studies investigating expressed emotion in families have appeared. They found studies from North America, England, Denmark, Italy, France, Spain, Germany, Taiwan, India, Egypt, and Australia. In the United States, studies have been made of Anglo Americans, Mexican Americans, and African Americans. The authors note that despite differences in the ways that people of different cultures perceive mental illness and express themselves, expressed emotion does not seem to be a culture-bound phenomenon. Two elements appear to be common to all cultures: critical comments and emotional overinvolvement. If these elements are present in families of schizophrenics at low levels, patients are likely to recover quickly; if they are present at high levels, patients are less likely to recover quickly.

Jenkins and Karno also found that expressed emotion tends to be higher in industrialized cultures (like that of the United States and many other Western cultures) than in nonindustrialized cultures. In other words, people in nonindustrialized countries are more supportive of family members with schizophrenia than are people in industrialized countries. The reasons for this difference appear to center on the role that individuals play in the two environments. For example, people in industrialized countries are generally raised with the idea that they will find a meaningful job that pays well. But people with schizophrenia who live in industrialized nations often find it hard to gain employment simply because so many jobs require specialized skills. As a result, they may be criticized for not contributing to the family income. In contrast, people with schizophrenia who live in nonindustrialized nations may find less specialized jobs in agriculture or in the family business—they can still find a way to contribute to the family's economic well-being. In addition, people living in nonindustrialized countries often live with an extended family where many people are contributing to the family economy. The loss or reduction in wages by a family member with schizophrenia may be partially compensated by other family members. Another advantage of living with an extended family is that there are more people who can share in the care of the family member with schizophrenia.

Interim Summary

Schizophrenic Disorders

The main positive symptoms of schizophrenia include thought disorders; delusions of persecution, grandeur, and control; and hallucinations. The main negative symptoms include withdrawal, apathy, and poverty of speech. The DSM-IV classifies schizophrenia into several subtypes, including undifferentiated, catatonic, paranoid, and disorganized. But the distinctions between process and reactive schizophrenia and between positive and negative symptoms also seem to be important.

People who develop chronic, process schizophrenia appear to be different from other people even as children, which suggests that the disorder takes root early in life. The diathesis-stress model accurately describes the course of schizophrenia: Some people seem to inherit a predisposition for the disorder, which is expressed when environmental stressors outweigh their attempts to cope with them. Recent research suggests that a low level of expressed emotion (including critical comments and emotional overinvolvement) on the part of family members facilitates the recovery of a patient with schizophrenia.

Positive symptoms of schizophrenia can be produced in normal people or made worse in schizophrenics by drugs that stimulate dopamine synapses (cocaine and amphetamine) and can be reduced or eliminated by drugs that block dopamine receptors (antipsychotic drugs). These findings have led to the dopamine hypothesis, which states that schizophrenia is caused by an inherited biochemical defect that causes dopamine neurons to be overactive.

More recent studies indicate that schizophrenia can best be conceived of as two different disorders. The positive symptoms are produced by overactivity of dopamine neurons and can be treated with antipsychotic drugs. The negative symptoms, which do not respond to these drugs, are caused by brain damage. Investigators have found direct evidence of brain damage by inspecting CT scans of living patients' brains.

Researchers have suggested three possible causes of the brain damage—and the corresponding negative symptoms—that accompanies schizophrenia: a virus that triggers an autoimmune disease, which causes brain damage later in life; a virus that damages the brain early in life; and birth trauma. Heredity presumably interacts with the first two factors—many people may be exposed to the virus, but the virus will cause brain damage only in people with a genetic sensitivity.

People born during the winter months are more likely to develop schizophrenia later in life than are people born at other times of the year. The causal factor seems likely to be seasonal variations in nutritional factors, toxins, and infectious agents. This effect is especially prevalent among the urban poor, who are at the greatest risk for viral infections.

Thought Questions

- Imagine that you are a clinical psychologist. A client of yours complains of hearing voices. You suspect that

---

expressed emotion Expressions of criticism, hostility, and emotional overinvolvement by family members toward a person with schizophrenia.

this individual may be schizophrenic, but you wish to gather more information before you make your diagnosis. What sorts of information about this person do you need before you can make your diagnosis? How would you gather it?

■ Suppose that a friend of yours, who acts a little strange at times, is diagnosed as being schizophrenic. Suppose further that this diagnosis is actually wrong—he truly is not schizophrenic. Your friend knows that the diagnosis is incorrect, but nobody believes him because his strange behavior makes the diagnosis seem believable. What would your friend have to say or do to convince you that he is normal?

Mood Disorders

Everyone experiences moods varying from sadness to happiness to elation. We're excited when our team wins a big game, saddened to learn that a friend's father has had a heart attack, thrilled at news of a higher-than-expected raise at work, and devastated by the death of a loved one. Such are the emotions from which the fabric of our lives are woven. Some people, though, experience more dramatic mood changes than these. Significant shifts or disturbances in mood that affect normal perception, thought, and behavior are called **mood disorders.** They may be characterized by a deep, foreboding depression or by a combination of depression and euphoria.

Description

In contrast to schizophrenia, whose principal symptom is thought disorders, the mood disorders are primarily disorders of emotion. The most severe mood disorders are bipolar disorder and major depression. **Bipolar disorder** is characterized by alternating periods of *mania* (wild excitement) and *depression.* **Major depression** involves persistent and severe feelings of sadness and worthlessness accompanied by changes in appetite, sleeping, and behavior. The lifetime prevalence rates for major depression are about 13 percent for males and about 21 percent for females (Kessler et al., 1994).

A less severe form of depression is called *dysthymic disorder* (pronounced *dis-thigh-mik*). The term comes from the Greek words *dus*, "bad," and thymos, "spirit." The primary difference between this disorder and major depression is its relatively low severity. Similarly, *cyclothymic disorder* resembles bipolar disorder but is much less severe.

Mania

Mania (the Greek word for "madness") is characterized by wild, exuberant, unrealistic activity unprecipitated by envi-ronmental events. During manic episodes, people are usually elated and self-confident; however, contradiction or interference tends to make them very angry. Their speech (and, presumably, their thought processes) becomes very rapid. They tend to flit from topic to topic and are full of grandiose plans, but their thoughts are not as disorganized as those of people with schizophrenia. Manic patients also tend to be restless and hyperactive, often pacing around ceaselessly. They often have delusions and hallucinations—typically of a nature that fits their exuberant mood. Davison and Neale (1990) recorded a typical interaction:

> *Therapist:* Well, you seem pretty happy today.
>
> *Client:* Happy! Happy! You certainly are a master of understatement, you rogue! (Shouting, literally jumping out of seat.) Why I'm ecstatic. I'm leaving for the West Coast today, on my daughter's bicycle. Only 3100 miles. That's nothing, you know. I could probably walk, but I want to get there by next week. And along the way I plan to contact a lot of people about investing in my fish equipment. I'll get to know more people that way—you know, Doc, "know" in the biblical sense (leering at the therapist seductively). Oh, God, how good it feels. It's almost like a nonstop orgasm. (Davison and Neale, p. 222)

The usual response that manic speech and behavior evokes in another person is one of sympathetic amusement. In fact, when an experienced clinician finds himself or herself becoming amused by a patient, the clinician begins to suspect the presence of mania. Because very few patients exhibit only mania, the DSM-IV classifies all cases in which mania occurs as bipolar disorder. Patients with bipolar disorder usually experience alternate periods of mania and depression. Each of these periods lasts from a few days to a few weeks, usually with several days of relatively normal behavior in between. Many therapists have observed that there is often something brittle and unnatural about the happiness during the manic phase, as though the patient is making himself or herself be happy to ward off an attack of depression. Indeed, some manic patients are simply hyperactive and irritable rather than euphoric.

mood disorder A disorder characterized by significant shifts or disturbances in mood that affect normal perception, thought, and behavior. Mood disorders may be characterized by deep, foreboding depression, or a combination of the depression and euphoria.

bipolar disorder Alternating states of depression and mania separated by periods of relatively normal affect.

major depression Persistent and severe feelings of sadness and worthlessness accompanied by changes in appetite, sleeping, and behavior.

mania Excessive emotional arousal and wild, exuberant, unrealistic activity.

Jim's reaction to Mark's statements reinforce Mark's feelings of worthlessness.

"Nobody likes me. I'm not good at anything."

"Mark's really negative. I don't like to be around people like that. Next time he calls, I'm going to avoid him."

Mark

Jim

Negative attitudes and statements of an individual with depression

Withdrawal reaction to negative attitudes and statements of others

Figure 17.7

Depression and strained interpersonal relationships. Depressed individuals are often caught in a vicious circle. They make negative self-statements that cause others to withdraw or fail to initiate social support, which, in turn, reinforces the depressed individual's negative self-statements.

Depression

Depressed people are extremely sad and are usually full of self-directed guilt, but not because of any particular environmental event. Depressed people cannot always state why they are depressed. Beck (1967) identified five cardinal symptoms of depression: (1) a sad and apathetic mood, (2) feelings of worthlessness and hopelessness, (3) a desire to withdraw from other people, (4) sleeplessness and loss of appetite and sexual desire, and (5) change in activity level, to either lethargy or agitation. Most people who are labeled "depressed" have a dysthymic disorder; a minority have a severe mood disorder. Major depression must be distinguished from grief, such as that caused by the death of a loved one. People who are grieving feel sad and depressed but do not fear losing their minds or have thoughts of self-harm. Because many people who do suffer from major depression or the depressed phase of bipolar disorder commit suicide, these disorders are potentially fatal. The fatality rate by suicide for major depression is estimated at 15 percent (Guze and Robins, 1970).

People with severe depression often have delusions, especially that their brains or internal organs are rotting away. Sometimes, they believe that they are being punished for unspeakable and unforgivable sins, as in the following statement, reported by Coleman (1976):

My brain is being eaten away.... If I had any willpower I would kill myself.... I don't deserve to live.... I have ruined everything...and it's all my fault.... I have been unfaithful to my wife and now I am being punished...my health is ruined...there's no use going on ...(sigh)....I have ruined everything...my family... and now myself....I bring misfortune to everyone....I am a moral leper...a serpent in the Garden of Eden. (Coleman, p. 346)

Possible Causes

The possible causes of mood disorders center on four variables: faulty cognition, heredity, brain biochemistry, and sleep/wake cycles.

Cognitive Causes

People with mood disorders don't have the same outlook on life as others. Specifically, they make negative statements about themselves and their abilities: "Nobody likes me." "I'm not good at anything." "What's the point in even trying, I'll just screw up anyway." Because they are so negative about themselves, depressed people are particularly unpleasant to be around. (See *Figure 17.7.*) The problem is that the depressed individual is caught in a vicious circle: Negative statements strain interpersonal relationships, which result in others withdrawing or failing to initiate social support, which, in turn, reinforces the depressed individual's negative statements (Klerman and Weissman, 1986).

The symptoms of major depression include apathy, feelings of worthlessness, social withdrawal, changes in sleeping and eating patterns, and lethargy or agitation.

Beck (1967, 1991) suggested that the changes in affect seen in depression are not primary but instead are secondary to changes in cognition. That is, the primary disturbance is a distortion in the person's view of reality. For example, a depressed person may see a scratch on the surface of his or her car and conclude that the car is ruined. Or a person whose recipe fails may see the unappetizing dish as proof of his or her unworthiness. Or a nasty letter from a creditor is seen as a serious and personal condemnation. According to Beck, depressed people's thinking is characterized by self-blame (things that go wrong are always their fault), overemphasis on the negative aspects of life (even small problems are blown out of proportion), failure to appreciate positive experiences (pessimism). This kind of pessimistic thinking involves negative thoughts about the self, about the present, and about the future, which Beck collectively referred to as the *cognitive triad*. In short, depressed people blame their present miserable situation on their inadequacies. And because of these inadequacies, they see no hope for improving the situation in the future.

In contrast with psychoanalytical theory, which emphasizes the role of the unconscious in the emergence of mental disorder, Beck's theory emphasizes the role of a person's judgment in contributing to his or her own emotional state. This theory has served a useful function in alerting therapists to the importance of considering the thought processes, as well as the feelings, of a patient with a severe mood disorder. Of course, if we observe an association between faulty cognition and depression, we cannot necessarily conclude that the faulty cognition causes the depression; in fact, the reverse could be true. In any event, Beck's method of treatment, based on his theory, has proved to be effective, as we shall see in Chapter 18.

Another causal factor in depression appears to involve the *attributional style* of the depressed person (Abramson, Seligman, and Teasdale, 1978; Abramson, Matelsky, and Alloy, 1989). According to this idea, it is not merely experiencing negative events that causes people to become depressed. What is actually more important are the attributions people make about why those events occur. People who are most likely to become depressed are those who attribute negative events and experiences to their own shortcomings and who believe that their life situations are never going to get any better. A person's attributional style, then, serves as a predisposition or diathesis for depression. In other words, people prone to depression tend to have *hopeless outlooks* on their lives—"I am not good at anything I try to do and it will never get any better. I am always going to be a lousy person." According to this view, depression is most likely when people with pessimistic attributional styles encounter significant or frequent life stressors (Abramson et al. 1989). The pessimistic attributions are then generalized to other, perhaps smaller, stressors, and eventually, a deep sense of hopelessness and despair sets in.

Such people also appear to suffer a double dose of hopelessness. Not only do they perceive negative outcomes as being their own fault, they also perceive positive outcomes as being due to circumstance or to luck. In addition, they apply pessimistic attributions to a wide range of events and experiences and apply positive attributions only to a very narrow range of events and experiences, if any.

Genetic Causes

Like schizophrenia, the mood disorders appear to have a genetic component. People who have first-degree relatives with a serious mood disorder are ten times more likely to develop these disorders than are people without afflicted relatives (Rosenthal, 1970). Furthermore, the concordance rate for bipolar disorder is 72 percent for monozygotic twins, compared with 14 percent for dizygotic twins. For major depression, the figures are 40 percent and 11 percent, respectively (Allen, 1976). Thus, bipolar disorder appears to be more heritable than major depression, and the two disorders appear to have different genetic causes.

Physiological Causes—Biochemical Factors

Two forms of medical treatment that have proved successful in alleviating the symptoms of severe depression are *electroconvulsive therapy* and *antidepressant drugs*. Their success indicates that physiological disorders may underlie these conditions. I will defer discussion of electroconvulsive and drug treatments until Chapter 18.

Currently, two types of antidepressant drugs are in widespread use. One type of antidepressant drug, **lithium carbonate**, is effective in treating bipolar disorder, though as yet no one knows why. Lithium carbonate is a simple inorganic com-

lithium carbonate A simple salt effective in treating bipolar disorder.

pound. Its active ingredient is the element lithium, a metal that is closely related to sodium, which is found in ordinary table salt. (In fact, lithium chloride was used as a sodium-free salt substitute until it was found to be toxic in large doses.) Lithium carbonate has been called the "wonder drug" of psychiatry; it is effective in treating most cases of bipolar disorder and it has few side effects as long as the dosage is carefully controlled. Many people who are being treated with lithium carbonate are leading perfectly normal lives.

The other type of drug includes the *antidepressant drugs*, such as *imipramine*. Experiments on laboratory animals have shown that these drugs have stimulating effects on synapses that use two transmitter substances, norepinephrine and serotonin.

Other drugs, including *reserpine*, which is used to treat high blood pressure, can *cause* episodes of depression. Reserpine lowers blood pressure by blocking the release of norepinephrine in muscles in the walls of blood vessels, thus causing the muscles to relax. However, because the drug also blocks the release of norepinephrine and serotonin in the brain, a common side effect is depression. This side effect strengthens the argument that biochemical factors in the brain play an important role in depression.

Several studies have found evidence for biochemical abnormalities in the brains of people with mood disorders. Taking samples of transmitter substances directly from the living brain is not possible. But when transmitter substances are released, a small amount gets broken down by enzymes in the brain, and some of the breakdown products accumulate in the cerebrospinal fluid or pass into the bloodstream and collect in the urine. Investigators have analyzed cerebrospinal fluid and urine for these substances.

For example, Träskmann et al. (1981) measured the level of a compound (5-HIAA) produced when serotonin is broken down in the cerebrospinal fluid of depressed people who had attempted suicide. The level of this compound was significantly lower than that of control subjects; this finding implies that there was less activity of serotonin-secreting neurons in the brains of the depressed subjects. In fact, 20 percent of the subjects with levels below the median subsequently killed themselves, whereas none of the subjects with levels above the median committed suicide. Taube et al. (1978) obtained evidence for decreased activity of neurons that secrete norepinephrine; they found low levels of a compound (MHPG) produced when this transmitter substance is broken down in the urine of patients with mood disorders. Thus, decreased activity of serotonin- and norepinephrine-secreting neurons appears to be related to depression. Presumably, antidepressant drugs alleviate the symptoms of depression by increasing the activity of these neurons.

Although the brain biochemistry of patients with mood disorders appears to be abnormal, we cannot be certain that a biochemical imbalance is the first event in a sequence that leads to depression. Environmental stimuli may cause the depression, which then leads to biochemical changes in the brain. For example, the brain levels of norepinephrine are lower in dogs who have been presented with an inescapable electrical shock and have developed *learned helplessness* (Miller, Rosellini, and Seligman, 1977). The dogs certainly did not inherit the low norepinephrine levels; they acquired them as a result of their experience. The findings so far suggest that a tendency to develop serious mood disorders is heritable and that low levels of norepinephrine and serotonin are associated with these disorders. However, the cause-and-effect relations have yet to be worked out.

Physiological Causes—Relation to Sleep Cycles

A characteristic symptom of mood disorders is sleep disturbances. Usually, people with a severe mood disorder have little difficulty falling asleep, but they awaken early and are unable to get back to sleep again. (In contrast, people with dysthymic disorder are more likely to have trouble falling asleep and getting out of bed the next day.) Kupfer (1976) reported that depressed patients tend to enter REM sleep sooner than normal people do and spend an increased time in this state during the last half of sleep. Noting this fact, Vogel, Vogel, McAbee, and Thurmond (1980) deprived depressed patients of REM sleep by awakening them whenever the EEG showed signs that they were entering this stage. Remarkably, the deprivation decreased their depression. These findings are supported by the observation that treatments that alleviate depression, such as electroconvulsive therapy and antidepressant drugs, profoundly reduce REM sleep in cats (Scherschlicht et al., 1982).

Ehlers, Frank, and Kupfer (1988) have proposed an intriguing hypothesis that integrates behavioral and biological evidence. They suggest that depression is triggered environmentally, through loss of *social zeitgebers*. A **zeitgeber** (from the German word for "time giver") is a stimulus that synchronizes daily biological rhythms, which are controlled by an internal biological clock located in the hypothalamus. The most important zeitgeber is light; each morning, our biological clocks are synchronized ("reset to the time zero") by daylight. These clocks control sleep and waking cycles, cycles of hormone secretion and body temperature, and many other physiological systems that fluctuate each day.

Ehlers and her colleagues note that in humans, social interactions, as well as light, may serve as zeitgebers. For example, people tend to synchronize their daily rhythms to those of their spouses. After loss of a spouse, people's daily schedules are usually disrupted, and, of course, many widows and widowers become depressed. Flaherty et al. (1987) studied recently widowed people and found that the individuals who were the most depressed were those who had the greatest re-

zeitgeber   Any stimulus, such as light, that synchronizes daily biological rhythms.

duction in number of social contacts and regular daily activities. Ehlers et al. (1988) suggest that some people may be more susceptible to the disruptive effects of changes in social contacts and regular daily routines. This susceptibility represents the genetic contribution toward developing mood disorders. Almost everyone becomes depressed, at least for a period of time, after the loss of a loved one. Other events that change a person's daily routine, such as the birth of an infant or the loss of a job, can also precipitate a period of depression. Perhaps people who "spontaneously" become depressed are reacting to minor changes in their daily routine that disrupt their biological rhythms. Clearly, this interesting hypothesis deserves further research.

Yet another phenomenon relates depression to sleep and waking—or, more specifically, to the phenomena responsible for daily rhythms. Some people become depressed during the winter season, when days are short and nights are long. The symptoms of this form of depression, called **seasonal affective disorder**, are slightly different from those of major depression. Both forms include lethargy and sleep disturbances, but seasonal depression includes a craving for carbohydrates and an accompanying weight gain. (As you will recall, people with major depression tend to lose their appetites.)

Seasonal affective disorder can be treated by exposing people to bright light for several hours a day (Rosenthal et al., 1985). Possibly, people with seasonal affective disorder require a stronger-than-normal zeitgeber to synchronize their biological clocks with the day-night cycle.

Several investigators have noticed that the symptoms of seasonal affective disorder resemble the behavioral characteristics of hibernation: carbohydrate craving, overeating and weight gain, oversleeping, and lethargy (Rosenthal et al., 1986). Animals who hibernate do so during the winter, and the behavior is triggered by a combination of short day length and cooler temperature. Thus, some of the brain mechanisms involved in hibernation may also be responsible for the mood changes associated with the time of year. This hypothesis has some support. Zvolsky et al. (1981) found that imipramine, an antidepressant drug, suppressed hibernation in hamsters.

As we saw, specific deprivation of REM sleep also has an antidepressant effect. *Total* sleep deprivation has an antidepressant effect. However, the effects are quite different. REM sleep deprivation takes several weeks to reduce depression and produces relatively long-lasting effects. Total sleep deprivation produces immediate effects—but the effects are short-lived (Wu and Bunney, 1990). Figure 17.8 shows the mood rating of

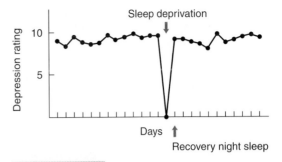

Figure 17.8

Sleep deprivation and depression. Changes in the depression rating of a depressed patient produced by a single night's total sleep deprivation.
(From Wu, J.C., and Bunney, W.E. The biological basis of an antidepressant response to sleep deprivation and relapse: Review and hypothesis. American Journal of Psychiatry, *1990, 147, 14–21. Copyright 1990, the American Psychiatric Association. Reprinted by permis-*

a patient who stayed awake one night. As you can see, the depression was lifted by the sleep deprivation but returned the next day, after a normal night's sleep. (See *Figure 17.8.*)

The data in Figure 17.9 are taken from eight different studies (cited by Wu and Bunney, 1990) and show self-ratings of depression of people who did and did not respond to sleep deprivation. (Total sleep deprivation improves the mood of patients with severe depression approximately two-thirds of the time.) People who responded to the sleep deprivation started the day depressed, but their mood gradually improved. This improvement continued through the sleepless night and during the following day. The next night, they were permitted to sleep normally, and their depression was back the next morning. Wu and Bunney suggest that a *depressogenic* ("depression-producing") substance is produced during sleep but disappears during waking. (See *Figure 17.9.*)

Why do some depressed people profit from total sleep deprivation while others do not? Although we cannot yet answer this question, an interesting study by Reinink et al. (1990) found that one can *predict* a person's responsiveness from his or her circadian pattern of mood. Most people feel better at a particular time of day—generally, either the morning or the evening. Depressed people, too, show these fluctuations in mood. Reinink and his colleagues found that the depressed people who were most likely to show an improvement in mood after a night of total sleep deprivation were those who felt worst in the morning and best in the evening. Perhaps these people are most sensitive to the hypothetical depressogenic substance produced during sleep. This substance makes them feel worst in the morning. As the day progresses, the chemical is metabolized and they start feeling better. A night without sleep simply prolongs this improvement in mood.

seasonal affective disorder A mood disorder characterized by depression, lethargy, sleep disturbances, and craving for carbohydrates. This disorder generally occurs during the winter, when the amount of daylight, relative to the other seasons, is low. This disorder can be treated with exposure to bright lights.

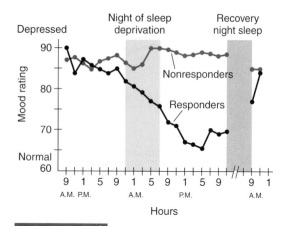

Figure 17.9

Self-ratings of depression and sleep deprivation. Mean mood rating of responding and nonresponding patients deprived of one night's sleep as a function of the time of day.

(From Wu, J.C., and Bunney, W.E. The biological basis of an antidepressant response to sleep deprivation and relapse: Review and hypothesis. American Journal of Psychiatry, 1990, 147, 14–21. Copyright 1990, the American Psychiatric Association. Reprinted by permis-

At the present time, total sleep deprivation does not provide a practical way of reducing people's depression (people cannot stay awake indefinitely). Fortunately, partial sleep deprivation, even if only for a few hours, seems to help.

Interim Summary

Mood Disorders

The serious mood disorders are primarily disorders of emotion, although delusions are also characteristically present. Bipolar disorder consists of alternating periods of mania and depression, whereas major depression consists of depression alone. The mood states of people with these disorders are not precipitated by environmental events; there is no external reason for these people to feel sad or elated. Beck has noted that although mood disorders involve emotional reactions, these reactions may be, at least in part, based on faulty cognition.

Heritability studies strongly suggest a biological component to mood disorders. This possibility receives support from the finding that biological treatments effectively reduce the symptoms of these disorders, while reserpine, a drug used to treat hypertension, can cause depression. Biological treatments include lithium carbonate for bipolar disorder and electroconvulsive therapy, antidepressant drugs, and REM sleep deprivation for depression. These findings, along with evidence from biochemical analysis of the breakdown prod-

ucts of norepinephrine and serotonin in depressed patients, suggest that depression results from underactivity of neurons that secrete norepinephrine or serotonin. However, the discovery that stress can reduce the amount of norepinephrine produced in an animal's brain warns us to be careful in making inferences about cause and effect.

Evidence also suggests that the primary physiological disorder in depression may manifest itself in terms of abnormalities in sleep/waking rhythms. Studies have shown that REM sleep deprivation alleviates the symptoms of depression, and all known biological treatments for depression themselves reduce REM sleep. Possibly, an important environmental trigger of depression may be events that disrupt a person's daily routine and social contacts. A specific form of depression, seasonal affective disorder, can be treated by exposure to bright light, which synchronizes the biological clock with the day-night cycle. In addition, total sleep deprivation temporarily reduces the symptoms of depression, particularly in people who tend to feel less depressed at the end of the day.

Let me close with a final thought. Besides having to simplify disorders that are typically complex, I have had to exaggerate the distinction between normalcy and mental disorder. I must emphasize again that no sharp line divides normal from abnormal behavior. At the extremes, there is no mistaking a person with, say, a phobic disorder, schizophrenia, or a mood disorder for a normal person. But most people do not fall at the extremes, and all of us recognize aspects of our own behavior in many of the descriptions of people with mental disorders.

Thought Questions

- Suppose that you have a friend whose mother has been diagnosed as having major depression. In addition to being concerned about her mother, your friend also worries that she may become depressed because she has heard that this disorder is genetic. Knowing that you are taking a course in psychology, she asks you to tell her more about the disorder and the likelihood that she, too, will develop it. What do you tell her?

- Medical students often self-diagnose themselves as having the symptoms of the diseases and disorders they are studying. In fact, though, their studies have simply made them more sensitive to even the slightest deviations from their normal level of physical health. While reading the section on mood disorders, did a similar thing happen to you—did you become more sensitive to your mood and to deviations from your normal mood? Can you trace the origins of these deviations to specific environmental events, or does there seem to be no reason for these perturbations in mood?

Suggestions for Further Reading

Carson, R.C., Butcher, J.N., and Mineka, S. *Abnormal Psychology and Modern Life*, 10th ed. New York: HarperCollins, 1996.

A highly readable, upper-division undergraduate text about psychological disorders, including their causes and treatment.

North, C.N. *Welcome, Silence.* New York: Simon and Schuster, 1987.

Vonnegut, M. *The Eden Express: A Personal Account of Schizophrenia.* New York: Praeger, 1975.

Both of these books are excellent, first-hand accounts of what it is like to suffer from schizophrenia.

Goodwin, D.W., and Guze, S.B. *Psychiatric Diagnosis,* 4th ed. New York: Oxford University Press, 1989.

This short book describes the characteristics of the most important mental disorders and what is known about their causes.

Cleckley, H. *The Mask of Sanity,* 5th ed. St. Louis: C.V. Mosby, 1976.

Cleckley's book is the definitive volume on antisocial personality disorder (psychopathy). Along with a thorough discussion of the disorder, it contains several detailed case studies.

Chapter 18

The Treatment of Mental Disorders

Chapter Outline

Mental Disorders and Psychotherapy

Early Treatment of Mental Disorders • The Development of Psychotherapy

People with mental disorders were once greatly misunderstood and treated inhumanely. Today, many forms of treatment are available for many different types of psychological problems. Therapists often use different methods or combine two or more methods to treat different problems.

Insight Therapies

Psychoanalysis and Modern Psychodynamic Approaches • Humanistic Therapy • Evaluation of Insight Psychotherapies

Insight therapies are based on the idea that a person's psychological problems can best be solved by talking about them with a specially trained therapist. Psychoanalytic and psychodynamic therapy attempt to get people to discover the unconscious and conscious forces that may be at the root of their problems. Humanistic therapy focuses more on the contribution of current thinking and emotions to maladaptive behavior. Gestalt therapy focuses on teaching people to confront their feelings as they are presently experienced—little emphasis is placed on past experiences. An important limitation to all insight therapies is that they are mainly relevant to mild mental disorders and not to more serious disorders, such as schizophrenia.

Behavior and Cognitive-Behavior Therapies

Therapies Based on Classical Conditioning • Therapies Based on Operant Conditioning • Maintaining Behavioral Change • Cognitive-Behavior Therapies • Evaluation of Behavior and Cognitive-Behavior Therapies

Therapies derived from the basic principles of classical and operant conditioning are effective in reducing anxiety and fear in people with anxiety disorders and phobias. Cognitive-behavior therapy is also effective in changing behavior, but in this case, the emphasis is placed on changing faulty cognitions as well as environmental conditions. Despite their effectiveness, applications of these therapies are limited by ethical considerations.

Group Therapy and Community Psychology

Family Therapy and Couples Therapy • Community Psychology • Evaluation of Group Therapy and Community Psychology • *Biology and Culture: Cultural Belief Systems and Indigenous Healing Therapies* • *Evaluating Scientific Issues: Assessing the Effectiveness of Psychotherapy*

Group therapies, including family and couples therapies, provide the opportunity for the therapist to observe people's interactions with each other and to suggest ways that those people may learn more adaptive responses. Community psychology stresses public education, social change, and prevention of psychological problems as strategies for teaching more effective behavior; it also provides important support services to those people who might otherwise be institutionalized for their problems.

Biological Treatments

Drug Therapy • Electroconvulsive Therapy • Psychosurgery • Evaluation of Biological Treatments

Certain classes of drugs have been found to be highly effective in treating the symptoms of schizophrenia, depression, bipolar disorder, and anxiety-related disorders. Severe depression is often effectively treated—as a last resort—by passing electrical current through the brain and inducing a seizure. Brain surgery is no longer a common treatment of mental disorders, although one form of it is sometimes used to treat people with severe obsessive-compulsive disorder.

Ethical and Legal Issues in Psychotherapy

Ethical Considerations in Practicing Psychotherapy • Legal Issues in Practicing Psychotherapy

Because the therapeutic relationship can be exploited and abused, a detailed set of ethical standards has evolved to guide therapists in their practices. Therapists must also be aware of the legal aspects of their work to avoid compromising their responsibilities to their profession, to their clients, and to society.

Selecting a Therapist

When selecting a therapist, one should look for someone who is licensed to practice therapy, knowledgeable about mental disorders, ethical, and supportive.

I f you were to meet my friend Molly, you would probably get the strong impression that she is mature, self-confident, witty, and happy. And you would be right—she is all these things.

But she hasn't always been this way. If you had met Molly two or three years ago, you would probably have gotten just the opposite impression—that she was immature, indecisive, and unhappy, perhaps even depressed.

As a friend, I have had the opportunity to watch her go through some incredible changes—changes that I am not sure I would have believed possible had I not witnessed them personally. Let me tell you a little more about Molly.

Molly is an only child—the result of an unplanned pregnancy. Both her parents are extremely bright and hard-working and both have very successful business careers. Molly's parents spent large amounts of time working away from home—on the road or at the office—to ensure their continued financial success. Other than during holidays and a few short "working vacations," she did not spend much time with her parents. She was basically raised by a series of nannies hired by her parents to look after her in their stead.

Molly grew up feeling unloved by her parents. She felt that something was wrong with her—that she was "defective" in some way. Why else would her parents avoid her so? She saw that her high school friends had parents who loved them and spent time with them, and she wanted the same for herself. But her parents were always too busy—they missed her first steps, her first day at school, her high school graduation, and the countless other precious moments that help give meaning to a young person's life.

When I first met Molly, she was a student in my introductory psychology class. She introduced herself to me one day after class and asked if she could speak to me during my office hours. I said sure.

During her visit with me, she told me her story and revealed her feelings about herself, her family, and her life. I could see that she was lonely and in considerable mental pain. She seemed lost. She said she had no friends and didn't feel that she could do anything right. She needed help.

I recommended that she see another friend of mine, a clinical psychologist in private practice. She did, and for the next year or so, the two of them worked very hard to improve her self-concept and to make her happier. The therapist taught Molly to replace her negative thoughts and self-statements with positive ones and to be more assertive in making friends and in asking her parents for more attention. The therapist also taught Molly to realize that her value as a human being wasn't dependent on other people's opinions of her, including her parents'.

Gradually, Molly's self-concept and level of self-confidence improved. She still gets sad when she thinks about her childhood, but now she also realizes that she has much to look forward to and that what happens now in her life is up to her. Her parents, who participated in several therapy sessions with Molly, are now aware of how ignoring their daughter affected her—and them. They, too, have come to feel a deep sense of loss and regret. As a result, they are now paying more attention to Molly and see her often. Needless to say, Molly is now much happier and more confident than when I first met her.

Keep in mind, though, that therapy is not always so successful. Recall Rick, my alcoholic friend to whom I introduced you in the opening vignette in Chapter 16. He spent several sessions in therapy with the same psychologist who treated Molly. He ended up drinking again and quitting therapy.

Therapy is a complex process whose outcome depends to a large extent on the relationship that the client and therapist are able to form. This chapter describes four basic approaches to the treatment of mental disorders: insight psychotherapies, behavior therapy and cognitive-behavior therapies, treatment of groups (including treatment of couples and the development of outreach programs that serve the community), and biological treatments. The final section of the chapter examines some ethical and legal issues involved in practicing therapy and some practical considerations to take into account when selecting a therapist. But before we discuss the different forms of therapy, let us first briefly consider the development of psychotherapy.

Mental Disorders and Psychotherapy

We live in a period during which mental disorders are often viewed as illnesses, much the same as physical diseases, like cancer. Psychologists agree that maladaptive behavior should be treated humanely. The person whose behavior is maladaptive needs help, and the emergence of techniques to provide such help has become a hallmark of psychology. As we shall soon see, though, the history of humankind's treatment of people with mental disorders and psychological problems has not always been so enlightened.

Early Treatment of Mental Disorders

Mental disorders have been with us since human existence began. For most of that time, people suffering from these disorders have been regarded with awe or fear. Sometimes, people whom we would now probably classify as paranoid schizophrenics were regarded as prophets; they were seen as instruments through whom gods or spirits were speaking. More often, they were considered to be occupied by devils or evil spirits and were made to suffer accordingly. The earliest known attempts to treat mental disorders involved **trephining**, or drilling holes in a person's skull. Presumably, the opening was made to permit evil spirits to leave the victim's head. In prehistoric times, this procedure was performed with a sharp-edged stone; later civilizations, such as the Egyptians, refined the practice. Signs of healing at the edges of the holes in prehistoric skulls indicate that some people survived these operations. (See *Figure 18.1.*)

Many painful and degrading practices were directed at people's presumed possession by evil spirits. People thought to be unwilling hosts for evil spirits were subjected to curses or insults designed to persuade the demons to leave. If this approach had no effect, exorcism was tried to make the person's body an unpleasant place for devils to reside. Other rituals included beatings, starving, near drowning, and the drinking of foul-tasting concoctions. The delusional schemes of psychotics often include beliefs of personal guilt and un-

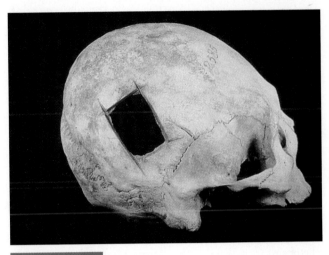

Figure 18.1

Among the earliest biological approaches to the treatment of mental disorders was the ancient practice of trephining, in which a hole was made in the skull to allow evil spirits to escape the person's head.

worthiness. In a society that accepted the notion that there were witches and devils, these people were ready to imagine themselves as evil. They confessed to unspeakable acts of "sorcery" and welcomed their own persecution and punishment.

Until the eighteenth century, many Europeans accepted the idea that devils and spirits were responsible for peculiar behaviors in some people. But a few people believed that these disorders reflected diseases and that they should be treated medically, with compassion for the victim. Johann Wier, a sixteenth-century physician, was among the first to challenge the practice of witchcraft. He argued that most people who were being tortured and burned for practicing witchcraft in fact suffered from mental illness. The Church condemned his writings as heretical and banned them. (Only in this century did they reemerge.) However, even within the Church some people began to realize that the prevailing beliefs and practices were wrong.

trephining A surgical procedure in which a hole is made in the skull of a living person.

As belief in witchcraft and demonology waned, the clergy, the medical authorities, and the general public began to regard people with mental disorders as ill. Torture and persecution eventually ceased. However, the lives of mentally ill people did not necessarily become better. Undoubtedly, many people with mental disorders were regarded as strange but harmless and managed to maintain a marginal existence in society. Others were sheltered by their families. The unfortunate ones were consigned to various "asylums" established for the care of the mentally ill. Most of these mental institutions were inhumane. Patients were often kept in chains and sometimes wallowed in their own excrement. Those who displayed bizarre catatonic postures or who had fanciful delusions were exhibited to the public for a fee. Many of the treatments designed to cure mental patients were little better than the tortures that had previously been used to drive out evil spirits. Patients were tied up, doused in cold water, bled, made to vomit, spun violently in a rotating chair, and otherwise assaulted. (See *Figure 18.2.*)

Mistreatment of the mentally ill did not go unnoticed by humanitarians. A famous and effective early reformer was Philippe Pinel (1745–1826), a French physician. In 1793, Pinel was appointed director of La Bicêtre, a mental hospital in Paris. Pinel believed that most mental patients would respond well to kind treatment. As an experiment, he removed the chains from some of the patients, took them out of dungeons, and allowed them to walk about the hospital grounds. The experiment was a remarkable success; an atmosphere of

peace and quiet replaced the previous noise, stench, and general aura of despair. Many patients were eventually discharged. Pinel's success at La Bicêtre was repeated when he was given charge of Salpêtrière Hospital. Some mentally ill people eventually recover—or at least get much better—without any treatment at all. But if a person was put in a mental institution that existed prior to Pinel's time, he or she had little chance to show improvement.

Pinel's success encouraged similar reforms elsewhere. In the United States, Dorothea Dix (1802–1887) led the campaign for humane treatment of mental patients. She raised millions of dollars for the construction of mental hospitals and spurred the reform of many mental health facilities. The process took a long time. Until very recently, some large mental hospitals were little more than warehouses for the mentally ill, who received little or no treatment but were merely provided with the necessities of life. Today there is much greater emphasis on treatment. The discovery of antipsychotic drugs has freed many people who otherwise would have spent their lives in institutions.

The Development of Psychotherapy

The modern history of specific treatments for mental disorders probably began with Franz Anton Mesmer (1734–1815), an Austrian physician who practiced in Paris in the late eighteenth and early nineteenth centuries. He devised a theory of "magnetic fluxes" according to which he attempted to effect cures by manipulating iron rods and bottles of chemicals. In reality, he hypnotized his patients and thereby alleviated some of their symptoms. As a result, hypnosis was first known as *mesmerism*.

A French neurologist, Jean Martin Charcot (1825–1893), began his investigations of the therapeutic uses of hypnosis when one of his students hypnotized a woman and induced her to display the symptoms of a conversion reaction (*hysteria*). Charcot examined her and concluded that she was a hysterical patient. The student then woke the woman, and her symptoms vanished. Charcot had previously believed that hysteria had an organic basis, but this experience changed his opinion, and he began investigating its psychological causes.

Just before Freud began private practice, he studied with Charcot in Paris and observed the effects of hypnosis on hysteria. Freud's association with Charcot, and later with Breuer, started him on his life's study of the determinants of personality and the origins of mental illness. (These topics were discussed in Chapters 14 and 17.) He created the practice of psychoanalysis. Some modern psychiatrists and psychologists still use some of his therapeutic methods to treat their clients.

As we will see in this chapter, other psychologists devised therapies based on their own theoretical views of maladaptive behavior and its causes. Some of these therapies, such as the humanistic and Gestalt therapies, are built on little or no scientific footing, while others, such as cognitive-behavior ther-

Figure 18.2

The "tranquilizing chair" devised by Benjamin Rush.

apy and drug therapy, rest on considerably more solid scientific foundations.

Regardless of whether the therapies they practice are empirically validated or not, all therapists have in common a strong commitment to helping people solve their problems—be they a matter of coping with everyday stressors or of more significant psychological disorders, such as schizophrenia or depression. Some psychotherapists adopt approaches to treatment that fit their own views of why people behave the way they do. For example, therapists who believe that behavior is strongly influenced by environmental contingencies, and people's perceptions of them, are likely to use cognitive-behavioral approaches to treating their clients' problems. Therapists who believe that behavior is strongly influenced by biological factors are likely to use a combination of drug therapy and psychotherapy in treating their clients' problems.

However, most therapists adopt a more general, eclectic approach. The **eclectic approach** (from the Greek *eklegein*, to "single out") involves the therapist using whatever methods he or she feels will work best for a particular client at a particular time. Such therapists are not strongly wed to particular theoretical orientations. Instead, they seek the particular form of therapy that will best solve a particular client's problems. This often means *combining* aspects of several different treatment approaches according to a particular client's problem and personal circumstances. For example, Acierno, Hersen, and Van Hasselt (1993) have shown that combinations of behavior and cognitive-behavior therapies are more effective in treating panic disorder than is either one alone. The opening vignette described a client whose therapist used several techniques to improve her self-concept and level of confidence (a combination of replacing negative thoughts with positive ones, teaching her to be more assertive and to realize her value as a human does not depend on what others think of her, and family therapy).

The reasons why people seek therapy are as varied as the people themselves. Some need help in adjusting to everyday problems at home, at work, or at school. Others face more serious problems such as the death of a loved one, their own approaching death, or difficulties in getting along with other people. Still others enter therapy or are placed in therapy by mental health agencies for very serious psychological problems such as schizophrenia, major depression, or drug abuse. Like Molly in the opening vignette, these people are at a low point in their lives. They feel that their own efforts are insufficient and that family and friends cannot provide the help they need to solve their problems. Almost anyone may benefit by seeing a therapist when problems seem overwhelming. Therapy is not just for people suffering from major psychological problems.

eclectic approach A form of therapy in which the therapist uses whatever method he or she feels will work best for a particular client at a particular time.

Interim Summary

Mental Disorders and Psychotherapy

At different times, people suffering from emotional or behavioral problems were believed to be possessed by demons or were accused of being witches. They were often subjected to unspeakable torture, including trephining, in which a small hole was punctured in the skull of the afflicted person to allow demonic spirits to escape. Even when not being physically harmed, mental patients in sixteenth- and seventeenth-century asylums encountered abject humiliation. Philippe Pinel, a French physician, is often credited with changing the asylum environment in the late eighteenth century.

Today, people seeking therapy have many treatment options—from psychoanalysis to drug treatment. In many cases, a person seeking therapy may find that his or her therapist uses an eclectic approach—borrowing methods from different treatments and blending them in a way that will work best in treating the patient's problem. Certainly, such options would not be available were it not for the modern view that people should have the chance to improve their level of functioning. People seeking therapy are perhaps even more diverse than those providing therapy. Although people seek therapy for many reasons, the one element they share is that they are at a low point at life in which alternative solutions, such as trying to solve the problem alone or with the help of friends and family, have failed.

Thought Questions

- What is your reaction toward people with mental disorders? Have you known anyone who has been diagnosed with a mental disorder? If so, what was your feeling about that person when you learned that fact?
- Would you ever seek help from a psychotherapist to help you with your problems? If so, describe what you might imagine psychotherapy to be like and how it might help you. If not, describe the reasons why you would not seek help.

Insight Therapies

Practitioners of *insight therapy* assume that people are essentially normal but learn maladaptive thought patterns and emotions, which are revealed in maladaptive behaviors. In other words, insight therapies view behavior as a symptom of deeper underlying psychological problems. Once a patient understands the causes of his or her problems, the problems—and the maladaptive behaviors—will cease. Insight will lead to a cure. In this section, we will take a close look at the insight therapies: psychoanalysis, client-centered therapy, and Gestalt therapy.

The insight therapies include a variety of treatments that emphasize talk between the therapist and the client as a means of discovering the reasons for the client's problems. Insight into these reasons presumably helps the client solve the problems. Some insight therapies, such as psychoanalysis, emphasize causes in the client's past. Others, such as client-centered and Gestalt therapies, emphasize the present; they attempt to get the client to see the effects of his or her maladaptive thoughts and emotions and to find more adaptive ways of living.

Psychoanalysis and Modern Psychodynamic Approaches

Sigmund Freud is given credit for developing **psychoanalysis**, a form of therapy aimed at providing the client insight into his or her unconscious motivations and impulses. Recall from Chapter 14 that Freud's theory of personality suggests that unconscious conflicts based on the competing demands of the id (representing biological urges), the superego (representing the moral dictates of society), and the ego (representing reality) often lead to anxiety. The source of these conflicts, according to Freud, can usually be traced back to unacceptable, often sexually based, urges from early childhood: repressed impulses and feelings that lead to conscious anxiety. As Freud (1933, p. 26) explained:

> One of the tasks of psychoanalysis . . . is to lift the veil of amnesia which hides the earliest years of childhood and to bring to conscious memory the manifestations of early infantile sexual life which are contained in them.

This veil is not easily lifted in the early stages of therapy because both the analyst and the client are unaware of the underlying conflicts. The repression of these conflicts is seldom complete, though, and they frequently intrude into consciousness in subtle ways. By encouraging the client to talk, the analyst tries to to bring these conflicts into view. The obscurity of the conflicts requires the analyst to interpret them in order to uncover their true meaning and gradually weave together a complete picture of the unconscious.

The purpose of therapy is to create a setting in which clues about the origins of intrapsychic conflicts are most likely to be revealed by the client. These clues are revealed in clients' dreams, physical problems, memory (or failure to remember certain things), manner of speech, and cognitive and emotional reactions to therapy. Then, by exposing the client to these clues, he or she will gain insight into the problem.

The primary function of the psychoanalyst is to *interpret* the clues about the origins of intrapsychic conflict given by the client. Although clients may provide their own interpretations of these phenomena, Freud argued that people are biased observers of their own problems and thus their interpretations cannot be accurate. Instead, accurate interpretation is best accomplished by undergoing therapy with a specially trained therapist. Even today therapists who practice psychoanalysis (or one of its modern forms) emphasize interpretation as the basic means of uncovering the root causes of their clients' problems.

While the psychoanalyst's primary role is interpretation, the client's main job is to provide the psychoanalyst something to interpret: descriptions of his or her fears, anxieties, thoughts, or repressed memories. This is not an easy task for the client to accomplish because the client unconsciously invokes one or more defense mechanisms, which, as you recall from Chapter 14, prevent anxiety-provoking memories and ideas from reaching conscious awareness. Together, the psychoanalyst and client work for insight into the client's problems.

The moment that insight is achieved, the "veil of amnesia" of which Freud spoke lifts and the client begins to understand the true nature of his or her problems. For some clients, insight is a sudden rush of profound understanding—sort of an "Ah-ah, so that's what was causing the problem!" experience. For other clients, perhaps the majority who undergo long-term therapy, the feeling may be more one of quiet accomplishment, such as that which comes after a long struggle that finally ends with success.

Psychoanalytic Techniques

Freud used **free association** to encourage the client to speak freely, without censoring possibly embarrassing or socially unacceptable thoughts. Freud achieved this goal in two ways. First, the client was encouraged to report any thoughts or images that came to mind, without worrying about their meaning. Second, Freud attempted to minimize any authoritative influence over the client's disclosures by eliminating eye contact. He usually sat in a chair at the head of a couch on which the client reclined.

Among the topics clients are encouraged to discuss are their dreams. *Dream interpretation*, the evaluation of the underlying meaning of dream content, is a hallmark of psychoanalysis (Freud, 1900). But even dream content is subject to some censoring, according to Freud, so that the analyst must be able to distinguish between the dream's *manifest* and *latent contents*. Recall that the manifest content of a dream is the actual images and events that occur within the dream; latent content is the hidden meaning or significance of the dream. The manifest content masks the latent content because the latent content is anxiety-provoking and causes the person psychological discomfort. Thus, the analyst must be especially skilled in recognizing the symbolic nature of dreams, for things are not always as they appear. For example, the client may relate the image of a growling, vicious dog chasing him or her down the street. The dog may actually symbolize an

psychoanalysis A form of therapy aimed at providing the client insight into his or her unconscious motivations and impulses.

free association A psychoanalytic procedure in which the client is encouraged to speak freely, without censoring possibly embarrassing or socially unacceptable thoughts or ideas.

Freud refined his practice of psychoanalysis in this office, where he asked his patients to recline on the couch (far right) and to tell him about their childhood experiences, their dreams, and their anxieties. Freud's goal was to discover his patients' unconscious motivations for the problems they were experiencing.

angry parent or spouse. The idea of a parent or spouse being angry and upset upset may be so painful to the client that it has been disguised within the dream. Bringing the client to an appreciation of the latent content of the dream is an important step toward insight and thus toward solving the client's psychological problems.

Insight is not achieved quickly, nor do clients always find it easy to disclose private aspects of their personal lives. In fact, there is something of a paradox involved in achieving insight, for the often painful or threatening knowledge resulting from insight is precisely what led to its repression in the first place. For example, a client may have to confront the reality of being abused as a child, or of being unloved, or of feeling peculiar, inferior, or out of place. Although the client wishes to be cured, he or she does not look forward to the anxiety and apprehension that may result from recalling painful memories. The client often becomes defensive at some point during therapy, unconsciously attempting to halt further insight by censoring his or her true feelings, a process Freud called **resistance**.

A psychoanalyst may conclude that resistance is operating when the client tries to change the topic, begins to miss appointments for therapy, or suddenly forgets what he or she was about to say. The skilled therapist, who is not burdened by the client's resistance, recognizes such diversions and redirects the discussion to the sensitive topics while minimizing the pain of rediscovery.

Over a period of months or even years of therapy sessions taking place as often as several times a week, the client gradually becomes less inhibited, and the discussion begins to drift away from recent events to the more distant shores of early childhood. As the client relives aspects of childhood, he or she may begin to project powerful attitudes and emotions onto the therapist, a process called **transference**. The client may come to love or hate the therapist with the same intensity of the powerful emotions experienced in childhood toward parents or siblings.

Originally, Freud thought of transference as an impediment to therapy, a distraction from the real issues at hand. But he soon realized that the experience of transference was essential to the success of therapy (Erdelyi, 1985). Whereas free association uncovers many of the relevant events and facts of the client's life, transference provides the means for reliving significant early experiences. The therapist contributes to this experience by becoming a substitute for the real players in the client's life and so becomes a tool for illuminating the conflicts of the unconscious.

Freud reasoned that the analyst, being human too, could just as easily project his or her emotions onto the client, a process he called **countertransference**. Unlike transference, Freud believed countertransference to be unhealthy and undesirable. To be effective, the analyst must remain emotionally detached and objective in his or her appraisal of the client's disclosures. For this reason, he argued that the analyst, in order to understand his or her own unconscious conflicts, should undergo complete analysis with another therapist.

Although Freud was not the first to talk about the unconscious mind, he was the first to develop a significant theory of abnormal behavior (which I described in Chapter 14). He also developed an equally influential therapy designed to provide the client with insight into the unconscious motives that underlie behavior. Psychoanalysis remains a force among contemporary therapeutic practices even a century after its founding, although its practice has undergone substantial modification.

Modern Psychodynamic Therapy

Psychoanalysis is now often referred to as *psychodynamic therapy* to reflect differences between modern psychoanalytic approaches and the original form of Freudian psychoanalysis. For example, although modern forms of psychodynamic therapies still focus on achieving insight into the unconscious, they tend to place less emphasis on sexual factors during development and more upon social and interpersonal experiences. Contemporary therapists also are more likely to address concerns and issues in the client's present life than to examine childhood experiences exclusively.

resistance A development during therapy in which the client becomes defensive, unconsciously attempting to halt further insight by censoring his or her true feelings.

transference The process by which a client begins to project powerful attitudes and emotions onto the therapist.

countertransference The process by which the therapist projects his or her emotions onto the client.

Modern psychodynamic therapists also view the ego as playing a more active role in influencing a person's thoughts and actions. Instead of viewing the ego as functioning merely to seek ways to satisfy the demands of the id and superego, they believe it to be a proactive component in one's overall psychological functioning. In other words, compared to Freud, modern psychodynamic therapists see the ego as having more control over the psyche. Thus, people receiving psychodynamic therapy are seen as being less constrained by the mind's unconscious forces than Freud thought them to be.

Although Freud considered analysis to be extremely involved and demanding, often requiring years to complete, today's therapists feel much can be gained by shortening the process, for example, by minimizing the client's dependence on the therapist. Psychodynamic therapy, as presently practiced, does not always take years to complete.

For example, one modern form of psychodynamic therapy, *time-limited therapy*, takes about twenty-five to thirty sessions with the therapist to complete (Strupp, 1993). The goal of time-limited therapy is to understand and improve the client's interpersonal skills through interpretation of transference processes. This therapy is based on Freud's belief that our early experiences with others influence the dynamics of our current relationships. Time-limited therapy focuses on the schemas that a client has about interpersonal relationships and attempts to modify those that are incorrect or that otherwise prevent the client from developing fulfilling relationships with others.

All forms of psychodynamic therapy share in common an interest in unconscious processes. There is an important corollary that attaches itself to this emphasis: Behavior or overt action is seldom important by itself. Rather, behavior is only important to the extent that it serves as a manifestation of the real, underlying motive or conflict. But, as we will see in next section, not all therapists agree with this idea.

Humanistic Therapy

The aim of **humanistic therapy** is to provide the client with a greater understanding of his or her unique potential for personal growth and self-actualization. Humanistic therapies proceed from the assumption that people are good and have innate worth. Psychological problems reflect some type of blocking of one's potential for personal growth; humanistic therapy is aimed at realizing this potential. The two major forms of humanistic therapy are client-centered therapy and Gestalt therapy.

Client-Centered Therapy

In the 1940s, Carl Rogers (1902–1987) developed the first humanistic therapy, creating a major alternative to psychoanalysis. Rogers found the formalism of psychoanalysis too confining and its emphasis on intrapsychic conflict too pessimistic (Tobin, 1991). His discontent led him to develop his own theory of personality, abnormal behavior, and therapy. His **client-centered therapy** is so named because of the respect given the client during therapy: The client decides what to talk about without direction or judgment from the therapist. The client takes ultimate responsibility for resolving his or her problems. The client, not a method or theory, is the focus of the therapy.

Rogers believed that the cause of many psychological problems can be traced to people's perceptions of themselves as they actually are (their *real selves*) as differing from the people they would like to be (their *ideal selves*). Rogers called this discrepancy between the real and the ideal perceptions of the self **incongruence**. The goal of client-centered therapy is to reduce incongruence by fostering experiences that will make attainment of the ideal self possible.

Because the client's and not the therapist's thoughts direct the course of therapy, the therapist strives to make those thoughts, perceptions, and feelings more noticeable to the client. This is frequently done through *reflection*, sensitive rephrasing or mirroring of the client's statements. For example:

> *Client:* I get so frustrated at my parents. They just don't understand how I feel. They don't know what it's like to be me.
>
> *Therapist:* You seem to be saying that the things that are important to you aren't very important to your parents. You'd like them now and then to see things from your perspective.

By reflecting the concerns of the client, the therapist demonstrates *empathy*, or the ability to perceive the world from another's viewpoint. The establishment of empathy is key in encouraging the client to deal with the incongruence between the real and the ideal selves.

For Rogers (1951, p. 20), the "worth and significance of the individual" is a basic ground rule of therapy. This theme is represented in therapy through **unconditional positive regard**, in which the therapist tries to convey to the client that his or her worth as a human being is not dependent on anything he or she thinks, does, or feels. Recall that in the opening vignette, one of the things that the therapist taught Molly was that her value as a human being did not depend on her parents' opinion of her or on how they treated her.

humanistic therapy A form of therapy focusing on the person's unique potential for personal growth and self-actualization.

client-centered therapy A form of therapy in which the client is allowed to decide what to talk about without strong direction and judgment from the therapist.

incongruence A discrepancy between a client's real and ideal selves.

unconditional positive regard According to Rogers, the therapeutic expression that a client's worth as a human being is not dependent on anything that he or she does, says, feels, or thinks.

In client-centered therapy, the therapist totally and unconditionally accepts the client and approves of him or her as a person so that the client can come to understand that his or her feelings are worthwhile and important. Once the client begins to pay attention to these feelings, a self-healing process begins. For example, a client usually has difficulty at first expressing feelings verbally. The therapist tries to understand the feelings underlying the client's confused state and to help him or her put them into words. Through this process, the client learns to understand and heed his or her own drive toward self-actualization. Consider the following example:

> *Alice:* I was thinking about this business of standards. I somehow developed a sort of knack, I guess, of—well—habit—of trying to make people feel at ease around me, or to make things go along smoothly. . . .
>
> *Counselor:* In other words, what you did was always in the direction of trying to keep things smooth and to make other people feel better and to smooth the situation.
>
> *A:* Yes. I think that's what it was. Now the reason why I did it probably was—I mean, not that I was a good little Samaritan going around making other people happy, but that was probably the role that felt easiest for me to play. I'd been doing it around the home so much. I just didn't stand up for my own convictions, until I don't know whether I have any convictions to stand up for.
>
> *C:* You feel that for a long time you've been playing the role of kind of smoothing out the frictions or differences or what not. . . .
>
> *A:* M-hum.
>
> *C:* Rather than having any opinion or reaction of your own in the situation. Is that it?
>
> *A:* That's it. Or that I haven't been really honestly being myself, or actually knowing what my real self is, and that I've been just playing a sort of false role. Whatever role no one else was playing, and that needed to be played at the time, I'd try to fill it in. (Rogers, 1951, pp. 152–153)

As this example illustrates, in Rogers's view, the therapist should not manipulate events but should create conditions under which the client can make his or her own decisions independently.

Gestalt Therapy

As we have seen, the development of client-centered therapy owes much to its founder's disenchantment with classical psychoanalysis. For much the same reason, Fritz Perls (1893–1970), though trained in Freudian techniques, disengaged himself from orthodox psychoanalysis and founded Gestalt therapy (Perls, 1969). **Gestalt therapy** emphasizes the unity of mind and body by teaching the client to "get in touch" with bodily sensations and emotional feelings long hidden from awareness. Gestalt therapy places exclusive emphasis upon present experience—not on the past—and the Gestalt therapist will often be quite confrontive, challenging the client to deal honestly with his or her emotions.

Like Freud, Perls believed that dreams are a rich source of information and that one must be able to understand their symbolism. In Gestalt therapy, the therapist will often have the client adopt the perspective of some person or even some object in the dream in an empathic manner.

In addition, the therapist often uses the *empty chair technique*, in which the client imagines that he or she is talking to someone sitting in the chair beside him or her. For example, a woman may be asked to say the things that she always wanted to say to her deceased father but didn't while he was alive. The empty chair technique allows her to experience in the here and now the feelings and perceptions that she may have suppressed while her father was alive. It also allows her to express these feelings and to gain insight into how these feelings have influenced her perception of herself and her world. This technique derives from Perls's belief that, for all of us, our memories, fears, and feelings of guilt affect our relationships with others.

The Gestalt therapist also encourages the client to gain a better understanding of his or her feelings by talking to his or herself (to different parts of his or her personality) and to inanimate objects. Any attempt by the client to avoid the reality of his or her situation is challenged by the therapist, who constantly attempts to keep the client's attention focused on present problems and tries to guide the client toward an honest confrontation with these problems. Perls (1967, p. 331) argued, "In the safe emergency of the therapeutic situation, the neurotic discovers that the world does not fall to pieces if he or she gets angry, sexy, joyous, mournful."

Evaluation of Insight Psychotherapies

In Chapter 14, we learned that psychoanalysis has little scientific support. But even though the theory cannot be confirmed, we should be able to assess the effectiveness of the psychoanalytic method—after all, it is results that count. However, evaluating the effectiveness of psychoanalysis or psychodynamic therapy is difficult because only a small proportion of people with mental disorders qualify for this method of treatment. To participate in this kind of therapy, a client must be intelligent, articulate, and motivated enough to spend three or more hours a week working hard to uncover unconscious conflicts. In addition, he or she must be able to afford the therapist's fees, which are high. These qualifications rule out most psychotics, as well as people who lack the time or money to devote to such a long-term project. Furthermore, many people who enter this kind of therapy become dissatisfied with their progress and leave. In other cases, the therapist

---

Gestalt therapy A form of therapy emphasizing the unity of mind and body by teaching the client to "get in touch" with unconscious bodily sensations and emotional feelings.

encourages a client to leave if he or she decides that the client is not cooperating fully. Thus, those who actually complete a course of therapy do not constitute a random sample, and we cannot conclude that this kind of therapy works just because a high percentage of this group is happy with the results. Those who have dropped out cannot be counted.

Another problem in evaluating psychoanalysis and psychodynamic therapy is that therapists have a way to "explain" their failures: They can blame them on the client. If the client appears to accept an insight into his or her behavior but the behavior does not change, the insight is said to be merely "intellectual." This escape clause makes the argument for the importance of insight completely circular and, therefore, illogical: If the client gets better, the improvement is due to insight; but if the client's behavior remains unchanged, real (as opposed to "intellectual") insight did not occur. An equivalent logic is to argue that wearing a charm (and sincerely believing in it) will cure cancer. If some people who wear the charm get better, the charm obviously works; if other people who wear the charm die, they obviously were not sincere believers.

Unlike many other clinicians, who prefer to rely on their own judgments concerning the effectiveness of their techniques, Rogers himself stimulated a considerable amount of research on the effectiveness of client-centered therapy. He recorded therapeutic sessions so that various techniques could be evaluated. One researcher, Charles Truax (1966), obtained permission from Rogers (and his clients) to record some therapy sessions, and he classified the statements made by the clients into several categories. One of the categories included statements of improving mental health, such as "I'm feeling better lately" or "I don't feel as depressed as I used to." After each of the patients' statements, Truax noted Rogers's reaction to see whether he gave a positive response. Typical positive responses were "Oh, really? Tell me more" or "Uh-huh. That's nice" or just a friendly "Mm." Truax found that of the eight categories of client statements, only those that indicated progress were regularly followed by a positive response from Rogers. Not surprisingly, during their therapy, the clients made more and more statements indicating progress.

This study attests to the power of social reinforcement and its occurrence in unexpected places. Rogers was an effective and conscientious psychotherapist, but he had not intended to single out and reinforce his clients' realistic expressions of progress in therapy. (Of course, he did not uncritically reinforce exaggerated or unrealistic positive statements.) This finding does not discredit client-centered therapy. Rogers simply adopted a very effective strategy for altering a person's behavior. He used to refer to his therapy as *nondirective*; however, when he realized that he was reinforcing positive statements, he stopped referring to it as nondirective because it obviously was not.

Like psychoanalysis, neither client-centered therapy nor Gestalt therapy is appropriate for serious problems such as psychoses. They are most effective for people who are motivated enough to want to change and who are intelligent

Carl Rogers (top right) taught his clients that personal growth is best achieved through the use of unconditional positive regard.

enough to be able to gain some insight concerning their problems. Some of these problems include coping with everyday stressors as well as experiencing excessive anxiety and fear.

Humanistic therapies are much more affordable and less time-consuming than traditional psychoanalysis. Many people would probably enjoy and profit from talking about their problems with a person as sympathetic as Carl Rogers or as direct and honest as Fritz Perls. Rogers's insights into the dynamics of the client-therapist relationship have had a major impact on the field of psychotherapy.

Interim Summary

Insight Psychotherapies

Insight psychotherapies are based primarily on conversation between therapist and client. The oldest form of insight psychotherapy, psychoanalysis, was devised by Freud. Psychoanalysis attempts to discover the forces that are warring in the client's psyche and to resolve these inner conflicts by bringing to consciousness his or her unconscious drives and the defenses that have been established against them. Insight is believed to be the primary source of healing.

Whereas psychoanalysis regards human behavior as motivated by intrapsychic conflict and biological urges, humanistic therapy emphasizes conscious, deliberate mental processes. Client-centered therapy is based on the premise that people are basically healthy and good and that their problems result from faulty thinking. Instead of evaluating themselves in terms of their own self-concepts, they judge themselves by other people's standards. This tendency is rectified by providing an environment of unconditional positive regard in which clients can find their own way to good mental health. Gestalt therapy focuses on convincing clients that they must deal honestly with their present feelings in order to become more mentally healthy. According to Gestalt therapists, the key to becoming happier is to confront one's fears and guilt and to keep one's emotions in proper perspective.

Among the shortcomings of insight psychotherapies is the narrow range of people that may benefit by undergoing such therapy. In general, the people who seem most likely to benefit from insight psychotherapy are those who are intelligent and able to articulate their problems. Insight psychotherapies are not effective with persons with serious mental disorders, such as schizophrenia. Psychoanalysis is also beset with problems related to evaluating its effectiveness in improving people's mental health.

Thought Questions

■ If you had some personal psychological problems, which kind of therapy—psychodynamic or humanistic—would you choose to resolve them? What factors would influence your choice?

■ Suppose that you were able to interview Freud, Rogers, and Perls. What sorts of questions would you ask each of them, and why would their answers to those questions be of interest to you?

Behavior and Cognitive-Behavior Therapies

Insight psychotherapies are based on the assumption that understanding leads to behavioral change. Once a person gains insight into the causes of his or her maladaptive behavior, that behavior will cease and will be replaced by adaptive behavior. In reality, however, insight is *not* often followed by behavioral change.

In contrast, the fundamental assumption made by behavior therapists is that people learn maladaptive or self-defeating behavior in the same way that they learn adaptive behavior. Undesirable behavior, such as nail biting or alcohol abuse, *is* the problem, not just a reflection of the problem. The methods that behavior therapists use to induce behavior change are extensions of classical and operant conditioning principles. Quite literally, Pavlov's study of the conditional salivary reflex in dogs and Skinner's research on operant behavior in pigeons and rats have yielded effective techniques for improving the quality of life for many people.

systematic desensitization A method of treatment in which the client is trained to relax in the presence of increasingly fearful stimuli.

Therapies Based on Classical Conditioning

Remember that in classical conditioning, a previously neutral stimulus (ultimately the CS) comes to elicit the same response as a stimulus (UCS) that naturally elicits that response because the CS reliably predicts the UCS. According to Joseph Wolpe (1958), one of the founders of behavior therapy, many of our everyday fears and anxieties become associated with neutral stimuli through coincidence. Consider an example: Suppose that you are involved in a car accident, and although you are not seriously hurt, you are upset for some time afterwards. When you get into a car for the first time after the accident, a sudden feeling of terror comes over you. You begin to perspire and breathe heavily, you feel like you are about to pass out, and it's all you can do to get out of the car without screaming. Your anxiety in response to getting into a car may be due to classical conditioning in which the pain and fear associated with the accident (the UCS) is associated with cars (CS).

Systematic Desensitization

One behavior therapy technique, developed by Wolpe, has been especially successful in eliminating some kinds of fears and phobias. This technique, called **systematic desensitization**, is designed to remove the unpleasant emotional response produced by the feared object or situation and replace it with an incompatible one—relaxation.

The client is first trained to achieve complete relaxation. The essential task is to learn to respond quickly to suggestions to feel relaxed and peaceful so that these suggestions can elicit an immediate relaxation response. Next, client and therapist construct a *hierarchy* of anxiety-related stimuli. Table 18.1 presents a hierarchy constructed with a subject who had an intense fear of spiders (Thorpe and Olson, 1990). The situations provoking the least amount of fear are at the top. (See *Table 18.1.*)

Finally, the conditional stimuli (fear-eliciting situations) are paired with stimuli that elicit the learned relaxation response. For example, a person with a fear of spiders is instructed to relax and then to imagine hearing from a neighbor that she saw a spider in her garage. If the client reports no anxiety, he or she is instructed to move to the next item in the hierarchy and to imagine hearing a neighbor say that there is a tiny spider across the street; and so on. Whenever the client begins feeling anxious, he or she signals to the therapist with some predetermined gesture—say, by raising a finger. The therapist instructs the client to relax and, if necessary, describes a less threatening scene. The client is not permitted to feel severe anxiety at any time. Gradually, over a series of sessions (the average is eleven), the client is able to get through the entire list, vicariously experiencing even the most feared encounters.

Scientific evaluations of systematic desensitization have been positive, and several experiments have found that all el-

Table 18.1

Sample Fear Hierarchy for Phobia of Spiders

1. Abbie [neighbor] tells you she saw one in her garage.
2. Abbie sees you, crosses the street, says there's a tiny one across the street.
3. Betty [at work] says there's one downstairs.
4. Friends downstairs say they saw one outside their apartment and disposed of it.
5. Carrie [daughter] returns from camp; says the restrooms were inhabited by spiders.
6. You see a small, dark spot out of the corner of your eye; you have a closer look; it isn't a spider.
7. You are with your husband. You see a tiny spider on a thread outside, but you can't see it very clearly.
8. You are alone. You see a tiny spider on a thread outside, but you can't see it very clearly.
9. You are reading the paper, and you see a cartoonist's caricature of a spider (with a human-like face and smile).
10. You are reading an article about the Brown Recluse.
11. You see a clear photograph of a spider's web in the newspaper.
12. You see a spider's web on the stairs at work.
13. You suddenly see a loose tomato-top in your salad.
14. You open a kitchen cabinet and suddenly see a large spider.

Source: Thorpe, G.L., and Olson, S.L. *Behavior Therapy: Concepts, Procedures, and Applications.* Boston: Allyn and Bacon, 1990. Reprinted by permission.

ements of the procedure are necessary for its success. For example, a person will not get rid of a phobia merely by participating in relaxation training or by constructing hierarchies of fear-producing situations. Only *pairings* of the anxiety-producing stimuli with instructions to relax will reduce the fear. One testimonial to this technique comes from a study by Johnson and Sechrest (1968), which attempted to reduce the fear of taking examinations in a group of college students. Students who underwent systematic desensitization received significantly higher grades on their final examination in a psychology course than did control subjects who were also taking the course but who received either no treatment or relaxation training alone.

Whereas practitioners of systematic desensitization are careful not to permit their clients to become too anxious, practitioners of a procedure called **implosion therapy** at-

tempt to rid their clients of their fears by arousing them intensely until their responses diminish through habituation and they learn that nothing bad happens. The therapist describes, as graphically as possible, the most frightening encounters possible with the object of a client's phobia. The client tries to imagine the encounter and to experience intense fear. In some cases, the client actually encounters the object of his or her fear, in which case the treatment is called *in vivo* (live) *implosion therapy.* Of course, the client is protected from any adverse effects of the encounter (or the encounter is imaginary), so there are no dangerous consequences. Eventually, the fear response begins to subside, and the client learns that even the worst imaginable encounter can become tolerable. In a sense, the client learns not to fear his or her own anxiety attack, and avoidance responses begin to extinguish.

Aversion Therapy

Sometimes people are attracted by stimuli that most of us would ignore, and they engage in maladaptive behavior as a result of this attraction. Fetishes, such as sexual attraction to women's shoes, are the most striking examples. A behavior technique called aversive therapy is effective in helping people change these behaviors. In **aversion therapy**, a negative reaction to a neutral stimulus is caused by pairing it with an aversive stimulus (UCS). Aversion therapy attempts to establish an unpleasant response (such as a feeling of fear or disgust) to the object that produces the undesired behavior. For example, a person with a fetish for women's shoes might be given painful electrical shocks while viewing color slides of women's shoes. Aversive therapy has also been used to treat drinking, smoking, transvestism, exhibitionism, and overeating. This technique has been shown to be moderately effective (Kanfer and Phillips, 1970). However, because the method involves pain or

People who are treated with systematic desensitization for their phobias often show remarkable positive changes in their behavior, for example, this person who has overcome an intense fear of snakes.

implosion therapy A form of therapy that attempts to rid people of fears by arousing them intensely until their responses diminish through habituation and they learn that nothing bad happens.

aversion therapy A form of treatment in which the client is trained to respond negatively to a neutral stimulus that has been paired with an aversive stimulus.

nausea, the client's participation must be voluntary, and the method should be employed only if other approaches fail or are impractical.

Therapies Based on Operant Conditioning

Behavior modification, a general term describing therapy based on operant conditioning principles, involves altering maladaptive behavior by rearranging the contingencies between behavior and its consequences. Increases in desirable behavior can be brought about through either positive or negative reinforcement and undesirable behavior can be reduced through either extinction or punishment.

In its infancy, behavior modification was applied chiefly to schizophrenic patients and the mentally retarded (Lindsley, 1956; Ayllon and Azrin, 1968; Neisworth and Madle, 1982). In the past three decades, however, use of operant principles has been extended to a wide array of behaviors and circumstances, for example; weight management, anorexia nervosa, bedwetting, smoking, and compliance with medical regimens (Kazdin, 1994).

Reinforcement of Adaptive Behaviors

Behavioral techniques are often used to alter the behavior of mentally retarded or emotionally disturbed people with whom communication is difficult. Reinforcement, which was described in Chapter 5, can be a powerful method of behavioral change. If the therapist has established a warm relationship with the client, he or she can use ordinary social reinforcers, such as signs of approval (friendly smiles and nods of the head), to encourage positive behavioral change. As we saw in the section on client-centered therapy, even nonbehavioral psychologists use reinforcement—deliberately or inadvertently—to produce behavioral change.

Token Economies

The behavior-analytic approach has been used on a large scale in mental institutions with generally good success. Residents are often asked to do chores to engage them in active participation in their environment. In some instances, other specific behaviors are also targeted as desirable and therapeutic, such as helping residents who have more severe problems. To promote these social behaviors, therapists have designed **token economies**: A list of tasks is compiled, and residents receive tokens as rewards for performing the tasks; later, they can exchange these tokens for snacks, other desired articles, or various privileges. The tokens become conditioned reinforcers for desirable and appropriate behaviors. Figure 18.3 shows the strong effects of the contingencies of a pay scale used in a token economy established by Ayllon and Azrin (1968). The amount of time spent performing the desirable behaviors was high when reinforcement contingencies were imposed and low when they were not. (See *Figure 18.3.*)

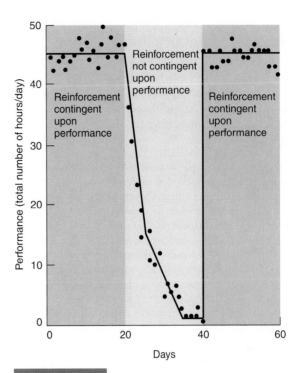

Figure 18.3

The effectiveness of a token economy. The effects of a token economy system of reinforcement on patients' performance of specified chores.
(From Teodoro Ayllon and Nathan Azrin, The Token Economy: A Motivational System for Therapy and Rehabilitation, *© 1968, pp. 249–250, 252. Reprinted by permission of Prentice-Hall, Inc., Englewood Cliffs, N.J.)*

Although token economies are based on a simple principle, they are very difficult to implement. A mental institution includes patients, caretakers, housekeeping staff, and professional staff. If a token economy is to be effective, all staff members who deal with residents must learn how the system works; ideally, they should also understand and agree with its underlying principles. A token economy can easily be sabotaged by a few people who believe that the system is foolish, wrong, or in some way threatening to themselves. If these obstacles can be overcome, token economies work very well.

Modeling

Humans (and many other animals) have the ability to learn without directly experiencing an event. People can imitate

behavior modification Behavior therapy based on the principles of operant conditioning.

token economy A program often used in institutions in which a person's adaptive behavior is reinforced with tokens that are exchangeable for desirable goods or special privileges.

the behavior of other people, watching what they do and, if the conditions are appropriate, performing the same behavior. This capability provides the basis for the technique of modeling. Behavior therapists have found that clients can make much better progress when they have access to a model providing samples of successful behaviors to imitate. Bandura (1971) described a modeling session with people who had a phobic fear of snakes:

> The therapist himself performed the fearless behavior at each step and gradually led subjects into touching, stroking, and then holding the snake's body with gloved and bare hands while the experimenter held the snake securely by head and tail. If a subject was unable to touch the snake following ample demonstration, she was asked to place her hand on the experimenter's and to move her hand down gradually until it touched the snake's body. After subjects no longer felt any apprehension about touching the snake under these secure conditions, anxieties about contact with the snake's head area and entwining tail were extinguished. The therapist again performed the tasks fearlessly, and then he and the subject performed the responses jointly; as subjects became less fearful, the experimenter gradually reduced his participation and control over the snake, until eventually subjects were able to hold the snake in their laps without assistance, to let the snake loose in the room and retrieve it, and to let it crawl freely over their bodies. Progress through the graded approach tasks was paced according to the subjects' apprehensiveness. When they reported being able to perform one activity with little or no fear, they were eased into a more difficult interaction. (p. 680)

This treatment eliminated fear of snakes in 92 percent of the subjects who participated. Modeling is successful for several reasons. Subjects learn to make new responses by imitating those of the therapist and their behavior of doing so is reinforced. When they observe a confident person approaching and touching a feared object without showing any signs of emotional distress, they probably experience a vicarious extinction of their own emotional responses. In fact, Bandura (1971) reports that "having successfully overcome a phobia that had plagued them for most of their lives, subjects reported increased confidence that they could cope effectively with other fear-provoking events" (p. 684), including encounters with other people.

Modeling has been used to establish new behaviors as well as to eliminate fears. Sex therapists have used specially prepared films or videotapes showing explicit sexual acts to help clients overcome inhibitions that are interfering with their sexual relations with their partners. Other therapists have acted out examples of useful, appropriate social exchanges for clients whose maladaptive behaviors usually prevent such interactions. As we shall see in a later section, modeling is an important aspect of almost all forms of group therapy.

Assertiveness Therapy

Assertiveness therapy is a procedure for developing coping skills in interpersonal situations in which a client might feel anxiety or is unable to function as effectively as he or she would like. In the opening vignette, Molly's therapist taught her how to be more assertive in seeking her parents' attention and in making friends. Assertiveness therapy is often used to help clients who feel frustrated at not being able to speak up to defend their rights, especially in those situations in which others are trying to take advantage of them or to otherwise compromise their values or moral standards.

The first step in assertiveness therapy is to identify the variables that are causing the client to feel distressed. For instance, the client's boss may be taking advantage of her and she is afraid to speak up for fear of losing her job. Once the variables controlling the situation are identified, the client practices assertive behaviors in the confines of therapy. For example, the client may practice confronting her boss with her feelings and requesting that he treat her more respectfully. Once the assertive behaviors are well practiced, the therapist encourages the client to apply her new skills to real-life situations. At the same time, the client is also encouraged to develop more effective interpersonal skills. Thus, rather than merely taking more abuse from her boss, the client would learn to approach her boss tactfully to let him know her feelings. For example, if her boss makes a rude remark toward her, she may say, "Are you feeling okay today? Has something made you upset?" With this response, the client has carefully centered the situation on the boss in a nonthreatening way (Carson et al., 1996).

Assertive behavior is believed to be incompatible with anxious behavior. That is, behaving assertively appears to inhibit anxious behaviors, leading to the development of more effective interpersonal skills. In those situations when people experience frustration, failure, and anxiety due to their inability to speak up for themselves or otherwise get their points across, assertiveness therapy is particularly effective.

Extinction of Maladaptive Behaviors

Recall that *extinction* is the process through which behavior is eliminated by removing previously available reinforcers. While it is seldom used by itself to combat undesirable behavior, extinction is often combined with other methods in behavior modification programs. For example, extinction might be used to eliminate a child's tantrum behaviors. If the tantrum behaviors have been reinforced—parents or caretakers have given in to the child's wishes—extinction might include ignoring the child's undesirable behavior.

There are two potential problems with using extinction. One is *extinction burst*. When a reinforcer that has previously followed a behavior is no longer forthcoming, that behavior will often intensify. You can imagine, for example, how a child whose tantrum behavior usually meets with social attention

A treatment strategy that is often effective in reducing tantrum behaviors in children is extinction—simply ignoring the behaviors.

will likely increase his or her efforts to obtain these reinforcers during the early stages of extinction. Fortunately, extinction burst is temporary, and if the extinction procedure is carried out, behavior generally diminishes.

The other problem with using extinction is that it is not always possible to eliminate the reinforcer that maintains undesirable behavior. For example, aggressive behavior in the classroom may be reinforced by the peer group, so attempts by a teacher to extinguish aggression may be only minimally effective. Extinction is also not the technique of choice when the client has direct control of the reinforcer, such as in thumb sucking.

Punishment of Maladaptive Behaviors

In general, punishment is not nearly as good a treatment method as positive reinforcement. For one thing, the person who is being punished may learn to fear or dislike the person who administers the punishment. If this person is the therapist, such an occurrence will probably interfere with other aspects of therapy. Second, there is a tendency to *overgeneralize*—to avoid performing a whole class of responses related to the response that is specifically being punished. For example, a child might not tell her father any more lies after being punished for doing so, but she might also stop sharing her secrets with him. Unfortunately, it is usually easier to punish a response than it is to figure out how to reinforce other responses that will replace the undesirable one. And when we are angry, we often find that it is satisfying to punish someone.

However, in some therapeutic situations, especially those in which the undesirable response is clearly harmful to the client, punishment is the most effective technique for eliminating an undesirable behavior. Cowart and Whaley (1971) reported the case of an emotionally disturbed child who per-

sisted in self-mutilation. He banged his head against the floor until it was a swollen mass of cuts and bruises. As a result, he had to be restrained in his crib in a hospital. The consequences of such confinement are serious for a child's development. After conventional techniques had failed, the therapist attached a pair of wires to the child's leg and placed him in a room with a padded floor. The child immediately began battering his head against the floor, and the therapist administered an electrical shock through the wires. The shock, which was certainly less damaging than the blows to the head, stopped the child short. He seemed more startled than anything else. He started banging his head against the floor again and received another shock. After a few repetitions of this sequence, the boy stopped his self-mutilation and could safely be let out of his crib.

The use of aversive methods raises ethical issues, particularly when the individual is so severely impaired that he or she is unable to give informed consent to a particular therapeutic procedure. Carr and Lovaas (1983) state that aversive methods involving stimuli such as electric shock should be used as the last resort. They should be used only when the patient's behavior poses a serious threat to his or her own well-being and after the following methods have been employed unsuccessfully: reinforcing other behaviors, attempting to extinguish the maladaptive behaviors, temporarily removing the patient from the environment that reinforces the maladaptive behaviors (a method called *time-out*), and trying to arrange for the patient to perform behaviors that are incompatible with the maladaptive ones.

Sometimes, the appropriate response need not actually be performed in the presence of the therapist but can be practiced vicariously. In a method called **covert sensitization**, instead of experiencing an actual punishing stimulus after performing an actual behavior, the client imagines that he or she is performing an undesirable behavior and then imagines receiving an aversive stimulus. For example, Thorpe and Olson (1990) describe the case of Frank, a man in his late twenties with a variety of social problems, including exhibitionism. He would drive far from his home town and expose his genitals to unsuspecting strangers. Although he derived sexual pleasure from this practice, he was disturbed by it and wanted desperately to be able to stop.

The therapist used a variety of methods to help the client improve his social skills and reduce his anxiety. In addition, the therapist used covert sensitization to eliminate the exhibitionism. The client was encouraged to imagine vivid scenes such as the following:

> He was driving around in his car, looking for a suitable victim. A woman, walking alone, appeared. Frank stopped the car and got out. He began to loosen his

covert sensitization A method used by behavior therapists in which a client imagines the aversive consequences of his or her inappropriate behavior.

clothing. He was feeling strongly aroused sexually. Suddenly a police car pulled up, its lights flashing and its siren wailing. The officers looked on Frank with contempt as they handcuffed him. At the same time one of Frank's workmates arrived on the scene. This workmate was the biggest gossip at the factory. News of Frank's arrest would soon be all over town. He would obviously lose his job. His crime would be reported in the local newspaper. Frank felt physically sick with shame. He thought ahead to the prospect of a long jail sentence in protective custody as a sex offender. (Thorpe and Olson, 1990, p. 17)

The client was indeed able to imagine scenes such as this one, and doing so made him feel very uncomfortable. Over several weeks, his impulse to expose himself declined.

Maintaining Behavioral Change

One of the problems with behavior therapy is that behaviors learned under one set of conditions may fail to occur in different environments; that is, the behavioral change may not generalize to other situations. This problem is especially acute in the treatment of alcohol addiction. Addicts may abstain from drinking in a treatment facility but go on a binge as soon as they leave it.

Behavior therapists have designed specific methods to ensure that positive behavioral change generalizes to situations outside a clinic or the therapist's office. As we saw in Chapter 5, intermittent reinforcement increases resistance to extinction. Thus, it is more effective to reinforce desirable responses intermittently than it is to reinforce every desirable response the client makes.

Another useful method that helps maintain behavioral change is *self-observation*, in which the client is taught to recognize when his or her behavior is appropriate. For example, Drabman, Spitalnik, and O'Leary (1973) rewarded a group of disruptive boys for performing desirable behaviors such as participating in classroom activities like reading. The reinforcement was effective; the frequency of disruptive behaviors declined and academic activity increased. To make the change as permanent as possible, the experimenters also reinforced the boys' behavior when the ratings of their own behaviors agreed with those of their teacher. In other words, they were trained to evaluate their behaviors in terms of those that should be reinforced and those that should not be. The assumption was that the self-evaluations would become conditioned reinforcers because they would initially be paired with actual reinforcement. Thus, the process of self-evaluation

would continue to reinforce the boys' behavior even after the period of training was over. Judging from the excellent results, the procedure succeeded.

Therapists also frequently ask friends and members of a client's family to become participants in the process of behavior therapy. These "adjunct therapists" are taught to encourage and reward desirable behaviors and to discourage or ignore undesirable ones. By these means, a client does not shuttle back and forth between two different types of environments—one in which the therapist selectively reinforces good behaviors and one in which reinforcement is haphazard or even inappropriate. For example, a person with behavioral problems may receive attention from the family only when he or she "acts up." Clearly, the best results will be obtained when other family members make an effort to ignore such outbursts and reinforce instances of good behavior instead.

Cognitive-Behavior Therapies

The first attempts at developing psychotherapies based on altering or manipulating cognitive processes emerged during the 1970s. These attempts were undertaken by behavior therapists who suspected that maladaptive behavior, or, for that matter, adaptive behavior, could be due to more than only environmental variables. They began exploring how their clients' thoughts, perceptions, expectations, and self-statements might interact with environmental factors in the development and maintenance of maladaptive behavior.

The focus of **cognitive-behavior therapy** is on changing the client's maladaptive thoughts, beliefs, and perceptions. This form of therapy is widely practiced today and has been shown to be effective in treating many kinds of psychological problems and mental disorders (Antonuccio, 1995; Munoz et al., 1994). Like behavior therapists—and unlike most insight psychotherapists—cognitive-behavior therapists are not particularly interested in events that occurred in the client's childhood. They are interested in the here and now and in altering the client's behavior so that it becomes more functional. Although they employ many methods used by behavior therapists, they believe that when behaviors change, they do so because of changes in cognitive processes.

Most of the practitioners of cognitive-behavior therapy use the methods of behavior therapy that I have just described. But in addition, they have developed some special methods designed to change the maladaptive patterns of cognition that they believe underlie maladaptive patterns of behavior. The attempt to change these patterns of cognition is referred to as **cognitive restructuring**. In the opening vignette, we saw that Molly's therapist taught her how to restructure her thinking by replacing negative thoughts and self-statements with more positive ones.

Rational-Emotive Therapy

The first form of cognitive restructuring, called rational-emotive therapy, was developed in the 1950s by Albert Ellis, a

---

cognitive-behavior therapy A treatment method that focuses on altering the client's thoughts, beliefs, and perceptions.

cognitive restructuring The process of replacing the client's maladaptive thoughts with more constructive ways of thinking.

clinical psychologist. **Rational-emotive therapy** is based on the belief that psychological problems are caused by how people think about upsetting events and situations. In contrast to the other forms of cognitive-behavior therapy, rational-emotive therapy did not grow out of the tradition of behavior therapy. For many years, Ellis was regarded as being outside the mainstream of psychotherapy, but now his methods are being practiced by a substantial number of therapists. Ellis asserts that psychological problems are the result of faulty cognitions; therapy is therefore aimed at changing people's beliefs. Rational-emotive therapy is highly directive and confrontational. The therapist tells his or her clients what they are doing wrong and how they should change.

According to Ellis and his followers, emotions are the products of cognition. A *significant activating event* (A) is followed by a *highly charged emotional consequence* (C), but it is not correct to say that A has caused C. Rather, C is a result of the *person's belief system* (B). Therefore, inappropriate emotions (such as depression, guilt, and anxiety) can be abolished only if a change occurs in the person's belief system. It is the task of the rational-emotive therapist to dispute the person's beliefs and to convince him or her that they are inappropriate. Ellis tries to show his clients that irrational beliefs are impossible to satisfy, that they make little logical sense, and that adhering to them creates needless anxiety, self-blame, and self-doubt. The following are examples of the kinds of ideas that Ellis (1973) believes to be irrational:

> The idea that it is a necessity for an adult to be loved or approved by virtually every significant person in the community.
>
> The idea that one should be thoroughly competent, adequate, and goal-oriented in all possible respects if one is to consider oneself as having worth.
>
> The idea that human unhappiness is externally caused and that people have little or no ability to control their lives.
>
> The idea that one's past is an all-important determinant of one's present behavior.
>
> The idea that there is invariably a right, precise, and perfect solution to human problems and that it is catastrophic if this perfect solution is not found. (pp. 152–153)

The excerpt below, taken from a therapy session with one of Ellis's own clients—a twenty-three-year-old woman who felt guilty about her relationship with her parents—shows how Ellis challenges clients to examine their irrational beliefs (Ellis, 1989).

> *Client:* The basic problem is that I am worried about my family. I'm worried about money. And I never seem to be able to relax.
>
> *Ellis:* Why are you so worried about your family? Let's go into that, first of all. What's to be concerned about? They have certain demands that you don't want to adhere to.

> *C:* I was brought up to think that I mustn't be selfish.
>
> *E:* Oh, we'll have to knock that out of your head!
>
> *C:* I think that that is one of my basic problems.
>
> *E:* That's right, you were brought up to be Florence Nightingale.
>
> *C:* Yes, I was brought up in a family of would-be Florence Nightingales, now that I realize the whole pattern of my family history. . . . My father became really alcoholic sometime when I was away in college. My mother developed breast cancer, and she had a breast removed. Nobody is healthy.
>
> *E:* How is your father now?
>
> *C:* Well, he's doing much better. . . . He spends quite a bit of money every week on pills. And if he misses a day of pills, he is absolutely unlivable. My mother feels that I shouldn't have left home—that my place is with them. There are nagging doubts about what I should—
>
> *E:* That's a *belief.* Why do you have to keep believing that—at your age? . . . Your parents indoctrinated you with this nonsense, because it is *their* belief. But why do you still have to believe that one should not be self-interested, that one should be self-sacrificial? Who needs that philosophy? All it's gotten you, so far, is guilt. And that's all it ever *will* get you. (pp. 234–235)

Although rational-emotive therapy is much more directive than client-centered therapy, there are some similarities. Just as Rogers emphasized unconditional positive regard, Ellis and his followers attempt to engender a feeling of full self-acceptance in their clients. They teach that self-blame is the core of emotional disturbance and that people can learn to stop continuously rating their own personal worth and measuring themselves against impossible standards. They emphasize that people will be happier if they can learn to see failures as unfortunate events, not as disastrous ones that confirm the lack of their own worth. Unlike a Rogerian therapist, a rational-emotive therapist will vigorously argue with his or her client, attacking beliefs that the therapist regards as foolish and illogical. This approach also differs from the client-centered approach in that the therapist does not need to be especially empathetic in order to be an effective teacher and guide.

In a review of research evaluating the effectiveness of rational-emotive therapy, Haaga and Davison (1989) concluded that the method has been shown to reduce general anxiety, test anxiety, and unassertiveness. Rational-emotive therapy has appeal and potential usefulness for those who can enjoy and profit from intellectual teaching and argumentation. The people who are likely to benefit most from this form of therapy are those who are self-demanding and who feel guilty for not living up to their own standards of perfection. People with serious anxiety disorders or with severe thought disorders, such as schizophrenia and other psy-

rational-emotive therapy Therapy based on the belief that psychological problems are caused not by upsetting events but by how people think about them.

choses, are unlikely to respond to an intellectual analysis of their problems.

Many therapists who adopt an eclectic approach use some of the techniques of rational-emotive therapy with some of their clients. In its advocacy of rationality and its eschewal of superstition, the therapy proposes a common-sense approach to living. However, many psychotherapists disagree with Ellis's denial of the importance of empathy in the relationship between therapist and client.

Cognitive Therapy for Depression

Aaron Beck (1967) has developed a therapy for depression that shares with Ellis's therapy an emphasis on the client's beliefs, interpretations, and perceptions. Beck's cognitive therapy, however, focuses more on faulty logic than on the beliefs themselves. The negative beliefs are seen as conclusions based on faulty logic. A depressed person concludes that he or she is "deprived, frustrated, humiliated, rejected or punished ('losers,' in the vernacular)" (Beck et al., 1979, p. 120). Beck views the cognitions of the depressed individual in terms of a *cognitive triad*: a negative view of the self ("I am worthless"), of the outside world ("The world makes impossible demands on me"), and of the future ("Things are never going to get better").

Even when confronted with evidence that contradicts their negative beliefs, depressed individuals often find an illogical means of interpreting good news as bad news (Lewinsohn, Mischel, Chaplin, and Barton, 1980). For example, a student who receives an A on an exam might attribute the high grade to an easy, unchallenging exam rather than to his or her own mastery of the material. The fact that few others in the class received As does little to convince the depressed person that he or she deserves congratulations for having done well. The depressed student goes on believing, against contrary evidence, that the good grade was not really deserved.

Once the faulty logic is recognized for what it is, therapy entails exploring means for correcting the distortions. Consider the following example from an actual therapy session.

A woman who complained of severe headaches and other somatic disturbances was found to be very depressed. When asked about the cognitions that seemed to make her unhappy, she said, "My family doesn't appreciate me"; "Nobody appreciates me, they take me for granted"; "I am worthless." As an example, she stated that her adolescent children no longer wanted to do things with her. Although this particular statement could very well have been accurate, the therapist decided to determine whether it was true. He pursued the "evidence" for the statement in the following interchange:

Patient: My son doesn't like to go to the theater or to the movies with me anymore.

Therapist: How do you know he doesn't want to go with you?

P: Teenagers don't actually like to do things with their parents.

In Aaron Beck's view, a person who is depressed has a negative view of him or herself, of his or her environment, and of his or her future.

T: Have you actually asked him to go with you?

P: No, as a matter of fact, he did ask me a few times if I wanted him to take me . . . but I didn't think he really wanted to go.

T: How about testing it out by asking him to give you a straight answer?

P: I guess so.

T: The important thing is not whether or not he goes with you but whether you are deciding for him what he thinks instead of letting him tell you.

P: I guess you are right but he does seem to be inconsiderate. For example, he is always late for dinner.

T: How often has that happened?

P: Oh, once or twice . . . I guess that's really not all that often.

T: Is he coming late for dinner due to his being inconsiderate?

P: Well, come to think of it, he did say that he had been working late those two nights. Also, he has been considerate in a lot of other ways. (Beck et al., 1979, pp. 155–156)

Actually, as the patient later found, her son was willing to go to the movies with her.

This example shows that the therapist does not accept the client's conclusions and inferences at their face value. Instead, those conclusions resulting from faulty logic are discussed so that the client may understand them from another perspective, changing his or her behavior as a result.

Evaluation of Behavior and Cognitive-Behavior Therapies

Psychotherapists of traditional orientations have criticized behavior therapy for its focus on the symptoms of a psychological problem to the exclusion of its root causes. Some psychoanalysts even argue that treatment of just the symptoms is dangerous. In their view, the removal of one symptom of an intrapsychic conflict will simply produce another, perhaps more serious, symptom through a process called *symptom substitution.*

There is little evidence that symptom substitution occurs. It is true that many people's behavioral problems are caused by conditions that existed in the past, and often these problems become self-perpetuating. Yet behavior therapy can, in many cases, eliminate the problem behavior without delving into the past. For example, a child may, for one reason or another, begin wetting the bed. The nightly awakening irritates the parents, who must change the bed sheets and the child's pajamas. The disturbance often disrupts family relationships. The child develops feelings of guilt and insecurity and wets the bed more often. Instead of analyzing the sources of family conflict, a therapist who uses behavior therapy would install a device in the child's bed that rings a bell when he or she begins to urinate. The child awakens and goes to the bathroom to urinate and soon ceases to wet the bed. The elimination of bedwetting causes rapid improvement in the child's self-esteem and in the entire family relationship. Symptom substitution does not appear to occur (Baker, 1969).

On the other hand, there are some situations in which behavior therapy should not be used. For example, a person who is involuntarily confined to an institution should not be subjected to aversive techniques unless he or she clearly wants to participate or unless the benefits far outweigh the discomfort. The decision to use aversive techniques must not rest only with people who are directly in charge of the patients, lest the procedures eventually be used merely for the sake of convenience. The decision must involve a committee that includes people who serve as advocates for patients.

Although cognitive-behavior therapists believe in the importance of unobservable constructs such as feelings, thoughts, and perceptions, they do not believe that good therapeutic results can be achieved by focusing on cognitions alone. They, like their behavior-analytic colleagues, insist that it is not enough to have their clients introspect and analyze their thought patterns. Instead, therapists must help clients to change their behavior. Behavioral changes can cause cognitive changes. For example, when a client observes that he or she is now engaging in fewer maladaptive behaviors and more adaptive behaviors, the client's self-perceptions and self-esteem are bound to change as a result. But cognitive-behavior therapists say that therapy can be even more effective when specific attention is paid to cognitions as well as to behaviors.

Because cognitive behavior therapists talk about unobservable cognitive processes, we must consider the differences between them and insight therapists, who also deal with unobservable processes. Unlike insight therapists, cognitive-behavior therapists concern themselves with conscious thought processes, not with unconscious motives. They are also more interested in the present determinants of the client's thoughts and behaviors rather than in his or her past history.

And because they come from the tradition of experimental psychology, they use rigorous empirical methods to evaluate the effectiveness of their techniques and to infer the nature and existence of cognitive processes.

Interim Summary

Behavior and Cognitive-Behavior Therapies

Behavior therapists attempt to use the principles of classical and operant conditioning to modify behavior—they try to eliminate fears or replace maladaptive behaviors with adaptive ones. Systematic desensitization uses classical conditioning procedures to condition relaxation to stimuli that were previously producing fear. In contrast, implosion therapy attempts to extinguish fear and avoidance responses. Aversion therapy attempts to condition an unpleasant response to a stimulus with which the client is preoccupied, such as a fetish.

Whereas classical conditioning involves automatic approach and avoidance responses to particular stimuli, operant conditioning involves reinforcement, extinction, or punishment of particular behaviors in particular situations. The most formal system involves token economies, which arrange contingencies in the environment of people who reside in institutions; in this case, the system of payment and reward is obvious to the participants. But not all instances of reinforcement and punishment are overt; they can also be vicarious. With the guidance of therapists, people can imagine their own behavior with its consequent reinforcement or punishment. Modeling has been used as an important adjunct to operant conditioning; therapists who use this effective technique provide specific examples of desirable behaviors.

Although some people view behavior therapy as a simple and rigid application of the principles of conditioning, therapists must be well-trained, sensitive people if the techniques are to be effective. The major problem with behavior therapy is people's tendency to discriminate the therapeutic situation from similar ones in the outside world, thus failing to generalize their behavior to situations outside the therapeutic setting. Techniques to promote generalization include the use of intermittent reinforcement and recruitment of family and friends as adjunct therapists.

With the exception of rational-emotive therapy, cognitive-behavior therapies grew out of the tradition of behavior therapy. These therapies attempt to change overt behavior, but they also pay attention to unobservable cognitive processes. Rational-emotive therapy is based on the assumption that people's psychological problems stem from faulty cognitions. Its practitioners use many forms of persuasion, including confrontation, to encourage people to abandon faulty cognitions in favor of logical and healthy ones.

Other forms of cognitive-behavior therapy involve systematic behavioral approaches to clients' problems, but their practitioners pay close attention to thinking and private verbal behavior. For example, Beck has developed ways to help depressed people correct errors of cognition that perpetuate self-defeating thoughts.

Some critics have accused behavior and cognitive-behavior therapists of doing nothing more than treating the symptoms of a disorder and ignoring its basic causes. However, there is no evidence to support the idea that symptom substitution occurs in people who undergo behavior or cognitive-behavior therapy.

Application of behavior and cognitive-behavior therapy can raise ethical concerns, particularly when aversive stimuli are used. If aversive techniques are the best solution, the client's participation must be voluntary or patient advocates must participate in the decision to use this form of therapy.

Thought Questions

- Think of the stimulus—either a thing or a situation—that you fear most. Based on what you learned about systematic desensitization, create a hierarchy of fear. Think about the hierarchy you have created for a few minutes and consider how you might find ways to relax as you imagine those aspects that elicit the least amount of fear. How successful are your efforts at relaxation as you progress through the hierarchy?

- Think again of your hierarchy of fear. Now, instead of applying efforts to relax, try to reconfigure your cognitions regarding the stimulus you fear. Are there cognitive aspects of your fear that are irrational or illogical? If so, how might you change these faulty cognitions so that your anxiety concerning the feared stimulus is reduced?

Group Therapy and Community Psychology

So far, I have been discussing individual forms of psychotherapy, in which a single client meets with a therapist. But in many cases, clients meet as a group, either because therapy is more effective that way or because it is more convenient or economical. In this section, I will discuss group and community therapies.

Group psychotherapy, in which two or more clients meet simultaneously with a therapist to discuss problems, became common during World War II. The stresses of combat produced psychological problems in many members of the armed

group psychotherapy Therapy in which two or more clients meet simultaneously with a therapist, discussing problems within a supportive and understanding environment.

forces, and the demand for psychotherapists greatly exceeded the supply. What began as an economic necessity became an institution once the effectiveness of group treatment was recognized.

Because most psychological problems involve interactions with other people, treating these problems in a group setting may be worthwhile. Group therapy provides four advantages that are not found in individual therapy:

1. The group setting permits the therapist to observe and interpret actual interactions without having to rely on clients' descriptions, which may be selective or faulty.

2. A group can bring social pressure to bear on the behaviors of its members. If a person receives similar comments about his or her behavior from all the members of a group, the message is often more convincing than if a psychotherapist delivers the same comments in a private session.

3. The process of seeing the causes of maladaptive behavior in other people often helps a person gain insight into his or her own problems. People can often can learn from the mistakes of others.

4. Knowing that other people have problems similar to one's own can bring comfort and relief. People discover that they are not alone.

The structure of group therapy sessions can vary widely. Some sessions are little more than lectures, in which the therapist presents information about a problem common to all members of the group, followed by discussion. For example, in a case involving a person with severe mental or physical illness, the therapist explains to family members the nature, treatment, and possible outcomes of the disorder. Then the therapist answers questions and allows people to share their feelings about what the illness has done to their family. Other groups are simply efficient ways to treat several clients at the same time. But most types of group therapy involve interactions among the participants.

Family Therapy and Couples Therapy

Family therapy and couples therapy have become important techniques for clinical psychologists. Very often dealing with the problems of an individual is not enough. People are products of their environments, and the structure of a person's family is a crucial part of that environment. Consequently, helping an unhappy person frequently means also restructuring his or her relationship with other family members. In addition, problems in the relations between members of a couple—with or without children—can often lead to stress and unhappiness. Recall that in the opening vignette, Molly's therapist held several sessions in which her parents participated. The therapist had felt that Molly's current relationship

Family therapy approaches mental disorders from the perspective that the structure of relationships within the family is part of the problem and that by restructuring those relationships people will become happier.

with her parents needed to be restructured. As it turned out, Molly's therapist was right.

In many cases, a family therapist meets with all the members of a client's family and analyzes the ways individuals interact with each other. The therapist attempts to get family members to talk to each other instead of addressing all comments and questions to him or her. As much as possible, the family therapist tries to collect data about the interactions—how individuals sit in relation to each other, who interrupts whom, who looks at whom before speaking—in order to infer the nature of interrelationships within the family. For example, there may be barriers between certain family members; perhaps a father is unable to communicate with one of his children. Or two or more family members may be so dependent on each other that they cannot function independently; they constantly seek each other's approval and, through overdependence, make each other miserable.

For example, consider the approach developed by Salvador Minuchin (1974), **structural family therapy**. He observes a family's interactions and draws simple diagrams of the relationships he infers from the behavior of family members. He identifies the counterproductive relationships and attempts to restructure the family in more adaptive ways. For example, he might diagram a family structure with father (F) on one side and mother (M) on the other side, allied with son (S) but estranged from daughter (D):

$$\frac{F}{MS|D}$$

He would then attempt to restructure the family as follows:

$$\frac{HW}{SD}$$

Husband (H) and wife (W) would replace mother and father, emphasizing that their primary relationship should be the one between spouses. The healthiest family interactions stem from an effectively functioning *marital subsystem*, consisting of husband and wife. A marriage that is completely child-oriented is always dysfunctional (Foley, 1979). And alliances between one parent and one or more children are almost always detrimental to the family.

After inferring the family structure, the therapist attempts to restructure it by replacing maladaptive interactions with more effective, functional ones. He or she suggests that perhaps all members of the family must change if the client is to make real improvement. The therapist gets family members to "actualize" their transactional patterns—to act out their everyday relationships—so that the maladaptive interactions will show themselves. Restructuring techniques include forming temporary alliances between the therapist and one or more of the family members, increasing tension in order to trigger changes in unstable structures, assigning explicit tasks and homework to family members (for example, making them interact with other members), and providing general support, education, and guidance. Sometimes, the therapist visits the family at home. For example, if a child in a family refuses to eat, the therapist will visit during mealtime in order to see the problem acted out as explicitly as possible.

Behavior therapists have also applied their methods of analysis and treatment to families. This approach focuses on the social environment provided by the family and on the ways that family members reinforce or punish each other's behavior. The strategy is to identify the maladaptive behaviors of the individuals and the ways these behaviors are inadvertently reinforced by the rest of the family. Then the therapist helps the family members find ways to increase positive exchanges and reinforce each other's adaptive behaviors. A careful analysis of the social dynamics of a family often reveals that changes need to be made not in the individual showing the most maladaptive behaviors but in the other members of the family.

All couples will find that they disagree on some important issues. These disagreements necessarily lead to conflicts. For example, they may have to decide whether to move to accommodate the career of one of the partners, they will have to decide how to spend their money, and they will have to decide how to allocate household chores. Their ability to resolve conflict is one of the most important factors that affects the quality and durability of their relationship (Schwartz and Schwartz, 1980).

When dealing with families and couples, which consist of people with long-established, ongoing personal relations, therapists have learned that changes in the nature of the rela-

structural family therapy A form of family therapy in which the maladaptive relationships among family members is inferred from their behavior and attempts are made to restructure these behaviors into more adaptive ones.

tions can have unforeseen consequences—and that they must be alert for these consequences. For example, LoPiccolo and Friedman (1985) describe treatment of a couple with a sexual problem. At first, the problem appeared to belong to the man.

> A couple with a marriage of twenty years duration sought treatment for the male's problem of total inability to have an erection. This had been a problem for over nineteen of their twenty years of marriage. Successful intercourse had only taken place in the first few months of the marriage. . . . [The wife] reported that she greatly enjoyed sex and was extremely frustrated by her husband's inability to have an erection.

The therapists used techniques developed by Masters and Johnson (1970) to treat the man's impotence, which succeeded splendidly. Within ten weeks the couple were able to have sexual intercourse regularly, and both had orgasms. However, even though the problem appeared to have been cured, and despite the physical gratification they received from their sexual relations, they soon stopped having them. In investigating this puzzling occurrence, the therapists discovered

> . . . that the husband had a great need to remain distant and aloof from his wife. He had great fears of being overwhelmed and controlled by her, and found closeness to be very uncomfortable. . . . For him, the inability to have an erection served to keep his wife distant from him, and to maintain his need for privacy, separateness, and autonomy in the relationship. (LoPiccolo and Friedman, 1985, p. 465)

The therapists also found that the wife had reasons to avoid sexual contact. For one thing, she apparently had never resolved the antisexual teachings imparted to her as a child by her family. In addition,

> . . . over the nineteen years of her husband being unable to attain an erection, she had come to have a very powerful position in the relationship. She very often reminded her husband that he owed her a lot because of her sexual frustration. Thus, she was essentially able to win all arguments with him, and to get him to do anything that she wanted. (LoPiccolo and Friedman, 1985, p. 465)

The therapists were able to address these issues and to help the couple resolve them. Eventually, they were able to alter the structure of their marriage and resumed their sexual relations.

This case illustrates the fact that a couple is not simply a collection of two individuals. Long-standing problems bring adjustments and adaptations (some of which may not be healthy). Even if the original problems are successfully resolved, the adjustments to these problems may persist and cause problems of their own.

You can appreciate how difficult the family therapist's job is. The task is formidable, as was recognized by Freud (1912) himself who stated, "When it comes to the treatment of relationships I must confess myself utterly at a loss and I have altogether little faith in any individual therapy of them." Of course, the modern therapist enjoys the benefit of several decades of research, theory, and practice not available to Freud. There is some optimism today concerning the effectiveness of family and couples therapy.

Community Psychology

So far, my discussion has been confined to therapists who wait for people with problems to approach them or who treat people committed to institutions. Another approach involves actively seeking out people with problems or the attempt to prevent problems before they begin. Therapists who participate in prevention are practicing **community psychology**, a form of treatment and education whose goal is to address psychological problems through an assessment of the *sociocultural* context in which they develop. Community psychology treats individuals and groups, establishes educational programs, and designs programs whose goal is to promote mental health by changing the environment.

Several different kinds of community treatment programs have been developed. One example is the *community mental health center*, a form of treatment sponsored by the United States Congress in the early 1960s and designed to supplement the care provided by mental hospitals. Instead of confining patients to an institution, community mental health centers provide outpatient care within the community. Some centers also provide *inpatient* care—the client may receive treatment while living full time on the premises for a short while.

A related type of community treatment program is the *halfway house*, a transitional setting where patients discharged from mental hospitals may receive outpatient care as they gradually become reintegrated into the community. Using the halfway house as their base, clients may take on part-time jobs, return to school, or just spend more time with their families and friends.

Deinstitutionalization

The process of allowing previously hospitalized patients to return to their communities for treatment is called **deinstitutionalization**. For the most part, this movement has been viewed as an important advance by community psychologists. Deinstitutionalization has reduced the number of per-

community psychology A form of treatment and education whose goal is to address psychological problems through an assessment of the sociocultural context in which they develop.

deinstitutionalization The process of returning previously hospitalized patients to their communities for treatment of psychological problems and mental disorders.

sons confined to mental institutions from over 500,000 people in 1950 to approximately 100,000 in the early 1990s (Lerman, 1981; Narrow et al., 1993).

However, deinstitutionalization has often proceeded more rapidly than has the funding and development of adequate community care programs and facilities (Grob, 1994). Many former residents of mental institutions had no families to look after them and "board and care" facilities were not adequately staffed and prepared to house these individuals. In fact, deinstitutionalization appears to have contributed significantly to the number of homeless people in the United States. One researcher has estimated that about a third of homeless people have chronic mental problems and another third have substance abuse problems (Rossi, 1990). Another researcher has estimated that about 130,000 schizophrenic individuals live on the streets or in public shelters, and only about 60,000 remain in traditional mental hospitals (Torrey, 1987).

Carson et al. (1996) reported the case of one individual, in his late forties, who was released and placed in a board and care facility after having been hospitalized for twenty-five years. At first, he seemed to be adapting well to life "on the outside." But after about two weeks, he turned up missing from the board and care facility. The police eventually found him living at the city dump. He had apparently stopped taking his antipsychotic medication and his mental condition deteriorated. He was immediately placed back in a public mental institution.

Community psychologists argue that the resolution to this sort of problem involves more careful screening of people who are being considered for deinstitutionalization and increased funding and development of community centers. But the problems posed by deinstitutionalization are not likely to be solved any time soon. Their successful resolution will require a strong and concerted effort by governmental agencies to provide money and support for the proper care of people suffering from mental disorders. Unfortunately, caring for the mentally ill has not been a top budgetary priority. And in today's tight fiscal climate, prospects for the necessary funding seem bleak. Perhaps this is why so many psychologists today advocate the *prevention* of mental disorders, which we will discuss next.

Preventive Psychology

Increasingly, community psychologists have been stressing treatment strategies aimed at forestalling the development of psychological problems (Seidman, 1991). This emphasis on treating the sociocultural variables predictive of psychological distress is called **preventive psychology**. A useful metaphor for describing preventive psychology is that individual therapy for psychological problems can be seen as similar to rescuing people from a river (Rappaport, 1977). Each person rescued is a life saved. But a more effective solution would be to go upstream and correct the problem that is causing people to fall into the river in the first place.

For example, consider a long-term follow-up study conducted by Gillham and her colleagues (1995). This study involved teaching cognitive skills to a large group of ten-to-twelve-year-old children who were at risk for depression. These skills included learning to identify negative and pessimistic beliefs and to replace them with more realistic and optimistic ones. The children were also taught to focus on accomplishing their goals, to make decisions by considering the pluses and minuses of their options, and to think about ways that certain kinds of problems might be solved.

The researchers compared the levels of depression for children who received this training to another group of similarly aged children who were also at risk for depression but who did not receive any prevention training. The results showed that the researchers' prevention program was successful—children who received the cognitive and social skills training were less depressed than were children who did not receive any training, even two years after undergoing the training. The researchers suggested that all children entering puberty are likely to benefit from the "psychological immunization against depression" that is provided by cognitive and social skills training.

Community psychologists distinguish between two kinds of prevention, primary and secondary. *Primary prevention* is any effort to eliminate the conditions responsible for psychological problems and to simultaneously bring about conditions that contribute to adaptive behavior. For example, providing children with educational materials concerning the dangers of taking drugs while encouraging healthy recreation and exercise represents an attempt to prevent experimentation with drugs. *Secondary prevention*, on the other hand, refers to prompt identification of problems and immediate intervention to minimize development of these problems. Suicide hotlines, which are staffed twenty-four hours a day by trained volunteers, are examples of secondary prevention measures.

Community mental health centers provide individual and group therapy and counseling to members of the communities in which they are located—most often, communities in which people are too poor to afford private mental health care. The goal of such centers is to provide immediate, accessible outpatient care for people who might otherwise find it difficult to get help. However, many community mental health centers are understaffed and underfunded, which limits the number of people who may be treated as well as the quality of care that can be offered. But to the extent that these centers can provide any effective mental health care at all—even for only small numbers of people—they are certainly a step in the right direction. The problem is not with the community mental health centers themselves. It is the inadequate

preventive psychology Any attempt to forestall the development of psychological problems by altering the sociocultural variables predictive of psychological distress.

resources many of them are provided, given the large numbers of people who require their services.

Such centers are generally staffed by psychologists, psychiatrists, social workers, and nurses. But they often also employ the services of paraprofessionals who have roots in the community. The use of paraprofessionals has many advantages. People from culturally deprived backgrounds frequently have difficulty relating to—and communicating with—middle-class therapists. However, if paraprofessionals having the same social and ethnic backgrounds are available, they may be able to gain the trust and confidence of clients and enable them to profit from the help that is available. Also, having faced similar problems, the paraprofessionals may be able to provide useful advice and to serve as role models for clients. Modeling is more effective when the model resembles the client.

Evaluation of Group Therapy and Community Psychology

Group and community therapies and family and couples therapy have filled important gaps in the treatment of mental disorders. Because group therapy is less expensive than private therapy, people who could not otherwise afford psychotherapy have a reasonable alternative to not getting any help. However, for those people who cannot afford private therapy and who are reticent to expose their problems to others, group therapy is not a good alternative. For these people, long-term treatment of any kind is generally not available.

Biology and Culture

Cultural Belief Systems and Indigenous Healing Therapies

Suppose that you are a clinical psychologist working in a community mental health center located in the heart of a large metropolitan area. One of your new clients is a young man, an immigrant from Jamaica, who is depressed. He blames his lethargy and unhappiness on *Obeah*—sorcery. Quite literally, this young man believes that someone has put a "hex," or curse, on him (Wedenoja, 1995). The problem you face, of course, is how to treat this individual—what sort of therapy would be the most effective?

As with all your clients, you must now determine what kind of treatment program will be most effective. However, this case poses a special problem because you know from your initial contacts that you and your client have different cultural belief systems about the cause of mental disorders. Your training represents a Western point of view, but this man knows little, if anything, about Western psychology or psychotherapy. His only experiences stem from his native culture and he wholeheartedly accepts and believes them.

If you treat him using one of the therapies discussed in this chapter, you are apt to make little progress in helping him. A better choice might be to choose to *cotreat* him with a traditional Jamaican healer, who is experienced in removing hexes. Many psychologists and psychiatrists whose clientele include persons with strong folk beliefs based on the customs and folklore of a particular culture have found such cotreatment to be very effective. For example, consider the following case involving a man treated at the New Horizons Community Mental Health Center in Miami, Florida (Lefley, 1984, 1994):

> A Haitian man diagnosed with schizophrenia failed to respond to ten days of inpatient therapy and drug therapy. He believed that he was cursed. The Health Center staff contacted a *houngan*—a *voodoo* priest—who performed an exorcism ritual on him. The man quickly calmed down, the medication soon reduced his symptoms, and he was released shortly thereafter.

The use of non-Western, culture-bound approaches to psychological (and medical) problems is called **indigenous healing** (or sometimes *ethnopsychiatry* or *ethnomedicine*). Indigenous healing therapies are quite common in many countries and within specific subcultures in North America, for example, among Native Americans, Asian Americans, Latino Americans, and African Americans of West Indian or Western African descent (Aponte, Rivers, and Wohl, 1995). Indigenous healing therapies are specific to each of these cultures—different cultures have different belief systems and methods of treatment for specific problems. However, all such approaches seem to have two elements in common:

1. The belief that the psychological problem is caused by factors external to the individual, such as a hex; by conduct that is considered immoral relative to culture standards for behavior; or by bad luck.
2. The problem is treated by ritual, often involving special incantations, herbal medicine, and spiritual forces and agents. Generally, these rituals involve calling upon these spiritual forces to remove the curse, to supplant the spiritual forces causing the problem, or to replace bad luck with good luck.

By understanding the belief systems of their non-Western clients and by incorporating aspects of these belief systems into their treatment plans, psychologists often produce successful results, as suggested by the example of the Haitian man given above. In fact, in some colleges and universities, clinical psychologists and psychiatrists in training receive specific instruction regarding the cultural belief systems and indigenous healing therapies they are

indigenous healing Non-Western, culture-bound approaches to the treatment of psychological and medical problems.

People in many non-Western cultures seek indigenous healing treatment approaches to their psychological problems.

liable to encounter in their work with clients (Zatrick and Lu, 1991). Such training would appear to sensitize them to those aspects of their clients' belief systems that are likely to impede therapy and to put them in a better position to understand the nature of their clients' problems and worries.

Have you thought any more about how you might treat your young Jamaican man who had been hexed? Consider how a similar case was handled by the New Horizons Community Mental Health Center:

> An African-American woman of Bahamian ancestry came to the center complaining of depression caused by a hex placed on her by her boyfriend's lover. She reported that the hex had caused problems for her at work and with her children. While undergoing counseling at the mental health center, she also sought out an *obeahman* because her boyfriend's girlfriend had used one to place the hex on her. The *obeahman* "cleansed her with special perfumes, oils, and herbs, and gave her special tasks that would align her with the benign forces of the universe. To finalize the therapeutic intervention, the healer took [her] to a cemetery at midnight, lowered her into an unfilled grave, and sprinkled her with grave dirt." Soon thereafter she got a raise at work, her children's behavior improved, and she broke off the relationship with her boyfriend. She continued, though, with the counseling sessions at the mental health center. (Lefley, 1994, p. 186)

We do not yet know the scientific explanation of why some people appear to be "cured" by indigenous healing or a mixture of indigenous healing and traditional psychotherapy but not by traditional psychotherapy alone. As you have learned, one of the most important qualities of successful therapists is their ability to form a warm and understanding relationship with their clients. Perhaps the familiar techniques of indigenous healing enable the client to feel more comfortable and open with the therapist and to establish a trusting relationship.

Evaluating Scientific Issues

Assessing the Effectiveness of Psychotherapy

Evaluation of therapies and therapists is a very important issue. It has received much attention, but almost everyone who is involved agrees that too little is known about the efficacy of psychotherapeutic methods, partially because psychotherapeutic effectiveness is difficult to study.

■ Why Is Psychotherapy Difficult to Evaluate?

Several factors make it extremely difficult to evaluate the effectiveness of a particular form of therapy or an individual therapist. One factor is the problem of *measurement.* Measuring a person's dysfunction is difficult; there are no easily applied, commonly agreed-upon criteria for mental health. Therefore, one usually cannot make valid before-and-after measurements. Most studies rely on ratings by the clients or the therapists to determine whether a therapy has succeeded. These two measures are obviously correlated, because therapists primarily base their ratings on what their clients say to them. Few studies interview friends or family members to obtain independent evaluations of the clients' condition—and those that do generally find a poor correlation between these ratings and those of clients and therapists (Sloane et al., 1975).

Ethics also sometimes prevent clinicians from using a purely scientific method of evaluation, which requires that experimental and control groups be constituted in equivalent ways. Leaving a person who appears to be suicidal untreated so that comparisons can be made with similar people who receive therapy presents risks that therapists consider unacceptable.

Self-selection—the fact that clients choose whether to enter therapy, what type of therapy to engage in, and how long to stay in therapy—makes it nearly impossible to establish either a stable sample population or a control group. That is, self-selection means that certain kinds of people are more likely than others to enter a particular therapy and stick with it, which produces a biased sample. Lack of a stable sample and lack of a control group makes it difficult to compare the effectiveness of various kinds of therapies. Many patients change therapists or leave therapy altogether. What conclusions can we make about the effectiveness of a therapy by looking only at the progress made by the clients who remain with it?

Yet another problem with scientific evaluation of psychotherapy is the question of an appropriate *control group.* You may recall from Chapter 2 that the effects of therapeutic drugs must be determined through comparison with the effects of *placebos* (inocuous pills that have no effects on people's thoughts and behavior) to be sure that the improvement has not occurred merely because the patient *thinks* that a pill has done some good. Placebo effects can also occur in psychotherapy: People know that they are being treated and get better because they *believe* that the treatment should lead to improvement. Most studies that evaluate psychotherapeutic techniques do not include control groups for these placebo effects. To do so, the investigator would have to design "mock therapy" sessions, during which the therapist does nothing therapeutic but convinces the patient that therapy is taking place; obviously, this goal is not easily achieved.

■ What Evidence Is There?

In a pioneering paper on psychotherapeutic evaluation, Eysenck (1952) examined nineteen studies assessing the effectiveness of psychotherapy. He reported that of the people who remained in psychoanalysis as long as their therapists thought they should, 66 percent showed improvement. Similarly, 64 percent of patients treated eclectically showed an improvement. However, 72 percent of patients who were treated only custodially (receiving no psychotherapy) in institutions showed improvement. In other words, people got better just as fast by themselves as they did in therapy.

Subsequent studies were not much more optimistic. Some investigators, including Eysenck, concluded that it is unethical to charge a person for psychotherapy because there is little scientific evidence that it is effective. Others said that the problems involved in performing scientific research are so great that we must abandon the attempt to evaluate therapies: Validation of the effectiveness of therapy must rely on the therapist's clinical judgment. Many forms of therapy have never been evaluated objectively because their practitioners are convinced that the method works and deem objective confirmation unnecessary.

Figure 18.4 summarizes Smith, Glass, and Miller's (1980) well-known meta-analysis of 475 studies comparing the outcome effectiveness of psychodynamic, Gestalt, client-centered, systematic desensitization, behavior modification, and cognitive behavior therapies. (See *Figure 18.4.*) A **meta-analysis** is a statistical procedure for estimating the magnitude of experimental effects reported by published studies. Relative to no therapy, each of these therapies was shown to be superior in helping people with their problems. As you can see, behavioral and cognitive therapies tended to exceed others in effectiveness, although these differences were often small. More recent research has confirmed these results, indicating that almost all people who enter behavior or cognitive-behavior therapy tend to improve with respect to the reason that brought them to therapy (Robinson et al., 1990). Keep in

mind that these data reflect hundreds of studies and thousands of clients. No conclusions can be drawn from studies like this as to the effectiveness of a particular therapy for any *one* client.

A very ambitious study sponsored by the U.S. National Institute of Mental Health compared the effectiveness of two forms of psychotherapy and drug treatment for treating depression (Elkin et al., 1985). The two forms of psychotherapy were cognitive therapy and a psychodynamic therapy. The therapists were carefully selected and received additional training over the course of two years to be certain that the application of the therapeutic approaches was of the highest standard possible. The sessions were videotaped and scrutinized to be certain that the high standard was maintained throughout the therapy. The drug (imipramine, an antidepressant medication) was not simply handed to the patient. The clients in this group met regularly with their physician, who provided a warm, supportive atmosphere; however, the physicians did not specifically practice psychotherapy. A control group received no therapy, only a placebo and the same type of support that the drug group received. The participants were evaluated before treatment, at several points during treatment, at the end of treatment, and at six-month, twelve-month, and eighteen-month follow-up periods.

Patients in all four groups, including the control group, improved over the course of the study (Elkin et al., 1989; Hirshfeld, 1990). Treatment with the antidepressant drug produced the most improvement, followed by the two psychotherapies. For moderately depressed patients, the differences between the three active treatments were not statistically significant. For severely depressed patients, the differences among the three treatments were significant. The recovery rate was approximately 70 percent for those who received imipramine, compared with 40 to 50 percent for those who received the psychotherapies and only 10 to 20 percent for subjects in the control group.

In 1995, the popular magazine *Consumer Reports* published its findings on the effectiveness of psychotherapy and drug therapy. Each year, the editors of *Consumer Reports* send a large-scale survey—concerning consumer satisfaction with a tremendous range of goods and services—to its subscribers. The 1994 survey included 26 questions about treatment for mental disorders. About 7000 readers responded to this portion of the survey, 2900 of whom had seen mental health professionals for help in coping with stress or emotional problems during the previous three years. The majority (59 percent) of these people had consulted either a psychologist or a psychiatrist; the remaining people had consulted a social worker, marriage counselor, or some other mental health professional.

In general, the results from this survey showed that people benefited greatly from psychotherapy. People who had undergone long-term treatment improved more than those who had undergone short-term treatment. In addi-

meta-analysis A statistical procedure by which the results of many studies are combined to estimate the magnitude of a particular effect.

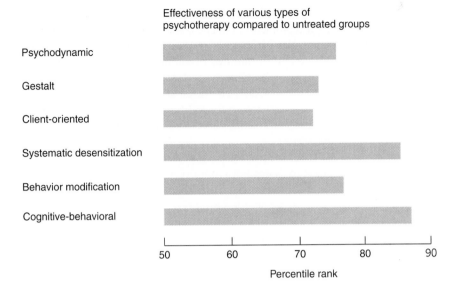

Figure 18.4

Effectiveness of psychotherapy. The results of Smith et al.'s meta-analysis comparing the effectiveness of different therapies.

tion, all forms of psychotherapy were found to be effective at making people feel better, regardless of the disorder from which they were suffering. And, in contrast to earlier studies, psychotherapy was found to be as effective as psychotherapy plus drug therapy in treating mental disorders.

A more detailed report, written by Martin Seligman, who served as a consultant for this project, was published that same year in the *American Psychologist*. Seligman noted that the results from the *Consumer Reports* survey complement the existing body of data—assembled up until now only by mental health professionals—that shows that psychotherapy appears to be beneficial. He suggested that its large-scale nature, combined with its lack of bias in surveying people who seek treatment and its sampling of treatment methods as they are actually practiced in the field, represents an innovative approach to assessing psychotherapy effectiveness. To the question "Do people have fewer symptoms and a better life after therapy than they did before?" Seligman and the *Consumer Reports* survey responded with a conclusive yes (Seligman, 1995). Keep in mind, though, that this study involved self-reports and thus cannot conclusively identify cause-and-effect relationships. For example, we cannot be certain that factors other than therapy in the respondents' lives did not have therapeutic effect on their mental states.

■ What Factors Influence Outcome?

An interesting study by Luborsky et al. (1971) investigated the factors that influence the outcome of psychotherapy, independent of the particular method used. They examined both patient variables and therapist variables. The important *patient variables* were psychological health at the beginning of the therapy, adequacy of personality, the patient's motivation for change, level of in-

telligence, level of anxiety (more anxious patients tended to do better), level of education, and socioeconomic status. Some of the variables seem to be self-confirming: If you are in fairly good psychological shape to begin with, you have a better chance of improving. In addition, if you are well educated and have adequate social and financial resources, your condition will probably improve. The finding that anxiety is a good sign probably indicates a motivation to improve.

Several *therapist variables* were significant. These variables were the number of years the therapist had been practicing, similarity in the personality of therapist and client, and the ability of the therapist to communicate empathy to the client. The finding that the more experienced therapists had more success with their clients is very encouraging; it suggests that therapists learn something from their years of experience, which in turn implies that *there is something to learn*. Thus, we have reason to believe that the process of psychotherapy is worthwhile.

Several studies have suggested that the ability to form understanding, warm, and empathetic relationships is one of the most important traits that distinguish an effective therapist from an ineffective one. For example, Strupp and Hadley (1979) enlisted a group of college professors on the basis of their reputations as warm, trustworthy, empathetic individuals. The professors (from the departments of English, history, mathematics, and philosophy) were asked to hold weekly sessions to counsel students with psychological difficulties. Another group of students was assigned to professional psychotherapists, both psychologists and psychiatrists, and a third group received no treatment at all. Most of the students showed moderate depression or anxiety.

Although there was much variability, with some individual students showing substantial improvement, students who met with the professors did as well as those who met with the professional therapists. Both groups did significantly better than the control subjects who received no treatment. These results suggest that sympathy and understanding are the most important ingredients in the psychotherapeutic process, at least for treatment of mild anxiety or depression. In such cases, the therapists' theories of how mental disorders should be treated may be *less* important than their ability to establish warm, understanding relationships with their clients.

■ What Should We Conclude?

This chapter has tried to convey the ingenuity shown by clinicians in their efforts to help people with psychological problems. The magnitude of the task is formidable. One encouraging outcome of evaluative research is its implication that therapy is effective. Experienced and empathetic therapists are likely to help their clients get better. Another encouraging outcome is the general success achieved in behavior and cognitive-behavior therapy, even though its goals are often circumscribed. Finally, although clinical psychologists are not responsible for the development of the biological therapies, they can take heart from several studies showing that psychotherapy significantly improves the mental health of clients who are also receiving drug therapy, which we will discuss later in this chapter.

Interim Summary

Group Therapy and Community Psychology

Many types of group therapy have been developed in response to the belief that certain problems can be treated more efficiently and more effectively in group settings. Practitioners of family therapy, couples therapy, and some forms of group behavior therapy observe people's interactions with others and attempt to help them learn how to establish more effective patterns of behavior. Treatment of groups, including families and couples, permits the therapist to observe clients' social behaviors, and it uses social pressures to help convince clients of the necessity for behavioral change. It permits clients to learn from the mistakes of others and observe that other people have similar problems, which often provides reassurance.

Community psychology involves psychologists' attempts to reach out to a community to try to establish readily available treatment facilities or provide crisis intervention to keep problems from becoming worse. It also tries to educate the public and promote social changes in order to prevent problems from occurring in the first place.

Indigenous healing therapies are based on belief systems regarding the causes and cures of psychological problems specific to a given culture. Although indigenous healing therapies often involve the use of special incantations and rit-

uals, they are effective in reducing the symptoms of psychological problems in the people who use them. For this reason, many North American psychologists and psychiatrists use a blending of traditional psychotherapy and indigenous healing therapy to treat immigrants from certain cultures. This method appears to be more effective than using only psychotherapy because the indigenous healing therapy provides the basis for making contact with the individual's cultural belief system.

The effectiveness of psychotherapeutic methods is difficult to assess, but given the immense expense of problems associated with mental disorders, we must do our best to evaluate these methods. Outcomes are difficult to measure objectively, ethical considerations make it hard to establish control groups for some types of disorders, and self-selection and dropouts make it impossible to compare randomly selected groups of subjects. However, what research there is suggests that some forms of psychotherapy—particularly behavior therapy and cognitive-behavior therapy—are effective. The effectiveness of drug therapy is easier to demonstrate because experimenters can construct double-blind studies using placebos. Several experiments assessing both drug treatment and psychotherapy have found that a combined approach is the most beneficial. The most ambitious study has found that antidepressant medication, delivered in a warm, caring atmosphere, was more effective than cognitive-behavior therapy or interpersonal therapy alone in treating severe depression; no significant differences were seen in less severe cases. The *Consumer Reports* study found that people do indeed benefit from therapy and that, contrary to the findings of earlier studies, psychotherapy alone appears to be as effective as the combination of psychotherapy and drug therapy in treating mental disorders.

The most important characteristic of a good psychotherapist appears to be the ability to form a warm, understanding relationship with a client. Perhaps when the therapist is empathetic, the client grows to care about the therapist's opinions, which allows the therapist to become a potent source of social reinforcement. In addition, the client may be more willing to model his or her behavior on the behavior of a caring therapist.

Table 18.2 summarizes the assumptions, primary goals, and methods involved in each of the traditional forms of psychotherapy I have discussed. (See *Table 18.2.*)

Thought Questions

■ How effective might group therapy be in helping you cope with your problems, anxieties, or fears? Would you feel comfortable telling others about these sorts of things? In what ways might you benefit from hearing others discuss their problems and worries?

■ It is a common practice for people to visit their physicians once a year for a check-up. It is also routine for people to visit their dentists twice a year to have their teeth cleaned and examined for cavities and other problems. Why don't people take the same preventive

Table 18.2

Summary of the Basic Assumptions, Goals, and Methods Involved in Traditional Forms of Psychotherapy

Type of Therapy	Basic Assumptions	Primary Goals	Typical Method of Analysis or Intervention
Psychoanalysis	Behavior is motivated by intrapsychic conflict and biological urges.	Discover the sources of conflict and resolve them through insight.	Free association, dream interpretation, interpretation of transference, resistance, memory, and manner of speech.
Psychodynamic	Behavior is motivated by both unconscious forces and interpersonal experiences.	Understand and improve interpersonal skills.	Interpretation of transference and modification of client's inappropriate schemas about interpersonal relationships.
Humanistic and Gestalt	People are good and have innate worth.	To promote personal growth and self-actualization and to enhance clients' awareness of bodily sensations and feelings.	Reduce incongruence through reflection, empathy, unconditional positive regard, and techniques to enhance personal awareness and feelings of self-worth.
Behavior and cognitive-behavior	Behavior is largely controlled by environmental contingencies, people's perception of them, or their combination.	To change maladaptive behavior and thinking patterns.	Manipulate environmental variables, restructure thinking patterns, and correct faulty thinking or irrational beliefs
Family/couples	Problems in relationships entail everybody involved in them.	To discover how interactions influence problems in individual functioning.	Analysis of patterns of family/couples' interaction and how others reinforce maladaptive and adaptive thinking and behaving.

approach to their mental health? Suppose that you were a clinical psychologist. How might you establish or set up such a preventive exam (what would the exam consist of; what kinds of problems would you look for; and how would you consider treating a problem if you found one)?

Biological Treatments

As we saw in Chapter 17, an important method for treating the symptoms of schizophrenia and mood disorders is medication. Besides drug therapy, there are two other forms of biological treatment: electroconvulsive therapy and psychosurgery.

Drug Therapy

Drug therapy, often called **pharmacotherapy,** is the treatment of psychological problems with chemical agents and is the most widely used form of biomedical therapy. Although

abuses have occurred, drug therapy created a revolution in the treatment of psychological disorders and is a highly active area of medical and psychological research today. Table 18.3 lists some of the more common drugs used to improve psychological functioning, their generic names, and their more recognizable trade names. (See *Table 18.3.*) There are four classes of drugs used to treat mental disorders: antipsychotic drugs, antidepressant drugs, antimanic drugs, and antianxiety drugs.

Antipsychotic Drugs

The development of **antipsychotic drugs** has had a profound effect on the treatment of schizophrenia. Many people who are treated with antipsychotic drugs, such as my father, are able to lead happy and productive lives. My father is able to live on his own, work, and enjoy life—just like people who do not other-

pharmacotherapy The treatment of psychological problems with chemical agents.

antipsychotic drugs Drugs used to treat psychotic disorders such as schizophrenia.

Table 18.3			

Drugs Commonly Used to Treat Mental Disorders

Therapeutic Function	Class of Drugs	Generic Name	Trade Name
Antipsychotic	Soporific	Chlorpromazine	Thorazine
	Nonsoporific	Acetophenazine	Tindal
	Phenothiazines	Thioridazine	Mellaril
		Fluphenazine	Permitil
		Trifluoperazine	Stelazine
		Perphenazine	Trilafon
	Butyrophenones	Haloperidol	Haldol
Antidepressant	Tricyclics	Imipramine	Tofranil
	Monoamine oxidase inhibitors	Amitryptiline	Elavil
		Phenelzine	Nardil
	Serotonin reuptake inhibitors	Fluoxetine	Prozac
			Miltown
Antianxiety	Propanediols	Meprobamate	Librium
	Benzodiazepines	Chlordiazepoxide	Valium
		Diazapam	
Antimanic	Lithium salts	Lithium carbonate	Eskalith

wise suffer from a serious mental illness. As long as my father takes his medication as prescribed, he functions very well. However, if for some reason he fails to do so, then symptoms of schizophrenia return and he begins experiencing serious problems, even in carrying out his normal daily routine.

Antipsychotic drugs thus do not cure schizophrenia. Instead, they simply reduce the severity of its most prominent positive symptoms—delusions and hallucinations—apparently by blocking dopamine receptors in the brain. Presumably, overactivity of dopamine synapses is responsible for the positive symptoms of schizophrenia. Although dopamine-secreting neurons are located in several parts of the brain, most researchers believe that the ones involved in the symptoms of schizophrenia are located in the cerebral cortex and parts of the limbic system near the front of the brain.

A different system of dopamine-secreting neurons in the brain is involved in the control of movement. Occasionally, this system of neurons degenerates in older people, producing Parkinson's disease. Symptoms of this disorder include tremors, muscular rigidity, loss of balance, difficulty in initiating movement, and impaired breathing that makes speech indistinct. In severe cases the person is bedridden.

The major problem with antipsychotic drugs is that they do not discriminate between these two systems of dopamine-

secreting neurons. The drugs interfere with the activity of both the circuits involved in the symptoms of schizophrenia and the circuits involved in the control of movements. Consequently, when a person with schizophrenia begins taking an antipsychotic drug, he or she often exhibits a movement disorder. Fortunately, the disorder is usually temporary and soon disappears. However, after taking the antipsychotic drug for several years, some people develop a different—more serious—movement disorder known as **tardive dyskinesia** (*tardive* means "late developing"; *dyskinesia* refers to a disturbance in movement), an often irreversible and untreatable syndrome characterized by continual involuntary lip smacking, grimacing, and drooling (Cumming and Wirshing, 1989). Severely affected people have difficulty talking, and occasionally, the movements interfere with breathing. The risk of developing this syndrome increases with age, dose, and duration of use (Hughes and Pierattini, 1992). For example, approximately 20 percent of older people develop tardive dyskinesia. The symptoms can temporarily be alleviated by *increasing* the dose of the antipsychotic drug, but doing so only serves to increase and perpetuate the person's dependence on the medication (Baldessarini and Tarsy, 1980).

Fortunately, an antischizophrenic drug has been developed that does not produce movement disorders. This drug, called *clozapine*, is also more effective than other antipsychotic drugs in helping hard-to-treat people (Kane et al., 1988). It improves the symptoms of about 30 to 50 percent of those people who have not responded to traditional antipsychotic drugs. Unfortunately, because about 2 percent of those

tardive dyskinesia　A serious movement disorder that can occur when a person has been treated with antipsychotic drugs for an extended period.

taking clozapine suffer an inhibition of white blood cell production, which can be fatal, weekly blood tests have to be conducted. People with schizophrenia have not yet received clozapine for a long enough time for researchers to be sure that the drug will not eventually produce tardive dyskinesia, but the results so far seem promising.

Antidepressant and Antimanic Drugs

Antidepressant drugs are a class of drugs used to treat the symptoms of major depression. **Antimanic drugs** are used to treat the symptoms of bipolar disorder and mania. The earliest used antidepressant drugs were derived from the family of chemicals known as tricyclics, which refers to their "three-ring" chemical structure (Lickey and Gordon, 1983). Because their chemical structure is similar to that of antipsychotic drugs, tricyclics were used in the belief that they might provide an effective treatment for schizophrenia. Although their use as an antipsychotic was quickly dismissed, researchers observed that these drugs did tend to elevate mood, suggesting their potential as an antidepressant.

Although the biology of depression is not well understood, the most widely accepted theory is that depression may result from a deficiency of the catecholamine neurotransmitters, norepinephrine and serotonin. Each of these neurotransmitters may be involved in different types of depression, although researchers are not sure how. Antidepressant drugs seem to slow down the reuptake of these neurotransmitters by presynaptic axons. Although tricyclics do not work for all people, about 60 to 80 percent of those whose depression has brought despair to their lives gradually return to normal after having been placed on tricyclics for two to six weeks (Hughes and Pierattini, 1992; Prien, 1984). Unfortunately, tricyclics have many side effects, including dizziness, sweating, weight gain, constipation, increased pulse, poor concentration, and dry mouth.

Another class of antidepressants is the monoamine oxidase inhibitors (MAOIs), which take one to three weeks to begin alleviating depression. MAOIs prevent enzymes in the synaptic gap from destroying dopamine, norepinephrine, and serotonin that have been released by presynaptic neurons. Although these drugs too can have many side effects—including high blood pressure (which can be fatal after the ingestion of certain foods—some wines, milk products, coffee, and chocolate), hyperthermia, blurred vision, impotence, insomnia, and nausea—MAOIs also have been shown to be more effective in treating atypical depressions such as those involving hypersomnia (too much sleep) or mood swings (Hughes and Pierattini, 1992).

A relatively new drug, *fluoxetine*, or *Prozac*, is having a tremendous impact on pharmacotherapy for depression. Prozac inhibits the reuptake of serotonin, leaving more of that neurotransmitter in the synaptic cleft to stimulate postsynaptic receptors. Prozac produces fewer negative side effects than do tricyclics and the MAOIs, although some persons have reported experiencing suicidal thoughts while being treated

with the drug. Moreover, because of its fewer side effects, Prozac can be taken in larger dosages, which generally results in more substantial reductions in depression relative to that produced by other antidepressants.

Lithium carbonate is most effective in the treatment of bipolar disorders or simple mania. People's manic symptoms usually decrease as soon as their blood level of lithium reaches a sufficiently high level (Gerbino, Oleshansky, and Gershon, 1978). In bipolar disorder, once the manic phase is eliminated, the depressed phase does not return. People with bipolar disorder have remained free of their symptoms for years as long as they have continued taking lithium carbonate. This drug can have some side effects, such as a fine tremor or excessive urine production; but in general, the benefits far outweigh the adverse symptoms. However, an overdose of lithium is toxic, which means that the person's blood level of lithium must be monitored regularly.

The major difficulty with treating bipolar disorder is that people with this disorder often miss their "high." When medication is effective, the mania subsides along with the depression. But most people enjoy at least the initial phase of their manic periods, and some believe that they are more creative at that time. In addition, many of these people say that they resent having to depend on a chemical "crutch." As a consequence, many people suffering from bipolar disorder stop taking their medication. Not taking their medication endangers the lives of these people because the risk of death by suicide is particularly high during the depressive phase of bipolar disorder.

Antianxiety Drugs

Antianxiety drugs are used in the treatment of everyday anxiety, phobias, obsessions, compulsions, panic attacks, and other anxiety related problems. The extreme popularity of antianxiety drugs, or minor tranquilizers as they are sometimes called, is indicated by the large numbers of prescriptions filled for these drugs in the United States and Europe. The most popular, most effective, and most abused of these drugs are the *benzodiazepines*, often known by their trade names, including Librium, Valium, and Xanax (Julien, 1992). Benzodiazepines appear to exert their effect by activating what is called the *benzodiazepine receptor*, which, in turn, produces activity in receptors sensitive to *gamma-aminobutyric acid* (GABA), an inhibitory neurotransmitter. More specifically, benzodiazepines appear to enhance the attachment of GABA molecules to the postsynaptic neuron by reconfiguring the shape of GABA receptors, thereby producing more neural activity.

antidepressant drugs Drugs used to treat depression.

antimanic drugs Drugs used to treat bipolar disorder and mania.

antianxiety drugs Drugs used to treat anxiety-related disorders.

Before the benzodiazepines were synthesized in the early 1960s, the major effective antianxiety drugs had been the barbiturates. The immediate success of Valium and Librium was due in part to the false belief that these newer drugs have a lower risk for abuse and are safer in cases of overdose (Lickey and Gordon, 1983). Although they are the safest of antianxiety drugs, researchers now know that the benzodiazepines can also produce physical tolerance and withdrawal when removed. Some individuals find it very difficult to stop using benzodiazepines because of the withdrawal syndrome and, thus, show an addiction to the drug. Taken in low dosages and for short periods, though, Valium and Librium can be effective means of reducing anxiety without incurring a high risk of physical dependence.

Besides being effective in treating depression, antidepressant drugs have also been used successfully to treat several anxiety disorders, including panic disorder and agoraphobia (Klein, Zitrin, Woerner, and Ross, 1983). These drugs appear to reduce the incidence of panic attacks, including those that accompany severe agoraphobia. However, antidepressant drugs do not reduce the anticipatory anxiety that a person feels between panic attacks.

Double-blind studies have found a particular antidepressant drug, *clomipramine*, to be useful in treating obsessive-compulsive disorder (Leonard et al., 1989). Because obsessive-compulsive disorder is so difficult to treat, and because it can be so disabling, this drug brings welcome relief to people whose lives have been disrupted by it. Other antidepressant drugs, which alleviate the symptoms of depression, have no effect on obsessive-compulsive disorder. Thus, the drug-induced biological changes that alleviate obsessive-compulsive disorder appear not to be the same as the ones that alleviate depression.

Although the antidepressants and other drugs are useful in alleviating the symptoms of certain anxiety disorders, they do not cure any of these conditions. Because the disorders are at least partly heritable, as we saw in Chapter 17, they may have some biological causes at their root. While drug therapy is helpful, the most permanent and long-lasting treatment is cognitive-behavior therapy. The drugs may be very useful in reducing the patients' symptoms so that they can participate effectively in therapy, but they do not provide a long-term solution.

Electroconvulsive Therapy

Electroconvulsive therapy (ECT) involves applying a pair of electrodes to a person's head and then passing a brief surge of electrical current through them. (See *Figure 18.5.*) The jolt produces a seizure—a storm of electrical activity in the brain

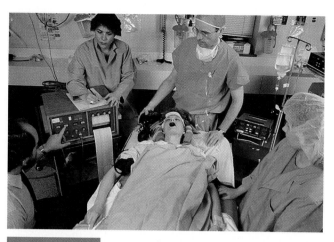

Figure 18.5

A patient being prepared for electroconvulsive therapy.

that renders the person unconscious. The wild firing of neurons that control movement produces convulsions—muscular rigidity and trembling, followed by rhythmic movements of the head, trunk, and limbs. After a few minutes, the person falls into a deep sleep. Today, people are anesthetized and temporarily paralyzed before the current is turned on. This procedure eliminates the convulsion but not the seizure, which is what causes the therapeutic effect. The seizure is believed to cause the brain to release higher than normal amounts of GABA, which decreases brain activity.

Electroconvulsive therapy has a bad reputation among many clinicians because it has been used to treat disorders such as schizophrenia, on which it has no useful effects, and because people have received excessive numbers of ECT treatments—as many as hundreds. Originally, ECT was thought to alleviate the symptoms of schizophrenia because schizophrenic people who also had epilepsy often appeared to improve just after a seizure. Subsequent research has shown that ECT has little or no effect on the symptoms of schizophrenia. However, it has been shown to be singularly effective in treating severe depression. Although no one knows for certain why ECT alleviates depression, possibly it does so by reducing REM sleep. As we saw in Chapter 17, people with major depression engage in abnormally large amounts of REM sleep, and REM sleep deprivation is an effective antidepressant therapy.

A case report by Fink (1976) illustrates the response of a depressed patient to a course of ECT. A forty-four-year-old widow had been hospitalized for three months for severe depression. A course of three ECT treatments per week was prescribed for her by her therapist's supervisor. Unknown to her therapist (a trainee), the first twelve treatments were subthreshold; that is, the intensity of the electrical current was too low to produce seizures. (The treatments could be regarded as placebo treatments.) Although both the woman and her therapist expected her to show some improvement, none was seen. In the next fourteen treatments, the current was raised to

electroconvulsive therapy (ECT) Treatment of severe depression that involves passing small amounts of electric current through the brain to produce seizure activity.

a sufficient level to produce seizures. After five actual seizures, both the woman and the therapist noticed an improvement. The woman began to complain less about various physical symptoms, to participate in hospital activities, and to make more positive statements about her mood. She became easier to talk with, and the therapist's notes of their conversations immediately proliferated. The fact that these responses occurred only after several actual seizures suggests that improvement stemmed from the biological treatment and not simply from the therapist's or the woman's expectations.

Some people with depression do not respond to antidepressant drugs, but a substantial percentage of these people improve after a few sessions of ECT. Because antidepressant medications are generally slow acting, taking ten days to two weeks for their therapeutic effects to begin, severe cases of depression are often treated with a brief course of ECT to reduce the symptoms right away. These people are then maintained on an antidepressant drug. Electroconvulsive therapy is also useful in treating pregnant women who have severe depression. Because the procedure does not involve long-term administration of drugs, the danger to the fetus is minimized (Goodwin and Guze, 1984). And because a depressed person runs a 15 percent chance of dying by suicide, the use of ECT may be justified in such cases.

There are several problems with ECT treatments. An excessive number of ECT treatments will produce permanent memory loss (Squire, Slater, and Miller, 1981) and other cognitive deficits. Nowadays, ECT is usually administered only to the right hemisphere, in order to minimize damage to people's verbal memories. Nevertheless, it is likely that even a small number of treatments cause at least some permanent brain damage. Therefore, the potential benefits of ECT must be weighed against its potential damage. Electroconvulsive therapy must be used only when the patient's symptoms justify it. Because ECT undoubtedly achieves its effects through the biochemical consequences of the seizure, pharmacologists may discover new drugs that can produce rapid therapeutic effects without ECT's deleterious ones. Once this breakthrough occurs, ECT can be discarded.

Psychosurgery

One other biological treatment for mental disorders is even more controversial than electroconvulsive therapy: **psychosurgery**, which is the treatment of a mental disorder, in the absence of obvious organic damage, through brain surgery. In contrast, brain surgery to remove a tumor or diseased neural tissue or to repair a damaged blood vessel is not psychosurgery, and there is no controversy about these procedures.

You may recall from Chapter 13 that prefrontal lobotomies were found to have serious side effects, such as apathy and severe blunting of emotions, intellectual impairments, and deficits in judgment and planning ability. Nevertheless, the procedure was once used for a variety of conditions, most of which were not improved by the surgery. Approximately

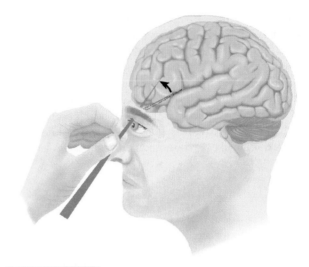

Figure 18.6

"Ice pick" prefrontal lobotomy. The sharp metal rod is inserted under the eyelid and just above the eye so that it pierces the skull and enters the base of the frontal lobe.

(Adapted with permission from Freeman, W. Proceedings of the Royal Society of Medicine, *1949, 42 (suppl.), 8–12.)*

forty thousand prefrontal lobotomies were performed in the United States alone, most of them from 1935 to 1955. A simple procedure, called "ice pick" prefrontal lobotomy by its critics, was even performed on an outpatient basis. (See *Figure 18.6.*) The development of antipsychotic drugs and the increasing attention paid to the serious side effects of prefrontal lobotomy led to a sharp decline in the use of this procedure during the 1950s. Today it is no longer performed (Valenstein, 1986).

A few surgeons have continued to refine the technique of psychosurgery and now perform a procedure called a **cingulotomy**, which involves cutting the cingulum bundle, a small band of nerve fibers that connects the prefrontal cortex with parts of the limbic system (Ballantine et al., 1987). Cingulotomies have been shown to be effective in helping some people who suffer from severe compulsions (Tippin and Henn, 1982). In a recent study, Baer and his colleagues (1995) conducted a long-term follow-up study of eighteen people who underwent cingulotomy for severe obsessive-compulsive disorder. For each of these people, other forms of therapy—drug therapy and behavior therapy—had been unsuccessful in treating the symptoms of this disorder. However, after their

psychosurgery Unalterable brain surgery used to relieve the symptoms of psychological disorders.

cingulotomy The surgical destruction of the cingulum bundle, which connects the prefrontal cortex with the limbic system; helps to reduce intense anxiety and the symptoms of obsessive-compulsive disorder.

surgeries, the people in Baer's study showed marked improvements in their functioning, decreased symptoms of depression and anxiety, and few negative side effects.

I must stress that psychosurgery should be used only as a last resort and never on a patient who cannot consent to treatment. The effects of psychosurgery are permanent; there is no way to reverse a brain lesion. All mental health professionals hope that more effective behavioral techniques and new drug treatments will make psychosurgical procedures obsolete.

Evaluation of Biological Treatments

There can be no doubt that drug therapy is the preferred biological treatment for mental disorders. Drug therapy, though, represents only a treatment option; it is not a cure. Usually, the drugs are effective only to the extent that the people for whom they are prescribed actually use them. In some cases, people forget to take their drugs, only to have the disordered symptoms return. In other cases, people take their drugs, get better, and stop taking the drugs because they feel that they are no longer "sick." In this case, too, the symptoms soon return. For some people, this cycle repeats itself over and over.

Thus, while drug therapy is an effective treatment option, it is not a panacea. But no cures for mental illness are on the horizon. And until one appears, research will continue on the development of new and more effective drugs and on finding ways to encourage people to follow their prescription regimens more closely.

Interim Summary

Biological Treatments

Biological treatments for mental disorders include drugs, electroconvulsive therapy, and psychosurgery. Research has shown that treatment of the positive symptoms of schizophrenia with antipsychotic drugs, of major depression with antidepressant drugs, and of bipolar disorder with lithium carbonate are the most effective ways to alleviate the symptoms of these disorders. Tricyclic antidepressant drugs can also alleviate severe anxiety that occurs during panic attacks and agoraphobia and can reduce the severity of obsessive-compulsive disorder. The antianxiety drugs help reduce anticipatory anxiety that occurs between panic attacks. Although electroconvulsive therapy is an effective treatment for depression, its use is reserved for cases in which rapid relief is critical because the seizures may produce brain damage. The most controversial treatment, psychosurgery, is rarely performed today. Its only presently accepted use, in the form of cingulotomy, is for treatment of crippling compulsions that cannot be reduced by more conventional means.

Thought Questions

- Suppose that you had a friend who was about to begin drug therapy for a mental disorder. Suppose further that you were able to accompany your friend to one of his or her pretreatment sessions with a psychiatrist (at present, only psychiatrists, not clinical psychologists, can prescribe drugs). What kind of questions would you think to ask the psychiatrist about the particular kind of drug therapy he or she was recommending for your friend? Would the questions you ask differ, depending on the kind of problem your friend was experiencing?
- Suppose that your friend had been treated for depression with tricyclics and the treatment failed—your friend is still extremely depressed. The psychiatrist now recommends ECT. What is your response? What sort of advice can you offer his or her family about following or not following the psychiatrist's recommendation?

Ethical and Legal Issues in Psychotherapy

The special relationship that exists between the therapist and the client is duplicated in few other places in society. With the possible exception of the traditional role of religious leaders, few people earn their living by listening to others describe the deeply intimate details of their lives. Unfortunately, the same characteristics that give the therapeutic relationship its potential for healing may also lead to abuses. For this reason, psychologists have developed a set of ethical standards to guide their professional activities, and legislatures and courts have provided additional regulations concerning the practice of therapy.

Ethical Considerations in Practicing Psychotherapy

The ethical standards for psychologists were formally defined by the publication of the *Ethical Standards of the American Psychological Association* (1979, 1981). One important standard is the *sexuality restraint*, which specifies that sexual intimacies with clients are unethical. A therapist who suggests such intimacy to a client or who allows himself or herself to be approached sexually by the client is unquestionably violating this standard. In some states, this matter has gone beyond ethical considerations to become a matter of law—sexual intimacies with a client, even with consent, can be considered a felony (APA, 1988). Nonetheless, the problem of sexual relations between therapist and client, although rare, remains an issue in psychotherapy (Pope, Tabachnick, and Keith-Spiegel, 1987).

Another ethical standard is the *confidentiality restraint*, which states that any information obtained about the client during therapy is confidential. This confidentiality extends to members of the client's family. As we will see next, in cases when a client has violent tendencies, the confidentiality restraint can be a difficult principle to follow.

Legal Issues in Practicing Psychotherapy

Because ethical principles are stated in absolute terms, problems and inconsistencies often arise in their application. For example, the confidentiality restraint sometimes leads to a dilemma in which any course of action leads to a violation of an ethical principle. Consider the 1969 Tarasoff case. A male student at the University of California at Berkeley began dating a fellow student, Tatiana Tarasoff. He fell in love with her, but she felt differently about him. Being upset by her rebuff, he entered therapy, where he explicitly stated to the therapist his intentions to purchase a gun and injure or kill Tatiana. The therapist then faced the dilemma of deciding whether to breach confidentiality and report the threat to the police, or to respect confidentiality and allow the possibility of harm.

The therapist contacted the campus police, who interviewed the student and released him. Shortly thereafter, the student went to Tatiana's home, shot her with a pellet gun, and then repeatedly and fatally stabbed her. Tatiana's parents sued the university, the campus police, and the therapist—and won. The California Supreme Court ruled in 1974 that the therapist, in addition to informing the police, should have further breached confidentiality and warned the victim. Further rulings in other cases have since established that the therapist can be liable for the violent behavior of a client even if the client does not specifically threaten anyone.

The resolution of this ethical dilemma for therapists is particularly difficult given that no method exists for accurately predicting violent behavior. To avoid legal liability, the therapist would have to warn others of the threat of danger every time violence is remotely probable. Given the impracticality of applying the court rulings literally, further legislation will be required to clarify the therapist's legal responsibilities. There is partial evidence that some therapists are simply not discussing violent thoughts or fantasies with their clients to reduce their liability (Wise, 1978).

Another dilemma that therapists encounter concerns the rights of hospitalized people. In an effort to avoid the abuses of the past, institutionalized people are now afforded many rights not available to others earlier in the century. One of the advantages of these rights is that frequent attempts are made at rehabilitation. The combination of fewer people being kept for long periods in mental hospitals and our current inadequacies in predicting violent behavior, however, makes for an extremely volatile social problem. For example, a potentially dangerous person may be released too early because the therapist may be worried about liability for retaining him or her for too long. Of course, the therapist and his or her institution can also be held liable if the person later commits acts of vio-

lence. Thus, the therapist would seem to be enmeshed in a no-win situation, having to be concerned about protecting himself or herself, the client, and the general public—all without the means to predict violence accurately or the means to control factors in the person's environment that might trigger it.

These and other legal and ethical issues make the practice of therapy a delicate balancing act. Not only do therapists assume responsibility for bringing effective methods of treatment to bear on the problems of the client, but also he or she must weigh the potential consequences of therapy for the family and friends of the client and for society in general.

Interim Summary

Ethical and Legal Issues in Psychotherapy

To enhance and protect the therapist-client relationship, the American Psychological Association has developed a set of ethical standards to guide the practice of therapy. Two especially important standards involve restraint of sexual relations between therapist and client and confidentiality.

However, problems can arise in the applications of some standards to real therapist-client situations. For example, serious questions arise with respect to confidentiality when the client is violent and threatens to harm someone. Should the therapist keep the client's violent tendencies private, respecting confidentiality, or should he or she warn the appropriate persons of the threat the client poses? The confidentiality standard points the therapist in one direction and recent court decisions, in which therapists have been held responsible for not issuing warnings, point in the other direction. There is no easy way for therapists to resolve this ethical dilemma.

Thought Question

■ Suppose that you have been asked by your psychology teacher to give a class presentation on the topic of "ethical issues in psychotherapy." During the presentation, one of your fellow students asks you to provide some examples of the different ways that a therapist could breach the confidentiality restraint. What is your response?

Selecting a Therapist

Chances are good that you or a close friend will become worried, anxious, or depressed. In most cases, people get through these times in their lives by talking with sympathetic friends, relatives, teachers, or members of the clergy. But sometimes, problems persist despite this help, and the person in distress thinks about seeking professional help. How can you tell that you need to consult a therapist, and how do you go about finding a good one?

In general, if you have a problem that makes you unhappy and that persists for several months, you should seriously consider getting professional advice. If the problem is very severe, you should not wait but should look for help immediately. For example, if you experience acute panic attacks, find yourself contemplating suicide, or hear voices that you know are not there, do not wait to see if the problems go away. You should also think about consulting a professional for specific problems, such as unhealthy habits like smoking, or specific fears, such as fear of flying. You do not have to be "mentally ill" to seek psychological help.

If you are a student at a college or university, the best place to turn is to the counseling service. If you are not sure what mental health support is available on campus, someone in the psychology department will certainly be able to tell you where to go. In larger universities, the psychology department often operates its own clinic. If you are not a student, you should ask your physician or call the local Mental Health Association and ask for advice. Or call the psychology department at a local college or university; you will surely find someone who will help you find professional help.

Table 18.4 describes some of the more common types of therapists, training, and degree credentials and the general types of responsibilities each type of therapist assumes. (See *Table 18.4.*) As you can see, the training and the types of professional duties assumed by therapists vary considerably. In addition, therapists often conduct therapy from particular theoretical orientations, as you saw earlier in this chapter. However, research suggests that the orientation of the therapist may not be a very important factor to consider when choosing a therapist, as each orientation has both its advantages and limitations (Smith and Glass, 1977).

But be careful. Not mentioned in Table 18.4, because he or she is not a legitimate practitioner, is the *charlatan*, or quack, who pretends to have knowledge of something—in this case treatment of psychological disorders—but does not. Some charlatans may attempt to treat their clients' problems through psychic healing, astrology, palm reading, or other unscientific or false approaches. Other charlatans may use more respectable approaches, such as "psychotherapy" but lack knowledge of mental disorders and therapeutic skills.

Charlatans can be found in almost every community swindling unsuspecting clients out of thousands of dollars each year. They are generally very good liars, leading people to believe that they have the requisite therapeutic skills. In addition, many people seeking therapy are not very wise consumers. They don't know what to look for in a genuine therapist.

Here are three reasonable questions that you should ask when you feel that you need to seek help from a therapist:

1. Is the therapist licensed to practice therapy in the state in which he or she is practicing?

2. What kind of formal training does the therapist have? From what academic institution does the therapist hold advanced degrees? Did the therapist fulfill an internship during which he or she learned therapeutic techniques under the supervision of licensed practitioners?

3. What kind of reputation does the therapist have? Is he or she known for practicing therapy using one or more of the unscientific approaches mentioned above?

If a therapist is not licensed to practice, has little or no formal training in therapy, and is known to practice therapy

---

Table 18.4

Types of Therapists, Their Degree Credentials, and Their Training and Professional Responsibilities

Title	Degree	Training Background and Professional Duties
Clinical psychologist	Ph.D. or Psy.D.	Graduate training in research, diagnosis, and therapy plus one year clinical internship. Conducts assessment, therapy, and clinical research; teaches in a college or university setting.
Counseling Psychologist	Ph.D., Psy.D. or Ed.D.	Graduate training in counseling. Conducts educational, vocational, and personal counseling.
Psychoanalyst	M.D.	Medical training plus specialized training in psychoanalysis. Conducts psychoanalytic therapy.
Psychiatrist	M.D.	Medical training plus psychiatry residency. Conducts diagnosis and biomedical therapy and psychotherapy.
Social Worker	M.S.W.	Graduate work in counseling and community psychology. Conducts psychotherapy; helps patients return to community.

using unscientific approaches, then he or she is very likely to be a charlatan, and you should avoid consulting with this person for therapy of any sort.

You should also talk with the therapist before committing yourself to a course of therapy. Do you like the person? Do you find the person sympathetic? If not, look elsewhere. Do not be impressed by an authoritative manner or glib assurances that he or she knows best what you need. Look for someone who asks good questions about your problems and needs and who helps you formulate a specific and realistic set of goals. Find out whether the therapist specializes in your type of problem. For example, if you want to overcome a specific fear or break a specific habit, you may not want to embark on a series of sessions in which you are expected to talk about the history of your relations with other family members. On the other hand, if your problem is with family relations, then a family therapist may be the best person to consult.

What about fees? Research on this topic indicates that the amount of money a person pays has no relation to the benefits he or she receives. Ask the therapist about how much the services will cost. Find out whether your health insurance will cover the fees. Do some comparison shopping. And be aware of the fact that therapists will often adjust their fees according to the ability of the client to pay.

How long should therapy continue? In some cases, the therapist will suggest a fixed number of sessions. In other cases, the duration is determined by the insurance company that pays for the services or by the policy of the clinic in which the therapist practices. But how do you decide when to quit in those cases when the duration is indefinite? Here are some guidelines. If you do not make progress within a reasonable amount of time, find someone else. If the therapist seems to be trying to exploit you—for example, by suggesting that sexual relations with him or her would benefit you—run, do not walk, away. The person is violating laws and ethical guidelines and is undoubtedly not someone who should be entrusted with your problems. If you find that therapy becomes the most important part of your life, or if you have become so dependent on your therapist that you feel unable to decide for yourself, think about quitting. If your therapist seems to want you to stay on even though your original problems have been solved, it is time to cut the cord.

Always remember that the therapist is someone *you* consult for professional advice and help. You do not owe the therapist anything other than frankness and a good-faith attempt to follow his or her advice. If you do not like the person or the advice, do not worry about hurting the therapist's feelings—look for someone else. Most people who consult therapists are glad that they did so; they usually find experienced, sympathetic people that they can trust who really do help them with their problems.

Interim Summary

Selecting a Therapist

Most of us experience a time in life when we are plagued by a persistent personal problem that makes us unhappy. In this situation, seeking professional help is usually a good idea. Counseling services, mental health centers, and psychologists and psychiatrists can generally be found in almost any city or town.

Finding a therapist who is right for you requires that you do some homework. As a rule, a good therapist will be licensed to practice therapy, have specific training in the treatment of psychological problems and mental disorders, and have a good reputation for being an empathetic and supportive therapist. If the therapist you choose turns out to be unsuitable for your needs, do not hesitate to look for a different therapist. The majority of people who seek therapy benefit by it and are happy that they sought help for their problems.

Thought Questions

- Sometimes people shy away from seeking therapy because of the stigma that they think will be attached to them if they do seek therapy. After reading this chapter, what suggestions might you have for these people to encourage them to seek therapy?
- Other than the fee paid to a therapist, what is the difference between a therapist and a friend? After all, doesn't a friend serve some of the same functions as a therapist: confidant, problem-solver, and source of empathy, warmth, and support?

Suggestions for Further Reading

Aponte, J.F., Rivers, R.Y., and Wohl, J. *Psychological Interventions and Cultural Diversity*. Boston: Allyn and Bacon, 1995.

This book addresses general issues faced by practitioners who deal with diverse ethnic and racial populations as well as specific types of interventions used for specific minority groups and problems.

Carson, R.C., Butcher, J.N., and Mineka, S. *Abnormal Psychology and Modern Life*, 10th ed. New York: HarperCollins, 1996.

A highly readable upper-division undergraduate text about psychological disorders, including their causes and treatment. The last four chapters deal exclusively with the assessment, treatment, and prevention of mental disorders.

Freud, S. *The Interpretation of Dreams*. London: Allen and Unwin, 1900.

This classic book is recommended to those who wish to understand better Freud's emphasis on dreams as the "royal road" to understanding unconsciousness.

Kazdin, A.E. *Behavior Modification in Applied Settings.* Pacific Grove, CA: Brooks/Cole, 1994.

Thorpe, G.L., and Olson, S.L. *Behavior Therapy: Concepts, Procedures, and Applications.* Boston: Allyn and Bacon, 1990.

These two texts provide excellent summaries of the development and uses of behavior modification.

Rogers, C.R. *Client-Centered Therapy.* New York: Houghton Mifflin, 1951.

Written by the founder of the humanistic movement in psychology, this book outlines the major features of client-centered therapy.

Wedding, D., and Corsini, R. *Case Studies in Psychotherapy.* Itasca, IL: Peacock, 1989.

A collection of twelve case studies involving different varieties of cognitive-behavioral, humanistic, and psychoanalytic therapies. In each case study, a client's problem and the means by which it was addressed is discussed. Highly interesting reading.

References

Abramson, L. Y., Metalsky, G. I., and Alloy, L. B. Hopelessness depression: A theory-based subtype. *Psychological Review*, 1989, *96*, 358–372.

Abramson, L. Y., Seligman, M. E. P., and Teasdale, J. D. Learned helplessness in humans: Critique and reformulation. *Journal of Abnormal Psychology*, 1978, *87*, 49–74.

Acierno, R. E., Hersen, M., and Van Hasselt, V. B. Interventions for panic disorder: A critical review of the literature. *Clinical Psychology Review*, 1993, *18*, 561–578.

Adamec, R. E., and Stark-Adamec, C. Limbic hyperfunction, limbic epilepsy, and interictal behavior: Models and methods of detection. In *The Limbic System*, edited by B. K. Doane and K. E. Livingston. New York: Raven Press, 1986.

Adams, D. B., Gold, A. R., and Burt, A. D. Rise in female-initiated sexual activity at ovulation and its suppression by oral contraceptives. *New England Journal of Medicine*, 1978, *299*, 1145–1150.

Adey, W. R., Bors, E., and Porter, R. W. EEG sleep patterns after high cervical lesions in man. *Archives of Neurology*, 1968, *19*, 377–383.

Adler, A. *Social Interest: A Challenge to Mankind.* New York: Putnam, 1939.

Aiken, L. R. *Dying, Death and Bereavement.* Boston: Allyn and Bacon, 1994.

Ainslie, G. Species reward: A behavioral theory of impulsiveness and impulse control. *Psychological Bulletin*, 1975, *82*, 463–496.

Ainsworth, M. D. S. *Infancy in Uganda: Infant Care and the Growth of Love.* Baltimore: Johns Hopkins University Press, 1967.

Ainsworth, M. D. S. The development of infant–mother attachment. In *Review of Child Development Research, Vol. 3*, edited by B. M. Caldwell and H. R. Ricciuti. Chicago: University of Chicago Press, 1973.

Ainsworth, M. D. S., Blehar, M. C., Waters, E., and Wall, S. *Patterns of Attachment.* Hillsdale, NJ: Lawrence Erlbaum Associates, 1978.

Ainsworth, M. D. S., and Bowlby, J. An ethological approach to personality development. *American Psychologist*, 1991, *46*, 333–341.

Albright, L., Kenny, D. A., and Malloy, T. E. Consensus in personality judgments at zero acquaintance. *Journal of Personality and Social Psychology*, 1988, *55*, 387–395.

Alexander, G. M., Sherwin, B. B., Bancroft, J., and Davidson, D. W. Testosterone and sexual behavior in oral contraceptive users and nonusers: A prospective study. *Hormones and Behavior*, 1990, *24*, 388–402.

Al-Issa, I. Culture and mental illness in an international perspective. In *Handbook of Culture and Mental Illness: An International Perspective*, edited by I. Al-Issa. Madison, CT: International Universities Press, 1995.

Allen, L. S., and Gorski, R. A. Sexual orientation and the size of the anterior commissure in the human brain. *Proceedings of the National Academy of Sciences*, 1992, *89*, 7199–7202.

Allen, M. G. Twin studies of affective illness. *Archives of General Psychiatry*, 1976, *33*, 1476–1478.

Allison, P., and Furstenberg, F. How marriage dissolution affects children: Variations by age and sex. *Developmental Psychology*, 1989, *25*, 540–549.

Allport, G. W. The historical background of modern social psychology. In *The Handbook of Social Psychology, Vol. 1*, edited by G. Lindzey and E. Aronson. Reading, MA: Addison-Wesley, 1968.

Allport, G. W., and Odbert, H. S. Trait-names: A psycholexical study. *Psychological Monographs*, 1936, *47* (1, Whole No. 211).

Ambrosio, A. L., and Sheehan, E. P. The just world belief and the AIDS epidemic. *Journal of Social Behavior and Personality*, 1991, *6*, 163–170.

American Psychological Association. *Ethical Standards of Psychologists.* Washington, DC: American Psychological Association, 1979.

American Psychological Association. Ethical principles of psychologists. *American Psychologist*, 1981, *36*, 633–638.

American Psychological Association. Trends in ethics cases, common pitfalls, and published resources. *American Psychologist*, 1988, *43*, 564–572.

Anderson, D. R., and Collins, P. A. *The Impact on Children's Education: Television's Influence on Cognitive Development.* Washington, DC: U.S. Department of Education, 1988.

Anderson, D. R., and Field, D. Children's attention to television: Implications for production. In *Children and the Formal Features of Television*, edited by M. Meyer. Munich: Saur, 1983.

Anderson, D. R., Field, D., Collins, P., Lorch, E., and Nathan, J. Estimates of young children's time with television: A methodological comparison of parent reports with time-lapse video home observation. *Child Development*, 1985, *56*, 1345–1357.

Anderson, D. R., and Lorch, E. Looking at television: Action or reaction? In *Children's Understanding of Television: Research on Attention and Comprehension*, edited by J. Bryant and D. R. Anderson. New York: Academic Press, 1983.

Anderson, R. H., Fleming, D. E., Rhees, R. W., and Kinghorn, E. Relationships between sexual activity, plasma testosterone, and the volume of the sexually dimorphic nucleus of the preoptic area in prenatally stressed and non-stressed rats. *Brain Research*, 1986, *370*, 1–10.

Andreasen, N. C., and Olsen, S. A. Negative vs. positive schizophrenia: Definition and validation. *Archives of General Psychiatry*, 1982, *39*, 789–794.

Angrist, B. J., Rotrosen, J., and Gershon, S. Positive and negative symptoms in schizophrenia–Differential response to amphetamine and neuroleptics. *Psychopharmacology*, 1980, *72*, 17–19.

Annau, Z., and Kamin, L. J. The conditioned emotional response as a function of intensity of the UCS. *Journal of Comparative and Physiological Psychology*, 1961, *54*, 428–432.

Anonymous. Effects of sexual activity on beard growth in man. *Nature*, 1970, *226*, 867–870.

Antonuccio, D. Psychotherapy for depression: No stronger medicine. *American Psychologist*, 1995, *50*, 450–452.

Aponte, J. F., Rivers, R. Y., and Wohl, J. *Psychological Interventions and Cultural Diversity.* Boston: Allyn and Bacon, 1995

Archer, S. L., and Waterman, A. S. Varieties of identity diffusions and foreclosures: An exploration of subcategories of the identity status. *Journal of Adolescent Research*, 1990, *5*, 96–111.

Arenberg, D. Cognition and aging: Verbal learning, memory, and problem solving. In *The Psychology of Adult Development and Aging,* edited by C. Eisdorfer and M. P. Lawton. Washington, DC: American Psychological Association, 1973.

Arnett, J. The young and the reckless: Adolescent reckless behavior. *Current Directions in Psychological Science*, 1995, *4*, 67–71.

Aronson, E., and Mills, J. The effects of severity of initiation on liking for a group. *Journal of Abnormal and Social Psychology*, 1959, *59*, 177–181.

Artmann, H., Grau, H., Adelman, M., and Schleiffer, R. Reversible and non-reversible enlargement of cerebrospinal fluid spaces in anorexia nervosa. *Neuroradiology*, 1985, *27*, 103–112.

Asch, S. E. Forming impressions of personality. *Journal of Abnormal and Social Psychology*, 1946, *41*, 258–290.

Asch, S. E. Effects of group pressure upon the modification and distortion of judgment. In *Groups, Leadership, and Men,* edited by H. Guetzkow. Pittsburgh: Carnegie, 1951.

Asch, S. E. *Social Psychology.* New York: Prentice-Hall, 1952.

Asch, S. E. Opinions and social pressure. *Scientific American*, 1955, *193*, 31–35.

Astley, S. J., Clarren, S. K., Little, R. E., Sampson, P. D., and Daling, J. R. Analysis of facial shape in children gestationally exposed to marijuana, alcohol, or cocaine. *Pediatrics*, 1992, *89*, 67–77.

Atkinson, R. C., and Shiffrin, R. M. Human memory: A proposed system and its control processes. In *The Psychology of Learning and Motivation: Advances in Research and Theory, Vol. 2,* edited by K. W. Spence and J. T. Spence. New York: Academic Press, 1968.

Axel, R. The molecular logic of smell. *Scientific American*, 1995, *273*, 154–159.

Ayllon, T., and Azrin, N. H. *The Token Economy: A Motivational System for Therapy and Rehabilitation.* New York: Appleton-Century-Crofts, 1968.

Babkin, B. P. *Pavlov: A Biography.* Chicago: University of Chicago Press, 1949.

Badcock, C. *Evolution and Individual Behavior: An Introduction to Human Sociobiology.* Cambridge, MA: Blackwell, 1991.

Baddeley, A. Working memory and conscious awareness. In *Theories of Memory,* edited by A. F. Collins, S. E. Cathercole, M. A. Conway, and P. E. Morris. Hillsdale, NJ: Erlbaum, 1993.

Baddeley, A. D. Domains of recollection. *Psychological Review*, 1982, *89*, 708–729.

Baddeley, A. D. *Working Memory.* Oxford: Clarendon Press, 1986.

Baenninger, M. A., Baenninger, R., and Houle, D. Attractiveness, attentiveness, and perceived male shortage: Their influence on the perceptions of other females. *Ethology and Sociobiology*, 1993, *14*, 293–304.

Baer, D. M., Peterson, R. F., and Sherman, J. A. Development of imitation by reinforcing behavioral similarity to a model. *Journal of the Experimental Analysis of Behavior*, 1967, *10*, 405–416.

Bahrick, H. P. The cognitive map of a city–50 years of learning and memory. In *The Psychology of Learning and Memory,* edited by G. Bower. New York: Academic Press, 1983.

Bahrick, H. P. Semantic memory content in permastore: Fifty years of memory for Spanish learned in school. *Journal of Experimental Psychology: General*, 1984a, *113*, 12–29.

Bahrick, H. P. Long-term memories: How durable, and how enduring? *Physiological Psychology*, 1984b, *12*, 53–58.

Bailey, A. J. The biology of autism. *Psychological Medicine*, 1993, *23*, 7–11.

Bailey, J. M., and Pillard, R. C. A genetic study of male sexual orientation. *Archives of General Psychiatry*, 1991, *48*, 1089–1096.

Bailey, J. M., Pillard, R. C., Neale, M. C., and Agyei, Y. Heritable factors influence sexual orientation in women. *Archives of General Psychiatry*, 1993, *50*, 217–223.

Bain, J. Hormones and sexual aggression in the male. *Integrative Psychiatry*, 1987, *5*, 82–89.

Baker, B. L. Symptom treatment and symptom substitution in enuresis. *Journal of Abnormal Psychology*, 1969, *74*, 42–49.

Baker, R. A. *They Call It Hypnosis.* Buffalo, NY: Prometheus Books, 1990.

Baldessarini, R. J., and Tarsy, D. Dopamine and the pathophysiology of dyskinesias induced by antipsychotic drugs. *Annual Review of Neuroscience*, 1980, *3*, 23–41.

Ball, K., and Sekuler, R. A specific and enduring improvement in visual motion discrimination. *Science*, 1982, *218*, 697–698.

Ballantine, H. T., Bouckoms, A. J., Thomas, E. K., and Giriunas, I. E. Treatment of psychiatric illness by stereotactic cingulotomy. *Biological Psychiatry*, 1987, *22*, 807–819.

Balon, R., Jordan, M., Pohl, R., and Yeragani, V. K. Family history of anxiety disorders in control subjects with lactate-induced panic attacks. *American Journal of Psychiatry*, 1989, *146*, 1304–1306.

Baltes, P., and Schaie, K. Aging and IQ: The myth of the twilight years. *Psychology Today,* October 1974, pp. 35–38.

Bandura, A. Psychotherapy based upon modeling principles. In *Handbook of Psychotherapy and Behavior Change,* edited by A. E. Bergin and S. L. Garfield. New York: John Wiley & Sons, 1971.

Bandura, A. *Aggression: A Social Learning Analysis.* Englewood Cliffs, NJ: Prentice-Hall, 1973.

Bandura, A. The self system in reciprocal determinism. *American Psychologist*, 1978, *33*, 344–358.

Bandura, A. Self-efficacy mechanism in human agency. *American Psychologist*, 1982, *37*, 122–147.

Bandura, A. *Social Foundations of Thought and Action: A Social-Cognitive Theory.* Englewood Cliffs, NJ: Prentice-Hall, 1986.

Bandura, A., and Menlove, F. L. Factors determining vicarious extinction of avoidance behavior through symbolic modeling. *Journal of Personality and Social Psychology*, 1968, *8*, 99–108.

Banks, M. S., Aslin, R. N., and Letson, R. D. Sensitive period for the development of human binocular vision. *Science*, 1975, *190*, 675–677.

Barash, D. *Sociobiology and Behavior.* London: Hodder and Stoughton, 1982.

Barber, T. X. Responding to "hypnotic" suggestions: An introspective report. *American Journal of Clinical Hypnosis*, 1975, *18*, 6–22.

Barber, T. X. Suggested ("hypnotic") behavior: The trance paradigm versus an alternative paradigm. In *Hypnosis: Developments in Research and New Perspectives,* edited by E. Fromm and R. E. Shor. Chicago: Aldine Press, 1979.

Barclay, C. D., Cutting, J. E., and Kozlowski, L. T. Temporal and spatial factors in gait perception that influence gender recognition. *Perception and Psychophysics*, 1978, *23*, 145–152.

Barnas, M. V., Pollina, J., and Cummings, E. M. Life-span attachment: Relations between attachment and socioemotional functioning in women. *Genetic, Social, and General Psychology Monographs*, 1991, *89*, 177–202.

Baron, A., and Galizio, M. Instructional control of human operant behavior. *Psychological Record*, 1983, *33*, 495–520.

Baron, A., Perone, M., and Galizio, M. Analyzing the reinforcement process at the human level: Can application and behavioristic interpretation replace laboratory research? *The Behavior Analyst*, 1991, *14*, 79–117.

Baron, R. A., and Byrne, D. *Social Psychology: Understanding Human Interaction.* Boston: Allyn and Bacon, 1994.

Bartlett, F. C. *Remembering: An Experimental and Social Study.* Cambridge: Cambridge University Press, 1932.

Bastiaans, J. Psychological factors in the development of cancer. In *Cancer Campaign. Vol. 19: The Cancer Patient—Illness and Recovery,* edited by E. Grundemann. Stuttgart: Gustav Fischer Verlag, 1985.

Bates, E., Camaioni, L., and Volterra, V. The acquisition of performatives prior to speech. *Merrill-Palmer Quarterly*, 1975, *21*, 205–224.

Bauer, P. J. What do infants recall of their lives? Memory for specific events by one- to two-year-olds. *American Psychologist*, 1996, *51*, 29–41.

Baumrind, D. Rejoinder to Lewis' reinterpretation of parental firm control effects: Are authoritative families really harmonious? *Psychological Bulletin*, 1983, *94*, 132–142.

Beauvois, M.-F., and Dérouesné, J. Phonological alexia: Three dissociations. *Journal of Neurology, Neurosurgery and Psychiatry*, 1979, *42*, 1115–1124.

Beck, A. T. *Depression: Clinical, Experimental and Theoretical Aspects.* New York: Harper and Row, 1967.

Beck, A. T. Cognitive therapy: A thirty-year retrospective. *American Psychologist*, 1991, *46*, 368–375.

Beck, A. T., Rush, A. J., Shaw, B. F., and Emery, G. *Cognitive Therapy of Depression.* New York: Guilford Press, 1979.

Begleiter, H., and Kissin, B. *The Genetics of Alcoholism.* New York: Oxford University Press, 1995.

Beilin, H. Piaget's theory: Alive and more vigorous than ever. *Human Development*, 1990, *33*, 362–365.

Bell, A. P., and Weinberg, M. S. *Homosexualities: A Study of Diversity among Men and*

Women. New York: Simon & Schuster, 1978.

Bell, A. P., Weinberg, M. S., and Hammersmith, S. K. *Sexual Preference: Its Development in Men and Women.* Bloomington: Indiana University Press, 1981.

Bellugi, U., and Klima, E. S. The roots of language in the sign talk of the deaf. *Psychology Today,* June 1972, pp. 61–76.

Belsky, J., and Rovine, M. J. Nonmaternal care in the first year of life and the security of infant–parent attachment. *Child Development,* 1988, *59,* 157–167.

Bem, D., and Allen, A. On predicting some of the people some of the time: The search for cross-situational consistencies in behavior. *Psychological Review,* 1974, *81,* 506–520.

Bem, D. J. Self-perception theory. In *Advances in Experimental Social Psychology, Vol. 6,* edited by L. Berkowitz. New York: Academic Press, 1972.

Benson, D. F., and Geschwind, N. The alexias. In *Handbook of Clinical Neurology, Vol. 4,* edited by P. Vinken and G. Bruyn. Amsterdam: North-Holland, 1969.

Berk, L. E. *Infants, Children, and Adolescents.* Boston: Allyn and Bacon, 1993.

Berk, L. E. *Child Development, 3rd Edition.* Boston: Allyn and Bacon, 1994.

Berkowitz, L. Aggressive cues in aggressive behavior and hostility catharsis. *Psychological Review,* 1964, *71,* 104–122.

Berlin, B., and Kay, P. *Basic Color Terms: Their Universality and Evolution.* Berkeley: University of California Press, 1969.

Berlyne, D. E. Motivational problems raised by exploratory and epistemic behavior. In *Psychology: A Study of a Science, Vol. 5,* edited by S. Koch. New York: McGraw-Hill, 1966.

Bermant, G., and Davidson, J. M. *Biological Bases of Sexual Behavior.* New York: Harper & Row, 1974.

Bernstein, I. L. Learned taste aversion in children receiving chemotherapy. *Science,* 1978, *200,* 1302–1303.

Bernstein, I. L. Aversion conditioning in response to cancer and cancer treatment. *Clinical Psychology Review,* 1991, *11,* 183–191.

Bernstein, I. L., Webster, M. M., and Bernstein, I. D. Food aversions in children receiving chemotherapy for cancer. *Cancer,* 1982, *50,* 2961–2963.

Bernstein, W. M., Stephenson, B. O., Snyder, M. L., and Wicklund, R. A. Causal ambiguity and heterosexual affiliation. *Journal of Experimental Social Psychology,* 1983, *19,* 78–92.

Berry, J. W. Towards a universal psychology of cognitive competence. In *Changing Conceptions of Intelligence and Intellectual Functioning,* edited by P. S. Fry. Amsterdam: North-Holland, 1984.

Berry, J. W., Poortinga, Y. H., Segall, M. H., and Dasen, P. R. *Cross-cultural Psychology: Research and Applications.* Cambridge: Cambridge University Press, 1992.

Bickel, W. K., and DeGrandpre, R. J. Modeling drug abuse policy in the behavioral economics laboratory. In *Advances in Behavioral Economics, Vol. 3,* edited by J. H. Kegal and L. Green. Norwood, NJ: Ablex, 1994.

Biederman, I. Recognition-by-components: A theory of human image interpretation. *Psychological Review,* 1987, *94,* 115–147.

Biederman, I. Higher-level vision. In *An Invitation to Cognitive Science. Vol. 2: Visual Cognition and Action.* Cambridge, MA: MIT Press, 1990.

Biernat, M., and Wortman, C. B. Sharing of home responsibilities between professionally employed women and their husbands. *Journal of Personality and Social Psychology,* 1991, *60,* 844–860.

Binet, A., and Henri, V. La psychologie individuelle. *Année Psychologique,* 1896, *2,* 411–465.

Bird, G., Bird, G., and Scruggs, M. Determinants of family task sharing: A study of husbands and wives. *Journal of Marriage and Family Therapy,* 1984, *46,* 345–355.

Birren, J. E., and Morrison, D. F. Analysis of the WISC subtests in relation to age and education. *Journal of Gerontology,* 1961, *16,* 363–369.

Bishop, G. D. Lay disease representations and responses to victims of disease. *Basic and Applied Social Psychology,* 1991a, *12,* 115–132.

Bishop, G. D. Understanding the understanding of illness. In *Mental Representation in Health and Illness,* edited by J. A. Skelton and R. T. Croyle. New York: Springer-Verlag, 1991b.

Bishop, G. D. *Health Psychology: Integrating Mind and Body.* Boston: Allyn and Bacon, 1994.

Bishop, G. D., Madey, S., Salinas, J., Massey, J., and Tudyk, D. The role of the availability heuristic in disease perception. *International Journal of Psychology,* 1992, *27,* 637.

Blaxton, T. A. Investigating dissociations among memory measures: Support for a transfer appropriate processing framework. Journal of Experimental Psychology: *Learning, Memory, and Cognition,* 1989, *15,* 657–668.

Bliss, E. L. Multiple personalities: A report of 14 cases with implications for schizophrenia and hysteria. *Archives of General Psychiatry,* 1980, *37,* 1388–1397.

Bloom, L. *Language Development: Form and Function in Emerging Grammars.* Cambridge, MA: MIT Press, 1970.

Blum, K., Noble, E. P., Sheridan, P. J., Montgomery, A., and Ritchie, T. Allelic association of human dopamine D2 receptor gene in alchoholism. *Journal of the American Medical Association,* 1990, *263,* 2055–2060.

Boaz, N. T. Origins of Hominidae. In *Milestones in Human Evolution* edited by A. J. Manyak and A. Manyak. Prospect Heights, IL: Waveland Press, 1993.

Bogatz, G., and Ball, S. *The Second Year of Sesame Street: A Continuing Evaluation.* Princeton, NJ: Educational Testing Service, 1972.

Bohannan, P. *How Culture Works.* New York: The Free Press, 1995.

Bohannon, J. N. Theoretical approaches to language acquisition. In *The Development of Language,* edited by J. B. Gleason. New York: Macmillan, 1993.

Bohannon, J. N., and Stanowicz, L. The issue of negative evidence: Adult responses to children's language errors. *Developmental Psychology,* 1988, *24,* 684–689.

Bohman, M., Cloninger, C. R., and Sigvardsson, S. Maternal inheritance of alcohol abuse: Cross-fostering analysis of adoptive women. *Archives of General Psychiatry,* 1981, *38,* 965–969.

Boller, F., and Dennis, M. (eds.). *Auditory Comprehension: Clinical and Experimental Studies with the Token Test.* New York: Academic Press, 1979.

Bolles, R. C. Species-specific defense reactions and avoidance learning. *Psychological Review,* 1970, *77,* 32–48.

Bolles, R. C. *Learning Theory.* New York: Holt, Rinehart and Winston, 1979.

Bonvillian, J., Nelson, K. E., and Charrow, V. Languages and language-related skills in deaf and hearing children. *Sign Language Studies,* 1976, *12,* 211–250.

Borgida, E., and Nisbett, R. E. The differential viewpoint of abstract vs. concrete information on decisions. *Journal of Applied Social Psychology,* 1977, *7,* 258–271.

Borysenko, J. Z. Behavioural-physiological factors in the development and management of cancer. *General Hospital Psychiatry,* 1982, *3,* 69–74.

Bosarge, L. Educating college students about sexually transmitted diseases, AIDS, and safe-sex practices. Unpublished master's thesis, Auburn University, 1989.

Botwinick, J., and Storandt, M. *Memory, Related Functions and Age.* Springfield, IL: Charles C. Thomas, 1974.

Bouchard, T. J., and McGue, M. Familial studies of intelligence: A review. *Science,* 1981, *212,* 1055–1059.

Bouchard, T. J., and Propping, P. (Eds.). *Twins as a Tool of Behavior Genetics.* Chichester, England: Wiley, 1993.

Bower, G. H. Mood and memory. *American Psychologist,* 1981, *36,* 129–148.

Bower, G. H., and Clark, M. C. Narrative stories as mediators for serial learning. *Psychonomic Science,* 1969, *14,* 181–182.

Bowlby, J. *Attachment and Loss. (Vol. 1). Attachment.* New York: Basic Books, 1969.

Bowlby, J. *Attachment and Loss (Vol. 2).* New York: Basic Books, 1973.

Bowlby, J. Attachment and loss: Retrospect and prospect. *American Journal of Orthopsychiatry,* 1982, *52,* 664–678.

Boynton, R. M. *Human Color Vision.* New York: Holt, Rinehart and Winston, 1979.

Boysson-Bardies, B., Sagart, L., and Durand, C. Discernible differences in the babbling of infants according to target language. *Journal of Child Language,* 1984, *11,* 1–15.

Brady, J. P., and Lind, D. L. Experimental analysis of hysterical blindness. *Archives of General Psychiatry,* 1961, *4,* 331–359.

Bransford, J. D., and Johnson, M. K. Contextual prerequisites for understanding: Some investigations of comprehension and recall. *Journal of Verbal Learning and Verbal Behavior,* 1972, *11,* 717–726.

Breitmeyer, B. G. *Visual Masking: An Integrative Approach.* New York: Oxford University Press, 1980.

Brickner, R. M. *The Intellectual Functions of the Frontal Lobe. A Study Based Upon Observations of a Man After Partial Frontal Lobectomy.* New York: Macmillan, 1936.

Briggs, S. R. Shyness: Introversion or Neuroticism? *Journal of Research in Personality,* 1988, *22,* 290–307.

Broadbent, D. E. *Perception and Communication.* London: Pergamon Press, 1958.

Broberg, D. J., and Bernstein, I. L. Candy as a scapegoat in the prevention of food aversions in children receiving chemotherapy. *Cancer,* 1987, *60,* 2344–2347.

Brooks-Gunn, J. Antecedents and consequences of variations in girls' maturational timing. *Journal of Adolescent Health Care,* 1988, *9,* 365–373.

Brooks-Gunn, J. Pubertal processes and the early adolescent transition. In *Child Development Today and Tomorrow,* edited by W. Damon. San Francisco: Jossey-Bass, 1989.

Brooks-Gunn, J., and Furstenberg, F. F. Adolescent sexual behavior. *American Psychologist,* 1989, *44,* 249–257.

Broverman, I. K., Vogel, S. R., Broverman, D. M., Clarkson, F. E., and Rosenkrantz, P. S. Sex role stereotypes: A current appraisal. *Journal of Social Issues,* 1972, *28,* 59–78.

Brown, A. S. A review of the tip-of-the-tongue experience. *Psychological Bulletin,* 1991, *109,* 204–223.

Brown, G. W. The discovery of expressed emotion: Induction or deduction? In *Expressed Emotion in Families,* edited by J. Leff and C. Vaughn. New York: Guilford Press, 1985.

Brown, G. W., Bone, M., Dalison, B., and Wing, J. K. *Schizophrenia and Social Care.* London: Oxford University Press, 1966.

Brown, J. D. Staying fit and staying well: Physical fitness as a moderator of life stress. *Personality Processes and Individual Differences,* 1991, *60,* 455–461.

Brown, J. D., and Rogers, R. J. Self-serving attributions: The role of physiological arousal. *Personality and Social Psychology Bulletin,* 1991, *17,* 501–506.

Brown, R., and Bellugi, U. Three processes in the child's acquisition of syntax. *Harvard Education Review,* 1964, *34,* 133–151.

Brown, R., and Hanlon, C. Derivational complexity and order of acquisition in child speech. In *Cognition and the Development of Language,* edited by J. R. Hayes. New York: John Wiley & Sons, 1970.

Brown, R., and McNeill, D. The "tip-of-the-tongue" phenomenon. *Journal of Verbal Learning and Verbal Behavior,* 1966, *5,* 325–337.

Brown, R. W., and Kulik, J. Flashbulb memories. *Cognition,* 1977, *5,* 73–99.

Brownell, K. D., Greenwood, M. R. C., Stellar, E., and Shrager, E. E. The effects of repeated cycles of weight loss and regain in rats. *Physiology and Behavior,* 1986, *38,* 459–464.

Buck, L., and Axel, R. A novel multigene family may encode odorant receptors: A molecular basis for odor recognition. *Cell,* 1991, *65,* 175–187.

Buck, R. W. Nonverbal communication of affect in children. *Journal of Personality and Social Psychology,* 1975, *31,* 644–653.

Buck, R. W. Nonverbal communication accuracy in preschool children: Relationships with personality and skin conductance. *Journal of Personality and Social Psychology,* 1977, *33,* 225–236.

Buri, J. R., Louiselle, P. A., Misukanis, T. M., and Mueller, R. A. Effects of parental authoritarianism and authoritativeness on self-esteem. *Personality and Social Psychology Bulletin,* 1988, *14,* 271–282.

Burt, C. The concept of consciousness. *British Journal of Psychology,* 1962, *53,* 229–242.

Buskist, W., and Miller, H. L. Interaction between rules and contingencies in the control of human fixed-interval performance. *Psychological Record,* 1986, *36,* 109–116.

Buss, A. H. *Personality: Temperament, Social Behavior, and the Self.* Boston: Allyn and Bacon, 1995.

Buss, D. M. The evolution of human intrasexual competition: Tactics of mate attraction. *Journal of Personality and Social Psychology,* 1988, *54,* 616–628.

Buss, D. M. Sex differences in human mate preferences: Evolutionary hypotheses tested in 37 cultures. *Behavioral and Brain Sciences,* 1989, *12,* 1–49.

Buss, D. M. International preferences in selecting mates: A study of 37 societies. *Journal of Cross-Cultural Psychology,* 1990, *21,* 5–47.

Buss, D. M. Mate preferences mechanisms: Consequences for partner choice and intrasexual competition. In *The Adapted Mind: Evolutionary Psychology and the Generation of Culture,* edited by J. H. Barkow, L. Cosmides, and J. Tooby. New York: Oxford University Press, 1992.

Cacioppo, J. T., Petty, R. E., and Crites, S. L. Attitude change. In *Encyclopedia of Human Behavior,* edited by V. S. Ramachandran. San Diego, CA: Academic Press, 1993.

Campfield, L. A., Smith, F. J., Guisez, Y., Devos, R., and Burn, P. Recombinant mouse OB protein: Evidence for a peripheral signal linking adiposity and central neural networks. *Science,* 1995, *269,* 546–549.

Cannon, W. B., and Washburn, A. L. An explanation of hunger. *American Journal of Physiology,* 1912, *29,* 444–454.

Carlson, N. R. *Foundations of Physiological Psychology,* 3rd ed. Boston: Allyn and Bacon, 1995.

Carpenter, P. A., and Just, M. A. What your eyes do while your mind is reading. In *Eye Movements in Reading: Perceptual and Language Processes,* edited by K. Rayner. New York: Academic Press, 1983.

Carpenter, P. A., Miyake, A., and Just, M. A. Language comprehension: Sentence and discourse processing. *Annual Review of Psychology,* 1995, *46,* 91–120.

Carr, E. G., and Lovaas, O. J. Contingent electric shock as a treatment for severe behavior problems. In *The Effect of Punishment on Human Behavior,* edited by S. Axelrod and J. Apsche. New York: Academic Press, 1983.

Carson, R. C., Butcher, J. N., and Mineka, S. (1996). *Abnormal Psychology and Modern Life, Tenth Edition.* New York: HarperCollins.

Carver, C. S., and Scheier, M. F. *Perspectives on Personality,* 2nd ed. Boston: Allyn and Bacon, 1992.

Case, R. *Intellectual Development: A Systematic Reinterpretation.* New York: Academic Press, 1985.

Case, R. *The Mind's Staircase.* Hillsdale, NJ: Erlbaum, 1992.

Cavanaugh, J. C. *Adult Development and Aging.* Belmont, CA: Wadsworth, 1990.

Centers for Disease Control. *Smoking, Tobacco, and Health: A Fact Book.* Washington, DC: U.S. Government Printing Office, 1987.

Cerruti, D. Discrimination theory of rule-governed behavior. *Journal of the Experimental Analysis of Behavior,* 1990, *54,* 129–153.

Chaiken, S. Communicator's physical attractiveness and persuasion. *Journal of Personality and Social Psychology,* 1979, *37,* 1387–1397.

Chapman, K. L., Leonard, L. B., and Mervis, C. B. The effect of feedback on young children's inappropriate word usage. *Journal of Child Language,* 1986, *13,* 101–117.

Chasdi, E. H. *Culture and Human Development: The Selected Papers of John Whiting.* New York: Cambridge University Press, 1994.

Chassin, L., Presson, C. C., Sherman, S. J., and Edwards, D. A. The natural history of cigarette smoking: Predicting young-adult smoking outcomes from adolescent patterns. *Health Psychology,* 1990, *9,* 710–716.

Cherry, E. C. Some experiments on the recognition of speech, with one and with two ears. *Journal of the Acoustical Society of America,* 1953, *25,* 975–979.

Chomsky, N. *Syntactic Structure.* The Hague: Mouton Publishers, 1957.

Chomsky, N. *Aspects of the Theory of Syntax.* Cambridge, MA: MIT Press, 1965.

Christianson, S., and Loftus, E. F. Remembering emotional events: The fate of detailed information. *Cognition and Emotion,* 1991, *5,* 81–108.

Cialdini, R. B. *Influence: Science and Practice,* 3rd ed. New York: HarperCollins, 1993.

Cialdini, R. B., Borden, R. J., Thorne, A., Walker, M. R., Freeman, S., and Sloan, L. R. Basking in reflected glory: Three (football) field studies. *Journal of Personality and Social Psychology,* 1976, *34,* 366–375.

Cialdini, R. B, Petty, R. E., and Cacioppo, J. T. Attitude and attitude change. *Annual Review of Psychology,* 1981, *32,* 357–404.

Clark, J. D. The African tinderbox: The spark that ignited our cultural heritage. In *Milestones in Human Evolution,* edited by A. J. Almquist and A. Manyak. Prospect Heights, IL: Waveland Press, 1993.

Clarke-Stewart, A. And daddy makes three: The father's impact on mother and young child. *Child Development,* 1978, *49,* 466–479.

Clarke-Stewart, K. A., and Fein, G. G. Early childhood programs. In *Handbook of Child Psychology. Vol. 2: Infancy and Developmental Psychobiology,* edited by P. H. Mussen. New York: John Wiley & Sons, 1983.

Cleckley, H. *The Mask of Sanity.* St. Louis: C. V. Mosby, 1976.

Cloninger, C. R. Neurogenetic adaptive mechanisms in alcoholism. *Science,* 1987, *236,* 410–416

Cloninger, C. R., Bohman, M., and Sigvardsson, S. Inheritance of alcohol abuse: Cross-fostering analysis of adoptive men. *Archives of General Psychiatry,* 1981, *38,* 861–868.

Cloninger, C. R., Bohman, M., Sigvardsson, S., and von Knorring, A. -L. Psychopathology in adopted-out children of alcoholics. The Stockholm Adoption Study. *Recent Developments in Alcoholism,* 1985, *7,* 235.

Cobb, S., and Rose, R. M. Hypertension, peptic ulcer, and diabetes in air traffic controllers. *Journal of the American Medical Association,* 1973, *224,* 489–492.

Coe, W. C., Kobayashi, K., and Howard, M. L. Experimental and ethical problems in evaluating the influence of hypnosis in antisocial conduct. *Journal of Abnormal Psychology,* 1973, *82,* 476–482.

Cohen, L. A. Diet and cancer. *Scientific American,* 1987, *102,* 42–48.

Cohen, M., and Davis, N. *Medication Errors: Causes and Prevention.* Philadelphia: G. F. Stickley, 1981.

Cohen, M. E., Robins, E., Purtell, J. J., Altmann, M. W., and Reid, D. E. *Journal of the American Medical Association,* 1953, *151,* 977–986.

Colegrove, F. W. Individual memories. *American Journal of Psychology,* 1899, *10,* 228–255.

Coleman, J. C. *Abnormal Psychology and Modern Life,* 5th ed. Glenview, IL: Scott, Foresman, 1976.

Coles, C. D., Platzman, K. A., Smith, I., James, M. E., and Falek, A. Effects of cocaine and alcohol use in pregnancy on neonatal growth and neurobehavioral status. *Neurotoxicology and Teratology,* 1992, *14,* 23–33.

Collins, A. M., and Quillian, M. R. Retrieval time from semantic memory. *Journal of Verbal Learning and Verbal Behavior,* 1969, *8,* 240–248.

Condry, J., and Condry, S. Sex differences: A study of the eye of the beholder. *Child Development,* 1976, *47,* 812–819.

Conner, R. L., and Levine, S. Hormonal influences on aggressive behaviour. In *Aggressive Behaviour,* edited by S. Garattine and E. B. Sigg. New York: John Wiley & Sons, 1969.

Conrad, R. Acoustic confusions in immediate memory. *British Journal of Psychology,* 1964, *55,* 75–83.

Conrad, R. Short-term memory processes in the deaf. *British Journal of Psychology,* 1970, *61,* 179–195.

Cooper, K. Running without risk. *Runner's World,* 1985, *20,* 61–64.

Cooper, K. H. *Aerobics.* New York: Evans and Company, 1968.

Cooper, K. H. *The New Aerobics.* New York: Evans and Company, 1970.

Cooper, M. L., Russell, M., and George, W. H. Coping, expectancies, and alcohol abuse: A test of social learning foundations. *Journal of Abnormal Psychology,* 1988, *97,* 218–230.

Cooper, R. M., and Zubek, J. P. Effects of enriched and restricted early environments on the learning ability of bright and dull rats. *Canadian Journal of Psychology,* 1958, *12,* 159–164.

Coover, G. D., Murison, R., and Jellestad, F. K. Subtotal lesions of the amygdala: The rostral central nucleus in passive avoidance and ulceration. *Physiology and Behavior,* 1992, *51,* 795–803.

Corbetta, M., Miezin, F. M., Doobmeyer, S., Shulman, G. L., and Petersen, S. E. Selective and divided attention during visual discriminations of shape, color, and speed: Functional anatomy by positron emission tomography. *Journal of Neuroscience,* 1991, *11,* 2383–2402.

Corkin, S., Sullivan, E. V., Twitchell, T. E., and Grove, E. The amnesic patient H. M.: Clinical observations and test performance 28 years after operation. *Society for Neuroscience Abstracts,* 1981, *7,* 235.

Corteen, R., and Williams, T. Television and reading skills. In *The Impact of Television: A Natural Experiment in Three Communities,* edited by T. M. Williams. New York: Academic Press, 1986.

Coryell, W. A blind family history study of Briquet's syndrome. Further validation of the diagnosis. *Archives of General Psychiatry,* 1980, *37,* 1266–1269.

Costa, P. T., and McCrae, R. R. Still stable after all these years: Personality as a key to some issues in adulthood and old age. In *Life-Span Development and Behavior,* edited by P. B. Baltes. New York: Academic Press, 1980.

Cotton, N. S. The familial incidence of alcoholism. A review. *Journal of Studies in Alcohol,* 1979, *40,* 89–116.

Cowart, J., and Whaley, D. Punishment of self-mutilation behavior. Unpublished manuscript cited by Whaley, D. L., and Malott, R. W. *Elementary Principles of Behavior.* New York: Appleton-Century-Crofts, 1971.

Cowley, D. S., and Arana, G. W. The diagnostic utility of lactate sensitivity in panic disorder. *Archives of General Psychiatry,* 1990, *47,* 277–284.

Cox, J. R., and Griggs, R. A. The effects of experience on performance in Wason's selection task. *Memory and Cognition,* 1982, *10,* 496–502.

Cox, R. H. Intervention strategies. *Stress and Coping: An Anthology,* edited by A. Monat and R. S. Lazarus, New York: Columbia University Press, 1991.

Craik, F. I. M., and Lockhart, R. S. Levels of processing: A framework for memory research. *Journal of Verbal Learning and Verbal Behavior,* 1972, *11,* 671–684.

Craik, F. I. M., and Tulving, E. Depth of processing and the retention of words in episodic memory. *Journal of Experimental Psychology: General,* 1975, *104,* 268–294.

Crick, F., and Mitchison, G. The function of dream sleep. *Nature,* 1983, *304,* 111–114.

Cromwell, P. F., Marks, A., Olson, J. N., and Avery, D. W. Group effects on decision-making by burglars. *Psychological Reports,* 1991, *69,* 579–588.

Crosby, F. J. *Juggling: The Unexpected Advantages of Balancing Career and Home for Women and Their Families.* New York: The Free Press, 1991.

Crow, T. J. Molecular pathology of schizophrenia: More than one disease process? *British Medical Journal,* 1980, *280,* 66–68.

Crowe, R. R., Noyes, R., Pauls, D. L., and Slymen, D. A family study of panic disorder. *Archives of General Psychiatry,* 1983, *40,* 1065–1069.

Crowne, D., and Marlowe, D. *The Approval Motive.* New York: John Wiley & Sons, 1964.

Croyle, R. T., and Cooper, J. Dissonance arousal: Physiological evidence. *Journal of Personality and Social Psychology,* 1983, *45,* 782–791.

Csikszentmihalyi, M., and Larson, R. *Being Adolescent: Conflict and Growth in the Teenage Years.* New York: Basic Books, 1984.

Culebras, A., and Moore, J. T. Magnetic resonance findings in REM sleep behavior disorder. *Neurology,* 1989, *39,* 1519–1523.

Cummings, J. L., and Wirshing, W. C. Recognition and differential diagnosis of tardive dyskinesia. *International Journal of Psychiatry in Medicine,* 1989, *19,* 133–144.

Curtiss, S. Issues in language acquisition relevant to cochlear implants in young children. In *Cochlear Implants in Young Deaf Children,* edited by E. Owens and D. K. Kessler. Boston: College-Hill Press, 1989.

Dabbs, J. M., Frady, R. L., Carr, T. S., and Besch, N. F. Saliva testosterone and criminal violence in young adult prison inmates. *Psychosomatic Medicine,* 1987, *49,* 174–182.

Dabbs, J. M., Ruback, J. M., Frady, R. L., and Hopper, C. H. Saliva testosterone and criminal violence among women. *Personality and Individual Differences,* 1988, *9,* 269–275.

Dale, P. S. *Language Development: Structure and Function,* 2nd ed. New York: Holt, Rinehart and Winston, 1976.

Daly, M., and Wilson, M. *Sex, Evolution, and Behavior.* North Scituate, MA: Duxbury Press, 1978.

Damasio, A. R., Tranel, D., and Damasio, H. Face agnosia and the neural substrates of memory. *Annual Review of Neuroscience,* 1990, *13,* 89–109.

Damasio, H. Neuroimaging contributions to the understanding of aphasia. In *Handbook of Neuropsychology, Vol. 2,* edited by F. Boller and J. Grafman. Amsterdam: Elsevier, 1989.

Damon, W., and Hart, D. Self-understanding and its role in social and moral development. In *Developmental Psychology: An Advanced Textbook,* edited by M. H. Bornstein and M. E. Lamb. Hillsdale, NJ: Erlbaum, 1992.

Daniels, P., and Weingarten, K. *Sooner or Later: The Timing of Parenthood in Adult Lives.* New York: Norton, 1982.

Darley, J. M., and Latané, B. Bystander intervention in emergencies: Diffusion of responsibility. *Journal of Personality and Social Psychology,* 1968, *8,* 377–383.

Darrach, B. The war on aging. *Life,* 1992, *15,* 32–43.

Darwin, C. *The Expression of the Emotions in Man and Animals.* Chicago: University of Chicago Press, 1872/1965.

Darwin, C. J., Turvey, M. T., and Crowder, R. G. An auditory analogue of the Sperling partial report procedure: Evidence for brief auditory storage. *Cognitive Psychology,* 1972, *3,* 255–267.

Darwin, F. *Charles Darwin's Autobiography.* New York: Henry Schuman, 1950/1887.

Dashiell, J. F. Experimental studies of the influence of social situations on the behavior of individual human adults. In *A Handbook of Social Psychology,* edited by C. Murcheson. Worcester, MA: Clark University Press, 1935.

Davidson, J. M., Camargo, C. A., and Smith, E. R. Effects of androgen on sexual behavior in hypogonadal men. *Journal of Clinical Endocrinology and Metabolism,* 1979, *48,* 955–958.

Davis, J. D., and Campbell, C. S. Peripheral control of meal size in the rat: Effect of sham feeding on meal size and drinking rats. *Journal of Comparative and Physiological Psychology,* 1973, *83,* 379–387.

Davis, J. M. A two-factor theory of schizophrenia. *Journal of Psychiatric Research,* 1974, *11,* 25–30.

Davis, M. The role of the amygdala in fear-potentiated startle: Implications for animal models of anxiety. *Trends in Pharmacological Sciences,* 1992, *13,* 35–41.

Davis, W. L., and Phares, E. J. Internal-external control as a determinant of information-seeking in a social influence situation. *Journal of Personality,* 1967, *35,* 547–561.

Davison, G. C., and Neale, J. M. *Abnormal Psychology,* 5th ed. New York: John Wiley & Sons, 1990.

Dawes, R. M., Faust, D., and Meehl, P. E. Clinical versus actuarial judgment. *Science,* 1989, *243,* 1668–1674.

Dawkins, R. *The Blind Watchmaker.* New York: Norton, 1986.

Deaux, K. Sex and gender. *Annual Review of Psychology,* 1985, *36,* 49–81.

DeCasper, A. J., and Fifer, W. P. Of human bonding: Newborns prefer their mothers' voices. *Science,* 1980, *208,* 1175–1176.

DeCasper, A. J., and Spence, M. Prenatal maternal speech influences newborns' perception of speech sounds. *Infant Behavior and Development,* 1986, *9,* 133–150.

deGroot, A. D. *Thought and Choice in Chess.* The Hague: Mouton Publishers, 1965.

Dekaban, A. *Neurology of Early Childhood.* Baltimore: Williams & Wilkins, 1970.

Dellas, M., and Jernigan, L. P. Affective personality characteristics associated with undergraduate ego identity formation. *Journal of Adolescent Research,* 1990, *5,* 306–324.

DeLongis, A., Folkman, S., and Lazarus, R. S. The impact of daily stress on health and mood: Psychological and social resources as mediators. *Journal of Personality and Social Psychology,* 1988, *54,* 486–495.

Dement, W. C. *Some Must Watch While Some Must Sleep.* San Francisco: W. H. Freeman, 1974.

Dennis, W. *Children of the Creche.* New York: Appleton-Century-Crofts, 1973.

DePue, R. A., and Monroe, S. M. Conceptualization and measurement of human disorder in life-stress research: The problem of chronic disturbance. *Psychological Bulletin,* 1986, *99,* 36–51.

Desimone, R., and Duncan, J. Neural mechanisms of selective visual attention. *Annual Review of Neuroscience,* 1995, *18,* 193–222.

Deutsch, J. A., Young, W. G., and Kalogeris, T. J. The stomach signals satiety. *Science,* 1978, *201,* 165–167.

Deutscher, I. The quality of postparental life. In *Middle Age and Aging,* edited by B. L. Neugarten. Chicago: University of Chicago Press, 1968.

Devane, W. A., Hanus, L., Breuer, A., Pertwee, R. G., Stevenson, L. A., Griffin, G., Gibson, D., Mandelbaum, A., Etinger, A., and Mechoulam, R. Isolation and structure of a brain constituent that binds to the cannabinoid receptor. *Science,* 1992, *258,* 1946–1949.

deVilliers, J. G., and deVilliers, P. A. *Language Acquisition.* Cambridge, MA: Harvard University Press, 1978.

Diener, F. Deindividuation: The absence of self-awareness and self-regulation in group members. In *Psychology of Group Influence,* edited by P. B. Paulus. Hillsdale, NJ: Erlbaum, 1979.

Dimsdale, J. E. A perspective on type A behavior and coronary disease. *The New England Journal of Medicine,* 1988, *318,* 110–112.

Dion, K., Berscheid, E., and Walster, E. What is beautiful is good. *Journal of Personality and Social Psychology,* 1972, *24,* 285–290.

Donenberg, G. R., and Hoffman, L. W. Gender differences in moral development. *Sex Roles,* 1988, *18,* 701–717.

Dooling, D. J., and Lachman, R. Effects of comprehension on retention of prose. *Journal of Experimental Psychology,* 1971, *88,* 216–222.

Drabman, R. S., Spitalnik, R., and O'Leary, K. D. Teaching self-control to disruptive children. *Journal of Abnormal Psychology,* 1973, *82,* 10–16.

Dérousné, J., and Beauvois, M. -F. Phonological processing in reading: Data from alexia. *Journal of Neurology, Neurosurgery, and Psychiatry,* 1979, *42,* 1125–1132.

Druckman, D., and Bjork, R. A. *In the Mind's Eye: Enhancing Human Performance.* Washington, DC: National Academy Press, 1991.

Dunn, J., Bretherton, I., and Munn, P. Conversations about feeling states between mothers and their young children. *Developmental Psychology,* 1987, *23,* 132–139.

Durham, W. H. *Coevolution: Genes, Culture, and Human Diversity.* Stanford, CA: Stanford University Press, 1991.

Dutton, D. G., and Aron, A. P. Some evidence for heightened sexual attraction under conditions of high anxiety. *Journal of Personality and Social Psychology,* 1974, *30,* 510–517.

D'Zurilla, T. Recall efficiency and mediating cognitive events in "experimental repression." *Journal of Personality and Social Psychology,* 1965, *1,* 253–257.

Eagly, A. H. The science and politics of comparing women and men. *American Psychologist,* 1995, *50,* 145–158.

Eagly, A. H., and Karau, S. J. Gender and the emergence of leaders: A meta-analysis. *Journal of Personality and Social Psychology,* 1991, *60,* 685–710.

Eddy, N. B., Halbach, H., Isbell, H., and Seevers, M. H. Drug dependence: Its significance and characteristics. *Bulletin of the World Health Organization,* 1965, *32,* 721–733.

Ehlers, C. L., Frank, E., and Kupfer, D. J. Social zeitgebers and biological rhythms. *Archives of General Psychiatry,* 1988, *45,* 948–952.

Eich, J., Weingartner, H., Stillman, R., and Gillin, J. State-dependent accessibility of retrieval cues and retention of a categorized list. *Journal of Verbal Learning and Verbal Behavior,* 1975, *14,* 408–417.

Eimas, P. D., Siqueland, E. R., Jusczyk, P., and Vigorito, J. Speech perception in infants. *Science,* 1971, *171,* 303–306.

Eisenberg, N., Fabes, R. A., Schaller, M., Miller, P., Carlo, G., Poulin, R., Shea, C., and Shell, R. Personality and socialization: Correlates of vicarious emotional responding. *Journal of Personality and Social Psychology,* 1991, *61,* 459–470.

Ekman, P. *The Face of Man: Expressions of Universal Emotions in a New Guinea Village.* New York: Garland STPM Press, 1980.

Ekman, P., and Friesen, W. V. Nonverbal leakage and clues to deception. *Psychiatry,* 1969, *32,* 88–105.

Ekman, P., and Friesen, W. V. Detecting deception from body or face. *Journal of Personality and Social Psychology,* 1974, *29,* 288–298.

Ekman, P., and Friesen, W. V. *Unmasking the Face.* Englewood Cliffs, NJ: Prentice-Hall, 1975.

Ekman, P., Friesen, W. V., and Ellsworth, P. *Emotion in the Human Face: Guidelines for Research and a Review of Findings.* New York: Pergamon Press, 1972.

Elder, G. H. Appearance and education in marriage mobility. *American Sociological Review,* 1969, *34,* 519–533.

Elias, M. Serum cortisol, testosterone and testosterone binding globulin responses to competitive fighting in human males. *Aggressive Behavior,* 1981, *7,* 215–224.

Elkin, I., Parloff, M. B., Hadley, S. W., and Autry, J. H. NIMH Treatment of Depression Collaborative Research Program. *Archives of General Psychiatry,* 1985, *42,* 305–316.

Elkin, I., Shea, M. T., Watkins, J. T., Imber, S. D., Sotsky, S. M., Collins, J. F., Glass, D. R., Pilkonis, P. A., Leber, W. R., Docherty, J. P., Fiester, S. J., and Parloff, M. B. National Institute of Mental Health Treatment of Depression Collaborative Research Program: General Effectiveness of Treatments. *Archives of General Psychiatry,* 1989, *46,* 971–982.

Ellenberger, H. F. The story of "Anna O": A critical review with new data. *Journal of the History of the Behavioral Sciences,* 1972, *8,* 267–279.

Ellis, A. Rational-emotive therapy. In *Current Psychotherapies,* edited by R. Corsini. Itasca, IL: Peacock, 1973.

Ellis, A. A twenty-three-year-old woman guilty about not following her parents' rules. In *Case Studies in Psychotherapy,* edited by D. Wedding and R. J. Corsini. Itasca, IL: Peacock, 1989.

Elms, A. C. Obedience in retrospect. *Journal of Social Issues,* 1995, *51,* 21–32.

Emde, R. N., Plomin, R., Robinson, J., DeFries, J., Reznick, J. S., Campos, J., Kagan, J., and Zahn-Waxler, C. Temperament, emotion, and cognition at fourteen months: The MacArthur longitudinal twin study. *Child Development,* 1992, *63,* 1437–1455.

Emmons, R. A., Diener, E., and Larsen, R. J. Choice and avoidance of everyday situations and affect congruence: Two models of reciprocal interactionism. *Journal of Personality and Social Psychology,* 1986, *51,* 815–826.

Engel, L. Darwin and the Beagle. In *The Voyage of the Beagle,* edited by L. Engel. Garden City, NY: Doubleday, 1962.

Entwisle, D. To dispel fantasies about fantasy-based measures of achievement motivation. *Psychological Bulletin,* 1972, *77,* 377–391.

Epstein, R. The spontaneous interconnection of three repertoires. *The Psychological Record,* 1985, *35,* 131–141.

Epstein, R. The spontaneous interconnection of four repertoires of behavior in a pigeon (*Columba livia*). *Journal of Comparative Psychology,* 1987, *101,* 197–201.

Epstein, R., Kirshnit, C., Lanza, R. P., and Rubin, L. Insight in the pigeon: Antecedents and determinants of an intelligent performance. *Nature,* 1984, *308,* 61–62.

Epstein, S. The stability of behavior. I. On predicting most of the people much of the time. *Journal of Personality and Social Psychology,* 1979, *37,* 1097–1126.

Epstein, W. The influence of syntactical structure on learning. *American Journal of Psychology,* 1961, *74,* 80–85.

Erdelyi, M. H. *Psychoanalysis: Freud's Cognitive Psychology.* San Francisco: W. H. Freeman, 1985.

Erickson, M. F., Sroufe, L. A., and Egeland, B. The relationship between quality of attachment and behavior problems in preschool in a high-risk sample. *Monographs of the Society for Research in Child Development,* 1985, *50(1–2, Serial No. 209).*

Ernulf, K. E., Innala, S. M., and Whitam, F. L. Biological explanation, psychological explanation, and tolerance of homosexuals: A cross-national analysis of beliefs and attitudes. *Psychological Reports,* 1989, *248,* 183–188.

Eron, L. D. A normative study of the thematic apperception test. *Psychological Monographs,* 1950, *64,* Whole No. 315.

Erting, C. J., Johnson, R. C., Smith, D. L., and Snider, B. D. *The Deaf Way: Perspectives from the International Conference on Deaf Culture.* Washington, DC: Gallaudet University Press, 1989.

Eslinger, P. J., and Damasio, A. R. Severe disturbance of higher cognition after bilateral frontal lobe ablation: Patient EVR. *Neurology,* 1985, *35,* 1731–1741.

Evans, R. I., Raines, B. E., and Hanselka, L. Developing data-based communications in social psychological research: Adolescent smoking prevention. *Journal of Applied Social Psychology,* 1984, *14,* 289–295.

Eysenck, H. J. The effects of psychotherapy: An evaluation. *Journal of Consulting Psychology,* 1952, *16,* 319–324.

Eysenck, H. J. *The Structure of Human Personality,* 3rd ed. London: Methuen, 1970.

Eysenck, H. J. Personality, stress and cancer: Prediction and prophylaxis. *British Journal of Medical Psychology,* 1988, *61,* 57–75.

Eysenck, H. J. Dimensions of personality: 16, 5, or 3?–Criteria for a taxonomic paradigm. *Personality and Individual Differences,* 1991, *12,* 773–790.

Eysenck, H. J., and Eysenck, M. W. *Personality and Individual Differences: A Natural Science Approach.* New York: Plenum Press, 1985.

Fabes, R. A., and Eisenberg, N. Young children's coping with interpersonal anger. *Child Development,* 1992, *63,* 116–128.

Fadda, F., Mosca, E., Colombo, G., and Gessa, G. L. Alcohol-preferring rats: Genetic sensitivity to alcohol-induced stimulation of dopamine metabolism. *Physiology and Behavior,* 1990, *47,* 727–729.

Fagot, B. I., and Hagan, R. I. Observations of parent reactions to sex-stereotyped behaviors: Age and sex differences. *Child Development,* 1991, *62,* 617–628.

Farmer, A., McGuffin, P., and Gottesman, I. Twin concordance in DSM-III schizophrenia. *Archives of General Psychiatry,* 1987, *44,* 634–641.

Feather, N. T., and McKee, I. R. Global self-esteem and attitudes toward the high achiever for Australian and Japanese students. *Social Psychology Quarterly,* 1993, *56,* 65–76.

Feeney, J. A., and Noller, P. Attachment style and verbal descriptions of romantic partners. *Journal of Social and Personal Relationships,* 1991, *8,* 187–215.

Feigenbaum, S. L., Masi, A. T., and Kaplan, S. B. Prognosis in rheumatoid arthritis: A longitudinal study of newly diagnosed younger adult patients. *American Journal of Medicine,* 1979, *66,* 377–384.

Feingold, A. Cognitive gender differences: A developmental perspective. *Sex Roles,* 1993, *29,* 91–112.

Feldman, R. D. *Whatever Happened to the Quiz Kids?* Chicago: Chicago Review Press, 1982.

Feshbach, S., and Singer, R. D. *Television and Aggression.* San Francisco: Jossey-Bass, 1971.

Festinger, L. *A Theory of Cognitive Dissonance.* Stanford: Stanford University Press, 1957.

Festinger, L., and Carlsmith, J. M. Cognitive consequences of forced compliance. *Journal of Abnormal and Social Psychology,* 1959, *58,* 203–210.

Festinger, L., Schachter, S., and Back, K. *Social Pressures in Informal Groups: A Study of a Housing Community.* New York: Harper & Row, 1950.

Feynman, R. P. *Surely You're Joking, Mr. Feynman!.* New York: Bantam Books, 1985.

Field, T. Individual differences in the expressivity of neonates and young infants. In *Development of Nonverbal Behavior in Children,* edited by R. S. Feldman. New York: Springer-Verlag, 1982.

Fields, L. Forward: Special issue on stimulus equivalence. *The Psychological Record,* 1993, *43,* 543–546.

Fields, L., Landon-Jimenez, V., Buffington, D. M., and Adams, B. J. Maintained nodal-distance effects in equivalence classes. *Journal of the Experimental Analysis of Behavior,* 1995, *64,* 129–146.

Fink, M. Presidential address: Brain function, verbal behavior, and psychotherapy. In *Evaluation of Psychological Therapies: Psychotherapies, Behavior Therapies, Drug Therapies, and Their Interactions,* edited by R. L. Spitzer and D. F. Klein. Baltimore: Johns Hopkins University Press, 1976.

Fischer, K. W., and Farrar, M. J. Generalizations about generalizations: How a theory of skill development explains both generality and specificity. *International Journal of Psychology,* 1987, *22,* 643–677.

Fischer, K. W., and Pipp, S. L. Processes of cognitive development: Optimal level and skill development. In *Mechanisms of Cognitive Development,* edited by R. Sternberg. New York: Freeman, 1984

Fiske, S. T. Controlling other people: The impact of power on stereotyping. *American Psychologist,* 1993, *48,* 621–628.

Flaherty, J., Frank, E., Hoskinson, K., Richman, J., and Kupfer, D. Social zeitgebers and bereavement. Paper presented at the 140th Annual Meeting of the American Psychiatric Association, Chicago, May 1987.

Flanagan, O. *Consciousness Reconsidered.* Cambridge, MA: Bradford Books, 1992.

Flavell, J. H., Everett, B. H., Croft, K., and Flavell, E. R. Young children's knowledge about visual perception: Further evidence for the level 1–level 2 distinction. *Developmental Psychology,* 1981, *17,* 99–103.

Flay, B. R., Ryan, K. B., Best, J. A., Brown, K. S., Kersell, M. W., d'Avernas, J. R., and Zanna, M. P. Are social-psychological smoking prevention programs effective? The Waterloo Study. *Journal of Behavioral Medicine,* 1985, *8,* 37–59.

Flexser, A. J., and Tulving, E. Retrieval independence in recognition and recall. *Psychological Review,* 1978, *85,* 153–171.

Foley, V. D. Family therapy. In *Current Psychotherapies,* 2nd ed., edited by R. J. Corsini. Itasca, IL: R. E. Peacock, 1979.

Folkman, S., and Lazarus, R. S. Coping and emotion. In *Stress and Coping: An Anthology,* edited by A. Monat and R. S. Lazarus. New York: Columbia University Press, 1991.

Forsyth, D. R. *Group Dynamics.* Pacific Grove, CA: Brooks/Cole, 1990.

Fouts, R. S. Chimpanzee language and elephant tails: A theoretical synthesis. In *Language in Primates: Perspectives and Implications,* edited by J. de Luce and H. T. Wilder. New York: Springer-Verlag, 1983.

Fouts, R. S., Hirsch, A., and Fouts, D. Cultural transmission of a human language in a chimpanzee mother/infant relationship. In *Psychological Perspectives: Child Nurturance Series, Vol. III,* edited by H. E. Fitzgerald, J. A. Mullins, and P. Page. New York: Plenum Press, 1983.

Frank, S. L., Pirsch, L. A., and Wright, V. C. Late adolescents' perceptions of their relationships with their parents: Relationships among deidealization, autonomy, relatedness, and insecurity and implications for adolescent adjustment and ego identity status. *Journal of Youth and Adolescence,* 1990, *19,* 571–588.

Fraser, J. G. Selection of patients. In *Cochlear Implants,* edited by R. F. Gray. London: Croom Helm, 1985.

Freedman, J. L., and Fraser, S. C. Compliance without pressure: The foot-in-the-door technique. *Journal of Personality and Social Psychology,* 1966, *4,* 195–203.

Freud, S. *The Interpretation of Dreams.* London: George Allen and Unwin Ltd, 1900.

Freud, S. *Recommendations for Physicians on the Psychoanalytic Method of Treatment.* (J. Riviere, Trans.), Zentralblatt, Bd. II. Reprinted in Sammlung, Vierte Folge, 1912.

Freud, S. *New Introductory Lectures on Psychoanalysis* (J. Strachey, Trans.). New York: Norton, 1933.

Friedman, M., and Rosenman, R. H. Association of specific overt behavior patterns with blood and cardiovascular findings—Blood cholesterol level, blood clotting time, incidence of arcus senilis, and clinical coronary artery disease. *Journal of the American Medical Association,* 1959, *162,* 1286–1296.

Friedman, M. I., Tordoff, M. G., and Kare, M. R. *Chemical Senses. Vol. 4: Appetite and Nutrition.* New York: Dekker, 1991.

Friedman, M. I., Tordoff, M. G., and Ramirez, I. Integrated metabolic control of food intake. *Brain Research Bulletin,* 1986, *17,* 855–859.

Fries, J. F., Bloch, D. A., Sharp, J. T., McShane, D. J., Spitz, P., Bluhm, G. B., Forrester, D., Genant, H., Gofton, P., and Richman, S. Assessment of radiologic progression in rheumatoid arthritis: A randomized, controlled trial. *Arthritis and Rheumatology,* 1986, *29,* 1–9.

Friesen, W. V. Cultural Differences in Facial Expression in a Social Situation: An Experimental Test of the Concept of Display Rules. Doctoral dissertation, University of California, San Francisco, 1972.

Fromkin, V. *Speech Errors as Linguistic Evidence.* The Hague: Mouton Publishers, 1973.

Fuhrman, W., Rahe, D. F., and Hartup, W. W. Rehabilitation of socially withdrawn preschool children through mixed-age and same-age socialization. *Child Development,* 1979, *50,* 915–922.

Fulker, D. W., and Cardon, L. R. What can twin studies tell us about the structure and correlates of cognitive abilities? In *Twins as a Tool of Behavior Genetics* edited by T. J. Bouchard and P. Propping. Chichester, England: Wiley, 1993.

Fulton, J. F. *Functional Localization in Relation to Frontal Lobotomy.* New York: Oxford University Press, 1949.

Furnham, A. Just world beliefs in twelve societies. *The Journal of Social Psychology,* 1992, *133,* 317–329.

Furrow, D., and Nelson, K. A further look at the motherese hypothesis: A reply to Gleitman, Newport & Gleitman. *Journal of Child Language,* 1986, *13,* 163–176.

Furrow, D., Nelson, K., and Benedict, H. Mothers' speech to children and syntactic development: Some simple relationships. *Journal of Child Language,* 1979, *6,* 423–442.

Fuson, K. C., and Kwon, Y. Korean children's understanding of multidigit addition and subtraction. *Child Development,* 1992, *63,* 491–506.

Fuster, J. M. *Memory in the Cerebral Cortex: An Empirical Approach to Neural Networks in the Human and Nonhuman Primate.* Cambridge, MA: MIT Press, 1995.

Gabrieli, J. D. E., Cohen, N.J., and Corkin, S. The impaired learning of semantic knowledge following bilateral medial temporal-lobe resection. *Brain and Cognition,* 1988, *7,* 157–177.

Galaburda, A., and Kemper, T. L. Observations cited by Geschwind, N. Specializations of the human brain. *Scientific American,* 1979, *241,* 180–199.

Galaburda, A. M. Neurology of developmental dyslexia. *Current Opinion in Neurobiology,* 1993, *3,* 237–242.

Galaburda, A. M., Menard, M. T., and Rosen, G. D. Evidence for aberrant auditory anatomy in developmental dyslexia. *Proceedings of the National Academy of Sciences,* 1994, *91,* 8010–8013.

Galaburda, A. M., Sherman, G. F., Rosen, G. D., Aboitiz, F., and Geschwind, N. Developmental dyslexia: Four consecutive patients with cortical anomalies. *Annals of Neurology,* 1985, *18,* 222–233.

Galizio, M. Contingency-shaped and rule-governed behavior: Instructional control of human loss avoidance. *Journal of the Experimental Analysis of Behavior,* 1979, *31,* 53–70.

Galton, F. *Hereditary Genius: An Inquiry into Its Laws and Consequences.* Cleveland, OH: World Publishing, 1869.

Ganong, W. F. Phonetic categorization in auditory word perception. *Journal of Experimental Psychology: Human Perception and Performance,* 1980, *6,* 110–125.

Garcia, J., and Koelling, R. Relation of cue to consequence in avoidance learning. *Psychonomic Science,* 1966, *4,* 123–124.

Gardner, H. *Frames of Mind.* New York: Basic Books, 1983.

Gardner, R. A., and Gardner, B. T. Teaching sign language to a chimpanzee. *Science,* 1969, *165,* 664–672.

Gardner, R. A., and Gardner, B. T. Early signs of language in child and chimpanzee. *Science,* 1975, *187,* 752–753.

Gardner, R. A., and Gardner, B. T. Comparative psychology and language acquisition. *Annals of the New York Academy of Sciences,* 1978, *309,* 37–76.

Garrett, V., Brantly, P., Jones, G., and McNight, G. The relation between daily stress and Crohn's disease. *Journal of Behavioral Medicine,* 1991, *34,* 187–196.

Garrity, L. I. Electromyography: A review of the current status of subvocal speech research. *Memory and Cognition,* 1977, *5,* 615–622.

Gatchel, R. J., Baum, A., and Krantz, D. S. *An Introduction to Health Psychology,* 2nd ed. New York: Newbery Award Records, 1989.

Gazzaniga, M. S. *The Bisected Brain.* New York: Appleton-Century-Crofts, 1970.

Gazzaniga, M. S., and LeDoux, J. E. *The Integrated Mind.* New York: Plenum Press, 1978.

Geary, D. C. Reflections of evolution of culture in children's cognition: Implications for mathematical development and instruction. *American Psychologist,* 1995, *50,* 24–37.

Geiselman, R. E., Fisher, R. P., Firstenberg, I., Hutton, L. A., Sullivan, S., Avetissian, L., and Prosk, A. Enhancement of eyewitness memory: An empirical evaluation of the cognitive interview. *Journal of Police Science and Administration,* 1984, *12,* 74–80.

Geller, D. M., Goodstein, L., Silver, M., and Sternberg, W. C. On being ignored: The effects of the violation of implicit rules of social interaction. *Sociometry,* 1974, *37,* 541–556.

Geller, E. S. Seatbelt psychology. *Psychology Today,* 1985, *19,* 12–13.

Gelman, R. Logical capacity of very young children: Number invariance rules. *Child Development,* 1972, *43,* 75–90.

Gerbino, L., Oleshansky, M., and Gershon, S. Clinical use and mode of action of lithium. In *Psychopharmacology: A Generation of Progress,* edited by M. A. Lipton, A. DiMascio, and K. F. Killam. New York: Raven Press, 1978.

Gerlernter, J., Goldman, D., and Risch, N. The A1 allele at the D2 dopamine gene and alcoholism. *Journal of the American Medical Association,* 1993, *269,* 1673–1677.

Gerrard, M. Are men and women really different? In *Females, Males, and Sexuality,* edited by K. Kelley. Albany, NY: SUNY Press, 1986.

Geschwind, N., Quadfasel, F. A., and Segarra, J. M. Isolation of the speech area. *Neuropsychologia,* 1968, *6,* 327–340.

Geschwind, N. A., and Behan, P. O. Laterality, hormones, and immunity. In *Cerebral Dominance: The Biological Foundations,* edited by N. Geschwind and A. M. Galaburda. Cambridge, MA: Harvard University Press, 1984.

Gibson, E. J., and Walk, R. R. The "visual cliff." *Scientific American,* 1960, *202,* 2–9.

Gil, T. E. Psychological etiology to cancer: Truth or myth? *Israel Journal of Psychiatry and Related Sciences,* 1989, *26,* 164–185.

Gilligan, C. F. In a different voice: Women's conceptions of self and morality. *Harvard Educational Review,* 1977, *47,* 481–517.

Gilligan, C. F. *In a Different Voice.* Cambridge, MA: Harvard University Press, 1982.

Gironell, A., de la Calzada, M. D., Sagales, T., and Barraquer-Bordas, L. Absence of REM sleep and altered non-REM sleep caused by a haematoma in the pontine tegmentum. *Journal of Neurology, Neurosurgery and Psychiatry,* 1995, *59,* 195–196.

Gladwin, T. *East Is a Big Bird.* Cambridge, MA: Harvard University Press, 1970.

Glaser, R., Rice, J., Sheridan, J., Post, A., Fertel, R., Stout, J., Speicher, C. E., Kotur, M., and Kiecolt-Glaser, J. K. Stress-related immune suppression: Health implications. *Brain, Behavior, and Immunity,* 1987, *1,* 7–20.

Glenberg, A. M., Meyer, M., and Lindem, K. Mental models contribute to foregrounding during text comprehension. *Journal of Memory and Language,* 1987, *26,* 69–83.

Gluck, M. A., and Myers, C. E. Representation and association in memory: A neurocomputational view of hippocampal function. *Current Directions in Psychological Science,* 1995, *4,* 23–29.

Godden, D. R., and Baddeley, A. D. Context-dependent memory in two natural environments: On land and under water. *British Journal of Psychology,* 1975, *66,* 325–331.

Goldberg, L. R. Simple models or simple processes? Some research on clinical judgments. *American Psychologist,* 1968, *23,* 483–496.

Goldberg, L. R. The structure of phenotypic personality traits. *American Psychologist,* 1993, *48,* 26–34.

Goldin-Meadow, S., and Feldman, H. The development of language-like communication without a language model. *Science,* 1977, *197,* 401–403.

Goldstone, R. L., Medink, D. L., and Gentner, D. Relational similarity and the nonindependence of features in similarity judgments. *Cognitive Psychology,* 1991, *23,* 222–262.

Golstein, M. J., and Strachan, A. M. The family and schizophrenia. In *Family Interaction and Psychopathology: Theories, Methods, and Findings,* edited by T. Jacob. New York: Plenum, 1987.

Goodglass, H. Agrammatism. In *Studies in Neurolinguistics,* edited by H. Whitaker and H. A. Whitaker. New York: Academic Press, 1976.

Goodwin, D. W. *Phobias: The Facts.* London: Oxford University Press, 1983.

Goodwin, D. W., and Guze, S. B. *Psychiatric Diagnosis,* 3rd ed. New York: Oxford University Press, 1984.

Gottesman, I. I. *Schizophrenia Genesis. The Origins of Madness.* New York: Freeman, 1991.

Gottesman, I. I., and Bertelsen, A. Confirming unexpressed genotypes for schizophrenia. *Archives of General Psychiatry,* 1989, *46,* 867–872.

Gottesman, I. I., and Shields, J. *Schizophrenia: The Epigenetic Puzzle.* Cambridge: Cambridge University Press, 1982.

Gottfries, C. G. Alzheimer's disease and senile dementia: Biochemical characteristics and aspects of treatment. *Psychopharmacology,* 1985, *86,* 27–41.

Gould, S. J. *Ever Since Darwin: Reflections in Natural History.* New York: Norton, 1977.

Gould, S. J. *The Flamingo's Smile.* New York: Norton, 1985.

Graf, P., and Mandler, G. Activation makes words more accessible, but not necessarily more retrievable. *Journal of Verbal Learning and Verbal Behavior,* 1984, *23,* 553–568.

Graf, P., Squire, L. R., and Mandler, G. The information that amnesic patients do not forget. *Journal of Experimental Psychology: Learning, Memory, and Cognition,* 1984, *10,* 164–178.

Graham, J. R. *MMPI-2: Assessing Personality and Psychopathology.* New York: Oxford University Press, 1990.

Grant, P. R. *Ecology and Evolution of Darwin's Finches.* Princeton, NJ: Princeton University Press, 1986.

Gray, J. A. *The Psychology of Fear and Stress,* 2nd ed. Cambridge, England: Cambridge University Press, 1987.

Green, D. M., and Swets, J. A. *Signal Detection Theory and Psychophysics.* New York: Krieger, 1974.

Greenberg, R., and Pearlman, C. A. Cutting the REM nerve: An approach to the adaptive role of REM sleep. *Perspectives in Biology and Medicine,* 1974, *17,* 513–521.

Greenough, W. T., and Volkmar, F. R. Pattern of dendritic branching in occipital cortex of rats reared in complex environments. *Experimental Neurology,* 1973, *40,* 491–504.

Greenwald, A. G., Pratkanis, A. R., Leippe, M. R., and Baumgardner, M. H. Under what conditions does theory obstruct research progress? *Psychological Review,* 1986, *93,* 216–229.

Greenwald, D. F. An external construct validity study of Rorschach personality variables. *Journal of Personality Assessment,* 1990, *55,* 768–780.

Griffiths, M., and Payne, P. R. Energy expenditure in small children of obese and non-obese mothers. *Nature,* 1976, *260,* 698–700.

Griffiths, R. R., Bigelow, G. E., and Henningfield, J. E. Similarities in animal and human drug-taking behavior. In *Advances in Substance Abuse, Vol. 1,* edited by N. K. Mello. Greenwich, CT: JAI Press, 1980.

Grob, G. N. Mad, homeless, and unwanted: A history of the care of the chronically mentally ill in America. *Psychiatric Clinician of North America,* 1994, *17,* 541–558.

Grossarth-Maticek, R., Bastiaans, J., and Kanazir, D. T. Psychosocial factors as strong predictors of mortality from cancer, ischaemic heart disease and stroke: The Yugoslav prospective study. *Journal of Psychosomatic Research,* 1985, *29,* 167–176.

Grossarth-Maticek, R., and Eysenck, H. J. Personality, stress and disease: Description and validation of a new inventory. *Psychological Reports,* 1990, *66,* 355–373.

Guerin, B. Social behavior as a discriminative stimulus and consequence in social anthropology. *The Behavior Analyst,* 1992, *15,* 31–41.

Guerin, B. Generalized social consequences, ritually reinforced behaviors, and the difficulties of analyzing social contingencies in the real world. *Experimental Analysis of Human Behavior Bulletin,* 1995, *13,* 11–14.

Guilmette, T. J., Faust, D., Hart, K., and Arkes, H. R. A national survey of psychologists who offer neuropsychological services. *Archives of Clinical Neuropsychology,* 1990, *5,* 373–392.

Gustafson, G. E., and Harris, K. L. Women's responses to young infants' cries. *Developmental Psychology,* 1990, *26,* 144–152.

Gustavson, C. R., and Gustavson, J. C. Predation control using conditioned food aversion methodology: Theory, practice, and implications. *Annals of the New York Academy of Sciences,* 1985, *443,* 348–356.

Guze, S. B., and Robins, E. Suicide and primary affective disorders. *British Journal of Psychiatry,* 1970, *117,* 437–438.

Guze, S. B., Wolfgram, E. D., McKinney, J. K., and Cantwell, D. P. Psychiatric illness in the families of convicted criminals. A study of 519 first-degree relatives. *Disorders of the Nervous System,* 1967, *28,* 651–659.

Guze, S. B., Woodruff, R. A., and Clayton, P. J. Secondary affective disorder: A study of 95 cases. *Psychological Medicine,* 1971, *1,* 426–428.

Haaga, D. A., and Davison, G. C. Cognitive change methods. In *Helping People Change,* 3rd ed., edited by A. P. Goldstein and F. H. Kanfer. New York: Pergamon Press, 1989.

Haberlandt, K. *Cognitive Psychology.* Boston: Allyn and Bacon, 1994

Haenny, P. E., Maunsell, J. H., and Schiller, P. H. State dependent activity in monkey visual cortex. II. Retinal and extraretinal factors in V4. *Experimental Brain Research,* 1988, *69,* 245–259.

Hagan, F. E. *Research Methods in Criminal Justice and Criminology.* New York: Macmillan, 1982.

Hake, D. F. The basic-applied continuum and the possible evolution of human operant social and verbal research. *The Behavior Analyst,* 1982, *5,* 21–28.

Halaas, J. L., Gajiwala, K. S., Maffei, M., and Cohen, S. L. Weight-reducing effects of the plasma protein encoded by the obese gene. *Science,* 1995, *269,* 543–546.

Halford, G. S. Is children's reasoning logical or analytical? *Human Development,* 1990, *33,* 356–361.

Hall, C. S., and Nordby, V. J. *A Primer of Jungian Psychology.* New York: New American Library, 1973.

Hall, E. T. *The Hidden Dimension.* New York: Doubleday, 1966.

Halliday, M. A. K. *Learning How to Mean: Explorations in the Development of Language.* London: Edward Arnold, 1975.

Halmi, K. A. Anorexia nervosa: Recent investigations. *Annual Review of Medicine,* 1978, *29,* 137–148.

Hamilton, W. D. The genetical evolution of social behaviour: I and II. *Journal of Theoretical Biology,* 1964, *7,* 1–52.

Hamilton, W. D. Selfish and spiteful behavior in an evolutionary model. *Nature,* 1970, *228,* 1218–1220.

Hanson, J. W., Jones, K. L., and Smith, D. W. Fetal alcohol syndrome: Experience with 41 patients. *Journal of the American Medical Association,* 1976, *235,* 1458–1466.

Hare, R. D. Temporal gradient of fear arousal in psychopaths. *Journal of Abnormal Psychology,* 1965, *70,* 442–445.

Harkins, S. G., and Petty, R. E. Effects of task difficulty and task uniqueness on social loafing. *Journal of Personality and Social Psychology,* 1982, *43,* 1214–1229.

Harlow, H. *Learning to Love.* New York: J. Aronson, 1974.

Harris, M. *Cultural Anthropology,* 3rd ed. New York: HarperCollins, 1991.

Hartshorne, H., and May, M. A. *Studies in Deceit.* New York: Macmillan, 1928.

Harwood, R. L., Miller, J. G., and Irizarry, N. L. *Culture and Attachment: Perceptions of the Child in Context.* New York: Guilford, 1995.

Hatfield, E. Passionate and compassionate love. In *The Psychology of Love,* edited by R. J. Sternberg and M. L. Barnes. New Haven, CT: Yale University Press, 1988.

Hatfield, E., and Sprecher, S. *Mirror, Mirror . . . The Importance of Looks in Everyday Life.* Albany, NY: SUNY Press, 1986.

Hayes, C. *The Ape in Our House.* London: Gollancz, 1952.

Hayes, S. C. *Rule-governed Behavior: Cognition, Contingencies, and Instructional Control.* New York: Plenum, 1989.

Heath, A. C., Meyer, J. M., and Martin, N. G. Inheritance of alcohol consumption patterns in the Australian twin survey, 1981. In *Genetics and Biology of Alcoholism,* edited by C. R. Cloninger and H. Begleiter. Plainview, NY: Cold Spring Harbor Laboratory Press, 1990.

Hebb, D. O. *The Organization of Behaviour.* New York: Wiley-Interscience, 1949.

Hebb, D. O. Drives and the C. N. S. (conceptual nervous system). *Psychological Review,* 1955, *62,* 243–254.

Hebb, D. O., Lambert, W. E., and Tucker, G. R. A DMZ in the language war. *Psychology Today,* April 1973, pp. 55–62.

Heckler, M. M. *Fifth Special Report to the U.S. Congress on Alcohol and Health.* Washington, DC: U.S. Government Printing Office, 1983.

Heider, E. R. "Focal" color areas and the development of color names. *Developmental Psychology,* 1971, *4,* 447–455.

Heider, E. R. Universals in color naming and memory. *Journal of Experimental Psychology,* 1972, *93,* 10–20.

Heider, F. *The Psychology of Interpersonal Relations.* New York: John Wiley & Sons, 1958.

Hellhammer, D. H., Hubert, W., and Schurmeyer, T. Changes in saliva testosterone after psychological stimulation in men. *Psychoneuroendocrinology,* 1985, *10,* 77–81.

Helmer, D. C., Ragland, D. R., and Syme, S. L. Hostility and coronary artery disease.

American Journal of Epidemiology, 1991, *133,* 112–122.

Helzer, J. E., and Canino, G. J. *Alcoholism in North America, Europe, and Asia.* New York: Oxford University Press, 1992.

Henderson, N. D. Human behavior genetics. *Annual Review of Psychology,* 1982, *33,* 403–440.

Henke, P. G. The telencephalic limbic system and experimental gastric pathology: A review. *Neuroscience and Biobehavioral Reviews,* 1982, *6,* 381–390.

Herdt, G., and Lindenbaum, S. (Eds.). *Social Analyses in the Time of AIDS.* Newbury Park, CA: Sage, 1992.

Herrnstein, R. J., and Loveland, D. H. Complex visual concept in the pigeon. *Science,* 1964, *146,* 549–551.

Herrnstein, R. J., and Murray, C. *The Bell Curve.* New York: Free Press, 1994.

Higgins, E. T., Rholes, W. S., and Jones, C. R. Category accessibility and impression formation. *Journal of Experimental Social Psychology,* 1977, *13,* 141–154.

Higgins, S. T., Budney, A. J., and Bickel, W. K. Applying behavioral concepts and principles to the treatment of cocaine dependence. *Drug and Alcohol Dependence,* 1994, *7,* 19–38.

Higgins, S. T., Hughes, J. R., and Bickel, W. K. Effects of d-amphetamine on choice in social versus monetary reinforcement: A discrete trial test. *Pharmacology, Biochemistry, and Behavior,* 1989, *34,* 297–301.

Hilgard, E. R. Divided consciousness in hypnosis: The implications of the hidden observer. In *Hypnosis: Developments in Research and New Perspectives,* edited by E. Fromm and R. E. Shor. Chicago: Aldine Press, 1979.

Hintzman, D. L. Articulatory coding in short-term memory. *Journal of Verbal Learning and Verbal Behavior,* 1967, *6,* 312–316.

Hirschfeld, M. A. Comment. *Archives of General Psychiatry,* 1990, *47,* 685–686.

Hobson, J. A. *The Dreaming Brain.* New York: Basic Books, 1988.

Hofling, C. K. *Textbook of Psychiatry for Medical Practice.* Philadelphia: J. B. Lippincott, 1963.

Hofman, M. A., and Swaab, D. F. Sexual dimorphism of the human brain: Myth and reality. *Experimental and Clinical Endocrinology,* 1991, *98,* 161–170.

Hohman, G. W. Some effects of spinal cord lesions on experienced emotional feelings. *Psychophysiology,* 1966, *3,* 143–156.

Hollander, E., Schiffman, E., Cohen, B., Rivera-Stein, M. A., Rosen, W., Gorman, J. M., Fyer, A. J., Papp, L., and Liebowitz, M. R. Signs of central nervous system dysfunction in obsessive-compulsive disorder. *Archives of General Psychiatry,* 1990, *47,* 27–32.

Hollenbeck, A. R. Television viewing patterns of families with young infants. *Journal of Social Psychology,* 1978, *105,* 259–264.

Hollis, K. L. Pavlovian conditioning of signal-centered action patterns and autonomic behavior: A biological analysis of function. *Advances in the Study of Behavior,* 1982, *12,* 1–64.

Hollis, K. L., Cadieus, E. L., and Colbert, M. M. The biological function of pavlovian conditioning: A mechanism for mating success in the blue gourami (*Trichogaster trichopterus*). *Journal of Comparative Psychology,* 1989, *103,* 115–121.

Holmes, T. H., and Rahe, R. H. The social readjustment rating scale. *Journal of Psychosomatic Research,* 1967, *11,* 213, 218.

Holyoak, K. J., and Spellman, B. A. Thinking. *Annual Review of Psychology,* 1993, *44,* 265–315.

Holyoak, K. J. Problem solving. In *An Invitation to Cognitive Science. Vol. 3: Thinking,* edited by D. N. Osherson and E. E. Smith. Cambridge, MA: MIT Press, 1990.

Horn, J. L. Human ability systems. In *Life Span Development, Vol. 1,* edited by P. B. Baltes. New York: Academic Press, 1978.

Horn, J. L. The theory of fluid and crystallized intelligence in relation to concepts of cognitive psychology and aging in adulthood. In *Aging and Cognitive Processes,* edited by F. I. M. Craik and S. Trehub. New York: Plenum Press, 1982.

Horn, J. L., and Cattell, R. B. Refinement and test of the theory of fluid and crystallized ability intelligences. *Journal of Educational Psychology,* 1966, *57,* 253–270.

Horne, J. A. A review of the biological effects of total sleep deprivation in man. *Biological Psychology,* 1978, *7,* 55–102.

Horne, J. A., and Minard, A. Sleep and sleepiness following a behaviourally "active" day. *Ergonomics,* 1985, *28,* 567–575.

Horney, K. *Neurosis and Human Growth.* New York: Norton, 1950.

Hornik, R. Out-of-school television and schooling: Hypothesis and methods. *Review of Educational Research,* 1981, *51,* 199–214.

Hovland, C. I., and Weiss, W. The influence of source credibility on communication effectiveness. *Public Opinion Quarterly,* 1951, *15,* 635–650.

Howard, J. H., Cunningham, D. A., and Rechnitzer, P. A. Health patterns associated with type A behavior: A managerial population. *Journal of Human Stress,* 1976, *2,* 24–31.

Howard, R. W. *Learning and Memory: Major Ideas, Principles, Issues, and Applications.* Westport, CT: Praeger, 1995.

Howlett, A. C. Reverse pharmacology applied to the cannabinoid receptor. *Trends in Pharmacological Sciences,* 1990, *11,* 395–397.

Hoyenga, K. B., and Hoyenga, K. T. *Gender-Related Differences: Origins and Outcomes.* Boston: Allyn and Bacon, 1993.

Hubel, D. H., and Wiesel, T. N. Functional architecture of macaque monkey visual cortex. *Proceedings of the Royal Society of London, Series B,* 1977, *198,* 1–59.

Hubel, D. H., and Wiesel, T. N. Brain mechanisms of vision. *Scientific American,* 1979, *241,* 150–162.

Hughes, J. R., and Pierattini, R. An introduction to pharmacotherapy. In *Psychopharmacology: Basic Mechanisms and Applied Interventions: Master Lectures in Psychology,* edited by J. Grabowski and G. R. Vandenbos. Washington, DC: American Psychological Association, 1992.

Hulit, L. M., and Howard, M. R. *Born to Talk: An Introduction to Speech and Language Development.* New York: Merrill/Macmillan, 1993.

Humphrey, N. K. Species and individuals in the perceptual world of monkeys. *Perception,* 1974, *3,* 105–114.

Hunt, E. Verbal ability. In *Human Abilities: An Information-Processing Approach,* edited by R. J. Sternberg. New York: W. H. Freeman, 1985.

Hunt, M. *Sexual Behavior in the 1970s.* Chicago: Playboy, 1974.

Huston, A. C. Sex-typing. In *Handbook of Child Psychology: Vol. 4. Socialization, Personality, and Social Development,* edited by E. M. Hetherington. New York: Wiley, 1983.

Huston, A. C., Watkins, B. A., and Kunkel, D. Public policy and children's television. *American Psychologist,* 1989, *44,* 424–433.

Huston, A. C., Wright, J. C., Rice, M. L., Kerkman, D., and St. Peters, M. Development of television viewing patterns in early childhood: A longitudinal investigation. *Developmental Psychology,* 1990, *26,* 409–420.

Hyde, T. S., and Jenkins, J. J. The differential effects of incidental tasks on the organization of recall of a list of highly associated words. *Journal of Experimental Psychology,* 1969, *82,* 472–481.

Hymes, R. W., Leinart, M., Rowe, S., and Rogers, W. Acquaintance rape: The effect of race of the defendant and the race of the victim on white juror decisions. *The Journal of Social Psychology,* 1993, *133,* 627–634.

Hyten, C., and Reilly, M. P. The renaissance of the experimental analysis of human behavior. *The Behavior Analyst,* 1992, *15,* 109–114.

Ickes, W., Patterson, M. L., Rajecki, D. W., and Tanford, S. Behavioral and cognitive consequences of reciprocal versus compensatory responses to pre-interaction expectancies. *Social Cognition,* 1982, *1,* 160–190.

Inglefinger, F. J. The late effects of total and subtotal gastrectomy. *New England Journal of Medicine,* 1944, *231,* 321–327.

Inoue, M., Koyanagi, T., Nakahara, H., Hara, K., Hori, E., and Nakano, H. Functional development of human eye movement in utero assessed quantitatively with real time ultrasound. *American Journal of Obstetrics and Gynecology,* 1986, *155,* 170–174.

Irvine, J., Garner, D. M., Craig, H. M., and Logan, A. G. Prevalence of type A behavior in untreated hypertensive individuals. *Hypertension,* 1991, *18,* 72–78.

Irwin, C. J. The evolution of ethnocentrism. In *The Sociobiology of Ethnocentrism,* edited by V. Reynolds, V. Falger, and I. Vine. London: Croom Helm, 1987.

Isabella, R. A., and Belsky, J. Interactional synchrony and the origins of infant-mother attachment: A replication study. *Child Development,* 1991, *62,* 373–384.

Isenberg, D. J. Group polarization: A critical review and meta-analysis. *Psychological Bulletin,* 1986, *50,* 1141–1151.

Izard, C. E. *The Face of Emotion.* New York: Appleton-Century-Crofts, 1971.

Jacklin, C. N., and Maccoby, E. E. Issues of gender differentiation in normal development. In *Developmental-Behavioral Pediatrics,* edited by M. D. Levine, W. B. Carey, A. C. Crocker, and R. T. Gross. Philadelphia: Saunders, 1983.

Jacob, F. Evolution and tinkering. *Science,* 1977, *196,* 1161–1166.

Jacobsen, C. F., Wolf, J. B., and Jackson, T. A. An experimental analysis of the functions of the frontal association areas in primates. *Journal of Nervous and Mental Disease,* 1935, *82,* 1–14.

Jaffe, J. H. Drug addiction and drug abuse. In *The Pharmacological Basis of Therapeutics, Vol. 7,* edited by L. S. Goodman and A. Gilman. New York: Macmillan, 1985.

James, W. What is an emotion? *Mind,* 1884, *9,* 188–205.

James, W. *Principles of Psychology.* New York: Henry Holt, 1890.

James, W. *The Principles of Psychology: Vol. 1.* New York: Holt, 1893.

James, W. P. T., and Trayhurn, P. Thermogenesis and obesity. *British Medical Bulletin,* 1981, *37,* 43–48.

Janis, I. L. *Victims of Groupthink.* Boston: Houghton Mifflin, 1972.

Janis, I. L. *Groupthink: Psychological Studies of Policy Decisions and Fiascoes.* Boston: Houghton Mifflin, 1982.

Javal, E. Essai sur la physiologie de la lecture. *Annales D'Oculistique,* 1879, *82,* 242–253.

Jaynes, J. The problem of animate motion in the seventeenth century. *Journal of the History of Ideas,* 1970, *6,* 219–234.

Jeffcoate, W. J., Lincoln, N. B., Selby, C., and Herbert, M. Correlations between anxiety and serum prolactin in humans. *Journal of Psychosomatic Research,* 1986, *30,* 217–222.

Jenkins, J. G., and Dallenbach, K. M. Oblivescence during sleep and waking. *American Journal of Psychology,* 1924, *35,* 605–612.

Jenkins, J. H., and Karno, M. The meaning of expressed emotion: Theoretical issues raised by cross-cultural research. *American Journal of Psychiatry,* 1992, *149,* 9–21.

Jensen, A. R. The nature of the black-white difference on various psychometric tests: Spearman's hypothesis. *Behavioral and Brain Sciences,* 1985, *8,* 193–263.

Jensen, T., Genefke, I., and Hyldebrandt, N. Cerebral atrophy in young torture victims. *New England Journal of Medicine,* 1982, *307,* 1341.

Jeste, D. V., Del Carmen, R., Lohr, J. B., and Wyatt, R. J. Did schizophrenia exist before the eighteenth century? *Comprehensive Psychiatry,* 1985, *26,* 493–503.

Johansson, G. Visual perception of biological motion and a model for its analysis. *Perception and Psychophysics,* 1973, *14,* 201–211.

Johnson, J. H., Butcher, J. N., Null, C., and Johnson, K. N. Replicated item level factor analysis of the full MMPI. *Journal of Personality and Social Psychology,* 1984, *47,* 105–114.

Johnson, J. S., and Newport, E. L. Critical period effects in second language learning: The influence of maturational state on the acquisition of English as a second language. *Cognitive Psychology,* 1989, *21,* 60–99.

Johnson, S. B., and Sechrest, L. Comparison of desensitization and progressive relaxation in treating test anxiety. *Journal of Consulting and Clinical Psychology,* 1968, *32,* 280–286.

Johnson-Laird, P. N. *Mental Models.* Cambridge, MA: Harvard University Press, 1983.

Johnson-Laird, P. N. Deductive reasoning ability. In *Human Abilities: An Information-Processing Approach,* edited by R. J. Sternberg. New York: W. H. Freeman, 1985.

Johnson-Laird, P. N., and Byrne, R. M. J. *Deduction.* Hillsdale, NJ: Erlbaum Associates, 1991.

Johnson-Laird, P. N., Byrne, R. M. J., and Schaeken, W. Propositional reasoning by model. *Psychological Review,* 1992, *99,* 418–439.

Johnston, W. A., and Dark, V. J. Selective attention. *Annual Review of Psychology,* 1986, *37,* 43–76.

Johnstone, E. C., Crow, T. J., Frith, C. D., Stevens, M., Kreel, L., and Husband, J. The dementia of dementia praecox. *Acta Psychiatrica Scandinavica,* 1978, *57,* 305–324.

Jones, D. C. Friendship satisfaction and gender: An examination of sex differences in contributors to friendship satisfaction. *Journal of Social and Personal Relationships,* 1991, *8,* 167–185.

Jones, D. T., and Reed, R. R. G$_{olf}$: An olfactory neuron specific-G protein involved in odorant signal transduction. *Science,* 1989, *244,* 790–795.

Jones, E. E. *Interpersonal Perception.* New York: W. H. Freeman, 1990.

Jones, E. E., and Nisbett, R. E. The actor and observer: Divergent perceptions of the causes of behavior. In *Attribution: Perceiving the Causes of Behavior,* edited by E. E. Jones, D. E. Kamouse, H. H. Kelley, R. E. Nisbett, S. Valins, and B. Weiner. Morristown, NJ: General Learning Press, 1971.

Jones, M. C., and Bayley, N. Physical maturing among boys as related to behavior. *Journal of Educational Psychology,* 1950, *41,* 129–184.

Jouvet, M. The role of monoamines and acetylcholine-containing neurons in the regulation of the sleep-waking cycle. *Ergebnisse der Physiologie,* 1972, *64,* 166–307.

Julesz, B. Texture and visual perception. *Scientific American,* 1965, *212,* 38–48.

Julien, R. M. *A Primer of Drug Action.* New York: Freeman, 1992.

Just, M. A., and Carpenter, P. A. A theory of reading: From eye fixations to comprehension. *Psychological Review,* 1980, *87,* 329–354.

Just, M. A., and Carpenter, P. A. *The Psychology of Reading and Language Comprehension.* Boston: Allyn and Bacon, 1987.

Just, M. A., Carpenter, P. A., and Wu, R. *Eye Fixations in the Reading of Chinese Technical Text* (Technical Report). Pittsburgh: Carnegie-Mellon University, 1983.

Justice, A. Review of the effects of stress on cancer in laboratory animals: Importance of time of stress application and type of tumor. *Psychological Bulletin,* 1985, *98,* 108–138.

Kagan, J., Kearsley, R. B., and Zelazo, P. R. *Infancy: Its Place in Human Development.* Cambridge, MA: Harvard University Press, 1978.

Kagan, J., Reznick, J. S., and Snidman, N. Biological bases of childhood shyness. *Science,* 1988, *240,* 167–171.

Kales, A., Scharf, M. B., Kales, J. D., and Soldatos, C. R. Rebound insomnia: A potential hazard following withdrawal of certain benzodiazepines. *Journal of the American Medical Association,* 1979, *241,* 1692–1695.

Kalish, R. A. Death and dying in a social context. In *Handbook of Aging and the Social Sciences,* edited by R. H. Binstock and E. Shanas. New York: Van Nostrand Reinhold, 1976.

Kane, J., Honigfeld, G., Singer, J., Meltzer, H., and the Clozaril Collaborative Study Group. Clozapine for the treatment-resistant schizophrenic: A double-blind comparison with chlorpromazine. *Archives of General Psychiatry,* 1988, *45,* 789–796.

Kanfer, F. H., and Phillips, J. S. *Learning Foundations of Behavior Therapy.* New York: John Wiley & Sons, 1970.

Kaplan, E. L., and Kaplan, G. A. The prelinguistic child. In *Human Development and Cognitive Processes,* edited by J. Eliot. New York: Holt, Rinehart and Winston, 1970.

Kapp, B. S., Gallagher, M., Applegate, C. D., and Frysinger, R. C. The amygdala central nucleus: Contributions to conditioned cardiovascular responding during aversive Pavlovian conditioning in the rabbit. In *Conditioning: Representation of Involved Neural Functions,* edited by C. D. Woody. New York: Plenum Press, 1982.

Karau, S. J., and Williams, K. D. Social loafing: Research findings, implications, and future directions. *Current Directions in Psychological Science,* 1995, *4,* 134–139.

Karbe, H., Herholz, K., Szelies, B., Pawlik, G., Wienhard, K., et al. Regional metabolic correlates of token test results in cortical and subcortical left hemispheric infarction. *Neurology,* 1989, *39,* 1083–1088.

Karbe, H., Szelies, B., Herholz, K., and Heiss, W. D. Impairment of language is related to left parieto-temporal glucose metabolism in aphasic stroke patients. *Journal of Neurology,* 1990, *237,* 19–23.

Katerndahl, D. A., and Realini, J. P. Lifetime prevalence rates of panic states. *American Journal of Psychiatry,* 1993, *150,* 246–249.

Katz, D. *The World of Colour.* London: Kegan Paul, Trench, Trubner, 1935.

Kausler, D. H. *Learning and Memory in Normal Aging.* New York: Academic Press, 1994.

Kay, P. Synchronic variability and diachronic changes in basic color terms. *Language in Society,* 1975, *4,* 257–270.

Kazdin, A. E. *Behavior Modification in Applied Settings.* Pacific Grove, CA: Brooks/Cole, 1994.

Keller, S. E., Weiss, J. M., Schleifer, S. J., Miller, N. E., and Stein, M. Stress-induced suppression of immunity in adrenalectomized rats. *Science,* 1983, *221,* 1301–1304.

Kelley, H. H. Attribution theory in social psychology. In *Nebraska Symposium on Motivation, Vol. 15,* edited by D. Levine. Lincoln: University of Nebraska Press, 1967.

Kelley, H. H., and Michela, J. L. Attribution theory and research. *Annual Review of Psychology,* 1980, *31,* 457–501.

Kenrick, D. T., and Cialdini, R. B. Romantic attraction: Misattribution versus reinforcement explanations. *Journal of Personality and Social Psychology,* 1977, *35,* 381–391.

Kenrick, D. T., Groth, G., Trost, M. R., and Sadalla, E. K. Integrating evolutionary and social exchange perspectives on relationships: Effects of gender, self-appraisal, and involvement level in mate selection. *Journal of Personality and Social Psychology*, 1993, *64*, 951–969.

Kenrick, D. T., Neuberg, S. L., Zierk, K. L., and Krones, J. M. Evolution and social cognition: Contrast effects as a function of sex, dominance, and physical attractiveness. *Personality and Social Psychology Bulletin*, 1994, *20*, 210–217.

Kertesz, A. Anatomy of jargon. In *Jargonaphasia*, edited by J. Brown. New York: Academic Press, 1981.

Kessler, R. C., McGonagle, K. A., Zhao, S., Nelson, C., Hughes, M., Eshleman, S., Wittchen, H., and Kendler, K. Lifetime and 12–month prevalence of DSM-III-R psychiatric disorders in the United States. *Archives of General Psychiatry*, 1994, *51*, 8–19.

Kety, S. S., Rosenthal, D., Wender, P. H., and Schulsinger, F. The types and prevalence of mental illness in the biological and adoptive families of adopted schizophrenics. In *The Transmission of Schizophrenia*, edited by D. Rosenthal and S. S. Kety. Elmsford, NY: Pergamon Press, 1968.

Keyes, D. *The Minds of Billy Milligan*. New York: Bantam, 1981.

Khachaturian, Z. S., and Blass, J. P. *Alzheimer's Disease: New Treatment Strategies.* New York: Dekker, 1992.

Kiang, N. Y. -S. *Discharge Patterns of Single Nerve Fibers in the Cat's Auditory Nerve.* Cambridge, MA: MIT Press, 1965.

Kiecolt-Glaser, J. K., Glaser, R., Shuttleworth, E. C., Dyer, C. S., Ogrocki, P., and Speicher, C. E. Chronic stress and immunity in family caregivers of Alzheimer's disease victims. *Psychosomatic Medicine*, 1987, *49*, 523–535.

Kihlstrom, J. F. Hypnosis. *Annual Review of Psychology*, 1985, *36*, 385–418.

Kimura, D. Are men's and women's brains really different? *Canadian Psychology*, 1987, *28*, 133–147.

Kinsey, A., Pomeroy, W. B., and Martin, C. E. *Sexual Behavior in the Human Male.* Philadelphia: Saunders, 1948.

Kinsey, A., Pomeroy, W. B., Martin, C. E. and Gebhard, P. H. *Sexual Behavior in the Human Female.* Philadelphia: Saunders, 1953.

Kirasic, K. C. Spatial cognition and behavior in young and elderly adults: Implications for learning new environments. *Psychology and Aging*, 1991, *6*, 10–18.

Kirasic, K. C., and Bernicki, M. R. Acquisition of spatial knowledge under conditions of temporospatial discontinuity in young and elderly adults. *Psychological Research*, 1990, *52*, 76–79.

Kissen, D. M. Personality characteristics in males conducive to lung cancer. *British Journal of Medical Psychology*, 1963, *36*, 27–36.

Kitayama, S., and Markus, H. R. Construal of self as cultural frame: Implications for internalizing psychology. Paper presented at Symposium on Internalization and Higher Education, Ann Arbor, MI, May 1992.

Klein, D. F., Zitrin, C. M., Woerner, M. G., and Ross, D. C. Treatment of phobias. II. Behavior therapy and supportive psychotherapy: Are there any specific ingredients? *Archives of General Psychiatry*, 1983, *40*, 139–145.

Kleitman, N. The nature of dreaming. In *The Nature of Sleep*, edited by G. E. W. Wolstenholme and M. O'Connor. London: J.&A. Churchill, 1961.

Kleitman, N. Basic rest-activity cycle—22 years later. *Sleep*, 1982, *4*, 311–317.

Klerman, G. L., and Weissman, M. M. The interpersonal approach to understanding depression. In *Contemporary Directions in Psychopathology: Toward the DMS-IV*, edited by T. Millon and G. L. Klerman. New York: Guilford Press, 1986.

Kline, M. V. The production of antisocial behavior through hypnosis: New clinical data. *International Journal of Clinical and Experimental Hypnosis*, 1972, *20*, 80–94.

Kluft, R. P. An introduction to multiple personality disorder. *Psychiatric Annals*, 1984, *7*, 9–29.

Knowlton, B. J., Ramus, S., and Squire, L. R. Normal acquisition of an artificial grammar by amnesic patients. *Society for Neuroscience Abstracts*, 1991, *17*, 4.

Knox, R. E., and Inkster, J. A. Postdecision dissonance at post time. *Journal of Personality and Social Psychology*, 1968, *8*, 310–323.

Kobasa, S. C. Stress life events, personality, and health: An inquiry into hardiness. *Journal of Personality and Social Psychology*, 1979, *42*, 168–177.

Koch, J. L. A. *Leitfaden der Psychiatrie*, 2nd ed. Ravensburg, Austria: Dorn, 1889.

Köhler, W. *The Mentality of Apes*, 2nd ed. New York: Liveright, 1927/1973.

Kolb, B., and Whishaw, I. W. *Fundamentals of Human Neuropsychology*. New York: W. H. Freeman, 1990.

Konner, M. J. Aspects of the developmental ethology of a foraging people. In *Ethological Studies of Child Behaviour*, edited by N. Blurton Jones. Cambridge: Cambridge University Press, 1972.

Kosslyn, S. M. Scanning visual images: Some structural implications. *Perception and Psychophysics*, 1973, *14*, 90–94.

Kosslyn, S. M. Evidence for analogue representation. Paper presented at the Conference on Theoretical Issues in Natural Language Processing, Massachusetts Institute of Technology, Cambridge, MA, July 1975.

Kozlowski, L. T., and Cutting, J. E. Recognizing the sex of a walker from a dynamic point-light display. *Perception and Psychophysics*, 1977, *21*, 575–580.

Kozulin, A., and Falik, L. Dynamic cognitive assessment of the child. *Current Directions in Psychological Science*, 1995, *4*, 192–196.

Kral, J. G. Surgical treatment of obesity. *Medical Clinics of North America*, 1989, *73*, 251–264.

Kramer, F. M., Jeffery, R. W., Forster, J. L., and Snell, M. K. Long-term follow-up of behavioral treatment for obesity: Patterns of weight regain among men and women. *International Journal of Obesity*, 1989, *13*, 123–136.

Kraut, R. E., and Johnston, R. Social and emotional messages of smiling: An ethological approach. *Journal of Personality and Social Psychology*, 1979, *37*, 1539–1553.

Kroger, W. S., and Doucé, R. G. Hypnosis in criminal investigation. *International Journal of Clinical and Experimental Hypnosis*, 1979, *27*, 358–374.

Krueger, T. H. *Visual Imagery in Problem Solving and Scientific Creativity.* Derby, CT: Seal Press, 1976.

Krull, D. S., and Erickson, D. J. Inferential hopscotch: How people draw social inferences from behavior. *Current Directions in Psychological Science*, 1995, *4*, 35–38.

Kubitz, K. A., and Landers, D. M. The effects of aerobic exercise on cardiovascular responses to mental stress: An examination of underlying mechanisms. *Journal of Sport and Exercise Physiology*, 1993, *15*, 326–337.

Kubler-Ross, E. *On Death and Dying.* New York: Macmillan, 1969.

Kubler-Ross, E. *Living with Death and Dying.* New York: Macmillan, 1981.

Kuhl, P. K., Williams, K. A., Lacerda, F., Stevens, K. N., and Lindblom, B. Linguistic experience alters phonetic perception in infants by 6 months of age. *Science*, 1992, *255*, 606–608.

Kulka, R. A., and Kessler, J. R. Is justice really blind? The effect of litigant physical attractiveness on judicial judgment. *Journal of Applied Social Psychology*, 1978, *4*, 336–381.

Kulka, R. A., Schlenger, W. E., Fairbank, J. A., Hough, R. L., Jordan, B. K., Marmar, C. R., and Weiss, D. S. *Trauma and the Vietnam War Generation: Report of Findings from the National Vietnam Veterans Readjustment Study.* New York: Brunner/Mazel, 1990.

Kunst-Wilson, W. R., and Zajonc, R. B. Affective discrimination of stimuli that cannot be recognized. *Science*, 1980, *207*, 557–558.

Kupfer, D. J. REM latency: A psychobiologic marker for primary depressive disease. *Biological Psychiatry*, 1976, *11*, 159–174.

Ladame, P. L. L'hypnotisme et la médecine légale. *Archives d l'Anthropologie Criminelle et des Sciences Pénales*, 1887, *2*, 293–335; 520–559.

Lakoff, G., and Turner, M. *More Than Cool Reason: The Power of Poetic Metaphor.* Chicago: University of Chicago Press, 1989.

Lange, C. G. *Über Gemüthsbewegungen.* Leipzig, East Germany: T. Thomas, 1887.

Langer, E. J., and Abelson, R. P. A patient by any other name . . . : Clinician group difference in labeling bias. *Journal of Consulting and Clinical Psychology*, 1974, *42*, 4–9.

Langer, E. J., Bashner, R. S., and Chanowitz, B. Decreasing prejudice by increasing discrimination. *Journal of Personality and Social Psychology*, 1985, *49*, 113–120.

Langlois, J. H., and Downs, A. C. Mothers, fathers, and peers as socialization agents of sex-typed play behaviors in young children. *Child Development*, 1980, *51*, 1237–1247.

Lankenau, H., Swigar, M. E., Bhimani, S., Luchins, D., and Quinlon, D. M. Cranial CT scans in eating disorder patients and controls. *Comprehensive Psychiatry*, 1985, *26*, 136–147.

LaPiere, R. T. Attitudes and actions. *Social Forces*, 1934, *13*, 230–237.

Latané, B., and Darley, J. M. *The Unresponsive Bystander: Why Doesn't He Help?* New York: Appleton-Century-Crofts, 1970.

Lauer, R. H. *Social Problems and the Quality of Life.* Dubuque, IA: W. C. Brown, 1989.

Laurence, J. -R., and Perry, C. *Hypnosis, Will, and Memory: A Psycho-Legal History.* New York: Guilford Press, 1988.

Lauter, J., Herscovitch, P., Formby, C., and Raichle, M. E. Tonotopic organization in human auditory cortex revealed by positron emission tomography. *Hearing Research,* 1985, *20,* 199–205.

Lavie, P., Pratt, H., Scharf, B., Peled, R., and Brown, J. Localized pontine lesion: Nearly total absence of REM sleep. *Neurology,* 1984, *34,* 1118–1120.

Lazarus, A. A. *Behavior Therapy and Beyond.* New York: McGraw-Hill, 1971.

Lazarus, R. S. Thoughts on the relations between emotion and cognition. In *Approaches to Emotion,* edited by K. R. Scherer and P. Ekman. Hillsdale, NJ: Lawrence Erlbaum Associates, 1984.

Lazarus, R. S., and Folkman, S. *Stress, Appraisal, and Coping.* New York: Springer, 1984.

LeDoux, J. E. Brain mechanisms of emotion and emotional learning. *Current Opinion in Neurobiology,* 1992, *2,* 191–197.

LeDoux, J. E. Emotion: Clues from the brain. *Annual Review of Psychology,* 1995, *46,* 209–235.

Lee, Y. T. Ingroup preference and homogeneity among African American and Chinese American students. *Journal of Social Psychology,* 1993, *133,* 225–235.

Leech, S., and Witte, K. L. Paired-associate learning in elderly adults as related to pacing and incentive conditions. *Developmental Psychology,* 1971, *5,* 180.

Lefkowitz, M. M., Eron, L. D., Walder, L. O., and Huesmann, L. R. *Growing Up to Be Violent: A Longitudinal Study of the Development of Aggression.* New York: Pergamon Press, 1977.

Lefley, H. P. Delivering mental health services across cultures. In *Mental Health Services: The Cross-Culture Perspective,* edited by P. B. Pedersen, N. Sartorius, and A. Marsella. Beverly Hills, CA: Sage, 1984

Lefley, H. P. Mental health treatment and service delivery in cross-cultural perspective. In *Cross-Cultural Topics in Psychology,* edited by L. L. Adler and U. P. Gielen. Westport, CT: Praeger, 1994.

Leger, D. W. *Biological Foundations of Behavior.* New York: HarperCollins, 1991.

Leli, D. A., and Filskov, S. B. Clinical detection of intellectual deterioration associated with brain damage. *Journal of Clinical Psychology,* 1984, *40,* 1435–1441.

Lennenberg, E. *Biological Foundations of Language.* New York: Wiley, 1967.

Leon, G. R. *Case Histories of Deviant Behavior,* 2nd ed. Boston: Allyn and Bacon, 1977.

Leonard, H. L., Swedo, S. E., Rapoport, J. L., Koby, E. V., Lenane, M. C., Cheslow, D. L., and Hamburger, S. D. Treatment of obsessive-compulsive disorder with clomipramine and desipramine in children and adolescents: A double-blind crossover comparison. *Archives of General Psychiatry,* 1989, *46,* 1088–1092.

Lerman, P. *Deinstitutionalization: A Cross-Problem Analysis.* Rockville, MD: U.S. Department of Health and Human Services, 1981.

Lerner, M. J. The unjust consequences of the need to believe in a just world. Paper pre-

sented at the meeting of the American Psychological Association, 1966.

LeShan, L. L., and Worthington, R. E. Personality as a factor in the pathogenesis of cancer: A review of literature. *British Journal of Medical Psychology,* 1956, *29,* 49–56.

LeVay, S. A difference in hypothalamic structure between heterosexual and homosexual men. *Science,* 1991, *253,* 1034–1037.

Levinson, D. J., Darrow, C. N., Klein, E. B., Levinson, M. H., and McKee, B. *The Seasons of a Man's Life.* New York: Alfred A. Knopf, 1978.

Lewinsohn, P. M., Mischel, W., Chaplin, W., and Barton, R. Social competence and depression: The role of illusory self-perceptions. *Journal of Abnormal Psychology,* 1980, *89,* 194–202.

Lewis, M., Young, G., Brooks, J., and Michalson, L. The beginning of friendship. In *Friendship and Peer Relations,* edited by M. Lewis and L. A. Rosenblum. New York: John Wiley & Sons, 1975.

Liberman, A. M., Cooper, F. S., Shankweiler, D. P., and Studdert-Kennedy, M. Perception of the speech code. *Psychological Review,* 1967, *74,* 431–461.

Lickey, M. E., and Gordon, B. *Drugs for Mental Illness.* New York: Freeman, 1983.

Lidz, T., Fleck, S., and Cornelison, A. R. *Schizophrenia and the Family.* New York: International Universities Press, 1965.

Liégeois, J. Rapports de la suggestion et du somnambulisme avec la jurisprudence et la médecine légale: La responsabilité dans les états hypnotiques. In *Premier Congrès International de l'Hypnotisme Expérimentale et Thérapeutique: Comptes Rendus.* Paris: Octave Doin, 1889.

Light, K. A., and Girdler, S. S. Cardiovascular health and women. In *The Health Psychology of Women,* edited by C. A Niven and D. Carroll. Chur, Switzerland: Harwood Press, 1993.

Lindsley, O. R. Operant conditioning methods applied to research in chronic schizophrenia. *Psychiatric Research Reports,* 1956, *24,* 289–291.

Linsky, A. S., Bachman, R., and Straus, M. A. *Stress, Culture, and Aggression.* New Haven, CT: Yale University Press, 1995.

Linville, P. W. The complexity-extremity effect and age-based stereotyping. *Journal of Personality and Social Psychology,* 1982, *42,* 183–211.

Linville, P. W., Fischer, G. W., and Salovey, P. Perceived distributions of the characteristics of in-group and out-group members: Empirical evidence and a computer simulation. *Journal of Personality and Social Psychology,* 1989, *57,* 165–188.

Lipsitz, A., Brake, G., Vincent, E. J., and Winters, M. Another round for the brewers: Television ads and children's alcohol expectancies. *Journal of Applied Social Psychology,* 1993, *23,* 439–450.

Lisker, L., and Abramson, A. The voicing dimension: Some experiments in comparative phonetics. In *Proceedings of Sixth International Congress of Phonetic Sciences, Prague, 1967.* Prague: Academia, 1970.

Livingstone, M. S., and Hubel, D. Segregation of form, color, movement, and depth:

Anatomy, physiology, and perception. *Science,* 1988, *240,* 740–749.

Locke, J. L. *The Child's Path to Spoken Language.* Cambridge, MA: Harvard University Press, 1993.

Loeb, G. E. Cochlear prosthetics. *Annual Review of Neuroscience,* 1990, *13,* 357–371.

Loehlin, J. C. *Genes and Environment in Personality Development.* London: Sage Publications, 1992.

Loehlin, J. C., and Nichols, R. C. *Heredity, Environment, and Personality.* Austin: University of Texas Press, 1976.

Loftus, E. F. *Eyewitness Testimony.* Cambridge, MA: Harvard University Press, 1979.

Loftus, E. F., and Palmer, J. C. Reconstruction of automobile destruction: An example of the interaction between language and memory. *Journal of Verbal Learning and Verbal Behavior,* 1974, *13,* 585–589.

Loftus, E. F., and Zanni, G. Eyewitness testimony: The influence of the wording of a question. *Bulletin of the Psychonomic Society,* 1975, *5,* 86–88.

Lombardo, R., and Carreno, L. Relationship of type A behavior pattern in smokers to carbon monoxide exposure and smoking topography. *Health Psychology,* 1987, *6,* 445–452.

Loomis, W. F. Skin pigment regulation of vitamin-D biosynthesis in man. *Science,* 1967, *157,* 501–506.

LoPiccolo, J., and Friedman, J. M. Sex therapy: An integrated model. In *Contemporary Psychotherapies: Models and Methods,* edited by S. J. Lynn and J. P. Garskee. New York: Merrill, 1985.

Lorenz, K. *On Aggression.* New York: Harcourt Brace Jovanovich, 1966.

Lowe, C. F. Determinants of human operant behavior. In *Advances in the Analysis of Behavior: Vol. 1: Reinforcement and the Organization of Behaviour,* edited by M. D. Zeiler and P. Harzem. Chichester, England: Wiley, 1979.

Lowe, C. F., Beasty, A., and Bentall, R. P. The role of verbal behavior in human learning: Infant performance on fixed-interval schedules. *Journal of the Experimental Analysis of Behavior,* 1983, *39,* 157–164.

Luborsky, L., Chandler, M., Auerbach, A. H., Cohen, J., and Bachrach, H. M. Factors influencing the outcome of psychotherapy: A review of quantitative research. *Psychological Bulletin,* 1971, *75,* 145–185.

Luck, S., Chelazzi, L., Hillyard, S., and Desimone, R. Effects of spatial attention on responses of V4 neurons in the macaque. *Society for Neuroscience Abstracts,* 1993, *69,* 27.

Lumeng, L., Murphy, J. M., McBride, W. J., and Li, T. Genetic influences on alcohol preferences in animals. In *The Genetics of Alcoholism,* edited by H. Begleiter and B. Kissin. New York: Oxford University Press, 1995.

Lundy, A. C. The reliability of the Thematic Apperception Test. *Journal of Personality Assessment,* 1985, *49,* 141–145.

Lundy, A. C. Instructional set and thematic apperception test validity. *Journal of Personality Assessment,* 1988, *52,* 309–320.

Lupfer, M. B., Clark, L. F., and Hutcherson, H. W. Impact of context on spontaneous trait and situational attributions. *Journal of*

Personality and Social Psychology, 1990, *58,* 239–249.

Lutsky, N. When is "obedience" obedience? Conceptual and historical commentary. *Journal of Social Issues,* 1995, *51,* 55–66.

Lykken, D. T. *A Tremor in the Blood: Uses and Abuses of the Lie Detector.* New York: McGraw-Hill, 1981.

Lykken, D. T. The case against polygraph testing. In *The Polygraph Test: Lies, Truth and Science,* edited by A. Gale. London: Sage Publications, 1988.

Lynn, R. Ethnic and racial differences in intelligence: International comparisons. In *Human Variation: The Biopsychology of Age, Race and Sex,* edited by R. T. Osborne, C. E. Noble, and N. Weyl. New York: Academic Press, 1978.

Lytton, H., and Romney, D. M. Parents' sex-related differential socialization of boys and girls: A meta-analysis. *Psychological Bulletin,* 1991, *109,* 267–296.

Lytton, W. W., and Brust, J. C. M. Direct dyslexia: Preserved oral reading of real words in Wernicke's aphasia. *Brain,* 1989, *112,* 583–594.

Maccoby, E. E. *Social Development: Psychological Growth and the Parent-Child Relationship.* New York: Harcourt Brace Jovanovich, 1980.

Maccoby, E. E., and Jacklin, C. N. *The Psychology of Sex Differences.* Stanford: Stanford University Press, 1974.

Mace, F. C., Lalli, J. S., Shea, M. C., Lalli, E. P., West, B. J., Roberts, M., and Nevin, J. A. The momentum of behavior in a natural setting. *Journal of the Experimental Analysis of Behavior,* 1990, *54,* 163–172.

Machon, R. A., Mednick, S. A., and Schulsinger, F. The interaction of seasonality, place of birth, genetic risk and subsequent schizophrenia in a high risk sample. *British Journal of Psychiatry,* 1983, *143,* 383–388.

MacLeod, C. M. Half a century of research on the Stroop effect: An integrative review. *Psychological Bulletin,* 1991, *109,* 163–203.

MacLeod, C. M. The Stroop task: The "gold standard" of attentional measures. *Journal of Experimental Psychology: General,* 1992, *38,* 421–439.

Maddi, S. R., and Kobasa, S. C. The development of hardiness. In *Stress and Coping,* edited by A. Monat and R. S. Lazarus. New York: Columbia University Press, 1991.

Maffei, M., Halaas, J., Ravussin, E., Pratley, R. E., Lee, G. H., Zhang, Y., Fei, H., Kim, S., Lallone, R., and Ranganathan, S. Leptin levels in human and rodent: Measurement of plasma leptin and ob RNA in obese and weight-reduced subjects. *Nature Medicine,* 1995 *11,* 1155–1161.

Magai, C., and McFadden, S. H. *The Role of Emotions in Social and Personality Development.* New York: Plenum, 1995

Magnus, H. Untersuchungen über den Farbensinn der Naturvölker. *Physiologische Abhandlungen,* 1880, Ser. 2, no. 7.

Maier, S. F., and Seligman, M. E. Learned helplessness: Theory and evidence. *Journal of Experimental Psychology: General,* 1976, *105,* 3–46.

Malpass, R. S., and Devine, P. G. Guided memory in eyewitness identification. *Journal of Applied Psychology,* 1981, *66,* 343–350.

Manuck, S. B., Kaplan, J. R., and Clarkson, T. B. Behaviorally-induced heart rate reactivity and atherosclerosis in cynomolgous monkeys. *Psychosomatic Medicine,* 1983, *45,* 95–108.

Manuck, S. B., Kaplan, J. R., and Matthews, K. A. Behavioral antecedents of coronary heart disease and atherosclerosis. *Arteriosclerosis,* 1986, *6,* 1–14.

Marcel, A. J. Conscious and unconscious perception: Experiments on visual masking and word recognition. *Cognitive Psychology,* 1983, *15,* 197–237.

Marcia, J. E. Ego identity crisis: Relationship to change in self-esteem, "general maladjustment," and authoritarianism. *Journal of Personality,* 1967, *25,* 118–133.

Marcia, J. E. Identity in adolescence. In *Handbook of Adolescent Psychology,* edited by J. Adelson. New York: Wiley, 1980.

Margolin, D. I., Friedrich, F. J., and Carlson, N. R. Visual agnosia-optic aphasia: Continuum or dichotomy? Paper presented at the meeting of the International Neuropsychology Society, 1985.

Margolin, D. I., Marcel, A. J., and Carlson, N. R. Common mechanisms in dysnomia and post-semantic surface dyslexia: Processing deficits and selective attention. In *Surface Dyslexia: Neuropsychological and Cognitive Studies of Phonological Reading.* London: Lawrence Erlbaum Associates, 1985.

Marks, G. A., Shaffery, J. P., Oksenberg, A., Speciale, S. G., and Roffward, H. P. A functional role for REM sleep in brain maturation. *Behavioural Brain Research,* 1995, *69,* 1–11.

Markus, H. R., and Kitayama, S. Culture and the self: Implications for cognition, emotion, and motivation. *Psychological Review,* 1991, *98,* 224–253.

Markus, H. R., and Nurius, P. Possible selves. *American Psychologist,* 1986, *41,* 954–969.

Marlatt, G. A., Baer, J. S., Donovan, D. M., and Kivlahan, D. R. Addictive behaviors: Etiology and treatment. *Annual Review of Psychology,* 1986, *39,* 223–252.

Marler, P. The filtering of external stimuli during instinctive behaviour. In *Current Problems in Animal Behaviour,* edited by W. H. Thorpe and O. L. Zangwill. Cambridge: Cambridge University Press, 1961.

Marshall, J. C., and Newcombe, F. Patterns of paralexia: A psycholinguistic approach. *Journal of Psycholinguistic Research,* 1973, *2,* 175–199.

Marshark, M., Richman, C. L., Yuille, J. C., and Hunt, R R. The role of imagery in memory: On shared and distinctive information. *Psychological Bulletin,* 1987, *102,* 28–41.

Martens, R. Palmar sweating and the presence of an audience. *Journal of Experimental Social Psychology,* 1969, *5,* 371–374.

Masling, J. The influence of situational and interpersonal variables in projective testing. *Psychological Bulletin,* 1960, *57,* 65–85.

Maslow, A. H. *Religions, Values, and Peak-Experiences.* New York: Viking Press, 1964.

Maslow, A. H. *Motivation and Personality,* 2nd ed. New York: Harper & Row, 1970.

Masters, W. H., and Johnson, V. E. *Human Sexual Inadequacy.* Boston: Little, Brown, 1970.

Mattes, R. D., Arnold, C., and Boraas, M. Learned food aversions among cancer chemotherapy patients: Incidence, nature and clinical implications. *Cancer,* 1987, *60,* 2576–2580.

Mawson, A. R. Anorexia nervosa and the regulation of intake: A review. *Psychological Medicine,* 1974, *4,* 289–308.

Mayer, J. Regulation of energy intake and the body weight: The glucostatic theory and the lipostatic hypothesis. *Annals of the New York Academy of Science,* 1955, *63,* 15–43.

Maynard Smith, J. Group selection and kin selection. *Nature,* 1964, *210,* 1145–1147.

Mayr, E. Behavior programs and evolutionary strategies. *American Scientist,* 1974, *34,* 650–659.

Mayr, E. Evolution. *Scientific American,* 1978, *239,* 46–55.

Mazur, A., and Lamb, T. Testosterone, status, and mood in human males. *Hormones and Behavior,* 1980, *14,* 236–246.

Mazur, J. E. *Learning and Behavior.* Englewood Cliffs, NJ: Prentice-Hall, 1994.

Mazziotta, J. C., Phelps, M. E., Carson, R. E., and Kuhl, D. E. Tomographic mapping of human cerebral metabolism: Auditory stimulation. *Neurologym,* 1982, *32,* 921–937.

McAlister, A., Perry, C., Killen, L. A., Slinkard, L. A., and Maccoby, N. Pilot study of smoking, alcohol, and drug abuse prevention. *American Journal of Public Health,* 1980, *70,* 719–721.

McCann, I. L., and Holmes, D. S. Influence of aerobic exercise on depression. *Journal of Personality and Social Psychology,* 1984, *46,* 1142–1147.

McCarthy, R. A., and Warrington, E. K. *Cognitive Neuropsychology: A Clinical Introduction.* San Diego: Academic Press, 1990.

McClanahan, K. K., Gold, J. A., Lenney, E., Ryckman, R. M., and Kulberg, G. E. Infatuation and attraction to a dissimilar other: Why is love blind? *The Journal of Social Psychology,* 1990, *130,* 433–445.

McClelland, J. L., and Romelhart, D. E. An interactive activation model of context effects in letter perception: Part 1. An account of basic findings. *Psychological Review,* 1981, *88,* 375–407.

McClintock, M. K., and Adler, N. T. The role of the female during copulation in wild and domestic Norway rats (*Rattus norvegicus*). *Behaviour,* 1978, *67,* 67–96.

McCrae, R. R., and Costa, P. T. Updating Norman's "adequate taxonomy": Intelligence and personality dimensions in natural language and in questionnaires. *Journal of Personality and Social Psychology,* 1985, *49,* 710–712.

McCrae, R. R., and Costa, P. T. Validation of the five-factor model of personality across instruments and observers. *Journal of Personality and Social Psychology,* 1987, *52,* 81–90.

McCrae, R. R., and Costa, P. T. *Personality in Adulthood.* New York: Guilford Press, 1990.

McCrae, R. R., Costa, P. T., and Busch, C. M. Evaluating comprehensiveness in personality systems: The California Q-Set and the five-factor model. *Journal of Personality,* 1986, *54,* 430–446.

McCue, M., Bacon, S., and Lykken, D. T. Personality stability and change in early adulthood: A behavior genetic analysis. *Developmental Psychology,* 1993, *29,* 96–109.

McGinty, D. J., and Sterman, M. B. Sleep suppression after basal forebrain lesions in the cat. *Science,* 1968, *160,* 1253–1255.

McGue, M., Pickens, R. W., and Svikis, D. S. Sex and age effects on the inheritance of alcohol problems: A twin study. *Journal of Abnormal Psychology,* 1992, *101,* 3–17

McKay, D. C. Aspects of the theory of comprehension, memory and attention. *Quarterly Journal of Experimental Psychology,* 1973, *25,* 22–40.

McKim, W. A. *Drugs and Behavior: An Introduction to Behavior Pharmacology,* 2nd ed. Englewood Cliffs, NJ: Prentice-Hall, 1991.

McNeal, J. Children as customers. *American Demographics,* 1990, *12(9),* 36–39.

McNeil, E. B. *The Quiet Furies: Man and Disorder.* Englewood Cliffs, NJ: Prentice-Hall, 1967.

McNeill, D. *The Acquisition of Language: The Study of Developmental Psycholinguistics.* New York: Harper & Row, 1970.

McReynolds, W. T. Learned helplessness as a schedule-shift effect. *Journal of Research in Personality,* 1980, *14,* 139–157.

Mednick, S. A., Gabrielli, W. F., and Hutchings, B. Genetic influences in criminal behavior: Some evidence from an adoption cohort. In *Prospective Studies of Crime and Delinquency,* edited by K. T. VanDusen and S. A. Mednick. Hingham, MA: Martinus Nyhoff, 1983.

Mednick, S. A., Machon, R. A., and Huttunen, M. O. An update on the Helsinki influenza project. *Archives of General Psychiatry,* 1990, *47,* 292.

Meehl, P. E. *Clinical Versus Statistical Prediction.* Minneapolis: University of Minnesota Press, 1954.

Meehl, P. E. Causes and effects of my disturbing little book. *Journal of Personality Assessment,* 1986, *50,* 370–375.

Mehler, J., Jusczyk, P., Lambertz, G., Halsted, N., Bertoncini, J., and Amiel-Tison, C. A precursor of language acquisition in young infants. *Cognition,* 1988, *29,* 143–178.

Meichenbaum, D. *Stress Innoculation Training.* New York: Pergamon Press, 1985.

Meichenbaum, D. H. *Cognitive-Behavior Modification: An Integrative Approach.* New York: Plenum Press, 1977.

Meindl, J. R., and Lerner, M. J. Exacerbation of extreme responses to an out-group. *Journal of Personality and Social Psychology,* 1985, *47,* 71–84.

Melzak, R. Phantom limbs. *Scientific American,* 1992, *266(4),* 120–126.

Menn, L., and Stoel-Gammon, C. Phonological development: Learning sounds and sound patterns. In *The Development of Language,* edited by J. B. Gleason. New York: Macmillan, 1993.

Mentkowski, T. Why I am what I am. *The Florida School Herald,* 1983, *82,* 1–2, 5, 12. Cited by Schein, J. D. *At Home Among Strangers.* Washington, DC: Gallaudet University Press, 1989.

Merikle, P. M. Subliminal auditory messages: An evaluation. *Psychology and Marketing,* 1988, *5,* 355–372.

Mervis, C. B., and Rosch, E. Categorization of natural objects. *Annual Review of Psychology,* 1981, *32,* 89–116.

Metter, E. J. Brain-behavior relationships in aphasia studied by positron emission tomography. *Annals of the New York Academy of Sciences,* 1991, *620,* 153–164.

Metter, E. J., Hanson, W. R., Jackson, C. A., Kempler, D., Van Lancker, D., Mazziotta, J. C., and Phelps, M. E. Temporoparietal cortex in aphasia: Evidence from positron emission tomography. *Archives of Neurology,* 1990, *47,* 1235–1238.

Meyer, R. G., and Osborne, Y. V. *Case Studies in Abnormal Behavior.* Boston: Allyn and Bacon, 1982.

Mikulincer, M., and Solomon, Z. Attributional style and combat-related posttraumatic stress disorder. *Journal of Abnormal Psychology,* 1988, *97,* 308–313

Miles, H. L. Apes and language: The search for communicative competence. In *Language in Primates: Perspectives and Implications,* edited by J. de Luce and H. T. Wilder. New York: Springer-Verlag, 1983.

Milgram, S. Behavioral study of obedience. *Journal of Abnormal and Social Psychology,* 1963, *67,* 371–378.

Milgram, S. *Obedience to Authority.* New York: Harper & Row, 1974.

Miller, G. A. The magical number seven plus or minus two: Some limits on our capacity for processing information. *Psychological Review,* 1956, *63,* 81–97.

Miller, G. A., Galanter, E., and Pribram, K. *Plans and the Structure of Behavior.* New York: Holt, Rinehart, and Winston, 1960.

Miller, G. A., Heise, G. A., and Lichten, W. The intelligibility of speech as a function of the context of the test materials. *Journal of Experimental Psychology,* 1951, *41,* 329–335.

Miller, G. A., and Taylor, W. G. The perception of repeated bursts of noise. *Journal of the Acoustical Society of America,* 1948, *20,* 171–182.

Miller, J. L., and Eimas, P. D. Speech perception: From signal to word. *Annual Review of Psychology,* 1995, *46,* 467–492.

Miller, N. E. Behavioral medicine: Symbiosis between laboratory and clinic. *Annual Review of Psychology,* 1983, *34,* 1–31.

Miller, R. J., Hennessy, R. T., and Leibowitz, H. W. The effect of hypnotic ablation of the background on the magnitude of the Ponzo perspective illusion. *International Journal of Clinical and Experimental Hypnosis,* 1973, *21,* 180–191.

Miller, W. R., Rosellini, R. A., and Seligman, M. E. P. Learned helplessness and depression. In *Psychopathology: Experimental Models,* edited by J. D. Maser and M. E. P. Seligman. San Francisco: W. H. Freeman, 1977.

Milner, B. Memory and the temporal regions of the brain. In *Biology of Memory,* edited by K. H. Pribram and D. E. Broadbent. New York: Academic Press, 1970.

Minuchin, S. *Families and Family Therapy.* Cambridge, MA: Harvard University Press, 1974.

Mirmiran, M. The function of fetal/neonatal rapid eye movement sleep. *Behavioural Brain Research,* 1995, *69,* 13–22.

Mischel, W. *Personality and Assessment.* New York: John Wiley & Sons, 1968.

Mischel, W. *Introduction to Personality,* 2nd ed. New York: Holt, Rinehart and Winston, 1976.

Mischel, W. The interaction of person and situation. In *Personality at the Crossroads: Current Issues in Interactional Psychology,* edited by D. Magnusson and N. S. Endler. Hillsdale, NJ: Lawrence Erlbaum Associates, 1977.

Mischel, W. On the interface of cognition and personality: Beyond the person-situation debate. *American Psychologist,* 1979, *34,* 740–754.

Mischel, W. Convergences and challenges in the search for consistency. *American Psychologist,* 1984, *39,* 351–364.

Mistry, J., and Rogoff, B. Remembering in a cultural context. In *Psychology and Culture,* edited by W. J. Lonner and Malpass. Boston: Allyn and Bacon, 1994.

Mogg, K., Bradley, B. P., Williams, R., and Matthews, A. Subliminal processing of emotional information in anxiety and depression. *Journal of Abnormal Psychology,* 1993, *102,* 304–311.

Money, J., and Ehrhardt, A. *Man & Woman, Boy & Girl.* Baltimore: Johns Hopkins University Press, 1972.

Money, J., Schwartz, M., and Lewis, V. G. Adult erotosexual status and fetal hormonal masculinization and demasculinization: 46,XX congenital virilizing adrenal hyperplasia and 46,XY androgen-insensitivity syndrome compared. *Psychoneuroendocrinology,* 1984, *9,* 405–414.

Monroe, S., Thase, M., and Simons, A. Social factors and psychobiology of depression: Relations between life stress and rapid eye movement sleep latency. *Journal of Abnormal Psychology,* 1992, *101,* 528–537.

Montagu, A. *Sociobiology Examined.* New York: Oxford University Press, 1980.

Montemayor, R. Children's performance in a game and their attraction to it as a function of sex-typed labels. *Child Development,* 1974, *45,* 152–156.

Moody, K. *Growing Up on Television: The TV Effect.* New York: Time Books, 1980.

Moore, C. L. The role of maternal stimulation in the development of sexual behavior and its neural basis. *Annals of the New York Academy of Sciences,* 1992, *662,* 160–177.

Moray, N. Attention in dichotic listening: Affective cues and the influence of instructions. *Quarterly Journal of Experimental Psychology,* 1959, *11,* 56–60.

Morris, N. M., Udry, J. R., Khan-Dawood, F., and Dawood, M. Y. Marital sex frequency and midcycle female testosterone. *Archives of Sexual Behavior,* 1987, *16,* 27–37.

Morris, T. A. "Type C" for cancer? Low trait anxiety in the pathogenesis of breast cancer. *Cancer Detection and Prevention,* 1980, *3,* 102.

Morton, J. Word recognition. In *Psycholinguistics 2: Structures and Processes.* Cambridge, MA: MIT Press, 1979.

Moss, C. S. *Hypnosis in Perspective.* New York: Macmillan, 1965.

Munoz, R. F., Hollon, S. D., McGrath, E., Rehm, L. P., and VandenBos, G. R. On the *AHCPR Depression in Primary Care* guidelines: Further consideration for practitioners. *American Psychologist*, 1994, *49*, 42–61.

Murray, D. M., Pirie, P., Luepker, R. V., and Pallonen, U. Five-and six-year follow-up results from four seventh-grade smoking prevention strategies. *Journal of Behavioral Medicine*, 1989, *12*, 207–218.

Myers, D. G., and Bishop, G. D. Discussion effects on racial attitudes. *Science*, 1970, *169*, 778–789.

Naeser, M. A., Palumbo, C. L., Helm-Estabrooks, N., Stiassny-Eder, D., and Albert, M. L. Severe nonfluency in aphasia: Role of the medial subcallosal fasciculus and other white matter pathways in recovery of spontaneous speech. *Brain*, 1989, *112*, 1–38.

Nafe, J. P., and Wagoner, K. S. The nature of pressure adaptation. *Journal of General Psychology*, 1941, *25*, 323–351.

Narrow, W. E., Regier, D. A., Rae, D. S., Manderscheid, R. W., and Locke, B. Z. Use of services by persons with mental and addictive disorders: Findings from the National Institute of Mental Health Epidemiologic Catchment Area Program. *Archives of General Psychiatry*, 1993, *50*, 95–107.

Navarick, D. J., Bernstein, D. J., and Fantino, E. The experimental analysis of human behavior (editorial). *Journal of the Experimental Analysis of Behavior*, 1990, *54*, 159–162.

Neal, A. M., and Turner, S. M. Anxiety Disorders Research with African Americans: Current status. *Psychological Bulletin*, 1991, *109*, 400–410.

Neisser, U. Visual search. *Scientific American*, 1964, *210*, 94–102.

Neisser, U. *Cognitive Psychology*. New York: Appleton-Century-Crofts, 1967.

Neisser, U. *Memory Observed*. San Francisco: W. H. Freeman, 1982.

Neisser, U. Selective reading: A method for the study of visual attention. Paper presented at the 19th International Congress of Psychology, London, 1969.

Neisser, U., and Becklen, R. Selective looking: Attending to visually significant events. *Cognitive Psychology*, 1975, *7*, 480–494.

Neisworth, J. T., and Madle, R. A. Retardation. In *International Handbook of Behavior Modification and Therapy*, edited by A. S. Bellack, M. Hersen, and A. E. Kazdin. New York: Plenum Press, 1982.

Nelson, L. J., and Miller, D. T. The distinctiveness effect in social categorization: You are what makes you unusual. *Psychological Science*, 1995, *6*, 246–249.

Neugarten, B. L. The roles we play. In American Medical Association, *Quality of Life: The Middle Years*. Acton, MA: Publishing Sciences Group, 1974.

Nevin, J. A. Behavioral momentum and the partial reinforcement effect. *Psychological Bulletin*, 1988, *103*, 44–56.

Newell, A., and Simon, H. A. *Human Problem Solving*. Englewood Cliffs, NJ: Prentice-Hall, 1972.

Newport, E. L. Motherese: the speech of mothers to young children. San Diego: University of California, Center for Human Information Processing, 1975.

Newport, E. L., Gleitman, H. R., and Gleitman, L. Mother I'd rather do it myself: Some effects and noneffects of maternal speech

style. In *Talking to Children: Language Input and Acquisition*, edited by C. E. Snow and C. A. Ferguson. Cambridge, England: Cambridge University Press, 1977.

Newport, E. L., and Supalla, R. A critical period effect in the acquisition of a primary language. Unpublished manuscript cited by J. S. Johnson and E. L. Newport. Critical period effects in second language learning: The influence of maturational state on the acquisition of English as a second language. *Cognitive Psychology*, 1989, *21*, 60–99.

Nicholl, C. S., and Russell, R. M. Analysis of animal rights literature reveals the underlying motives of the movement: Ammunition for counter offensive by scientists. *Endocrinology*, 1990, *127*, 985–989.

Nicolaus, L. K., Hoffman, T. E., and Gustavson, C. R. Taste aversion conditioning in free ranging raccoons *(Procyon lotor)*. *Northwest Science*, 1982, *56*, 165–169.

Nicolaus, L. K., and Nellis, D. W. The first evaluation of the use of conditioned taste aversion to control predation by mongooses upon eggs. *Applied Animal Behaviour Science*, 1987, *17*, 329–346.

Nielsen, A. C. *Annual Nielsen report on television: 1990*. New York: Nielsen Media Research, 1990.

Nielsen, L. L., and Sarason, I. G. Emotion, personality, and selective attention. *Journal of Personality and Social Psychology*, 1981, *41*, 945–960.

Nisbett, R. E., and Schachter, S. Cognitive manipulation of pain. *Journal of Experimental Social Psychology*, 1966, *2*, 227–236.

Nisbett, R. E., and Wilson, T. D. Telling more than we can know: Verbal reports on mental processes. *Psychological Review*, 1977, *84*, 231–259.

Noland, M. P., Kryscio, R. J., Riggs, R. S., Linville, L. H., Perritt, L. J., and Tucker, T. C. Use of snuff, chewing tobacco, and cigarettes among adolescents in a tobacco-producing area. *Addictive Behaviors*, 1990, *15*, 517–530.

Norman, W. T. Toward an adequate taxonomy of personality attributes: Replicated factor structure in peer nomination personality ratings. *Journal of Abnormal and Social Psychology*, 1963, *66*, 574–583.

North, C. N. *Welcome, Silence*. New York: Simon & Schuster, 1987.

Novak, M. A., and Harlow, H. F. Social recovery of monkeys isolated for the first year of life. 1. Rehabilitation and therapy. *Developmental Psychology*, 1975, *11*, 453–465.

Offer, D., and Sabshin, M. *Normality and the Life Cycle: A Critical Integration*. New York: Basic Books, 1984.

O'Haire, H. AIDS and population: Think again. *Populi*, 1994, *20/21*, 8–10.

Öhman, A., Erixon, G., and Löfberg, I. Phobias and preparedness: Phobic versus neutral pictures as conditional stimuli for human autonomic responses. *Journal of Abnormal Psychology*, 1975, *84*, 41–45.

Okagaki, L., and Sternberg, R. J. Putting the distance into students' hands: Practical intelligence for school. In *The Development and Meaning of Psychological Distance*, edited by R. R. Cocking and K. A. Renninger. Hillsdale, NJ: Erlbaum Associates, 1993.

Oldenburg, D. Hidden messages. *The Washington Post*, April 3, 1990.

Olton, D. S., Collison, C., and Werz, M. A. Spatial memory and radial arm maze performance in rats. *Learning and Motivation*, 1977, *8*, 289–314.

Olton, D. S., and Samuelson, R. J. Remembrance of places past: Spatial memory in rats. *Journal of Experimental Psychology: Animal Behavior Processes*, 1976, *2*, 97–116.

Orne, M. T. The nature of hypnosis: Artifact and essence. *Journal of Abnormal and Social Psychology*, 1959, *58*, 277–299.

Orne, M. T., and Evans, F. J. Social control in the psychological experiment: Antisocial behavior and hypnosis. *Journal of Personality and Social Psychology*, 1965, *1*, 189–200.

Orne, M. T., Whitehouse, W. G., Dinges, D. F., and Orne, E. C. Reconstructing memory through hypnosis. In *Hypnosis and Memory*, edited by H. M. Pettinati. New York: Guilford Press, 1988.

Orvis, B. R., Kelley, H. H., and Butler, D. Attributional conflict in young couples. In *New Directions in Attribution Research, Vol. 1*, edited by J. H. Harvey, W. J. Ickes, and R. F. Kidd. Hillsdale, NJ: Erlbaum, 1976.

Overmeier, J. B., and Seligman, M. E. P. Effects of inescapable shock upon subsequent escape and avoidance responding. *Journal of Comparative and Physiological Psychology*, 1967, *63*, 28–33.

Owens, R. E. *Language Development: An Introduction*. New York: Merrill/Macmillan, 1992.

Ozer, D. J. Correlation and the coefficient of determination. *Psychological Bulletin*, 1985, *97*, 307–315.

Paffenbarger, R. S., Hyde, J. T., Wing, A. L., and Hsieh, C. C. Physical activity, all-cause mortality, and longevity of college alumni. *New England Journal of Medicine*, 1986, *314*, 605–612.

Paikoff, R. L., and Brooks-Gunn, J. Do parent-child relationships change during puberty? *Psychological Bulletin*, 1991, *110*, 47–66.

Palmer, S. E. The effects of contextual scenes on the identification of objects. *Memory and Cognition*, 1975, *3*, 519–526.

Park, B., and Rothbart, M. Perception of outgroup homogeneity and levels of social categorization: Memory for the subordinate attributes of in-group and out-group members. *Journal of Personality and Social Psychology*, 1982, *42*, 1051–1068.

Parke, R. D., and Collmer, C. W. Child abuse: An interdisciplinary analysis. In *Review of Child Development Research, Vol. 5*, edited by E. M. Hetherington. Chicago: University of Chicago Press, 1975.

Parke, R. D., and Tinsley, B. R. The father's role in infancy: Determinants of involvement in caregiving and play. In *The Role of the Father in Child Development*, edited by M. E. Lamb. New York: John Wiley & Sons, 1981.

Parkin, A. J., Blunden, J., Rees, J. E., and Hunkin, N. M. Wernicke-Korsakoff syndrome of nonalcoholic origin. *Brain and Cognition*, 1991, *15*, 69–82.

Patterson, F. G., and Linden, E. *The Education of Koko*. New York: Holt, Rinehart and Winston, 1981.

Patton, G. The course of anorexia nervosa. *British Medical Journal*, 1989, *299*, 139–140.

Patton, J., Stinard, T., and Routh, D. Where do children study? *Journal of Educational Research,* 1983, *76,* 280–286.

Pauls, D. L., and Leckman, J. F. The inheritance of Gilles de la Tourette's syndrome and associated behaviors. *New England Journal of Medicine,* 1986, *315,* 993–997.

Pavlov, I. P. *Conditioned Reflexes.* Oxford, England: Oxford University Press, 1927.

Pearson, J. C., Turner, L. H., and Todd-Mancillas, W. *Gender and Communication.* Dubuque, IA: Brown, 1991.

Pease, D. M., Gleason, J. B., and Pan, B. A. Learning the meaning of words: Semantic development and beyond. In *The Development of Language,* edited by J. B. Gleason. New York: Macmillan, 1993.

Pelleymounter, M. A., Cullen, M. J., Baker, M. B., Hecht, R., et al. Effects of the obese gene product on body weight regulation in ob/ob mice. *Science,* 1995, *269,* 540–543.

Penfield, W., and Jasper, H. *Epilepsy and the Functional Anatomy of the Human Brain.* Boston: Little, Brown, 1954.

People v. Kempinski. No. W80CF 352 (Circuit Court, 12th District, Will County, Illinois, October 21, 1980).

Perlmutter, M., and Hall, E. *Adult Development and Aging.* New York: Wiley, 1985.

Perls, F. S. Group vs. individual therapy. *ETC: A Review of General Semantics,* 1967, *34,* 306–312.

Perls, F. S. *Gestalt Therapy Verbatim.* Lafayette, CA: Real People Press, 1969.

Persky, H., Lief, H. I., Strauss, D., Miller, W. R., and O'Brien, C. P. Plasma testosterone level and sexual behavior of couples. *Archives of Sexual Behavior,* 1978, *7,* 157–173.

Pert, C. B., Snowman, A. M., and Snyder, S. H. Localization of opiate receptor binding in presynaptic membranes of rat brain. *Brain Research,* 1974, *70,* 184–188.

Pervin, L. A. *Personality: Theory, Assessment, and Research.* New York: John Wiley & Sons, 1975.

Peskin, J. Measuring household production for the GNP. *Family Economics Review,* 1982, *3,* 16–25.

Peters, R. K., Cady, L. D., Bischoff, D. P., Bernstein, L., and Pile, M. C. Physical fitness and subsequent myocardial infarction in healthy workers. *Journal of the American Medical Association,* 1983, *249,* 3052–3056.

Petersen, S. E., and Fiez, J. A. The processing of single words studied with positron emission tomography. *Annual Review of Neurosience,* 1993, *16,* 509–530.

Petersen, S. E., Fox, P. T., Posner, M. I., Mintin, M., and Raichle, M. E. Positron emission tomography studies of the cortical anatomy of single-word processing. *Nature,* 1988, *331,* 585–589.

Petersen, S. E., Fox, P. T., Snyder, A. Z., and Raichle, M. E. Activation of extrastriate and frontal cortical areas by visual words and word-like stimuli. *Science,* 1990, *249,* 1041–1044.

Peterson, A. C., and Ebata, A. T. Developmental transitions and adolescent problem behavior: Implications for prevention and intervention. In *Social Prevention and Intervention,* edited by K. Herrelmann. New York: De Gruyter, 1987.

Peterson, L. R., and Peterson, M. J. Short-term retention of individual verbal items. *Journal of Experimental Psychology,* 1959, *58,* 193–198.

Peterson, R. Pubertal development as a cause of disturbance: Myths, realities, and unanswered questions. *Genetic, Social, and General Psychology Monographs,* 1985, *111,* 205–232.

Petre-Quadens, O., and De Lee, C. Eye movement frequencies and related paradoxical sleep cycles: Developmental changes. *Chronobiologia,* 1974, *1,* 347–355.

Petty, R. E., and Cacioppo, J. T. The elaboration likelihood model of persuasion. In *Advances in Experimental Social Psychology,* 1986, *19,* 123–205.

Pfefferbaum, A., Zipursky, R. B., Lim, K. O., Zatz, L. M., Stahl, S. M., and Jernigan, T. L. Computed tomographic evidence for generalized sulcal and ventricular enlargement in schizophrenia. *Archives of General Psychiatry,* 1988, *45,* 633–640.

Phares, E. J. *Clinical Psychology: Concepts, Methods, and Profession.* Homewood, IL: Dorsey Press, 1979.

Phares, E. J. *Introduction to Personality.* Columbus, OH: Merrill, 1984.

Piaget, J. *The Origins of Intelligence in Children.* Translated by M. Cook. New York: International Universities Press, 1952.

Piaget, J. Intellectual evolution from adolescence to adulthood. *Human Development,* 1972, *15,* 1–12.

Picariello, M. L., Greenberg, D. N., and Pillemer, D. B. Children's sex-related stereotyping of colors. *Child Development,* 1990, *61,* 1453–1460.

Pickens, R. W., Svikis, D. S., McGue, M., Lykken, D. T., Heston, L. L., and Clayton, P. J. Heterogeneity in the inheritance of alcoholism: A study of male and female twins. *Archives of General Psychiatry,* 1991, *48,* 19–28.

Pilleri, G. The blind Indus dolphin, *Platanista indi. Endeavours,* 1979, *3,* 48–56.

Pinker, S. Language acquisition. In *An Invitation to Cognitive Science. Vol. 1: Language,* edited by D. N. Osherson and H. Lasnik. Cambridge, MA: MIT Press, 1990.

Plomin, R. The nature and nurture of cognitive abilities. In *Advances in the Psychology of Human Intelligence,* edited by R. Sternberg. Hillsdale, NJ: Lawrence Erlbaum Associates, 1988.

Plomin, R. *Nature and Nurture: An Introduction to Behavioral Genetics.* Pacific Grove, CA: Brooks/Cole, 1990.

Plomin, R., and Bergeman, C. S. The nature of nurture: Genetic influence on "environmental" measures. *Behavioral and Brain Sciences,* 1991, *14,* 373–427.

Plomin, R., and Rende, R. Human behavioral genetics. *Annual Review of Psychology,* 1991, *43,* 161–190.

Poggio, G. F., and Poggio, T. The analysis of stereopsis. *Annual Review of Neuroscience,* 1984, *7,* 379–412.

Pollack, I., and Pickett, J. M. Intelligibility of excerpts from fluent speech: Auditory vs. structural context. *Journal of Verbal Learning and Verbal Behavior,* 1964, *3,* 79–84.

Pomerleau, O. F. Smoking treatment comes of age. *Psychopharmacology and Substance Abuse Newsletter,* 1992, *24,* 3.

Poole, M. E., Langan-Fox, J., and Omodei, M. Sex differences in perceived career success. *Genetic, Social and General Psychology Monographs,* 1991, *117,* 155–174.

Pope, K. S., Tabachnick, B. G., and Keith-Spiegel, P. Ethics of practice: The beliefs and behaviors of psychologists as therapists. *American Psychologist,* 1987, *42,* 993–1006.

Porter, C., Markus, H., and Nurius, P. S. Conceptions of possibility among people in crisis. Unpublished manuscript. University of Michigan, Ann Arbor, 1984.

Posner, M. I., Snyder, C. R. R., and Davidson, B. J. Attention and the detection of signals. *Journal of Experimental Psychology: General,* 1980, *109,* 160–174.

Potts, G. R. Information processing strategies used in the encoding of linear orderings. *Journal of Verbal Learning and Verbal Behavior,* 1972, *11,* 727–740.

Powell, K. E., Thompson, P. D., Caspersen, C. J., and Kendrick, J. S. Physical activity and the incidence of coronary heart disease. *Annual Review of Public Health,* 1987, *8,* 253–287.

Pratkanis, A. R., Breckler, S. H., and Greenwald, A. G. *Attitude Structure and Function.* Hillsdale, NJ: Lawrence Erlbaum Associates, 1989.

Pratkanis, A. R., Eskenazi, J., and Greenwald, A. G. What you expect is what you believe, but not necessarily what you get: On the effectiveness of subliminal self-help audiotapes. Paper presented at the annual convention of the Western Psychological Association, Los Angeles, 1990. (Cited by Druckman and Bjork, 1990.)

Premack, D. Language and intelligence in ape and man. *American Scientist,* 1976, *64,* 674–683.

Prichard, J. C. *A Treatise on Insanity and Other Disorders Affecting the Mind.* London: Sherwood, Gilbert, and Piper, 1835.

Propping, P., Kruger, J., and Janah, A. Effect of alcohol on genetically determined variants of the normal electroencephalogram. *Psychiatry Research,* 1980, *2,* 85–98.

Propping, P., Kruger, J., and Mark, N. Genetic disposition to alcoholism: An EEG study in alcoholics and their relatives. *Human Genetics,* 1981, *59,* 51–59.

Rachlin, H. *Modern Behaviorism.* New York: Freeman, 1970.

Rachman, S., and Hodgson, R. J. Experimentally-induced "sexual fetishism": Replication and development. *Psychological Record,* 1968, *18,* 25–27.

Rachman, S. J., and Wilson, G. T. Using direct and indirect measures to study perception without awareness. *Perception and Psychophysics,* 1980, *44,* 563–575.

Ragland, D. R., and Brand, R. J. Type A behavior and mortality from coronary heart disease. *New England Journal of Medicine,* 1988, *318,* 65–69.

Rahe, R. H., and Arthur, R. J. Life changes and illness reports. In *Life Stress and Illness,* edited by K. E. Gunderson and R. H. Rahe. Springfield, IL: Thomas, 1978.

Rajecki, D. J. *Attitudes,* 2nd ed. Sunderland, MA: Sinauer Associates, 1989.

Ramey, C. Abecedarian project. In *Encyclopedia of Human Intelligence,* edited by R. J. Sternberg. New York: Macmillan, 1994.

Rappaport, J. *Community Psychology: Values, Research and Action.* New York: Holt, Rinehart and Winston, 1977.

Ray, O., and Ksir, C. *Drugs, Society, and Human Behavior,* 5th ed. St. Louis: Times Mirror, 1990.

Raybin, J. B., and Detre, T. P. Sleep disorder and symptomatology among medical and nursing students. *Comprehensive Psychiatry,* 1969, *10,* 452–467.

Rayner, K., and Pollatsek, A. *The Psychology of Reading.* Englewood Cliffs, NJ: Prentice-Hall, 1989.

Reber, A. A., and Allen, R. Analogical and abstraction strategies in synthetic grammar learning: A functionalist interpretation. *Cognition,* 1978, *6,* 189–221.

Reber, A. S. The cognitive unconscious: An evolutionary perspective. *Consciousness and Cognition,* 1992, *1,* 93–133.

Regan, D. T. Effects of a favor and liking on compliance. *Journal of Experimental Social Psychology,* 1971, *7,* 627–639.

Regier, D. A., Boyd, J. H., Burke, J. D., Rae, D. S., Myers, J. K., Kramer, M., Ropins, L. N., George, L. K., Karno, M., and Locke, B. Z. One-month prevalence of mental disorders in the United States. *Archives of General Psychiatry,* 1988, *45,* 977–986.

Reinink, E., Bouhuys, N., Wirz-Justice, A., and van den Hoofdakker, R. Prediction of the antidepressant response to total sleep deprivation by diurnal variation of mood. *Psychiatry Research,* 1990, *32,* 113–124.

Reinke, B. J., Holmes, D. S., and Harris, R. L. The timing of psychosocial changes in women's lives: The years 25 to 45. *Journal of Personality and Social Psychology,* 1985, *48,* 1353–1364.

Reiser, M., and Nielsen, M. Investigative hypnosis: A developing specialty. *American Journal of Clinical Hypnosis,* 1980, *23,* 75–83.

Rescorla, R. A. Predictability and number of pairings in Pavlovian fear conditioning. *Psychonomic Science,* 1966, *4,* 383–384.

Rescorla, R. A. Associative relations in associative learning. The Eighteenth Bartlett Memorial Lecture. *The Quarterly Journal of Experimental Psychology,* 1991, *43,* 1–23.

Rest, J. R. *Development in Judging Moral Issues.* Minneapolis: University of Minnesota Press, 1979.

Review Panel. Coronary-prone behavior and coronary heart disease: A critical review. *Circulation,* 1981, *673,* 1199–1215.

Reynolds, A. G., and Flagg, P. W. *Cognitive Psychology,* 2nd ed. Boston: Little, Brown, 1983.

Rheingold, H. L., and Eckerman, C. O. Fear of the stranger: A critical examination. In *Advances in Child Development and Behavior, Vol. 8,* edited by H. W. Reese. New York: Academic Press, 1973.

Rice, M. L., Huston, A. C., Truglio, R., and Wright, J. Words from "Sesame Street": Learning vocabulary while viewing. *Developmental Psychology,* 1990, *26,* 421–428.

Riggs, L. A., Ratliff, F., Cornsweet, J. C., and Cornsweet, T. N. The disappearance of steadily fixated visual test objects. *Journal of the Optical Society of America,* 1953, *43,* 495–501.

Rips, L. J., Shoben, E. J., and Smith, E. E. Semantic distance and the verification of semantic relations. *Journal of Verbal Learning and Verbal Behavior,* 1973, *12,* 1–20.

Rischer, C. E., and Easton, T. A. *Focus on Human Biology.* New York: HarperCollins, 1992.

Ris-Stalpers, C., Kuiper, G. G. J. M., Faber, P. W., Schweikert, H. U., Van Rooij, H. C. J., Zegers, N. D., Hodgins, M. B., Degenhart, H. J., Trapman, J., and Brinkmann, A. O. Aberrant splicing of androgen receptor mRNA results in synthesis of a nonfunctional receptor protein in a patient with androgen insensitivity. *Proceedings of the National Academy of Sciences,* 1990, *87,* 7866–7870.

Ritter, R. C., Brenner, L., and Yox, D. P. Participation of vagal sensory neurons in putative satiety signals from the upper gastrointestinal tract. In *Neuroanatomy and Physiology of Abdominal Vagal Afferents,* edited by S. Ritter, R. C. Ritter, and C. D. Barnes. Boca Raton, FL: CRC Press, 1992.

Ritter, S., and Taylor, J. S. Capsaicin abolishes lipoprivic but not glucoprivic feeding in rats. *American Journal of Physiology,* 1989, *256,* R1232–R1239.

Rittle, R. H. Changes in helping behavior: Self- versus situational perceptions as mediators of the foot-in-the-door effect. *Personality and Social Psychology Bulletin,* 1981, *7,* 431–437.

Robbins, L. N., Helzer, J. E., Weissman, M. M., Orvaschel, H., Gruenberg, E., Burke, J. D., and Regier, D. A. Lifetime prevalence of specific psychiatric disorders in three sites. *Archives of General Psychiatry,* 1984, *41,* 949–958.

Robins, L. N., and Regier, D. A. (Eds.). *Psychiatric Disorders in America.* New York: The Free Press, 1994.

Robinson, L. A., Berman, J. S., and Neimeyer, R. A. Psychotherapy for the treatment of depression: A comprehensive review of controlled outcome research. *Psychological Bulletin,* 1990, *108,* 30–49.

Rock, I., and Gutman, D. The effect of inattention on form perception. *Journal of Experimental Psychology: Human Perception and Performance,* 1981, *7,* 275–285.

Rodin, J., Schank, D., and Striegel-Moore, R. Psychological features of obesity. *Medical Clinics of North America,* 1989, *73,* 47–66.

Roediger, H. L. Implicit memory: Retention without remembering. *American Psychologist,* 1990, *45,* 1043–1056.

Roff, J. D., and Knight, R. Family characteristics, childhood symptoms, and adult outcome in schizophrenia. *Journal of Abnormal Psychology,* 1981, *90,* 510–520.

Roffwarg, H. P., Muzio, J. N., and Dement, W. C. Ontogenetic development of human sleep-dream cycle. *Science,* 1966, *152,* 604–619.

Rogers, C. R. *On Becoming a Person.* Boston: Houghton Mifflin, 1961.

Rogers, C. T. *Client-centered Therapy.* Boston: Houghton Mifflin, 1951.

Rogers, M. P., Trentham, D. E., McCune, W. J., Ginsberg, B. I., Rennke, H. G., Reike, P., and David, J. R. Effect of psychological stress on the induction of arthritis in rats. *Arthritis and Rheumatology,* 1980, *23,* 1337–1342.

Rogoff, B. *Apprenticeship in Thinking: Cognitive Development in Social Context.* New York: Oxford University Press, 1990.

Rogoff, B., and Chavajay, P. What's become of research on the cultural basis of cognitive development. *American Psychologist,* 1995, *50,* 859–877.

Rogoff, B., and Waddell, K. J. Memory for information organized in a scene by children from two cultures. *Child Development,* 1982, *53,* 1224–1228.

Rollins, B. C., and Feldman, H. Marital satisfaction over the life cycle. *Journal of Marriage and the Family,* 1970, *32,* 20–28.

Rosch, E. On the internal structure of perceptual and semantic categories. In *Cognitive Development and the Acquisition of Language,* edited by R. E. Moore. New York: Academic Press, 1973.

Rosch, E. H. Cognitive representations of semantic categories. *Journal of Experimental Psychology: General,* 1975, *104,* 192–233.

Rosch, E. H., Mervis, C. B., Gray, W. D., Johnson, D. M., and Boyes-Braem, P. Basic objects in natural categories. *Cognitive Psychology,* 1976, *8,* 382–439.

Rose, G. A., and Williams, R. T. Metabolic studies of large and small eaters. *British Journal of Nutrition,* 1961, *15,* 1–9.

Rose, R. J. Genetic and environmental variance in content dimensions of the MMPI. *Journal of Personality and Social Psychology,* 1988, *55,* 302–311.

Rose, R. J. Genes and human behavior. *Annual Review of Psychology,* 1995, *46,* 625–654.

Rosenblatt, J. S., and Aronson, L. R. The decline of sexual behavior in male cats after castration with special reference to the role of prior sexual experience. *Behaviour,* 1958, *12,* 285–338.

Rosenman, R. H., Brand, R. J., Jenkins, C. D., Friedman, M., Straus, R., and Wurm, M. Coronary heart disease in the Western Collaborative Group Study: Final follow-up experience of 8 1/2 years. *Journal of the American Medical Association,* 1975, *233,* 872–877.

Rosenthal, D. *Genetic Theory and Abnormal Behavior.* New York: McGraw-Hill, 1970.

Rosenthal, N. E., Genhart, M., Jacobson, F. M., Skwerer, R. G., and Wehr, T. A. Disturbances of appetite and weight regulation in seasonal affective disorder. *Annals of the New York Academy of Sciences,* 1986, *499,* 216–230.

Rosenthal, N. E., Sack, D. A., James, S. P., Parry, B. L., Mendelson, W. B., Tamarkin, L., and Wehr, T. A. Seasonal affective disorder and phototherapy. *Annals of the New York Academy of Sciences,* 1985, *453,* 260–269.

Rosenthal, R., and Fode, K. L. The effect of experimental bias on the performance of the albino rat. *Behavioral Science,* 1963, *8,* 183–187.

Rosenzweig, M. R. Experience, memory, and the brain. *American Psychologist,* 1984, *39,* 365–376.

Ross, G., Nelson, K., Wetstone, H., and Tanouye, E. Acquisition and generalization of novel object concepts by young language learners. *Journal of Child Language,* 1986, *13,* 67–83.

Ross, L. The intuitive psychologist and his shortcomings: Distortions in the attribution process. In *Advances in Experimental Social Psychology,* edited by L. Berkowitz. New York: Academic Press, 1977.

Ross, L. D., Amabile, T. M., and Steinmetz, J. L. Social roles, social control, and biases in social-perception processes. *Journal of Personality and Social Psychology,* 1977, *35,* 485–494.

Rosser, R. *Cognitive Development: Psychological and Biological Perspectives.* Boston: Allyn and Bacon, 1994.

Rossi, P. H. The old homeless and the new homeless. *American Psychologist,* 1990, *45,* 954–959.

Roth, E. M., and Mervis, C. B. Fuzzy set theory and class inclusion relations in semantic categories. *Journal of Verbal Learning and Verbal Behavior,* 1983, *22,* 509–525.

Rothkopf, E. Z. Incidental memory for location of information in text. *Journal of Verbal Learning and Verbal Behavior,* 1971, *10,* 608–613.

Rotter, J. B. *Social Learning and Clinical Psychology.* Englewood Cliffs, NJ: Prentice-Hall, 1954.

Rotter, J. B. Generalized expectancies for internal versus external control of reinforcement. *Psychological Monographs,* 1966, *80* (1, Whole No. 609).

Rowland, L. J. Will hypnotized persons try to harm themselves or others? *Journal of Abnormal and Social Psychology,* 1939, *34,* 114–117.

Rubin, Z. *Liking and Loving: An Invitation to Social Psychology.* New York: Holt, Rinehart and Winston, 1973.

Rumelhart, D. E., McClelland, J. L., and the PDP Research Group. *Parallel Distributed Processing: Explorations in the Microstructure of Cognition.* Cambridge, MA: MIT Press, 1986.

Rushing, W. A. *The AIDS Epidemic: Social Dimensions of an Infectious Disease.* Boulder, CO: Westview Press, 1995.

Russell, G. F. M., and Treasure, J. The modern history of anorexia nervosa: An interpretation of why the illness has changed. *Annals of the New York Academy of Sciences,* 1989, *575,* 13–30.

Russell, P. J. *Genetics.* New York: HarperCollins, 1992.

Ryback, R. S., and Lewis, O. F. Effects of prolonged bed rest on EEG sleep patterns in young, healthy volunteers. *Electroencephalography and Clinical Neurophysiology,* 1971, *31,* 395–399.

Rymer, R. A silent childhood. *The New Yorker,* 1992 (April 23), pp. 41–81.

Sachs, J. The emergence of intentional communication. In *The Development of Language,* edited by J. B. Gleason. New York: Macmillan, 1993.

Sachs, J. S. Recognition memory for syntactic and semantic aspects of connected discourse. *Perception and Psychophysics,* 1967, *2,* 437–442.

Sachs, O. *Seeing Voices: A Journey into the World of the Deaf.* Berkeley, CA: University of California Press, 1989.

Sackheim, H. A., Paulus, D., and Weiman, A. L. Classroom seating and hypnotic susceptibility. *Journal of Abnormal Psychology,* 1979, *88,* 81–84.

Saegert, S. C., Swap, W., and Zajonc, R. B. Exposure, context, and interpersonal attraction. *Journal of Personality and Social Psychology,* 1973, *25,* 234–242.

Saffran, E. M., Marin, O. S. M., and Yeni-Komshian, G. H. An analysis of speech perception in word deafness. *Brain and Language,* 1976, *3,* 209–228.

Saffran, E. M., Schwartz, M. F., and Marin, O. S. M. Evidence from aphasia: Isolating the components of a production model. In *Language Production,* edited by B. Butterworth. London: Academic Press, 1980.

Sakai, F., Meyer, J. S., Karacan, I., Derman, S., and Yamamoto, M. Normal human sleep: Regional cerebral haemodynamics. *Annals of Neurology,* 1979, *7,* 471–478.

Salapatek, P. Pattern perception in early infancy. In *Infant Perception: From Sensation to Cognition, Vol. 1,* edited by L. B. Cohen and P. Salapatek. New York: Academic Press, 1975.

Salmon, U. J., and Geist, S. H. Effect of androgens upon libido in women. *Journal of Clinical Endocrinology and Metabolism,* 1943, *172,* 374–377.

Salthouse, T. A. Effects of age and skill in typing. *Journal of Gerontology,* 1984, *113,* 345–371.

Salthouse, T. A. Cognitive aspects of motor functioning. In *Central Determinants of Age-Related Declines in Motor Function,* edited by J. A. Joseph. New York: New York Academy of Sciences, 1988.

Sande, G. N., Goethals, G. R., and Radloff, C. E. Perceiving one's own traits and others: The multifaceted self. *Journal of Personality and Social Psychology,* 1988, *54,* 13–20.

Sandven, K., and Resnick, M. Informal adoption among black adolescent mothers. *American Journal of Orthopsychiatry,* 1990, *60,* 210–224.

Sanna, L. J., and Shorland, R. L. Valence of anticipated evaluation and social facilitation. *Journal of Experimental Social Psychology,* 1990, *26,* 82–92.

Santos, M. D., Leve, C., and Pratkanis, A. R. Hey buddy, can you spare seventeen cents? Mindful persuasion and the pique technique. *Journal of Applied Social Psychology,* 1994, *24,* 755–764.

Sapolsky, R. Glucocorticoid toxicity in the hippocampus: Reversal by supplementation with brain fuels. *Journal of Neuroscience,* 1986, *6,* 2240–2244.

Sapolsky, R. M., Krey, L. C., and McEwen, B. S. The neuroendocrinology of stress and aging: The glucocorticoid cascade hypothesis. *Endocrine Reviews,* 1986, *7,* 284–301.

Sarason, I., and Sarason, B. *Abnormal Psychology: The Problem of Maladaptive Behavior,* 7th ed. Englewood Cliffs, NJ: Prentice-Hall, 1993.

Savage-Rumbauch, E. S. Language acquisition in a nonhuman species: Implications for the innateness debate. *Development Psychobiology,* 1990, *23,* 599–620.

Scarr, S., Webber, P. L., Weinberg, A., and Wittig, M. A. Personality resemblance among adolescents and their parents in biologically related and adoptive families. *Journal of Personality and Social Psychology,* 1981, *40,* 885–898.

Scarr, S., and Weinberg, R. A. IQ Performance of black children adopted by white families. *American Psychologist,* 1976, *31,* 726–739.

Scarr, S., and Weinberg, R. A. The influence of "family background" on intellectual attainment. *American Sociological Review,* 1978, *43,* 674–692.

Schachter, S. The interaction of cognitive and physiological determinants of emotional state. In *Psychobiological Approaches to Social Behavior,* edited by P. H. Liederman and D. Shapiro. Stanford, CA: Stanford University Press, 1964.

Schachter, S., and Singer, J. E. Cognitive, social and physiological determinants of emotional state. *Psychological Review,* 1962, *69,* 379–399.

Schaie, K. W. Cognitive development in aging. In *Language and Communication in the Elderly,* edited by L. K. Obler and M. L. Martin. Lexington, MA: Heath, 1980.

Schaie, K. W. Intellectual development in adulthood. In *Handbook of the Psychology of Aging,* 3rd ed., edited by J. E. Birren and K. W. Schaie. San Diego: Academic Press, 1990.

Schaie, K. W., and Strother, C. R. A cross-sequential study of age changes in cognitive behavior. *Psychological Bulletin,* 1968, *70,* 661–684.

Schaie, K. W., and Willis, S. L. *Adult Development and Learning,* 3rd ed. New York: HarperCollins, 1992.

Schanberg, S. M., and Field, T. M. Sensory deprivation stress and supplemental stimulation in the rat pup and preterm human neonate. *Child Development,* 1987, *58,* 1431–1447.

Schank, R., and Abelson, R. P. *Scripts, Plans, Goals, and Understanding.* Hillsdale, NJ: Lawrence Erlbaum Associates, 1977.

Schein, J. D. *At Home Among Strangers.* Washington, DC: Gallaudet University Press, 1989.

Schenck, C. H., Bundlie, S. R., Ettinger, M. G., and Mahowald, M. W. Chronic behavioral disorders of human REM sleep: A new category of parasomnia. *Sleep,* 1986, *9,* 293–308.

Scherschlicht, R., Polc, P., Schneeberger, J., Steiner, M., and Haefely, W. Selective suppression of rapid eye movement sleep (REMS) in cats by typical and atypical antidepressants. In *Typical and Atypical Antidepressants: Molecular Mechanisms,* edited by E. Costa and G. Racagni. New York: Raven Press, 1982.

Schiano, D. J., and Watkins, M. J. Speech-like coding of pictures in short-term memory. *Memory and Cognition,* 1981, *9,* 110–114.

Schleifer, S. J., Keller, S. E., Camerino, M., Thornton, J. C., and Stein, M. Suppression of lymphocyte stimulation following bereavement. *Journal of the American Medical Association,* 1983, *15,* 374–377.

Schmauk, F. J. Punishment, arousal, and avoidance learning in sociopaths. *Journal of Abnormal Psychology,* 1970, *122,* 509–522.

Schneider, D. J. Social cognition. *Annual Review of Psychology,* 1991, *42,* 527–561.

Schwab, J. The Sandalu bachelor ritual among the Laiapu Enga (Papua, New Guinea). *Anthropos,* 1995, *90,* 27–47.

Schwartz, M. F., Marin, O. S. M., and Saffran, E. M. Dissociations of language function in dementia: A case study. *Brain and Language,* 1979, *7,* 277–306.

Schwartz, M. F., Saffran, E. M., and Marin, O. S. M. The word order problem in agrammatism. I. Comprehension. *Brain and Language,* 1980, *10,* 249–262.

Schwartz, R., and Schwartz, L. J. *Becoming a Couple.* Englewood Cliffs, NJ: Prentice-Hall, 1980.

Schwarzkopf, S. B., Nasrallah, H. A., Olson, S. C., Coffman, J. A., and McLaughlin, J. A. Perinatal complications and genetic loading in schizophrenia: Preliminary findings. *Psychiatry Research,* 1989, *27,* 233–239.

Scoville, W. B., and Milner, B. Loss of recent memory after bilateral hippocampal lesions. *Journal of Neurology, Neurosurgery and Psychiatry,* 1957, *20,* 11–21.

Scribner, S. Modes of thinking and ways of speaking: Culture and logic reconsidered. In *Thinking: Readings in Cognitive Science,* edited by P. N. Johnson-Laird and P. C. Wason. Cambridge, England: Cambridge University Press, 1977.

Segall, M. H., Campbell, D. T., and Herskovits, M. J. *The Influence of Culture on Visual Perception.* Indianapolis, IN: Bobbs-Merrill, 1966.

Seidman, E. Growing up the hard way. *American Journal of Community Psychology,* 1991, *19,* 173–205.

Seligman, M. E. P. Phobias and preparedness. *Behavior Therapy,* 1971, *2,* 307–320.

Seligman, M. E. P. *Helplessness.* San Francisco: W. H. Freeman, 1975.

Seligman, M. E. P. The effectiveness of psychotherapy: The *Consumer Reports* Study. *American Psychologist,* 1995, *50,* 965–974.

Seligman, M. E. P., and Schulman, P. Explanatory style as a predictor of productivity and quitting among life insurance sales agents. *Journal of Personality and Social Psychology,* 1986, *50,* 832–838.

Selkoe, D. J. Biochemistry of altered brain proteins in Alzheimer's disease. *Annual Review of Neuroscience,* 1989, *12,* 463–490.

Selye, H. *The Stress of Life.* New York: McGraw-Hill, 1956.

Selye, H. *The Stress of Life.* New York: McGraw-Hill, 1976.

Selye, H. History and present status of the stress concept. In *Stress and Coping,* edited by A. Monat and R. S. Lazarus. New York: Columbia University Press, 1991.

Selye, H., and Tuchweber, B. Stress in relation to aging and disease. In *Hypothalamus, Pituitary and Aging,* edited by A. Everitt and J. Burgess. Springfield, IL: Charles C. Thomas, 1976.

Shaffer, D. R. *Developmental Psychology: Childhood and Adolescence,* 2nd ed. Belmont, CA: Brooks/Cole, 1989.

Shakin, E. J., and Holland, J. Depression and pancreatic cancer. *Journal of Pain and Symptom Management,* 1988, *3,* 194–198.

Shatz, M., and Gelman, R. The development of communication skills: Modifications in the speech of young children as a function of listener. *Monographs of the Society for Research in Child Development,* 1973, *38* (Serial no. 152).

Shavit, Y., Depaulis, A., Martin, F. C., Terman, G. W., Pechnick, R. N., Zane, C. J., Gale, R. P., and Liebeskind, J. C. Involvement of brain opiate receptors in the immune-suppressive effect of morphine. *Proceedings of the National Academy of Sciences, USA,* 1986, *83,* 7114–7117.

Shavit, Y., Lewis, J. W., Terman, G. W., Gale, R. P., and Liebeskind, J. C. Opioid peptides mediate the suppressive effect of stress on natural killer cell cytotoxicity. *Science,* 1984, *223,* 188–190.

Shepard, R. N., and Metzler, J. Mental rotation of three-dimensional objects. *Science,* 1971, *171,* 701–703.

Shepher, J. *Incest: The Biosocial View.* Cambridge, MA: Harvard University Press, 1983.

Sherif, M. *The Psychology of Social Norms.* New York: Harper, 1936.

Sherif, M., Harvey, O. J., White, B. J., Hood, W. E., and Sherif, C. W. *Intergroup Conflict and Cooperation: The Robbers Cave Experiment.* Norman, OK: Institute of Group Relations, 1961.

Sherman, S. J., Presson, C. C., and Chassin, L. Mechanisms underlying the false consensus effect: The special role of threats to the self. *Personality and Social Psychology Bulletin,* 1984, *10,* 127–138.

Shibley Hyde, J., and Plant, E. A. Magnitude of psychological gender differences: Another side to the story. *American Psychologist,* 1995, *50,* 159–161.

Shipley, E. F., Smith, C. S., and Gleitman, L. R. A study in the acquisition of language: Free responses to commands. *Language,* 1969, *45,* 322–342.

Shock, N. Systems integration. In *Handbook of the Biology of Aging,* edited by C. Finch and L. Hayflick. New York: Van Nostrand Reinhold, 1977.

Shotland, R. L., and Heinold, W. D. Bystander response to arterial bleeding: Helping skills, the decision-making process, and differentiating the helping response. *Journal of Personality and Social Psychology,* 1985, *49,* 347–356.

Sidman, M., and Tailby, W. Conditional discrimination versus matching to sample: An expansion of the testing paradigm. *Journal of the Experimental Analysis of Behavior,* 1982, *37,* 5–22.

Silverman, I. Inclusive fitness and ethnocentrism. In *The Sociobiology of Ethnocentrism,* edited by V. Reynolds, V. Falger, and I. Vine. London: Croom Helm, 1987.

Simons, R. C., and Hughes, C. C. Culture-bound syndromes. In *Culture, Ethnicity, and Mental Illness,* edited by A. C. Gaw. Washington, DC: American Psychiatric Press, 1993.

Singer, D. G., and Singer, J. L. *The House of Make-Believe.* Cambridge, MA: Harvard University Press, 1990.

Sirevaag, A. M., Black, J. E., Shafron, D., and Greenough, W. T. Direct evidence that complex experience increases capillary branching and surface area in visual cortex of young rats. *Developmental Brain Research,* 1988, *43,* 299–304.

Sivacek, J., and Crano, W. D. Vested interest as a moderator of attitude-behavior consistency. *Journal of Personality and Social Psychology,* 1982, *43,* 210–221.

Skarin, K. Cognitive and contextual determinants of stranger fear in six- and eleven-month-old infants. *Child Development,* 1977, *48,* 537–544.

Skinner, B. F. *Walden Two.* New York: Macmillan, 1948.

Skinner, B. F. *Science and Human Behavior.* New York: Macmillan, 1953.

Skinner, B. F. *Beyond Freedom and Dignity.* New York: Vantage, 1971.

Skinner, B. F. Why I am not a cognitive psychologist. *Behaviorism,* 1978, *5,* 1–10.

Skinner, B. F. Selection by consequences. *Science,* 1981, *213,* 501–504.

Skinner, B. F. The evolution of verbal behavior. *Journal of the Experimental Analysis of Behavior,* 1986, *45,* 115–122.

Skinner, B. F. *Upon Further Reflection.* Englewood Cliffs, NJ: Prentice-Hall, 1987.

Skinner, B. F. Can psychology be a science of mind? *American Psychologist,* 1990, *45,* 1206–1210.

Sloane, R. B., Staples, F. R., Cristol, A. H., Yorkston, N. J., and Whipple, K. *Psychoanalysis Versus Behavior Therapy.* Cambridge, MA: Harvard University Press, 1975.

Smith, G. H., and Engel, R. Influence of a female model on perceived characteristics of an automobile. *Proceedings of the 76th Annual Convention of the American Psychological Association,* 1968, *3,* 681–682.

Smith, M. L., and Glass, G. V. Meta-analysis of psychotherapy outcome studies. *American Psychologist,* 1977, *32,* 752–760.

Smith, M. L., Glass, G. V., and Miller, T. I. *Benefits of Psychotherapy.* Baltimore: Johns Hopkins University Press, 1980.

Snow, C. E. Mothers' speech to children learning language. *Child Development,* 1972a, *43,* 549–565.

Snow, C. E. Young children's responses to adult sentences of varying complexity. Paper presented at the Third International Congress of Applied Linguistics, Copenhagen, August 1972b.

Snow, C. E. Mothers' speech research: From input to interaction. In *Talking to Children: Language Input and Acquisition,* edited by C. E. Snow and C. Ferguson. Cambridge: Cambridge University Press, 1977.

Snow, C. E. Conversations with children. In *Language Acquisition,* 2nd ed., edited by P. Fletcher and M. Garman. Cambridge: Cambridge University Press, 1986.

Snow, C. E., Arlman-Rupp, A., Hassing, Y., Jobse, J., Joosten, J., and Vorster, J. Mothers' speech in three social classes. *Journal of Psycholinguistic Research,* 1976, *5,* 1–20.

Snow, C. E., and Goldfield, B. A. Building stories: The emergence of information structures from conversation. In *Analyzing Discourse: Text and Talk,* edited by D. Tannen. Washington, DC: Georgetown University Press, 1982.

Snow, M. E., Jacklin, C. N., and Maccoby, E. E. Sex-of-child differences in father-child interaction at one year of age. *Child Development,* 1983, *54,* 227–232.

Snow, W. G., and Weinstock, J. Sex differences among non-brain-damaged adults on the Wechsler Adult Intelligence Scales: A review of the literature. *Journal of Clinical and Experimental Neuropsychology,* 1990, *12,* 873–886.

Snyder, M., Tanke, E. D., and Berscheid, E. Social perception and interpersonal behavior: On the self-fulfilling nature of social stereotypes. *Journal of Personality and Social Psychology,* 1977, *35,* 656–666.

Snyder, S. H. *Madness and the Brain.* New York: McGraw-Hill, 1974.

Sobesky, W. E. The effects of situational factors on moral judgments. *Child Development,* 1983, *54,* 575–584.

Solkoff, N., and Matuszak, D. Tactile stimulation and behavioral development among low-birthweight infants. *Child Psychiatry and Human Development,* 1975, *6,* 33–37.

Solkoff, N., Yaffe, S., Weintraub, D., and Blase, B. Effects of handling on the subsequent development of premature infants. *Developmental Psychology,* 1969, *4,* 765–768.

Solomon, G. F. Psychoneuroimmunology: Interactions between central nervous system and immune system. *Journal of Neuroscience Research,* 1987, *18,* 1–9.

Spanos, N. P., Weekes, J. R., and Bertrand, L. D. Multiple personality: A social psychological perspective. *Journal of Abnormal Psychology,* 1985, *94,* 362–376.

Spear, N. E., and Riccio, D. C. *Memory: Phenomena and Principles.* Boston: Allyn and Bacon, 1994.

Spearman, C. *The Abilities of Man.* London: Macmillan, 1927.

Spears, R., van der Pligt, J., and Eiser, J. R. Illusory correlation in the perception of group attitudes. *Journal of Personality and Social Psychology,* 1985, *48,* 863–875.

Sperling, G. A. The information available in brief visual presentation. *Psychological Monographs,* 1960, *74* (no. 498).

Sperry, R. W. Brain bisection and consciousness. In *Brain and Conscious Experience,* edited by J. Eccles. New York: Springer-Verlag, 1966.

Spiegel, D., Bloom, J., and Yalom, I. D. Group support for patients with metastatic breast cancer. *Archives of General Psychiatry,* 1981, *38,* 527–533.

Spiegel, D., Bloom, J. R., Kraemer, H. C., and Gottheil, E. Effect of psychosocial treatment on survival of patients with metastatic breast cancer. *Lancet,* 1989, *2,* 888–891.

Spinelli, D. H., and Jensen, F. E. Plasticity: The mirror of experience. *Science,* 1979, *203,* 75–78.

Spinelli, D. H., Jensen, F. E., and DiPrisco, G. V. Early experience effect on dendritic branching in normally reared kittens. *Experimental Neurology,* 1980, *62,* 1–11.

Spirduso, W. W., and MacRae, P. G. Motor performance and aging. In *Handbook of the Psychology of Aging,* 3rd ed., edited by J. E. Birren and K. W. Schaie. San Diego: Academic Press, 1990.

Spiro, M. F. *Children of the Kibbutz.* Cambridge, MA: Harvard University Press, 1958.

Spiro, R. J. Remembering information from text: The "state of schema" approach. In *Schooling and the Acquisition of Knowledge,* edited by R. C. Anderson, R. J. Spiro, and W. E. Montague. Hillsdale, NJ: Lawrence Erlbaum Associates, 1977.

Spiro, R. J. Accommodative reconstruction in prose recall. *Journal of Verbal Learning and Verbal Behavior,* 1980, *19,* 84–95.

Spitzer, R. L., Skodol, A. E., Gibbon, M., and Williams, J. B. W. *Diagnostic and Statistical Manual of Mental Disorders Case Book.* Washington, DC: American Psychiatric Association, 1981.

Squire, L. R. *Memory and Brain.* Oxford, England: Oxford University Press, 1987.

Squire, L. R., Slater, P. C., and Miller, P. L. Retrograde amnesia following ECT: Long-term follow-up studies. *Archives of General Psychiatry,* 1981, *38,* 89–95.

Sroufe, L. A., Cooper, R. G., and DeHart, G. B. *Child and Adolescent Development.* New York: McGraw-Hill, 1992.

Staats, A. W., and Staats, C. K. Attitudes established by classical conditioning. *Journal of Abnormal and Social Psychology,* 1958, *57,* 37–40.

Staats, C. K., and Staats, A. W. Meaning established by classical conditioning. *Journal of Experimental Psychology,* 1957, *54,* 74–80.

Standing, L. Learning 10,000 pictures. *Quarterly Journal of Experimental Psychology,* 1973, *25,* 207–222.

Stebbins, W. C., Miller, J. M., Johnsson, L.- G., and Hawkins, J. E. Ototoxic hearing loss and cochlear pathology in the monkey. *Annals of Otology, Rhinology, and Laryngology,* 1969, *78,* 1007–1026.

Steen, S. N., Oppliger, R. A., and Brownell, K. D. Metabolic effects of repeated weight loss and regain in adolescent wrestlers. *Journal of the American Medical Association,* 1988, *260,* 47–50.

Sterman, M. B., and Clemente, C. D. Forebrain inhibitory mechanisms: Cortical synchronization induced by basal forebrain stimulation. *Experimental Neurology,* 1962a, *6,* 91–102.

Sterman, M. B., and Clemente, C. D. Forebrain inhibitory mechanisms: Sleep patterns induced by basal forebrain stimulation in the behaving cat. *Experimental Neurology,* 1962b, *6,* 103–117.

Stern, J. A., Brown, M., Ulett, G. A., and Sletten, I. A comparison of hypnosis, acupuncture, morphine, Valium, aspirin, and placebo in the management of experimentally induced pain. In *Hypnosis and Relaxation: Modern Verification of an Old Equation.* New York: Wiley-Interscience, 1977.

Stern, M., and Karraker, K. H. Sex stereotyping of infants: A review of gender labeling studies. *Sex Roles,* 1989, *20,* 501–522.

Stern, W. *The Psychological Methods of Testing Intelligence.* Baltimore: Warwick and York, 1914.

Sternberg, R. J. *Beyond IQ: A Triarchic Theory of Human Intelligence.* Cambridge: Cambridge University Press, 1985.

Sternberg, R. J. Triangulating love. In *The Psychology of Love,* edited by R. J. Sternberg and M. L. Barnes. New Haven, CT: Yale University Press, 1988.

Sternberg, R. J. For whom the bell curve tolls: A review of *The Bell Curve. Psychological Science,* 1995, *6,* 257–261.

Sternberg, R. J., Conway, B. E., Ketron, J. L., and Bernstein, M. People's conceptions of intelligence. *Journal of Personality and Social Psychology,* 1981, *41,* 37–55.

Sternberger, L. G., and Burns, G. L. Obsessions and compulsions: Psychometric properties of the Padua inventory with an American college population. *Behavior Research and Therapy,* 1990, *28,* 341–345.

Stevens, J. R. Schizophrenia and multiple sclerosis. *Schizophrenia Bulletin,* 1988, *14,* 231–241.

Stich, S. P. Rationality. In *An Invitation to Cognitive Science. Vol. 3: Thinking,* edited by D. N. Osherson and E. E. Smith. Cambridge, MA: MIT Press, 1990.

Stine, E. L., and Bohannon, J. N. Imitations, interactions, and language acquisition. *Journal of Child Language,* 1983, *10,* 589–603.

Stokoe, W. C. Apes who sign and critics who don't. In *Language in Primates: Perspectives and Implications,* edited by J. de Luce and H. T. Wilder. New York: Springer-Verlag, 1983.

Stone, A. A., Cox, D. S., Valdimarsdottir, H., Jandorf, L., and Neale, J. M. Evidence that secretory IgA antibody is associated with daily mood. *Journal of Personality and Social Psychology,* 1987, *52,* 988–993.

Stone, A. A., Reed, B. R., and Neale, J. M. Changes in daily event frequency precede episodes of physical symptoms. *Journal of Human Stress,* 1987, *13,* 70–74.

Strickland, B. R. Internal-external expectancies and cardiovascular functioning. In *Choice and Perceived Control,* edited by L. C. Perlmutter and R. A. Monty. Hillsdale, NJ: Erlbaum, 1979.

Stroop, J. R. Studies of interference in serial verbal reactions. *Journal of Experimental Psychology,* 1935, *18,* 743–762.

Strupp, H. H. The Vanderbilt psychotherapy studies: Synopsis. *Journal of Consulting and Clinical Psychology,* 1993, *61,* 431–433.

Strupp, H. H., and Hadley, S. W. Specific vs. nonspecific factors in psychotherapy. *Archives of General Psychiatry,* 1979, *36,* 1125–1136.

Stunkard, A. J., Sørenson, T. I., Harris, C., Teasdale, T. W., Chakraborty, R., Schull, W. J., and Schulsinger, F. An adoption study of human obesity. *New England Journal of Medicine,* 1986, *314,* 193–198.

Suddath, R. L., Christison, G. W., Torrey, E. F., Casanova, M. F., and Weinberger, D. R. Anatomical abnormalities in the brains of monozygotic twins discordant for schizophrenia. *New England Journal of Medicine,* 1990, *322,* 789–794.

Sullivan, R. M., Taborsky-Barba, S., Mendoza, R., Itano, A., Leon, M., Cotman, C. W., Payne, T. F., and Lott, I. Olfactory classical conditioning in neonates. *Pediatrics,* 1991, *87,* 511–518.

Suzdak, P. D., Glowa, J. R., Crawley, J. N., Schwartz, R. D., Skolnick, P., and Paul, S. M. A selective imidazobenzodiazepine antagonist of ethanol in the rat. *Science,* 1986, *234,* 1243–1247.

Swaab, D. F., and Hofman, M. A. An enlarged suprachiasmatic nucleus in homosexual men. *Brain Research,* 1990, *537,* 141–148.

Symons, D. *The Evolution of Human Sexuality.* New York: Oxford University Press, 1979.

Szasz, T. S. The myth of mental illness. *American Psychologist,* 1960, *15,* 113–118.

Szasz, T. S. *Insanity: The Idea and Its Consequences.* New York: Wiley, 1987.

Szymusiak, R., and McGinty, D. Sleep-related neuronal discharge in the basal forebrain of cats. *Brain Research,* 1986, *370,* 82–92.

Talmon, Y. *Family and Community in the Kibbutz.* Cambridge, MA: Harvard University Press, 1972.

Tanenhaus, M. K. *Psycholinguistics: An Overview.* Cambridge: Cambridge University Press, 1988.

Taras, H. L., Sallis, J. F., Patterson, T. L., Nader, P. R., and Nelson, J. A. Television's influence on children's diet and physical activity. *Journal of Developmental and Behavioral Pediatrics*, 1989, *10*, 176–180.

Tartaglia, L. A., Dembski, M., Weng, X., Deng, N. H., Culpepper, J., Devos, R., Richards, G. J., Campfield, L. A., Clark, F. T., Deeds, J., Muir, C., Sanker, S., Moriarty, A., Moore, K. J., Smutko, J. S., Mays, G. G., Woolf, E. A., Monroe, C. A., and Tepper, R. I. Identification and expression cloning of a leptin receptor, OB-R. *Cell*, 1995, *83*, 1263–1271.

Taube, S. L., Kirstein, L. S., Sweeney, D. R., Heninger, G. R., and Maas, J. W. Urinary 3–methoxy-4–hydroxyphenyleneglycol and psychiatric diagnosis. *American Journal of Psychiatry*, 1978, *135*, 78–82.

Tavris, C., and Sadd, S. *The Redbook Report on Female Sexuality*. New York: Delacorte Press, 1977.

Taylor, S. E. *Introduction to Health Psychology*. New York: McGraw-Hill, 1991.

Taylor, S. E., Peplau, L. A., and Sears, D. O. *Social Psychology*. Englewood Cliffs, NJ: Prentice-Hall, 1994.

Telch, M. J., Broouillard, M., Telch, C. F., Agras, W. S., and Taylor, C. B. Role of cognitive appraisal in panic-related avoidance. *Behaviour Research and Therapy*, 1989, *27*, 373–383.

Temoshok, L. Personality, coping style, emotion and cancer: Towards an integrative model. *Cancer Surveys*, 1987, *6*, 545–567.

Temoshok, L., Heller, B. W., Sagebiel, R. W., Blois, M. S., Sweet, D. M., DiClemente, R. J., and Gold, M. L. The relationship of psychosocial factors to prognostic indicators in cutaneous malignant melanoma. *Journal of Psychosomatic Research*, 1985, *29*, 139–153.

Terenius, L., and Wahlström, A. Morphine-like ligand for opiate receptors in human CSF. *Life Sciences*, 1975, *16*, 1759–1764.

Terrace, H. S., Petitto, L. A., Sanders, R. J., and Bever, T. G. Can an ape create a sentence? *Science*, 1979, *206*, 891–902.

Terry, R. D., and Davies, P. Dementia of the Alzheimer type. *Annual Review of Neuroscience*, 1980, *3*, 77–96.

Thelen, E. Motor development: A new synthesis. *American Psychologist*, 1995, *50*, 79–95.

Thibadeau, R., Just, M. A., and Carpenter, P. A. A model of the time course and content of reading. *Cognitive Science*, 1982, *6*, 157–203.

Thompson, T., and Schuster, C. R. *Behavioral Pharmacology*. Englewood Cliffs, NJ: Prentice-Hall, 1968.

Thorndike, E. L. *The Elements of Psychology*. New York: Seiler, 1905.

Thorpe, G. L., and Olson, S. L. *Behavior Therapy: Concepts, Procedures, and Applications*. Boston: Allyn and Bacon, 1990.

Thurstone, L. L. *Primary Mental Abilities*. Chicago: University of Chicago Press, 1938.

Tienari, P., Sorri, A., Lahti, I., Naarala, M., Wahlberg, K.- E., Moring, J., Pohjola, J., and Wynne, L. C. Genetic and psychosocial factors in schizophrenia: The Finnish adoptive family study. *Schizophrenia Bulletin*, 1987, *13*, 476–483.

Tippin, J., and Henn, F. A. Modified leukotomy in the treatment of intractable obsessional neurosis. *American Journal of Psychiatry*, 1982, *139*, 1601–1603.

Tobin, S. A. A comparison of psychoanalytic self-psychology and Carl Rogers's person-centered therapy. *Journal of Humanistic Psychology*, 1991, *31*, 9–33.

Tomasello, M., and Farrar, J. Joint attention and early language. *Child Development*, 1986, *57*, 1454–1463.

Tong, Y. C., Busby, P. A., and Clark, G. M. Perceptual studies on cochlear implant patients with early onset of profound hearing impairment prior to normal development of auditory, speech and language skills. *Journal of the Acoustical Society of America*, 1988, *84*, 951–962.

Tooby, J., and Cosmides, L. Evolutionary psychology and the generation of culture, Part I: Theoretical considerations. *Ethology and Sociobiology*, 1989, *10*, 39–49.

Tooby, J., and Cosmides, L. On the universality of human nature and the uniqueness of the individual: The role of genetics and adaptation. *Journal of Personality*, 1990, *58*, 17–67.

Tootell, R. B., Reppas, J. B., Dale, A. M., and Look, R. B. Visual motion aftereffect in human cortical area MT revealed by functional magnetic resonance imaging. *Nature*, 1995, *375*, 139–141.

Torgerson, S. Genetic factors in anxiety disorders. *Archives of General Psychiatry*, 1983, *40*, 1085–1089.

Torrey, E. F. *Surviving Schizophrenia: A Family Manual*. New York: Harper & Row, 1988.

Torrey, E. F., Torrey, B. B., and Peterson, M. R. Seasonality of schizophrenic births in the United States. *Archives of General Psychiatry*, 1977, *34*, 1065–1070.

Tourney, G. Hormones and homosexuality. In *Homosexual Behavior*, edited by J. Marmor. New York: Basic Books, 1980.

Treisman, A. M. Contextual cues in selective listening. *Quarterly Journal of Experimental Psychology*, 1960, *12*, 242–248.

Treisman, A. M. Features and objects: The fourteenth Bartlett Memorial Lecture. *Quarterly Journal of Experimental Psychology*, 1988, *40A*, 201–237.

Triplett, N. The dynamogenic factors in pacemaking and competition. *American Journal of Psychology*, 1897, *9*, 507–533.

Trivers, R. L. The biology of reciprocal altruism. *Quarterly Review of Biology*, 1971, *46*, 35–57.

Trivers, R L. Parental investment and sexual selection. In *Sexual Selection and the Descent of Man*, edited by B. Campbell. Chicago: Aldine, 1972.

Tronick, E., Als, H., Adamson, L., Wise, S., and Brazelton, T. B. The infant's response to entrapment between contradictory messages in face-to-face interaction. *Journal of the American Academy of Child Psychiatry*, 1978, *17*, 1–13.

Träskmann, L., Åsberg, M., Bertilsson, L., and Sjöstrand, L. Monoamine metabolites on CSF and suicidal behavior. *Archives of General Psychiatry*, 1981, *38*, 631–636.

Truax, C. B. Reinforcement and nonreinforcement in Rogerian psychotherapy. *Journal of Abnormal Psychology*, 1966, *71*, 1–9.

Tulving, E. Episodic and semantic memory. In *Organization of Memory*, edited by E. Tulving and W. Donaldson. New York: Academic Press, 1972.

Tulving, E. *Elements of Episodic Memory*. Oxford: Oxford University Press, 1983.

Tulving, E. Precis of *Elements of Episodic Memory*. *The Behavioral and Brain Sciences*, 1984, *7*, 223–268.

Tulving, E., and Osler, S. Effectiveness of retrieval cues in memory for words. *Journal of Experimental Psychology*, 1968, *77*, 593–601.

Tupes, E. C., and Christal, R. E. Recurrent personality factors based on trait ratings. USAF ASD Technical Report, 1961, 61–97.

Turner, A. M., and Greenough, W. T. Differential rearing effects on rat visual cortex synapses. I. Synaptic and neuronal density and synapses per neuron. *Brain Research*, 1985, *329*, 195–203.

Turner, S. M., Beidel, D. C., and Nathan, R. S. Biological factors in obsessive-compulsive disorders. *Psychological Bulletin*, 1985, *97*, 430–450.

Tversky, A., and Kahneman, D. Judgment under uncertainty: Heuristics and biases. In *Judgment Under Uncertainty*, edited by D. Kahneman, P. Slovic, and A. Tversky. New York: Cambridge University Press, 1982.

Tyrell, J. B., and Baxter, J. D. Glucocorticoid therapy. In *Endocrinology and Metabolism*, edited by P. Felig, J. D. Baxter, A. E. Broadus, and L. A. Frohman. New York: McGraw-Hill, 1981.

Tyron, R. Genetic differences in maze-learning ability in rats. *Yearbook of the National Society for the Study of Education*, 1940, *39*, 111–119.

Ullman, L. P., and Krasner, L. *Psychological Approach to Abnormal Behavior*. Englewood Cliffs, NJ: Prentice-Hall, 1969.

Ungerleider, L. G., and Mishkin, M. Two cortical visual systems. In *Analysis of Visual Behavior*, edited by D. J. Ingle, M. A. Goodale, and R. J. W. Mansfield. Cambridge, MA: MIT Press, 1982.

Uno, H., Tarara, R., Else, J. G., Suleman, M. A., and Sapolsky, R. M. Hippocampal damage associated with prolonged and fatal stress in primates. *The Journal of Neuroscience*, 1989, *9*, 1705–1711.

Vaillant, G. E., and Milofsky, E. S. The etiology of alcoholism. *American Psychologist*, 1982, *37*, 494–503.

Valenstein, E. S. *Great and Desperate Cures: The Rise and Decline of Psychosurgery and Other Radical Treatments for Mental Illness*. New York: Basic Books, 1986.

Vecera, S. P., and Farrah, M. J. Does visual attention select objects or locations? *Journal of Experimental Psychology*, 1994, *123*, 146–160.

Vernon, P. E. *Intelligence: Heredity and Environment*. San Francisco: W. H. Freeman, 1979.

Vogel, G. W., Vogel, F., McAbee, R. S., and Thurmond, A. G. Improvement of depression by REM sleep deprivation. *Archives of General Psychiatry*, 1980, *37*, 247–253.

von Békésy, G. *Experiments in Hearing*. New York: McGraw-Hill, 1960.

Von Wright, J. M., Anderson, K., and Stenman, U. Generalization of conditioned GSRs in dichotic listening. In *Attention and Performance, Vol. V*, edited by P. M. A. Rabbitt and S. Dornic. London: Academic Press, 1975.

Vygotsky, L. S. Thinking and speech. In *The Collected Works of L. S. Vygotsky: Vol. 1. Problems of General Psychology,* edited by R. W. Rieber and A. S. Carton and translated by N. Minick. New York: Plenum. (Original work published in 1934.)

Wade, C., and Tavris, C. The longest war: Gender and culture. In *Psychology and Culture,* edited by W. J. Lonner and R. Malpass. Boston: Allyn and Bacon, 1994.

Wade, G. N., and Gray, J. M. Gonadal effects on food intake and adiposity: A metabolic hypothesis. *Physiology and Behavior,* 1979, *22,* 583–593.

Wagner, A. R., Siegal, S., Thomas, E., and Ellison, G. D. Reinforcement history and the extinction of a conditioned salivary response. *Journal of Comparative and Physiological Psychology,* 1964, *58,* 354–358.

Wagner, R. K., and Sternberg, R. J. Executive control of reading, 1983. Cited by Sternberg, R. J. *Beyond IQ: A Triarchic Theory of Human Intelligence.* Cambridge: Cambridge University Press, 1985.

Walker, E., and Lewine, R. J. Prediction of adult-onset schizophrenia from childhood home movies of the patients. *American Journal of Psychiatry,* 1990, *147,* 1052–1056.

Walker, L. J. A longitudinal study of moral reasoning. *Child Development,* 1989, *60,* 157–166.

Wallen, K. Desire and ability: Hormones and the regulation of female sexual behavior. *Neuroscience and Biobehavioral Reviews,* 1990, *14,* 233–241.

Wallen, K., Mann, D. R., Davis-DaSilva, M., Gaventa, S., Lovejoy, J. C., and Collins, D. C. Chronic gonadotropin-releasing hormone agonist treatment suppresses ovulation and sexual behavior in group-living female rhesus monkeys (*macaca mulatta*). *Animal Behaviour,* 1986, *36,* 369–375.

Walster, E., Aronson, V., Abrahams, D., and Rottman, L. Importance of physical attractiveness in dating behavior. *Journal of Personality and Social Psychology,* 1966, *4,* 508–516.

Walster, E., and Berscheid, E. Adrenaline makes the heart grow fonder. *Psychology Today,* June 1971, pp. 47–62.

Wann, D. L., and Dolan, T. J. Spectators' evaluations of rival and fellow fans. *The Psychological Record,* 1994, *44,* 351–358.

Ward, I. Prenatal stress feminizes and demasculinizes the behavior of males. *Science,* 1972, *175,* 82–84.

Wason, P. Reasoning about a rule. *Quarterly Journal of Experimental Psychology,* 1968, *20,* 273–281.

Wason, P. C., and Johnson-Laird, P. N. *Psychology of Reasoning: Structure and Content.* Cambridge, MA: Harvard University Press, 1972.

Waters, E., Wippman, J., and Sroufe, L. A. Attachment, positive affect, and competence in the peer group: Two studies in construct validation. *Child Development,* 1979, *50,* 821–829.

Watkins, C. E. What have surveys taught us about the teaching and practice of psychological assessment? *Journal of Personality Assessment,* 1991, *56,* 426–437.

Watson, D. L., and Tharp, R. G. *Self-directed Behavior: Self-modification for Personal Adjustment,* 4th ed. Monterey, CA: Brooks/Cole, 1972.

Watson, J. B. *Behaviorism,* rev. ed. New York: W. W. Norton, 1930.

Watson, J. S., and Ramey, C. T. Reactions to responsive contingent stimulation in early infancy. *Merrill-Palmer Quarterly,* 1972, *18,* 219–227.

Waugh, N. C., and Norman, D. A. Primary memory. *Psychological Review,* 1965, *72,* 89–104.

Wedenjoa, W. Social and cultural psychiatry of Jamaicans, at home and abroad. In *Handbook of Culture and Mental Illness: An International Perspective,* edited by I. Al-Issa. Madison, CT: International Universities Press, 1995.

Weidner, G., Sexton, G., McLellarn, R., Connor, S. L., and Matarazzo, J. D. The role of type A behavior and hostility in an elevation of plasma lipids in adult women and men. *Psychosomatic Medicine,* 1987, *49,* 136–145.

Weigel, R. H., Vernon, D. T. A., and Tognacci, L. N. Specificity of the attitude as a determinant of attitude-behavior congruence. *Journal of Personality and Social Psychology,* 1974, *30,* 724–728.

Weinberger, D. R., Bigelow, L. B., Kleinman, J. E., Klein, S. T., Rosenblatt, J. E., and Wyatt, R. J. Cerebral ventricular enlargement in chronic schizophrenia: An association with poor response to treatment. *Archives of General Psychiatry,* 1980, *37,* 11–13.

Weinberger, D. R., and Wyatt, J. R. Brain morphology in schizophrenia: *In vivo* studies. In *Schizophrenia as a Brain Disease,* edited by F. A. Henn and G. A. Nasrallah. New York: Oxford University Press, 1982.

Weir, W. Another look at subliminal "facts." *Advertising Age,* 1984, *55,* 46.

Weisner, T. S., and Wilson-Mitchell, J. E. Non-conventional family life-styles and sex typing in six-year-olds. *Child Development,* 1990, *61,* 1915–1933.

Weiss, J. M. Effects of coping responses on stress. *Journal of Comparative and Physiological Psychology,* 1968, *65,* 251–260.

Weitzman, E. D. Sleep and its disorders. *Annual Review of Neuroscience,* 1981, *4,* 381–418.

Weltzin, T. E., Hsu, L. K. G., Pollice, C., and Kaye, W. H. Feeding patterns in bulimia nervosa. *Biological Psychiatry,* 1991, *30,* 1093–1110.

Werner, H. Studies on contour. *American Journal of Psychology,* 1935, *37,* 40–64.

Wernicke, K. *Der Aphasische Symptomenkomplex.* Breslau, Poland: Cohn & Weigert, 1874.

Wertheimer, M. Psychomotor co-ordination of auditory-visual space at birth. *Science,* 1961, *134,* 1692.

White, G. L. Physical attractiveness and courtship progress. *Journal of Personality and Social Psychology,* 1980, *39,* 660–668.

Whitehead, R. G., Rowland, M. G. M., Hutton, M., Prentice, A. M., Müller, E., and Paul, A. Factors influencing lactation performance in rural Gambian mothers. *Lancet,* 1978, *2,* 178–181.

Whorf, B. L. Science and linguistics. In *Language, Thought and Reality: Selected Writings of Benjamin Lee Whorf,* edited by J. B. Carroll. Cambridge, MA: MIT Press, 1956.

Wiesel, T. N. Postnatal development of the visual cortex and the influence of environment. *Nature,* 1982, *299,* 583–592.

Wilcoxon, H. C., Dragoin, W. B., and Kral, P. A. Illness-induced aversions in rat and quail: Relative salience of visual and gustatory cues. *Science,* 1971, *171,* 826–828.

Williams, K., Harkins, S., and Latané, B. Identifiability as a deterrent to social loafing: Two cheering experiments. *Journal of Personality and Social Psychology,* 1981, *40,* 303–311.

Williams, R. B., Hanel, T. L., Lee, K. L., and Kong, Y. H. Type A behavior, hostility, and coronary atherosclerosis. *Psychosomatic Medicine,* 1980, *42,* 539–549.

Wilson, E. O. *On Human Nature.* Cambridge, MA: Harvard University Press, 1978.

Wise, E., Hadar, U., Howard, D., and Patterson, K. Language activation studies with positron emission tomography. In *Exploring Brain Functional Anatomy with Positron Emission Tomography,* edited by D. Chadwick and J. Whelan. Chichester, England: Wiley, 1991.

Wise, R. Where the public peril begins: A survey of psychotherapists to determine the effects of Tarasoff. *Stanford Review,* 1978, *31,* 165–190.

Woerner, P. L., and Guze, S. B. A family and marital study of hysteria. *British Journal of Psychiatry,* 1968, *114,* 161–168.

Wolfe, L. The sexual profile of that cosmopolitan girl. *Cosmopolitan,* 1980, pp. 254–265.

Wolff, P. H. Crying and vocalization in early infancy. In *Determinants of Infant Behaviour, Vol. 4,* edited by B. M. Foss. London: Methuen, 1969.

Wolpe, J. *Psychotherapy by Reciprocal Inhibition.* Stanford, CA: Stanford University Press, 1958.

Wood, D. L., Sheps, S. G., Elveback, L. R., and Schirder, A. Cold pressor test as a predictor of hypertension. *Hypertension,* 1984, *6,* 301–306.

Woodall, K. L., and Matthews, K. A. Changes in and stability of hostile characteristics: Results from a 4-year longitudinal study of children. *Journal of Personality and Social Psychology,* 1993, *63,* 491–499.

Woodruff, R. A., Guze, S. B., and Clayton, P. J. Anxiety neurosis among psychiatric outpatients. *Comprehensive Psychiatry,* 1972, *13,* 165–170.

Woods, S. W., Charney, D. S., Goodman, W. K., and Heninger, G. R. Carbon dioxide-induced anxiety. *Archives of General Psychiatry,* 1988, *45,* 43–52.

Woodworth, R. S., and Schlosberg, H. *Experimental Psychology.* New York: Holt, Rinehart and Winston, 1954.

Worchel, F. F., Aaron, L. L., and Yates, D. F. Gender bias on the Thematic Apperception Test. *Journal of Personality Assessment,* 1990, *55,* 593–602.

Wu, J. C., and Bunney, W. E. The biological basis of an antidepressant response to sleep deprivation and relapse: Review and hypothesis. *American Journal of Psychiatry,* 1990, *147,* 14–21.

Yates, W. R., Perry, P., and Murray, S. Aggression and hostility in anabolic steroid users. *Biological Psychiatry*, 1992, *31*, 1232–1234.

Young, A., Stokes, M., and Crowe, M. Size and strength of the quadriceps muscles of old and young women. *European Journal of Clinical Investigation*, 1984, *14*, 282–287.

Youniss, J., and Smollar, J. Adolescent relations with mothers, fathers, and friends. Chicago: University of Chicago Press, 1985.

Zajonc, R. B. Attitudinal effects of mere exposure. *Journal of Personality and Social Psychology, Monograph Supplement*, 1968, *9*, 1–27.

Zajonc, R. B. On primacy of affect. In *Approaches to Emotion*, edited by K. R. Scherer and P. Ekman. Hillsdale, NJ: Lawrence Erlbaum Associates, 1984.

Zatrick, D. F., and Lu, F. G. The ethnic/minority focus unit as a training site in transcultural psychiatry. *Academic Psychiatry*, 1991, *15*, 218–225.

Zeki, S. *A Vision of the Brain.* Oxford: Blackwell Scientific Publications, 1993.

Zihl, J., von Cramon, D., Mai, N., and Schmid, C. Disturbance of movement vision after bilateral posterior brain damage: Further evidence and follow up observations. *Brain*, 1991, *114*, 2235–2252.

Zimbardo, P. G. The human choice: Individuation, reason, and order versus deindividuation, impulse, and chaos. In *Nebraska Symposium on Motivation*, edited by W. J. Arnold and D. Levine. Lincoln: University of Nebraska Press, 1970.

Zola, D. Redundancy and word perception during reading. *Perception and Psychophysics*, 1984, *36*, 277–284.

Zuckerman, M. *Psychobiology of Personality.* Cambridge: Cambridge University Press, 1991.

Zvolsky, P., Jansky, L., Vyskocilova, J., and Grof, P. Effects of psychotropic drugs on hamster hibernation: Pilot study. *Progress in Neuropsychopharmacology*, 1981, *5*, 599–602.

Name Index

Subject Index

Note: Page numbers in *italic* type indicate figures; those followed by t indicate tables. **Boldface** type indicates key terms and concepts.

Credits

CHAPTER 1

P. 1, Joseph Nettis/Tony Stone Images; p. 3, left, Jeff Corwin/Tony Stone Images; p. 3, right, Phil Borges/Tony Stone Images; p. 8, top, Corbis-Bettmann; p. 10, Fig. 1.1, Stock Montage, Inc.; p. 11, National Library of Medicine; p. 12, National Library of Medicine; p. 13, National Library of Medicine; p. 15 National Library of Medicine; p. 16, bottom, Corbis-Bettmann; p. 16, top, Archives of the History of American Psychology/ University of Akron; p. 17, right, John Lawrence/Tony Stone Images.

CHAPTER 2

P. 51, Gavin Hellier/Tony Stone Images; p. 25, top, Tony Stone Worldwide; p. 25, bottom, Harcourt/Anthro-Photo File; p. 31, George Zimbel/Monkmeyer Press Photo Service; p. 35, Lawrence Migdale/Tony Stone Images; p. 37, Fig. 2.9, UPI/Corbis-Bettmann; p. 40, Hank Morgan/Photo.

Researchers, Inc.; p. 41, left, David Austen/Stock, Boston; p. 41, right, Photo Researchers, Inc./National Snow and Ice Data Center/Science Photo Library; p. 48, Don Spiro/Tony Stone Images.

CHAPTER 3

P. 51, Phil Borges/Tony Stone Images; p. 54, Northwind Picture Archives; p. 59, left, John Reader/Science Photo Library/Photo Researchers, Inc.; p. 59, center, Topham/ The Image Works; p. 59, right, Robert E. Daemmrich/Tony Stone Images; p. 62, top, CNRI/Science Photo Library/Photo Researchers, Inc.; p. 62, bottom, David Phillips/Photo Researchers, Inc.; p. 68, Will & Deni McIntyre/Photo Researchers, Inc.; p. 69, Owen Franken/Stock, Boston; p. 73, Barag Schuler/Anthro-Photo; p. 74, David Madison/Tony Stone Images; p. 75, SuperStock; p. 79, David Wells/The Image Works.

CHAPTER 4

P. 83, Glyn Kirk/Tony Stone Images; p. 99, Fig. 4.19, Larry Mulvehill/Rainbow.

CHAPTER 5

P. 123, Abe Rezny/The Image Works; p. 125, Charles Thatcher/Tony Stone Images; p. 129, Bob Daemmrich/The Image Works; p. 132, Bob Daemmrich/Stock, Boston; p. 134, David Young Wolff/Tony Stone Images; p. 136, L. Kolvoord/ The Image Works; p. 137, Bob Daemmrich/ Stock, Boston; p. 139, Bob Daemmrich/The Image Works; p. 141, Fred Jewel/AP Photo; p. 143, Bob Daemmrich/Stock, Boston; p. 145, Dion Ogust/The Image Works; p. 147, Robert E. Daemmrich/Tony Stone Worldwide; p. 154, Fig. 5.20, SuperStock International, Inc.

CHAPTER 6

P. 159, Charles Thatcher/Tony Stone Images; p. 161, John Marmaras/Woodfin Camp & Associates, Inc.; p. 162, Lonnie Duka/Tony Stone Worldwide; p. 165, SuperStock; p. 171, left & right, Richard Elliot/Tony Stone Images; p. 175, Gary Yeowell/Tony Stone Images; p. 181, The Image Works; p. 186, Photo Researchers, Inc.; p. 188, Four By Five; p. 190, Omikron/Photo Researchers, Inc.; p. 195, Photo Researchers, Inc./Gerard Vandystadt/Agence Vandystadt.

CHAPTER 7

P. 199, Geoff Dore/Tony Stone WorldWide; p. 209, Patricia Thomson/Tony Stone Images; p. 210, Sarah Stone/Tony Stone Worldwide; p. 213, Simon Fraser, New Castle University/ Photo Researchers, Inc.; p. 220, Fig. 7.30, Bohdan Hrynewych/Stock, Boston; p. 220, Fig. 7.31, SuperStock; p. 222, left, SuperStock; p. 222, right, Tony Stone Images; p. 226, John Ficara/ Woodfin Camp & Associates, Inc.; p. 229, Art Resource/Prentice-Hall Photo Archives.

CHAPTER 8

P. 231, SuperStock; p. 234, Chad Ehlers/Tony Stone Images; p. 234, Ron Sherman/Stock,

Boston; p. 240, SuperStock; p. 246, left & right, Ogust/The Image Works; p. 249, The Image Works/First Image; p. 251, left, Charles Gupton/Stock, Boston; p. 251, right, Robert Yager/Tony Stone Images; p. 252, Karl Weatherly/Tony Stone Images; p. 258, Jim Harrison/Stock, Boston; p. 260, left, Eastcott/ Momatiuk/Woodfin Camp & Associates, Inc. p. 260, top right, Betty Press/Woodfin Camp & Associates, Inc.; p. 260, bottom right, Mark S. Wexler/Woodfin Camp & Associates, Inc.; p. 261, Grantpix/Photo Researchers, Inc.

CHAPTER 9

P. 269, Andrew Errington/Tony Stone Images; p. 271, S. Lousada/Petit Format/Photo Researchers, Inc.; p. 274, Cary Wolinsky/Stock, Boston; p. 279, bottom right, Adam Woolfitt/ Woodfin Camp & Associates, Inc.; p. 280, Chris Noble/Tony Stone Images; p. 285, Philippe Platilly/Science Photo Library/Photo Researchers, Inc.; p. 288, Corbis-Bettmann; p. 291, Fig. 9.13, Michael Heron/Woodfin Camp & Associates, Inc.; p. 294, SuperStock; p. 295, Ken Heyman/Woodfin Camp & Associates, Inc.; p. 298, Courtesy of the Sleep Disorders Foundation, Stanford University.

CHAPTER 10

P. 301, Owen Franken/Stock, Boston; p. 303, N. R. Rowan/The Images Works; p. 310, Peter Poulides/Tony Stone WorldWide; p. 313, Michael Ventura/Tony Stone Images; p. 316, Lawrence Migdale/Tony Stone WorldWide; p. 319, Frank Pedrick/The Image Works; p. 321, Fig. 10.17, Courtesy of Dr. Patricia Kuhl, University of Washington; p. 322, Fig. 10.18, James Wilson/Woodfin Camp & Associates; p. 330, Courtesy of CNN.

CHAPTER 11

P. 333, James Balog/Tony Stone Images; p. 335, Nicholas DeVore/Tony Stone WorldWide; p. 340 Nigel Dickinson/Tony Stone Images; p. 345, Bob Daemmrich/The Image Works; p. 348, Greenlar/

The Image Works; p. 353, left, Charles Gupton/ Tony Stone Images; p. 353, right, Marc Pokempner/Tony Stone Images; p. 355, Pat Sullivan/AP Photo; p. 360, WideWorld Photos; p. 364, Michael Rosenfeld/Tony Stone Images.

CHAPTER 12
P. 369, David Madison/Tony Stone Images; p. 372, Neil Harding/Tony Stone Images; p. 376, Courtesy of J. Campos, B. Bertenthal, & R. Kermoran; p. 378, Bob Daemmrich/Stock, Boston; p. 379, Jean Claude LeJeune/Stock, Boston; p. 385, McLaughlin/The Image Works; p. 387, Owen Franken/Stock, Boston; p. 394, left, Peter Cade/Tony Stone Images; p. 394, right, Kindra Clineff/Tony Stone Images; p. 404, Tom McCarthy/Rainbow; p. 405, Fig. 12.11, Alfred Pasieka/Science Photo Library/Photo Researchers, Inc.; p. 408, Kim Newton/Woodfin Camp & Associates, Inc.

CHAPTER 13
P. 413, David Madison/Tony Stone Images; p. 418, Eastcott/The Image Works; p. 420, Wayne Eastep/Tony Stone Images; p. 425, Tony Stone WorldWide; p. 428, Steven Weinberg/Tony Stone Images; p. 436, Brian Seed/Tony Stone Images; p. 439, top, Tom Walker/Stock, Boston.

CHAPTER 14
P. 447, Chris Windsor/Tony Stone Images; p. 488, left & right, D. Gorton/Time Magazine; p. 450, Fig. 14.1, The Bettmann Archive; p. 451,

Jon Riley/Tony Stone Images; p. 493, Frank Siteman/Stock, Boston; p. 458, Sue Ann Miller/Tony Stone Images; p. 460, Paula Lerner/Saga Agency; p. 466, Andy Sacks/Tony Stone Images; p. 468, Phil Degginger/Tony Stone Images; p. 472, Topham; p. 473, SuperStock; p. 479, Ziggy Kaluzny/Tony Stone Images; p. 480, SuperStock.

CHAPTER 15
P. 483, Anthony Cassidy/Tony Stone Images; p. 487, Keren Su/Tony Stone Images; p. 489, Lawrence Migdale/Stock, Boston; p. 493, Robert E. Daemmrich/Tony Stone Images; p. 500, B. Daemmrich/The Image Works; p. 503, Nat Antman/The Image Works; p. 505, John Doman/AP WideWorld Photos; p. 506, Paula Lerner/Woodfin Camp & Associates, Inc.; p. 511, WideWorld Photos, Inc.; p. 516, Catherine Karnow/Woodfin Camp & Associates, Inc.; p. 518, left, Nicholas DeVore/Tony Stone WorldWide; p. 518, right, Michael Busselle/Tony Stone Images.

CHAPTER 16
P. 523, Keren Su/Tony Stone Images; p. 524, Robert Frerck/Woodfin Camp & Associates, Inc.; p. 529, Jacques Chenet/Woodfin Camp & Associates, Inc.; p. 535, A. Ramey/Woodfin Camp & Associates, Inc.; p. 528, Michael Abramson/Woodfin Camp & Associates, Inc.; p. 539, Okoniewski/The Image Works; p. 544, Enrico Dagino/Woodfin Camp & Associates,

Inc.; p. 545, Andrejs Liepins/Science Photo Library/Photo Researchers, Inc.; p. 550, James Wilson/Woodfin Camp & Associates, Inc.; p. 553, Patrick Ward/Stock, Boston.

CHAPTER 17
P. 559, Ian Shaw, Tony Stone Images; p. 561, R. Daemmrich/The Image Works; p. 562, Betty Press/Woodfin Camp & Associates, Inc.; p. 563, Peter Southwick/Stock, Boston; p. 568, Frank Siteman/Stock, Boston; p. 570, Bill Horsman/ Stock, Boston; p. 577, Susan Greenwood/Maison Agency; p. 578, John Eastcott/YVA Momatiuk/ Woodfin Camp & Associates, Inc.; p. 581, AP/World Wide Photos; p. 584, Roswell Angier/Stock, Boston; p. 587, Grunnitus/ Monkmeyer; p. 595, Matthew McVay/Tony Stone WorldWide.

CHAPTER 18
P. 601, Andrea Booker/Tony Stone Images; p. 603, Fig. 18.1, Loren McIntyre/Woodfin Camp & Associates, Inc.; p. 604, Fig. 18.2, Corbis-Bettmann; p. 607, Photo Researchers, Inc.; p. 610, Michael Rougier/Life Magazine © Time Warner, Inc.; p. 612, Jerry Howard/Stock, Boston; p. 615, Paula Lerner/Woodfin Camp & Associates, Inc.; p. 618, Oscar Burriel/Latin Stock/Science Photo/Photo Researchers, Inc.; p. 621, Joseph Nettis/Photo Researchers, Inc.; p. 625, Bruce Hands/Tony Stone Images; p. 632, James Wilson/Woodfin Camp & Associates, Inc.